Higher Learning. Forward Thinking.™

McGraw-Hill
Ryerson

...ning Centre

For the Student

Online Study Guide

Do you understand the material? You'll know after working through this comprehensive Online Student Study Guide. Try the Multiple Choice and True/False questions for each chapter and work through the journal entries to maximize your time spent reviewing text concepts. They're auto-graded with feedback and the option to send results directly to faculty.

Web Links

This section references various Web sites, including all company Web sites linked from the text.

Microsoft® PowerPoint® Presentations

View and download presentations created for each text. Great for pre-class preparation and post-class review.

Internet Application Questions

Go online to learn how companies use the Internet in their day-to-day activities. Answer questions based on current organization Web sites and strategies.

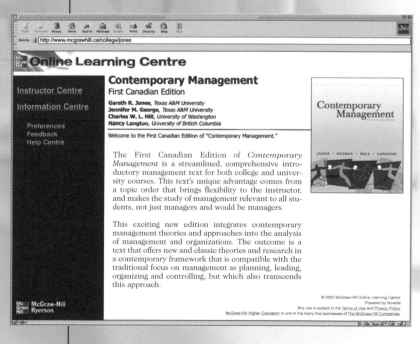

Netsite: http://www.mcgrawhill.ca/college/jones

Online Learning Centre

Instructor Centre
Information Centre

Preferences
Feedback
Help Centre

Contemporary Management
First Canadian Edition

Gareth R. Jones, *Texas A&M University*
Jennifer M. George, *Texas A&M University*
Charles W. L. Hill, *University of Washington*
Nancy Langton, *University of British Columbia*

Welcome to the First Canadian Edition of "Contemporary Management."

The First Canadian Edition of *Contemporary Management* is a streamlined, comprehensive introductory management text for both college and university courses. This text's unique advantage comes from a topic order that brings flexibility to the instructor, and makes the study of management relevant to all students, not just managers and would be managers.

This exciting new edition integrates contemporary management theories and approaches into the analysis of management and organizations. The outcome is a text that offers new and classic theories and research in a contemporary framework that is compatible with the traditional focus on management as planning, leading, organizing and controlling, but which also transcends this approach.

© 2002 McGraw-Hill Online Learning Centre
Powered by Novelis
Any use is subject to the Terms of Use and Privacy Policy.
McGraw-Hill Higher Education is one of the many fine businesses of The McGraw-Hill Companies.

McGraw-Hill
Ryerson

Your Internet companion to the most exciting educational tools on the Web!

The Online Learning Centre can be found at:

www.mcgrawhill.ca/college/jones

Contemporary
Management
First Canadian Edition

Contemporary Management

First Canadian Edition

Gareth R. Jones
Texas A&M University

Jennifer M. George
Texas A&M University

Charles W. L. Hill
University of Washington

Nancy Langton
University of British Columbia

McGraw-Hill Ryerson

Toronto   Montréal   Boston   Burr Ridge, IL   Dubuque, IA   Madison, WI   New York   San Francisco
St. Louis   Bangkok   Bogotá   Caracas   Kuala Lumpur   Lisbon   London   Madrid   Mexico City   Milan
New Delhi   Santiago   Seoul   Singapore   Sydney   Taipei

McGraw-Hill
Ryerson Limited

A Subsidiary of The **McGraw·Hill** *Companies*

Contemporary Management
First Canadian Edition

ISBN: 0-07-089372-1

1 2 3 4 5 6 7 8 9 10   TCP   0 9 8 7 6 5 4 3 2

Printed and bound in Canada.

Care has been taken to trace ownership of copyright material contained in this text; however, the publisher will welcome any information that enables them to rectify any reference or credit for subsequent editions.

Vice President and Editorial Director: Patrick Ferrier
Sponsoring Editor: Lenore Gray Spence
Developmental Editors: Su Mei Ku/Kim Brewster
Senior Marketing Manager: Jeff MacLean
Copy Editor: Laurel Sparrow
Production Coordinator: Emily Hickey
Photo and Literary Permissions: Alison Derry, Permissions Plus
Composition: Bookman Typesetting Co. Inc.
Cover Design: Dianna Little
Cover Image Credit: © Lisa Henderling/Stock Illustration Source
Author photo: Gary Schwartz
Printer: Transcontinental Printing Group

Canadian Cataloguing in Publication Data

Main entry under title:
    Contemporary management

1st Canadian ed.
Includes bibliographical references and index.
ISBN 0-07-089372-1

1. Management.   I. Jones, Gareth R.

HD31.C638 2001   658   C2001-903152-1

Brief Contents

Preface   xv
Acknowledgments   xxiii

Part One
Management   1

Chapter 1
Managers and Managing   2

Chapter 2
The Evolution of Management Theory   32

Part Two
The Environment of Management   59

Chapter 3
The Organizational Environment   60

Chapter 4
The Global Environment   90

Chapter 5
Ethics, Social Responsibility, and
Diversity   120

Part Three
Managing Decision Making and
Planning   153

Chapter 6
The Manager as a Decision Maker   154

Chapter 7
The Manager as a Planner and
Strategist   188

Part Four
Managing Organizational Architecture   221

Chapter 8
Managing Organizational Structure   222

Chapter 9
Organizational Control and Culture   254

Chapter 10
Human Resource Management   286

Part Five
Managing Individuals and Groups   321

Chapter 11
The Manager as a Person   322

Chapter 12
Motivation   348

Chapter 13
Leadership   378

Chapter 14
Groups and Teams   408

Chapter 15
Communication   442

Chapter 16
Organizational Conflict, Negotiation,
and Politics   474

Chapter 17
Organizational Change   500

Contents

Preface   xv

Acknowledgments   xxiii

Part One
Management   1

Chapter 1
Managers and Managing   2

A Case in Contrast

WestJet Brings Back its First CEO   3

What is Management?   5
Achieving High Performance: A Manager's Goal   5

Management Insight
How to Be an Effective Mine Manager   6

Managerial Functions   7
Planning   7
Organizing   8
Leading   8
Controlling   9
Types of Managers   10
Levels of Management   10
Recent Changes in Managerial Hierarchies   12

Management Insight
Managing from the Bottom at WestJet   14

Tips for Managers
Managing Resources   15
Managerial Roles and Skills   15
Managerial Roles Identified by Mintzberg   15
Managerial Skills   17

Tips for Managers
Tasks and Roles   19
Challenges for Management in the
Canadian Environment   19
Organizational Size   19
The Types of Organizations   19
The Political and Legal Climate   20
Managing a Diverse Workforce   20

Focus on Diversity
Canadian Armed Forces Faces Diversity   21

Challenges for Management in a
Global Environment   21
Building a Competitive Advantage   22

Managing Globally
How Mountain Equipment Co-op Faces the
Globalization Challenge   24
Maintaining Ethical Standards   24

Ethics in Action
How to Destroy a Charity's Reputation   25
Utilizing New Information Systems and
Technologies   25

Management Insight
Can the Information Revolution Change Canadian
Healthcare?   25
Summary and Review   26
Management in Action   27
The Challenges of Heading the CBC   29
Managers Crucial to Curbing Turnover   30

Chapter 2
The Evolution of Management Theory   32

A Case in Contrast

Changing Ways of Making Cars   33

Scientific Management Theory   35
Job Specialization and the Division of Labour   36
F.W. Taylor and Scientific Management   36

Ethics in Action
Fordism in Practice   39
The Gilbreths   40
Administrative Management Theory   40
The Theory of Bureaucracy   41
Fayol's Principles of Management   42
Behavioural Management Theory   43

Management Insight
How to Discourage Employees   43
The Work of Mary Parker Follett   44
The Hawthorne Studies and Human Relations   45
Theory X and Theory Y   46
Management Science Theory   47
Organizational Environment Theory   48
The Open-Systems View   48

Contingency Theory 49

Managing Globally
Philips' Organic Structure Works 51

Tips for Managers
Applying Management Principles 52
Summary and Review 52
Management in Action 54
A Shake-Up at Eastman Kodak 56
Mr. Edens Profits from Watching His Workers'
Every Move 57

Part Two

The Environment of Management 59

Chapter 3

The Organizational Environment 60

A Case in Contrast
From Crown Corporation to Privatization 61

What is the Organizational Environment? 63
The Task Environment 64
Suppliers 64
Distributors 65
Customers 65
Competitors 66

Management Insight
It's Hard to Get Into the Lottery Ticket Printing Business 67
The Industry Life Cycle 68
The General Environment 70
Economic Forces 70
Technological Forces 71

Management Insight
Computer-Aided Design Makes a Difference at
Algonquin Automotive 72
Sociocultural Forces 72
Demographic Forces 73
Political and Legal Forces 74

Management Insight
NB Power Faces Deregulation 74

Ethics in Action
Chapters' Code of Conduct 75
Global Forces 76

Tips for Managers
Forces in the Environment 76
Managing the Organizational
Environment 76
Reducing the Impact of Environmental Forces 77
Creating an Organizational Structure and
Control Systems 78

Boundary-Spanning Roles 79

Managing Diversity
Canadian Companies Mentor Aboriginal Businesses 81
Managers as Agents of Change 82

Tips for Managers
Managing the Organizational Environment 83
Summary and Review 83
Management in Action 84
The Brewing Industry 86
Levi's is Hiking Up its Pants 87

Chapter 4

The Global Environment 90

A Case in Contrast
Responding to NAFTA 91

The Changing Global Environment 93
Declining Barriers to Trade and Investment 93
Declining Barriers of Distance and Culture 94
Effects of Free Trade on Managers 95

Management Insight
The BC Wine Industry and the Free Trade Agreement 96
The Global Task Environment 97
Suppliers 98

Managing Globally
Spectramind Phones You From New Delhi 99
Distributors 99
Customers 100
Competitors 100
The Global General Environment 101
Political and Legal Forces 101
Economic Forces 102

Managing Globally
CoolBrands Takes Ice Cream to North Korea 103
Changes in Political and Legal and Economic
Forces 103
Sociocultural Forces 105

Tips for Managers
Understanding the Global Environment 108
Choosing a Way to Expand Internationally 108
Importing and Exporting 108
Licensing and Franchising 109
Strategic Alliances 109

Managing Globally
How Scotiabank Moved to Latin America 110
Wholly Owned Foreign Subsidiaries 111
Impediments to an Open Global
Environment 111
Government-Imposed Impediments 112
Self-Imposed Ethical Impediments 112

Ethics in Action
Maiwa Handprints Pays Third World Artisans More   113

Tips for Managers
Managing the Global Environment   114
Summary and Review   114
Management in Action   115
The Road Not Taken   117
Predictable Trade Regimes Essential For
Small Business   118

Chapter 5

Ethics, Social Responsibility,
and Diversity   120

A Case in Contrast
**Ethical Stances at Pembina and
Bridgestone**   121

Ethics and Stakeholders   123
Sources of an Organization's Code of Ethics   125

Managing Globally
Should Canadians Be Doing Business in Sudan?   127

Ethics in Action
How to Make Profits and Harm Clients   128
What Behaviours Are Ethical?   129

Ethics in Action
Is it Right to Use Child Labour?   130
Why Would Managers Behave Unethically
Toward Other Stakeholders?   131
Promoting Ethics   132

Tips for Managers
Championing Ethical Behaviour   133
Social Responsibility   133
Approaches to Social Responsibility   134
Why Be Socially Responsible?   135
Managing an Increasingly Diverse
Workforce   136
The Ethical Imperative to Manage Diversity
Effectively   137

Focus on Diversity
Sex Discrimination at BioChem Pharma Inc.   138
Effectively Managing Diversity Makes Good
Legal Sense   139
Effectively Managing Diversity Makes Good
Business Sense   139
Why Are Diverse Employees Sometimes
Treated Unfairly?   140
How to Manage Diversity Effectively   142
Increasing Diversity Awareness   142
Increasing Diversity Skills   142
Techniques for Increasing Diversity
Awareness and Skills   143

The Importance of Top-Management
Commitment to Diversity   144

Focus on Diversity
Sweetgrass Comes to the RCMP   144

Tips for Managers
Managing an Increasingly Diverse Workforce   145
Sexual Harassment   146
Forms of Sexual Harassment   146
Steps Managers Can Take to Eradicate
Sexual Harassment   147
Summary and Review   148
Management in Action   149
Mentoring Diverse Employees Pays Off   151
Stuff Your Gold Watch   152

Part Three

Managing Decision Making and
Planning   153

Chapter 6

The Manager as a Decision Maker   154

A Case in Contrast
**A Tale of Two Decisions at Calling
Systems International**   155

The Nature of Managerial Decision
Making   157
Programmed and Nonprogrammed
Decision Making   158
The Classical Model   159
The Administrative Model   159

Management Insight
Marketing Beavis and Butt-Head Trading Cards   162
Steps in the Decision-Making Process   163
Recognize the Need for a Decision   163
Generate Alternatives   164
Assess Alternatives   164
Choose Among Alternatives   165
Implement the Chosen Alternative   166
Learn from Feedback   166

Tips for Managers
Managing the Decision-Making Process   166
Cognitive Biases and Decision Making   167
Prior Hypothesis Bias   167

Management Insight
Turning Pestilence Into Profit   168
Representativeness Bias   168
Illusion of Control   168
Escalating Commitment   168

Be Aware of Your Biases   169
Group Decision Making   169
  The Perils of Groupthink   169
  Devil's Advocacy and Dialectical Inquiry   170
  Diversity Among Decision Makers   171

Focus on Diversity
Kids Help Improve Decision Making at The BrainStore   171
Organizational Learning and Creativity   172
  Creating a Learning Organization   172
  Promoting Individual Creativity   173
  Promoting Group Creativity   174
  Promoting Creativity at the Global Level   175

Managing Globally
Building Cross-Cultural Creativity   176

Tips for Managers
Improving Decision Making   177
Information and the Manager's Job   177
  Attributes of Useful Information   177
  Information Systems and Technology   179
  Information and Decisions   179
The Information Technology Revolution   180
Summary and Review   180
Management in Action   182
  CP Wants to be Leaner, Meaner: To Sell Off
    Core Business   184
  How Disney Keeps Ideas Coming   185

Chapter 7

The Manager as a Planner and
Strategist   188

A Case in Contrast
  Gerald Pencer Starts a Cola War   189

An Overview of the Planning Process   191
  Levels of Planning   192
  Who Plans?   194
  Time Horizons of Plans   194
  Standing Plans and Single-Use Plans   195
  Why Planning is Important   195
  Scenario Planning   196

Tips for Managers
Planning   197
Determining the Organization's Vision,
Mission and Goals   197
  Defining the Business   197

Focus on Diversity
Native Healing Centre Comes to General Hospital   198
  Establishing Major Goals   198
Formulating Strategy   199
  SWOT Analysis   200

Management Insight
Finning Narrows its Focus   201
  The Five Forces Model   202
Formulating Corporate-Level Strategies   203

Managing Globally
E.D. Smith Wants to Expand to the United States   203
  Concentration on a Single Business   204
  Diversification   204
  International Expansion   206
  Vertical Integration   207

Managing Globally
McDonald's Vertically Integrates to Preserve Quality   209
Formulating Business-Level Strategies   210
  Low-Cost Strategy   210
  Differentiation Strategy   210
  "Stuck in the Middle"   211
  Focused Low-Cost and Focused
    Differentiation Strategies   211
Formulating Functional-Level Strategies   212
Planning and Implementing Strategy   214

Tips for Managers
Strategy   214
Summary and Review   215
Management in Action   216
  De Zen and the Art of Home Maintenance   218
  Holding its Own   220

Part Four

Managing Organizational
Architecture   221

Chapter 8

Managing Organizational Structure   222

A Case in Contrast
  **Altamira Moves from its Entrepreneurial
  Roots to a Team Structure**   223

Designing Organizational Structure   225
  The Organizational Environment   226
  Strategy   226
  Technology   226
  Human Resources   228
Grouping Tasks Into Jobs: Job Design   228
  Job Enlargement and Job Enrichment   230
  The Job Characteristics Model   230
Grouping Jobs Into Functions and
Divisions   232

Tips for Managers
Designing Structure and Jobs   232

Functional Structure   232

Divisional Structures: Product, Market, and Geographic   234

Management Insight
Cascades Inc.'s Product Structure   236

Management Insight
From Geographic to Market Structure at Royal Bank   238

Matrix and Product Team Designs   238

Hybrid Structure   241

Coordinating Functions and Divisions   241

Allocating Authority   241

Managing Globally
Procter & Gamble's New World Hierarchy   244

Strategic Alliances and Network Structure   245

Focus on Diversity
Membertou Development Seeks Jobs for the Mi'kmaq   246

Management Insight
Ryder Creates Teams Through Outsourcing   247

Tips for Managers
Choosing a Structure   248

Summary and Review   248

Management in Action   249

The Organizing Approach at Microsoft   252

Survival of the Fittest   253

Chapter 9

Organizational Control and Culture   254

A Case in Contrast
Different Approaches to Output Control Create Different Cultures   255

What is Organizational Control?   257

The Importance of Organizational Control   257

Managing Globally
Skoda—A Laughingstock No More   259

Control Systems   259

The Control Process   260

Management Insight
Nacan Products Promotes Safety   263

Management Insight
WestJet's Employees Control Costs   264

Output Control   265

Financial Measures of Performance   265

Organizational Goals   266

Operating Budgets   267

Problems with Output Control   268

Ethics in Action
ScotiaMcLeod Looks to Become a Conservative Blue-Chip Safe House   269

Behaviour Control   269

Direct Supervision   269

Management by Objectives   270

Bureaucratic Control   271

Problems with Bureaucratic Control   271

Tips for Managers
Control   272

Organizational Culture and Clan Control   273

Creating a Strong Organizational Culture   273

Management Insight
Ray Kroc: McDonald's Hero   277

Culture and Managerial Action   278

Summary and Review   280

Management in Action   281

Mutual Life Goes Public, and Becomes Clarica   283

Fostering Corporate Culture   284

Chapter 10

Human Resource Management   286

A Case in Contrast
Training and Development at Comtek and TD Canada Trust   287

Strategic Human Resource Management   289

Overview of the Components of HRM   289

Management Insight
At Greenarm Management, Family Comes First   290

The Legal Environment of HRM   291

Recruitment and Selection   292

Human Resource Planning   292

Focus on Diversity
Amusement Parks Hire Seniors   293

Job Analysis   294

External and Internal Recruitment   295

Management Insight
Recruiting Challenges at Two Small Companies   295

The Selection Process   297

Management Insight
Broadening the Pre-Employment Interview   298

Ethics in Action
The Costs of Withholding Negative Information in References   300

Tips for Managers
Recruitment and Selection   301

Training and Development   301

Types of Training   301

Types of Development   303

Issues in Career Development   303

The Organization's Responsibilities   304

The Employee's Responsibilities   304
Performance Appraisal and Feedback   305
Types of Performance Appraisal   306

Management Insight
Using Appraisals to Manage Training   307
Who Appraises Performance?   309
Effective Performance Feedback   310

Tips for Managers
Performance Appraisal   311
Pay and Benefits   312
Pay Level   312
Pay Structure   312
Benefits   313
Labour Relations   314
Unions   314
Collective Bargaining   315
Summary and Review   315
Management in Action   317
Human Resource Management in an Era
of Downsizing   319
The Blessed: Under 30, They Are
the Darlings of the Industry–
But They Want More   320

Part Five
Managing Individuals and Groups   321

Chapter 11
The Manager as a Person   322

A Case in Contrast
**Three Ways to Run a Bank: Insensitive,
Charismatic, or Consensual**   323

**Enduring Characteristics: Personality
Traits**   325
The Big Five Personality Traits   325

Focus on Diversity
Openness to Experience Useful at Any Age   327
Other Personality Traits That Affect
Managerial Behaviour   328
Values, Attitudes, and Moods   329
Values: Terminal and Instrumental   330

Managing Globally
Values of the Overseas Chinese   331
Attitudes   332
Moods   333
Perceptions   334

Focus on Diversity
Exercisers are "Better" People   334

Factors That Influence Perception   335
Ways to Ensure Accurate Perceptions   336

Tips for Managers
Perception   336
Stress   336
Consequences of Stress   336
Sources of Managerial Stress   337
Coping With Stress   338

Management Insight
Life Balance Improves Performance   339

Tips for Managers
Stress   340
Summary and Review   341
Management in Action   342
Stamina: Who Has It, Why It's Important,
and How to Get It   344
In Her Father's Footsteps   345

Chapter 12
Motivation   348

A Case in Contrast
**Motivating Employees at Eastman Kodak
and Mars**   349

The Nature of Motivation   351
Need Theories   353
Maslow's Hierarchy of Needs   353
Alderfer's ERG Theory   354
Herzberg's Motivator–Hygiene Theory   355

Management Insight
Treating People Right at Pazmac Enterprises   356
Expectancy Theory   356
Expectancy   356
Instrumentality   357
Valence   358
Bringing it All Together   358

Managing Globally
Motorola Promotes High Motivation in Malaysia   359
Goal-Setting Theory   360
Reinforcement Theory   361

Management Insight
Maple Leaf Raffles Trucks   362
Equity Theory   363
Equity   364
Inequity   365
Ways to Restore Equity   365

Tips for Managers
Expectancy and Equity Theories   366
Pay and Motivation   367

Management Insight
Paying Workers Well is Not Enough   368
Basing Merit Pay on Individual, Group, or
Organizational Performance   368
Salary Increase or Bonus?   368

Management Insight
Failed Performance Rewarded?   369
Examples of Merit Pay Plans   370

Management Insight
Semiconductors Simplify the Administration of
Piece-Rate Pay   370
Summary and Review   372
Management in Action   373
Motivating with Stretch Targets   375
Telus Gives Stock Options to all its Employees   376

Chapter 13

Leadership   378

A Case in Contrast
**Levy Fosters Growth While Irwin
Fosters Decline**   379

The Nature of Leadership   381
Personal Leadership Style and Managerial Tasks   381
Leadership Styles Across Cultures   382
Power: The Key to Leadership   383

Ethics in Action
Curtailing Coercive Power Makes Good Business Sense   384
Empowerment: An Ingredient in Modern
Management   386
Trait and Behaviour Models of Leadership   387
The Trait Model   387
The Behaviour Model   388

Management Insight
Consideration and Customer Service at Staples and
Chiat/Day   388
Contingency Models of Leadership   389
Fiedler's Contingency Model   390
Hersey–Blanchard's Situational Leadership Theory   392
Path–Goal Theory   392

Management Insight
Turnaround in the Forestry Industry   393
The Leader Substitutes Model   394
Bringing it All Together   395

Tips for Managers
Contingency Models of Leadership   395
Transactional and Transformational
Leadership   396

Managing Globally
Transformational Leadership in South Korea   399

Tips for Managers
Transformational Leadership   400
Gender and Leadership   400
Summary and Review   402
Management in Action   403
Cynthia Trudell: Leading in a Man's World   405
M&M Founder Carving Bigger Slice
of Market: Specialty Meats   406

Chapter 14

Groups and Teams   408

A Case in Contrast
**Teams Work Wonders at Willow
Manufacturing**   409

Groups, Teams, and Organizational
Effectiveness   410
Groups and Teams as Performance Enhancers   411

Management Insight
Creating Workplaces That Encourage Teamwork   412
Groups, Teams, and Responsiveness
to Customers   412
Teams and Innovation   413

Managing Globally
Cross-Cultural Team's Innovation Yields the
1996 Honda Civic   413
Groups and Teams as Motivators   414
Types of Groups and Teams   415
The Top-Management Team   415
Research and Development Teams   416
Command Groups   416
Task Forces   416
Self-Managed Work Teams   416

Management Insight
Self-Managed Teams at Langley Memorial Reduce
Management Costs   417
Virtual Teams   418

Management Insight
Virtual Teams Require Planning   418
Beware! Teams Aren't Always the Answer   419
Group Dynamics   419
Group Size, Tasks, and Roles   420
Group Leadership   424
Group Development Over Time   424
Group Norms   426
Group Cohesiveness   428

Focus on Diversity
Promoting Cohesiveness in a Diverse Team at
Mercedes-Benz   430
Managing Groups and Teams for High
Performance   432

Motivating Group Members to Achieve
Organizational Goals 432
Preventing Groupthink 432
Reducing Social Loafing in Groups 433
Helping Groups to Manage Conflict
Effectively 434

Tips for Managers
Group Dynamics and Managing Groups and Teams
for High Performance 434
Summary and Review 435
Management in Action 436
Teams Manage AES (With the Help of a Few
Managers) 438
Team Building Adventures More Than Game 439

Chapter 15

Communication 442

A Case in Contrast
**The Importance of Good Communication
Skills** 443

Communication in Organizations 445
The Importance of Good Communication 445

Management Insight
TD Canada Trust's New Boss Likes to Talk 446
The Communication Process 446
The Role of Perception in Communication 447
The Dangers of Ineffective Communication 448
Information Richness and Communication
Media 449
Face-to-Face Communication 450
Spoken Communication Electronically
Transmitted 451
Personally Addressed Written Communication 451

Ethics in Action
Eavesdropping on Voice Mail and E-mail 453
Impersonal Written Communication 454
Communication Networks 454
Communication Networks in Groups
and Teams 454
Organizational Communication Networks 456
Technical Advances in Communication 457
The Internet 457
Intranets 457
Groupware 458

Management Insight
Is Anybody Out There? 458

Tips for Managers
Information Richness and Communication Media 459
Developing Communication Skills 459
Communication Skills for Senders 460

Focus on Diversity
Options in Communication Media for the Deaf 461
Communication Skills for Receivers 462
Understanding Linguistic Styles 464

Tips for Managers
Sending and Receiving Messages 467
Summary and Review 467
Management in Action 469
Stinging Office E-Mail Lights "Firestorm" 471
Out of Sight, Not Out of Mind 472

Chapter 16

Organizational Conflict, Negotiation, and Politics 474

A Case in Contrast
The Power of Political Skills 475

Organizational Conflict 477

Management Insight
Conflict at McCain Foods 477
Types of Conflict 479

Ethics in Action
Cayoosh Resort 480
Sources of Conflict 481
Conflict Management Strategies 482

Tips for Managers
Handling Conflict 485
Negotiation Strategies for Integrative
Bargaining 486

Management Insight
Debra McPherson and the BC Nurses' Union 487

Tips for Managers
Negotiation 488
Organizational Politics 488
The Importance of Organizational Politics 488
Political Strategies for Increasing Power 489
Political Strategies for Exercising Power 491

Tips for Managers
Political Strategies 493
Summary and Review 494
Management in Action 495
Unions Find Fertile Ground at Newspapers 497
Half a Loaf at Blimpie 498

Chapter 17

Organizational Change 500

A Case in Contrast
Facing the Winds of Change 501

Managing Organizational Change   503
   Assessing the Need for Change   503
   Lewin's Three-Stage Model of Change   504
Resistance to Change   505

Focus on Diversity
Deloitte & Touche Looks for a More Humane Workplace   505
   Individual Resistance to Change   506

Management Insight
IMMI Overcomes Resistance to Change   507
   Organizational Resistance to Change   507
Overcoming Resistance to Change   508

Management Insight
Conducting Change in a Unionized Environment   509
Changing the Production System   511
Managing Change By Improving
Quality   511
   Total Quality Management   512
   Putting TQM Into Action: The Management
     Challenge   513
Managing Change by Improving
Efficiency   514
   Total Quality Management and Efficiency   515
   Just-in-Time Inventory and Efficiency   515

Managing Globally
The *Kanban* System in Japan   515
   Kaizen (Continuous Improvement) and Efficiency   517
   Process Reengineering and Efficiency   517

Tips for Managers
Changing the Production System   518
Changing Production Systems: Some
Remaining Issues   518

Ethics in Action
The Human Cost of Improving Productivity   519
Changing Organizational Culture   519
Summary and Review   520
Management in Action   522
   Applying *Kaizen* to Improve Production
     at Ventra   524
   In the Clutches of a Slowdown   525

Integrated Cases   529
Glossary   535
Endnotes   549
Photo Credits   576
Index   577

Preface

Welcome to the first Canadian edition of *Contemporary Management*. This book has received a favourable reception and level of support in its American version, and I am delighted at the opportunity to introduce a product of such high quality to the Canadian market. This book is innovative in its attempt to integrate contemporary management theories and approaches into the analysis of management and organizations. Our goal has been to distill new and classic theorizing and research into a contemporary framework that is compatible with the traditional focus on management as planning, organizing, leading, and controlling, but which transcends this traditional approach.

Users and reviewers of previous editions report that students appreciate and enjoy *Contemporary Management's* presentation of management, a presentation that makes its relevance obvious even to those who lack exposure to a "real-life" management context. Students like both the book's content and the way we relate management theory to real-life examples to drive home the message that management matters both because it determines how well organizations perform, and because managers and organizations affect the lives of people who work inside them and people outside the organization, such as customers and shareholders.

The contemporary nature of our approach can be seen most clearly by our approach to writing about the subject: the study of management is not just for managers and would-be managers; it helps everyone who works in an organization understand how and why priorities get set. As you examine our Table of Contents and peruse our treatment of management issues, you will see why *Contemporary Management* outshines other management books. The concepts and theories we discuss show how managers deal with the many new issues and challenges they face, such as promoting and sustaining a competitive advantage, managing new information technology, developing big global organizations, and managing a diverse workforce. We also show how this happens in the Canadian environment, where managers are more likely to face the challenges of unionization and public sector organizations.

Unique Coverage

As you will see, we have some chapters and material that are not contained in any other Canadian management book. Chapter 9, for example, "Organizational Control and Culture," has the strongest coverage of culture among competing texts. As another example, Chapter 11, "The Manager as a Person," discusses managers as real people with their own personalities, strengths, weaknesses, opportunities, and problems. From this chapter, students will relate to managers as people similar to themselves. Students will also appreciate the challenges managers face and how, as future managers, they can successfully meet them. Chapter 15, "Communication," offers a broad overview of the communication process and then discusses the skills one needs to be a better communicator *and* listener. Another unique chapter for a management book is Chapter 16, "Organizational Conflict, Politics, and Negotiation." While some other management texts cover conflict, we go much further in also exploring how managers can successfully manage organizational politics and negotiation.

Emphasis on Applied Management

Our contemporary approach means that we have gone to great lengths to bring the manager back into the subject matter of management. That is, we have written our chapters from the perspective of current or future managers to illustrate, in a hands-on way, the problems and opportunities they face and how they can effectively meet them. For example, in Chapter 5 we provide an integrated treatment of ethics, diversity, and sexual harassment that clearly explains their significance to practising managers. In Chapter 7, on planning and strategy, we provide an integrated treatment of highlighting the choices managers face as they go about performing the planning role. In Chapter 8, on organizational structure, we discuss how managers make decisions about the appropriate organizational form in which to structure the organization. And in both Chapter 10, on human resources management, and Chapter 17, on organizational change, we look at how managers have met the challenges of unionization, a particularly important question to Canadian managers. These are just some of the examples of applied management. Throughout the text, we emphasize important issues managers face and how management theory, research, and practice can help them and their organizations be effective.

Rich and Relevant Examples

An important feature of our book is the way we use real-world examples and stories about managers and companies to drive home the applied lessons to students. Our reviewers were unanimous in their praise of the sheer range and depth of the rich, interesting examples we use to illustrate the chapter material and make it come alive. We've included coverage of large and small firms, from a variety of industries in both the public sector and the private sector, and from all of the provinces and territories.

A CASE IN CONTRAST Each chapter opens with a feature called "A Case in Contrast," which contrasts the behaviours and actions of two managers and organizations to help demonstrate the uncertainty and challenges surrounding the management process. We cover such organizations as Calgary-based WestJet and Petro-Can; Saint-Laurent, Quebec-based Gildan Activewear; Toronto-based Altamira Investment Services, Willow Manufacturing, and Moore Business Corporation; and Vancouver-based QLT and Vancouver's City Hall.

TIPS FOR MANAGERS Each chapter contains the feature "Tips for Managers," which distills the lessons that students can take from the chapter and use to develop their management skills.

much time developing and assessing alternatives that decisions take a long time to make, and even when decisions are made, it often is not clear exactly what has been decided. The German scientists complain that the North American scientists will not accept advice and criticism. The Japanese scientists complain that they are not involved in the main decision-making process. Moreover, each group of scientists has complained that the other groups are hoarding information and ideas to protect their individual and their company's interests, thus undermining the joint creative process.[16]

Despite these problems, the project continues. However, the major breakthroughs that the three companies hope to achieve by bringing their scientists together have not yet occurred. Managers directing the joint venture have observed that, for the most part, cooperation and brainstorming are occurring not among the different groups of scientists but within each group. Managers believe that creativity will be further enhanced by increasing cooperation across the groups—the original goal of the project—and they are planning to develop more group training programs to break down cross-cultural barriers and encourage a truly cross-national approach to problem solving.

Tips for Managers

Improving Decision Making

1. Be aware of the operation of cognitive biases and test the assumptions managers use to frame problems, select alternatives, and make decisions.
2. Recognize the advantages of using diverse decision making groups.
3. Use devil's advocacy and dialectical inquiry to guard against groupthink.
4. Take all possible steps to promote creativity at the individual and group level and make a technique like brainstorming a routine part of the problem-solving process.

Information and the Manager's Job

Managers cannot make decisions—let alone plan, organize, lead, and control effectively—unless they have access to information. Information is the source of the knowledge and intelligence that they need to make the right decisions. ...ation, however, is not the ...e data.[17] **Data** are ... summarized, and ... and unor... ...cts such as ... er of ...

data Raw, unsummar...

will be used when e-mail abuse is suspected and the consequences that will result when e-mail abuse is confirmed. The increasing use of voice mail and e-mail in companies large and small has led to some ethical concerns, as depicted in the following "Ethics in Action."

Ethics in Action

Eavesdropping on Voice Mail and E-Mail

Should managers listen to their subordinates' voice mail messages? Should they read their employees e-mail? Many employees who currently use voice mail and e-mail would probably answer this question with an emphatic "No!" Just as workers do not expect their bosses to eavesdrop on their telephone conversations, intercepting voice mail messages without the consent of the receiver seems to be unethical and an invasion of privacy. Some managers evidently feel differently, however. Over 20 percent of managers contacted for a recent survey indicated that they monitored their subordinates' voice mail, e-mail, or computer files. Some of these managers contend that because the systems the employees are using are company owned or are paid for with company funds, managers should have access to the information contained on them.

National Post writer Jonathan Kay recently interviewed an employee who was fired for forwarding dirty jokes to clients via e-mail.[31] Kay called the man Fred Jones, since he didn't want to be identified. Jones sold network computers for a living and during this employment had received consistently good performance reviews and always received top bonuses. Jones believed he sent the jokes only to the clients he thought would like them, and assumed that a client would tell him if he or she did not. Unbeknownst to him, however, a client had complained to the company about the dirty jokes and after the company investigated, they fired Jones. Jones still doesn't completely understand why he was fired. He feels his e-mail was private, and no different from telling jokes at the water cooler.

Current law may be on the side of employers, however, at least in some instances. In Canada, employee information, including e-mails they send, is not necessarily private. The Federal Privacy and Access to Information Acts, in place since 1983, apply to all federal government departments, most federal ...cies, and some federal cro... ...orations. The... ...collection, ...disclosure of p... ...ls right...

ETHICS IN ACTION The chapters also contain various kinds of boxes: The boxes entitled "**Management Insights**" illustrate the topics of the chapter, and the "**Ethics in Action**," "**Managing Globally**," and "**Focus on Diversity**" boxes examine the chapter topic from each of these perspectives. These are not "boxes" in the traditional sense, meaning they're not disembodied from the chapter narrative. These thematic applications are fully integrated into the reading so that they will engage students while illustrating the chapter material. Through access to low-cost foreign sources of inputs. This approach allows managers to keep costs low.

Strategic alliances can be formed for other purposes than entering foreign markets, however. Sault Ste. Marie-based Algoma Steel was looking for a strategic alliance in Spring 2001, as it was emerging from creditor protection. Company president Sandy Adam acknowledged that an alliance would help defray the costs of entering new markets. Hamilton, ON-based Dofasco Inc. developed key strategic alliances with National Steel of Japan and France's Usinor to develop higher-quality steels that result in better financial returns. The "Focus on Diversity" highlights an alliance formed between the Mi'kmaq in Nova Scotia and a number of Canadian companies.

Focus on Diversity

Membertou Development Seeks Jobs for the Mi'kmaq

Starting in early 2001, leaders of the Cape Breton Mi'kmaq reserve signed joint venture agreements with SNC-Lavalin Group, Sodexho Marriott Services, Ledgers Canada, Georgia-Pacific and Clearwater Fine Foods through the Membertou Development Corporation.

The parties signed what they called joint venture agreements. For the 1000-person band, with an unemployment rate of 50 percent, the agreements should mean more jobs. The companies will find it easier to bid on government contracts, since their use of native workers will be viewed favourably.

Bernd Christmas, head of Halifax-based Membertou Development Corp., explained what he saw as the key benefit of the partnerships. "We have to develop our own revenue streams and get away from dependency on the federal government. That's the only way to true self-government."

Clearwater Fine Foods will be able to buy all the snow crab of Membertou fishermen, and has agreed to hire 20 native workers for its processing line, which represents a third of the plant's workforce. The Georgia-Pacific agreement is expected to bring jobs in the mining sector, and Ledgers Canada will work with the band to provide financial consulting services. The SNC-Lavalin agreement with Membertou says it will "explore jointly mutually beneficial collaborative efforts to develop projects in the Maritime provinces."

Sodexho Marriott believes that its agreement with Membertou will give it an advantage...

these boxes, students will learn about such organizations as Vancouver-based Mountain Equipment Co-op and Maiwa Handprints; Prince George, BC-based Eagleye Log Homes; Calgary-based Talisman Energy Inc. and Calaway Park; Edmonton-based Finning Ltd.; Winnipeg-based Pollard Banknote; The Native Healing Centre at Regina's General Hospital; Markham, Ontario-based CoolBrands International; Montreal-based BioChem Pharma Inc. and PEAK Investment; Kingsey Falls, Quebec-based Cascades Inc.; Winona, Ontario-based E.D. Smith & Sons Ltd.; New Brunswick-based Greenarm Management; and Halifax-based Membertou Development Corporation.

Each chapter also contains two "Management Cases." Some of the cases were written specifically for this textbook, while others are taken directly from the pages of Canadian print media, including the *National Post*, *The Globe and Mail*, the *Ottawa Citizen*, and *The Vancouver Sun*. The cases taken from the media show students fully detailed real-world examples of relevant managerial action. Through both kinds of end-of-chapter cases, students will be introduced to organizations such as the CBC; Guelph, Ontario-based Sleeman Breweries Ltd.; Moncton, New Brunswick-based Amcor PET Packaging; Toronto-based The Brothers Markle Inc. and Magna Corporation; and such Canadian managers as Belinda Stronach, Cynthia Trudell, Vic De Zen of Royal Group Technologies Ltd., and Mac Voisin of M and M Meat Shops.

These organizations represent only a small sample of the breadth and depth of organizational coverage in *Contemporary Management*. The large, well-known companies of Canada, and their CEOs and managers are also covered in some detail. Coverage is not confined to Canada, however, so students will also be exposed to management practices in other parts of the world, through additional examples provided.

Finally, the book contains two "Integrative Cases" to help instructors and students alike apply a broad range of theory to the organizational and managerial problems of Canadian Tire and Kooshies Baby Products.

Flexible Organization

Another factor of interest to instructors concerns the way we have designed the grouping of chapters to allow instructors to teach the chapter material in the order that best suits their needs. For example, the more micro-oriented instructor can follow Chapters 1 and 2 with 11 through 16 and then do the more macro chapters. The more macro-oriented professor can follow Chapters 1 and 2 with 3 through 7, jump to 17 and then do the micro Chapters 11–16. Our sequencing of parts and chapters gives the instructor considerable freedom to design the course that best suits him or her. Instructors are not tied to the planning, organizing, leading, controlling framework, even though our presentation remains consistent with this approach.

Experiential Learning Features

We have given considerable time and attention to developing state-of-the-art experiential end-of-chapter learning exercises that we hope will also drive home the meaning of management to students. Grouped together at the end of each chapter in the section called Management in Action, they include:

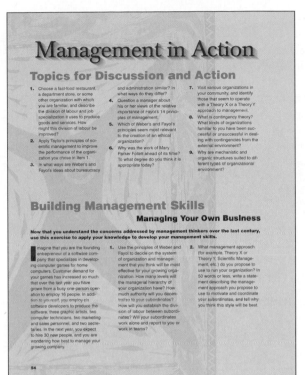

TOPICS FOR DISCUSSION AND ACTION A set of chapter-related questions and points for reflection, some of which ask students to research actual management issues and learn first-hand from practicing managers.

BUILDING MANAGEMENT SKILLS A self-development exercise that asks students to apply what they have learned to their own experience of organizations and managers or to the experiences of others.

SMALL GROUP BREAKOUT EXERCISE This unique exercise is designed to allow instructors in large classes to utilize interactive experiential exercises in groups of 3–4 students. The instructor calls on students to break up into small groups—simply by turning to people around them—and all students participate in the exercise in class. A mechanism is provided for the different groups to share what they have learned with each other.

EXPLORING THE WORLD WIDE WEB Two Internet exercises designed to draw students into the Web and give them experience with the new information systems, while applying what they have learned.

MANAGEMENT CASE   A case for discussion, drawing on contemporary, real-world managers and organizations, which we have written to highlight chapter themes and issues.

MANAGEMENT CASE IN THE NEWS   An actual article from a business publication like *The Globe and Mail* or *National Post* that shows how practising managers are facing the issues students have just learned about.

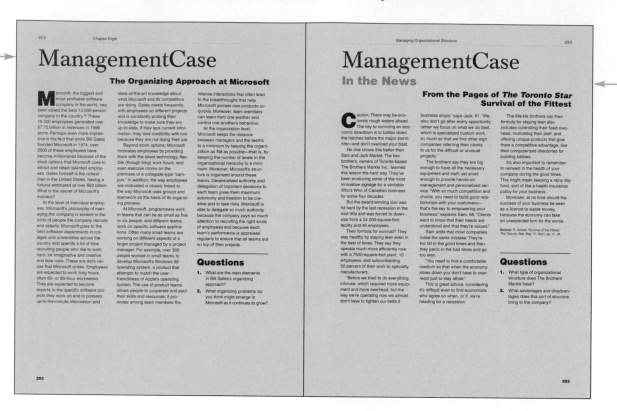

Our idea is that instructors can select from these exercises and vary them over the semester so that students can learn the meaning of management through many different avenues. These exercises complement the chapter material and have been class tested to add to the overall learning experience, and students report that they both learn from them and enjoy them.

Integrated Learning System

Great care was used in the creation of the supplemental materials to accompany *Contemporary Management.* The textbook authors were involved in the entire process to ensure quality and consistency with the textbook. Whether you are a seasoned professor or a newly minted instructor, you'll find our support materials to be the most thorough and thoughtful ever created!

Student Resources

STUDENT STUDY GUIDE   adapted by Nancy Langton. Access to this online interactive study guide is free to purchasers of new copies of the textbook. It includes an outline of each of the chapters; multiple choice and true/false application questions; Internet application questions; a "Student Journal"; and Video exercises. This comprehensive learning aid will assist students in their under-standing of key concepts, and help them prepare for exams.

WEB SITE AND ONLINE LEARNING CENTRE   at http://www.mcgraw hill.ca/college/jones. A resource for faculty and students, the *Contemporary Management* Web site contains information for lecture and learning enhancement. Along with features of the text and author biographical information, you'll find CBC Video Cases, Web exercises, outside research assignments, links to national and international news, a career area for students, and other course-enhancing materials.

Instructor Resources

INSTRUCTOR'S RESOURCE MANUAL   Revised by Nancy Langton, contains:

- Detailed chapter outlines
- Detailed answers on all the Management in Action (i.e., end-of-chapter) material
- Teaching Notes on CBC Video Cases
- Several lecture enhancers per chapter

CBC VIDEO CASES   selected by Nancy Langton. Available on VHS and from the Web site, these CBC Video Cases present management decision making in the Canadian environment. The CBC Video Teaching Notes are in the Instructor's Resource Manual.

TEST BANK   by Jeff Young of Mount Saint Vincent University. This volume contains over 100 test items per chapter, including multiple choice, true/false, ap-plied, and essay. Each question is ranked in terms of difficulty and page-referenced to the textbook.

BROWNSTONE DIPLOMA COMPUTERIZED TEST GENERATION SYSTEM   available on the Instructor's CD-ROM. An easy-to-use computer-ized version of the test bank available in Windows format. This easy-to-use soft-ware allows for quick and easy generation of tests, exams and pop quizzes. Instructors can generate multiple versions of the same quiz and an accompanying answer key for each version. Help-desk support is provided to text adopters through an exclusive McGraw-Hill Ryerson toll-free number.

POWERPOINT® CLASSROOM PRESENTATION SOFTWARE adapted by Nancy Langton. Over 300 images, including all significant figures and tables from the text, for use in the classroom or as handouts are packaged ready-to-run with Windows installation program and a slide viewer. No additional soft-ware is required, but slides can be modified with Microsoft® PowerPoint® for Windows. Speaker's notes are included for each PowerPoint slide. The slides are available on the Instructor's CD-ROM and also from the Instructor's Centre on the Web site.

PROFILES IN MANAGEMENT VIDEO SERIES   These US videos are available to Canadian text adopters and contain ten segments profiling the man-agement styles and practices of real managers on the job. Students will get real insight into the job of managers at various levels within an organization, and among very different types of businesses. Companies profiled include: Second City, Handy Andy, Specialized Bicycle, Tellabs, Washburn Guitars, Southwest

Airlines, and 1st Chicago Bank. For more information on these, contact your local sales representative.

SUPPLEMENTARY VIDEO CASES AND NOTES   The 17 videos that accompanied the US version of the textbook are also available to Canadian text adopters. These 7–12 minute video segments tie concepts from the text directly to a real company profile. Cases and additional instructional material is provided on the instructor area of the Online Learning Centre, allowing for ultimate flexibility for faculty. For more information on these, contact your local sales representative.

INSTRUCTOR PRESENTATION CD-ROM   This is state-of-the-art technology that provides a single resource for faculty to customize in-class presentations. This CD-ROM contains:

- Instructor's Resource Manual
- Test Bank and Computerized Test Bank
- PowerPoint Classroom Presentation Software
- Student Study Quizzes
- CBC and US Video Clips
- Special Presentation Platform that allows faculty to build classroom presentations in sequence using the resources from the CD.

WEB SITE AND ONLINE LEARNING CENTRE   at http://www.mcgraw hill.ca/college/jones, as detailed above, the Web site contains an Instructor Centre with materials and resources to enhance classroom instruction, including: PowerPoint materials including masters for all significant figures from the text, CBC Video Cases and Teaching Notes, Teaching Notes for US Video Cases, *Profiles in Management* Video Teaching Notes, and other teaching resources.

Acknowledgments

When Pat Ferrier, Vice President and Editorial Director at McGraw-Hill Ryerson, first approached me about Canadianizing *Contemporary Management*, I took a very deep breath. I had worked with Pat and a number of people currently at McGraw on my very first book project, with another publisher. I wondered whether we were up for the challenge of working together again. This product shows how much all of us have learned about working together in the intervening years.

In making my acknowledgments, I would be remiss if I did not thank Gareth Jones, Jennifer George, and Charles Hill for providing a truly excellent vehicle for adaptation. Without their strong foundation, I would not have been able to bring to the Canadian market a management book that is up-to-date, innovative, and full of Canadian examples, research, and statistics.

The McGraw-Hill Ryerson team has been exceptionally outstanding throughout the production of this book. From the moment I expressed interest in pursuing this project, the support, encouragement, and willingness to go above and beyond by every member of the team has been heartwarming. There is always the fear that in mentioning people by name, someone will get left off inadvertently, so I apologize for that possibility in advance. Pat Ferrier, Lenore Gray-Spence (Sponsoring Editor), Kim Brewster ("in-house" Developmental Editor), and Kelly Dickson (Manager, Editorial Services) provided a very strong core team of support in ways too numerous to mention. Dianna Little (Art Director) helped me realize my design ambitions for the book, and Jeff MacLean (Senior Marketing Manager) helped get the sales reps behind the project with extra bonuses. I enjoyed being reunited with a former DE, Lesley Mann, who continued her role as supplier of "not to be missed" news articles, even though she was not part of my official team. Lesley has an uncanny sense for knowing the kinds of background material I need for my book projects. Members of the McGraw sales team also lent a much needed hand supplying newspaper articles from hometowns, ensuring broad Canadian coverage for my examples. Four reps in particular deserve special mention for their help: Megan Farrell, Bruce McIntosh, Tracy Sawchuck, and Milton Vacon. The sales team's involvement and encouragement as I wrote was an unexpected source of support, and one that was definitely appreciated.

There are two people on this team for whom I'd like to express particular appreciation. Su Mei Ku, my very talented "day-to-day" Developmental Editor, and another repeat team player, put in long and exhausting hours helping me to get the manuscript in order. She knew and understood how to make things easier for me so that I could concentrate fully on the writing and research process. And she was always available, cheerleading all the way. I have already told her of my plans to appoint her my developmental editor for life. The other person I want to particularly acknowledge is Mike Ryan, Sales Manager at McGraw-Hill Ryerson. Mike has been a part of all of my book projects to date, formerly serving as my Acquisitions Editor at another publisher. It is really my friendship with and respect for Mike that led me to take on this project. His unwavering faith in my writing ability has challenged me to reach further than I might have imagined on each of my projects to date. I am especially grateful for his support, encouragement, and willingness to listen.

One of the key things I learned in working with this entire team was actually a reminder: different organizations have different cultures, and the same people, placed in different organizations, can respond quite differently to similar situations. These are important things for all managers and students of human behaviour to learn. Another thing I learned was the value of chocolate as a motivator. I would not be able to count the number of boxes of chocolate shipped my way—to soothe despair or exhaustion, to reward deadlines made, to keep me going through the next stage. There were flowers, kind notes and other treats as well. I could not have felt more valued or supported as an author, and I appreciated that experience. It made all of the hard work of producing this book under challenging deadlines that much easier. In short, the McGraw-Hill Ryerson team has set a new standard for showing authors that they matter.

There are additional supporting players who helped make the project go smoothly. Alison Derry did yeoman work while maintaining a sense of humour in getting the photos that you see, as well as acquiring myriad permissions. The library and photo department at the *National Post* deserve special mention for their help, most specifically, Theresa Butcher (*National Post* librarian) and Julie Nicholson (*National Post* photo department) who helped Alison a lot during this project. Laurel Sparrow was my copyeditor, and dedicated herself to the task of eliminating the numerous inconsistencies and misspellings that can crop up in a book of this length. To both Alison and Laurel, a job well done!

While the team at McGraw-Hill Ryerson was an important part of my writing experience, I also have to thank my UBC colleagues for all of their support and encouragement. Dan Muzyka, my dean, has been very supportive of my desire to write textbooks. More generally, my Organizational Behaviour and Human Resources Division colleagues can be counted on to bring various things to my attention, from newspaper articles to research reports, and to engage in various discussions with me about appropriate presentation of material. They also encouraged my writing efforts. I would like to thank them publicly for their support: Brian Bemmels, Peter Frost, Dev Jennings, Tom Knight, Sally Maitlis, Dave McPhillips, Sandra Robinson, Dan Skarlicki, Mark Thompson, and Skip Walter. Our divisional secretary, Irene Khoo, deserves special mention for helping to keep the project on track, doing some of the word processing, managing the courier packages and faxes, and always being attentive to detail. I could not ask for a better, more dedicated, or more cheerful assistant. She really helps keep everything together.

I don't think one could be an author without having good friends to encourage, and to pull one away from work. Again, I'll just single out a few. John Fleming, who introduced me to the world of writing books, continues to provide a strong mentoring role, while being perhaps the most amusing and dedicated correspondent I know. His excellent recommendations for "light" reading provided much needed breaks from writing. Pat, Alan and Nicole Carlson provided a much needed home away from home when I took short breaks in between intense periods of writing. Their hospitality helped me catch my breath each time before starting up again. The members of the Carnavaron Quilt Guild provided Monday night breaks from writing sessions, and always asked how things were going and encouraged me along the way. And finally Rob Gareau solved the problem of all those chocolates: endless workouts! His training sessions and friendship keep me in shape physically and mentally.

Reviewers of the Canadian Edition

Finally, I want to acknowledge the many reviewers of this Canadian edition for their detailed, helpful, and timely comments. They made a number of great suggestions that helped improve this textbook:

Lewis Callahan, Lethbridge College

Sherry Campbell, BCIT

Monica Diochon, St. Francis Xavier University

Gary Docherty, St. Clair College

Burt Fraughton, Nova Scotia Community College

Judy Koch, Grant MacEwan College

Louis Masson, SAIT

Colleen McKey, McMaster University

Don Smith, Georgian College

Terry Sulis, Nova Scotia Community College

Frank Vuo, Lethbridge College

Vic de Witt, Red River College

Jeff Young, Mount Saint Vincent University

I dedicate this book to my father, Peter X. Langton. He was a man of many talents, and he would have been amused beyond words to watch me write a text on management. To my family I give silent acknowledgment for everything else.

Nancy Langton
October 2001

Authors

Gareth Jones is a Professor of Management in the Lowry Mays College and Graduate School of Business at Texas A&M University. He received both his B.A. and Ph.D. from the University of Lancaster, U.K. He previously held teaching and research appointments at the University Warwick, Michigan State University, and the University of Illinois at Urbana–Champaign.

He specializes in both strategic management and organizational theory and is well known for his research that applies transaction cost analysis to explain many forms of strategic behaviour. He is currently interested in strategy process and issues concerning the development of trust and the role of affect in the strategic decision making process. He has published many articles in leading journals of the field and his recent work has appeared in the *Academy of Management Review, Journal of International Business Studies, Human Relations*, and the *Journal of Management*. One of his articles won the *Academy of Management Journal* Best Paper Award, and he is one of the most prolific authors in the *Academy of Management Review*. He is serving or has served on the editorial boards of the *Academy of Management Review*, the *Journal of Management*, and *Management Inquiry*. In addition to his academic achievements, Gareth is co-author on three other major textbooks in the management discipline, including organizational behaviour, organizational theory, and strategic management.

Jennifer George is a Professor of Management in the Lowry Mays College and Graduate School of Business at Texas A&M University. She received her B.A. in Psychology/Sociology from Wesleyan University, her M.B.A. in Finance from New York University, and her Ph.D. in Management and Organizational Behaviour from New York University.

She specializes in Organizational Behaviour and is well known for her research on affect and mood, their determinants, and their effects on various individual and group level work outcomes. She is the author of many articles in leading peer-reviewed journals, and her recent work has appeared in the *Academy of Management Review*, the *Journal of Management*, and *Human Relations*. One of her papers won the Academy of Management's Organizational Behavior Division Outstanding Competitive Paper Award. She is, or has been, on the editorial review boards of the *Journal of Applied Psychology, Academy of Management Journal, Journal of Management*, and *Journal of Managerial Issues* and was a consulting editor for the *Journal of Organizational Behavior*. She is a Fellow in the American Psychological Association, the American Psychological Society, and the Society for Industrial and Organizational Psychology.

With her husband, Gareth Jones, she has written a leading textbook in organizational behaviour. They have also collaborated on two children, Nicholas, who is seven, and Julia, who is six.

Charles W. L. Hill is the Hughes M. Blake Professor of International Business at the School of Business, University of Washington. Professor Hill received his Ph.D. in industrial organization economics in 1983 from the University of Manchester's Institute of Science and Technology (UMIST). In addition to the University of Washington, he has served on the faculties of UMIST, Texas A&M University, and Michigan State University. He has published many articles in peer-reviewed academic journals. He has also published two college textbooks, one on strategic management and the other on international business, both market leaders. Professor Hill is, or has served, on the editorial boards of several academic journals, such as the *Academy of Management Journal* and the *Strategic Management Journal* and was a consulting editor at the *Academy of Management Review*.

Professor Hill teaches in the undergraduate M.B.A. and executive M.B.A. programs at the University of Washington and has received awards for teaching excellence in these programs.

Nancy Langton received her Ph.D. from Stanford University. Since completing her graduate studies, Professor Langton has taught at the University of Oklahoma and the University of British Columbia. Currently Chair of the Organizational Behaviour and Human Resources division in the Faculty of Commerce, University of British Columbia, she teaches at the undergraduate, MBA, and Ph.D. level and conducts executive programs on working in a dot-com world, attracting and retaining employees, time management, as well as women and management issues. Professor Langton has received several major three-year research grants from the Social Sciences and Humanities Research Council of Canada (SSHRC), and her research interests have focused on human resource issues in the workplace, including pay equity, gender equity, and leadership and communication styles. She is currently conducting longitudinal research with entrepreneurs in the Greater Vancouver Region, looking specifically at their human resource practices. She is the Academic Director of the newly established International Business Family Centre at UBC, which will be dedicated to studying issues important to the survival of family businesses and business families. Her research has appeared in such journals as *Administrative Science Quarterly, American Sociological Review, Sociological Quarterly, Journal of Management Education,* and *Gender, Work and Organizations.* She has won Best Paper commendations from both the Academy of Management and the Administrative Sciences Association of Canada. She has also published two textbooks on organizational behaviour.

Professor Langton routinely wins high marks from her students for teaching. She has been nominated many times for the Commerce Undergraduate Society Awards, and has won several honourable mention plaques. In 1998 she won the University of British Columbia Faculty of Commerce's most prestigious award for teaching innovation, The Talking Stick. The award was given for Professor Langton's redesign of the undergraduate organizational behaviour course as well as the many activities that were a spin-off of these efforts. At heart, Professor Langton enjoys being a teacher. But she also is a quilter, and an accomplished pizza maker. She wishes she had more time for these latter two activities.

Part 1

MANAGEMENT

Chapter 1
Managers and Managing

Chapter 2
The Evolution of
Management Theory

Chapter one

Managers and Managing

Learning Objectives

1. Describe what management is, what managers do, what organizations are for, and how managers utilize organizational resources efficiently and effectively to achieve organizational goals.

2. Distinguish among planning, organizing, leading, and controlling (the four principal managerial functions), and explain how managers' ability to handle each one can affect organizational performance.

3. Differentiate among three levels of management, and understand the responsibilities of managers at different levels in the organizational hierarchy.

4. Identify the roles managers perform and the skills they need to execute those roles effectively.

5. Explain the key challenges managers face in the Canadian environment.

6. Discuss the principal challenges managers face in today's increasingly competitive global environment.

A Case in Contrast

WestJet Brings Back its First CEO

When Clive Beddoe was honoured at the end of 2000 with a national Entrepreneur of the Year award cosponsored by *Canadian Business*, he was in his second stint as CEO and president of Calgary-based WestJet (www.westjet.com).[1] Beddoe founded the airline in 1996 with Don Bell, Mark Hill, and Tim Morgan, but stepped aside to be executive chairman when Steve Smith, formerly of Air Canada, was appointed CEO in early 1999. The two men could not have been more different in their management styles.

Beddoe started WestJet having no experience running an airline. However, he and his co-founders had a solid business plan. Their intention was to copy the successful Dallas, Texas-based discount carrier, Southwest Airlines. They would do this by running a low-cost operation, with short flights on selected routes, with very low fares and high customer service.

WestJet is the fastest-growing airline ever launched in Canada and one of the most profitable in North America. Beddoe insists, however, that it's not the business plan but WestJet's corporate culture that accounts for the airline's extraordinary performance. "The entire environment is conducive to bringing out the best in people," he says. "It's the culture that creates the passion to succeed."

Beddoe's leadership strength is that he understands how to manage people. Or more precisely, he understands how to get his employees to manage themselves. WestJet sets performance goals for employees, but workers have the freedom to do their jobs without interference from supervisors.

Many of WestJet's job applicants come from outside the airline industry. "We prefer it that way," says Beddoe. "This is a new culture, a new vision. It's better to start with a clean slate."

Clive Beddoe, CEO of WestJet (second from right), won the 2000 National Entrepreneur of the Year for his success in managing the company he founded with (from left to right) Donald Bell, Tim Morgan, and Mark Hill.

Steve Smith did not work out as CEO of WestJet, and was forced to resign. However, he will have a second chance to run an airline: Air Canada chose him in August 2001 to lead its new discount airline.

WestJet employees are expected to have enthusiasm and a sense of humour. One thing Beddoe doesn't want is employees who want to be part of a union.

Therefore, he created the Pro-Active Communication Team (PACT, for short), an employee association that helps management address employee concerns before they become a problem. Everyone at WestJet belongs to PACT; there are chapters representing the different work groups. Representatives from each chapter sit on a council and deal with personnel issues and help set salary scales. Beddoe feels that PACT works because, "It takes away the opportunity for conflict. Employees are part of the solution, not the problem." One industry observer notes that because of the way PACT is structured, WestJet will always be union-free. "That's a very important element of WestJet's corporate structure, given Canada's propensity for strong labour movements," says the observer. Beddoe sees PACT more positively: "It took me two years to convince our people to embrace the concept of PACT because everyone here is so antiunion. But the staff voted 92 percent in favour of it. We have since had some extremely successful resolutions to issues that have cropped up."

In early 1999, Beddoe decided he no longer wanted to run the day-to-day business of the carrier, preferring to take on the role of executive chair. WestJet hired Steve Smith, a well-respected executive in the aviation community with more than 20 years' experience, to become WestJet's second CEO. The co-founders thought that Smith—who was running Air Canada's regional airline, Air Ontario—was well suited to take WestJet from a private concern into a public company. WestJet's board also liked Smith's amiable, energetic personality.

However, his experience at Air Ontario, where he frequently dealt with hostile unions, left Smith with more of a top-down management style. Beddoe says that Smith "treated PACT like a union, and they resented that immediately. He came from a background where you just weren't open and straightforward, [where] you don't play all your cards at once. Well, we don't do that."

About 18 months after Smith was hired, WestJet's board asked for his resignation because of "a difference in philosophy as to management style." Beddoe described WestJet as having a "culture that trusts people, and by trusting them they in turn trust you. And that gives people a sense of accomplishment at the end of the day." Smith's style was different; according to Julius Maldutis, an analyst at CIBC World Markets: "Steve Smith came from a more formal culture and preferred stringent controls—top-down management style. Consequently, employees became agitated, morale suffered and the culture that built the airline was at risk."

To underscore that it really was his managerial philosophy that cost Smith his job, it should be noted that during his tenure there was a sharp increase in earnings, and a 120-percent rise in share price during his last year, including a three-for-two stock split. Thus, from a bottom-line perspective, Smith was successful, although by the time of his dismissal, some of the core senior executives were threatening to quit. Smith rarely comments on his departure from WestJet, but he did acknowledge that his management style didn't mesh with WestJet's collaborative approach. ●

Overview

The story of WestJet's two CEOs illustrates many of the challenges facing people who become managers: Managing a company is a complex activity, and managers must learn the skills and acquire the knowledge necessary to become effective managers. Management is clearly more an art form than a science. Even effective managers make mistakes, and success at one company does not necessarily guarantee success at another.

In this chapter, we look at what managers do and what skills and abilities they must develop if they are to manage their organizations successfully over time. We also identify the different kinds of managers that organizations need, and the skills and abilities they must develop if they are to be successful. Finally, we identify some of the challenges that Canadian managers must address if their organizations are to grow and prosper. ●

What is Management?

When you think of a manager, what kind of person comes to mind? Do you see someone who, like Clive Beddoe, can determine the future prosperity of a large for-profit company? Or do you see the administrator of a not-for-profit organization such as a school, library, healthcare organization or charity? Or do you think of the person in charge of your local McDonald's restaurant or Wal-Mart store? Do you realize that even employees are being asked to assume some managerial functions, and that management occurs even in informal groups? In other words, these days almost everyone is called upon to manage, although the scope of that responsibility will vary. What, then, does management mean?

Management takes place in **organizations**, which are collections of people who work together and coordinate their actions to achieve a wide variety of goals.[2] **Management** is the planning, organizing, leading, and controlling of resources to achieve goals effectively and efficiently. **Resources** are assets such as people, machinery, raw materials, information, skills, and financial capital. A **manager** is a person responsible for supervising the use of a group or organization's resources to achieve its goals.

Achieving High Performance: A Manager's Goal

Organizational performance is a measure of how efficiently and effectively managers use resources to satisfy customers and achieve organizational goals. For instance, the principal goal of Steve Jobs is to manage Apple Computer so that it produces personal computers that customers are willing to buy; the principal goal of doctors, nurses, and hospital administrators is to increase their hospital's ability to make sick people well; the principal goal of each McDonald's restaurant manager is to produce burgers, fries, and shakes that people want to eat and pay for. Organizational performance increases in direct proportion to increases in efficiency and effectiveness (see Figure 1.1).

Efficiency is a measure of how well or how productively resources are used to achieve a goal.[3] Organizations are efficient when managers minimize the amount of input resources (such as labour, raw materials, and component parts) or the amount of time needed to produce a given output of goods or services. For example, McDonald's recently developed a more efficient fat fryer that not only reduces (by 30 percent) the amount of oil used in cooking but also speeds up the cooking of french fries. A manager's responsibility is to ensure that an organization and its members perform, as efficiently as possible, all the activities that are needed to provide goods and services to customers.

Effectiveness is a measure of the appropriateness of the goals that managers have selected for the organization to pursue, and of the degree to which the organization achieves those goals. Organizations are effective when managers choose appropriate goals and then achieve them. Some years ago, for example, managers at McDonald's decided on the goal of providing breakfast service to attract more customers. This goal has proven to be a very smart choice, for sales of breakfast food now account for over 30 percent of McDonald's revenues. High-performing organizations like Campbell Soup, McDonald's, Wal-Mart, Intel, Home Depot, Arthur Andersen, and the March of Dimes are simultaneously efficient and effective, as shown in Figure 1.1.

organizations Collections of people who work together and coordinate their actions to achieve goals.

management The planning, organizing, leading, and controlling of resources to achieve organizational goals effectively and efficiently.

resources Assets such as people, machinery, raw materials, information, skills, and financial capital.

manager A person who is responsible for supervising the use of an organization's resources to achieve its goals.

organizational performance A measure of how efficiently and effectively a manager uses resources to satisfy customers and achieve organizational goals.

efficiency A measure of how well or productively resources are used to achieve a goal.

effectiveness A measure of the appropriateness of the goals an organization is pursuing and of the degree to which the organization achieves those goals.

Figure 1.1
Efficiency, Effectiveness, and Performance in an Organization

EFFICIENCY

	LOW	HIGH
HIGH	Low efficiency/ High effectiveness Manager chooses the right goals to pursue, but does a poor job of using resources to achieve these goals. Result: A product that customers want, but that is too expensive for them to buy.	High efficiency/ High effectiveness Manager chooses the right goals to pursue and makes good use of resources to achieve these goals. Result: A product that customers want at a quality and price that they can afford.
LOW	Low efficiency/ Low effectiveness Manager chooses wrong goals to pursue and makes poor use of resources. Result: A low-quality product that customers do not want.	High efficiency/ Low effectiveness Manager chooses inapppropriate goals, but makes good use of resources to pursue these goals. Result: A high-quality product that customers do not want.

EFFECTIVENESS

High-performing organizations are efficient *and* effective.

Managers who are effective are those who choose the right organizational goals to pursue and have the skills to utilize resources efficiently. Consider, for example, the way in which Kjell Larsson, the mine manager at Myra Falls copper and zinc mine, turned a hostile situation around in a unionized workplace.

Management Insight

How to Be an Effective Mine Manager

Vancouver Island's Myra Falls copper and zinc mine has a history of rough management–union relations, even for the mining industry.[4] Work stoppages preceded the last two union contracts. While the current agreement came after just a one-day strike, the previous contract was an arbitrated decision after a bitter 16-month strike–lockout. Even though the mine is under new ownership, the bitterness still lingers.

Swedish-controlled Boliden bought the mine in 1998. Immediately the company sent Kjell Larsson over to be the mine manager. Larsson asked every one of the miners how the mine's operation could be improved. Together, the miners and the managers identified five key problem areas and then formed teams to figure out how to solve the problems.

"To me, that kind of set the stage for cooperation," says Claude Pelletier, the union leader who led the miners through the 16-month strike in 1998. "Larsson was a confident enough manager to share information and accept proposals, and none of the 'Boliden outsiders' bashed the … unions."

Larsson and Boliden represent a new form of management, particularly in a unionized environment. The company stresses communication, team problem

Boliden Limited
www.boliden.se/

solving, worker empowerment and responsibility, and the union is involved in everything from training to strategic planning. The company refers to it as "co-management." "The leadership we recognize here are management and union," says Dave Bazowsky, who has worked in human resources at Myra Falls. Everyone was involved during budget discussions and information about the company—such as tonnes mined each day, percentage of ore, extract shipped, progress against budget, and safety—is readily shared with employees.

Managerial Functions

What do managers do?

The job of management is to help an organization make the best use of its resources to achieve its goals. How do managers accomplish this objective? They do so by performing four essential managerial functions: *planning, organizing, leading,* and *controlling* (see Figure 1.2). French manager Henri Fayol first outlined the nature of these managerial activities around the turn of the twentieth century in *General and Industrial Management,* a book that remains the classic statement of what managers must do to create a high-performing organization.[5]

Managers at all levels and in all departments—whether in small or large organizations, for-profit or not-for-profit organizations, or organizations that operate in one country or throughout the world—are responsible for performing these four functions, and we will look at each in turn. How well managers perform them determines how efficient and effective their organization is. Individuals who are not managers can also be involved in planning, organizing, leading and controlling, so understanding these processes is important for everyone.

Planning

planning Identifying and selecting appropriate goals and courses of action; one of the four principal functions of management.

Planning is a process used to identify and select appropriate goals and courses of action. There are three steps in the planning process: (1) deciding which goals the organization will pursue, (2) deciding what courses of action to adopt to attain those goals, and (3) deciding how to allocate organizational resources to attain

Figure 1.2
Four Functions of Management

those goals. How well managers plan determines how effective and efficient their organization is—its performance level.[6]

As an example of planning in action, consider the dilemma facing Dave Orton, president and chief operating officer of Thornhill, ON-based ATI Technologies Inc., a graphics computer chip maker in early 2001.[7] ATI once had as much as 29 percent of the chip market, but by late 2000, its share was about 20 percent, with rival Nvidia at 19 percent. Intel had 35 percent of the market share. In 1999, Orton tried to change strategy by acquiring contracts with General Instrument, Sony, and Vestel that were expected to take ATI into new markets beyond supplying graphics chips for personal computers. This did not work out, and by 2001, the decline in personal computer sales was cutting away even more of ATI's potential market. Orton's strategy to supply chips for boxes that sit atop television sets had also met with some setbacks. Some of the company investors wondered whether being sold to Nvidia might be ATI's best strategy.

The outcome of planning is a **strategy**, a cluster of decisions concerning what organizational goals to pursue, what actions to take, and how to use resources to achieve goals. For instance, WestJet's strategy is to be a low-cost provider in the Canadian discount airline market. Planning is a difficult activity because, normally, which goals an organization should pursue and how best to pursue them—which strategies to adopt—is not immediately clear. Managers take risks when they commit organizational resources to pursue a particular strategy. Either success or failure is a possible outcome of the planning process. The failure of many of the dot-coms is attributable to managers trying to make money quickly, without business plans or long-term vision. In Chapter 7, we focus on the planning process and on the strategies organizations can select to respond to opportunities or threats.

Organizing

Organizing is a process used to establish a structure of working relationships that allow organizational members to work together to achieve organizational goals. Organizing involves grouping people into departments according to the kinds of job-specific tasks they perform. In organizing, managers also lay out the lines of authority and responsibility between different individuals and groups, and they decide how best to coordinate organizational resources, and in particular, human resources.

The outcome of organizing is the creation of an **organizational structure**, a formal system of task and reporting relationships that coordinates and motivates organizational members so that they work together to achieve organizational goals. Organizational structure determines how an organization's resources can best be used to create goods and services.

We examine the organizing process in Chapters 8 through 10. In Chapter 8, we consider the organizational structures that managers can use to coordinate and motivate people and other resources. In Chapter 9, we look at the important roles that an organization's culture, values, and norms play in binding people and departments together so that they work toward organizational goals. In Chapter 10, we discuss ways in which managers can develop and enhance the value of their employees through activities such as selection, training, and performance appraisal.

Leading

In **leading**, managers articulate a clear vision for organizational members to follow, and they energize and enable organizational members so that they understand the part they play in achieving organizational goals. Leadership depends on

ATI Technologies Inc.
www.ati.com/

strategy A cluster of decisions about what goals to pursue, what actions to take, and how to use resources to achieve goals.

organizing Structuring working relationships in a way that allows organizational members to work together to achieve organizational goals; one of the four principal functions of management.

organizational structure A formal system of task and reporting relationships that coordinates and motivates organizational members so that they work together to achieve organizational goals.

leading Articulating a clear vision and energizing and enabling organizational members so that they understand the part they play in achieving organizational goals; one of the four principal functions of management.

the use of power, influence, vision, persuasion, and communication skills, both to coordinate the behaviours of individuals and groups so that their activities and efforts are in harmony and to encourage employees to perform at a high level. The outcome of leadership is a high level of motivation and commitment among organizational members.

We discuss the issues involved in managing and leading individuals and groups in Chapters 11 through 16. In Chapter 11, we consider what managers are like as people and the personal challenges managers face as they try to perform their jobs effectively. In Chapters 12 and 13, we examine theories about and models of the best ways to motivate and lead employees to encourage high motivation and commitment. In Chapter 14, we look at the way groups and teams can contribute to achieving organizational goals, and the coordination problems that can arise when people work together in groups and teams. In Chapters 15 and 16, we consider how communication and coordination problems can arise between people and functions, and how managers can try to manage these problems through bargaining and negotiation and by creating appropriate information networks. Understanding how to manage and lead effectively is an important skill. You might be interested to know that CEOs have only a few short months to prove to investors that they are able to communicate a vision and carry it out. Recent studies suggest that CEOs are given 14–18 months by investors and analysts to show results.[8]

Controlling

controlling Evaluating how well an organization is achieving its goals and taking action to maintain or improve performance; one of the four principal functions of management.

In **controlling**, managers evaluate how well an organization is achieving its goals and take action to maintain or improve performance. For example, managers monitor the performance of individuals, departments, and the organization as a whole to see whether they are meeting desired performance standards. If standards are not being met, managers take action to improve performance. Individuals working in groups also have the responsibility of controlling, i.e., making sure the group achieves its goals and actions.

The outcome of the control process is the ability to measure performance accurately and regulate organizational efficiency and effectiveness. In order to exercise control, managers must decide which goals to measure—perhaps goals pertaining to productivity, quality, or responsiveness to customers—and then they must design information and control systems that will provide the data they need to assess performance. These mechanisms provide feedback to the manager, and the manager provides feedback to employees. The controlling function also allows managers to evaluate how well they themselves are performing the other three functions of management—planning, organizing, and leading—and to take corrective action.

We cover the most important aspects of the control function in Chapter 9, where we outline the basic process of control and examine some control systems that managers can use to monitor and measure organizational performance.

Finally, in Chapter 17, we look at how managers can effectively engage in changing the organization to improve effectiveness in planning, organizing, leading, and controlling. We'll discuss how managers can create specific control systems to improve quality and efficiency. We will also consider ways in which managers can change the organization's culture.

The four managerial functions—planning, organizing, leading, and controlling—are essential to a manager's job. At all levels in a managerial hierarchy, and across all departments in an organization, effective management means making decisions and managing these four activities successfully.

Types of Managers

To perform efficiently and effectively, organizations traditionally employ three types of managers–first-line managers, middle managers, and top managers–arranged in a hierarchy (see Figure 1.3). Typically, first-line managers report to middle managers, and middle managers report to top managers. Managers at each level have different but related types of responsibilities for utilizing organizational resources to increase efficiency and effectiveness. These three types of managers are grouped into departments according to their specific job responsibilities. A **department**–such as manufacturing, accounting, or engineering–is a group of people who work together and possess similar skills or use the same kind of knowledge, tools, or techniques to perform their jobs. As Figure 1.3 indicates, first-line, middle, and top managers, who differ from one another by virtue of their job-specific responsibilities, are found in each of an organization's major departments. Below, we examine the reasons why organizations use a hierarchy of managers and group them into departments. We then examine some recent changes that have been taking place in managerial hierarchies.

department A group of people who work together and possess similar skills or use the same knowledge, tools, or techniques to perform their jobs.

Levels of Management

As just discussed, organizations normally have three levels of management: first-line managers, middle managers, and top managers.

FIRST-LINE MANAGERS   At the base of the managerial hierarchy are **first-line managers** (often called *supervisors*). They are responsible for the daily supervision and coordination of the nonmanagerial employees who perform many of the specific activities necessary to produce goods and services. First-line managers may be found in all departments of an organization.

first-line managers Managers who are responsible for the daily supervision of nonmanagerial employees.

Examples of first-line managers include the supervisor of a work team in the manufacturing department of a car plant, the head nurse in the obstetrics department of a hospital, and the chief mechanic overseeing a crew of mechanics in the service department of a new car dealership.

MIDDLE MANAGERS   Supervising the first-line managers are **middle managers**, who have the responsibility of finding the best way to organize human and other resources to achieve organizational goals. To increase efficiency, middle managers try to find ways to help first-line managers and nonmanagerial employees better utilize resources in order to reduce manufacturing costs or improve the way services are provided to customers. To increase effectiveness, middle managers are responsible for evaluating whether the goals that the organization is pursuing are appropriate and for suggesting to top managers ways in which goals should be changed. Very often, the suggestions that middle managers make to top managers can dramatically increase organizational performance, as we explain in Chapter 7. A major part of the middle manager's job is to develop and fine-tune skills and know-how, such as manufacturing or marketing expertise, that allow the organization to be efficient and effective. Middle managers also coordinate resources across departments and divisions. Middle managers make the thousands of specific decisions that go into the production of goods and services: which first-line supervisors should be chosen for this particular project? Where can we find the highest-quality resources? How should employees be organized to allow them to make the best use of resources?

middle managers Managers who supervise first-line managers and are responsible for finding the best way to use resources to achieve organizational goals.

Behind a first-class sales force, look for the middle managers responsible for training, motivating, and rewarding salespeople. Behind a committed staff of secondary school teachers, look for the principal who energizes them to look for ways to obtain the resources they need to do an outstanding and innovative job in the

Figure 1.3
Management Hierarchy

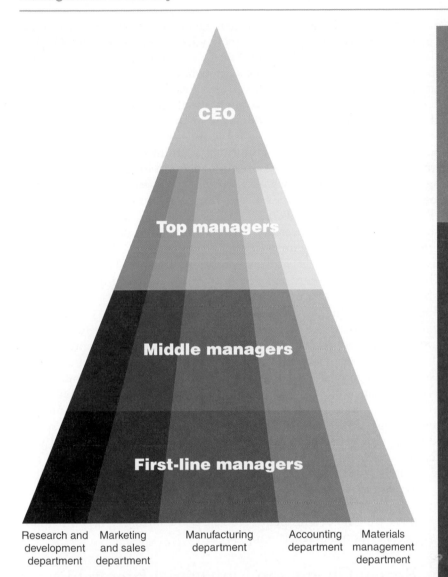

CEO

Top managers

Middle managers

First-line managers

Research and
development
department

Marketing
and sales
department

Manufacturing
department

Accounting
department

Materials
management
department

An entrepreneur founds an organization, takes the role of Chief Executive Officer (CEO) and begins the management task of organizing.

As more and more employees are hired, the CEO realizes the need to create a hierarchy of managers.

Top managers are hired and together with the CEO become responsible for planning, identifying, and selecting appropriate goals and courses of action.

Middle managers are hired and become responsible for the effective management of organizational resources.

First-line managers are hired and take on the day-to-day burden of leading and controlling human and other resources to help the organization perform efficiently.

At the same time that the organization is dividing vertically into hierarchical levels, it also divides horizontally into departments: groups of people who work together and possess similar skills or use the same knowledge, tools, or techniques to perform their jobs. Managers and employees become members of a particular department, such as manufacturing, marketing, or research and development.

The final result of this division vertically and horizontally is an organizational structure.

classroom. Kjell Larsson, the Myra Falls mine manager discussed earlier, is a good example of a committed middle manager.

top managers Managers who establish organizational goals, decide how departments should interact, and monitor the performance of middle managers.

TOP MANAGERS   In contrast to middle managers, **top managers** are responsible for the performance of all departments.[9] They have *cross-departmental responsibility* and they're responsible for connecting the parts of the organization together. Top managers help carry out the organizational vision; they establish organizational goals, such as which goods and services the company should produce; they decide how the different departments should interact; and they monitor how well middle managers in each department utilize resources to achieve goals.[10] Top managers are ultimately responsible for the success or failure of an organization, and their performance is continually scrutinized by people inside and outside the organization, such as other employees and investors.[11]

Top managers report to a company's *chief executive officer*–such as WestJet CEO Clive Beddoe, Shaw Communications CEO Jim Shaw, and Quebecor CEO Pierre Karl Péladeau–or to the *president* of the organization, who is second-in-command, such as Falconbridge president Oyvind Hushovd or CBC president Robert Rabinovitch. In some organizations one person holds the title of both CEO and president, such as Paul Godfrey, president and CEO of the Toronto Blue Jays. The CEO and president are responsible for developing good working relationships among the top managers who head the various departments (manufacturing and marketing, for example), and who usually have the title *vice-president.* A central concern of the CEO is the creation of a smoothly functioning **top-management team**, a group composed of the CEO, the president, and the department heads most responsible for helping to achieve organizational goals.[12] The CEO also has the responsibility of setting the vision for the organization.

top-management team A group composed of the CEO, the president, and the heads of the most important departments.

restructuring Downsizing an organization by eliminating the jobs of large numbers of top, middle, and first-line managers and nonmanagerial employees.

The relative importance of planning, organizing, leading, and controlling–the four managerial functions–to any particular manager depends on the manager's position in the managerial hierarchy.[13] The amount of time that managers spend planning and organizing resources to maintain and improve organizational performance increases as they move higher in the hierarchy (see Figure 1.4). Top managers devote most of their time to planning and organizing, the functions that are so crucial to determining an organization's long-term performance. The lower a manager's position is in the hierarchy, the more time he or she spends leading and controlling first-line managers or nonmanagerial employees.

Andrea Jung—CEO of Avon, the famous cosmetic producer—advanced to that rank after first serving as the company's president and chief operating officer.

Recent Changes in Managerial Hierarchies

The tasks and responsibilities of managers at different levels have been changing dramatically in recent years. Increasingly, top managers are encouraging lower-level managers to look beyond the goals of their own departments and take a cross-departmental view to find new opportunities to improve organizational performance. Stiff competition for resources from organizations both at home and abroad has put increased pressure on all managers to improve efficiency, effectiveness, and organizational performance. To respond to these pressures, many organizations have been changing the managerial hierarchy.[14]

RESTRUCTURING   To decrease costs, CEOs and their top-management teams have been restructuring organizations to reduce the number of employees on the payroll. **Restructuring** can involve flattening the organization through eliminating some hierarchical layers, reducing the number of departments or the

Figure 1.4
Relative Amount of Time That Managers Spend on the
Four Managerial Functions

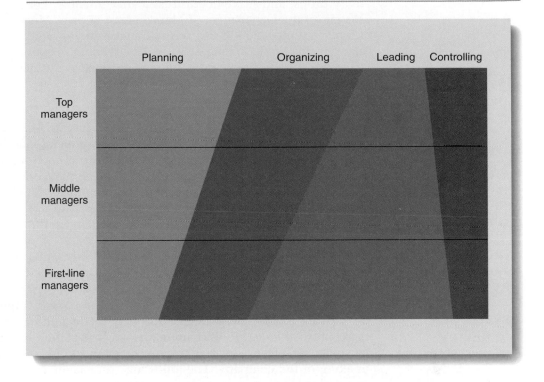

number or types of product lines, selling off parts of the business, closing plants, or even deciding to outsource some of the functions within the organization. Often, restructuring involves downsizing, or eliminating the jobs of large numbers of top, middle, or first-line managers and nonmanagerial employees. Downsizing has been a frequent event in Canada recently, as seen in the layoff announcements of Monday, January 29, 2001: DaimlerChrysler cut 3100 jobs in Canada; JDS Uniphase laid off 700 contract workers in Ottawa; and *The Toronto Star* cut 200 jobs. Restructuring promotes efficiency by reducing costs and allowing the organization to make better use of its remaining resources. Large for-profit organizations today typically employ 10 percent fewer managers than they did 10 years ago. Canadian National Railway, Nortel Networks Corporation, General Motors, and many other organizations have eliminated several layers of middle management. The middle managers who still have jobs at these companies have had to assume additional responsibilities and are under increasing pressure to perform. For instance, when Indigo Books & Music, Inc. removed a layer of management from all its stores in May 2000, each store's general manager had to handle the responsibilities of the marketing, purchasing, and operations managers who had previously reported to the general manager.

Does restructuring work?   Not everyone agrees that restructuring has a positive impact on society at large. For instance, Industry Minister John Manley believes, "It's part of my job to push the corporate sector and urge them to take into account the enormous damage it does when you cast people aside instead of retraining them."[15] Moreover, when polled, 58 percent of Canadians did not find it acceptable for profitable corporations to lay off workers.[16] Len Brooks, executive director of the Clarkson Centre for Business Ethics at the University of Toronto, says laying off employees to maximize profit and improve cash flow "is really a dumb idea. Only a third of its prac-

Clarkson Centre
for Business Ethics
www.mgmt.utoronto.ca/
CCBE/

titioners achieve their financial objectives while paying a huge price as employee morale craters."[17] Many studies show that "surviving employees become narrow-minded, self-absorbed, and risk averse [after downsizing]. Morale sinks, productivity drops, and survivors distrust management."[18] For instance, Professor Terry Wagar, of the Department of Management at Saint Mary's University in Halifax, surveyed almost 2000 firms across Canada and found that companies that downsized during the 1990s suffered a variety of negative consequences. These included decreases in efficiency and employee satisfaction and less favourable employer–employee relations.[19]

EMPOWERMENT AND SELF-MANAGED TEAMS   Another major change in management has taken place at the level of first-line managers, who typically supervise the employees engaged in producing goods and services. Many organizations have taken two steps to reduce costs and improve quality. One is the **empowerment** of the workforce, expanding employees' tasks and responsibilities so that they have more authority and accountability. The other is the creation of **self-managed teams**—groups of employees who are given responsibility for supervising their own activities and for monitoring the quality of the goods and services they provide.

Under both empowerment and self-managed teams, employees assume many of the responsibilities and duties previously performed by first-line managers.[20] What is the role of the first-line manager in this new work context? First-line managers act as coaches or mentors whose job is not to tell employees what to do, but to provide advice and guidance and help teams find new ways to perform their tasks more efficiently.[21] The unionized workers at the Myra Falls copper mine are an example of empowered employees who are asked to share in the decision making of the company. The following "Management Insight" provides another example of management tasks and responsibilities being given to employees with no formal managerial role.

empowerment
Expanding employees' tasks and responsibilities.

self-managed teams
Groups of employees who supervise their own activities and monitor the quality of the goods and services they provide.

Management Insight

Managing from the Bottom at WestJet

Clive Beddoe, president and CEO of Calgary-based WestJet Airlines Ltd. (www.westjet.com), believes that letting employees manage themselves is the key to WestJet's success.[22] When Beddoe first founded WestJet, he realized that he faced a difficult management problem: his employees were spread all over the country, working in airports, hangars, or inflight. "What occurred to me," says Beddoe, "is we had to overcome the inherent difficulty of trying to manage people and to hone the process into one where people wanted to manage themselves."

Thus, Beddoe created a company that is managed from the bottom. Workers are encouraged to perform their jobs without interference from supervisors. "I don't direct things," says Beddoe. "We set some standards and expectations, but [I] don't interfere in how our people do their jobs." For instance, flight attendants are asked to serve customers in a caring, positive and cheerful manner. How they do that is left up to them.

Beddoe notes that letting employees manage themselves results in substantial benefits. He avoids the cost of employing a large layer of supervisory people. And productivity per person is much higher. WestJet operates with about 59 people per aircraft, compared with more than 140 at a typical full-service airline such as Air Canada. Beddoe believes that his management from the bottom gives workers pride in what they do. "They are the ones making the decisions about what they're doing and how they're doing it," says Beddoe.

Tips for Managers

Managing Resources

1. Talk to customers to assess whether the goods or services that an organization provides adequately meet their needs and how they might be improved.

2. Analyze how an organization can better obtain or use resources to increase efficiency and effectiveness.

3. Critically assess how the skills and know-how of departments are helping an organization to achieve a competitive advantage. Take steps to improve skills whenever possible.

4. Count the number of managers at each level in the organization and analyze how to increase efficiency and effectiveness of the workforce.

Managerial Roles and Skills

How important are intuition and emotion for managers?

Though we might like to think that a manager's job is highly orchestrated and that management is a logical, orderly process in which managers make a concerted effort to make rational decisions, being a manager often involves acting emotionally and relying on gut feelings. Quick, immediate reactions to situations rather than deliberate thought and reflection are an important aspect of managerial action.[23] Often, managers are overloaded with responsibilities, do not have time to spend in analyzing every nuance of a situation, and therefore make decisions in uncertain conditions without being sure which outcomes will be best.[24] Moreover, for top managers in particular, the current situation is constantly changing, and a decision that seems right today may prove to be wrong tomorrow.

Despite all of this flux, however, it is important to note that the roles managers need to play and the skills they need to utilize have changed little since the early 1970s, when McGill University professor Henry Mintzberg detailed 10 specific roles that effective managers undertake. A **role** is a set of specific tasks that a person is expected to perform because of the position he or she holds in an organization. Although the roles that Mintzberg described overlap with Fayol's model, they are useful because they focus on what managers do in a typical hour, day, or week in an organization, as they go about the business of managing.[25] Below, we discuss these roles and then examine the skills effective managers need to develop.

role The specific tasks that a person is expected to perform because of the position he or she holds in an organization.

Managerial Roles Identified by Mintzberg

Mintzberg reduced to 10 roles the specific tasks that managers need to perform as they plan, organize, lead, and control organizational resources.[26] Managers assume each of these roles in order to influence the behaviour of individuals and groups inside and outside the organization. People inside the organization include other managers and employees. People outside the organization include shareholders, customers, suppliers, the local community in which an organization is located, and any local or government agency that has an interest in the organization and what it does.[27] Mintzberg grouped the 10 roles into three broad categories: *interpersonal, informational,* and *decisional* (see Table 1.1). Managers often perform several of these roles simultaneously.

McGill University:
Henry Mintzberg
www.management.mcgill.ca/
people/faculty/profiles/
mintzber.htm

INTERPERSONAL ROLES   Managers assume interpersonal roles in order to coordinate and interact with organizational members and provide direction and supervision both for employees and for the organization as a whole. A manager's first interpersonal role is to act as a *figurehead*–the person who symbolizes an

Table 1.1

Managerial Roles Identified by Mintzberg

Type of Role	Specific Role	Examples of Role Activities
INTERPERSONAL	Figurehead	Outline future organizational goals to employees at company meetings; open a new corporate headquarters building; state the organization's ethical guidelines and the principles of behaviour employees are to follow in their dealings with customers and suppliers.
	Leader	Provide an example for employees to follow; give direct commands and orders to subordinates; make decisions concerning the use of human and technical resources; mobilize employee support for specific organizational goals.
	Liaison	Coordinate the work of managers in different departments; establish alliances between different organizations to share resources to produce new goods and services.
INFORMATIONAL	Monitor	Evaluate the performance of managers in different functions and take corrective action to improve their performance; watch for changes occurring in the external and internal environment that may affect the organization in the future.
	Disseminator	Inform employees about changes taking place in the external and internal environment that will affect them and the organization; communicate to employees the organization's vision and purpose.
	Spokesperson	Launch a national advertising campaign to promote new goods and services; give a speech to inform the local community about the organization's future intentions.
DECISIONAL	Entrepreneur	Commit organizational resources to develop innovative goods and services; decide to expand internationally to obtain new customers for the organization's products.
	Disturbance handler	Move quickly to take corrective action to deal with unexpected problems facing the organization from the external environment, such as a crisis like an oil spill, or from the internal environment, such as producing faulty goods or services.
	Resource allocator	Allocate organizational resources among different functions and departments of the organization; set budgets and salaries of middle and first-level managers.
	Negotiator	Work with suppliers, distributors, and labour unions to reach agreements about the quality and price of input, technical, and human resources; work with other organizations to establish agreements to pool resources to work on joint projects.

organization or a department. Assuming the figurehead role, the chief executive officer determines the direction or mission of the organization and informs employees and other interested parties about what the organization is seeking to achieve. Managers at all levels act as figureheads and role models who establish the appropriate and inappropriate ways to behave in the organization. Steve Jobs is a manager who excels at performing the figurehead role at Apple Computer.

A manager's role as a *leader* is to encourage subordinates to perform at a high level and to take steps to train, counsel, and mentor subordinates to help them reach their full potential. A manager's power to lead comes both from formal authority due to his or her position in the organization's hierarchy and from his or her personal qualities, including reputation, skills, or personality. The personal behaviour of a leader affects employee attitudes and behaviour; indeed, subordinates' desire to perform at a high level—and even whether they desire to arrive at work on time and not to be absent often—depends on how satisfied they are with working for the organization.

In performing as a *liaison*, managers link and coordinate the activities of people and groups both inside and outside the organization. Inside the organization, managers are responsible for coordinating the activities of people in different departments to improve their ability to cooperate. Outside the organization, managers are responsible for forming linkages with suppliers or customers or with the organization's local community in order to obtain scarce resources. People outside an organization often come to equate the organization with the manager they are dealing with, or with the person they see on television or read about in the newspaper. For example, Ted Rogers personifies Rogers Communications to most Canadians.

INFORMATIONAL ROLES Informational roles are closely associated with the tasks necessary to obtain and transmit information. First, a manager acts as a *monitor* and analyzes information from inside and outside the organization. With this information, a manager can effectively organize and control people and other resources. Acting as a *disseminator*, the manager transmits information to other members of the organization to influence their work attitudes and behaviour. In the role of *spokesperson*, a manager uses information to promote the organization so that people inside and outside the organization respond positively to it.

DECISIONAL ROLES Decisional roles are closely associated with the methods managers use to plan strategy and utilize resources. In the role of *entrepreneur*, a manager must decide which projects or programs to initiate and how to invest resources to increase organizational performance. As a *disturbance handler*, a manager assumes responsibility for handling an unexpected event or crisis that threatens the organization's access to resources. In this situation, a manager must also assume the roles of figurehead and leader to mobilize employees to help secure the resources needed to avert the problem.

Under typical conditions, an important role a manager plays is that of *resource allocator*, deciding how best to use people and other resources to increase organizational performance. While engaged in that role, the manager must also be a *negotiator*, reaching agreements with other managers or groups claiming the first right to resources, or with the organization and outside groups such as shareholders or customers.

Managerial Skills

To successfully perform their roles, managers must have certain skills. Research has shown that formal education, training and experience help managers to acquire three principal types of skills: *conceptual, human,* and *technical*.[28] As you might expect, the level of these skills that a manager needs depends on his or her level in the managerial hierarchy (see Figure 1.5).

conceptual skills
The ability to analyze and diagnose a situation and to distinguish between cause and effect.

CONCEPTUAL SKILLS Conceptual skills are demonstrated by the ability to analyze and diagnose a situation and to distinguish between cause and effect. Planning and organizing require a high level of conceptual skill, as does performing the managerial roles discussed above. Top managers require the best conceptual skills, because their primary responsibilities are planning and organizing.[29] Conceptual skills allow managers to understand the big picture confronting an organization. The ability to focus on the big picture lets the manager see beyond the situation immediately at hand and consider choices while keeping the organization's long-term goals in mind.

human skills The ability to understand, alter, lead, and control the behaviour of other individuals and groups.

HUMAN SKILLS Human skills include the ability to understand, alter, lead, and control the behaviour of other individuals and groups. The ability to communicate and give feedback, to coordinate and motivate people, to give recognition, and to mold individuals into a cohesive team distinguishes effective from ineffective managers. By all accounts, Clive Beddoe of WestJet and Kjell Larsson of the Myra Falls mine possess human skills.

To manage interpersonal interactions effectively, each person in an organization needs to learn how to empathize with other people—to understand their

Figure 1.5

Conceptual, Human, and Technical Skills Needed by
Three Levels of Management

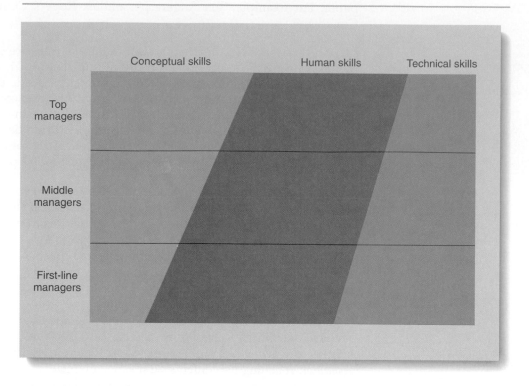

viewpoints and the problems they face. One way to help managers understand
their personal strengths and weaknesses is to have their superiors, peers, and subordinates provide feedback about their performance in the roles identified by
Mintzberg. Thorough and direct feedback allows managers to develop their
human skills.

technical skills Job-
specific knowledge and
techniques that are
required to perform an
organizational role.

*Do you think technical
skills are enough
qualification to be a
manager?*

TECHNICAL SKILLS   **Technical skills** are the job-specific knowledge and
techniques that are required to perform an organizational role. Examples include
a manager's specific manufacturing, accounting, or marketing skills. Managers
need a range of technical skills to be effective. The array of technical skills a person needs depends on his or her position in the organization. The manager of a
restaurant, for example, may need cooking skills to fill in for an absent cook,
accounting and bookkeeping skills to keep track of receipts and costs and to
administer the payroll, and aesthetic skills to keep the restaurant looking attractive
for customers.

Effective managers need all three kinds of skills—conceptual, human, and technical. The absence of even one type can lead to failure. Michael Kavanagh, human
resources director for Vancouver-based Crystal Decisions, highlights this point. He
says that at Crystal, a large computer software company, "We place a lot of emphasis on behavioural (human) skills. It's the difference between who gets hired and
who doesn't. Your technical skills get you in the door, but your behavioural
skills are increasingly a criteria in enhancing your employment opportunities."
Management skills, roles, and functions are closely related, and wise managers or
prospective managers are constantly in search of the latest educational contributions to help them develop the conceptual, human, and technical skills they need
to function in today's changing and increasingly competitive environment.

Tips for Managers

Tasks and Roles

1. Estimate how much time managers spend performing each of the four tasks of planning, organizing, leading, and controlling. Decide if managers are spending the right amount of time on each task.

2. Decide which of Mintzberg's 10 managerial roles managers are performing well or poorly.

3. Based on this analysis, take steps to ensure that managers possess the right levels of conceptual, technical, and human skills to perform their jobs effectively.

Challenges for Management in the Canadian Environment

Managing in Canada presents a number of unique challenges and opportunities. Though these will be addressed throughout the textbook, we will identify them briefly here.

Organizational Size

publicly held organizations

Companies whose shares are available on the stock exchange for public trading by brokers/dealers.

It is important to recognize that managers don't just manage in large organizations. There are management responsibilities in organizations of every size. You may think of managers managing large manufacturing operations, but you might not realize that only 16.7 percent of Canadians work in manufacturing organizations. Most Canadians (around 75 percent) work in the service sector of the economy. You might think that most people work in large **publicly held organizations** like Ford Motor Company of Canada Limited or Nortel Networks. However, large organizations represent only 3 percent of the organizations in Canada. Of the 928 000 organizations in Canada in 1996, 97 percent of these employed fewer than 50 people. Big business employs just over 40 percent of all workers in Canada, while small businesses employ about 34 percent of all workers.[30] Moreover, the government is a large employer in Canada. For instance, Canada Post, a crown corporation, is the sixth largest employer in Canada, behind only George Weston Ltd., Onex Corp., Nortel Networks, Laidlaw Inc., and Hudson's Bay Company. In 1998, about 18 percent of the labour force was self-employed, meaning that these people were managing themselves.

Canada Post
www.canadapost.ca/

The Types of Organizations

privately held organizations

Companies whose shares are not available on the stock exchange but are privately held.

Large organizations are often publicly held, so that the managers report to a board of directors who are responsible to shareholders. This represents one form of organization in Canada. There are also numerous **privately held organizations**, both large and small. Privately held organizations can be individually owned, family owned, or owned by some other group of individuals. Other organizational forms, such as partnerships and cooperatives, also require managers.

Many managers work in the public sector as civil servants, for municipal, provincial, and federal governments. The challenges of managing within government departments can be quite different from the challenges of managing in publicly held organizations. Critics argue that governments have no measurable performance objectives, and therefore employees feel less accountable for their actions. In addition to working directly for the government, some managers and employees work for crown corporations. These are structured like private-sector corporations, with boards of directors, CEOs, and so on. Rather than being owned by shareholders, however, they are owned by governments. The employees of a crown corporation are not civil servants. Managers in crown corporations are more independent than the senior bureaucrats who manage government departments.

Many of Canada's larger organizations are actually subsidiaries of American parent organizations (e.g., Sears, Safeway, General Motors and Ford Motor Company). This means that managers in these companies often report to American top managers, and are not always free to set their own goals and targets. Conflicts can arise between Canadian managers and the American managers to whom they report about how things should be done.

The Political and Legal Climate

Some 30 percent of Canadian employees are unionized, and this presents an additional challenge to management. In unionized organizations, managers must learn to work with unions and their managers to create a positive work climate. Organizations with unionized employees are governed by the collective agreements negotiated between management and the union(s).

Competition Bureau
www.competition.ic.gc.ca/

Canadian organizations are affected by Canadian law at a number of levels. The Competition Bureau determines whether there is too little competition in an industry, and rules on what companies must do to increase competition. For instance, the Competition Bureau recently ruled that Chapters Inc. and Indigo Books & Music, Inc. would have to sell 13 superstores and refrain from opening new stores for two years if they were to merge, which they did on June 13, 2001 under the Chapters Inc. name. This ruling affects the plans that the managers of Chapters Inc. can make in the next couple of years.

Canadian companies are also affected by interprovincial trade rules, marketing boards, and whether they are in the regulated sector (which includes agriculture, telecommunication, utilities, and transportation, for example). Canada has greater regulation of firms than does either the United States or the United Kingdom.[31] These rules and regulations can affect the products that firms are able to provide, or the prices at which they must offer goods. Thus they impact managers' abilities to make decisions freely for firms affected by these regulations.

Canadian organizations are also affected by trade barriers from other countries. These are discussed more fully in Chapter 4.

Managing a Diverse Workforce

The face of Canada has changed considerably in the last 20 years, and thus another challenge for managers is to recognize the need to treat human resources in a fair and equitable manner. In the past, white male employees dominated the ranks of management, but today the workplace comprises women, First Nations peoples, Asian Canadians, African Canadians, and Indo-Canadians in addition to white males. Moreover, today's workplace is much more likely to include gays and lesbians, the elderly, and people with disabilities. Managers must recognize the performance-enhancing possibilities of a diverse workforce, such as the ability to take advantage of the skills and experiences of different kinds of people.[32] When managers fail to understand how diversity might affect the workplace, they can encounter difficulties such as those experienced by the Canadian Armed Forces.

Focus on Diversity

Canadian Armed Forces Faces Diversity

A recent report by a special advisory board set up by Defence Minister Art Eggleton found that women, visible minorities, and Aboriginals remain underrepresented in the Canadian Armed Forces, with the army lagging behind both the navy and the air force.[33] "The board found a lot of positive initiatives underway within the (Forces) and the department," said Sandra Perron, a former infantry officer who heads the group. "We also found quite a few deficiencies."

The report said that the army tended to have a poor attitude toward women: both participants and instructors in combat training centres and battle schools claimed that "women are too weak to be in the combat arms." In addition, many soldiers believe that physical standards have been lowered so women can qualify. Perhaps the biggest problem, however, is that "soldiers tended to dismiss diversity training as a waste of time."

The army sponsors a Leadership in a Diverse Army program, but its graduates seem unconvinced of the need for integration. By contrast, "Air and Maritime Commands seem to have greater awareness and acceptance of concepts of diversity." Women make up 5.6 percent of the total enlistment and 8.8 percent of the officers in the navy and 7.9 percent of the air force. However, only 1 percent of combat officers and 2.5 percent of combat soldiers are female.

The board recommended that army leadership lead by example on integration questions. It also suggested that the military improve recruiting materials, do a better job of attracting women and minorities and make fitness tests "less a measure of mere strength and more a gauge of ability to perform tasks." The latter might help to fight the view that there was a double standard in fitness tests.

Even though some managers resist diversity initiatives, managers who value their diverse employees are the managers who best succeed in promoting performance over the long run.[34] Today, more and more organizations are realizing that people are their most important resource and that developing and protecting human resources is an important challenge for management in a competitive global environment. Introducing cultural sensitivity into the workplace is one of the many tasks managers have to face. We discuss many of the issues surrounding the management of a diverse Canadian workforce in Chapter 5.

Challenges for Management in a Global Environment

global organizations

Organizations that operate and compete in more than one country.

Canadian firms are less likely to operate only within their own borders these days. Not only do firms face competition domestically, but they also face global competition. The rise of **global organizations**, organizations that operate and compete in more than one country, has put severe pressure on many organizations to improve their performance and to identify better ways to use their resources. The successes of German chemical companies Schering and Hoescht, Italian furniture manufacturer Natuzzi, Korean electronics companies Samsung and Lucky Goldstar, and Brazilian plane maker Empresa Brasileira de Aeronautica SA (Embraer) are putting pressure on organizations in other countries to raise their level of performance in order to compete successfully with these global companies.

Canada has been slow historically to face the global challenge. In the list of the Top 100 Global Companies of 1998, not one Canadian firm appears. The majority are American, but there are several entries from Switzerland, as well as the

United Kingdom, France and Sweden. Today, managers who make no attempt to learn and adapt to changes in the global environment find themselves reacting rather than innovating, and their organizations often become uncompetitive and fail.[35] Three major challenges stand out for Canadian managers in today's global economy: building a competitive advantage, maintaining ethical standards, and utilizing new kinds of information systems and technologies.

Building a Competitive Advantage

competitive advantage The ability of one organization to outperform other organizations because it produces desired goods or services more efficiently and effectively than competitors do.

If Canadian managers and organizations are to reach and remain at the top of the competitive environment, they must build a competitive advantage. **Competitive advantage** is the ability of one organization to outperform other organizations because it produces desired goods or services more efficiently and effectively than its competitors. The four building blocks of competitive advantage are superior *efficiency, quality, innovation,* and *responsiveness to customers* (see Figure 1.6).

INCREASING EFFICIENCY   Organizations increase their efficiency when they reduce the quantity of resources (such as people and raw materials) they use to produce goods or services. In today's competitive environment, organizations are constantly seeking new ways to use their resources to improve efficiency. Many organizations are training their workers in new skills and techniques to increase their ability to perform many new and different tasks. Canada could do more on the training front, however: Japanese and German companies invest far more in training employees than do Canadian companies.

In addition to training employees, organizations sometimes partner together to increase efficiency. For instance, Montreal-based Radio-Canada and *La Presse* signed a partnership agreement in early 2001 to combine their efforts in such areas as the Internet, special events, and marketing. Guy Crevier, president and publisher of *La Presse*, noted that the agreement would "increase the efficiency of the partners." They also plan to share the infrastructure costs for foreign bureaus and the cost and results of public opinion polls.[36]

Figure 1.6
Building Blocks of Competitive Advantage

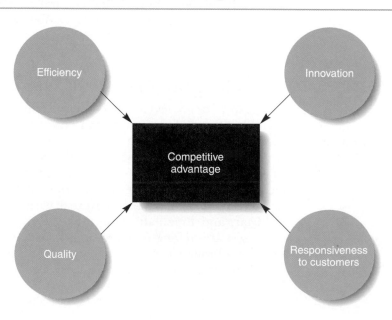

Today's steel rolling mills are almost all under the control of highly skilled employees who use state-of-the-art, computer-controlled production systems to increase operating efficiency.

Managers must improve efficiency if their organizations are to compete successfully with companies operating in Mexico, Malaysia, and other countries where employees are paid comparatively low wages. New methods must be devised either to increase efficiency or to gain some other competitive advantage—higher-quality goods, for example—if the loss of jobs to low-cost countries is to be prevented.

INCREASING QUALITY The challenge from global organizations such as Korean electronics manufacturers, Mexican agricultural producers, and European marketing and financial firms has also increased pressure on companies to improve the quality of goods and services delivered. One major thrust to improve quality has been to introduce the quality-enhancing techniques known as *total quality management (TQM)*. Employees involved in TQM are often organized into quality control teams and are given the responsibility of continually finding new and better ways to perform their jobs; they also are given the responsibility for monitoring and evaluating the quality of the goods they produce. TQM is based on a significant new philosophy of managing behaviour in organizations, and we thoroughly discuss this approach, and ways of managing TQM successfully, in Chapter 17.

innovation The process of creating new goods and services or developing better ways to produce or provide goods and services.

INCREASING INNOVATION Innovation—the process of creating new goods and services that customers want, or developing better ways to produce or provide goods and services—poses a special challenge. Managers must create an organizational setting in which people are encouraged to be innovative. Typically, innovation takes place in small groups or teams; management decentralizes control of work activities to team members and creates an organizational culture that rewards risk taking. Understanding and managing innovation and creating a work setting that encourages risk taking are among the most difficult managerial tasks. As we saw earlier in the chapter, WestJet has accomplished innovation by its management from the bottom policy.

INCREASING RESPONSIVENESS TO CUSTOMERS Organizations use their products and services to compete for customers, so training employees to be responsive to customers' needs is vital for all organizations, but particularly for service organizations. Retail stores, banks, and restaurants, for example, depend entirely on their employees to perform behaviours that result in high-quality service at a reasonable cost.[37] As Canada and other countries move toward a more service-based economy (in part because of the loss of manufacturing jobs to China, Malaysia, and other countries with low labour costs), managing behaviour in service organizations is becoming increasingly important. Many organizations are empowering their customer service employees and giving them the authority to take the lead in providing high-quality customer service. As noted previously, the empowering of nonmanagerial employees changes the role of first-line managers and often leads to the more efficient use of organizational resources. The following "Managing Globally" feature discusses how Vancouver-based Mountain Equipment Co-op faces challenges in trying to be more responsive to co-op members while increasing efficiency, quality, and innovation.

Managing Globally

How Mountain Equipment Co-op Faces the Globalization Challenge

At Vancouver-based Mountain Equipment Co-op (MEC) (www.mec.ca), determining the appropriate strategy for running a business in a global economy raises more questions than solutions.[38] MEC prides itself on being about values, while it sells fleece, Goretex, and crampons, and keeps its eye on the bottom line.

The co-op also uses workers in Asian factories to produce about 20 percent of its goods. Originally, MEC aimed to produce all of its goods in Canada, but with company growth and concern about prices, some of the production had to be moved to lower-wage countries like China and Vietnam. CEO Peter Robinson notes that, "We're getting good at looking at conditions in our manufacturing facilities, but now we want to look at conditions in that country."

At the annual general meeting in April 2001, co-op members voted on whether MEC should stop contracting work to China. Robinson, a human rights activist, was sympathetic to the resolution proposed. "It gives us an opportunity to talk about where we came from and where we are going. We have to talk about what we can do beyond the factory."

MEC's official attitude is that it does business with companies, not countries. Therefore, it concerns itself more with conditions on the factory floor than with what the country's government is doing. Producing in China presents a dilemma to the idealistic members concerned about China's human rights progress, however. Robinson feels that trying to produce all products in Canada is impractical, though—not only because of higher wages, but "Asian plants are often technologically superior to those in North America and are able to better meet MEC's need for a high volume of quality goods completed on time."

Globalization does not necessarily mean that companies are abandoning superior conditions at home in order to save money in low-cost countries, either. MEC ended contracts with three Vancouver factories because of labour or technological conditions. Nevertheless, globalization does force companies to wrestle with the challenge of being politically correct while providing affordable merchandise to their customers.

Maintaining Ethical Standards

Why might it be hard to maintain ethical standards?

While mobilizing organizational resources, managers at all levels are under considerable pressure to increase the level at which their organizations perform. For example, top managers receive pressure from shareholders to increase the performance of the entire organization in order to boost the stock price, improve profits, or raise dividends. In turn, top managers may then pressure middle managers to find new ways to use organizational resources to increase efficiency or quality in order to attract new customers and earn more revenues.

Pressure to increase performance can be healthy for an organization because it causes managers to question the organization's operations and encourages them to find new and better ways to plan, organize, lead, and control. However, too much pressure to perform can be harmful.[39] It may induce managers to behave unethically in dealings with individuals and groups both inside and outside the organization.[40] For example, a purchasing manager for a large retail chain might buy inferior clothing as a cost-cutting measure, or, to secure a large foreign contract, a sales manager in a large defence company might offer bribes to foreign officials. In spring 2001, supervisory procedures at BMO Nesbitt Burns were investigated by the Manitoba Securities Commission and the Investment Dealers Association after a number of client complaints against brokers in the Winnipeg office. Among other charges, brokers were alleged to have churned client accounts to increase

Manitoba Securities
Commission
www.msc.gov.mb.ca/

their own personal commissions.[41] Another example illustrating unethical managerial behaviour is described in the following "Ethics in Action" feature.

Ethics in Action

How to Destroy a Charity's Reputation

In September 2000, William Townsend, executive director of the BC Lions Society for Children with Disabilities (www.lionsocietybc.bc.ca) for the previous 20 years, resigned amid a growing scandal.[42] In recent years, the society had made a $50 000 loan to a psychic for an international tour that subsequently collapsed, paid $65 000 to a former society director for farm equipment unsuitable for the society's purposes, lost $3.86 million on a Hawaiian cruise ship venture, and invested a total of $1.2 million to build and operate a funeral services business in Salmon Arm.

No reason was given for Townsend's resignation, but he noted that the executive board "felt someone should be responsible and I'm the one." He also acknowledged responsibility for anything that had gone wrong. As a result of all of this negative publicity, the society cancelled the annual Timmy's Christmas Telethon for December 2000. The program had aired on CBC Television for 23 years.

When managers act unethically, some individuals or groups may obtain short-term gains, but in the long run the organization and people inside and outside the organization will pay. In Chapter 5, we discuss the nature of ethics and the importance of managers and all members of an organization behaving ethically as they pursue organizational goals.

Utilizing New Information Systems and Technologies

Another important challenge facing Canadian managers is the pressure to increase performance through new information systems and technologies.[43] Canadian companies have been slower to adopt new technologies than their American counterparts, lagging behind the United States by two decades when it comes to corporate and government spending on information technology, a recent Conference Board of Canada report found. As a result, the United States enjoys higher productivity and economic growth rates.[44] The importance of information systems and technologies is discussed in greater detail in Chapters 6 and 15. Consider here how hospitals might be able to use new information technologies to improve their performance.

Conference Board
of Canada
www.conferenceboard.ca/

Management Insight

Can the Information Revolution Change Canadian Healthcare?

Canada faces a critical shortage of healthcare professionals.[45] With the aging of Canadian physicians, decreases in medical school enrolments since the early 1990s, loss of physicians to the United States and changes in younger physicians' lifestyles, the doctor shortage is not easily solved. The number of nurses is also too low to provide adequate healthcare in this country.

However, if the productivity of healthcare professionals could increase, the system might face less strain than predicted. Might technology, which has been responsible for the sustained economic growth experienced across North America, offer a partial answer to the healthcare crisis?

Chapter Summary

WHAT IS MANAGEMENT?

• Achieving High
  Performance: A
  Manager's Goal

MANAGERIAL FUNCTIONS

• Planning

• Organizing

• Leading

• Controlling

TYPES OF MANAGERS

• Levels of
  Management

• Recent Changes
  in Managerial
  Hierarchies

MANAGERIAL ROLES AND SKILLS

• Managerial Roles
  Identified by
  Mintzberg

• Managerial Skills

CHALLENGES FOR MANAGEMENT IN THE CANADIAN ENVIRONMENT

• Organizational Size

• The Types of
  Organizations

• The Political and
  Legal Climate

• Managing a Diverse
  Workforce

CHALLENGES FOR MANAGEMENT IN A GLOBAL ENVIRONMENT

• Building a Competitive Advantage

• Maintaining Ethical
  Standards

• Utilizing New
  Information Systems
  and Technologies

FedEx can track a parcel anywhere around the globe, as can its customers, using the company's Web site. The same type of technology could be used to track a patient's "progress across the continuum of care through well-defined, best-practice care protocols." The Internet could also be used to provide an integrated view of patient records across all care providers. Patient information in different hospitals, homecare agencies, community provider organizations, and doctors' offices could be linked under the patient's authorization and transmitted to care providers.

These possibilities are not available in the Canadian healthcare sector at the moment, because only about 2 percent of its annual budget goes towards information technology. Many for-profit firms devote 5 to 15 percent of annual expenditures to information technology. But healthcare managers may want to consider ways that technology could make the entire system more productive.

Summary and Review

WHAT IS MANAGEMENT?   A manager is a person responsible for supervising the use of an organization's resources to meet its goals. An organization is a collection of people who work together and coordinate their actions to achieve a wide variety of goals. Management is the process of using organizational resources to achieve organizational goals effectively and efficiently through planning, organizing, leading, and controlling. An efficient organization makes the most productive use of its resources. An effective organization pursues appropriate goals and achieves these goals by using its resources to create the goods or services that customers want.

MANAGERIAL FUNCTIONS   According to Fayol, the four principal managerial functions are planning, organizing, leading, and controlling. Managers at all levels of the organization and in all departments perform these functions. Effective management means managing these activities successfully.

TYPES OF MANAGERS   Organizations typically have three levels of management. First-line managers are responsible for the day-to-day supervision of nonmanagerial employees. Middle managers are responsible for developing and utilizing organizational resources efficiently and effectively. Top managers have cross-departmental responsibility. The top managers' job is to establish appropriate goals for the entire organization and to verify that department managers are utilizing resources to achieve those goals. To increase efficiency and effectiveness, some organizations have altered their managerial hierarchies by restructuring, by empowering their workforces, and by utilizing self-managed teams.

MANAGERIAL ROLES AND SKILLS   According to Mintzberg, managers play 10 different roles: figurehead, leader, liaison, monitor, disseminator, spokesperson, entrepreneur, disturbance handler, resource allocator, and negotiator. Three types of skills help managers perform these roles effectively: conceptual, human, and technical skills.

CHALLENGES FOR MANAGEMENT IN THE CANADIAN ENVIRONMENT   Canada's environment presents many interesting challenges to managers: a variety of different types and sizes of organizations; a number of national and international laws; handling unions; and managing a diverse workforce.

CHALLENGES FOR MANAGEMENT IN A GLOBAL ENVIRONMENT Today's competitive global environment presents many interesting challenges to managers: to build a competitive advantage by increasing efficiency, quality, innovation, and responsiveness to customers; to behave ethically toward people inside and outside the organization; and to utilize new information systems and technologies.

Management in Action

Topics for Discussion and Action

1. Describe the difference between efficiency and effectiveness, and identify real organizations that you think are, or are not, efficient and effective.

2. In what ways can managers at each of the three levels of management contribute to organizational efficiency and effectiveness?

3. Identify an organization that you believe is high performing and one that you believe is low performing, using the criteria of effectiveness and efficiency. Give 10 reasons why you think the performance levels of the two organizations differ so much.

4. Choose an organization such as a school or a bank; visit it; then list the different kinds of organizational resources it uses.

5. Visit an organization, and talk to first-line, middle, and top managers about their respective management roles in the organization and what they do to help the organization be efficient and effective.

6. Ask a middle or top manager, perhaps someone you already know, to give examples of how he or she performs the managerial functions of planning, organizing, leading, and controlling. How much time does he or she spend in performing each function?

7. Like Mintzberg, try to find a cooperative manager who will allow you to follow him or her around for a day. List the types of roles the manager plays, and indicate how much time he or she spends performing them.

8. What are the building blocks of competitive advantage? Why is obtaining a competitive advantage important to managers?

9. What are some of the challenges that Canadian managers face? To what extent are these challenges specific to Canada?

10. In what ways do you think managers' jobs have changed the most over the last 15 years? Why have these changes occurred?

Building Management Skills

Thinking About Managers and Management

Think of an organization that has provided you with work experience and the manager to whom you reported (or talk to someone who has had extensive work experience); then answer these questions.

1. Think of your direct supervisor. If he or she belongs to a department, of what department is he or she a member? At what level of management is this person?

2. How do you characterize your supervisor's approach to management? For example, which particular management functions and roles does this person perform most often? What kinds of management skills does this manager have?

3. Do you think the functions, roles, and skills of your supervisor are appropriate for the particular job he or she performs? How could this manager improve his or her task performance?

4. How did your supervisor's approach to management affect your attitudes and behaviour? For example, how well did you perform as a subordinate, and how motivated were you?

5. Think of the organization and its resources. Do its managers utilize organizational resources effectively? Which resources contribute most to the organization's performance?

6. Describe how the organization treats its human resources. How does this treatment affect the attitudes and behaviours of the workforce?

7. If you could give your manager one piece of advice or change one management practice in the organization, what would it be?

8. How attuned are the managers in the organization to the need to increase efficiency, quality, innovation, or responsiveness to customers? How well do you think the organization performs its prime goals of providing the goods or services that customers want or need the most?

Small Group Breakout Exercise

Opening a New Restaurant

Form groups of three or four people, and appoint one group member as the spokesperson who will communicate your findings to the entire class when called on by the instructor. Then discuss the following scenario.

You and your partners have decided to open in your local community a large, full-service restaurant that will be open from 7 a.m. to 10 p.m. to serve breakfast, lunch, and dinner. Each of you is investing $75 000 in the venture, and together you have secured a bank loan for $450 000 more to begin operations. You and your partners have little experience in managing a restaurant beyond serving meals or eating in restaurants, and you now face the task of deciding how you will manage the restaurant and what your respective roles will be.

1. Decide what your respective managerial roles in the restaurant will be. For example, who will be responsible for the necessary departments and specific activities? Describe your managerial hierarchy.

2. Which building blocks of competitive advantage do you need to establish to help your restaurant succeed? What criteria will you use to evaluate how successfully you are managing the restaurant?

3. Discuss the most important decisions that must be made about (a) planning, (b) organizing, (c) leading, and (d) controlling, to allow you and your partners to utilize organizational resources effectively and build a competitive advantage.

4. For each managerial function, list the issue that will contribute the most to your restaurant's success.

Exploring the World Wide Web

Specific Assignment

Enter Magna International's Web site (www.magnaint.com/), and click on "Company Info." From there, click on both "Corporate Constitution" and "Employee's Charter." You should print out both documents. Also click on "Our Founder."

1. What expectations does Magna International have for its employees and managers?

2. What is Frank Stronach's "Fair Enterprise" system?

General Assignment

Search for the Web site of a company in which a manager discusses his or her approach to planning, organizing, leading, or controlling. What is that manager's approach to managing? What effects has this approach had on the company's performance?

ManagementCase

The Challenges of Heading the CBC

When Robert Rabinovitch was appointed president at the CBC in November 1999, the announcement was greeted with enthusiasm by friends and CBC employees alike. Ted Johnson, a senior executive with Power Corp., remarked: "This is a man with remarkable people skills, strategic vision and understanding of technology. But no one should be fooled by the charm—he is as tough as he has to be."

In his early months, he was a popular president with the employees because of his clear, passionate vision for the corporation. CBC staff were excited when he opposed new licence conditions imposed by the Canadian Radio-Television and Telecommunications Commission (CRTC) shortly after he took over. The CRTC wanted the CBC to stop broadcasting foreign blockbuster films, produce more regional programming and reduce professional sports coverage. Rabinovitch refused, saying, "There's no way the CBC can implement these decisions." He projected that these changes would cost the CBC $50 million in revenue.

By spring 2001, Rabinovitch's honeymoon with his employees was clearly over. A study completed then shows that morale among CBC staff had dropped significantly during the previous two years, and much of their unhappiness was directed at senior management. Employees felt that management was untrustworthy, and lacked competence and a clear direction.

Managing an organization like the CBC is not easy. The CBC has had sharp drops in its viewing and listening audiences, deep budget cuts, huge layoffs and an often-hostile relationship with the prime minister's office. Rabinovitch's predecessor, Perrin Beatty, faced numerous battles with the CBC's chairwoman, Guylaine Saucier, who is well connected with the Liberal party. She wanted Prime Minister Jean Chretien to fire Beatty, and when he didn't, she undermined Beatty's authority, making it difficult for him to run the company.

Almost three-quarters of the corporation's annual budget of $1.2 billion comes from the federal government. The rest comes from commercial revenue, and not everyone believes that the CBC should be running commercials. Between 1990 and 2000, $414 million was cut from the CBC's budget.

Management at CBC struggle to balance the books because, by law, the corporation has to break even every year. To cope, the CBC has engaged in numerous rounds of layoffs. Between 1990 and early 2000, the CBC cut 1740 employees. "The corporation has been through so many of these layoffs that they have become routine," says Mike Sullivan, national representative of the Communications Energy and Paperworkers Union of Canada, which represents 2100 CBC technicians. "To CBC management, it's like eating candy. They think, 'It's so easy, why would we look at other ways of saving money?'"

The broadcaster has made numerous programming changes in the last few years, most of which employees didn't understand. The changes seemed to be made for no obvious reason. "Senior managers seem to be addicted to this sort of organizational change," one source said. "It doesn't help that they seem to score points for it."

Rabinovitch is trying to figure out how to reduce costs and create a more viable CBC. He faces a lot of challenges. The government dictates many of the policies with regard to programming that the CBC must make. Meanwhile the corporation faces competition from cable companies and television networks in the United States and Canada that produce their own programming. Another challenge facing Rabinovitch is labour unions. More than 90 percent of the CBC's costs come from union contracts. This takes away some of Rabinovitch's flexibility to replace underperforming staff with creative younger talent.

Source: C. Cobb, "Mistrust Reigns at CBC: Survey," *National Post*, May 22, 2001, pp. A1, A8; M. Fraser, "This Dish May be Too Hot to Handle: CBC's Bold Plan to Sell Off Infrastructure Faces Stiff Opposition," *Financial Post (National Post)*, February 5, 2001, p. C2; A. Clark, "Remaking the CBC: The Public Broadcaster Faces More Job Losses," *Maclean's*, February 14, 2000, p. 57; A. Wilson-Smith, "The CBC's New Boss: Bob Rabinovitch Says Canada's Beleaguered Public Broadcaster Must Build on its Strengths, and Not Try to be All Things to All People," *Maclean's*, November 1, 1999, p. 30.

Questions

1. How might Robert Rabinovitch's approach to management be affected by conditions at the CBC?
2. What can Rabinovitch do to build a competitive advantage at CBC?

ManagementCase

In the News

From the Pages of *The Globe and Mail*
Managers Crucial to Curbing Turnover

Ernst and Young is putting its managers under the microscope with a confidential employee poll.

The professional services firm is hoping to cull candid information from its workers to help its managers become more effective and help curb turnover.

"People leave managers. They don't leave organizations," says Keith Bowman, the company's director of human resources.

"For the last five years, people have had an incredible number of work opportunities. They are more likely to look for other jobs and leave. The role of the manager is absolutely fundamental to keeping people from leaving."

Starting next month, Ernst and Young employees will be asked about their managers: "How well does the individual foster a positive work environment and help our people grow?"

Staff can respond electronically to one of several preselected ratings, from not well to extremely well. All responses are anonymous.

This approach comes at a time when the working world is under siege by an employee retention crisis—one that observers say will only get more severe in the years to come as an impending labour shortage of almost one million workers is expected across all industries in Canada.

As a result, organizations are desperate to understand how to keep top talent from job-hopping.

Their desperation is well founded, given that one in three workers will resign from his job in the next two years, according to a new survey by The Hay Group.

Ineffective managers are a major factor in the increasing rates of departure, says the research company, which interviewed over one million employees in 330 organizations around the world.

"Poor managers have a huge impact on employee turnover. Management's inability to adapt to the times will continue to contribute dramatically to sustaining high levels of turnover," says Ron Grey, managing director of The Hay Group Canada.

"We have seen significant problems with senior managers who have not recognized the changing relationship with workers and continue to operate using historical methods," he says.

As the workplace becomes more team-based and virtual, the role of managers must also change, Mr. Bowman says.

"If you have the right people, you do not need to manage them. More work is team-based. More work is done from home. Managers should look for results and output, not whether their people are in the office at 9 a.m."

The Hay Group survey found the main reason workers left was that they felt their skills weren't being used. The second-most cited reason was the inability of top managers to be effective leaders.

For instance, only 30 to 40 percent of workers surveyed said they felt their bosses were eager to help advance their careers.

Managers were also criticized for tolerating workers who under perform—creating a key source of dissatisfaction among their peers, Mr. Grey says. Over half of the employees surveyed said their employers routinely accept poor performers who shirk responsibility. Many top workers respond by leaving.

To add insult to injury, Mr. Grey says, managers often don't understand why so many people are eager to leave and change jobs.

"Managers have a degree of blind loyalty that makes it difficult for them to understand the views of other employees," Mr. Grey says.

Workplace consultants urge managers to become better communicators, to treat employees as individuals and help foster career development.

KMPG's chief human resources officer, Lorne Burns, says many of the firm's employees leave because they are "cherry-picked" by their clients, not because of bad management. The company has started rerecruiting former employees who may want to return.

Still, Mr. Burns says, old-style management techniques that rely on close supervision, hierarchy and paternalistic methods are the most common reasons organizations are given for high turnover.

"People feel trapped. They are unhappy with the working relationship they have with their managers and want to get out."

Source: N. Southworth, "Managers Crucial to Curbing Turnover," *The Globe and Mail*, May 30, 2001, p. M1.

Questions

1. How does management style affect turnover?

2. What can managers do to make sure that employees are less likely to quit their jobs?

Chapter two

The Evolution of Management Theory

1. Describe how the need to increase organizational efficiency and effectiveness has guided the evolution of management theory.

2. Explain the principle of job specialization and division of labour, and tell why the study of person–task relationships is central to the pursuit of increased efficiency.

3. Identify the principles of administration and organization that underlie effective organizations.

4. Trace the changes that have occurred in theories about how managers should behave in order to motivate and control employees.

5. Explain the contributions of management science to the efficient use of organizational resources.

6. Explain why the study of the external environment and its impact on an organization has become a central issue in management thought.

A Case in Contrast

Changing Ways of Making Cars

Car production has changed dramatically over the years as managers have applied different views or philosophies of management to organize and control work activities. Prior to 1900, workers worked in small groups, cooperating to hand-build cars with parts that often had to be altered and modified to fit together. This system, a type of small-batch production, was very expensive; assembling just one car took considerable time and effort; and workers could produce only a few cars in a day. To reduce costs and sell more cars, managers of early car companies needed better techniques to increase efficiency.

Henry Ford revolutionized the car industry. In 1913, Ford opened the Highland Park car plant in Detroit to produce the Model T. Ford and his team of manufacturing managers pioneered the development of mass-production manufacturing, a system that made the small-batch system almost obsolete overnight. In mass production, moving conveyor belts bring the car to the workers.

Each individual worker performs a single assigned task along a production line, and the speed of the conveyor belt is the primary means of controlling their activities. Ford experimented to discover the most efficient way for each individual worker to perform an assigned task. The result was that each worker performed one

In 1913, Henry Ford revolutionized the production process of a car by pioneering mass-production manufacturing, a production system in which a conveyor belt brings each car to the workers, and each individual worker performs a single task along the production line. Even today, cars are built using this system, as shown in this photo of workers along a computerized automobile assembly line.

This photo, taken in 1904 inside Daimler Motor Co., is an example of the use of small-batch production, a production system in which small groups of people work together and perform all the tasks needed to assemble a product.

specialized task, such as bolting on the door or attaching the door handle, and jobs in the Ford car plant became very repetitive.[1]

Ford's management approach increased efficiency and reduced costs so much that by 1920 he was able to reduce the price of a car by two-thirds and sell over two million cars a year.[2] Ford Motor Company (www.ford.com) became the leading car company in the world, and many competitors rushed to adopt the new mass-production techniques. Two of these companies, General Motors (GM) (www.gm.com) and Chrysler (www.chryslercorp.com), eventually emerged as Ford's major competitors.

The CEOs of GM and Chrysler—Alfred Sloan and Walter Chrysler—went beyond simple imitation of the Ford approach by adopting a new strategy: offering customers a wide variety of cars to choose from. To keep costs low, Henry Ford had offered customers only one car—the Model T. The new strategy of offering a wide range of models was so popular that Ford was eventually forced to close his factory for seven months in order to reorganize his manufacturing system to widen his product range. Due to his limited vision of the changing car market, his company lost its competitive advantage. During the early 1930s, GM became the market leader.

The next revolution in car production took place not in the United States but in Japan. A change in management thinking occurred there when Ohno Taiichi, a Toyota production engineer, pioneered the development of lean manufacturing in the 1960s after touring the US plants of the Big Three car companies. The management philosophy behind lean manufacturing is to continuously find methods to improve the efficiency of the production process in order to reduce costs, increase quality, and reduce car assembly time.

In lean manufacturing, workers work on a moving production line, but they are organized into small teams, each of which is responsible for a particular phase of car assembly, such as installing the car's transmission or electrical wiring system. Each team member is expected to learn all the tasks of all members of his or her team, and each work group is charged with the responsibility not only to assemble cars but also to continuously find ways to increase quality and reduce costs. By 1970, Japanese managers had applied the new lean production system so efficiently that they were producing higher-quality cars at lower prices than their US counterparts, and by 1980 Japanese companies were dominating the global car market.

To compete with the Japanese, managers at the Big Three car makers visited Japan to learn lean production methods. In recent years, Chrysler Canada has been the North American model for speed in automobile production. Chrysler's Windsor, Ontario assembly plant opened in 1928, and over 54 years built its first five million vehicles. Less than 11 years later, in 1994, the plant reached the eight-million mark.[3]

Canadian Auto Workers
www.caw.ca/

Chrysler's Windsor facility has made a reputation for itself as "the biggest single experiment with flexible manufacturing methods at one site."[4] In the last 20 years, the plant has been so successful that Ken Lewenza, president of Local 444 of the Canadian Auto Workers, describes it as "Chrysler's high-pressure plant, always expected to meet peak demand for the firm's most popular products."[5] On July 24, 2000, the plant reopened its doors after being shut down for just two weeks to retool for the newest generation of DaimlerChrysler AG minivans, due in dealers' showrooms a month later. That was by far Windsor's quickest turnover, but flexible manufacturing procedures introduced in 1983 have enabled the plant to display North America's speediest production turnovers. In 1982–83, the plant shut down for 16 weeks to retool from making sedans to the first models of the Chrysler minivan, and then in 1995, it closed for 12 weeks for retooling to produce the next generation of minivans.

While the Windsor facility has been a model for quick turnarounds, Canada's auto industry in general has fared well with the advancements in lean production methods. One analyst suggested that Canada is "in the golden era of the auto sector in Canada," with a chance to outpace Michigan as early as 2001.[6] ●

Overview

As this sketch of the evolution of global car manufacturing suggests, changes in management practices occur as managers, theorists, researchers, and consultants seek new ways to increase organizational efficiency and effectiveness. The driving force behind the evolution of management theory is the search for better ways to utilize organizational resources. Advances in management theory typically occur as managers and researchers find better ways to perform the principal management tasks: planning, organizing, leading, and controlling human and other organizational resources.

In this chapter, we examine how management theory concerning appropriate management practices has evolved in modern times, and look at the central concerns that have guided its development. First, we examine the so-called classical management theories that emerged around the turn of the twentieth century. These include scientific management, which focuses on matching people and tasks to maximize efficiency; and administrative management, which focuses on identifying the principles that will lead to the creation of the most efficient system of organization and management. Next, we consider behavioural management theories, developed both before and after the Second World War, which focus on how managers should lead and control their workforces to increase performance. Then we discuss management science theory, which developed during the Second World War and which has become increasingly important as researchers have developed rigorous analytical and quantitative techniques to help managers measure and control organizational performance. Finally, we discuss business in the 1960s and 1970s and focus on the theories that were developed to help explain how the external environment affects the way organizations and managers operate.

By the end of this chapter, you will understand the ways in which management theory has evolved over time. You will also understand how economic, political, and cultural forces have affected the development of these theories and the ways in which managers and their organizations behave. Figure 2.1 summarizes the chronology of the management theories that are discussed in this chapter.   ●

Scientific Management Theory

The evolution of modern management began in the closing decades of the nineteenth century, after the industrial revolution had swept through Europe, Canada, and the United States. In the new economic climate, managers of all types of

Figure 2.1

The Evolution of Management Theory

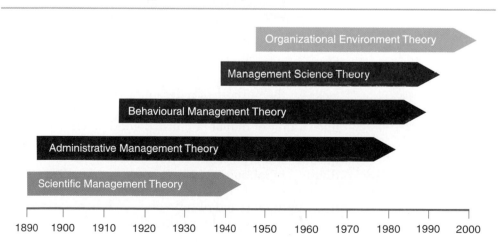

organizations–political, educational, and economic–were increasingly trying to find better ways to satisfy customers' needs. Many major economic, technical, and cultural changes were taking place at this time. The introduction of steam power and the development of sophisticated machinery and equipment changed the way in which goods were produced, particularly in the weaving and clothing industries. Small workshops run by skilled workers who produced hand-manufactured products (a system called *crafts production*) were being replaced by large factories in which sophisticated machines controlled by hundreds or even thousands of unskilled or semiskilled workers made products.

Owners and managers of the new factories found themselves unprepared for the challenges accompanying the change from small-scale crafts production to large-scale mechanized manufacturing. Many of the managers and supervisors had only a technical orientation, and were unprepared for the social problems that occur when people work together in large groups (as in a factory or shop system). Managers began to search for new techniques to manage their organizations' resources, and soon they began to focus on ways to increase the efficiency of the worker–task mix.

Job Specialization and the Division of Labour

The Adam Smith Institute
www.adamsmith.org.uk/

The famous economist Adam Smith was one of the first to look at the effects of different manufacturing systems.[7] He compared the relative performance of two different manufacturing methods. The first was similar to crafts-style production, in which each worker was responsible for all of the 18 tasks involved in producing a pin. The other had each worker performing only 1 or a few of the 18 tasks that go into making a completed pin.

Smith found that factories in which workers specialized in only 1 or a few tasks had greater performance than factories in which each worker performed all 18 pin-making tasks. In fact, Smith found that 10 workers specializing in a particular task could, between them, make 48 000 pins a day, whereas those workers who performed all the tasks could make only a few thousand at most.[8] Smith reasoned that this difference in performance was due to the fact that the workers who specialized became much more skilled at their specific tasks, and, as a group, were thus able to produce a product faster than the group of workers who each had to perform many tasks. Smith concluded that increasing the level of **job specialization**–the process by which a division of labour occurs as different workers specialize in different tasks over time–increases efficiency and leads to higher organizational performance.[9]

job specialization

The process by which a division of labour occurs as different workers specialize in different tasks over time.

Based on Adam Smith's observations, early management practitioners and theorists focused on how managers should organize and control the work process to maximize the advantages of job specialization and the division of labour.

F.W. Taylor and Scientific Management

scientific management

The systematic study of relationships between people and tasks for the purpose of redesigning the work process to increase efficiency.

Frederick W. Taylor (1856–1915) is best known for defining the techniques of **scientific management**, the systematic study of relationships between people and tasks for the purpose of redesigning the work process to increase efficiency. Taylor believed that if the amount of time and effort that each worker expended to produce a unit of output (a finished good or service) could be reduced by increasing specialization and the division of labour, then the production process would become more efficient. Taylor believed that the way to create the most efficient division of labour could best be determined by means of scientific management techniques, rather than intuitive or informal rule-of-thumb knowledge. Based on his experiments and observations as a manufacturing manager in a variety of settings, he developed four principles to increase efficiency in the workplace:[10]

- Principle 1: *Study the way workers perform their tasks, gather all the informal job knowledge that workers possess, and experiment with ways of improving the way tasks are performed.*

  To discover the most efficient method of performing specific tasks, Taylor studied in great detail and measured the ways different workers went about performing their tasks. One of the main tools he used was a time-and-motion study, which involves the careful timing and recording of the actions taken to perform a particular task. Once Taylor understood the existing method of performing a task, he tried different methods of dividing and coordinating the various tasks necessary to produce a finished product. Usually this meant simplifying jobs and having each worker perform fewer, more routine tasks, as at the pin factory or on Ford's car assembly line. Taylor also sought ways to improve each worker's ability to perform a particular task—for example, by reducing the number of motions workers made to complete the task, by changing the layout of the work area or the type of tool workers used, or by experimenting with tools of different sizes.

- Principle 2: *Codify the new methods of performing tasks into written rules and standard operating procedures.*

  Once the best method of performing a particular task was determined, Taylor specified that it should be recorded so that the procedures could be taught to all workers performing the same task. These rules could be used to standardize and simplify jobs further—essentially, to make jobs even more routine. In this way, efficiency could be increased throughout an organization.

- Principle 3: *Carefully select workers so that they possess skills and abilities that match the needs of the task, and train them to perform the task according to the established rules and procedures.*

  To increase specialization, Taylor believed workers had to understand the tasks that were required and be thoroughly trained in order to perform the tasks at the required level. Workers who could not be trained to this level were to be transferred to a job where they were able to reach the minimum required level of proficiency.[11]

- Principle 4: *Establish a fair or acceptable level of performance for a task, and then develop a pay system that provides a reward for performance above the acceptable level.*

  To encourage workers to perform at a high level of efficiency, and to provide them with an incentive to reveal the most efficient techniques for performing a task, Taylor advocated that workers should benefit from any gains in performance. They should be paid a bonus and receive some percentage of the performance gains achieved through the more efficient work process.

Why might scientific management lead to an increase in labour union participation?

By 1910, Taylor's system of scientific management had become known and, in many instances, faithfully and fully practised.[12] However, managers in many organizations chose to implement the new principles of scientific management selectively. This decision ultimately resulted in problems. For example, some managers using scientific management obtained increases in performance, but rather than sharing performance gains with workers through bonuses as Taylor had advocated, they simply increased the amount of work that each worker was expected to do. Many workers experiencing the reorganized work system found that as their performance increased, managers required them to do more work for the same pay. Workers also learned that increases in performance often meant fewer jobs and a greater threat of layoffs, because fewer workers were needed. In addition, the specialized, simplified jobs were often monotonous and repetitive, and many workers became dissatisfied with their jobs.

Scientific management brought many workers more hardship than gain, and left them with a distrust of managers who did not seem to care about their well-being.[13] These dissatisfied workers resisted attempts to use the new scientific

Charlie Chaplin tries to extricate a fellow employee from the machinery of mass production in this clip from *Modern Times*. The complex machinery is meant to represent the power that machinery has over the worker in the new work system.

management techniques and at times even withheld their job knowledge from managers to protect their jobs and pay.

Unable to inspire workers to accept the new scientific management techniques for performing tasks, some organizations increased the mechanization of the work process. For example, one reason for Henry Ford's introduction of moving conveyor belts in his factory was the realization that when a conveyor belt controls the pace of work (instead of workers setting their own pace), workers can be pushed to perform at higher levels—levels that they may have thought were beyond their reach. Charlie Chaplin captured this aspect of mass production in one of the opening scenes of his famous movie, *Modern Times* (1936). In the film, Chaplin caricatured a new factory employee fighting to work at the machine-imposed pace but losing the battle to the machine. Henry Ford also used the principles of scientific management to identify the tasks that each worker should perform on the production line and thus to determine the most effective way to create a division of labour to suit the needs of a mechanized production system.

From a performance perspective, the combination of the two management practices—(1) achieving the right mix of worker–task specialization and (2) linking people and tasks by the speed of the production line—makes sense. It produces the huge savings in cost and huge increases in output that occur in large, organized work settings. For example, in 1908, managers at the Franklin Motor Company redesigned the work process using scientific management principles, and the output of cars increased from 100 cars a *month* to 45 cars a *day*; workers' wages increased by only 90 percent, however.[14] From other perspectives, though, scientific management practices raise many concerns. The definition of the workers' rights not by the workers themselves but by the owners or managers as a result of the introduction of the new management practices raises an ethical issue, which we examine in this "Ethics in Action."

Ethics in Action

Fordism in Practice

From 1908 to 1914, through trial and error, Henry Ford's talented team of production managers pioneered the development of the moving conveyor belt and thus changed manufacturing practices forever. Although the technical aspects of the move to mass production were a dramatic financial success for Ford and for the millions of Americans who could now afford cars, for the workers who actually produced the cars, many human and social problems resulted.

With simplification of the work process, workers grew to hate the monotony of the moving conveyor belt. By 1914, Ford's car plants were experiencing huge employee turnover—often reaching levels as high as 300 or 400 percent per year as workers left because they could not handle the work-induced stress.[15] Henry Ford recognized these problems and made an announcement: From that point on, to motivate his workforce, he would reduce the length of the workday from nine hours to eight hours, and the company would double the basic wage from US$2.50 to US$5.00 per day. This was a dramatic increase, similar to an announcement today of an overnight doubling of the minimum wage. Ford became an internationally famous figure, and the word "Fordism" was coined for his new approach.[16]

Ford's apparent generosity was matched, however, by an intense effort to control the resources—both human and material—with which his empire was built. He employed hundreds of inspectors to check up on employees, both inside and outside his factories. In the factory, supervision was close and confining. Employees were not allowed to leave their places at the production line, and they were not permitted to talk to one another. Their job was to concentrate fully on the task at hand. Few employees could adapt to this system, and they developed ways of talking out of the sides of their mouths, like ventriloquists, and invented a form of speech that became known as the "Ford Lisp."[17] Ford's obsession with control brought him into greater and greater conflict with managers, who were often fired when they disagreed with him. As a result, many talented people left Ford to join his growing rivals.

Outside the workplace, Ford went so far as to establish what he called the "Sociological Department" to check up on how his employees lived and the ways in which they spent their time. Inspectors from this department visited the homes of employees and investigated their habits and problems. Employees who exhibited behaviours contrary to Ford's standards (for instance, if they drank too much or were always in debt) were likely to be fired. Clearly, Ford's effort to control his employees led him and his managers to behave in ways that today would be considered unacceptable and unethical, and in the long run would impair an organization's ability to prosper.

Despite the problems of worker turnover, absenteeism, and discontent at Ford Motor Company, managers of the other car companies watched Ford reap huge gains in efficiency from the application of the new management principles. They believed that their companies would have to imitate Ford if they were to survive. They followed Taylor and used many of his followers as consultants to teach them how to adopt the techniques of scientific management. In addition, Taylor elaborated his principles in several books, including *Shop Management* (1903) and *The*

A scene from *Cheaper by the Dozen* illustrating how "efficient families," such as the Gilbreths, use formal family courts to solve problems of assigning chores to different family members and to solve disputes when they arise.

Principles of Scientific Management (1911), which explain in detail how to apply the principles of scientific management to reorganize the work system.[18]

Taylor's work has had an enduring effect on the management of production systems. Managers in every organization, whether it produces goods or services, now carefully analyze the basic tasks that must be performed and try to devise the work systems that will allow their organizations to operate most efficiently.

The Gilbreths

Two prominent followers of Taylor were Frank Gilbreth (1868–1924) and Lillian Gilbreth (1878–1972), who refined Taylor's analysis of work movements and made many contributions to time-and-motion study.[19] Their aims were to (1) break up into each of its component actions and analyze every individual action necessary to perform a particular task, (2) find better ways to perform each component action, and (3) reorganize each of the component actions so that the action as a whole could be performed more efficiently—at less cost of time and effort.

The Gilbreths often filmed a worker performing a particular task and then separated the task actions, frame by frame, into their component movements. Their goal was to maximize the efficiency with which each individual task was performed so that gains across tasks would add up to enormous savings of time and effort. Their attempts to develop improved management principles were captured—at times quite humorously—in the movie *Cheaper by the Dozen*, which depicts how the Gilbreths (with their 12 children) tried to live their own lives according to these efficiency principles and apply them to daily actions such as shaving, cooking, and even raising a family.[20]

Eventually, the Gilbreths became increasingly interested in the study of fatigue. They studied how the physical characteristics of the workplace contribute to job stress that often leads to fatigue and thus poor performance. They isolated factors—such as lighting, heating, the colour of walls, and the design of tools and machines—that result in worker fatigue. Their pioneering studies paved the way for new advances in management theory.

In workshops and factories, the work of the Gilbreths, Taylor, and many others had a major effect on the practice of management. In comparison with the old crafts system, jobs in the new system were more repetitive, boring, and monotonous as a result of the application of scientific management principles, and workers became increasingly dissatisfied. Frequently, the management of work settings became a game between workers and managers: Managers tried to initiate work practices to increase performance, and workers tried to hide the true potential efficiency of the work setting in order to protect their own well-being.[21]

Administrative Management Theory

administrative management The study of how to create an organizational structure that leads to high efficiency and effectiveness.

Side by side with scientific managers studying the person–task mix to increase efficiency, other researchers were focusing on **administrative management**, the study of how to create an organizational structure that leads to high efficiency and effectiveness. Organizational structure is the system of task and authority relationships that control how employees use resources to achieve the organization's goals. Two of the most influential views regarding the creation of efficient systems of organizational administration were developed in Europe. Max Weber, a German professor of sociology, developed one theory. Henri Fayol, the French manager who developed a model of management introduced in Chapter 1, developed the other.

The Theory of Bureaucracy

Max Weber (1864–1920) wrote at the turn of the twentieth century, when Germany was undergoing its industrial revolution.[22] To help Germany manage its growing industrial enterprises at a time when it was striving to become a world power, Weber developed the principles of **bureaucracy**–a formal system of organization and administration designed to ensure efficiency and effectiveness. A bureaucratic system of administration is based on five principles (summarized in Figure 2.2).

bureaucracy A formal system of organization and administration designed to ensure efficiency and effectiveness.

authority The power to hold people accountable for their actions and to make decisions concerning the use of organizational resources.

* Principle 1: *In a bureaucracy, a manager's formal authority derives from the position he or she holds in the organization.*

  Authority is the power to hold people accountable for their actions and to make decisions concerning the use of organizational resources. Authority gives managers the right to direct and control their subordinates' behaviour to achieve organizational goals. In a bureaucratic system of administration, obedience is owed to a manager, not because of any personal qualities that he or she might possess–such as personality, wealth, or social status–but because the manager occupies a position that is associated with a certain level of authority and responsibility.[23]

* Principle 2: *In a bureaucracy, people should occupy positions because of their performance, not because of their social standing or personal contacts.*

  This principle was not always followed in Weber's time and is often ignored today. Some organizations and industries are still affected by social networks in which personal contacts and relations, not job-related skills, influence hiring and promotional decisions.

* Principle 3: *The extent of each position's formal authority and task responsibilities, and its relationship to other positions in an organization, should be clearly specified.*

  When the tasks and authority associated with various positions in the organization are clearly specified, managers and workers know what is expected of them

Figure 2.2
Weber's Principles of Bureaucracy

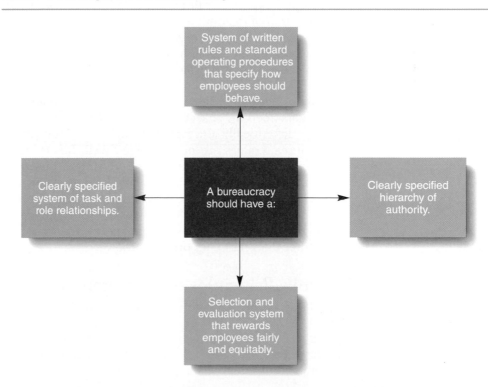

Christie Hefner, the daughter of Playboy founder Hugh Hefner, now runs Playboy Enterprises. Do you think Ms. Hefner earned this position based on her performance or knowledge, or received it based on her relationship to Hugh Hefner? Do you consider her gender an opportunity or barrier for her success in the industry?

rules Formal written instructions that specify actions to be taken under different circumstances to achieve specific goals.

standard operating procedures Specific sets of written instructions about how to perform a certain aspect of a task.

norms Unwritten rules and informal codes of conduct that prescribe how people should act in particular situations.

and what to expect from each other. Moreover, an organization can hold all its employees strictly accountable for their actions when each person is completely familiar with his or her responsibilities.

* Principle 4: *So that authority can be exercised effectively in an organization, positions should be arranged hierarchically, so employees know whom to report to and who reports to them.*[24]

Managers must create an organizational hierarchy of authority that makes it clear who reports to whom and to whom managers and workers should go if conflicts or problems arise. This principle is especially important in the armed forces, CSIS, RCMP, and other organizations that deal with sensitive issues involving possible major repercussions. It is vital that managers at high levels of the hierarchy be able to hold subordinates accountable for their actions.

* Principle 5: *Managers must create a well-defined system of rules, standard operating procedures, and norms so that they can effectively control behaviour within an organization.*

Rules are formal written instructions that specify actions to be taken under different circumstances to achieve specific goals (for example, if *A* happens, do *B*). **Standard operating procedures** (**SOPs**) are specific sets of written instructions about how to perform a certain aspect of a task. A rule might state that at the end of the workday employees are to leave their machines in good order, and a set of SOPs then specifies exactly how they should do so, itemizing which machine parts must be oiled or replaced. **Norms** are unwritten, informal codes of conduct that prescribe how people should act in particular situations. For example, an organizational norm in a restaurant might be that waiters should help each other if time permits.

Rules, SOPs, and norms provide behavioural guidelines that improve the performance of a bureaucratic system because they specify the best ways to accomplish organizational tasks. Companies such as McDonald's and Wal-Mart have developed extensive rules and procedures to specify the types of behaviours that are required of their employees, such as, "Always greet the customer with a smile."

Weber believed that organizations that implement all five principles will establish a bureaucratic system that will improve organizational performance. The specification of positions and the use of rules and SOPs to regulate how tasks are performed make it easier for managers to organize and control the work of subordinates. Similarly, fair and equitable selection and promotion systems improve managers' feelings of security, reduce stress, and encourage organizational members to act ethically and further promote the interests of the organization.[25]

If bureaucracies are not managed well, however, many problems can result. Sometimes, managers allow rules and SOPs–"bureaucratic red tape"–to become so cumbersome that decision making becomes slow and inefficient and organizations are unable to change. When managers rely too much on rules to solve problems and not enough on their own skills and judgment, their behaviour becomes inflexible. A key challenge for managers is to use bureaucratic principles to benefit, rather than harm, an organization.

Fayol's Principles of Management

Working at the same time as Weber but independently of him, Henri Fayol (1841–1925), the CEO of Comambault Mining, identified 14 principles (summarized in Table 2.1) that he believed to be essential to increasing the efficiency of the management process.[26] Some of the principles that Fayol outlined have faded from contemporary management practices, but most have endured.

Table 2.1
Fayol's 14 Principles of Management

Division of Labour   Job specialization and the division of labour should increase efficiency, especially if managers take steps to lessen workers' boredom.

Authority and Responsibility   Managers have the right to give orders and the power to exhort subordinates for obedience.

Unity of Command   An employee should receive orders from only one superior.

Line of Authority   The length of the chain of command that extends from the top to the bottom of an organization should be limited.

Centralization   Authority should not be concentrated at the top of the chain of command.

Unity of Direction   The organization should have a single plan of action to guide managers and workers.

Equity   All organizational members are entitled to be treated with justice and respect.

Order   The arrangement of organizational positions should maximize organizational efficiency and provide employees with satisfying career opportunities.

Initiative   Managers should allow employees to be innovative and creative.

Discipline   Managers need to create a workforce that strives to achieve organizational goals.

Remuneration of Personnel   The system that managers use to reward employees should be equitable for both employees and the organization.

Stability of Tenure of Personnel   Long-term employees develop skills that can improve organizational efficiency.

Subordination of Individual Interests to the Common Interest   Employees should understand how their performance affects the performance of the whole organization.

Esprit de Corps   Managers should encourage the development of shared feelings of comradeship, enthusiasm, or devotion to a common cause.

The principles that Fayol and Weber set forth still provide a clear and appropriate set of guidelines that managers can use to create a work setting that makes efficient and effective use of organizational resources. These principles remain the bedrock of modern management theory; recent researchers have refined or developed them to suit modern conditions. For example, Weber's and Fayol's concerns for equity and for establishing appropriate links between performance and reward are central themes in contemporary theories of motivation and leadership.

Behavioural Management Theory

behavioural management The study of how managers should behave in order to motivate employees and encourage them to perform at high levels and be committed to the achievement of organizational goals.

The **behavioural management** theorists writing in the first half of the twentieth century all espoused a theme that focused on how managers should personally behave in order to motivate employees and encourage them to perform at high levels and be committed to the achievement of organizational goals. The "Management Insight" indicates how employees can become demoralized when managers do not treat their employees properly.

Management Insight

How to Discourage Employees

Catherine Robertson, owner of Vancouver-based Robertson Telecom Inc., made headlines in February 2001 for her management policies.[27] Robertson is a government contractor whose company operates Enquiry BC, which gives British Columbians toll-free telephone information and referral services about all provincial government programs.

Female telephone operators at Robertson Telecom must wear skirts or dresses even though they never come in contact with the public. Not even dress pants are allowed. As Gillian Savage, a former employee, notes, "This isn't a suggested thing, it's an order: No pants." Brad Roy, another former employee, claims a female Indo-Canadian employee was sent home to change when she arrived at work wearing a Punjabi suit (a long shirt over pants).

The no-pants rule is not the only concern of current and former employees. Roy also said, "I saw some people being reprimanded for going to the washroom." While Robertson denied Roy's allegation regarding washrooms, she did confirm that company policy included the no-pants rule, that employees were not allowed to bring their purses or other personal items to their desks, and that they were not allowed to drink coffee or bottled water at their desks. The company does not provide garbage cans for the employees.

A group of current and former employees recently expressed concern with the number of rules Robertson has in place, and claimed that the rules have led to high turnover and poor morale. A current employee claims that many workers do not care whether they give out the right government phone numbers.

Robertson said that she knew of no employees who were discontent, and was shocked that the policies had caused distress among employees. She defended the dress code as appropriate business attire.

Robertson may have to make some adjustments in her management style. The cabinet minister responsible for Enquiry BC, Catherine MacGregor, ordered an investigation of the contractor after being contacted by *The Vancouver Sun* about the allegations. She noted that the skirts-only rule for women is not appropriate, and that, "All of our contractors are expected to fully comply with the Employment Standards Act, Workers Compensation rules and human rights legislation."

Additionally, Mary-Woo Sims, head of the BC Human Rights Commission, said dress codes can't be based on gender. Thus, an employer can't tell men they must wear pants (as Robertson does), but tell women they can't. "On the face of it, it would appear to be gender discriminatory," Sims said.

BC Employment
Standards Branch
www.labour.gov.bc.ca/esb/

BC Human Rights
Commission
www.bchrc.gov.bc.ca/

Why is it important to think about the human side of management?

The Work of Mary Parker Follett

If F.W. Taylor is considered to be the father of management thought, Mary Parker Follett (1868–1933) serves as its mother.[28] Much of her writing about management and about the way managers should behave toward workers was a response to her concern that Taylor was ignoring the human side of the organization. She pointed out that management often overlooks the multitude of ways in which employees can contribute to the organization when managers allow them to participate and exercise initiative in their everyday work lives.[29] Taylor, for example, relied on time-and-motion experts to analyze workers' jobs for them. Follett, in contrast, argued that because workers know the most about their jobs, they should be involved in job analysis and managers should allow them to participate in the work development process.

Follett proposed that, "Authority should go with knowledge ... whether it is up the line or down." In other words, if workers have the relevant knowledge, then workers, rather than managers, should be in control of the work process itself, and managers should behave as coaches and facilitators—not as monitors and supervisors. In making this statement, Follett anticipated the current interest in self-managed teams and empowerment. She also recognized the importance of having managers in different departments communicate directly with each other to speed decision making. She advocated what she called "cross-functioning": members of different departments working together in cross-departmental teams to accomplish projects—an approach that is increasingly utilized today.[30]

Fayol also mentioned expertise and knowledge as important sources of managers' authority, but Follett went further. She proposed that knowledge and expertise, and not managers' formal authority deriving from their position in the hierarchy, should decide who would lead at any particular moment. She believed, as do many management theorists today, that power is fluid and should flow to the person who can best help the organization achieve its goals. Follett took a horizontal view of power and authority, in contrast to Fayol, who saw the formal line of authority and vertical chain of command as being most essential to effective management. Follett's behavioural approach to management was very radical for its time.

The Hawthorne Studies and Human Relations

Hawthorne Studies
http://management
learning.com/topi/
mngthwth.html

Probably because of its radical nature, Follett's work was unappreciated by managers and researchers until quite recently. Instead, researchers continued to follow in the footsteps of Taylor and the Gilbreths. One focus was on how efficiency might be increased through improving various characteristics of the work setting, such as job specialization or the kinds of tools workers used. One series of studies was conducted from 1924 to 1932 at the Hawthorne Works of the Western Electric Company.[31] This research, now known as the Hawthorne studies, began as an attempt to investigate how characteristics of the work setting–specifically the level of lighting or illumination–affect worker fatigue and performance. The researchers conducted an experiment in which they systematically measured worker productivity at various levels of illumination.

The experiment produced some unexpected results. The researchers found that regardless of whether they raised or lowered the level of illumination, productivity increased. In fact, productivity began to fall only when the level of illumination dropped to the level of moonlight, a level at which presumably workers could no longer see well enough to do their work efficiently.

The researchers found these results puzzling and invited a noted Harvard psychologist, Elton Mayo, to help them. Subsequently, it was found that many other factors also influence worker behaviour, and it was not clear what was actually influencing the Hawthorne workers' behaviour. However, this particular effect–which became known as the **Hawthorne effect**–seemed to suggest that workers' attitudes toward their managers affect the level of workers' performance. In particular, the significant finding was that a manager's behaviour or leadership approach can affect performance. This finding led many researchers to turn their attention to managerial behaviour and leadership. If supervisors could be trained to behave in ways that would elicit cooperative behaviour from their subordinates, then productivity could be increased. From this view emerged the **human relations movement**, which advocates that supervisors be behaviourally trained to manage subordinates in ways that elicit their cooperation and increase their productivity.

Hawthorne effect The finding that a manager's behaviour or leadership approach can affect workers' level of performance.

human relations movement Advocates of the idea that supervisors be behaviourally trained to manage subordinates in ways that elicit their cooperation and increase their productivity.

The importance of behavioural or human relations training became even clearer to its supporters after another series of experiments–the bank wiring room experiments. In a study of workers making telephone switching equipment, researchers Elton Mayo and F.J. Roethlisberger discovered that the workers, as a group, had deliberately adopted a norm of output restriction to protect their jobs. Workers who violated this informal production norm were subjected to sanctions by other group members. Those who violated group performance norms and performed above the norm were called "ratebusters"; those who performed below the norm were called "chiselers."

The experimenters concluded that both types of workers threatened the group as a whole. Ratebusters threatened group members because they revealed to managers how fast the work could be done. Chiselers were looked down on because they were not doing their share of the work. Work-group members disciplined both ratebusters and chiselers in order to create a pace of work that the workers (not the managers) thought was fair. Thus, a work group's influence over output can be as great as the supervisors' influence. Since the work group can influence the behaviour of its members, some management theorists argue that supervisors should be trained to behave in ways that gain the goodwill and cooperation of workers so that supervisors, not workers, control the level of work-group performance.

One of the main implications of the Hawthorne studies was that the behaviour of managers and workers in the work setting is as important in explaining the level of performance as the technical aspects of the task. Managers must understand the workings of the **informal organization**, the system of behavioural rules and norms that emerge in a group, when they try to manage or change behaviour in organizations. Many studies have found that, as time passes, groups often develop elaborate procedures and norms that bond members together, allowing unified action either to cooperate with management in order to raise performance or to restrict output and thwart the attainment of organizational goals.[32] The Hawthorne studies demonstrated the importance of understanding how the feelings, thoughts, and behaviour of work-group members and managers affect performance. It was becoming increasingly clear to researchers that understanding behaviour in organizations is a complex process that is critical to increasing performance.[33] Indeed, the increasing interest in the area of management known as **organizational behaviour**, the study of the factors that have an impact on how individuals and groups respond to and act in organizations, dates from these early studies.

informal organization
The system of behavioural rules and norms that emerge in a group.

organizational behaviour The study of the factors that have an impact on how individuals and groups respond to and act in organizations.

Theory X and Theory Y

Several studies after the Second World War revealed how assumptions about workers' attitudes and behaviour affect managers' behaviour. Perhaps the most influential approach was developed by Douglas McGregor. He proposed that two different sets of assumptions about work attitudes and behaviours dominate the way managers think and affect how they behave in organizations. McGregor named these two contrasting sets of assumptions *Theory X* and *Theory Y* (see Figure 2.3).[34]

THEORY X According to the assumptions of **Theory X**, the average worker is lazy, dislikes work, and will try to do as little as possible. Moreover, workers have little ambition and wish to avoid responsibility. Thus, the manager's task is to counteract workers' natural tendencies to avoid work. To keep workers' performance at a high level, the manager must supervise them closely and control their behaviour by means of "the carrot and stick"–rewards and punishments.

Managers who accept the assumptions of Theory X design and shape the work setting to maximize their control over workers' behaviours and minimize workers'

Theory X Negative assumptions about workers that lead to the conclusion that a manager's task is to supervise them closely and control their behaviour.

Figure 2.3
Theory X Versus Theory Y

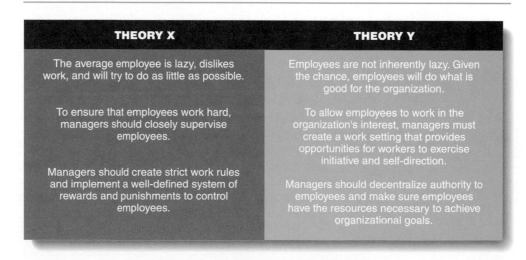

THEORY X	THEORY Y
The average employee is lazy, dislikes work, and will try to do as little as possible.	Employees are not inherently lazy. Given the chance, employees will do what is good for the organization.
To ensure that employees work hard, managers should closely supervise employees.	To allow employees to work in the organization's interest, managers must create a work setting that provides opportunities for workers to exercise initiative and self-direction.
Managers should create strict work rules and implement a well-defined system of rewards and punishments to control employees.	Managers should decentralize authority to employees and make sure employees have the resources necessary to achieve organizational goals.

control over the pace of work. These managers believe that workers must be made to do what is necessary for the success of the organization, and they focus on developing rules, SOPs, and a well-defined system of rewards and punishments to control behaviour. They see little point in giving workers autonomy to solve their own problems because they think that the workforce neither expects nor desires cooperation. Theory X managers see their role as to closely monitor workers to ensure that they contribute to the production process and do not threaten product quality. Henry Ford, who closely supervised and managed his workforce, fits McGregor's description of a manager who holds Theory X assumptions.

Theory Y Positive assumptions about workers that lead to the conclusion that a manager's task is to create a work setting that encourages commitment to organizational goals and provides opportunities for workers to be imaginative and to exercise initiative and self-direction.

THEORY Y In contrast, **Theory Y** assumes that workers are not inherently lazy, do not naturally dislike work, and, if given the opportunity, will do what is good for the organization. According to Theory Y, the characteristics of the work setting determine whether workers consider work to be a source of satisfaction or punishment; and managers do not need to control workers' behaviour closely in order to make them perform at a high level, because workers will exercise self-control when they are committed to organizational goals. The implication of Theory Y, according to McGregor, is that "the limits of collaboration in the organizational setting are not limits of human nature but of management's ingenuity in discovering how to realize the potential represented by its human resources."[35] It is the manager's task to create a work setting that encourages commitment to organizational goals and provides opportunities for workers to be imaginative and to exercise initiative and self-direction.

When managers design the organizational setting to reflect the assumptions about attitudes and behaviour suggested by Theory Y, the characteristics of the organization are quite different from those of an organizational setting based on Theory X. Managers who believe that workers are motivated to help the organization reach its goals can decentralize authority and give more control over the job to workers, both as individuals and in groups. In this setting, individuals and groups are still accountable for their activities, but the manager's role is not to control employees but to provide support and advice, to make sure employees have the resources they need to perform their jobs, and to evaluate them on their ability to help the organization meet its goals. Henri Fayol's approach to administration more closely reflects the assumptions of Theory Y, rather than Theory X.

Management Science Theory

management science theory An approach to management that uses rigorous quantitative techniques to help managers make maximum use of organizational resources.

Management science theory is a contemporary approach to management that focuses on the use of rigorous quantitative techniques to help managers make maximum use of organizational resources to produce goods and services. In essence, management science theory is a contemporary extension of scientific management, which, as developed by Taylor, also took a quantitative approach to measuring the worker–task mix in order to raise efficiency. There are many branches of management science; each of them deals with a specific set of concerns:

- *Quantitative management* utilizes mathematical techniques—such as linear and nonlinear programming, modelling, simulation, queuing theory, and chaos theory—to help managers decide, for example, how much inventory to hold at different times of the year, where to locate a new factory, and how best to invest an organization's financial capital.

- *Operations management (or operations research)* provides managers with a set of techniques that they can use to analyze any aspect of an organization's production system to increase efficiency.

- *Total quality management (TQM)* focuses on analyzing an organization's input, conversion, and output activities to increase product quality.[36]

- *Management information systems (MIS)* help managers design information systems that provide information about events occurring inside the organization as well as in its external environment—information that is vital for effective decision making.

All these subfields of management science provide tools and techniques that managers can use to help improve the quality of their decision making and increase efficiency and effectiveness.

Organizational Environment Theory

organizational environment The set of forces and conditions that operate beyond an organization's boundaries but affect a manager's ability to acquire and utilize resources.

An important milestone in the history of management thought occurred when researchers went beyond the study of how managers can influence behaviour within organizations to consider how managers control the organization's relationship with its external environment, or **organizational environment**—the set of forces and conditions that operate beyond an organization's boundaries but affect a manager's ability to acquire and utilize resources. Resources in the organizational environment include the raw materials and skilled people that an organization requires to produce goods and services, as well as the support of groups including customers who buy these goods and services and provide the organization with financial resources. One way of determining the relative success of an organization is to consider how effective its managers are at obtaining scarce and valuable resources.[37] The importance of studying the environment became clear after the development of open-systems theory and contingency theory during the 1960s.

The Open-Systems View

open system A system that takes in resources from its external environment and converts them into goods and services that are then sent back to that environment for purchase by customers.

One of the most influential views of how an organization is affected by its external environment was developed by Daniel Katz, Robert Kahn, and James Thompson in the 1960s.[38] These theorists viewed the organization as an **open system**—a system that takes in resources from its external environment and converts or transforms them into goods and services that are then sent back to that environment, where they are bought by customers (see Figure 2.4).

At the *input stage*, an organization acquires resources such as raw materials, money, and skilled workers to produce goods and services. Once the organization has gathered the necessary resources, conversion begins. At the *conversion stage*, the organization's workforce, using appropriate tools, techniques, and machinery, transforms the inputs into outputs of finished goods and services such as cars, hamburgers, or flights to Hawaii. At the *output stage*, the organization releases finished goods and services to its external environment, where customers purchase and use them to satisfy their needs. The money the organization obtains from the sales of its outputs allows the organization to acquire more resources so that the cycle can begin again.

closed system A system that is self-contained and thus not affected by changes that occur in its external environment.

entropy The tendency of a system to lose its ability to control itself and thus to dissolve and disintegrate.

The system just described is said to be "open" because the organization draws from and interacts with the external environment in order to survive; in other words, the organization is open to its environment. A closed system, in contrast, is a self-contained system that is not affected by changes that occur in its external environment. Organizations that operate as **closed systems**, that ignore the external environment and that fail to acquire inputs, are likely to experience **entropy**, the tendency of a system to lose its ability to control itself and thus to dissolve and disintegrate.

Management theorists can model the activities of most organizations by using the open-systems view. Manufacturing companies like Ford and General Electric, for example, buy inputs such as component parts, skilled and semiskilled labour, and robots and computer-controlled manufacturing equipment; then, at the con-

Figure 2.4

The Organization as an Open System

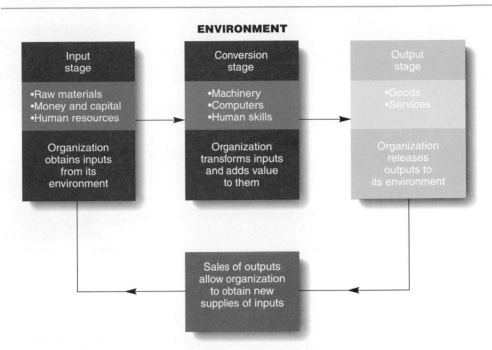

version stage, they use their manufacturing skills to assemble inputs into outputs of cars and computers. As we discuss in later chapters, competition between organizations for resources is one of several major challenges to managing the organizational environment.

Researchers using the open-systems view are also interested in how the various parts of a system work together to promote efficiency and effectiveness. Systems theorists like to argue that "the parts are more than the sum of the whole"; they mean that an organization performs at a higher level when its departments work together rather than separately. **Synergy**, the performance gains that result when individuals and departments coordinate their actions, is possible only in an organized system. The recent interest in using teams comprising people from different departments reflects systems theorists' interest in designing organizational systems to create synergy and thus increase efficiency and effectiveness.

synergy Performance gains that result when individuals and departments coordinate their actions.

Contingency Theory

contingency theory The idea that managers' choice of organizational structures and control systems depends on—is contingent on—characteristics of the external environment in which the organization operates.

Another milestone in management theory was the development of **contingency theory** in the 1960s by Tom Burns and G.M. Stalker in the United Kingdom and Paul Lawrence and Jay Lorsch in the United States.[39] The crucial message of contingency theory is that *there is no one best way to organize*: The organizational structures and the control systems that managers choose depend on—are contingent on—characteristics of the external environment in which the organization operates. According to contingency theory, the characteristics of the environment affect an organization's ability to obtain resources. To maximize the likelihood of gaining access to resources, managers must allow an organization's departments to organize and control their activities in ways most likely to allow them to obtain resources, given the constraints of the particular environment they face. In other words, how managers design the organizational hierarchy, choose a control system, and lead and motivate their employees is contingent on the characteristics of the organizational environment (see Figure 2.5).

Figure 2.5
Contingency Theory of Organizational Design

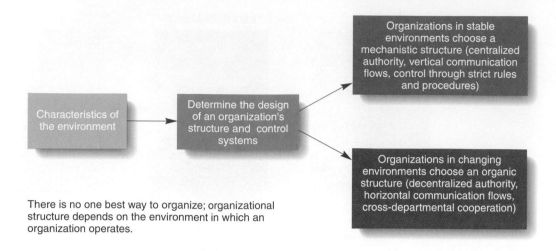

There is no one best way to organize; organizational structure depends on the environment in which an organization operates.

An important characteristic of the external environment that affects an organization's ability to obtain resources is the degree to which the environment is changing. Changes in the organizational environment include: changes in technology, which can lead to the creation of new products (such as compact discs) and result in the obsolescence of existing products (eight-track tapes); the entry of new competitors (such as foreign organizations that compete for available resources); and unstable economic conditions. In general, the more quickly the organizational environment is changing, the greater are the problems associated with gaining access to resources and the greater is the manager's need to find ways to coordinate the activities of people in different departments in order to respond to the environment quickly and effectively.

The basic idea behind contingency theory—that there is no one best way to design or lead an organization—has been incorporated into other areas of management theory, including leadership theories.

MECHANISTIC AND ORGANIC STRUCTURES   Drawing on Weber's and Fayol's principles of organization and management, Burns and Stalker proposed two basic ways in which managers can organize and control an organization's activities to respond to characteristics of its external environment: They can use a *mechanistic structure* or an *organic structure*.[40] As you will see, a mechanistic structure typically rests on Theory X assumptions, and an organic structure typically rests on Theory Y assumptions.

When the environment surrounding an organization is stable, managers tend to choose a mechanistic structure to organize and control activities and make employee behaviour predictable. In a **mechanistic structure**, authority is centralized at the top of the managerial hierarchy, and the vertical hierarchy of authority is the main means used to control subordinates' behaviour. Tasks and roles are clearly specified, subordinates are closely supervised, and the emphasis is on strict discipline and order. Everyone knows his or her place, and there is a place for everyone. A mechanistic structure provides the most efficient way to operate in a stable environment because it allows managers to obtain inputs at the lowest cost, giving an organization the most control over its conversion processes and enabling the most efficient production of goods and services with the smallest expenditure of resources. McDonald's restaurants operate with a mechanistic

mechanistic structure

An organizational structure in which authority is centralized, tasks and rules are clearly specified, and employees are closely supervised.

structure. Supervisors make all important decisions; employees are closely supervised and follow well-defined rules and standard operating procedures.

In contrast, when the environment is changing rapidly, it is difficult to obtain access to resources, and managers need to organize their activities in a way that allows them to cooperate, to act quickly to acquire resources (such as new types of inputs to produce new kinds of products), and to respond effectively to the unexpected. In an **organic structure**, authority is decentralized to middle and first-line managers to encourage them to take responsibility and act quickly to pursue scarce resources. Departments are encouraged to take a cross-departmental or functional perspective, and, as in Mary Parker Follett's model, authority rests with the individuals and departments best positioned to control the current problems the organization is facing. In an organic structure, control is much looser than it is in a mechanistic structure, and reliance on shared norms to guide organizational activities is greater.

Managers in an organic structure can react more quickly to a changing environment than can managers in a mechanistic structure. However, an organic structure is generally more expensive to operate, so it is used only when needed—when the organizational environment is unstable and rapidly changing. To facilitate global expansion, managers at Philips (a Dutch electronics company) were forced to change from a mechanistic to an organic structure, and their experience illustrates the different properties of these structures.

organic structure
An organizational structure in which authority is decentralized to middle and first-line managers and tasks and roles are left ambiguous to encourage employees to cooperate and respond quickly to the unexpected.

Managing Globally

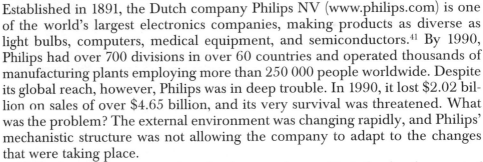

Philips' Organic Structure Works

Established in 1891, the Dutch company Philips NV (www.philips.com) is one of the world's largest electronics companies, making products as diverse as light bulbs, computers, medical equipment, and semiconductors.[41] By 1990, Philips had over 700 divisions in over 60 countries and operated thousands of manufacturing plants employing more than 250 000 people worldwide. Despite its global reach, however, Philips was in deep trouble. In 1990, it lost $2.02 billion on sales of over $4.65 billion, and its very survival was threatened. What was the problem? The external environment was changing rapidly, and Philips' mechanistic structure was not allowing the company to adapt to the changes that were taking place.

Philips' environment was changing in several ways. First, the development of the European Union had increased competition from other European electronics companies, such as the United Kingdom's General Electric. Second, competition from Sony, Matsushita, and other low-cost Japanese companies had increased. Third, advances in technology in the form of new and more powerful computer chips and lasers had ushered in a new era of global competition. Philips' organizational structure was preventing managers from responding quickly to these challenges.

Over the years, decision making at Philips had become extremely centralized; all significant new product decisions were made in the Netherlands at the company's Eindhoven headquarters. At Eindhoven, 3000 corporate managers supervised the 2500 middle managers who were responsible for coordinating product development on a global scale. Decisions made by these 5500 managers were communicated to managers in Philips' 700 divisions spread across 60 countries, who then made decisions for their respective countries. Philips' tall, centralized, mechanistic structure slowed communication and decision making and undermined the company's ability to respond to the global changes taking place. Moreover, very little communication was occurring between managers on the same hierarchical level but in different divisions (such horizontal communication is critical to speeding up the development of new products and reducing costs).

Top managers realized they had to change the organizational structure to allow the company to respond better to its environment. They began by dividing the organization into four product groups—lighting, consumer electronics, electronic components, and telecommunication. They gave each product group global responsibility for all aspects of its own activities—research, sales, and manufacturing.[42] In other words, they decentralized authority to the managers of the product groups. In this way, Philips tried to create a flatter, more flexible organic structure at a global level—a structure in which managers close to the action, not top managers at distant corporate headquarters, made decisions. Throughout the 1990s, the change to an organic structure produced major success for Philips. Costs fell, the speed of new product development increased sharply, and Philips made record profits. Nevertheless, low-cost competition from countries such as China, Korea, and Malaysia is still forcing managers to search continuously for better, more efficient ways to meet the challenges of the global environment.

Because the managers of many global organizations have been facing problems similar to those of Philips, researchers' interest in managers' attempts to deal with the organizational environment both at home and abroad has increased rapidly. Part Three of this book is devoted to strategic management, the study of the relationship between organizations and their external environment and of the strategies organizations adopt to manage that environment.[43]

Tips for Managers

Applying Management Principles

1. Analyze whether an organization's division of labour is meeting its current needs. Consider ways to change the level of job specialization to increase performance.

2. Examine the way an organization works in reference to Weber and Fayol's principles. Decide if the distribution of authority in the hierarchy best meets the organization's needs. Similarly, decide if the right system to discipline or remunerate employees is being used.

3. Examine organizational policies to see if managers are consistently behaving in an equitable manner and whether these policies lead to ethical employee behaviour.

Summary and Review

In this chapter, we examined the evolution of management theory and research over the last century. Much of the material in the rest of this book stems from developments and refinements of this work.

SCIENTIFIC MANAGEMENT THEORY   The search for efficiency started with the study of how managers could improve person–task relationships to increase efficiency. The concept of job specialization and division of labour remains the basis for the design of work settings in modern organizations. New developments like lean production and total quality management are often viewed as advances on the early scientific management principles developed by Taylor and the Gilbreths.

Chapter Summary

SCIENTIFIC MANAGEMENT THEORY

- Job Specialization and the Division of Labour
- F.W. Taylor and Scientific Management
- The Gilbreths

ADMINISTRATIVE MANAGEMENT THEORY

- The Theory of Bureaucracy
- Fayol's Principles of Management

BEHAVIOURAL MANAGEMENT THEORY

- The Work of Mary Parker Follett
- The Hawthorne Studies and Human Relations
- Theory X and Theory Y

MANAGEMENT SCIENCE THEORY

ORGANIZATIONAL ENVIRONMENT THEORY

- The Open-Systems View
- Contingency Theory

ADMINISTRATIVE MANAGEMENT THEORY   Max Weber and Henri Fayol outlined principles of bureaucracy and administration that are as relevant to managers today as when they were written at the turn of the twentieth century. Much of modern management research refines these principles to suit contemporary conditions. For example, the increasing interest in the use of cross-departmental teams and the empowerment of workers are issues that managers also faced a century ago.

BEHAVIOURAL MANAGEMENT THEORY   Researchers have described many different approaches to managerial behaviour, including Theories X and Y. Often, the managerial behaviour that researchers suggest reflects the context of their own historical era and culture. Mary Parker Follett advocated managerial behaviours that did not reflect accepted modes of managerial behaviour at the time, but her work was largely ignored until conditions changed.

MANAGEMENT SCIENCE THEORY   The various branches of management science theory provide rigorous quantitative techniques that give managers more control over their organization's use of resources to produce goods and services.

ORGANIZATIONAL ENVIRONMENT THEORY   The importance of studying the organization's external environment became clear after the development of open-systems theory and contingency theory during the 1960s. A main focus of contemporary management research is to find methods to help managers improve the way they utilize organizational resources and compete successfully in the global environment. Strategic management and total quality management are two important approaches intended to help managers make better use of organizational resources.

Management in Action

Topics for Discussion and Action

1. Choose a fast-food restaurant, a department store, or some other organization with which you are familiar, and describe the division of labour and job specialization it uses to produce goods and services. How might this division of labour be improved?

2. Apply Taylor's principles of scientific management to improve the performance of the organization you chose in Item 1.

3. In what ways are Weber's and Fayol's ideas about bureaucracy and administration similar? In what ways do they differ?

4. Question a manager about his or her views of the relative importance of Fayol's 14 principles of management.

5. Which of Weber's and Fayol's principles seem most relevant to the creation of an ethical organization?

6. Why was the work of Mary Parker Follett ahead of its time? To what degree do you think it is appropriate today?

7. Visit various organizations in your community, and identify those that seem to operate with a Theory X or a Theory Y approach to management.

8. What is contingency theory? What kinds of organizations familiar to you have been successful or unsuccessful in dealing with contingencies from the external environment?

9. Why are mechanistic and organic structures suited to different types of organizational environment?

Building Management Skills

Managing Your Own Business

Now that you understand the concerns addressed by management thinkers over the last century, use this exercise to apply your knowledge to develop your management skills.

Imagine that you are the founding entrepreneur of a software company that specializes in developing computer games for home computers. Customer demand for your games has increased so much that over the last year you have grown from a busy one-person operation to employ 16 people. In addition to yourself, you employ six software developers to produce the software, three graphic artists, two computer technicians, two marketing and sales personnel, and two secretaries. In the next year, you expect to hire 30 new people, and you are wondering how best to manage your growing company.

1. Use the principles of Weber and Fayol to decide on the system of organization and management that you think will be most effective for your growing organization. How many levels will the managerial hierarchy of your organization have? How much authority will you decentralize to your subordinates? How will you establish the division of labour between subordinates? Will your subordinates work alone and report to you or work in teams?

2. What management approach (for example, Theory X or Theory Y, Scientific Management, etc.) do you propose to use to run your organization? In 50 words or less, write a statement describing the management approach you propose to use to motivate and coordinate your subordinates, and tell why you think this style will be best.

Small Group Breakout Exercise

Modelling an Open System

Form groups of three to five people, and appoint one group member as the spokesperson who will communicate your findings to the class when called on by the instructor. Then discuss the following scenario.

Think of an organization with which you are all familiar, such as a local restaurant, store, or bank. After choosing an organization, model it from an open-systems perspective. Identify its input, conversion, and output processes, and identify forces in the external environment that help or hurt the organization's ability to obtain resources and dispose of its goods or services.

Exploring the World Wide Web

Specific Assignment

Investigate the history of Ford Motor Company by utilizing the extensive resources of Ford's historical library. Research Ford's Web site (www.ford.com), and locate and read the material on Ford's history and evolution over time.

1. What kinds of management concerns have occupied Ford's top managers from its beginnings to today?

2. Do these concerns seem to have changed over time?

General Assignment

Search for a Web site that contains the time line or a short history of a company, detailing the way the organization has developed over time. What are the significant stages in the company's development, and what problems and issues have confronted managers at these stages?

ManagementCase

A Shake-Up at Eastman Kodak

Eastman Kodak Company was incorporated in New Jersey on October 24, 1901, as successor to Eastman Dry Plate Company, the business originally established by George Eastman in 1880. The Dry Plate Company had been formed to mass-produce the dry plates needed for early cameras. After George Eastman developed silver-halide paper-based photographic film and invented the first portable camera, he formed his new company to capitalize on his inventions.

From the beginning, Eastman was aware of the need to reduce costs to bring his products to the mass market, and he quickly adopted scientific management principles to improve production efficiency. Eastman also developed a people-oriented approach. Over the years, Eastman Kodak became known as "Mother Kodak" because of the bonds that developed between the organization and its members. Until the 1980s, Kodak never had layoffs and turnover was very low. It was quite common for both managers and workers to spend their entire working careers with Kodak, and for whole families or successive generations of families to be employed by the company at its Rochester, New York headquarters and manufacturing plants.

With success, however, decision making became centralized at the top of the organization. A group of long-term managers made all significant operating decisions and then communicated the decisions down a very tall hierarchy to managers at lower levels. When it came time to decide who would be promoted, seniority and loyalty to Mother Kodak were more important than a person's performance; fitting in and being a member of the "Kodak Team" were the keys to success.

This management approach worked well while Kodak had a virtual monopoly of the photographic products market, but it became a liability when Kodak faced stiff competition from foreign competitors like Germany's Agfa and Japan's Fuji Film. These companies, having found new ways to produce film and paper at costs lower than Kodak's, began to challenge Kodak's dominance. Managers at Kodak were slow to respond to the challenge. The organization's tall, centralized structure slowed decision making, and its conservative orientation made managers reluctant to change. In the 1980s, things went from bad to worse for Kodak as its share of the market and profits fell. Top management had to address the problems.

After much soul searching, top managers decided they had to totally change Kodak's organizational structure to make the company more competitive. They divided the company into four separate product divisions and began a massive downsizing of the workforce. Kodak's policy of lifetime employment was discontinued as managers announced the first layoffs in its history. Top management's goal was to flatten the organization's hierarchy and push authority and responsibility to employees at lower levels. Top management hoped that decentralized authority would help lower-level managers become more entrepreneurial and more inclined to search for new ways to cut costs.

These changes helped Kodak, but were not enough to reverse its decline. In 1994, in a break with the past, Kodak appointed a CEO from outside the company to change the organization further. George Fisher, former CEO of Motorola, took charge. Fisher was renowned for creating a climate of innovation at Motorola and for helping that company to become a market leader in the cellular telephone industry. To increase the rate of new product development and to help the company regain market share, he has been striving to change Kodak managers' conservative management style into an entrepreneurial approach. Fisher also has continued to restructure the company, laying off thousands more employees and managers and selling many of Kodak's divisions. The Kodak of today is very different from the Kodak of 10 years ago, and a new set of principles guides managers and workers.

Questions

1. What was the source of the problems facing Kodak in the 1980s?

2. Using the chapter material as a base, discuss the way Kodak altered its organization and management approach to deal with its problems.

ManagementCase
In the News

From the pages of *The Wall Street Journal*
Mr. Edens Profits from Watching His Workers' Every Move

Control is one of Ron Edens's favorite words. "This is a controlled environment," he says of the blank brick building that houses his company, Electronic Banking System Inc.

Inside, long lines of women sit at spartan desks, slitting envelopes, sorting contents and filling out "control cards" that record how many letters they have opened and how long it has taken them. Workers here, in "the cage," must process three envelopes a minute. Nearby, other women tap keyboards, keeping pace with a quota that demands 8500 strokes an hour.

The room is silent. Talking is forbidden. The windows are covered. Coffee mugs, religious pictures and other adornments are barred from workers' desks.

In his office upstairs, Mr. Edens sits before a TV monitor that flashes images from eight cameras posted through the plant. "There's a little bit of Sneaky Pete to it," he says, using a remote control to zoom in on a document atop a worker's desk. "I can basically read that and figure out how someone's day is going."

This day, like most others, is going smoothly, and Mr. Edens's business has boomed as a result. "We maintain a lot of control," he says. "Order and control are everything in this business."

Mr. Edens's business belongs to a small but expanding financial service known as "lockbox processing." Many companies and charities that once did their paperwork in-house now "out-source" clerical tasks to firms like EBS, which processes donations to groups such as Mothers Against Drunk Driving, the Doris Day Animal League, Greenpeace and the National Organization for Women.

More broadly, EBS reflects the explosive growth of jobs in which workers perform low-wage and limited tasks in white-collar settings. This has transformed towns like Hagerstown—a blue-collar community hit hard by industrial layoffs in the 1970s—into sites for thousands of jobs in factory-sized offices.

Many of these jobs, though, are part-time and most pay far less than the manufacturing occupations they replaced. Some workers at EBS start at the minimum wage of US$4.25 an hour and most earn about US$6 an hour. The growth of such jobs—which often cluster outside major cities—also completes a curious historic circle. During the Industrial Revolution, farmers' daughters went to work in textile towns like Lowell, Mass. In post-industrial America, many women of modest means and skills are entering clerical mills where they process paper instead of cloth (coincidentally, EBS occupies a former garment factory).

"The office of the future can look a lot like the factory of the past," says Barbara Garson, author of *The Electronic Sweatshop* and other books on the modern workplace. "Modern tools are being used to bring nineteenth-century working conditions into the white-collar world."

The time–motion philosophies of Frederick Taylor, for instance, have found a 1990s correlate in the phone, computer and camera, which can be used to monitor workers more closely than a foreman with a stopwatch ever could. Also, the nature of the work often justifies a vigilant eye. In EBS workers handle thousands of dollars in cheques and cash, and Mr. Edens says cameras help deter would-be thieves. Tight security also reassures visiting clients. "If you're disorderly, they'll think we're out of control and that things could get lost," says Mr. Edens, who worked as a financial controller for the National Rifle Association before founding EBS in 1983.

But tight observation also helps EBS monitor productivity and weed out workers who don't keep up. "There's multiple uses," Mr. Edens says of surveillance. His desk is covered with computer printouts recording the precise toll of keystrokes tapped by each data-entry worker. He also keeps a day-to-day tally of errors. The work floor itself resembles an enormous classroom in the throes of exam period. Desks point toward the front, where a manager keeps watch from a raised platform that workers call "the pedestal" or "the birdhouse." Other supervisors are positioned toward the back of the room. "If you want to watch someone," Mr. Edens explains, "it's easier from behind because they don't know you're watching." There also is a black globe hanging from the ceiling, in which cameras are positioned.

Mr. Edens sees nothing Orwellian about this omniscience. "It's not a Big Brother attitude," he says. "It's more of a calming attitude."

But studies of workplace monitoring suggest otherwise. Experts say that surveillance can create a hostile environment in which workers feel pressured, paranoid and prone to stress-related illness. Surveillance also can be used punitively, to intimidate workers or to justify their firing.

Following a failed union drive at EBS, the National Labour Relations Board filed a series of complaints against the company, including charges that EBS threatened, interrogated and spied on workers. As part of an out-of-court settlement, EBS reinstated a fired worker and posted a notice that it would refrain from illegal practices during a second union vote, which also failed.

"It's all noise," Mr. Edens says of the unfair labour charges. As to the pressure that surveillance creates, Mr. Edens sees that simply as "the nature of the beast." He adds: "It's got to add stress when everyone knows their production is being monitored. I don't apologize for that."

Mr. Edens also is unapologetic about the Draconian work rules he maintains, including one that forbids all talk unrelated to the completion of each task. "I'm not paying people to chat. I'm paying them to open envelopes," he says. Of the blocked windows, Mr. Edens adds: "I don't want them looking out—it's distracting. They'll make mistakes."

This total focus boosts productivity but it makes many workers feel lonely and trapped. Some try to circumvent the silence rule, like kids in a school library. "If you don't turn your head and sort of mumble out of the side of your mouth, supervisors won't hear you most of the time," Cindy Kesselring explains during her lunch break. Even so, she feels isolated and often longs for her former job as a waitress. "Work is your social life, particularly if you've got kids," says the 27-year-old mother.

"Here it's hard to get to know people because you can't talk."

During lunch, workers crowd the parking lot outside, chatting nonstop. "Some of us don't eat much because the more you chew the less you can talk," Ms. Kesselring says. There aren't other breaks and workers aren't allowed to sip coffee or eat at their desks during the long stretches before and after lunch. Hard candy is the only permitted desk snack.

New technology, and the breaking down of labour into discrete, repetitive tasks, also have effectively stripped jobs such as those at EBS of whatever variety and skills clerical work once possessed. Workers in the cage (an antiquated banking term for a money-handling area) only open envelopes and sort contents, those in the audit department compute figures, and data-entry clerks punch in the information that the others have collected. If they make a mistake, the computer buzzes and a message such as "check digit error" flashes on the screen.

"We don't ask these people to think—the machines think for them," Mr. Edens says. "They don't have to make any decisions." This makes the work simpler but also deepens its monotony. In the cage, Carol Smith says she looks forward to envelopes that contain anything out of the ordinary, such as letters reporting that the donor is deceased. Or she plays mental games. "I think to myself, *A* goes in this pile, *B* goes here and *C* goes there—sort of like Bingo." She says she sometimes feels "like a machine," particularly when she fills out the "control card" on which she lists "time in" and "time out" for each tray of envelopes. In a slot marked "cage operator," Ms. Smith writes her code number, 3173. "That's me," she says.

Barbara Ann Wiles, a keyboard operator, also plays mind games to break up the boredom. Tapping in the names and addresses of new donors, she tries to imagine the

faces behind the names, particularly the odd ones. "Like this one, Mrs. Fittizzi," she chuckles. "I can picture her as a very stout lady with a strong accent, hollering on a street corner." She picks out another: "Doris Angelroth—she's very sophisticated, a monocle maybe, drinking tea on an overstuffed mohair couch."

It is a world remote from the one Ms. Wiles inhabits. Like most EBS employees, she must juggle her low-paying job with childcare. On this Friday, for instance, Ms. Wiles will finish her eight-hour shift at about 4 p.m., go home for a few hours, then return for a second shift from midnight to 8 a.m. Otherwise, she would have to come in on Saturday to finish the week's work. "This way I can be home on the weekend to look after my kids," she says.

Others find the work harder to leave behind at the end of the day. In the cage, Ms. Smith says her husband used to complain because she often woke him in the middle of the night. "I'd be shuffling my hands in my sleep," she says, mimicking the motion of opening envelopes.

Her cage colleague, Ms. Kesselring, says her fiancé has a different gripe. "He dodges me for a couple of hours after work because I don't shut up—I need to talk, talk, talk," she says. And there is one household task she can no longer abide.

"I won't pay bills because I can't stand to open another envelope," she says. "I'll leave letters sitting in the mailbox for days."

Source: T. Horwitz, "Mr. Edens Profits from Watching His Workers' Every Move," *The Wall Street Journal*, December 1, 1994.

Questions

1. Which of the management theories described in the chapter does Ron Edens make most use of?

2. What is your view of Edens' management approach?

Part 2

THE ENVIRONMENT OF MANAGEMENT

Chapter 3
The Organizational Environment

Chapter 4
The Global Environment

Chapter 5
Ethics, Social Responsibility, and Diversity

Chapter three

The Organizational Environment

Learning Objectives

1. Explain why the ability to perceive, interpret, and respond appropriately to the organizational environment is crucial for managerial success.

2. Identify the main forces in an organization's task and general environments, and describe the challenges that each force presents to managers.

3. Discuss the main ways in which managers can manage the organizational environment.

4. Explain why boundary-spanning activities are important.

A Case in Contrast

From Crown Corporation to Privatization

Calgary-based Petro-Canada (Petrocan) (www.petro-canada.ca) was established in 1975 by the Liberal government under Pierre Trudeau to provide Canadians with "a window on the energy industry." Petrocan was to bring some Canadian ownership to the energy sector, which was dominated at the time by foreign companies. It has been called "a money pit for Canadian taxpayers in its early years".[1] Moreover, it was viewed with suspicion by others in the energy industry, "as both a spy agency and unfair competition."[2]

Ian Doig, who writes an energy newsletter, says of that time: "There was never any love lost between the industry in those days and Petro-Canada ... a company owned by the state inside a red building."[3]

Petrocan, as a crown corporation, did not face the same financial realities as other oil firms. It was allowed to engage in widespread explo-

ration opportunities, including the East coast, the Arctic and the untested oilsands. It also engaged in a series of corporate acquisitions to increase cash flow, resulting very shortly in creating a huge debt, something most private corporations would not have been able to withstand.

Wilbert (Bill) Hopper was the chairman and CEO of Petro-Canada from its inception until 1993. He had a "divide-and-conquer management strategy, flattering people to their faces and then denigrating them behind their backs."[4] Moreover, he "used to boast that he was nearly impossible to fire."[5]

Unlike what generally occurs at public corporations, Hopper didn't face challenges from his board of directors regarding his management of the company. The sole shareholder of the company from 1976 to 1991 was the government.

Hopper's first real challenge to his management practices came in 1991, when privatization

Wilburt (Bill) Hopper was the first CEO of Petro-Canada. Hopper's management style did not survive Petrocan's privatization.

Jim Stanford, chairman and CEO of Petro-Canada from 1993 to 1999, successfully oversaw much of the privatization of Petrocan.

brought a change in Petrocan's governance structure. Between 1991 and 1993, the government sold a 30-percent interest in the company. The first shares were offered for $13; a year later, the second issue, at $8.25, did not sell out. Nearly a year later, the price was down to $7.25. The move toward privatization was not as successful as had been hoped.

To understand why Petrocan might have had difficulties with privatization, one should note that for many years the company benefited from large subsidies and favouritism from the government. At the same time, while most oil and gas companies were aggressively reducing debt, non-performing assets, and employees, Petrocan's debt increased.

As a manager, Hopper did not easily adapt to the new environment facing Petrocan, but tended to resist the changes that were necessary to make the company profitable. While he engaged in some corporate downsizing, he found it easier to get rid of employees than corporate assets.

Finally, in January 1993, a group of disgruntled directors voted to remove him. They were concerned that Hopper was depressing the long-term value of Petrocan, because of his "refusal to cut waste and reduce the company's payroll."[6]

Jim Stanford, a long-time Petrocan employee, replaced Hopper. He immediately began to cut costs. Eight months after he took over, Petrocan's publicly traded shares were trading at $12.50.

The environment that Stanford faced was very much different from that of Hopper. Stanford says, "The major turning point [making it possible for his success] was when the company ceased to be a crown corporation and the federal government started selling its stock."[7] Stanford also oversaw further privatization of the company. In the fall of 1995, the government sold an additional 52 percent of its shares at $14.65 per share.

Stanford is credited with turning Petro-Canada "from a staid crown corporation into a profitable, dynamic energy giant."[8] At the end of 1999, Stanford stepped down, and Rob Brenneman, former head of corporate planning at Exxon Corp., took over as chief executive officer. Stanford's final year was one of the most profitable in Petro-Canada's history, because of high oil prices.

At the time that Stanford stepped down, Duncan Mathieson, an analyst at Scotia Capital Markets in Toronto, noted, "Compared to what it was five years ago, it's a massively different company."[9] The company is also viewed with a lot less suspicion. Alan MacFadyen, a professor of economics at the University of Calgary, says that Calgarians now view Petrocan "as being independent, and of functioning with much the same objectives as other companies. And that's what people in the industry here feel comfortable with."[10] ●

Overview

Bill Hopper and Jim Stanford faced very different environments during the time that each was CEO at Petro-Canada. They also took different actions that had different outcomes. In the organizational environment, all managers face a rich array of forces that they must recognize and respond to quickly and appropriately if their organizations are to survive and prosper. The external environment is uncertain and unpredictable because it is complex and constantly changing. Managers must position their organizations to deal efficiently and effectively with new developments. Hopper saw no need to make his company profitable, because it was a crown corporation. When the environment changed, and the company started to privatize, he was not prepared to make the necessary changes. As a result, he lost his job. Stanford rose to the challenge of privatization by taking appropriate action, and turning Petrocan into a very successful and profitable operation. Petrocan's growth continues.

In this chapter, we examine the organizational environment in detail. We describe it and identify the principal forces–both task and general–that create pressure and influence managers and thus affect the way in which organizations operate. We conclude with a study of several methods that managers can use to help organizations adjust and respond to forces in the organizational environment. By the end of the chapter, you will understand the steps managers must take to ensure that organizations adequately address and appropriately respond to their external environment.   ●

What is the Organizational Environment?

organizational environment The set of forces and conditions that operate beyond an organization's boundaries but affect a manager's ability to acquire and utilize resources.

The **organizational environment** is a set of forces and conditions, such as technology and competition, that are outside the organization's boundaries and have the potential to affect the way the organization operates, and the way managers engage in planning and organizing.[11] These forces change over time and thus present managers with *opportunities* and *threats*. We generally divide the organization's **external environment** into two major categories: the task environment and the general environment. These are depicted in Figure 3.1.

external environment The forces operating outside an organization that affect how the organization functions.

The **task environment** is a set of external forces and conditions that originate with suppliers, distributors, customers, and competitors and affect an organization's ability to obtain inputs and dispose of its outputs, because they pressure and influence managers on a daily basis. When managers turn on the radio or television,

task environment The set of forces and conditions that originate with suppliers, distributors, customers, and competitors and affect an organization's ability to obtain inputs and dispose of its outputs, because they influence managers on a daily basis.

Figure 3.1
Forces in the Organizational Environment

arrive at their offices in the morning, open their mail, or look at their computer screens, they are likely to learn about problems facing them because of changing conditions in their organization's task environment.

general environment
The wide-ranging economic, technological, sociocultural, demographic, political and legal, and global forces that affect an organization and its task environment.

The **general environment** is a wide-ranging set of external factors including economic, technological, sociocultural, demographic, political and legal, and global forces that affect the organization and its task environment directly or indirectly. For the individual manager, opportunities and threats resulting from changes in the general environment are often more difficult to identify and respond to than are events in the task environment. In Chapter 7, we examine how managers analyze their environment, using SWOT (strengths, weaknesses, opportunities, and threats) analysis.

Some changes in the external environment, such as the introduction of new technology or the opening of foreign markets, create opportunities for managers to obtain resources or enter new markets and thereby strengthen their organizations. In contrast, the rise of new competitors, an economic recession, or an oil shortage poses a threat that can devastate an organization if managers are unable to obtain resources or sell the organization's goods and services. The quality of managers' understanding of forces in the organizational environment, and their ability to respond appropriately to those forces, are critical factors affecting organizational performance.

In this chapter, we explore the nature of these forces and consider how managers can respond to them. A detailed discussion of the way the external environment affects the planning and organizing processes is presented in Parts Three and Four. Our focus now is on understanding the organizational environment and its impact on managers and organizations.

internal environment
The forces operating within an organization and stemming from the organization's structure and culture.

Some management theorists refer to another kind of environment, the **internal environment**, that managers must understand and control. The internal environment consists of forces operating within an organization and stemming from the organization's structure and culture. Although the task, general, and internal environments influence each other, we leave detailed discussion of how to manage structure and culture until Part Four (particularly, Chapter 9, "Organizational Control and Culture") and concentrate here on forces in the task and general environments and their effects on organizations.

The Task Environment

Forces in the task environment result from the actions of suppliers, distributors, customers, and competitors (see Figure 3.1). These four groups affect a manager's ability to obtain resources and dispose of outputs on a daily, weekly, and monthly basis and thus have a significant impact on short-term decision making.

Suppliers

suppliers Individuals and organizations that provide an organization with the input resources that it needs to produce goods and services.

Suppliers are the individuals and organizations that provide an organization with the input resources (such as raw materials, component parts, or employees) that it needs to produce goods and services. In return, the supplier receives compensation for those goods and services. An important aspect of a manager's job is to ensure a reliable supply of input resources.

A computer company such as Dell Canada, for example, has hundreds of suppliers. There are suppliers of component parts such as microprocessors (Intel and AMD) and disk drives (Quantum and Seagate Technologies). There are also suppliers of preinstalled software, including the operating system (Microsoft) and specific applications software (Quicken, Symantec, and America Online). Dell's providers of capital, such as banks and financial institutions, are also important suppliers.

There are several suppliers of labour to Dell and other companies. One is the group of educational institutions that train future Dell employees and therefore provide the company with skilled workers. In some industries, trade unions—organizations that represent employee interests and can control the supply of labour by exercising the right of unionized workers to strike—could be considered suppliers. Unions also can influence the terms and conditions under which labour is employed. In organizations and industries where unions are very strong, an important part of a manager's job is to negotiate and administer agreements with unions and their representatives.

Changes in the nature, numbers, or types of suppliers result in forces that produce opportunities and threats to which managers must respond if their organizations are to prosper. Often, when managers do not respond to a threat, they put their organization at a competitive disadvantage.

Another major supplier-related threat that confronts managers arises when suppliers' bargaining position with an organization is so strong that they can raise the prices of the inputs they supply to the organization. A supplier's bargaining position is especially strong if (1) the supplier is the sole source of an input and (2) the input is vital to the organization.[12] For example, one of the complaints against Microsoft was that it unfairly used its monopoly in computer operating systems to require a number of computer manufacturers and distributors to install other Microsoft products on computers they sold. In contrast, when an organization has many suppliers for a particular input, it is in a relatively strong bargaining position with those suppliers and can demand low-cost, high-quality inputs from them.

In addition to raising prices, suppliers can make operations difficult for an organization by restricting its access to important inputs. For example, provincial governments supply financial resources to Canada's universities and colleges and, in recent years, have often seriously hindered the operations of those institutions by reducing funding. This resource scarcity has forced programs at the colleges and universities to eliminate perceived operating inefficiencies (such as small classes) and actively pursue other sources of outside revenues—for instance, by increasing fees to students or by soliciting gifts from alumni.

Distributors

distributors
Organizations that help other organizations sell their goods or services to customers.

Distributors are organizations that help other organizations sell their goods or services to customers. The decisions that managers make about how to distribute products to customers can have important effects on organizational performance. For many years, Apple Computer refused to let others sell its computers, which meant that customers had to buy directly from Apple. Thus, potential customers who shopped at large computer stores with a variety of products were less likely to buy an Apple computer, since it would not be sold there.

The changing nature of distributors and distribution methods can also bring opportunities and threats for managers. If distributors are so large and powerful that they can control customers' access to a particular organization's goods and services, they can threaten the organization by demanding that it reduce the prices of its goods and services.[13] For example, before Chapters was recently taken over by Indigo Books & Music, publishers complained that Chapters had used its market share to force them into dropping their wholesale prices to the book retailer. Because Chapters was the largest distributor of books to customers in Canada, publishers felt compelled to comply with Chapters' demands.

Chapters/Indigo
www.chapters.indigo.ca/

In contrast, the power of a distributor may be weakened if there are many options. Demand for service from regional phone companies has declined greatly with the advent of cell phones and the larger number of service providers.

Customers

customers Individuals and groups that buy the goods and services that an organization produces.

Customers are the individuals and groups that buy the goods and services that an organization produces. Dell Canada's customers can be segmented into several distinct groups: (1) individuals who purchase PCs for home use, (2) small companies, (3) large companies, (4) government agencies, and (5) educational institutions. Changes in the numbers and types of customers or changes in customers' tastes and needs also result in opportunities and threats. An organization's success depends on its response to customers. When Eaton's failed in the late 1990s, much of the reason for its failure was its lack of responsiveness to changing customer needs. Managers' ability to identify an organization's main customers and produce the goods and services they want is a crucial factor affecting organizational and managerial success.

Competitors

competitors
Organizations that produce goods and services that are similar to a particular organization's goods and services.

potential competitors
Organizations that presently are not in a task environment but could enter if they so chose.

★ **barriers to entry**
Factors that make it difficult and costly for an organization to enter a particular task environment or industry.

★ **economies of scale**
Cost advantages associated with large operations.

One of the most important forces that an organization confronts in its task environment is competitors. **Competitors** are organizations that produce goods and services that are similar to a particular organization's goods and services. In other words, competitors are organizations that are vying for the same customers. Dell Canada's competitors include other domestic manufacturers of PCs (such as Apple, Compaq, and IBM) as well as foreign competitors (such as NEC and Toshiba in Japan and Group Bull in France).

Rivalry between competitors is potentially the most threatening force that managers must deal with. A high level of rivalry often results in price competition, and falling prices reduce access to resources and cause profits to decrease. Today, competition in the personal computer industry is intense as all the major players battle to increase their market share by offering customers better-equipped machines at lower prices.

Although the rivalry between existing competitors is a major threat, so is the potential for new competitors to enter the task environment. **Potential competitors** are organizations that are not presently in a task environment but could enter if they so chose. Hewlett-Packard, for example, is not currently in the wireless communication industry, but it could enter this industry if HP managers decided that doing so would be profitable. When new competitors enter an industry, competition increases and prices decrease.

In general, the potential for new competitors to enter a task environment (and thus boost the level of competition) is a function of barriers to entry.[14] **Barriers to entry** are factors that make it difficult and costly for an organization to enter a particular task environment or industry.[15] In other words, the more difficult and costly it is to enter the task environment, the higher are the barriers to entry. The higher the barriers to entry, the smaller is the number of competitors in an organization's task environment and thus the lower is the threat of competition. With fewer competitors, it is easier to obtain customers and keep prices high. Montreal-based Air Canada operates as a near monopoly because of the high cost of establishing an airline. In 2001 alone, Royal Airlines and CanJet were swallowed up by Canada 3000, and Roots Air was bought out by Air Canada after only one month of operation.

Barriers to entry result from two main sources: *economies of scale* and *brand loyalty* (see Figure 3.2). **Economies of scale** are the cost advantages associated with large operations. Economies of scale result from factors such as being able to manufacture products in very large quantities, buy inputs in bulk, or make more effective use of organizational resources than competitors by fully utilizing employees' skills and knowledge. If organizations already in the task environment are large and enjoy significant economies of scale, then their costs are lower than the costs of potential entrants will be, and newcomers will find it very expensive to enter the industry. In the Management Case

Frank Stronach, chair of Toronto-based Magna Entertainment Corp., thinks that the Canadian government should not be limiting competition as it did by granting the Ontario Jockey Club a monopoly over slot machines at race tracks in Toronto. Stronach would like to open a race track in Ontario, but not without lucrative slot machines onsite.

Figure 3.2
Barriers to Entry and Competition

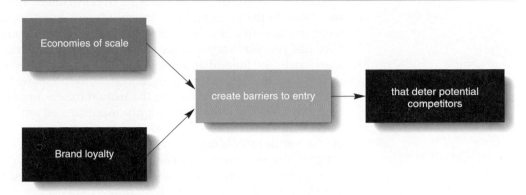

at the end of the chapter, we discuss Sleeman Breweries, where the production of premium beers does not allow for the economies of scale faced by Molson and Labatt.

brand loyalty Customers' preference for the products of organizations currently existing in the task environment.

Brand loyalty is customers' preference for the products of organizations currently existing in the task environment. If established organizations enjoy significant brand loyalty, then a new entrant will find it extremely difficult and costly to obtain a share of the market. Newcomers must bear the huge advertising costs of building customer awareness of the good or service they intend to provide.[16] In 1999, two years after the federal government opened up competition in local telephone rates, a number of companies looked to attract new customers. Bell tried to attract customers from the west while Telus ventured east. Both had the benefit of brand recognition that upstart companies did not. By 2001, few of the many new companies that were created to deliver local phone service survived, while Bell and Telus were still in fierce competition. Brand loyalty does not always work, however. Toronto-based Roots Canada was hoping its customers' loyalty to its clothing line would carry over to flying on Roots Air, but after a month it became obvious that brand loyalty only went so far.

In some cases, government regulations function as a barrier to entry. For example, until the late 1980s, government regulations prohibited third parties from reselling long-distance service in this country. This restriction prevented competition with the established long-distance companies—Bell Canada, SaskTel, and NBTel. When the regulation was amended to allow other companies to compete, the opportunities and threats facing companies in the telephone industry changed. Even more competition opened up when the CRTC allowed for competition in long-distance calls to destinations outside of Canada. Healthcare in Canada is another area where the government has established regulations that make it difficult to establish private hospitals.

One company that has benefited from high barriers to entry is Winnipeg-based Pollard Banknote, which is profiled in the following "Management Insight."

Management Insight

It's Hard to Get Into the Lottery Ticket Printing Business

Because of high entry barriers, there are basically only three companies in the world that print all of the lottery and gaming tickets that are produced: two are in the United States and the third is Winnipeg-based Pollard Banknote.[17] Pollard Banknote employs more than 900 people at production facilities in Canada, the United States, and France. It can produce six billion lottery tickets annually, and serves customers in 40 jurisdictions. The company has gone from $5 million in sales in the early years to a projected $125 million for 1998.

Laurie Pollard, the company's owner, attributes his success to deciding to specialize in the printing business, and then taking first-mover advantage. "We were the first in Canada to develop break-open or pull-tab tickets," he says. "We had markets very quickly in Saskatchewan, Alberta and Ontario." Shortly afterwards, the federal and provincial governments became vitally interested in developing lotteries themselves, and so Pollard met with government people to get the contract to supply all of the instant lottery products. Pollard's first challenge was to produce a "very highly sophisticated and very secure document."

Having succeeded at that, his next step was to guarantee security of the tickets, so vendors would have no way of knowing whether or not they had winning tickets. A sample of every batch of tickets goes through rigorous testing twice: once at Pollard's inhouse laboratory, and then at the independent lab of the client's choice, at Pollard Banknote's expense.

These days, Pollard Banknote can count on brand loyalty for its continuing success. "We know before a game even goes out of here that they're all right. And we haven't been proven wrong yet," says Pollard. In addition, there is strict plant security, and staff members are trained to uphold the high security standards.

In summary, high barriers to entry create a task environment that is highly threatening and causes difficulty for managers trying to gain access to the customers and other resources an organization needs. Conversely, low barriers to entry result in a task environment where competitive pressures are more moderate and managers have greater opportunities to acquire the customers and other resources they need for their organizations to be effective.

Not only for-profit organizations but also not-for-profit organizations have customers, suppliers, and competitors that influence and pressure managers because of the opportunities and threats they create. Consider one of Canada's business schools. The customers of the business school are the organizations that hire its graduates, society at large (which benefits from an educated workforce), and the students themselves. Competitors of the business school include other business schools, both inside and outside the province, and inhouse corporate education programs, such as CIBC's "Leadership Centre" in King City north of Toronto, which produces customized programs that satisfy many of CIBC's immediate business education needs. Suppliers include the federal and provincial governments, both of which supply financial resources to the business school, as well as donors targeted in fund-raising activities. The ultimate suppliers of these resources, of course, are taxpayers.

CIBC
www.cibc.com/

The Industry Life Cycle

An important determinant of the nature and strength of the forces in an organization's task environment (and thus of the nature of opportunities and threats) is the **industry life cycle**–the changes that take place in an industry as it goes through the stages of birth, growth, shakeout, maturity, and decline (see Figure 3.3). Each stage in the life cycle is associated with particular kinds of forces in the task environment. Managers need to understand which life-cycle stage their organization is in, if they are to accurately perceive the opportunities and threats that it faces.

industry life cycle
The changes that take place in an industry as it goes through the stages of birth, growth, shakeout, maturity, and decline.

BIRTH   The birth stage of an industry is characterized by competition among companies to develop the winning technology–the one that will allow them to provide the goods or services that customers want. Early in an industry's evolu-

Figure 3.3
Stages in the Industry Life Cycle

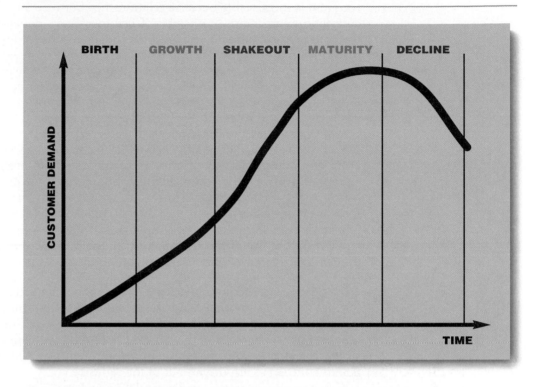

How might an industry's life cycle affect managerial decisions?

tion, managers of new organizations experiment with different ways of producing the product or delivering it to customers. In the early years of the videocassette recorder industry, for example, there were three competing technological standards: the Betamax standard produced by Sony, the VHS standard produced by Matsushita, and the V2000 standard produced by Philips NV. Today, in what is now a mature industry, just one technology is available: the VHS standard. In the birth stage, an organization's relationships with its suppliers, distributors, and customers are fluid and likely to change quickly, making the environment uncertain and difficult to predict and control.

GROWTH   The growth stage begins at the point when a product gains customer acceptance and an influx of consumers enters the market. Rapid growth in customer demand attracts many new organizations into the industry, increasing the level of competition. The newcomers often pioneer new varieties of the industry's products and improved ways of producing and delivering those products to customers. This is occurring in the cellular phone and wireless communication industry today. These changes lead to a complex set of forces in the task environment as the relationships among suppliers, distributors, and competitors all change rapidly.

SHAKEOUT   Near the end of the growth stage, there is a marked change in an industry's task environment because slowing customer demand for the industry's product raises the level of competition in the industry. In response, organizations often reduce their prices, and the result can be a price war, which causes prices to fall rapidly. In the shakeout stage, the least-efficient companies are driven out of the industry; consequently, there is significant uncertainty until the shakeout is complete.

MATURITY By the time an industry reaches maturity, most customers have bought the product and demand is growing slowly or is constant. The task environment is more stable because relationships between suppliers, distributors, and competitors are more predictable. Customers have developed brand loyalty for the products of certain companies, and managers have developed good working relationships with suppliers and distributors. A few large companies usually dominate mature industries, so the level of competition is lower, or at least more predictable, because each company can predict how its competitors will behave. Finally, organizations that have survived into maturity are often protected from new competition by relatively high barriers to entry.

This stable situation may persist for a long time, allowing companies to enjoy high profits. In a mature industry with low barriers to entry, competitors may enter the market, however, and if this happens, rapid change may occur. For example, prior to 1973, the Canadian automobile industry was a stable, mature industry dominated by General Motors, Ford, and Chrysler. However, a rapid increase in the price of oil in 1973 opened the door to Japanese producers. By selling small, fuel-efficient cars, the Japanese producers were able to capture market share from the Big Three auto makers. In the process, they dramatically changed the competitive environment in the auto industry.

DECLINE In the final stage in the evolution of an industry, customer demand for the industry's product decreases. Falling demand typically leads to a situation in which organizations in the industry are making more of the product than customers want to buy. As in the shakeout period, companies often respond to this situation by cutting prices, and competition increases. Once again, the most inefficient companies are driven out of the industry.

Effective managers must understand the way forces in the task environment change over time as a result of changes in the industry environment. The quality of managers' planning, organizing, and decision making depends on their ability to perceive correctly and understand the forces operating in the task and general environments.

The General Environment

Economic, technological, sociocultural, demographic, political and legal, and global forces in an organization's general environment can have profound effects on the organization's task environment, effects that may not be evident to managers. For example, technology in the telecommunications industry has made it possible for companies to offer their customers a variety of products. Thus, while in the past consumers simply chose the cheapest long-distance package or the best telephone system, now they're looking at enhanced communication products—such as local calling, cellular, long distance, Internet access, and videoconferencing—that are offered as part of the package. Telephone providers who failed to expand their range of offerings have had difficulty maintaining their customer base.

Managers must constantly analyze forces in the general environment because these forces affect long-term decision making and planning. In Chapter 7, we examine one of the major tasks involved in planning–the careful and thorough analysis of forces in the general environment. Here, however, we look next at each of the major forces in the general environment in turn, exploring their impact on managers and on the organization's task environment, and examining how managers can deal with them.

Economic Forces

economic forces
Interest rates, inflation, unemployment, economic growth, and other factors that affect the general health and well-being of a nation or the regional economy of an organization.

Economic forces affect the general health and well-being of a nation or the regional economy of an organization. They include interest rates, inflation, unemployment, and economic growth. Economic forces produce many opportunities and threats for managers. Low levels of unemployment and falling interest rates mean a change in the customer base: more people have more money to spend, and as a result organizations have an opportunity to sell more goods and services. Good economic times affect supplies: resources become easier to acquire, and organizations have an opportunity to flourish.

In contrast, worsening macroeconomic conditions pose a threat because they limit managers' ability to gain access to the resources their organization needs. Profit-oriented organizations such as retail stores and hotels have fewer customers for their goods and services during economic downturns. Not-for-profit organizations such as charities and colleges receive fewer donations during economic downturns. Even a moderate deterioration in national or regional economic conditions can seriously affect performance. Beginning in the late 1980s and continuing through much of the 1990s, economic growth in Canada slowed down. This recession reduced the demand for all kinds of goods and services. Many companies reported large losses, and thousands of workers lost their jobs as companies downsized and closed entire factories. Organizations started to recover slowly in the mid-1990s as the economy started to recover from the recession.

Poor economic conditions make the environment more complex and managers' jobs more difficult and demanding. Managers may need to reduce the number of individuals in their departments and increase the motivation of remaining employees, and managers and workers alike may need to identify ways to acquire and utilize resources more efficiently. Successful managers realize the important effects that economic forces have on their organizations and they pay close attention to what is occurring in the national and regional economy in order to respond appropriately.

Technological Forces

technology The combination of skills and equipment that managers use in the design, production, and distribution of goods and services.

technological forces Outcomes of changes in the technology that managers use to design, produce, or distribute goods and services.

Technology is the combination of skills and equipment that managers use in the design, production, and distribution of goods and services. **Technological forces** are outcomes of changes in the technology that managers use to design, produce, or distribute goods and services. Technological forces have increased in magnitude since the Second World War because the overall pace of technological change has accelerated so greatly.[18]

Technological forces can have profound implications for managers and organizations. Technological change can make established products obsolete overnight—for example, eight-track tapes and black and white televisions—forcing managers to find new products to make. Although technological change can threaten an organization, it also can create a host of new opportunities for designing, making, or distributing new and better kinds of goods and services. Telephone companies and the cable industry in Canada have competed in recent years to offer high-speed Internet access to consumers. As of 1999, however, "there (wasn't) a single incumbent telco in North America that (was) deploying DSL (digital subscriber line technology) effectively. Meanwhile, cable operators have signed up more than 330 000 Canadians to their high-speed service."[19]

Managers must move quickly to respond to such changes if their organizations are to survive and prosper.

Changes in information technology also are changing the very nature of work itself within organizations and, in addition, the manager's job. Telecommuting along the information superhighway and teleconferencing are now everyday activities that provide opportunities for managers to supervise and coordinate geographically dispersed employees. Salespeople in many companies work from home offices and commute electronically to work. Salespeople communicate with other employees through companywide electronic mail networks and use video cameras attached to PCs for "face-to-face" meetings with fellow workers who may be many miles away. Managers at Algonquin Automotive have utilized advances in information technology in a different way—to revolutionize the way the company designs and builds automotive accessories.

Management Insight

Computer-Aided Design Makes a Difference at Algonquin Automotive

Huntsville, Ontario's Algonquin Automotive is a full-service supplier of automotive accessories (e.g., running boards, towing products, and skid plates), selling exclusively to auto manufacturers, such as Ford, DaimlerChrysler, Toyota, Nissan and General Motors.[20] In 1997, its development costs for a typical product were $59 680, the design cycle was 21 weeks, and the product launch took 75 weeks. Today, costs have been reduced to $26 420, the design cycle is only nine weeks, and product launch takes less than a year.

This change came about when they stopped using physical models (made out of clay, wood and fibreglass), and started using virtual prototypes with the help of I-DEAS software to develop their products.

To reduce cycle time and costs, Algonquin Automotive's management decided to re-engineer the design process so that more was done through software, and less through building physical prototypes. This had significant benefits. Before they started their re-engineering, it had taken them 75 weeks to develop the 1997 Sienna running board. The time to develop and produce the 1998 Land Cruiser running board was 50 weeks, and then just 42 weeks for the GM running board.

"Many factors affect launch time," says Dan Christian, Algonquin Automotive's engineering coordinator, "but one of the reasons we now get a product to market eight months sooner is the quality of the surface data we create [through the software]. It is so much better that our tool-makers don't waste time reworking the data. Any way we look at it, the replacement of physical models with virtual prototypes has been beneficial for us."

Sociocultural Forces

sociocultural forces
Pressures emanating from the social structure of a country or society or from the national culture.

social structure
The arrangement of relationships between individuals and groups in a society.

Sociocultural forces are pressures emanating from the social structure of a country or society or from the national culture. Pressures from both sources can either constrain or facilitate the way organizations operate and managers behave. **Social structure** is the arrangement of relationships between individuals and groups in a society. Societies differ substantially in social structure. In societies that have a high degree of social stratification, there are many distinctions among individuals and groups. Caste systems in India and Tibet and the recognition of numerous social classes in the United Kingdom and France produce a multilayered social structure in each of those countries. In contrast, social stratification is lower in relatively egalitarian New Zealand and in Canada, and the social structure reveals fewer distinctions among people. Most top managers in France come from the upper classes of French society, but top managers in Canada come from all strata of Canadian society.

Societies also differ in the extent to which they emphasize the individual over the group. For example, the United States emphasizes the primacy of the individual, and Japan emphasizes the primacy of the group. Canada falls somewhere between these two extremes. These differences may dictate the methods managers need to use to motivate and lead employees.

national culture

The set of values that a society considers important and the norms of behaviour that are approved or sanctioned in that society.

National culture is the set of values that a society considers important and the norms of behaviour that are approved or sanctioned in that society. Societies differ substantially in the values and norms that they emphasize. For example, in Canada and the United States individualism is valued, and in Korea and Japan individuals are expected to conform to group expectations.[21] National culture also affects the way managers motivate and coordinate employees and the way organizations do business. Ethics, an important aspect of national culture, is discussed in detail in Chapter 5.

Social structure and national culture not only differ across societies but also change within societies over time. In the 1960s and 1970s in Canada, there were changes in attitudes about the roles of women, love, sex, and marriage. Many people in Asian countries such as Hong Kong, Singapore, Korea, and Japan think that the younger generation is far more individualistic and "North American-like" than previous generations. Similarly, throughout much of eastern Europe, new values that emphasize individualism and entrepreneurship are replacing communist values based on collectivism and obedience to the state.

Individual managers and organizations must be responsive to changes in, and differences among, the social structures and national cultures of all the countries in which they operate. In today's increasingly integrated global economy, managers are likely to interact with people from several countries, and many live and work abroad. Effective managers are sensitive to differences between societies and adjust their behaviours accordingly.

Managers and organizations also must respond to social changes within a society. During the 1970s and 1980s, for example, Canadians became more interested in their personal health and fitness. Managers who recognized this trend early and exploited the opportunities that resulted from it were able to reap significant gains for their organizations. PepsiCo used the opportunity presented by the fitness trend and took market share from arch rival Coca-Cola by being the first to introduce diet colas and fruit-based soft drinks. The health trend did not offer opportunities to all companies, however; to some, it posed a threat. Tobacco companies are under pressure due to consumers' greater awareness of negative health impacts from smoking.

Demographic Forces

demographic forces

Outcomes of changes in, or changing attitudes toward, the characteristics of a population, such as age, gender, ethnic origin, race, sexual orientation, and social class.

Demographic forces are outcomes of changes in, or changing attitudes toward, the characteristics of a population, such as age, gender, ethnic origin, race, sexual orientation, and social class. Like the other forces in the general environment, demographic forces present managers with opportunities and threats and can have major implications for organizations. Over the last 25 years, for example, women have entered the workforce in increasing numbers. Between 1973 and 1998, the percentage of working-age women in the workforce increased from 48 to 77 percent in Canada and from 50 to 77 percent in the United States.[22] The dramatic increase in the number of working women has brought to the forefront of public concern issues such as equal pay for equal work and sexual harassment at work. Managers must address these issues if they are to attract and make full use of the talents of female workers. We discuss the important issue of workforce diversity at length in Chapter 5.

Changes in the age distribution of a population are another example of a demographic force that affects managers and organizations. Currently, most industrialized nations are experiencing the aging of their populations as a consequence of falling birth and death rates and the aging of the baby-boom generation. In Germany, for example, the percentage of the population over age 65 is expected to rise from 15.4 percent in 1990 to 20.7 percent in 2010. Comparable figures for Canada are 11.4 and 14.4 percent; for Japan, 11.7 and 19.5 percent; and for the

Government policy regarding whether publications such as *The National Post* are owned by Canadians affects whether advertisers can deduct the cost of an ad from their taxes. So when Conrad Black renounced his Canadian citizenship, Hollinger International had to restructure its ownership to be sure that at least three-quarters of the paper was owned by Canadians.

political and legal forces Outcomes of changes in laws and regulations, such as the deregulation of industries, the privatization of organizations, and increased emphasis on environmental protection.

United States, 12.6 and 13.5 percent.[23] The aging of the population is increasing opportunities for organizations that cater to older people; the home healthcare and recreation industries, for example, are seeing an upswing in demand for their services.

The aging of the population also has several implications for the workplace. Most significant are a relative decline in the number of young people joining the workforce and an increase in active employees willing to postpone retirement past the traditional retirement age of 65. These changes suggest that organizations will need to find ways to motivate and utilize the skills and knowledge of older employees, an issue that many Western societies have yet to tackle.

Political and Legal Forces

Political and legal forces result from political and legal developments within society and significantly affect managers and organizations. Political processes shape a society's laws; for instance, demands for more environmental consciousness by corporations have strengthened pollution laws in this country. Laws constrain the operations of organizations and managers and thus create both opportunities and threats.[24] For example, throughout much of the industrialized world there has been a strong trend toward deregulation of industries previously controlled by the state and privatization of organizations once owned by the state. The "Case in Contrast" discussed the effects of privatization on Petro-Canada. In the "Management Insight," the dilemmas facing managers at NB Power as New Brunswick sets out to deregulate energy are uncovered.

Management Insight

NB Power Faces Deregulation

In January 2001, New Brunswick Premier Bernard Lord and Energy Minister Jeannot Volpe outlined a 10-year plan for the future of electricity and natural gas production in the province.[25] Recognizing that deregulation has a bad name, particularly after the recent energy crisis in California, the two talked about "restructuring" and "reregulating" instead. Explained Volpe, "The policy does not mean deregulation. It's a change in regulation to allow the province to participate in a competitive energy market."

Analysts who have studied the plan say that it lays the groundwork for deregulation, and encourages market-based rates for electricity. Large industries would have the opportunity to "generate their own power or shop for cheap power on the North American grid."

Managers at NB Power (www.nbpower.com) must figure out how they will operate in this new environment, which will take effect in April 2003. The crown corporation has had a power generation and transmission monopoly since the 1920s. NB Power's nuclear power plant at Point Lepreau is aging, and needs to be either refurbished or closed. Either decision would mean a multimillion-dollar expense. The corporation's hydroelectric dam at Mactaquac is also deteriorating, and in need of action.

NB Power's large industrial customers—like the Irving group of companies, McCain Foods Ltd., and pulp and paper producers—will most certainly explore alternatives for cheaper sources of energy when the new policy goes into place.

Thus managers are faced with a number of critical decisions in the next two years on how to manage in a less regulated environment.

Deregulation and privatization are just two examples of political and legal forces that can create challenges for organizations and managers. Others include increased emphasis on environmental protection and the preservation of endangered species, and increased emphasis on safety in the workplace. In 1986, the federal government enacted the Employment Equity Act, and provincial governments have their own equity acts that cover discrimination on the basis of race, gender, or age. Successful managers carefully monitor changes in laws and regulations in order to take advantage of the opportunities they create and counter the threats they pose in an organization's task environment. For example, when changes in Canadian law allowed competition in first long-distance and then later local telephone service, this was great news for consumers. However, managers at Bell and the other provincial phone companies faced huge challenges. Between 1992 and 1999, they lost about a third of their long-distance customers to competition. At the same time, revenue per call plummeted. Managers at Bell Canada were facing losing up to 30 percent of their business customers when the competition for local calls heated up.[26]

The Competition Act of 1986 provides more legislation that affects how companies may operate. Under this Act, the Bureau of Competition Policy acts to maintain and encourage competition in Canada. For example, if two major competing companies consider merging, they face intense scrutiny from the Bureau. When Heather Reisman and Gerry Schwartz bought Chapters in 2001, they had to receive approval before they could merge Chapters with their Indigo bookstores. The Bureau imposed a number of conditions before approving the merger, including the sale or closure of 20 stores and a Code of Conduct for dealing with publishers, which is shown in "Ethics in Action."

Employment
Equity Act
http://laws.justice.gc.ca/
en/E-5.401/

Competition
Act
http://laws.justice.gc.ca/
en/C-34/

Ethics in Action

Chapters' Code of Conduct[27]

1. Chapters may not demand publisher discounts (off the suggested retail price) of more than 45 to 46 percent for "trade books" (most books consumers buy) and 46 to 47 percent for mass market (small-sized) paperbacks.

2. Chapters must pay publishers in a timely manner: within 110 days for the first 12 months after the merger is approved; 100 days for the next 24 months; 90 days afterward.

3. Chapters has between 3 and 12 months to return unsold books, although extensions may be granted if requested in writing. Returned books must be in "usable condition" and those returned that are damaged or out of print will be shipped back to Chapters at its expense.

4. Chapters cannot return more than 42 percent of the books purchased in the 12 months after the merger is approved, and no more than 30 percent afterward.

5. Chapters must not shut superstores without advising publishers at least 60 days in advance. The bookseller should try to minimize returns by moving inventory to other stores.

6. Chapters book purchase decisions must be based on "commercial considerations such as the quality and salability of the book"; and "under no circumstances" can Chapters discriminate against a book simply because the publisher has not agreed to participate in a related promotion.

Chapters was forced to accept this Code of Conduct because of complaints about the way the company had treated publishers in the past. These rules restrict the way that Chapters can do business until 2006.

Global Forces

Global forces are outcomes of changes in international relationships, changes in nations' economic, political, and legal systems, and changes in technology. The global environment is the subject of Chapter 4, so here we are limiting our discussion to a few introductory comments. Perhaps the most important global force affecting managers and organizations is the increasing economic integration of countries around the world.[28] Free-trade agreements such as those enforced by the World Treaty Organization (WTO) and the North American Free Trade Agreement (NAFTA), and the growth of the European Union (EU), have led to a lowering of barriers to the free flow of goods and services between nations.[29]

Falling trade barriers have created enormous opportunities for organizations in one country to sell goods and services in other countries. But by allowing foreign companies to compete for an organization's domestic customers, falling trade barriers also pose a serious threat, because they increase competition in the task environment. One of the major challenges facing Canadian managers after the North American Free Trade Agreement (NAFTA) was how to compete successfully against American companies moving into Canada. Zellers and The Bay, for instance, faced strong challenges from Wal-Mart, as well as smaller boutique operations.

Tips for Managers

Forces in the Environment

1. List the forces in an organization's task environment that affect it the most. Analyze changes taking place that may result in opportunities or threats for the organization.

2. List the forces in the general environment that affect an organization the most. Analyze changes taking place that may result in opportunities or threats for the organization.

3. Devise a plan indicating how your managers propose to take advantage of opportunities or counterthreats that arise from environmental forces and what kinds of resources they will need to do so.

Managing the Organizational Environment

As previously discussed, an important task for managers is to understand how forces in the task and general environments generate opportunities for, and threats to, their organizations. To analyze the importance of opportunities and threats in the organizational environment, managers must measure (1) the level of complexity in the environment and (2) the rate at which the environment is changing. With this information, they can plan appropriately and choose the best goals and courses of action.

The complexity of the organizational environment is a function of the number and potential impact of the forces to which managers must respond in both the task and general environments. A force that seems likely to have a significant negative impact is a potential threat to which managers must devote a high level of organizational resources. A force likely to have a marginal impact poses little threat to an organization and requires only a minor commitment of managerial time and attention. A force likely to make a significant positive impact warrants a considerable commitment of managerial time and effort to take advantage of the opportunity.

In general, the larger an organization is, the greater is the number of environmental forces that managers must respond to. Compare, for example, the organizational environment facing the manager of a small country diner with that facing top managers at Taco Bell's headquarters. At the local level, the main concern of a diner manager is to ensure an adequate supply of inputs, such as food supplies and restaurant employees, to provide customers with fast and efficient service. In contrast, top managers at Taco Bell must determine: how to distribute food supplies to restaurants in the most efficient ways; how to ensure that the organization's practices do not discriminate against any ethnic groups or older workers; how to respond to customers' new preference for tacos made with low-fat cheese and sour cream; and how to deal with competition from McDonald's, which has reduced the cost of its hamburgers to compete with Taco Bell's low-cost tacos and burritos. Clearly, the more forces managers must deal with, the more complicated is the management process.

Environmental change is the degree to which forces in the task and general environments change and evolve over time. Change is problematic for an organization and its managers because the consequences of change can be difficult to predict.[30] For example, managers in the computer and telecommunications industries know that technological advances such as the increasing power and falling cost of microprocessors and the development of the information superhighway will produce dramatic changes in their task environments, but they do not know what the magnitude or effects of those changes will be. Managers can attempt to forecast or simply guess about future conditions in the task environment, such as where and how strong the new competition may be. But, confronted with a complex and changing task environment, managers cannot be sure that decisions and actions taken today will be appropriate in the future. This uncertainty makes their jobs especially challenging. It also makes it vitally important for managers to understand the forces that shape the organizational environment.

As a first step in managing the organizational environment, managers need to list the types and relative strengths of the forces that affect their organization's task and general environments the most. Second, they need to analyze the way changes in these forces may result in opportunities or threats for their organizations. Third, they need to draw up a plan indicating how they propose to take advantage of those opportunities or counter those threats, and what kinds of resources they will need to do so. An understanding of the organizational environment is necessary so that managers can anticipate how the task environment might look in the future and decide on the actions to pursue if the organization is to prosper.

Reducing the Impact of Environmental Forces

Often, managers can counter threats in the task environment by reducing the potential impact of forces in that environment. In the 1980s, for example, managers at Xerox Corporation dealt with over 3000 different suppliers and employed an army of managers to purchase inputs. To reduce costs and simplify dealings with suppliers, top managers at Xerox decided to reduce the number of the company's suppliers. Today, fewer than 300 suppliers provide Xerox with high-quality inputs at a much lower cost than in the past.

Finding ways to reduce the number and potential impact of forces in the organizational environment is the job of all managers in an organization. The principal task of the CEO and top-management team is to devise strategies that will allow an organization to take advantage of opportunities and counter threats in its general and task environments (see Part Three for a discussion of this vital topic).

Taco Bell Corp.
www.tacobell.com/

environmental change

The degree to which forces in the task and general environments change and evolve over time.

Xerox Corporation
www.xerox.com/

Middle managers in an organization's departments collect relevant information about the task environment, such as (1) the future intentions of the organization's competitors, (2) the identity of new customers for the organization's products, and (3) the identity of new suppliers of crucial or low-cost inputs. First-line managers find ways to use resources more efficiently to hold costs down or to get close to customers and learn what they want.

Creating an Organizational Structure and Control Systems

Another way to respond to a complex and changing organizational environment is to increase the complexity of the organization's structure and its control systems. (We discuss organizational structure and control systems in detail in Part Four.) To do this, top managers have different departments deal with the various forces affecting the task and general environments (see Figure 3.4). For example, the sales and service departments develop the skills and knowledge necessary to handle relationships with customers. The research and development department is responsible for identifying changes in technology that will impact the organization and for using that technology to develop new goods and services to attract customers. The finance and accounting departments are responsible for scanning and monitoring economic forces and assessing their impact on the organization.

As discussed in Chapter 2, another important action that managers can take to organize and control an organization's activities in response to characteristics of the organizational environment is designing a mechanistic structure or an organic structure. In stable environments with low levels of complexity and competition, managers have relatively few problems in accessing resources and can effectively use a mechanistic structure to coordinate their activities. In a *mechanistic structure*, authority is centralized at the top of the hierarchy, and tasks and roles are clearly

Figure 3.4

How Managers Use Functions to Manage Forces in the Task and General Environments

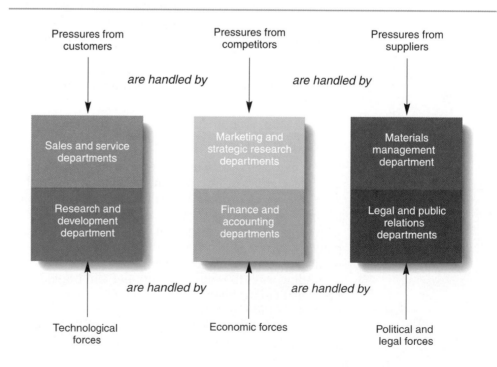

specified. Mechanistic structures help the organization to utilize its resources efficiently and effectively in a stable environment.

In contrast, when the environment is changing rapidly and there is a high level of complexity, an organic structure is more appropriate. In an organic structure, authority is decentralized to the middle and first-line managers close to the scene of the action. Roles and tasks are deliberately left ambiguous to encourage employees to cooperate and find creative responses to new and emerging situations that are continually arising. Organic structures allow managers to respond better to unpredictable and uncertain events or contingencies.

Middle managers within an organization's departments are responsible for identifying what is happening in the environment as it relates to their functional area and for forecasting how environmental forces are likely to affect their departments and the organization as a whole. The ability of department managers to (1) develop the skills they need to manage the segment of the environment they are responsible for and (2) work with other departments in an organic fashion determines organizational performance—the organization's ability to acquire and utilize resources efficiently and effectively. Effective organizations have departments that are able to respond quickly and appropriately to unforeseen situations and to take advantage of unexpected opportunities. Ineffective organizations lack the ability to respond to changes in the task and general environments and the skills needed to secure scarce and valuable resources.

In essence, managers must develop *internal* structure and control systems that allow them to respond appropriately to the specific forces and conditions in the *external* environment. Managing the match between the organization and its environment so that the organization's structure and control systems respond well to the forces in the task and general environments is a vital management task. In the long run, the ability of managers to perform this task is one key factor that separates high-performing from low-performing organizations.

Boundary-Spanning Roles

How might boundary-spanning roles affect organizational performance?

The ability of managers to gain access to the information they need to forecast the future and choose appropriate goals and courses of action is critical to successful management in times of uncertainty. This was evident in the "Case in Contrast" at the beginning of this chapter. Bill Hopper's perception of Petro-Canada's environment as it moved towards privatization was inaccurate, and, as a result, the Petro-Canada CEO did not take the action necessary to reposition his organization in the more competitive energy industry of the 1990s. In contrast, his successor, Jim Stanford, more correctly perceived the changes taking place in Petro-Canada's task environment and took appropriate action to improve the company's performance.

The history of organizations is marked by numerous once-great organizations whose managers did not recognize and respond to significant changes taking place in the task and general environments. Examples include now-defunct Eaton's (though it has re-emerged, after a fashion) and Canadian Airlines, which was not able to be competitive against Air Canada.

boundary spanning
Interacting with individuals and groups outside the organization to obtain valuable information from the task and general environments.

Managers can learn to perceive, interpret, and appreciate their organizations' task and general environments better by practising **boundary spanning**—interacting with individuals and groups outside the organization to obtain valuable information from the task and general environments.[31] Managers who engage in boundary-spanning activities seek ways not only to respond to forces in the external environment but also to *influence directly and manage* the perceptions of stakeholders in that environment to increase their organizations' access to resources. Thus boundary spanning is a way of adapting or responding to the organization's environment.

How does boundary spanning work? (See Figure 3.5.) A manager in a boundary-spanning role in Organization *X* establishes a link with a manager in a boundary-spanning role in Organization *Y*. The two managers communicate and share information that helps both of them understand the changing forces and conditions in the industry environment. These managers then share this information with other managers in their respective organizations so that all managers become better informed about events outside their own organization's boundaries. As a result, the managers in both organizations can make more appropriate decisions.

For an example of a manager performing a boundary-spanning role, consider the situation of a purchasing manager for Taco Bell. The purchasing manager is charged with finding the lowest-cost supplier of low-fat cheese and sour cream. To perform this task, the manager could write to major food companies and ask for price quotes. Or the manager could phone food company managers personally, develop an informal yet professional relationship with them, and, over time, learn from them which food companies are active in the low-fat food area and what they envision for the future. By developing such a relationship, the purchasing manager will be able to provide Taco Bell with valuable information that will allow Taco Bell's purchasing department to make well-informed choices. This flow of information from the task environment may, in turn, allow marketing to develop more effective sales campaigns or product development to produce better-looking and better-tasting tacos.

What would happen if managers in all of an organization's departments performed boundary-spanning roles? The richness of the information available to managers throughout the organization would probably lead to an increase in the quality of managers' decision making and planning, enabling them to produce goods and services that customers prefer or to create advertising campaigns that attract new customers. Managers can engage in many kinds of boundary-spanning activities; some of them were identified by Henry Mintzberg (see Table 1.1). Four of the most important ones are discussed next.

REPRESENTING AND PROTECTING THE ORGANIZATION

Managers, by their actions alone, can shape the perceptions of outsiders—individuals, groups, and other organizations—to make them view an organization favourably.[32] For example, a manager who speaks in public is representing his or her organization, and the public often judges an organization by what its managers say.

Figure 3.5
The Nature of Boundary-Spanning Roles

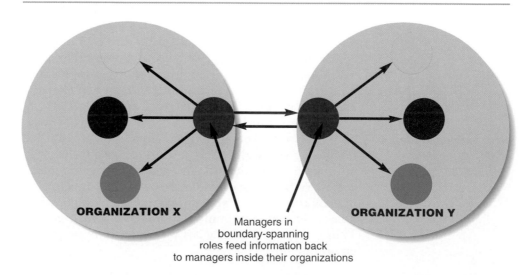

ORGANIZATION X   ORGANIZATION Y

Managers in
boundary-spanning
roles feed information back
to managers inside their organizations

Organizations in many industries form and fund political action committees (PACs) and employ lobbyists to influence legislators to pass laws favouring their interests.

In times of crisis, managers can protect their organizations by acting quickly and appropriately across the organizational boundary to head off or respond to problems effectively. For example, the speed at which executives at Exxon or Shell respond to an oil spill affects the way the public views their companies, as Exxon found out to its detriment when it was accused of being slow to react to the Exxon Valdez disaster in Alaska in 1989.

SCANNING AND MONITORING THE ENVIRONMENT   Searching for and collecting information to understand how trends and forces in the task and general environments are changing is an important boundary-spanning activity. Many organizations employ researchers whose only job is to scan professional journals, trade association publications, and newspapers to identify changes in technology, government regulations, fashion trends, and so on, that will affect the way their organization operates. Managers regularly go to conferences, industry association meetings, and exhibitions to monitor and learn about changes taking place in the part of the task environment that they are responsible for.

gatekeeping Deciding what information to allow into the organization and what information to keep out.

GATEKEEPING AND INFORMATION PROCESSING   Merely collecting information is not enough for the boundary-spanning manager. He or she must interpret what the information means and then practise **gatekeeping**, deciding what information to allow into the organization and what information to keep out. The nature of the information that the gatekeeper chooses to pass on to other managers will influence the decisions they make. Thus, accurate information processing is vital. Sometimes, however, managers pass on only the information that supports their interests or makes their job easier, or the information that they think other managers want to hear. Such selectivity obscures rather than clarifies the situation and undermines the quality of decision making. Poor information processing delayed the responses of many once-dominant companies, such as IBM, General Motors, and Eaton's, to radical changes taking place in their organizational environments.[33]

ESTABLISHING INTERORGANIZATIONAL RELATIONSHIPS   In today's culturally diverse world and integrated global environment, it is more important than ever for organizations to develop alliances and agreements with other organizations domestically and around the world to help themselves obtain and utilize resources. Alliances and agreements are developed when managers meet and develop personal relationships with one another, and establishing these *interorganizational relationships* is an increasingly important boundary-spanning task. An example of how managers are engaging in boundary-spanning activities with Aboriginal businesses with great success follows in this "Managing Diversity" feature.

Managing Diversity

Canadian Companies Mentor Aboriginal Businesses

A number of Canadian companies have been forming strategic alliances and other relationships with Aboriginal businesses, in an effort to help these businesses become more successful.[34] More than 20 000 North American Indians, Métis, and Inuit in Canada have their own businesses. A recent survey by Statistics Canada found that many reported having difficulty with access to capital. They also reported problems common to many Canadian businesses, including the needs to improve management skills, increase productivity, become innovative, and expand their markets.

Syncrude Canada, Placer Dome, Toronto-Dominion Bank, PCL, the Alberta Energy Company, Diavik Diamond Mines, Weldwood of Canada, SaskEnergy, Cameco, Weyerhaeuser, Manitoba Hydro and the Royal Bank have assisted Aboriginal companies in a variety of ways. These include providing financial investments, coordinating joint ventures between newly formed Aboriginal companies and established non-Aboriginal firms, and providing Aboriginal companies with business, financial and technical expertise. The Aboriginal businesses involved in mentoring experienced increased business growth and expansion.

One of the benefits to the companies that mentor Aboriginal firms is that they gain quality goods and services from local suppliers, increased market access to the Aboriginal community, and improved relations with the communities. Meanwhile, the communities gain from increased employment opportunities and economic development.

Managers as Agents of Change

It is important to note that, although much of the change that occurs in the organizational environment is independent of a particular organization (for example, basic advances in biotechnology or plastics), a significant amount of environmental change is the direct consequence of actions taken by managers within organizations.[35] As explained in Chapter 2 (see Figure 2.4), an organization is an open system: It takes in inputs from the environment and converts them into goods and services that are sent back to the environment. Thus, change in the environment is a two-way process (see Figure 3.6). Many times, however, the choices that managers make about which products to produce, and even about how to compete with other organizations, affect the environment in many ways.

Consider how actions taken by managers at Nortel in 1971 helped turn Nortel into a global leader in the telecommunications industry, where it remained for 30 years. The decision, considered risky at the time, was to make a big investment in digital technology. Treating phone signals as digital information enabled such things as voice mail and call display. Soon other telecommunications companies followed suit, and a variety of new products were offered to the market. However, no company has been able to capture Nortel's lead. "By grabbing an early lead in the digital switching market, Nortel grew to US$8 billion in sales from US$600 million in 20 years."[36]

Figure 3.6

Change in the Environment as a Two-Way Process

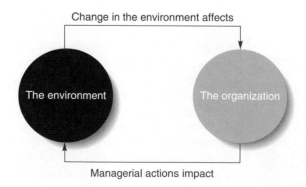

Change in the environment affects

The environment

The organization

Managerial actions impact

Tips for Managers

Managing the Organizational Environment

1. To assess the level of uncertainty in the environment, analyze its level of complexity and rate of change.

2. Once the number and importance of the forces in the environment have been determined, decide how to build and develop departments to respond to them.

3. After analyzing your customers, competitors, and suppliers, decide which managers should be responsible for identifying and responding to their needs.

4. Once the rate of change in the task and general environment has been determined, decide whether a mechanistic or an organic structure is most appropriate for the organization.

Chapter Summary

WHAT IS THE ORGANIZATIONAL ENVIRONMENT?

THE TASK ENVIRONMENT

- Suppliers
- Distributors
- Customers
- Competitors
- The Industry Life Cycle

THE GENERAL ENVIRONMENT

- Economic Forces
- Technological Forces
- Sociocultural Forces
- Demographic Forces
- Political and Legal Forces
- Global Forces

MANAGING THE ORGANIZATIONAL ENVIRONMENT

- Reducing the Impact of Environmental Forces
- Creating an Organizational Structure and Control Systems
- Boundary-Spanning Roles
- Managers as Agents of Change

Summary and Review

WHAT IS THE ORGANIZATIONAL ENVIRONMENT? The organizational environment is the set of forces and conditions that operate beyond an organization's boundaries but affect a manager's ability to acquire and utilize resources. The organizational environment has two components: the task environment and the general environment.

THE TASK ENVIRONMENT The task environment is the set of forces and conditions that originate with suppliers, distributors, customers, and competitors and that influence managers on a daily basis.

THE GENERAL ENVIRONMENT The general environment includes wider-ranging economic, technological, sociocultural, demographic, political and legal, and global forces that affect an organization and its task environment.

MANAGING THE ORGANIZATIONAL ENVIRONMENT Two factors affect the nature of the opportunities and threats that organizations face: (1) the level of complexity in the environment and (2) the rate of change in the environment. Managers must learn how to analyze the forces in the environment in order to respond effectively to opportunities and threats. The principal way in which managers increase their organization's ability to manage the environment is by creating an organizational structure and control systems to allow managers throughout the organization to deal with the specific parts of the environment for which they are responsible. Developing an organizational structure involves building departmental skills and resources, giving authority to managers at all levels to allow them to respond quickly, and choosing a mechanistic or an organic structure, depending on the complexity and rate of change in the task and general environments. Managers also can help their organization adapt to its general and task environments by engaging in boundary-spanning activities. Such activities include representing and protecting the organization, scanning and monitoring the environment, gatekeeping and information processing, and establishing interorganizational relationships.

Management in Action

Topics for Discussion and Action

1. Why is it important for managers to understand the nature of the environmental forces that are acting on them and their organization?

2. Choose an organization, and ask a manager in that organization to list the types and strengths of forces in the organization's task environment. Ask the manager to pay particular attention to identifying opportunities and threats that result from pressures and changes in customers, competitors, and suppliers.

3. Read the business section of your local newspaper, to get an idea of task and general forces that affect the organizations in your community. What local conditions have a major impact on organizations in your area?

4. Which organization is likely to face the most complex task environment: a biotechnology company trying to develop a cure for cancer, or a large retailer like Zellers or The Bay? Why?

5. The population is aging because of declining birth rates, declining death rates, and the aging of the baby-boom generation. What might some of the implications of this demographic trend be for (a) a pharmaceutical company, (b) the home construction industry, and (c) the agenda of political parties?

6. Currently, most households and businesses in Canada, the United Kingdom, the United States, and a number of other countries do not have a choice of electricity supplier. But as a result of deregulation, within a decade the average business and household will be able to choose from among several competing suppliers. How might this development alter the task environment facing a manager in an electric utility?

7. In what different ways can managers design an organization's structure to allow the organization to respond to its task environment?

8. Choose an organization, and ask its managers to describe the organizational structure and control systems that help the organization respond to its environment. Do you think managers in this organization are doing a good job of matching the organization to its task and general environments?

9. What is the purpose of boundary-spanning roles? List five ways in which managers in a biotechnology company can help their company by engaging in boundary-spanning activities.

Building Management Skills

Analyzing an Organization's Task and General Environments

Pick an organization with which you are familiar. It can be an organization in which you have worked or currently work, or it can be an organization that you interact with regularly as a customer (such as the college or university that you are currently attending). For this organization do the following.

1. Describe the main forces in the task environment that are affecting the organization.

2. Describe the main forces in the general environment that are affecting the organization.

3. Try to determine whether the organization's task and general environments are relatively stable or changing rapidly.

4. Explain how environmental forces affect the job of an individual manager within this organization. How do they determine the opportunities and threats that its managers must confront?

Small Group Breakout Exercise

How to Enter the Copying Business

Form groups of three to five people, and appoint one group member as the spokesperson who will communicate your findings to the whole class when called on by the instructor. Then discuss the following scenario.

You and your partners have decided to open a small printing and copying business in a college town of 100 000 people. Your business will compete with companies like Kinko's. You know that over 50 percent of small businesses fail in their first year, so to increase your chances of success, you have decided to do a detailed analysis of the task environment of the copying business in order to analyze the opportunities and threats you will encounter. As a group:

1. Decide what you must know about (a) your future customers, (b) your future competitors, and (c) other critical forces in the task environment, if you are to be successful.

2. Evaluate the main barriers to entry into the copying business.

3. Based on this analysis, list some of the steps you will take to help your new copying business succeed.

Exploring the World Wide Web

Specific Assignment

Examine the environment that the communications company Nortel Networks faces as it pursues its activities around the globe. Explore Nortel's Web site (www.nortel.com), and click on "Corporate Information" and "Corporate Citizenship". Explore these locations and other relevant ones for information about Nortel's environment.

1. What major forces in the task and general environments present opportunities and threats for Nortel?

2. How are Nortel's managers managing these forces?

General Assignment

Search for the Web site of a company that has a complex, rapidly changing environment. What forces in its organizational environment are creating the strongest opportunities and threats? How are managers attempting to respond to these opportunities and threats?

ManagementCase

The Brewing Industry

For many years now, the Canadian brewing industry has effectively been a duopoly, dominated by Labatt Brewing Co. and Molson Inc., which together control some 90 percent of the market.[37] The only other national figure in the industry is Guelph, ON-based Sleeman Breweries Ltd., which has gained 5 percent of the national market since its 1988 revival, with niche brands like Stroh, Okanagan Spring, Upper Canada and Frosted Frog.

As a new competitor, Sleeman has worked cautiously to build up its market share, working in partnership with more experienced breweries. It started in 1988 with the help of former Detroit-based Stroh Brewery Co., which purchased 20 percent of the shares and offered its expertise as one of the biggest US breweries. From that beginning, Sleeman has steadily expanded as a regional maker of premium craft beers.

Sleeman's strategy for growth has been to buy up "craft beer makers that had a reputation for making high-quality natural brews in small quantities."[38] Purchases include Okanagan Spring Brewery in Vernon, BC, Upper Canada Brewing in Toronto, Montreal's La Brasserie Seigneuriale, and the bankrupt Maritime Beer Co. in Dartmouth, NS. With these and other purchases, Sleeman has become a national beer maker.

In 2000, Sleeman started its entrance into the US market, by teaming up with Boston Beer Co. to market its Samuel Adams brand in Canada, in exchange for which Boston will market Sleeman's products in the United States. Sleeman also acquired the Canadian rights to Stroh's low-priced American beers, including Old Milwaukee, Rainier and Stroh's. Of this move, John Sleeman, chair and CEO, said, "This will counterbalance the premium-priced beers [Sleeman] has specialized in, providing extra volume for the plants and insulating the company from the vagaries of the domestic beer market."[39] Sleeman tries to avoid competing directly with Molson and Labatt: "We compete with them in the value-priced segment, but they don't have strong entries in the premium categories."[40]

With the concentration of sales in the hands of just three major Canadian players, Canada's small brewers are asking for help from the federal government. In September 2000, about 70 of them from across the country asked Ottawa for a reduction in the excise tax charged by Ottawa. "This industry is threatened," said Pierre Paquin, general manager of the newly formed Canadian Council of Regional Brewers. "We're not saying give us handouts. We're saying, give us a field where we can play too."[41] The craft-brewing industry employs about 3300 people directly and indirectly in Canada. Industry members see themselves as small business owners who should not have to pay the same rate of excise tax as Canadian beer giants Molson Inc. and Labatt Brewing Co. "Canadian brewers, regardless of size, pay about $2.30 in excise tax on a case of beer," said Donald Ross of Granville Island Brewing, chair of the Craft Brewers Association of British Columbia. "But it costs a small brewer as much as $260 to make a hectolitre, about 12 cases of beer, compared with $128 for the big breweries"[42] Craft breweries rely on employees rather than machines to produce their beer, and thus their labour costs are considerably higher. Other countries extract less tax from small brewers. "In the United States, for instance, the big brewers pay about Cdn$1.88 a case in excise taxes while the small brewers pay about 74 cents," said Ross.

John Wiggins of Creemore Springs Brewery Ltd., chairman of the Ontario Small Brewers Association, claims that the current excise tax situation "creates an uneven playing field. By dumping us into the same pot as the large brewers and charging us the same amount, it's actually making us non-competitive. It's punitive to our section of the industry."[43]The success of the large brewers resulted from two factors. First, economies of scale allowed them to keep the costs of making beer low and to make higher profits as their market increased. At the same time, their national presence permitted them to engage in large-scale advertising campaigns and develop national brand names for their beers. The smaller brewers have higher costs and primarily regional customers.

Even the Canadian giants in the industry are impacted by a number of different forces, however. First, sales of beer are flat in Canada because many customers have switched to wine or wine coolers. Second, social attitudes toward drinking, and in particular toward drinking and driving, have changed. Concern over the health effects of drinking alcohol have increased, and organizations such as MADD (Mothers Against Drunk Driving) and SADD (Students Against Destructive

Decisions) have lobbied for tighter control over sales of alcohol to minors and for strengthening legal penalties for drunk driving. One of the most interesting forces affecting the large brewers has been an increase in competition from small regional beer makers and import beer makers who are capitalizing on Canadian customers' demands for new tastes and higher beer quality.

Questions

1. What are the principal forces in the organizational environment facing the major brewers?

2. How has the level of uncertainty changed over time in the brewing industry? What is the source of these changes?

ManagementCase
In the News

From the Pages of *Business Week*
Levi's is Hiking Up its Pants

Back in September, Levi Strauss & Co. was all set to ship to retailers its newest invention: a line of blue jeans called Special Reserve. Samples had been made. Stores had placed orders. Levi's had even handed out T-shirts with the Special Reserve logo at an August sales meeting in Palm Springs, Calif.

But weeks before the debut, an unprecedented thing occurred. Thomas A. Fanoe—two months into his reign as president of Levi's USA—pulled the plug on the launch and sent nearly a year's worth of work into the circular file. Why? Because Special Reserve, which was likely to appeal to consumers 25 years and up, didn't solve Levi's core problem: teenage indifference.

That's quite a turnabout for a brand once synonymous with rebellious youth. While Levi retains its hold over the baby boomers who built the brand into mythic proportions, the company has neglected the whims of the latest crop of teens. "They missed all the kids, and those are your future buyers," says Bob Levy, owner of Dave's Army & Navy Store in New York, which devotes 50 percent of its shelves to Levi products.

The oversight has cost it dearly. With shrinking teen sales one of the key factors in the erosion of its once dominant market share, Levi Strauss was forced to announce on Nov. 3 that it would shutter 11 of its US plants and lay off one-third of its North American workforce. The news followed a similar announcement in February in which Levi's said it would lay off 1000 salaried US employees.

Of course, increased competition added to Levi's tight fit. But the San Francisco clothing giant's biggest problem is plummeting market share: In 1990, Levi Strauss had 30.9 percent of the US blue jeans market, but it has just 18.7 percent today, according to estimates by Tactical Retail Solutions Inc., a researcher in New York. Most troubling has been the drop among consumers aged 15 to 19. Levi says it enjoyed a 33 percent share of their jeans dollars in 1993, vs. about 26 percent now.

Missing those buyers can be a long-term mistake. "It's very important that you attract this age group," says Gordon Harton, vice-president for the Lee brand at rival VF Corp. "By the time they're 24, they've adopted brands that they will use for the rest of their lives. Worse, since teens set fashion trends that influence even older shoppers, the defection to other brands affects sales all down the product line."

Caught with its pants down, the US$7 billion company is scrambling to get back on track. Top management is giving virtually every aspect of the Levi's brand the once-over. Some products are being repositioned, while others are being scrapped altogether. Hiring policies are being reviewed to cultivate new talent and bring in fresh ideas. And marketing initiatives, including the company's 67-year-old relationship with ad agency Foote, Cone & Belding, are being completely revamped. "We are examining every element of the marketing, big M, of the Levi's brand," says Fanoe. "That means product, distribution, advertising, public relations, customer service. Everything."

How did the undisputed king of denim get into this hole? Levi Chairman and CEO Robert D. Haas says it was, in part, the classic corporate goof: taking your eyes off the ball. Projects during the last decade, such as expanding the casual clothing line Dockers and launching its upscale cousin Slates distracted executives from the threat to Levi's core jeans brand. "When you try to take on too many things, you are not as attentive to the warning signs," he concedes.

The warning signs became sirens at a July 31 meeting, when top US managers learned the results of a yearlong research project into what the kids of baby boomers—called the Echo Boom generation—think of the world's largest branded-apparel maker. The news wasn't good.

For half a day, executive product managers, and marketers of the Levi's brand in the US watched teen after teen on video talking about the blue-jeans king as if it were a has-been. Levi's, they said, was uncool, more suitable for their parents or older siblings than for fashion-conscious kids. "That was scary," recalls Stephen Goldstein, vice-president for marketing and research for Levi's USA. "Kids say they love the Levi's brand. But if you ask them whether it's 'with it,' they'll say no."

Meanwhile, the competition had made inroads. Top-end designers such as Tommy Hilfiger and Ralph Lauren have squeezed Levi on one end, while private labels sold by low-priced retailers such as J.C. Penney Co. and Sears, Roebuck & Co. have come on strong from the other direction. Trends such as wide-legged and baggy jeans took hold without response from Levi. "Levi Strauss was zagging when the world was zigging," says retail consultant Alan Millstein. "The company totally missed the significance of the inner city and the huge impact it has on trends. It tells me they're sleepy in their marketing."

But Levi execs seem to be waking up. The decision to scrap Special Reserve came in tandem with a move to pump up Levi's Silver Tab brand, the eight-year-old jeans line

that is considered more stylish among young consumers. Indeed, the median age of those who buy Silver Tab apparel is 18, compared with about 25 for other Levi's products. With its baggier fits and use of more than just denim fabrics, kids tag Silver Tab as Levi's hippest clothes. So the company plans to expand the line to include more tops, more trendy styles, and new khaki pants.

To catch teens' attention, Levi plans to spend five times as much in 1998 as it did this year on promoting Silver Tab. And for all its brands, it's also increasing marketing aimed specifically at teens. For instance, Levi is sponsoring concerts in New York and San Francisco for up-and-coming bands playing music known as Electronica. It's also outfitting characters on hot TV shows, such as Friends and Beverly Hills 90210. "As the Echo Boom generation goes, so goes Levi Strauss & Co.," says Goldstein. "We have to be relevant to this population."

The quest to jazz up Levi's image has also left the company searching for a new ad agency: A review, which includes longtime agency Foote, Cone & Belding, is under way. Although Levi has attempted to target teens in its latest ads, so far that hasn't translated into improved sales. Levi says its most recent TV campaign—featuring images such as a young man driving through a car wash with the windows down—has logged positive response from young consumers on the company's Web site. But when kids hit the stores and found them stocked mostly with traditional styles, Goldstein concedes, they didn't buy.

Another way Levi hopes to overcome that problem is by working over its retail presentation and the packaging and labelling of all its goods. In 1998, the company says it will come out with jazzier, more colourful packaging aimed at giving its products a more exciting, youthful look. And Levi has ditched plans to open more than 100 new stores in

malls around the country. Instead, it will follow Nike Inc.'s retail approach and open a handful of grand flagship stores in big cities. The first one is set to open in San Francisco in 1999.

But marketing and products aren't all that's getting a makeover. The company is also shaking up management. Now, Levi is considering a plan calling for 30 percent of all new management jobs to be filled by outsiders. Critics argue that one reason Levi appears to be losing touch with what's happening in the marketplace is that it doesn't recruit enough outside executives or solicit enough independent opinions. "It has always been insular, paternalistic, and, quite frankly, a little smug," says Isaac Lagnado, president of Tactical Retail Solutions.

Will this work? Most industry experts believe that the 140-year-old apparel giant can right itself—given its vast resources and still formidable market presence. But it's likely to be a difficult, multiyear process. Retailer Levy says the wake-up call comes none too soon. "They are facing the problem," he says. "That's important because they weren't doing it before." No one is more confident than Haas. "From time to time, any brand is likely to have periods of great strength and relevancy and periods of regrouping and refocusing," he says. "We're going to restore the Levi's brand with consumers." The trick will be to keep the generation that grew up on Bob Dylan, while understanding the new age of Electronica.

Source: L. Himelstein, "Levi's is Hiking Up its Pants," *Business Week*, December 1, 1997, pp. 71, 75.

Questions

1. What factors in its environment are giving rise to opportunities and threats for Levi Strauss?

2. How are Levi's managers trying to manage these opportunities and threats?

Chapter four

The Global Environment

Learning Objectives

1. Explain why the global environment is becoming more open and competitive and why barriers to the global transfer of goods and services are falling, increasing the opportunities, complexities, and challenges that managers face.

2. Identify each of the forces in the global task environment, and explain why they create opportunities and threats for global managers.

3. Describe the way in which political, legal, economic, and socio-cultural forces in the general environment can affect managers and the way in which global organizations operate.

4. List the impediments to the development of a more open global environment.

A Case in Contrast

Responding to NAFTA

Greg and Glenn Chamandy, co-founders and owners of Saint-Laurent, QC-based Gildan Activewear Inc. (www.gildan.com) have found a winning formula for thriving in the competitive T-shirt business. With Greg as CEO and Glenn as president, Gildan has become a global shirt empire supplying more than 1000 different styles, sizes, and colours to the silk screen printing business.

The brothers credit the free trade agreement with forcing them to think through their business options. They had already concluded that they couldn't manage both their late grandfather's children's wear company and their own knitting business. The looming North American Free Trade Agreement (NAFTA) would open new markets to them, but it was also going to wipe out the tariffs that had protected their grandfather's business. They decided to close their grandfather's business and get into the T-shirt business.

To build their business, "Gildan focused on building a low-cost infrastructure so they could compete on price," says Andrea Harbour, an analyst with Toronto's Sprott Securities Ltd.

"They're instrumental in maintaining the price at a level that keeps the pressure on competitors."[1]

Using the latest machinery, the material for the T-shirts is knitted and dyed in the Montreal area. However, right from the start the Chamandys decided to use inexpensive offshore labour to sew their shirts. The shirt-assembly work is then shipped to several sites in Central America and the Caribbean. Offshore labour may seem obvious today, but back in 1992 most of Gildan's US competitors were not even considering such a move. Instead, they were continuing to do most of their sewing in the United States.

Gildan also uses technology to its advantage. For instance, lasers are used to detect minute defects in material, and fabric is dyed using an automated process. Some competitors still have workers manually mix and match coloured dyes by hand. Montreal also has cheaper hydro rates than most of its US competitors.

Gildan sells through 38 wholesale distributors in Canada and the United States, and the company has recently signed up 21 distributors in Europe.[2] Using distributors limits financial risk,

Employees of Gildan Activewear model one of their company's products.

Fruit of the Loom has had difficulty dealing with the arrival of NAFTA, and has struggled to position itself as a result.

raises efficiency, and reduces costs, according to Greg. "But our competitors are willing to cut out their distributors," he says. "Since the distributors don't compete with each other, or us, they're more loyal to us."[3]

By the late 1990s, Gildan had established a name for itself as a supplier of inexpensive, good quality T-shirts. Their competitors have been unable to keep pace.

Fruit of the Loom was one of Gildan's biggest competitors. The company was started 150 years ago, and its name has always been virtually synonymous with T-shirts. Bill Farley, Fruit of the Loom's CEO from 1985 to 1999, is known as a flamboyant, charismatic deal maker. In the 1980s, he built a mini-empire of apparel companies with $4.5 billion in debt, most of it junk-bond financing from Drexel Burnham Lambert Inc.[4] For a while, he controlled both Fruit of the Loom and West Point–Pepperell Inc. He once appeared in Fruit of the Loom TV ads doing sit-ups in a tank top, and he even briefly considered running for US president. However, he faced liquidation in 1991 and West Point–Pepperell Inc. was sold off to reassert itself as a highly successful shirt manufacturer several years later under new management. Meanwhile, Farley continued to head Fruit of the Loom, which he managed with good success in the early 1990s.

Fruit of the Loom decided to ignore NAFTA for three years. Only 12 percent of manufacturing for the company was done offshore during most of the 1990s. The company instead relied on its network of plants in the American South to manufacture its products. Finally, in 1998, Farley moved his operations south of the US border, shifting 95 percent of Fruit of the Loom's manufacturing offshore in just 12 months.[5]

Farley's offshore strategy was fraught with errors. In setting up plants quickly, Fruit of the Loom employed untrained labourers to work in its factories. This made it difficult to compete with Gildan, which had "steadily assembled an army of skilled workers using spanking new equipment."[6] Moreover, putting Americans out of work and giving jobs to Mexicans did not generate positive publicity for Fruit of the Loom.

In 2000, Gildan's market share increased to 27 percent, from 14.8 percent in 1998. Meanwhile, Fruit of the Loom filed for Chapter 11 bankruptcy protection on December 30, 1999. Many analysts suggest that Farley's move was too little, too late. ●

Overview

global organization

An organization that operates and competes in more than one country.

Just a decade ago, many Canadian and US managers and organizations, not just Farley and Fruit of the Loom, decided against investing in the global environment because of the problems associated with expanding abroad. Instead, they chose to operate as if Canada and the United States were closed systems, detached from the rest of the world. Events of the last 10 years, however, have shown managers of organizations large and small, for-profit and not-for-profit, that they cannot afford to ignore the forces in the global environment. Many organizations and managers have concluded that, in order to survive in the twenty-first century, they need to adopt a global perspective. Most organizations must become **global organizations**, organizations that operate and compete in more than one country.

If organizations are to adapt to the global environment, their managers must learn to understand the global forces that operate in it and how these forces give rise to opportunities and threats. In this chapter, we examine why the global environment is becoming more open, vibrant, and competitive. We examine how forces in the global task and general environments affect global organizations and their managers. We examine the different ways in which organizations can expand internationally. We also examine impediments to the creation of an even more open global environment. By the end of this chapter, you will appreciate the changes that have been taking place in the global environment and understand why it is important for managers to develop a global perspective as they strive to increase organizational efficiency and effectiveness. ●

The Changing Global Environment

Until relatively recently, many managers did not regard the global environment as a significant source of opportunities and threats. Traditionally, managers regarded the global environment as *closed*–that is, as a set of distinct national markets and countries that were isolated physically, economically, and culturally from one another. As a result, they did not think much about global competition, exporting, obtaining inputs from foreign suppliers, or the challenges of managing in a foreign culture. These issues were simply outside the experience of the majority of managers, whose organizations remained firmly focused on competing at home, in the domestic marketplace.

Today, more and more managers regard the global environment as a source of important opportunities and threats to which they must respond. Managers now view the global environment as *open*–that is, as an environment in which they and their organizations are free to buy goods and services from, and sell goods and services to, whichever countries they choose. An open environment is also one in which global organizations are free not only to compete against each other to attract customers but also to establish foreign subsidiaries to become the strongest competitors throughout the world.

In this section, we explain why the global environment is becoming more open and competitive and why this development is so significant for managers today. We examine how economic changes such as the lowering of barriers to trade and investment have led to greater interaction and exchanges between organizations and countries. We discuss how declines in barriers of distance and culture have increased the interdependencies between organizations and countries. In addition, we consider the specific implications of these changes for managers and organizations.

Declining Barriers to Trade and Investment

During the 1920s and 1930s, many countries erected formidable barriers to international trade and investment in the belief that this was the best way to promote their economic well-being. Many of these barriers were high tariffs on imports of manufactured goods. A **tariff** is a tax that a government imposes on imported or, occasionally, on exported goods. The aim of import tariffs is to protect domestic industries and jobs, such as those in the auto industry, from foreign competition by raising the price of goods from abroad. The application of tariffs by competing countries can have unintended consequences, however. In early 2001, Canada and Brazil were locked in battle over whether each country was subsidizing exports for its own jet producers, Montreal-based Bombardier Inc. and Empresa Brasileira de Aeronautica SA (Embraer), respectively. Canada applied for a WTO investigation, and suggested tariffs on Brazilian products ranging from shoes to beef. Canadian shoe stores, for instance, could be caught in a trade war not of their doing, to support the production of jets in Canada.

Very often, when one country imposes an import tariff, others follow suit and the result is a series of retaliatory moves as countries progressively raise tariff barriers against each other. In the 1920s, this behaviour depressed world demand and helped usher in the Great Depression of the 1930s and massive unemployment. In short, rather than protecting jobs and promoting economic well-being, governments of countries that resort to raising high tariff barriers ultimately reduce employment and undermine economic growth.[7]

THE RISE OF FREE TRADE, GATT, AND THE WTO Having learned from the Great Depression, advanced Western industrial countries after the Second World War committed themselves to the goal of removing barriers to the free flow of resources between countries. This commitment was reinforced by

tariff A tax that a government imposes on imported or, occasionally, exported goods.

free-trade doctrine
The idea that if each country specializes in the production of the goods and services that it can produce most efficiently, this will make the best use of global resources.

GATT General Agreement on Tariffs and Trade, signed by a number of countries in 1947 to help reduce trade barriers through lower tariffs. By 1994, 117 countries were party to the agreement.

WTO World Treaty Organization, comprising 125 countries, determines and enforces policies regarding trade among member nations.

acceptance of a principle that predicted that free trade, rather than tariff barriers, was the best way to foster a healthy domestic economy and low unemployment.[8]

The **free-trade doctrine** predicts that if each country agrees to specialize in the production of the goods and services that it can produce most efficiently, this will make the best use of global resources and will result in lower prices. For example, if Indian companies are highly efficient in the production of textiles and Canadian companies are highly efficient in the production of computer software, then under a free-trade agreement production of textiles would shift to India and computer software to Canada. Under these conditions, prices of textiles and software should fall because both goods are being produced in the location where they can be made at the lowest cost, benefiting consumers and making the best use of scarce resources.

Countries that accepted this free-trade doctrine set as their goal the removal of barriers to the free flow of goods between countries. They attempted to achieve this through an international treaty known as the General Agreement on Tariffs and Trade (**GATT**), signed in 1947. In the half-century since the Second World War, there were eight rounds of GATT negotiations aimed at lowering tariff barriers. The last round, the Uruguay Round, involved 117 countries and was formally completed in April 1994. This round succeeded in lowering tariffs by over 30 percent from the previous level. The average decline in tariff barriers achieved among the governments of developed countries since 1947 is more than 94 percent (similar in theory to a 94-percent reduction in taxes on imports).

Perhaps the most important outcome of the Uruguay Round was the creation of a new international organization, the World Trade Organization (**WTO**). The WTO supersedes all institutional aspects of GATT, and "can be viewed as an umbrella organization embracing GATT and a number of other agreements covering a wide range of international issues."[9] The WTO has 125 member countries, the significant exceptions being China and most members of OPEC (the Organization of Petroleum Exporting Countries). The discussion of whether to allow membership to China has been a significant issue because of the country's rapid economic growth and its position on human rights.

Declining Barriers of Distance and Culture

Barriers of distance and culture also "closed" the global environment and kept managers looking inward. The management problems that Unilever, a large British soap and detergent maker, experienced at the turn of the twentieth century illustrate the effect of these barriers.

Unilever
www.unilever.com/

Founded in London during the 1880s by William Lever, Unilever had a worldwide reach by the early 1900s and operated subsidiaries in most major countries of the British Empire, including India, Canada, and Australia. Lever had a very hands-on, autocratic management style and found his far-flung business empire difficult to control. The reason for Lever's control problems was that communication over great distances was difficult. It took six weeks to reach India by ship from England, and international telephone and telegraph services were very unreliable.

Another problem that Unilever encountered was the difficulty of doing business in societies that were separated from the United Kingdom by barriers of language and culture. Different countries have different sets of national beliefs, values, and norms, and Lever found that a management approach that worked in the United Kingdom did not necessarily work in India or Persia (now Iran). As a result, management practices had to be tailored to suit each unique national culture. After Lever's death in 1925, top management at Unilever decentralized decision-making authority to the managers of the various national subsidiaries so that they could develop a management approach that suited the country in which they were operating. One result of this strategy was that the subsidiaries grew distant and remote from one another.[10]

In the middle of a maize field, villagers in Niger, Africa, gather to view worldwide news and events on their village's communal television.

Since the end of the Second World War, major advances in communications and transportation technology have been reducing the barriers of distance and culture that affected Unilever and other global organizations. Over the last 30 years, global communications have been revolutionized by developments in satellites, digital switching, and optical fibre telephone lines. Satellites and optical fibres can carry hundreds of thousands of messages simultaneously.[11] As a result of such developments, reliable and instantaneous communication is now possible with nearly any location in the world. Fax machines in Sri Lanka, cellular phones in the Brazilian rain forest, satellite dishes in Russia, video phones in Manhattan, and videoconferencing facilities in Japan are all part of the communications revolution that is changing the way the world works. This revolution has made it possible for a global organization—a tiny garment factory or a huge company such as Unilever—to do business anywhere, anytime, and to search out customers and suppliers from around the world.

Several major innovations in transportation technology since the Second World War also have made the global environment more open. Most significant, the growth of commercial jet travel has reduced the time it takes to get from one location to another.

In addition to making travel faster, modern communications and transportation technologies have also helped reduce the cultural distance between countries. Canadians do not necessarily view this as a good thing, however, as it means that US culture seems to be building a dominant force internationally. US television networks such as CNN, MTV, and HBO can now be received in many countries around the world, and Hollywood films are shown around the globe. The Canadian government continues to protect Canadian culture content in the broadcasting and publishing industries in particular.

Effects of Free Trade on Managers

In what ways has free trade been either a positive or a negative factor for Canadian businesses?

The lowering of barriers to trade and investment and the decline of distance and culture barriers have created enormous opportunities for organizations to expand the market for their goods and services through exports and investments in foreign countries. Not only has the shift toward a more open global economy created more opportunities to sell goods and services in foreign markets; it also has created the opportunity to buy more from foreign countries. Indeed, the success of companies such as Gap and Toys 'R' Us has been based in part on their managers' willingness to import low-cost clothes and toys from foreign manufacturers. Other companies such as Nortel Networks, CN and Ford Motor Company have set up operations in Asia-Pacific that provide services to these customers and their clients. What these activities show is that any service that can be delivered by phone, fibre or satellite can now be outsourced.

The manager's job is also more challenging in a dynamic global environment because of the increased intensity of competition that goes hand in hand with the lowering of barriers to trade and investment. Thus, the job of the average manager in one of the Big Three automobile manufacturers became a lot harder from the mid-1970s on as a result of the penetration of the automobile market by efficient Japanese and German competitors and the increase in competition that resulted from it. In addition, the application of tariffs by competing countries has added to the challenge of a manager's job. As we saw earlier, a number of Canadian companies are doing business in Brazil, and are thus affected by the trade battle in jetliners between the two countries. Canada's softwood lumber industry has faced punishing tariffs from the United States because of US beliefs that the Canadian government subsidizes the industry.

NAFTA The North American Free Trade Agreement, which became effective on January 1, 1994, was designed to abolish the tariffs on 99 percent of the goods traded between Canada, the United States and Mexico by 2004.

NAFTA　The growth of regional trade agreements such as the North American Free Trade Agreement (**NAFTA**) also presents opportunities and threats for managers and their organizations. NAFTA, which became effective on January 1, 1994, will abolish within 10 years the tariffs on 99 percent of the goods traded between Mexico, Canada, and the United States. NAFTA also removes most barriers on the cross-border flow of resources, giving, for example, financial institutions and retail businesses in Canada and the United States unrestricted access to the Mexican marketplace. During NAFTA's first six years, trade between Mexico and Canada increased by almost 15 percent annually, reaching $14 billion in 2000. Canada has also increased its investment in Mexico considerably, investing $3.5 billion in 2000.[12] Westcoast Energy, Scotiabank, and BCE are just a few examples of Canadian companies that have expanded their operations in Mexico.

The establishment of free-trade areas creates an opportunity for manufacturing organizations because it allows them to reduce their costs. They can do this either by shifting production to the lowest-cost location within the free-trade area (for example, textile companies shifting production to Mexico) or by serving the whole region from one location, rather than establishing separate operations in each country.

Some managers might see regional free-trade agreements as a threat, however, because they expose a company based in one member country to increased competition from companies based in the other member countries. Managers in Mexico, Canada, and the United States are experiencing this now that NAFTA is here. For the first time, Mexican managers find themselves facing a threat: head-to-head competition in some industries against efficient Canadian and US organizations. But the opposite is true as well: Canadian and US managers are experiencing threats in labour-intensive industries, such as the textile industry, where Mexican businesses have a cost advantage. Despite the challenges, some clear success stories have come from freer trade agreements, as the "Management Insight" shows.

Management Insight

The BC Wine Industry and the Free Trade Agreement

When the Canada–United States Free Trade Agreement (FTA)–the precursor to NAFTA–was signed in early 1988, many Canadians worried about the impact of the agreement on the country's industries. The BC wine industry is an example of an industry that was seriously affected by the agreement. Prior to the FTA, the industry was heavily protected by the BC Liquor Control Board, which charged high markups on foreign wines. BC wines were able to dominate the low-price segment of the industry. BC wines were not known for their quality: "Dating from the 1920s, the BC wine industry used low-quality BC grapes, often mixed with grape concentrate from California, to produce cheap low-quality wine."[13] While there were some attempts throughout the 1960s, 1970s, and 1980s to improve the quality of wine, the industry targeted the low-quality protected sector.

During the negotiation of the FTA, BC wineries were quite concerned that they would face destruction, since they would not be able to compete with superior California wines. At the same time, a GATT ruling reduced the protection that Canada could provide against wines from other countries. After the agreement was signed, many BC wine grape growers sold their farms, accepting compensation under the FTA adjustment assistance program. However, other growers planted high-quality grapes, and a number of wineries accepted the challenge to produce high-quality wines so that they could compete.

Today, the BC wine industry is a model of success under competition. It has become a major exporter of wine, and BC wines have won numerous international awards in recent years. Sales have even improved in the domestic market. In addition, the BC wine regions have become significant tourist destinations for those wanting to tour the wineries and taste the wines.

Not all industries have necessarily prospered as a result of trade liberalization, but managers should not assume that stronger competition will always result in failure of their business or industry.

FTAA A possible extension of NAFTA was discussed recently. The Summit of the Americas closed April 22, 2001 with the leaders of 34 countries calling for a free-trade zone across the western hemisphere by 2005, to be called the Free Trade Agreement of the Americas (**FTAA**). Member countries would have to be democratic, which currently excludes only communist-ruled Cuba. The treaty would remove trade barriers across the Americas from the Arctic Circle to Cape Horn. All countries are expected to ratify a completed pact by 2005. US President George W. Bush called the proposed Free Trade Agreement of the Americas a "logical extension" of the North American Free Trade Agreement, which took effect in 1994. It is too early to tell whether all countries will sign the agreement, and it is not clear to what extent Canada will gain additional trading partners or markets as a result of this agreement. Most of the other markets are quite small compared to Mexico and the United States.

Nevertheless, the shift toward a more open, competitive global environment has increased both the opportunities that managers can take advantage of and the threats they must respond to in performing their jobs effectively. Next, we look in detail at the forces in the global task and general environments to see where these opportunities and threats are arising.

FTAA The Free Trade Agreement of the Americas, seen as a logical extension of NAFTA, is intended to remove trade barriers across the Americas from the Arctic Circle to Cape Horn. The agreement is expected to be completed by 2005.

The Global Task Environment

As managers operate in the global environment, they confront forces that differ from country to country and from world region to world region.[14] In this section, we examine some of the forces in the global task environment that increase opportunities or threats for managers. The major forces in the global task environment are similar to those introduced in Chapter 3: suppliers, distributors, customers, and competitors (see Figure 4.1).

Figure 4.1
Forces in the Global Task Environment

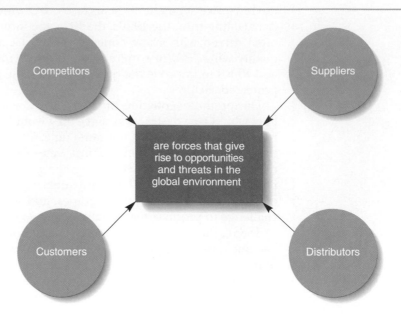

Suppliers

At a global level, managers have the opportunity to buy products from foreign suppliers or to become their own suppliers and manufacture their own products abroad. For example, as noted in the "Case in Contrast," to lower costs, Gildan went offshore to manufacture its T-shirts. This enabled Gildan to charge its Canadian and US customers lower prices than either Fruit of the Loom or Hanes. Companies are increasingly engaging in **global outsourcing**, the process by which organizations purchase inputs from other companies or produce inputs themselves throughout the world, to lower their production costs and improve the quality or design of their products. While Nike sends manufacturing contracts to Indonesia, companies such as Nortel Networks, CN and Ford Motor Company export the provision of services to foreign countries. Services that can be delivered by phone, fibre, or satellite can be outsourced. While we talk about this as a North American "problem," because it takes jobs away from our citizens, even countries like Japan are starting to shift manufacturing offshore to reduce costs. Japan's Yamaha Motor Co., Aiwa Co., and Fujitsu Ltd. have started to manufacture their products in cheaper locations such as Taiwan, China, and Southeast Asia.

A common problem facing managers of large global organizations such as Nortel, Ford, Procter & Gamble, and IBM is the development of a global network of suppliers that will allow their companies to keep costs down and quality high. For example, Boeing relies on 545 different suppliers from around the world.[15] Boeing buys at least $700 million worth of products annually from 200 Canadian suppliers. For instance, Richmond, BC-based parts supplier Avcorp Industries gets 30 percent of its $50 million in sales from Boeing.[16] Eight Japanese suppliers make parts for the Boeing 777's fuselage, doors, and wings; a Singaporean supplier makes the doors for the plane's forward landing gear; and three Italian suppliers manufacture wing flaps. Boeing's rationale for buying so many inputs from foreign suppliers is that these suppliers are the best in the world at performing their particular activity, and doing business with them helps Boeing to produce a high-quality final product, a vital requirement given the need for aircraft safety and reliability.[17] Of course, the suppliers are affected when either a company such as

global outsourcing

The purchase of inputs from foreign suppliers, or the production of inputs abroad, to lower production costs and improve product quality or design.

Boeing
www.boeing.com/

Boeing suffers problems, or the world economy suffers a downturn. Still, small organizations must be alert to global opportunities to buy or manufacture low-cost products abroad in order to prosper. Not only manufacturing can be carried out overseas, however. Increasingly, companies are relying on low-cost suppliers of labour to carry out service jobs, as the "Managing Globally" shows. While companies in Third World countries face a variety of obstacles in providing services, they are figuring out ways to meet the challenge.

Managing Globally

Spectramind Phones You From New Delhi

The phone rings during dinner and it's a cellphone company trying to sell you a new, improved cellphone plan.[18] You might logically assume that the call is coming from somewhere in Canada, perhaps New Brunswick, which is known for its high concentration of call centres. But the call may just as easily be coming from New Delhi, India.

Raman Roy, chief executive of New Delhi-based Spectramind eServices (Pvt.) Ltd. (www.spectramind.com), knows that cost is only one factor when North American companies are looking for service operations where they might outsource call servicing. The foreign employees need to be able to make personal connections with North American customers if their sales pitch is to be successful. "We also have to acclimatize the staff with the environment of the caller. When someone says, 'What about the game the Titans played last night?' our people must know how to answer.'"

Call servicing centres can be set up easily in the Third World because of technology that makes distance irrelevant. The centres in India can provide the same service as a North American firm for less than half the cost. And the quality of the employee is often better. "At Spectramind we employ graduates with 12 years of schooling who, because India's real unemployment is very high, are not transient. As a result when they join a company, they stay," says Roy.

While the employees might have never been to North America, they're expected to be up to speed on North American events. Therefore, employees are expected to read newspapers or scan the Internet to find out such things as scores of games, entertainment news, and political developments.

While India can provide a highly educated workforce, companies like Spectramind still face problems with the country's infrastructure. For instance, Spectramind "has two sources of electricity and three back-up generators... [and] five different telecommunications systems, including [a] direct satellite link to cover itself for any problem that might crop up in delivering services."

Distributors

Toys 'R' Us
http://inc.toysrus.com/

Another force that creates opportunities and threats for global managers is the nature of a country's distribution system. As Toys 'R' Us discovered in Japan, the traditional means by which goods and services are distributed and sold to customers can present challenges to managers of organizations pursuing international expansion. Traditionally, Japanese toy manufacturers sold their products through wholesalers who added their own price markup, which made it difficult for Toys 'R' Us to enjoy its competitive advantage of price discounting in Japan. Though Toys 'R' Us insisted on buying directly from Japanese manufacturers, the manufacturers refused. It was not until Japan's deep recession in the early 1990s that the manufacturers were willing to deal with Toys 'R' Us directly.[19] Therefore, as Toys

'R' Us' experience shows, managers must identify the hidden problems surrounding the distribution and sale of goods and services—such as anticompetitive government regulations—in order to discover hidden threats early and find ways to overcome them before significant resources are invested.

Customers

The most obvious opportunity associated with expanding into the global environment is the prospect of selling goods and services to new customers.

Today, once-distinct national markets are merging into one huge global marketplace where the same basic product can be sold to customers worldwide. This consolidation is occurring both for consumer goods and for business products and has created enormous opportunities for managers. The global acceptance of Coca-Cola, Levi's blue jeans, Sony Walkmans, McDonald's hamburgers, and Motorola pagers and flip phones is a sign that the tastes and preferences of consumers in different countries are beginning to become more similar.[20] Likewise, large global markets currently exist for business products such as telecommunications equipment, electronic components, computer services, and financial services. Thus, Motorola sells its telecommunications equipment, Intel its microprocessors, and Computer Associates its business systems management software, to customers throughout the world.

Nevertheless, despite evidence that the same goods and services are receiving acceptance from customers worldwide, it is important not to place too much emphasis on this development. Because national cultures differ in many ways, significant differences between countries in consumer tastes and preferences still remain. These differences often require managers to customize goods and services to suit the preferences of local consumers. For example, despite McDonald's position as a leading global organization, its management has recognized a need for local customization. In Brazil, McDonald's sells a soft drink made from the guarana, an exotic berry that grows along the Amazon River (in 1996, Pepsi announced that it was test-marketing a drink made from this berry in the United States). In Malaysia, McDonald's sells milkshakes flavoured with durian, a strong-smelling fruit that local people consider an aphrodisiac.[21] Similarly, when Mattel decided to begin selling Barbie dolls in Japan, it had to redesign the doll's appearance (colour of hair, facial features, and so on) to suit the tastes of its prospective customers.

Two newly affluent Chinese consumers enjoy a drink of Coca-Cola, a global brand whose recipe has nevertheless been specially altered to satisfy the tastes of Chinese consumers.

Competitors

Although finding less-expensive or higher-quality supplies and attracting new customers are global opportunities for managers, entry into the global environment also leads to major threats in the form of increases in competition both at home and abroad. Canadian managers in foreign markets, for example, face the problem of competing against local companies that are familiar with the local market and have generated considerable brand loyalty. As a result, Canadian managers might find it difficult to break into a foreign market and obtain new customers. Of course, foreign competitors trying to enter a Canadian company's domestic market face the same challenges. Canadian and US car companies faced strong global competition at home in the 1970s, when foreign competitors aggressively entered the Canadian and US market. In the global environment, the level of competition can increase rapidly, and managers must be alert to the changes taking place in order to respond appropriately.

The Global General Environment

Despite evidence that countries are becoming more similar to one another and that the world is on the verge of becoming a "global village," countries still differ across a range of political, legal, economic, and cultural dimensions. When an organization operates in the global environment, it confronts in the global general environment a series of forces that differ from country to country and world region to world region. In this section, we consider how forces in the global general environment—such as political and legal, economic, and sociocultural forces—create opportunities and threats for managers of global organizations (see Figure 4.2).

Political and Legal Forces

Global political and legal forces result from the diverse and changing nature of various countries' political and legal systems. The global range of political systems includes everything from representative democracies to totalitarian regimes, and in order to manage global organizations effectively, managers must understand how these different political systems work.

In **representative democracies**, such as the United Kingdom, Canada, Germany, and the United States, citizens periodically elect individuals to represent their interests. These elected representatives form a government whose function is to make decisions on behalf of the electorate. To guarantee that voters can hold elected representatives legally accountable for their actions, an ideal representative democracy incorporates a number of safeguards into the law. These include: (1) an individual's right to freedom of expression, opinion, and organization; (2) free media; (3) regular elections in which all eligible citizens are allowed to vote; (4) limited terms for elected representatives; (5) a fair court system that is independent from the political system; (6) a nonpolitical police force and armed service; and (7) relatively free access to state information.[22]

In contrast, in **totalitarian regimes** a single political party, individual, or group of individuals holds all political power. Typically, totalitarian regimes neither recognize nor permit opposition from individuals or groups. Most of the

representative democracy A political system in which representatives elected by citizens and legally accountable to the electorate form a government whose function is to make decisions on behalf of the electorate.

totalitarian regime A political system in which a single party, individual, or group holds all political power and neither recognizes nor permits opposition.

Figure 4.2
Forces in the Global General Environment

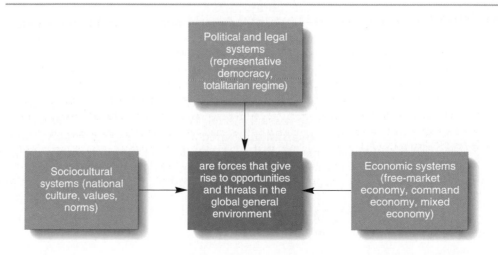

constitutional guarantees on which representative democracies are based are denied to the citizens of totalitarian states. In most totalitarian countries, political repression is widespread. Those who question the policies of the rulers and their right to rule find themselves imprisoned or worse. Totalitarian regimes are found in countries such as China, Iraq, and Iran.

Why must managers be concerned about the political makeup of a foreign country in which they are doing business? First, stable democratic countries with a high degree of political freedom tend to be characterized by economic freedom and a well-defined legal system. In turn, economic freedom and a well-defined legal system protect the rights of individuals and corporations and are conducive to business.[23] Second, totalitarian regimes' lack of respect for human rights raises the question of whether it is ethical to trade with, or invest in, those countries (we examine the ethical issues of operating globally in Chapter 5).

Economic Forces

Economic forces are caused by the changing nature of countries' economic systems. Around the globe, economic systems range from free-market economies to command economies, and managers must learn how different economic systems work in order to understand the opportunities and threats associated with them.

free-market economy

An economic system in which private enterprise controls production, and the interaction of supply and demand determines which and how many goods and services are produced and how much consumers pay for them.

In a **free-market economy**, the production of goods and services is left in the hands of *private* (as opposed to *government*) enterprise. The goods and services that are produced, and the quantities that are produced, are not specified by a central authority. Rather, production is determined by the interaction of the forces of supply and demand. If demand for a product exceeds supply, the price of the product will rise, prompting managers and organizations to produce more. If supply exceeds demand, prices will fall, causing managers and organizations to produce less. In a free-market economy, the purchasing patterns of consumers, as signalled to managers by changes in demand, determine what and how much is produced.

command economy

An economic system in which the government owns all businesses and specifies which and how many goods and services are produced and the prices at which they are sold.

In a **command economy**, the goods and services that a country produces, the quantity in which they are produced, and the prices at which they are sold are all planned by the government. In a pure command economy, all businesses are government owned and private enterprise is forbidden. As recently as 1989–1991, the communist countries of eastern Europe and the Soviet Union had command economies, as did other communist countries such as China and Vietnam. The overall failure of these economies to perform as well as the free-market-oriented systems of western Europe, North America, and areas of the Pacific Rim helped precipitate the collapse of communism in many of these countries and the subsequent dismantlement of command economies. Even in China and Vietnam, which remain communist controlled, there has been a marked shift away from a command economy.

mixed economy

An economic system in which some sectors of the economy are left to private ownership and free-market mechanisms and others are owned by the government and subject to government planning.

Between free-market economies on the one hand, and command economies on the other, are mixed economies. In a **mixed economy**, certain sectors of the economy are left to private ownership and free-market mechanisms, and other sectors are characterized by significant government ownership and government planning. Mixed economies are most commonly found in the democratic countries of western Europe, but they are disappearing as these countries shift toward the free-market model. For example, in the United Kingdom in the early 1980s, the government owned a majority stake in many important industries, including airlines, healthcare, steel, and telecommunications. Since then, following a trend toward privatization, the British government has sold its airline, steel, and telecommunications interests to private investors, and a significant private healthcare sector has emerged to compete with government-provided healthcare. Similar privatization efforts have been undertaken in other western European countries.

The manager of a global organization generally prefers a free-market system, for two reasons. First, because much of the economy is in private hands, there tend to be few restrictions on organizations that decide to invest in countries with free-market economies. For example, Canadian companies face fewer impediments to investing in the United Kingdom, with its largely free-market system, than they do in China, where a free market is allowed only in certain sectors of the economy. Second, free-market economies tend to be more economically developed and have higher rates of economic growth than command or mixed economies, so their citizens tend to have higher per capita incomes and more spending power.[24] As a result, for companies attempting to export or to establish foreign subsidiaries, they are more attractive markets than are mixed economies or command economies, which are closely regulated by government. One company that has tried to figure out a way to survive in a command economy is Markham, ON-based CoolBrands International, described in "Managing Globally."

Managing Globally

CoolBrands Takes Ice Cream to North Korea

CoolBrands International (www.yogenfruz.com), based in Markham, Ontario, is best known for selling Yogen Fruz, Bresler's and Eskimo Pie ice cream products to Canadians.[25] Recently the company has decided to open two side-by-side operations in North Korea, to sell Canadian-made ice cream. One will be a Swensen's Ice Cream outlet and the other will be an I Can't Believe It's Yogurt outlet.

Not many Canadian companies do business in North Korea, which has "a reputation for being 'difficult' to deal with." North Korea and Canada only established diplomatic relations in February 2001, so there is no Canadian embassy to help manage the challenge of doing business in North Korea if something goes wrong. Michael Serruya, CoolBrands' co-chair and CEO, believes that it's worth getting a foot in the door before anyone else tries to do so, despite possible risks.

A spokesperson for North Korea based at the United Nations in New York said that it is rare for foreigners to open businesses in his country, but noted that "it is possible if the company has good relations with certain institutions in our country." To ease its entry into North Korea, CoolBrands has followed the lead of several other companies, and formed an alliance with South Korea's Korea Fruz Inc., which is also opening ice cream shops in South Korea. South Koreans have had an easier time moving into North Korea than Westerners have.

André Schmid, a professor of East Asian studies at the University of Toronto, notes that doing business in North Korea carries multiple risks, including a lack of infrastructure and no guarantees under local law. The North Korean government has reneged on millions of dollars in Western bank loans back to the 1970s.

As the example of CoolBrands illustrates, managers who want to take advantage of the opportunities created by changing global, political and legal, and economic forces face a major challenge.

Changes in Political and Legal and Economic Forces

In recent years, two large and related shifts in political and economic forces have occurred globally (see Figure 4.3).[26] One—the shift away from totalitarian dictatorships and toward more democratic regimes—has been most dramatic in Eastern

Figure 4.3
Changes in Political and Economic Forces

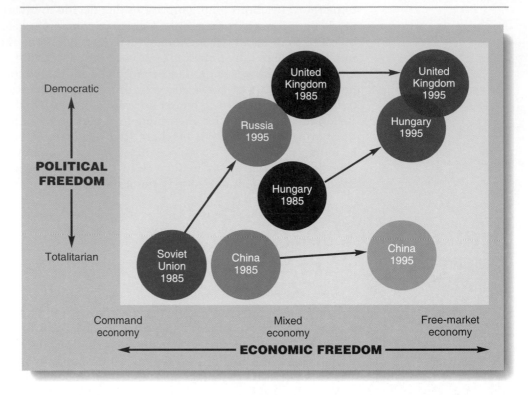

Europe and the former Soviet Union, where totalitarian communist regimes collapsed during the late 1980s and early 1990s. The other—the shift toward representative democracy—has occurred from Latin America to Africa. For the most part, the movement toward democracy has been precipitated by the failure of totalitarian regimes with command or mixed economies to improve the well-being of their citizens. This failure has been particularly noticeable in comparisons of these countries with democratic, free-market countries such as Canada, Germany, Japan, and the United States.

Accompanying this change in political forces has been a worldwide shift away from command and mixed economies and toward the free-market model, as noted previously.[27] This economic shift was triggered by the realization that government involvement in economic activity often impedes economic growth. Thus, a wave of privatization and deregulation has swept over the world, from the former communist countries to Latin America, Asia, and western Europe. Governments have sold off government-owned organizations to private investors and have dismantled regulations that inhibit the operation of the free market.

These trends are good news for managers of global organizations because they result in the expansion of opportunities for exporting and investment abroad. A decade ago, few Western companies exported to or invested in eastern Europe because the combination of totalitarian political regimes and command economies created a hostile environment for Western businesses. Since 1990, however, the environment in eastern Europe has become far more favourable for Western businesses; from 1990 to 1993, Western businesses invested $23 billion in eastern Europe.[28] A similar story is unfolding in China, where, despite the continued presence of a totalitarian communist regime, a move toward greater economic freedom has occurred and has produced a surge of Western and Japanese business activity in this region of the world. From 1990 to 1993, foreign companies invested nearly $62 billion in China.[29]

The managers of many Western companies have experienced considerable difficulty in their attempts to establish business operations in eastern Europe and China, however. For example, when the Chiquita banana company entered the Czech Republic in 1990, the company was hoping to take advantage of that nation's rapid move toward a free-market economy. However, Chiquita found that the premium bananas it sold in the West could not be marketed in the Czech Republic. After decades of communism, Czech citizens apparently had difficulty understanding why something of better quality should cost more. Chiquita was forced to switch to lower-quality bananas after discovering that consumers were unwilling to pay higher prices for superior bananas.[30]

Sociocultural Forces

What is interesting about the experiences of a company like Chiquita in the Czech Republic is that many of the problems are the result of critical differences in the values, norms, and attitudes of Western cultures and of eastern European cultures conditioned by communism and a command economy. **National culture** is an important sociocultural force that global managers must take into account when they do business in foreign countries. National culture includes the values, norms, knowledge, beliefs, moral principles, laws, customs, and other practices that unite the citizens of a country.[31] National culture shapes individual behaviour by specifying appropriate and inappropriate behaviour and interaction with others. People learn national culture in their everyday lives by interacting with those around them. This learning starts at an early age and continues throughout a person's life.

VALUES AND NORMS The basic building blocks of national culture are values and norms. **Values** are ideas about what a society believes to be good, right, desirable, or beautiful. They provide the basic underpinnings for notions of individual freedom, democracy, truth, justice, honesty, loyalty, social obligation, collective responsibility, the appropriate roles for men and women, love, sex, marriage, and so on. Values are more than merely abstract concepts; they are invested with considerable emotional significance. People argue, fight, and even die over values such as "freedom."

Though deeply embedded in society, values are not static—although change in a country's values is likely to be slow and painful. For example, the value systems of many formerly communist states, such as Russia, are undergoing significant changes as those countries move away from a value system that emphasizes the state and toward one that emphasizes individual freedom. Social turmoil often results when countries undergo major changes in their values.

Norms are unwritten rules and codes of conduct that prescribe appropriate behaviour in particular situations and shape the behaviour of people toward one another. Two types of norms play a major role in national culture: folkways and mores. **Folkways** are the routine social conventions of everyday life. They concern customs and practices such as dressing appropriately for particular situations, good social manners, eating with the correct utensils, and neighbourly behaviour. Although folkways define the way people are expected to behave, violation of folkways is not a serious or moral matter. People who violate folkways are often thought to be eccentric or ill mannered, but they are not usually considered to be evil or bad. In many countries, foreigners may be excused initially for violating folkways because they are unaccustomed to local behaviour, but repeated violations will not be excused because foreigners are expected to learn appropriate behaviour.

Mores are norms that are considered to be central to the functioning of society and to social life. They have much greater significance than folkways. Accordingly, the violation of mores can be expected to bring serious retribution. Mores include proscriptions against theft, adultery, and incest. In many societies, mores have

Chiquita
www.chiquita.com/

national culture The set of values that a society considers important and the norms of behaviour that are approved or sanctioned in that society.

values Ideas about what a society believes to be good, right, desirable, or beautiful.

norms Unwritten rules and informal codes of conduct that prescribe how people should act in particular situations.

folkways The routine social conventions of everyday life.

mores Norms that are considered to be central to the functioning of society and to social life.

been enacted into law. Thus, all advanced societies have laws against theft and incest. However, there are many differences in mores from one society to another.[32] In North America, for example, drinking alcohol is widely accepted; in Saudi Arabia, the consumption of alcohol is viewed as a violation of social mores and is punishable by imprisonment.

HOFSTEDE'S MODEL OF NATIONAL CULTURE   Researchers have spent considerable time and effort identifying similarities and differences in the values and norms of different countries. One model of national culture was developed by Gert Hofstede.[33] As a psychologist for IBM, Hofstede collected data on employee values and norms from more than 100 000 IBM employees in 64 countries. Based on his research, Hofstede developed five dimensions along which national cultures can be placed (see Figure 4.4).

INDIVIDUALISM VERSUS COLLECTIVISM   **Individualism** is a worldview that values individual freedom and self-expression and adherence to the principle that people should be judged by their individual achievements rather than by their social background. In Western countries, individualism usually includes admiration for personal success, a strong belief in individual rights, and high regard for individual entrepreneurs.[34]

In contrast, **collectivism** is a worldview that values subordination of the individual to the goals of the group and adherence to the principle that people should be judged by their contribution to the group. Collectivism was widespread in communist countries but has become less prevalent since the collapse of communism in those countries. Japan is a noncommunist country where collectivism is highly valued.

POWER DISTANCE   By **power distance**, Hofstede meant the degree to which societies accept the idea that inequalities in the power and well-being of their citizens are acceptable. Societies in which inequalities are allowed to persist or grow over time have *high power distance.* In contrast, in societies with *low power distance*, large inequalities between citizens are not allowed to develop.

Advanced Western countries such as the United States, Germany, the Netherlands, and the United Kingdom have relatively low power distance and high individualism. Canada ranks higher on power distance than does the United States. Economically poor Latin American countries such as Guatemala and

---

individualism

A worldview that values individual freedom and self-expression and adherence to the principle that people should be judged by their individual achievements rather than by their social background.

collectivism A worldview that values subordination of the individual to the goals of the group and adherence to the principle that people should be judged by their contribution to the group.

power distance

The degree to which societies accept the idea that inequalities in the power and well-being of their citizens are due to differences in individuals' physical and intellectual capabilities and heritage.

Figure 4.4
Hofstede's Model of National Culture

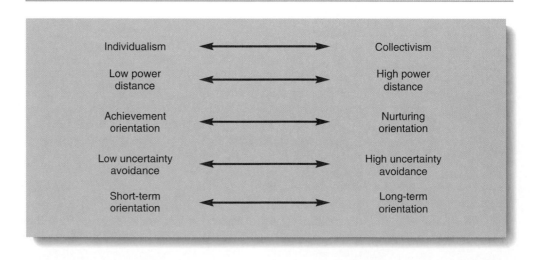

Panama, and Asian countries such as Malaysia and the Philippines, have high power distance and low individualism.[35] These findings suggest that the cultural values of richer countries emphasize protecting the rights of individuals and, at the same time, providing a fair chance of success to every member of society.

ACHIEVEMENT VERSUS NURTURING ORIENTATION   Societies that have an **achievement orientation** value assertiveness, performance, success, competition, and results. Societies that have a **nurturing orientation** value the quality of life, warm personal relationships, and services and care for the weak. Canada, Japan, and the United States tend to be achievement oriented; the Netherlands, Sweden, and Denmark are more nurturing oriented.

achievement orientation A worldview that values assertiveness, performance, success, and competition.

nurturing orientation A worldview that values the quality of life, warm personal friendships, and services and care for the weak.

UNCERTAINTY AVOIDANCE   Societies as well as individuals differ in their tolerance for uncertainty and risk. Societies low on **uncertainty avoidance** (such as the United States and Hong Kong) are easygoing, value diversity, and tolerate differences in personal beliefs and actions. Canada ranks higher on power distance than does the United States, although it gets only a moderate score on this scale. Societies high on uncertainty avoidance (such as Japan and France) are more rigid and skeptical about people whose behaviours or beliefs differ from the norm. In these societies, conformity to the values of the social and work groups to which a person belongs is the norm, and structured situations are preferred because they provide a sense of security.

uncertainty avoidance The degree to which societies are willing to tolerate uncertainty and risk.

LONG-TERM VERSUS SHORT-TERM ORIENTATION   The last dimension that Hofstede described is orientation toward life and work.[36] A national culture with a **long-term orientation** rests on values such as thrift (saving) and persistence in achieving goals. A national culture with a **short-term orientation** is concerned with maintaining personal stability or happiness and living for the present. Societies with a long-term orientation include Taiwan and Hong Kong, well known for their high rate of per capita savings. Canada, the United States, and France have a short-term orientation, and their citizens tend to spend more and save less.

long-term orientation A worldview that values thrift and persistence in achieving goals.

short-term orientation A worldview that values personal stability or happiness and living for the present.

NATIONAL CULTURE AND GLOBAL MANAGEMENT   Differences among national cultures have important implications for managers. First, because of cultural differences, management practices that are effective in one country might be troublesome in another. GE managers learned this while trying to manage Tungsram, GE's Hungarian subsidiary. Often, management practices must be tailored to suit the cultural contexts within which an organization operates. An approach effective in Canada might not work in Japan, Hungary, or Mexico, because of differences in national culture. For example, pay-for-performance systems used in Canada, which emphasize the performance of individuals alone, might not work well in Japan, where individual performance in pursuit of group goals is the value that receives emphasis.

Managers doing business with individuals from another country must be sensitive to the value systems and norms of that country and behave accordingly. For example, Friday is the Islamic Sabbath. Thus, it would be impolite and inappropriate for a Canadian manager to schedule a busy day of activities for Saudi Arabian managers visiting on a Friday.

A culturally diverse management team can be a source of strength for an organization participating in the global marketplace. Organizations that employ managers from a variety of cultures appreciate better how national cultures differ than do organizations with culturally homogeneous management teams, and they tailor their management systems and behaviours to the differences.

culture shock The feelings of surprise and disorientation that people experience when they do not understand the values, folkways, and mores that guide behaviour in a culture.

Culture shock is a phrase that sums up the feelings of surprise and disorientation that people experience when they enter a foreign culture and do not understand the values, folkways, and mores that guide behaviour in that culture. Many managers and their families experience culture shock when they move abroad. If they have received no training, they may not understand how to do business in a foreign country or how local stores and school systems operate. Learning a different culture takes time and effort, and global organizations must devote considerable resources to helping **expatriate managers** (managers who go abroad to work for a global organization) adapt to local conditions and learn the local culture.

expatriate managers
Managers who go abroad to work for a global organization.

Tips for Managers

Understanding the Global Environment

1. Carefully analyze forces in the global task environment to identify opportunities and threats, and then select the most appropriate way to operate in that task environment.

2. Find opportunities to take advantage of the global environment by, for example, finding new kinds of customers to export goods and services to, or new avenues for investment in foreign countries, or new ways to buy and make products overseas.

3. Identify the threats in the global environment, such as strong foreign companies poised to invade the home market or powerful suppliers who might withhold inputs.

4. Be sensitive to the differences between countries, and carefully analyze their political, economic, and sociocultural systems to find the best way to operate in those countries.

5. Recognize the need to become internationally and cross-culturally aware.

Choosing a Way to Expand Internationally

What's the best way to expand internationally?

As we have discussed, the trend toward a more open, competitive global environment has proven to be both an opportunity and a threat for organizations and managers. The opportunity is that organizations that expand globally are able to open new markets and reach more customers and gain access to new sources of raw materials and to low-cost suppliers of inputs. The threat is that organizations that expand globally are likely to encounter new competitors in the foreign countries they enter, and must respond to new political, economic, and cultural conditions.

Before setting up foreign operations, managers of companies need to analyze the forces in a particular country's environment (such as in Korea or Brazil) in order to choose the right method to expand and respond to those forces in the most appropriate way. In general, there are four basic ways to operate in the global environment: importing and exporting, licensing and franchising, strategic alliances, and wholly owned foreign subsidiaries. We briefly discuss each one, moving from the lowest level of foreign involvement and investment required of a global organization and its managers, and the least amount of risk, to the high end of the spectrum (see Figure 4.5).[37]

Importing and Exporting

The least complex global operations are exporting and importing. A company engaged in **exporting** makes products at home and sells them abroad. An organization might sell its own products abroad or allow a local organization in the foreign country to distribute its products. Compaq and Microsoft, for example,

exporting Making products at home and selling them abroad.

Figure 4.5
Four Ways of Expanding Internationally

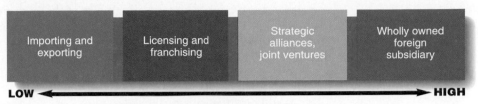

Level of foreign involvement and investment
and degree of risk

control the distribution of their products to foreign computer retailers; makers of many luxury products, such as producers of French wine and spirits, allow local organizations to take responsibility for distribution activities. Few risks are associated with exporting because a company does not have to invest in developing manufacturing facilities abroad. It can further reduce its investment abroad if it allows a local company to distribute its products.

importing Selling at home products that are made abroad.

A company engaged in **importing** sells products at home that are made abroad (products it makes itself or buys from other companies). For example, most of the products that Pier 1 Imports and The Bombay Company sell to their customers are made abroad. In many cases, the appeal of a product—such as Irish glass, French wine, Italian furniture, or Indian silk—is that it is made abroad.

Licensing and Franchising

licensing Allowing a foreign organization to take charge of manufacturing and distributing a product in its country or world region in return for a negotiated fee.

In **licensing**, a company (the licenser) allows a foreign organization (the licensee) to take charge of both manufacturing and distributing one or more of its products in the licensee's country or world region in return for a negotiated fee. Chemical maker DuPont might license a local factory in India to produce nylon or Teflon. The advantage of licensing is that the licenser does not have to bear the development costs associated with opening up in a foreign country; the licensee bears the costs. The risks associated with this strategy are that the company granting the license has to give its foreign partner access to its technological know-how and so risks losing control over its secrets.

franchising Selling to a foreign organization the rights to use a brand name and operating know-how in return for a lump-sum payment and a share of the profits.

Whereas licensing is pursued primarily by manufacturing companies, **franchising** is pursued primarily by service organizations. In franchising, a company (the franchiser) sells to a foreign organization (the franchisee) the rights to use its brand name and operating know-how in return for a lump-sum payment and share of the franchiser's profits. Hilton Hotels might sell a franchise to a local company in Chile to operate hotels under the Hilton name in return for a franchise payment. The advantage of franchising is that the franchiser does not have to bear the development costs of overseas expansion and avoids the many problems associated with setting up foreign operations. The downside is that the organization that grants the franchise may lose control over the way in which the franchisee operates and product quality may fall. In this way, franchisers, such as Hilton, Avis, and McDonald's, risk losing their good names. Canadian customers who buy McDonald's hamburgers in Korea may reasonably expect those burgers to be as good as the ones they get at home. If they are not, McDonald's reputation will suffer over time.

Strategic Alliances

One way to overcome the loss-of-control problems associated with exporting, licensing, and franchising is to expand globally by means of a strategic alliance. In

strategic alliance
An agreement in which managers pool or share their organization's resources and know-how with another company, and the two organizations share the rewards and risks of starting a new venture.

a **strategic alliance**, managers pool or share their organization's resources and know-how with those of another company, and the two organizations share the rewards or risks of starting a new venture. Sharing resources allows a Canadian company, for example, to take advantage of the high-quality skills of foreign manufacturers and the specialized knowledge of foreign managers about the needs of local customers, and to reduce the risks involved in a venture. At the same time, the terms of the alliance give the Canadian company more control over how the good or service is produced or sold in the foreign country than it would have as a franchiser or licenser.

A strategic alliance can take the form of a written contract between two or more companies to exchange resources, or it can result in the creation of a new organization. A **joint venture** is a strategic alliance between two or more companies that agree to establish jointly and share the ownership of a new business.[38] An organization's level of involvement increases in a joint venture because it normally involves a capital investment in production facilities in order to produce goods or services. Risk, however, is usually reduced. "Managing Globally" looks at some of the risks Scotiabank encountered in entering the Latin American market through strategic alliances in recent years.

joint venture A strategic alliance among two or more companies that agree to establish jointly and share the ownership of a new business.

Managing Globally

How Scotiabank Moved to Latin America

The Bank of Nova Scotia (www.scotiabank.com) has undertaken a strategy very different from many of its Canadian rivals in recent years.[39] While Bank of Montreal and TD Canada Trust, among others, are investing heavily in the United States, Scotiabank has been building a network of banks stretching from Argentina to Mexico.

Scotiabank calls itself Canada's most international bank. Founded in Nova Scotia in 1832, it had a branch in Jamaica before having one in Toronto. However, it moved its head office to Toronto in 1900. Today it has 1700 offices in 53 countries.

The bank has used a rather cautious strategy in Latin America, spreading its investments around to minimize risk in moving into this region. It forms strategic alliances by buying minority stakes in second-tier banks. Rick Waugh, Scotiabank's vice-chairman in charge of international banking, sees the bank's approach as part of a "diversified, integrated strategy."

Not everyone agrees that Scotiabank's investment in Latin America is wise. "There are not a whole lot of positive things coming out of this strategy, and a whole lot of risk," said Tanya Azarchs, a debt analyst with the New York-based bond rating agency Standard and Poor's. The agency downgraded Scotiabank's debt one notch because of its Latin moves, which will increase the bank's borrowing costs.

Critics note that Scotiabank has suffered because of instability in the region and Mexico's monetary crisis in the mid-1990s. In addition, Scotiabank often has minority holdings in these banks, so its managers have less say over setting policy. Moreover, these Latin American banks are often controlled by tightly knit families used to doing business their own way. In Banco Quilmes in Argentina, Scotiabank had to increase its stake in a bank when other shareholders wanted out, and it faced the same thing at a bank in Chile.

"The problem with minority interests is that when things go well and you want to increase your stake, the owners don't want to sell," said Pat Boucher, senior bank analyst with Spanish banking giant Santander, who worked for Scotiabank for four years. "When things go bad you don't want to put more money in but you are often forced to or pull out, but you don't want to pull out because you might never be able to come back in."

How important are strategic alliances to Canadian companies? The head of Bank of Montreal's Chicago-based subsidiary, Harris Bank, recently emphasized the need for Canadian banks to look beyond mergers and joint ventures at home if they want to improve their financial viability. Al McNally, chairman and CEO, suggests that, "To thrive and prosper, success at home must be matched and multiplied by success in the United States. It's also the only way to ensure that Canada continues to grow as an important financial services provider—creating thousands of good jobs, and substantial foreign income, for Canadians."[40]

Wholly Owned Foreign Subsidiaries

wholly owned foreign subsidiary Production operations established in a foreign country independent of any local direct involvement.

When managers decide to establish a **wholly owned foreign subsidiary**, they invest in establishing production operations in a foreign country independent of any local direct involvement. Many Japanese car component companies, for example, have established their own operations in Canada and the United States to supply Canadian- and American-based Japanese car makers such as Toyota with high-quality inputs. Many of the larger companies operating in Canada, including GM Canada, Procter & Gamble Canada, and McDonald's Canada, are actually subsidiaries of American corporations. Generally the Canadian subsidiaries set their own targets and goals, and manage their operations, but they also report to a head office in the United States. A number of factors have made Canada a good investment opportunity for American firms. The low Canadian dollar results in lower cost structures and higher productivity. Because of Canada's healthcare system, employers in Canada pay far less for health premiums for their workers than they would in the United States. Jim Stanford, an economist with the Canadian Auto Workers union in Toronto, suggests that, "Medicare gives Canadian plants a savings of $6 per hour per worker over the United States."[41]

Operating alone, without any direct involvement from foreign companies, a wholly owned foreign subsidiary receives all of the rewards and bears all of the risks associated with operating abroad.[42] This method of international expansion is much more expensive than the others because it requires a higher level of foreign investment and presents managers with many more threats. However, investment in a foreign subsidiary or division offers significant advantages: It gives an organization high potential returns because the organization does not have to share its profits with a foreign organization, and it reduces the level of risk because the organization's managers have full control over all aspects of their foreign subsidiary's operations. Moreover, this type of investment allows managers to protect their technology and know-how from foreign organizations. Large, well-known companies like DuPont, General Motors, and Arthur Andersen, which have plenty of resources, make extensive use of wholly owned subsidiaries.

Impediments to an Open Global Environment

To this point, we have emphasized the trend toward the creation of a more open, competitive global environment and the advantages that result from this, such as access to more customers or to higher-quality or cheaper inputs. However, as every manager of a global organization knows, we live in an imperfect world, and significant barriers to cross-border exchanges between countries continue to make global expansion risky and expensive.

Government-Imposed Impediments

World Trade
Organization/GATT
www.gatt.org/

One reason why barriers exist is that governments have ways of getting around free-trade agreements such as the GATT. GATT aims primarily to lower tariff barriers, but there are various nontariff barriers to trade that governments can erect. In other words, there are many loopholes in the GATT that countries can exploit. One class of nontariff impediments to international trade and investment is known as administrative barriers. Administrative barriers are government policies that, in theory, have nothing to do with international trade and investment but, in practice, have the intended effect of limiting imports of goods and inward investment by foreign corporations.

One example of an administrative trade barrier is Japan's Large Scale Retail Store Law, which prior to 1991 allowed small retailers to block the establishment of a large retail establishment for up to 10 years. This law was used to slow the entry of Toys 'R' Us into the Japanese market. Another kind of administrative trade barrier prevents Dutch companies from exporting tulip bulbs to Japan. Why do Dutch companies export tulip bulbs to almost every country in the world except Japan? Japanese customs inspectors insist on checking every tulip bulb by cutting the stems vertically down the middle, and even Japanese ingenuity cannot put them back together.[43]

Self-Imposed Ethical Impediments

What recommendations might you make for investing in countries with questionable human rights practices?

Organizations impose on themselves other impediments to cross-border trade and investment. Why would managers choose to limit their own options for engaging in international trade and investment? In many countries, human rights, workers' rights, and environmental protection are of such low priority that managers decline to have their organizations trade with, or invest in, these countries on ethical grounds.

The human rights issue has recently been raised in both Canada and the United States in connection with importing goods from China. China is not a democracy, and its human rights record is poor. Some of the goods imported into Canada and the United States from China are made with prison labour. Many prisoners in China are political prisoners, locked up because of their opposition to the communist-controlled state. Learning of this use of prisoners, many organizations broke off their ties with Chinese companies.

A number of Canadian and US citizens have questioned the wisdom of investing in Mexico, given the country's poor environmental record and labour laws. The critics argue that Canadian and US businesses investing in Mexico are doing so to take advantage of that nation's lax (by US standards) environmental and labour laws. Concern is raised, for instance, about the poor wages in the *maquiladoras* where items are produced for export. Mexico's new president, Vicente Fox, has a different take on the *maquiladoras*. "The minimum wage in Mexico is seven dollars a day, and people working in *maquiladoras* get four times that," he said. "We'd love to have the kind of standard of living that Canada has, but we don't. That's why we're working on trade agreements and … on investment. We are trying to improve our situation."[44] There are additional arguments given in favour of investing in countries that have poor records on human rights, environmental protection, and workers' rights. One goes like this: Rich countries tend to have better records in these areas than poor countries; economic growth increases a country's concern for human rights, environmental protection, and workers' rights; so trade or investment in a poor country eventually might improve its stance on human rights, environmental protection, and workers' rights.[45] One manager using trade and investment to improve conditions in poor countries is Charllotte Kwon, founder of Maiwa Handprints. As illustrated in the following "Ethics in Action," Kwon believes in paying craftspeople from developing countries a fair price for their products. She tries to improve the welfare of people in less-developed countries while at the same time giving Maiwa Handprints products for its store.

Ethics in Action

Maiwa Handprints Pays Third World Artisans More

Charllotte Kwon is owner and CEO of Vancouver-based Maiwa Handprints (www.maiwa.com).[46] The business, which includes two retail stores that sell clothing and bedding, a production studio in East Vancouver, and an office and warehouse in Mumbai, India, employs 12 people in Vancouver. Maiwa grossed $1 million last year.

Kwon mainly sells imported textiles, and though she could pay 30-40 percent less than she does to artisans in Third World countries, she does not believe in buying low and selling high, if that means exploiting workers. When Kwon goes on buying trips to remote Third World villages, she encourages artisans to raise their prices. When she first started doing this, artisans in India were both amazed and distrustful. "She's going the wrong way. She's bidding up. She doesn't know how to negotiate," Kwon reports they said to each other.

To get the artisans to understand her prices, she shows the local people price stickers from her store, and then translates the Canadian-dollar prices into rupees. To further increase the workers' understanding, she explains to them, "This is what I sell for. This is what it costs me to move it from your village to Mumbai. This is what it costs to ship it to Vancouver. This is how much I pay Canada Customs. This is what I pay my employees, this is my rent on the store, this is what I pay in tax—and this is what I can pay you."

Kwon generally pays the artisans substantially more than what others pay them. She is trying to protect craftspeople so that more art of this type can be produced. She also notes that she doesn't need to pay the minimum to survive: "I live okay. I don't need anything more."

Kwon sources her products right at the village level. She says she does not deal with the Indian government or cooperatives run by it. She also does not deal with agents, feeling this is where corruption begins. By dealing with the artisans directly, she knows that they get full payment, and she knows that she can count on a continuing supply of product.

Kwon also works with villagers to help them improve their production standards. For instance, in a village called Ntuma, in the northeastern state of Naga-

Charllotte Kwon, owner and CEO of Vancouver-based Maiwa Handprints, is committed to improving the lives of Indian workers who make cloth for sale at Maiwa.

land, she has 30 weavers. However, for the first three years, the products didn't meet her standards. Nevertheless, she saw the potential, and paid for every shipment she rejected. Her persistence paid off, and now she receives what she calls "perfect product."

Kwon sees herself as a link between artisans who couldn't find markets in their own countries, and buyers in this country who are happy to have well-produced textiles. By building these relationships, she improves the welfare of poor people, and helps the economies of local villages. She believes that offering fair prices for the work makes for a better business relationship for Maiwa. Kwon also feels responsible for her craftspeople. In January 2001, an earthquake caused great devastation for the Kutch desert area of Northwest India. Maiwa has organized several fundraisers to help the community rebuild, and is donating money of its own as well.

Tips for Managers

Chapter Summary

THE CHANGING GLOBAL ENVIRONMENT

• Declining Barriers to Trade and Investment

• Declining Barriers of Distance and Culture

• Effects of Free Trade on Managers

THE GLOBAL TASK ENVIRONMENT

• Suppliers

• Distributors

• Customers

• Competitors

THE GLOBAL GENERAL ENVIRONMENT

• Political and Legal Forces

• Economic Forces

• Changes in Political and Legal and Economic Forces

• Sociocultural Forces

CHOOSING A WAY TO EXPAND INTERNATIONALLY

• Importing and Exporting

• Licensing and Franchising

• Strategic Alliances

• Wholly Owned Foreign Subsidiaries

IMPEDIMENTS TO AN OPEN GLOBAL ENVIRONMENT

• Government-Imposed Impediments

• Self-Imposed Ethical Impediments

Managing the Global Environment

1. Identify the ways that the shift to a more open global environment has resulted in a more complex, competitive, and changing environment and how this affects a manager's job.

2. Analyze the changes taking place in relations between countries and world regions to forecast where new opportunities and threats may come from.

3. Try to foresee the way that impediments to trade and investment will make doing business in other countries difficult. Develop a plan to overcome these impediments.

Summary and Review

THE CHANGING GLOBAL ENVIRONMENT In recent years, there has been a marked shift away from a closed global environment, in which countries are cut off from each other by barriers to international trade and investment and by barriers of distance and culture, toward a more open global environment. The emergence of an open global environment and the reduction of barriers to the free flow of goods, services, and investment owe much to the rise of global trade agreements such as GATT; to the growing global acceptance of a free-market philosophy; and to the poor performance of countries that protected their markets from international trade and investment.

THE GLOBAL TASK ENVIRONMENT Forces in the global task environment are more complex than those inside only one country, and thus present managers with greater opportunities and threats. Managers must analyze forces in their global task environment to determine how best to operate abroad. In doing so, they determine how best to work with suppliers, distributors, customers and competitors.

THE GLOBAL GENERAL ENVIRONMENT In the general environment, managers must recognize the substantial differences that exist among countries' political, legal, economic, and sociocultural systems. Political, legal, and economic differences range from democratic states with free-market systems to totalitarian states with mixed or command economies. These differences impact on the attractiveness of a nation as a trading partner or as a target for foreign investment. Substantial differences in national culture can also be observed, such as those described in Hofstede's model of national culture. Management practices must be tailored to the particular culture in which they are to be applied. What works in Canada, for example, might not be appropriate in France, Peru, or Vietnam.

CHOOSING A WAY TO EXPAND INTERNATIONALLY Managers can decide to expand internationally through importing and exporting, licensing and franchising, strategic alliances, and wholly owned foreign subsidiaries. Licensing involves the least direct costs to a company, while a wholly owned foreign subsidiary receives all of the rewards and bears all of the risks of operating abroad.

IMPEDIMENTS TO AN OPEN GLOBAL ENVIRONMENT Despite the shift toward a more open, competitive global environment, many impediments to international trade and investment still remain. Some are imposed by governments; others are self-imposed by organizations.

Management in Action

Topics for Discussion and Action

1. In what ways does a more open global environment increase opportunities and threats in the global task environment?

2. How do political, legal, and economic forces shape national culture? What characteristics of national culture do you think have the most important effect on how successful a country is in doing business abroad?

3. Ask an expatriate manager about the most important problems and challenges that he or she confronted during an assignment abroad.

4. The textile industry has a labour-intensive manufacturing process that utilizes unskilled and semiskilled workers. What are the implications of the shift to a more open global environment for textile companies whose manufacturing operations are based in high-wage countries such as Australia, Canada, and the United States?

5. "Over the next decade we will see the emergence of enormous global markets for standardized products such as cars, blue jeans, food products, and recorded music." In your view, is this an accurate statement or an exaggeration?

6. After the passage of the North American Free Trade Agreement, some Canadian companies shifted production operations to Mexico to take advantage of lower labour costs and lower standards for environmental and worker protection. As a result, they cut their costs and were better able to survive in an increasingly competitive global environment. Was their behaviour ethical—that is, did the ends justify the means?

7. Go to the library and gather information that allows you to compare and contrast the political, economic, and cultural systems of the United States, Mexico, and Canada. In what ways are the countries similar? How do they differ? How might the similarities and differences influence the activities of managers at an enterprise such as Wal-Mart, which does business in all three countries?

Building Management Skills

Studying a Global Organization

Pick one of the following companies—Nortel, Bombardier, Procter & Gamble, or IBM. Collect information about the company from its annual reports or from articles in business magazines such as *Report on Business* or *Canadian Business*; then do the following.

1. Identify the three largest foreign markets in which the company operates.

2. List the forces in the global task environment that you think have most affected the company's organization, and try to determine how its managers have responded to those forces.

3. Identify the political, economic, and sociocultural forces that have the most effect on the company, paying particular attention to differences in national culture. What implications, if any, do such differences have for the way in which this company sells its product in different national markets?

4. Determine how the shift toward a more open global environment has affected the opportunities and threats facing managers in the company.

Small Group Breakout Exercise

How to Become Globally Aware

Form groups of three to five people, and appoint one group member as the spokesperson who will communicate your findings to the whole class when called on by the instructor. Then discuss the following scenario.

You are store managers who work for a large Canadian retailer that is planning to open a chain of new stores in France. Each of you has been given the responsibility to manage one of these stores, and you are meeting to develop a plan of action to help you and your families adjust to the conditions that you will encounter in France. As a group, do the following.

1. Decide which forces in the environment will most affect your ability and your family's ability to adjust to the French culture.

2. Identify the best ways to gather information about the French business and social environment to enable you to understand these forces.

3. Decide what steps you and your family can take before you leave for France to smooth your transition into the French culture and help you avoid culture shock.

Exploring the World Wide Web

Specific Assignment

This exercise deals with the global activities of Goodyear Tire and Rubber Company. Research Goodyear's Web site (www.goodyear.com), and click on "Corporate," then on "The Corporation" and "Strategic Business Units" and "Worldwide Facilities" to access information about Goodyear's global presence. Also, click on "Investor Relations" to find the 2000 annual report, where you can examine the section on strategic developments.

1. What is Goodyear's method of expanding into the global environment, and why do you think this approach was chosen?

2. How will declining barriers of distance and culture affect the way in which Goodyear operates?

General Assignment

Search for the Web site of a company with a strong global presence. What are the main forces in the task and general global environments that most affect the way this company operates?

ManagementCase

In the News

From the pages of *The Globe and Mail*
The Road Not Taken

When we began our study of the Canadian economy in 1990, Canada was the third-richest country in the world (in GDP per capita) and had a dollar valued at US$0.85. We released our report, *Canada at the Crossroads*, in 1991 and, a decade later, Canada is the fifth-richest country in the world and has a dollar valued at US$0.65, a 23-percent international pay cut for all Canadians.

Why the substantial decline? Faced with two paths in 1991, the economy overall chose the less favourable path. This path hewed closely to the Canadian tradition of competing on the basis of lower-cost labour or raw materials and pursuing company strategies of replicating competitors elsewhere.

There is an alternative path—competing on the basis of uniqueness and innovation—which is the only path toward rising relative prosperity for Canada in the global economy. There is no question that Canadian firms can succeed at it. However, lulled by a steadily declining dollar, Canadian firms still face strong temptations toward more of the same.

Perhaps nothing could illustrate the contrast better than the trajectories of two industries that we studied in 1991, newsprint and telecommunications switches. In 1991, newsprint was one of Canada's leading export industries, with both impressive size ($5.5 billion in sales), and leading world export share (62 percent). The Canadian industry featured seven large companies, including the world's largest

player, Abitibi-Price. The strength of the industry depended on three advantages: low wood fibre cost, low energy costs, and proximity to the world's largest market.

But these static advantages quickly came under pressure with the development of thermomechanical pulping, which facilitated the efficient use of low-cost fibre found in abundant supply in the southern US and Latin America. Moreover, Canada lagged by a decade or more in implementing new processing technologies. Historically lax environmental regulation had also left firms unprepared for the heightening of environmental concerns about the forest products sector worldwide.

Since 1991, prices in the newsprint industry have drifted downward. In terms of world paper production, newsprint has dropped from 39 percent to 30 percent, as value-added grades of paper have grown. Meanwhile, Asia's growing appetite for newsprint has spurred investment in Asian production.

Winners in coping with these changes have been the Scandinavian firms, who invested heavily to upgrade themselves and their home industry through the 1990s. At home, they worked together through industry associations and universities to promote innovation. The average worker in the Scandinavian industry has a related university degree. Abroad, they invested heavily in North American assets.

Norway's Norske Skog purchased Canadian newsprint player Fletcher Challenge Canada and is in the

process of acquiring Pacifica Papers, another Canadian newsprint company. Swedish/Finnish firm Stora Enso and Finland's UPM-Kymmene also made major acquisitions abroad.

Unlike the Scandinavian industry, the Canadian pulp and paper sector, exemplified by newsprint, focused primarily on domestic consolidation rather than upgrading and globalizing. It also maintained its focus on the lowest-value-added, slowest-growing part of the marketspace: standard newsprint. And so, one of Canada's historical core industries has lost nine points of global share since 1991.

Today, the newsprint industry depends largely on the devalued Canadian dollar to stay profitable—shaky competitive ground indeed. At US$0.65, the Canadian newsprint industry is right at the average of industry cost-competitiveness worldwide. At US$0.85, Canada would be the least cost-competitive country in the world by far!

Contrast Canadian newsprint to the telecommunications switch industry. In 1991, the industry was Canada's most important high-technology sector. Nortel enjoyed the leading global market share in the important digital switch segment. Although things looked good for the industry back at the beginning of the 1990s, it was a target for worldwide competitors.

Yet the decade surprised us all. The market was transformed from digital switches for handling voice traffic for traditional phone companies such as Bell Canada, to optical transmission systems for handling data and Internet protocol traffic over alternative carrier networks, such as Qwest Corporation's all-fibre network.

Nortel and other members of the nascent Canadian cluster in 1991 could have continued a narrow definition of the industry and focused financial and managerial energy on consolidating it. Had it done so, the Canadian industry would have experienced a drift downward, as did newsprint.

However, the industry acted boldly and aggressively to innovate. Rather than attempt to maintain current positions—through replicating competitors and better management of the status quo—Canadian firms boldly chose innovative strategies with global aspirations, exploiting entirely new markets. They did well

thanks to intense R & D, branding and managerial boldness. Despite the current capital markets challenges, Nortel, JDS Uniphase, Celestica and others are positioned to lead the next wave of innovation in the telecommunications equipment market.

At the turn of the millennium, Canada once again faces a fork in the road. If we are to compete and win on the world stage in the coming century, Canadian firms and governments must turn their backs on a culture of replication, and strive instead for uniqueness and innovation.

Innovation is the key today to global competitive advantage. Government at all levels must enhance Canada's commitment to creating a superior macroeconomic and microeconomic context for competitiveness. And our firms must

develop more distinctive strategies based on relentless innovation.

If we all set our aspirations higher, Canada can not only prosper and succeed, but can become a leader in the global economy.

Roger Martin is dean of the Joseph L. Rotman School of Management at the University of Toronto. Michael E. Porter is Bishop William Lawrence University Professor at the Harvard Business School.

Source: R. Martin and M. Porter, "The Road Not Taken," *The Globe and Mail*, April 26, 2001, p. A19.

Questions

1. How did the global environment affect the different strategies of companies in the newsprint and telecommunication industries?

2. What kinds of problems do you think Canadian managers are likely to encounter if they ignore the impact of globalization?

ManagementCase
In the News

From the pages of the *National Post*
Predictable Trade Regimes
Essential For Small Business

As the rhetoric intensifies in Quebec City, and in light of Canada's announcement that we have entered into a new round of multilateral negotiations on international trade in services, I want to share a few thoughts as the owner of a small technology business. From my perspective, Canada urgently needs a new trade framework where international rules are clear, fair and predictable for service-oriented companies.

Our company, Domosys Corporation, has 51 employees

and exports control networking technology to more than 40 countries around the world, including the United States and Japan. IBM, Nokia, General Electric, and Ingersoll Rand are some of our clients. Last year, the company brought in about $3 million in revenues. In our business, we would not be able to prosper and to provide highly skilled jobs in Canada if we could not grow outside this country. Size matters. Expanding access to international markets is urgent for our company and the many others like ours that

are the backbone of Canada's knowledge-based economy.

Over the years, in the pursuit of global opportunities, we have been challenged by needless difficulties, from nontariff trade barriers to cumbersome visa requirements, through discriminatory regulations and unpredictable customs officials. Wherever the regulations are subject to interpretation, you ask five lawyers and you are going to get five different answers. That level of unpredictability creates tremendous risk for small businesses.

A good example is the navigation of approvals for the certification of new technologies. In the United States, we recently submitted for approval an innovative technology for telecommunications. Initially, it was approved, only to be rejected months later. It was ultimately decided that the original approval was flawed because the regulations did not apply to this new technology. In fact, the technology was so new, no one was certain which regulations applied.

Numerous other examples fall under the arcane regulations governing the delivery of onsite engineering services. Typically these regulations differ in each market. Equally disconcerting and all too common are the arbitrary application or interpretation of the movement of our people across borders. One day we can send a team into a foreign market to solve a customer's problem. However, we never know if the next time that same team will be prohibited from the same market to undertake the same task.

Naturally, our customers expect us to support their operations wherever they may be. Arbitrary regulations that reduce our ability to rapidly deploy people and to resolve technical problems directly impact our ability to compete effectively. Our nationality is not important unless it means we cannot deliver reliably to a foreign customer. Then the potential cost to that customer becomes too great.

Intellectual property is another important concern to us. Trademark and patent applications designed to protect intellectual property must be registered separately in different jurisdictions, each with their different set of rules. Registration is a long and expensive process. When legal challenges arise and we must retain the services of specialized legal counsel in the specific jurisdiction, the costs escalate rapidly. Yet in the absence of clear international rules on intellectual property, we have no choice but to protect our investment in our unique product offering.

For the communications industry in particular, various national or supra-national bodies have regulatory authority. They govern the allocation of the spectrum and its use. Principally, they aim to ensure clear, nonconflicting and equitable distribution of this asset between different users. In our four main markets (United States, EU, Japan, and Canada), four different sets of regulations govern the use of the same medium for the same applications. This creates significant costs in designing products to meet such a large number of requirements and then running each through the official certification process.

In addition, there can be significant subjectivity exercised by the various "official test houses" in the certification process. The cost of this uncertainty, both to the company selling the technology and to the local buyer, can kill a deal.

These examples of impediments to doing business internationally can be prohibitive to a smaller firm and tend to stifle ingenuity and growth. The present system is not working well and, in my experience, is biased against small and medium-sized companies that lack the resources to challenge arbitrary decisions or to develop the knowledge of unwritten rules required to successfully compete in foreign markets.

After the creation of the World Trade Organization in 1995, everyone recognized the need to establish clear international rules to govern and facilitate the growing trade in services. To ensure that all countries, whatever their size or strength, could freely participate on an equal basis in the trade in services, the member countries, including Canada, agreed to establish the General Agreement on Trade in Services (GATS).

Clear, nondiscriminatory and predictable international trade rules are essential. For this reason, all Canadians have a vested interest in ensuring that Canada, alongside economic giants like the United States, the European Union and Japan, participates in the GATS negotiations. We must ensure our voice is heard.

Evan Price is the president and CEO of Domosys Corporation, a provider of control networking technology, based in Quebec City.

Source: E. Price, "Predictable Trade Regimes Essential for Small Business," *Financial Post (National Post)*, April 21, 2001, p. D11.

Questions

1. What is Evan Price's (the author of this article) view of trade rules?

2. What difficulties do small businesses face when they expand globally?

Chapter five

Ethics, Social Responsibility, and Diversity

Learning Objectives

1. Describe the concept of ethics, and detail the ways that ethics develop.

2. Explain how different ethical models affect managerial decisions about the right or proper way to behave when dealing with various organizational stakeholders.

3. Describe the concept of social responsibility, and detail the ways in which organizations can promote both ethical and socially responsible behaviour by their employees.

4. Define diversity, and explain why the effective management of diverse employees is both an ethical issue and a means for an organization to improve its performance.

5. Identify instances of sexual harassment, and discuss how to prevent its occurrence.

A Case in Contrast

Ethical Stances at Pembina and Bridgestone

When an oil pipeline running between Taylor and Prince George, BC ruptured in the early hours of August 2, 2000, Calgary-based Pembina Pipeline (www.pembina.com) had a nightmare in the making on its hands. Pembina was the owner of the pipeline, which spilled approximately one million litres of light crude oil into the Pine River. It was the largest-ever spill on a river in Western Canada, and there were threats to the drinking water supply of the local area.

Pembina immediately issued a barebones news release, and then hired Calgary-based Communication Incorporated (CI) to handle its media relations. CI told Pembina's CEO, Bob Michaleski, to "Talk about as much as you can, give as much information as you can and never lie."[1]

Michaleski certainly could have tried to place the blame elsewhere. He had purchased the pipeline that burst just 12 hours before the spill occurred. So he could have laid blame on someone else's shoulders. Instead, Michaleski remained steadfast in accepting responsibility by continuing to say: "It's our pipeline, our spill and our responsibility." That earned Pembina big credibility points with media and public alike.

Even though the oil spill caused widespread environmental damage to the river, Mayor Charlie Lasser of Chetwynd, BC, the small town whose drinking water was affected by this spill, proclaimed five months later, "We turned a liability into an asset." The town brought in a dowser, who helped to find sources for two new wells that have since been drilled within a kilometre of the district's reservoir on the banks of the Pine River. Pembina Pipeline paid to find and develop the new wells.

After one of its pipelines burst in Chetwynd, BC, Pembina Pipeline quickly got to work on cleaning up the spill, and making things right for the small community.

Masatoshi Ono, CEO of Bridgestone, was slow to admit fault after his company's Firestone tires were linked to an unusually high number of accidents.

Pembina also paid millions of dollars for cleanup and repairs, while facing a production curtailment at the Husky Oil Refinery in Prince George until the pipeline could be repaired.

At almost the same time that Pembina was facing its oil spill crisis, Japanese tire-maker Bridgestone (www.bridgestone-firestone.com) was facing a public relations disaster of its own making. Its Firestone Tires subsidiary faced a voluntary recall of 6.5 million tires in August 2000 and a mandated recall of another 1.4 million by the United States National Highway Traffic Safety Administration. The tires were linked to 46 deaths in Venezuela and 88 deaths in the United States as a result of shredding, peeling or blowouts in accidents mainly involving Ford Motor Co.'s Explorer sport-utility vehicle.

As the Bridgestone crisis unfolded in September 2000, Bridgestone engaged in progressive acts of damage control, rather than admitting responsibility for the tire failures. For instance, Yoichiro Kaizaki, Bridgestone's president, told a news conference that he had learned as early as May that the tires were linked to an unusually high number of accidents. He also admitted that the company's headquarters in Tokyo was slow to take action after learning about the accidents.[2]

Masatoshi Ono, CEO of Bridgestone Corp., testified before the United States Congress that he did not know the reason for the Firestone tire failures. Meanwhile, John Lampe, executive vice-president of Bridgestone's US operations, suggested that it was not its tires, but the tendency of Ford Motor Co.'s Explorer to roll over that was responsible for many of the fatal crashes being reviewed by regulators.[3]

Still, most investors saw the major problem as a tire issue. Richard Hilgert, an analyst with Fahnestock and Co., noted that, "The consumer seems to have voted with its pocketbook and they're buying Ford vehicles. They are comfortable with the Explorer product as long as it's equipped with tires other than Firestone."

The effect on Bridgestone was enormous. Profits plunged 80 percent in 2000.[4] The recall cost the company US$510 million at its Firestone subsidiary in the United States. Kaizaki stepped down in March 2001, acknowledging that his company's image was badly hurt and that there was no telling when the damage would end. However, he denied that his resignation was related to the recent crisis. "I am not resigning to take responsibility for the recall. I decided on this move to strengthen our management in a rapidly changing global environment and to win back the trust of our customers and shareholders," he said.[5]

Ford's US operations also took a hit as a result of the tire scandal, with decreased sales and profits, although Oakville, ON-based Ford Canada's "operational highlights included 283 000 new car and truck sales in 2000, making it the second-best sales year since 1989," noted Bob Girard, Ford Canada's vice-president, general sales.[6] "We're pleased to see that Canadians continue to have confidence in our vehicles," said Ford spokesperson Lauren More.[7] Consumers may have been more sympathetic to Ford, which immediately tried to help its customers get tire replacements, while providing clearer information about the cause of the crisis.

Bridgestone's managers seem to have put what they erroneously thought were the interests of their company ahead of their customers' interests. Managers at Pembina Pipeline put the local community's interests first. Bridgestone's stance has led many to wonder if the company will be able to recover its good name. Meanwhile, among the residents of Chetwynd and those of BC more broadly, Pembina gained a reputation for being socially responsible.   ●

Overview

As the behaviour of Pembina's and Bridgestone's managers suggests, managers may interpret their responsibilities to their customers and to their organizations in very different ways. Pembina accepted responsibility immediately, and then helped to restore the water supply. Bridgestone's managers postponed action and, to safeguard the profits of their company, did not confront the fact that their product was defective and dangerous. As a result, car companies such as Ford continued to buy Bridgestone's tires, and the potential for accidents increased.

The ways in which managers view their responsibilities to the individuals and groups that are affected by their actions are central to the discussion of ethics and social responsibility, and to the discussion of organizational performance as well. In this chapter, we explore what it means to behave ethically. We describe how managers and organizations can behave in a socially responsible way toward the individuals and groups in their organizational environment.

We then focus on one particular dimension of ethical behaviour that is receiving increasing attention today: how to manage diversity to ensure that all of the people whom an organization employs are fairly and equitably treated. Managers' ability and desire to behave ethically and to manage diversity effectively are central concerns in today's complex business environment. Increasingly, if managers ignore these issues or fail to act appropriately, their organizations are unlikely to prosper in the future.

We also discuss sexual harassment, a behaviour that is both unethical and illegal, and which is another critical issue that managers and organizations—military as well as civilian—must confront and respond to in a serious manner. In 1998, the Canadian Armed Forces was reeling from reports of widespread sexual harassment of female recruits by their male training officers. By the end of the chapter, you will appreciate why ethics, diversity, and sexual harassment are issues that make a manager's job both more challenging and more complex.   ●

Ethics and Stakeholders

organizational stakeholders

Shareholders, employees, customers, suppliers, and others who have an interest, claim, or stake in an organization and in what it does.

The individuals and groups that have an interest, claim, or stake in an organization and in what it does are known as organizational stakeholders.[8] **Organizational stakeholders** include shareholders, managers, nonmanagerial employees, customers, suppliers, the local community in which an organization operates, and even citizens of the country in which an organization operates. In order to survive and prosper, an organization must effectively satisfy its stakeholders.[9] Stockholders want dividends, managers and workers want salaries and stable employment, and customers want high-quality products at reasonable prices. If stakeholders do not receive these benefits, they may withdraw their support for the organization: Stockholders will sell their stock, managers and workers will seek jobs in other organizations, and customers will take their business elsewhere.

Managers are the stakeholder group that determines which goals an organization should pursue to benefit stakeholders most, and how to make the most efficient use of resources to achieve those goals. In making such decisions, managers frequently have to juggle the interests of different stakeholders, including themselves.[10] The following examples describe managerial decisions that helped or harmed different stakeholders:

How do you decide whether a decision is ethical?

- In early 2001, Brampton, ON-based Nortel Networks decided to terminate 20 000 employees after losing about $280 billion in stock market value when the telecommunications market collapsed. This represented 21 percent of Nortel's workforce.

- After a loss of over $65 million in market value over 13 years, the board of directors of Newfoundland's Fishery Producers International Ltd. (FPI) faced ouster in the spring of 2001. The board was criticized for its decisions over the years. "FPI was given a huge opportunity," said John Risley, president of Nova Scotia-based Clearwater Foods Ltd. "It had a huge pool of assets, $100 million in cash, and no debt. Thirteen years later, what you have is a company with a

Pacific Gas and
Electric Company
www.pge.com/

Levi Strauss & Co.
www.levi.com/

market value of $35 million. It has been managed in a bureaucratic way."[11] Risley led the group of dissident shareholders trying to gain control of FPI.

- When Martin Putman, a lawyer employed by Pacific Gas and Electric Company (PG&E), experienced a period of severe depression, the quality of his work declined and PG&E fired him for poor performance. Putman sued and won $1.2 million because he claimed (and the court agreed) that PG&E should have made an attempt to accommodate his illness to allow him to perform acceptably.[12]

- In 1995, managers at Levi Strauss, the jeans maker, announced that, because of declining jeans sales, the company would close two plants in San Antonio, Texas, and lay off over 1200 workers to save over $600 million a year in salaries and other costs. Because Levi's was one of the largest employers in San Antonio, this decision had a serious impact on the prosperity of the local community.

In each of those examples, some stakeholders (managers and stockholders) benefited, while others (individual workers and local communities) were harmed. Managerial decisions that may benefit some stakeholder groups and harm others involve questions of ethics.

ethics Moral principles or beliefs about what is right or wrong.

Ethics are moral principles or beliefs about what is right or wrong. These beliefs guide individuals in their dealings with other individuals and groups (stakeholders) and provide a basis for deciding whether behaviour is right and proper.[13] Ethics help people determine moral responses to situations in which the best course of action is unclear.

Managers often experience an ethical dilemma when they confront a situation that requires them to choose between two courses of action, especially if each decision is likely to serve the interests of one particular stakeholder group to the detriment of the other.[14] To make an appropriate decision, managers must weigh the competing claims or rights of the various stakeholder groups. Sometimes, making a decision is easy because some obvious standard, value, or norm of behaviour applies. In other cases, managers have trouble deciding what to do.

Philosophers have debated for centuries about the specific criteria that should be used to determine whether decisions are ethical or unethical. Three models of what determines whether a decision is ethical—the *utilitarian*, *moral rights*, and *justice* models—are summarized in Table 5.1.[15] In theory, each model offers a different and complementary way of determining whether a decision or behaviour is ethical, and all three models should be used to sort out the ethics of a particular course of action. Ethical issues are seldom clear-cut, however, and the interests of different stakeholders often conflict, so it is frequently extremely difficult for a decision maker to use these models to ascertain the most ethical course of action. For this reason, many experts on ethics propose this practical guide to determine whether a decision or behaviour is ethical.[16] A decision is probably acceptable on ethical grounds if a person can answer "yes" to each of these questions:

1. Does my decision fall within the accepted values or standards that typically apply in the organizational environment?

2. Am I willing to see the decision communicated to all stakeholders affected by it—for example, by having it reported in newspapers or on television?

3. Would the people with whom I have a significant personal relationship, such as family members, friends, or even managers in other organizations, approve of the decision?

ethical decision A decision that reasonable or typical stakeholders would find acceptable because it aids stakeholders, the organization, or society.

unethical decision A decision that a manager would prefer to disguise or hide from other people because it enables a company or a particular individual to gain at the expense of society or other stakeholders.

From an organizational perspective, an **ethical decision** is a decision that reasonable or typical stakeholders would find acceptable because it aids stakeholders, the organization, or society. By contrast, an **unethical decision** is a decision that a person would prefer to disguise or hide from other people because it enables a company or a particular individual to gain at the expense of society or other stakeholders.

Table 5.1
Utilitarian, Moral Rights, and Justice Models of Ethics

Utilitarian Model An ethical decision is a decision that produces the greatest good for the greatest number of people.

Managerial Implication Managers should compare and contrast alternative courses of action based on the benefits and costs of those alternatives for different organizational stakeholder groups. They should choose the course of action that provides the most benefits to stakeholders. For example, managers should locate a new manufacturing plant at the place that will most benefit its stakeholders.

Problems for Managers How do managers decide on the relative importance of each stakeholder group? How are managers to measure precisely the benefits and harms to each stakeholder group? For example, how do managers choose between the interests of stockholders, workers, and customers?

Moral Rights Model An ethical decision is a decision that best maintains and protects the fundamental rights and privileges of the people affected by it. For example, ethical decisions protect people's rights to freedom, life and safety, privacy, free speech, and freedom of conscience.

Managerial Implications Managers should compare and contrast alternative courses of action based on the effect of those alternatives on stakeholders' rights. They should choose the course of action that best protects stakeholders' rights. For example, decisions that would involve significant harm to the safety or health of employees or customers are unethical.

Problems for Managers If a decision will protect the rights of some stakeholders and hurt the rights of others, how do managers choose which stakeholder rights to protect? For example, in deciding whether it is ethical to snoop on an employee, does an employee's right to privacy outweigh an organization's right to protect its property or the safety of other employees?

Justice Model An ethical decision is a decision that distributes benefits and harms among stakeholders in a fair, equitable, or impartial way.

Managerial Implications Managers should compare and contrast alternative courses of action based on the degree to which the action will promote a fair distribution of outcomes. For example, employees who are similar in their level of skill, performance, or responsibility should receive the same kind of pay. The allocation of outcomes should not be based on arbitrary differences such as gender, race, or religion.

Problems for Managers Managers must learn not to discriminate between people because of observable differences in their appearance or behaviour. Managers must also learn how to use fair procedures to determine how to distribute outcomes to organizational members. For example, managers must not give people they like bigger raises than they give to people they do not like or bend the rules to help their favourites.

Sources of an Organization's Code of Ethics

codes of ethics Formal standards and rules, based on beliefs about right or wrong, that managers can use to help themselves make appropriate decisions with regard to the interests of their stakeholders.

Codes of ethics are formal standards and rules, based on beliefs about right or wrong, that managers can use to help themselves make appropriate decisions with regard to the interests of their stakeholders.[17] Ethical standards embody views about abstractions such as justice, freedom, equity, and equality (see Table 5.1). An organization's code of ethics derives from three principal sources in the organizational environment: *societal* ethics, *professional* ethics, and the *individual* ethics of the organization's top managers (see Figure 5.1). Shell Canada's Code of Ethics states the following:

Shell Canada's reputation and credibility are based upon its total commitment to ethical business practices. To safeguard the Shell reputation, employees must conduct themselves in accordance with the highest ethical standards and also be perceived to be acting ethically at all times.[18]

The company's ethics Web page (www.shell.ca/code/values/ethics/ethics.html) describes in some detail how different stakeholders are to interpret the code of ethics.

societal ethics Standards that govern how members of a society are to deal with each other on issues such as fairness, justice, poverty, and the rights of the individual.

SOCIETAL ETHICS **Societal ethics** are standards that govern how members of a society deal with each other in matters involving issues such as fairness, justice, poverty, and the rights of the individual. Societal ethics emanate from a society's laws, customs, and practices, and from the unwritten values and norms

Figure 5.1
Sources of an Organization's Code of Ethics

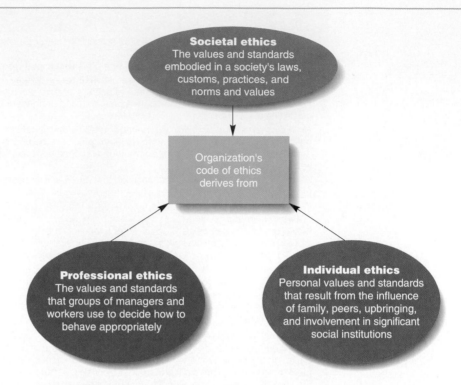

that influence how people interact with each other. People in a particular country may automatically behave ethically because they have internalized values and norms that specify how they should behave in certain situations. Not all values and norms are internalized, however. The typical ways of doing business in a society and laws governing the use of bribery and corruption are the result of decisions made and enforced by people with the power to determine what is appropriate.

Societal ethics vary among societies. For example, ethical standards accepted in Canada and the United States are not accepted in all other countries. In many economically poor countries, bribery is standard practice to get things done—such as getting a telephone installed or a contract awarded. In Canada and many other Western countries, bribery is considered unethical and often illegal. A recent study examining corruption in Asia found that some Asian governments were far more tolerant of corruption than others. Singapore (0.83 out of a possible grade of 10, with 10 being the worst), Japan (2.5) and Hong Kong (3.77) scored relatively low on corruption, while Vietnam, Indonesia, India, the Philippines and Thailand scored as the most corrupt of the 12 Asian countries surveyed.[19]

Should Canada as a country do more to promote ethical actions by businesses?

While Canada has no national laws regarding codes of ethics, in 1997 a coalition of Canadian companies developed a new international code of ethics. The code is voluntary and deals with issues such as the environment, human rights, business conduct, treatment of employees and health and safety standards. Those supporting the Canadian code include the Alliance of Manufacturers & Exporters Canada as well as the Conference Board of Canada and the Business Council on National Issues. Alcan Aluminum Ltd. and Shell Canada Ltd. are among the companies that have signed the code. Former Foreign Affairs Minister Lloyd Axworthy hailed the code as a way of putting Canadian values into the international arena.[20] Interpretation of what Canadian companies should be doing is not always clear, however, as the "Managing Globally" shows.

Managing Globally

Should Canadians Be Doing Business in Sudan?

During 1999 and 2000, Calgary-based Talisman Energy Inc. came under increasing fire from church and human rights organizations and the United States for its stake in an oil project in Sudan.[21] Critics said Sudan uses oil revenues to fund its civil war.

Though the Canadian government backed off from its threat to impose sanctions in February 2000, at the same time the United States slapped sanctions on the consortium operating the Sudan project, of which Talisman owns 25 percent. In order to shield itself from the US sanctions, Talisman flowed its investments in Sudan through a Dutch subsidiary.

The United States justified its sanctions by noting that Talisman "provided a new source of hard currency for a regime that has been responsible for massive human-rights abuses—including slavery—and sponsoring terrorism outside Sudan."[22]

Jim Buckee, president and chief executive, in responding to sanctions by the United States defended Talisman's actions, noting that his company isn't in the business of peacemaking "and shouldn't be expected to take on the dirty work of governments."[23]

Foreign Affairs Minister Lloyd Axworthy, responding to the US sanctions, said that, "Other countries have no business making laws for Canadian companies." He also suggested that Talisman needs to make its own decisions, but did not support Canadian intervention in the company's policies. "They could look seriously at some monitoring agency on human rights abuses. These are company decisions," Axworthy said.[24]

professional ethics

Standards that govern how members of a profession are to make decisions when the way they should behave is not clear-cut.

PROFESSIONAL ETHICS Professional ethics are standards that govern how members of a profession, managers or workers, make decisions when the way in which they should behave is not clear-cut.[25] Medical ethics govern the way doctors are to treat patients. Doctors are expected to perform only necessary medical procedures and to act in a patient's interest and not in their own. Nurses in Canada have their own ethical standards, separate from those of the medical profession, through the Canadian Nurses Association and the provincial regulatory bodies. The ethics of scientific research require scientists to conduct their experiments and present their findings in ways that ensure the validity of their conclusions. Like society at large, most professional groups can impose punishments for violations of ethical standards. Doctors and lawyers can be prevented from practising their professions if they disregard professional ethics and put their own interests first, as managers at Bridgestone did.

Within an organization, professional rules and norms often govern how employees such as lawyers, researchers, and accountants make decisions and act in certain situations, and these rules and norms may become part of the organization's code of ethics. When they do, workers internalize the rules and norms of their profession (just as they do those of society) and often follow them automatically when deciding how to behave.[26] Because most people tend to follow established rules of behaviour, people often take ethics for granted. However, when professional ethics are violated, such as when scientists fabricate data to disguise the harmful effects of products, ethical issues rise to the forefront. The failure to discipline a broker after numerous customer complaints led to big image problems for Toronto-based BMO Nesbitt Burns.

Ethics in Action

How to Make Profits and Harm Clients

Brokerage firms sometimes skirt a fine line between complying with industry regulations and trying to generate profits.[27] At the Winnipeg office of BMO Nesbitt Burns (www.bmonesbittburns.com), broker Randolph McDuff was investigated in March 1999 for trading irregularities. Lorne Switzer, the head of compliance at Nesbitt Burns' head office in Toronto, recommended that McDuff be fired.

During the investigation, McDuff admitted that he made unauthorized trades in client accounts. Bill Haldane, a compliance officer for the firm, noted: "McDuff did not seem to understand that a client must be contacted prior to a trade being executed."

Despite Switzer's recommendation, McDuff was not fired. Instead, he was fined $2000 and warned that that "any further occurrences may result in termination of employment."

The fine might give the impression that McDuff's behaviour was a one-time thing. However, his behaviour had been under discussion at head office at least since the beginning of 1998. An internal document dated January 28, 1999 noted that "we have experienced a large increase in the amount of settlements [anticipated and settled]" regarding McDuff.

Nevertheless, Tom Waitt, senior vice-president of BMO Nesbitt Burns' Prairie division and McDuff's supervisor in Manitoba, urged the head office to avoid taking drastic action, but rather simply to keep McDuff under close supervision. A memo that McDuff wrote to his supervisor in September 1999 may explain why the Winnipeg office was so interested in keeping him on: "I know there is this great big cloud over my head and that head office wants me out of here. Does head office forget about my contributions to this firm over the years? In addition to providing for more than 15 percent of the office revenue consistently over the past five years, I have been an advocate of Nesbitt Burns. … Rookies and marketers are still amazed at my work ethic. Some have said that it inspires them to work harder."

BMO Nesbitt Burns' lack of action against McDuff eventually resulted in very bad publicity in the national newspapers. Moreover, by spring 2001 the company was facing investigations on several fronts. The Manitoba Securities Commission fined Waitt and BMO Nesbitt Burns a total of $160 000, though Waitt was only given a reprimand, rather than a suspension. The Investment Dealers Association (IDA) was reviewing the supervisory procedures at Nesbitt Burns' head office. The IDA's probe will investigate how Nesbitt Burns deals with client complaints and how it reviews and audits sales staff. Finally, the Canadian Banking Ombudsman was probing McDuff's activities as well as the "general situation in Winnipeg."

individual ethics

Personal standards that govern how individuals interact with other people.

INDIVIDUAL ETHICS   **Individual ethics** are personal standards and values that govern how individuals interact with other people.[28] Sources of individual ethics include the influence of one's family, peers, and upbringing in general. The experiences gained over a lifetime—through membership in significant social institutions such as schools and religions, for example—also contribute to the development of the personal standards and values that a person applies to decide what is right or wrong and whether to perform certain actions or make certain decisions.

Many decisions or behaviours that one person finds unethical, such as using animals for cosmetics testing, may be acceptable to another person. If decisions or behaviours are not illegal, individuals may agree to disagree about their ethical beliefs, or they may try to impose their beliefs on other people and make their own ethical beliefs the law.[29] Within an organization, the individual ethics of top managers are especially important in shaping the organization's code of ethics.

Societal, professional, and individual ethics factor into the development of organizational codes of ethics—codes that influence how managers and workers make decisions affecting the interests of other organizational stakeholders. In 2000, KPMG reported that of the 154 public- and private-sector firms they surveyed, 86 percent had a written document outlining their values and principles, while 73 percent had programs or initiatives focusing on promoting ethical practices.[30]

To understand how an organization's code of ethics affects the choices of its managers, it is useful to examine some managers' behaviour toward different stakeholder groups.

What Behaviours Are Ethical?

Should shareholders receive more consideration than other stakeholders when managers make decisions for their companies?

A key ethical decision facing managers is how to apportion harms and benefits among stakeholder groups.[31] Suppose a company has a few very good years and makes high profits. Who should receive these profits—managers, workers, stockholders, or customers? As oil prices soared throughout the world in 2000 and 2001, Canadian oil industry profits reached record highs. Customers, who saw their heating bills rise considerably over that same period, suggested that rebates should be given to them.

The decision about how to divide profits among managers, workers, stockholders, and even customers might not seem to be an ethical issue, but it is—and in the same manner as how to apportion harms or costs among stakeholders when things go wrong.[32] For instance, it is not unusual for companies to engage in restructurings, resulting in massive layoffs, to improve their bottom line. Are layoffs of managers and workers ethical? Managers at some companies try to make the layoffs less painful by introducing generous early retirement programs that give workers full pension rights if they retire early. Employees are sometimes paid a month's or several months' salary for each year of service to the company.

In Canada, severance payments are not required by law, so the decision to pay layoff benefits is typically an ethical choice made by a company's top managers in light of their organization's code of ethics. Many managers believe that employees who have worked for long periods of time for a company should receive layoff payments because they have made an investment in the company—providing their skills and loyalty—just as a stockholder invests in a company by providing capital. Workers, however, have a weaker claim on a company than do stockholders because they usually have no legally enforceable ownership rights in the company. Stockholders are the legal owners of a corporation. Moreover, when top managers decide to give layoff benefits to workers, the decision can harm stockholders, whose dividend payments may be reduced. Thus, deciding how to distribute organizational resources becomes an ethical issue. Top managers must choose the right or proper way to balance the interests of their different stakeholders, and their code of ethics helps them to do so.

Ethical issues loom large when a manager's decision is not governed by legal requirements and it is up to the manager to determine the appropriate actions to take. In Western Europe, organizations are required by law to give employees layoff payments based on their years of service. Germany, France, and the United Kingdom specify how much managers and workers are entitled to receive if they are laid off. Managers in these organizations simply follow the rules in deciding how to behave.

In general, the poorer a country is, the more likely are employees to be treated with little regard. One issue of particular ethical concern on a global level is whether it is ethical to use child labour.

★ link between poverty and labour standards.

Ethics in Action

Is it Right to Use Child Labour?

In recent years, the number of Canadian and US companies that buy their inputs from low-cost foreign suppliers has been growing, and concern about the ethics associated with employing young children in factories has been increasing. In Pakistan, children as young as six work long hours in deplorable conditions to make rugs and carpets for export to Western countries. Some children in poor countries throughout Africa, Asia, and South America work in similar conditions.

Opinions about the ethics of child labour vary widely. Some believe that the practice is totally reprehensible and should be outlawed on a global level. Another view, championed by *The Economist* magazine (www.economist.com), is that, although nobody wants to see children employed in factories, citizens of rich countries need to recognize that in poor countries children are often a family's only breadwinner. Thus, denying children employment would cause whole families to suffer, and correcting one wrong (child labour) might produce a greater wrong (poverty). Instead, *The Economist* favours regulating the conditions under which children are employed and hopes that over time, as poor countries become richer, the need for child employment will disappear.

Many Canadian and US retailers buy their clothing from low-cost foreign suppliers, and managers in these companies have had to take their own ethical stance on child labour. In Chapter 1, we discussed how Mountain Equipment Co-op (www.mec.ca) was facing demands from some of its members to discontinue manufacturing clothing in China. Wal-Mart Canada (www.walmart.com) has been criticized for its policy of doing business with third party suppliers—such as Hampton Industries, Sutton Creations, Global Gold, Stretch-O-Rama, Cherry Stix and By Design—that import goods from Myanmar (formerly Burma), which engages in forced labour, including that of children. In defence of the company's actions, Wal-Mart Canada spokesman Andrew Pelletier noted, "We have a policy we are looking at, of monitoring vendors sourcing from other countries.... For other corporations, our expectation is that they would take their direction from the Canadian government, that's what we would recommend they would do."

At present, the Canadian government, unlike the US government, does not have regulations governing the use of child labour in foreign countries by Canadian companies. Clearly, if Canadian retailers are to be true to their ethical stance on this troubling issue, they cannot ignore the fact that they are buying clothing made by children, and they must do more to regulate the conditions under which these children work.

Managers also face ethical dilemmas when choosing how to deal with certain stakeholders. For example, suppliers provide an organization with its inputs and expect to be paid within a reasonable amount of time. Some managers, however, consistently delay payment to make the most use of their organization's money. This practice can hurt a supplier's cash flow and threaten its very survival.

An organization that is a powerful customer and buys large amounts of particular suppliers' products is in a position to demand that suppliers reduce their prices. If an organization does this, suppliers earn lower profits and the organization earns more. Is this behaviour just "business as usual," or is it unethical?

Before it was bought out by Heather Reisman of Indigo Books & Music, Inc. and Gerry Schwartz of Onex Corporation, Toronto-based Chapters controlled between 40 and 70 percent of the Canadian retail book market.[33] It owned its own wholesale distribution company, and because of its volume, Chapters demanded

Publishers hoped that Heather Reisman, the CEO of Chapters, would be more friendly to the publishing industry than former CEO Larry Stephenson.

BC Hydro
www.bchydro.com/

the lowest unit costs from publishers, usually a 50-percent discount, "or else."[34] Some publishers were relieved when Reisman took over as CEO of Chapters, viewing her as more friendly to the publishing industry, and less likely to demand such steep discounts from already struggling publishers.

Sometimes it is suppliers who can take advantage of situations in the market to gain higher profits. After California's energy crisis in 2000 and 2001, a report was filed with the US Federal Energy Regulatory Commission claiming that BC Hydro "reaped US$176 million in 'excessive' profits by price gouging California utilities."[35] BC Hydro was accused of offering "power at a range of high prices and sometimes in large amounts when the state was most desperate."[36] BC Hydro officials "acknowledge they did anticipate periods of severe power shortages and planned for them by letting their reservoirs rise overnight and then opening them to create hydro electricity, which could be produced inexpensively but sold for a premium." But BC Hydro officials say they played by the rules of the electricity trade marketplace. "It was the marketplace that determined what the price of electricity would be at any given time," said BC Hydro spokesman Ian Cousins. One can readily raise the question: Was this good business, or was this unethical behaviour?

In addition to suppliers and distributors, customers are a critical stakeholder group because, as noted in Chapter 1, organizations depend on them for their very survival. Customers have the right to expect an organization to provide goods and services that will not harm them. As well, local communities and the general public also have an interest or stake in whether the decisions that managers make are ethical. The quality of a city's school system or police department, the economic health of its downtown area, and its general level of prosperity all depend on choices made by managers of organizations.

In sum, managers face many ethical choices as they deal with the different and sometimes conflicting interests of organizational stakeholders. Deciding what behaviour is ethical is often a difficult task that requires managers to make tough choices that will benefit some stakeholders and harm others.

Why Would Managers Behave Unethically Toward Other Stakeholders?

Typically, *unethical behaviour*–behaviour that falls outside the bounds of accepted standards or values–occurs because managers put their personal interests above the interests of other organizational stakeholders or choose to ignore the harm that they are inflicting on others.[37] Managers confront ethical dilemmas every time they have to balance the claims of one stakeholder group against the claims of another, and they might feel tempted to engage in unethical acts if the harm done to stakeholders is indirect or seems insignificant relative to the benefits that the managers themselves or their organization will receive from the unethical activity.[38]

In some countries, but not in Canada or the United States, bribing foreign officials to get business is an acceptable practice. Suppose that bribery will ensure that a Canadian expatriate manager can secure for her company a large contract that in turn will net her a huge bonus and promotion. Bribery is not illegal in the country in which she is doing business; her competitors are actively engaging in it, and nobody really gets hurt. Is such bribery really unethical behaviour, and does the Canadian government really have the right to say that for Canadian citizens living abroad it is illegal? Similarly, if all members of a company's sales force routinely pad their expense accounts, is this behaviour really unethical, since it is the common practice in the company? As discussed previously, family, upbringing, and religion help teach people how to distinguish between right and wrong behaviour and to be productive members of society. Managers who let self-interest take control of their decision making in such situations and ignore societal ethics as well are often those who have a poor or undeveloped code of individual ethics.[39]

Beyond the pursuit of ruthless self-interest, managers or workers may have other reasons to act unethically, such as feeling pressured by the situation they are in.[40] Sometimes the behaviour of other managers (particularly superiors) may cause managers to behave unethically. Often, managers who find themselves under intense pressure to perform and to help their organization succeed encourage subordinates to act in ethically dubious ways, such as bribing foreign officials, overcharging customers, or delivering substandard products. An example of this type of activity occurred in 1992 when Sears was accused of consistently overcharging customers for car repairs.[41] Apparently, to improve a very weak financial position, Sears created a bonus system that encouraged its car repair employees to convince customers that they needed repairs that actually were unnecessary. Subsequently, Sears changed its bonus system, but only after considerable harm had been done to the company's reputation.

Promoting Ethics

A 2000 ethics survey by KPMG found that nearly two-thirds of Canadian firms promote values and ethical practices. However, more than half of the companies surveyed have not designated a senior manager who is responsible for ethical issues. Only 14 percent evaluate their employees in terms of ethical performance.[42] Despite a seeming lack of commitment to concrete actions by Canada's companies, there are many ways in which managers can communicate their desire for employees at all levels to behave ethically toward organizational stakeholders.

ESTABLISHING ETHICAL CONTROL SYSTEMS   Perhaps the most important step to encourage ethical behaviour is to develop a code of ethics that is given to every employee and published regularly in company newsletters and annual reports. The Integrity Program at Calgary-based Nexen Inc. (formerly Canadian Occidental Petroleum Ltd.) covers such things as business conduct, employee and human rights, and the environment. Each division at Nexen has an integrity leader who is supposed to make sure that the message about the company's commitment to ethics spreads throughout the organization.[43] At UPS Canada, employees must develop an action plan around their codes of conduct. Managers are assessed on matters such as integrity and fair treatment.[44]

The next step is to provide a visible means of support for ethical behaviour. Increasingly, organizations are creating the role of ethics officer, or **ethics ombudsman**, to monitor their ethical practices and procedures. The ethics ombudsman is responsible for communicating ethical standards to all employees, for designing systems to monitor employees' conformity to those standards, and for teaching managers and nonmanagerial employees at all levels of the organization how to respond to ethical dilemmas appropriately.[45] Because the ethics ombudsman has organizationwide authority, organizational members in any department can discuss instances of unethical behaviour by their managers or co-workers without fear of retribution. This arrangement makes it easier for everyone to behave ethically. In addition, ethics ombudsmen can provide guidance when organizational members are uncertain about whether an action is ethical. Some organizations have an organizationwide ethics committee to provide guidance on ethical issues and help write and update the company code of ethics.

Nexen Inc. Integrity Program
www.cdnoxy.com/about/integ.htm

ethics ombudsman
An ethics officer who monitors an organization's practices and procedures to be sure they are ethical.

DEVELOPING AN ETHICAL CULTURE An organization can also communicate its position on ethics and social responsibility to employees by making ethical values and norms a central part of its organizational culture. A number of companies try to encourage ethical behaviour through their corporate culture, emphasizing such values as honesty, trust, respect and fairness. We discuss organizational culture in depth in Chapter 9. Here, it is important to note that when organizational members abide by the organization's values and norms, those values and norms become part of each individual's personal code of ethics. Thus, an employee who faces an ethical dilemma automatically responds to the situation in a manner that reflects the ethical standards of the organization. High standards and strong values and norms help individuals resist self-interested action and recognize that they are part of something bigger than themselves.[46]

Managers' role in developing ethical values and standards in other employees is very important. Employees naturally look to those in authority to provide leadership, and managers become ethical role models whose behaviour is scrutinized by their subordinates. If top managers are not ethical, their subordinates are not likely to behave in an ethical manner. They may think that if it's alright for a top manager to engage in ethically dubious behaviour, it's alright for them too.

Ethical control systems such as codes of ethics and regular training programs help employees learn an organization's ethical values. However, KPMG reported in 2000 that 61 percent of Canadian companies surveyed gave no ethics training at all, and a third of Canadian businesses provide managers with less than one hour of training per year.[47]

Tips for Managers

Championing Ethical Behaviour

1. Analyze the way stakeholders will be affected by managerial decisions and ensure that managers make decisions in such a way that they can defend them to all of those who will be affected by their actions.

2. Develop a written code of ethics for an organization and encourage members of different functions to develop specific guidelines that will help them know how to behave when confronted by an ethical dilemma.

3. Ensure that all managers are responsible for helping their subordinates learn how to determine whether an action is unethical or not and to discover instances of unethical behaviour.

4. Ensure that managers serve as role models and always act ethically and with integrity.

Social Responsibility

social responsibility

A manager's duty or obligation to make decisions that promote the welfare and well-being of stakeholders and society as a whole.

There are many reasons why it is important for managers and organizations to act ethically and to do everything possible to avoid harming stakeholders. However, what about the other side of the coin? What responsibility do managers have to provide benefits to their stakeholders and to adopt courses of action that enhance the well-being of society at large? The term **social responsibility** refers to a manager's duty or obligation to make decisions that nurture, protect, enhance, and promote the welfare and well-being of stakeholders and society as a whole. Many kinds of decisions signal an organization's interest in being socially responsible (see Table 5.2).

Table 5.2

Forms of Socially Responsible Behaviour

Managers are being socially responsible and showing their support for their stakeholders when they:
- Provide severance payments to help laid-off workers make ends meet until they can find another job;
- Provide workers with opportunities to enhance their skills and acquire additional education so they can remain productive and do not become obsolete because of changes in technology;
- Allow employees to take time off when they need to and provide extended healthcare and pension benefits for employees;
- Contribute to charities or support various civic-minded activities in the cities or towns in which they are located;
- Decide to keep open a factory whose closure would devastate the local community;
- Decide to keep a company's operations in Canada to protect the jobs of Canadian workers rather than move abroad;
- Decide to spend money to improve a new factory so that it will not pollute the environment;
- Decline to invest in countries that have poor human rights records;
- Choose to help poor countries develop an economic base to improve living standards.

Approaches to Social Responsibility

obstructionist approach Disregard for social responsibility; willingness to engage in and cover up unethical and illegal behaviour.

The strength of organizations' commitment to social responsibility ranges from low to high (see Figure 5.2).[48] At the low end of the range is an **obstructionist approach**. Obstructionist managers choose not to behave in a socially responsible way. Instead, they behave unethically and illegally and do all they can to prevent knowledge of their behaviour from reaching other organizational stakeholders and society at large.

defensive approach Minimal commitment to social responsibility; willingness to do what the law requires and no more.

A **defensive approach** indicates at least a commitment to ethical behaviour. Managers adopting this approach do all they can to ensure that their employees behave legally and do not harm others. But when making ethical choices, these managers put the claims and interests of their shareholders first, at the expense of other stakeholders.

Some economists believe that managers in a capitalist society should always put stockholders' claims first, and that if these choices are not acceptable to other members of society and are considered unethical, then society must pass laws and create rules and regulations to govern the choices managers make.[49] From a defensive perspective, it is not managers' responsibility to make socially responsible choices; their job is to abide by the rules that have been legally established.

accommodative approach Moderate commitment to social responsibility; willingness to do more than the law requires if asked.

An **accommodative approach** is an acknowledgment of the need to support social responsibility. Accommodative managers agree that organizational members ought to behave legally and ethically, and they try to balance the interests of different stakeholders against one another so that the claims of stockholders are

Figure 5.2

Approaches to Social Responsibility

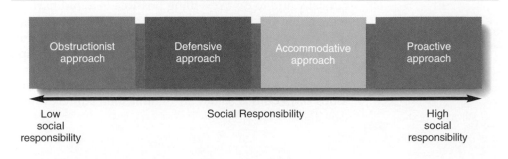

seen in relation to the claims of other stakeholders. Managers adopting this approach want to make choices that are reasonable in the eyes of society and want to do the right thing when called on to do so.

Managers taking a **proactive approach** actively embrace the need to behave in socially responsible ways, go out of their way to learn about the needs of different stakeholder groups, and are willing to utilize organizational resources to promote not only the interests of stockholders but those of the other stakeholders.

proactive approach

Strong commitment to social responsibility; eagerness to do more than the law requires and to use organizational resources to promote the interests of all organizational stakeholders.

Why Be Socially Responsible?

Several advantages are argued to result when managers and organizations behave in a socially responsible manner. First, workers and society benefit directly because organizations (rather than the government) bear some of the costs of helping workers. Second, it has been said that if all organizations in a society were socially responsible, the quality of life as a whole would be higher. Indeed, several management experts have argued that the way in which organizations behave toward their employees determines many of a society's values and norms and the ethics of its citizens. It has been suggested that if all organizations adopted a caring approach and agreed that their responsibility was to promote the interests of their employees, a climate of caring would pervade the wider society.[50] Experts point to Japan, Sweden, Germany, the Netherlands, and Switzerland as countries where organizations are very socially responsible and where, as a result, crime and unemployment rates are relatively low, the literacy rate is relatively high, and sociocultural values promote harmony between different groups of people. Other reasons for being socially responsible are that it is the right thing to do and that companies that act responsibly toward their stakeholders benefit from increasing business and see their profits rise.[51]

McDonald's is one of the many global organizations that has declared its commitment to be socially responsible—it supports a proactive stance on the issues and wants its customers to support this stance too.

Given these advantages, why would anyone quarrel over the pursuit of social responsibility by organizations and their managers? One issue that comes up is that although some stakeholders benefit from managers' commitment to social responsibility, other stakeholders, particularly shareholders, may think they are being harmed when organizational resources are used for socially responsible courses of action. Some people argue that business has only one kind of responsibility: to use its resources for activities that increase its profits and thus reward its stockholders.[52]

How should managers decide which social issues they will respond to, and to what extent their organizations should trade profits for social gain? Obviously, illegal behaviour should not be tolerated, and all managers and workers should be alert to its occurrence and report it promptly. The term **whistle-blower** is used to refer to a person who reports illegal or unethical behaviour and takes a stand against unscrupulous managers or other stakeholders who are pursuing their own ends.[53] Unlike the United States, Canada does not have universal laws to protect whistle-blowers. Canadian jurisdictions bring in this legislation at their own discretion. For instance, in late 1993, the Ontario NDP government passed a bill to protect employees who blew the whistle on their polluting employers.[54] Beyond the need to behave legally, there are some criteria that managers may use to help themselves choose which social actions to undertake. A **social audit** allows managers to take into consideration both the private or organizational and the social effects of particular decisions. They rank various alternative courses of action according to both their profitability and their social benefits.

Evidence suggests that, in the long run, managers who behave in a socially responsible way will most benefit all organizational stakeholders (including stockholders). It appears that socially responsible companies, in comparison with less responsible competitors, are less risky investments, tend to be somewhat more profitable, have a more loyal and committed workforce, and have better **reputations**; these qualities encourage stakeholders (including customers and suppliers) to establish long-term business relationships with the companies.[55] Socially responsible companies are also sought out by communities, which encourage such organizations to locate in their cities and offer them incentives such as property-tax reductions and the construction of new roads and free utilities for their plants. Thus, there are many reasons to believe that, over time, strong support of social responsibility confers the most benefits on organizational stakeholders (including stockholders) and on society at large.

whistle-blower A person who reports illegal or unethical behaviour.

social audit A tool that allows managers to analyze the profitability and social returns of socially responsible actions.

reputation The esteem or high repute that individuals or organizations gain when they behave ethically.

Managing an Increasingly Diverse Workforce

One of the most important issues in management to emerge over the last 30 years has been the increasing diversity of the workforce. In Chapter 4, we addressed issues of diversity that result from organizations' expansion into the global environment. Here, we address diversity as it occurs closer to home—in an organization's workforce. **Diversity** is dissimilarity—differences—among people due to age, gender, race, ethnicity, religion, sexual orientation, socioeconomic background, and capabilities/disabilities (see Figure 5.3). Diversity raises important ethical issues and social responsibility issues as well. It is also a critical issue for organizations, one that if not handled well can surely bring an organization to its knees, especially in our increasingly global environment.

Canada has become a truly diverse country, although this might not be apparent to everyone. According to the 1996 census, the visible minority population makes up about 11 percent of the total population. In Toronto and Vancouver it is above 30 percent, however, while in Quebec and St. John's, only 1 percent of the population has visible minority status. There are many more women and minorities—including people with disabilities and gays and lesbians—in the workforce than ever before, and most experts agree that diversity is steadily increasing.

diversity Differences among people in age, gender, race, ethnicity, religion, sexual orientation, socioeconomic background, and capabilities/disabilities.

Figure 5.3
Sources of Diversity in the Workforce

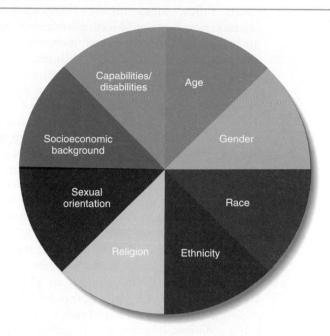

How much attention do you think companies should pay to creating diversity initiatives?

Why is diversity such a pressing issue both in the popular press and for managers and organizations? There are several reasons:

- There is a strong ethical imperative in many societies that all people receive equal opportunities and be treated fairly and justly. Unfair treatment is also illegal.

- Effectively managing diversity can improve organizational effectiveness. When managers manage diversity effectively, they not only encourage other managers to treat diverse members of an organization fairly and justly, but also realize that diversity is an important organizational resource that can help an organization to gain a competitive advantage.

- Embracing diversity encourages more participation and accordingly encourages differences of opinions/ideas that are beneficial to the organization.

what do these studies/stats really tell us? What do they really measure/observe?

- There is substantial evidence that diverse individuals continue to experience unfair treatment in the workplace as a result of *biases, stereotypes,* and *overt discrimination.* In one study, résumés of equally qualified men and women were sent to high-priced restaurants (where potential earnings are high). Though equally qualified, men were more than twice as likely as women to be called for a job interview and more than five times as likely to receive a job offer.[56] White men are most likely to head Canadian corporations. In August 1999, only 13 of Canada's largest companies had women as CEOs.[57] Overall, only two percent of the Financial Post 500 companies were headed by female CEOs in 2000.

In the rest of this section, we examine each of these issues in detail. Then we look at the steps that managers can take to manage diversity effectively in their organizations.

The Ethical Imperative to Manage Diversity Effectively

Effectively managing diversity not only makes good business sense, but it is an ethical imperative in Canadian society. Two moral principles provide managers with guidance in their efforts to meet this imperative: distributive justice and procedural justice.

distributive justice

A moral principle calling for the distribution of pay raises, promotions, and other organizational resources to be based on meaningful contributions that individuals have made and not on personal characteristics over which they have no control.

DISTRIBUTIVE JUSTICE   The principle of **distributive justice** dictates that the distribution of pay raises, promotions, job titles, interesting job assignments, office space, and other organizational resources among members of an organization be fair. The distribution of these outcomes should be based on the meaningful contributions that individuals have made to the organization (such as time, effort, education, skills, abilities, and performance levels) and not on irrelevant personal characteristics over which individuals have no control (such as gender, race, or age).[58] Managers have an obligation to ensure that distributive justice exists in their organizations. This does not mean that all members of an organization receive identical or similar outcomes; rather it means that members who receive more outcomes than others have made substantially higher or more significant contributions to the organization.

Is distributive justice common in organizations in corporate Canada? Probably the best way to answer this question is to say that things are getting better. Fifty years ago, overt discrimination against women and minorities was not uncommon; today, organizations are inching closer toward the ideal of distributive justice. Statistics comparing the treatment of women and minorities with the treatment of white men suggest that most managers would need to take a proactive approach in order to achieve distributive justice in their organizations.

Women, for example, make up 51 percent of the Canadian population and 45 percent of the Canadian labour force, but only 15 percent of senior manager positions, and 34 percent of manager and administrator positions. Some organizations do much better at promoting women than others, however. For instance, since 1991, Toronto-based Bank of Montreal has worked diligently to advance women through the ranks, after discovering that while 75 percent of its employees were women, 91 percent of them were in nonmanagement positions.[59] After a number of management-introduced initiatives, women held 23 percent of the executive positions at the Bank of Montreal in 1997.

In many countries, managers have not only an ethical obligation to strive to achieve distributive justice in their organizations, but also a legal obligation to treat all employees fairly, and they risk being sued by employees who feel that they are not being fairly treated.

procedural justice

A moral principle calling for the use of fair procedures to determine how to distribute outcomes to organizational members.

PROCEDURAL JUSTICE   The principle of **procedural justice** requires managers to use fair procedures to determine how to distribute outcomes to organizational members.[60] This principle applies to typical procedures such as appraising subordinates' performance, deciding who should receive a raise or a promotion, and deciding whom to lay off when an organization is forced to downsize. Procedural justice exists, for example, when managers (1) carefully appraise a subordinate's performance, (2) take into account any environmental obstacles to high performance beyond the subordinate's control, such as lack of supplies, machine breakdowns, or dwindling customer demand for a product, and (3) ignore irrelevant personal characteristics such as the subordinate's age or ethnicity. Like distributive justice, procedural justice is necessary not only to ensure ethical conduct but also to avoid costly lawsuits, as illustrated in this "Focus on Diversity."

Focus on Diversity

Sex Discrimination at BioChem Pharma Inc.

Kathryn MacDougall, a former director of legal affairs at Montreal-based BioChem Pharma Inc., sued the company for $12 million in July 2000, citing gender discrimination and gender harassment.[61] MacDougall, who worked for the company from 1993 and 1997, was the first woman ever on Biochem's management committee. She requested reinstatement, and that she be named vice-president, legal affairs, with corresponding salary, stock options and benefits. MacDougall claimed "the drug company denied her a title, position, salary, benefits, vacations and compensation package equal to those given to men working at the same level, even though she was involved in every legal aspect of BioChem's business." In effect, she claimed that the company violated procedural justice in its treatment of her.

BioChem maintained that its treatment of MacDougall was appropriate and planned to defend itself vigorously in court.

Effectively Managing Diversity Makes Good Legal Sense

A variety of legislative acts affect diversity management in Canada. Under the Canadian Human Rights Act, it is against the law for any employer or provider of service that falls within federal jurisdiction to make unlawful distinctions based on the following prohibited grounds: race, national or ethnic origin, colour, religion, age, sex (including pregnancy and childbirth), marital status, family status, mental or physical disability (including previous or present drug or alcohol dependence), pardoned conviction, or sexual orientation. Employment with the following employers and service providers is covered by the Human Rights Act: federal departments, agencies and crown corporations; Canada Post; chartered banks; national airlines; interprovincial communications and telephone companies; interprovincial transportation companies; and other federally regulated industries, such as certain mining operations.

In addition to the Human Rights Act, Canada's Employment Equity Act of 1995 lists four protected categories of employees: Aboriginal peoples (persons who are Indians, Inuit or Métis); persons with disabilities; members of visible minorities (non-Caucasian in race or non-white in colour); and women. The reasoning behind the Employment Equity Act is that individuals should not face employment barriers due to being a woman, a person with a disability, an Aboriginal person, or a member of a visible minority. Thus the Federal legislation aims at ensuring that members of these four "designated groups" are treated equitably. Employers affected by the Canadian Human Rights Act are also covered by the Employment Equity Act.

A number of provinces have their own legislation, including employment equity acts, that governs within-province employers. Many companies have difficulty complying with equity acts, as recent audits conducted by the Canadian Human Rights Commission show. In an audit of 180 companies, only Status of Women Canada; Elliot Lake, ON-based AJ Bus Lines, National Parole Board, Canadian Transportation Agency, Les-Méchins, QC-based Verreault Navigation, and Nortel Networks were compliant on their first try.[62]

Effectively Managing Diversity Makes Good Business Sense

Though organizations are compelled to follow the law, the diversity of organizational members can be a source of competitive advantage in more than a legal sense, as it helps an organization to provide customers with better goods and services.[63] The variety of points of view and approaches to problems and opportunities that diverse employees provide can improve managerial decision making. Just as the workforce is becoming increasingly diverse, so too are the customers who buy an organization's goods or services.

Diverse members of an organization are likely to be attuned to what goods and services diverse segments of the market want and do not want. Major car companies, for example, are increasingly assigning women to their design teams to

Human Rights Act
http://laws.justice.gc.ca/en/H-6/

Employment Equity Act
http://laws.justice.gc.ca/en/E-5.401/

ensure that the needs and desires of female customers (a growing segment of the market) are taken into account in new car design.

Effectively managing diversity makes good business sense for another reason. More and more, consumer and civil rights organizations are demanding that companies think about diversity issues from a variety of angles. For instance, Toronto-based Royal Bank of Canada found its efforts to acquire North Carolina-based Centura Banks Inc. under fire by Inner City Press/Community on the Move (ICP), a US civil rights group. In April 2001, the group asked American and Canadian regulators to delay approval of the acquisition to allow further investigation of alleged abusive lending practices carried out by Centura. "Centura's normal interest rate lending disproportionately denies and excludes credit applications from people of colour," said Matthew Lee, ICP executive director.[64] ICP alleges that, in two American cities, Centura denied applications for home purchase from black people three times more frequently than applications from white people. The group wants Royal Bank to guarantee that it will end the alleged unfair lending practices.

Being aware of diversity issues extends beyond just employees however, to consider the issues of suppliers, clients and customers. Nestlé Canada recently announced that it was planning to do away with its nut-free products because trying to keep the production area free of nut products seemed more costly than it was beneficial. Nestlé Canada was soon deluged with protests from Canadian families who had relied upon such products as Kit Kat, Mirage, Coffee Crisp, and Aero chocolate bars and Smarties. One to two percent of all Canadians, and perhaps as many as eight percent of children are allergic to peanuts and/or other nuts, which is why the protest was so vocal. Within a month, Nestlé Canada announced that it would go back to producing these candies in a nut-free facility to appease its consumers with this particular disability. Nestlé's initial decision factored in "a growing public demand for chocolate with nuts, as well as the need to protect jobs at its Toronto plant."[65] Nestlé senior vice-president Graham Lute still wants to expand Nestlé's manufacturing in Canada, but says, "We'll just execute it in a different way, but not as attractive a way as it would have been before, from a sheer business point of view."[66] In other words, the attention to this particular diversity issue has caused the company to rethink part of its business strategy.

Nestlé Canada
www.nestle.ca/english/

Why are Diverse Employees Sometimes Treated Unfairly?

Even though most people would agree that distributive justice and procedural justice are desirable goals, diverse organizational members are still sometimes treated unfairly, as previous examples illustrate. Why is this problem occurring? Three factors may induce some managers to act unethically, unfairly, or even illegally toward diverse organizational members: biases, stereotypes, and overt discrimination.

bias The systematic tendency to use information about others in ways that result in inaccurate perceptions.

BIASES   **Biases** are systematic tendencies to use information about others in ways that result in inaccurate perceptions. Because of the way biases operate, people often are unaware that their perceptions of others are inaccurate. There are several types of biases.

The *similar-to-me effect* is the tendency to perceive others who are similar to ourselves more positively than we perceive people who are different.[67] The similar-to-me effect is summed up by the saying "Birds of a feather flock together." It can lead to unfair treatment of diverse employees simply because they are different from the managers who are perceiving them, evaluating them, and making decisions that will affect their future in the organization.

Managers in larger corporations (particularly top managers) are likely to be white men. Although these managers may endorse the principles of distributive and procedural justice, they may unintentionally fall into the trap of perceiving other white men more positively than they perceive women and minorities. This is the similar-to-me effect. Being aware of this bias and using objective information about employees' capabilities and performance as much as possible in decision making about job assignments, pay raises, promotions and other outcomes can help managers avoid the similar-to-me effect.

Social status, a person's real or perceived position in a society or an organization, can be the source of another bias. The *social status effect* is the tendency to perceive individuals with high social status more positively than we perceive those with low social status. A high-status person may be perceived as smarter and more believable, capable, knowledgeable, and responsible than a low-status person, even in the absence of objective information about either person.

Imagine being introduced to two people at a company Christmas party. Both are in their late thirties, and you learn that one is a member of the company's top-management team and the other is a supervisor in the mailroom. From this information alone, you are likely to assume that the top manager is smarter, more capable, more responsible, and even more interesting than the mailroom supervisor. Because women and minorities have traditionally had lower social status than white men, the social status effect may lead some people to perceive women and minorities less positively than they perceive white men.

Have you ever stood out in a crowd? Maybe you were the only man in a group of women, or maybe you were dressed differently from everyone else (you were dressed formally for a social gathering, and everyone else was in jeans). Salience—conspicuousness—is another source of bias. The *salience effect* is the tendency to focus attention on individuals who are conspicuously different from us. When people are salient, they often feel as though all eyes are watching them, and this perception is not too far off the mark. Salient individuals are more often the object of attention than are other members of a work group, for example. A manager who has six male subordinates and one female subordinate reporting to him may inadvertently pay more attention to the female in group meetings because of the salience effect.

Individuals who are salient are often perceived to be primarily responsible for outcomes and operations and are evaluated more extremely, in either a positive or a negative direction.[68] Thus, when the female subordinate does a good job on a project, she receives excessive praise, and when she misses a deadline, she is excessively chastised.

stereotype Simplistic and often inaccurate beliefs about the typical characteristics of particular groups of people.

STEREOTYPES   **Stereotypes**, the second factor that can cause managers to treat diverse employees unfairly, are simplistic and often inaccurate beliefs about the typical characteristics of particular groups of people. Stereotypes are usually based on a highly visible characteristic, such as a person's age, gender, or race.[69] Managers who allow stereotypes to influence their perceptions assume erroneously that a person possesses a whole host of characteristics simply because of being an Asian woman, a white man, or a lesbian, for example. A manager who accepts stereotypes might, for example, decide not to promote a highly capable young mother into a management position that requires a lot of travel because the manager is certain that she will not want to be away from her small children for extended periods of time.

overt discrimination Knowingly and willingly denying diverse individuals access to opportunities and outcomes in an organization.

OVERT DISCRIMINATION   **Overt discrimination** is the third factor that can cause managers to treat diverse employees unfairly. It occurs when managers knowingly and willingly deny diverse individuals access to opportunities and outcomes in an organization. Overt discrimination is not only unethical but also illegal. Unfortunately, just as some managers steal from their organizations, others engage in overt discrimination. For example, in 1997, after an investigation by the Canadian

Human Rights Commission, Health Canada was cited for overt discrimination against "what one senior manager called 'colonials' in the federal department."[70] The Rights Commission's report found a number of practices that had a "disproportionately negative effect on visible minorities in Health Canada." As examples of discrimination, the report quoted one senior manager "as telling an East Indian doctor that 'colonials' didn't interact well with others and that 'good brainy guys had to come from the UK.'" Another senior manager was reported "as greeting his Trinidadian subordinate with 'Hello darkness, my old friend,' and 'Blackie.'"

Overt discrimination and decisions based on stereotypes are clear violations of the principles of distributive and procedural justice. But sometimes even managers who are committed to these principles treat diverse members of an organization unfairly because of the operation of biases. Simple awareness of these biases is the first step toward overcoming their effects. We next consider proactive steps that managers and organizations can take to ensure that the effects of biases and stereotypes are minimal and diverse members receive the respect and opportunities they deserve.

How to Manage Diversity Effectively

Effectively managing diversity ought to be a top priority for managers in all organizations, large and small, public and private, for-profit and not-for-profit. Managers need to ensure that they and their subordinates appreciate the value that diversity brings to an organization, understand why diversity should be celebrated rather than ignored, and have the ability to interact and work effectively with men and women who are physically challenged or are of a diverse race, age, gender, ethnicity, nationality, or sexual orientation. The effective management of diversity will help an organization to gain a competitive advantage. In this section, we describe how managers can increase diversity awareness and diversity skills in their organizations, and we explain the importance of top-management commitment to diversity.

Increasing Diversity Awareness

It is natural for you to view other people from your own perspective, because your feelings, thoughts, attitudes, and experiences guide how you perceive and interact with others. The ability to appreciate diversity, however, requires people to become aware of other perspectives and the various attitudes and experiences of others. Many diversity awareness programs in organizations strive to increase managers' and workers' awareness of (1) their own attitudes, biases, and stereotypes and (2) the differing perspectives of diverse managers, subordinates, coworkers, and customers. Diversity awareness programs often have these goals:[71]

- Providing organizational members with accurate information about diversity;
- Uncovering personal biases and stereotypes;
- Assessing personal beliefs, attitudes, and values and learning about other points of view;
- Overturning inaccurate stereotypes and beliefs about different groups;
- Developing an atmosphere in which people feel free to share their differing perspectives and points of view;
- Improving understanding of others who are different from oneself.

Increasing Diversity Skills

Efforts to increase diversity skills focus on improving the way in which managers and their subordinates interact with each other and on improving their ability to work with different kinds of people.[72]

Why are communication and understanding important in dealing with diversity?

UNDERSTANDING HOW CULTURAL DIFFERENCES AFFECT WORKING STYLES
Educating managers and their subordinates about why and how people differ in their ways of thinking, communicating, and approaching business and work can help all members of an organization to develop a healthy respect for diversity, and, at the same time, facilitate mutual understanding. When Canadian and Japanese managers interact, for example, the Canadians often feel frustrated by what they view as indecisiveness in the Japanese, and the Japanese are often frustrated by what they perceive as hasty, shortsighted decision making by the Canadians. If Japanese and Canadian managers realize that these different approaches to decision making are by-products of cultural differences and recognize the relative merits of each approach, they may be more likely to adopt a decision-making style that both groups are comfortable with, one that incorporates the advantages of each approach and minimizes the disadvantages.

BEING ABLE TO COMMUNICATE EFFECTIVELY WITH DIVERSE PEOPLE
Diverse organizational members may differ in style of communication, language fluency, word use, nonverbal signals sent through facial expression and body language, and the way in which they perceive and interpret information. Managers and their subordinates must learn to communicate effectively with one another if an organization is to take advantage of the skills and abilities of its diverse workforce. Educating organizational members about differences in ways of communicating is often a good starting point.

Organizational members should also feel comfortable enough to "clear the air" and solve communication difficulties and misunderstandings as they occur, rather than letting problems grow and fester without acknowledgment. Take the case of Mary Cramer, a working mother with four children who is employed by a large bank. Her newly hired manager, Alicia Fuller, who is single, recently commented that she did not know how Cramer managed to juggle her multiple responsibilities at work and at home. Cramer took offence at this comment. She felt that Fuller was questioning her ability to be a top performer at work and that Fuller was implying that Cramer could not possibly manage her home and work responsibilities effectively. For several weeks, Cramer brooded about this apparent criticism and avoided interacting with Fuller as much as possible. Then one day one of her co-workers told her how impressed Fuller was with her work, and Cramer realized that she may have misinterpreted Fuller's remarks.

Diversity education can help managers and subordinates gain a better understanding of how people may interpret certain kinds of comments. Diversity education also can help employees learn how to resolve misunderstandings. For example, both Cramer and Fuller should have felt free to try to clear up their misunderstanding on the spot. If Cramer had immediately mentioned her concerns, Fuller could have explained that she intended her comments to be a compliment, not the implied criticism that Cramer misunderstood them to be. Cramer would have been spared all the stress that this small incident caused her, and her relationship with Fuller would have gotten off to a better start.

BEING FLEXIBLE
Managers and their subordinates must learn how to be open to different approaches and ways of doing things. This does not mean that organizational members have to suppress their personal styles. Rather, it means that they must be open to, and not feel threatened by, different approaches and perspectives, and they must have the patience and flexibility needed to understand and appreciate diverse perspectives.

Techniques for Increasing Diversity Awareness and Skills

Many managers use a multipronged approach to increase diversity awareness and skills in their organizations: films and printed materials are supplemented by experiential exercises to uncover hidden biases and stereotypes. Sometimes simply providing a forum for people to learn about and discuss their differing attitudes, values, and experiences can be a powerful means for increasing awareness. Also useful are role-playing exercises in which people act out problems resulting from lack of awareness and indicate the increased understanding that comes from appreciating others' viewpoints. Accurate information and training experiences can debunk stereotypes. Group exercises, role-plays, and diversity-related experiences can help organizational members develop the skills they need to work effectively with a variety of people.

Managers sometimes hire outside consultants to provide diversity training. For instance, Trevor Wilson, president of Toronto-based Omnibus Consulting, has presented employment equity programs to such clients as IBM Canada Ltd., Molson Co. Ltd., and National Grocers Co. Ltd.[73] Some organizations have their own diversity experts inhouse, such as Maureen Geddes at Chatham, ON-based Union Gas.

The Importance of Top-Management Commitment to Diversity

When top management is truly committed to diversity, top managers embrace diversity through their actions and example, spread the message that diversity can be a source of competitive advantage, deal effectively with diverse employees, and are willing to commit organizational resources to managing diversity. That last step alone is not sufficient. If top managers commit resources to diversity (such as providing money for training programs) but as individuals do not value diversity, any initiatives they undertake are likely to fail.

Some organizations recruit and hire women for first-level and middle-management positions, but after being promoted into middle management, some of these female managers quit to start their own businesses. A major reason for their departure is their belief that they will not be promoted into top-management positions because of a lack of commitment to diversity among members of the top-management team. As Professor David Sharp of the Richard Ivey School of Business notes, "It seems that some Canadian women entrepreneurs are neither born, nor made. They are pushed."[74] The Bank of Montreal is an example of an organization that has been very proactive in making sure women won't leave, through its efforts to aggressively promote women to upper-management positions.

By now, it should be clear that managers can take a variety of steps to manage diversity effectively. Many companies and their managers continue to develop and experiment with new diversity initiatives to meet this ethical and business imperative. Although some initiatives prove to be unsuccessful, it is clear that managers must make a long-term commitment to diversity. Training sessions oriented toward the short term are doomed to failure: Participants quickly slip back into their old ways of doing things. The effective management of diversity, like the management of the organization as a whole, is an ongoing process: It never stops and never ends. The "Focus on Diversity" shows how the RCMP is working with Aboriginal cadets to make them feel more included.

Focus on Diversity

Sweetgrass Comes to the RCMP

To help Aboriginal cadets engage in spiritual practices while in training, the RCMP training academy in Regina created an Aboriginal Heritage Room, with cedar walls, Plains Indian artifacts, and reproductions of old photographs of Aboriginal Canadians.[75]

At the opening ceremony in December 2000, Elder Art Kaiswatum used the sweet-smelling smoke of burning buffalo sage to cleanse the room. The

RCMP Commander Giuliano Zaccardelli (right) wafts buffalo sage smoke during a smudging ceremony while Timothy Kaiswatum from Piapot First Nations holds the sage. The smudging was part of the opening ceremonies of the Aboriginal Heritage Room at the RCMP training academy in Regina.

Heritage Room makes it possible for Aboriginal cadets to practise ceremonies, meet with elders, and discuss their culture. Cadet Dustin Ward, from the Micmac reserve in New Brunswick, finds the Heritage Room "one more sign that the RCMP welcomes First Nations Mounties. It shows the children hope that they can come here some day and be an RCMP cadet."

Saskatchewan-born Aboriginal Pauline Busch worked alongside the Commanding Officer's Aboriginal Advisory Committee at the academy for two years to get the Heritage Room established. She remembered the decision in the late 1980s to allow Aboriginal Mounties to wear their hair in braids, if they wanted. "There's nothing that warms a child's heart and pride as seeing another Aboriginal person in the red serge, fully outlined with the braids."

Tips for Managers

Managing an Increasingly Diverse Workforce

1. Make sure that managerial decision making conforms to the values of distributive and procedural justice.

2. Be careful that managers do not treat subordinates who are similar to them more favourably than those who are different.

3. Help managers to understand their stereotypes and why they are likely to be inaccurate.

4. Clearly communicate to subordinates your managerial commitment to effective diversity management.

5. Provide ongoing diversity training for subordinates.

Sexual Harassment

There have been several notable cases of sexual harassment in recent years. For instance, the Canadian Armed Forces was subject to intense media scrutiny during 1998 for alleged cover-ups of sexual harassment. Similarly, Sears Canada had a notorious incident in 1996 that led to the death of two employees in Chatham, Ontario. Theresa Vince, a human resources supervisor, was killed by her store manager, Russell Davis, who'd been sexually harassing her. Davis then killed himself. University campuses across Canada have seen a dramatic increase in the number of sexual harassment complaints, according to Paddy Stamp, sexual harassment officer at the University of Toronto.[76] Sexual harassment is apparently pervasive in the workplace: a survey conducted by York University in 1999 found that 48 percent of working Canadian women reported that they had experienced some form of sexual harassment in the previous year.

Although women are the most frequent victims of sexual harassment—particularly those in male-dominated occupations, or those who occupy positions stereotypically associated with certain gender relationships (such as a female secretary reporting to a male boss)—men can also be victims of sexual harassment. Several male employees at Jenny Craig in the United States said that they were subject to lewd and inappropriate comments from female co-workers and managers.[77] To date, there have been no media reports of women sexually harassing either men or women in Canada.

Sexual harassment seriously damages both the people who are harassed and the reputation of the organization in which it occurs. Sexual harassment is not only unethical; it is also illegal. Beyond the negative publicity, sexual harassment also can cost organizations large amounts of money. Managers have an ethical obligation to ensure that they, their co-workers, and their subordinates never engage in sexual harassment, even unintentionally.

sexual harassment
Unwelcome behaviour of a sexual nature in the workplace that negatively affects the work environment or leads to adverse job-related consequences for the employee.

The Supreme Court of Canada defines **sexual harassment** as unwelcome behaviour of a sexual nature in the workplace that negatively affects the work environment or leads to adverse job-related consequences for the employee. In 1987, the court ruled that employers will be held responsible for harassment by their employees. The court also said that the employers should promote a workplace that is free of it. The court recommended that employers have clear guidelines to prevent harassment, including procedures to investigate complaints.

Typically, sexual harassment complaints that are not resolved in the workplace are heard by a provincial or territorial human rights tribunal. However, in an effort to provide more venues for hearing sexual harassment complaints, the Ontario Labour Relations Board conceded in August 1997 that sexual harassment is a health and safety issue, and thus could be addressed by that board.[78] This may lead to other provinces making similar moves.

Forms of Sexual Harassment

There are two basic forms of sexual harassment: quid pro quo sexual harassment and hostile work environment sexual harassment. **Quid pro quo sexual harassment** occurs when a harasser asks or forces an employee to perform sexual favours to keep a job, receive a promotion, receive a raise, obtain some other work-related opportunity, or avoid receiving negative consequences such as demotion or dismissal.[79] This "Sleep with me, honey, or you're fired" form of harassment is the more extreme form of harassment and leaves no doubt in anyone's mind that sexual harassment has taken place.[80] A study connected by York University in 1999 found that only three percent of working Canadian women reported quid pro quo sexual harassment.[81]

quid pro quo sexual harassment Asking or forcing an employee to perform sexual favours in exchange for some reward or to avoid negative consequences.

hostile work environment sexual harassment Telling lewd jokes, displaying pornography, making sexually oriented remarks about someone's personal appearance, and other sex-related actions that make the work environment unpleasant.

Hostile work environment sexual harassment is more subtle. **Hostile work environment sexual harassment** occurs when organizational members are faced with an intimidating, hostile, or offensive work environment because of their sex.[82] Lewd jokes, sexually oriented comments, displays of pornography, displays or distribution of sexually oriented objects, and sexually oriented remarks about one's physical appearance are examples of hostile work environment sexual harassment. About 45 percent of working Canadian women reported this form of harassment in the recent study at York University. Barbara Orser, a researcher with the Conference Board of Canada, noted that "sexual harassment is more likely to occur in workplace environments that tolerate bullying, intimidation, yelling, innuendo and other forms of discourteous behaviour."[83]

A hostile work environment interferes with organizational members' ability to perform their jobs effectively and has been deemed illegal by the courts. Managers who engage in hostile work environment harassment or allow others to do so risk costly lawsuits for their organizations, as evidenced by the experience of Markham, ON-based Magna International Inc. A former saleswoman in the parts maker's Detroit sales office brought a sexual harassment case against the company, alleging that she faced harassment in the office.[84] She also alleged that her male co-workers regularly entertained customers at area strip clubs. That case is still under investigation, though auto industry executives and observers acknowledge that some purchasing executives for the auto makers are entertained at strip clubs.[85]

Steps Managers Can Take to Eradicate Sexual Harassment

Managers have an ethical obligation to eradicate sexual harassment in their organizations. There are many ways to accomplish this objective. Here are four initial steps that managers can take to deal with the problem.[86]

- *Develop and clearly communicate a sexual harassment policy endorsed by top management.* This policy should include prohibitions against both quid pro quo and hostile work environment sexual harassment. It should contain: (1) examples of types of behaviour that are unacceptable, (2) a procedure for employees to use to report instances of harassment, (3) a discussion of the disciplinary actions that will be taken when harassment has taken place, and (4) a commitment to educate and train organizational members about sexual harassment.

- *Use a fair complaint procedure to investigate charges of sexual harassment.* Such a procedure should: (1) be managed by a neutral third party, (2) ensure that complaints are dealt with promptly and thoroughly, (3) protect and fairly treat victims, and (4) ensure that alleged harassers are fairly treated.

- *When it has been determined that sexual harassment has taken place, take corrective actions as soon as possible.* These actions can vary depending on the severity of the harassment. When harassment is extensive, prolonged over a period of time, of a quid pro quo nature, or severely objectionable in some other manner, corrective action may include firing the harasser.

- *Provide sexual harassment education and training to organizational members, including managers.* Managers at DuPont, for example, developed DuPont's "A Matter of Respect" program to help educate employees about sexual harassment and eliminate its occurrence.

Barbara Orser, a researcher with the Conference Board of Canada, noted that most large Canadian organizations have harassment policies on paper. However, many lack a clear resolution process.

The Conference Board of Canada www.conferenceboard.ca/

Chapter Summary

ETHICS AND STAKEHOLDERS

- **Sources of an Organization's Code of Ethics**

- **What Behaviours Are Ethical?**

- **Why Would Managers Behave Unethically Toward Other Stakeholders?**

- **Promoting Ethics**

SOCIAL RESPONSIBILITY

• Approaches to Social Responsibility

• Why Be Socially Responsible?

MANAGING AN INCREASINGLY DIVERSE WORKFORCE

• The Ethical Imperative to Manage Diversity Effectively

• Effectively Managing Diversity Makes Good Legal Sense

• Effectively Managing Diversity Makes Good Business Sense

• Why Are Diverse Employees Sometimes Treated Unfairly?

HOW TO MANAGE DIVERSITY EFFECTIVELY

• Increasing Diversity Awareness

• Increasing Diversity Skills

• Techniques for Increasing Diversity Awareness and Skills

• The Importance of Top-Management Commitment to Diversity

SEXUAL HARASSMENT

• Forms of Sexual Harassment

• Steps Managers Can Take to Eradicate Sexual Harassment

Summary and Review

ETHICS AND STAKEHOLDERS   Ethics are moral principles or beliefs about what is right or wrong. These beliefs guide people in their dealings with other individuals and groups (stakeholders) and provide a basis for deciding whether behaviour is right and proper. Many organizations have a formal code of ethics derived primarily from societal ethics, professional ethics, and the individual ethics of the organization's top managers. Managers can apply ethical standards to help themselves decide on the proper way to behave toward organizational stakeholders.

SOCIAL RESPONSIBILITY   Social responsibility refers to a manager's duty to make decisions that nurture, protect, enhance, and promote the welfare and well-being of stakeholders and society as a whole. Managers generally take one of four approaches to the issue of socially responsible behaviour: obstructionist, defensive, accommodative, or proactive. Promoting ethical and socially responsible behaviour is a major managerial challenge.

MANAGING AN INCREASINGLY DIVERSE WORKFORCE   Diversity is differences among people due to age, gender, race, ethnicity, religion, sexual orientation, socioeconomic background, and capabilities/disabilities. Effectively managing diversity is an ethical imperative that makes good business sense. The effective management of diversity can be accomplished if top management is committed to principles of distributive and procedural justice, values diversity as a source of competitive advantage, and is willing to devote organizational resources to increasing employees' diversity awareness and diversity skills.

HOW TO MANAGE DIVERSITY EFFECTIVELY   Effectively managing diversity ought to be a top priority for managers in all organizations. Managers need to ensure that they and their subordinates appreciate the value that diversity brings to an organization, understand why diversity should be celebrated rather than ignored, and have the ability to interact and work effectively with men and women who are physically challenged or are of a diverse race, age, gender, ethnicity, nationality, or sexual orientation.

SEXUAL HARASSMENT   Two forms of sexual harassment are quid pro quo sexual harassment and hostile work environment sexual harassment. Steps that managers can take to eradicate sexual harassment include development and communication of a sexual harassment policy endorsed by top management, use of fair complaint procedures, prompt corrective action when harassment occurs, and sexual harassment training and education for organizational members.

Management in Action

Topics for Discussion and Action

1. Why is it important for people and organizations to behave ethically?

2. Ask a manager to describe an instance of ethical behaviour that she or he observed and an instance of unethical behaviour. What caused these behaviours, and what were the outcomes?

3. Search business magazines such as *Report on Business* or *Canadian Business* for an example of ethical or unethical behaviour, and use the material in this chapter to analyze it.

4. Which stakeholder group should managers be most concerned about when they decide on their approach to social responsibility? Why?

5. Discuss why violations of the principles of distributive and procedural justice continue to occur in modern organizations. What can managers do to uphold these principles in their organizations?

6. Discuss an occasion when you may have been treated unfairly because of stereotypical thinking. What stereotypes were applied to you? How did they result in your being unfairly treated?

7. Choose a National Post Business 500 company not mentioned in the chapter. Conduct library research to determine what steps this organization has taken to effectively manage diversity and eliminate sexual harassment.

Building Management Skills

Solving Diversity-Related Problems

Think about the last time that you (1) were treated unfairly because you differed from a decision maker on a particular dimension of diversity or (2) observed someone else being treated unfairly because that person differed from a decision maker on a particular dimension of diversity. Then answer these questions.

1. Why do you think the decision maker acted unfairly in this situation?

2. In what ways, if any, were biases, stereotypes, or overt discrimination involved in this situation?

3. Was the decision maker aware that he or she was acting unfairly?

4. What could you or the person who was treated unfairly have done to improve matters and rectify the injustice on the spot?

5. Was any sexual harassment involved in this situation? If so, what kind was it?

6. If you had authority over the decision maker (for example, if you were his or her manager or supervisor), what steps would you take to ensure that the decision maker no longer treated diverse individuals unfairly?

Small Group Breakout Exercise

What Is Ethical Behaviour?

Form groups of three to five people, and appoint one group member as the spokesperson who will communicate your findings to the class when called on by the instructor. Then discuss the following scenario.

You are the managers of the functions of a large hospital, and you have been charged with the responsibility to develop a code of ethics to guide the members of your organization in their dealings with stakeholders. To guide you in creating the ethical code, do the following.

1. Discuss the various kinds of ethical dilemmas that hospital employees—doctors, nurses, pharmacists—may encounter in their dealings with stakeholders such as patients or suppliers.

2. Identify a specific behaviour that the 3 kinds of hospital employees mentioned in Item 1 might exhibit, and characterize the behaviour as ethical or unethical.

3. Based on this discussion, identify 3 standards or values that you will incorporate into your personal ethical code to help yourself determine whether a behaviour is ethical or unethical.

Exploring the World Wide Web

Specific Assignment

This exercise looks at how Procter & Gamble Canada describes its stance on workplace diversity. Explore Procter & Gamble's Web site (www.pg.com/canada) and, in particular, look under the section "Working at Procter & Gamble" to find the company's statement on diversity, and some words of wisdom. Also look under the section "Introduction to Procter & Gamble" located on the home page and follow the links to find out about the company's purpose, values and principles.

1. In what ways does Procter & Gamble show its support for a diverse workforce?

2. To what extent do you think the company's policies on diversity contribute to supporting Procter & Gamble's purpose, values, and principles?

General Assignment

Search for a company Web site that has an explicit statement of the company's approach to workplace diversity. What is its approach, and how does this approach support the company's main goals?

ManagementCase

Mentoring Diverse Employees Pays Off

Many successful managers today have had the help of a mentor at some point in their careers. A mentor is an experienced member of an organization who provides advice, guidance, and potential opportunities to a less-experienced member (the mentee) and helps the mentee learn the ropes and how to advance up the corporate ladder. Diverse employees often have a hard time finding mentors because experienced organizational members are different from them. For instance, research studies indicate that managers are more likely to mentor people who are similar to them rather than those who are different.[87] The similar-to-me effect helps explain this phenomenon because it can lead managers and employees to perceive those who are similar to themselves more positively than they perceive those who are different.

When individuals do mentor employees different from themselves, however, both the mentee and the mentor stand to benefit. Take the case of GE Plastics executive Jay Pomeroy and Gen-Xer Amelia Burkhart. Burkhart, global manager of e-plastics.com, GE Plastics' online division brought Pomeroy up to speed on the Internet, and even showed him how to conduct a virtual meeting. Their relationship was a form of reverse mentoring, with a younger techie teaching a senior executive how to become more computer savvy. At the same time, the younger employee gets mentoring from the senior employee. Burkhart, for instance, says that Pomeroy gave her tips on managing her career, shared knowledge of the company, and became a close contact she can consult when issues come up.

Another example of diverse mentoring is Wesley von Shack, chief executive of DQE Corporation, a small, conservative Pittsburgh utility managed predominantly by white men, and Diana Green, a former vice-president of Xerox Corporation and an African American. Von Shack recruited Green to DQE almost 10 years ago to manage DQE's human resources department. They seemed to have a similar approach to managing, and they had certain values in common (such as frankness, loyalty, devotion to career, and commitment to community service). He thought, too, that she would be able to help him make DQE more innovative and attractive to talented prospective employees and customers. In short, von Shack believed that Green could make a substantial contribution to his organization. Nevertheless, he realized the obstacles she might face in an organization in which (when she first joined the company) white men held practically all middle- and upper-management positions. How would first-line managers who had never reported to any woman feel about reporting to an African American woman?

Von Shack took an active role in mentoring Green so that she would have the opportunity to help his company change, improve, and gain a competitive advantage. He made sure that she had an understanding of DQE's conservative corporate culture when she first started out. Von Shack took great pains to make sure that employees at DQE realized the contributions that Green was making to the company. He and his family even attended community affairs that Green was involved with to show his support of and admiration for her. He praised her capabilities to top managers outside DQE and thereby helped her gain positions on the boards of directors of other companies.

Von Shack was not content to keep Green in charge of human resources (a department that in many companies turns out to be limbo for many female and minority managers). He believed that she could make a more wide-ranging contribution to the organization, and he gave her the opportunities to do so. She now manages purchasing, transportation, customer service, real estate, materials management, and public affairs for DQE. Green is one of DQE's four top managers, and von Shack remains impressed with her ability to meet the challenges he presents her.

While von Shack's mentoring has helped Green advance to her current top-management position, it also has helped von Shack run his company. In Green, he has a valuable top manager on whom he often tests out his ideas because he knows she will give him an honest reaction.

Deloitte & Touche Canada uses mentoring as a way to keep talented people, and help them move into leadership roles. Carol Paradine, a partner in Deloitte & Touche's Ottawa office, is mentored by Don Craig, who is on the board of directors and a managing partner for southwest Ontario. They talk every three months, usually in a face-to-face two-hour meeting. Paradine finds that the mentoring program gives her access to top management. Craig provides guidance on a variety of issues: "Sometimes there are challenges I'm facing and I tell him how I plan to approach them and ask his opinion."[88]

Questions

1. Why are top and middle managers often reluctant to mentor diverse lower-level managers and nonmanagers, even when such mentoring relationships can have tremendous payoffs?

2. What steps can managers take to mentor diverse organizational members?

3. What steps can a top manager take to encourage other top and middle managers to mentor diverse organizational members?

ManagementCase

In the News

From the Pages of *Canadian Business*
Stuff Your Gold Watch

In many cultures, the elderly are respected, even revered, by younger generations. Senior citizens are trusted advisers, admired for their wisdom. Sir Winston Churchill was 66 when he first became prime minister of Britain in 1940 and 81 when he retired. South Africans elected 76-year-old Nelson Mandela as president in 1994.

Our very own prime minister is old enough to have been collecting old age pension cheques at 24 Sussex for a couple of years now, and senior citizen CEOs run some of the country's most powerful corporations: Ken Thomson is 76; Jimmy Pattison is 71; Izzy Asper is 67. I guess owning the joint helps, because what do the rest of us schmoes get for our 65th birthdays? Not reverence, that's for sure—more like a swift kick in the ass as we carry the vestiges of our working lives out the door.

It's really quite shocking that, in a time when human rights laws protect child pornography buffs, it hasn't occurred to lawmakers that mandatory retirement is a blatant display of discrimination. Of course some professions, such as law enforcement and the military, necessarily retire their employees at a younger age. But time and time again, the Supreme Court of Canada has ruled in favor of forced retirement. (An interesting sidenote: the mandatory retirement age for Supreme Court justices is 75, not 65.)

Not all the top judges have agreed, however, that mental competence, adaptability and energy magically disappear once you hit the arbitrary age of 65. Madame Justice Claire L'Heureux-Dubé, herself 73, wrote about the case of a Vancouver doctor who was forced to resign his hospital post: "One is no less competent the day after one's 65th birthday, than the day before. Fundamentally it is a question of personal dignity and fairness."

Not all the provinces are guilty. In Quebec and Manitoba, employers have to come up with rationale other than age for giving employees their pink slips. In the US, it's illegal to force anyone into retirement as long as they are willing and able to work. But the Ontario Human Rights Commission (OHRC), perhaps prompted by the United Nations' declaration of 1999 as the International Year of Older Persons, only recently decided to launch a public policy review into age discrimination. "Aging," notes an OHRC discussion paper released this past July, "is something that all individuals who do not die prematurely will eventually experience."

And with premature deaths at an all-time low—senior citizens now account for 12% of Canada's population and by 2030 will make up 23%— mandatory retirement is bound to be a big-ticket issue. Ontario's provincewide public consultations will be held in November, and you can bet a fair number of its 1.5 million seniors will descend on the hearings, along with more than a few aging boomers indignant—and terrified—at the thought of being unceremoniously given the boot in a few years.

And rightly so. While more and more people are retiring to lives of leisure in their 50s, many don't have enough savings or large enough pensions to allow them to quit at 65. Others simply don't relish the thought of 15 or 20 years of arts and crafts or helping kiddies cross the street at lunchtime.

There are, of course, a couple of valid arguments in favor of mandatory retirement. A favorite of youngsters everywhere is that forced retirement makes way for a whole new generation to move up the ranks. Don't pull out the knitting needles just yet, though: according to a study conducted by the Canada Pension Plan, people are far more likely to die in their first year of retirement than in subsequent years. But with a full 41 working years stretching ahead of me, I'm willing to take my chances. Any seniors out there willing to swap their CPP cheques for an exciting new career in journalism, give me a call.

Dawn Calleja is a staff writer with *Canadian Business*.

Source: D. Calleja, "Stuff Your Gold Watch: Why Hasn't it Occurred to Canadian Lawmakers That Forced Retirement is Blatant Discrimination?" *Canadian Business*, October 16, 2000, p. 131.

Questions

1. How are different stakeholder groups affected by mandatory retirement policies?

2. What kinds of ethical issues does mandatory retirement raise?

Part 3

**MANAGING
DECISION
MAKING AND
PLANNING**

Chapter 6
The Manager as a
Decision Maker

Chapter 7
The Manager as a
Planner and Strategist

Chapter six

The Manager as a Decision Maker

Learning Objectives

1. Differentiate between programmed and nonprogrammed decisions, and explain why nonprogrammed decision making is a complex, uncertain process.

2. Describe the six steps that managers should take to make the best decisions.

3. Explain how cognitive biases can affect decision making and lead managers to make poor decisions.

4. Identify the advantages and disadvantages of group decision making, and describe techniques that can improve it.

5. Explain the role that organizational learning and creativity play in helping managers to improve their decisions.

6. Differentiate between data and information, and list the attributes of useful information.

7. Describe three reasons why managers must have access to information to perform their tasks and roles effectively.

A Case in Contrast

A Tale of Two Decisions at Calling Systems International

August 14, 2000, 9:30 a.m.: Sharon Eastman glances one last time at her presentation slides. "This new product proposal looks unbeatable," she thinks. "I've covered every base and looked at the issue from every angle. I know the technology; I can handle any question that Redland throws at me. He has to approve this."

Sharon Eastman is the marketing manager at Calling Systems International (CSI), a 350-employee, Halifax-based company that makes computer-controlled telephone calling and answering equipment. CSI was the creation of Alan Redland, an energetic man with a domineering personality and seemingly unlimited faith in his own vision. Redland had founded CSI five years earlier. Already the company had made the *Profit* magazine list of the 100 fastest-growing small companies in Canada. Sharon was hired 12 months ago as a newly minted MBA. Prior to getting her MBA, she had worked as a computer systems engineer for IBM.

Sharon's responsibilities as marketing manager at CSI include looking for new product

Finding the right way to frame your arguments is an important part of the process of convincing others to take your ideas seriously and support your position. Managing the perceptions of individuals and groups is an important part of the decision-making process.

opportunities. She has found what she thinks is a gem. Three months earlier, Sharon was visiting the credit collection department of a large bank to which CSI was trying to sell its equipment. The staff of this department tries to collect bad debts from delinquent loan customers over the phone. Sharon noticed that many of the employees spend an enormous amount of time dialing phone numbers, getting busy signals, or getting no answer at all. Little of their time is spent actually talking to delinquent customers.

"Wow," thought Sharon. "It should be possible to predict how often a telephone operator gets no answer, or a busy signal. We could also find out how long, on average, an operator talks to someone over the phone. We could write a computer program that takes this into account. This program could be used to control an automated dialing system. We could use a mathematical algorithm to predict when an operator will come free and how much time will be needed to get a 'live' person on the other end of the phone line. The dialing system, let's call it a predictive dialing system, would then know when to dial in order to match up a free telephone operator with a 'live' person. The result? Telephone operators would waste no time dialing, listening to busy signals, or getting no answer. Brilliant!"

Over the past three months, Sharon had worked on the idea with two engineers at CSI. She concluded that the idea not only was technically feasible, but could be a commercial gold mine. Now she had to present her new product proposal to CSI's executive committee, which is composed of Redland and three other senior managers. They could OK the idea or kill it.

August 14, 2000, 11:00 a.m.: An angry and dejected Sharon bursts through her office and flings her presentation slides against the opposite wall. Her office mate, Ron, looks up and raises an eyebrow. "I gather things didn't go too well then?"

"It was awful, a complete disaster. Redland has just come back from some seminar at the University of Alberta on the information superhighway. He has decided that the company has to become involved in that area. He thinks he has seen the future, and we should be part of it. He wouldn't even let me explain my idea. He just kept asking me, 'How does this fit with our information superhighway strategy?' What information superhighway strategy? I didn't know we had one!"

"Didn't any of the other executive committee members speak up on your behalf?" asks Ron. "I know that Mike Kidder and John Matsuka were excited by the idea. They told me so."

"They just hung on every word Redland said and nodded in agreement," replies Sharon.

March 12, 2001, 9:30 a.m.: Sharon sits waiting for the summons from the executive team. "Here we go again, Predictive Dialing Systems Proposal Mark II," thinks Sharon. "It should be different this time."

Sharon's faith was not ill placed. Two months earlier, CSI had been taken over by a large telecommunications company. Redland and the rest of the executive team had left and been replaced by a team of managers from the acquiring company.

March 12, 2001, 3:30 p.m.: An exhausted-looking Sharon stumbles into her office and slumps into her chair. "Where on earth have you been?" asks Ron.

"With the new executive team," replies Sharon. "They have been quizzing me for hours about the project. We didn't stop for lunch. They wanted to know absolutely everything. How big was the potential market? How much would the predictive dialing system sell for? What were my data sources? What were my assumptions? They challenged every single assumption I made! How did I know that this was technically feasible? How long would it take to get a predictive dialing system to market? And on and on and on!"

"And?" asks Ron.

Sharon takes a deep breath, "And, they liked the idea, but not enough to give me the go-ahead yet. They want some specific information on various topics. But they said that if things do check out, they will invest in the project. And if they do, I get to head it!"[1] •

Overview

The "Case in Contrast" describes how two different management teams approached the same decision—namely, whether to pursue Sharon Eastman's new product idea. The first team dismissed Eastman's proposal without exploring it because it was not the brainchild of Alan Redland, the company's domineering CEO. The second management team not only listened to Sharon Eastman but bombarded her with questions, vigorously challenging the assumptions behind her proposal to determine its validity.

The purpose of this chapter is to examine how managers make decisions, and to explore how individual, group, and organizational factors affect the quality of the decisions they make and thus determine organizational performance. We discuss the nature of managerial decision making and examine some models of the decision-making process that help reveal the complexities of successful decision making. Then we outline the main steps of the decision-making process; in addition, we explore the biases that may cause capable managers to make poor decisions both as individuals and as members of a group. Finally, we examine how managers can promote organizational learning and creativity and improve the quality of their decision making. By the end of this chapter, you will understand the crucial role decision making plays in creating a high-performing organization. •

decision making

The process by which managers respond to opportunities and threats by analyzing options and making determinations about specific organizational goals and courses of action.

The Nature of Managerial Decision Making

Every time a manager acts to plan, organize, direct, or control organizational activities, he or she makes a stream of decisions. In opening a new restaurant, for example, managers have to decide where to locate it, what kinds of food to provide to customers, what kinds of people to employ, and so on. In Chapter 1, where we considered Mintzberg's managerial roles, we described four decision-making roles managers have. We also noted in Chapter 1 the importance of managers having conceptual skills. Decision making is a basic part of every task in which a manager is involved, and in this chapter we study how decisions are made.

As we discussed in the previous three chapters, one of the main tasks facing a manager is to manage the organizational environment. Forces in the external environment give rise to many opportunities and threats for managers and their organizations. In addition, inside an organization managers must address many opportunities and threats that may arise during the course of utilizing organizational resources. To deal with these opportunities and threats, managers must make decisions—that is, they must select one solution from a set of alternatives. **Decision making** is the process by which managers analyze the options facing them and make determinations, or decisions, about specific organizational goals and courses of action. A good decision results in the selection of appropriate goals and courses of action that increase organizational performance; bad decisions result in lower performance.

When Belinda Stronach took over as CEO of Magna International in February 2001, one of her first major decisions was to realign the company along four product lines: Magna Steyr Tesma, InTier, Decoma and Cosma. This structure will give each management team greater flexibility and autonomy in making decisions. Stronach's father, Frank Stronach (shown with her here), founded the company.

Microsoft
www.microsoft.com/

Magna International
www.magnaint.com/

Managers are always searching for ways to improve their decision making in order to improve organizational performance. At the same time, they do their best to make sure that they make no costly mistakes that will hurt organizational performance. Examples of spectacularly good decisions include two made by Bill Gates and Frank Stronach. Bill Gates decided to buy a computer operating system for $78 000 from a small company in Seattle and sell it to IBM for the new IBM personal computer—a decision that resulted in Gates and Microsoft becoming the richest man and richest software company, respectively, in the United States. Frank Stronach decided to move to Canada from Austria in 1954 with $200 in his pocket, and started Multimatic Investments Ltd., a small automotive tool-and-die shop, just two years later in the east end of Toronto. Today, that shop is Toronto-based Magna International, an auto-parts giant that employs 28 000 workers and has annual sales in excess of $6 billion. In 1998, Stronach was paid $26.5 million for running Magna.

Examples of spectacularly bad decisions include: the decision by managers at NASA and Morton Thiokol to launch the *Challenger* space shuttle—a decision that resulted in the deaths of six astronauts in 1986; the decision of the Canadian Red Cross in 1986 that testing for non-A, non-B hepatitis would prevent only a small number of cases and cost too much money (up to $20 million in the first year), a decision which eventually cost taxpayers $1.5 billion in compensation to Hepatitis C victims; and the 1994 decision of former BC Premier Glen Clark to create the fast-ferry project which cost BC taxpayers more than $500 million to build three ferries that in the end were not suitable in BC's waters. Buyers for the ferries still have not been found.

Programmed and Nonprogrammed Decision Making

Regardless of the specific decision that a manager is responsible for, the decision-making process is either programmed or nonprogrammed.[2]

programmed decision making Routine, virtually automatic decision making that follows established rules or guidelines.

PROGRAMMED DECISION MAKING   **Programmed decision making** is a routine, virtually automatic process. Programmed decisions are decisions that have been made so many times in the past that managers have been able to develop rules or guidelines to be applied when certain situations inevitably occur. Programmed decision making takes place for much of the day-to-day running of an organization, such as: when a school principal asks the school board to hire a new teacher whenever student enrollment increases by 40 students; when a manufacturing supervisor hires new workers whenever existing workers' overtime increases by more than 10 percent; and when an office manager orders basic office supplies, such as paper and pens, whenever the inventory of supplies on hand drops below a certain level. Furthermore, in the last example, the office manager probably orders the same amount of supplies each time. This decision making is called programmed because the office manager, for example, does not need to make judgments continually about what should be done. He or she can rely on long-established decision rules such as these:

- *Rule 1:* When the storage shelves are three-quarters empty, order more copy paper.
- *Rule 2:* When ordering paper, order enough to fill the shelves.

Managers can develop rules and guidelines to regulate all kinds of routine organizational activities. Programmed decision making is possible when managers have the information they need to create rules that will guide decision making. There is little ambiguity to overcome when assessing whether the stockroom is empty or when counting the number of new students in class.

nonprogrammed decision making
Nonroutine decision making that occurs in response to unusual, unpredictable opportunities and threats.

NONPROGRAMMED DECISION MAKING **Nonprogrammed decision making** occurs when there are no ready-made decision rules that managers can apply to a situation. Why are there no rules? The situation is unexpected, and managers lack the information they would need to develop rules to cover it. Examples of nonprogrammed decision making include decisions to invest in a new kind of technology, to develop a new kind of product, to launch a new promotional campaign, to enter a new market, or to expand internationally.

How do managers make decisions in the absence of decision rules? First they must search for information about alternative courses of action; then they must rely on intuition and judgment to choose wisely among alternatives. **Intuition** is a person's ability to make sound decisions based on past experience and immediate feelings about the information at hand. **Judgment** is a person's ability to develop a sound opinion because of the way he or she evaluates the importance of the information available in a particular context. "Exercising" one's judgment is a more rational process than "going with" one's intuition. For reasons that we examine later in this chapter, both intuition and judgment are often flawed and can result in poor decision making. Thus, the likelihood of error is much greater in *nonprogrammed* decision making than in programmed decision making.[3] In the remainder of this chapter, when we talk about decision making, we are referring to nonprogrammed decision making because it is the type of decision making that causes the most problems for managers.

intuition Ability to make sound decisions based on one's past experience and immediate feelings about the information at hand.

judgment Ability to develop a sound opinion based on one's evaluation of the importance of the information at hand.

The classical and the administrative decision-making models reveal many of the assumptions, complexities, and pitfalls that affect decision making. These models help reveal the factors that managers and other decision makers must be aware of in order to improve the quality of their decision making. It is important to remember that the classical and administrative models are just that—guides that can help managers understand the decision-making process. In real life, the process is typically not cut-and-dried; these models can help guide a manager through it, however.

The Classical Model

classical decision-making model A prescriptive approach to decision making based on the assumption that the decision maker can identify and evaluate all possible alternatives and their consequences and rationally choose the most appropriate course of action.

One of the earliest models of decision making, the **classical model**, is *prescriptive*, which means that it specifies how decisions *should* be made. Managers using the classical model make a series of simplifying assumptions about the nature of the decision-making process (see Figure 6.1). The premise of the classical model is that once managers recognize the need to make a decision, they should be able to generate a complete list of *all* alternatives and consequences, from which they then can make the best choice. In other words, the classical model assumes that managers have access to *all* the information they need to make the **optimum decision**, which is the most appropriate decision possible in light of what they believe to be the most desirable future consequences for their organization. Furthermore, the classical model assumes that managers can easily list their own preferences for each alternative and rank them from least to most preferred in order to make the optimum decision.

optimum decision The most appropriate decision in light of what managers believe to be the most desirable future consequences for their organization.

The Administrative Model

administrative model An approach to decision making that explains why decision making is inherently uncertain and risky and why managers usually make satisficing rather than optimum decisions.

James March and Herbert Simon disagreed with the underlying assumptions of the classical model of decision making. In contrast, they proposed that managers in the real world do not have access to all the information they need to make a decision. Moreover, they pointed out that even if all information were readily available, many managers would lack the mental or psychological ability to absorb and evaluate it correctly. As a result, March and Simon developed the **administrative model** of decision making to explain why decision making is

Figure 6.1
The Classical Model of Decision Making

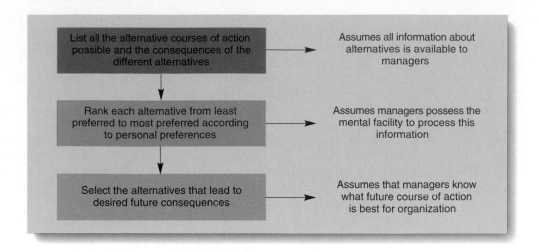

always an inherently uncertain and risky process—and why managers can rarely make decisions in the manner prescribed by the classical model. The administrative model is based on three important concepts: *bounded rationality*, *incomplete information*, and *satisficing*.

BOUNDED RATIONALITY   March and Simon pointed out that human decision-making capabilities are bounded by people's limitations in their ability to interpret, process, and act on information.[4] These limitations constrain the ability of decision makers to determine the optimum decision. **Bounded rationality** thus describes the situation in which the number of alternatives and the amount of information are so great that it is difficult for the manager to evaluate it all before making a decision.[5]

INCOMPLETE INFORMATION   Even if managers did have an unlimited ability to evaluate information, they still would not be able to arrive at the optimum decision because they would have incomplete information. Information is incomplete because the full range of decision-making alternatives is unknowable in most situations, and the consequences associated with known alternatives are uncertain.[6] In other words, information is incomplete because of risk and uncertainty, ambiguity, and time constraints (see Figure 6.2).

Risk is the degree of probability a manager assigns to a particular course of action. Under **uncertainty**, however, the probabilities of alternative outcomes cannot be determined, and future outcomes are *unknown*: Managers are working blind, the probability of a given outcome occurring is *not* known, and managers have little information to use in making a decision.

A second reason why information is incomplete is that much of the information that managers have at their disposal is **ambiguous information**. Its meaning is not clear—it can be interpreted in multiple and often conflicting ways.[7] Take a look at Figure 6.3. Do you see a young woman or an old woman? In a similar fashion, different managers often interpret the same piece of information differently and make different decisions based on their own interpretations.

The third reason why information is incomplete is that managers have neither the time nor the money to search for all possible alternative solutions and evaluate all the potential consequences of those alternatives. Consider the situation confronting a purchasing manager at Ford Motor Company who has one month

bounded rationality
Cognitive limitations that constrain one's ability to interpret, process, and act on information.

risk The degree of probability that the possible outcomes of a particular course of action will occur.

uncertainty
Unpredictability.

ambiguous information
Information that can be interpreted in multiple and often conflicting ways.

Figure 6.2
Why Information Is Incomplete

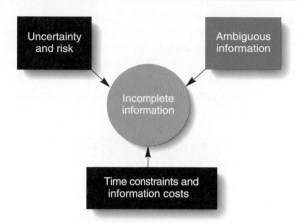

to choose a supplier for a small engine part. There are thousands of potential suppliers for this part. There is simply no way for the purchasing manager to contact all potential suppliers and ask each for its terms. Even if the time were available, the costs of obtaining the information, including the manager's own time, would be prohibitive.

SATISFICING   Faced with bounded rationality, an uncertain future, unquantifiable risks, considerable ambiguity, time constraints, and high information costs, March and Simon argue, managers do not attempt to discover every alternative. Rather, they use a strategy known as **satisficing**, exploring a limited sample of all potential alternatives.[8] When managers satisfice, they search for and choose acceptable, or satisfactory, ways to respond to problems and opportunities, rather than trying to make the optimum decision.[9] In the case of the Ford purchasing manager, limited search involves asking a limited number of suppliers for their

satisficing Searching for and choosing an acceptable, or satisfactory, response to problems and opportunities, rather than trying to make the best decision.

Figure 6.3
Ambiguous Information: Young Woman or Old Woman?

terms, trusting that they are representative of suppliers in general, and making a choice from that set. Although this course of action is reasonable from the perspective of the purchasing manager, it may mean that a potentially superior supplier is overlooked.

March and Simon pointed out that managerial decision making is often more art than science. In the real world, managers must rely on their intuition and judgment to make what seems to them to be the best decision in the face of uncertainty and ambiguity.[10] Consider, for example, the crucial decisions that Bill Jemas, a vice-president of entertainment and business development at Fleet Corporation, a leading trading-card company, has to make.

Management Insight

Marketing Beavis and Butt-Head Trading Cards

As usual, Bill Jemas is under pressure. He must quickly make several crucial decisions about the marketing strategy for a new line of Beavis and Butt-Head trading cards to be launched by the Fleet Corporation (Beavis and Butt-Head are cartoon characters from a popular MTV show). At 10:00 a.m., two other managers, Lisa Weiner and Donna Johnson (production manager and assistant production manager respectively), enter Jemas's office to discuss the launch strategy. The trio begins a serious discussion about the cards' design and where the Fleet logo will appear. While two possible designs are being considered, the question of how to set the retail price for the cards is raised. The trio quickly arrives at a decision. Beavis and Butt-Head are extremely popular characters, they reason, so the cards should command a premium price—$2.75 per pack.[11] After agreeing on the price, they return to the design issue. By 10:15 a.m., it too has been settled.

Jemas and the others then turn their attention to advertising. A six-figure advertising budget has already been assigned to the project, and the trio has to decide where to spend the money. The target market group is primarily teenage boys, and the trio quickly decides to place advertisements in publications that serve this audience, including *Tough Stuff* and *Metal Edge.* Then a more involved discussion takes place about whether to advertise in *Rolling Stone* magazine, which covered Beavis and Butt-Head in a 1993 issue. *Rolling Stone* is considered an expensive alternative for the company, but the trio is leaning toward advertising with the magazine, particularly since the cards will be sold in record stores. "I heard that they [referring to the Beavis and Butt-Head cover issue] were *Rolling Stone*'s top-selling issue last year," offers Lisa. Jemas likes the idea, but a final decision will have to wait a day or two. A larger advertising budget may be required.

It's now 10:30 a.m. and representatives from Daniel Edelman Inc., a New York public relations firm, enter the office. The conversation turns to the PR campaign that Edelman has planned for the Beavis and Butt-Head line. A decision has to be made about sampling (sampling involves sending out samples of the line—in this case to magazine writers). The group debates the pros and cons of sampling. "I think people just like to get stuff," says Jemas. It's agreed—a pack of cards will be sent to writers at all relevant magazines. At 11:50 a.m. the meeting ends with a swift discussion of Edelman's bill. Time for lunch.

Two things may surprise you about the previous example. First, the managers made a number of critical decisions very quickly. Two decisions, one about pricing and one about design, were made in 15 minutes. The pricing decision appeared to be almost an afterthought. A third decision, about advertising media, was made in the next 15 minutes. The final decision, about sampling, took longer to make, partly because the Edelman people required time to present examples of their work. Nevertheless, four crucial decisions were made in under two hours.

The second fact that stands out is that for each of their decisions, these managers were clearly satisficing. Knowing they had incomplete information, they did not try to discover all possible solutions and get involved in a detailed analysis of the pros and cons of different alternatives. Instead, they relied on their experience in this business and used their judgment to satisfice and reach an acceptable decision on crucial issues.

The Beavis and Butt-Head example illustrates that managerial decision making is often fast paced, as managers use their experience and judgment to make crucial decisions under conditions of incomplete information. Although there is nothing wrong with this approach, decision makers should be aware that human judgment is often flawed. As a result, even the best managers sometimes make poor decisions.[12] Later in this chapter, we discuss cognitive and other factors that tend to skew decision making.

Steps in the Decision-Making Process

What is the process for making a decision?

Using the work of March and Simon as a basis, researchers have developed a step-by-step model of the decision-making process and the issues and problems that managers confront at each step. There are six steps that managers should consciously follow to make a good decision (see Figure 6.4).[13] We review them in the remainder of this section.

Recognize the Need for a Decision

The first step in the decision-making process is to recognize the need for a decision. Some stimuli usually spark the realization that there is a need to make a decision. These stimuli often become apparent because changes in the organizational environment result in new kinds of opportunities and threats.

Figure 6.4

Six Steps in Decision Making

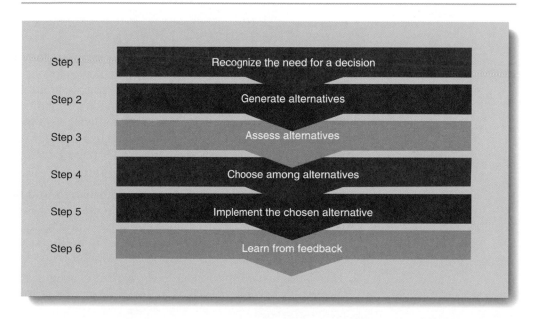

Step 1 Recognize the need for a decision

Step 2 Generate alternatives

Step 3 Assess alternatives

Step 4 Choose among alternatives

Step 5 Implement the chosen alternative

Step 6 Learn from feedback

The stimuli that spark decision making are as likely to result from the actions of managers inside an organization as they are from changes in the external environment.[14] An organization possesses a set of skills, competencies, and resources in its employees and in departments such as marketing, manufacturing, and research and development. Managers who actively pursue opportunities to use these competencies create the need to make decisions. For example, Sharon Eastman, described in the "Case in Contrast," was on the lookout to find an opportunity to use Calling Systems International's competency to develop a new kind of telephone answering system, and she forced the company's managers to recognize that they needed to make a decision. Managers thus can be reactive or proactive in recognizing the need to make a decision, but the important issue is that they must recognize this need and respond in a timely and appropriate way.[15] Once the decision maker recognizes the need to make a decision, the person will need to diagnose the issue or problem, in order to determine the underlying factors that accompany the problem.

Generate Alternatives

Having recognized the need to make a decision, a manager must generate a set of feasible alternative courses of action to take in response to the opportunity or threat. Management experts cite failure to properly generate and consider different alternatives as one reason why managers sometimes make bad decisions.[16]

One major problem is that managers may find it difficult to come up with creative alternative solutions to specific problems. Perhaps some of them are used to seeing the world from a single perspective—they have a certain "managerial mindset." Many managers find it difficult to view problems from a fresh perspective. According to best-selling management author Peter Senge, we all are trapped within our personal mental models of the world—our ideas about what is important and how the world works.[17] Generating creative alternatives to solve problems and take advantage of opportunities may require that we abandon our existing mindsets and develop new ones—something that usually is difficult to do.

The importance of getting managers to set aside their mental models of the world and generate creative alternatives is reflected in the growth of interest in the work of authors such as Peter Senge and Edward de Bono, who have popularized techniques for stimulating problem solving and creative thinking among managers.[18] Later in this chapter, we discuss the important issues of organizational learning and creativity in detail.

Assess Alternatives

Once managers have generated a set of alternatives, they must evaluate the advantages and disadvantages of each one.[19] The key to a good assessment of the alternatives is to define the opportunity or threat exactly and then specify the criteria that *should* influence the selection of alternatives for responding to the problem or opportunity. One reason for bad decisions is that managers often fail to specify the criteria that are important in reaching a decision.[20] In general, successful managers use four criteria to evaluate the pros and cons of alternative courses of action (see Figure 6.5):

1. *Practicality:* Managers must decide whether they have the capabilities and resources required to implement the alternative, and they must be sure that the alternative will not threaten the attainment of other organizational goals. At first glance, an alternative might seem to be economically superior to other alternatives, but if managers realize that it is likely to threaten other important projects, they might decide that it is not practical after all.

2. *Economic feasibility:* Managers must decide whether the alternatives are economically feasible—that is, whether they can be accomplished, given the orga-

Figure 6.5
General Criteria for Evaluating Possible Courses of Action

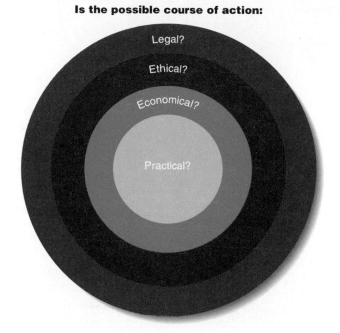

Is the possible course of action:

nization's performance goals. Typically, managers perform a cost–benefit analysis of the various alternatives to determine which one is likely to have the best net financial payoff.

3. *Ethicalness:* Managers must ensure that a possible course of action is ethical and that it will not unnecessarily harm any stakeholder group. Many of the decisions that managers make may help some organizational stakeholders and harm others (see Chapter 5). When examining alternative courses of action, managers need to be very clear about the potential effects of their decisions.

4. *Legality:* Managers must ensure that a possible course of action is legal and that they will not be in violation of any domestic and international laws or government regulations.

Very often, a manager must consider these four criteria simultaneously. Some of the worst managerial decisions can be traced to poor assessment of the alternatives. Selecting the right set of criteria by which to assess alternatives is never easy. Often it becomes necessary to collect additional information in order to make a satisfactory evaluation.

Choose Among Alternatives

Once the set of alternative solutions has been carefully evaluated, the next task is to rank the various alternatives (using the criteria discussed in the previous section) and make a decision. When ranking alternatives, managers must be sure that all of the available information is brought to bear on the problem or issue at hand. Identifying all *relevant* information for a decision does not mean that the manager has *complete* information, however; in most instances, information is incomplete.

Perhaps more serious than the existence of incomplete information is the often-documented tendency of managers to ignore critical information even when it is available. We discuss this tendency in detail when we examine the operation of cognitive biases and groupthink.

The disastrous launch of the Challenger space shuttle illustrates the importance of bringing all available information to bear on the decision-making process and making sure the alternative courses of action are evaluated using all relevant criteria.

Implement the Chosen Alternative

Once a decision has been made and an alternative has been selected, the alternative must be implemented and many subsequent and related decisions must be made. Once a course of action has been decided (for example, to develop a new line of women's clothing), thousands of subsequent decisions are necessary to implement it (such as decisions to recruit dress designers, obtain fabrics, find high-quality manufacturers, and sign contracts with clothing stores to sell the new line).

Although the need to make subsequent decisions to implement the chosen course of action may seem obvious, many managers make a decision and then fail to act on it. This is the same as not making a decision at all. To ensure that a decision is implemented, top managers must assign to middle managers the responsibility for making the follow-up decisions necessary to achieve the goal. They must give middle managers sufficient resources to achieve the goal, and they must hold the middle managers accountable for their performance. If the middle managers are successful at implementing the decision, they should be rewarded; if they fail, they should be subject to sanctions.

Learn from Feedback

The final step in the decision-making process is learning from feedback. Effective managers always conduct a retrospective analysis to see what they can learn from past successes or failures. Managers who do not evaluate the results of their decisions do not learn from experience; instead, they stagnate and are likely to make the same mistakes again and again.[21] To avoid this problem, managers must establish a formal procedure with which they can learn from the results of past decisions. The procedure should include these steps:

1. Compare what actually happened to what was expected to happen as a result of the decision.

2. Explore why any expectations for the decision were not met.

3. Develop guidelines that will help in future decision making.

Individuals who always strive to learn from past mistakes and successes are likely to continuously improve the decisions they make.

Tips for Managers

Managing the Decision-Making Process

1.   Recognize that it is impossible for managers to make the optimum decision and orient their actions to making the best decision possible.

2.   To make the best decision possible, learn to use intuition and judgment to uncover acceptable alternatives and to choose between them.

3.   Constantly monitor changes in organizational performance and in the environmental forces to discover if there are any opportunities or threats that need to be addressed.

4. Create a set of clearly defined criteria to frame opportunities and threats and apply these criteria consistently.

5. Encourage managers at all levels to make problem solving a major part of their jobs and to generate as many feasible alternatives as possible.

6. Be aware of the role people's preferences and interests play in generating alternative courses of action and learn how to manage coalitions to promote effective decision making.

7. Once an alternative course of action has been chosen, take steps to implement the decision. Request periodic updates on the situation from the managers responsible for implementing the chosen alternative.

8. Learn from your successes and mistakes and use this information to improve your next decision.

Cognitive Biases and Decision Making

heuristics Rules of thumb that simplify decision making.

In the 1970s, two psychologists, Daniel Kahneman and Amos Tversky, suggested that because all decision makers are subject to bounded rationality, they tend to use **heuristics**, rules of thumb that simplify the process of making decisions.[22] Kahneman and Tversky argued that rules of thumb are often useful because they help decision makers make sense of complex, uncertain, and ambiguous information. Sometimes, however, the use of heuristics can lead to systematic errors in the way decision makers process information about alternatives and make decisions. **Systematic errors** are errors that people make over and over and that result in poor decision making. Because of cognitive biases, which are caused by systematic errors, otherwise capable managers may end up making bad decisions.[23] Four sources of bias that can adversely affect the way managers make decisions are prior hypotheses, representativeness, the illusion of control, and escalating commitment (see Figure 6.6).

systematic errors Errors that people make over and over and that result in poor decision making.

Prior Hypothesis Bias

prior hypothesis bias A cognitive bias resulting from the tendency to base decisions on strong prior beliefs even if evidence shows that those beliefs are wrong.

Decision makers who have strong prior beliefs about the relationship between two variables tend to make decisions based on those beliefs *even when presented with evidence that their beliefs are wrong*. In doing so, they are falling victim to **prior hypothesis bias**. Moreover, decision makers tend to seek and use information that is consistent with their prior beliefs and to ignore information that contradicts those beliefs. At Calling Systems International (CSI), profiled in the "Case in Contrast," we saw CEO Alan Redland reject Sharon Eastman's new product proposal because it was not consistent with his prior beliefs about what CSI should be doing.

The prior hypothesis bias is also evident in the actions of the BC forestry products industry in this "Management Insight." One company, Eagleye Log Homes, went against the prior hypothesis bias of the industry, however, and gained a market edge as a result.

Figure 6.6

Sources of Cognitive Bias at the Individual and Group Levels

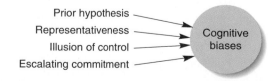

Management Insight

Turning Pestilence Into Profit

When the mountain pine beetle struck millions of hectares of prime northern BC forests recently, the forest industry viewed it as a disaster.[24] The beetle carries a fungus that stains the trees blue. The industry knew the biases of their customers. "Nobody wants blue stain in their wood and just having a tree with something called a fungus is not to most people's liking," says Larry Pedersen, BC's chief forester. The industry watched in alarm as the Japanese, their largest market, rejected the lumber. Meanwhile, the forest products industry faces a shortage of uninfected Japan-grade lumber.

Log-home builders Dean and Lori Gunderson, owners of Prince George, BC-based Eagleye Log Homes, didn't let assumptions about customer biases get in their way. Instead, they discovered that when the blue-stained logs dry, they turn gold, creating a tiger-stripe motif to their log homes. They started marketing the logs to US clients. It turns out that Americans much prefer these logs over the non-infected logs. It definitely gives us a market edge," says Lori Gunderson. "They don't understand why this is salvage wood. This is a unique phenomenon and they think it is beautiful."

Representativeness Bias

representativeness bias A cognitive bias resulting from the tendency to generalize inappropriately from a small sample or from a single vivid event or episode.

Many decision makers inappropriately generalize from a small sample or even from a single vivid case or episode. An interesting example of the **representativeness bias** occurred as more and more investors invested in dot-com companies that had no serious business plan after perceiving that Amazon.com was going to be the next great business model. The investors made the mistake of thinking that marketing on the Internet would be good for any new company.

Illusion of Control

illusion of control A source of cognitive bias resulting from the tendency to overestimate one's own ability to control activities and events.

Other errors in decision making result from the **illusion of control**, the tendency of decision makers to overestimate their ability to control activities and events. Top-level managers seem to be particularly prone to this bias. Having worked their way to the top of an organization, they tend to have an exaggerated sense of their own worth and are overconfident about their ability to succeed and to control events.[25] The illusion of control causes managers to overestimate the odds of a favourable outcome and, consequently, to make inappropriate decisions. For example, in the 1980s, Nissan was run by Katsuji Kawamata, an autocratic manager who thought he had the skills to run the car company alone. He made all the decisions—decisions that resulted in a series of spectacular mistakes, including changing the company's name from Datsun to Nissan—and Nissan's share of the North American market fell dramatically.

Escalating Commitment

escalating commitment A source of cognitive bias resulting from the tendency to commit additional resources to a project even if evidence shows that the project is failing.

Having already committed significant resources to a course of action, some managers commit more resources to the project *even if they receive feedback that the project is failing.*[26] Feelings of personal responsibility for a project apparently bias the analysis of decision makers and lead to **escalating commitment**. They decide to increase their investment of time and money in a course of action and ignore evidence that it is illegal, unethical, uneconomical, or impractical (see Figure 6.5). Often, the more appropriate decision would be to "cut and run."

A tragic example of where escalating commitment can lead is the Challenger disaster. Apparently, managers at both NASA and Morton Thiokol were so anxious to keep the shuttle program on schedule that they ignored or discounted any evidence that would slow the program down. Thus, the information offered by two engineers at Thiokol, who warned about O-ring failure in cold weather, was discounted, and the shuttle was launched on a chilly day in January 1986.

Be Aware of Your Biases

How can managers avoid the negative effects of cognitive biases and improve their decision-making and problem-solving abilities? Managers must become aware of biases and their effects, and they must identify their own personal style of making decisions.[27] One useful way for managers to analyze their decision-making style is to review two decisions that they made recently—one decision that turned out well and one that turned out poorly. Problem-solving experts recommend that a manager start by determining how much time he or she spent on each of the decision-making steps, such as gathering information to identify the pros and cons of alternatives or ranking the alternatives, to make sure that sufficient time is being spent on each step.[28]

Another recommended technique for examining decision-making style is for managers to list the criteria they typically use to assess and evaluate alternatives—the heuristics (rules of thumb) they typically employ, their personal biases, and so on—and then critically evaluate the appropriateness of these different factors.

Many individual managers are likely to have difficulty identifying their own biases, so it is often advisable for managers to scrutinize their own assumptions by working with other managers to help expose weaknesses in their decision-making style. In this context, the issue of group decision making becomes important.

Group Decision Making

Do groups make decisions differently than individuals?

Many, perhaps most, important organizational decisions are made by groups of managers rather than by individuals. Group decision making is superior to individual decision making in several respects. When managers work as a team to make decisions and solve problems, their choices of alternatives are less likely to fall victim to the biases and errors discussed previously. They are able to draw on the combined skills, competencies, and accumulated knowledge of group members, and thereby improve their ability to generate feasible alternatives and make good decisions. Group decision making also allows managers to process more information and to correct each other's errors. In the implementation phase, all managers affected by the decisions agree to cooperate. When a group of managers makes a decision (as opposed to one top manager making a decision and imposing it on subordinate managers), the probability that the decision will be implemented successfully increases. (We discuss how to encourage employee participation in decision making in Chapter 15.)

Nevertheless, some disadvantages are associated with group decision making. Groups often take much longer than individuals to make decisions. Getting two or more managers to agree to the same solution can be difficult because managers' interests and preferences are often different. In addition, just like decision making by individual managers, group decision making can be undermined by biases. A major source of group bias is groupthink.

groupthink A pattern of faulty and biased decision making that occurs in groups whose members strive for agreement among themselves at the expense of accurately assessing information relevant to a decision.

The Perils of Groupthink

Groupthink is a pattern of faulty and biased decision making that occurs in groups whose members strive for agreement among themselves at the expense of accurately assessing information relevant to a decision.[29] When managers are subject to groupthink, they collectively embark on a course of action without developing appropriate criteria to evaluate alternatives. Typically, a group rallies around one central manager, such as the CEO, and the course of action that the manager supports. Group members become blindly committed to that course of action without evaluating its merits. Commitment is often based on an emotional, rather than an objective, assessment of the optimal course of action.

In the "Case in Contrast," groupthink was probably at work when the first executive team at Calling Systems International, headed by Alan Redland, dismissed Sharon Eastman's new product proposal. Despite previously expressing support for Eastman's idea, two members of the executive team merely nodded their agreement with Redland when he criticized the proposal—a sure sign that pressures toward agreement were at work in this group. Pressures for agreement and harmony within a group have the unintended effect of discouraging individuals from raising issues that run counter to majority opinion. This same process preceded the Challenger disaster, as managers at NASA and Morton Thiokol fell victim to groupthink, convincing each other that all was well and that there was no need to delay the launch of the shuttle.

While there is considerable anecdotal evidence to suggest the negative implications of groupthink in organizational settings, very little empirical work has been conducted in organizations on the subject of groupthink.[30] In fact, more recently, groupthink has been criticized for overestimating the link between the decision-making process and its outcome[31] and for suggesting that its effect is uniformly negative.[32] A 1999 study of groupthink in five large corporations reported that elements of groupthink may affect decision making differently. For instance, the illusion of vulnerability, belief in inherent group morality and the illusion of unanimity were positively associated with team performance, counter to what the original groupthink proposals suggest.[33]

Devil's Advocacy and Dialectical Inquiry

The existence of cognitive biases and groupthink raises the question of how to improve the quality of group and individual decision making so that managers make decisions that are realistic and based on a thorough evaluation of alternatives. Two techniques known to counteract groupthink and cognitive biases are devil's advocacy and dialectical inquiry (see Figure 6.7).[34]

Devil's advocacy is a critical analysis of a preferred alternative to ascertain its strengths and weaknesses before it is implemented.[35] Typically, one member of the decision-making group plays the role of devil's advocate. The devil's advocate cri-

devil's advocacy Critical analysis of a preferred alternative made by a group member who, playing the role of devil's advocate, defends unpopular or opposing alternatives for the sake of argument.

Figure 6.7
Devil's Advocacy and Dialectical Inquiry

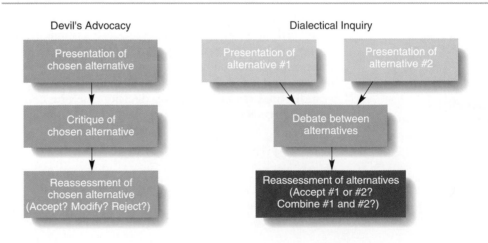

tiques and challenges the way the group evaluated alternatives and chose one over the others. The purpose of devil's advocacy is to identify all the reasons that might make the preferred alternative unacceptable after all. In this way, decision makers can be made aware of the possible perils of recommended courses of action.

dialectical inquiry
Critical analysis of two preferred alternatives in order to find an even better alternative for the organization to adopt.

Dialectical inquiry goes one step further. Two groups of managers are assigned to a problem, and each group is responsible for evaluating alternatives and selecting one of them.[36] Top managers hear each group present its preferred alternative, and then each group critiques the other's position. During this debate, top managers challenge both groups' positions to uncover potential problems and perils associated with their solutions. The goal is to find an even better alternative course of action for the organization to adopt.

Both devil's advocacy and dialectical inquiry can help counter the effects of cognitive biases and groupthink.[37] In practice, devil's advocacy is probably the easier method to implement because it involves less commitment of managerial time and effort than does dialectical inquiry.

Diversity Among Decision Makers

Another way to improve group decision making is to promote diversity in decision-making groups.[38] Bringing together managers of both genders and from various ethnic, national, and functional backgrounds, and so on, broadens the range of life experiences and opinions that group members can draw from as they generate, assess, and choose among alternatives. Moreover, diverse groups are sometimes less prone to groupthink because group members already differ from each other and thus are less subject to pressures for uniformity. The Swiss firm, The BrainStore, profiled in the following "Focus on Diversity," takes advantage of diversity to improve decision making.

Focus on Diversity

Kids Help Improve Decision Making at The BrainStore

The BrainStore, an "idea factory" in Biel, Switzerland, recognizes the importance of diversity in putting together creative ideas.[39] It uses an international network of kids to help the company brainstorm for its most challenging projects.

The BrainStore sees itself as an "idea factory," a factory that manufactures and sells ideas. Their clients include: the pharmaceuticals giant Novartis AG, which was looking for ideas for new food products; the Swiss Cancer Association, which wanted ideas on how to promote the use of sun-protection products; and a 70-year-old woman who wanted ideas to help her fall in love again.

Markus Mettler, 33, and Nadja Schnetzler, 27, founded the company with the idea that one should "approach the manufacturing of ideas with as much rigour and as much discipline as you apply to the manufacturing of assembly-line products."

Whenever The BrainStore faces a truly big creative challenge, it calls in the BrainNet, a 1500-person global network made up of mainly young people aged 13 to 20. The young people help the company by scouring the world for new trends and offbeat sources of inspiration. "We're not looking for average ideas," says Mr. Mettler. "We're looking for crazy ideas. We use kids to find those ideas, because they know how to talk without letting their thinking get in the way."

The young people mix with members of The BrainStore's client teams during creative workshops. "One of the ideas behind the company was to blend the professionalism of experts with the unbridled enthusiasm of kids," says

Schnetzler. The company has teens working with such clients as Nestlé SA and the Swiss railway.

Recently, nine kids helped five executives from Credit Suisse Group, one of the country's top banks, to brainstorm ideas for phasing out a passbook-savings plan that Swiss families had cherished for years, but that bank employees had come to see as obsolete. The cross-generational teams developed a set of raw ideas. The ideas now have to go through the remaining steps in The BrainStore assembly line: "compression (in which a team of in-house employees and outside experts sorts through ideas and picks out the best ones); testing (research and prototype); and finishing (marketing campaigns and positioning strategies)." Mettler suggests that it is this assembly-line process that keeps innovation flowing, by making sure that all parts of the decision-making process get carried out.

Organizational Learning and Creativity

The quality of managerial decision making ultimately depends on innovative responses to opportunities and threats. How can managers increase their ability to make nonprogrammed decisions, decisions that will allow them to adapt to, modify, and even drastically alter their task environments so that they can continually increase organizational performance? The answer is, by encouraging organizational learning.[40]

organizational learning
The process through which managers seek to improve employees' desire and ability to understand and manage the organization and its task environment.

learning organization
An organization in which managers try to maximize the ability of individuals and groups to think and behave creatively and thus maximize the potential for organizational learning to take place.

creativity A decision maker's ability to discover original and novel ideas that lead to feasible alternative courses of action.

Organizational learning is the process through which managers seek to improve employees' desire and ability to understand and manage the organization and its task environment so that employees can make decisions that continuously raise organizational effectiveness.[41] A **learning organization** is one in which managers do everything possible to maximize the ability of individuals and groups to think and behave creatively and thus maximize the potential for organizational learning to take place. At the heart of organizational learning is **creativity**, the ability of a decision maker to discover original and novel ideas that lead to feasible alternative courses of action. Encouraging creativity among managers is such a pressing organizational concern that many organizations hire outside experts to help them develop programs to train their managers in the art of creative thinking and problem solving.

Creating a Learning Organization

How do managers go about creating a learning organization? Learning theorist Peter Senge identified five principles for creating a learning organization (see Figure 6.8).[42]

1. For organizational learning to occur, top managers must allow every person in the organization to develop a sense of *personal mastery*. Managers must empower employees and allow them to experiment and create and explore what they want.

2. As part of attaining personal mastery, organizations need to encourage employees to develop and use *complex mental models*–sophisticated ways of thinking that challenge them to find new or better ways of performing a task–to deepen their understanding of what is involved in a particular activity. Senge argues that managers must encourage employees to develop a taste for experimenting and risk taking.[43]

3. Managers must do everything they can to promote group creativity. Senge thinks that *team learning* (learning that takes place in a group or team) is more important than individual learning in increasing organizational learning. He points out that most important decisions are made in subunits such as groups, functions, and divisions.

Figure 6.8
Senge's Principles for Creating a Learning Organization

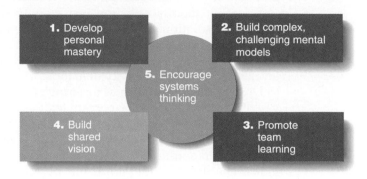

4. Managers must emphasize the importance of *building a shared vision*—a common mental model that all organizational members use to frame problems or opportunities.

5. Managers must encourage *systems thinking* (a concept drawn from systems theory, discussed in Chapter 2). Senge emphasizes that, in order to create a learning organization, managers must recognize the effects of one level of learning on another. Thus, for example, there is little point in creating teams to facilitate team learning if managers do not also take steps to give employees the freedom to develop a sense of personal mastery.

Building a learning organization requires managers to change their management assumptions radically. Developing a learning organization is neither a quick nor an easy process. Senge has been working with Ford Motor Company for almost 15 years to help Ford managers make theirs a learning organization. Why does Ford want this? Top management believes that to compete successfully in the twenty-first century, Ford must improve its members' ability to be creative and make the right decisions. Next, we look at some specific ways in which managers can promote creativity at the individual, group, and global levels.[44] Increasing creativity in Canada may well be an important and challenging endeavour. A 2001 report based on two years of research concluded that "while there are pockets of innovation in Canadian industry and schools, most of the country might as well be declared creatively AWOL."[45]

Promoting Individual Creativity

Can people become more creative?

Research suggests that individuals are most likely to be creative when certain conditions are met. First, as just discussed, people must be given the opportunity and freedom to generate new ideas. Creativity declines when managers look over the shoulders of talented employees and try to "hurry up" a creative solution. How would you feel if your boss said you had one week to come up with a new product idea to beat the competition? Creativity results when individuals have an opportunity to experiment, to take risks, and to make mistakes and learn from them. Highly innovative companies in Canada include Brampton, ON-based Nortel Networks, Montreal-based Bombardier and London, ON-based 3M Co. Companies that have a lot of innovation foster that through their formal structure and expectations. For instance, in one recent year, 3M launched more than 200 new products. To encourage this level of development, managers are told that 30 percent of sales are expected to come from products less than four years old.[46]

Once managers have generated alternatives, creativity can be fostered by providing them with constructive feedback so that they know how well they are doing. Ideas that seem to be going nowhere can be eliminated and creative energies refocused in other directions. Ideas that seem promising can be promoted, and help from other managers can be obtained as well.[47]

It is also important for top managers to stress the importance of looking for alternative solutions and to visibly reward employees who come up with creative ideas. Being creative can be demanding and stressful. Employees who believe that they are working on important, vital issues will be motivated to put forth the high levels of effort that creativity demands.

Despite the importance of fostering creativity in organizations, in a recent survey of 500 CEOs, only six percent felt that they were doing a great job at managing their creative people. John Macdonald, the founder of Richmond, BC-based MacDonald Dettwiler & Associates (MDA) suggests that "managing creative people is a bit like riding herd on a thousand prima donnas. They are all highly individual people who don't follow the herd, so managing them is a challenge," says Macdonald.[48]

MacDonald
Dettwiler and
Associates
www.mda.ca/

Promoting Group Creativity

To encourage creativity at the group level, organizations can make use of group problem-solving techniques that promote creative ideas and innovative solutions. These techniques can also be used to prevent groupthink and to help managers uncover biases. Here, we look at three group decision-making techniques: *brainstorming*, the *nominal group technique*, and the *Delphi technique*.

BRAINSTORMING   **Brainstorming** is a group problem-solving technique in which individuals meet face-to-face to generate and debate a wide variety of alternatives from which to make a decision.[49] Generally, from 5 to 15 managers meet in a closed-door session and proceed like this:

brainstorming A group problem-solving technique in which individuals meet face-to-face to generate and debate a wide variety of alternatives from which to make a decision.

- One person describes in broad outline the problem the group is to address.
- Group members then share their ideas and generate alternative courses of action.
- As each alternative is described, group members are not allowed to criticize it, and everyone withholds judgment until all alternatives have been heard. One member of the group records the alternatives on a flip chart.
- Group members are encouraged to be as innovative and radical as possible. Anything goes; and the greater the number of ideas put forth, the better. Moreover, group members are encouraged to "piggyback"–that is, to build on each other's suggestions.
- When all alternatives have been generated, group members debate the pros and cons of each and develop a short list of the best alternatives.

Brainstorming is very useful in some problem-solving situations–for example, when trying to find a new name for a perfume or for a model of car. But sometimes individuals working alone can generate more alternatives. The main reason for this loss of productivity appears to be **production blocking**, which occurs because group members cannot always simultaneously make sense of all the alternatives being generated, think up additional alternatives, and remember what they were thinking.[50]

production blocking
A loss of productivity in brainstorming sessions due to the unstructured nature of brainstorming.

Electronic brainstorming, with people interacting on computers to generate ideas, is the newest form of brainstorming. For example, Calgary-based Tarragon Oil and Gas hired Calgary-based Jerilyn Wright and Associates for help with electronic brainstorming to design its new workspace.[51] Queen's University's Executive Decision Centre is "one of the first electronic [decision-making] facilities in North America and the first to be made accessible to the public."[52] Glaxo Wellcome, Bombardier, DuPont, Imperial Oil, the Department of National

Defence, the Canadian Security and Intelligence Service, and the United Way have all used these facilities. Mississauga, ON-based DuPont Canada uses the system regularly for focused creativity sessions with both employees and customers. Whitby, ON-based McGraw-Hill Ryerson Canada became a regular user after finding that one of its divisions experienced a surge in sales after visiting the Queen's Centre.

NOMINAL GROUP TECHNIQUE To avoid production blocking, the **nominal group technique** is often used. It provides a more structured way of generating alternatives in writing and gives each manager more time and opportunity to generate alternative solutions. The nominal group technique is especially useful when an issue is controversial and when different managers might be expected to champion different courses of action. Generally, a small group of managers meets in a closed-door session and adopts the following procedures:

nominal group technique A decision-making technique in which group members write down ideas and solutions, read their suggestions to the whole group, and discuss and then rank the alternatives.

- One manager outlines the problem to be addressed, and 30 or 40 minutes are allocated for each group member to write down ideas and solutions. Group members are encouraged to be innovative.

- Managers take turns reading their suggestions to the group. One manager writes the alternatives on a flip chart. No criticism or evaluation of alternatives is allowed until all alternatives have been read.

- The alternatives are then discussed, one by one, in the sequence in which they were first proposed. Group members can ask for clarifying information and critique each alternative to identify its pros and cons.

- When all alternatives have been discussed, each group member ranks all the alternatives from most preferred to least preferred, and the alternative that receives the highest ranking is chosen.[53]

DELPHI TECHNIQUE Both nominal group technique and brainstorming require managers to meet together to generate creative ideas and engage in joint problem solving. What happens if managers are in different cities or in different parts of the world and cannot meet face-to-face? Videoconferencing is one way to bring distant managers together to brainstorm. Another way is to use the **Delphi technique**, a written approach to creative problem solving.[54] The Delphi technique works like this:

Delphi technique A decision-making technique in which group members do not meet face-to-face but respond in writing to questions posed by the group leader.

- The group leader writes a statement of the problem and a series of questions to which participating managers are to respond.

- The questionnaire is sent to the managers and departmental experts who are most knowledgeable about the problem; they are asked to generate solutions and mail the questionnaire back to the group leader.

- A team of top managers records and summarizes the responses. The results are then sent back to the participants, with additional questions to be answered before a decision can be made.

- The process is repeated until a consensus is reached and the most suitable course of action is apparent.

Promoting Creativity at the Global Level

The Delphi technique is particularly useful when managers are separated by barriers of time and distance, a situation that is common in the global environment. Today, organizations are under increasing pressure to reduce costs and develop global products. To do so, they typically centralize their research and development (R&D) expertise by bringing R&D managers together at one location. Encouraging creativity among teams of R&D experts from different countries poses special problems, however. First, R&D experts often have difficulty communicating their ideas to one another because of language problems and because of cultural differences in their approaches to problem solving. Second, the decision-making process differs from country to country. In Japan, for example, decisions tend to be made in a very participative manner, and the group as a whole must agree on a course of action before a decision gets made. In contrast, decision making is very centralized in Mexico; top managers decide what to do, with little input from subordinates.

Managers must take special steps to encourage creativity among people from different countries who are supposed to be working together. They must develop training programs that promote awareness and understanding so that diverse individuals can cooperate and brainstorm new ideas and approaches to problems, opportunities, and threats. They must also understand that different cultures have different approaches to creativity. For example, Terry Graham, president and CEO of Scarborough, ON-based Image Processing Systems Inc., saw brainstorming backfire when doing business in China. He says that meetings with Chinese businesspeople "are definitely not for brainstorming. We learned this lesson the hard way. Our team thought we could show our creativity by placing fresh alternatives in front of an important manager. It was two years before the company would talk to us again."[55] The story of how IBM, Siemens, and Toshiba established a strategic alliance to design a new computer chip illustrates other issues involved in managing creativity on a global level.

Managing Globally

Building Cross-Cultural Creativity

In 1993, the US computer giant IBM (www.pc.ibm.com) joined with two other global computer companies, Siemens AG of Germany (www.siemens.com) and Toshiba of Japan (www.toshiba.com), to establish a joint venture to build the next generation of computer chips–chips capable of handling 16 times as much information as the most advanced computer chips available today. The joint venture was formed, and each company did not try to develop its own chip, because of the huge cost of developing a new chip–typically billions of dollars. Although each company has a world-class research and development program, top managers were hoping that pooling the talents of their best R&D scientists would enable all three organizations to reap the benefits of synergy and achieve major product breakthroughs quickly and efficiently.

The three companies brought together 100 of their best scientists at an IBM facility in East Fishkill, New York; there they worked together until 1998, developing the new chip. The companies have taken several steps to bridge the obvious cultural gaps among the scientists and to foster creativity. Various language training programs have been developed to help the Japanese and Germans speak colloquial English so that they and the Americans can better brainstorm with one another. Team-building programs have been designed to build cooperative relationships among the scientists assigned to each of the many different departments involved in various aspects of the project. For example, IBM established a buddy system whereby IBM scientists are responsible for introducing their Japanese and German counterparts to the intricacies of IBM's computer system.

Despite these efforts, fostering creativity and cooperation among the American, German, and Japanese scientists has proven to be difficult. The problem can be attributed in large part to cultural differences related to three different national approaches to problem solving and decision making. The North American scientists complain that the Japanese scientists like to spend so much time developing and assessing alternatives that decisions take a long time to make, and even when decisions are made, it often is not clear exactly what has been decided. The German scientists complain that the North American scientists will not accept advice and criticism. The Japanese scientists complain that they are not involved in the main decision-making process. Moreover, each group of scientists has complained that the other groups are hoarding information and ideas to protect their individual and their company's interests, thus undermining the joint creative process.[56]

Despite these problems, the project continues. However, the major break-throughs that the three companies hope to achieve by bringing their scientists together have not yet occurred. Managers directing the joint venture have observed that, for the most part, cooperation and brainstorming are occurring not among the different groups of scientists but within each group. Managers believe that creativity will be further enhanced by increasing cooperation across the groups–the original goal of the project–and they are planning to develop more group training programs to break down cross-cultural barriers and encourage a truly cross-national approach to problem solving.

Tips for Managers

Improving Decision Making

1. Be aware of the operation of cognitive biases and test the assumptions managers use to frame problems, select alternatives, and make decisions.

2. Recognize the advantages of using diverse decision making groups.

3. Use devil's advocacy and dialectical inquiry to guard against groupthink.

4. Take all possible steps to promote creativity at the individual and group level and make a technique like brainstorming a routine part of the problem-solving process.

Information and the Manager's Job

data Raw, unsummarized, and unanalyzed facts.

information Data that are organized in a meaningful fashion.

Managers cannot make decisions–let alone plan, organize, lead, and control effectively–unless they have access to information. Information is the source of the knowledge and intelligence that they need to make the right decisions. Information, however, is not the same as data.[57] **Data** are raw, unsummarized, and unanalyzed facts such as volume of sales, level of costs, or number of customers. **Information** is data that are organized in a meaningful fashion, such as in a graph showing the change in sales volume or costs over time. Alone, data do not tell managers anything; information, in contrast, can communicate a great deal of useful knowledge to the person who receives it–such as a manager who sees sales falling or costs rising. The distinction between data and information is important because one of the uses of information technology is to help managers transform data into information in order to make better managerial decisions.

Attributes of Useful Information

Four factors determine the usefulness of information to a manager: quality, timeliness, completeness, and relevance (see Figure 6.9).

QUALITY Accuracy and reliability determine the quality of information.[58] The greater the accuracy and reliability are, the higher is the quality of information. For an information system to work well, the information that it provides must be of high quality. If managers conclude that the quality of information provided by

Figure 6.9
Factors Affecting the Usefulness of Information

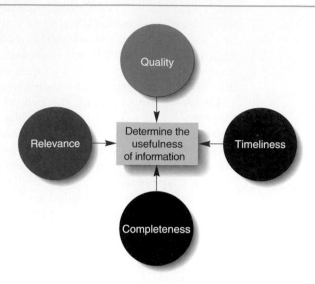

their information system is low, they are likely to lose confidence in the system and stop using it. Alternatively, if managers base decisions on low-quality information, poor and even disastrous decision making can result. For example, the partial meltdown of the nuclear reactor at Three Mile Island in Pennsylvania during the 1970s was the result of poor information caused by an information system malfunction. The information system indicated to engineers controlling the reactor that there was enough water in the reactor core to cool the nuclear pile, although this was in fact not the case. The consequences included the partial meltdown of the reactor and the release of radioactive gas into the atmosphere.

TIMELINESS   Information that is timely is available when it is needed for managerial action, not after the decision has been made. In today's rapidly changing world, the need for timely information often means that information must be available on a real-time basis.[59] **Real-time information** is information that reflects current conditions. In an industry that experiences rapid changes, real-time information may need to be updated frequently. Airlines use real-time information on the number of flight bookings and competitors' prices to adjust their prices on an hour-to-hour basis to maximize their revenues.

real-time information
Frequently updated information that reflects current conditions.

COMPLETENESS   Information that is complete gives managers all the information they need to exercise control, achieve coordination, or make an effective decision. We have already noted that because of uncertainty, ambiguity, and bounded rationality, managers have to make do with incomplete information.[60] One of the functions of information systems is to increase the completeness of the information that managers have at their disposal.

RELEVANCE   Information that is relevant is useful and suits a manager's particular needs and circumstances. Irrelevant information is useless and may actually hurt the performance of a busy manager who has to spend valuable time determining whether information is relevant. Given the massive amounts of information that managers are now exposed to and humans' limited information-processing capabilities, the people who design information systems need to make sure that managers receive only relevant information.

Information Systems and Technology

information system

A system for acquiring, organizing, storing, manipulating, and transmitting information.

management information system

An information system that managers plan and design to provide themselves with the specific information they need.

information technology

The means by which information is acquired, organized, stored, manipulated, and transmitted.

An **information system** is a system for acquiring, organizing, storing, manipulating, and transmitting information.[61] A **management information system (MIS)** is an information system that managers plan and design to provide themselves with the specific information they need to perform their roles effectively. Information systems have existed for as long as there have been organizations—a long time indeed. Before the computer age, most information systems were paper based. Clerks recorded important information on documents (often in duplicate or triplicate) in the form of words and numbers, sent a copy of the document to superiors, customers, or suppliers, as the case might be, and stored other copies in files for future reference.

Information technology is the means by which information is acquired, organized, stored, manipulated, and transmitted. Rapid advances in the power of information technology—specifically, through the use of computers—are having a fundamental impact on information systems and on managers and their organizations.[62] Managers need information for three reasons: to make effective decisions; to control the activities of the organization; and to coordinate the activities of the organization.

Information and Decisions

Much of management (planning, organizing, leading, and controlling) is about making decisions. For example, the marketing manager must decide what price to charge for a product, what distribution channels to use, and what promotional messages to emphasize. The manufacturing manager must decide how much of a product to make and how to make it. The purchasing manager must decide from whom to purchase inputs and what inventory of inputs to hold. The human relations manager must decide how much employees should be paid, how they should be trained, and what benefits they should be given. The engineering manager must make decisions about new product design. Top managers must decide how to allocate scarce financial resources among competing projects, how best to structure and control the organization, and what business-level strategy the organization should be pursuing. In addition, regardless of their functional orientation, all managers have to make decisions about matters such as what performance evaluation to give to a subordinate.

Decision making cannot be effective in an information vacuum. To make effective decisions, managers need information, both from inside the organization and from external stakeholders. When deciding how to price a product, for example, the marketing manager needs information about how consumers will react to different prices. She needs information about unit costs because she does not want to set the price below the costs of production. In addition, she needs information about competitive strategy, since pricing strategy should be consistent with an organization's competitive strategy. Some of this information will come from outside the organization (for example, from consumer surveys) and some from inside the organization (information about unit production costs comes from manufacturing). As this example suggests, managers' ability to make effective decisions rests on their ability to acquire and process information.

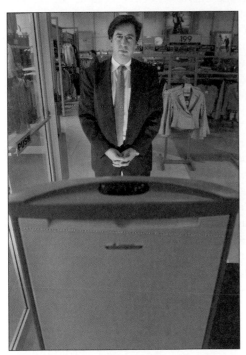

Jeffrey Worstman, CEO of Toronto-based Danier Leather, Inc., uses information technology to itemize inventory on a weekly basis in each store. Doing so allows him to make decisions about how to handle problems with missing inventory. The information lets him know pretty quickly whether he's dealing with employee theft or a rash of thieves.

When WestJet tries to determine how many tickets from each fare class should be assigned to future flight schedules, it analyzes historical booking patterns on every flight. "We have seasonality models, event models, time-of-day models, and all of those run through our forecast every night and are optimized nightly based on that day's sales," said Brenda Crockstad, WestJet's director of revenue and scheduling.[63]

The Information Technology Revolution

The advances in management information systems and technology have had important effects on managers and organizations. By improving the ability of managers to coordinate and control the activities of the organization, and by helping managers make more effective decisions, modern computer-based information systems have become a central component of any organization's structure. The rapid rise of computer-based information systems has been associated with a "delayering" (flattening) of the organizational hierarchy and a move toward greater decentralization and horizontal information flows within organizations.[64] By electronically providing managers with high-quality, timely, relevant, and relatively complete information, modern management information systems have reduced the need for tall management hierarchies. Moreover, because of e-mail and the ability to share documents, information is more available to everyone within an organization, not just to managers.

The result of this greater flow of information should be improved performance, for achieving superior efficiency, quality, innovation, and customer responsiveness that requires managers to break down the barriers between departments. For all of their usefulness, information systems have some limitations, however. A serious potential problem is that, in all of the enthusiasm for management information systems, electronic communication by means of a computer network, and the like, a vital *human* element of communication might be lost. Some kinds of information cannot be aggregated and summarized on an MIS report.

Electronic communication should be used to support face-to-face communication, not to replace it. For example, it would be wrong to make a judgment about an individual's performance merely by "reading the numbers" provided by a management information system. Instead, the numbers should be used to alert managers to individuals who may have a performance problem. The nature of this performance problem should then be explored in a face-to-face meeting, during which more detailed information can be gathered. As a top Boeing manager has noted, "In our company, the use of e-mail and videoconferencing has not reduced the need to visit people at other sites; it has increased it. E-mail has facilitated the establishment of communications channels between people who previously would not communicate, which is good, but direct visits are still required to cement any working relationships that evolve out of these electronic meetings."[65]

Summary and Review

THE NATURE OF MANAGERIAL DECISION MAKING Programmed decisions are routine decisions that are made so often that managers have developed decision rules to be followed automatically. Nonprogrammed decisions are made in response to situations that are unusual or novel; they are nonroutine decisions. The classical model of decision making assumes that decision makers have complete information, are able to process that information in an objective, rational manner, and make optimum decisions. March and Simon argue that managers are boundedly rational, rarely have access to all the information they need

Chapter Summary

THE NATURE OF MANAGERIAL DECISION MAKING

- Programmed and Nonprogrammed Decision Making
- The Classical Model
- The Administrative Model

STEPS IN THE DECISION-MAKING PROCESS

- Recognize the Need for a Decision
- Generate Alternatives
- Assess Alternatives
- Choose Among Alternatives
- Implement the Chosen Alternative
- Learn from Feedback

COGNITIVE BIASES AND DECISION MAKING

- Prior Hypothesis Bias
- Representativeness Bias
- Illusion of Control
- Escalating Commitment
- Be Aware of Your Biases

GROUP DECISION MAKING

- The Perils of Groupthink
- Devil's Advocacy and Dialectical Inquiry
- Diversity Among Decision Makers

ORGANIZATIONAL LEARNING AND CREATIVITY

- Creating a Learning Organization
- Promoting Individual Creativity
- Promoting Group Creativity
- Promoting Creativity at the Global Level

INFORMATION AND THE MANAGER'S JOB

- Attributes of Useful Information
- Information Systems and Technology
- Information and Decisions

THE INFORMATION TECHNOLOGY REVOLUTION

to make optimum decisions, and consequently satisfice and rely on their intuition and judgment when making decisions.

STEPS IN THE DECISION-MAKING PROCESS   When making decisions, managers should take these six steps: recognize the need for a decision, generate alternatives, assess alternatives, choose among alternatives, implement the chosen alternative, and learn from feedback.

COGNITIVE BIASES AND DECISION MAKING   Most of the time, managers are fairly good decision makers. On occasion, however, problems result because human judgment is adversely affected by the operation of cognitive biases that result in poor decisions. Cognitive biases are caused by systematic errors in the way decision makers process information and make decisions. Sources of these errors include prior hypotheses, representativeness, the illusion of control, and escalating commitment. Managers should undertake a personal decision audit to become aware of their biases in order to improve their decision making.

GROUP DECISION MAKING   Many advantages are associated with group decision making, but there are also several disadvantages. One major source of poor decision making is groupthink. Afflicted decision makers collectively embark on a dubious course of action without questioning the assumptions that underlie their decision. Managers can improve the quality of group decision making by using techniques such as devil's advocacy and dialectical inquiry, and by increasing diversity in the decision-making group.

ORGANIZATIONAL LEARNING AND CREATIVITY   Organizational learning is the process through which managers seek to improve employees' desire and ability to understand and manage the organization and its task environment so that employees can make decisions that continuously raise organizational effectiveness. Managers must take steps to promote organizational learning and creativity at the individual and group levels to improve the quality of decision making.

INFORMATION AND THE MANAGER'S JOB   Computer-based information systems are central to the operation of most organizations. By providing managers with high-quality, timely, relevant, and relatively complete information, properly implemented information systems can improve managers' ability to coordinate and control the operations of an organization and to make effective decisions. Moreover, information systems can help the organization to attain a competitive advantage through their beneficial impact on productivity, quality, innovation, and responsiveness to customers. Thus, modern information systems are becoming an indispensable management tool.

THE INFORMATION TECHNOLOGY REVOLUTION   In recent years, there have been rapid advances in the power, and rapid declines in the cost, of information technology. Falling prices, wireless communication, computer networks, and software developments have all increased the potential for information technology to radically improve the power and efficacy of computer-based information systems. Modern information systems and technology have changed organizational structure by making it flatter and by encouraging more cross-functional communication. In turn, this has helped organizations achieve a competitive advantage. However, despite their usefulness, information systems have some limitations—the most serious of which is loss of the human element.

Management in Action

Topics for Discussion and Action

1. What are the main differences between programmed decision making and nonprogrammed decision making?

2. In what ways do the classical and administrative models of decision making help managers appreciate the complexities of real-world decision making?

3. Ask a manager to recall the best and the worst decisions he or she ever made. Try to determine why these decisions were so good or so bad.

4. Why do capable managers sometimes make bad decisions? What can individual managers do to improve their decision-making skills?

5. In what kinds of groups is groupthink most likely to be a problem? When is it least likely to be a problem? What steps can group members take to ward off groupthink?

6. What is organizational learning, and how can managers promote it?

7. To be useful, information must be of high quality, timely, relevant, and as complete as possible. Describe the negative impact that a tall management hierarchy, when used as an information system, can have on these desirable attributes.

8. Ask a manager to describe the main kinds of information systems that he or she uses on a routine basis at work.

9. Because of the growth of high-powered, low-cost computing, wireless communications, and technologies such as videoconferencing, many managers soon may not need to come into the office to do their jobs. They will be able to work at home. What are the pros and cons of such an arrangement?

Building Management Skills

How Do You Make Decisions?

Pick a decision that you made recently that has had important consequences for you. This decision may be your decision about which college or university to attend, which major to select, whether to take a part-time job, or which part-time job to take. Using the material in this chapter, analyze the way in which you made the decision.

1. Identify the criteria you used, either consciously or unconsciously, to guide your decision making.

2. List the alternatives you considered. Were these all possible alternatives? Did you unconsciously (or consciously) ignore some important alternatives?

3. How much information did you have about each alternative? Did you base the decision on complete or incomplete information?

4. Try to remember how you reached the decision. Did you sit down and consciously think through the implications of each alternative, or did you make the decision on the basis of intuition? Did you use any rules of thumb to help you make the decision?

5. In retrospect, do you think that your choice of alternative was shaped by any of the cognitive biases discussed in this chapter?

6. Having answered those five questions, do you think in retrospect that you made a reasonable decision? What, if anything, might you do to improve your ability to make good decisions in the future?

Small Group Breakout Exercise

Brainstorming

Form groups of three or four people, and appoint one member as the spokesperson who will communicate your findings to the whole class when called on by the instructor. Then discuss the following scenario.

You and your partners are trying to decide which kind of restaurant to open in a centrally located shopping centre that has just been built in your city. The problem confronting you is that the city already has many restaurants that provide different kinds of food in all price ranges. You have the resources to open any type of restaurant. Your challenge is to decide which type is most likely to succeed.

Use the brainstorming technique to decide which type of restaurant to open. Follow these steps.

1. As a group, spend 5 or 10 minutes generating ideas about the alternative kinds of restaurants that you think will be most likely to succeed. Each group member should be as innovative and creative as possible, and no suggestion should be criticized.

2. Appoint one group member to write down the alternatives as they are identified.

3. Spend the next 10 or 15 minutes debating the pros and cons of the alternatives. As a group, try to reach a consensus on which alternative is most likely to succeed.

4. After making your decision, discuss the pros and cons of the brainstorming method, and decide whether any production blocking occurred.

5. When called on by the instructor, the spokesperson should be prepared to share your group's decision with the class, as well as the reasons you made your decision.

Exploring the World Wide Web

Specific Assignment

This exercise examines the decisions facing Nortel Networks with the plummet in stock prices that happened in 2001.

Scan Nortel's Web site (www.nortelnetworks.com) to get a feel for this innovative company. In particular, from the home page click on "Corporate Information," and "News and Events," and read the stories about current decisions being made at Nortel.

1. What opportunities and threats do John Roth (or his successor) and Nortel currently face?

2. What kinds of decisions does Roth (or his successor) need to make at the present time?

General Assignment

Search for a Web site that describes a company whose managers have just made a major decision. What was the decision? Why did they make it? How successful has it been?

ManagementCase

In the News

From the Pages of the *National Post*
CP Wants to be Leaner, Meaner: To Sell off Core Business

Canadian Pacific Ltd. is looking to divest at least one of its five core businesses this year, says David O'Brien, the company's chairman, president and chief executive.

During a conference call with analysts to discuss year-end results yesterday, Mr. O'Brien said the conglomerate is determined to reduce the range of its businesses, but he did not elaborate on how this would be done.

"I would have to say that our highest priority within the next 12 months is to further narrow the focus of Canadian Pacific, so that would be strategic priority number one," he said.

Investors have long complained CP suffers from a holding company discount in which the market value of the conglomerate is lower than the value of the parts individually.

For example, analysts say that CP's 91% stake in PanCanadian Petroleum has a market value of $8 billion, while CP itself has a market capitalization of $13.4 billion. The rail unit, Canadian Pacific Railway Co., is valued at $4 billion to $5 billion by some analysts, leaving its extensive coal, hotel and shipping arm with negligible stock market value.

Mr. O'Brien disputed analyst methods of reckoning the value of the individual units in a November interview. He said the discount is exaggerated and is really only 12%. However, he did concede at the time that something has to go.

"We're obviously not going to build five global businesses, we don't have the financial capacity to do that nor the intention. But we do think we can build a couple of global businesses," he said.

Figuring out what CP might keep or sell has become a parlour game for analysts and other industry observers.

Most agree the railway is a likely candidate for divestiture because Mr. O'Brien himself has said it is too small to be a buyer in the expected coming consolidation of the railway industry in North America.

Yesterday, he quashed rumours that CP was contemplating a sale of the unit to Canadian National Railway Co. "We have not had any discussions with CN, are not having any discussions with respect to a merger or sale to CN, nor are we contemplating a sale to any other party," he said.

Seizing on comments made by Mr. O'Brien in the past that CP has a bias toward energy and hotels, many analysts expect shipping and the railway units will be put on the block.

Mr. O'Brien cautioned against such speculation in November. However, he also conceded at the time that energy and hotels offer the best growth opportunities for the company.

Source: P. Fitzpatrick, "CP Wants to be Leaner, Meaner: To Sell Off Core Business," *Financial Post (National Post)*, January 23, 2001, pp. C1, C8.

Questions

1. Evaluate O'Brien's actions in terms of the six-step decision-making process described in this chapter (see Figure 6.4).

2. Do you think O'Brien might be suffering from any of the cognitive biases described in the chapter? Which ones?

3. Do you think O'Brien has charted the right course for Canadian Pacific? What new opportunities and threats might be on the horizon?

ManagementCase

In the News

From the Pages of *Fortune*
How Disney Keeps Ideas Coming

Starting with *The Little Mermaid*, a string of animated blockbusters has earned the Walt Disney Co. some US$5 billion since 1989. By any count, that's a tribute to how Disney not only sates its own notorious appetite for ever fatter profits but also gets the best out of that often-prickly-but-you-can't-live-without-'em bunch of folks, "the creatives." Most important, Disney sees to it that good ideas keep coming from all directions and that movies meet their deadlines. Peter Schneider, 45, president of feature animation, tells how a Gong Show for all his staffers—not to mention Ping-Pong with CEO Michael Eisner, who knows how to lose a game—helps the process.

How does a Gong Show get you the best ideas? We have people thinking about what we should do next all the time. But lots of other people in the building, including secretaries, want to present their ideas too. So three times a year they get to do just that, pitching what they think would make a good animated film, to me, Michael Eisner, Roy Disney, and my executive VP, Tom Schumacher.

Isn't that a pretty scary audience? Well, people with ideas get some help from their co-workers. Development helps them shape their pitch, for instance, so that it can be presented in three to five minutes, and coaches them on things such as the sort of visuals they could use. And if you're scared to death, someone else will hold your hand when you're up there. On the day of the Gong Show, it's very formal. The four of us all sit at a table and the room is full of people with ideas they want to

submit. That way everybody gets to hear all of the ideas. It's not as though you're pitching alone. There's a group supporting you. We usually have about 40 presenters. That morning we pick names at random, so there's no advance order, but each person knows when it's his or her turn.

Still, it must be tough for people to get up and say what they think to Michael Eisner. That's key, though. You have to create an environment where people feel safe about their ideas. And you do that by setting the example. Senior management has to take on the responsibility of saying, "Michael, you're wrong." When people see us saying that, it gives them permission to say it too.

Once all the ideas are presented, the four of us talk about which ones we liked and what aspects we liked about some of the others. Somebody may have a great concept, but the story may not be very good. Or somebody may have a great title. What we can't do is say, "Oh, that's fabulous. Great pitch, guys!" and when they leave, mumble, "What an idea! That was awful!" You must have immediate communication and not worry about people's egos and feelings and how to do it gently enough. You have to tell people why an idea didn't work. We don't pull our punches. If you do that enough, and people don't get fired or demoted, they begin to understand that no matter how good, bad, or indifferent the idea, it can be expressed, accepted, and thought about.

What films came out of the Gong Show? Most of Disney's animated features, in fact. In the case of *Hercules*, an animator came up with the central idea that a man is judged

by his inner strength and not his outer strength. The title was also his idea, but we didn't go for his story line. In the end that came from the two guys who became the directors of the film.

Did the guy with the original idea get paid for it? If we buy the pitch, the presenter usually gets what we'd pay for a first treatment. [Schneider would not give specifics, but a US$20 000 payment, spread over the period between an accepted pitch and a movie's release, is not unusual.]

How does a good idea become a business? First we come up with a core value for each story. I hate calling anything a mission statement, but I suppose it could be called that. The core value puts process in creativity. It's written down, and we all talk about it. It's not mysterious or ethereal. It's a value that we hang on to in terms of judging whether we're doing a good job. Are we telling the story we agreed to tell? You can't manage anything that doesn't have agreed-upon goals and direction.

How do you reach an agreement? It's a very collective approach to our work. We spend a lot of time in meetings arguing, discussing, and trying to come to a consensus. For instance, there was a lot of initial debate about what story we were telling with *The Hunchback of Notre Dame*. People thought we could never make it work. So we went back to the book and asked questions. What was the fundamental value of the book? What could the story be? What should it be? We discussed what changes we were going to make to have it tell our tale. As everybody gave their input, the debate moved along a little bit and

185

changed. We eventually decided that our story would be about discovering self-value.

But there's a time to talk and a time to start making the film. Yes, and that's the dilemma. As soon as you make the process concrete, it's wrong—but you have to lock things up or you can't go forward. You want to keep things in flux, in change, in chaos, until everybody says, "Gosh, that's exactly right." At the same time, there has to be a system and a certain amount of expectation. You have to say, "Within these boundaries, you will create. This is the budget. This is as big as it gets. These are your limitations. Make it work within this framework." And then be open to the judgment of, "My God, the framework's not right. Let's change it."

Do deadlines help you draw boundaries and do they play a role in managing creativity? They're a key ingredient to creativity. If you let people work on blank canvases with no rules, they tend to think too much. A deadline says, "By five o'clock tomorrow, you will have this up on storyboard, good, bad, or indifferent"—because we'll all come in and talk about it. We'll have something to react to. It'll spark the next idea.

Who sets the deadlines? Who's in charge? It's unclear who really is in charge of our process. Certainly the directors and the producers are the day-to-day point people. But there's a lot of give and take with Michael, Roy, Tom, and myself. The four of us are always asking if we're telling the story, if it's correct, if it's good. It's the dialogue that makes it work. At the end of the day, I think the idea of Disney animation is in charge. There's never really a possessiveness in terms of a particular person. I think you can assign it to a group of people.

But there must be some sort of hierarchy? I'm a very big believer in hierarchy, one that is not too structured. I don't think you can create things without it. When I first came here ten years ago, it was very flat. There was no real acknowledgment

in the animation ranks of who was good and who was not so good. Now it's very clear who the top five people in our business are. It gives people a sense of what they're progressing toward creatively.

The other kind of hierarchy is clearly that you have directors, an art director, a head of background. Each of these people is charged with leadership in terms of their troops. By and large we try to choose someone who is a great manager and a great artist. Those are very hard skills to find together. There has to be a certain sense of judgment, of quality, of speed, and the ability to say, "This is not good enough, not fast enough. You can do more. I expect more." Or to say, "Take your time. This is really important. Go slow." A real sense of judgment and an ability to communicate it.

How much autonomy do you give those who lead a Disney project? It's about putting the pieces together to allow people to do their job. It's about people clicking. So you want leadership to pick leadership. You want directors to pick their own art directors, the art directors to pick their head of background, heads of background to pick their own crew. You want people to have a sense of being chosen and wanted on a picture, not assigned, transferred, or exiled to it. You want people to say, "God, they want me."

How often can you do that? Seventy-five percent of the time. The other times we arrogantly say, even to directors, "Just do it." On one of our most successful projects, we told the director to shut up and do it. He was a very talented man but a bit indecisive in terms of where he wanted to go with his career. He didn't know if it was the right project. I said to him, "You've been offered to direct a major animated movie. Do it." He said, "But I don't think I like this and that." "Then change it," I said, "Get in there and start working." He did, and he became ecstatic about the work. But it was the process of it, not that he came in

saying, "I know what to do with this movie." It was the process: Going to work, drawing the drawing, talking about it, arguing about it, fighting about it, redoing it, being there.

But aren't you always going to have tension between the production side of the business and the creative side? Always is right. But it's very healthy. Production's job is to ask whether every decision is worth it. We recently discussed making a small change at the end of *Hunchback*. We were in our last weeks, and the final four shots didn't quite fire off. We were talking about 30 feet of film, which is a significant change. Production said, "Guys, it's 30 feet." And we said, "Yeah, but it doesn't work." They finally agreed, but we didn't go with our first choice, which was time-consuming and expensive, and figured out a way to make the change faster and for less money.

People are getting more comfortable with the idea that this is not about us and them. One of our managers organized a Ping-Pong tournament during lunch hours last year, and the winners played a final game with Michael Eisner and [president] Mike Ovitz. They said, "Oh, my God, Michael Eisner's playing Ping-Pong in our building. Wow, I'm important." I'm not sure they say that directly. But where else would the CEO be playing Ping-Pong with an hourly artist? The big guys lost the game, which goes to show people didn't feel they had to let Eisner win. The lines of hierarchy are so blurred that it makes no difference who you are to get access.

Source: J. McGowan, "How Disney Keeps Ideas Coming," *Fortune*, April 1, 1996, pp. 131–33.

Questions

1. How does the Walt Disney Company try to encourage its employees to be creative and innovative?

2. How would you describe Disney's approach to decision making?

Chapter seven

The Manager as a
Planner and Strategist

Learning Objectives

1. Describe the three steps of the planning process.

2. Explain the relationship between planning and strategy.

3. Explain the role of planning in predicting the future and in mobilizing organizational resources to meet future contingencies.

4. Outline the main steps in SWOT analysis.

5. Differentiate among corporate-, business-, and functional-level strategies.

6. Describe the vital role that strategy implementation plays in determining managers' ability to achieve an organization's mission and goals.

A Case in Contrast

Gerald Pencer Starts a Cola War

Coca-Cola (www.coca-cola.com) and Pepsi-Cola (www.pepsi.com) are household names worldwide. In 1995, together they controlled over 70 percent of the global soft-drink market and over 75 percent of the US soft-drink market. Their success can be attributed in part to the overall strategy that Coca-Cola and PepsiCo developed to produce and promote their products. Both companies decided to build global brands by manufacturing the soft-drink concentrate that gives cola its flavour and then selling the concentrate in syrup form to bottlers throughout the world. Coca-Cola and PepsiCo charge the bottlers a premium price for the syrup; they then invest part of the proceeds in advertising to build and maintain brand awareness. The bottlers are responsible for producing and distributing the actual cola. They add carbonated water to the syrup, package the resulting drink, and distribute it to vending machines, supermarkets, restaurants, and other retail outlets.

The bottlers leave all the advertising to Coca-Cola and PepsiCo. In addition, the bottlers must sign an exclusive agreement that prohibits them from distributing competing cola brands. A Coke or Pepsi bottler cannot bottle any other cola drink. This strategy has two major advantages for Coca-Cola and PepsiCo. First, it forces bottlers to enter into exclusive agreements, which create a high barrier to entry into the industry; any potential competitors that might want to produce and distribute a new cola product must create their own distribution network rather than use the existing network. Second, the large amount of money spent on advertising (in 2000, Coca-Cola spent $2.55 billion, and PepsiCo

Which of these colas tastes the best? That depends on your personal preferences. However, there is no doubt which cola costs the least, that produced by the Cott Corporation, which makes cola for organizations such as Safeway Canada and Loblaw's, including its President's Choice brand pictured here.

$1.95 billion) to develop a global brand name has helped Coca-Cola and PepsiCo differentiate their products so that consumers are more likely to buy a Coke or a Pepsi rather than a lesser-known cola. Moreover, brand loyalty allows both companies to charge a premium or comparatively high price for what is, after all, merely coloured water and flavouring. This differentiation strategy has made Coca-Cola and PepsiCo two of the most profitable companies in the world.

The global environment may be undergoing a change, however, because of Gerald Pencer, a Canadian entrepreneur who in the early 1990s came up with a new plan for competing in the cola market and created a new strategy to attract customers. Pencer's strategy was to produce a low-priced cola, manufactured and bottled by his own company, the Toronto-based Cott Corporation, and sell directly to major retail establishments (such as supermarket chains) as a private-label "house brand," thus bypassing the bottlers. He implemented this plan first in Canada and then quickly expanded into the United States because of interest in his product. Retailers are attracted to Cott's cola because its low cost allows them to make 15 percent more profit than they receive from selling Coke or Pepsi.[1]

To implement his strategy, Pencer planned to do no advertising (so that he could charge a low price for his cola) and to take advantage of efficient national distribution systems that retailers such as Toronto-based Loblaw's have created in recent years. This low-cost strategy enables Cott to circumvent the barrier to entry created by the exclusive distribution agreements that Coca-Cola and PepsiCo have signed with their bottlers. Cott delivers its products to the regional distribution centres of stores such as Loblaw's, and then Loblaw's and others handle distribution and advertising from that point on.

Pencer went on to supply an international network of bottlers by offering to sell cola concentrate for as little as one-sixth of the price that Coca-Cola and PepsiCo charge. In April 1994, for example, Cott launched a cola product in the United Kingdom for Sainsbury's, the United Kingdom's biggest food retailer. Sold as "Sainsbury's Classic Cola," the product was priced 30 percent below Coke and Pepsi. Within four weeks of the launch, Cott's cola had won a 60-percent share of Sainsbury's cola sales, equal to a quarter of the United Kingdom's entire take-home cola market! Cott also scored big in its home province of Ontario, where Cott's private-label brands now account for 31 percent of the entire cola market. Building on this success, by mid-1994, Cott had signed supply agreements with 90 retail chains around the world, including major retailers in the United Kingdom, France, Spain, Japan, and the United States.

By 1999, Pepsi had virtually conceded the "cola war," relying instead on its Frito-Lay snack division. Even though Coke faced serious global problems in 1999, it lost no market share to Pepsi, where it commands 51 percent internationally to Pepsi's 21 percent. Pepsi is stronger in the United States, but its market share was generally static at about 31 percent during the entire 1990s, while Coke's increased to 44 percent from 40 percent.[2] Cott, meanwhile, had to go through two years of painful restructuring in 1998–2000, following the death of founder Gerald Pencer. Despite this, the company remains the world's largest retailer-brand beverage supplier with three core markets: Canada, the United States and the United Kingdom.[3] ●

Overview

As the "Case in Contrast" suggests, there is more than one way to compete in an industry, and to find a viable way to enter and compete in an industry, managers must study the way other organizations behave and identify their strategies. By studying the strategies of Coca-Cola and PepsiCo, Gerald Pencer was able to devise a strategy that allowed him to enter the cola industry and take on these global giants. So far, Cott has had considerable success.

In an uncertain competitive environment, managers must engage in thorough planning to find a strategy that will allow them to compete effectively. This chapter explores the manager's role both as planner and as strategist. We discuss the different elements involved in the planning process, including its three major steps: (1) determining an organization's mission and major goals, (2) choosing strategies to realize the mission and goals, and (3) selecting the appropriate way of organizing resources to implement the strategies. We also discuss scenario planning and SWOT analysis, important techniques that managers use to analyze their current situation. By the end of this chapter, you will understand the role managers play in the planning and strategy-making process to create high-performing organizations. ●

An Overview of the Planning Process

planning Identifying and selecting appropriate goals and courses of action; one of the four principal functions of management.

strategy A cluster of decisions about what goals to pursue, what actions to take, and how to use resources to achieve goals.

vision statement A broad declaration of the big picture of the organization and/or a statement of its dreams for the future.

mission statement A broad declaration of an organization's purpose that identifies the organization's products and customers and distinguishes the organization from its competitors.

goal A desired future outcome that an organization strives to achieve.

Planning, as we noted in Chapter 1, is a process that managers use to identify and select appropriate goals and courses of action for an organization.[4] The organizational plan that results from the planning process details the goals of the organization and specifies how managers intend to attain those goals. The cluster of decisions and actions that managers take to help an organization attain its goals is its **strategy**. Thus, planning is both a goal-making and a strategy-making process.

In most organizations, planning is a three-step activity (see Figure 7.1). The first step is determining the organization's vision, mission and goals. A **vision statement** reveals the big picture of the organization, its dream for the future. When Bill Gates founded Microsoft, his vision was "a computer on every desk, in every home and in every office." Steve Ballmer, Microsoft's current CEO, sees this vision as insufficient in today's high-tech world, and has developed a new vision: "Empower people anytime, anywhere, on any device."[5] A **mission statement** is a broad declaration of an organization's overriding purpose; this statement is intended to identify an organization's products and customers, as well as to distinguish the organization in some way from its competitors. A **goal** is a desired future outcome that an organization strives to achieve. Generally the goals are set based on the vision and mission of the organization.

The second step is formulating strategy. Managers analyze the organization's current situation and then conceive and develop the strategies necessary to attain the organization's mission and goals.

Figure 7.1
Three Steps in Planning

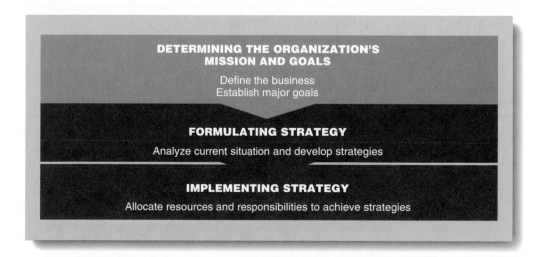

DETERMINING THE ORGANIZATION'S MISSION AND GOALS
Define the business
Establish major goals

FORMULATING STRATEGY
Analyze current situation and develop strategies

IMPLEMENTING STRATEGY
Allocate resources and responsibilities to achieve strategies

Even non-profit organizations have vision and mission statements. For instance, the vision statement of the Girl Guides of Canada is "Every girl in Canada wants to be and can be a member of Girl Guides of Canada–Guides du Canada: a vibrant, dynamic movement for girls, shaping a finer world." Their mission statement is "Girl Guides of Canada–Guides du Canada is a movement for girls, led by women. It challenges girls to reach their potential and empowers them to give leadership and service as responsible citizens of the world."

division A business unit that has its own set of managers and functions or departments and competes in a distinct industry.

divisional managers Managers who control the various divisions of an organization.

corporate-level plan Top management's decisions pertaining to the organization's mission, overall strategy, and structure.

corporate-level strategy A plan that indicates in which industries and national markets an organization intends to compete.

business-level plan Divisional managers' decisions pertaining to divisions' long-term goals, overall strategy, and structure.

The third step is implementing strategy. Managers decide how to allocate the resources and responsibilities required to implement those strategies between people and groups within the organization.[6] In subsequent sections of this chapter, we look in detail at the specifics of each of these steps. But first we examine the general nature and purpose of planning, one of the four managerial functions identified by Fayol.

Before going on to learn more about planning, you might want to consider the words of Ron Zambonini, CEO of Ottawa-based Cognos, who notes that planning seems to have gone out of fashion in the last five years. Speaking of dot-com founders, he said: "You see them in California, and, to a certain extent, here too. They work … 90 hours a week, but the whole goal they have is not to build a business or a company. [All they really want is] someone to buy them out."[7] Unfortunately, many of those companies folded, and were not bought out. Planning may have helped them be more successful.

Levels of Planning

In large organizations, planning usually takes place at three levels of management: corporate, business or division, and department or functional. Figure 7.2 shows the link between the three steps in the planning process and these three levels. To understand this model, consider how Toronto-based Rogers Communications Inc., a large organization that includes many businesses, operates.[8] Rogers Communications has three main levels of management: corporate level, business level, and functional level. At the corporate level are president and CEO Ted Rogers, senior vice-presidents Charles E. Hoffman, Ronan D. McGrath, John H. Tory, and Anthony P. Viner, and their corporate support staff. Below the corporate level is the business level. At the business level are the different **divisions** of the company. Rogers divisions include Rogers AT&T Wireless, Rogers Cable,

Figure 7.2
Levels and Types of Planning

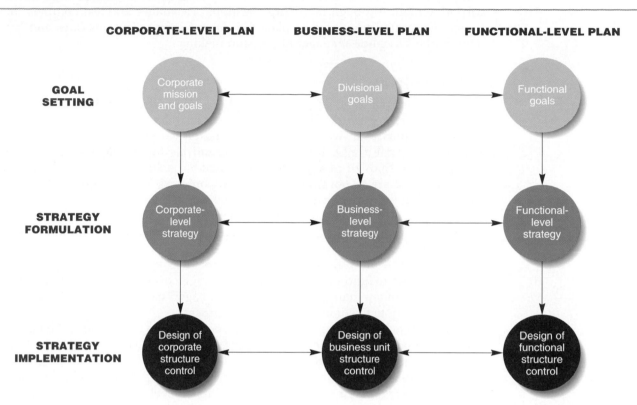

figure diagram

CORPORATE-LEVEL PLAN   BUSINESS-LEVEL PLAN   FUNCTIONAL-LEVEL PLAN

GOAL SETTING — Corporate mission and goals / Divisional goals / Functional goals

STRATEGY FORMULATION — Corporate-level strategy / Business-level strategy / Functional-level strategy

STRATEGY IMPLEMENTATION — Design of corporate structure control / Design of business unit structure control / Design of functional structure control

---

business-level strategy A plan that indicates how a division intends to compete against its rivals in an industry.

function A unit or department in which people have the same skills or use the same resources to perform their jobs.

functional managers Managers who supervise the various functions, such as manufacturing, accounting, and sales, within a division.

functional-level plan Functional managers' decisions pertaining to the goals that functional managers propose to pursue to help the division attain its business-level goals.

functional-level strategy A plan that indicates how a function intends to achieve its goals.

and Rogers Media. Each division has its own set of **divisional managers**. In turn, each division has its own set of functions or departments—manufacturing, marketing, human resource management, R&D, and so on. Thus, Rogers Cable has its own marketing function, as do Rogers AT&T Wireless and Rogers Media.

At Rogers Communications, as at other large organizations, planning takes place at each level. The **corporate-level plan** contains top management's decisions pertaining to the organization's mission and goals, overall (corporate-level) strategy, and structure (see Figure 7.2). **Corporate-level strategy** indicates in which industries and national markets an organization intends to compete.

The corporate-level plan provides the framework within which divisional managers create their business-level plans. At the business level, the managers of each division create a **business-level plan** that details (1) long-term goals that will allow the division to meet corporate goals and (2) the division's business-level strategy and structure. **Business-level strategy** states the methods a division or business intends to use to compete against its rivals in an industry.

A **function** is a unit or department in which people have the same skills or use the same resources to perform their jobs. Examples include manufacturing, accounting, and sales. The business-level plan provides the framework within which **functional managers** devise their plans. A **functional-level plan** states the goals that functional managers propose to pursue to help the division attain its business-level goals, which, in turn, will allow the organization to achieve its corporate goals. A **functional-level strategy** sets forth the actions that managers intend to take at the level of departments such as manufacturing, marketing, and R&D to allow the organization to attain its goals.

An important issue in planning is ensuring *consistency* in planning across the three different levels. Functional goals and strategies should be consistent with divisional goals and strategies, which in turn should be consistent with corporate goals and strategies, and vice versa. Once complete, each function's plan is normally linked to its division's business-level plan, which, in turn, is linked to the corporate plan. Although many organizations are smaller and less complex than Rogers Communications, most plan as Rogers Communications does and have written plans to guide managerial decision making.

Who Plans?

In general, corporate-level planning is the primary responsibility of top managers.[9] At Nortel Networks, the corporate-level goal that Nortel be the first to market with products that will contribute to a faster, easier-to-use Internet was first articulated by the CEO, John Roth. Roth and his top-management team also decided what kinds of new products to pursue to achieve this goal. Corporate-level managers are responsible for approving business- and functional-level plans to ensure that they are consistent with the corporate plan.

Corporate planning decisions are not made in a vacuum. Other managers have input to corporate-level planning. At Nortel and many other companies, divisional and functional managers are encouraged to submit proposals for new business ventures to the CEO and top managers, who evaluate the proposals and decide whether to fund them.[10] Thus, even though corporate-level planning is the responsibility of top managers, lower-level managers can be and usually are given the opportunity to become involved in the process.

This approach is common not only at the corporate level but also at the business and functional levels. At the business level, planning is the responsibility of divisional managers, who also review functional plans. Functional managers also typically participate in business-level planning. Similarly, although the functional managers bear primary responsibility for functional-level planning, they can and do involve their subordinates in this process. Thus, although ultimate responsibility for planning may lie with certain select managers within an organization, all managers and many nonmanagerial employees typically participate in the planning process.

Time Horizons of Plans

time horizon

The intended duration of a plan.

Plans differ in their **time horizon**, or intended duration. Managers usually distinguish among long-term plans with a horizon of five years or more, intermediate-term plans with a horizon between one and five years, and short-term plans with a horizon of one year or less.[11] Typically, corporate- and business-level goals and strategies require long- and intermediate-term plans, and functional-level goals and strategies require intermediate- and short-term plans.

Although most organizations operate with planning horizons of five years or more, it would be inaccurate to infer from this that they undertake major planning exercises only once every five years and then "lock in" a specific set of goals and strategies for that time period. Most organizations have an annual planning cycle, which is usually linked to their annual financial budget (although a major planning effort may be undertaken only every few years).

Although a corporate- or business-level plan may extend over five years or more, it is typically treated as a *rolling plan*, a plan that is updated and amended every year to take account of changing conditions in the external environment. Thus, the time horizon for an organization's 2001 corporate-level plan might be 2006; for the 2002 plan it might be 2007; and so on. The use of rolling plans is essential because of the high rate of change in the environment and the difficulty of predicting competitive conditions five years in the future. Rolling plans allow managers to make midcourse corrections if environmental changes warrant, or to change the thrust of the plan altogether if it no longer seems appropriate. The use of rolling plans allows managers to plan flexibly, without losing sight of the need to plan for the long term.

Standing Plans and Single-Use Plans

Another distinction often made between plans is whether they are standing plans or single-use plans. Managers create standing and single-use plans to help achieve an organization's specific goals. *Standing plans* are used in situations in which programmed decision making is appropriate. When the same situations occur repeatedly, managers develop policies, rules, and standard operating procedures (SOPs) to control the way employees perform their tasks. A *policy* is a general guide to action; a *rule* is a formal, written guide to action; and a *standard operating procedure* is a written instruction describing the exact series of actions that should be followed in a specific situation. For example, an organization may have a standing plan about ethical behaviour by employees. This plan includes a policy that all employees are expected to behave ethically in their dealings with suppliers and customers; a rule that requires any employee who receives from a supplier or customer a gift larger than $10 to report the gift; and an SOP that obliges the recipient of the gift to make the disclosure in writing within 30 days.

In contrast, *single-use plans* are developed to handle nonprogrammed decision making in unusual or one-of-a-kind situations. Examples of single-use plans include *programs*, which are integrated sets of plans for achieving certain goals, and *projects*, which are specific action plans created to complete various aspects of a program. One of NASA's major programs was to reach the moon, and one project in this program was to develop a lunar module capable of landing on the moon and returning to Earth.

Why Planning is Important

Do managers have to plan?

Essentially, planning is ascertaining where an organization is at the present time and deciding where it should be in the future and how to move it forward. When managers plan, they must consider the future and forecast what may happen in order to take action in the present and mobilize organizational resources to deal with future opportunities and threats. As we have discussed in previous chapters, however, the external environment is uncertain and complex, and managers typically must deal with incomplete information and bounded rationality. This is one reason why planning is so complex and difficult.

Almost all managers engage in planning, and all should participate because they must try to predict future opportunities and threats. The absence of a plan often results in hesitation, false steps, and mistaken changes of direction that can hurt an organization or even lead to disaster. Planning is important for four main reasons:

1. Planning is a useful way of getting managers to participate in decision making about the appropriate goals and strategies for an organization. Effective planning gives all managers the opportunity to participate in decision making. At Intel, for example, top managers, as part of their annual planning process, regularly request input from lower-level managers to determine what the organization's goals and strategies should be.

2. Planning is necessary to give the organization a sense of direction and purpose.[12] A plan states what goals an organization is trying to achieve and what strategies it intends to use to achieve them. Without the sense of direction and purpose that a formal plan provides, managers may interpret their own tasks and roles in ways that best suit themselves. The result will be an organization that is pursuing multiple and often conflicting goals, and a set of managers who do not cooperate and work well together. By stating which organizational goals and strategies are important, a plan keeps managers on track so that they use the resources under their control effectively.

3. A plan helps coordinate managers of the different functions and divisions of an organization to ensure that they all pull in the same direction. Without a good plan, it is possible that the members of the manufacturing function will produce

Intel Corporation
www.intel.com/

more products than the members of the sales function can sell, resulting in a mass of unsold inventory. Implausible as this might seem, according to Lee Iacocca, the former chairman of Chrysler Corporation, this situation prevailed at Chrysler in the late 1970s. Iacocca described how Chrysler's planning process had broken down because of power struggles and political infighting among managers. One result was that sales managers and manufacturing managers simply did not communicate with each other—each function acted alone without regard for the other.[13]

4. A plan can be used as a device for controlling managers within an organization. A good plan specifies not only which goals and strategies the organization is committed to, but also who is responsible for putting the strategies into action to attain the goals. When managers know that they will be held accountable for attaining a goal, they are motivated to do their best to make sure the goal is achieved.

Tracy Jeffrey, founder of Saskatoon-based The Grocery Go-Pher, found out the hard way how important planning is. Though her business is doing well, she regrets not having created a business plan when she started her business. "I really didn't understand what a business plan was for," she says.[14] "When you don't do a business plan, you end up in a situation where you're five years down the road and you don't know what your main objective as a business is."

Henri Fayol, the originator of the model of management we discussed in Chapter 1, said that effective plans should have four qualities: unity, continuity, accuracy, and flexibility.[15] *Unity* means that at any one time only one central, guiding plan is put into operation to achieve an organizational goal; more than one plan to achieve a goal would cause confusion and disorder. *Continuity* means that planning is an ongoing process in which managers build and refine previous plans and continually modify plans at all levels—corporate, business, and functional—so that they fit together into one broad framework. *Accuracy* means that managers need to make every attempt to collect and utilize all available information at their disposal in the planning process. Of course, managers must recognize the fact that uncertainty exists and that information is almost always incomplete (for reasons we discussed in Chapter 6). Despite the need for continuity and accuracy, however, Fayol emphasized that the planning process should have enough *flexibility* so that plans can be altered if the situation changes; managers must not be bound to a static plan.

Scenario Planning

One way in which managers can try to create plans that have the four qualities that Fayol described is by utilizing scenario planning, one of the most widely used planning techniques. **Scenario planning** (also known as *contingency planning*) is the generation of multiple forecasts of future conditions followed by an analysis of how to respond effectively to each of those conditions.

As noted previously, planning is about trying to forecast and predict the future in order to be able to anticipate future opportunities and threats. The future, however, is inherently unpredictable. How can managers best deal with this unpredictability? This question preoccupied managers at Royal Dutch Shell in the 1970s. Managers at Shell, one of the largest global oil and gas producers, came to the conclusion that because the future is unpredictable the only reasonable approach to planning is first to generate "multiple futures"—or scenarios of the future—based on different assumptions about conditions in the world oil market that *might prevail* in the future, and then to develop different plans that detail what the company *should do* in the event that any of these scenarios actually occurs. Accordingly, Shell's managers used scenario planning to generate different future scenarios of conditions in the oil market, asked divisional managers how they would respond to these opportunities and threats if such a scenario occurred, and then developed a set of plans based on these responses.

scenario planning

The generation of multiple forecasts of future conditions followed by an analysis of how to respond effectively to each of those conditions; also called contingency planning.

Shell
www.shell.com/

Managers at Shell believe that the advantage of scenario planning was not only the plans that were generated but also the ability to educate managers at all levels about the dynamic and complex nature of Shell's environment and the breadth of strategies available to Shell. Indeed, Shell's top managers now see scenario planning as a learning tool that raises the quality of the planning process and brings real benefits to the organization.[16]

Shell's success with scenario planning influenced many other companies to adopt similar systems. The great strength of scenario planning is its ability not only to anticipate the challenges of an uncertain future but also to educate managers to think about the future—to think strategically.

Tips for Managers

Planning

1. Think ahead by using exercises like scenario planning on a regular basis.

2. See plans as a guide to action. Don't feel straitjacketed by plans that may no longer be appropriate in a changing environment.

3. Make sure that the plans created at each of the three organizational levels are compatible with one another and that managers at all levels recognize how their actions fit into the overall corporate plan. Give managers at all levels the opportunity to participate in the planning process to best analyze an organization's present situation and the future scenarios that may affect it.

Determining the Organization's Vision, Mission and Goals

Determining the organization's vision, mission and goals is the first step of the planning process. Once these are agreed upon and formally stated in the corporate plan, they guide the next steps by defining which strategies are appropriate and which are inappropriate.[17]

Defining the Business

Vision differs from other forms of organizational direction setting in several ways:

"A vision has clear and compelling imagery that offers an innovative way to improve, which recognizes and draws on traditions, and connects to actions that people can take to realize change. Vision taps people's emotions and energy. Properly articulated, a vision creates the enthusiasm that people have for sporting events and other leisure time activities, bringing that energy and commitment to the workplace."[18]

The organization's vision is generally set by the CEO.

The organization's mission is supposed to flow from the vision for the organization. To determine an organization's mission, managers must first define its business so that they can identify what kind of value they will provide to customers. To define the business, managers must ask three questions:[19] (1) Who are our customers? (2) What customer needs are being satisfied? (3) How are we satisfying customer needs? They ask these questions to identify the customer needs that the organization satisfies and the way the organization satisfies those needs. Answering these questions helps managers to identify not only what customer needs they are satisfying now but what needs they should try to satisfy in the future and who their true competitors are. All of this information helps managers plan and establish appropriate goals.

Workers'
Compensation
Board of BC
www.worksafebc.com/

For example, the mission of the Workers' Compensation Board (WCB) of British Columbia is the safety, protection, and health of workers. Based on this mission, the WCB has established the following goals:[20]

- Creation of workplaces that are safe and secure from injury and disease;
- Successful rehabilitation and return-to-work of injured workers;
- Fair compensation for workers suffering injury or illness on the job;
- Sound financial management to ensure a viable WCB system;
- Protection of the public interest.

The case of Regina General Hospital's Native Healing Centre shows the important role that defining the business had in its planning process.

Focus on Diversity

Native Healing Centre Comes to General Hospital

Regina's General Hospital spent four years planning for the opening of its Native Healing Centre in December 1999.[21] "The Native Healing Centre and other initiatives were identified during needs assessment planning," said Anita Bergman, chair of the Regina District Health Board. The hospital recognized that the services it provided did not necessarily meet the needs of patients from the Aboriginal community who felt challenged by being from a minority culture, did not speak English, and had different beliefs about how to deal with personal well-being. Therefore, it developed a strategy to expand its services by working with those in the Aboriginal community to create a healing centre for Aboriginals.

The Native Health Centre at General Hospital includes an enclosed, circular healing room that is used for prayer, feasts and talking circles. The healing room may also be used for burning sweetgrass and holding healing ceremonies. The circular design is in keeping with the traditional medicine wheel or circle, an ancient symbol used by almost all the Native people of North and South America. The $312 000 facility also houses a family lounge and offices for the nine full-time staff who provide counselling, cross-cultural training and referrals to other agencies for Aboriginal people. The staff also follows up with the patients in the community.

There is only one other facility like this in Canada, and that is also in Saskatchewan. Jim Saunders, interim chief executive officer of the Regina Health District, says that, "The healing centre enables us to understand their culture and their health needs and it allows us to meet those needs much more effectively than in any other setting."

The role of the centre is to build trust and respect with patients. Staff members work as intermediaries between the hospital and its clients, helping the patients to understand hospital policies and procedures, while being knowledgeable and respectful of the Aboriginal culture's traditional healing approach.

"Through the creation of the Native Healing Centres, the Regina Health District is pleased to continue its strong relationship and long-term partnership with the Aboriginal community," said Saunders. "This is a unique project that enables us to respond to the needs of the Aboriginal community in the most efficient and effective way."

Establishing Major Goals

Once the business is defined, managers must establish a set of primary goals to which the organization is committed. Developing these goals gives the organization a sense of direction or purpose. In most organizations, articulating major goals is the job of the CEO, although other managers have input into the process. Thus, as noted previously, under the leadership of Jack Welch, General Electric has operated with the primary goal that it be first or second in every business in which it competes.

Gildan Activewear
www.gildan.com/

The best statements of organizational goals are ambitious—that is, they stretch the organization and require managers to improve its performance capabilities.[22] For example, as we saw in Chapter 4, when Saint-Laurent, QC-based Gildan Activewear Inc. started its T-shirt business in 1992, it was facing well-known rivals Hanes and Fruit of the Loom. However, the two founders, brothers Greg and Glenn Chamandy, were determined to win in the American market, while headquartered in Quebec. Fruit of the Loom recently declared bankruptcy and Gildan is very close to Hanes' market share. Gildan's managers' vision of the mission and goals of their company, and those of Bombardier and Nortel, are presented in Figure 7.3.

Although goals should be challenging, they should be realistic. Challenging goals give managers an incentive to look for ways to improve an organization's operation, but a goal that is unrealistic and impossible to attain may prompt managers to give up.[23] For example, in 2000, Nortel grew 42 percent, and became a $46.5 billion company. John Roth was looking at $62 billion on the horizon. However, with the plunge of the technology stocks at the end of that year, Nortel's future was not looking so bright. Continuing with that goal in the short run would most likely be demoralizing for the company's managers. In April 2001, Roth was working on new, achievable goals for Nortel.

The time period in which a goal is expected to be achieved should be stated. Time constraints are important because they emphasize that a goal must be attained within a reasonable period; they inject a sense of urgency into goal attainment and act as a motivator.

Formulating Strategy

strategy formulation

Analysis of an organization's current situation followed by the development of strategies to accomplish its mission and achieve its goals.

Strategy formulation involves managers in analyzing an organization's current situation and then developing strategies to accomplish its mission and achieve its goals.[24] Strategy formulation begins with managers analyzing the factors within an organization and outside, in the task and general environments, that affect or may affect the organization's ability to meet its goals now and in the future. SWOT

Figure 7.3
Three Mission Statements

COMPANY	MISSION STATEMENT
Bombardier	Bombardier's mission is to be the leader in all the markets in which it operates. This objective will be achieved through excellence in the fields of aerospace, rail transportation equipment, recreational products, financial services and services related to its products and core businesses.
Nortel Networks	Delivering greater value for customers worldwide through integrated network solutions spanning data and telephony.
Gildan Activewear	Gildan Activewear is dedicated to being the lowest-cost manufacturer and leading marketer of branded basic activewear to wholesale channels of distribution both in North America and internationally. To attain this goal, we will deliver the best in quality, service and price to our customers and, ultimately, to the end-users of our activewear products.

analysis and the five forces model are two techniques managers use to analyze these factors.

SWOT Analysis

SWOT analysis is a planning exercise in which managers identify organizational strengths (S) and weaknesses (W), and environmental opportunities (O) and threats (T). Based on a SWOT analysis, managers at the different levels of the organization select the corporate-, business-, and functional-level strategies to best position the organization to achieve its mission and goals (see Figure 7.4). Because SWOT analysis is the first step in strategy formulation at any level, we consider it first, before turning specifically to corporate-, business-, and functional-level strategies.

In Chapters 3 and 4, we discussed forces in the task and general environments that have the potential to affect an organization. We noted that changes in these forces can produce opportunities that an organization might take advantage of and threats that may harm its current situation. The first step in SWOT analysis is to identify an organization's strengths and weaknesses. Table 7.1 lists many important strengths (such as high-quality skills in marketing and in research and development) and weaknesses (such as rising manufacturing costs and outdated technology). The task facing managers is to identify the strengths and weaknesses that characterize the present state of their organization.

The second step in SWOT analysis begins when managers embark on a full-scale SWOT planning exercise to identify potential opportunities and threats in the environment that affect the organization at the present or may affect it in the future. Examples of possible opportunities and threats that must be anticipated (many of which were discussed in Chapter 3) are listed in Table 7.1.

With the SWOT analysis completed, and strengths, weaknesses, opportunities, and threats identified, managers can begin the planning process and determine strategies for achieving the organization's mission and goals. The resulting strategies should enable the organization to attain its goals by taking advantage of opportunities, countering threats, building strengths, and correcting organizational weaknesses. To appreciate how managers use SWOT analysis to formulate strategy, consider how James Shepard, CEO of Finning, used it to select strategies to try to turn Finning around.

Figure 7.4
Planning and Strategy Formulation

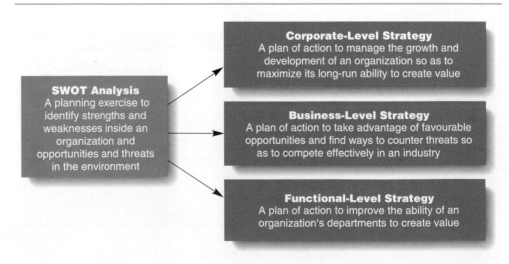

Table 7.1
Questions for SWOT Analysis

Potential Strengths	Potential Opportunities	Potential Weaknesses	Potential Threats
Well-developed strategy?	Expand core business(es)?	Poorly developed strategy?	Attacks on core business(es)?
Strong product lines?	Exploit new market segments?	Obsolete, narrow product lines?	Increase in domestic competition?
Broad market coverage?	Widen product range?	Rising manufacturing costs?	Increase in foreign competition?
Manufacturing competence?	Extend cost or differentiation advantage?	Decline in R&D innovations?	Change in consumer tastes?
Good marketing skills?	Diversify into new growth businesses?	Poor marketing plan?	Fall in barriers to entry?
Good materials management systems?	Expand into foreign markets?	Poor materials management systems?	Rise in new or substitute products?
R&D skills and leadership?	Apply R&D skills in new areas?	Loss of customer goodwill?	Increase in industry rivalry?
Human resource competencies?	Enter new related businesses?	Inadequate human resources?	New forms of industry competition?
Brand-name reputation?	Vertically integrate forward?	Loss of brand name?	Potential for takeover?
Cost of differentiation advantage?	Vertically integrate backward?	Growth without direction?	Changes in demographic factors?
Appropriate management style?	Overcome barriers to entry?	Loss of corporate direction?	Changes in economic factors?
Appropriate organizational structure?	Reduce rivalry among competitors?	Infighting among divisions?	Downturn in economy?
Appropriate control systems?	Apply brand-name capital in new areas?	Loss of corporate control?	Rising labour costs?
Ability to manage strategic change?	Seek fast market growth?	Inappropriate organizational structure and control systems?	Slower market growth?
Others?	Others?	High conflict and politics?	Others?
		Others?	

Management Insight

Finning Narrows its Focus

Edmonton-based Finning Ltd. used SWOT analysis in the early 1990s to determine its future strategy.[25] The company sells and services Caterpillar, the world's finest heavy-duty construction, forestry, and mining equipment. Faced with drops in revenues and profits when the economic cycle turned downward, they downsized and divested. However, these actions did not address where they should go when the next growth cycle occurred.

Finning's executive group, a team of seven key decision makers, found through their analysis that Finning "had significant strengths but also some notable weaknesses," said James Shepard, Finning's CEO at the time. "The same was true for threats and opportunities."

The team started by defining their business, which took days, and hours of heated discussion. This discussion, based on the company's strengths, clearly articulated for Finning the business they were in. Specifically, they realized that their customers were businesspeople, not retail customers.

Having arrived at the definition of their business, the Finning managers then set out to determine their distinctive excellence. Together the statements on business and distinctive excellence led to Finning's vision statement: "We provide best solutions by building relationships based on an intimate understanding of each customer's problem."

Two weaknesses Finning identified in its analysis were not communicating well with its employees, and safety management results that were not very good. The company put policies in place to address both of these issues.

Finning's strategic planning paid off in a number of ways. It showed a marked improvement in safety and increased employee satisfaction. In addition, over the next several years they had record increases in revenue and net income.

Finning also attributes its success with its 1993 purchase of Gildemeister S.A.C., the Caterpillar dealership in Chile, to its strategic planning. When Finning bought the dealership, "It had poor market share, was underperforming and lacked the direction needed to excel." Less than three years later, the company was a leader in the market, with over 70 percent market share in the mining sector. As Shepard explains, "It would have been possible to go into Chile and succeed without our new corporate strategy, but it would have taken longer. With an aggressive application of our vision, we took the company from a weak second in market share to a commanding lead in a relatively short time."

Ventures West
www.ventureswest.com/

Many of the dot-com companies that failed in recent years did not have an apparent strategy to guide them. Some planned on advertising revenues that would flow from people simply visiting their sites, but were not clear on how to develop customers who paid money for products. Robin Lewis, president of Vancouver-based venture capital firm Ventures West, wondered briefly if his company was out of touch when it refused to join the rush to fund dot-com companies. But now he's certain he made the right decision: "We couldn't find one where we thought we understood the business and the business model well enough to commit our money."[26] The strategies presented to Ventures West did not merit venture capital.

The Five Forces Model

What kinds of threats do organizations face?

Michael Porter's five forces model is a well-known model that helps managers isolate particular forces in the external environment that are potential threats. Porter identified five factors (the first four are also discussed in Chapter 3) that are major threats because they affect how much profit organizations competing within the same industry can expect to make:

- *The level of rivalry among organizations in an industry.* The more that companies compete against one another for customers–for example, by lowering the prices of their products or by increasing advertising–the lower is the level of industry profits (low prices mean less profit).

- *The potential for entry into an industry.* The easier it is for companies to enter an industry–because, for example, barriers to entry, such as brand loyalty, are low (see Chapter 3)–the more likely it is for industry prices and therefore industry profits to be low.

- *The power of suppliers.* If there are only a few suppliers of an important input, then (as discussed in Chapter 3) suppliers can drive up the price of that input, and expensive inputs result in lower profits for the producer.

- *The power of customers.* If only a few large customers are available to buy an industry's output, they can bargain to drive down the price of that output. As a result, producers make lower profits.

- *The threat of substitute products.* Often, the output of one industry is a substitute for the output of another industry (plastic may be a substitute for steel in some applications, for example). Companies that produce a product with a known substitute cannot demand high prices for their products, and this constraint keeps their profits low.

Porter argued that when managers analyze opportunities and threats, they should pay particular attention to these five forces because they are the major threats that an organization will encounter. It is the job of managers at the corporate, business, and functional levels to formulate strategies to counter these threats so that an organization can respond to its tasks and general environments, perform at a high level, and generate high profits.

Knowledge House
www.knowledge
house.net/

Examining and possibly altering a company's strategy to better reflect a changing environment can have big payoffs. For 17 years, Halifax-based Knowledge House had operated as a small, moderately successful software publisher in the medical education market. In 1999, CEO John Chambers decided on a new strategy, to become a full service provider of technology-enabled education programs. By 2001, the company had gone from $800 000 in sales to $18 million, and from 4 employees to over 170.[27]

Formulating Corporate-Level Strategies

Corporate-level strategy is a plan of action concerning which industries and countries an organization should invest its resources in to achieve its mission and goals. In developing a corporate-level strategy, managers ask: How should the growth and development of the company be managed in order to increase its ability to create value for its customers (and thus increase performance) over the long run? Managers of most organizations have the goal to grow their companies and actively seek out new opportunities to use the organization's resources to create more goods and services for customers.

In addition, some managers must help their organizations respond to threats due to changing forces in the task or general environment. For example, customers may no longer be buying the kinds of goods and services a company is producing (manual typewriters, eight-track tapes, black and white televisions), or other organizations may have entered the market and attracted customers away (this happened to Xerox when its patents expired and many companies rushed into the market to sell photocopiers). Or the markets may become saturated, as happened in the telecommunications industry recently, when more high-speed fibre optics networks were built than the market demanded. Top managers aim to find the best strategies to help the organization respond to these changes and improve performance.

The principal corporate-level strategies that managers use to help a compa grow, to keep it on top of its industry, and to help it retrench and reorganiz order to stop its decline are (1) concentration on a single business, (2) divers tion, (3) international expansion, and (4) vertical integration. These four stra are all based on one idea: An organization benefits from pursuing any one only when the strategy helps *further increase the value of the organization's f services for customers.* To increase the value of goods and services, a corpo strategy must help an organization, or one of its divisions, differentia value to its products either by making them unique or special or by l costs of value creation. Sometimes formulation of a corporate-level sents difficult challenges, as this "Management Insight" indicates.

Managing Globally

E.D. Smith Wants to Expand to the United States

E.D. Smith & Sons Ltd., famous for its jams and pie
a strategy that makes sense for the Winona, ON-based co.
Smith, chair and CEO, is the third-generation Smith to run the bu
has annual sales of about $140 million a year. Smith says the compan, too
big to be a regional player and too small to be taken seriously by the big multinational buyers."

Most companies that face this problem take one of two paths: sell out to a big multinational, or buy another company to grow in size and compete with the multinationals. The third option, just to wait and hope for the best, is the one that Smith dismisses: "If we don't do anything, if we don't expand, we'll become a small regional player. That is not an option. We'll be left behind."

Smith is looking for a buyer, although his preference would be to form an alliance that would help him meet his goal of being a significant player in the US market. Right now, most US supermarket chains don't even know of Smith's company, and so don't call him for products to stock their shelves. And even if they did, Smith is not sure that he would be successful at meeting demand. To do so, he would have to ramp up production, set up warehouses across the United States, and be able to supply an entire supermarket chain at once.

If a buyer does come along, he knows he may have to sell his shares, and hand over control of the family-owned business to someone else. However, he insists that any potential buyer must be willing to acquire the entire E.D. Smith operation, including the 380 employees. If a buyer or partner doesn't come along soon, Smith will probably buy a company that has the relationships and warehouses he needs. He's not as pleased with this option, however. "Our safest route is to link with [or sell to] a company that has the logistics and customer relationships. If that is not possible, we'll make acquisitions on our own, go down a road that is riskier."

Concentration on a Single Business

Most organizations begin their growth and development with a corporate-level strategy aimed at concentrating resources in one business or industry in order to develop a strong competitive position within that industry. For example, McDonald's began as one restaurant in California, but its managers' long-term goal was to focus its resources in the fast-food business and use those resources to expand quickly across the United States. Winnipeg-based Peak of the Market recently bought Winnipeg-based Stella Produce because it would allow the co-operative to increase its packaging capacity while adding another recognized brand name.[29] This decision by Peak of the Market's president and CEO, Larry McIntosh, continued the company's concentration on a single business while bringing it new growth opportunities.

Sometimes, concentration on a single business becomes an appropriate corporate-level strategy when managers see the need to reduce the size of their organizations in order to increase performance. Managers may decide to get out of certain industries, for example, when particular divisions lose their competitive advantage. Managers may sell off those divisions, lay off workers, and concentrate remaining organizational resources in another market or business to try to improve performance. After Lucent Technology's disastrous year in 2000, the company spun off its microelectronics and enterprise-networks divisions by creating Agere Systems Inc. and Avaya Inc. and putting them up for sale. Lucent's managers made a decision to focus their strategy on "competing directly with Nortel Networks in optical, data and wireless networking."[30] By ridding itself of its enterprise-networks division, Lucent signalled that it would no longer try to compete with Cisco Systems Inc. By disposing of its microelectronics division, Lucent stopped supplying some of its competitors. In contrast, when organizations are performing effectively, they often decide to enter new industries in which they can use their resources to create more value.

Lucent Technology
www.lucent.com/

Diversification

diversification

Expanding operations into a new business or industry and producing new goods or services.

Diversification is the strategy of expanding operations into a new business or industry and producing new goods or services.[31] Examples of diversification include PepsiCo's diversification into the snack-food business with the purchase of Frito-Lay, Seagram's diversification into the entertainment industry with the acquisition of MCA Universal, and Quebecor's move into broadcasting with its acquisition of Videotron. There are two main kinds of diversification: related and unrelated.

related diversification
Entering a new business or industry to create a competitive advantage in one or more of an organization's existing divisions or businesses.

synergy Performance gains that result when individuals and departments coordinate their actions.

Procter & Gamble
www.pg.com/

RELATED DIVERSIFICATION   **Related diversification** is the strategy of entering a new business or industry to create a competitive advantage in one or more of an organization's existing divisions or businesses. Related diversification can add value to an organization's products if managers can find ways for its various divisions or business units to share their valuable skills or resources so that synergy is created.[32] **Synergy** is obtained when the value created by two divisions cooperating is greater than the value that would be created if the two divisions operated separately. For example, suppose two or more divisions within a diversified company can utilize the same manufacturing facilities, distribution channels, advertising campaigns, and so on. Each division that shares resources has to invest less in the shared functions than it would have to invest if it had full responsibility for the activity. In this way, related diversification can be a major source of cost savings.[33] Similarly, if one division's R&D skills can be used to improve another division's products, the second division's products may receive a competitive advantage.

Procter & Gamble's disposable diaper and paper towel businesses offer one of the best examples of the successful production of synergies. These businesses share the costs of procuring inputs such as paper and developing new technology to reduce manufacturing costs. In addition, a joint sales force sells both products to supermarkets, and both products are shipped by means of the same distribution system. This resource sharing has enabled both divisions to reduce their costs, and as a result, they can charge lower prices than their competitors and thus attract more customers.[34]

In pursuing related diversification, managers often seek to find new businesses where they can use the existing skills and resources in their departments to create synergies, add value to the new business, and hence improve the competitive position of the company. Alternatively, managers may acquire a company in a new industry because they believe that some of the skills and resources of the *acquired* company might improve the efficiency of one or more of their existing divisions. If successful, such skill transfers can help an organization to lower its costs or better differentiate its products, because they create synergies between divisions.

One way to achieve diversification is by forming partnerships, something *The Toronto Star* recently announced it would do with the CBC. The two companies intend to maintain editorial independence while pooling some editorial, promotions and Internet activity.

unrelated diversification Entering a new industry or buying a company in a new industry that is not related in any way to an organization's current businesses or industries.

UNRELATED DIVERSIFICATION   Managers pursue **unrelated diversification** when they enter new industries or buy companies in new industries that are not related in any way to their current businesses or industries. One main reason for pursuing unrelated diversification is that, sometimes, managers can buy a poorly performing company, transfer their management skills to that company, turn its business around, and increase its performance, all of which creates value.

Another reason for pursuing unrelated diversification is that purchasing businesses in different industries lets managers engage in *portfolio strategy*, which is apportioning financial resources among divisions to increase financial returns or spread risks among different businesses, much as individual investors do with their own portfolios. For example, managers may transfer funds from a rich division (a "cash cow") to a new and promising division (a "star") and, by allocating money appropriately between divisions, create value. Though used as a popular explanation in the 1980s for unrelated diversification, portfolio strategy ran into increasing criticism in the 1990s.[35]

Today, many companies and their managers are abandoning the strategy of unrelated diversification because there is evidence that too much diversification can cause managers to lose control of their organization's core business. For instance, Seagram's venture into the entertainment business ultimately led it to sell off its original core business, the alcoholic-drinks division, and bring an end to a longstanding Canadian family business. Pepsi's CEO sold its restaurant businesses–Kentucky Fried Chicken, Pizza Hut, and Taco Bell–in 1997, because these did not fit its strategy of being in the snack industry. Management experts suggest that although unrelated diversification might initially create value for a company, managers sometimes use portfolio strategy to expand the scope of their organization's businesses too much. When this happens, it becomes difficult for top managers to be knowledgeable about all of the organization's diverse businesses. Managers do not have the time to process all of the information that is required to assess the strategy and performance of each division adequately and objectively, and organizational performance often suffers.

Thus, although unrelated diversification can create value for a company, research evidence suggests that many diversification efforts have reduced value rather than created it.[36] As a consequence, since the 1990s, there has been a trend among many diversified companies to divest many of their unrelated divisions. Managers sold off divisions and concentrated organizational resources on their core business and focused more on related diversification.[37] For instance, Toronto-based George Weston Ltd., the food processing and supermarket giant, announced in February 2001 that it would sell Georgetown, ON-based Neilson Dairy, Canada's fourth-largest dairy, and Black's Harbour, NB-based Connors Bros., a fish processing operation, so that it could acquire Bestfoods Baking Co. Chairman Galen Weston explained that the move would allow the company "to go forward in the baking and the supermarket business."[38] The company did not feel that it held a competitive advantage in either the dairy or the fish processing industries.

International Expansion

As if planning the appropriate level of diversification were not a difficult enough decision, corporate-level managers also must decide on the appropriate way to compete internationally. A basic question confronts the managers of any organization that competes in more than one national market: To what extent should the organization customize features of its products and marketing campaign to different national conditions?[39]

If managers decide that their organization should sell the same standardized product in each national market in which it competes, and use the same basic marketing approach, they adopt a **global strategy**.[40] Such companies undertake very little, if any, customization to suit the specific needs of customers in different countries. But if managers decide to customize products and marketing strategies to specific national conditions, they adopt a **multidomestic strategy**. Matsushita has traditionally pursued a global strategy, selling the same basic TVs and VCRs in every market in which it does business and often using the same basic marketing approach. Unilever, the European food and household products company, has pursued a multidomestic strategy. Thus, to appeal to German customers, Unilever's German division sells a different range of food products and uses a different marketing approach than its North American division. Even McDonald's has had to customize its food products for the global market. When McDonald's went to India, it had to sell chicken burgers and mutton burgers rather than beef burgers.

Both global and multidomestic strategies have advantages and disadvantages. The major advantage of a global strategy is the significant cost savings associated with not having to customize products and marketing approaches to different national conditions. For example, in the 1980s Levi Strauss paid an advertising

global strategy Selling the same standardized product and using the same basic marketing approach in each national market.

multidomestic strategy Customizing products and marketing strategies to specific national conditions.

M&M/Mars, the candy maker, previously used a multidomestic strategy and sold its candy under different brand names in the different countries in which it operates. Now it has changed to a global strategy to reduce costs and sells the candy under the same name throughout the world, as this billboard in Russia suggests.

agency $775 000 to produce a series of TV commercials to promote its 501 jeans. By using the same series in many countries and simply changing the language, Levi was able to save a significant amount of money and keep its prices low.[41]

The major disadvantage of pursuing a global strategy is that, by ignoring national differences, managers may leave themselves vulnerable to local competitors that do differentiate their products to suit local tastes. This occurred in the British consumer electronics industry. Amstrad, a British computer and electronics company, got its start by recognizing and responding to local consumer needs. Amstrad captured a major share of the British audio market by ignoring the standardized inexpensive music centres marketed by companies pursuing a global strategy, such as Sony and Matsushita. Instead, Amstrad's product was encased in teak rather than metal and featured a control panel tailor-made to appeal to British consumers' preferences. To remain competitive in this market, Matsushita had to increase its emphasis on local customization.

The advantages and disadvantages of a multidomestic strategy are the opposite of those of a global strategy. The major advantage of a multidomestic strategy is that, by customizing product offerings and marketing approaches to local conditions, managers may be able to gain market share or charge higher prices for their products. The major disadvantage is that customization raises production costs and puts the multidomestic company at a price disadvantage because it often has to charge prices higher than the prices charged by competitors pursuing a global strategy. Obviously, the choice between these two strategies calls for trade-offs.

Vertical Integration

When an organization is doing well in its business, managers often see new opportunities to create value by either producing their own inputs or distributing their own outputs. Managers at E. & J. Gallo Winery, for example, realized that they could lower Gallo's costs if they produced their own wine bottles rather than buying them from a glass company. As a result, Gallo established a new division to produce glass bottles.

vertical integration

A strategy that allows an organization to create value by producing its own inputs or distributing and selling its own outputs.

Vertical integration is the corporate-level strategy through which an organization becomes involved in producing its own inputs (backward vertical integration) or distributing and selling its own outputs (forward vertical integration).[42] A steel company that supplies its iron ore needs from company-owned iron ore mines is engaging in backward vertical integration. When Steve Jobs announced in 2001 that Apple Computer would open 25 retail stores to sell Macintosh machines directly to consumers, he showed that Apple was engaging in forward vertical integration.

Figure 7.5 illustrates the four main stages in a typical raw-materials-to-consumer value chain; value is added at each stage. Typically, the primary operations of an organization take place in one of these stages. For a company based in the assembly stage, backward integration would involve establishing a new division in intermediate manufacturing or raw-material production, and forward integration would involve establishing a new division to distribute its products to wholesalers or to sell directly to customers. A division at one stage receives the product produced by the division in the previous stage, transforms it in some way—adding value—and then transfers the output at a higher price to the division at the next stage in the chain.

As an example of how the value chain works, consider the cola segment of the soft-drink industry, discussed in the "Case in Contrast." Raw-materials suppliers include sugar companies and G.D. Searle, manufacturer of the artificial sweetener NutraSweet, which is used in diet colas. These companies sell their products to companies that make concentrate—such as Coca-Cola, PepsiCo, and Cott Corporation—which mix these inputs with others to produce the cola concentrate that they market. In the process, they add value to these inputs. The concentrate producers then sell the concentrate to bottlers, who add carbonated water to the concentrate and package the resulting drink—again adding value to the concentrate. Next, the bottlers sell the packaged product to various distributors, including retail stores such as Costco and Safeway, and fast-food chains such as McDonald's. These distributors add value by making the product accessible to customers. Thus, value is added by companies at each stage in the raw-materials-to-consumer chain.

A major reason why managers pursue vertical integration is that it allows them either to add value to their products by making them special or unique or to lower the costs of value creation. For example, Coca-Cola and PepsiCo, in a case of forward vertical integration to build brand loyalty and enhance the differentiated appeal of their colas, decided to buy up their major bottlers to increase control over marketing and promotion efforts—which the bottlers had been handling.[43] An example of using forward vertical integration to lower costs is Matsushita's decision

Figure 7.5
Stages in a Vertical Value Chain

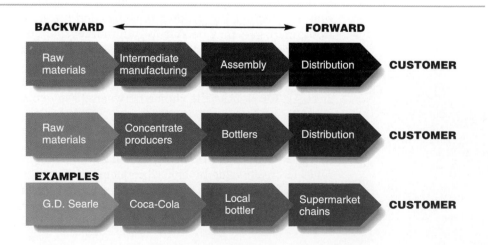

to open company-owned stores to sell its own products and thus keep the profit that independent retailers otherwise would earn.[44] The way in which McDonald's has used vertical integration to increase value is profiled in this "Managing Globally."

Managing Globally

McDonald's Vertically Integrates to Preserve Quality

McDonald's (www.mcdonalds.com) has been expanding into foreign markets ever since the mid-1970s, when managers became worried that a maturing market for fast food in the United States would limit growth opportunities. By the mid-1990s, McDonald's managers had operations in over 50 countries, and one-third of McDonald's revenues were generated by foreign sales.

When McDonald's enters a foreign market, managers try to apply the same basic approach to business that has proven successful in the United States and Canada. The main features of McDonald's restaurants worldwide are essentially the same, the food in particular. To achieve this uniformity, McDonald's builds close relationships with the suppliers of key restaurant and food inputs—such as potatoes, hamburger meat, and hamburger buns.

McDonald's, however, has found that it cannot always get the supplies it needs in foreign countries. In the United States and Canada, suppliers are fiercely loyal to McDonald's because their fortunes are closely linked to McDonald's fortunes. McDonald's maintains rigorous specifications for all the inputs it uses, and these standards have been the key to its consistency and quality control. Outside the United States and Canada, however, McDonald's has found that suppliers are far less willing or able to meet McDonald's input specifications. As a result, managers in some countries have found it necessary to vertically integrate backward and produce their own inputs.

In the United Kingdom, for example, McDonald's managers had problems persuading local bakeries to produce hamburger buns to the company's specifications. After quality problems were experienced with two local bakeries, McDonald's allocated resources to build a bakery in the United Kingdom to supply its own restaurants.

A more extreme problem faced the McDonald's Canada managers who made the decision to open the first McDonald's restaurant in Russia. There, the Canadians found that local suppliers simply lacked the capability to produce high-quality inputs. Managers were forced to vertically integrate through the local food industry on a heroic scale, importing potato seeds and indirectly managing dairy farms, cattle ranches, and vegetable plots. They ultimately ended up constructing the world's largest food-processing plant at a cost of $40 million. The restaurant itself cost only $4.5 million.[45] However, McDonald's Canada's managers expect a big payoff for these investments in the future.

Although vertical integration can help an organization to grow rapidly, it can be a problem when forces in the organizational environment counter the strategies of the organization and make it necessary for managers to reorganize or retrench. Vertical integration can reduce an organization's flexibility in responding to changing environmental conditions. For example, IBM used to produce most of its own components for mainframe computers. Doing this made sense in the 1960s, but it become a major handicap for the company in the fast-changing computer industry of the 1990s. The rise of organizationwide networks of personal computers has meant slumping demand for mainframes. As demand fell, IBM found itself with an excess-capacity problem, not only in its mainframe

IBM
www.ibm.com/

assembly operations but also in component operations. Closing down this capacity cost IBM over $7.75 billion in 1993 and clearly limited the company's ability to pursue other opportunities.[46] When considering vertical integration as a strategy to add value, managers must be careful because sometimes vertical integration actually reduces an organization's ability to create value when the environment changes.

One thing that managers need to consider when deciding on possible expansion strategies is the human costs of consolidating operations. While Air Canada initially projected $880 million in "synergies" from merging with Canadian Airlines, that figure was going to be at least $150 million less because of the difficulty of bringing the two employee groups together. CEO Robert Milton noted that it was "an emotionally charged process" that is "perceived to create winners and losers."[47] Management from the two merged companies can also clash, creating political struggles, as was seen in the public battling between the management of pulp and paper giant Montreal-based Abitibi Consolidated, and Montreal-based Quebecor.

Formulating Business-Level Strategies

Michael Porter, the researcher who developed the five forces model discussed earlier, also formulated a theory of how managers can select a business-level strategy, a plan to gain a competitive advantage in a particular market or industry.[48] According to Porter, managers must choose between the two basic ways of increasing the value of an organization's products: differentiating the product to add value or lowering the costs of value creation. Porter also argues that managers must choose between serving the whole market or serving just one segment or part of a market. Given those choices, managers choose to pursue one of four business-level strategies: low cost, differentiation, focused low cost, or focused differentiation (see Table 7.2). As you read about the different strategies below, you may want to consider the strategies of the newsprint and telecommunications industries that were discussed in the "Management Case" in Chapter 4.

Table 7.2

Porter's Business-level Strategies

Strategy	Number of Market Segments Served	
	Many	Few
Low cost	✓	
Focused low cost		✓
Differentiation	✓	
Focused differentiation		✓

Low-Cost Strategy

low-cost strategy

Driving the organization's costs down below the costs of its rivals.

With a **low-cost strategy**, managers try to gain a competitive advantage by focusing the energy of all the organization's departments or functions on driving the organization's costs down below the costs of its rivals. This strategy requires manufacturing managers to search for new ways to reduce production costs, R&D managers to focus on developing new products that can be manufactured more cheaply, and marketing managers to find ways to lower the costs of attracting customers. According to Porter, organizations pursuing a low-cost strategy can sell a product for less than their rivals sell it and yet still make a profit because of their lower costs. Thus, organizations that pursue a low-cost strategy hope to enjoy a competitive advantage based on their low prices. "A Case in Contrast" in Chapter 4 discussed the low-cost strategy of Saint-Laurent, QC-based Gildan Activewear Inc.

Differentiation Strategy

differentiation strategy

Distinguishing an organization's products from the products of competitors in dimensions such as product design, quality, or after-sales service.

With a **differentiation strategy**, managers try to gain a competitive advantage by focusing all the energies of the organization's departments or functions on distinguishing the organization's products from those of competitors in one or more

John Sleeman, CEO of Sleeman Breweries, which produces premium-priced beer, uses a differentiation strategy to distinguish his company from the low-cost beer strategies of Molson and Labatt.

important dimensions, such as product design, quality, or after-sales service and support. Often, the process of making products unique and different is expensive. This strategy, for example, often requires managers to increase spending on product design or R&D to differentiate the product, and costs rise as a result. However, organizations that successfully pursue a differentiation strategy may be able to charge a *premium price* for their products, a price usually much higher than the price charged by a low-cost organization. The premium price allows organizations pursuing a differentiation strategy to recoup their higher costs.

Coca-Cola and PepsiCo, profiled in the "Case in Contrast," are clearly pursuing a strategy of differentiation. Both companies spend enormous amounts of money on advertising to differentiate, and create a unique image for, their products. The Cott Corporation, in contrast, is pursuing a low-cost strategy. A major reason for Cott's low costs is the fact that the company does not advertise, which allows Cott to underprice both Coke and Pepsi.

"Stuck in the Middle"

According to Porter's theory, managers cannot simultaneously pursue both a low-cost strategy and a differentiation strategy. Porter identified a simple correlation: Differentiation raises costs and thus necessitates premium pricing to recoup those high costs. For example, if Cott Corporation suddenly began to advertise heavily to try to build a strong brand image for its products, Cott's costs would rise. Cott could then no longer make a profit simply by pricing its cola lower than Coca-Cola or Pepsi. According to Porter, managers must choose between a low-cost strategy and a differentiation strategy. He says that managers and organizations that have not made this choice are "stuck in the middle." According to Porter, organizations stuck in the middle tend to have lower levels of performance than do those that pursue a low-cost or a differentiation strategy. To avoid being stuck in the middle, top managers must instruct departmental managers to take actions that will result in either low cost or differentiation.

However, exceptions to this rule can be found. In many organizations, managers have been able to drive costs down below those of rivals and simultaneously differentiate their products from those offered by rivals.[49] For example, Toyota's production system is reportedly the most efficient in the world. This efficiency gives Toyota a low-cost strategy vis à vis its rivals in the global car industry. At the same time, Toyota has differentiated its cars from those of rivals on the basis of superior design and quality. This superiority allows the company to charge a premium price for many of its popular models.[50] Thus, Toyota seems to be simultaneously pursuing both a low-cost and a differentiated business-level strategy. This example suggests that although Porter's ideas may be valid in most cases, very well-managed companies such as Toyota, McDonald's, and Compaq may have both low costs and differentiated products.

Focused Low-Cost and Focused Differentiation Strategies

focused low-cost strategy Serving only one segment of the overall market and being the lowest-cost organization serving that segment.

Both the differentiation strategy and the low-cost strategy are aimed at serving most or all segments of the market. Porter identified two other business-level strategies that aim to serve the needs of customers in only one or a few market segments.[51] A company pursuing a **focused low-cost strategy** serves one or a few segments of the overall market and aims to be the lowest-cost company serving that segment. This is the strategy that Cott Corporation adopted. Cott focuses on large retail chains and strives to be the lowest-cost company serving that segment of the market.

By contrast, a company pursuing a **focused differentiation strategy** serves just one or a few segments of the market and aims to be the most differentiated company serving that segment. BMW pursues a focused strategy, producing cars exclusively for higher-income customers. By contrast, Toyota pursues a differentiation strategy and produces cars that appeal to consumers in all segments of the car market, from basic transportation (Toyota Tercel), through the middle of the market (Toyota Camry), to the high-income end of the market (Lexus).

As these examples suggest, companies pursuing either of these focused strategies have chosen to specialize in some way—by directing their efforts at a particular kind of customer (such as serving the needs of babies or affluent customers) or even the needs of customers in a specific geographical region (customers on the east or west coast).

focused differentiation strategy Serving only one segment of the overall market and trying to be the most differentiated organization serving that segment.

Formulating Functional-Level Strategies

How can managers of departments add value to the organization?

As discussed earlier in the chapter, a functional-level strategy is a plan of action to improve the ability of an organization's departments to create value. It is concerned with the actions that managers of individual departments (such as manufacturing or marketing) can take to add value to an organization's goods and services and thereby increase the value customers receive. The price that customers are prepared to pay for a product indicates how much they value an organization's products. The more customers value a product, the more they are willing to pay for it.

There are two ways in which departments can add value to an organization's products:

1. Departmental managers can lower the costs of creating value so that an organization can attract customers by keeping its prices lower than its competitors' prices.

2. Departmental managers can add value to a product by finding ways to differentiate it from the products of other companies.

If customers see more value in one organization's products than in the products of its competitors, they may be willing to pay premium prices. Thus, there must be a fit between functional- and business-level strategies if an organization is to achieve its mission and goal of maximizing the amount of value it gives customers. The better the fit between functional- and business-level strategies, the greater will be the organization's competitive advantage—its ability to attract customers and the revenue they provide.

Each organizational function has an important role to play in lowering costs or adding value to a product (see Table 7.3). Manufacturing can find new ways to lower production costs or to build superior quality into the product to add value. Marketing, sales, and after-sales service and support can add value by, for example, building brand loyalty (as Coca-Cola and PepsiCo have done in the soft-drink industry) and finding more effective ways to attract customers. Human resource management can lower the costs of creating value by recruiting and training a highly productive workforce. The R&D function can lower the costs of creating value by developing more efficient production processes. Similarly, R&D can add value by developing new and improved products that customers value over established product offerings. Managers can lower the costs of creating value and can add value through their effective leadership and coordination of the whole organization (see Chapter 13).

Table 7.3
How Functions Can Lower Costs and Create Value or Add Value to Create a Competitive Advantage

Value-creating Function	Ways to Lower the Cost of Creating Value (Low-cost Advantage)	Ways to Add Value (Differentiation Advantage)
Sales and marketing Materials management Research and development Manufacturing Human resource management	• Find new customers • Find low-cost advertising methods • Use just-in-time inventory system/computerized warehousing • Develop long-term relationships with suppliers and customers • Improve efficiency of machinery and equipment • Design products that can be made more cheaply • Develop skills in low-cost manufacturing • Reduce turnover and absenteeism • Raise employee skills	• Promote brand-name awareness and loyalty • Tailor products to suit customers' needs • Develop long-term relationships with suppliers to provide high-quality inputs • Reduce shipping time to customers • Create new products • Improve existing products • Increase product quality and reliability • Hire highly skilled employees • Develop innovative training programs

In trying to add value or lower the costs of creating value, all functional managers should attend to these four goals:[52]

1. *To attain superior efficiency.* Efficiency is a measure of the amount of inputs required to produce a given amount of outputs. The fewer the inputs required to produce a given output, the higher is the efficiency and the lower the cost of outputs. For example, a 1990 study of the automobile industry found that it took the average Japanese auto company 16.8 employee-hours to build a car, while the average American auto company took 25.1 employee-hours. These numbers suggest that Japanese companies at that time were more efficient and had lower costs than their American rivals.[53]

2. *To attain superior quality.* Here, quality means producing goods and services that are reliable—they do the job they were designed for and do it well.[54] Providing high-quality products creates a brand-name reputation for an organization's products. In turn, this enhanced reputation allows the organization to charge a higher price. In the automobile industry, for example, not only does Toyota have an efficiency-based cost advantage over many American and European competitors, but the higher quality of Toyota's products has also enabled the company to earn more money because customers are willing to pay a premium price for its cars.

3. *To attain superior innovation.* Anything new or unusual about the way in which an organization operates or the goods and services it produces is the result of innovation. Innovation leads to advances in the kinds of products, production processes, management systems, organizational structures, and strategies that an organization develops. Successful innovation gives an organization something unique that its rivals lack. This uniqueness may enhance value added and thereby allow the organization to differentiate itself from its rivals and attract customers who will pay a premium price for its product. For example, Toyota is widely credited with pioneering a number of critical innovations in the way cars are built, and these innovations have helped Toyota achieve superior productivity and quality—the basis of Toyota's competitive advantage.

4. *To attain superior responsiveness to customers.* An organization that is responsive to customers tries to satisfy their needs and give them exactly what they want. An

organization that treats customers better than its rivals treats them provides a valuable service for which customers may be willing to pay a higher price.

Attaining superior efficiency, quality, innovation, and responsiveness to customers requires the adoption of many state-of-the-art management techniques and practices, such as total quality management, flexible manufacturing systems, just-in-time inventory, self-managing teams, cross-functional teams, process reengineering, and employee empowerment. It is the responsibility of managers at the functional level to identify these techniques and develop a functional-level plan that contains the strategies necessary to develop them. We discuss these techniques in Part Five, where we focus on the management of operations and processes. The important issue to remember here is that all of these techniques can help an organization achieve a competitive advantage by lowering the costs of creating value or by adding value above and beyond that offered by rivals.

Planning and Implementing Strategy

After identifying appropriate strategies to attain an organization's mission and goals, managers confront the challenge of putting those strategies into action. Strategy implementation is a five-step process:

1. Allocating responsibility for implementation to the appropriate individuals or groups;
2. Drafting detailed action plans that specify how a strategy is to be implemented;
3. Establishing a timetable for implementation that includes precise, measurable goals linked to the attainment of the action plan;
4. Allocating appropriate resources to the responsible individuals or groups;
5. Holding specific individuals or groups responsible for the attainment of corporate, divisional, and functional goals.

As an example of how strategy implementation works in practice, consider again the case of Finning. While analyzing its strengths and weaknesses (during a SWOT analysis), Finning's managers discovered that safety management results were not very good. To address this, the managers created a Health, Safety and Environment Committee at the board of directors' level. The company then appointed a safety manager to monitor progress on all safety statistics quarterly. All operations (Canadian, European, and Chilean) report directly to the committee on their progress on safety and environmental issues. As the case of Finning illustrates, the planning process goes beyond the mere identification of strategies; it also includes actions taken to ensure that the organization actually implements its strategies. It should be noted that the plan for implementing a strategy may require radical redesign of the structure of the organization, the development of new control systems, and the adoption of a program for changing the culture of the organization. We address these issues in the next three chapters.

Tips for Managers

Strategy

1. Periodically define an organization's business to determine how well it is achieving its mission. Use this planning exercise to determine its future goals.
2. Make SWOT analysis an integral part of the planning process.
3. Always be alert for opportunities to increase the value of an organization's goods and services so it can better serve its customers' needs.

Chapter Summary

AN OVERVIEW OF THE PLANNING PROCESS

• Levels of Planning

• Who Plans?

• Time Horizons of Plans

• Standing Plans and Single-Use Plans

• Why Planning is Important

• Scenario Planning

DETERMINING THE ORGANIZATION'S VISION, MISSION AND GOALS

• Defining the Business

• Establishing Major Goals

FORMULATING STRATEGY

• SWOT Analysis

• The Five Forces Model

FORMULATING CORPORATE-LEVEL STRATEGIES

• Concentration on a Single Business

• Diversification

• International Expansion

• Vertical Integration

FORMULATING BUSINESS-LEVEL STRATEGIES

• Low-Cost Strategy

• Differentiation Strategy

• "Stuck in the Middle"

• Focused Low-Cost and Focused Differentiation Strategies

FORMULATING FUNCTIONAL-LEVEL STRATEGIES

PLANNING AND IMPLEMENTING STRATEGY

4. Ensure that functional managers focus on finding new ways in which to lower the costs of value creation or to add value to products so that an organization can pursue both a low-cost and a differentiation strategy.

5. Carefully assess the costs and benefits associated with using a corporate-level strategy and only enter a new business when it can be clearly demonstrated that it will increase the value of a product(s).

Summary and Review

AN OVERVIEW OF THE PLANNING PROCESS Planning is a three-step process: (1) determining an organization's mission and goals, (2) formulating strategy, and (3) implementing strategy. Managers use planning to identify and select appropriate goals and courses of action for an organization and to decide how to allocate the resources they need to attain those goals and carry out those actions. A good plan builds commitment for the organization's goals, gives the organization a sense of direction and purpose, coordinates the different functions and divisions of the organization, and controls managers by making them accountable for specific goals. In large organizations, planning takes place at three levels: corporate, business or division, and department or functional. Although planning is typically the responsibility of a well-defined group of managers, the subordinates of those managers should be given every opportunity to have input into the process and to shape the outcome. Long-term plans have a time horizon of five years or more; intermediate-term plans, between one and five years; and short-term plans, one year or less.

DETERMINING THE ORGANIZATION'S MISSION AND GOALS AND FORMULATING STRATEGY Determining the organization's mission requires managers to define the business of the organization and establish major goals. Strategy formulation requires managers to perform a SWOT analysis and then choose appropriate strategies at the corporate, business, and functional levels. At the corporate level, organizations use strategies such as concentration on a single business, diversification, international expansion, and vertical integration to help increase the value of the goods and services provided to customers. At the business level, managers are responsible for developing a successful low-cost or differentiation strategy, either for the whole market or for a particular segment of it. At the functional level, departmental managers strive to develop and use their skills to help the organization either to add value to its products by differentiating them or to lower the costs of value creation.

PLANNING AND IMPLEMENTING STRATEGY Strategy implementation requires managers to allocate responsibilities to appropriate individuals or groups, draft detailed action plans that specify how a strategy is to be implemented, establish a timetable for implementation that includes precise, measurable goals linked to the attainment of the action plan, allocate appropriate resources to the responsible individuals or groups, and hold individuals or groups accountable for the attainment of goals.

Management in Action

Topics for Discussion and Action

1. Describe the three steps of planning. Explain how they are related.

2. How can scenario planning help managers predict the future?

3. Ask a manager about the kinds of planning exercises he or she regularly uses. What are the purposes of these exercises, and what are their advantages or disadvantages?

4. What is the role of divisional and functional managers in the formulation of strategy?

5. Why is it important for functional managers to have a clear grasp of the organization's mission when developing strategies within their departments?

6. What is the relationship among corporate-, business-, and functional-level strategies, and how do they create value for an organization?

7. Ask a manager to identify the corporate-, business-, and functional-level strategies used by his or her organization.

Building Management Skills

How to Analyze a Company's Strategy

Pick a well-known business organization that has received recent press coverage and for which you can get a number of years' annual reports from your school library or on the Internet. For this organization, do the following.

1. From the annual reports, identify the main strategies pursued by the company over a 10-year period.

2. Try to identify why the company pursued these strategies. What reason was given in the annual reports, press reports, and elsewhere? What goals and objectives did the company say it had?

3. Document whether and when any major changes in the strategy of the organization occurred. If changes did occur, try to identify the reason for them.

4. If changes in strategy occurred, try to determine the extent to which they were the result of long-term plans and the extent to which they were responses to unforeseen changes in the company's task environment.

5. What is the main industry that the company competes in?

6. What business-level strategy does the company seem to be pursuing in this industry?

7. What is the company's reputation with regard to productivity, quality, innovation, and responsiveness to customers in this industry? If the company has attained an advantage in any of these areas, how has it done so?

8. What is the current corporate-level strategy of the company? What is the company's stated reason for pursuing this strategy?

9. Has the company expanded internationally? If it has, identify its largest international market. How did the company enter this market? Did its mode of entry change over time?

Small Group Breakout Exercise

Low Cost or Differentiation?

Form groups of three or four people, and appoint one member as spokesperson who will communicate your findings to the class when called on by the instructor. Then discuss the following scenario.

You are a team of managers of a major national clothing chain, and you have been charged with finding a way to restore your organization's competitive advantage. Recently, your organization has been experiencing increasing competition from 2 sources. First, discount stores such as Zeller's and Target have been undercutting your prices because they buy their clothes from low-cost foreign manufacturers while you buy most of yours from high-quality domestic suppliers. Discount stores have been attracting those of your customers who buy at the low end of the price range. Second, small boutiques opening in malls provide high-price designer clothing and are attracting away your customers at the high end of the market. Your company has become stuck in the middle, and you have to decide what to do: Should you start to buy abroad so that you can lower your prices and start to pursue a low-cost strategy? Should you focus on the high end of the market and become more of a differentiator? Or should you try to do both and pursue both a low-cost and a differentiation strategy?

1. Using scenario planning, analyze the pros and cons of each alternative.
2. Think about the various clothing retailers in your local malls and city, and analyze the choices they have made about how to compete with one another along the low-cost and differentiation dimensions.

Exploring the World Wide Web

Specific Assignment

This exercise follows up on the activities of McDonald's Corporation (www.mcdonalds.com), which is vertically integrating on a global level. Research McDonald's Web site to get a feel for this global giant. In particular, focus on McDonald's most recent annual report and its descriptions of the company's goals and objectives.

1. What are the main elements of McDonald's strategy at the corporate, business, and functional levels?
2. How successful has the company been recently?
3. Has McDonald's Canada's strategy been any different than its parent operation's?

General Assignment

Search for a Web site that contains a good description of a company's strategy. What is the company's mission? Use the concepts and terminology of this chapter to describe the company's strategy to achieve its mission.

ManagementCase

In the News

From the Pages of the *Financial Post Daily*
De Zen and the Art of Home Maintenance

He's the plastic version of Magna Inc.'s Frank Stronach, but that's not to say Vic De Zen is a cheap imitation. Like Stronach, De Zen, the chairman, president and chief executive of Royal Group Technologies Ltd., arrived in Canada as a poor immigrant tool and die maker and went on to establish an empire. But where Stronach made his fortune as an auto parts magnate, De Zen, 56, has built an $850-million-a-year company in the plastics business.

And today, he's embarking on an ambitious plan to extend Royal's domain further by housing the world in its revolutionary plastic homes.

"If you have an operation on your heart, it's plastic. And in your knee, it's plastic. Without plastic, we're going to die," says De Zen during a kinetic interview at his company's Woodbridge, Ont. head office.

Twice during the rapid-fire conversation he springs from his chair— once to fetch a bottle of Crown Royal as a gift for a visitor and another time to drag him by the sleeve to a window looking out on a 75-hectare field that will soon be home to a giant warehouse.

Like its boss, Royal is a company on the move, with plans to add 180 000 square metres of manufacturing space to its existing 495 000 square metres around the world.

Much of this expansion is being driven by demand for plastic window frames, blinds and siding, which have yielded compound annual revenue growth averaging 21.8% over the past five years.

Earnings hit $97.5 million ($1.21 a share) in 1997, for 33% compounded annual growth over five years.

"The guy is driven. He sets the tone for his company and all those ideas that flow come from him. He's a great ideas man," says Farras Shammas of the Canadian Plastics Industry Association. "I guess it's one man's vision. Put simply, Vic is a visionary, there's no doubt about it."

Analysts are keen on the stock, valuing it like a growth stock rather than a building materials company. Even if, as expected, the building materials division slows down with a cooling economy and rising interest rates, the burgeoning housing division is expected to continue strong.

Investors have been equally positive, bidding Royal stock up from a low of $30 last year to a 52-week high of $48 this spring. Yesterday, the shares (RYG/TSE) closed at $44, up 5 cents.

Royal's results are evident even in the company's parking lot, which looks like a Mercedes dealership.

It's made De Zen, who owns 20% of the shares and 80% of the votes, a rich man. He gets around on a Canadair regional jet and hanging in the boardroom is a picture of him linking arms with Prime Minister Jean Chretien.

But it hasn't always been so cushy. De Zen was born near Venice and apprenticed in Switzerland before coming to Canada in 1962 with $20. Legend has it he was at work an hour later putting up TV antennas with his brother.

After repeated disappointments with bad bosses, in 1970 he and two partners pooled $58 000 in savings to set up a line of plastic extrusion machines that was Royal Plastics. His take-home pay was $35 a week.

Among the many lessons learned was self-reliance. De Zen still remembers the frustration of looking for someone to repair equipment whenever there were problems. "I had no spare parts and I didn't know what to do. I had very little money and every time I called somebody in they overcharged me," he says. "If nobody is feeding you, you have to grow your own food."

Today, Royal is totally vertically integrated. Its various units are involved in every stage of the business, from providing chemicals and compounding to designing and making machinery, building its own plants and transporting its products with a 250-truck fleet that picks up scrap for recycling.

In April, it went a step further, agreeing to pay $82 million for a polyvinyl chloride resin plant in Sarnia, Ont., from Imperial Oil Ltd.

In an age when many companies are outsourcing work to concentrate on core businesses, De Zen has no qualms about Royal's strategy. For him, outsourcing is like leasing a car when you can afford to buy it.

Moreover, he says, integration allows the company to control quality, respond more quickly to customer needs and develop new ideas in months rather than years.

"How can you compete in world markets today? The Americans are big and they are super businessmen. If you cannot make it faster than them and better, customers won't deal with you," he says.

All this sets up Royal for its newest and biggest venture yet, the construction of plastic houses through the Royal Building System.

In some ways, plastic houses are an old idea. When Disneyland opened its Tomorrowland theme park in 1955, among the exhibits were plastic houses set not too far from the Moonliner. Since then, multinationals such as General Electric Co. have tried to build plastic houses and failed. Royal's houses, developed after $50 million in spending and seven prototypes since 1990, may change that.

The building system works somewhat like a giant Lego set. Instead of blocks, though, it uses hollow panels that slot together and are then filled with cement. Once finished with brick or siding, the resulting house looks like a regular home, only it feels more solid inside. It's also cheaper and faster to build, with three semi-skilled workers able to put up a 550-square-foot home in three days for about US$16 000.

"With the building system they don't cut down any more trees, it's maintenance-free, very competitive and it lasts over 200 years," says De Zen.

Home sales could grow to 40% of Royal's total revenue by 2002 from less than 10% in 1997, he expects.

Royal sees the potential market as vast, having received building code approval in about 25 countries. It has made sales throughout the world, including in South America, Russia, Eastern Europe, Taiwan and the southern U.S., where termites and damp weather feast on traditional wooden structures.

Among the big sales last year were a $40-million, 800-home project in Russia, a $10-million, 2160-home complex in the Philippines, a $14-million, 460-unit resort and casino in St. Kitts, and a $5-million, 400-home deal in Argentina.

In Canada, the homes are also beginning to gain acceptance, with sales to such diverse customers as remote First Nations groups and the luxury condo market.

The system has commercial applications too, with Shell Oil Co. using it to erect at least 70 car washes and a 2000-square-metre office in Houston. Royal has formed a 50-50 joint venture with Shell Chemical Holdings Inc. to develop the market for Royal structures for such things as convenience stores, service centres, research facilities and office buildings.

De Zen himself doesn't live in a plastic house—his wife refuses to move from their home in the country —but his son is building an 1800-square-metre plastic monster home for himself.

Despite the growing financial returns—the backlog for homes is about $150 million—De Zen says the greatest satisfaction comes from helping shelter the poor.

This was brought home when he toured Antigua after a hurricane in 1995 destroyed most houses but left standing homes and a school built with the Royal System.

"People were kissing me, they thought I was like the Pope," he recalls. "They called me in. 'Come on, eat and drink with us,' they said. 'My friend is dead, but I'm alive.'"

Source: P. Fitzpatrick, "De Zen and the Art of Home Maintenance," *The Financial Post Daily*, May 13, 1998, p. 10.

Questions

1. Use Porter's five forces model to analyze the nature of competition in Royal Group Technologies' industry.

2. What business- and functional-level strategies is Vic De Zen pursuing to compete in this industry?

ManagementCase
In the News

From the Pages of *Canadian Plastics*
Holding its Own

This New Brunswick-based operation, one of Amcor PET Packaging's five bottle manufacturing plants in Canada, has seen a number of changes in the Atlantic Canada bottling market in recent years. One of the company's long-time customers, Coca Cola, pulled out of the Maritimes when it decided to consolidate its operations in Quebec. While soft drink beverage bottles still form the bulk of the Moncton plant's business, bottled water now accounts for 15 to 20 percent of sales and has seen significant growth during the last few years.

"We've been very encouraged by the growth of the water market," says plant manager David Kinnear. The plant is currently supplying a number of companies with water bottles in 355 mL, 500 mL, 1 L and 1.5 L sizes. It is also looking to secure more bottled water business in the near future. As the bottled water market has grown, large beverage companies have also entered the market, Kinnear says, noting that Pepsi sponsors the Aquafina label and Coca Cola has the Desani brand.

The company's main customers in the beverage business are Pepsi, Cott, Big 8 and Cassidy beverages, for which it supplies bottles in sizes ranging from 250 mL to 2 L. It makes bottles in clear and green, which are made from pre-colored PET. It also has the capability to make a blue-tinted bottle for water using color concentrate.

The facility has three Husky injection molding machines for making pre-forms, and three Krupp Coroplast machines, as well as one Milacron machine, for stretch-blowing the pre-forms into bottles. Blow machines run at a rate of between 2700 and 10 100 bottles per hour. Palletized bottles are usually aged 72 hours before shipping and stored in a high-ceilinged warehouse capable of accommodating three-high pallet stacking.

The Moncton operation has its own budget, and, as well, is empowered to meet its production targets and develop new business. As a member of the Amcor PET Packaging family, however, the facility receives considerable R&D and marketing support at the corporate level, Kinnear stresses. All resin pricing is negotiated through Amcor's central corporate offices.

There is a high priority placed on reducing costs at the company, as there is in the bottling industry as a whole, notes Kinnear. Designing bottles that are lighter in weight is one strategy used to cut raw material costs. For instance, in 1981 a 2 L bottle weighed about 68 g, compared with 47 g today. As bottles become lighter, the goal to take out still more weight and meet all the performance criteria required for bottles becomes more of a challenge. Amcor, and as it was once known, Twinpak, have been at the forefront in the use of advanced technology to build lighter, stronger bottles through investment in corporate research and development.

At the plant level, employees are encouraged to suggest and implement ways to cut costs and improve efficiencies. The plant's maintenance staff often manufactures parts that frequently need to be replaced in production equipment, thus saving the premium on parts bought from dealers. Kinnear says the stable, mature workforce of 53 employees contributes to the facility's ability to control costs and maintain an edge on competitors.

While allowing with typical Maritime modesty that the plant's goal is to maintain the business it has, Kinnear says it is always on patrol for new business and growth. "We are always looking for new opportunities. Every day we ask ourselves what steps we can take to find new business and customers."

Source: M. LeGault, "Holding its Own: Growth in the Bottled Water Business has Enabled Amcor PET Packaging's Moncton Plant to Maintain its Position as the Leading Bottle Manufacturer in Atlantic Canada," *Canadian Plastics*, December 2000, p. 16.

Questions

1. What strategies did David Kinnear use to increase the profitability of the Moncton plant?

2. What kinds of control systems does Kinnear use with his employees? How does the control system support productivity?

3. What kinds of corporate- and business-level strategies is Kinnear working on to help increase Amcor's performance?

Part 4

MANAGING ORGANIZATIONAL ARCHITECTURE

Chapter 8
Managing Organizational Structure

Chapter 9
Organizational Control and Culture

Chapter 10
Human Resource Management

Chapter eight

Managing Organizational Structure

Learning Objectives

1. Identify the factors that influence managers' choice of an organizational structure.

2. Explain how managers group tasks into jobs that are motivating and satisfying for employees.

3. Describe the organizational structures managers can design, and explain why they choose one structure over another.

4. Explain why there is a need to both centralize and decentralize authority.

5. Explain why managers who seek new ways to increase efficiency and effectiveness are using strategic alliances and network structures.

A Case in Contrast

Altamira Moves from its Entrepreneurial Roots to a Team Structure

Altamira Investment Services (www.altamira.com) was the poster child for the Canadian mutual fund industry from 1987 to the mid-1990s. Founded in the late 1960s in Toronto, the company had developed an entrepreneurial style that served it well in its early years. By the early 1990s, Altamira was seen as the little no-load company that could, because it was one of the hottest firms in the no-load sector and was attracting lots of money from investors.

By the mid-1990s, however, the company's entrepreneurial style was not working as well. Altamira had grown too large, too fast, and little consideration had been given to adjusting the organizational structure to suit the new times. The environment for mutual fund companies had changed considerably over the company's 30-year history: regulations were being rewritten, new market entrants were using e-business, established companies were making new alliances to increase their global capacities, and consumers were demanding a more integrated approach to their wealth management needs.[1]

The company was also facing internal problems: there had been a bitter battle for ownership of Altamira; the company's flagship mutual fund was not doing well; one of its star performers had resigned under a cloud of suspicion; and clients had become impatient and taken millions of dollars elsewhere.

In early 1998, Altamira named Gordon Cheesbrough as CEO to turn the company around. Cheesbrough had been chief executive at ScotiaMcLeod Inc., the investment dealer

Gordon Cheesbrough, CEO of Altamira Investment Services, instituted more of a team structure at the company when he arrived in 1998.

When Frank Mersch, formerly the "star" fund manager at Altamira, departed the company, the need for structural changes in the organization became obvious.

arm of the Bank of Nova Scotia. Though Altamira was struggling when Cheesbrough arrived, he immediately recognized that there were a number of things that
the company did well. These included having a smart group of people who were
"loyal to the company and committed to putting it back on top."[2] The company also
had a good reputation for direct-to-client services and a history of innovation.

He also saw a number of things that had to change. One serious problem was that
the lagging performance of the Altamira Equity Fund was affecting the entire company. Because it represented 35 percent of the company's mutual fund assets, the
fund's performance had a large impact on everyone's morale. Frank Mersch had been
the fund manager for Altamira Equity for a number of years, and was considered a
star. In fact, Mersch was the face of Altamira during the 1980s and early 1990s.

However, with the departure of Mersch as the result of being disciplined by the
Ontario Securities Commission for trading in a penny stock, it became obvious that
Altamira's largest organizational structure problem was its star system of portfolio
management. "If Altamira hadn't invented it, we certainly had put our name on it,"
said Cheesbrough. While that system had greatly benefited Altamira for a number
of years, Cheesbrough did not see it as the way to move the company forward. "One
person cannot carry a company on his or her shoulders. The star system … inhibits
team-building. It hampers succession planning and expansion into new areas that
require new skills. And it affects the morale of employees who live in the star's
shadow."[3]

Cheesbrough's goal was to create a team-based corporate structure for Altamira,
while keeping the unique qualities and spirit that had made the company successful
in the past. Creating a team was not an easy task, however. When Cheesbrough
arrived, there were 14 highly talented, highly competitive portfolio managers. The
competitive drive was directed at each other, however, rather than toward the competition. "So I quickly called the managers together and told them that, from now on,
we would be fighting the competition and not each other," said Cheesbrough.[4]

Building the team was not always easy. As Cheesbrough noted, communication
wasn't open or frequent at the company when he started there. Often, employees
found out important company news by reading it in the newspaper. So he insisted
that people had to be treated as team members, not as competitors. The company
began weekly meetings so that portfolio managers could share market information
and develop ideas for new products. "In short, we started thinking about maximizing our performance and service capabilities as a fund family, not just as individual
funds," says Cheesbrough.[5]

TA Associates Inc., which bought 35 percent of Altamira in 1997, feels that
Cheesbrough did the right thing by moving to a team structure. "[Mersch's depar-
ture] made room to do what needed to be done anyway, which was to move more
to a team management approach. … You've got a lot more cooperation than ever
before and the investment results are, I think, starting to show that," said Andrews
McLane, TA's managing director.[6]

Altamira was considering an IPO in late 2000, although because of market conditions the company has decided not to pursue this for the time being. But its fortunes are certainly better than when Gordon Cheesbrough first arrived. The team
structure seems to be making a difference for Altamira. ●

Overview

As the "Case in Contrast" suggests, the challenge facing Altamira Investment
Services was to identify the best way to operate in the new, more competitive
industry environment. Under Gordon Cheesbrough, Altamira radically changed

the way it organized its employees and other resources to meet that challenge, and the company has improved.

In Part Four, we examine how managers can organize and control human and other resources to create high-performing organizations. To organize and control (two of the four functions of management identified in Chapter 1), managers must design an organizational architecture that makes the best use of resources to produce the goods and services customers want. **Organizational architecture** is the combination of the organizational structure, control systems, culture, and human resource management system that determines how efficiently and effectively organizational resources are used.

By the end of this chapter, you will be familiar not only with various organizational structures but also with various factors that determine the organizational design choices that managers make. Then in Chapters 9 and 10, we examine issues surrounding the design of an organization's control systems, culture, and human resource management systems. ●

organizational architecture The organizational structure, control systems, culture, and human resource management system that together determine how efficiently and effectively organizational resources are used.

Designing Organizational Structure

organizational structure A formal system of task and reporting relationships that coordinates and motivates organizational members so that they work together to achieve organizational goals.

organizational design The process by which managers make specific organizing choices that result in a particular kind of organizational structure.

Organizing is the process by which managers establish the structure of working relationships among employees to allow them to achieve organizational goals efficiently and effectively. **Organizational structure** is the formal system of task and reporting relationships that determines how employees use resources to achieve organizational goals.[7] **Organizational design** is the process by which managers make specific organizing choices that result in the construction of a particular organizational structure.[8]

As noted in Chapter 2, according to contingency theory, managers design organizational structures to fit the factors or circumstances that are affecting the company the most and causing them the most uncertainty.[9] Thus, there is no "best" way to design an organization: Design reflects each organization's specific situation. Four factors are important determinants of organizational structure: the nature of the organizational environment, the type of strategy the organization pursues, the technology the organization uses, and the characteristics of the organization's human resources (see Figure 8.1).[10]

Figure 8.1
Factors Affecting Organizational Structure

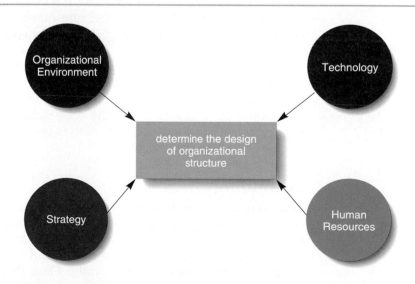

The Organizational Environment

In general, the more quickly the external environment is changing and the greater the uncertainty within it, the greater are the problems facing managers trying to gain access to scarce resources. In this situation, to speed decision making and communication and make it easier to obtain resources, managers typically make organizing choices that bring flexibility to the organizational structure.[11] They are likely to decentralize authority and empower lower-level employees to make important operating decisions. In contrast, if the external environment is stable, if resources are readily available, and if uncertainty is low, then less coordination and communication among people and functions is needed to obtain resources, and managers can make organizing choices that bring more formality to the organizational structure. Managers in this situation prefer to make decisions within a clearly defined hierarchy of authority and use extensive rules and standard operating procedures to govern activities.

As we discussed in Chapters 3 and 4, change is rapid in today's marketplace, and increasing competition both at home and abroad is putting greater pressure on managers to attract customers and increase efficiency and effectiveness. Consequently, interest in finding ways to structure organizations–such as through empowerment and self-managed teams–to allow people and departments to behave flexibly has been increasing. The "Case in Contrast" shows how Altamira moved toward a more flexible structure through its use of teams.

Strategy

As discussed in Chapter 7, once managers decide on a strategy, they must choose the right means to implement it. Different strategies often call for the use of different organizational structures. For example, a differentiation strategy aimed at increasing the value customers perceive in an organization's goods and services usually succeeds best in a flexible structure. Flexibility facilitates a differentiation strategy because managers can develop new or innovative products quickly–an activity that requires extensive cooperation among functions or departments. In contrast, a low-cost strategy that is aimed at driving down costs in all functions usually fares best in a more formal structure, which gives managers greater control over the expenditures and actions of the organization's various departments.[12]

In addition, at the corporate level, when managers decide to expand the scope of organizational activities by, for example, vertical integration or diversification, they need to design a flexible structure to provide sufficient coordination among the different business divisions.[13] As discussed in Chapter 7, many companies have been divesting businesses because managers have been unable to create a competitive advantage to keep them up to speed in fast-changing industries. By moving to a more flexible structure, such as a product division structure, divisional managers gain more control over their different businesses.

Finally, expanding internationally and operating in many different countries challenges managers to create organizational structures that allow organizations to be flexible on a global level.[14] As we discuss later, managers can group their departments or functions and divisions in several ways to allow them to pursue an international strategy effectively.

Technology

Technology is the combination of skills, knowledge, tools, machines, computers, and equipment that are used in the design, production, and distribution of goods and services. As a rule, the more complicated the technology that an organization uses, the more difficult it is for managers and workers to impose strict control on technology or to regulate it efficiently. Thus, the more complicated the technology, the greater is the need for a flexible structure to enhance managers' ability to respond to unexpected situations and give them the freedom to work out new solutions to the problems they encounter. In contrast, the more routine the technology, the more appropriate a formal structure is, because tasks are simple and the steps needed to produce goods and services have been worked out in advance.

What makes a technology routine or complicated? One researcher who investigated this issue, Charles Perrow, argued that two factors determine how complicated or nonroutine technology is: task variety and task analyzability.[15] *Task variety* is the number of new or unexpected problems or situations that a person or function encounters in performing tasks or jobs. *Task analyzability* is the degree to which programmed solutions are available to people or functions to solve the problems they encounter. Nonroutine or complicated technologies (such as the work of scientists in a research and development laboratory who develop new products or discover new drugs) are characterized by high task variety and low task analyzability. This means that many varied problems occur, and that solving these problems requires significant nonprogrammed decision making. In contrast, routine technologies (such as typical mass-production or assembly operations or fast-food operations) are characterized by low task variety and high task analyzability. This means that the problems encountered do not vary much and are easily resolved through programmed decision making.

The extent to which producing or creating goods and services depends on people or machines also determines how nonroutine a technology is. The more the technology used to produce goods and services is based on the skills, knowledge, and abilities of people working together on an ongoing basis and not on automated machines that can be programmed in advance, the more complex the technology is. Joan Woodward, a professor who investigated the relationship between technology and organizational structure, differentiated among three kinds of technology on the basis of the relative contribution made by people or machines.[16]

small-batch technology Technology that is used to produce small quantities of customized, one-of-a-kind products and is based on the skills of people who work together in small groups.

Small-batch technology is used to produce small quantities of customized, one-of-a-kind products based on customer demand. Production is carried out by skilled people who work together in small groups. Examples of goods and services produced by small-batch technology include custom-built cars, such as Ferraris and Rolls-Royces, highly specialized metals and chemicals that are produced by the pound rather than by the ton, and the process of auditing in which a small team of auditors is sent to a company to evaluate and report on its accounts. Because small-batch goods or services are customized and unique, workers need to respond to each situation as required; thus, a structure that decentralizes authority to employees and allows them to respond flexibly is most appropriate with small-batch technology.

mass-production technology Technology that is based on the use of automated machines that are programmed to perform the same operations over and over.

Woodward's second kind of technology, **mass-production technology**, is based primarily on the use of automated machines that are programmed to perform the same operations time and time again. Individuals perform a repetitive task, there is little need for flexibility, and a formal organizational structure gives managers the most control over the production process. Mass production results in an output of large quantities of standardized products such as washing machines and services such as car washes or dry cleaning.

continuous-process technology Technology that is almost totally mechanized and is based on the use of automated machines working in sequence and controlled through computers from a central monitoring station.

The third kind of technology that Woodward identified, **continuous-process technology**, is almost totally mechanized. Products are produced by automated machines working in sequence and controlled through computers from a central monitoring station. Examples of continuous-process technology include chemical plants such as Saskatoon Chemicals and Shell Canada's polypropylene plant in Sarnia, Ontario. Other examples are large steel mills, oil refineries, nuclear power stations, and large-scale brewing operations. Workers watch for breakdowns or other problems that may occur unexpectedly and cause dangerous or even deadly situations. If an unexpected situation does occur, employees must be able to respond quickly and appropriately to prevent a disaster from resulting (such as an explosion in a chemical complex). The need for a flexible response makes a flexible organizational structure the preferred choice with this kind of technology.

In summary, the nature of an organization's technology is an important determinant of its structure. Today, with the increasing use of computer-controlled production, and the movement toward using self-managed teams (groups of workers who are given the responsibility for supervising their own activities and for monitoring the quality of the goods and service they provide) to promote innovation, increase quality, and reduce costs, many companies are trying to make their structures more flexible to take advantage of the value-creating benefits of complex technology.

Human Resources

A final important factor affecting an organization's choice of structure is the characteristics of the human resources it employs. In general, the more highly skilled an organization's workforce is and the more people are required to work together in groups or teams to perform their tasks, the more likely is the organization to use a flexible, decentralized structure. Highly skilled employees or employees who have internalized strong professional values and norms of behaviour as part of their training usually desire freedom and autonomy and dislike close supervision. Accountants, for example, have learned the need to report company accounts honestly and impartially, and doctors and nurses have absorbed the obligation to give patients the best care possible.

Flexible structures, characterized by decentralized authority and empowered employees, are well suited to the needs of highly skilled people. Similarly, when people work in teams, they must be allowed to interact freely, which also is possible in a flexible organizational structure. Thus, when designing an organizational structure, managers must pay close attention to the workforce and to the work itself.

In summary, an organization's external environment, strategy, technology, and human resources are the factors to be considered by managers seeking to design the best structure for an organization. The greater the level of uncertainty in an organization's environment, the more complex its strategy and technology, and the more highly qualified and skilled its workforce, the more likely are managers to design a structure that is flexible. The more stable an organization's environment, the less complex and more well understood its strategy or technology, and the less skilled its workforce, the more likely are managers to design an organizational structure that is formal and controlling.

How do managers design a structure to be either flexible or formal? The way an organization's structure works depends on the organizing choices managers make about four issues:

• How to group tasks into individual jobs;
• How to group jobs into functions and divisions;
• How to allocate authority in the organization among jobs, functions, and divisions;
• How to coordinate or integrate jobs, functions, and divisions.

Grouping Tasks Into Jobs: Job Design

job design The process by which managers decide how to divide tasks into specific jobs.

The first step in organizational design is **job design**, the process by which managers decide how to divide into specific jobs the tasks that have to be performed to provide customers with goods and services. Managers at McDonald's, for example, have decided how best to divide the tasks required to provide customers with fast, cheap food in each McDonald's restaurant. After experimenting with different job arrangements, McDonald's managers decided on a basic division of labour among chefs and food servers. Managers allocated all the tasks involved in actually cooking the food (putting oil in the fat fryers, opening packages of frozen french fries, putting beef patties on the grill, making salads, and so on) to the job of chef. They allocated all the tasks involved in giving the food to customers (such as greeting customers, taking orders, putting fries and burgers into bags, adding salt, pepper, and serviettes, and taking money) to food servers. In addition, they created other jobs—the job of dealing with drive-through customers, the job of keeping the restaurant clean, and the job of shift manager responsible for overseeing employees and responding to unexpected events. The result of the job design process is a *division of labour* among employees, one that McDonald's and other managers have discovered through experience is most efficient.

Establishing an appropriate division of labour among employees is a critical part of the organizing process, one that is vital to increasing efficiency and effectiveness. At McDonald's, the tasks associated with chef and food server were split into different jobs because managers found that, for the kind of food McDonald's serves, this approach was most efficient. It is efficient because when each employee is given fewer tasks to perform (so that his or her job becomes more specialized), employees become more productive at performing the tasks that constitute their job.

At Subway sandwich shops, however, managers chose a different kind of job design. At Subway, there is no division of labour among the people who make the sandwiches, wrap the sandwiches, give them to customers, and take the money. The roles of chef and food server are combined into one role. This different division of tasks and jobs is efficient for Subway and not for McDonald's because Subway serves a limited menu of mostly submarine-style sandwiches that are prepared to order. Subway's production system is far simpler than McDonald's, because McDonald's menu is much more varied and its chefs must cook many different kinds of foods.

Managers of every organization must analyze the range of tasks to be performed and then create jobs that best allow the organization to give customers the

McDonald's
www.mcdonalds.com/

Subway
www.subway.com/

Workers at Subway follow the carefully designed work procedures that allow the company to provide a large variety of sandwiches to customers quickly at peak times.

job simplification
Reducing the number of tasks that each worker performs.

goods and services they want. In deciding how to assign tasks to individual jobs, however, managers must be careful not to take **job simplification**, the process of reducing the number of tasks that each worker performs, too far.[17] Too much job simplification may reduce efficiency rather than increase it if workers find their simplified jobs boring and monotonous, become demotivated and unhappy, and as a result perform at a low level.

Job Enlargement and Job Enrichment

In an attempt to create a division of labour and design individual jobs to encourage workers to perform at a higher level and be more satisfied with their work, several researchers have proposed ways other than job simplification to group tasks into jobs: job enlargement and job enrichment.

job enlargement
Increasing the number of different tasks in a given job by changing the division of labour.

Job enlargement is increasing the number of different tasks in a given job by changing the division of labour.[18] For example, because Subway food servers make the food as well as serve it, their jobs are "larger" than the jobs of McDonald's food servers. The idea behind job enlargement is that increasing the range of tasks performed by a worker will reduce boredom and fatigue and may increase motivation to perform at a high level—increasing both the quantity and the quality of goods and services provided.

job enrichment
Increasing the degree of responsibility a worker has over his or her job.

Job enrichment is increasing the degree of responsibility a worker has over his or her job by, for example, (1) empowering workers to experiment to find new or better ways of doing the job, (2) encouraging workers to develop new skills, (3) allowing workers to decide how to do the work and giving them the responsibility for deciding how to respond to unexpected situations, and (4) allowing workers to monitor and measure their own performance.[19] The idea behind job enrichment is that increasing workers' responsibility increases their involvement in their jobs and thus increases their interest in the quality of the goods they make or the services they provide.

In general, managers who make design choices that increase job enrichment and job involvement are likely to increase the degree to which workers behave flexibly rather than rigidly or mechanically. Narrow, specialized jobs are likely to lead people to behave in predictable ways; workers who perform a variety of tasks and who are allowed and encouraged to discover new and better ways to perform their jobs are likely to act flexibly and creatively. Thus, managers who enlarge and enrich jobs create a flexible organizational structure, and those who simplify jobs create a more formal structure. If workers are also grouped into self-managed work teams, the organization is likely to be flexible because team members provide support for each other and can learn from one another.

The Job Characteristics Model

What factors make jobs more interesting and motivating?

J.R. Hackman and G.R. Oldham's job characteristics model is an influential model of job design that explains in detail how managers can make jobs more interesting and motivating.[20] Hackman and Oldham's model (see Figure 8.2) also describes the likely personal and organizational outcomes that will result from enriched and enlarged jobs.

According to Hackman and Oldham, every job has five characteristics that determine how motivating the job is. These characteristics determine how employees react to their work and lead to outcomes such as high performance and satisfaction and low absenteeism and turnover:

- *Skill variety:* The extent to which a job requires an employee to use a wide range of different skills, abilities, or knowledge. *Example:* The skill variety required by the job of a research scientist is higher than that called for by the job of a McDonald's food server.

Figure 8.2
The Job Characteristics Model

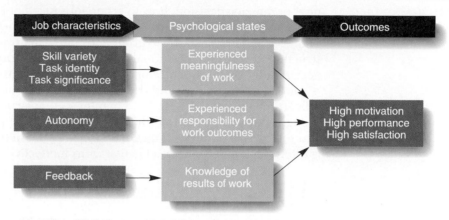

Source: Adapted from J.R. Hackman and G.R. Oldham, *Work Redesign* (Reading, MA: Addison-Wesley, 1980).

- *Task identity:* The extent to which a job requires a worker to perform all the tasks required to complete the job from the beginning to the end of the production process. *Example:* A craftworker who takes a piece of wood and transforms it into a custom-made piece of furniture such as a desk has higher task identity than does a worker who performs only one of the numerous operations required to assemble a television.

- *Task significance:* The degree to which a worker feels his or her job is meaningful because of its effect on people inside the organization such as co-workers or outside the organization such as customers. *Example:* A teacher who sees the effect of his or her efforts in a well-educated and well-adjusted student enjoys higher task significance than does a dishwasher who monotonously washes dishes as they come to the kitchen.

- *Autonomy:* The degree to which a job gives an employee the freedom and discretion needed to schedule different tasks and decide how to carry them out. *Example:* Salespeople who have to plan their schedules and decide how to allocate their time among different customers have relatively high autonomy compared to assembly-line workers whose actions are determined by the speed of the production line.

- *Feedback:* The extent to which actually doing a job provides a worker with clear and direct information about how well he or she has performed the job. *Example:* An air traffic controller whose mistakes may result in a midair collision receives immediate feedback on job performance; a person who compiles statistics for a business magazine often has little idea of when he or she makes a mistake or does a particularly good job.

Hackman and Oldham argue that those five job characteristics affect an employee's motivation because they affect three critical psychological states (see Figure 8.2). The more employees feel that their work is meaningful and that they are *responsible for work outcomes* and *responsible for knowing how those outcomes affect others*, the more motivating work becomes and the more likely employees are to be satisfied and to perform at a high level. Moreover, employees who have jobs that are highly motivating are called on to use their skills more and to perform more tasks, and they are given more responsibility for doing the job. All of the foregoing are characteristic of jobs and employees in flexible structures where authority is decentralized and where employees commonly work with others and must learn new skills to complete the range of tasks for which their group is responsible.

Grouping Jobs Into Functions and Divisions

Once managers have decided which tasks to allocate to which jobs, they face the next organizing decision: how to group jobs together to best match the needs of the organization's environment, strategy, technology, and human resources. Most top-management teams decide to group jobs into departments and develop a functional structure to use organizational resources. As the organization grows, managers design a divisional structure or a more complex matrix or product team structure.

Choosing a structure and then designing it so that it works as intended is a significant challenge. As noted in Chapter 7, managers reap the rewards of a well-thought-out strategy only if they choose the right type of structure to implement and execute the strategy. The ability to make the right kinds of organizing choices is often what differentiates effective from ineffective managers.

Tips for Managers

Designing Structure and Jobs

1. Carefully analyze an organization's environment, strategy, technology, and human resources to decide which type of organizational structure to use.

2. To create a more formal structure, carefully define the limits of each worker's job, create clear job descriptions, and evaluate each worker on his or her individual job performance.

3. To create a more flexible structure, enlarge and enrich jobs and allow workers to expand their jobs over time. Also, encourage workers to work together and evaluate both individual and group performance.

4. Use the job characteristics model to guide job design and recognize that most jobs can be enriched to make them more motivating and satisfying.

Functional Structure

A *function* is a group of people, working together, who possess similar skills or use the same kind of knowledge, tools, or techniques to perform their jobs. Manufacturing, sales, and research and development are often organized into functional departments. A **functional structure** is an organizational structure composed of all the departments that an organization requires to produce its goods or services. Figure 8.3 shows the functional structure that Pier 1 Imports, a home furnishings company, uses to supply its customers with a range of goods from around the world to satisfy their desires for new and innovative products.

Pier 1's main functions are finance and administration, merchandising (purchasing the goods), stores (managing the retail outlets), logistics (managing product distribution), marketing, human resources, and real estate. Each job inside a function exists because it helps the function perform the activities necessary for high organizational performance. Thus, within the logistics department are all the jobs necessary to distribute and transport products efficiently to stores, and inside the marketing department are all the jobs (such as promotion, photography, and visual communication) that are necessary to increase the appeal of Pier 1's products to customers.

There are several advantages to grouping jobs according to function. First, when people who perform similar jobs are grouped together, they can learn from observing one another and thus become more specialized and can perform at a higher level. The tasks associated with one job often are related to the tasks associated to another job, which encourages cooperation within a function. In Pier 1's marketing department, for example, the person designing the photography pro-

functional structure

An organizational structure composed of all the departments that an organization requires to produce its goods or services.

Pier 1
www.pier1.com/

Figure 8.3
The Functional Structure of Pier 1 Imports

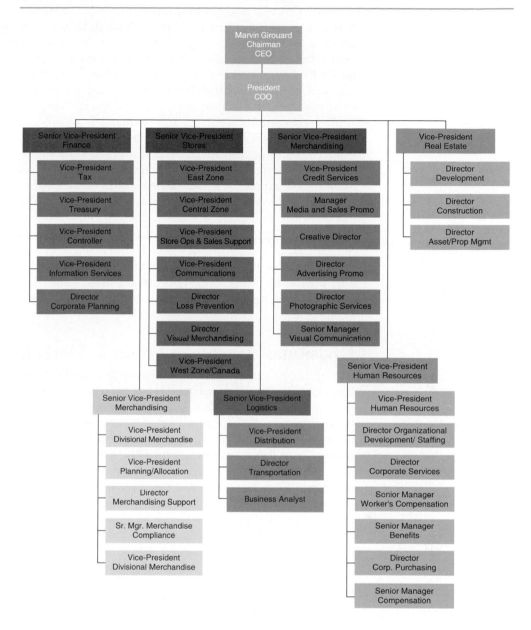

gram for an ad campaign works closely with the person responsible for designing store layouts and with visual communication experts. As a result, Pier 1 is able to develop a strong, focused marketing campaign to differentiate its products.

Second, when people who perform similar jobs are grouped together, it is easier for managers to monitor and evaluate their performance.[21] Imagine if marketing experts, logistics experts, and real-estate experts were grouped together in one function and supervised by a manager from merchandising. Obviously, the merchandising manager would not have the expertise to evaluate all these different people appropriately. A functional structure, however, allows co-workers to evaluate how well other co-workers are performing their jobs, and if some co-workers are performing poorly, more experienced co-workers can help them develop new skills.

Finally, as we saw in Chapter 3, managers appreciate functional structure because it allows them to create the set of functions they need in order to scan and monitor the task and general environments.[22] With the right set of functions in place, managers are in a good position to develop a strategy that allows the organization to respond to its particular situation. Employees in marketing can specialize in monitoring new marketing developments that will allow Pier 1 to better target its customers. Employees in merchandising can monitor all potential suppliers of home furnishings both at home and abroad to find the goods most likely to appeal to Pier 1's customers.

As an organization grows, and particularly as its task environment and strategy change because it is beginning to produce a wider range of goods and services for different kinds of customers, several problems can make a functional structure less efficient and effective.[23] First, managers in different functions may find it more difficult to communicate and coordinate with one another when they are responsible for several different kinds of products, especially as the organization grows both domestically and internationally. Second, functional managers may become so preoccupied with supervising their own specific departments and achieving their departmental goals that they lose sight of organizational goals. If that happens, organizational effectiveness will suffer because managers will be viewing issues and problems facing the organization only from their own, relatively narrow, departmental perspectives.[24] Both of these problems can reduce efficiency and effectiveness.

Divisional Structures: Product, Market, and Geographic

As the problems associated with growth and diversification increase over time, managers must search for new ways to organize their activities to overcome the problems associated with a functional structure. Most managers of large organizations choose a **divisional structure** and create a series of business units to produce a specific kind of product for a specific kind of customer. Each *division* is a collection of functions or departments that work together to produce the product. The goal behind the change to a divisional structure is to create smaller, more manageable units within the organization. There are three forms of divisional structure (see Figure 8.4).[25] When managers organize divisions according to the type of good or service they provide, they adopt a *product* structure. When managers organize divisions according to the area of the country or world they operate in, they adopt a *geographic* structure. When managers organize divisions according to the types of customers they focus on, they adopt a *market* structure.

divisional structure
An organizational structure composed of separate business units within which are the functions that work together to produce a specific product for a specific customer.

PRODUCT STRUCTURE   Imagine the problems that managers at Pier 1 would encounter if they decided to diversify into producing and selling cars, fast food, and health insurance—in addition to home furnishings—and tried to use their existing set of functional managers to oversee the production of all four kinds of products. No manager would have the necessary skills or abilities to oversee those four products. Consequently, if managers decide to diversify into new industries or to expand their range of products, they commonly design a product structure to organize their operations (see Figure 8.4A).

Using a **product structure**, managers place each distinct product line or business in its own self-contained division and give divisional managers the responsibility for devising an appropriate business-level strategy to allow the division to compete effectively in its industry or market.[26] Each division is self-contained because it has a complete set of all the functions—marketing, R&D, finance, and so on—that it needs to produce or provide goods or services efficiently and effectively. Functional managers report to divisional managers, and divisional managers report to top or corporate managers.

product structure
An organizational structure in which each product line or business is handled by a self-contained division.

Figure 8.4
Product, Market, and Geographic Structures

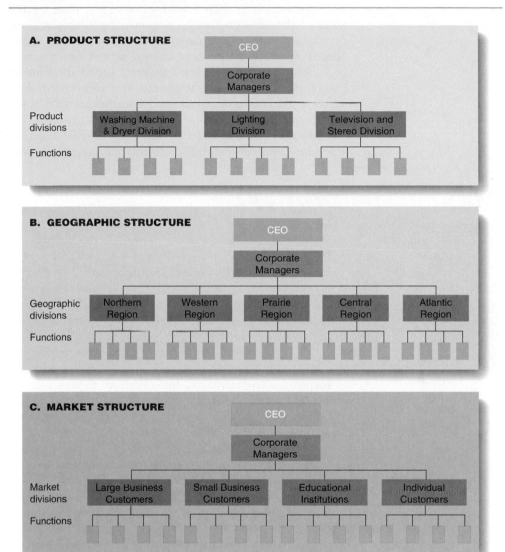

Grouping functions into divisions focused on particular products has several advantages for managers at all levels in the organization. First, a product structure allows functional managers to specialize in only one product area, so they are able to build expertise and fine-tune their skills in this particular area. Second, each division's managers can become experts in their industry; this expertise helps them choose and develop a business-level strategy to differentiate their products or lower their costs while meeting the needs of customers. Third, a product structure frees corporate managers from the need to supervise each division's day-to-day operations directly; this latitude allows corporate managers to create the best corporate-level strategy to maximize the organization's future growth and ability to create value. Corporate managers are likely to make fewer mistakes about which businesses to diversify into or how best to expand internationally, for example, because they are able to take an organizationwide view.[27] Corporate managers also are likely to better evaluate how well divisional managers are doing, and they can intervene and take corrective action as needed.

The extra layer of management, the divisional management layer, can improve the use of organizational resources. Moreover, a product structure puts divisional managers close to their customers and lets them respond quickly and appropriately to the changing task environment. Organizations sometimes change their divisional strategy because of market changes. For instance, Brampton, ON-based Nortel Networks announced its new product structure in early 2001. The divisions include: Optical Inter-City Products; Local Internet Products; Wireless Internet Products; Photonics Components; and Other, which would include certain customer premises-based voice and data networking solutions, certain narrowband and broadband access products and a few other products. These divisions reflect Nortel's new product strategy. The way in which Cascades Inc.'s managers created a product structure is profiled in this "Management Insight."

Management Insight

Cascades Inc.'s Product Structure

Laurent Lemaire, president and CEO of Kingsey Falls, QC-based Cascades Inc. (www.cascades.com), Canada's second-largest pulp and paper company, is known for his acquisitions in the pulp and paper products industry.[28] Cascades has more than 80 mills and plants in Canada, the United States, France, Germany and Sweden. The company's strength has been absorbing and turning around money-losing acquisitions. While Laurent Lemaire is president and CEO, his two brothers Bernard and Alain are also a part of the business.

Cascades has four publicly traded subsidiaries, including Paperboard Industries International Inc., Perkins Papers Ltd., Rolland, and Boralex Inc. The first three are in the pulp and paper business, producing tissues, containerboard packaging, boxboard packaging, and fine papers. Boralex is an energy producer headed by brother Bernard. Each of the companies is treated as a separate entity, based on product.

The Lemaires emphasize decentralized, entrepreneurial management, a style once viewed as unwieldy and complicated. However, other Canadian forest products companies, such as Avenor Inc. and Domtar, are now following Cascades' lead and decentralizing their operations. Under Cascades' novel corporate structure, each subsidiary company operates like a federation of small and medium-sized businesses. In fact, each mill within a subsidiary operates as a separate business unit, accountable for its own bottom line. The company uses profit sharing to motivate its employees (Cascades paid out $26 million in 1997), but employees get to share only in the profits generated by the mill they work for. The product structure managers at each individual operation have to be both more responsible and more accountable for operations, while encouraging employees to take more ownership of their job performance.

GEOGRAPHIC STRUCTURE When organizations expand rapidly both at home and abroad, functional structures can create special problems, because managers in one central location may find it increasingly difficult to deal with the different problems and issues that may arise in each region of a country or area of the world. In these cases, a **geographic structure**, in which divisions are broken down by geographical location, is often chosen (see Figure 8.4B). To achieve the corporate mission of providing next-day mail service, Fred Smith, CEO of Federal Express, chose a geographic structure and divided up operations by creating a division in each region. Large retailers often use a geographic structure. Since the needs of retail customers differ by region—for example, umbrellas in Vancouver and down-filled parkas in the Prairies and the East—a geographic structure gives

geographic structure
An organizational structure in which each region of a country or area of the world is served by a self-contained division.

retail regional managers the flexibility they need to choose products that best meet the needs of regional customers.

In adopting a *global geographic structure*, such as shown in Figure 8.5A, managers locate different divisions in each world region in which the organization operates. Managers are most likely to do this when they pursue a multidomestic strategy, because customer needs vary widely by country or world region. For example, if products that appeal to Canadian customers do not sell in Europe, the Pacific Rim, or South America, then managers must customize the products to meet the needs of customers in those different world regions; a *global geographic structure* with global divisions will allow them to do this.

In contrast, to the degree that customers abroad are willing to buy the same kind of product or slight variations thereof, managers are more likely to pursue a global strategy. In this case, they are likely to use a *global product structure*, perform most important functional activities at home, and export the final product abroad. In a *global product structure*, managers create an international division, which takes responsibility for selling the different divisions' products in foreign countries (see Figure 8.5B). Often, managers in the international division create foreign subsidiaries to distribute and sell their products to customers in these foreign countries. DaimlerChrysler AG, for example, designs and manufactures its Mercedes line of cars in Germany, and managers in DaimlerChrysler AG's international division take responsibility for shipping these cars to the company's foreign subsidiaries. As we noted at the beginning of this chapter, an organization's strategy is a major determinant of its structure both at home and abroad.

Figure 8.5

Global Geographic and Global Product Structures

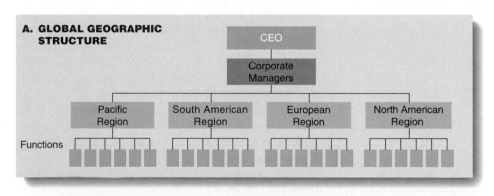

MARKET STRUCTURE   Sometimes, the pressing issue facing managers is to group functions according to the type of customer buying the product, in order to tailor the organization's products to each customer's unique demands. Burnaby-based TELUS is structured around six customer-focused business units: Consumer Solutions, focused on households and individuals; Business Solutions, focused on small to medium-sized businesses and entrepreneurs; Client Solutions, focused on multinational business with complex telecommunications needs; Global Trading & Partner Solutions, focused on wholesale and international customers; Wireless Solutions, focused on people and businesses on the go; and QuébecTel, a TELUS Company for the Quebec marketplace.

market structure

An organizational structure in which each kind of customer is served by a self-contained division; also called customer structure.

To satisfy the needs of diverse customers, TELUS adopts a **market structure** (also called a *customer structure*), which groups divisions according to the particular kinds of customers they serve (see Figure 8.4C). A market structure allows managers to be responsive to the needs of their customers and allows them to act flexibly to make decisions in response to customers' changing needs, as the experience of Royal Bank/Dominion Securities suggests in this "Management Insight."

Management Insight

From Geographic to Market Structure at Royal Bank

Recently, Toronto-based Royal Bank/Dominion Securities (www.rbcds.com) announced a new global banking division responsible for all corporate relationships to be headed by Michael Norris, former head of investment banking (Canada).[29] The restructuring seeks to handle the major tasks of global banking in a more integrative fashion. These two tasks are (1) getting the business (origination) and (2) executing the business (debt products). Previously, clients were contacted by both a corporate banker and an investment banker who would try to get new business. Under the restructuring, there will be one relationship officer responsible for debt, equity, or advisory services. The 200 relationship officers will be divided into eight industry groups: communications and technology, diversified industries, energy, financial institutions, mining, forest products, real estate and the public sector.

Corporate clients will now have industry specialists serving their needs, whereas previously the divisions were made according to geographic regions. Under the previous structure, customers were not getting the level of personalized service they required. Meanwhile, the bankers' talents were stretched thin because clients from different industries had different needs. As a result, Royal Bank/DS decided to redesign the organization, changing from a geographic to a market structure to make it easier for the salesforce to serve its customers.

Gordon Nixon, the CEO at Royal Bank, explains that the change seeks to accommodate the needs of clients who want services and products delivered as efficiently as possible. Adds Norris, "The important message here is that we have eliminated geographies [as a way of dividing the business], [and] we have focused our business on global lines." The restructuring means that there will be a single accountability for all of the products Royal/DS delivers to clients.

Matrix and Product Team Designs

Moving to a product, market, or geographic divisional structure allows managers to respond more quickly and flexibly to the particular set of circumstances they confront. However, when the environment is dynamic and is changing rapidly, and uncertainty is high, even a divisional structure may not provide managers with enough flexibility to respond to the environment quickly. When customer needs or technology is changing rapidly and the environment is very uncertain, managers must design the most flexible organizational structure available: a matrix structure or a product team structure (see Figure 8.6).

matrix structure
An organizational structure that simultaneously groups people and resources by function and by product.

MATRIX STRUCTURE   In a **matrix structure**, managers group people and resources in two ways simultaneously: by function and by product.[30] Employees are grouped into *functions* to allow them to learn from one another and become more skilled and productive. In addition, employees are grouped into *product teams*, teams in which members of different functions work together to develop a specific product. The result is a complex network of reporting relationships among product teams and functions that makes the matrix structure very flexible (see Figure 8.6A). Each person in a product team reports to two bosses: (1) a functional

Figure 8.6
Matrix and Product Team Structures

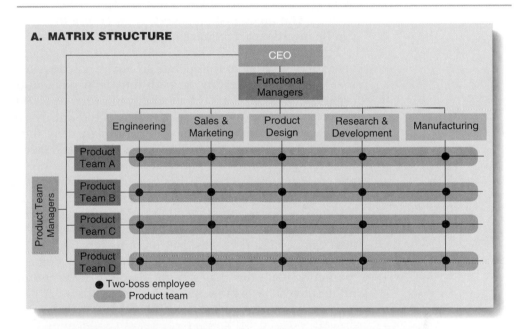

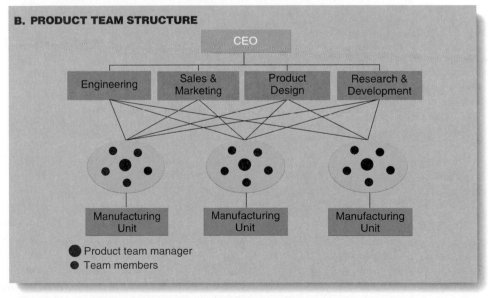

boss, who assigns individuals to a team and evaluates their performance from a functional perspective, and (2) the boss of the product team, who evaluates their performance on the team. Thus, team members are known as *two-boss employees* because they report to two different managers.

The functional employees assigned to product teams change over time as the specific skills that the team needs change. At the beginning of the product development process, for example, engineers and R&D specialists are assigned to a product team because their skills are needed to develop new products. When a provisional design has been established, marketing experts are assigned to the team to gauge how customers will respond to the new product. Manufacturing personnel join when it is time to find the most efficient way to produce the product. As their specific jobs are completed, team members leave and are reassigned to new teams. In this way, the matrix structure makes the most use of human resources.

To keep the matrix structure flexible, product teams are empowered and team members are responsible for making the most of the important decisions involved in product development.[31] The product team manager acts as a facilitator, controlling the financial resources and trying to keep the project on time and within budget. The functional managers try to ensure that the product is the best that it can be in order to maximize its differentiated appeal.

High-tech companies have been using matrix structures successfully for many years. These companies operate in environments where new product developments take place monthly or yearly and the need to innovate quickly is vital to the organization's survival. The flexibility afforded by a matrix structure allows managers to keep pace with a changing and increasingly complex environment. For this reason, matrixes also have been designed by managers seeking to control international operations as they move abroad and face problems of coordinating their domestic and foreign divisions.[32] Motorola, for example, operates a global matrix structure because it hopes to obtain synergies from cooperation among its worldwide divisions.

A global matrix structure allows an organization's domestic divisions to supply its foreign divisions quickly with knowledge about new R&D advances in order to help the foreign divisions gain a competitive advantage in their local markets. Likewise, the foreign divisions can transmit to domestic divisions new product marketing ideas that may give the domestic divisions an advantage in the domestic market. The expression "Think locally but act globally" describes the way managers in global matrix structures should behave.[33]

PRODUCT TEAM STRUCTURE   The dual reporting relationships that are at the heart of a matrix structure have always been difficult for managers and employees to deal with. Often, the functional boss and the product boss make conflicting demands on team members, who do not know which boss to satisfy first. Also, functional and product team bosses may come into conflict over precisely who is in charge of which team members and for how long. To avoid these problems, managers have devised a way of organizing people and resources that still allows an organization to be flexible but makes its structure easier to operate: a product team structure.

The **product team structure** differs from a matrix structure in two ways: (1) It does away with dual reporting relationships and two-boss managers, and (2) functional employees are permanently assigned to a cross-functional team that is empowered to bring a new or redesigned product to market. A **cross-functional team** is a group of managers brought together from different departments to perform organizational tasks. When managers are grouped into cross-departmental teams, the artificial boundaries between departments disappear, and a narrow focus on departmental goals is replaced with a general interest in working together to achieve organizational goals. The results of such changes have been dramatic:

product team structure An organizational structure in which employees are permanently assigned to a cross-functional team and report only to the product team manager or to one of his or her direct subordinates.

cross-functional team A group of managers from different departments brought together to perform organizational tasks.

For example, Chrysler Canada's use of cross-functional teams has reduced the time it takes to retool for a new product to just weeks.

Members of a cross-functional team report only to the product team manager or to one of his or her direct subordinates. The heads of the functions have only an informal, advisory relationship with members of the product teams. The role of functional managers is only to counsel and help team members, share knowledge among teams, and provide new technological developments that can help improve each team's performance (see Figure 8.6B).[34]

Managers at Chrysler, Hallmark Cards, Rubbermaid, Hewlett-Packard, Microsoft, Lexmark, and other large companies have moved to product team structures in recent years to try to make their organizations work more flexibly. Many of these companies have had considerable success with this structure. Increasingly, organizations are making empowered cross-functional teams an essential part of their organizational architecture to help them gain a competitive advantage in fast-changing organizational environments.

Hybrid Structure

hybrid structure
The structure of a large organization that has many divisions and simultaneously uses many different organizational structures.

A large organization that has many divisions and simultaneously uses many different structures has a **hybrid structure**. Most large organizations use product division structures and create self-contained divisions; then each division's managers select the structure that best meets the needs of the particular environment, strategy, and so on. Thus, one product division may choose to operate with a functional structure, another may choose a geographic structure, and a third may choose a product team structure because of the nature of the division's products or the desire to be more responsive to customers' needs.

Organizational structure may be likened to the layers of an onion. The outer layer provides the overarching organizational framework—most commonly a product division structure—and each inner layer is the structure that each division selects for itself in response to the contingencies it faces. The ability to break a large organization into smaller units or divisions makes it much easier for managers to change structure when the need arises—for example, when a change in technology or an increase in competition in the environment necessitates a change from a functional to a product team structure.

Coordinating Functions and Divisions

In organizing, managers' first task is to group functions and divisions and create the organizational structure best suited to the contingencies they face. Managers' next task is to ensure that there is sufficient coordination among functions and divisions so that organizational resources are used efficiently and effectively. Having discussed how managers divide organizational activities into jobs, functions, and divisions to increase efficiency and effectiveness, we now look at how they put the parts back together.

Allocating Authority

authority The power to hold people accountable for their actions and to make decisions concerning the use of organizational resources.

hierarchy of authority
An organization's chain of command, specifying the relative authority of each manager.

As organizations grow and produce a wider range of goods and services, the size and number of their functions and divisions increase. To coordinate the activities of people, functions, and divisions and to allow them to work together effectively, managers must develop a clear hierarchy of authority.[35] **Authority** is the power vested in a manager to make decisions and use resources to achieve organizational goals by virtue of his or her position in an organization. The **hierarchy of authority** is an organization's chain of command—the relative authority that each manager has—extending from the CEO at the top, down through the middle

span of control

The number of subordinates who report directly to a manager.

managers and first-line managers, to the nonmanagerial employees who actually make goods or provide services. Every manager, at every level of the hierarchy, supervises one or more subordinates. The term **span of control** refers to the number of subordinates who report directly to a manager.

TALL AND FLAT ORGANIZATIONS   As an organization grows in size (normally measured by the number of its managers and employees), its hierarchy of authority normally lengthens, making the organizational structure taller. A *tall* organization has many levels of authority relative to company size; a *flat* organization has fewer levels relative to company size (see Figure 8.7).[36] As a hierarchy becomes taller, problems may result that make the organization's structure less flexible and that slow managers' response to changes in the organizational environment.

For instance, communication problems may arise. When an organization has many levels in the hierarchy, it can take a long time for the decisions and orders of upper-level managers to reach managers farther down in the hierarchy, and it can take a long time for top managers to learn how well their decisions worked out. Feeling out of touch, top managers may want to verify that lower-level man-

Figure 8.7

Tall and Flat Organizations

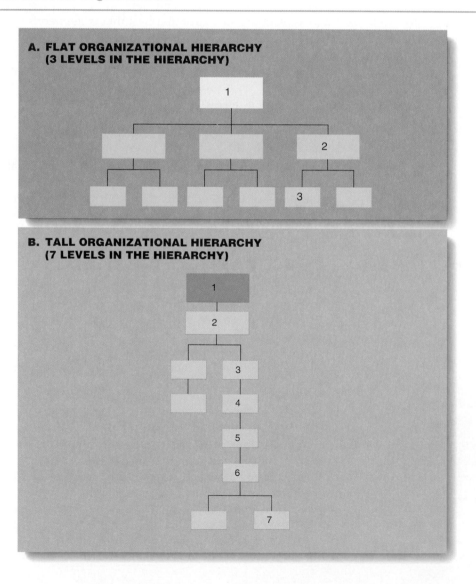

A. FLAT ORGANIZATIONAL HIERARCHY
   (3 LEVELS IN THE HIERARCHY)

B. TALL ORGANIZATIONAL HIERARCHY
   (7 LEVELS IN THE HIERARCHY)

agers are following orders and may require written confirmation from them. Middle managers, who know they will be held strictly accountable for their actions, start devoting more time to the process of making decisions in order to improve their chances of being right. They might even try to avoid responsibility by making top managers decide what actions to take.

Another communication problem that can result is the distortion of commands and orders being transmitted up and down the hierarchy, which causes managers at different levels to interpret differently what is happening. Distortion of orders and messages can be accidental, occurring because different managers interpret messages from their own narrow functional perspectives. Or it can be intentional, occurring because managers low in the hierarchy decide to interpret information to increase their own personal advantage.

Another problem with tall hierarchies is that they usually indicate that an organization is employing many managers, and managers are expensive. Managerial salaries, benefits, offices, and secretaries are a huge expense for organizations. Large companies such as IBM and General Motors pay their managers billions of dollars a year. Throughout the 1990s, hundreds of thousands of middle managers were laid off as companies attempted to reduce costs by restructuring and downsizing their workforces.

THE MINIMUM CHAIN OF COMMAND To ward off the problems that result when an organization becomes too tall and employs too many managers, top managers need to ascertain whether they are employing the right number of middle and first-line managers, and to see whether they can redesign their organizational architecture to reduce the number of managers. Top managers might well follow a basic organizing principle—the principle of the minimum chain of command—which states that top managers should always construct a hierarchy with the fewest levels of authority necessary to use organizational resources efficiently and effectively.

Effective managers constantly scrutinize their hierarchies to see whether the number of levels can be reduced—for example, by eliminating one level and giving the responsibilities of managers at that level to managers above and empowering employees below. This practice has become increasingly common in Canada and the United States as companies that are battling low-cost foreign competitors search for new ways to reduce costs.

One organization that is trying to empower staff is Ducks Unlimited of Oak Hammock Marsh, Manitoba, a not-for-profit organization devoted to preserving wetland wildlife.[37] The company recently went through a reorganization, flattening its management structure. The 330 staff members have been divided into groups to focus on different areas critical to the future of the organization. They are examining such issues as performance, development and job classification.

Gary Goodwin, director of human resources, explains that "the reorganization was essentially to help empower employees, making it easier for people working in the field to make decisions quickly without having to go up and down the proverbial power ladder."

CENTRALIZATION AND DECENTRALIZATION OF AUTHORITY Another way in which managers can keep the organizational hierarchy flat is to decentralize authority to lower-level managers and nonmanagerial employees.[38] If managers at higher levels give lower-level employees the responsibility to make

Ducks Unlimited
www.ducks.org/

Sam Markle, left, and brother Jack, owners of Toronto-based The Brothers Markle Inc., keep their company lean, even in good times. With 10 employees, and heavy reliance on subcontracting, their organizational structure is flat.

important decisions and only manage by exception, then the problems of slow and distorted communication noted previously are kept to a minimum. Moreover, fewer managers are needed because their role is not to make decisions but to act as coach and facilitator and to help other employees make the best decisions. In addition, when decision making is low in the organization and near the customer, employees are better able to recognize and respond to customer needs.

Decentralizing authority allows an organization and its employees to behave flexibly even as the organization grows and becomes taller. This is why managers are so interested in empowering employees, creating self-managed work teams, establishing cross-functional teams, and even moving to a product team structure. These design innovations help keep the organizational architecture flexible and responsive to complex task and general environments, complex technologies, and complex strategies.

Although more and more organizations are taking steps to decentralize authority, too much decentralization has certain disadvantages. If divisions, functions, or teams are given too much decision-making authority, they may begin to pursue their own goals at the expense of organizational goals. Managers in engineering design or R&D, for example, may become so focused on making the best possible product that they fail to realize that the best product may be so expensive that few people will be willing or able to buy it. Also, with too much decentralization, lack of communication among functions or among divisions may prevent possible synergies among them from ever materializing, and organizational performance suffers. As the "Case in Contrast" shows, Altamira's lack of communication among the portfolio managers under the star system resulted in a great deal of competition that was not helpful to the company as a whole when the internal and external environment of the company started to change.

Top managers must seek the balance between centralization and decentralization of authority that best meets the four major contingencies an organization faces (see Figure 8.1). If managers are in a stable environment, using well-understood technology, and producing staple kinds of products (such as cereal, canned soup, books, or televisions), then there is no pressing need to decentralize authority, and managers at the top can maintain control of much of the organizational decision making.[39] However, in uncertain, changing environments where high-tech companies are producing state-of-the-art products, top managers must empower employees and allow teams to make important strategic decisions so that the organization can keep up with the changes taking place. An interesting example of a company that has faced the issue of how best to distribute authority on a global level is Procter & Gamble, the US consumer products company.

Managing Globally

Procter & Gamble's New World Hierarchy

In 1995, top managers at Procter & Gamble (P&G) took a long, hard look at the company's global operations and decided that they could make much better use of organizational resources if they altered the balance among centralized and decentralized decision making. Until 1995, managers in each P&G division, in each country in which the company operated, were more or less free to make their own decisions. Thus, managers in charge of the soap and detergent division in the United Kingdom operated independently from managers in the soap and detergent divisions in France and Germany. Moreover, even within the United Kingdom, the soap and detergent division operated independently from other British Procter & Gamble divisions such as the healthcare and beauty products divisions. Top managers saw that this highly decentralized global decision making was resulting in the loss of possible synergies to be obtained from cooperation both among managers of the same kind of division in the different countries (soap and detergent divisions throughout Europe) and among managers in different divisions operating in the same country or world region. So Procter & Gamble's top managers pioneered a new organizational structure.

They divided P&G's global operations into four main areas—North America, Europe, the Middle East and Africa, and Asia. In each area, they created a new position—global executive vice-president—and made the person in that position responsible for overseeing the operation of all the divisions within his or her world region. Procter & Gamble had never attempted this approach before.[40] Each global executive vice-president is responsible for getting the various divisions within his or her area to cooperate and to share information and knowledge that will lead to synergies; thus, authority is centralized at the world area level. All of these new executive vice-presidents report directly to the president of Procter & Gamble, further centralizing authority.

In another change to centralize authority, P&G's top managers grouped together divisions operating in the same area and put them under the control of one manager. For example, the manager of the British soap and detergent division took control over soap and detergent operations in the United Kingdom, Ireland, Spain, and Portugal, and became responsible for obtaining synergies among them so the company could reduce costs and innovate products more quickly across Europe.

Procter & Gamble is delighted with its new balance between centralized and decentralized authority. Top managers believe they are making much better use of organizational resources to meet customers' needs, and they believe Procter & Gamble is poised to become the dominant consumer goods company in the world, not merely in the United States.

strategic alliance
An agreement in which managers pool or share their organization's resources and know-how with a foreign company, and the two organizations share the rewards and risks of starting a new venture.

joint venture A strategic alliance among two or more companies that agree to establish jointly and share the ownership of a new business.

network structure
A series of strategic alliances that an organization creates with suppliers, manufacturers, and distributors to produce and market a product.

Strategic Alliances and Network Structure

Recently, innovations in organizational architecture pioneered by Japanese companies—strategic alliances, joint ventures, and network structures—have been sweeping through Canadian, American, and European business. While many use the terms *strategic alliance* and *joint venture* interchangeably, technically, they are different. A **strategic alliance** is a formal agreement that commits two or more companies to exchange or share their resources in order to produce and market a product.[41] A **joint venture** is a strategic alliance among two or more companies that agree to establish jointly and share the ownership of a new business. A **network structure** is a series of strategic alliances that an organization creates with suppliers, manufacturers, and distributors to produce and market a product.

Japanese car companies such as Toyota and Honda have formed a series of strategic alliances with suppliers of inputs such as car axles, gearboxes, and air-conditioning systems. Network structures allow an organization to bring resources (workers especially) together on a long-term basis in order to find new ways to reduce costs and increase the quality of products—without incurring the high costs of operating a complex organizational structure (such as the costs of employing many managers). More and more Canadian, American, and European organizations are relying on strategic alliances to gain

Two Winnipeg-based firms—Cardinal Capital Management (whose president and CEO, Tim Burt, is shown here) and Lawton Partners Financial Planning Services—formed a strategic alliance to strengthen each of their businesses. Cardinal will provide investment management for Lawton's clients, and Lawton will provide financial planning, estate planning and tax-advantaged planning strategies. Clients of both companies will thus have a broader array of services available to them.

access to low-cost foreign sources of inputs. This approach allows managers to keep costs low.

Strategic alliances can be formed for other purposes than entering foreign markets, however. Sault Ste. Marie-based Algoma Steel was looking for a strategic alliance in Spring 2001, as it was emerging from creditor protection. Company president Sandy Adam acknowledged that an alliance would help defray the costs of entering new markets. Hamilton, ON-based Dofasco Inc. developed key strategic alliances with National Steel of Japan and France's Usinor to develop higher-quality steels that result in better financial returns. The "Focus on Diversity" highlights an alliance formed between the Mi'kmaq in Nova Scotia and a number of Canadian companies.

Focus on Diversity

Membertou Development Seeks Jobs for the Mi'kmaq

Starting in early 2001, leaders of the Cape Breton Mi'kmaq reserve signed joint venture agreements with SNC-Lavalin Group, Sodexho Marriott Services, Ledgers Canada, Georgia-Pacific and Clearwater Fine Foods through the Membertou Development Corporation.[42]

The parties signed what they called joint venture agreements. For the 1000-person band, with an unemployment rate of 50 percent, the agreements should mean more jobs. The companies will find it easier to bid on government contracts, since their use of native workers will be viewed favourably.

Bernd Christmas, head of Halifax-based Membertou Development Corp., explained what he saw as the key benefit of the partnerships. "We have to develop our own revenue streams and get away from dependency on the federal government. That's the only way to true self-government."

Clearwater Fine Foods will be able to buy all the snow crab of Membertou fishermen, and has agreed to hire 20 native workers for its processing line, which represents a third of the plant's workforce. The Georgia-Pacific agreement is expected to bring jobs in the mining sector, and Ledgers Canada will work with the band to provide financial consulting services. The SNC-Lavalin agreement with Membertou says it will "explore jointly mutually beneficial collaborative efforts to develop projects in the Maritime provinces."

Sodexho Marriott believes that their agreement with Membertou will give them a competitive advantage in providing catering and housekeeping services to oil rigs off the East Coast. They would hire and train Mi'kmaq employees to do that work.

While these ventures won't immediately solve all the problems of the reserve, Christmas believes that they provide a start. "Our biggest challenge is to educate the business community and the Canadian public about how a community like Membertou works. We are learning how we can maintain our rights and engage in community activity and keep up with it all."

boundaryless organization An organization whose members are linked by computers, faxes, computer-aided design systems, and video teleconferencing and who rarely, if ever, see one another face to face.

The ability of managers to develop a network structure to produce or provide the goods and services customers want, rather than creating a complex organizational structure to do so, has led many researchers and consultants to popularize the idea of a **boundaryless organization** composed of people who are linked by computers, faxes, computer-aided design systems, and video teleconferencing and who rarely, if ever, see one another face to face. People are utilized when their services are needed, much as in a matrix structure, but they are not formal members of an organization. They are functional experts who form an alliance with an organization, fulfill their contractual obligations, and then move on to the next project.

outsourcing Using outside suppliers and manufacturers to produce goods and services.

The use of **outsourcing** and the development of network structures is increasing rapidly as organizations recognize the many opportunities that the approaches offer to reduce costs and increase organizational flexibility. Canadian companies spent almost $49 billion on outsourcing in 1999.[43] Toronto-based The Brothers Markle Inc., a sign making company, outsources over 50 percent of its work. Why the management team does this is described in this chapter's "Management Case In the News."

Companies that specialize in outsourced work, such as EDS—which manages the information systems of large organizations like Xerox and Eastman Kodak—are major beneficiaries of this new approach. Similarly, on a global level, the development of a global network of strategic alliances among companies is an alternative to the use of the complex global matrix structure. A global matrix is far more difficult to manage because an organization performs all the functional activities itself and thus must coordinate and integrate among them.

Designing organizational architecture is becoming an increasingly complex management function. To maximize efficiency and effectiveness, managers must carefully assess the relative benefits of having their own organization perform a functional activity versus forming an alliance with another organization to perform the activity. The "Management Insight" shows some of the advantages and concerns that Mississauga, ON-based Ryder Integrated Logistics faces in providing outsourcing services to its clients.

Management Insight

Ryder Creates Teams Through Outsourcing

Outsourcing has become more popular as companies decide to focus more closely on their core activities. Companies such as Ryder Integrated Logistics in Mississauga, Ontario provide outsourced logistics for such blue-chip clients as General Motors, Chrysler, Northern Telecom and Hewlett-Packard.

Doug Harrison, Ryder's vice-president and managing director, says the move towards more outsourcing has transformed his company. "Instead of the typical up–down organizational structure, Ryder is organized into virtual teams in order to serve clients. Managers are responsible for everyone in their teams, rather than just the people in their own department."[44] The result is quicker response time to the market, and "we don't have to worry about following these departmental hierarchies," Harrison says. In addition, there's less worry about politics within the organization.

To do their work, Ryder employees work with their counterparts in the customer's operations, which means that each team has members from both companies working together. Management at Ryder had to stop thinking about preserving the hierarchy of the organization and start thinking about working in a team environment. Corporate clients have to rethink their structures too: "The key for the corporate client is to convert the time, energy and commitment it formerly used to manage the people, assets and procedures inhouse, to managing the relationship with the outsourcer," notes Jim Kilpatrick, who is with the Deloitte & Touche Consulting Group in Toronto.[45]

Ryder's new structure is apparently working well. According to Harrison, growth in the first half of 1998 was up 54 percent from the same period in 1997.[46]

Tips for Managers

Choosing a Structure

1. If an organization begins to produce a wider range of products, and especially if it enters new businesses or industries, evaluate whether a move to a product structure will keep the organization organic.

2. If your organization grows and expands regionally or nationally, evaluate whether a move to a geographic structure will keep the organization organic.

3. If an organization begins to serve different kinds of customers, evaluate whether or not a move to a market structure will keep the organization organic.

4. To increase efficiency, quality, innovation or responsiveness to customers, consider moving to a matrix or product team structure and find ways of decentralizing authority and empowering employees.

5. No matter what kind of structure an organization uses, periodically analyze its hierarchy of authority and keep the number of levels in the hierarchy to a minimum.

6. Analyze if strategic alliances or a network structure are organizing choices that will help keep an organization flatter and more organic.

Chapter Summary

DESIGNING ORGANIZATIONAL STRUCTURE

• The Organizational Environment

• Strategy

• Technology

• Human Resources

GROUPING TASKS INTO JOBS: JOB DESIGN

• Job Enlargement and Job Enrichment

• The Job Characteristics Model

GROUPING JOBS INTO FUNCTIONS AND DIVISIONS

• Functional Structure

• Divisional Structures: Product, Market, and Geographic

• Matrix and Product Team Designs

• Hybrid Structure

COORDINATING FUNCTIONS AND DIVISIONS

• Allocating Authority

STRATEGIC ALLIANCES AND NETWORK STRUCTURE

Summary and Review

DESIGNING ORGANIZATIONAL STRUCTURE The four main determinants of organizational structure are the external environment, strategy, technology, and human resources. In general, the higher the level of uncertainty associated with these factors, the more appropriate is a flexible, adaptable structure as opposed to a formal, rigid one.

GROUPING TASKS INTO JOBS: JOB DESIGN Job design is the process by which managers group tasks into jobs. To create more interesting jobs, and to get workers to act flexibly, managers can enlarge and enrich jobs. The job characteristics model provides a useful tool that managers can use to measure how motivating or satisfying a particular job is.

GROUPING JOBS INTO FUNCTIONS AND DIVISIONS Managers can choose from many kinds of organizational structures to make the best use of organizational resources. Depending on the specific organizing problems they face, managers can choose from functional, product, geographic, market, matrix, and product team structures.

COORDINATING FUNCTIONS AND DIVISIONS No matter which structure managers choose, they must decide how to distribute authority in the organization, how many levels to have in the hierarchy of authority, and what balance to strike between centralization and decentralization to keep the number of levels in the hierarchy to a minimum. As organizations grow, managers must increase integration and coordination among functions and divisions.

STRATEGIC ALLIANCES AND NETWORK STRUCTURE To avoid many of the communication and coordination problems that emerge as organizations grow, managers are attempting to develop new ways of organizing. In a strategic alliance, managers enter into a contract with another organization to provide inputs or to perform a functional activity. If managers enter into a series of these contracts and a substantial number of activities are performed outside their organization, they have created a network structure.

Management in Action

Topics for Discussion and Action

1. Would a flexible or a more formal structure be appropriate for these organizations: (a) a large department store, (b) a Big Five accountancy firm, (c) a biotechnology company? Explain your reasoning.

2. Using the job characteristics model as a guide, discuss how a manager can enrich or enlarge subordinates' jobs.

3. How might a salesperson's job or a secretary's job be enlarged or enriched to make it more motivating?

4. When and under what conditions might managers change from a functional structure to (a) a product, (b) a geographic, or (c) a market structure?

5. How do matrix structure and product team structure differ? Why is product team structure more widely used?

6. Find a manager and identify the kind of organizational structure that his or her organization uses to coordinate its people and resources. Why is the organization using that structure? Do you think a different structure would be more appropriate? Which one?

7. With the same or another manager, discuss the distribution of authority in the organization. Does the manager think that decentralizing authority and empowering employees is appropriate?

8. Compare the pros and cons of using a network structure to perform organizational activities, and performing all activities inhouse or within one organizational hierarchy.

Building Management Skills

Understanding Organizing

Think of an organization with which you are familiar, perhaps one you have worked in—such as a store, restaurant, office, church, or school. Then answer the following questions.

1. Which contingencies are most important in explaining how the organization is organized? Do you think it is organized in the best way?

2. Using the job characteristics model, how motivating do you think the job of a typical employee in this organization is? Can you think of any ways in which a typical job could be enlarged or enriched?

3. What kind of organizational structure does the organization use? If it is part of a chain, what kind of structure does the entire organization use? What other structures discussed in the chapter might allow the organization to operate more effectively? For example, would the move to a product team structure lead to greater efficiency or effectiveness? Why or why not?

4. How many levels are there in the organization's hierarchy? Is authority centralized or decentralized? Describe the span of control of the top manager and of middle or first-line managers.

5. Is the distribution of authority appropriate for the organization and its activities? Would it be possible to flatten the hierarchy by decentralizing authority and empowering employees?

6. What are the principal integrating mechanisms used in the organization? Do they provide sufficient coordination among individuals and functions? How might they be improved?

7. Now that you have analyzed the way in which this organization is organized, what advice would you give its managers to help them improve the way it operates?

Small Group Breakout Exercise

Bob's Appliances

Form groups of three or four people, and appoint one member as the spokesperson who will communicate your findings to the whole class when called on by the instructor. Then discuss the following scenario.

Bob's Appliances sells and services household appliances such as washing machines, dishwashers, stoves, and refrigerators. Over the years, the company has developed a good reputation for the quality of its customer service, and many local builders patronize the store. Recently, some new appliance retailers, including Circuit City and Future Shop, have opened stores that also provide numerous appliances. In addition to appliances, however, to attract more customers these stores carry a complete range of consumer electronics products like televisions, stereos, and computers. Bob Lange, the owner of Bob's Appliances, has decided that if he is to stay in business he must widen his product range and compete directly with the chains.

In 2001, he decided to build a new 20 000-square-foot store and service centre, and he is now hiring new employees to sell and service the new line of consumer electronics. Because of his company's increased size, Lange is not sure of the best way to organize the employees. Currently, he uses a functional structure; employees are divided into sales, purchasing and accounting, and repair. Bob is wondering whether selling and servicing consumer electronics is so different from selling and servicing appliances that he should move to a product structure (see figure) and create separate sets of functions for each of his two lines of business.[47]

You are a team of local consultants that Bob has called in to advise him as he makes this crucial choice. Which structure do you recommend? Why?

FUNCTIONAL STRUCTURE

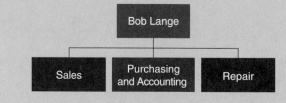

PRODUCT STRUCTURE

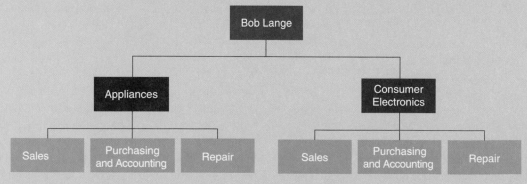

Exploring the World Wide Web

Specific Assignment

Enter the Web site of the German publishing company Bertelsmann (www.bertelsmann.com). Click on the English language version. Click on "Profile," then on "At a Glance" and "Activities" to examine the "Entrepreneurial Leadership and Organization" section.

1. What are Bertelsmann's mission and corporate goals?

2. What kind of organizational structure does Bertelsmann have?

3. What is Bertelsmann's approach to managing its structure (its approach to decentralization, delegation, and so on)?

General Assignment

Search for a Web site that tells the story of how an organization changed its structure in some way to increase its efficiency and effectiveness.

ManagementCase

The Organizing Approach at Microsoft

Microsoft, the biggest and most profitable software company in the world, has been called the best 15 000-person company in the country.[48] These 15 000 employees generated over $7.75 billion in revenues in 1996 alone. Perhaps even more impressive is the fact that since Bill Gates founded Microsoft in 1974, over 2000 of these employees have become millionaires because of the stock options that Microsoft uses to attract and retain talented employees. Gates himself is the richest man in the United States, having a fortune estimated at over $93 billion. What is the secret of Microsoft's success?

At the level of individual employees, Microsoft's philosophy of managing the company is evident in the sorts of people the company recruits and selects. Microsoft goes to the best software departments in colleges and universities across the country and spends a lot of time recruiting people who like to work hard, be imaginative and creative, and take risks. These are work values that Microsoft prizes. Employees are expected to work long hours, often 60- or 80-hour workweeks. They are expected to become experts in the specific software projects they work on and to possess up-to-the-minute information and state-of-the-art knowledge about what Microsoft and its competitors are doing. Gates meets frequently with employees on different projects and is constantly probing their knowledge to make sure they are up-to-date. If they lack current information, they lose credibility with him because they are not doing their job.

Beyond stock options, Microsoft motivates employees by providing them with the latest technology, flexible (though long) work hours, and even exercise rooms on the premises of a collegiate-type "campus." In addition, the way employees are motivated is closely linked to the way Microsoft uses groups and teamwork as the basis of its organizing process.

At Microsoft, programmers work in teams that can be as small as five or six people, and different teams work on specific software applications. Often many small teams are working on different aspects of a larger project managed by a project manager. For example, over 300 people worked in small teams to develop Microsoft's Windows 98 operating system, a product that attempts to match the user-friendliness of Apple's operating system. The use of product teams allows people to cooperate and pool their skills and resources; it promotes among team members the intense interactions that often lead to the breakthroughs that help Microsoft pioneer new products so quickly. Moreover, team members can learn from one another and control one another's behaviour.

At the organization level, Microsoft keeps the distance between managers and the teams to a minimum by keeping the organization as flat as possible—that is, by keeping the number of levels in the organizational hierarchy to a minimum. Moreover, Microsoft's structure is organized around these teams. Decentralized authority and delegation of important decisions to each team gives them maximum autonomy and freedom to be creative and to take risks. Microsoft is able to delegate so much authority because the company pays so much attention to recruiting the right kinds of employees and because each team's performance is appraised regularly to ensure that all teams are on top of their projects.

Questions

1. What are the main elements in Bill Gates's organizing approach?

2. What organizing problems do you think might emerge in Microsoft as it continues to grow?

ManagementCase

In the News

From the Pages of *The Toronto Star*
Survival of the Fittest

Caution: There may be economic rough waters ahead. The key to surviving an economic slowdown is to batten down the hatches before the major storm hits—and don't overload your boat.

No one knows this better than Sam and Jack Markle. The two brothers, owners of Toronto-based The Brothers Markle Inc., learned this lesson the hard way. They've been producing some of the most innovative signage for a veritable Who's Who of Canadian business for some four decades.

But the award-winning duo was hit hard by the last recession in the mid-'90s and was forced to downsize from a 24 000-square-foot facility and 40 employees.

Their formula for survival? They stay healthy by staying lean even in the best of times. They say they operate much more efficiently now with a 7500-square-foot plant, 10 employees, and subcontracting 50 percent of their work to specialty manufacturers.

"Before we tried to do everything inhouse, which required more equipment and more overhead, but the way we're operating now we almost don't have to tighten our belts if business drops," says Jack, 61. "We also don't go after every opportunity; rather we focus on what we do best, which is specialized custom work, so much so that we find other sign companies referring their clients to us for the difficult or unusual projects."

The brothers say they are big enough to have all the necessary equipment and staff, yet small enough to provide hands-on management and personalized service. "With so much competition and choice, you need to build good relationships with your customers— that's the key to empowering your business," explains Sam, 68. "Clients want to know that their needs are understood and that they're valued."

Sam adds that most companies make the same mistake: They're too fat in the good times and then they panic in the bad times and go too lean.

"You need to find a comfortable medium so that when the economy slows down you don't have to over-react just to stay afloat."

This is great advice, considering it's difficult even to find economists who agree on when, or if, we're heading for a recession.

The Markle brothers say their formula for staying lean also includes controlling their fixed overhead, motivating their staff, and offering unique products that give them a competitive advantage, like their computerized directories for building lobbies.

It's also important to remember to reinvest in the health of your company during the good times. This might mean keeping a rainy day fund, sort of like a health insurance policy for your business.

Moreover, at no time should the success of your business be seen as a licence to waste money, because the economy can take an unexpected turn for the worse.

Source: R. Gotlieb "Survival of the Fittest," *The Toronto Star*, May 17, 2001, pp. J1, J8.

Questions

1. What type of organizational structure does The Brothers Markle have?

2. What advantages and disadvantages does this sort of structure bring to the company?

Chapter nine

Organizational Control and Culture

Learning Objectives

1. Define organizational control, and describe the four steps of the control process.

2. Identify the main output controls, and discuss their advantages and disadvantages as means of coordinating and motivating employees.

3. Identify the main behaviour controls, and discuss their advantages and disadvantages as means of coordinating and motivating employees.

4. Explain the role of organizational culture in creating effective organizational architecture.

A Case in Contrast

Different Approaches to Output Control Create Different Cultures

Giddings and Lewis (www.giddings.com)—the well-known manufacturer of automated factory equipment for companies such as General Motors (www.gm.com), Boeing (www.boeing.com), and Ford (www.ford.com)—was in trouble when CEO William J. Fife took control of the company. Fife had been given the responsibility to turn the company's performance around; it had been suffering because of rising costs and falling sales. Fife began the turnaround by embarking on a program to develop new products to widen the company's product range. Moreover, he coupled innovation with a focus on responsiveness to customers; indeed, he personally flew all over the United States to talk to customers to make sure that the products being developed would suit their needs.[1]

To motivate Giddings and Lewis's managers to raise the company's performance, Fife established exacting performance targets and goals. For example, managers were told to achieve goals such as "a 20-percent increase in sales"

or "a 20-percent reduction in costs," and their bonuses were closely tied to their ability to reach their goals. Periodically, Fife met with his managers and reviewed their progress toward meeting the goals. Measured by his managers' success in achieving their goals, Fife's turnaround program was successful. In five years, Giddings and Lewis was the most profitable firm in its industry.

Informix (www.informix.com), a high-tech company based in Menlo Park, California, specialized in creating software to link networks of workstations.[2] Informix's CEO, Philip White, also learned about the importance of establishing specific performance goals for managers when his company experienced deteriorating performance after its acquisition of another software company. After the acquisition, Informix was paying two different workforces, including two different salesforces and two sets of programmers; its soaring operating costs resulted in a loss of almost $50 million. White realized that

Differing performance goals, and delivery of those performance goals, can often have positive effects on the outcomes, but different effects on managers and workers within the organizations. Both William J. Fife and Philip White were successful in turning their organizations around, but Fife destroyed the work values, norms, and culture of Giddings and Lewis in the process.

he had to get costs back under control. Like Fife at Giddings and Lewis, White created an exacting set of performance goals that forced his managers to make some tough decisions.

To get manufacturing costs under control, White gave manufacturing managers a detailed budget that forced them to streamline their workforces to cut costs and find more efficient ways to make products. Within four years, manufacturing costs dropped from 13 percent of revenue to 5 percent. White developed tough performance goals in other functional areas as well, and set revenue and profit targets that the managers of each product line were expected to achieve. As at Giddings and Lewis, the result of using tough performance goals at Informix was the launch of a large number of successful new products that made the company an industry leader.

Both CEOs seem to have had considerable success in using performance goals to turn their organizations around and control their managers, but the ways in which each CEO implemented these goals had very different effects on managers and workers within the organizations. At Informix, White adopted a participatory approach to setting goals and measuring performance. White's managers felt involved in the goal-setting process, and they were challenged by the goals he set and motivated to mobilize organizational resources to achieve them. Moreover, Informix's managers were told to create challenging goals for their subordinates, so, over time, Informix developed a goal-driven culture based on values and norms that reinforced managers' drive to make the company the best in its industry.

Fife's use of goals at Giddings and Lewis resulted in the emergence of a very different set of values and norms. Fife alone dictated the goals that his managers were expected to achieve. When the results did not please him (that is, when a manager did not meet his or her goals), Fife verbally abused the offending manager in front of other managers, who were forced to sit through the attacks in embarrassed silence. Managers began to claim that Fife's use of goals to control behaviour was creating competitive rather than cooperative work values and norms and was destroying Giddings and Lewis's culture. Giddings and Lewis's board of directors took the managers' side and asked Fife to resign. ●

Overview

As the "Case in Contrast" suggests, the different ways in which Fife and White decided to control the behaviour of their managers had very different effects on the way those managers behaved. White adopted a participatory approach and involved his managers in setting goals and targets. Fife alone established the performance standards that managers at Giddings and Lewis were expected to achieve, and he closely monitored their progress. As a result of their different ways of controlling their employees, Fife and White created very different cultures in their organizations. When managers make choices about how to influence and regulate their subordinates' behaviour and performance, they establish the second foundation of organizational architecture, organizational control. A major source of control is culture.

As discussed in Chapter 8, the first task facing managers is to establish the structure of task and reporting relationships that will allow organizational members to use resources most efficiently and effectively. Structure alone, however, does not provide the incentive or motivation for people to behave in ways that help achieve organizational goals. The purpose of organizational control is to provide managers with a means of motivating subordinates to work toward achieving organizational goals, and to provide managers with specific feedback on how well an organization and its members are performing. Organizational structure pro-

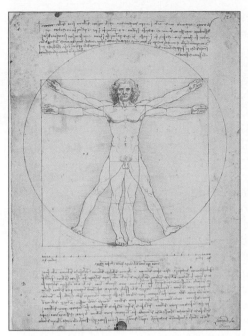

This famous Leonardo da Vinci drawing illustrates the artist's concern for understanding how the human body controls its own movements and how the different parts of the body work together to maintain the body's integrity. The interconnection of the body is similar to the way in which various departments operate in an organization.

vides an organization with a skeleton; organizational control and culture provide the muscles, sinews, nerves, and sensations that allow managers to regulate and govern the organization's activities. The managerial functions of organizing and controlling are inseparable, and effective managers must learn to make them work together in a harmonious way.

In this chapter, we look in detail at the nature of organizational control and describe the steps in the control process. We discuss three types of control available to managers for controlling and influencing organizational members—output control, behaviour control, and clan control (which operates through the values and norms of an organization's culture).[3] By the end of this chapter, you will appreciate the rich variety of control systems available to managers and understand why developing an appropriate control system is vital to increasing the performance of an organization and its members. ●

What is Organizational Control?

As noted in Chapter 1, *controlling* is the process whereby managers monitor and regulate how efficiently and effectively an organization and its members are performing the activities necessary to achieve organizational goals. As discussed in previous chapters, in *planning* and *organizing*, managers develop the organizational strategy and structure that they hope will allow the organization to use resources most effectively to create value for customers. In *controlling*, managers monitor and evaluate whether their organization's strategy and structure are working as intended, how they could be improved, and how they might be changed if they are not working.

Control, however, does not just mean reacting to events after they have occurred. It also means keeping an organization on track and anticipating events that might occur. Control is concerned with keeping employees motivated, focused on the important problems confronting the organization, and working together to take advantage of opportunities that will help an organization perform more highly over time.

The Importance of Organizational Control

To understand the importance of organizational control, consider Tom Waitt, a Winnipeg branch manager of Nesbitt Burns, and head of the firm's operations in Alberta. In May 2001, the Manitoba Securities Commission accused him of failing to detect problems in the accounts of three of his sales representatives, and investigated him for possible punitive action. The Securities Commission did not feel that Waitt had exercised sufficient control over employees to prevent complaints from clients and possible unethical or illegal behaviour. Control helps managers to achieve superior efficiency, quality, responsiveness to customers, and innovation—the four building blocks of competitive advantage.

To determine how *efficiently* they are using their resources, managers must be able to measure accurately how many units of inputs (raw materials, human resources, and so on) are being used to produce a unit of output. Managers must also be able to measure how many units of outputs (goods and services) are being produced. A control system contains the measures or yardsticks that allow managers to assess how efficiently the organization is producing goods and services. Moreover, if managers experiment with changing the way the organization produces goods and services to find a more efficient way of producing them, these measures tell managers how successful they have been. Thus, for example, when managers at Chrysler decided to change to a product team structure to design, engineer, and manufacture new cars, they used measures such as time taken to design a new car and cost savings per car produced to evaluate how well the new structure worked in comparison with the old structure. They found that the new one performed better. Without a control system in place, managers have no idea how well their organization is performing and how its performance can be improved—information that is becoming increasingly important in today's highly competitive environment.

Why would control be important to a manager?

Today, much of the competition among organizations revolves around increasing the *quality* of goods and services. In the car industry, for example, cars within each price range compete against one another in features, design, and reliability. Thus, whether a customer will buy a Ford Taurus, GM Cavalier, Chrysler Intrepid, Toyota Camry, or Honda Accord depends significantly on the quality of each product. Organizational control is important in determining the quality of goods and services because it gives managers feedback on product quality. If managers of an organization such as Chrysler consistently measure the number of customer complaints and the number of new cars returned for repairs, or if the principal of a school measures how many students drop out of school or how achievement scores on nationally based tests vary over time, they have a good indication of how much quality they have built into their product—be it an educated student or a car that does not break down. Effective managers create a control system that consistently monitors the quality of goods and services so that they can make continuous improvements to quality—an approach that can give them a competitive advantage.

Managers can also help make their organizations more *responsive to customers* if they develop a control system that allows them to evaluate how well employees with customer contact are performing their jobs. Monitoring employee behaviour can help managers find ways to increase employees' performance levels, perhaps by revealing areas in which skill training can help employees or by finding new procedures that allow employees to perform their jobs better. When employees know that their behaviours are being monitored, they may also have more incentive to be helpful and consistent in their interaction with customers. To improve customer service, for example, Toyota Canada's customer service centres regularly survey customers about their experiences with particular Toyota dealers. If a dealership receives too many customer complaints, Toyota's managers investigate the dealership to uncover the sources of the problems and suggest solutions. If necessary, they might even threaten to reduce the numbers of cars a dealership receives to force the dealer to improve the quality of its customer service.

Toyota Canada
www.toyota.ca/

Finally, controlling can raise the level of *innovation* in an organization. Successful innovation takes place when managers create an organizational setting in which employees feel empowered to be creative and in which authority is decentralized to employees so that they feel free to experiment and take risks. Deciding on the appropriate control systems to encourage risk taking is an important management challenge; organizational culture (discussed later in this chapter) becomes important in this regard. At Chrysler, to encourage high performance in each product team, top managers monitored each team's performance separately—by examining how each team reduced costs or increased quality, for example—and used a performance-related bonus system to pay each team. The product team manager then evaluated each team member's individual performance, and the most innovative employees received promotions and rewards based on their superior performance. The "Managing Globally" describes how Volkswagen transformed Skoda automobiles from a laughingstock to Car of the Year, by imposing controls on the formerly communist-run manufacturer.

Managing Globally

Skoda—A Laughingstock No More

"The reason a Skoda came equipped with a rear-window defroster, according to the old joke about Czechoslovakia's communist-era clunker, was so drivers could keep their hands warm while pushing it."[4] That was how many thought of the car for many years, but more recently, The Czech Republic's Skoda Auto company has been a survivor. While most other Eastern European car manufacturers have either shut down or done poorly, Skoda Auto has become central Europe's biggest auto maker.

So what made the difference? The most important factor was that Skoda became a subsidiary of Volkswagen AG; with that came the introduction of German precision into the company's operations. Volkswagen is known for its culture of innovation and desire to be market leader, traits that Skoda didn't have. At over 100 years old, Skoda was involved in many different businesses, from nuclear engineering to water purification, before Volkswagen took over. And though the company was a near-monopoly in its own country, few of the divisions were economically viable. They didn't have to be in a centrally planned economy: the government subsidized the company to keep it going. Volkswagen's management changed that by demanding profitability.

Volkswagen also dealt with the problem of the poor quality of local supplies. Skoda brought many of the suppliers inhouse so that management could watch what the contractors were making and give input when things needed to be changed. This brought a measure of *feedforward, concurrent* and *feedback control* to dealing with supplies, while also saving transportation costs.

The word *skoda* in the Czech language roughly translates as "what a shame." And for many years, that was an adequate description of the car. The influence of its parent company's management style has made a difference, however. "There was a massive transfer of know-how from Volkswagen, and we have accepted VW's corporate culture," said Vratislav Kulhanek, Skoda's CEO, a Czech. Skoda's newest model, the Fabia, has been winning awards. Two British trade magazines—*What Car?* and *Auto Express*—named it Car of the Year for 2000, and in Germany it won the prestigious Golden Steering Wheel award.

Control Systems

control systems Formal target-setting, monitoring, evaluation, and feedback systems that provide managers with information about how well the organization's strategy and structure are working.

Control systems are formal target-setting, monitoring, evaluation, and feedback systems that provide managers with information about whether the organization's strategy and structure are working efficiently and effectively.[5] Effective control systems alert managers when something is going wrong and give them time to respond to opportunities and threats. An effective control system has three characteristics: (1) It is flexible enough to allow managers to respond as necessary to unexpected events; (2) It provides accurate information and gives managers a true picture of organizational performance; and (3) It provides managers with the information in a timely manner because making decisions on the basis of outdated information is a recipe for failure.

feedforward control
Control that allows managers to anticipate problems before they arise.

Control systems are developed to measure performance at each stage in the conversion of inputs into finished goods and services (see Figure 9.1). At the *input stage*, managers use **feedforward control** to anticipate problems before they arise in order to avoid problems later, during the conversion process.[6] For example, by giving stringent product specifications to suppliers in advance (a form of performance target), an organization can control the quality of the inputs it receives from its suppliers and thus avoid potential problems at the conversion stage. Similarly, by screening job applicants and using several interviews to select the most highly

Figure 9.1
Three Types of Control

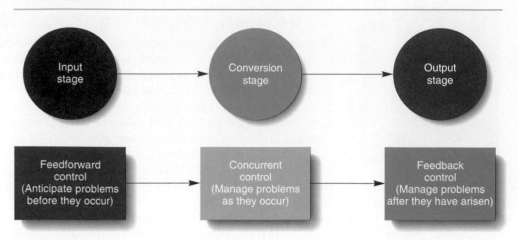

skilled people, managers can lessen the chance that they will hire people who lack the skills or experience needed to perform effectively. Another form of feedforward control is the development of management information systems that provide managers with timely information about changes in the task and general environments that may impact their organization later on. Effective managers always monitor trends and changes in the external environment to try to anticipate problems. (We briefly discussed management information systems in Chapter 6.)

At the *conversion stage*, **concurrent control** gives managers immediate feedback on how efficiently inputs are being transformed into outputs so that managers can correct problems as they arise. Concurrent control alerts managers to the need for quick reaction to the source of the problem, be it a defective batch of inputs, a machine that is out of alignment, or a worker who lacks the skills necessary to perform a task efficiently. Concurrent control is at the heart of total quality management programs (discussed in Chapter 17), in which workers are expected to constantly monitor the quality of the goods or services they provide at every step of the production process and inform managers as soon as they discover problems. One of the strengths of Toyota's production system, for example, is that individual workers are given the authority to push a button to stop the assembly line whenever they discover a quality problem. When all problems have been corrected, the result is a finished product that is much more reliable.

At the *output stage*, managers use **feedback control** to provide information about customers' reactions to goods and services so that corrective action can be taken if necessary. For example, a feedback control system that monitors the number of customer returns alerts managers when defective products are being produced, and a system that measures increases or decreases in product sales alerts managers to changes in customer tastes so they can increase or reduce the production of specific products.

concurrent control

Control that gives managers immediate feedback on how efficiently inputs are being transformed into outputs so that managers can correct problems as they arise.

feedback control

Control that gives managers information about customers' reactions to goods and services so that corrective action can be taken if necessary.

The Control Process

The control process, whether at the input, conversion, or output stage, can be broken down into four steps: establishing standards of performance, then measuring, comparing, and evaluating actual performance (see Figure 9.2).[7]

- Step 1: *Establish the standards of performance, goals, or targets against which performance is to be evaluated.*

  At Step 1 in the control process, managers decide on the standards of performance, goals, or targets that they will use to evaluate the performance of the entire

Figure 9.2
Four Steps in Organizational Control

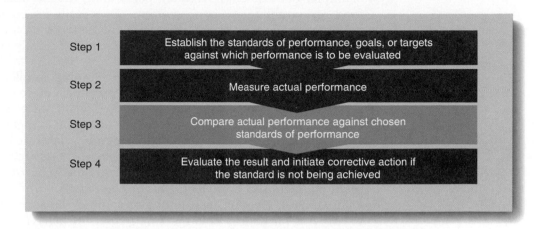

organization or some part of it, such as a division, a function, or an individual. The standards of performance that managers select measure efficiency, quality, responsiveness to customers, and innovation.[8] If managers decide to pursue a low-cost strategy, for example, then they need to measure efficiency at all levels in the organization.

How do managers achieve control?

At the corporate level, a standard of performance that measures efficiency is *operating costs*, the actual costs associated with producing goods and services, including all employee-related costs. Top managers might set a corporate goal of "reducing operating costs by 10 percent for the next three years" to increase efficiency. Corporate managers might then evaluate divisional managers for their ability to reduce operating costs within their respective divisions, and divisional managers might set cost-savings targets for functional managers. Thus, performance standards selected at one level affect those at the other levels, and ultimately individual managers are evaluated for their ability to reduce costs. For example, S.I. Newhouse, the owner of Condé Nast, publisher of magazines such as *GQ, Vanity Fair*, and *Mademoiselle*, started an across-the-board attempt to reduce costs to reverse the company's losses and instructed all divisional managers to begin a cost-cutting program. When Newhouse decided to retire, he chose as the new CEO Steven T. Florio, the division head who had been most successful in reducing costs and increasing efficiency at *The New Yorker* magazine.

Managers can set a variety of standards, including time, output, quality, and behaviour standards. Time standards refer to how long it is supposed to take to complete a task. Some companies, for instance, instruct staff that all e-mails must be answered within 24 hours. Output standards refer to the quantity of the service or product the employee is to produce. Quality standards refer to the level of quality expected in the delivery of goods or services. For instance, a company might set what it considers an acceptable level of defects. Or a retail store might set a standard of one complaint per thousand customers served. Finally, a company might set behaviour standards, which can govern things like hours worked, dress code, or how one interacts toward others.

- Step 2: *Measure actual performance.*

Once managers have decided which standards or targets they will use to evaluate performance, the next step in the control process is to measure actual performance. In practice, managers can measure or evaluate two things: (1) the actual *outputs* that result from the behaviour of their members and (2) the *behaviours* themselves (hence the terms *output control* and *behaviour control*).[9]

Sometimes both outputs and behaviours can be easily measured. Measuring outputs and evaluating behaviour are relatively easy in a fast-food restaurant, for example, because employees are performing routine tasks. Managers of a fast-food restaurant can measure outputs quite easily by counting how many customers their employees serve and how much money customers spend. Managers can easily observe each employee's behaviour and quickly take action to solve any problems that may arise.

When an organization and its members perform complex, nonroutine activities that are intrinsically difficult to measure, it is much more difficult for managers to measure outputs or behaviour.[10] It is very difficult, for example, for managers in charge of R&D departments at Merck or Microsoft to measure performance or to evaluate the performance of individual members because it can take 5 or 10 years to determine whether the new products that scientists are developing are going to be profitable. Moreover, it is impossible for a manager to measure how creative a research scientist is by watching his or her actions.

In general, the more nonroutine or complex organizational activities are, the harder it is for managers to measure outputs or behaviours.[11] Outputs, however, are usually easier to measure than behaviours because they are more tangible and objective. Therefore, the first kind of performance measures that managers tend to use are those that measure outputs. Then managers develop performance measures or standards that allow them to evaluate behaviours to determine whether employees at all levels are working toward organizational goals. Some simple behaviour measures are: Do employees come to work on time? Do employees consistently follow the established rules for greeting and serving customers? Each type of output and behaviour control and the way it is used at the different organizational levels—corporate, divisional, functional, and individual—is discussed in detail later in the chapter.

- Step 3: *Compare actual performance against chosen standards of performance.*
  During Step 3, managers evaluate whether—and to what extent—performance deviates from the standards of performance chosen in Step 1. If performance is higher than expected, managers might decide that they set performance standards too low and may raise them for the next time period to challenge their subordinates.[12] Managers at Japanese companies are well known for the way they try to raise performance in manufacturing settings by constantly raising performance standards to motivate managers and workers to find new ways to reduce costs or increase quality.

  However, if performance is too low and standards were not reached, or if standards were set so high that employees could not achieve them, managers must decide whether to take corrective action.[13] If managers are to take any form of corrective action, Step 4 is necessary.

- Step 4: *Evaluate the result and initiate corrective action if the standard is not being achieved.*
  The final step in the control process is to evaluate the results. Whether performance standards have been met or not, managers can learn a great deal during this step. If managers decide that the level of performance is unacceptable, they must try to solve the problem. Sometimes, performance problems occur because the standard was too high—for example, a sales target was too optimistic and impossible to achieve. In this case, adopting more realistic standards can reduce the gap between actual performance and desired performance. However, if managers determine that something in the situation is causing the problem, then to raise performance they will need to change the way in which resources are being utilized.[14] Perhaps the latest technology is not being used; perhaps workers lack the advanced training they need to perform at a higher level; perhaps the organization

needs to buy its inputs or assemble its products abroad to compete against low-cost rivals; perhaps it needs to restructure itself or reengineer its work processes to increase efficiency. If managers decide that the level has been achieved or exceeded, they can consider whether the standard set was too low. However, they might also consider rewarding employees for a job well done.

Establishing targets and designing measurement systems can be difficult for managers. Because of the high level of uncertainty in the organizational environment, managers rarely know what might happen. Thus, it is vital for managers to design control systems to alert them to problems so that these can be dealt with before they become threatening. Another issue is that managers are not just concerned with bringing the organization's performance up to some predetermined standard; they want to push that standard forward, to encourage employees at all levels to find new ways to raise performance. The "Management Insight" shows how Collingwood, ON-based Nacan Products Ltd. uses a variety of mechanisms to ensure that safety is taken seriously at the starch manufacturing plant.

Management Insight

Nacan Products Promotes Safety

Collingwood, ON-based Nacan Products Ltd., a starch manufacturer, reached one million hours without a lost-time claim at the beginning of 2001.[15] The company is understandably pleased with its safety record. The potential safety hazards in the company include high-speed machinery, forklifts, and accidental slips, trips and falls. Safety is an important concern at Nacan. Plant manager Terry Gates says that "All management personnel have safety [activities] in their development goals that [are] reviewed and used in their performance assessment to a weighted level of 25 percent of their overall salary increase." Employees who show a strong commitment to safety also get salary increases.

The company has a series of controls in place to make sure that safety gets carried out. Each month, a new safety topic is discussed on the shop floor. There is a full-time safety coordinator who assists with safety initiatives. The company conducts safety audits to ensure compliance with all safety, environmental and procedural regulations. Supervisors and staff conduct training programs.

Nacan benchmarks itself agains DuPont Canada, "which is hands down the top safety organization," says Gates. DuPont Canada has gone 23.6 million hours without a lost-time injury. Gates thinks Nacan can duplicate DuPont's record because of the company's incentive programs. "Safety initiatives at our company don't just mean we walk the walk or talk the talk," says Gates. "It's also attached to our pay cheques."

In the following sections, we consider the three most important types of control that managers use to coordinate and motivate employees to ensure that they pursue superior efficiency, quality, innovation, and responsiveness to customers: *output control*, *behaviour control*, and *organizational culture* or *clan control* (see Figure 9.3). Managers use all three to govern and regulate organizational activities, no matter what specific organizational structure is in place. At some companies, however, employees are also made more responsible for efficiency, quality, innovation and responsiveness to customers. This is most likely to happen when employees are made shareholders of the organization. For intance, at WestJet, Clive Beddoe comments that he's got "1400 sets of sharp eyes belonging to employees watching costs."[16]

Figure 9.3
Three Organizational Control Systems

Type of control	Mechanisms of control
Output control	Financial measures of performance Organizational goals Operating budgets
Behaviour control	Direct supervision Management by objectives Rules and standard operating procedures
Organizational culture/clan control	Values Norms Socialization

Management Insight

WestJet's Employees Control Costs

WestJet's strategy is to keep costs low, thus generating profit margins that are considerably higher than rival airlines', especially those of Air Canada.[17] To keep those costs low, the airline uses only one type of aircraft (the 125-seat 737), encourages customers to buy tickets over the Internet, does not provide paper tickets, has minimal in-flight service and no meals on board.

Despite these measures, Clive Beddoe, WestJet's CEO, says it's really his employees who contribute the most to cost-cutting. He wanted to make sure that employees felt responsible for the profitability of the airline, so he introduced a generous profit-sharing plan. Through this, employees can earn up to the equivalent of 30 percent of their annual salary. A stock plan will match up to 20 percent of an employee's wages that are invested. The benefit to this for employees is large: some customer service agents have made as much as $400 000 on WestJet stock.

The company's accountants say that the profit-sharing plan turns each employee into 'a cost cop' who is always looking for waste and savings. "We are one of the few companies that has to justify [to employees] its Christmas party every year," Derek Payne, treasury director, boasted and lamented.

WestJet encourages teamwork amongst its employees. There are no rigid job descriptions for positions, so employees have a lot of freedom to determine and carry out their day-to-day duties. However, all employees are required to help with all tasks. Sometimes even pilots load baggage.

When a plane lands, all employees on the flight, even those flying on their own time, are expected to prepare the plane for its next takeoff. This saves the company $2.5 million annually in cleaning costs. It also means that planes get turned around within about a half-hour, usually, although they have been able to do it in as little as six minutes.

All of this shows that WestJet doesn't need to use bureaucratic control to make sure employees keep the company's costs low. "There's peer pressure among themselves. They recognize who buys into this program and who doesn't, and peer pressure is an amazing thing," said Sandy Campbell, the chief financial officer.

Output Control

All managers, like William Fife and Philip White (profiled in the "Case in Contrast"), develop a system of output control for their organizations. First, they choose the goals or output performance standards or targets that they think will best measure efficiency, quality, innovation, and responsiveness to customers. Then they measure to see whether the performance goals and standards are being achieved at the corporate, divisional or functional, and individual levels of the organization. In the "Management Insight" we saw how Nacan Products counts days without a lost-time injury to determine whether managers and employees are meeting safety standards. The three main mechanisms that managers use to assess output or performance are financial measures, organizational goals, and operating budgets.

Financial Measures of Performance

Top managers are most concerned with overall organizational performance and use various financial measures to evaluate performance. The most common are profit ratios, liquidity ratios, leverage ratios, and activity ratios. They are discussed below and summarized in Table 9.1.[18]

- *Profit ratios* measure how efficiently managers are using the organization's resources to generate profits. *Return on investment (ROI)*, an organization's net income before taxes divided by its total assets, is the most commonly used financial performance measure because it allows managers of one organization to compare performance with that of other organizations. ROI allows managers to assess an organization's competitive advantage. *Gross profit margin* is the

Table 9.1

Four Measures of Financial Performance

Profit Ratios		
Return on investment	$= \dfrac{\text{Net profit before taxes}}{\text{Total assets}}$	Measures how well managers are using the organization's resources to generate profits.
Gross profit margin	$= \dfrac{\text{Sales revenue} - \text{cost of goods sold}}{\text{Sales revenue}}$	The difference between the amount of revenue generated from the product and the resources used to produce the product.
Liquidity Ratios		
Current ratio	$= \dfrac{\text{Current assets}}{\text{Current liabilities}}$	Do managers have resources available to meet claims of short-term creditors?
Quick ratio	$= \dfrac{\text{Current assets} - \text{inventory}}{\text{Current liabilities}}$	Can managers pay off claims of short-term creditors without selling inventory?
Leverage Ratios		
Debt-to-assets ratio	$= \dfrac{\text{Total debt}}{\text{Total assets}}$	To what extent have managers used borrowed funds to finance investments?
Times-covered ratio	$= \dfrac{\text{Profit before interest and taxes}}{\text{Total interest charges}}$	Measures how far profits can decline before managers cannot meet interest charges. If ratio declines to less than 1, the organization is technically insolvent.
Activity Ratios		
Inventory turnover	$= \dfrac{\text{Cost of goods sold}}{\text{Inventory}}$	Measures how efficiently managers are turning inventory over so excess inventory is not carried.
Days sales outstanding	$= \dfrac{\text{Accounts receivable}}{\text{Total Sales}} \div 360$	Measures how efficiently managers are collecting revenues from customers to pay expenses.

difference between the amount of revenue generated by a product and the resources used to produce the product. This measure provides managers with information about how efficiently an organization is utilizing its resources and about how attractive customers find the product. It also provides managers with a way to assess how well an organization is building a competitive advantage.

- *Liquidity ratios* measure how well managers have protected organizational resources so as to be able to meet short-term obligations. The *current ratio* (current assets divided by current liabilities) tells managers whether they have the resources available to meet the claims of short-term creditors. The *quick ratio* tells whether they can pay these claims without selling inventory.

- *Leverage ratios* such as the *debt-to-assets ratio* and the *times-covered ratio* measure the degree to which managers use debt (borrow money) or equity (issue new shares) to finance ongoing operations. An organization is highly leveraged if it uses more debt than equity. Debt can be very risky when profits fail to cover the interest on the debt.

- *Activity ratios* provide measures of how well managers are creating value from organizational assets. *Inventory turnover* measures how efficiently managers are turning inventory over so that excess inventory is not carried. *Days sales outstanding* provides information on how efficiently managers are collecting revenue from customers to pay expenses.

The objectivity of financial measures of performance is the reason why so many managers use them to assess the efficiency and effectiveness of their organizations. When an organization fails to meet performance standards such as ROI, revenue, or stock price targets, managers know that they must take corrective action. Thus, financial controls tell managers when a corporate reorganization might be necessary, when they should sell off divisions and exit from businesses, or when they should rethink their corporate-level strategies.[19] For example, Nortel Networks, JDS Uniphase Corp., and Lucent were all trying to rethink corporate strategies in the spring and summer of 2001 after their stock prices tumbled precipitously.

Although financial information is an important output control, financial information by itself does not provide managers with all the information they need about the four building blocks of competitive advantage. Financial results inform managers about the results of decisions they have already made; they do not tell managers how to find new opportunities to build competitive advantage in the future. To encourage a future-oriented approach, top managers must establish organizational goals that encourage middle and first-line managers to achieve superior efficiency, quality, innovation, and responsiveness to customers.

Organizational Goals

How are organizational goals linked to control?

Once top managers, after consultation with lower-level managers, have set the organization's overall goals, they then establish performance standards for the divisions and functions. These standards specify for divisional and functional managers the level at which their units must perform if the organization is to achieve its overall goals.[20] Each division is given a set of specific goals to achieve (see Figure 9.4). Divisional managers then develop a business-level strategy (based on achieving superior efficiency or innovation) that they hope will allow them to achieve that goal.[21] In consultation with functional managers, they specify the functional goals that the managers of different functions need to achieve to allow the division to achieve its goals. Sales managers might be evaluated for their ability to increase sales; materials management managers for their ability to increase the quality of inputs or lower their costs; R&D managers for the number of products they innovate or the number of patents they receive. In turn, functional managers establish goals that first-line managers and nonmanagerial employees need to achieve to allow the function to achieve its goals.

Figure 9.4
Organizationwide Goal Setting

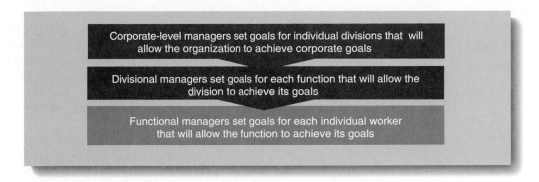

Corporate-level managers set goals for individual divisions that will allow the organization to achieve corporate goals

Divisional managers set goals for each function that will allow the division to achieve its goals

Functional managers set goals for each individual worker that will allow the function to achieve its goals

Output control is used at every level of the organization, and it is vital that the goals set at each level harmonize with the goals set at other levels so that managers and other employees throughout the organization work together to attain the corporate goals that top managers have set.[22] It is also important that goals be set appropriately so that managers are motivated to accomplish them. If goals are set at an impossibly high level, managers might work only half-heartedly to achieve them because they are certain they will fail. In contrast, if goals are set so low that they are too easy to achieve, managers will not be motivated to use all their resources as efficiently and effectively as possible. Research suggests that the best goals are *specific difficult goals*–goals that will challenge and stretch managers' ability but are not out of reach and will not require an impossibly high expenditure of managerial time and energy. Such goals are often called *stretch goals*. Nacan Products seeks to mimic the safety record of DuPont Canada, which has the best safety record of any company in Canada.

Deciding what is a specific difficult goal and what is a goal that is too difficult or too easy is a skill that managers must develop. Based on their own judgment and work experience, managers at all levels must assess how difficult a certain task is, and they must assess the ability of a particular subordinate manager to achieve the goal. If they do so successfully, challenging interrelated goals–goals that reinforce one another and focus on achieving overall corporate objectives–will energize the organization (this is what Philip White achieved at Informix, profiled in the "Case in Contrast").

Operating Budgets

operating budget

A budget that states how managers intend to use organizational resources to achieve organizational goals.

Once managers at each level have been given a goal or target to achieve, the next step in developing an output control system is to establish operating budgets that regulate how managers and workers attain those goals. An **operating budget** is a blueprint that states how managers intend to use organizational resources to achieve organizational goals efficiently. Typically, managers at one level allocate to subordinate managers a specific amount of resources to use to produce goods and services. Once they have been given a budget, these lower-level managers must decide how to allocate money for different organizational activities. They are then evaluated for their ability to stay within the budget and to make the best use of available resources. It would appear that many dot-com companies focused more on spending whatever money came in (i.e., had a high "burn rate") without consideration of developing and then staying within a budget. This practice proved to be disastrous when investors decided to stop pouring money into these companies after they had little in the way of performance that they could show investors.

Large organizations often treat each division as a singular or stand-alone responsibility centre. Corporate managers then evaluate each division's contribution to corporate performance. Managers of a division may be given a fixed budget for resources and evaluated for the amount of goods or services they can produce using those resources (this is a *cost* or *expense* budget approach). Or managers may be asked to maximize the revenues from the sales of goods and services produced (a revenue budget approach). Or managers may be evaluated on the difference between the revenues generated by the sales of goods and services and the budgeted cost of making those goods and services (a *profit* budget approach). Japanese companies' use of operating budgets and challenging goals to increase efficiency is instructive in this context.

In summary, three components—objective financial measures, challenging goals and performance standards, and appropriate operating budgets—are the essence of effective output control. Most organizations develop sophisticated output control systems to allow managers at all levels to maintain an accurate picture of the organization so that they can move quickly to take corrective action as needed.[23] Output control is an essential part of management.

Problems with Output Control

What are the pitfalls of output control?

When designing an output control system, managers must be careful to avoid some pitfalls. First, they must be sure that their output standards motivate managers at all levels and do not cause managers to behave in inappropriate ways to achieve organizational goals.

Suppose that top managers give divisional managers the goal of doubling profits over a three-year period. This goal seems challenging and reachable when it is jointly agreed upon, and in the first two years profits go up by 70 percent. In the third year, however, an economic recession hits and sales plummet. Divisional managers think it is increasingly unlikely that they will meet their profit goal. Failure will mean losing the substantial monetary bonus tied to achieving the goal. How might managers behave to try to preserve their bonus?

One course of action they might take is to find ways to reduce costs, since profit can be increased either by raising revenues or by reducing costs. Thus, divisional managers might cut back on expensive research and development activities, delay maintenance on machinery, reduce marketing expenditures, and lay off middle managers and workers to reduce costs so that at the end of the year they will make their target of doubling profits and will receive their bonus. This tactic might help them achieve a short-run goal—doubling profits—but such actions could hurt long-term profitability or ROI (because a cutback in R&D can reduce the rate of product innovation, a cutback in marketing will lead to the loss of customers, and so on).

The long term is what corporate managers should be most concerned about. Thus, top managers must consider carefully how flexible they should be when using output control. If conditions change (as they will because of uncertainty in the task and general environments), it is probably better for top managers to communicate to managers lower in the hierarchy that they are aware of the changes taking place and are willing to revise and lower goals and standards. Indeed, most organizations schedule yearly revisions of their five-year plan and goals.

Second, the inappropriate use of output control systems can lead lower-level managers and workers to behave unethically. If goals are too challenging, employees may be motivated to behave unethically toward customers, as sometimes happens in brokerage firms. As discussed in the following "Ethics in Action," ScotiaMcLeod is trying to change the way in which its brokers are rewarded in order to reduce potential ethical conflicts.

Ethics in Action

ScotiaMcLeod Looks to Become a Conservative Blue-Chip Safe House

For decades, retail brokerage ScotiaMcLeod's output control system rewarded brokers by giving them a commission for every trade they made.[24] This type of reward ensured that brokers would actively trade in client accounts, thus increasing their commissions. However, in recent years it has also created "churning", advising clients to trade too much, and this has led to investigations by regulatory bodies, as well as fines and discipline against the brokerages and individual brokers.

James Werry, who runs Toronto-based ScotiaMcLeod, wants brokers to be more accountable for the performance of the portfolios they manage. Under the commission system it was the number of trades that generated income for the brokers, not how well the portfolio did. Now he wants brokers to generate fee-based accounts instead, where investors pay a quarterly or annual fee based on the size of their accounts. Accounts that are managed well by brokers will grow larger, so both the investor and the broker gain.

Werry is also trying to change the image of ScotiaMcLeod, and sees its new output control system as the way to do this. The new image he wants to project is ScotiaMcLeod as a conservative, blue-chip safe house. To do this, however, Scotia's brokers can't be under investigation for churning accounts. By developing a user-friendly brokerage firm and instituting a fee-based system, Werry hopes that ScotiaMcLeod will gain a competitive advantage over other brokerage houses still using commissions to reward brokers.

The message is clear: Although output control is a useful tool for keeping managers and employees at all levels motivated and the organization on track, it is only a guide to appropriate action. Managers must be sensitive to how they use output control and constantly monitor its effects at all levels in the organization.

Behaviour Control

Organizational structure by itself does not provide any mechanism that motivates managers and nonmanagerial employees to behave in ways that make the structure work or even improve the way it works—hence the need for control. Put another way, managers can develop an elegant organizational structure with highly appropriate task and reporting relationships, but it will work as designed only if managers also establish control systems that allow them to motivate and shape employee behaviour.[25] Output control is one method of motivating employees; behaviour control is another method. In this section, we examine three mechanisms of behaviour control that managers can use to keep subordinates on track and make organizational structures work as they are designed to work: direct supervision, management by objectives, and rules and standard operating procedures (see Figure 9.3).

Direct Supervision

The most immediate and potent form of behaviour control is direct supervision by managers who actively monitor and observe the behaviour of their subordinates, teach subordinates the behaviours that are appropriate and inappropriate, and intervene to take corrective action as needed. When managers personally supervise subordinates, they lead by example and in this way can help subordinates develop and increase their own skill levels (leadership is the subject of Chapter 13). Thus, control through personal supervision can be a very effective way of motivating employees and promoting behaviours that increase efficiency and effectiveness.[26]

Nevertheless, certain problems are associated with direct supervision. First, it is very expensive because a manager can personally manage only a small number of subordinates effectively. Therefore, if direct supervision is the main kind of control being used in an organization, a lot of managers will be needed and costs will increase. For this reason, output control is usually preferred to behaviour control; indeed, output control tends to be the first type of control that managers at all levels use to evaluate performance.

Second, direct supervision can demotivate subordinates if they feel that they are under such close scrutiny that they are not free to make their own decisions. Moreover, subordinates may start to pass the buck and avoid responsibility if they feel that their manager is waiting in the wings ready to reprimand anyone who makes the slightest error.

Third, as noted previously, for many jobs direct supervision is simply not feasible. The more complex a job is, the more difficult it is for a manager to evaluate how well a subordinate is performing. The performance of divisional and functional managers, for example, can be evaluated only over relatively long time periods (this is why an output control system is developed), so it makes little sense for top managers to monitor their performance continually.

Management by Objectives

To provide a framework within which to evaluate subordinates' behaviour and, in particular, to allow managers to monitor progress toward achieving goals, many organizations implement some version of management by objectives (MBO). **Management by objectives** is a system of evaluating subordinates for their ability to achieve specific organizational goals or performance standards and to meet operating budgets.[27] Most organizations make some use of management by objectives because it is pointless to establish goals and then fail to evaluate whether or not they are being achieved. Management by objectives involves three specific steps:

management by objectives A goal-setting process in which a manager and his or her subordinates negotiate specific goals and objectives for the subordinate to achieve and then periodically evaluate the extent to which the subordinate is achieving those goals.

- Step 1: *Specific goals and objectives are established at each level of the organization.*
  Management by objectives starts when top managers establish overall organizational objectives, such as specific financial performance targets. Objective setting then cascades down throughout the organization as managers at the divisional and functional levels set their objectives to achieve corporate objectives.[28] Finally, first-line managers and workers jointly set objectives that will contribute to achieving functional goals.

- Step 2: *Managers and their subordinates together determine the subordinates' goals.*
  An important characteristic of management by objectives is its participatory nature. Managers at every level sit down with the subordinate managers who report directly to them, and together they determine appropriate and feasible goals for the subordinate and bargain over the budget that the subordinate will need so as to achieve his or her goals. The participation of subordinates in the objective-setting process is a way of strengthening their commitment to achieve their goals and meet their budgets.[29] Another reason why it is so important for subordinates (both individuals and teams) to participate in goal setting is so they can tell managers what they think they can realistically achieve.[30]

- Step 3: *Managers and their subordinates periodically review the subordinates' progress toward meeting goals.*
  Once specific objectives have been agreed upon for managers at each level, managers are accountable for meeting those objectives. Periodically, they sit down with their subordinates to evaluate their progress. Normally, salary raises and promotions are linked to the goal-setting process, and managers who achieve their

goals receive greater rewards than those who fall short. (The issue of how to design reward systems to motivate managers and other organizational employees is discussed in Chapter 10.)

In companies that decentralize responsibility for the production of goods and services to empowered teams and cross-functional teams, management by objectives works somewhat differently. Managers ask each team to develop a set of goals and performance targets that the team hopes to achieve—goals that are consistent with organizational objectives. Managers then negotiate with each team to establish its final goals and the budget the team will need to achieve them. The reward system is linked to team performance, not to the performance of any one team member.

Bureaucratic Control

bureaucratic control

Control of behaviour by means of a comprehensive system of rules and standard operating procedures.

When direct supervision is too expensive and management by objectives is inappropriate, managers might turn to another mechanism to shape and motivate employee behaviour: bureaucratic control. **Bureaucratic control** is control by means of a comprehensive system of rules and standard operating procedures (SOPs) that shape and regulate the behaviour of divisions, functions, and individuals. In Chapter 2, we discussed Max Weber's theory of bureaucracy and noted that all organizations use bureaucratic rules and procedures but some use them more than others.[31]

Rules and SOPs guide behaviour and specify what employees are to do when they confront a problem that needs a solution. It is the responsibility of a manager to develop rules that allow employees to perform their activities efficiently and effectively. When employees follow the rules that managers have developed, their behaviour is *standardized*—actions are performed in the same way time and time again—and the outcomes of their work are predictable. In addition, to the degree that managers can make employees' behaviour predictable, there is no need to monitor the outputs of behaviour because standardized behaviour leads to standardized outputs.

Suppose a worker at Toyota comes up with a way to attach exhaust pipes that reduces the number of steps in the assembly process and increases efficiency. Always on the lookout for ways to standardize procedures, managers make this idea the basis of a new rule: "From now on, the procedure for attaching the exhaust pipe to the car is as follows ..." If all workers followed the rule to the letter, every car would come off the assembly line with its exhaust pipe attached in the new way, and there would be no need to check exhaust pipes at the end of the line. In practice, mistakes and lapses of attention do happen, so output control is used at the end of the line, and each car's exhaust system is given a routine inspection. However, the number of quality problems with the exhaust system is minimized because the rule (bureaucratic control) is being followed.

Service organizations such as retail stores and fast-food restaurants attempt to standardize the behaviour of employees by instructing them on the correct way to greet customers or the appropriate way to serve and bag food. Employees are trained to follow the rules that have proven to be most effective in a particular situation. The better trained the employees are, the more standardized is their behaviour, and the more trust managers can have that outputs (such as food quality) will be consistent.

Problems with Bureaucratic Control

How can bureaucratic control go wrong?

All organizations make extensive use of bureaucratic control because rules and SOPs effectively control routine organizational activities. With a bureaucratic control system in place, managers can manage by exception and intervene and take corrective action only when necessary. However, managers need to be aware of a number of problems associated with bureaucratic control, because they can reduce organizational effectiveness.[32]

First, establishing rules is always easier than discarding them. Organizations tend to become overly bureaucratic over time as managers do everything according to the rule book. If the amount of "red tape" becomes too great, decision making slows and managers react slowly to changing conditions. This sluggishness can imperil an organization's survival if agile new competitors emerge.

Second, because rules constrain and standardize behaviour and lead people to behave in predictable ways, there is a danger that people become so used to automatically following rules that they stop thinking for themselves. Thus, too much standardization can actually reduce the level of learning taking place in an organization and get the organization off track if managers and workers focus on the wrong issues. An organization thrives when its members are constantly thinking of new ways to increase efficiency, quality, and customer responsiveness. By definition, new ideas do not come from blindly following standardized procedures. Similarly, the pursuit of innovation implies a commitment by managers to discover new ways of doing things; innovation, however, is incompatible with the use of extensive bureaucratic control.

Managers must therefore be sensitive about the way they use bureaucratic control. It is most useful when organizational activities are routine and well understood and when employees are making programmed decisions such as in mass-production settings or in a routine service setting, for example restaurants and stores (e.g., Tim Horton's, Canadian Tire or Midas Muffler). Bureaucratic control is much less useful in situations where nonprogrammed decisions have to be made and managers have to react quickly to changes in the organizational environment.

To use output control and behaviour control, managers must be able to identify the outcomes they want to achieve and the behaviours they want employees to perform to achieve these outcomes. For many of the most important and significant organizational activities, however, output control and behaviour control are inappropriate for several reasons:

- A manager cannot evaluate the performance of workers such as doctors, research scientists, or engineers by observing their behaviour on a day-to-day basis.
- Rules and SOPs are of little use in telling a doctor how to respond to an emergency situation or a scientist how to discover something new.
- Output controls such as the amount of time a surgeon takes for each operation or the costs of making a discovery are very crude measures of the quality of performance, and could in fact harm performance.

How can managers attempt to control and regulate the behaviour of their subordinates when personal supervision is of little use, when rules cannot be developed to tell employees what to do, and when outputs and goals cannot be measured at all or can be measured usefully only over long periods? One source of control increasingly being used by organizations is a strong organizational culture.

Tips for Managers

Control

1. Identify the source(s) of an organization's competitive advantage (efficiency, quality, innovation, and customer responsiveness). Then design control systems that allow managers to evaluate how well they are building competitive advantage.

2. Involve employees in the goal-setting process and make MBO an organizationwide activity.

3. Choose the right balance of direct supervision and bureaucratic controls to allow managers to monitor progress toward goals and to take corrective action as needed.

4. Periodically evaluate the output and behaviour control system to keep it aligned with your current strategy and structure.

Organizational Culture and Clan Control

organizational culture A system of shared meaning, held by organization members, that distinguishes the organization from other organizations.

norms The standards of behaviour and common expectations that control the ways in which individuals and groups in an organization interact with each other and work to achieve organizational goals.

Organizational culture is another control system that regulates and governs employee attitudes and behaviour. **Organizational culture** refers to a system of shared meaning, held by organization members, that distinguishes the organization from other organizations.[33] Members of all organizations are influenced by the values and norms they learn from their managers and other employees. **Norms** are the standards of behaviour and common expectations that control the ways in which individuals and groups in an organization interact with each other and work to achieve organizational goals.

Culture can be viewed both as helping to make sense of the organization and as operating as a control mechanism that guides employee behaviour. In essence, culture defines the rules of the game:

Culture by definition is elusive, intangible, implicit, and taken for granted. But every organization develops a core set of assumptions, understandings, and implicit rules that govern day-to-day behaviour in the workplace. Until newcomers learn the rules, they are not accepted as full-fledged members of the organization. Transgressions of the rules on the part of high-level executives or front-line employees result in universal disapproval and powerful penalties. Conformity to the rules becomes the primary basis for reward and upward mobility.[34]

clan control Control exerted on individuals and groups in an organization by shared values, norms, standards of behaviour, and expectations.

William Ouchi used the term **clan control** to describe the control exerted on individuals and groups in an organization by shared values, norms, standards of behaviour, and expectations. Organizational culture is not an externally imposed system of constraints, such as direct supervision or rules and procedures. Rather, employees internalize organizational values and norms and then let those values and norms guide their decisions and actions. Just as people in society at large generally behave in accordance with socially acceptable values and norms, such as the norm that people should line up at the checkout counters in supermarkets, so are individuals in an organizational setting mindful of the force of organizational values and norms.

Organizational culture is an important source of control for two reasons. First, it makes control possible in situations where managers cannot use output or behaviour control. Second and more important, when a strong and cohesive set of organizational values and norms is in place, employees focus on thinking about what is best for the organization in the long run—all their decisions and actions become oriented toward helping the organization perform well. For example, a teacher spends personal time after school coaching and counselling students; an R&D scientist works 80 hours a week, evenings and weekends, to help speed up a late project; a sales clerk at a department store runs after a customer who left a credit card at the cash register. Many researchers and managers believe that employees of some organizations go out of their way to help their organization because the organization has a strong and cohesive organizational culture—a culture that controls employee attitudes and behaviours. Strong bureaucratic control is less likely to foster positive attitudes and behaviours that encourage employees to go above and beyond.

Creating a Strong Organizational Culture

Culture is created and sustained in three ways.[35] First, the founders and/or senior managers of the organization only hire and keep employees who think and feel the way they do. Second, the management indoctrinates and socializes these employees to their way of thinking and feeling. Finally, top managers serve as role models. By observing their behaviour, employees identify with them and thereby internalize their beliefs, values, and assumptions.

In an organization, values and norms inform organizational members about what goals they should pursue and how they should behave to reach those goals. Thus, values and norms perform the same function as formal goals, written rules, or direct supervision. In Chapter 4, we discussed values and norms in the context of national culture. *Values* are beliefs and ideas about the kinds of goals members of a society should pursue and about the kinds or modes of behaviour people should use to achieve these goals.[36] *Norms* are unwritten rules or guidelines that prescribe appropriate behaviour in particular situations. Norms emerge from values.[37]

Managers can influence the kinds of values and norms that develop in an organization. Some managers might cultivate values and norms that let subordinates know that they are welcome to perform their roles in innovative, creative ways and to be innovative and entrepreneurial, willing to experiment and go out on a limb even if there is a significant chance of failure. Top managers at organizations such as Nortel Networks, Lucent Technology, and 3M Canada encourage employees to adopt such values to support their commitment to innovation as a source of competitive advantage.

Other managers, however, might cultivate values and norms that let employees know that they should always be conservative and cautious in their dealings with others, should always consult with their superiors before making important decisions, and should always put their actions in writing so they can be held accountable for whatever happens. In any setting where caution is needed—nuclear power stations, large oil refineries, chemical plants, financial institutions, insurance companies—a conservative, cautious approach to making decisions might be highly appropriate.[38] In a nuclear power plant, for example, the catastrophic consequences of a mistake make a high level of supervision vital. Similarly, in a bank or mutual fund company, the risk of losing investors' money also makes a cautious approach to investing highly appropriate. Some managers encourage caution as a method of control, however, and this may stifle employees' ability to innovate.

Difficulties arise when two organizations merge and the managers of the companies have created different types of cultures. For instance, when Calgary-based TransCanada PipeLines merged with Nova Corporation, also of Calgary, in 1998, the companies' different cultures led to conflicts in bringing the two companies together. Nova and TransCanada treated their employees very differently. TransCanada had a more traditional, top-down management control structure. Nova relied on its culture of empowering its employees to govern their behaviour. "One Nova employee summed up the differences by describing the impending deal along the lines of 'GI Joe meets the Care Bears.'"[39] Three years later the two companies had not completely resolved their cultural differences.

The managers of different kinds of organizations may deliberately cultivate and develop the organizational values and norms that are best suited to their task and general environments, strategy, or technology. Organizational culture is transmitted to organizational members through the values of the founder, the process of socialization, ceremonies and rites, and stories and language (see Figure 9.5).

How important is the founder in creating organizational culture?

VALUES OF THE FOUNDER   One manager who has a very important impact on the kind of organizational culture that emerges in an organization is the founder. An organization's founder and his or her personal values and beliefs have a substantial influence on the values, norms, and standards of behaviour that develop over time within the organization.[40] Founders set the stage for the way cultural values and norms develop because they hire other managers to help them run their organizations. It is reasonable to assume that founders select managers who share their vision of the organization's goals and what it should be doing. In any case, new managers quickly learn from the founder what values and norms are appropriate in the organization and thus what is desired of them. Subordinates imitate the style of the founder and, in turn, transmit his or her values and norms to their subordinates. Gradually over time, the founder's values and norms permeate the organization.[41]

Figure 9.5
Factors Creating a Strong Organizational Culture

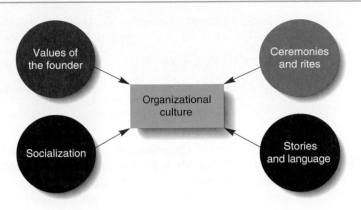

A founder who requires a great display of respect from subordinates and insists on proprieties such as formal job titles and formal modes of dress encourages subordinates to act in this way toward their subordinates. Often, a founder's personal values affect an organization's competitive advantage. Frank Stronach, founder of Toronto-based Magna Corporation, believes that his employees should show a "strong sense of ownership and entrepreneurial energy." He practises this belief by diverting 10 percent of pre-tax profit to profit-sharing programs for his employees. Similarly managers' salaries are deliberately set "below industry standards" so that managers will earn more through profit-sharing bonuses. To further emphasize managerial responsibility, Magna's managers are given considerable autonomy over buying, selling, and hiring. Through these policies of profit sharing and empowerment, Stronach has developed a workforce that has made Magna one of the largest and most profitable companies in the country. Similarly, Richard Branson of the Virgin Group, known for his entrepreneurial style, challenges his managers to act like him. All of his small companies are headed by managing directors who have a stake in the company they run. He wants his managers to operate the companies as if they were their own. Branson's style of management has made Virgin a success in a number of different markets it has entered.

SOCIALIZATION   Over time, organizational members learn from each other which values are important in an organization and the norms that specify appropriate and inappropriate behaviours. Eventually, organizational members behave in accordance with the organization's values and norms—often without realizing they are doing so. **Organizational socialization** is the process by which newcomers learn an organization's values and norms and acquire the work behaviours necessary to perform jobs effectively.[42] As a result of their socialization experiences, organizational members internalize an organization's values and norms and behave in accordance with them, not only because they think they have to but because they think that these values and norms describe the right and proper way to behave.[43]

Most organizations have some kind of socialization program to help new employees "learn the ropes"—the values, norms, and culture of their organization. The military, for example, is well known for the rigorous socialization process it uses to turn raw recruits into trained soldiers. Organizations such as Arthur Andersen also put new recruits through a rigorous training program to provide them with the knowledge they need not only to perform well in their jobs but also to represent the company to its clients. New recruits attend a six-week training program at Arthur Andersen's Chicago training centre, where they learn from

Virgin Group
www.virgin.com/

organizational socialization

The process by which newcomers learn an organization's values and norms and acquire the work behaviours necessary to perform jobs effectively.

Table 9.2

Organizational Rites

Type of Rite	Example of Rite	Purpose of Rite
Rite of passage	Induction and basic training	Learn and internalize norms and values
Rite of integration	Office Christmas party	Build common norms and values
Rite of enhancement	Presentation of annual award	Motivate commitment to norms and values

experienced organizational members how to behave and what they should be doing. Thus, through the organizational socialization program, the founder and top managers of an organization can transmit to employees the cultural values and norms that shape the behaviour of organizational members.

CEREMONIES AND RITES   Another way in which managers can attempt to create or influence an organizational culture is by developing organizational ceremonies and rites—formal events that recognize incidents of importance to the organization as a whole and to specific employees.[44] The most common rites that organizations use to transmit cultural norms and values to their members are rites of passage, of integration, and of enhancement (see Table 9.2).[45]

Rites of passage determine how individuals enter, advance within, or leave the organization. The socialization programs developed by military organizations (such as the Canadian Armed Forces) or by large accountancy firms (such as Arthur Andersen) described above are rites of passage. Likewise, the ways in which an organization prepares people for promotion or retirement are rites of passage.

Sometimes, rites of passage can get out of hand. Fraternities, sororities, sports teams, and even the military have been known to use hazing to initiate members. Activities can include "sleep deprivation, public nudity and childish pranks or, at worst, extreme drunkenness, gross racial slurs, even beatings."[46] The videotaped hazing rituals at CFB Petawawa caused the Airborne Regiment to be disbanded in 1995. Deborah Harrison, a sociologist at Brock University in St. Catharines, Ontario, argues that the videotaped hazing "is evidence of a military-wide problem of racism and macho-style bonding."[47] While the goal of the hazing might have been to desensitize new recruits to the brutality of war, many Canadians felt that the practice had gone too far.

Rites of integration, such as shared announcements of organizational successes, office parties, and company cookouts, build and reinforce common bonds among organizational members. Southwest Airlines is well known for its efforts to develop ceremonies and rituals to bond employees to the organization by showing them that they are valued members. Southwest holds cookouts in the parking lot of its Dallas headquarters, and CEO Herb Kelleher personally attends each employee Christmas party throughout the country. Because there are so many Christmas parties to attend, Kelleher often finds himself attending parties in July!

Rites of enhancement, such as awards dinners, newspaper releases, and employee promotions, let organizations

Flamboyant Southwest Airlines CEO Herb Kelleher, pictured here on a Harley-Davidson motorcycle given to him by his pilots, prepares to enjoy his company's annual Chili Cook-Off in Dallas. Such organizational rites and ceremonies help build his organization's culture.

publicly recognize and reward employees' contributions and thus strengthen their commitment to organizational values. By bonding members within the organization, rites of enhancement help promote clan control.

STORIES AND LANGUAGE   Stories and language also communicate organizational culture. Stories (whether fact or fiction) about organizational heroes and villains and their actions provide important clues about values and norms. Such stories can reveal the kinds of behaviours that are valued by the organization and the kinds of practices that are frowned on.[48] Stories about Ted Rogers, the person (hero) who made Rogers Communications the company it is today, shed light on many aspects of Rogers Communications' corporate culture. The "Management Insight" shows how McDonald's founder Ray Kroc was responsible for setting his organization's culture.

Management Insight

Ray Kroc: McDonald's Hero

McDonald's Corporation (www.mcdonalds.com) has a rich culture sustained by hundreds of stories that organizational members tell about founder Ray Kroc. Most of these stories have a common theme. They focus on how Kroc established the strict operating values and norms that are at the heart of McDonald's culture. Kroc was dedicated to achieving perfection in McDonald's quality, service, cleanliness, and value for money (QSC&V), and these four central values permeate McDonald's culture. The following story illustrates the way Kroc went about socializing McDonald's employees to these values.

One day, Ray and a group of regional managers from the Houston region were touring various restaurants. One of the restaurants was having a bad day operationally. Ray was incensed about the long lines of customers, and he was furious when he realized that the product customers were receiving that day was not up to his high standards. To address the problem, he jumped up and stood on the front counter and got the attention of all customers and operating crew personnel. He introduced himself, apologized for the long wait and cold food, and told the customers that they could have freshly cooked food or their money back—whichever they wanted. As a result, the customers left happy, and when Kroc checked on the restaurant later, he found that his message had gotten through to its managers and crew—performance had improved.

Other stories describe Kroc scrubbing dirty toilets and picking up litter inside or outside a restaurant. These and similar stories are spread around the organization by McDonald's employees. They are the stories that have helped establish Kroc as McDonald's hero.

McDonald's employees are expected to be extremely dedicated to the central values of McCulture, to work hard, and to be loyal to McFamily. If they do accept its culture, McFamily will take care of them. McDonald's needs employees to be dedicated to QSC&V in order to maintain its high standards and keep its competitive advantage. Stories about heroes can help create a strong culture and increase employee dedication.

Language—through slogans, symbols, and jargon—is used to help employees come to know expectations, while bonding with one another. Markham, ON-based Lucent Technologies Canada uses two acronyms to convey a set of expectations to employees. GROWS summarizes the behaviours expected for high performance: G is for global growth mind set; R is for results focus; O is for obsession with customers and competitors; W is for a workplace that is open, supportive, and

Lucent TOUCH
www.lucent.ca/intl/ca/
en/speeches/pdf/08.08.01_
speech.pdf

diverse; and S is for speed to market. Similarly, employees are evaluated for paying attention to Lucent Canada's TOUCH: T is for teamwork; O is for obsession with customers; U is for uncompromising quality; C is for cost effectiveness; and H is for helping others excel.[49]

MATERIAL SYMBOLS   The organization's layout, sizes of offices, whether individuals wear uniforms or there is a dress code, and what kinds of automobiles top executives are given, are examples of material symbols.[50] Material symbols convey to employees who is important, how much distance there is between top management and employees, and what kinds of behaviour are appropriate. For example, in "A Case in Contrast" in Chapter 14, we describe Toronto-based Willow Manufacturing, where everyone from the CEO down wears a uniform, to convey the message that everyone in the company is part of a team.

The president and chief executive officer of Ford Canada, Alain Batty, has the same huge desk in his office in Toronto as does Ford Motor Co. CEO Jacques Nassar and every other Ford divisional head. The office buildings for all of Ford's operations are also the same. Founder Henry Ford believed it was more efficient to organize office space this way.[51] At Bolton, ON-based Husky Injection Molding Systems, employees and management share the parking lot, dining room, and even washrooms, conveying the sense of an egalitarian workplace.

Husky Injection
Molding Systems
http://www.husky.ca/

The concept of organizational language encompasses not only spoken language but how people dress, the offices they occupy, the cars they drive, and the degree of formality they use when they address one another. IBM Canada, long known for its dark blue suits, introduced less formal clothing in 1993 so that customers would feel more comfortable when interacting with the company.[52] Formal business attire supports Arthur Andersen's conservative culture, which emphasizes the importance of conforming to organizational norms such as respect for authority and staying within one's prescribed role. When employees "speak" and understand the language of their organization's culture, they know how to behave in the organization and what attitudes are expected of them.

Culture and Managerial Action

Does culture really help managers perform their functions?

The way in which organizational culture shapes and controls employee behaviour is evident in the way managers perform their four main functions: planning, organizing, leading, and controlling. As we consider these functions, we continue to distinguish between two kinds of top managers: those who create organizational values and norms that encourage creative, *innovative* behaviour, and those who encourage a *conservative*, cautious approach by their subordinates. We noted earlier that both kinds of values and norms may be appropriate in different situations.

PLANNING   Top managers in an organization with an *innovative* culture are likely to encourage lower-level managers to participate in the planning process and develop a flexible approach to planning. They are likely to be willing to listen to new ideas and to take risks involving the development of new products. In contrast, top managers in an organization with *conservative* values are likely to emphasize formal top-down planning. Suggestions from lower-level managers are likely to be subjected to a formal review, which can significantly slow decision making. Although this deliberate approach may improve the quality of decision making in a nuclear power plant, it also can have unintended consequences. At conservative IBM, for example, before its more recent turnaround, the planning process became so formalized that managers spent most of their time assembling complex slide shows and overheads to defend their current positions rather than thinking about what they should be doing to keep IBM abreast of the changes taking place in the computer industry.

ORGANIZING   Valuing creativity, managers in an *innovative* culture are likely to try to create an organic structure, one that is flat, with few levels in the hierarchy, and in which authority is decentralized so that employees are encouraged to work together to find solutions to ongoing problems. A product team structure may be very suitable for an organization with an innovative culture. In contrast, managers in a *conservative* culture are likely to create a well-defined hierarchy of authority and establish clear reporting relationships so that employees know exactly to whom to report and how to react to any problems that arise.

LEADING   In an *innovative* culture, managers are likely to lead by example, encouraging employees to take risks and experiment. They are supportive regardless of whether employees succeed or fail. In contrast, managers in a *conservative* culture are likely to develop a rigid management by objectives system and to monitor constantly subordinates' progress toward goals, overseeing their every move. We examine leadership in detail in Chapter 13, when we look at the leadership styles that managers can adopt to influence and shape employee behaviour.

CONTROLLING   As this chapter makes clear, there are many control systems that managers can adopt to shape and influence employee behaviour. The control systems they choose reflect a choice about how they want to motivate organizational members and keep them focused on organizational goals. Managers who want to encourage the development of *innovative* values and norms that encourage risk taking choose output and behaviour controls that match this objective. They are likely to choose output controls that measure performance over the long run and develop a flexible MBO system suited to the long and uncertain process of innovation. In contrast, managers who want to encourage the development of *conservative* values choose the opposite combination of output and behaviour controls. They develop specific, difficult goals for subordinates, frequently monitor progress toward these goals, and develop a clear set of rules that subordinates are expected to adhere to. Sometimes managers who are hired by a company do not fit into the existing culture. Calgary-based WestJet fired CEO Steve Smith, who was far more controlling than the rest of the company's culture. WestJet's founders sent a strong message to the employees by firing Smith in a year when the company had done very well financially.

The values and norms of an organization's culture strongly affect the way managers perform their management functions. The extent to which managers buy into the values and norms of their organization shapes their view of the world and their actions and decisions in particular circumstances.[53] In turn, the actions that managers take can have an impact on the performance of the organization. Thus, organizational culture, managerial action, and organizational performance are linked together. Geoffrey Relph, IBM's director of services marketing, notes that his previous company (GE Appliances in Louisville, Kentucky) had a very different set of expectations than IBM Canada: "The priorities in GE are: 'Make the financial commitments. Make the financial commitments. Make the financial commitments.' At IBM, the company's attention is divided among customer satisfaction, employee morale, and positive financial results."[54] GE Appliances' focus on financial commitments may deter employees from also looking at customer satisfaction. It may also suggest that managers need to be concerned with employee morale.

Although organizational culture can give rise to managerial actions that ultimately benefit the organization, this is not always the case. Sometimes culture can become so much a part of the organization that it becomes difficult to improve performance.[55] For example, Wayne Sales, the new president and CEO of Canadian Tire, is trying desperately to revitalize customer service in the company's stores.

Canadian Tire
www.canadiantire.ca/

Canadians have become so used to poor service that employees don't necessarily see the need to change. However, with alternatives such as Home Hardware, Revy Home Centres, and Home Depot Canada, lack of customer service is likely to become an increasing issue as Sales sets out to "drive away the chain's 'crappy tire' image."[56]

Summary and Review

Chapter Summary

WHAT IS ORGANIZATIONAL CONTROL?

• The Importance of Organizational Control

• Control Systems

• The Control Process

OUTPUT CONTROL

• Financial Measures of Performance

• Organizational Goals

• Operating Budgets

• Problems with Output Control

BEHAVIOUR CONTROL

• Direct Supervision

• Management by Objectives

• Bureaucratic Control

• Problems with Bureaucratic Control

ORGANIZATIONAL CULTURE AND CLAN CONTROL

• Creating a Strong Organizational Culture

• Culture and Managerial Action

WHAT IS ORGANIZATIONAL CONTROL? Controlling is the process whereby managers monitor and regulate how efficiently and effectively an organization and its members are performing the activities necessary to achieve organizational goals. Controlling is a four-step process: (1) establishing performance standards, (2) measuring actual performance, (3) comparing actual performance against performance standards, and (4) evaluating the results and taking corrective action if needed.

OUTPUT CONTROL To monitor output or performance, managers choose goals or performance standards that they think will best measure efficiency, quality, innovation, and responsiveness to customers at the corporate, divisional, departmental or functional, and individual levels. The main mechanisms that managers use to monitor output are financial measures of performance, organizational goals, and operating budgets.

BEHAVIOUR CONTROL In an attempt to shape behaviour and induce employees to work toward achieving organizational goals, managers utilize direct supervision, management by objectives, and bureaucratic control by means of rules and standard operating procedures.

ORGANIZATIONAL CULTURE AND CLAN CONTROL Organizational culture is the set of values, norms, standards of behaviour, and common expectations that control the ways individuals and groups in an organization interact with each other and work to achieve organizational goals. Clan control is the control exerted on individuals and groups by shared values, norms, standards of behaviour, and expectations. Organizational culture is transmitted to employees through the values of the founder, the process of socialization, organizational ceremonies and rites, and stories and language. The way managers perform their management functions influences the kind of culture that develops in an organization.

Management in Action

Topics for Discussion and Action

1. What is the relationship between organizing and controlling?

2. How do output control and behaviour control differ?

3. Ask a manager to list the main performance measures that he or she uses to evaluate how well the organization is achieving its goals.

4. Ask the same or a different manager to list the main forms of output control and behaviour control that he or she uses to monitor and evaluate employee behaviour.

5. Why is it important for managers to involve subordinates in the control process?

6. What is organizational culture, and how does it affect the way employees behave?

7. Interview some employees of an organization, and ask them about the organization's values, norms, socialization practices, ceremonies and rites, and special language and stories. Referring to this information, describe the organization's culture.

8. What kind of controls would you expect to find most used in (a) a hospital, (b) the Armed Forces, (c) a city police force. Why?

Building Management Skills

Understanding Controlling

For this exercise, you will analyze the control systems used by a real organization such as a department store, restaurant, hospital, police department, or small business. It can be the organization that you investigated in Chapter 8 or a different one. Your objective is to uncover all the different ways in which managers monitor and evaluate the performance of the organization and employees.

1. At what levels does control take place in this organization?

2. Which output performance standards (such as financial measures and organizational goals) do managers use most often to evaluate performance at each level?

3. Does the organization have a management by objectives system in place? If it does, describe it. If it does not, speculate about why not.

4. How important is behaviour control in this organization? For example, how much of managers' time is spent directly supervising employees? How formal is the organization? Do employees receive a book of rules to instruct them about how to perform their jobs?

5. What kind of culture does the organization have? What are the values and norms? Do employees tell any particular stories that reveal the organization's norms and values? What effect does the organizational culture have on the way employees behave or treat customers?

6. Based on this analysis, do you think there is a fit between the organization's control systems and its culture? What is the nature of this fit? How could it be improved?

Small Group Breakout Exercise

How Best to Control the Sales Force?

Form groups of three or four people, and appoint one member as the spokesperson who will communicate your findings to the whole class when called on by the instructor. Then discuss the following scenario.

You are the regional sales managers of an organization that supplies high-quality windows and doors to building supply centres nationwide. Over the last three years, the rate of sales growth has slackened. There is increasing evidence that, to make their jobs easier, salespeople are primarily servicing large customer accounts and ignoring small accounts. In addition, the salespeople are not dealing promptly with customer questions and complaints, and this inattention has resulted in a drop in after-sales service. You have talked about these problems, and you are meeting to design a control system to increase both the amount of sales and the quality of customer service.

1. Design the control system that you think will best motivate salespeople to achieve these goals.

2. What relative importance do you put on (a) output control, (b) behaviour control, and (c) organizational culture in this design?

Exploring the World Wide Web

Specific Assignment

Enter Hewlett-Packard's Web site (www.hp.com). Click on "Company Information"; then click on "About HP," "Corporate Objectives and the HP Way," and "The HP Way."

1. What are the main elements of the HP Way?

2. How does the HP Way lead to an organizational culture that helps Hewlett-Packard to achieve its strategies?

3. How easy would it be to institute the HP Way and culture in other companies?

General Assignment

Search for the Web site of a company that actively uses organizational culture (or one of the other types of control) to build competitive advantage. What kind of values and norms is the culture based on? How does it affect employee behaviour?

ManagementCase

Mutual Life Goes Public, and Becomes Clarica

In June 1999, Waterloo, ON-based Mutual Life of Canada's policy-holders voted to accept a plan presented by the company's management team to go public. The company started issuing shares, and took on a new identity, as Clarica, to begin its life as a shareholder-owned company.

Bob Astley, Mutual's and now Clarica's president and CEO, told the policy-holders that the change to the company's operating procedures would be dramatic, and would include "Tough competition, new rules and a lot more people-watching."

Four of Canada's life insurers went public in recent years: Clarica, Sun Life Assurance Co., Manulife Financial Corp., and Canada Life Assurance Co. Doing so allowed the insurers to have opportunities similar to the banks, such as raising capital in the equity and debt markets. However, it also forced them to focus more on efficiency and profitability.

The trend to go public is the opposite of what some Canadian life insurers did in the 1950s and '60s. Back then the trend was to go from publicly traded companies to mutuals in order to be protected from possible foreign takeovers. Today, demutualization (i.e., becoming publicly traded) is a response to globalization and the need to raise capital for domestic or foreign expansion.

The shift from a mutual company to a publicly held company has had an impact on both Astley's way of managing and on his employees. The company used to make annual plans regarding strategy and performance. Now, Astley says, the pace has increased considerably. "We're on 90-day business planning and individuals have 90-day personal plans."

Working for a publicly traded company is a new experience for many of Clarica's employees. The pace is different, and there is more stress involved in meeting performance standards. As Astley explains, "The single-minded focus on profitability in each of the business segments has been sharpened as a result of the public disclosure, the need to report earnings on a quarterly basis and the need to satisfy investors."

Astley spends his day a lot differently as well. Being a CEO for a publicly listed company, he says has caused him "to be much more focused on results and probably more demanding of the people around me. I spend more of my time thinking about and meeting with investors and analysts, explaining the company. I delegate more and I pick my spots. I don't get involved in activities inside the company that I can't afford the time for."

Eighteen months after the name change, Astley expressed annoyance at the constant jokes that "Clarica sounds like a brand of toilet bowl cleanser." He acknowledged that the company still has a ways to go to become a household name. "The name Clarica had no meaning in itself. Our task was to infuse it with meaning. We're working at that. It takes many, many months, indeed years, to build up name awareness to the highest level that we'd all want to have. We're still on that path," says Astley.

Clarica faces a new legal environment from the one present when it first became a publicly listed company. New financial services legislation likely means that Clarica, the smallest of the four life insurance companies that went public in 1999 and 2000, probably faces "a strategic alliance, merger with another insurance company or outright acquisition by a bank."

So now Astley is trying to get his company ready for sale. "My goal in running the company is going to be to make us the most effective company we can, to have the highest share price we can, to be innovative and to continue to grow. I'm not going to just sit around and wait for December 31, 2001." And he may even consider acquiring another company, either in Canada or the United States, rather than being acquired.

Source: R. McQueen, "Polishing up Clarica Life: Sale Possible. Federal Legislation Would Make Insurer a Likely Target," *Financial Post (National Post)*, December 4, 2000, p. C6; S. Gordon, "En Garde! Insurance Companies are Taking on the Banks More Directly, in the Marketplace and in the Regulatory Arena," *Canadian Banker*, March 2000, pp. 20–24; M. Strathdee, "Mutual Group to Meet June 10 on Issuing Shares," *Canadian Press Newswire*, March 25, 1999.

Questions

1. How might going public affect the kinds of controls used at Clarica?

2. In what ways would you expect the culture at Clarica to change as it went through the transition to become a publicly traded company?

ManagementCase
In the News

Fostering Corporate Culture

When Brown University buddies Tom First and Tom Scott launched their juice company, Nantucket Nectars, six years ago, they deliberately made things as informal as possible.

No hierarchy. No dress code. No stodgy corporate culture.

The free-spirited attitude of the blond beach boys is flaunted throughout their Brighton-based company, from the dogs roaming the purple-toned offices to the naked man pictured jumping into the harbor on their juice labels.

But now, as juice sales approach US$20 million, Nantucket Nectars is outgrowing its fraternity house culture, and "Tom and Tom" (as they're known) are grappling with how to manage that growth without destroying the entrepreneurial spirit that has made the company special.

"It's one of my biggest fears," admits First, 29, whose baby face belies his intensity. "Once you start departmentalizing, you lose that."

Whether identified by purple walls or conservative blue suits, a company's culture has everything to do with its success—or failure.

That's especially true within start-up companies, where hard-driving employees typically put in long hours for relatively low pay.

IBM's paternalistic culture—often identified by its propensity toward blue suits and red ties—fostered deep employee loyalty with promises of good benefits, good pay and, until recently, a lifetime job.

Too often, company cultures—especially at start-up firms—are measured by what people wear to work or how much time they spend playing games in the corridors. But while blue jeans and Nerf basketball games might inspire creativity or relieve tension, they are not what make the culture.

A company's culture has more to do with its employees' behaviour, values and expectations. When employees understand and share a company's mission and values, specialists say, they are more productive, and the company is more prosperous.

So where does a company's culture come from?

Whether intentional or not, it's typically spawned by the founder early in the company's life.

First and Scott, 30, set the work ethic for Nantucket Nectars long before selling a single bottle of juice. During summers on Nantucket, they spent long hours selling supplies from a boat, shucking scallops, even walking dogs—anything to earn money and a reputation for service.

"Nantucket's a close-knit community. We needed to be respected as businesspeople, and not just seen as college kids passing through," First says.

Today, Nantucket Nectars's employees put in equally long hours. The office is lit up well past 8 P.M., and many staffers drop in on weekends to take care of business.

The founders didn't initially realize the example they were setting. About two months ago, First called the staff together and encouraged them to leave at 6 P.M. each night.

The problem, says staffer Wink Mleczko, is that employees thought they were guilty of being inefficient.

"I'm like a tornado," First confesses. "I have tunnel vision. People look at their leaders and I have to be real careful about the tone I set."

Whether or not the founder of a company thinks much about cultural issues during its start-up phase, those issues become critical as a company matures, specialists and entrepreneurs agree.

"How you maintain a culture during explosive growth is probably the No. 1 thing that I worry about," says Frank Ingari, chief executive of Shiva Corp., a US$118 million company that makes equipment and software for telecommuters.

In his view, a company's culture has to fit not only the employee, but the employee's family, too. Not surprisingly, then, Shiva encourages employees to work from home on flexible schedules, if it fits their lifestyle.

"I don't care whether people are working here or there, as long as they are self-starters, self-motivators and hard workers," Ingari says.

Pamela Reeve, president and chief executive of Lightbridge Inc., a Waltham-based provider of software for the cellular communications industry, shares Ingari's obsession with managing culture.

"You have to pay as much attention to cultural issues as you do to your financing or marketing. To me, it's one of the assets that has to be managed and fertilized and watered."

Without a clearly defined culture, employees may try to clone themselves in the image of the company's leader—by wearing similar clothes or adopting various personality traits—rather than embrace the leader's ideas and principles, says William Bygrave, director of the Center for Entrepreneurial Studies at Babson College.

Another problem as companies grow, adds Babson colleague Julian Lange, is that "people try to divine what's happening in the company by reading titles."

At Lightbridge, Reeve tried to head off that situation by giving her company a very flat organization. "We have very little structure," she says. "Sure, someone has to have spending responsibility and someone has to have responsibility for hiring and training. But that's all in the background. We're very team-oriented. I don't run the team. I'm just on it."

She compares the situation to her first whitewater rafting trip. The guide led the group through tumultuous waters, but he steered from the back of the boat.

To promote teamwork among the company's 300 employees, Lightbridge holds frequent brown bag lunches where goals are discussed, and ties performance incentives to companywide accomplishments, not individual ones.

When the company moved into larger office space at the end of a particularly stressful period of growth, Reeve invited art therapists in for a day to help employees design artwork that reflected the company's culture.

"We needed to put our soul in the building," she says.

In one exercise, each employee was assigned to paint a small area on a large canvas, which was their "home." The space between each area was their "neighborhood."

Together, employees decided how to paint those common areas. The result is an "eclectic mix of colorful abstract paintings displayed throughout Lightbridge's offices.

The art helps tie employees together, something that becomes more difficult as companies grow beyond the start-up phase.

At Nantucket Nectars, weekly staff meetings include a guest speaker—an employee "who has to stand up and talk about their whole life, and what inspires them," First says. "We're so busy, sometimes we don't respect what other people do. I wanted everyone to understand who the people are and how they're helping this company."

"You have to respect the fact that your employees are smart," says David Blohm, president of software company Virtual Entertainment, who has used similar teambuilding tactics.

At his last company, Mathsoft Inc., which he founded in 1985 and took public in 1993, Blohm made sure every employee was plugged in by requiring them to demonstrate the company's software products to colleagues.

"We wanted them to talk about the product benefits, like they were demonstrating them to their in-laws. We wanted them to talk about it at that level. That raises the level of understanding and empathy for the customer," Blohm says.

To produce the cultural flavour of a small company, many entrepreneurs search for ways to bring employees together, whether for Halloween parties, pizza and beer blasts, or summer barbecues.

At Molten Metal Technology Inc. in Waltham, it's breakfast. Each Friday, two of the company's most recent hires are responsible for preparing breakfast for the rest of their colleagues.

In the beginning, when there were only a dozen or so employees,

it was easy. "You just stopped and got a bag of bagels," says Ian Yates, vice-president of sales and market development for the environmental technology company.

Now, however, Molten Metal has 300 employees, including 150 at its Waltham headquarters. But the tradition continues, with some newcomers going all out, preparing everything from pancakes to such ethnic favorites as breakfast burritos. The company picks up the tab.

"It's a small price to pay for the benefit, which is bringing people together," says Yates. "We don't want the first chance for people to meet to be in a meeting or on a project. If you know someone first, you'd be surprised how much better you listen to them."

Another meeting place at Molten Metal is the fifth-floor atrium, where employees and executives talk over business issues, while shooting pool or playing table tennis or air hockey.

Having fun is actually part of the 7-year-old company's mission statement. But in the end, what makes any company's culture work is a shared sense of passion for the company's objectives.

"We're part of a team that is dedicated to changing the way the world deals with waste," Yates says. "We're pulling on the same end of the rope together. That's pretty powerful. It makes the time playing table tennis more fun."

Source: J. Muller, "Fostering Corporate Culture," *Boston Globe*, February 4, 1996, p. 73.

Questions

1. What factors influence the values and norms of Nantucket Nectars' culture?

2. What factors make it easy or difficult to create or change an organization's culture?

Chapter ten

Human Resource Management

Learning Objectives

1. Explain why strategic human resource management can help an organization gain a competitive advantage.

2. Describe the steps managers take to recruit and select organizational members.

3. Discuss the training and development options that ensure that organizational members can effectively perform their jobs.

4. Explain why performance appraisal and feedback is such a crucial activity, and list the choices managers must make in designing effective performance appraisal and feedback procedures.

5. Explain the issues managers face in determining levels of pay and benefits.

A Case in Contrast

Training and Development at Comtek and TD Canada Trust

Comtek Advanced Structures Ltd. (www.comtek advanced.com) of Burlington, Ontario is an aircraft-parts manufacturer.[1] Besides being a parts manufacturer, the company also repairs the parts it makes for airliners. For this task, the company needs experienced repair people.

"It's fairly specialized work, and we can only grow the business as fast as we have people available," says Patrick Whyte, president and CEO. Getting enough trained people has been so difficult that Whyte decided to take matters into his own hands. In 1995, he created a three-year part-time apprenticeship program for his employees. The program consists of 12 learning modules on the repair of different aircraft parts, and is taught inhouse. New employees can apply for the program after they've been with the firm for six months. Ontario's provincial government recognizes the program, and even supplies a certificate of accomplishment to graduates. The company, not the employee, pays for the program, which costs $15 000 per employee.

Whyte sees his investment in training as a good expenditure: the program attracts new hires, and it reduces turnover substantially. Employees stay with the company because they feel a sense of accomplishment through the course. "The return for us is that they may decide to spend the rest of their career here," he says. "People these days get a lot of their job satisfaction from the training."

Whyte's also been able to use the training to grow his business. When he started the company as a first-time CEO in 1994, the economy was booming and it was easy for the company to expand. Since 1994, Comtek has grown to more than 100 employees in 2001 from a start of 6. In 2000 alone, Comtek doubled the number

Both Comtek Advanced Structures and TD Canada Trust invest heavily in employee training and development. Both companies see this as an investment in their employees.

of its employees. Revenue grew more than 1500 percent to slightly more than $7 million between 1995 and 2000.

Though Comtek faces a downturn in 2001's turbulent environment, Whyte expects to be able to survive reasonably well. "If the economy slows down, regional airlines don't take on new airplanes, but they still have to repair the ones they have," he says. "I don't think in our sector we'd have any layoffs, but it's a question of growing more slowly." Whyte's training program may well be the key that keeps his company going.

Comtek is a small company, especially compared to something like TD Canada Trust Bank (TD) (www.tdcanadatrust.com). So how does training differ for a big corporation? Rather than an apprenticeship program, TD uses a classroom approach, using satellites to deliver programs to 300 sites.[2] Some of these sites are in training centres where 100 people can attend a course together, while other sites are the lunchrooms of remote branches. TD's approach, offering much greater face-to-face delivery of material, differs from that of the Bank of Montreal (BOM), which delivers almost 80 percent of its training through computer programs and similar activities. BOM finds that its method allows students to forge their own path of learning, at their own pace, while Jane Hutcheson, TD's vice-president of learning and development, suggests that the benefit of TD's approach is that, "You can interact in real time."

To find out what kinds of courses they should take, TD's employees log onto People Development@TD, a program that catalogues their strengths and also lets them see the skills required for all positions in the bank, including that of CEO. Employees are encouraged to sketch out a program with their manager to develop added competencies.

Like Whyte, Hutcheson sees training as an investment in employees, not a cost. She points out that employee education provides a 15-percent return to the bank. Although their means are dramatically different, both Comtek's training and TD's development programs are achieving similar goals: ensuring that the companies are building the human resources they need to be effective and gain a competitive advantage. Moreover, managers in both companies realize how valuable training and development are for employees at all hierarchical levels, from entry level to top management. ●

Overview

Managers are responsible for acquiring, developing, protecting, and utilizing the resources that an organization needs to be efficient and effective. One of the most important resources in all organizations is human resources—the people involved in the production and distribution of goods and services. Human resources include all members of an organization, ranging from top managers to entry-level employees. Effective managers like Patrick Whyte and Jane Hutcheson in the "Case in Contrast" realize how valuable human resources are and take active steps to make sure that their organizations build and fully utilize their human resources to gain a competitive advantage.

This chapter examines how managers can tailor their human resource management system to their organization's strategy and structure. We discuss in particular the major components of human resource management: recruitment and selection, training and development, performance appraisal, pay and benefits, and labour relations. By the end of this chapter, you will understand the central role that human resource management plays in creating a high-performing organization. ●

Strategic Human Resource Management

human resource management Activities that managers engage in to attract and retain employees and to ensure that they perform at a high level and contribute to the accomplishment of organizational goals.

strategic human resource management The process by which managers design the components of a human resource management system to be consistent with each other, with other elements of organizational architecture, and with the organization's strategy and goals.

Society for Human Resource Management www.shrm.org/

Human resource management (HRM) includes all the activities that managers engage in to attract and retain employees and to ensure that they perform at a high level and contribute to the accomplishment of organizational goals. **Strategic human resource management** is the process by which managers design the components of an HRM system to be consistent with each other, with other elements of organizational architecture, and with the organization's strategy and goals.[3] The objective of strategic HRM is the development of an HRM system that enhances an organization's efficiency, quality, innovation, and responsiveness to customers—the four building blocks of competitive advantage, which we discussed in Chapter 1.

Overview of the Components of HRM

An organization's human resource management system has five major components: recruitment and selection, training and development, performance appraisal and feedback, pay and benefits, and labour relations (see Figure 10.1). Managers use *recruitment and selection,* the first component of an HRM system, to attract and hire new employees who have the abilities, skills, and experiences that will help an organization achieve its goals. Microsoft Corporation, for example, has the goal of remaining the premier computer software company in the world. To achieve this goal, Bill Gates realized, it would be important to hire only the best software designers. When Microsoft hires new software designers, hundreds of highly qualified candidates with excellent recommendations are interviewed and rigorously tested; only the best are hired. This careful attention to selection has contributed to Microsoft's competitive advantage. Microsoft has little trouble recruiting top programmers because candidates know they will be at the forefront of the industry if they work for Microsoft, utilizing the latest technology and working with the

Figure 10.1

Components of a Human Resource Management System

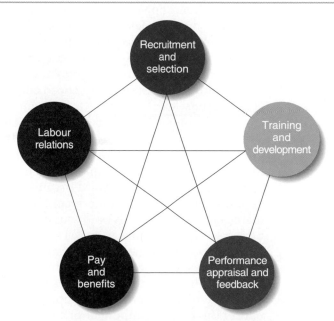

Each component of an HRM system influences
the others, and all five must fit together

best people.[4] The "Management Insight" shows how one Fredericton company selects employees for their focus on their families.

Management Insight

At Greenarm Management, Family Comes First

Earl Brewer, CEO of Greenarm Management, believes in hiring people who put people first.[5] "We don't want people working excessively and neglecting their families," he says. At the Fredericton, NB-based developer and property management firm, turnover is low. Brewer says its because they hire the right people: "They have to have passion for the job."

When *Atlantic Progress* surveyed the employees, they found that employees raved about working for the company. Their explanations for why Greenarm was such a great place to work included: "Its people. The company hires energetic, highly motivated people;" "It's an exciting, friendly atmosphere with many highly productive employees."

The employees also commented that senior management leads by example. Because senior management members find it important to balance work life and family life, employees feel comfortable doing the same. As one employee explains, "I tell people that my company expects hard, good quality work, but also expects me and others to have a family life and to be happy."

Greenarm, named a Best Company to Work For in Atlantic Canada in 2001, is also a successful company. It is New Brunswick's largest private sector property management company.

After recruiting and selecting employees, managers use the second component, *training and development*, to ensure that organizational members develop skills and abilities that will enable them to perform their jobs effectively in the present and the future. Training and development is an ongoing process; changes in technology and the environment, as well as in an organization's goals and strategies, often require organizational members to learn new techniques and ways of working. The "Case in Contrast" describes Patrick Whyte and Comtek's heavy investment in the development of repairpeople to ensure that they acquire the technical skills needed to find new ways to increase Comtek's revenues and profits. At Microsoft Corporation, newly hired program designers receive on-the-job training by joining small teams that include experienced employees who serve as mentors or advisers. New recruits learn firsthand from team members how to go about developing computer systems that are responsive to customers' programming needs.[6]

The third component, *performance appraisal and feedback*, serves two different purposes in HRM. First, performance appraisal can provide managers with the information they need to make good human resources decisions–decisions about how to train, motivate, and reward organizational members.[7] Thus, the performance appraisal and feedback component is a kind of *control system* that can be used with management by objectives (discussed in Chapter 9). Second, performance feedback from performance appraisal serves a developmental purpose for members of an organization. When managers regularly evaluate their subordinates' performance, they can provide subordinates with valuable information about their strengths and weaknesses and the areas in which they need to concentrate.

On the basis of performance appraisals, managers distribute *pay* to employees, part of the fourth component of an HRM system. By rewarding high-performing organizational members with pay raises, bonuses, and the like, managers increase the likelihood that an organization's most valued human resources are motivated to continue their high levels of contribution to the organization. Moreover, when pay is linked to performance, high-performing employees are more likely to stay with the organization, and managers are more likely to be able to fill open positions with highly talented individuals. *Benefits,* such as health insurance, are important outcomes that employees receive by virtue of their membership in an organization.

Last but not least, *labour relations* encompasses the steps that managers take to develop and maintain good working relationships with the labour unions that may represent their employees' interests. For example, an organization's labour relations component can help managers establish safe working conditions and fair labour practices in their offices and plants.

Managers must ensure that all five of these components fit together and complement their company's structure and control systems.[8] For example, if managers decide to decentralize authority and empower employees, they need to invest in training and development to ensure that lower-level employees have the knowledge and expertise they need to make the decisions that top managers would make in a more centralized structure.

Each of the five components of HRM influences the others (see Figure 10.1).[9] The kinds of people that the organization attracts and hires through recruitment and selection, for example, determine (1) the training and development that are necessary, (2) the way performance is appraised, and (3) the appropriate levels of pay and benefits. Managers at Microsoft ensure that their organization has highly qualified program designers by (1) recruiting and selecting the best candidates, (2) providing new hires with the guidance of experienced team members so that they learn how to be responsive to customers' needs when designing programs and systems, (3) appraising program designers' performance in terms of their individual contributions and their team's performance, and (4) basing programmers' pay on individual and team performance.

The Legal Environment of HRM

To what extent does the legal environment affect human resource practices?

In the rest of this chapter, we focus in detail on the choices managers must make in strategically managing human resources to attain organizational goals and gain a competitive advantage. Effectively managing human resources is a complex undertaking for managers, and we provide an overview of some of the major issues they face. Before we do, however, we need to look at how the legal environment affects human resource management.

The local, provincial, and federal laws and regulations that managers and organizations must abide by add to the complexity of HRM. For example, under the *Canadian Human Rights Act,* it is against the law for any employer or provider of service that falls within federal jurisdiction to make unlawful distinctions based on the following prohibited grounds: race, national or ethnic origin, colour, religion, age, sex (including pregnancy and childbirth), marital status, family status, mental or physical disability (including previous or present drug or alcohol dependence), pardoned conviction, or sexual orientation. Employment with the following employers and service providers is covered by the Human Rights Act: federal departments, agencies and crown corporations; Canada Post; chartered banks; national airlines; interprovincial communications and telephone companies; interprovincial transportation companies; and other federally regulated industries, such as certain mining operations.

The *Employment Equity Act* creates four "protected categories"—women, Aboriginal people, people with disabilities, and visible minorities—who must not be discriminated against in employment by federally regulated employers and all employers receiving federal contracts worth more than $200 000. The goal of employment equity is to ensure that all citizens have an equal opportunity to obtain employment regardless of their gender, race or ethnicity, or disabilities. Provincial governments also have equity legislation to which employers must respond. Thus human resource managers must comply with this legislation in the recruitment, selection and promotion of employees.

Contemporary challenges that managers face related to the legal environment include how to eliminate sexual harassment (see Chapter 5), how to make accommodations for disabled employees, how to deal with employees who have substance abuse problems, and how to manage HIV-positive employees and employees with AIDS.[10] HIV-positive employees are infected with the virus that causes AIDS, but they may show no AIDS symptoms and may not develop AIDS in the near future. Often, such employees are able to perform their jobs effectively, and managers must take steps to ensure that they are able to do so and are not discriminated against in the workplace.[11] Employees with AIDS may or may not be able to perform their jobs effectively, and, once again, managers need to ensure that they are not unfairly discriminated against.[12] Many organizations have instituted AIDS awareness training programs to educate organizational members about HIV and AIDS, dispel unfounded myths about how HIV is spread, and ensure that individuals infected with the virus are treated fairly and are able to be productive as long as they can be while not putting others at risk.[13]

Recruitment and Selection

recruitment Activities that managers engage in to develop a pool of qualified candidates for open positions.

selection The process that managers use to determine the relative qualifications of job applicants and their potential for performing well in a particular job.

human resource planning Activities that managers engage in to forecast their current and future needs for human resources.

Recruitment includes all the activities that managers engage in to develop a pool of qualified candidates for open positions.[14] **Selection** is the process by which managers determine the relative qualifications of job applicants and their potential for performing well in a particular job. Before actually recruiting and selecting employees, managers need to engage in two important activities: human resource planning and job analysis (see Figure 10.2).

Human Resource Planning

Human resource planning includes all the activities that managers engage in to forecast their current and future needs for human resources. Current human resources are the employees an organization needs today to provide high-quality goods and services to customers. Future human resources are the employees the organization will need at some later date to achieve its longer-term goals. As part of human resource planning, managers must make both demand forecasts and supply forecasts. *Demand forecasts* estimate the qualifications and numbers of employees an organization will need given its goals and strategies. *Supply forecasts* estimate the availability and qualifications of current employees now and in the future, and the supply of qualified workers in the external labour market.

The assessment of both current and future human resource needs helps managers determine whom they should be trying to recruit and select to achieve orga-

Figure 10.2
The Recruitment and Selection System

nizational goals now and in the future. Montreal-based BCE recently created a new position, "chief talent officer," and appointed Léo Houle to the post. Houle will report directly to BCE's CEO, Jean Monty. He will be responsible for executive recruitment, compensation and succession planning to make sure that BCE's companies have the right leadership and talent as BCE looks toward the future.[15]

When there is a shortage of available employees, managers sometimes need to be more creative in the types of employees they are willing to hire, as this "Focus on Diversity" indicates.

Focus on Diversity

Amusement Parks Hire Seniors

Toronto's Canada's Wonderland, Calgary's Calaway Park, and Vancouver's Pacific National Exhibition (PNE) used to hire only students to sell hot dogs, run the rides, and collect tickets each summer.[16] Now, they're looking to senior citizens for staffing needs as well.

Calaway Park's marketing director, Bob Williams, believes that senior citizens offer a good source of employees. "I think that the seniors market is more viable today than it was years ago. Seniors are hard workers. They're great workers."

Lowell Schrieder, spokesperson for Canada's Wonderland, agrees: "We're trying to break the perception that we wouldn't hire beyond students. Seniors are just as good as the young ones. They're very congenial."

John McGrath, a 71-year-old who has worked at the park for the last four years, explains that he found the job appealing after sitting at home for several years, just being "retired." "It takes me away from my rocking chair. It keeps my brain young."

Seniors often find it difficult to find jobs. Ann Watson, 62, who works at Calaway Park, didn't want to remain unemployed, "but because of my age, nobody wanted me." Sometimes, employers think that seniors won't want to work for the type of pay they offer for jobs that are considered to be entry level. The PNE solves this problem by offering extra perks, including complimentary tickets for family and friends, and occasionally gives out $500 prizes for the employees as well.

outsourcing Using outside suppliers and manufacturers to produce goods and services.

As a result of their human resource planning, managers sometimes use **outsourcing** to fill some of their human resource needs. Instead of recruiting and selecting employees to produce goods and services, managers contract with people who are not members of their organization to produce goods and services. Kelly Services is an organization that provides temporary typing, clerical, and secretarial workers to managers who want to use outsourcing to fill some of their human resource requirements in these areas. Outsourcing is increasingly being used on a global level. Managers in some Canadian computer software companies are outsourcing some of their programming work to programmers in India who are highly skilled but cost the companies substantially less than they would normally pay for the programming work to be done inhouse.

There are at least two reasons why human resource planning sometimes leads managers to outsource: flexibility and cost. First, outsourcing can give managers increased flexibility, especially when accurately forecasting human resource needs is difficult, human resource needs fluctuate over time, or finding skilled workers in a particular area is difficult. Second, outsourcing can sometimes allow managers to make use of human resources at a lower cost. When work is outsourced, costs may be lower for a number of reasons: The organization does not have to provide benefits to workers; managers are able to contract for work only when the work is needed; and managers do not have to invest in training. Outsourcing can be used for functional activities such as after-sales service on appliances and equipment, legal work, and the management of human resources or information systems. CIBC outsourced its human resources and technology operations to EDS Canada in the spring of 2001. Among other duties, EDS is responsible for administering the bank's payroll, benefits, and pensions; it provides a call centre for employees and managers, and runs CIBC's human resources systems. Joyce Phillips, CIBC executive vice-president of human resources, explained this move: "This move is aligned with CIBC's overall strategy to focus on its core businesses while using the expertise of leading providers to support our administrative needs."[17] The Bank of Canada, the Ontario government and the Canadian Pacific and Canadian National railways also outsource some of their operations to EDS. Scotiabank outsources the running of its computer system to IBM Canada.

Outsourcing does have its disadvantages, however. When work is outsourced, managers may lose some control over the quality of goods and services. Also, individuals performing outsourced work may have less knowledge of organizational practices, procedures, and goals and less commitment to an organization than regular employees. In addition, unions resist outsourcing because it has the potential to eliminate the jobs of some of their members.

Job Analysis

Job analysis is a second important activity that managers need to undertake prior to recruitment and selection.[18] **Job analysis** is the process of identifying (1) the tasks, duties, and responsibilities that make up a job (the *job description*), and (2) the knowledge, skills, and abilities needed to perform the job (the job specifications).[19] For each job in an organization, a job analysis needs to be done.

A job analysis can be done in a number of ways, including observing current employees as they perform the job or interviewing them. Often, managers rely on questionnaires completed by jobholders and their managers. The questionnaires ask about the skills and abilities needed to perform the job, job tasks and the amount of time spent on them, responsibilities, supervisory activities, equipment used, reports prepared, and decisions made.[20]

The Position Analysis Questionnaire (PAQ) is a comprehensive standardized questionnaire that many managers rely on to conduct job analyses.[21] It focuses on behaviours jobholders perform, working conditions, and job characteristics, and it can be used for a variety of jobs.[22] The PAQ contains 194 items organized into six divisions: (1) information input (where and how the jobholder acquires information to perform the job), (2) mental processes (reasoning, decision-making, planning, and information-processing activities that are part of the job), (3) work output (physical activities performed on the job and machines and devices used), (4) relationships with others (interactions with other people that are necessary to perform the job), (5) job context (the physical and social environment of the job), and (6) other job characteristics (such as work pace).[23] A trend in some organizations is toward flexible jobs in which tasks and responsibilities change and cannot be specified clearly in advance. For these kinds of jobs, job analysis focuses more on determining the skills and knowledge workers need to be effective and less on specific duties.

When managers have completed human resource planning and job analyses for all jobs in an organization, they will know their human resource needs and the jobs they need to fill. They also will know what knowledge, skills, and abilities potential employees will need to perform those jobs. At this point, recruitment and selection can begin.

job analysis Identifying the tasks, duties, and responsibilities that make up a job and the knowledge, skills, and abilities needed to perform the job.

Position Analysis
Questionnaire
www.paq.com/

External and Internal Recruitment

As noted earlier, recruitment is what managers use to develop a pool of qualified candidates for open positions.[24] They generally use two types of recruiting: external and internal.

What are the advantages and disadvantages of recruiting from outside the company?

EXTERNAL RECRUITING   When managers recruit externally to fill open positions, they look outside the organization for people who have not worked for the organization previously. There are multiple means through which managers can recruit externally—advertisements in newspapers and magazines, open houses for students, career counsellors at high schools and colleges or onsite at the organization, career fairs at colleges, recruitment meetings with groups in the local community, and notices on the Internet and World Wide Web.

Many large organizations send teams of interviewers to college campuses to recruit new employees. External recruitment can also take place through informal networks, such as when current employees inform friends about open positions in their companies or recommend people they know to fill vacant spots. Some organizations use employment agencies for external recruitment, and some external recruitment takes place simply through walk-ins—jobhunters coming to an organization and inquiring about employment possibilities.

With all the downsizings and corporate layoffs that have taken place in recent years, you might think that external recruiting would be a relatively easy task for managers. However, it often is not, because even though many people may be looking for jobs, many of the jobs that are opening up require skills and abilities that these jobhunters do not have. For example, Canada faces a large shortage of high-tech workers because there are not enough workers who have these particular skills, and many of them are wooed by US firms that can pay more for their skills.

External recruiting has both advantages and disadvantages for managers. Advantages include having access to a potentially large applicant pool, being able to attract people to an organization who have the skills, knowledge, and abilities the organization needs to achieve its goals, and being able to bring in newcomers who may have a fresh approach to problems and be up-to-date on the latest technology. These advantages have to be weighed against the disadvantages, however, including lower morale if current employees feel that there are individuals within the company who should be promoted. External recruitment also has high costs. Employees recruited externally lack knowledge about the inner workings of the organization and may need to receive more training than those recruited internally. InSystems uses its Web site to inform potential employees about its culture and strategic plans, as shown in the "Management Insight." Finally, when employees are recruited externally, there is always uncertainty about whether they actually will be good performers. Angiotech Pharmaceuticals solves this problem by working with potential employees years before they're ready to be hired, as the "Management Insight" illustrates.

Management Insight

Recruiting Challenges at Two Small Companies

William Hunter, chairman and CEO of Vancouver-based Angiotech Pharmaceuticals Inc. (www.angiotech.com), which has developed drugs to treat arthritis and multiple sclerosis, has the difficult problem of recruiting trained scientists for his company.[25] So he "grows" new employees in the lab.

Specifically, Angiotech spends about $250 000 a year on a research chair at the University of British Columbia and sponsors laboratories at other universities as well. "The money goes to grad students working on projects closely related to what we do," says Hunter. The money spent at UBC funds graduate student research, where they learn more about pharmacology, a core part of Angiotech's business. "When they graduate, we're one of the most obvious choices to work for," Hunter notes.

Hunter and Angiotech's chief scientific officer conduct research with the UBC students, generally over a three-year period. Thus they learn a lot about how the students think, and what their potential is. Though Angiotech also uses traditional methods of recruiting, developing employees in the lab is their preferred approach. And it is also successful: "I can honestly say there hasn't been a person out of those labs that we wanted to hire that didn't want to come and work for us."

Markham, ON-based InSystems uses technology to find its employees. Human Resources Director Diane Dowsett says the Internet is often the first contact the company has with potential employees. The company's Web site includes a career section that lists current job openings, and information on the company's philosophy and strategic plan. The site also includes information about the company's culture and testimonials from InSystems employees. Dowsett finds that job applicants always mention the Web site during interviews. The use of technology for recruiting doesn't stop with the firm's Web site, however. InSystems also uses a recruiting consultant to scan online job boards for potential hires, especially technical specialists.

INTERNAL RECRUITING   When recruiting is internal, managers turn to existing employees to fill open positions. Employees recruited internally are either seeking **lateral moves** (job changes that entail no major changes in responsibility or authority levels) or promotions. Internal recruiting has several advantages. First, internal applicants are already familiar with the organization (including its goals, structure, culture, rules, and norms). Second, managers already know internal candidates; they have considerable information about their skills and abilities and actual behaviour on the job. Third, internal recruiting can help boost levels of employee motivation and morale, both for the employee who gets the job and for other workers. Those who are not seeking a promotion or who may not be ready for a promotion can see that it is a possibility for the future; or a lateral move can alleviate boredom once a job has been fully mastered and also provide a useful way to learn new skills. Finally, internal recruiting is normally less time-consuming and expensive.

Given the advantages of internal recruiting, why do managers rely on external recruiting as much as they do? The answer is because there are disadvantages to internal recruiting—among them, a limited pool of candidates and a tendency among those candidates to be "set" in the organization's ways. Often, the organization simply does not have suitable internal candidates. Sometimes, even when suitable internal applicants are available, managers may rely on external recruiting to find the very best candidate or to help bring new ideas and approaches into the organization. When organizations are in trouble and performing poorly, external recruiting is often relied on to bring in managerial talent with a fresh approach. Thus, when Nortel Networks announced in October 2001 that it would promote the company's Chief Financial Officer, Frank Dunn, as the replacement for John Roth, some analysts expressed disappointment, because Dunn was a career number cruncher, not a dynamic strategist.

HONESTY IN RECRUITING   At times, when trying to recruit the most qualified applicants, managers may be tempted to paint overly rosy pictures of both the open positions and the organization as a whole. They may worry that if they are totally honest about advantages and disadvantages, they either will not be

lateral move A job change that entails no major changes in responsibility or authority levels.

able to fill positions or will have fewer or less-qualified applicants. A manager trying to fill a secretarial position, for example, may emphasize the high level of pay and benefits that the job offers and fail to mention the fact that the position is usually a dead-end job offering few opportunities for promotion.

Research suggests that painting an overly rosy picture of a job and organization is not a wise recruiting strategy. Recruitment is most likely to be effective when managers provide potential applicants with an honest assessment of both the advantages and the disadvantages of a job and organization. Such an assessment is called a **realistic job preview** (RJP).[26] RJPs can be effective because they reduce the number of new hires who quit because their jobs and organizations fail to meet their unrealistic expectations and they help applicants decide for themselves whether a job is right for them.

Professor Sandra Robinson of the Faculty of Commerce at UBC refers to the discrepancy between an employee's expectations and what management delivers as a breach in the **psychological contract** of employment. This unwritten agreement sets out mutual expectations—what management expects from workers, and vice versa.[27] Robinson's research shows that 55 percent of employees reported a significant contract breach by their employer in the last two years. Seventy-five percent of those reporting a contract violation also said they either *intended to quit* or *did quit* in the subsequent year. Those who did not quit reported a decreased sense of obligation to the company, and decreased performance.

The Selection Process

How do managers select employees?

Once managers develop a pool of applicants for open positions through the recruitment process, they need to find out whether each applicant is qualified for the position and whether he or she is likely to be a good performer. If more than one applicant meets these two conditions, managers must further determine which applicants are likely to be better performers than others. They have several selection tools to help them sort out the relative qualifications of job applicants and appraise their potential for being good performers in a particular job. Those tools include background information, interviews, tests, and references.[28]

BACKGROUND INFORMATION To aid in the selection process, managers obtain background information from job applications and from résumés. Such information might include highest levels of education obtained, college majors and minors, type of college or university attended, years and type of work experience, and mastery of foreign languages. Background information can be helpful both to screen out applicants who are lacking key qualifications (such as a college degree) and to determine which qualified applicants are more promising than others (for example, applicants with a B.Sc. may be acceptable, but those who also have an MBA are preferable).

INTERVIEWS Virtually all organizations use interviews during the selection process. Two general types of interviews are structured and unstructured. In a *structured interview*, managers ask each applicant the same standard questions (such as "What are your unique qualifications for this position?" and "What characteristics of a job are most important for you?"). Particularly informative questions may be those that prompt an interviewee to demonstrate skills and abilities needed for the job in answering the question. Sometimes called *situational interview questions*, these questions present interviewees with a scenario that they would likely encounter on the job and ask them to indicate how they would handle it.[29] For example, applicants for a sales job may be asked to indicate how they would respond to a customer who complains about waiting too long for service, a customer who is indecisive, and a customer whose order is lost.

realistic job preview An honest assessment of the advantages and disadvantages of a job and organization.

psychological contract An individual's beliefs or perceptions regarding the terms and conditions of an agreement to which that individual is party.

Earl Brewer, president of Greenarm Management, wants employees who have a passion for the job and who understand balance. In job interviews, one consideration is whether "family is first," something Brewer thinks is important in the people he hires.

An *unstructured interview* proceeds more like an ordinary conversation. The interviewer feels free to ask probing questions to discover what the applicant is like and does not ask a fixed set of questions prepared in advance. In general, structured interviews are superior to unstructured interviews because they are more likely to yield information that will help identify qualified candidates and they are less subjective. Also, evaluations based on structured interviews may be less likely to be influenced by the biases of the interviewer than evaluations based on unstructured interviews.

Even when structured interviews are used, however, there is always the potential for the biases of the interviewer to influence his or her judgments. Recall from Chapter 5 how the similar-to-me effect can cause people to perceive others who are similar to themselves more positively than they perceive those who are different and how stereotypes can result in inaccurate perceptions. It is important for interviewers to be trained to avoid these biases and sources of inaccurate perceptions as much as possible. Many of the approaches to increasing diversity awareness and diversity skills described in Chapter 5 can be used to train interviewers to avoid the effects of biases and stereotypes. In addition, using multiple interviewers can be advantageous, for their individual biases and idiosyncrasies may cancel one another out.[30]

When conducting interviews, managers have to be careful not to ask questions that are irrelevant to the job in question; otherwise their organizations run the risk of costly lawsuits. It is inappropriate and illegal, for example, to inquire about an interviewee's spouse or to ask questions about whether an interviewee plans to have children. Questions such as these, which are irrelevant to job performance, may be viewed as discriminatory and as violating human rights legislation. Thus, interviewers also need to be instructed in what is required under the legislation and informed about questions that may be seen as violating those laws.

While we often think of managers having sole responsibility for hiring, they need not be the only ones doing interviewing, as the "Management Insight" indicates.

Management Insight

Broadening the Pre-Employment Interview

At Montreal-based PEAK Investment (www.peakgroup.com), prospective job candidates are interviewed by everyone with whom the person might work, including potential subordinates.[31] "If a team is to work properly as a team, then they should have a say in who the other team members are," says CEO Robert Frances.

One advantage to PEAK's approach is that the team knows its strengths and weaknesses and can evaluate the candidate accordingly. If team members can't agree on the outcome of an interview, they are encouraged to compromise. However, if team members don't think they'll get along with the candidate, then the person is not hired.

Frances uses this approach to hiring because he wants to encourage team building. "If people don't have some control over the team-building process they become cynical and you've had it, you're doomed," he says.

The approach is also good for the new employee, particularly if he or she comes from a more traditional hierarchical corporate environment. The candidate gets to see, through the job interview, whether a more democratic approach to work appeals.

Yet another way of conducting interviews is to let the candidate interview the CEO. That's exactly what CEO Warren Kotler of Toronto-based Lunatex Inc. does. Kotler—whose company supplies corporate promotional products, premiums, and incentives to businesses—believes in the importance of personal relationships among employees. "It's like a partnership: we all work together. Nobody really works for me, so it's just as important that they know about me and the goings-on here, as that I know about them," Kotler says. The interview format shows that power and responsibility flow both ways at Lunatex.

TESTING Potential employees may be asked to take ability tests, personality tests, physical ability tests, or performance tests. Ability tests assess the extent to which applicants possess skills necessary for job performance, such as verbal comprehension or numerical skills.

Personality tests measure personality traits and characteristics relevant to job performance. Some retail organizations, for example, give job applicants honesty tests to determine how trustworthy they are. The use of personality tests (including honesty tests) for hiring purposes is controversial. Some critics maintain that honesty tests do not really measure honesty (that is, they are not valid) and can be subject to faking by job applicants. For jobs that require physical abilities—such as firefighting, garbage collecting, and package delivery—managers use as selection tools physical ability tests that measure physical strength and stamina.

Performance tests measure job applicants' performance on actual job tasks. Applicants for secretarial positions, for example, are typically required to complete a typing test that measures how quickly and accurately they are able to type. Applicants for middle- and top-management positions are sometimes given short-term projects to complete—projects that mirror the kinds of situations that arise in the job being filled—to assess their knowledge and problem-solving capabilities.[32]

REFERENCES Applicants for many jobs are required to provide references from former employers or other knowledgeable sources (such as a college instructor or adviser) who know the applicants' skills, abilities, and other personal characteristics. These individuals are asked to provide candid information about the applicant. References are often used at the end of the selection process to confirm a decision to hire. Yet the fact that many former employers are reluctant to provide negative information in references sometimes makes it difficult to interpret what a reference is really saying about an applicant.

In fact, several recent lawsuits filed by applicants who felt that they were unfairly denigrated or had their privacy invaded by unfavourable references from former employers have caused managers to be increasingly wary of providing any kind of negative information in a reference, even if it is accurate. For jobs in which the jobholder is responsible for the safety and lives of other people, however, failing to provide accurate, negative information in a reference does not just mean that the

Lisa Cedars grimaces as she hauls a 165-lb. dummy to the finish line during a physical fitness test for firefighting applicants. The physical test is just one of many used to determine the top candidates.

wrong person might get hired; it also may mean that other people's lives will be at stake, as indicated in this "Ethics in Action."

Ethics in Action

The Costs of Withholding Negative Information in References

In late 1994, an American Airlines (www.americanair.com) commuter plane crashed near Raleigh, North Carolina, because the pilot mistakenly thought there was engine failure. Subsequent inquiries indicated that the same pilot had been found unfit to fly on his previous job. Managers at American Airlines did not have access to this information when they hired him, however. Why? Airlines that in the past provided negative references and documented poor performance have been sued by former employees for invasion of privacy. The former employer of this particular pilot was unwilling to risk getting sued and thus failed to provide an accurate (and negative) reference.[33]

Is it ethical to withhold negative information when lives are at stake? Managers who withhold negative information from references often do so because they fear that their companies may be subject to costly lawsuits if they give a negative reference for a former employee, even if it is accurate.

Realizing the ethical dilemma faced by these managers and the potential risks to human life and well-being, legislators have taken steps to protect former employers who give accurate, negative information in references for former employees. Under defamation law, reference writers are protected by qualified privilege. "If you give a reference honestly, even if it's negative, even if it's wrong, you're protected," says Richard McEachin, president of Toronto-based McEachin and Associates, a research company specializing in "competitive intelligence" and background checking.[34]

For example, when anesthesiologist Dr. Pavel Straka's current employer, Toronto's Humber River Regional Hospital, refused to promote him to a full-time position, Straka asked Ontario Superior Court Justice Romaine W.M. Pitt to force his new employer to reveal the content of reference letters written by three of his former associates at Toronto's St. Michael's Hospital.[35] Straka was concerned that the letters contained negative information that Humber River was using to deny his promotion. When Justice Pitt refused Straka's request, he took it to the Ontario Court of Appeal, which also turned him down in late 2000. While Straka can use Section 37 of the Public Hospitals Act to see the letters, even if the letters do contain the negative information he suspects, he won't be able to sue the writers for libel in court to clear his name, because the letters' authors can use a defence of qualified privilege to argue that they had a moral or legal duty to disclose the information in the reference letters. Clearly, rights to privacy and protection against defamation are important societal values, but when human lives and well-being are at stake, former employers need to be able to provide accurate information in references, even if it is negative and prevents an applicant from obtaining a job.

THE IMPORTANCE OF RELIABILITY AND VALIDITY   Whatever selection tools a manager uses, they need to be both reliable and valid. **Reliability** is the degree to which a tool or test measures the same thing each time it is administered. Scores on a selection test should be very similar if the same person is assessed with the same test on two different days; if there is quite a bit of variability, the test is unreliable. For interviews, determining reliability is more complex because the dynamic is more one of personal interpretation. Suffice it to say here

reliability The degree to which a tool or test measures the same thing each time it is used.

that the reliability of interviews can be increased if two or more different qualified interviewers interview the same candidate. If the interviews are reliable, the interviewers should come to similar conclusions about the interviewee's qualifications.

validity The degree to which a tool or test measures what it purports to measure.

Validity is the degree to which a tool or test measures what it purports to measure—in the case of selection tests, that is the degree to which the test predicts performance on the tasks or job in question. Does a physical ability test used to select firefighters, for example, actually predict on-the-job performance? Do typing tests predict secretarial performance? These are questions of validity.

Managers have an ethical and legal obligation to use reliable and valid selection tools. Yet there are degrees of reliability and validity; they are not all-or-nothing characteristics. Thus, managers should strive to use selection tools in such a way that they can achieve the greatest degree of reliability and validity.

Tips for Managers

Recruitment and Selection

1. Prior to recruiting and selecting new employees, use human resource planning and job analysis to determine your human resource needs now and in the future.

2. Provide job applicants with an honest assessment of the advantages and disadvantages of a job.

3. Use other selection tools in addition to interviews to decide which applicants to hire.

4. Make sure that the selection tools you use are reliable and valid.

Training and Development

training Teaching organizational members how to perform their current jobs and helping them acquire the knowledge and skills they need to be effective performers.

development Building the knowledge and skills of organizational members so that they will be prepared to take on new responsibilities and challenges.

needs assessment An assessment of which employees need training or development and what type of skills or knowledge they need to acquire.

Training and development help to ensure that organizational members have the knowledge and skills they need to perform their jobs effectively, take on new responsibilities, and adapt to changing conditions. **Training** focuses primarily on teaching organizational members how to perform their current jobs and helping them acquire the knowledge and skills they need to be effective performers. **Development** focuses on building the knowledge and skills of organizational members so that they will be prepared to take on new responsibilities and challenges. Training tends to be used more frequently at lower levels of an organization; development tends to be used more frequently with professionals and managers. Comtek's apprenticeship program, described in the "Case in Contrast," focuses in large part on ensuring that entry-level workers have the skills they need to perform their jobs effectively. The program aims to ensure that when workers start their first jobs at Comtek, they have the knowledge and skills needed for good performance.

Before creating training and development programs, managers should perform a **needs assessment** in which they determine which employees need training or development and what type of skills or knowledge they need to acquire (see Figure 10.3).[36]

Types of Training

Employee training can be take place in several ways.

CLASSROOM INSTRUCTION Through classroom instruction, employees acquire knowledge and skills in a classroom setting. The instruction itself may take place within the organization or outside it, such as when employees are

Figure 10.3
Training and Development

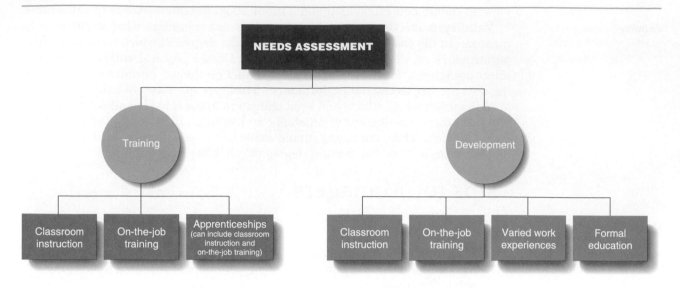

encouraged to take courses at local colleges and universities. Many organizations actually establish their own formal instructional divisions—some are even called "colleges"—to provide needed classroom instruction.

Classroom instruction frequently includes the use of videos and role-plays in addition to traditional written materials, lectures, and group discussions. *Videos* can be used to demonstrate appropriate and inappropriate job behaviours. For example, by watching an experienced salesperson effectively deal with a loud and angry customer in a video clip, inexperienced salespeople can develop skills in handling similar situations. During a *role-play*, trainees either directly participate in or watch others perform actual job activities in a simulated setting. At McDonald's Hamburger University, for example, role-playing is used to help franchisees acquire the knowledge and skills they need to manage their restaurants.

Simulations can also be used as part of classroom instruction, particularly on complicated jobs that require an extensive amount of learning and in which errors carry a high cost. In a simulation, key aspects of the work situation and job tasks are duplicated as closely as possible in an artificial setting. For example, air traffic controllers are trained by means of simulations because of the complicated nature of the work, the extensive amount of learning involved, and the very high costs of air traffic control errors.

McDonald's
Hamburger University
www.mcdonalds.com/
corporate/careers/hambuniv/

on-the-job training
Training that takes place in the work setting as employees perform their job tasks.

ON-THE-JOB TRAINING   In **on-the-job training**, learning occurs in the work setting as employees perform their job tasks. On-the-job training can be provided by co-workers or supervisors or occur simply as jobholders gain experience and knowledge from doing the work. Managers often use on-the-job training on a continuing basis to ensure that their subordinates keep up-to-date with changes in goals, technology, products, or customer needs and desires.

E-TRAINING   More companies are starting to rely on online training to help employees keep up with skills and new products. E-training can include online text, live presentations broadcast over the Internet, slide shows, taped lectures and video on demand. Employees can interact with instructors and take tests; employers can keep track of employees' progress. At Cisco Systems Canada, 80 percent of sales staff training is done online.[37] Cisco employees can get up to speed on Cisco's networking products and learn how to install the products in material

Bell Nexxia
www.bellnexxia.com/

offered online. At Bell Nexxia, a division of Bell Canada, employees can use their cellphones and handheld devices to access e-training. For companies, e-training reduces training costs and improves employee productivity. Bell Nexxia's $3 million training budget was cut by about $1.8 million because of savings in developing courses, as well as not having to provide employees with travel and accommodation as part of the training.

Types of Development

Although both classroom instruction and on-the-job training can be used for development purposes as well as for training, development often includes additional activities such as varied work experiences and formal education.

VARIED WORK EXPERIENCES Top managers need to develop an understanding of, and expertise in, a variety of functions, products and services, and markets. In order to develop executives who will have this expertise, managers frequently make sure that employees with high potential have a wide variety of job experiences, some in line positions and some in staff positions. Varied work experiences broaden employees' horizons and help them think in terms of the big picture. For example, a one-to-three-year stint overseas is increasingly being used to provide managers with international work experiences. With organizations becoming more global, managers need to develop an understanding of the different values, beliefs, cultures, regions, and ways of doing business in different countries.

FORMAL EDUCATION Many large corporations reimburse employees for tuition expenses they incur in taking college courses and obtaining advanced degrees. This is not just benevolence on the part of the employer or even a simple reward given to the employee; it is an effective way to develop employees who will be able to take on new responsibilities and more challenging positions. For similar reasons, corporations spend thousands of dollars sending managers to executive development programs such as executive MBA programs. In these programs, managers learn from experts the latest in business and management techniques and practices. To save time and travel costs, some managers are relying on *long-distance learning* to educate and develop employees formally.

Issues in Career Development

A career is "the evolving sequence of a person's work experiences over time."[38] As individuals progress through their lives, they may get promoted, or they may change employers, or even become self-employed. All of this constitutes one's career. There are benefits to effective career development: it improves satisfaction and self-esteem, reduces stress, and strengthens an individual's psychological and physical health.[39] It also helps the organization, because employees are better suited to meet organizational needs.

The issue of career development, and who is responsible for making sure it happens, has become a national issue. The federal government is predicting "a looming national employment crisis" because of an aging and shrinking labour force.[40] Within 10 to 15 years, there will not be enough young people to replace those who are retiring. There is also concern that employees need to develop more job-related skills due to the increase in technology and the demands of the information economy. There is no single answer as to who should take action to resolve the issue of skills training: the government, employers, or employees.

Human Resources Development Canada (HRDC) proposed in 2001 a plan to increase the skills of Canada's workforce. The plan's main proposals included:

Human Resources
Development Canada
www.hrdc-drhc.gc.ca/

encouraging individuals to retrain and pursue lifelong learning; giving incentives to private industry to make employee training a top priority; increasing the numbers of skilled immigrants and speeding up their accreditation; and bringing into the labour force traditionally unemployed groups. The HRDC proposal faced serious controversy and is only one way of trying to resolve the skills crisis in Canada.

There are benefits to organizations when they offer career development programs.[41] By doing so, they can make sure that the right people will be available for changing staffing needs, they can increase workforce diversity, and they can help employees get a better understanding of what is expected in various positions, that is, to have more realistic job expectations. Below, we describe both the organization's and employee's responsibilities for career development today.

The Organization's Responsibilities

What responsibility does the organization have for helping employees plan their careers?

What, if any, responsibility does the organization have for career development? Organizations take a variety of positions on this question. At Montreal-based Alcan Aluminum, employees are assessed annually, and then the employee's manager provides feedback regarding the potential for advancement and career prospects.[42] At the same time, employees discuss their career aspirations with their manager. High potential employees are brought to the attention of senior management so that divisions anywhere within Alcan have knowledge about employees and their skills. Alcan's managers also develop an annual five-year plan to examine their human resource needs so that appropriate individuals can be identified and given training. At Hewlett-Packard Canada, by contrast, employees are expected to develop their own career plans and seek out the development they need. This is done with encouragement by their managers.

Employers that have successful career development programs provide support for employees to continually add to their skills, abilities, and knowledge. This support includes:[43]

"**1.** *Clearly communicating the organization's goals and future strategies.* When people know where the organization is headed, they're better able to develop a personal plan to share in that future.

2. *Creating growth opportunities.* Employees should have the opportunity to get new, interesting, and professionally challenging work experiences.

3. *Offering financial assistance.* The organization should offer tuition reimbursement to help employees keep current.

4. *Providing the time for employees to learn.* Organizations should be generous in providing paid time off from work for off-the-job training. Additionally, workloads should not be so demanding that they preclude employees from having the time to develop new skills, abilities, and knowledge."

The Employee's Responsibilities

While it is to an organization's advantage to develop its employees, Canada's employers do not have a good reputation for employee training. The country ranks seventeenth in terms of private-sector employers placing a "high priority" on employee training, falling behind Sweden, Japan, Norway, Germany, Australia and the United States.[44] Therefore, it is wise for individuals to take a more entrepreneurial approach to their careers. By maintaining flexibility and keeping skills and knowledge up-to-date, individuals will have more job opportunities available to them. Barbara Moses makes the following suggestions for how to be a career activist, and take charge of your own career.[45]

BBM Human Resource Consultants (Barbara Moses) www.bbmcareerdev.com/

1. *Ensure your employability.* Make sure you have alternatives, in case you lose your job. Gain new skills; pursue opportunities that will stretch you.

2. *Have a fall-back position.* Have multiple options for your career, and try to see yourself in multiple roles. This means you could be an employee, a contract worker, or a freelance consultant using a broader set of skills.

3. *Know your key skills.* Know how to package your existing skills and experience in new ways (e.g., an architect who has a hobby as a gardener may start a business designing and building greenhouses). Identify your key talents and skills, and don't limit yourself to a job title.

4. *Market! Market! Market!* Always keep your eyes open for new work assignments, and position yourself for these. Let key people know your skills, and how you can bring value to the organization. Be sure to network. Be sure to treat everyone you meet as a potential client.

5. *Act Type A, be Type B.* While it is important to have the drive and achievement orientation of a Type A personality, it is also important to have the more relaxed Type B attitude of feeling good about yourself, even if you are not producing at a mile a minute. Your sense of self should not be completely tied to your job and the workplace.

6. *Stay culturally current.* Make sure that you're aware of world and cultural events. Being in the know helps you establish relationships with other people, and can help you manage your career effectively.

7. *Be a compelling communicator.* Everyone is busy these days, so it's important to communicate effectively and efficiently. You may be communicating with people halfway around the globe, or individuals who know little about the technical details of what you do. So being clear is important.

8. *Manage your finances.* If you have your finances in order, this will give you greater opportunities to explore change.

9. *Act like an insider, think like an outsider.* Work as a team player and be self-aware, and able to evaluate your performance with some objectivity. It is important to be able to think independently. Sometimes you will have to make decisions without the help of a group.

10. *Be capable of rewarding yourself.* With increased demands on everyone, you may not receive all of the external feedback you might like. Learn how to give yourself a pat on the back when you do things well. Celebrate your successes, and take time to nourish yourself.

Performance Appraisal and Feedback

performance appraisal
The evaluation of employees' job performance and contributions to their organization.

performance feedback
The process through which managers share performance appraisal information with subordinates, give subordinates an opportunity to reflect on their own performance, and develop, with subordinates, plans for the future.

The recruitment and selection and the training and development components of a human resource management system ensure that employees have the knowledge and skills they need to be effective now and in the future. Performance appraisal and feedback complement recruitment, selection, training, and development. **Performance appraisal** is the evaluation of employees' job performance and contributions to their organization. **Performance feedback** is the process through which managers share performance appraisal information with their subordinates, give subordinates an opportunity to reflect on their own performance, and develop, with subordinates, plans for the future. In order for there to be performance feedback, performance appraisal must take place. Performance appraisal could take place without providing performance feedback, but wise managers are careful to provide feedback because it can contribute to employee motivation and performance.

Performance appraisal and feedback contribute to the effective management of human resources in two ways. Performance appraisal gives managers important information on which to base human resources decisions.[46] Decisions about pay raises, bonuses, promotions, and job moves all hinge on the accurate appraisal of performance. Performance appraisal also can help managers determine which workers are candidates for training and development, and in what areas. Performance feedback encourages high levels of employee motivation and performance. It lets good performers know that their efforts are valued and appreciated and lets poor performers know that their lacklustre performance needs improvement. Performance feedback can provide both good and poor performers with insight into their strengths and weaknesses and ways in which they can improve their performance in the future.

Types of Performance Appraisal

Performance appraisal focuses on the evaluation of traits, behaviours, or results.[47]

Do some types of appraisals give clearer job performance information than others?

TRAIT APPRAISALS　　When trait appraisals are used, managers assess subordinates on personal characteristics that are relevant to job performance, such as skills, abilities, or personality. A factory worker, for example, may be evaluated for her ability to use computerized equipment and perform numerical calculations. A social worker may be evaluated for his empathy and communication skills.

Three disadvantages of trait appraisals often lead managers to rely on other appraisal methods. First, possessing a certain personal characteristic does not ensure that the personal characteristic will actually be used on the job and result in high performance. For example, a factory worker may possess superior computer and numerical skills but be a poor performer because of a low level of motivation. The second disadvantage of trait appraisals is linked to the first. Because traits do not always show a direct association with performance, workers and courts of law may view them as unfair and potentially discriminatory. The third disadvantage of trait appraisals is that they often do not enable managers to provide employees with feedback that they can use to improve performance. Because trait appraisals focus on relatively enduring human characteristics that change only over the long term, employees can do little to change their behaviour in response to performance feedback from a trait appraisal. Telling the social worker that he lacks empathy provides him with little guidance about how to improve his interactions with clients, for example. The disadvantages of trait appraisals suggest that managers should use them only when they can demonstrate that the traits assessed are accurate and important indicators of job performance.

BEHAVIOUR APPRAISALS　　Through behaviour appraisals, managers assess how workers perform their jobs–the actual actions and behaviours that workers exhibit on the job. Whereas trait appraisals assess what workers *are like*, behaviour appraisals assess what workers *do*. For example, with a behaviour appraisal, a manager might evaluate a social worker on the extent to which he looks clients in the eye when talking with them, expresses sympathy when they are upset, and refers them to community counselling and support groups geared toward the specific problem they are encountering. Behaviour appraisals are especially useful when *how* workers perform their jobs is important. In educational organizations such as high schools, for example, it is important not just how many classes and students are taught but also how they are taught or the methods teachers use to ensure that learning takes place.

Behaviour appraisals have the advantage of providing employees with clear information about what they are doing right and wrong and how they can improve their performance. In addition, because behaviours are much easier for employees to change than traits, performance feedback from behaviour appraisals is more likely to lead to performance improvements. The "Management Insight" shows how Montreal-based Proximi-T Technologies uses its appraisals to help determine training programs for its employees.

Management Insight

Using Appraisals to Manage Training

Montreal-based Proximi-T Technologies de l'information Inc., a business application software consulting firm, reviews its employees' performance every three months.[48] Employees are evaluated against a set of values important to the company. Team leaders evaluate their team members on such things as whether individuals are transparent, proactive, and balanced in their lives.

Proximi-T employees are also evaluated on 10 technical abilities, such as programming and change management, and personal qualities. For instance, employees are evaluated on how well they write and speak in English and French, how they deal with diversity, and what kind of leaders they are.

Proximi-T's evaluations may seem extensive, but president Yves Poire finds it necessary because of the difficult of hiring IT staff. "It's tough to get access to senior IT staff right now, people with experience, so we need to go with younger people, and that causes us a lot of training," explains Poire. By doing careful evaluations, the management at Proximi-T knows where it needs to invest in more training for the staff. This helps the company be at the leading edge in consulting.

RESULTS APPRAISALS For some jobs, *how* people perform the job is not as important as *what* they accomplish or the results they obtain. With results appraisals, managers appraise performance in terms of results or the actual outcomes of work behaviours.

Take the case of two new-car salespeople. One salesperson might strive to develop personal relationships with customers, spending hours talking to them and frequently calling them up to see how their decision-making process is going. The other salesperson might have a much more hands-off approach; although being very knowledgeable and answering customers' questions, doesn't approach them but waits for them to come to him or her. Both salespeople sell, on average, the same number of cars, and the customers of both are satisfied with the customer service they receive (customers respond to postcards that the dealership mails them to assess their satisfaction). The manager of the dealership appropriately uses results appraisals (sales and customer satisfaction) to evaluate the salespeople's performance because it does not matter which behaviour salespeople use to sell cars as long as they sell the desired number and satisfy customers. If one salesperson sells too few cars, however, the manager can give that salesperson performance feedback that he or she is not selling enough.

OBJECTIVE AND SUBJECTIVE APPRAISALS Whether managers appraise performance in terms of traits, behaviours, or results, the information they assess is either *objective* or *subjective*. **Objective appraisals** are based on facts and are likely to be numerical—the number of cars sold, the number of meals prepared, the number of times late, the number of audits completed. Managers often use objective appraisals when results are being appraised, because results tend to be easier to quantify than traits or behaviours. However, when the way in which workers perform their jobs is important, more subjective behaviour appraisals are more appropriate than results appraisals.

Subjective appraisals are based on managers' perceptions of traits, behaviours, or results. Because subjective appraisals rest on managers' perceptions, there is always the chance that they are inaccurate (we discuss managerial perception in more detail in the next chapter). It is for this reason that both researchers and managers have spent considerable time and effort in developing reliable and valid subjective measures of performance.

objective appraisal

An appraisal that is based on facts and is likely to be numerical.

subjective appraisal

An appraisal that is based on perceptions of traits, behaviours, or results.

Some popular subjective measures, such as the graphic rating scale, the behaviourally anchored rating scale (BARS), and the behaviour observation scale (BOS), are illustrated in Figure 10.4.[49] When graphic rating scales are used, performance is assessed along a continuum with specified intervals. With a BARS, performance is assessed along a scale with clearly defined scale points containing examples of specific behaviours. A BOS assesses performance in terms of how often specific behaviours are performed. Many managers use both objective and subjective appraisals. For example, a salesperson may be appraised in terms of the dollar value of sales (objective) and the quality of customer service (subjective).

Figure 10.4

Subjective Measures of Performance

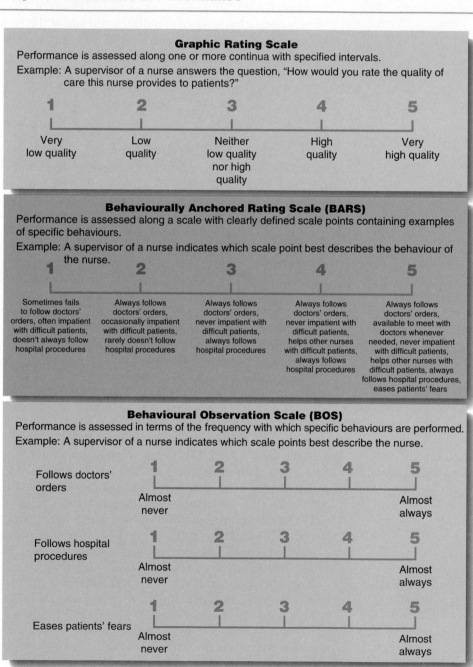

Who Appraises Performance?

We have been assuming that managers or the supervisors of employees evaluate performance. This is a pretty fair assumption, for supervisors are the most common appraisers of performance. Performance appraisal is an important part of most managers' job duties. It is managers' responsibility to motivate their subordinates to perform at a high level, and managers make many of the decisions that hinge on performance appraisals, such as decisions about pay raises or promotions. Appraisals by managers can, however, be usefully augmented by appraisals from other sources (see Figure 10.5).

SELF, PEERS, SUBORDINATES, AND CLIENTS   When self-appraisals are used, managers supplement their evaluations with an employee's assessment of his or her own performance. Peer appraisals are provided by an employee's co-workers. Especially when subordinates work in groups or teams, feedback from peer appraisals can motivate team members while providing managers with important information for decision making. A growing number of companies are having subordinates appraise their own managers' performance and leadership as well. Sometimes, customers or clients provide assessments of employee performance in terms of responsiveness to customers and quality of service.

Although appraisals from each of these sources can be useful, managers need to be aware of potential issues that may arise when they are used. Subordinates sometimes may be inclined to inflate self-appraisals, especially if organizations are downsizing and they are worried about their job security. Managers who are appraised by their subordinates may fail to take needed but unpopular actions for fear that their subordinates will appraise them negatively.

360-degree appraisal

A performance appraisal by peers, subordinates, superiors, and sometimes clients who are in a position to evaluate a manager's performance.

360-DEGREE PERFORMANCE APPRAISALS   To improve motivation and performance, some organizations include 360-degree appraisals and feedback in their performance appraisal systems, especially for managers. In a **360-degree appraisal**, a manager's performance is appraised by a variety of people, such as the manager himself or herself and the manager's peers or co-workers,

Figure 10.5
Who Appraises Performance?

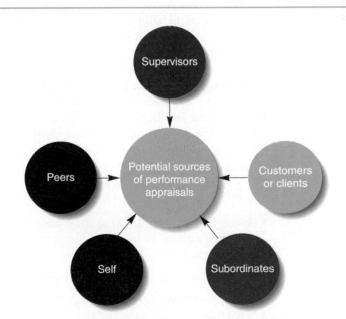

subordinates, superiors, and sometimes even customers or clients. The manager receives feedback based on evaluations from these multiple sources.

The growing number of companies using 360-degree appraisals and feedback includes Toronto-based Celestica, Markham, ON-based InSystems, Burnaby, BC-based Dominion Directory Information Services, and Hudsons' Bay. A 360-degree appraisal and feedback is not always as clear-cut as it might seem. On the one hand, some subordinates may try to get back at their bosses by giving managers negative evaluations, especially when evaluations are anonymous (to encourage honesty and openness). On the other hand, some managers may coach subordinates to give—or even threaten sanctions if they fail to give—positive evaluations.

Peers often are very knowledgeable about performance but may be reluctant to provide an accurate and negative appraisal of someone they like or a positive appraisal of someone they dislike. In addition, whenever peers, subordinates, or anyone else evaluates a worker's performance, managers must be sure that the evaluators are actually knowledgeable about the performance dimensions being assessed. For example, subordinates should not evaluate their supervisor's decision making if they have little opportunity to observe this dimension of his or her performance.

These potential problems with 360-degree appraisals and feedback do not mean that they are not useful. Rather, they suggest that in order for 360-degree appraisals and feedback to be effective, there has to be trust throughout an organization. More generally, trust is a critical ingredient in any performance appraisal and feedback procedure. In addition, managers using 360-degree appraisals and feedback have to consider carefully the pros and cons of using anonymous evaluations and of using the results of the appraisals for decision making about important issues such as pay raises.

Effective Performance Feedback

In order for the performance appraisal and feedback component of a human resource management system to encourage and motivate high performance, managers must provide their subordinates with performance feedback. To generate useful information to pass on to subordinates, managers can use both formal and informal appraisals. **Formal appraisals** are conducted at set times during the year and are based on performance dimensions and measures that have been specified in advance. A salesperson, for example, may be evaluated by his or her manager twice a year on the performance dimensions of sales and customer service, sales being objectively measured from sales reports and customer service being measured with a BARS (see Figure 10.4). **Informal appraisals**—unscheduled appraisals of ongoing progress and areas for improvement—may occur at the request of the employee.

An integral part of a formal appraisal is a meeting between the manager and the subordinate in which the subordinate is given feedback on his or her performance. Performance feedback shows subordinates areas in which they are excelling and areas in which they are in need of improvement; it should also provide them with guidance for improving performance. Canadian workers report that the practice of performance appraisals is not carried out well in many workplaces. A 1997 survey of 2004 Canadian workers from a variety of industrial sectors by Watson Wyatt Worldwide, an international consulting firm, found the following:[50]

- Only 60 percent said that they understood the measures used to evaluate their performance.
- Only 57 percent thought that their performance was rated fairly.
- Only 47 percent said that their managers clearly expressed goals and assignments.
- Only 42 percent reported regular, timely performance reviews.
- Only 39 percent reported that their performance review was helpful in improving their on-the-job performance.

formal appraisal

An appraisal conducted at a set time during the year and based on performance dimensions and measures that were specified in advance.

informal appraisal

An unscheduled appraisal of ongoing progress and areas for improvement.

- Only 19 percent reported a clear, direct, and compelling linkage between their performance and their pay.

Managers often dislike providing performance feedback, especially when the feedback is negative, but doing so is an important managerial activity. Here are some guidelines for effectively giving performance feedback that will contribute to employee motivation and performance:

How can managers improve the performance feedback they give employees?

- Be specific and focus on behaviours or outcomes that are correctable and within a worker's ability to improve. *Example:* Telling a salesperson that he or she is too shy when interacting with customers is likely to do nothing more than lower the person's self-confidence and prompt him or her to become defensive. A more effective approach is to give the salesperson feedback about specific behaviours to engage in—greeting customers as soon as they enter the department; asking customers whether they need help; volunteering to help customers find items if they seem to be having trouble.
- Approach performance appraisal as an exercise in problem solving and solution finding, not criticizing. *Example:* Rather than criticizing a financial analyst for turning reports in late, the manager helps the analyst determine why the reports are late and identify ways to better manage time.
- Express confidence in a subordinate's ability to improve. *Example:* Instead of being skeptical, a first-level manager tells a subordinate of confidence that the subordinate can increase quality levels.
- Provide performance feedback both formally and informally. *Example:* The staff of a preschool receives feedback from formal performance appraisals twice a year. The director of the school also provides frequent informal feedback, such as complimenting staff members on creative ideas for special projects, noticing when they do a particularly good job handling a difficult child, and pointing out when they provide inadequate supervision.
- Praise instances of high performance and areas of a job in which a worker excels. *Example:* Rather than focusing on just the negative, a manager discusses the areas the subordinate excels in as well as areas in need of improvement.
- Avoid personal criticisms, and treat subordinates with respect. *Example:* An engineering manager acknowledges subordinates' expertise and treats them as professionals. Even when the manager points out performance problems to subordinates, it is important to refrain from criticizing them personally.
- Agree to a timetable for performance improvements. *Example:* A first-level manager and subordinate decide to meet again in one month to determine whether quality has improved.

In following these guidelines, managers need to keep in mind *why* they are giving performance feedback: to encourage high levels of motivation and performance. Moreover, the information that managers gather through performance appraisal and feedback helps them determine how to distribute pay raises and bonuses.

Tips for Managers

Performance Appraisal

1. Supplement periodic formal performance appraisals with more frequent informal appraisals and give performance feedback often.

2. When high performance can be reached by different kinds of behaviours and how employees perform their jobs is not important, use results appraisals to evaluate performance and give feedback.

3. When providing performance feedback, focus on specific behaviours or outcomes, adopt a problem-solving mode, express confidence in

employees, praise instances of high performance, and agree to a timetable for improvements.

4. Avoid personal criticisms and treat employees with respect when providing feedback.

5. Provide performance feedback from both formal and informal performance appraisals.

Pay and Benefits

Pay includes employees' base salaries, pay raises, and bonuses and is determined by a number of factors, including characteristics of the organization and of the job and levels of performance. Employee benefits are based on membership in an organization (and not necessarily on the particular job held) and include sick days, vacation days, and medical and life insurance. In Chapter 12, we discuss the ways in which pay can be used to motivate organizational members to perform at a high level, as well as pay plans managers can use to help an organization achieve its goals and gain a competitive advantage. Here we focus on establishing an organization's pay level and pay structure.

Pay Level

pay level The relative position of an organization's pay incentives in comparison with those of other organizations in the same industry employing similar kinds of workers.

Pay level is a broad comparative concept that refers to how an organization's pay incentives compare, in general, to those of other organizations in the same industry employing similar kinds of workers. Managers must decide whether they want to offer relatively high wages, average wages, or relatively low wages. High wages help ensure that an organization is going to be able to recruit, select, and retain high performers, but high wages also raise costs. Low wages give an organization a cost advantage but may undermine the organization's ability to select and recruit high performers and motivate current employees to perform at a high level. Either of these situations may lead to inferior quality or inferior customer service.

In determining pay levels, managers should take their organization's strategy into account. A high pay level may prohibit managers from effectively pursuing a low-cost strategy. But a high pay level may be well worth the added costs in an organization whose competitive advantage lies in superior quality and excellent customer service. As one might expect, hotel and motel chains with a low-cost strategy, such as Days Inn and Hampton Inns, have lower pay levels than chains striving to provide high-quality rooms and services, such as Four Seasons and Hyatt Regency.

Pay Structure

pay structure
The arrangement of jobs into categories that reflect their relative importance to the organization and its goals, levels of skill required, and other characteristics.

After deciding on a pay level, managers have to establish a pay structure for the different jobs in the organization. A **pay structure** clusters jobs into categories that reflect their relative importance to the organization and its goals, levels of skill required, and other characteristics that managers consider to be important. Pay ranges are established for each job category. Individual jobholders' pay within job categories is then determined by factors such as performance, seniority, and skill levels.

Pay structure is quite a bit different in the public sector, compared to the private sector. On average, governments at all three levels (federal, provincial and local) pay a premium of about 9 percent to their employees, compared to private sector jobs. Public sector workers are also more likely to be covered by pension plans.

Stride Rite, the children's shoe maker, has established an intergenerational daycare centre for its employees in which the families of employees are encouraged to take an active interest in the care of employees' children.

Despite the seeming differences between public and private sector wages, it is generally women and less-skilled workers who get higher wages for working in the public sector. Managers, especially male managers, do not get paid much more for working in the public sector. Moreover, at the federal level, senior managers are paid less than they might earn in the private sector. There is also far more wage compression in the public sector. In the private sector, on average, individuals in managerial, administrative, or professional occupations are paid 41 percent more than those in service occupations. In the public sector, it is not uncommon for managers to be paid only 10 percent more than other employees.[51]

There are some interesting global differences in pay structures. Large corporations based in the United States tend to pay their CEOs and top managers higher salaries than do their Canadian, European, or Japanese counterparts. For instance, in 1997, the average Canadian CEO received $500 000, while the average American CEO received $1 million.[52]

Concerns have been raised over whether it is equitable or fair for CEOs of large companies in Canada to be making hundreds of thousands or even millions of dollars in years when their companies are restructuring and laying off a good portion of their workforces. Some also question the tenuous link between executive compensation and firm performance. In 1998, for example, the average pretax compensation for the 100 highest-paid Canadian executives was $3.4 million, up 26 percent from $2.7 million in 1997. Meanwhile, earnings at Canada's 135 biggest companies that year slumped 18 percent.[53] Questions were also raised after Nortel's shares lost $308 billion in less than a year, while CEO John Roth collected $154 million in 2000, including a bonus of $8.6 million.[54]

Benefits

Organizations are legally required to provide certain benefits to their employees, including workers' compensation, social insurance, and employment insurance. Workers' compensation provides employees with financial assistance if they become unable to work because of a work-related injury or illness. Social insurance provides financial assistance to retirees and disabled former employees. Employment insurance provides financial assistance to workers who lose their jobs through no fault of their own. The legal system in Canada views these three benefits as ethical requirements for organizations and thus mandates that they be provided.

Other benefits—such as extended health insurance, dental insurance, vacation time, pension plans, life insurance, flexible working hours, company-provided daycare, and employee assistance and wellness programs—are provided at the option of employers. Benefits mandated by public policy and benefits provided at the option of employers cost organizations a substantial amount of money.

In some organizations, top managers decide which benefits might best suit the organization and employees and offer the same benefit package to all employees. Other organizations, realizing that employees' needs and desires for benefits might differ, offer **cafeteria-style benefit plans** that let employees themselves choose the benefits they want, from among such things as flextime, tuition credits, and extended medical and dental plans. Some organizations have success with cafeteria-style plans; others find them difficult to manage.

cafeteria-style benefit plan A plan from which employees can choose the benefits that they want.

Labour Relations

labour relations The
activities that managers
engage in to ensure that
they have effective working
relationships with the labour
unions that represent their
employees' interests.

Labour relations are the activities that managers engage in to ensure that they have effective working relationships with the labour unions that represent their employees' interests. Although the federal and provincial governments have responded to the potential for unethical organizations and managers to treat workers unfairly—by creating and enforcing the Canada Labour Code, the Canadian Human Rights Act, and provincial Employment Standards laws—some workers believe that a union will help ensure that their interests are fairly represented in their organizations.

Unions

Unions exist to represent workers' interests in organizations. Given that managers have more power than rank-and-file workers and that organizations have multiple stakeholders, there is always the potential that managers might take steps that will benefit one set of stakeholders (such as shareholders) while hurting another (such as employees). For example, managers might decide to speed up a production line to lower costs and increase production in the hope of increasing returns to shareholders. This action could, however, hurt employees who are forced to work at a rapid pace, who may have increased risk of injuries as a result of the line speedup, and who receive no additional pay for the extra work they are performing. Unions represent workers' interests in scenarios such as this one.

Parliament passed the first significant piece of labour legislation in 1907; it was the Industrial Disputes Investigation Act. This act required workers and employers in the transportation, resources and utilities industries to submit disputes to a conciliation board before starting a strike or lockout. It was not until 1944, however, that Canadian workers were granted the right to join a union, bargain collectively, and strike, through bill *PC 1003*. Public sector workers in both the provincial and federal government were not given full collective bargaining rights until 1965, through the Public Service Staff Relations Act. In general, the provinces have drafted their own labour legislation, which follows in some way the federal labour legislation.

Employees might vote to have a union represent them for any number of reasons.[55] They may feel that their wages and working conditions are in need of improvement. They may feel that managers are not treating them with respect. They may think that their working hours are unfair or that they need more job security or a safer work environment. Or they may be dissatisfied with management and find it difficult to communicate their concerns to their bosses. Regardless of the specific reason, one overriding reason is power: A united group inevitably wields more power than an individual, and this type of power may be especially helpful to employees in some organizations.

Although these would seem to be potent forces for unionization, some workers are reluctant to join unions. Sometimes this reluctance is due to the perception that union leaders are corrupt. Some workers may simply feel that belonging to a union might not do them much good or might actually cause more harm than good while costing them money in membership dues. Employees also might not want to be "forced" into doing something they do not want to do (such as striking) because the union thinks it is in their best interest. Moreover, although unions can be a positive force in organizations, they sometimes can be a negative force, impairing organizational effectiveness. For example, when union leaders resist needed changes in an organization or are corrupt, organizational performance can suffer.

About 34 percent of Canadian workers are represented by unions today. Representation has remained fairly consistent for the last twenty years, a pattern very much unlike that of the United States. In the United States, about 14 percent of workers are covered by labour unions, and there has been a steady decline there since the 1960s. Union representation in the United States peaked in the 1950s at about 32 percent.

Union membership and leadership, traditionally dominated by white men, is also becoming increasingly diverse.

Collective Bargaining

collective bargaining

Negotiation between labour unions and managers to resolve conflicts and disputes about issues such as working hours, wages, benefits, working conditions, and job security.

Collective bargaining is negotiation between labour unions and managers to resolve conflicts and disputes about important issues such as working hours, wages, benefits, working conditions, and job security. Before sitting down with management to negotiate, union members sometimes go on strike to drive home their concerns to managers. Once an agreement that union members support has been reached (sometimes with the help of a neutral third party called a *mediator*), union leaders and managers sign a contract spelling out the terms of the collective bargaining agreement. We discuss conflict and negotiation in depth in Chapter 16, but some brief observations are in order here because collective bargaining is an ongoing consideration in labour relations.

The signing of a contract, for example, does not bring collective bargaining to a halt. Disagreement and conflicts can arise over the interpretation of the contract. In these cases, a neutral third party known as an *arbitrator* is usually called in to resolve the conflict. An important component of a collective bargaining agreement is a *grievance procedure* through which workers who feel they are not being fairly treated are allowed to voice their concerns and have their interests represented by the union. Workers who feel they were unjustly fired in violation of a union contract, for example, may file a grievance, have the union represent them, and get their jobs back if an arbitrator agrees with them.

Union members sometimes go on strike when managers make decisions that they feel will hurt them and are not in their best interests. This is precisely what happened in 1996 when General Motors' assembly plants in Canada and the United States were idle for 18 days. The strike, which originated in GM's Dayton, Ohio brake assembly plants, was due to management's decision to buy some parts from other companies rather than making them in GM's own plants.[56] Both the Canadian Auto Workers and the United Auto Workers called a strike because outsourcing threatens union members' jobs. The agreement reached by the union and management, bargaining collectively, allowed the outsourcing to continue but contained provisions for the creation of hundreds of new jobs as well as for improvements in working conditions.[57]

Summary and Review

STRATEGIC HUMAN RESOURCE MANAGEMENT   Human resource management (HRM) includes all the activities that managers engage in to ensure that their organizations are able to attract, retain, and effectively utilize human resources. Strategic HRM is the process by which managers design the components of a human resource management system to be consistent with each other, with other elements of organizational architecture, and with the organization's strategies and goals.

RECRUITMENT AND SELECTION   Before recruiting and selecting employees, managers must engage in human resource planning and job analysis. Human resource planning includes all the activities managers engage in to forecast their current and future needs for human resources. Job analysis is the process of

Chapter Summary

**STRATEGIC HUMAN
RESOURCE
MANAGEMENT**

• Overview of the
  Components of HRM

• The Legal
  Environment of HRM

**RECRUITMENT AND
SELECTION**

• Human Resource
  Planning

• Job Analysis

• External and
  Internal Recruitment

• The Selection
  Process

**TRAINING AND
DEVELOPMENT**

• Types of Training

• Types of Development

**ISSUES IN CAREER
DEVELOPMENT**

• The Organization's
  Responsibilities

• The Employee's
  Responsibilities

**PERFORMANCE
APPRAISAL AND
FEEDBACK**

• Types of Performance
  Appraisal

• Who Appraises
  Performance?

• Effective
  Performance
  Feedback

PAY AND BENEFITS

• Pay Level

• Pay Structure

• Benefits

LABOUR RELATIONS

• Unions

• Collective Bargaining

identifying (1) the tasks, duties, and responsibilities that make up a job and (2) the knowledge, skills, and abilities needed to perform the job. Recruitment includes all the activities that managers engage in to develop a pool of qualified applicants for open positions. Selection is the process by which managers determine the relative qualifications of job applicants and their potential for performing well in a particular job.

TRAINING AND DEVELOPMENT Training focuses on teaching organizational members how to perform effectively in their current jobs. Development focuses on broadening organizational members' knowledge and skills so that employees will be prepared to take on new responsibilities and challenges.

ISSUES IN CAREER DEVELOPMENT A career is the sum total of work-related experiences throughout a person's life. The stages in a linear career are preparation for work, organizational entry, early career, midcareer, and late career. Individuals face different tasks and challenges at each stage, and therefore have to manage their careers continually.

PERFORMANCE APPRAISAL AND FEEDBACK Performance appraisal is the evaluation of employees' job performance and contributions to their organization. Performance feedback is the process through which managers share performance appraisal information with their subordinates, give subordinates an opportunity to reflect on their own performance, and develop with subordinates plans for the future. Performance appraisal provides managers with useful information for decision making. Performance feedback can encourage high levels of motivation and performance.

PAY AND BENEFITS Pay level is the relative position of an organization's pay incentives in comparison with those of other organizations in the same industry employing similar kinds of workers. A pay structure clusters jobs into categories that reflect their relative importance to the organization and its goals, levels of skill required, and other characteristics. Pay ranges are established for each job category. Organizations are legally required to provide certain benefits to their employees; other benefits are provided at the discretion of employers.

LABOUR RELATIONS Labour relations are the activities that managers engage in to ensure that they have effective working relationships with the labour unions that may represent their employees' interests. Collective bargaining is the process through which labour unions and managers resolve conflicts and disputes and negotiate agreements.

Management in Action

Topics for Discussion and Action

1. Discuss why it is important for the components of the human resource management system to be in sync with an organization's strategy and goals and with each other.

2. Interview a manager in a local organization to determine how that organization recruits and selects employees.

3. Discuss why training and development is an ongoing activity for all organizations.

4. Describe the types of development activities that you think middle managers need most.

5. Evaluate the pros and cons of 360-degree performance appraisals and feedback. Would you like your performance to be appraised in this manner? Why or why not?

6. Discuss why two restaurants in the same community might have different pay levels.

7. Explain why union membership is becoming more diverse.

Building Management Skills

Analyzing Human Resource Systems

Think about your current job or a job that you had in the past. If you have never had a job, then interview a friend or family member who is currently working. Answer the following questions about the job you have chosen.

1. How are people recruited and selected for this job? Are the recruitment and selection procedures that the organization uses effective or ineffective? Why?

2. What training and development do people who hold this job receive? Is it appropriate? Why or why not?

3. How is performance of this job appraised? Does performance feedback contribute to motivation and high performance on this job?

4. What levels of pay and benefits are provided for this job? Are these levels of pay and benefits appropriate? Why or why not?

Small Group Breakout Exercise
Building a Human Resource Management System

Form groups of three or four people, and appoint one group member as the spokesperson who will communicate your findings to the whole class when called on by the instructor. Then discuss the following scenario.

You and your 2 or 3 partners are engineers with a business minor who have decided to start a consulting business. Your goal is to provide manufacturing-process engineering and other engineering services to large and small organizations. You forecast that there will be an increased use of outsourcing for these activities. You discussed with managers in several large organizations the services you plan to offer, and they expressed considerable interest. You have secured funding to start the business and are now building the HRM system. Your human resource planning suggests that you need to hire between 5 and 8 experienced engineers with good communication skills, 2 clerical/secretarial workers, and 2 MBAs who between them will have financial, accounting, and human resource skills. You are striving to develop an approach to building your human resources that will enable your new business to prosper.

1. Describe the steps you will take to recruit and select (a) the engineers, (b) the clerical/secretarial workers, and (c) the MBAs.

2. Describe the training and development the engineers, the clerical/secretarial workers, and the MBAs will receive.

3. Describe how you will appraise the performance of each group of employees and how you will provide feedback.

4. Describe the pay level and pay structure of your consulting firm.

Exploring the World Wide Web
Specific Assignment

Many companies take active steps to recruit and retain valuable employees. One such company is InSystems. Scan Insystems' Web site (http://www.insystems.com/index1.html) to learn more about this company, including clicking on "About Us." Then click on "Careers" and, under that, "Employee Development" and "Employee Testimonials" to find out more about what it's like for employees to work at InSystems.

1. What steps is InSystems taking to recruit and retain employees?

2. Do you think that its approach is effective? Why or why not?

General Assignment

Find Web sites of two companies that try to recruit new employees by means of the World Wide Web. Are their approaches to recruitment on the Web similar or different? What are the potential advantages of the approaches of each? What are the potential disadvantages?

ManagementCase

Human Resource Management in an Era of Downsizing

Managers face a balancing job between recruiting and retaining employees, and adjust their labour force size to maximize profits. When shareholder value goes down, employers start laying off their employees.[58] For instance, November 1999 saw the following layoff announcements (size of layoff in parentheses): Ottawa-based Newbridge (10 percent of workforce); Peterborough, ON-based General Electric (85 employees, after announcements in August and September of similar layoffs); Toronto-based Royal Bank (between 3000 and 6000 employees); and Halifax-based High Liner Foods (50 employees). Ottawa-based JDS Uniphase and Brampton, Ontario's Nortel Networks announced large layoffs in 2001.

Evidence suggests that layoffs are linked to increased earning. For instance, in 1995, General Motors of Canada reported a record profit for any Canadian company ($1.39 billion) but fired 2500 employees. Royal Bank, Toronto-Dominion Bank, Bank of Montreal, Scotiabank, and CIBC announced record collective profits between 1995 and 1998, but laid off thousands of people while doing so. Bell Canada, Inco, Imperial Oil, Petro-Canada, Maritime Telephone and Telegraph, CP Rail, and Shell Canada also showed increased profit but laid off employees.

There is some concern about the impact of these cuts on society. Industry minister John Manley noted: "I think it's part of my job to push the corporate sector and urge them to take into account the enormous damage it does when you cast people aside instead of retraining them."[59] Fifty-eight percent of Canadians who were asked about the acceptability of profitable corporations laying off workers said that they did not find this acceptable.

It's not clear that laying off employees to maximize profit and improve cash flow even works. Len Brooks, executive director of the Clarkson Centre for Business Ethics at the University of Toronto, says its "really a dumb idea. Only a third of its practitioners achieve their financial objectives while paying a huge price as employee morale craters."[60] Study after study shows that after downsizing "surviving employees become narrow-minded, self-absorbed, and risk averse. Morale sinks, productivity drops, and survivors distrust management."[61]

A study by the American Management Association (AMA) confirms Brooks' reflections.

Of 700 companies that had downsized between 1989 and 1994, productivity fell in 30 percent of the cases, and rose in 34 percent of the cases.[62] Profits fell 30 percent of the time, and rose 51 percent of the time. The biggest negative factor, though, was that employee morale fell in 83 percent of the companies.

Human resource managers can take other options rather than downsizing.[63] A number of Canadian corporations have developed options such as job sharing, voluntarily reduced work time, and phased-in retirement as ways to avoid downsizing. Companies engaging in such practices are trying to preserve employee morale.

Beyond company morale, however, companies are starting to realize that they are losing key human resources when they let their employees walk out the door. Michael Stern, president of executive-search firm Michael Stern Associates Inc. in Toronto, notes: "At the peak of the last recession, I do believe that older workers were at a disadvantage. But that's changing. Companies found out that when they let everybody over the age of 50 go, they lost not only experience and knowledge but also the wisdom they need to move the organization forward."[64]

Montreal-based Mutual Group, faced with the prospect of merging its 3500 employees with the 1700 employees of Metropolitan Life of Canada, is trying to avoid letting too much knowledge go out the door. Hubert Saint-Onge, Mutual's senior vice-president, strategic capability, says the company is proceeding strategically. "We are definitely not simply getting rid of people through early-retirement packages. ... We will also identify people we want to keep based on capability and talent. Our aim is to end up with a balanced workplace where there is room for youth as well as experienced workers. Certainly, we don't plan on getting rid of people because they are older. If anything, we see the experience and maturity of older workers as a plus."[65]

Questions

1. How can managers determine which employees to let go when they are involved in downsizing?

2. What advantages might there be for companies to hold on to some of their older workers, even as they are trying to figure out whom to lay off?

3. How might downsizing negatively affect employees who remain after a layoff?

ManagementCase

In the News

From the Pages of *The Ottawa Citizen*

The Blessed: Under 30, They Are the Darlings of the Industry—But They Want More

In the last three years, something momentous has been happening at Nortel Networks Corp. While an army of startups—not to mention archrival Cisco Systems Inc.—has been siphoning workers from the telecom giant, Nortel has been forced to remake itself in the image of its talent-snatching competitors. Quite simply, Canada's oldest technology company could no longer afford to appear stodgy and out-of-date, especially if it wanted to appeal to a new generation of engineering and business talent.

The Brampton-based corporation—which employs some 15 000 workers in Ottawa—embarked on a systematic overhaul. It boosted salaries, moved to merit-based pay, and doled out signing bonuses. It offered stock options to half of its 85 000 employees worldwide—a fivefold increase from the 10 percent that used to qualify. Taking a page from the rec-room atmosphere at many startups, Nortel experimented with informal, café-and-lounge work spaces. And it devised some clever ways to show staff they're appreciated. One employee recognition plan, rolled out last year, awards "Pride Points" that can be converted into all kinds of prizes, whether they be camcorders, bikes, gift certificates, or cold, hard cash.

"That's something that does wonders for motivation," says Jacqui McGillivray, who studies what Nortel employees want. While such perks aren't aimed specifically at Nortel's under-30 population, Linda Duxbury's [a professor at the School of Business, University of Carleton] research shows this crowd is hungry for recognition from their bosses. They want to know that their contributions are valued, and they want regular feedback from their bosses. What these newbies think and want is very important to their employers.

While only one in four tech workers is under 30, they are the undisputed darlings of the industry: companies not only want to hire them, but they do everything they can to keep them. Employers associate youth with enthusiasm, new ideas, and an endless capacity for work.

For their part, those under 30 are intensely loyal to their own career goals, and they work hard to be noticed by their employers. In particular, they spend more effort developing office relationships, and they're eager to learn from older colleagues. They also like to take on big responsibilities. For those reasons, they're driven less by money than by challenging work.

At Nortel, recruiters count on the company's reputation for cutting-edge technology to attract and keep their best people. "That's the number one reason people stay here," says McGillivray.

To prove themselves, young workers take advantage of training programs, special projects, and strong mentors—all of which companies seem happy to provide. It should come as no surprise, then, that these workers are generally satisfied with their work environment. But that doesn't mean they feel any loyalty to the company. Despite their employer's efforts to keep them happy, an overwhelming 9 out of 10 workers in this age group think about leaving their jobs. The main reason for this paradox appears to be frustration with career advancement. Those who simply can't wait around for promotions inevitably find other opportunities—ones that promise greater job responsibility, better pay, and more cutting-edge work.

If there is one source of job stress for the under-30 crowd, it's the fast pace of the industry. Seven out of ten workers in this age group feel the pressure of rapid product cycles, which force punishing project deadlines on them. The speed of technology trends also leaves many young workers worried that their skills will quickly be out of date. Duxbury believes companies don't do enough to help their younger employees manage this change. Indeed, in an economic slowdown, it's the young ones that feel the greatest pressure. As companies start cutting their workforce, it's usually the under-30s who are asked to do more with less, Duxbury adds. "Unlike their older colleagues, the young ones haven't yet learned the survival skills to cope with the pace, which is why many compensate by working long hours."

Source: P. Tam, "The Blessed: Under 30, They Are the Darlings of the Industry—But They Want More," *The Ottawa Citizen*, February 19, 2001, p. B3.

Questions

1. What is Nortel's approach to pay?
2. With the technology downturn that occurred in 2001, do you expect that Nortel will continue to use the same ways of rewarding its younger employees?

Part 5

MANAGING INDIVIDUALS AND GROUPS

Chapter 11
The Manager as a Person

Chapter 12
Motivation

Chapter 13
Leadership

Chapter 14
Groups and Teams

Chapter 15
Communication

Chapter 16
Organizational Conflict, Negotiation, and Politics

Chapter 17
Organizational Change

Chapter eleven

The Manager as a Person

Learning Objectives

1. Describe the various personality traits that affect how managers think, feel, and behave.

2. Explain what values, attitudes, and moods are, and describe their impact on managerial action.

3. Explain why managers' perceptions are central to decision making, why they are inherently subjective, and how they are formed.

4. Describe the consequences and sources of the stress that managers experience.

A Case in Contrast

Three Ways to Run a Bank: Insensitive, Charismatic, or Consensual

The Bank of Montreal (BMO) (www.bmo.com) has had three different CEOs since 1975, and each of them had very different personalities, which led to different ways of running the bank.[1] In 1975, William Mulholland was named president, appointed at a time when the bank was dubbed "The Worst" by analysts, after achieving in the 1930s the status of being Canada's oldest and biggest bank. In the first two years of his reign, Mulholland slashed 5000 jobs, invested a greater share of funds into higher-profit commercial loans, and moved quickly into the computer age, dominating other banks on the number of ATM installations.

Though Mulholland was successful at transforming BMO from "The Worst" back to first again, he was regarded as insensitive and arrogant by the bank's employees. At a speech in 1984 honouring three departing key executives, Mulholland spoke mainly of the day's newspaper editorial. He gave one of the executives a one-sentence mention, and said simply, "Bye, fellows," to the other two. The audience sat in stunned silence.

Mulholland possessed no end of self-assurance. Even after he retired, he continued to remind the world about his 1984 brainwave of buying Harris Bankcorp of Chicago, a manoeuvre envied by every Canadian bank. Despite this accomplishment, Mulholland was generally risk-averse, and did not pursue many of the real estate deals and international syndicates that other banks did during the 1980s.

Matthew Barrett followed Mulholland in 1989. Although Mulholland can be credited with the purchase of Harris, not all of his leadership turned out well. By the time Barrett took over, the bank "was known for treating workers as if they were barely human." Barrett was widely viewed as charismatic "and possessed an easy

Matthew Barrett (shown at top) and Tony Comper (shown at bottom) have led the Bank of Montreal. The men have very different personalities and personal lives, and these influenced how they ran the bank.

manner that was just the antidote needed to recover from Mulholland's machine-gun management style." Perhaps due to his charismatic nature, BMO became more profitable than ever before under Barrett, and also became known as a model employer.

Perhaps Barrett's most memorable, though failed, accomplishment was his proposal to merge Bank of Montreal and Royal Bank. Finance Minister Paul Martin forbade the merger, and many in the financial community attributed the failed merger to Barrett's arrogance. Before announcing the proposed merger, Barrett did not even consult with the federal government about his plan.

Tony Comper followed Barrett in 1999. His management style is the most consensual of the three men, and "he has neither the vanity of Mulholland nor the dominant personality of Barrett." Comper is also seen as more decisive than Barrett, who was sometimes regarded as a ditherer.

The personalities and lifestyles of Barrett and Comper are quite different. Barrett is viewed as flashy, "slick and silver-tongued," while Comper is seen as being sober, and is a "techno-whiz who speaks in jargon." Comper's student days were filled with reading English literature and he considered becoming a Roman Catholic priest. A devout Roman Catholic, he is still married to his first wife after 30 years. Barrett's second marriage was to a jet-setting, beautiful, younger woman and was billed as the social event for Toronto.

At the time of his appointment, Bay Street analysts were pleased that Comper had been named to BMO. Some analysts noted that "the Bank of Montreal does not need charisma now—it needs a hands-on innovator who can implement restructuring plans with the patience and wisdom of a would-be priest."

At first, it seemed that the analysts might be right about Comper, whose first year was marked by record earnings and aggressive cost-cutting. However, by early 2001, the picture was not so bright. The bank's first-quarter earnings had dipped disappointingly, at a time when rivals had double-digit growth. Overall, BMO had fallen to sixth of the Big Six in revenue growth and fifth in five-year shareholder returns, when only a few years previously it had been number two. Moreover, a recent customer-satisfaction survey had BMO come in dead last of all the big banks. Comper had previously announced his "strategy of simple steps" for moving the bank ahead. Even Comper acknowledged at his 2001 shareholders' meeting that his plans were "short on grandeur."

All in all, Mulholland, Barrett, and Comper illustrate how managers, even of the same company, can differ from each other in many ways. ●

Overview

In previous chapters, we discussed many of the challenges managers face as they seek to achieve organizational goals through planning, organizing, and controlling. Considering the multiple challenges managers face, one might almost start to think that effective managers must be superhuman. Managers are people, however, and like people everywhere they have their own distinctive personalities, ways of viewing things, personal challenges and disappointments, shortcomings, and the like.

In this chapter, we focus on the manager as a feeling, thinking human being; we look at managers like Mulholland, Barrett, and Comper, featured in the "Case in Contrast," what makes them tick, and what makes them act the way they do as managers. We start by describing enduring characteristics that seem to influence how managers "manage," as well as how they view other people, their organizations, and the world around them. We discuss as well how managers' values, attitudes, and moods may play out in organizations. We describe how all managerial action is based on managers' perceptions and the need for their perceptions to be as accurate as possible. We complete the picture of a manager as a feeling, thinking human being by discussing managerial careers and the stress managers experience in their daily lives. By the end of this chapter, you will have a good appreciation of how the personal characteristics of managers influence the process of management. ●

Enduring Characteristics: Personality Traits

personality traits
Enduring tendencies to feel, think, and act in certain ways.

All people have certain enduring characteristics that influence how they think, feel, and behave both on and off the job. These characteristics are **personality traits**, particular tendencies to feel, think, and act in certain ways that can be used to describe the personalities of all individuals—tendencies, for example, to be enthusiastic and flamboyant like Barrett or low-key like Comper, demanding or easy-going, excited or mellow, nervous or relaxed, risk-seeking like Barrett or risk-averse like Mulholland, outgoing or shy. It is important to understand the personalities of managers because their personalities influence their behaviour and their approach to management.

Canfor:
David Emerson
www.canfor.com/1400.asp

Some managers—like WestJet's former CEO, Steve Smith, whose top-down management style agitated employees and decreased morale—are efficient in their leadership, but not effective. As we noted in "A Case in Contrast" in Chapter 1, Smith was asked to step down because of his abrasiveness with employees.[2] Other managers—like Vancouver-based Canfor's CEO, David Emerson—may be as concerned about effectiveness and efficiency as highly critical managers but are easier to get along with and likable and frequently praise the people around them. Emerson is known for his open and democratic style. Both styles of management may produce excellent results, but their effects on employees are quite different. Do managers deliberately decide to adopt one or the other of these approaches to management? Although they may do so part of the time, in all likelihood their personalities also account for their different approaches.

The Big Five Personality Traits

We can think of an individual's personality as being composed of five general traits or characteristics: extroversion, negative affectivity, agreeableness, conscientiousness, and openness to experience.[3] Researchers often consider these the "Big Five" personality traits.[4] Each of them can be viewed as a continuum along which every individual or, more specifically, every manager falls (see Figure 11.1).

Some managers may be at the high end of one trait continuum, others may be at the low end, and still others somewhere in between. An easy way to understand how these traits can affect a person's approach to management is to describe what people are like at the high and low ends of each trait continuum. As will become evident as you read about each trait, there is no single "right" or "wrong" trait for being an effective manager; rather, effectiveness is determined by a complex interaction between characteristics of managers (including personality traits) and the nature of the job and organization in which they are working. Moreover, personality traits that enhance managerial effectiveness in one situation may impair it in another.

extroversion
The tendency to experience positive emotions and moods and to feel good about oneself and the rest of the world.

EXTROVERSION **Extroversion** is the tendency to experience positive emotions and moods and to feel good about oneself and the rest of the world. Individuals who are at the high end of the extroversion continuum (often called extroverts) tend to be sociable, affectionate, outgoing, and friendly. Individuals who are low on extroversion (often called *introverts*) tend to be less inclined toward social interaction and to have a less positive outlook. Being high on extroversion

Figure 11.1
The Big Five Personality Traits

Managers' personalities can be described by determining which point on each of the following dimensions best characterizes the manager in question:

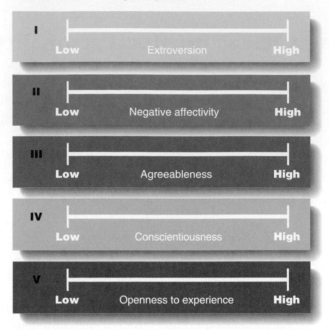

may be an asset for those whose jobs entail especially high levels of social interaction. Individuals who are low on extroversion may nevertheless be very effective and efficient, especially when their jobs do not require excessive social interaction. Their more "quiet" approach may enable them to accomplish quite a bit of work in a limited time.

negative affectivity

The tendency to experience negative emotions and moods, to feel distressed, and to be critical of oneself and others.

NEGATIVE AFFECTIVITY   **Negative affectivity** is the tendency to experience negative emotions and moods, feel distressed, and be critical of oneself and others. Individuals who are high on this trait continuum may often feel angry and dissatisfied and complain about their own and others' lack of progress. Individuals who are low on negative affectivity do not tend to experience many negative emotions and moods and are less pessimistic and critical of themselves and others. On the plus side, the "critical" approach of an individual high on negative affectivity may sometimes be effective if this trait spurs the individual and others to improve their performance. Nevertheless, it is probably more pleasant to work with someone who is low on negative affectivity; the better working relationships that such an individual is likely to cultivate can also be an important asset. William Mulholland was high on negative affectivity, which is why employee morale was low by the time he stepped down.

agreeableness

The tendency to get along well with other people.

AGREEABLENESS   **Agreeableness** is the tendency to get along well with others. Individuals who are high on the agreeableness continuum are likeable, tend to be affectionate, and care about other people. Individuals who are low on agreeableness may be somewhat distrustful of others, unsympathetic, uncooperative, and even at times antagonistic. Being high on agreeableness may be especially important for individuals whose responsibilities require them to develop good, close relationships with others.

conscientiousness
The tendency to be careful, scrupulous, and persevering.

CONSCIENTIOUSNESS   **Conscientiousness** is the tendency to be careful, scrupulous, and persevering. Individuals who are high on the conscientiousness continuum are organized and self-disciplined; those who are low on this trait might sometimes appear to lack direction and self-discipline. Conscientiousness has been found to be a good predictor of performance in many kinds of jobs, including managerial jobs in a variety of organizations.[5] CEOs of major companies, such as Lou Gerstner of IBM, often show signs of being high on conscientiousness—the long hours they work, their attention to detail, and their ability to handle their multiple responsibilities in an organized manner. Tom Bata, founder of the world's biggest shoemaking company, once based in Batawa, Ontario, demonstrated his conscientiousness to quality by ripping defective shoes to bits in front of shopfloor workers, to remind the employees to produce only high-quality goods.[6] Sonja Bata, Tom's wife and a partner in the business, also showed conscientiousness towards the employees. When Batawa finally had to be closed, she noted, "We always ran the company as if our employees were members of our family. This is why we didn't close it years ago. It had not been making money for years, but I think we, as employers, had a responsibility to our people in good and bad times."[7] The Batas balanced commitment to quality and their employees in making their decisions.

openness to experience The tendency to be original, have broad interests, be open to a wide range of stimuli, be daring, and take risks.

OPENNESS TO EXPERIENCE   **Openness to experience** is the tendency to be original, have broad interests, be open to a wide range of stimuli, be daring, and take risks.[8] Individuals who are high on this trait continuum may be especially likely to take risks and be innovative in their planning and decision making. Entrepreneurs who start their own businesses—like Bill Gates of Microsoft and Anita Roddick of The Body Shop—are, in all likelihood, high on openness to experience, which has contributed to their success as entrepreneurs and managers.

Individuals who are low on openness to experience may be less prone to take risks and more conservative in their planning and decision making. In certain kinds of organizations and positions, this tendency might be an asset. The manager of the fiscal office in a public university, for example, must ensure that all university departments and units follow the university's rules and regulations pertaining to budgets, spending accounts, and reimbursements of expenses.

Age stereotypes might lead one to think that as workers get older they may be less open to new experiences and taking risks. But that is exactly what baby boomers will have to do to survive in high-tech firms, as this "Focus on Diversity" indicates.

Focus on Diversity

Openness to Experience Useful at Any Age

Baby boomers who are not open to experience may be having trouble coping in today's new workplace.[9] Consider Dev Ramcharan of Primus Telecommunications Canada, a boomer who reports to Dave Lefebvre, a 30-something VP of network services. Lefebvre dresses casually and wears motorcycle boots in the office. He's pretty nonconformist in his views on how an executive is supposed to act.

Ramcharan says that members of "Generation X" or the "Nexus Generation" are different from the boomers, with a more straightforward frankness and little old-school mentality. "In the boomer days, there were many who tended to micro-manage their staff. They [were] firm and clear, and management was a separate culture from its staff. Now, there's less stress and more interaction," Ramcharan says.

Many suggest that Generation-X executives have brought to the workplace innovative ways and a more casual style of interaction. They are less likely to say "I am your VP; you are my servant," says Ramcharan.

Not everyone agrees that the new generation knows how to manage, however. Some venture capitalist firms are staying away from Gen-X led companies, feeling that the inexperience of many of those in charge led to the recent dot-com meltdown.

Baby boomers who want to get ahead are going to have to learn to work comfortably with Gen-Xers, according to University of Ottawa professor Vojtek Michalowski. "The high technology industry is a survival of the fittest contest. Those who adapt to change will be the eventual winners."

What can the "Big Five" model tell me?

By now, it should be clear that successful managers and employees occupy a variety of positions on the "Big Five" personality-trait continua. One highly effective manager may be high on extroversion and negative affectivity, another equally effective manager may be low on both these traits, and still another somewhere in between. It is important for members of an organization to understand these differences across individuals because they can shed light on how people behave and on their approach to planning, leading, organizing, and controlling. If subordinates realize, for example, that their manager is low on extroversion, they will not feel slighted when their manager seems to be aloof because they will realize that by nature he or she is simply not outgoing.

Managers themselves also need to be aware of their own personality traits and the traits of others, including their subordinates and fellow managers. A manager who is aware of a tendency to be highly critical of other people might try to tone down this negative approach. Similarly, a manager who realizes that a chronically complaining subordinate tends to be so negative because of personality may take the complaints with a grain of salt and realize that things probably are not as bad as this subordinate says they are.

In order for all members of an organization to work well together and with people outside the organization, such as customers and suppliers, it is important for them to understand each other. Such understanding comes, in part, from an appreciation of some of the fundamental ways in which people differ from one another—that is, from an appreciation of personality traits.

Other Personality Traits That Affect Managerial Behaviour

Many other specific traits, in addition to the Big Five, can be used to describe people's personalities. Here we look at some that are particularly important for understanding managerial effectiveness: locus of control, self-esteem, and the needs for achievement, affiliation, and power.

internal locus of control The tendency to locate responsibility for one's fate within oneself.

external locus of control The tendency to locate responsibility for one's fate within outside forces and to believe that one's own behaviour has little impact on outcomes.

LOCUS OF CONTROL   People differ in their views about how much control they have over what happens to and around them. The locus of control trait captures these beliefs.[10] People with an **internal locus of control** believe that they themselves are responsible for their own fate; they see their own actions and behaviours as being important and decisive determinants of important outcomes such as levels of job performance, promotion, or being turned down for a choice job assignment. Some managers with an internal locus of control see the success of a whole organization as resting on their shoulders, as did Mulholland and Barrett in the "Case in Contrast." People with an **external locus of control** believe that outside forces are responsible for what happens to and around them; they do not think that their own actions make much difference.

Unilever Canada:
Kevin Boyce
www.unilever.ca/
corporate/index.html

Managers need to have an internal locus of control because they are responsible for what happens in organizations; they need to believe that they can and do make a difference. Kevin Boyce was appointed president of Toronto-based Unilever Canada in the fall of 2000, just as Unilever decided to restructure, combining its three businesses, Lever Pond's, Lipton, and Good Humor–Breyers, into one company under the name Unilever Canada. Boyce believes he will be able to manage this big company, while "retain[ing] the focus to act small."[11] His internal locus of control disposes him to believe that he will be able to make sure that Unilever does not become bureaucratic as it combines the cultures of three very different businesses. CEOs like Boyce believe so strongly in their ability to influence what happens around them that they are confident they can improve the performance of organizations and carry out difficult tasks while doing so.

self-esteem The degree to which individuals feel good about themselves and their capabilities.

SELF-ESTEEM   **Self-esteem** is the degree to which individuals feel good about themselves and their capabilities. People with high self-esteem feel that they are competent, deserving, and capable of handling most situations, as do Barrett and Comper. People with low self-esteem have poor opinions of themselves, are unsure about their capabilities, and question their ability to succeed at different endeavours.[12] Research suggests that people tend to choose activities and goals that are consistent with their levels of self-esteem. High self-esteem is desirable for managers because it is likely to facilitate their setting and keeping high standards for themselves, to push them ahead on difficult projects, and to give them the confidence they need to make and carry out important decisions.

NEEDS FOR ACHIEVEMENT, AFFILIATION, AND POWER
Psychologist David McClelland has extensively researched the needs for achievement, affiliation, and power.[13] The **need for achievement** is the extent to which an individual has a strong desire to perform challenging tasks well and to meet personal standards for excellence. People with a high need for achievement often set clear goals for themselves and like to receive performance feedback. The **need for affiliation** is the extent to which an individual is concerned about establishing and maintaining good interpersonal relations, being liked, and having other people get along with each other. The **need for power** is the extent to which an individual desires to control or influence others.[14]

need for achievement
The extent to which an individual has a strong desire to perform challenging tasks well and to meet personal standards for excellence.

need for affiliation
The extent to which an individual is concerned about establishing and maintaining good interpersonal relations, being liked, and having other people get along.

need for power
The extent to which an individual desires to control or influence others.

Research suggests that high needs for achievement and for power are assets for first-line and middle managers and that a high need for power is especially important for upper managers.[15] One study found that US presidents with a relatively high need for power tended to be especially effective during their terms of office.[16] A high need for affiliation may not always be desirable in managers because it might lead them to try too hard to be liked by others (including subordinates) rather than doing all they can to ensure that performance is as high as it can and should be.

Taken together, the personality traits desirable in managers—an internal locus of control, high self-esteem, and high needs for achievement and power—suggest that managers need to be take-charge individuals who believe that their own actions are decisive in determining their own and their organization's fate, believe in their own capabilities, and have a personal desire for accomplishment and influence over others.

Values, Attitudes, and Moods

What are managers striving to achieve, how do they think they should behave, what do they think about their jobs and organizations, and how do they actually feel at work? Some answers to these questions can be found by exploring managers' values, attitudes, and moods.

Values, attitudes, and moods capture how managers experience their jobs as individuals. *Values* describe what managers are trying to achieve through work and how they think they should behave. *Attitudes* capture their thoughts and feelings about their specific jobs and organizations. *Moods* encompass how managers actually feel when they are managing. Although these three aspects of managers' work experience are highly personal, they also have important implications for understanding how managers behave, how they treat and respond to others, and how, through their efforts, they help contribute to organizational effectiveness through planning, leading, organizing, and controlling.

terminal value A personal conviction about lifelong goals or objectives that an individual seeks to achieve.

instrumental value A personal conviction about modes of conduct or ways of behaving that an individual seeks to follow.

Values: Terminal and Instrumental

There are two kinds of personal values—*terminal* and *instrumental*. A **terminal value** is a personal conviction about lifelong goals or objectives; an **instrumental value** is a personal conviction about desired modes of conduct or ways of behaving.[17] Milton Rokeach, one of the leading researchers in the area of human values, identified 18 terminal values and 18 instrumental values that describe each person's value system (see Figure 11.2).[18] By rank ordering the terminal values from 1 (most important as a guiding principle in one's life) to 18 (least important as a guiding principle in one's life) and then rank ordering the instrumental values from 1 to

Figure 11.2
Terminal and Instrumental Values

Terminal Values	Instrumental Values
A comfortable life (a prosperous life)	Ambitious (hard-working, aspiring)
An exciting life (a stimulating, active life)	Broad-minded (open-minded)
A sense of accomplishment (lasting contribution)	Capable (competent, effective)
A world at peace (free of war and conflict)	Cheerful (lighthearted, joyful)
A world of beauty (beauty of nature and the arts)	Clean (neat, tidy)
Equality (brotherhood, equal opportunity for all)	Courageous (standing up for beliefs)
Family security (taking care of loved ones)	Forgiving (willing to pardon others)
Freedom (independence, free choice)	Helpful (working for the welfare of others)
Happiness (contentedness)	Honest (sincere, truthful)
Inner harmony (freedom from inner conflict)	Imaginative (daring, creative)
Mature love (sexual and spiritual intimacy)	Independent (self-reliant, self-sufficient)
National security (protection from attack)	Intellectual (intelligent, reflective)
Pleasure (an enjoyable, leisurely life)	Logical (consistent, rational)
Salvation (saved, eternal life)	Loving (affectionate, tender)
Self-respect (self-esteem)	Obedient (dutiful, respectful)
Social recognition (respect, admiration)	Polite (courteous, well-mannered)
True friendship (close companionship)	Responsible (dependable, reliable)
Wisdom (a mature understanding of life)	Self-controlled (restrained, self-disciplined)

Source: M. Rokeach, *The Nature of Human Values* (New York: Free Press, 1973).

value system The terminal and instrumental values that are guiding principles in an individual's life.

18, a person gives a good picture of his or her **value system**—what he or she is striving to achieve in life and how he or she wants to behave.[19] (You can gain a good understanding of your own values by rank ordering first the terminal values and then the instrumental values listed in Figure 11.2.)

Several of the terminal values listed in Figure 11.2 seem to be especially important for managers—such as *a sense of accomplishment (a lasting contribution), equality (brotherhood, equal opportunity for all),* and *self-respect (self-esteem).* A manager who thinks a sense of accomplishment is of paramount importance might focus on making a lasting contribution to an organization by developing a new product line or opening a new foreign subsidiary. A manager who places equality at the top of his or her list of terminal values may be at the forefront of an organization's efforts to support, provide equal opportunities to, and capitalize on the many talents of an increasingly diverse workforce. The relative importance that managers place on each terminal value helps explain what they are striving to achieve in their organizations and what they will focus their efforts on.

Although much of Rokeach's research was based in the United States, the terminal and instrumental values he identified can be used to describe the values of people from other cultures as well, as indicated in this "Managing Globally."

Managing Globally

Values of the Overseas Chinese

Over 55 million Chinese people work outside China, manage much of the trade and investment in all East Asia (except for Korea and Japan), and now are expanding beyond Asia to Europe and the United States. Often referred to as the "Overseas Chinese," they are prominent in businesses such as real estate and investment in countries like Singapore and Malaysia.[20] They tend to be successful at what they do, so successful that some of them are now running multi-billion-dollar companies.

Y.C. Wang is the founder and chairman of the Taiwan-based Formosa Plastics Group, which established a $3.3 billion plastics manufacturing and petrochemical plant in Point Comfort, Texas, in 1994. Cheng Yu-tong, a Hong Kong-based real-estate manager, owns the Stouffer and Renaissance United States hotel chains and has taken control of some of Donald Trump's New York City real-estate ventures. President Enterprises, a Taiwanese food company, produces Girl Guide cookies in eight of its United States bakeries and also owns the bakery that makes Famous Amos chocolate chip cookies.

One distinguishing characteristic of some Overseas Chinese, whether they are managing a bank in Hong Kong or a truly global organization, is their values. Above all else, they seem to value hard work, ambition, strong family ties, family security, responsibility, self-control, and competence. Billionaire Y.C. Wang has never taken a day off, and Kao Chin-yen, vice-chairman of President Enterprises, says that he would feel sick if he had no work to do. Many of the businesses managed and owned by Overseas Chinese are family businesses, and parents work hard to ensure that their children have both the education and the experience they will need to assume responsible positions in their companies. That many Overseas Chinese are very disciplined and responsible managers who are highly competent is evident from their successes around the world.

Given these values, you might think that the Overseas Chinese are somewhat risk-averse, but they are not. They also consider being daring and being creative to be important guiding principles, as evidenced by their multimillion-dollar investments around the world. Y.C. Wang is building one of the largest manufacturing facilities in the world in Taiwan at an estimated cost of $14 billion.

Respect, admiration, and social recognition also are important for these entrepreneurial managers. Many of the business deals between organizations owned and managed by Overseas Chinese are conducted through networks of managers who have developed close relationships of mutual trust and respect over decades. Personal relationships and connections built on respect and admiration are called *guanxi* and are the modus operandi for many Overseas Chinese. Similarly, *xinyong*, having a good reputation and a good credit rating, is a most valued asset for many Overseas Chinese managers.[21]

All in all, managers' value systems signify what managers as individuals are trying to accomplish and be like in their personal lives and at work. Thus, a manager's value system is a fundamental guide to his or her behaviour and efforts at planning, leading, organizing, and controlling.

Attitudes

attitude A collection of feelings and beliefs.

An **attitude** is a collection of feelings and beliefs. Like everyone else, managers have attitudes about their jobs and organizations, and these attitudes affect how they approach their jobs. Two of the most important attitudes in this context are job satisfaction and organizational commitment.

job satisfaction
The collection of feelings and beliefs that managers have about their current jobs.

JOB SATISFACTION   Job satisfaction is the collection of feelings and beliefs that managers have about their current jobs. Managers who are high in job satisfaction generally like their jobs, feel that they are being fairly treated, and believe that their jobs have many desirable features or characteristics (such as interesting work, good pay and job security, autonomy, or nice co-workers). Levels of job satisfaction tend to increase as one moves up the hierarchy in an organization. Upper managers, in general, tend to be more satisfied with their jobs than entry-level employees. Managers' levels of job satisfaction can range from very low to very high and anywhere in between.

In general, it is desirable for managers and employees to be satisfied with their jobs, for at least two reasons. First, satisfied individuals may be more likely to go the extra mile for their organization or perform **organizational citizenship behaviours** (OCBs), behaviours that are not required of organizational members but that contribute to and are necessary for organizational efficiency, effectiveness, and gaining a competitive advantage.[22] Individuals who are satisfied with their jobs are more likely to perform these "above and beyond the call of duty" behaviours, which can range from putting in extra-long hours when needed, to coming up with truly creative ideas and overcoming obstacles to implement them (even when doing so is not part of the individual's job), to going out of one's way to help a co-worker, subordinate, or superior (even when doing so entails considerable personal sacrifice).[23]

organizational citizenship behaviours
Behaviours that are not required of organizational members but that contribute to and are necessary for organizational efficiency, effectiveness, and gaining a competitive advantage.

A second reason why it is desirable for individuals to be satisfied with their jobs is that satisfied individuals may be less likely to quit.[24] For instance, a manager who is highly satisfied may never even think about looking for another position; a dissatisfied manager may always be on the lookout for new opportunities. Turnover can hurt an organization because it results in the loss of the experience and knowledge that managers have gained about the company, industry, and the environment.

A growing source of dissatisfaction for many lower-level and middle managers, as well as for nonmanagerial employees, is the threat of unemployment and increased workloads from organizational downsizings. A recent study of 4300 workers conducted by Wyatt Co. found that 76 percent of the employees of expanding companies are satisfied with their jobs but only 57 percent of the employees of companies that have downsized are satisfied.[25] Organizations that try to improve their efficiency through restructuring often eliminate a sizable number of first-line and middle-management positions. This decision obviously hurts the managers who are laid off, and it can also reduce the job satisfaction of individuals who remain, who might fear that they will be the next to be let go. In addition, the workloads of the remaining employees, including managers, are often dramatically increased as a result of restructuring, which can also contribute to dissatisfaction.

organizational commitment The collection of feelings and beliefs that managers have about their organization as a whole.

Roche Macaulay & Partners Advertising www.rochemacaulay.com/

ORGANIZATIONAL COMMITMENT **Organizational commitment** is the collection of feelings and beliefs that managers have about their organization as a whole. Individuals who are committed to their organization believe in what their organization is doing, are proud of what the organization stands for, and feel a high degree of loyalty toward the organization. Committed individuals are more likely to go above and beyond the call of duty to help their company and are less likely to quit.[26] Of course, not everyone is so committed to their company that they would fire themselves as president, but that's exactly what Geoffrey Roche, of Toronto-based Roche Macaulay & Partners Advertising, did. He didn't see himself as a good president, and thought the company would grow better with someone else at the top. He intends to focus more on the creative aspects of the business. "The agency 'has been a little under the radar' for the past couple of years and the shakeup will help burnish its reputation for strong creativity," he explained.[27]

Moods

mood A feeling or state of mind.

Just as you are sometimes in a bad mood and at other times in a good mood, so too are managers. A **mood** is a feeling or state of mind. When people are in a positive mood, they feel excited, enthusiastic, active, or elated.[28] When people are in a negative mood, they feel distressed, fearful, scornful, hostile, jittery, or nervous.[29] People who are high on extroversion are especially likely to experience positive moods; people who are high on negative affectivity are especially likely to experience negative moods. Moods, however, are also determined by the situation or circumstances a person is in; receiving a raise is likely to put most people in a good mood regardless of their personality traits. People who are high on negative affectivity are not always in a bad mood, and people who are low on extroversion still experience positive moods.[30]

The actions of Geoffrey Roche, of Toronto-based Roche Macaulay & Partners Advertising, show strong organizational commitment. He fired himself as president because he thought the company would grow better with someone else at the top.

Research on the effects of mood on the behaviour of managers and other members of an organization has just begun. Preliminary studies suggest that the subordinates of managers who experience positive moods at work may perform at somewhat higher levels and be less likely to resign and leave the organization than the subordinates of managers who do not tend to be in a positive mood at work.[31] Other research suggests that creativity might be enhanced by positive moods.[32]

Nevertheless, sometimes negative moods can have their advantages. Some studies suggest that critical thinking and devil's advocacy may be promoted by a negative mood, and sometimes especially accurate judgments may be made by managers in negative moods.[33]

Managers and other members of an organization need to realize that how they feel affects how they treat others and how others respond to them, including their subordinates. For example, a subordinate may be more likely to approach a manager with a somewhat far-out but potentially useful idea if the subordinate thinks the manager is in a good mood. Likewise, when managers are in very bad moods, their subordinates might try to avoid them at all costs.

A recent study of 400 randomly selected executives from large Canadian companies looked at mood-swing tendencies of executives. The researchers found that only 3 percent of the executives in the study experienced mood-swing patterns that are considered normal; 57 percent of the respondents experienced slight elevations of mood, called "hypomania," which result in more energy, confidence and drive, less need for sleep and feelings of happiness and creativity. Those who experience hypomania can burn out, however, and they may put their employees and others around them under additional stress.[34]

Perceptions

Most people tend to think that the decisions people make in organizations and the actions they take are the result of some "objective" determination of the issues involved and the surrounding situation. However, an individual's interpretation of a situation or even of another person is precisely that–an interpretation. For example, different individuals may see the same nonconformist subordinate in different ways: One may see a creative maverick, while another may see a troublemaker. Different individuals may even view what appears to be an "objectively" negative event–such as declining sales of a major product line–in different ways: One may see it as a looming threat to the profitability of the division, while another may view it as an important opportunity to revamp and reorient the product line to increase revenues and market share.

perception The process through which people select, organize, and interpret what they see, hear, touch, smell, and taste, to give meaning and order to the world around them.

Perception is the process through which people select, organize, and interpret sensory input–what they see, hear, touch, smell, and taste–to give meaning and order to the world around them.[35] All decisions and actions that people take are based on their subjective perceptions. When these perceptions are relatively accurate–close to the true nature of what is actually being perceived–good decisions are likely to be made and appropriate actions taken. Managers of fast-food restaurant chains such as McDonald's, Pizza Hut, and Wendy's accurately perceived that their customers were becoming more health conscious in the 1980s and 1990s and added salad bars and low-fat entrées to their menus. Managers at Kentucky Fried Chicken, Jack-in-the-Box, and Burger King took much longer to perceive this change in what customers wanted.

When individuals' perceptions are relatively inaccurate, individuals are likely to make bad decisions and take inappropriate actions, which hurt organizational effectiveness. Bad decisions may range from providing products or services that customers do not want, to hiring unqualified people, to failing to promote top-performing subordinates who subsequently decide to take their skills to competing organizations. In the "Focus on Diversity" that follows, we investigate the results of a study conducted at McMaster University that revealed how students' perceptions led to decisions about what kinds of personalities individuals have. In reading this feature, you might consider how a manager's perceptions might affect judgments regarding an employee's work performance.

Focus on Diversity

Exercisers Are "Better" People

A recent study conducted by McMaster University professor Kathleen Martin revealed just how strongly stereotypes affect people's judgments of others.[36] Students were asked to compare their attitudes about men and women who were described in exactly the same way except for whether or not they were exercisers. Martin found that the students "made judgments about things that had nothing to do with exercise at all."

Based on the description, students were asked to evaluate "Tom" or "Mary" on 12 personality characteristics, including afraid or brave and has self-control or lacks self-control. They were also asked to evaluate eight physical characteristics, including fit or unfit, sickly or healthy, ugly or good looking. Included in the descriptions was whether the individual was someone who exercised or not. In some descriptions, no mention of exercise was made.

The students evaluated the non-exercisers more negatively on every personality and physical characteristic than they did those described as exercisers. In scenarios where exercise was not mentioned, the non-exercisers were rated more poorly on personality characteristics than those for whom no information about exercise was given. "When Mary and Tom were described as exercisers, they were considered to be harder workers, more confident, braver, smarter, neater, happier and more sociable than the non-exerciser."

This study shows that perceptions of individuals may not be accurate at all. Below, we consider how perceptions are formed and discuss ways to ensure that perceptions are accurate.

Factors That Influence Perception

Are perceptions the same as reality?

Individuals' perceptions of the same person, event, or situation are likely to differ because individuals are different from each other in personality, values, attitudes, and moods. Each of these factors can influence the way someone perceives a situation. An individual who is high on openness to experience is likely to perceive a risky new venture as a positive opportunity; an individual who is low on openness to experience may perceive the same venture as a threat. An individual who has high levels of job satisfaction and organizational commitment may perceive a job transfer to another geographic location as an opportunity to learn and develop new skills; a dissatisfied, uncommitted individual may perceive the same transfer as a demotion and unwanted extra work.

People's perceptions are also affected by their past experience and acquired knowledge about or biases toward people, events, and situations. Suppose a manager's past experience of computer experts suggests that they are intelligent, quiet, shy, not very athletic, and somewhat eccentric. When introduced to a computer software developer at a party, this manager uses this information to form a perception of the developer. The information causes the manager to notice that the developer is dressed casually while other partygoers are dressed up, to ignore the fact that the developer told a funny joke, to sense that the developer often seems to be at a loss for words, and to ignore the fact that the developer used to be a star soccer player in university even though this accomplishment came up in conversation.

Although this example is a bit extreme, it does show how people tend to perceive other people and events and situations in ways that are consistent with their past knowledge and experience. Managers are as likely as any other member of an organization to do this. A manager who has had a bad experience launching new products might perceive a proposal for a new product more negatively than necessary, because past experience suggests that new product launches are risky and often doomed to failure. Similarly, a manager who has always been successful in efforts to sell a domestically popular product in foreign countries might perceive that the product has great potential in India even though most of the available evidence suggests the opposite.

Reema Rafay, of Etobicoke, ON-based Innovative Staffing Solutions, has experienced the problems of perceptual bias first hand. She helps clients find employees. Because she's young, the older executives she meets with sometimes think she's a representative from her company, not its owner.

Ways to Ensure Accurate Perceptions

What can organizational members do to ensure that they perceive people and situations as they truly are? First, individuals should try to be open to other points of view and perspectives.[37] Individuals who are open to other perspectives put their own beliefs and knowledge to an important reality test and will be more inclined to modify or change them when necessary. Second, individuals should not be afraid to change their views about a person, issue, or event. In the case of a manager who has had negative experiences with new product launches, if other managers present convincing information that suggests a product looks like a winner, then the manager should not be afraid to reverse position. In fact, reversing position and supporting a new product that turns out to be a best-seller will help the manager develop a more balanced and accurate perception of the potential for success in new product launches.

Tips for Managers

Perception

1. Be open to points of view and perspectives different from your own.

2. Seek out opinions from others who have had different kinds of experiences than yourself.

3. Do not be afraid to change your views about a person, issue, or event.

4. When you have made what turns out to be a bad decision or have not performed up to expectations, try to determine if your perceptions were faulty.

Stress

stress A condition that individuals experience when they face important opportunities or threats and are uncertain about their ability to handle or deal with them effectively.

To round out the picture of managers as feeling and thinking human beings, we turn now to a challenge that both managers and nonmanagers face throughout their careers and lives—stress. People experience **stress** when they face important opportunities or threats and are uncertain about their ability to handle or deal with them effectively.[38] The nature of managerial jobs almost ensures that managers experience stress. Many opportunities in an organization and in the task and general environments give managers a chance to improve their organization's efficiency and effectiveness, and many threats jeopardize an organization's success and even survival. Whether a manager can successfully take advantage of opportunities and overcome threats is often uncertain. This uncertainty makes management a stressful business. In a recent study of 400 randomly selected executives from large Canadian companies conducted by researchers at Sudbury, Ontario's Laurentian University, respondents reported a great deal of stress. Professors Darren Larose and Bernadette Schell found that 88 percent of executives surveyed reported elevated levels of stress and/or a predisposition toward serious illnesses such as cancer and heart disease. These levels are far higher than those found in the general population.[39]

Consequences of Stress

High levels of stress can be damaging, especially when they last for a long time. Although reactions to stress differ across individuals, one way to understand the effect that incessant stress can have on managers is by considering the physiological, psychological, and behavioural consequences of stress.

PHYSIOLOGICAL CONSEQUENCES Physiological consequences of stress range from the mild to the severe. Sleep disturbances, sweaty palms, feeling flushed, headaches, stomachaches, backaches, and nausea are some physical reactions to stress, as are high blood pressure, heart attacks, and impaired functioning of the immune system. The relationship between levels of stress and these physiological consequences is complicated.[40] Some people tend to experience more of these physiological consequences than others, and different people experience different kinds of consequences. What does seem to be clear is that the most severe consequences of stress, such as high blood pressure and heart attacks, are likely to occur only when excessive levels of stress are experienced over an extended period of time.

PSYCHOLOGICAL CONSEQUENCES You are probably quite familiar with some of the psychological consequences of stress—being in a bad mood, feeling nervous, angry, or upset, or feeling scornful, bitter, or hostile.[41] These negative feelings carry over into work attitudes such as lower levels of job satisfaction and organizational commitment. At some point, all workers are likely to experience these psychological consequences. When stress levels become too high for too long a time, however, these negative feelings can become overwhelming.

BEHAVIOURAL CONSEQUENCES How can managers perform their many and varied duties when they are experiencing stress, especially given the stressful nature of their jobs? Stress does not necessarily impair job performance and in some cases actually enhances it. Just as the stress you may experience before an exam energizes you to study, or the stress a worker experiences trying to meet a tight deadline pushes him or her to make more efficient use of time, so too can the stress managers experience push them to do a good job. Facing an important opportunity to increase sales often propels marketing managers to develop innovative marketing campaigns that appeal to different segments of the customer base. The threat posed by the opening of a new Mexican restaurant a block away from what had been the only Mexican restaurant in a small university town may encourage the manager of the older restaurant to make some needed changes in the menu and advertise some specials in the local newspaper, and those steps may result in the restaurant being busier than it ever was before the new restaurant appeared on the scene. In these cases, stress has positive effects on performance.

Nevertheless, stress sometimes impairs performance. A student who experiences test anxiety draws a blank on material that was known well the day before the exam. The manager of a dry cleaning store who forgets to turn off the presses one day before closing the shop because of worry over dwindling profits is not functioning up to the usual level because of too much stress.

One way to understand the seemingly contradictory effects that stress can and does have on people's functioning and performance is to picture the relationship between stress and performance as an inverted U (see Figure 11.3). Stress up to a certain point (Point A in the figure) is positive in that it propels people to do their best. Once this point is reached, however, stress becomes negative; increases in stress detract from performance and are dysfunctional. When stress impairs performance, many people also experience some of the physiological and psychological consequences of stress.

Sources of Managerial Stress

There are many sources of managerial stress—individuals' jobs, organizations, and personal lives. Two particularly common sources within the workplace are *role conflict* and *role overload*. In Chapter 1, we described the multiple roles that managers play, such as spokesperson and figurehead (see Table 1.1). In

Figure 11.3
The Inverted-U Relationship Between Stress and Performance

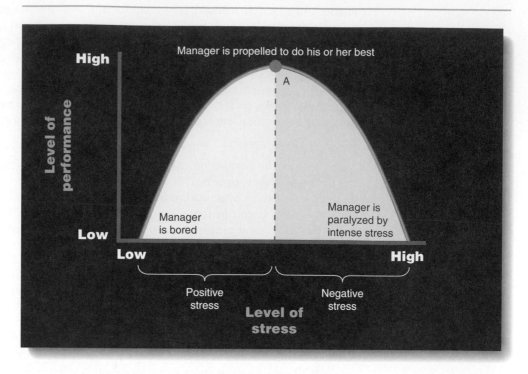

role conflict The conflict or friction that occurs when expected behaviours are at odds with each other.

performing these roles, managers are expected to demonstrate certain behaviours. **Role conflict** occurs when there is conflict or friction between expected behaviours.[42] In performing the roles of spokesperson and information disseminator, managers may find their responsibility to transmit accurate information to be at odds with their responsibility to promote a positive image for the organization in the eyes of the public. In performing the roles of leader and resource allocator, managers may experience conflict between their responsibility to motivate organizational members and reward high performance and their responsibility to allocate scarce resources (including money for raises and bonuses).

role overload The condition of having too many responsibilities and activities to perform.

Role overload occurs when managers have too many responsibilities and activities to perform.[43] At this point, you might be thinking that role overload is part and parcel of most managers' jobs. Managers do have multiple responsibilities, and at times these can become excessive, resulting in high levels of stress.

Coping With Stress

People manage or deal with stress in two basic ways: problem-focused coping and emotion-focused coping. **Problem-focused coping** includes the actions people take to deal directly with the source of their stress.[44] **Emotion-focused coping** includes the actions people take to deal with their stressful feelings and emotions.[45] Although individuals may cope with stress somewhat differently, here we look at two problem-focused strategies (time management and getting help from a mentor) and three emotion-focused strategies (exercise, meditation, and social support) that can be used.

problem-focused coping The actions people take to deal directly with the source of their stress.

emotion-focused coping The actions people take to deal with their stressful feelings and emotions.

PROBLEM-FOCUSED COPING

TIME MANAGEMENT Time management can be an especially useful strategy for individuals trying to cope with numerous and sometimes conflicting demands.

Time management includes various techniques that help people to make better use of, and accomplish more with, their time: making lists of what needs to be accomplished in a certain relatively short time period (such as a day or week), prioritizing tasks to clarify which ones are most important and which ones could be delegated or put off, and estimating how long it will take to accomplish tasks and dividing one's day(s) accordingly.[46]

GETTING HELP FROM A MENTOR   Seeking the advice and guidance of a mentor can be an effective problem-focused strategy. A **mentor** is an experienced member of an organization who provides advice and guidance to a less-experienced worker. The help that a mentor provides can range from advice about handling a tricky job assignment, dealing with a disagreement with a supervisor, and what kind of subsequent positions to strive for, to information about appropriate behaviour and what to wear in various situations. A mentor is likely to have faced a problem (threat or opportunity) similar to the problem the individual is currently facing and thus will be in a good position to comment on what are especially effective or ineffective ways of dealing with it. In any case, receiving advice from someone who has had more experience and also is less personally involved in the issue at hand can be helpful. Moreover, research has found that receiving help from a mentor is associated with an increase in pay, pay satisfaction, promotion, and feeling good about one's accomplishments.[47] The following "Management Insight" describes how Grace White, of Nova Scotia's CanJam Trading Ltd., learned to put more balance in her life to reduce stress by taking advice from a female mentor who was older and clearly exhibited serenity and a sense of peace.

mentor An experienced member of an organization who provides advice and guidance to a less-experienced worker.

Management Insight

Life Balance Improves Performance

Can a person build a $50 million-dollar business, and have a rewarding personal life? Grace White, president and CEO of Dartmouth, NS-based CanJam Trading Ltd., is living proof that it's possible.[48] Her company exports products "from fish to corn meal" to the United States, Japan, and China.

White received a Woman Entrepreneur of the Year award and, in 1999, CanJam was named one of Chatelaine's top 100 women-owned businesses in Canada. To do so, she led what became a pretty unbalanced life. "In 1992, when my husband died, I threw myself into work to cope with the pain," she says. "For a long time I was working seven days a week, and sometimes 15 or 16 hours a day."

In 1998, White decided that she didn't want to have that sort of life anymore, and met a mentor who inspired her to re-evaluate her priorities. "I realized that the order in my life should be God first, then my children, then my company, and my community," she says.

Despite moving to have more balance in her life, White hasn't lost her ambition. By 2005, she plans to be doing $100 million in sales. To achieve this goal, she recently purchased Atlantic Pearl, a Nova Scotia fish-processing plant. This gives CanJam more control over both pricing and delivery. White also believes in building relationships to help increase her business: "We have had customers become suppliers and suppliers become customers," she says. "We don't focus on our success. We focus on our customers' success."

EMOTION-FOCUSED COPING

EXERCISE   Many individuals jog, swim, or use exercise machines such as NordicTracks, rowing machines, or treadmills in their homes or offices. Physical exercise is among the most effective ways to deal with stressful feelings and emotions. Regular exercise can also improve cardiovascular functioning and contribute to a general sense of well-being and relaxation.

MEDITATION   Temporarily putting everyday cares aside by being in a quiet environment and focusing on some soothing mental or visual image or verbal phrase can also be an effective means of emotion-focused coping.[49] Akin to meditation are special breathing techniques that can be used to combat stressful feelings. In Japan, many managers practise special breathing techniques (such as breathing slowly and shallowly) in a variety of positions (such as standing, bending, and squatting) to improve their *Ki*, or life force and energy. They believe that doing this improves their health and stamina, alleviates stress, and allows them to remain in control and even to stay youthful.[50]

social support

Emotional support provided by other people such as friends, relatives, and co-workers.

SOCIAL SUPPORT   There is more than a grain of truth in the old saying that sometimes all you need is a shoulder to cry on. **Social support**, the availability of other people (such as friends, relatives, co-workers, or supervisors) to talk to, discuss problems with, or receive advice from, can alleviate stressful feelings and emotions.[51] Families or co-workers in similar kinds of positions are important sources of social support. Mentors can also be a good source of social support as well as practical advice for dealing with actual sources of stress. Grace White found that her mentor also became her friend, thus providing an additional source of social support.

When coping is successful, opportunities and threats responsible for stress are dealt with directly and stressful feelings and emotions do not get out of hand. Sometimes when people are unable to cope effectively with the stress they are experiencing, help from a trained expert such as a psychologist can be beneficial.

Tips for Managers

Stress

1. Take active steps to accommodate workers' multidimensional lives whenever possible.

2. If you are experiencing especially high levels of stress, try to make better use of your time, ask for advice from others who have been in similar situations, and consider trying to cut back on or delegate some of your less important responsibilities.

3. If you often feel anxious, nervous, worried, upset, or angry, consider exercising more regularly, or try to find some alternative way to cope with your stressful feelings—such as meditation or involvement in a hobby or leisure activity.

Chapter Summary

ENDURING CHARACTERISTICS: PERSONALITY TRAITS

- The Big Five Personality Traits
- Other Personality Traits That Affect Managerial Behaviour

VALUES, ATTITUDES, AND MOODS

- Values: Terminal and Instrumental
- Attitudes
- Moods

PERCEPTIONS

- Factors That Influence Perception
- Ways to Ensure Accurate Perceptions

STRESS

- Consequences of Stress
- Sources of Managerial Stress
- Coping With Stress

Summary and Review

ENDURING CHARACTERISTICS: PERSONALITY TRAITS Personality traits are enduring tendencies to feel, think, and act in certain ways. The Big Five general traits are extroversion, negative affectivity, agreeableness, conscientiousness, and openness to experience. Other personality traits that affect managerial behaviour are locus of control, self-esteem, and the needs for achievement, affiliation, and power.

VALUES, ATTITUDES, AND MOODS A terminal value is a personal conviction about lifelong goals or objectives; an instrumental value is a personal conviction about modes of conduct. Terminal and instrumental values have an impact on what managers try to achieve in their organization and the kinds of behaviours they engage in. An attitude is a collection of feelings and beliefs. Two attitudes important for understanding managerial behaviours include job satisfaction (the collection of feelings and beliefs that managers have about their jobs) and organizational commitment (the collection of feelings and beliefs that managers have about their organization). A mood is a feeling or state of mind. Managers' moods, or how they feel at work on a day-to-day basis, have the potential to impact their own behaviour and effectiveness as well as their subordinates'.

PERCEPTIONS Perception—the process through which managers select, organize, and interpret sensory input to give meaning and order to the world around them—is inherently subjective. Managers' personalities, values, attitudes, moods, knowledge, and past experience all have the potential to influence their perceptions. Accurate perceptions are a necessary ingredient for making good decisions.

STRESS People experience stress when they face important opportunities or threats and are uncertain about their ability to handle or deal with them effectively. Stress has physiological, psychological, and behavioural consequences. Two common sources of managerial stress are role conflict and role overload. People manage or deal with stress in two basic ways. Problem-focused coping strategies for managers include time management and getting help from a mentor. Emotion-focused coping strategies for managers include exercise, meditation, and social support.

Management in Action

Topics for Discussion and Action

1. Discuss why managers who have different types of personalities can be equally effective and successful.

2. Interview a manager in a local organization. Ask the manager to describe situations in which he or she is especially likely to act in accordance with his or her values. Ask the manager to describe situations in which he or she is less likely to act in accordance with his or her values.

3. Can managers be too satisfied with their jobs? Can they be too committed to their organizations? Why or why not?

4. Assume that you are a manager of a restaurant. Describe what it is like to work for you when you are in a negative mood.

5. Develop guidelines for managers to use to ensure that their perceptions are as accurate as possible.

6. Describe the steps that organizations can take to help managers and nonmanagers alike cope effectively with stress.

Building Management Skills

Diagnosing Stress

Everybody experiences stress in their daily lives. Think about your own life and the extent to which you are currently experiencing stress. Then answer the following questions.

1. What are the sources of the stress that you are currently experiencing?

2. Are you experiencing any physiological, psychological, or behavioural consequences of stress? If so, describe these consequences.

3. In what problem-focused ways are you coping with stress? Are these helping you deal with the sources of your stress?

4. In what emotion-focused ways are you coping with stress? Are these helping you deal with your stressful feelings and emotions?

5. Can you think of any other problem-focused and emotion-focused coping techniques that may help you deal with the stress that you are currently experiencing?

Small Group Breakout Exercise
Coping with Managerial Stress in Hard Times

Form groups of three or four people, and appoint one member as the spokesperson who will communicate your findings to the whole class when called on by the instructor. Then discuss the following scenario.

You are the top-management team of a medium-sized company that manufactures cardboard boxes, containers, and other kinds of cardboard packaging materials. Your company is facing increasing levels of competition for major corporate customer accounts. In an effort to cut costs and remain competitive, your company recently downsized. Approximately 25 percent of the production workers, 30 percent of the first-line managers, and 40 percent of the middle managers were laid off. You anticipated how stressful the downsizing would be for the production workers and took the appro-

priate steps to help both those who were laid off and those who kept their jobs to cope effectively with the stress that they were experiencing. However, you did not anticipate the high levels of stress that the first-line managers and the middle managers appear to be experiencing. The workloads of these managers have increased substantially, they are facing many changes in their and their subordinates' jobs, some have reported feeling guilty that co-workers were laid off, and their own sense of job security has been shattered. You are meeting today to address this problem.

1. Describe the likely sources of stress for the first-line managers.

2. Describe the likely sources of stress for the middle managers.

3. Develop a plan of action to help the first-line managers cope effectively with the stress that they are experiencing.

4. Develop a plan of action to help the middle managers effectively cope with the stress they are experiencing.

Exploring the World Wide Web
Specific Assignment

Many companies take active steps to ensure that their employees behave in a socially responsible and ethical manner. One such company is Vancouver-based VanCity Credit Union. Scan VanCity's Web site to learn more about this company (www.vancity.com). Read the section on "Doing What's Right" on the homepage and then click on "Corporate Social Responsibility" and "Social Auditing." Read the various documents available, including their "Social Report."

1. Which values does VanCity encourage its employees to abide by?

2. How might the production of an ethical audit and ethical guidelines influence employees' work attitudes and moods?

General Assignment

Find the Web site of a company that is undertaking initiatives to enhance levels of job satisfaction or organizational commitment among employees. What are those initiatives? Do you think they will be successful in promoting job satisfaction or organizational commitment? Why or why not?

ManagementCase

Stamina: Who Has It, Why It's Important, and How to Get It

Top managers put in longer hours and sleep less than most of us do. For example, Herb Kelleher, CEO of Southwest Airlines, works 90 hours a week and on average sleeps 5 hours a night, while Bill Gates, CEO of Microsoft, works 60 hours and sleeps 6. John Tory, CEO of Toronto-based Rogers Cablesystems, works 80 hours. Les Hammond is CEO of both ASEAN Holdings Inc. and Global Explorations Corp., based in Vancouver. When he's actually in Vancouver, he works about 75 hours a week. He's often abroad on business, however. Then, Hammond says, he sleeps "six hours times seven days, subtract that from the total hours ... [I work] about 120 hours."[52] How do they do it? They have stamina—a seemingly endless amount of energy that enables them to do more with less sleep than most people can each day.[53]

Stamina is not important just for managers at the top of an organization. Managers at all levels are under increasing pressure to take on more responsibility. Corporate downsizing and restructuring often double the workload of those remaining. An increasingly global economy is increasing the need to travel and communicate with associates around the world. Developments such as electronic communication and voice mail are keeping managers constantly informed and in touch. On a typical day, public relations manager Pam Alexander may rush from a press conference in California to the airport to travel to London for another press conference.

People with high levels of stamina seem to be especially optimistic about the future. William Morgan, who is director of the Sport Psychology Laboratory at the University of Wisconsin, suggests that people who are high on the personality trait of extroversion may be at somewhat of an advantage when it comes to stamina. He has found that when people are asked to perform stressful exercises in his laboratory, extroverts often describe the exercises as easier and less painful than introverts. Extroverts also may be more likely to derive support from those around them because of their outgoing nature.

Nevertheless, many extroverts might not have the stamina of some highly successful managers. How can people in general boost their stamina so that they too can gain an extra day for work or leisure per week by getting more done each day? You might not actually want to cut back too much on your sleep. Although some people are probably born with the ability to function on little sleep, sleep experiments have found that people generally tend to sleep eight hours a day, even when they are kept away from radios and TVs, clocks, windows, and anything else that would let them know whether it is night or day and what time it is. Timothy Monk, sleep researcher and professor at the University of Pittsburgh Medical Center, suggests that some people probably can comfortably cut back to around six hours a night (preferably with a 20-minute nap during the day).[54] Further cuts in sleep time might actually hurt a manager's ability to perform because lack of sleep can impair memory and short-term judgment, often without people being aware of what is happening.

Diet seems to have a considerable impact on stamina. Fatty foods are hard to digest and rob blood from the brain, causing sleepiness. Alcohol also robs one of stamina by dehydrating the body of important fluids and disturbing sleep. Ideally, two-thirds of one's diet should be composed of complex carbohydrates (grains, fruits, and vegetables). Carbohydrates increase levels of serotonin (nature's own tranquilizer) in the brain. If you are nervous during the day, a high-carbohydrate lunch can help calm you, but if you are already relaxed, you might want to indulge in four ounces of protein at lunchtime to be at your peak energy level the rest of the day.

Exercise is also a key contributor to stamina. Sports psychologist James Loehr suggests a routine of 100 stomach crunches (a variant of the sit-up entailing lying on the floor with your knees bent and lifting your shoulders a few inches from the floor). Loehr says that stomach crunches help one's posture and respiratory functioning, which contribute to stamina (and confidence as well). Interval training in which you raise and lower your heartbeat by, for example, running or cycling at different speeds also contributes to stamina. Loehr has helped speed skater Dan Jansen, tennis stars Jim Courier and Arantxa Sanchez Vicario, and boxer Ray Mancini increase their stamina and lower their levels of debilitating stress.

With all this advice, what about managers like Herb Kelleher, who, at age 63, smokes cigarettes, eats chicken-fried steak, and has been known to indulge in Wild Turkey and the like? Kelleher's energy and long working hours and the fact that he often has time left over for socializing are truly phenomenal.[55] Maybe he and others like him were just born with an exceptional amount of stamina. For the rest of us, diet and exercise might help.

Questions

1. Why might being high on the extroversion continuum contribute to stamina?

2. Might a manager with a lot of stamina nevertheless succumb to some of the negative consequences of too much stress? Why or why not?

3. What can organizations do to help their members increase their stamina?

4. What are some of the potential personal costs of working 60 or more hours per week?

ManagementCase

In the News

From the Pages of *The National Post*
In Her Father's Footsteps

Belinda Stronach is a multimillionaire's daughter who married a Norse god. She appears to have Fame, Fortune and Happiness in mythic proportions. She has just added Power to that list, assuring her place in the family dynasty by assuming control of Magna International Inc., the $10.5 billion car-parts colossus started by her father, Frank.

It seems that the blond-haired Ms. Stronach, soft-spoken and highly disciplined, has spent her entire life being groomed for this moment.

What really drives the 34-year-old, according to those who know her best, is not a love of money or influence but a defining relationship with her flamboyant father, combined with an extraordinarily strong social conscience she appears to have inherited from him.

Frank Stronach, a restless and fiercely ambitious man, arrived in Canada from his native Austria in 1954 with $54 in his pocket and the classic immigrant's dream of building a successful life for himself. Apprenticed to a tool-and-die maker

at 14, he started his life in the new world picking up golf balls at a Montreal course and washing dishes in a hospital in Kitchener, Ontario, before finding work making tools in an airplane plant.

Focused and frugal, it took him three years to save enough money to buy a garage on Dupont Street in midtown Toronto and open his own firm.

That was 44 years ago. The company Belinda Stronach is taking control of today has annual sales of $10.5 billion and employs some 60 000 people at 166 manufacturing divisions and 32 product development and engineering centres around the world.

Ms. Stronach is said to be like her father in many ways: intelligent, highly focused and a natural athlete who particularly loves skiing. Unlike her father, she did not have to scratch her way to the top. By the time she was born in 1966, he was well on the way to building the company that would be her inheritance. She has been described as the apple of his eye, and the two are

said to enjoy a close relationship. It seems there was never any question that she, not her brother Andy, would be the one working most closely by his side.

"What really drives Belinda? Aside from the love of the business, I think she has this very special love and respect for her dad," says Dennis Mills, a Liberal MP and long-time family friend. "I know that may sound old-fashioned but that is what I see.

"They have always had this special father-daughter relationship. Frank is more of a visionary but Belinda grasps the vision very fast. She is very sharp, she gets it. If you have someone around you—and especially if she's your daughter—and she grasps the vision, I think it makes for a pretty special relationship. And she is following in his footsteps in a way."

But Ms. Stronach appears to be temperamentally quite unlike her famous father in at least one notable respect. Mr. Stronach is undeniably flashy. One of the first purchases he made when he began making money was a brand-new Pontiac convertible, which he promptly shipped to Europe so he could drive it to his hometown of Wei and show people what a success he had become. Trophies have always been evident in the backdrop of his life: thoroughbred racehorses, private jets and buildings that look like Bavarian castles. Mr. Mills, who has known Ms. Stronach since she was 17, says she has always been very low-key despite her privileged upbringing, and mixes comfortably with people from all walks of life.

"She is very understated. There is not one ounce of pretentiousness in Belinda Stronach. She is what I would call very low-maintenance."

She joined the family firm in 1985 after spending a year at York University, becoming a member of Magna's board of directors in 1988, a vice-president in 1995 and executive vice-president in 1999. Her first husband, Don Walker, was a former General Motors executive who was Magna's president and CEO. When the couple—who have two children, a son, 10, and a daughter, 8—separated in 1995, Ms. Stronach returned to the "family compound," building a house next to her parents', a mansion that overlooks the company's turreted headquarters in Aurora, Ontario, near Toronto.

Ms. Stronach delicately sidesteps questions about ways in which she resembles her father, saying she prefers to talk about the important lessons she has learned at his knee.

"The special qualities I have learned from him involve fairness, decision making, entrepreneurship, definitely how to challenge and motivate people, and the importance of believing in an idea," she says, sounding decidedly weary after a long day of interviews and board meetings. Assuming the position of CEO (she is replacing Mr. Walker, her former husband, who will remain at Magna as CEO of the newly created Magna Interiors group) will give her the opportunity to step out of her father's shadow.

"I think it's a great opportunity to make my own mark, to establish a reputation as a competent leader," she says. "Magna has a great corporate culture that tries to balance the interests of the managers, the employees and investors, and this gives me an opportunity to help that philosophy evolve."

But as she steps out of the shadow, it will be straight into the spotlight. Until now, Ms. Stronach has managed to live a fairly private life, away from the media glare that follows her father. "I know that comes with the job, so it's something I'm prepared for," she says.

She came under intense scrutiny in 1999 when she married Johann Olav Koss, who is something of a national deity in Norway for winning three gold medals in the 1994 Lillehammer Olympics, setting three world speed-skating records along the way. Mr. Koss (nicknamed King Koss) is beloved not only for his sporting prowess but for his humanitarian efforts. A medical doctor, he donated his $31 000 winner's bonus to Olympic Aid, a humanitarian fund he helped found to help people in the war-torn city of Sarajevo, site of the 1984 Winter Olympics. He has worked hard to keep the organization going, and received many accolades for his efforts, including being named *Sports Illustrated* Sportsman of the Year in 1994 and one of 100 future world leaders by *Time*.

Humanitarianism is a subject dear to both their hearts. In lieu of wedding gifts, the couple requested donations to the Starlight Foundation, a charity that grants wishes to seriously ill children. She is active in many charities. A sense of social justice runs in the family. Ms. Stronach's grandfather was a factory worker and strong Communist supporter, and her father always instilled in his children the importance of giving back.

Mr. Stronach is one of the first businessmen in Canada to offer his employees profit-sharing, and when Ms. Stronach refers to the unique

corporate culture, she is referring in part to the "Magna Carta," the legally binding contract that guarantees Magna employees 10 percent of its pre-tax earnings: 3 percent in cash and 7 percent through a deferred profit-sharing plan. It is policies such as this that have helped Magna attract and retain top talent.

"Growing up in our household it was an important value," she says. "I come from a very fortunate background and financial situation. I think it's important for people like me to give back to society. It's much more difficult to think of which charity you're going to give to when you're thinking about where your next meal is going to come from."

Ms. Stronach, who is also president of the fashion house Misura Inc., does not appear daunted at running the day-to-day operations of one of the country's larger corporations, although she acknowledges her strengths are people skills, rather than the more traditional facility with numbers.

"I believe I understand what motivates people, managers and employees, and recently initiated and led a global restructuring of our human resources capabilities. But there's no question I have to have a strong appreciation of the numbers, and the legal issues; that's extremely important because that's what you're measured on at the end of the day, right? Do you have a successful, profitable business?"

Paul Godfrey, president and CEO of the Toronto Blue Jays, says he, for one, has no doubt Ms. Stronach will measure up by any yardstick.

"She is extremely smart and able to size up a situation very well. Her dad is one of the great entrepreneurs in Canadian business, and I think as time goes by, she is making all the right moves in the community in meeting the right people, doing the right things, and being involved in every aspect of life in Toronto.

"I'm a big, big fan of hers. She has great people skills, and listens very, very well. She doesn't have the experience her dad has but that's natural, because she hasn't got the years her dad has. She is more reserved, but will end up getting equal results. I think she's got 'winner' written all over her."

Source: S. Rubin, "In Her Father's Footsteps—But no Longer in His Shadow," *National Post,* February 23, 2001, p. A1.

Questions

1. How would you describe Frank Stronach's personality? Belinda Stronach's?

2. How would you compare the values, attitudes, and moods of father and daughter?

3. What factors might affect the perceptions that Frank Stronach has about his company and his employees? Would Belinda Stronach's perceptions be different from her father's? In what ways?

Chapter twelve

Motivation

Learning Objectives

1. Explain what motivation is and why managers need to be concerned about it.

2. Describe from the perspectives of expectancy theory and equity theory what managers should do to have a highly motivated workforce.

3. Explain how goals and needs motivate people and what kinds of goals are especially likely to result in high performance.

4. Explain why and how managers can use pay as a major motivation tool.

A Case in Contrast

Motivating Employees at Eastman Kodak and Mars

George Fisher, CEO of Eastman Kodak (www.kodak.com), the well-known photographic products company, and John and Forrest Mars, the brothers who run the privately owned candy company Mars Inc., could not have more different ways of motivating their employees.[1]

George Fisher's approach to motivation includes raising levels of responsibility at Kodak and encouraging employees to make decisions in a timely manner and to take risks in order to meet quality, customer satisfaction, and product development goals. Fisher sets specific, difficult goals for his employees to attain but gives them the responsibility to figure out how to meet them. In contrast, the Mars brothers like to call the shots and are reluctant to share responsibility, even with top managers. As one former manager at Mars put it, "Senior managers are scared of the Mars boys. They are like Russian czars, dictatorial in spirit and manner. There's a court around them. You don't pick a fight with John or Forrest."[2] The Mars brothers are so autocratic that not even high-level managers are motivated to take risks and come up with creative new ideas, because they are likely to get shot down by Forrest or John.

Fisher expresses confidence in his subordinates' ability to succeed. He expects high performance, has made it clear that shortfalls will not go unnoticed, and holds employees accountable for reaching their difficult goals. Forrest and John Mars not only do not express confidence in their subordinates but frequently criticize them and their capabilities and are prone to angry outbursts when things displease them. Former Mars managers suggest that Forrest and John are such difficult people to work for that they make other hard-hitting CEOs look like Barney, the pur-

ple dinosaur character for young children. Some Mars employees feel that the Mars brothers have little faith in employees' competence and capabilities, given their tendencies to be so critical.

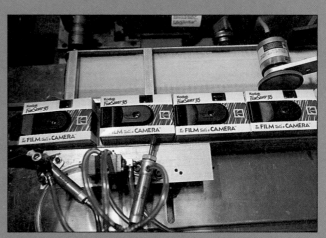

George Fisher, CEO of Kodak, and John and Forrest Mars, the brothers who run the candy company Mars Inc., have very different ways of motivating their employees. Fisher likes to give employees the responsibility of making decisions and the opportunity to take risks. The Mars brothers like to call the shots and are reluctant to share responsibility, even with top managers.

Fisher has an informal, approachable style; he practically never raises his voice or shows anger or displeasure. He treats employees so well that they want to do a good job to help him turn Kodak around. As Carl Kohrt, general manager of the $2.5 billion health sciences unit, says, "It's like talking to your father ... You don't want to disappoint him." The Mars brothers are anything but approachable. Their frequent angry outbursts and tirades motivate employees to avoid them whenever possible.

Positive feedback for a job well done is an integral part of Fisher's approach to motivation. He takes great pains to make sure that he is accessible to Kodak employees so that he can help spur them on and provide positive feedback and praise. For example, Fisher often visits with Kodak researchers for updates on their projects, and he praises their efforts. The only feedback the Mars brothers seem to provide is negative. They are impatient and use a variety of punishments on employees who disappoint them, including criticizing and berating them in front of their co-workers.

Consistent with his approachable style, Fisher is always available to talk to employees and has breakfast in the company cafeteria for this purpose. He encourages all employees to send him e-mail messages and some days receives as many as 30. His secretary prints out the messages, and Fisher personally responds to each one with a handwritten note on the printout, typically within a day. Fisher shows that he cares about what his employees think, gives them input on their ideas, and commends them for good suggestions. The Mars brothers do not welcome input from their employees. Managers and workers at all levels are afraid of them, are reluctant to stand up for what they believe in if it might not be what the brothers want to hear, and are reluctant to interact with them. "Fear of Forrest" causes many Mars employees to keep their opinions to themselves so as to avoid Forrest Mars' angry outbursts.

How are the Mars brothers able to attract employees despite what some former Mars executives claim is a very negative approach to motivation? They do it by paying salaries that are twice as large as the salaries paid by other companies in their industry. George Fisher also uses pay to motivate; he does it, however, by linking pay to performance levels. Even researchers in Kodak's labs are being held accountable for progress on their projects, including ensuring that projects are completed in a timely fashion.

How does the difference in Fisher's and the Mars brothers' styles of motivating employees affect their companies' performance? Kodak, under Fisher, performed better than it had for decades, and at the time of his retirement in 2000, Kodak remained the world's number-one film seller with 36 percent of the market. Meanwhile, Mars has been losing market share in the candy industry both in the United States and in western Europe. •

Overview

Even with the best strategy in place and an appropriate organizational architecture, an organization will be effective only if its members are motivated to perform at a high level. George Fisher clearly realizes this. One reason why leading is such an important managerial activity is that it entails ensuring that each member of an organization is motivated to perform highly and help the organization achieve its goals. When managers are effective, the outcome of the leading process is a highly motivated workforce. A key challenge for managers of organizations both large and small is to encourage employees to perform at a high level.

In this chapter, we describe what motivation is, where it comes from, and why managers need to promote high levels of it for an organization to be effective and achieve its goals. We examine important theories of motivation: need theories, expectancy theory, goal-setting theory, reinforcement theory, and equity theory.

Each provides managers with important insights about how to motivate organizational members. The theories are complementary in that each focuses on a somewhat different aspect of motivation. Considering all of the theories together will give managers a rich understanding of the many issues and problems involved in encouraging high levels of motivation throughout an organization. Last, we consider the use of pay as a motivation tool. By the end of this chapter, you will understand what it takes to have a highly motivated workforce. ●

The Nature of Motivation

motivation Psychological forces that determine the direction of a person's behaviour in an organization, a person's level of effort, and a person's level of persistence.

Motivation may be defined as psychological forces that determine the direction of a person's behaviour in an organization, a person's level of effort, and a person's level of persistence in the face of obstacles.[3] The *direction of a person's behaviour* refers to the many possible behaviours in which people could engage. For example, employees at Kodak have frequent interactions with their CEO, George Fisher; they even send him e-mail messages. In contrast, employees at Mars try to avoid John and Forrest Mars and often hold their tongues out of fear of displeasing them. *Effort* refers to how hard people work. Employees at Kodak exert high levels of effort to attain their difficult goals and help George Fisher get Kodak back on the right track. *Persistence* refers to whether, when faced with roadblocks and obstacles, people keep trying or give up. Researchers in Kodak's labs sometimes face what seem to be insurmountable problems, yet they persist in their efforts to complete their projects on a timely basis and meet their goals.

Motivation is so central to management because it explains why people behave the way they do in organizations—why employees at Kodak are striving to reach difficult goals and do not want to let George Fisher down, and why employees at Mars are afraid to stand up for what they believe. Motivation also explains why a waiter is polite or rude, why a kindergarten teacher really tries to get children to enjoy learning or just goes through the motions, and why some workers put forth twice the effort of others.

intrinsically motivated behaviour Behaviour that is performed for its own sake.

Motivation can come from *intrinsic* or *extrinsic* sources. **Intrinsically motivated behaviour** is behaviour that is performed for its own sake; the source of motivation is actually to perform the behaviour, and motivation comes from doing the work itself. Many managers are intrinsically motivated; they derive a sense of accomplishment and achievement from helping their organizations to achieve their goals and gain a competitive advantage. Jobs that are interesting and challenging or high on the five characteristics described by the job characteristics model (see Chapter 8) are more likely to lead to intrinsic motivation than are jobs that are boring or do not make use of a person's skills and abilities. An elementary school teacher who enjoys teaching children, a computer programmer who loves solving programming problems, and a commercial photographer who relishes taking creative photographs are all intrinsically motivated. For these individuals, motivation comes from performing their jobs, whether they be teaching children, finding bugs in computer programs, or taking pictures.

extrinsically motivated behaviour Behaviour that is performed to acquire material or social rewards or to avoid punishment.

Extrinsically motivated behaviour is behaviour that is performed to acquire material or social rewards or to avoid punishment; the source of motivation is the consequences of the behaviour, not the behaviour itself. Employees at Mars who keep their ideas to themselves and agree with whatever the Mars brothers tell them are extrinsically motivated; fear of punishment motivates them to behave in this manner. Similarly, a car salesperson who is motivated by receiving a commission on all cars sold, a lawyer who is motivated by the high salary and status that go along with the job, and a factory worker who is motivated by the opportunity to earn a secure income are all extrinsically motivated. Their motivation comes from the consequences they receive as a result of their work behaviours.

People can be intrinsically motivated, extrinsically motivated, or both intrinsically and extrinsically motivated. A top manager who derives a sense of accomplishment and achievement from managing a large corporation and strives to reach year-end targets to obtain a hefty bonus is both intrinsically and extrinsically motivated. Similarly, a nurse who enjoys helping and taking care of patients and is motivated by having a secure job with good benefits is both intrinsically and extrinsically motivated. Whether workers are intrinsically motivated, extrinsically motivated, or both depends on a wide variety of factors: workers' own personal characteristics (such as their personalities, abilities, values, attitudes, and needs), the nature of their jobs (such as whether they have been enriched or whether they are high or low on the five core characteristics of the job characteristics model), and the nature of the organization (such as its structure, its culture, its control systems, its human resource management system, and the ways in which rewards such as pay are distributed to employees).

Regardless of whether people are intrinsically or extrinsically motivated, they join and are motivated to work in organizations to obtain certain outcomes. An **outcome** is anything a person gets from a job or organization. Some outcomes, such as autonomy, responsibility, a feeling of accomplishment, and the pleasure of doing interesting or enjoyable work, result in intrinsically motivated behaviour. Other outcomes, such as pay, job security, benefits, and vacation time, result in extrinsically motivated behaviour.

Organizations hire people to obtain important inputs. An **input** is anything a person contributes to his or her job or organization, such as time, effort, education, experience, skills, knowledge, and actual work behaviours. Inputs such as these are necessary for an organization to achieve its goals. Managers strive to motivate members of an organization to contribute inputs—through their behaviour, effort, and persistence—that help the organization achieve its goals. How do managers do this? They ensure that members of an organization obtain the outcomes they desire when they make valuable contributions to the organization. Managers use outcomes to motivate people to contribute their inputs to the organization. Giving people outcomes when they contribute inputs and perform well aligns the interests of employees with the goals of the organization as a whole because when employees do what is good for the organization, they personally benefit.

This alignment between employees and organizational goals as a whole can be described by the motivation equation depicted in Figure 12.1. Managers seek to ensure that people are motivated to contribute important inputs to the organization, that these inputs are put to good use or focused in the direction of high per-

outcome Anything a person gets from a job or organization.

input Anything a person contributes to his or her job or organization.

Figure 12.1
The Motivation Equation

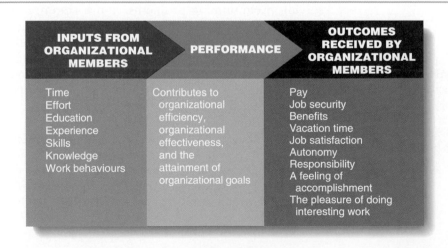

formance, and that high performance results in workers obtaining the outcomes they desire.

The main theories of motivation that we cover in this chapter fall into one of two categories: needs theories and process theories. Needs theories focus on the types of needs individuals have that will lead them to be motivated, while process theories explore how one actually motivates someone. Each of the theories of motivation we discuss focuses on one or more aspects of the motivation equation in Figure 12.1. Together, the theories provide a comprehensive set of guidelines for managers to follow to promote high levels of employee motivation. Effective managers such as George Fisher in the "Case in Contrast" tend to follow many of these guidelines, whereas ineffective managers often fail to follow them and seem to have trouble motivating organizational members.

Need Theories

need A requirement or necessity for survival and well-being.

need theories Theories of motivation that focus on what needs people are trying to satisfy at work and what outcomes will satisfy those needs.

A **need** is a requirement or necessity for survival and well-being. The basic premise of need theories is that people are motivated to obtain outcomes at work that will satisfy their needs. **Need theories** suggest that in order to motivate a person to contribute valuable inputs to a job and perform at a high level, a manager must determine what needs the person is trying to satisfy at work and ensure that the person receives outcomes that help to satisfy those needs when the person performs at a high level and helps the organization achieve its goals.

There are several different need theories. In Chapter 11, we discussed David McClelland's ideas about managers' needs for achievement, affiliation, and power. Here, we discuss Abraham Maslow's hierarchy of needs, Clayton Alderfer's ERG theory, and Frederick Herzberg's motivator–hygiene theory. These theories describe needs that people try to satisfy at work. In doing so, they provide managers with insights about what outcomes will motivate members of an organization to perform at a high level and contribute inputs to help the organization achieve its goals.

Maslow's hierarchy of needs An arrangement of five basic needs that, according to Maslow, motivate behaviour. Maslow proposed that the lowest level of unmet needs is the prime motivator and that only one level of needs is motivational at a time.

Maslow's Hierarchy of Needs

Psychologist Abraham Maslow proposed that all people seek to satisfy five basic kinds of needs: physiological needs, safety needs, belongingness needs, esteem needs, and self-actualization needs (see Table 12.1).[4] He suggested that these needs constitute a **hierarchy of needs**, with the most basic or compelling needs—physiological and safety needs—at the bottom. Maslow argued that these lowest-level needs must be met before a person will strive to satisfy needs higher up in the hierarchy, such as self-esteem needs. Once a need is satisfied, he proposed, it ceases to operate as a source of motivation. The lowest level of *unmet* needs in the hierarchy is the prime motivator of behaviour; if and when this level is satisfied, needs at the next highest level in the hierarchy motivate behaviour.

Although this theory identifies needs that are likely to be important sources of motivation for many people, research does not support Maslow's contention that there is a need hierarchy or his notion that only one level of needs is motivational at a time.[5] Nevertheless, a key conclusion can be drawn from Maslow's theory: People differ in what needs they are trying to satisfy at work. To have a motivated workforce, managers must determine which needs employees are trying to satisfy in organizations and

Vancouver-based Pazmac Enterprises owner Steve Scarlett recognizes that his employees have needs other than money. Scarlett hires a personal trainer to help his employees meet their fitness goals.

Table 12.1
Maslow's Hierarchy of Needs

	Needs	Description	Examples of How Managers Can Help People Satisfy These Needs at Work
Highest-level needs	Self-actualization needs	The needs to realize one's full potential as a human being	By giving people the opportunity to use their skills and abilities to the fullest extent possible
	Esteem needs	The needs to feel good about oneself and one's capabilities, to be respected by others, and to receive recognition and appreciation	By granting promotions and recognizing accomplishments
	Belongingness needs	Needs for social interaction, friendship, affection, and love	By promoting good interpersonal relations and organizing social functions such as company picnics and holiday parties
	Safety needs	Needs for security, stability, and a safe environment	By providing job security, adequate medical benefits, and safe working conditions
Lowest-level needs (most basic or compelling)	Physiological needs	Basic needs for things such as food, water, and shelter that must be met in order for a person to survive	By providing a level of pay that enables a person to buy food and clothing and have adequate housing

The lowest level of unsatisfied needs motivates behaviour; once this level of needs is satisfied, a person tries to satisfy the needs at the next level.

then make sure that individuals receive outcomes that will satisfy their needs when they perform at a high level and contribute to organizational effectiveness. By doing this, managers align the interests of individual members with the interests of the organization as a whole. By doing what is good for the organization (that is, performing at a high level), employees receive outcomes that satisfy their needs.

In addition, in an increasingly global economy it is important for managers to realize that citizens of different countries might differ in the needs they seek to satisfy through work.[6] Some research suggests, for example, that people in Greece and Japan are especially motivated by safety needs and that people in Sweden, Norway, and Denmark are motivated by belongingness needs.[7] In poor countries with low standards of living, physiological and safety needs are likely to be the prime motivators of behaviour. As countries become wealthier and have higher standards of living, it is likely that needs related to personal growth and accomplishment (such as esteem and self-actualization) become important as motivators of behaviour.

Alderfer's ERG Theory

Alderfer's ERG theory
The theory that three universal needs—for existence, relatedness, and growth—constitute a hierarchy of needs and motivate behaviour. Alderfer proposed that needs at more than one level can be motivational at the same time.

Clayton Alderfer's **ERG theory** collapses the five categories of needs in Maslow's hierarchy into three universal categories—existence, relatedness, and growth—also arranged in a hierarchy (see Table 12.2). Alderfer agrees with Maslow that as lower-level needs become satisfied, a person seeks to satisfy higher-level needs. Unlike Maslow, however, Alderfer believes that a person can be motivated by needs at more than one level at the same time. A cashier in a supermarket, for example, may be motivated both by existence needs and by relatedness needs. The existence needs motivate the cashier to come to work regularly and not make mistakes so that the job will be secure and he or she will be able to pay rent and buy food. The relatedness needs motivate the cashier to become friends with some of the other cashiers and have a good relationship with the store manager. Alderfer also suggests that when people experience need frustration or are unable

Table 12.2
Alderfer's ERG Theory

	Needs	Description	Examples of How Managers Can Help People Satisfy These Needs at Work
Highest-level needs	**Growth needs**	The needs for self-development and creative and productive work	By allowing people to continually improve their skills and abilities and engage in meaningful work
↕	**Relatedness needs**	The needs to have good interpersonal relations, to share thoughts and feelings, and to have open two-way communication	By promoting good interpersonal relations and by providing accurate feedback
Lowest-level needs	**Existence needs**	Basic needs for food, water, clothing, shelter, and a secure and safe environment	By promoting enough pay to provide for the basic necessities of life and safe working conditions

As lower-level needs are satisfied, a person is motivated to satisfy higher-level needs. When a person is unable to satisfy higher-level needs (or is frustrated), motivation to satisfy lower-level needs increases

to satisfy needs at a certain level, they will focus all the more on satisfying the needs at the next lowest level in the hierarchy.[8]

As with Maslow's theory, research does not tend to support some of the specific ideas outlined in ERG theory, such as the existence of the three-level need hierarchy that Alderfer proposed.[9] However, for managers, the important message from ERG theory is the same as that from Maslow's theory: Determine what needs your subordinates are trying to satisfy at work, and make sure that they receive outcomes that will satisfy those needs when they perform at a high level and help the organization achieve its goals.

Herzberg's Motivator–Hygiene Theory

Herzberg's motivator–hygiene theory A need theory that distinguishes between motivator needs (related to the nature of the work itself) and hygiene needs (related to the physical and psychological context in which the work is performed). Herzberg proposed that motivator needs must be met in order for motivation and job satisfaction to be high.

According to **Herzberg's motivator–hygiene theory**, people have two sets of needs or requirements: motivator needs and hygiene needs.[10] *Motivator needs* are related to the nature of the work itself and how challenging it is. Outcomes such as interesting work, autonomy, responsibility, being able to grow and develop on the job, and a sense of accomplishment and achievement help to satisfy motivator needs. In order to have a highly motivated and satisfied workforce, Herzberg suggested, managers should take steps to ensure that employees' motivator needs are being met.

Hygiene needs are related to the physical and psychological context in which the work is performed. Hygiene needs are satisfied by outcomes such as pleasant and comfortable working conditions, pay, job security, good relationships with co-workers, and effective supervision. According to Herzberg, when hygiene needs are not met, workers will be dissatisfied, and when hygiene needs are met, workers will not be dissatisfied. Satisfying hygiene needs will not, however, result in high levels of motivation or even high levels of job satisfaction. For motivation and job satisfaction to be high, hygiene needs *and* motivator needs must be met.

Many research studies have tested Herzberg's propositions, and, by and large, the theory fails to receive support.[11] Nevertheless, Herzberg's formulations have contributed to our understanding of motivation in at least two ways. First, Herzberg helped to focus researchers' and managers' attention on the important distinction between intrinsic motivation (related to motivator needs) and extrinsic motivation (related to hygiene needs), covered earlier in the chapter. Second, his theory helped to prompt researchers and managers to study how jobs can be designed or redesigned so that they are intrinsically motivating.

The "Management Insight" shows how the owner of Pazmac Enterprises uses insights from needs theories to motivate his employees.

Management Insight

Treating People Right at Pazmac Enterprises

Steve Scarlett, owner of Langley, BC-based Pazmac Enterprises, recognizes the importance of addressing employees' needs in order to motivate them.[12] The employees at Scarlett's machine shop enjoy perks often associated with employees in the high-tech industry: during the work week, they have access to personal trainers, a fully equipped exercise room, and a swimming pool. On weekends, the company organizes guided hikes, snowshoeing expeditions, and other activities as desired.

These are great extrinsic rewards, but Scarlett also provides intrinsic rewards. There are no job titles at the company so that there are fewer barriers, and relationships can more easily be formed among all employees. All employees are involved in decision making. "I believe business needs to be planned diplomatically … we talk things out," says Scarlett.

Scarlett is also concerned about employees' hygiene needs. Usually machine shops are noisy and messy, the floors are covered with oil, and employees wear dirty overalls. Pazmac, however, is spotlessly clean. The lunch room is tastefully designed, and the men's washroom is plush, with potpourri bowls and paintings on the walls.

"I treat people the way I'd want to be treated. At business school, you learn all about managing fixed assets and depreciation of equipment, but not a moment is spent on the value of people," Scarlett says. He tries very conscientiously to meet the needs of his employees to keep them motivated.

Needs theories address the different needs that individuals have that could be used to motivate them. Process theories, which we cover below, focus on the more concrete ways of actually motivating someone. Within the process theories, we cover expectancy theory and goal-setting theory.

Expectancy Theory

expectancy theory
The theory that motivation will be high when workers believe that high levels of effort will lead to high performance, and high performance will lead to the attainment of desired outcomes.

Expectancy theory, formulated by Victor H. Vroom in the 1960s, posits that motivation will be high when workers believe that high levels of effort will lead to high performance, and high performance will lead to the attainment of desired outcomes. Expectancy theory is one of the most popular theories of work motivation because it focuses on all three parts of the motivation equation: inputs, performance, and outcomes. Expectancy theory identifies three major factors that determine a person's motivation: *expectancy, instrumentality,* and *valence* (see Figure 12.2).[13]

Expectancy

expectancy In expectancy theory, a perception about the extent to which effort will result in a certain level of performance.

Expectancy is a person's perception about the extent to which effort (an input) will result in a certain level of performance. A person's level of expectancy determines whether he or she believes that a high level of effort will result in a high level of performance. People are motivated to put forth a lot of effort on their jobs only if they think that their effort will pay off in high performance—that is, if they have a high expectancy. Think about how motivated you would be to study for a test if you thought that, no matter how hard you tried, you would get a D. Think

Figure 12.2
Expectancy, Instrumentality, and Valence

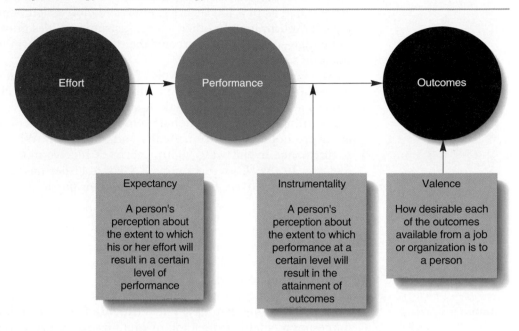

about how motivated a marketing manager would be who thought that, no matter how hard he or she worked, there was no way to increase sales of an unpopular product. In these cases, expectancy is low, so overall motivation is also low.

Members of an organization will be motivated to put forth a high level of effort only if they think that doing so will lead to high performance. In other words, in order for people's motivation to be high, expectancy must be high. Thus, in attempting to influence motivation, managers need to make sure that their subordinates believe that if they do try hard they actually can succeed. George Fisher actively encourages high levels of expectancy among Kodak employees by expressing confidence in their ability to perform at a high level, holding them to high standards, and giving them the responsibility to determine the best ways of achieving goals. As the "Case in Contrast" indicates, the Mars brothers' excessive criticism leads to relatively low levels of expectancy among Mars employees, who do not believe in their own ability to succeed and consequently have low motivation.

In addition to expressing confidence in subordinates, another way for managers to boost subordinates' expectancy levels and motivation is by providing training so that people have all the expertise they need for high performance. At Julius Blum GmbH, a manufacturing company that produces hinges in Hoechst, Austria, managers boost their employees' expectancy and motivation through a four-year apprenticeship program combining classroom-type and on-the-job instruction that costs practically $7.75 million a year. The program is well worth its cost, however. Blum has some of the best-trained employees in Austria, and the combination of their training and high expectancy and motivation has resulted in the company being very successful.[14]

Julius Blum GmbH
www.blum.com/

instrumentality

In expectancy theory, a perception about the extent to which performance will result in the attainment of outcomes.

Instrumentality

Expectancy captures a person's perceptions about the relationship between effort and performance. **Instrumentality**, the second major concept in expectancy theory, is a person's perception about the extent to which performance at a certain level will result in the attainment of outcomes (see Figure 12.2). According to expectancy theory, employees will be motivated to perform at a high level only if they think that high performance will lead to (or is *instrumental* to attaining) outcomes such as pay, job security, interesting job assignments, bonuses, or a feeling of accomplishment. In other words, instrumentalities must be high for motivation to be high—people must perceive that if they do perform highly, they will receive outcomes.

Managers promote high levels of instrumentality when they clearly link performance to desired outcomes. In addition, managers must clearly communicate this linkage to subordinates. By making sure that outcomes available in an organization are distributed to organizational members on the basis of their performance, managers promote high instrumentality and motivation. When outcomes are linked to performance in this way, high performers receive more outcomes than low performers. In the "Case in Contrast," George Fisher raised levels of instrumentality for Kodak employees by closely linking their pay to their performance.

Valence

valence In expectancy theory, how desirable each of the outcomes available from a job or organization is to a person.

Although it is important for all members of an organization to have high expectancies and instrumentalities, expectancy theory acknowledges that people differ in their preferences for outcomes. For many people, pay is the most important outcome of working. For others, a feeling of accomplishment or enjoying one's work is more important than pay. The term **valence** refers to how desirable each of the outcomes available from a job or organization is to a person. To motivate organizational members, managers need to determine which outcomes have high valence for them—are highly desired—and make sure that those outcomes are provided when members perform at a high level. From the "Case in Contrast," it appears that for many employees at Mars, pay that is twice the industry average has such high valence that it keeps them working for the demanding Mars brothers despite the presence of few other desirable outcomes.

Bringing it All Together

According to expectancy theory, high motivation results from high levels of expectancy, instrumentality, and valence (see Figure 12.3). If any one of these factors is low, motivation is likely to be low. No matter how tightly desired outcomes are linked to performance, if a person thinks that it is practically impossible for

Figure 12.3
Expectancy Theory

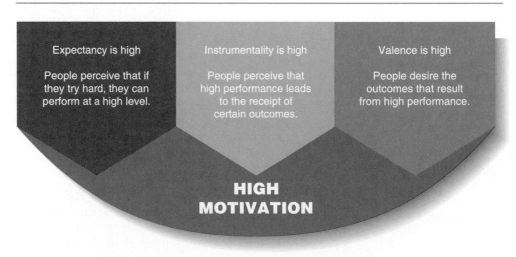

him or her to perform at a high level, then motivation to perform at a high level will be exceedingly low. Similarly, if a person does not think that outcomes are linked to high performance, or if a person does not desire the outcomes that are linked to high performance, then motivation to perform at a high level will be low.

Managers of successful companies often strive to ensure that employees' levels of expectancy, instrumentality, and valence are high so that they will be highly motivated, as is illustrated by Motorola's efforts at managing globally.

Managing Globally

Motorola Promotes High Motivation in Malaysia

Motorola (www.motorola.com) is a truly global organization with major operations in countries such as India and China.[15] At Motorola's plant in Penang, Malaysia, which produces walkie-talkies and cordless phones, workers have such high levels of motivation that managers are trying to transplant what goes on there to some of Motorola's US operations. Key to Motorola's success in Malaysia is the fact that employees in the Penang plant have high levels of expectancy, instrumentality, and valence, and are highly motivated.

What did managers do to motivate workers in Malaysia, a developing country in which managers in most organizations typically treat workers not as important contributors to the organization but as easily replaceable units of labour? First, Motorola's managers made a major commitment to boosting expectancy levels so that workers are confident that they can perform highly and make valuable contributions to the organization, not only in their actual job performance but also in the form of suggestions for ways to cut costs and boost quality. New employees have two days of classroom instruction in which they are taught about quality control, how to use statistical procedures, and how to work together in teams to come up with ideas to improve quality and cut costs. Employees then have, on average, 48 hours of classroom training per year to further hone their skills. The training boosts not only workers' skills and capabilities but also their confidence and expectancy levels. New employees are also assigned as a mentor a skilled worker who helps them and provides them with encouragement. Motorola pays for engineers in the plant to receive a master's degree, and the best production workers are selected for a two-year training program to become technicians.

Penang managers also took steps to boost instrumentality by making sure that employees' efforts lead to outcomes they desire. Workers who win quality competitions are given trophies and other forms of recognition. Workers who suggest at least 100 cost-saving ideas in a year and have at least 60 percent of them implemented become members of the prestigious "100 Club." Belonging to the club does not bring many material rewards, but the recognition alone is a highly valent outcome for workers.

Mariana Osman is a member of the 100 Club. She is responsible for reworking cordless phones that have quality defects and made over 150 suggestions for cutting costs and reducing defects in one year. Valent outcomes (in addition to the recognition) that Motorola provides to Osman for her high performance and valuable contributions are a salary that is relatively high in Malaysia ($287 per month), job security, promotional opportunities (which someday may lead to her being a manager or engineer), and the feeling that she is a valued member of Motorola. As Osman puts it, "I'm one of the family here ... I want to do what is best for the company."[16]

Employees like Osman are the norm rather than the exception at the Penang plant. So it is no wonder that Motorola is taking steps to boost expectancy, instrumentality, valence, and ultimately motivation at all of its plants by using some of the initiatives that Penang managers put into place, such as training to boost expectancy and linking valent outcomes to high performance.[17]

Goal-Setting Theory

goal-setting theory
A theory that focuses on identifying the types of goals that are most effective in producing high levels of motivation and performance and explaining why goals have these effects.

Edwin Locke
www.rhsmith.umd.edu/mao/elocke/

Gary Latham
www.mgmt.utoronto.ca/faculty/bios/latham.htm

Goal-setting theory, also a process theory, focuses on motivating workers to contribute their inputs to their jobs and organizations; in this way it is similar to expectancy theory and equity theory. But goal-setting theory takes this focus a step further by considering as well how managers can ensure that organizational members focus their inputs in the direction of high performance and the achievement of organizational goals.

Ed Locke and Gary Latham, the leading researchers on goal-setting theory, suggest that the goals that organizational members strive to attain are prime determinants of their motivation and subsequent performance. A *goal* is what a person is trying to accomplish through his or her efforts and behaviours.[18] Just as you may have a goal to get a good grade in this course, so do members of an organization have goals that they strive to meet. In the "Case in Contrast," we mentioned that researchers in Kodak's labs have goals for finishing their projects in a timely fashion. Similarly, salespeople at The Bay strive to meet sales goals, and top managers have market share and profitability goals.

Goal-setting theory suggests that in order to result in high motivation and performance, goals must be *specific* and *difficult*.[19] Specific goals are often quantitative–a salesperson's goal to sell $200 worth of merchandise per day, a scientist's goal to finish a project in one year, a CEO's goal to reduce debt by 40 percent and increase revenues by 20 percent, a restaurant manager's goal to serve 150 customers per evening. In contrast to specific goals, vague goals such as "doing your best" or "selling as much as you can" do not have much motivational force.

Difficult goals are hard but not impossible to attain. In contrast to difficult goals, easy goals are goals that practically everyone can attain, and moderate goals are goals that about one-half of the people can attain. Both easy and moderate goals have less motivational power than difficult goals.

Regardless of whether specific, difficult goals are set by managers, workers, or managers and workers together, they lead to high levels of motivation and performance. At Kodak, George Fisher sets specific, difficult goals for his employees but then leaves decisions about how to meet the goals up to them. When managers set goals for their subordinates, it is important that their subordinates accept the goals or agree to work toward them and also that they are committed to them or really want to attain them. Some managers find that having subordinates participate in the actual setting of goals boosts their acceptance of and commitment to the goals. In addition, it is important for organizational members to receive *feedback* about how they are doing; feedback can often be provided by the performance appraisal and feedback component of an organization's human resource management system (see Chapter 10).

As a part of George Fisher's attempt to motivate his workforce, he created teams of workers who were given responsibility for developing innovative new products quickly and cost effectively. Kodak's Zebra Team, so named because it is responsible for Kodak's black-and-white photographic products, has achieved major gains in productivity and profitability over the last two years.

Do difficult goals really motivate?

Specific, difficult goals affect motivation in two ways. First, they motivate people to contribute more inputs to their jobs. Specific, difficult goals cause people to put forth high levels of effort, for example. Just as you would study harder if you were trying to get an A in a course instead of a C, so too will a salesperson work harder to reach a $200 sales goal instead of a $100 goal. Specific, difficult goals also cause people to be more persistent when they run into difficulties than easy, moderate, or vague goals. A salesperson who is told to sell as much as possible might stop trying on a slow day, whereas having a specific, difficult goal to reach causes him or her to keep trying.

A second way in which specific, difficult goals affect motivation is by helping people focus their inputs in the right direction. These goals let people know what they should be focusing their attention on, be it increasing the quality of customer service or sales or lowering new product development times. The fact that the goals are specific and difficult also frequently causes people to develop *action plans* for reaching them.[20] Action plans can include the strategies that will be used to attain the goals, and timetables or schedules for the completion of different activities crucial to goal attainment. Like the goals themselves, action plans also help ensure that efforts are focused in the right direction and that people do not get sidetracked along the way.

Although specific, difficult goals have been found to increase motivation and performance in a wide variety of jobs and organizations both in Canada and abroad, recent research suggests that they may detract from performance under certain conditions. When people are performing complicated and very challenging tasks that require a considerable amount of learning, specific, difficult goals may actually impair performance.[21] All of a person's attention needs to be focused on learning complicated and difficult tasks. Striving to reach a specific, difficult goal may detract from performance on complex tasks because some of a person's attention is directed away from learning about the task and toward trying to figure out how to achieve the goal. Once a person has learned the task and it no longer seems complicated or difficult, then the assignment of specific, difficult goals is likely to have its usual effects.

Reinforcement Theory

reinforcement theory
A motivation theory based on the relationship between a given behaviour and its consequence.

reinforcement Anything that causes a given behaviour to be repeated or stopped.

positive reinforcement
Giving people outcomes they desire when they perform organizationally functional behaviours.

Reinforcement theory is a motivation theory that looks at the relationship between behaviour and its consequences. **Reinforcement** is defined as anything that causes a certain behaviour to be repeated or stopped. Four reinforcements are generally discussed in the theory: positive reinforcement, negative reinforcement, extinction and punishment.

POSITIVE REINFORCEMENT   **Positive reinforcement** gives people outcomes they desire when they perform organizationally functional behaviours. These outcomes, called positive reinforcers, include any outcomes that a person desires, such as pay, praise, or a promotion. Organizationally functional behaviours are behaviours that contribute to organizational effectiveness; they can include producing high-quality goods and services, providing high-quality customer service, and meeting deadlines. By linking positive reinforcers to the performance of functional behaviours, managers motivate people to perform the desired behaviours. In the "Case in Contrast," for example, George Fisher motivates Kodak employees to perform desired behaviours by giving them positive feedback and praise and by linking pay to performance levels. Maple Leaf Foods gives positive reinforcement to employees to encourage them to show up for work, as this "Management Insight" shows.

Management Insight

Maple Leaf Raffles Trucks

Employees at a hog slaughterhouse in Brandon, Manitoba are known for missing a lot of work.[22] "The job sucks. That's basically it," said Scott Oldenburger. "It's cold, you stand in one spot for hours on end, you're not allowed to take a p— unless it's on your scheduled break. It's gross." Oldenburger only worked there for about a month before he decided to quit. And he had one of the more pleasant jobs on the production line: cutting shoulders.

Managers at Maple Leaf Foods, which owns the slaughterhouse, offer a variety of incentives to encourage workers to show up for their shifts. They have even raffled off trucks to the bung flushers, head splitters, and kidney poppers at the plant. To be eligible for the draw, held every three months, employees have to show up for every one of their shifts during that period. Employees get bonuses of 75 cents an hour for perfect attendance during shorter periods. Regular wages range from $8.25 to $13.

The incentive program has paid off. Before Maple Leaf started giving out the rewards, 12 percent of the employees skipped work each day. Since the rewards, absenteeism is down to about 7 to 8 percent.

The plant processes 45 000 hogs per week. Employees work under assembly line conditions that are highly mechanized, with separate jobs for cutting off tongues, ears and tails.

The plant's human resources manager, Steve LeBlanc, suggests that the plant is not as unpleasant as it sounds, however. "Everything is very well-lit in our plant, it's clean and there is a lot of technology there. When people take a walk through our plant, they're usually pleasantly surprised. But it is work."

negative reinforcement
Eliminating or removing undesired outcomes when people perform organizationally functional behaviours.

NEGATIVE REINFORCEMENT   **Negative reinforcement** also can be used to encourage members of an organization to perform desired or organizationally functional behaviours. Managers using negative reinforcement actually eliminate or remove undesired outcomes once the functional behaviour is performed. These undesired outcomes, called *negative reinforcers*, can range from a manager's constant nagging or criticism, to unpleasant assignments, to the ever-present threat of losing one's job. When negative reinforcement is used, people are motivated to perform behaviours because they want to stop receiving or avoid undesired outcomes. Managers who try to encourage salespeople to sell more by threatening them with being fired are using negative reinforcement. In this case, the negative reinforcer is the threat of job loss, which is removed once the functional behaviours are performed.

Whenever possible, managers should try to use positive reinforcement. Negative reinforcement can make for a very unpleasant work environment and even a negative culture in an organization. No one likes to be nagged, threatened, or exposed to other kinds of negative outcomes. The use of negative reinforcement sometimes causes subordinates to resent managers and try to get back at them.

extinction Curtailing the performance of dysfunctional behaviours by eliminating whatever is reinforcing them.

EXTINCTION   Sometimes members of an organization are motivated to perform behaviours that actually detract from organizational effectiveness. One way for managers to curtail the performance of dysfunctional behaviours is to eliminate whatever is reinforcing the behaviours. This process is called **extinction**.

Suppose a manager has a subordinate who frequently stops by the office to chat—sometimes about work-related matters but at other times about various topics ranging from politics to last night's football game. Though the chats are fun, the manager ends up working late to catch up. To extinguish this behaviour, the manager stops acting interested in these non-work-related conversations and keeps responses polite and friendly but brief. No longer being reinforced with a pleasurable conversation, the subordinate eventually ceases to be motivated to interrupt the manager during working hours to discuss non-work-related issues.

PUNISHMENT Sometimes managers cannot rely on extinction to eliminate dysfunctional behaviours because they do not have control over whatever is reinforcing the behaviour or because they cannot afford the time needed for extinction to work. When employees are performing dangerous behaviours or behaviours that are illegal or unethical, the behaviour needs to be eliminated immediately. Therefore the manager will use **punishment**, administering an undesired or negative consequence to subordinates when they perform the dysfunctional behaviour. Punishments used by organizations range from verbal reprimands to pay cuts, temporary suspensions, demotions, and firings. Punishment, however, can have some unintended side effects—resentment, loss of self-respect, a desire for retaliation, etc.—and should be used only when absolutely necessary. The "Case in Contrast" relates how the Mars brothers' excessive use of punishment is dysfunctional for their company.

ORGANIZATIONAL BEHAVIOUR MODIFICATION When managers systematically apply operant conditioning techniques to promote the performance of organizationally functional behaviours and discourage the performance of dysfunctional behaviours, they are engaging in **organizational behaviour modification** (OB MOD).[23] OB MOD has been used successfully to improve productivity, efficiency, attendance, punctuality, compliance with safety procedures, and other important behaviours in a wide variety of organizations. The five basic steps in OB MOD are described in Figure 12.4.

OB MOD works best for behaviours that are specific, objective, and countable—such as attendance and punctuality, making sales, or putting telephones together—which lend themselves to careful scrutiny and control. OB MOD may be questioned because of its lack of relevance to certain kinds of work behaviours (for example, the many work behaviours that are not specific, objective, and countable). Some people also have questioned it on ethical grounds. Critics of OB MOD suggest that it is overly controlling and robs workers of their dignity, individuality, freedom of choice, and even their creativity. Supporters counter that OB MOD is a highly effective means of promoting organizational efficiency. Both sides of this argument have some merit. What is clear, however, is that when used appropriately, OB MOD provides managers with a technique to motivate the performance of at least some organizationally functional behaviours.

In trying to understand how these theories of motivation fit together, it may be helpful to remember that needs theories suggest that individuals have needs, and they will be motivated to have these needs met. Expectancy, goal-setting, and reinforcement theories show the processes by which individuals can be encouraged to behave in ways that earn rewards. Job design, which we discussed in Chapter 8, can also be a way of motivating individuals. Job rotation, job enlargement, and job enrichment can increase an employee's job satisfaction, and thus lead him or her to be more motivated in performing the job.

While we have covered some of the process theories of motivation, what still needs to be addressed is the issue of fairness in allocating rewards. Equity theory, which we discuss below, suggests that individuals evaluate and interpret rewards to assess whether they have been treated fairly compared to others.

Equity Theory

Equity theory is a theory of motivation that concentrates on people's perceptions of the fairness of their work *outcomes* relative to, or in proportion to, their work *inputs.* Equity theory complements need and expectancy theories by focusing on

punishment

Administering an undesired or negative consequence when dysfunctional behaviour occurs.

organizational behaviour modification

The systematic application of operant conditioning techniques to promote the performance of organizationally functional behaviours and discourage the performance of dysfunctional behaviours.

equity theory A theory of motivation that focuses on people's perceptions of the fairness of their work outcomes relative to their work inputs.

Figure 12.4
Five Steps in OB MOD

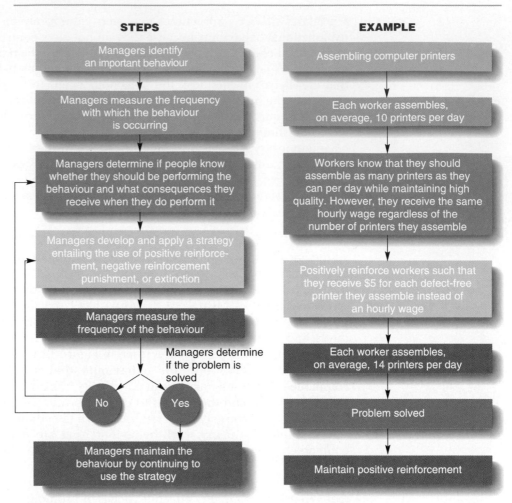

Source: Adapted from F. Luthans and R. Kreitner, *Organizational Behaviour Modification and Beyond* (Glenview, IL: Scott, Foresman, 1985).

how people perceive the relationship between the outcomes they receive from their jobs and organizations and the inputs they contribute. Equity theory was formulated in the 1960s by J. Stacy Adams, who stressed that what is important in determining motivation is the *relative* rather than the *absolute* level of outcomes a person receives and inputs a person contributes. Specifically, motivation is influenced by the comparison of one's own outcome/input ratio with the outcome/input ratio of a referent.[24] The *referent* could be another person or a group of people who are perceived to be similar to oneself; the referent also could be oneself in a previous job or one's expectations about what outcome/input ratios should be. In a comparison of one's own outcome/input ratio to a referent's outcome/input ratio, one's *perceptions* of outcomes and inputs (not any objective indicator of them) are key.

Equity

equity The justice, impartiality, and fairness to which all organizational members are entitled.

Equity exists when a person perceives his or her own outcome/input ratio to be equal to a referent's outcome/input ratio. Under conditions of equity (see Table 12.3), if a referent receives more outcomes than you receive, the referent

Table 12.3
Equity Theory

Condition	Person		Referent	Example
Equity	$\dfrac{\text{Outcomes}}{\text{Inputs}}$	$=$	$\dfrac{\text{Outcomes}}{\text{Inputs}}$	An engineer perceives that he contributes more inputs (time and effort), and receives proportionally more outcomes (a higher salary and choice job assignments), than his referent.
Underpayment inequity	$\dfrac{\text{Outcomes}}{\text{Inputs}}$	$<$ (less than)	$\dfrac{\text{Outcomes}}{\text{Inputs}}$	An engineer perceives that he contributes more inputs but receives the same outcomes as his referent.
Overpayment inequity	$\dfrac{\text{Outcomes}}{\text{Inputs}}$	$>$ (greater than)	$\dfrac{\text{Outcomes}}{\text{Inputs}}$	An engineer perceives that he contributes the same inputs but receives more outcomes than his referent.

contributes proportionally more inputs to the organization, so his or her outcome/input ratio still equals your outcome/input ratio. Maria Lau and Claudia King, for example, both work in a shoe store in a large mall. Lau is paid more per hour than King but also contributes more inputs, including being responsible for some of the store's bookkeeping, closing the store, and periodically depositing cash in the bank. When King compares her outcome/input ratio to Lau's (her referent's), she perceives the ratios to be equitable because Lau's higher level of pay (an outcome) is proportional to her higher level of inputs (bookkeeping, closing the store, and going to the bank).

Similarly, under conditions of equity, if you receive more outcomes than a referent, then your inputs are perceived to be proportionally higher. Continuing with our example, when Lau compares her outcome/input ratio to King's (her referent's) outcome/input ratio, she perceives them to be equitable because her higher level of pay is proportional to her higher level of inputs.

When equity exists, people are motivated to continue contributing their current levels of inputs to their organizations in order to receive their current levels of outcomes. Under conditions of equity, if people wish to increase their outcomes, they are motivated to increase their inputs.

Inequity

inequity Lack of fairness.

Inequity, lack of fairness, exists when a person's outcome/input ratio is not perceived to be equal to a referent's. Inequity creates pressure or tension inside people and motivates them to restore equity by bringing the two ratios back into balance.

There are two types of inequity: underpayment inequity and overpayment inequity (see Table 12.3). **Underpayment inequity** exists when a person's own outcome/input ratio is perceived to be *less* than that of a referent: In comparing yourself to a referent, you think that you are *not* receiving the outcomes you should be, given your inputs. **Overpayment inequity** exists when a person perceives that his or her own outcome/input ratio is *greater* than that of a referent: In comparing yourself to a referent, you think that the referent is receiving fewer outcomes than he or she should be, given his or her inputs.

underpayment inequity Inequity that exists when a person perceives that his or her own outcome/input ratio is less than the ratio of a referent.

overpayment inequity Inequity that exists when a person perceives that his or her own outcome/input ratio is greater than the ratio of a referent.

Ways to Restore Equity

According to equity theory, both underpayment inequity and overpayment inequity create tension that motivates most people to restore equity by bringing the ratios back into balance.[25] When people experience *underpayment* inequity, they may be motivated to lower their inputs by reducing their working hours, putting forth less effort on the job, or being absent, or they may be motivated to increase their outcomes by asking for a raise or a promotion. Susan Richie, a financial analyst at a large corporation, noticed that she was working longer hours and getting more work accomplished than a co-worker who had the same position, yet they both received the exact same pay and other outcomes. To restore equity, Richie decided to stop coming in early and staying late. Alternatively, she could have tried to restore equity by trying to increase her outcomes by, for example, asking her boss for a raise.

When people experience *overpayment* inequity, they may try to restore equity by changing their perceptions of their own or their referents' inputs or outcomes. Equity can be restored when people "realize" that they are contributing more inputs than they originally thought. Equity also can be restored by perceiving the referent's inputs to be lower or the referent's outcomes to be higher than one originally thought. When equity is restored in this way, actual inputs and outcomes are unchanged. What is changed is how people think about or view their own or the referent's inputs and outcomes. Mary McMann experienced overpayment inequity when she realized that she was being paid $2 an hour more than a co-worker who had the same job as she did in a record store and who contributed the same amount of inputs. McMann restored equity by changing her perceptions of her inputs. She "realized" that she worked harder than her co-worker and solved more problems that came up in the store.

Experiencing either overpayment or underpayment inequity, you might decide that your referent is not appropriate because, for example, the referent is too different from yourself. Choosing a more appropriate referent may bring the ratios back into balance.

Finally, when people experience *underpayment* inequity and other means of equity restoration fail, they may leave the organization.

Motivation is highest when as many people as possible in an organization perceive that they are being equitably treated—their outcomes and inputs are in balance. Top contributors and performers are motivated to continue contributing a high level of inputs because they are receiving the outcomes they deserve. Mediocre contributors and performers realize that if they want to increase their outcomes, they have to increase their inputs. Managers of effective organizations, like George Fisher at Eastman Kodak, realize the importance of equity for motivation and performance and continually strive to ensure that employees feel they are being equitably treated.

Tips for Managers

Expectancy and Equity Theories

1. Express sincere confidence in your subordinates' capabilities and let them know that you expect them to succeed.

2. Distribute outcomes based on important inputs and performance levels and clearly communicate to your subordinates that this is the case.

3. Determine which outcomes your subordinates desire and try to gain control over as many of these as possible (i.e., have the authority to distribute or withhold outcomes).

4. Provide clear information to your subordinates about which inputs are most valuable for them to contribute to their jobs and the organization in order to receive desired outcomes.

Pay and Motivation

In Chapter 10, we discussed how managers establish a pay level and structure for an organization as a whole. Here we focus on how, once a pay level and structure are in place, managers can use pay to motivate employees to perform at a high level and attain their work goals. Pay is used to motivate entry-level workers, first-line and middle managers, and even top managers such as CEOs. Pay can be used to motivate people to perform behaviours that will help an organization achieve its goals (as at Kodak in the "Case in Contrast"), and it can be used to motivate people to join and remain with an organization (as at Mars Inc.).

How does pay motivate? Each of the theories described in this chapter alludes to the importance of pay and suggests that pay should be based on performance:

- *Need theories:* People should be able to satisfy their needs by performing at a high level; pay can be used to satisfy several different kinds of needs.

- *Expectancy theory:* Instrumentality, the association between performance and outcomes such as pay, must be high for motivation to be high. In addition, pay is an outcome that has high valence for many people.

- *Goal-setting theory:* Outcomes such as pay should be linked to the attainment of goals.

- *Reinforcement theory:* The distribution of outcomes such as pay should be contingent on the performance of organizationally functional behaviours.

- *Equity theory:* Outcomes such as pay should be distributed in proportion to inputs (including performance levels).

As these theories suggest, to promote high motivation, managers should base the distribution of pay to organizational members on performance levels so that high performers receive more pay than low performers (other things being equal).[26]

In deciding whether to pay for performance, managers also have to determine whether to use salary increases or bonuses. Thus some pay-for-performance programs (particularly those that use bonuses) are variable-pay programs. With variable pay, earnings go up and down annually based on performance.[27] Thus, there is no guarantee that an individual will earn as much this year as last. In 1996, roughly two-thirds of non-management employees in Canada had some sort of variable-pay plan, up from one-third in 1992. The programs are more common for nonunionized workers than unionized ones. Prem Benimadhu from the Conference Board of Canada notes, "Canadian unions have been very allergic to variable compensation."[28] In addition to wage uncertainty, employees may object to pay for performance if they feel that factors out of their control might affect the extent to which bonuses are possible.

Pillsbury Canada
www.pillsbury.com/
world/Canada.asp

Markham, ON-based Pillsbury Canada Limited has a Value Incentive Plan under which employee performance is rewarded at three levels: corporate, team, and individual.[29] When corporate financial targets are met or exceeded, a percentage-of-pay bonus results. If teams meet their own cost reduction-based goals, and quality and profit improvement are above the corporate plan, employees can earn additional percentage-of-pay bonuses. Finally, when employees meet two or three key individual objectives, they can earn an equivalent percentage-of-pay bonus.

Not all organizations reward performance at all three levels, as does Pillsbury Canada or Toronto-based Canada Life. More usually, managers have to decide whether to base pay on individual, group, or organizational performance. Before considering that issue, however, the "Management Insight" suggests that managers also need to consider whether pay is the best motivator for their employees.

Management Insight

Paying Workers Well is Not Enough

Managers may not be giving enough consideration to what employees really want in terms of pay and benefits from the workplace.[30] According to a survey of 75 Canadian employers conducted between December 2000 and February 2001 by N. Winter Consulting, employers focus on compensation for their employees. Almost 60 percent of the companies said they had changed their reward strategy in recent years, giving salary increases, incentive pay, profit sharing and flexible benefits.

Meanwhile, surveys of employees show that they want "challenging work, continuous learning, flexible work arrangements and better communication with their employers." However, less than 10 percent of companies said they had recently introduced programs to help employees balance their work with their personal lives. Only 25 percent plan to introduce flexible hours, onsite childcare or subsidized fitness to their workplace in the next two years.

Companies in the survey said they were having difficulty attracting and retaining employees. Their reward plans may have something to do with this. "Paying competitively, whether through base pay or incentive pay, only puts employers on a level playing field to compete for talent. It's the price of entry but it's not enough," said Nadine Winter, president of N. Winter.

Companies may need to pay more attention to what their employees say that they want. Winter found that only 48 percent of the companies surveyed their employees to find out their needs, wants and values.

Basing Merit Pay on Individual, Group, or Organizational Performance

merit pay plan A compensation plan that bases pay on performance.

A compensation plan that bases pay on performance is often called a **merit pay plan**. Managers can base merit pay on individual, group, or organizational performance. When individual performance (such as the dollar value of merchandise a salesperson sells, the number of loudspeakers a factory worker assembles, or a lawyer's billable hours) can be accurately determined, individual motivation is likely to be highest when pay is based on individual performance.[31] When members of an organization work closely together and individual performance cannot be accurately determined (as in a team of computer programmers developing a single software package), pay cannot be based on individual performance, and a group- or organization-based plan must be used. When the attainment of organizational goals hinges on members working closely together and cooperating with each other (as in a small construction company that builds custom homes), group- or organization-based plans may be more appropriate than individual-based plans.[32]

It is possible to combine elements of an individual-based plan with a group- or organization-based plan to motivate each individual to perform highly while at the same time motivating all individuals to work well together, cooperate with each other, and help each other as needed. Pillsbury Canada's Value Incentive Plan is such a program. Employees of Pillsbury Canada are motivated to cooperate and help each other because when the firm as a whole performs well, everybody benefits by having a larger bonus fund. Employees also are motivated to contribute their inputs to the organization because their contributions determine their share of the bonus fund.

Salary Increase or Bonus?

Managers can distribute merit pay to people in the form of a salary increase or a bonus on top of regular salaries. Although the dollar amount of a salary increase or

To motivate middle managers, many organizations are returning to pay-for-performance incentive pay systems. Here, middle managers on a team at Yoplait, the yogurt maker, celebrate the results of their high performance—bonuses that will average more than $77 000 for each person.

bonus might be identical, bonuses tend to have more motivational impact for at least three reasons. First, salary levels are typically based on performance levels, cost-of-living increases, and so forth from the day that people start working in an organization, which means that the absolute level of the salary is based largely on factors unrelated to *current* performance. A five-percent merit increase in salary, for example, may seem relatively small in comparison to one's total salary. Second, a current salary increase may be affected by other factors in addition to performance, such as cost-of-living increases or across-the-board market adjustments. Third, because organizations rarely reduce salaries, salary levels tend to vary less than performance levels do. Related to this point is the fact that bonuses give managers more flexibility in distributing outcomes. If an organization is doing well, bonuses can be relatively high to reward employees for their contributions. However, unlike salary increases, bonus levels can be reduced when an organization's performance lags. All in all, bonus plans have more motivational impact than salary increases because the amount of the bonus can be directly and exclusively based on performance.[33] Toronto-based Molson, Ontario Hydro, and Bank of Montreal are examples of firms that use bonuses to pay their managers and employees.

While performance pay is becoming more common, Canada lags behind the United States in giving performance-based pay.[34] Several factors account for this: Canada has a more unionized economy, a relative lack of competition, and a large public sector. Federal and provincial government employees have not been covered by bonuses to any great extent. For instance, until recently the only bonus for federal civil servants was $800 for those in bilingual jobs. This is starting to change, however. For instance, the Alberta government, which already had performance bonuses for senior administrators and for colleges and universities, introduced them for public school teachers and administrators in March 1999.[35] Federal executives were introduced to a new bonus plan in August 1999, with their performance being evaluated against business plans and corporate priorities of their departments. Their pay will also depend on their "leadership qualities, ethics, values and how they treat their staff."[36] When British Columbia's premier, Gordon Campbell, was elected in 2001, he announced that he and all his cabinet ministers would have 20 percent of their ministerial stipend held back each year. Cabinet ministers would receive the rest of their stipend if they reached budgetary and service delivery goals and if the government as a whole met its objectives. Some may question whether federal and provincial governments are really ready to tie pay to performance, however, as this "Management Insight" points out. It is certainly worth considering what message a bonus sends to the public and to the managers when performance has been criticized.

Management Insight

Failed Performance Rewarded?

During 2000, a number of federal agencies were criticized for poor performance.[37] The Auditor General's office confirmed that there were "widespread, pervasive deficiencies" in the Human Resources Development Canada (HRDC) $1 billion grants and contributions programs. The Auditor General also found irregularities in how contracts were awarded at the Canadian International Development Agency (CIDA), which sometimes bent rules to do so. The agency was also criticized for its lack of supervision in "the executive phase of projects."

The Atlantic Opportunities Agency was criticized by the Auditor General for leasing space at an "excessive cost." The agency paid 20 to 30 percent higher leasing costs than it would have for buildings of better quality elsewhere. Transport Canada was criticized for "significant weaknesses" in how it turned over 18 of the country's largest airports to private managers. The agency "did not determine fair market value of the airports before the transfers."

Despite these findings, senior public servants at all of these agencies received large performance bonuses during 1999–2000. At HRDC, 92 percent of managers received bonuses. At CIDA, 94 of 95 managers received bonuses. At the Atlantic Opportunities Agency, all 35 managers received bonuses, while at Transport Canada 111 of 119 senior managers received bonuses.

Were the bonuses appropriate? Arguments were made on both sides. John Williams, an Alliance MP, said the government's performance bar is so low that "even bureaucrats who trip over it" can receive a bonus. A CIDA spokesperson said that "The Auditor General underlined one problem that occurred in one year, but it doesn't mean the rest of the job wasn't done well and that's why the managers and executives did receive their bonuses for 1999–2000."

Examples of Merit Pay Plans

Managers can choose among several merit pay plans, depending on the work that employees perform and other considerations. Using *piece-rate pay*, an individual-based merit plan, managers base employees' pay on the number of units each employee produces, whether televisions, computer components, or welded auto parts. Advances in technology are currently simplifying the administration of piece-rate pay in the farming industry, as indicated in this "Management Insight."

Management Insight

Semiconductors Simplify the Administration of Piece-Rate Pay

Agricultural workers have long been paid on a piece-rate basis—by the number of boxes of fruit or vegetables they pick. However, the traditional means of administering piece-rate pay for farm workers is time-consuming and tedious. For example, workers are often given a token or have a card punched for each box of produce they pack during the day. Then, at the end of the day, a manager counts the tokens or the punches on the cards and writes the number down. Figures for all workers are entered into a computer, and pay rates for the day are determined. Gary Parke, a manager and partner at Parkesdale Farms in Plant City, Florida, calls this type of system a "big payroll monster" because of the large amount of counting, record keeping, and computer entries required.

New metal buttons the size of a dime that farm workers clip to their shirts or put in their pockets have tamed the payroll monster while providing managers with important information for planning, such as how quickly a harvest is proceeding and which fields have the highest yields. The buttons are made by Dallas Semiconductor Corp.[38] and customized for use in farming by Agricultural Data Systems, based in Laguna Niguel, California. Each button contains a semiconductor that is linked to payroll computers by use of a wand-like probe in the field.[39] The wand relays the number of boxes of fruit or vegetables that each worker picks, as well as the type and quality of the produce picked, the location where it was picked, and the time and the date. The buttons are activated by touching them with the probe; hence, they are called Touch Memory Buttons.

Farm workers who pick strawberries at the Bob Jones Ranch in Oxnard, California were originally opposed to using the buttons and, after a trial period, were able to go back to the old punch card system. The workers' primary complaint was that the buttons were too controlling of their behaviour. However, according to Ann Woods, office manager at the ranch, being back on the old punch card system for just one day convinced the workers that the buttons were effective and actually saved them time as well.

Managers generally find that the buttons save time, improve accuracy, and provide valuable information about their crops and yields. Some workers have resisted the buttons because they are afraid that they give managers too much information about a worker's behaviour (detailed histories of work performance can be stored on computers). Nevertheless, the buttons have certainly helped managers to administer piece-rate pay more accurately and efficiently to farm workers while gathering useful information for planning and decision making.[40]

Using *commission pay*, another individual-based merit pay plan, managers base pay on a percentage of sales. Managers at the successful real-estate company Re/Max International Inc. use commission pay for their agents, who are paid a percentage of their sales. Many salespeople work on commission, particularly those who sell big-ticket items such as automobiles, major appliances and computers.

Examples of organization-based merit pay plans include gainsharing and profit sharing. *Gainsharing* focuses on improving productivity through reducing expenses or cutting costs. Organizational members are motivated to come up with and implement cost-cutting strategies because a percentage of the cost savings achieved during a specified period of time is distributed back to employees.[41] Gainsharing's popularity was initially limited to large unionized manufacturing companies,[42] such as Molson Breweries and Hydro-Québec. This has changed in recent years, with smaller companies (such as Delta, BC-based Avcorp Industries) and governments (such as Ontario's City of Ajax and Kingston Township) also introducing gainsharing.

Under *profit sharing*, employees receive a share of an organization's profits. The Conference Board of Canada reported in 1999 that 70 percent of companies offered incentive payouts to non-management employees in the form of cash bonuses, profit sharing and productivity gainsharing. In 1998, this represented 26 percent of base pay for executives and 7.4 percent of base pay for non-executives.[43] Regardless of the specific kind of plan that is used, managers should always strive to link pay to the performance of behaviours that help an organization achieve its goals.

Chapter Summary

THE NATURE OF MOTIVATION

NEED THEORIES

- Maslow's Hierarchy of Needs
- Alderfer's ERG Theory
- Herzberg's Motivator–Hygiene Theory

EXPECTANCY THEORY

- Expectancy
- Instrumentality
- Valence
- Bringing it All Together

GOAL-SETTING THEORY

REINFORCEMENT THEORY

EQUITY THEORY

- Equity
- Inequity
- Ways to Restore Equity

PAY AND MOTIVATION

- Basing Merit Pay on Individual, Group, or Organizational Performance
- Salary Increase or Bonus?
- Examples of Merit Pay Plans

Summary and Review

THE NATURE OF MOTIVATION   Motivation encompasses the psychological forces within a person that determine the direction of a person's behaviour in an organization, a person's level of effort, and a person's level of persistence in the face of obstacles. Managers strive to motivate people to contribute their inputs to an organization, to focus these inputs in the direction of high performance, and to ensure that people receive the outcomes they desire when they perform at a high level.

NEED THEORIES   Need theories suggest that in order to have a motivated workforce, managers should determine what needs people are trying to satisfy in organizations and then ensure that people receive outcomes that will satisfy these needs when they perform at a high level and contribute to organizational effectiveness.

EXPECTANCY THEORY   According to expectancy theory, managers can promote high levels of motivation in their organizations by taking steps to ensure that expectancy is high (people think that if they try, they can perform at a high level), instrumentality is high (people think that if they perform at a high level, they will receive certain outcomes), and valence is high (people desire these outcomes).

GOAL-SETTING THEORY   Goal-setting theory suggests that managers can promote high motivation and performance by ensuring that people are striving to achieve specific, difficult goals. It also is important for people to accept the goals, be committed to them, and receive feedback about how they are doing.

REINFORCEMENT THEORY   Reinforcement theory suggests that managers can motivate people to perform highly by using positive reinforcement or negative reinforcement (positive reinforcement being the preferred strategy). Managers can motivate people to avoid performing dysfunctional behaviours by using extinction or punishment.

EQUITY THEORY   According to equity theory, managers can promote high levels of motivation by ensuring that people perceive that there is equity in the organization or that outcomes are distributed in proportion to inputs. Equity exists when a person perceives that his or her own outcome/input ratio equals the outcome/input ratio of a referent. Inequity motivates people to try to restore equity.

PAY AND MOTIVATION   Each of the motivation theories discussed in this chapter alludes to the importance of pay and suggests that pay should be based on performance. Merit pay plans can be based on individual, group, or organizational performance and can entail the use of salary increases or bonuses.

Management in Action

Topics for Discussion and Action

1. Interview four people who have the same kind of job (such as salesperson, waiter/waitress, or teacher), and determine what kinds of needs they are trying to satisfy at work.

2. Discuss why two people with similar abilities may have very different expectancies for performing at a high level.

3. Describe why some people have low instrumentalities even when their managers distribute outcomes based on performance.

4. Describe three techniques or procedures that managers can use to determine whether a goal is difficult.

5. Discuss why managers should always try to use positive reinforcement instead of negative reinforcement.

6. Analyze how professors try to promote equity to motivate students.

Building Management Skills

Diagnosing Motivation

Think about the ideal job that you would like to obtain upon graduation. Describe this job, the kind of manager you would like to report to, and the kind of organization you would be working in. Then answer the following questions.

1. What would be your levels of expectancy and instrumentality on this job? Which outcomes would have high valence for you on this job? What steps would your manager take to influence your levels of expectancy, instrumentality, and valence?

2. Whom would you choose as a referent on this job? What steps would your manager take to make you feel that you were being equitably treated? What would you do if, after a year on the job, you experienced underpayment inequity?

3. What goals would you strive to achieve on this job? Why? What role would your manager play in determining your goals?

4. What needs would you strive to satisfy on this job? Why? What role would your manager play in helping you satisfy these needs?

Small Group Breakout Exercise

Increasing Motivation

Form groups of three or four people, and appoint one member as the spokesperson who will communicate your findings to the whole class when called on by the instructor. Then discuss the following scenario.

You are a group of partners who own a chain of 15 dry-cleaning stores in a medium-sized town. You are meeting today to discuss a problem in customer service that surfaced recently. When any one of you is spending the day or even part of the day in a particular store, clerks seem to be providing excellent customer service, spotters are making sure all stains are removed from garments, and pressers are doing a good job of pressing difficult items such as silk blouses. Yet during those same

visits customers complain to you about such things as stains not being removed and items being poorly pressed in some of their previous orders; indeed, several customers have brought garments in to be redone. Customers also sometimes comment on having waited too long for service on previous visits. You are meeting today to address this problem.

1. Discuss the extent to which you believe that you have a motivation problem in your stores.

2. Given what you have learned in this chapter, design a plan to increase the motivation of clerks to provide prompt service to customers even when they are not being watched by a partner.

3. Design a plan to increase the motivation of spotters to remove as many stains as possible even when they are not being watched by a partner.

4. Design a plan to increase the motivation of pressers to do a top-notch job on all clothes they press, no matter how difficult.

Exploring the World Wide Web

Specific Assignment

Many companies take active steps to recognize their employees for jobs well done. One such company is DuPont Canada. Scan DuPont Canada's Web site (www.dupont.ca) to learn more about this company. Then click on "People" and "Recognizing our People."

1. What kinds of rewards is Dupont Canada using to motivate its employees to perform at a high level?

2. How are attention to safety, health and work issues encouraged at DuPont Canada?

General Assignment

Find a Web site of a company that bases pay on performance for some or all of its employees. Describe the merit pay plan in use at this company. Which employees are covered by the plan? Do you think this pay plan will foster high levels of motivation? Why or why not?

ManagementCase

Motivating With Stretch Targets

Top managers of many organizations have discovered a powerful tool to increase motivation and performance: stretch targets. Stretch targets are goals that call for dramatic improvements in key aspects of organizational performance and effectiveness, such as extraordinary increases in revenues, reductions in costs, or increases in the rate at which new products are developed and brought to market.[44] Typically, organizational goals or objectives are incremental, involving changes such as a 10-percent reduction in inventory costs or a 5-percent increase in revenues. These goals seem to motivate members of an organization to achieve the specified increments in performance but often little more. Top managers who use stretch targets instead of incremental goals have a vision of how much better an organization could be performing and then choose a target to motivate members of the organization to achieve this high level of performance. Much careful planning goes into the establishment of stretch targets.

At 3M, for example, Desi DeSimone was concerned about a depressed market for some of the goods 3M produced, and was especially concerned about a lack of increase in revenues from new products. He decided to set a stretch target for employees to increase by 30 percent 3M's revenues from products that had been introduced within the last four years. Along with this stretch target came some changes in 3M's strategies. Rather than spending time developing products with modest potential that were akin to existing products on the market, 3M employees were encouraged to focus on developing major

new products with high sales potential. In addition, employees were urged to bring these potential bestsellers to market quickly. As a result of the specific, difficult goal DeSimone set, the newly introduced Scotch-Brite Never Rust soap pad gained 22 percent of the soap pad market from Brillo and SOS in its first 18 months on the market.

At Boeing, CEO Frank Shrontz was concerned about the slow and inefficient ways in which airplanes were produced. He decided to motivate his employees with an ambitious stretch target that would cut costs to such a great extent that Boeing would be able to lower its prices and sell more planes. After considerable planning and strategic analysis, the stretch target he decided on was a 25-percent reduction in the cost of producing a plane, while maintaining Boeing's high quality standards. At the same time, he implemented a second stretch target: reducing the amount of time it took to build a plane from 18 months to 8 months—again, while maintaining high quality. If achieved, this second stretch target would result in lower costs (due to less inventory expense) and more sales (due to decreased risk for airlines). Progress toward these stretch targets has been good: New, more efficient, and less costly methods of production are being implemented in practically all phases of airplane production at Boeing, and the time needed to complete a plane has already dropped to between 10 and 12 months.[45] Montreal-based Canadian National Railway's (CN) supply management department, GE, and Union Pacific Railroad are other examples of companies using stretch targets.

Stretch targets seem to be powerful motivators that result in organizations and their members achieving the unthinkable in performance and effectiveness improvements. Five key aspects of stretch targets and the ways that managers implement them in organizations can account for their stunning success.

First, stretch targets are specific, difficult goals, as illustrated by the examples above.

Second, managers who implement stretch targets do whatever they can to boost expectancy so employees believe they actually can reach the target. CEO Steven Mason, who has implemented stretch targets at Mead, a large paper manufacturer, suggests that one way to make sure that employees are confident that the targets are reachable is by concentrating "on things ... [they] can control."

Third, managers boost employees' self-confidence by demonstrating to them that other organizations have been able to reach the standards set by the stretch targets. Mason, for example, had his employees visit General Electric's successful light bulb and appliance divisions to see what other companies have done. Like Mead, those divisions operate in mature industries with stable prices, yet they have been more profitable than many of Mead's operations because of their constant drive to increase productivity. If those divisions of GE could increase productivity in a mature industry with stable prices, why, Mason asked, couldn't Mead?

Fourth, managers take advantage of opportunities for learning from others. At Boeing, for example, Shrontz sent teams of employees to top-performing manufacturing companies in diverse industries ranging from shipbuilding to computer manufacturing so that they could learn from and become motivated by these exemplary organizations.

Fifth, once managers set the stretch target and employees believe they can reach it, employees are given considerable autonomy in working to achieve it, setting intermediary goals, and so forth—that is, the employees control how they go about meeting the goal. For example, at CSX, a shipping and railroad company, CEO John Snow indicates that once stretch targets are set, "It's people in the field who find the right path."[46] Stretch targets certainly seem to be the right path for at least some top managers to take to motivate employees to achieve dramatic improvements in organizational performance.

Questions

1. Why do stretch targets result in high levels of motivation and performance?

2. How can or should managers respond to employees who complain that a stretch target is impossible to achieve?

3. In what kinds of situations might it be particularly appropriate for managers to implement stretch targets?

4. In what kinds of situations might stretch targets not be such a good idea?

ManagementCase

In the News

From the Pages of *The Vancouver Sun*
Telus Gives Stock Options to all its Employees

While employees at some struggling telecommunications companies are bracing for pink slips, 20 000 workers at Telus Corp. got an unexpected bonus Thursday—100 stock options, with another 200 on the way.

Team Telus Options, touted as the first plan to offer options to every employee of a Canadian telecom company, will help in efforts to create "a performance culture within Telus," chief executive Darren Entwistle said.

It gives employees an incentive to work hard to ensure Telus' stock price rises—and to stick with the company since workers can only exercise the options as employees.

The plan is also open to new employees, making Burnaby-based Telus a more appealing employer as it sets out to add 500 to 1000 workers in Ontario and Quebec during three years, Entwistle said.

"The demand for talent in this industry far outstrips supply."

Only about 6.5 per cent of mid-to-large-sized businesses in Canada currently provide universal employee stock options, the Conference Board of Canada says.

Telus executives, directors and managers, who have been part of a stock-option plan for several years, are ineligible for Team Telus Options.

Often reserved for high-level executives and employees of new companies, stock options give workers the right to buy or sell stock at a specified price, by a specific date.

In the Telus plan, the first 100 options are in non-voting shares, at an exercise price of $34.88.

In two years, employees will be able to exercise them. If the stock has reached $50 by then, for example, the 100 options will be worth $1512.

Employees will be granted another 100 options in one year,

and a further 100 in two years. The options must be exercised within 10 years after they are granted.

The granting of options is prominent in the computer and information-technology sector, the chemical and pharmaceutical sector and the telecommunications industry.

Pivotal Software of North Vancouver provides universal employee stock options.

"All our employees have had stock options since August of 1999, when we went public," company official Jacqueline Voci said. "It gives every employee an incentive to make the company succeed."

Crystal Decisions, formerly Seagate Software, has been giving employees stock options since the mid-1990s.

"Greg Kerfoot, the founder of the company, maintained that all employees should benefit from the growth and success of the company," Crystal official Alison MacDonald said. "We are a private company but if we go public down the road, employees can choose to exercise their options."

Consulting firm Towers Perrin says more than 90 per cent of the Fortune 1000 companies use stock options for their senior operating team.

In Canada, all but three of the top 100 companies on the TSE offer options to at least the senior management team.

However, universal employee stock option plans aren't widespread.

"It's not common for companies to offer options to every employee and it's not common enough," said Ross Birney, an associate with Rogers Group. "The companies that have done so in the past have been very successful. Why shouldn't an entry-level person benefit from the success of a company?"

The federal government relaxed tax rules on stock options last year.

The study said options not only benefit employees but help companies grow.

"Companies with a stock option plan are expected to expand up to 11 per cent faster than those without," it said.

Source: "Telus Gives Stock Options to all its Workers," *The Vancouver Sun*, March 2, 2001, pp. C7, C8.

Questions

1. To what extent does rewarding employees with stock options support the motivation theories presented in the chapter?

2. To what extent are lower-level employees likely to find stock options as motivating as upper management?

Chapter thirteen

Leadership

Learning Objectives

1. Describe what leadership is, when leaders are effective and ineffective, and the sources of power that enables managers to be effective leaders.

2. Identify the traits that show the strongest relationship to leadership, the behaviours leaders engage in, and the limitations of the trait and behaviour models of leadership.

3. Explain how contingency models of leadership enhance our understanding of effective leadership and management in organizations.

4. Describe what transformational leadership is, and explain how managers can engage in it.

5. Characterize the relationship between gender and leadership.

A Case in Contrast

Levy Fosters Growth While Irwin Fosters Decline

Dr. Julia Levy, president and CEO of Vancouver-based QLT (www.qltinc.com), has been credited with creating a company that is a world leader in photodynamic therapy, a field of medicine that uses light-activated drugs to treat disease.[1] In contrast, George Irwin, who was CEO of Toronto-based Irwin Toy Ltd. (www.irwintoy.com) until November 2000, has been credited with overseeing the demise of what was once the biggest toy company in Canada.

Many analysts attribute the differences in the companies' performances to their CEOs' different leadership styles.

Though Levy was named Pacific Entrepreneur of the Year by *Canadian Business* in 2000, she thinks of herself as an accidental entrepreneur and CEO. She was the company's chief scientific officer, and avoided the CEO role for 13 years until QLT's board offered it to her in 1995. She accepted the job only because she felt that QLT had a team of seasoned managers upon whom she could rely to overcome some of her own shortcomings.

Irwin grew up almost destined to become CEO of Irwin Toy. His grandfather had founded the company, and he was appointed president in 1990 after his father Macdonald and uncle Arnold, who had co-run the company for many years, decided that it was time for the next generation to take over. He was named CEO in 1994.

Levy is the ultimate team player when managing her company. She doesn't like to lead directly. Instead, she prefers to keep asking questions until people come up with the right answers themselves. She feels that this approach empowers her employees and gives them ownership of the solutions.

Dr. Julia Levy, president and CEO of QLT, believes in listening to all of her employees and being sensitive to their needs.

Irwin's employees found him more distant, by contrast. By the time of his departure, he had "lost the confidence of many employees and family members, … stopped listening to the input of those around him and failed to be an effective leader."

Levy works hard to establish trust amongst her employees. Despite the pressures of being

George Irwin, former CEO of Irwin Toy, used a more distant leadership style, which drove a number of key employees to quit.

Table 13.1
Some Thoughts About What it Means to be a Canadian Leader

Canadian ambassador to the United States Raymond Chretien:	I think our leadership is based upon what we are as a society. We have maintained our cohesion. We have maintained our capacity to build a tolerant, caring society that speaks to all aspects of our human development. This is why we are highly regarded.
Maclean's editor-in-chief Robert Lewis:	Recently, I sat beside an American CEO at a conference and, as the discussion unfolded, he started mumbling, "You Canadians are always trying to get some kind of consensus. Why don't you stop that and make some decisions?"
ABC news anchor Peter Jennings:	I think Canadian leadership, as we've already cited in peacekeeping operations, in international conventions, in international situations, is reflected in the notion that we've had to make our way somewhat more subtly on the world stage than the United States has ever been obliged to do.
Wi-LAN Inc. founder Hatim Zaghloul:	In high-tech, we Canadians often will take longer making a decision, whereas in Silicon Valley, they would advertise their product when it's just a concept, and then they would go and build it if someone bought it. In Canada, we only advertise once it's meeting 99.99 percent of our specifications.
Olympic gold-medal rower Marnie McBean:	Canadians just don't follow the person who's shouting the loudest. . . . And I think that's where this sense of a style of Canadian leadership comes from—not from being boastful or a braggart. It comes from being able to do the job. Just sort of putting the head down, doing the job and we get our respect from our actions and from our performance.

Source: R. Lewis, "The Canadian Way: There is a Confident Canadian Style of Leadership, and it is Making a Global Impact," *Maclean's*, July 1, 2000, p. 26.

leadership style was to make decisions himself even when those around him urged him to consider alternatives. Irwin therefore centralized authority and decision making at Irwin Toy (an organizing task), took major responsibility for strategy development (a planning task), and forced his uncle Bryan, cousin Scott, and younger brother David to leave the company when they no longer supported his performance (a control task).

Managers at all levels and in all kinds of organizations have their own personal leadership styles, which determine not only how they lead their subordinates but also how they perform the other management tasks. Derek Burney, who succeeded Doug Cowpland as CEO of Ottawa-based Corel in August 2000, was not viewed at the outset as the right person to head Corel. He was initially appointed interim CEO after Cowpland's resignation while the board searched for a permanent CEO. However, he immediately started negotiating with Microsoft to form an alliance (a planning task), something Cowpland would have never done, while quickly bringing together the employees to be more team-like (an organizing task). Thus he showed a balance between making decisions himself and working with his employees to build their confidence in him. Cowpland, who had been seen as remote and demanding, and whose senior managers never lasted long once they got to the top, had quite a difference style from Burney, who is credited with bringing energy and enthusiasm back to Corel.

Corel Corporation
www.corel.com/

Leadership Styles Across Cultures

Some evidence suggests that leadership styles vary not only among individuals but also among countries or cultures. Some research suggests that European man-

Samsung's managers have had to spend considerable time learning new leadership skills to influence and motivate Canadian and US employees. In these two countries, leaders need to be more directive as well as participative as compared to some Asian counterparts.

agers tend to be more humanistic or people oriented than both Japanese and American managers. The collectivistic culture in Japan places prime emphasis on the group rather than the individual, so the importance of individuals' own personalities, needs, and desires is minimized. Organizations in the United States tend to be very profit oriented and thus tend to downplay the importance of individual employees' needs and desires. Many countries in Europe have a more individualistic perspective than Japan and a more humanistic perspective than the United States, which may result in some European managers being more people oriented than their Japanese or American counterparts. European managers, for example, tend to be reluctant to lay off employees, and when a layoff is absolutely necessary, they take careful steps to make it as painless as possible.[3]

Another cross-cultural difference that has been noted is in time horizons. Managers in any two countries often differ in their time horizons, but there also may be cultural differences. Canadian and US organizations tend to have a short-run profit orientation, which results in a leadership style emphasizing short-run performance. Many of the investors and creators of the dot-com companies that failed in 2000 and 2001 demonstrated very short-term objectives, along the lines of "get rich quick." Many of these companies failed to have a business plan that would guide them in a long-term strategy. By contrast, Japanese organizations tend to have a long-run growth orientation, which results in Japanese managers' personal leadership styles emphasizing long-run performance. Justus Mische, a personnel manager at the European organization Hoechst suggests that "Europe, at least the big international firms in Europe, have a philosophy between the Japanese, long term, and the United States, short term."[4] Research on these and other global aspects of leadership is in its infancy, but as it continues, more cultural differences in managers' personal leadership styles may be discovered.

Power: The Key to Leadership

No matter what one's leadership style, a key component of effective leadership is found in the *power* the leader has to affect other people's behaviour and get them to act in certain ways.[5] There are several types of power: legitimate, reward, coercive, expert, and referent power (see Figure 13.1).[6] Effective leaders take steps to ensure that they have sufficient levels of each type and that they use the power they have in beneficial ways.

legitimate power

The authority that a manager has by virtue of his or her position in an organization's hierarchy.

LEGITIMATE POWER **Legitimate power** is the authority a manager has by virtue of his or her position in an organization's hierarchy. Personal leadership style often influences how a manager exercises legitimate power. Take the case of Carol Loray, who is a first-line manager in a greeting card company and leads a group of 15 artists and designers. Loray has the legitimate power to hire new employees, assign projects to the artists and designers, monitor their work, and appraise their performance. She uses this power effectively. She always makes sure that her project assignments match the interests of her subordinates as much as possible so they will enjoy their work. She monitors their work to make sure they are on track but does not engage in close supervision, which can hamper creativity. She makes sure her performance appraisals are developmental, providing concrete advice for areas where improvements could be made. Recently, Loray negotiated with her manager to increase her legitimate power, so now she can initiate and develop proposals for new card lines.

Figure 13.1
Sources of Managerial Power

reward power The ability of a manager to give or withhold tangible and intangible rewards.

REWARD POWER **Reward power** is the ability of a manager to give or withhold tangible rewards (pay raises, bonuses, choice job assignments) and intangible rewards (verbal praise, a pat on the back, respect). As you learned in Chapter 12, members of an organization are motivated to perform at a high level by a variety of rewards. Being able to give or withhold rewards based on performance is a major source of power that allows managers to have a highly motivated workforce.

Effective managers use their reward power in such a way that subordinates feel that their rewards signal that they are doing a good job and their efforts are appreciated. Ineffective managers use rewards in a more controlling manner (wielding the "stick" instead of offering the "carrot"), which signals to subordinates that the manager has the upper hand. Managers also can take steps to increase their reward power. Carol Loray had the legitimate power to appraise her subordinates' performance, but she lacked the reward power to distribute raises and end-of-year bonuses until she discussed with her own manager why this would be a valuable motivational tool for her to use. Loray now receives a pool of money each year for salary increases and bonuses and has the reward power to distribute them as she sees fit.

coercive power
The ability of a manager to punish others.

COERCIVE POWER **Coercive power** is the ability of a manager to punish others. Punishment can range from verbal reprimands, to reductions in pay or working hours, to actual dismissal. Punishment can have negative side effects such as resentment and retaliation and should be used only when necessary (for example, to curtail a dangerous behaviour). Managers who rely heavily on coercive power tend to be ineffective as leaders and sometimes even get fired themselves. Steve Smith, WestJet's former CEO featured in Chapter 1's "A Case in Contrast," was used to dealing coercively with unionized employees before he moved to WestJet. After a short time of his using that same approach at WestJet, employees and senior management were ready to quit. Smith was forced to resign.

Excessive use of coercive power seldom produces high performance and is questionable ethically. Sometimes it amounts to a form of mental abuse, robbing workers of their dignity and causing excessive levels of stress. Overuse of coercive power can even result in dangerous working conditions. Better results can be obtained with reward power, as indicated in this "Ethics in Action."

Ethics in Action

Curtailing Coercive Power
Makes Good Business Sense

Ricardo Semler was only 21 in 1979 when he took control of his family business, Semco, a Brazilian manufacturer of industrial products such as pumps, mixers, and propellers.[7] Use of coercive power had been the norm rather than the exception at Semco. Fear was rampant. Guards policed the factory, workers were frisked when they left for the day, their visits to the washroom were timed, and anyone who broke a piece of equipment had to pay for it. Though some other traditional Brazilian companies were and still are managed in a similar fashion, Semler found managing Semco in this manner to be so stressful that, after collapsing one day on a business trip, he vowed to make Semco "a true democracy, a place run on trust and freedom, not fear."[8] His goal was to create an ethical workplace in which all employees were treated with respect and dignity. By all reports, he has achieved his goal.

How did Semler achieve this feat? After careful planning and analysis, he decided to use reward power instead of coercive power to get things done. Workers are no longer closely monitored and can come and go when they want. Workers are allowed to choose their own bosses. A record 23 percent of Semco's profits are given back to employees for a job well done. Semler even rewards top managers by sharing his title as CEO. Semler rotates the CEO position among himself and six other managers every six months.[9]

Aside from creating more ethical working conditions that have lowered levels of fear, distrust, and stress for Semco employees, what have been the consequences of Semler's radical changes? When Semler took over the business in 1979, Semco had sales of $16 740 per employee (about half of the amount of its competitors in Brazil). In recent years, Semco's sales averaged around $209 250 per employee (four times the figures for its competitors). Nonmanagers and managers alike realize that Semler must be on the right track. The company receives 1000 job applications per open position, and managers from global organizations such as Mobil (www.mobil.com) and IBM (www.ibm.com) have traveled to Brazil to see firsthand what is happening at Semco.[10]

expert power Power that is based in the special knowledge, skills, and expertise that a leader possesses.

EXPERT POWER   **Expert power** is based in the special knowledge, skills, and expertise that a leader possesses. The nature of expert power varies, depending on the leader's level in the hierarchy. First-line and middle managers often have technical expertise relevant to the tasks that their subordinates perform. Their expert power gives them considerable influence over subordinates.

Some top managers derive expert power from their technical expertise. Julia Levy, described in the "Case in Contrast," is one of these. Her years of teaching science to undergraduates at the University of British Columbia gave her an edge when raising funds from investors for QLT—she was able to explain to investors what her biotech firm was doing. Many top-level managers lack technical expertise, however, and derive their expert power from their abilities as decision makers, planners, and strategists.

Effective leaders take steps to ensure that they do have an adequate amount of expert power to perform their leadership roles. They may obtain additional training or education in their fields, make sure they keep up-to-date with the latest developments and changes in technology, stay abreast of changes in their fields through involvement in professional associations, and read widely to be aware of momentous changes in the organization's task and general environments. Expert power tends to be best used in a guiding or coaching manner rather than in an arrogant, high-handed manner.

referent power Power that comes from subordinates' and co-workers' respect, admiration, and loyalty.

REFERENT POWER   **Referent power** is more informal than the other kinds of power. Referent power is a function of the personal characteristics of a leader; it is the power that comes from subordinates' and co-workers' respect, admiration, and loyalty. Leaders who are likeable and whom subordinates wish to use as a role model are especially likely to possess referent power.

In addition to being a valuable asset for top managers, referent power can help first-line and middle managers be effective leaders as well. Sally Carruthers, for example, is the first-line manager of a group of secretaries in the finance department of a large university. Carruthers' secretaries are known to be among the best in the university. Much of their willingness to go above and beyond the call of duty has been attributed to Carruthers' warm and caring nature, which makes each of them feel important and valued. Managers can take steps to increase their referent power, such as taking time to get to know their subordinates and showing interest in and concern for them.

Empowerment: An Ingredient in Modern Management

empowerment
Expanding employees' tasks and responsibilities.

More and more managers today are incorporating in their personal leadership styles an aspect that at first glance seems to be the opposite of being a leader. In Chapter 1, we described how **empowerment**–the process of giving employees at all levels in the organization the authority to make decisions, be responsible for their outcomes, improve quality, and cut costs–is becoming increasingly popular in organizations. When leaders empower their subordinates, the subordinates typically take over some of the responsibilities and authority that used to reside with the leader or manager, such as the right to reject parts that do not meet quality standards, the right to check one's own work, and the right to schedule work activities. Empowered subordinates are given the power to make some of the decisions that their leaders or supervisors used to make.

At first glance, empowerment might seem to be the opposite of effective leadership because managers are allowing subordinates to take a more active role in leading themselves. In actuality, however, empowerment can contribute to effective leadership for several reasons:

Does empowerment of employees decrease the power of managers?

- Empowerment increases a manager's ability to get things done because the manager has the support and help of subordinates who may have special knowledge of work tasks.

- Empowerment often increases workers' involvement, motivation, and commitment, which helps ensure that they will be working toward organizational goals.

- Empowerment gives managers more time to concentrate on their pressing concerns because they spend less time on day-to-day supervisory activities.

Effective managers like Julia Levy realize the benefits of empowerment; ineffective managers like George Irwin try to keep control over all decision making and force agreement from subordinates. The personal leadership style of managers who empower subordinates often entails developing subordinates so that they can make good decisions and being subordinates' guide, coach, and source of inspiration. Empowerment is a popular trend in Canada and the United States at companies as diverse as United Parcel Service (a package delivery company), Vancouver-based Dominion Directory (which publishes *The Yellow Pages*), and Langley, BC-based Redwood Plastics (a manufacturing company), and it is also taking off around the world.[11] Even companies in South Korea (such as Samsung, Hyundai, and Daewoo), in which decision making typically was centralized with the founding families, are empowering managers at lower levels to make decisions.[12]

Rotman School of
Management
www.mgmt.utoronto.ca/

Not every employee is a good candidate for empowerment, however. A recent study that Professor Jia Lin Xie, of the University of Toronto's Rotman School of Management, conducted with several others found that people who lack confidence can get ill from being put in charge of their own work. The researchers found that "workers who had high levels of control at work, but lacked confidence in their abilities or blamed themselves for workplace problems, were more likely to have lower antibody levels and experienced more colds and flus."[13]

Some of the difficulty with empowerment is that not all companies introduce it properly. Professor Dan Ondrack at the University of Toronto's Rotman School of Management notes that for employees to be empowered, four conditions need to be met: (1) There must be a clear definition of the values and mission of the company; (2) the company must help employees acquire the relevant skills; (3) employees need to be supported in their decision making, and not criticized when they try to do something extraordinary; and (4) workers need to be recognized for their efforts.[14]

Trait and Behaviour Models of Leadership

Leading is such an important process in all organizations—nonprofit organizations, government agencies, and schools as well as for-profit corporations—that it has been researched for decades. Early approaches to leadership, called the *trait model* and the *behaviour model*, sought to determine what effective leaders are like as people and what they do that makes them so effective.

The Trait Model

The trait model of leadership focused on identifying the personal characteristics that are responsible for effective leadership. Researchers thought that effective leaders must have certain personal qualities that set them apart from ineffective leaders and from people who never become leaders. Decades of research (beginning in the 1930s) and hundreds of studies indicate that certain personal characteristics do appear to be associated with effective leadership (see Table 13.2 for a list of these).[15] Notice that although this model is called the "trait" model, some of the personal characteristics that it identifies are not personality traits per se but rather are concerned with a leader's skills, abilities, knowledge, and expertise. As the "Case in Contrast" shows, Julia Levy certainly appears to possess many of these characteristics (such as intelligence, self-confidence, and integrity and honesty). Leaders who do not possess these traits may be ineffective.

Traits alone, however, are not the key to understanding leader effectiveness. Some effective leaders do not possess all of these traits, and some leaders who do possess them are not effective in their leadership roles. This lack of a consistent relationship between leader traits and leader effectiveness led researchers to shift their attention away from traits and to search for new explanations for effective leadership. Rather than focusing on what leaders are like (the traits they possess), researchers began to turn their attention to what effective leaders actually do—in other words, to the behaviours that allow effective leaders to influence their subordinates to achieve group and organizational goals.

Table 13.2

Traits and Personal Characteristics Related to Effective Leadership

TRAIT	DESCRIPTION
Intelligence	Helps managers understand complex issues and solve problems
Knowledge and expertise	Help managers make good decisions and discover ways to increase efficiency and effectiveness
Dominance	Helps managers influence their subordinates to achieve organizational goals
Self-confidence	Contributes to managers' effectively influencing subordinates and persisting when faced with obstacles or difficulties
High energy	Helps managers deal with the many demands they face
Tolerance for stress	Helps managers deal with uncertainty and make difficult decisions
Integrity and honesty	Help managers behave ethically and earn their subordinates' trust and confidence
Maturity	Helps managers avoid acting selfishly, control their feelings, and admit when they have made a mistake

The Behaviour Model

After extensive study, researchers at Ohio State University in the 1940s and 1950s identified two basic kinds of leader behaviours that many leaders in the United States, Germany, and other countries engaged in to influence their subordinates: *consideration* and *initiating structure*.[16]

consideration Behaviour indicating that a manager trusts, respects, and cares about subordinates.

CONSIDERATION   Leaders engage in **consideration** when they show their subordinates that they trust, respect, and care about them. Managers who truly look out for the well-being of their subordinates and do what they can to help subordinates feel good and enjoy their work perform consideration behaviours. In the "Case in Contrast," Julia Levy engages in consideration when she treats her subordinates with respect, and encourages a work/family balance for her employees; George Irwin's favouritism of an employee and disregard of other managers' concerns exemplifies a lack of consideration. Louis Hughes, CEO of General Motors Europe, learned German so that he could communicate with employees in Germany and show them that he truly cared.[17] With the increasing focus on the importance of high-quality customer service, many managers are realizing that when they are considerate to subordinates, subordinates are more likely to be considerate to customers and vice versa. The experiences of Staples, a discount office supply retailer, and the advertising agency Chiat/Day are consistent with this observation, as indicated in this "Management Insight."

Management Insight

Consideration and Customer Service at Staples and Chiat/Day

Staples (www.staples.com) is a top-performing retailer with annual percentage increases in sales and profits as high as 50 percent. Tom Stemberg, founder and CEO of Staples, has raised customer service to an art form. He is constantly on the lookout for new ways to please customers, and salespeople at Staples go out of their way to help customers no matter how large or small their orders are. Salespeople develop close, long-term relationships with customers and strive to provide innovative solutions to their office supply problems.

Other retailers also realize the value of high-quality customer service but have tended not to be as successful as Staples in actually providing it. One of Stemberg's guiding principles is that managers should treat subordinates in the way that they would like subordinates to treat customers. Stemberg goes out of his way to be considerate to the managers who report to him, and he encourages them to do likewise with their own subordinates. Rod Sargent, one of Stemberg's subordinates, recalls that when his newborn son was sick and in intensive care for a week, Stemberg called him every night to see how the baby was doing and provide support.[18]

Things could not have been more different at the Chiat/Day advertising agency (www.chiatday.com). Jay Chiat founded this unconventional company, which was responsible for such innovative ad campaigns as the Energizer bunny and Reebok's "U.B.U." campaign. Chiat, however, was not considerate to his employees, and they in turn were not considerate to the firm's customers. Former Chiat/Day vice-chair Jane Newman said that Jay Chiat "would terrorize people."[19] Chiat took away his employees' offices and gave them lockers, laptop computers, and cellular phones, claiming that they did not need offices to get their work done and should not be focused on their own egos. Even when things were going well in the agency, Chiat rarely offered a kind word to his subordinates, let alone showed any concern for their well-being.

In turn, Chiat/Day employees tended to be rude and inconsiderate to the agency's major corporate customers. Nike (www.nike.com), once one of Chiat/Day's clients, left the agency for this very reason. Nike creative director Peter Moore recalled, "They were arrogant. Our people were miserable having to deal with them."[20] The lack of consideration that Jay Chiat showed his employees and the lack of consideration that they showed Chiat/Day's clients played a major role in the decline of the agency. Key clients ultimately took their accounts elsewhere, Chiat/Day lost talented employees who were tired of not being treated well, and eventually the company was sold to Omnicom Group Inc., an advertising agency holding company.[21]

initiating structure

Behaviour that managers engage in to ensure that work gets done, subordinates perform their jobs acceptably, and the organization is efficient and effective.

INITIATING STRUCTURE   Leaders engage in **initiating structure** when they take steps to make sure that work gets done, subordinates perform their jobs acceptably, and the organization is efficient and effective. Assigning tasks to individuals or work groups, letting subordinates know what is expected of them, deciding how work should be done, making schedules, encouraging adherence to rules and regulations, and motivating subordinates to do a good job are all examples of initiating structure.[22]

Initiating structure and consideration are independent leader behaviours. Leaders can be high on both, low on both, or high on one and low on the other.

Leadership researchers have identified leader behaviours similar to consideration and initiating structure. Researchers at the University of Michigan, for example, identified two categories of leadership behaviours, *employee-centred behaviours* and *job-oriented behaviours*, that correspond roughly to consideration and initiating structure, respectively.[23] Models of leadership popular with consultants also tend to zero in on these two kinds of behaviours. For example, Robert Blake and Jane Mouton's Managerial Grid® focuses on *concern for people* (similar to consideration) and *concern for production* (similar to initiating structure). Blake and Mouton advise that effective leadership often requires both a high level of concern for people and a high level of concern for production.[24] As another example, Paul Hersey and Kenneth Blanchard's model focuses on *supportive behaviours* (similar to consideration) and *task-oriented behaviours* (similar to initiating structure). According to Hersey and Blanchard, leaders need to consider the nature of their subordinates when trying to determine the extent to which they should perform these two types of behaviours.[25]

You might expect that effective leaders and managers would perform both kinds of behaviours, but research has found that this is not necessarily the case. The relationship between performance of consideration and initiating structure behaviours and leader effectiveness is not clear-cut. Some leaders are effective even when they do not perform consideration behaviours or initiating structure behaviours, and some leaders are ineffective even when they do perform both kinds of behaviours. Like the trait model of leadership, the behaviour model alone cannot explain leader effectiveness. Realizing this, researchers began building more complicated models of leadership, models that focused not only on the leader and what he or she does but also on the situation or context in which leadership occurs.

Contingency Models of Leadership

Simply possessing certain traits or performing certain behaviours does not ensure that a manager will be an effective leader in all situations calling for leadership. Some managers who seem to possess the "right" traits and perform the "right" behaviours turn out to be ineffective leaders. Managers lead in a wide variety of situations and organizations and have various kinds of subordinates performing diverse tasks in many environmental contexts. Given the wide variety of situations in which leadership occurs, what makes a manager an effective leader in one situation (such as certain traits or certain behaviours) is not necessarily what that manager needs in order to be equally effective in a different situation. An effective army general might not be an effective university president, an effective manager of a restaurant might not be an effective manager of a clothing store, an effective coach of a football team might not be an effective manager of a fitness centre, and an effective first-line manager in a manufacturing company might not be an effective middle manager. The traits or behaviours that may contribute to a manager being an effective leader in one situation might actually result in the same manager being an ineffective leader in another situation.

Contingency models of leadership take into account the situation or context within which leadership occurs. According to contingency models, whether or not a manager is an effective leader is the result of the interplay between what the manager is like, what he or she does, and the situation in which leadership takes place. Contingency models propose that whether a leader who possesses certain traits or performs certain behaviours is effective depends on, or is contingent on, the situation or context. In this section, we discuss four prominent contingency models developed to shed light on what makes managers effective leaders: Fred Fiedler's contingency model, Hersey–Blanchard's situational leadership theory, Robert House's path–goal theory, and the leader substitutes model. As you will see, these leadership models are complementary; each focuses on a somewhat different aspect of effective leadership in organizations.

Fiedler's Contingency Model

Fred E. Fiedler was among the first leadership researchers to acknowledge that effective leadership is contingent on, or depends on, the characteristics of the leader *and* of the situation. Fiedler's contingency model helps explain why a manager may be an effective leader in one situation and ineffective in another; it also suggests which kinds of managers are likely to be most effective in which situations.[26]

LEADER STYLE   Like the trait approach, Fiedler hypothesized that personal characteristics can influence leader effectiveness. He used the term *leader style* to refer to a manager's characteristic approach to leadership, and he identified two basic leader styles: *relationship oriented* and *task oriented*. All managers can be described as having one style or the other.

relationship-oriented leaders Leaders whose primary concern is to develop good relationships with their subordinates and to be liked by them.

Relationship-oriented leaders are primarily concerned with developing good relationships with their subordinates and being liked by them. Relationship-oriented managers focus on having high-quality interpersonal relationships with subordinates. This does not mean, however, that the job does not get done when relationship-oriented leaders are at the helm. But it does mean that the quality of interpersonal relationships with subordinates is a prime concern for relationship-oriented leaders.

task-oriented leaders Leaders whose primary concern is to ensure that subordinates perform at a high level.

Task-oriented leaders are primarily concerned with ensuring that subordinates perform at a high level. Task-oriented managers focus on task accomplishment and making sure the job gets done.

SITUATIONAL CHARACTERISTICS   According to Fiedler, leadership style is an enduring characteristic; managers cannot change their style, nor can they adopt different styles in different kinds of situations. With this in mind, Fiedler identified three situational characteristics that are important determinants of how favourable a situation is for leading: leader–member relations, task structure, and position power. When a situation is favourable for leading, it is relatively easy for a manager to influence subordinates so that they perform at a high level and contribute to organizational efficiency and effectiveness. In a situation unfavourable for leading, it is much more difficult for a manager to exert influence.

LEADER–MEMBER RELATIONS   The first situational characteristic that Fiedler described, leader–member relations, is the extent to which followers like, trust, and are loyal to their leader. Situations are more favourable for leading when **leader–member relations** are good.

TASK STRUCTURE   The second situational characteristic that Fiedler described, **task structure**, is the extent to which the work to be performed is clear-cut so that a leader's subordinates know what needs to be accomplished and how to go about doing it. When task structure is high, situations are favourable for leading. When task structure is low, goals may be vague, subordinates may be unsure of what they should be doing or how they should do it, and the situation is unfavourable for leading.

POSITION POWER   The third situational characteristic that Fiedler described, **position power**, is the amount of legitimate, reward, and coercive power a leader has by virtue of his or her position in an organization. Leadership situations are more favourable for leading when position power is strong.

COMBINING LEADER STYLE AND THE SITUATION   By taking all possible combinations of good and poor leader–member relations, high and low task structure, and strong and weak position power, Fiedler identified eight leadership situations, which vary in their favourability for leading (see Figure 13.2). After extensive research, he determined that relationship-oriented leaders are most effective in moderately favourable situations (situations IV, V, VI, and VII in Figure 13.2) and task-oriented leaders are most effective in very favourable (situations I, II, and III) or very unfavourable situations (situation VIII).

PUTTING THE CONTINGENCY MODEL INTO PRACTICE   According to Fiedler, leader style is an enduring characteristic that managers cannot change. This suggests that, in order to be effective, managers need to be placed in leadership situations that fit their style, or situations need to be changed to suit the manager. Situations can be changed, for example, by giving a manager more position power or taking steps to increase task structure such as by clarifying goals.

Research studies tend to support Fiedler's model but also suggest that, like most theories, it is in need of some modifications.[27] Additionally, some researchers find fault with the model's premise that leaders cannot alter their styles.

leader–member relations The extent to which followers like, trust, and are loyal to their leader; a determinant of how favourable a situation is for leading.

task structure The extent to which the work to be performed is clear-cut so that a leader's subordinates know what needs to be accomplished and how to go about doing it; a determinant of how favourable a situation is for leading.

position power The amount of legitimate, reward, and coercive power that a leader has by virtue of his or her position in an organization; a determinant of how favourable a situation is for leading.

Figure 13.2
Fiedler's Contingency Theory of Leadership

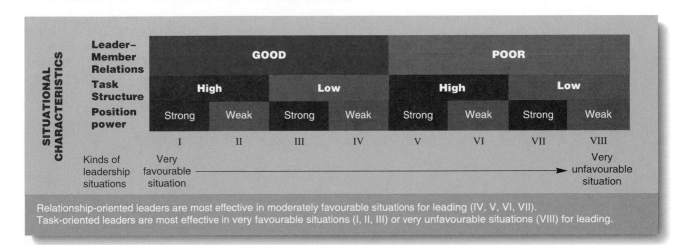

Relationship-oriented leaders are most effective in moderately favourable situations for leading (IV, V, VI, VII).
Task-oriented leaders are most effective in very favourable situations (I, II, III) or very unfavourable situations (VIII) for leading.

Hersey–Blanchard's Situational Leadership Theory

Paul Hersey and Ken Blanchard's **situational leadership theory** (SLT)[28] has been incorporated into leadership training programs at numerous Fortune 500 companies; over one million managers a year are taught its basic elements.[29]

SLT compares the leader–follower relationship to that between a parent and child. Just as parents needs to give more control to a child as the child becomes more mature and responsible, so too should leaders do this with employees. Hersey and Blanchard identify four specific leader behaviours that managers can use to lead their employees: highly directive to highly laissez-faire. Their theory is situationally based because the leader needs to choose a behaviour that will match the follower's ability and motivation. SLT says that if a follower is *unable* and *unwilling* to do a task, the leader needs to give clear and specific directions (in other words, the leader needs to be highly directive). If a follower is *unable* but *willing*, the leader needs to display both high task orientation and high relationship orientation. The high task orientation will compensate for the follower's lack of ability. The high relationship orientation will encourage the follower to "buy into" the leader's desires (in other words, the leader needs to "sell" the task). If the follower is *able* but *unwilling*, the leader needs to use a supportive and participative style. Finally, if the employee is both *able* and *willing*, the leader doesn't need to do much (in other words, a laissez-faire approach will work).

Path–Goal Theory

Developed by University of Toronto professor Martin Evans in the late 1960s, and subsequently expanded upon by Robert House (formerly at the University of Toronto, but now at the Wharton School of Business), **path–goal theory** focuses on what leaders can do to motivate their subordinates to achieve group and organizational goals.[30] The premise of path–goal theory is that effective leaders motivate subordinates to achieve goals by (1) clearly identifying the outcomes that subordinates are trying to obtain from the workplace, (2) rewarding subordinates with these outcomes for high performance and the attainment of work goals, and (3) clarifying for subordinates the paths leading to the attainment of work goals. Path–goal theory is a contingency model because it proposes that the steps that managers should take to motivate subordinates depend on both the nature of the subordinates and the type of work they do.

Based on the expectancy theory of motivation (see Chapter 12), path–goal theory provides managers with three guidelines to follow to be effective leaders:

1. *Find out what outcomes your subordinates are trying to obtain from their jobs and the organization.* These outcomes can range from satisfactory pay and job security to reasonable working hours and interesting and challenging job assignments. After identifying these outcomes, the manager should make sure that he or she has the reward power needed to distribute or withhold these outcomes.
2. *Reward subordinates for high performance and goal attainment with the outcomes they desire.*
3. *Clarify the paths to goal attainment for subordinates, remove any obstacles to high performance, and express confidence in subordinates' capabilities.* This does not mean that a manager needs to tell his or her subordinates what to do. Rather, it means that a manager needs to make sure that subordinates are clear about what they should be trying to accomplish and have the capabilities, resources, and confidence levels they need to be successful.

Path–goal theory identifies four kinds of behaviours that leaders can engage in to motivate subordinates:

- *Directive behaviours* are similar to initiating structure and include setting goals, assigning tasks, showing subordinates how to complete tasks, and taking concrete steps to improve performance.

- *Supportive behaviours* are similar to consideration and include expressing concern for subordinates and looking out for their best interests.
- *Participative behaviours* give subordinates a say in matters and decisions that affect them.
- *Achievement-oriented behaviours* motivate subordinates to perform at the highest level possible by, for example, setting very challenging goals, expecting that they be met, and believing in subordinates' capabilities.

Which of these behaviours should managers use to lead effectively? The answer to this question depends, or is contingent, on the nature of the subordinates and the kind of work they do.

Directive behaviours may be beneficial when subordinates are having difficulty completing assigned tasks, but they might be detrimental when subordinates are independent thinkers who work best when left alone. *Supportive* behaviours are often advisable when subordinates are experiencing high levels of stress. *Participative* behaviours can be particularly effective when subordinates' support of a decision is required. *Achievement-oriented* behaviours may increase motivation levels of highly capable subordinates who are bored from having too few challenges, but they might backfire if used with subordinates who are already pushed to their limit.

Effective managers seem to have a knack for determining the kinds of leader behaviours that are likely to work in different situations and result in increased efficiency and effectiveness, as indicated in this "Management Insight."

Management Insight

Turnaround in the Forestry Industry

When Tom Stephens took over as president and CEO of Vancouver-based Macmillan Bloedel (MacBlo) (www.weyerhaeuser.com) in September 1997, the company had spent three unsuccessful years trying to cut costs and improve productivity.[31] Within three months of his arrival, Stephens wrote a newsletter message accusing employees of giving up. "Collectively we're seen as losers— and that includes the 23rd-floor head office." With that, he announced that MacBlo would shed unprofitable operations.

At first, others thought that Stephens was simply using the same style as Al "Chainsaw" Dunlop, a familiar manager in the United States, who went into companies and fired thousands of employees to attain a quick corporate turn-around. Stephens said his style was more multi-layered than Dunlop's: "I can chew gum and walk at the same time."

Stephens proved true to his word. He did cut staff, but he also sold more than $1 billion worth of assets. He paid down debt, focused on the core business of solid wood products, and invested in a new mill in Saskatchewan. At the end of his first year, MacBlo showed a $42 million profit, compared to a $368 million loss the year before.

Stephens was not simply bottom-line oriented. For years, MacBlo had been a target of environmentalists, resisting pleas to abandon clear-cutting. Stephens started working to win over the environmentalists shortly after he arrived. Within a year he announced that MacBlo would end clear-cutting, going for a more selective approach to logging. "People want a more sensitive, less intrusive form of harvesting of their natural resources," he said. Greenpeace sent him a congratulatory bottle of champagne for his announcement.

In mid-June 1999, Weyerhaeuser Co., of Federal Way, Washington, offered $3.6 billion for MacMillan Bloedel Ltd., a sure sign of just how effective Stephens' leadership had been. Weyerhaeuser said it will honour the Canadian company's environmental promises.

Not every manager has been as successful at turnarounds in Canada as Tom Stephens, who was recruited from the United States because of his success at bringing Denver-based Manville Corp. out of bankruptcy. Retailer Millard Barron was brought north to turn Zellers Inc. around, and American Bill Fields was supposed to save Hudson's Bay Co. Neither could replicate their US experiences in Canada. Texas oilman J.P. Bryan was given the chance to restore to profitability two Canadian companies—Gulf Canada Resources Ltd. and Canadian 88 Energy Corp—and failed at both attempts.[32] These examples show the importance of understanding that one's leadership style may need to be adjusted for different companies and employees, and perhaps even for different countries.

The Leader Substitutes Model

leader substitute

Characteristics of subordinates or characteristics of a situation or context that act in place of the influence of a leader and make leadership unnecessary.

Can we just do away with leaders?

The leader substitutes model suggests that leadership is sometimes unnecessary because substitutes for leadership are present. A **leader substitute** is something that acts in place of the influence of a leader and makes leadership unnecessary. This model suggests that under certain conditions managers do not have to play a leadership role—that members of an organization sometimes can perform highly without a manager exerting influence over them.[33] The leader substitutes model is a contingency model because it suggests that in some situations leadership is unnecessary.

Take the case of David Cotsonas, who teaches English at a foreign language school in Cyprus, an island in the Mediterranean Sea. Cotsonas is fluent in Greek, English, and French, an excellent teacher, and highly motivated. Many of his students are businesspeople who have some rudimentary English skills and wish to increase their fluency to be able to conduct more of their business in English. He enjoys not only teaching them English but learning about the work they do, and he often keeps in touch with his students after they have finished his classes. Cotsonas meets with the director of the school twice a year to discuss semiannual class schedules and enrollments.

With practically no influence from a leader, Cotsonas is a highly motivated top performer at the school. In his situation, leadership is unnecessary because substitutes for leadership are present. Cotsonas's teaching expertise, his motivation, and his enjoyment of his work all are substitutes for the influence of a leader—in this case, the school's director. If the school's director were to try to exert influence over the way Cotsonas goes about performing his job, Cotsonas would probably resent this infringement on his autonomy, and it is unlikely that his performance would increase because he is already one of the school's best teachers.

As in Cotsonas' case, *characteristics of subordinates*—such as their skills, abilities, experience, knowledge, and motivation—can be substitutes for leadership.[34] *Characteristics of the situation or context*—such as the extent to which the work is interesting and enjoyable—also can be substitutes. When work is interesting and enjoyable, as it is for Cotsonas, jobholders do not need to be coaxed into performing because performing is rewarding in its own right. Similarly, when managers empower their subordinates or use *self-managed work teams* (discussed in detail in Chapter 14), the need for leadership influence from a manager is decreased because team members manage themselves.

Substitutes for leadership can increase organizational efficiency and effectiveness because they free up some of managers' valuable time and allow managers to focus their efforts on discovering new ways to improve organizational effectiveness. The director of the language school, for example, was able to spend much of his time making arrangements to open a second school in Rhodes, an island in the Aegean Sea, because of the presence of leadership substitutes not only in the case of Cotsonas but for most of the other teachers at the school as well.

Bringing it All Together

Effective leadership in organizations occurs when managers take steps to lead in a way that is appropriate for the situation or context in which leadership occurs and for the subordinates who are being led. The three contingency models of leadership discussed above help managers home in on the necessary ingredients for effective leadership. They are complementary in that each one looks at the leadership question from a different angle. Fiedler's contingency model explores how a manager's leadership style needs to be matched to the leadership situation that the manager is in for maximum effectiveness. Hersey–Blanchard's situational leadership theory examines the need for leaders to adjust their style to match their followers' ability and motivation. House's path–goal theory focuses on how managers should motivate subordinates and describes the specific kinds of behaviours that managers can engage in to have a highly motivated workforce. The leadership substitutes model alerts managers to the fact that sometimes they do not need to exert influence over subordinates and thus can free up their time for other important activities. Table 13.3 recaps these four contingency models of leadership.

Table 13.3
Contingency Models of Leadership

MODEL	FOCUS	KEY CONTINGENCIES
Fiedler's contingency model	Describes two leader styles, relationship-oriented and task-oriented, and the kinds of situations in which each kind of leader will be most effective	Whether or not a relationship-oriented or a task-oriented leader is effective is contingent on the situation
Hersey–Blanchard's situational leadership theory	Describes how leaders adjust their styles to match their followers' ability and motivation	The styles that managers should use are contingent on the ability and motivation of subordinates
House's path–goal theory	Describes how effective leaders motivate their followers	The behaviours that managers should engage in to be effective leaders are contingent on the nature of the subordinates and the work they do
Leader substitutes model	Describes when leadership is unnecessary	Whether or not leadership is necessary for subordinates to perform highly is contingent on characteristics of the subordinates and the situation

Tips for Managers

Contingency Models of Leadership

1. If you or one of your subordinates is relationship-oriented and in a very unfavourable situation for leading, try to increase the favourability of the situation by increasing task structure or position power or improving leader–member relations.

2. Determine what outcomes your subordinates are trying to obtain from their jobs, make sure you have reward power for these outcomes, and distribute the outcomes based on performance levels.

3. Express confidence in your subordinates' capabilities and do whatever you can to help them believe in their ability to succeed. Remove any obstacles to success.

4. Explore how you can take advantage of leadership substitutes to free up some of the time you spend supervising your subordinates.

Transactional and Transformational Leadership

transactional leadership Leaders who guide their subordinates toward expected goals with no expectation of exceeding expected behaviour.

The leadership theories presented thus far have concerned a transactional style of leadership. **Transactional leadership** occurs when managers guide or motivate their subordinates in the direction of established goals. Some transactional leaders use rewards and recognize appropriate behaviour. Under this kind of leadership, employees will generally meet performance expectations, though rarely will they exceed expectations.[35] Other transactional leaders emphasize correction and possibly punishment rather than rewards and recognition. This style "results in performance below expectations, and discourages innovation and initiative in the workplace."[36] While leaders should not ignore poor performance, effective leaders emphasize how to achieve expectations, rather than dwelling on mistakes.

Siemens AG
www.siemens.com/

An exciting new kind of leadership is sweeping the globe. The dramatic changes that Heinrich von Pierer, chief executive of the German electronics company Siemens AG, has made in his company exemplify what this new leadership is all about. When von Pierer took over in 1992, Siemens had a rigid hierarchy, was suffering from increased global competition, and was saddled with a conservative, perfectionist culture that stifled creativity and innovation and slowed decision making. Von Pierer's changes have been nothing short of revolutionary.[37] At the new Siemens, subordinates critique their managers, who receive training in how to be more democratic and participative and how to spur creativity. Employees are no longer afraid to speak their minds, and the quest for innovation is a driving force throughout the company.

transformational leadership Leadership that makes subordinates aware of the importance of their jobs and performance to the organization and aware of their own needs for personal growth and that motivates subordinates to work for the good of the organization.

Von Pierer is literally transforming Siemens and its thousands of employees to be more innovative and take the steps needed to gain a competitive advantage. When managers have such dramatic effects on their subordinates and on an organization as a whole, they are engaging in transformational leadership. **Transformational leadership** occurs when managers change (or transform) their subordinates in three important ways:[38]

1. *Transformational managers make subordinates aware of how important their jobs are for the organization and how necessary it is for them to perform those jobs as best they can so that the organization can attain its goals.* Von Pierer sent the message throughout Siemens that innovation, cost cutting, and increasing customer service and satisfaction were everyone's responsibilities and that improvements could be and needed to be made in these areas. For example, when von Pierer realized that managers in charge of microprocessor sales were not realizing the importance of their jobs and of performing them in a top-notch fashion, he had managers from Siemens' top microprocessor customers give the Siemens' microprocessor managers feedback about their poor service and unreliable delivery schedules. The microprocessor managers quickly realized how important it was for them to take steps to improve customer service.

2. *Transformational managers make their subordinates aware of the subordinates' own needs for personal growth, development, and accomplishment.* Von Pierer has made Siemens' employees aware of their own needs in this regard through numerous workshops and training sessions, through empowering employees throughout the company, through the development of fast-track career programs, and through increased reliance on self-managed work teams.[39]

3. *Transformational managers motivate their subordinates to work for the good of the organization as a whole, not just for their own personal gain or benefit.* Von Pierer's message to Siemens' employees has been clear: Dramatic changes in the way they perform their jobs are crucial for the future viability and success of Siemens. As von Pierer puts it, "We have to keep asking ourselves: Are we flexible enough? Are we changing enough?"[40] One way von Pierer has tried to get all employees thinking in these terms is by inserting self-addressed postcards in the company

magazine that is distributed to all employees; he urges employees to send their ideas for making improvements to him directly.

When managers transform their subordinates in these three ways, subordinates trust the manager, are highly motivated, and help the organization achieve its goals. As a result of von Pierer's transformational leadership, for example, a team of Siemens' engineers working in blue jeans in a rented house developed a tool control system in one-third the time and at one-third the cost of other similar systems developed at Siemens.[41] How do managers like von Pierer transform subordinates and produce dramatic effects in their organizations? There are at least three ways in which managers and other transformational leaders can influence their followers: by being a charismatic leader, by stimulating subordinates intellectually, and by engaging in developmental consideration. Table 13.4 outlines the differences between transactional and transformational leadership.

BEING A CHARISMATIC LEADER Transformational managers are **charismatic leaders**. They have a vision of how good things could be in their work groups and organizations that is in contrast with the status quo. Their vision usually entails dramatic improvements in group and organizational performance as a result of changes in the organization's structure, culture, strategy, decision making, and other critical processes and factors. This vision paves the way for gaining a competitive advantage.

charismatic leader
An enthusiastic, self-confident leader able to communicate clearly his or her vision of how good things could be.

Charismatic leaders are excited and enthusiastic about their vision and clearly communicate it to their subordinates. The excitement, enthusiasm, and self-confidence of a charismatic leader contribute to the leader's being able to inspire followers to enthusiastically support his or her vision.[42] As Mal Ransom, vice-president of marketing at Packard Bell Computers, puts it, "We all buy into the dream; we all buy into the vision."[43] People often think of charismatic leaders or managers as being "larger than life." The essence of charisma, however, is having a vision and enthusiastically communicating it to others. Thus, managers who appear to be quiet and earnest can also be charismatic.

The most comprehensive analysis of charismatic leadership was conducted by Professor Rabindra Kanungo at McGill University, together with Jay Conger.[44] Based on studies of managers from Canada, the United States, and India, they

Table 13.4
Characteristics of Transactional and Transformational Leaders

Transactional Leader

Contingent Reward: Contracts exchange of rewards for effort, promises rewards for good performance, recognizes accomplishments.

Management by Exception (active): Watches and searches for deviations from rules and standards, takes corrective action.

Management by Exception (passive): Intervenes only if standards are not met.

Laissez Faire: Abdicates responsibilities, avoids making decisions.

Transformational Leader

Charisma: Provides vision and sense of mission, instills pride, gains respect and trust.

Inspiration: Communicates high expectations, uses symbols to focus efforts, expresses important purposes in simple ways.

Intellectual Stimulation: Promotes intelligence, rationality, and careful problem solving.

Individualized Consideration: Gives personal attention, treats each employee individually, coaches, advises.

Source: B.M. Bass, "From Transactional to Transformational Leadership: Learning to Share the Vision," *Organizational Dynamics*, Winter 1990, p. 22. Reprinted by permission of the publisher. *American Management Association*, New York. All rights reserved.

Table 13.5

Key Characteristics of Charismatic Leaders

1. *Vision and articulation.* Has a vision—expressed as an idealized goal—that proposes a future better than the status quo; is able to clarify the importance of the vision in terms that are understandable to others.
2. *Personal risk.* Willing to take on high personal risk, incur high costs, and engage in self-sacrifice to achieve the vision.
3. *Environmental sensitivity.* Able to make realistic assessments of the environmental constraints and resources needed to bring about change.
4. *Sensitivity to follower needs.* Perceptive of others' abilities and responsive to their needs and feelings.
5. *Unconventional behaviour.* Engages in behaviours that are perceived as novel and counter to norms.

Source: Based on J.A. Conger and R.N. Kanungo, *Charismatic Leadership in Organizations* (Thousand Oaks, CA: Sage, 1998), p. 94.

identified five dimensions that characterize charismatic leadership. These are shown in Table 13-5.

Does charismatic leadership really make a difference? An unpublished study by Robert House and some colleagues looking at 63 American and 49 Canadian companies (including Nortel, Molson, Gulf Canada, and Manulife) found that "between 15 and 25 percent of the variation in profitability among the companies was accounted for by the leadership qualities of their CEO."[45] Charismatic leaders led more profitable companies.

One of the most cited studies of the effects of charismatic leadership was done at the University of British Columbia in the early 1980s by Jane Howell (now at the University of Western Ontario) and Peter Frost (still at the University of British Columbia).[46] The two found that those who worked under a charismatic leader generated more ideas, produced better results, reported higher job satisfaction, and showed stronger bonds of loyalty. Howell, in summarizing these results, says, "Charismatic leaders know how to inspire people to think in new directions."[47]

STIMULATING SUBORDINATES INTELLECTUALLY Transformational managers openly share information with their subordinates so that subordinates are aware of problems and the need for change. The manager causes subordinates to view problems in their groups and throughout the organization from a different perspective, consistent with the manager's vision. Whereas in the past subordinates may not have been aware of some problems, may have viewed problems as a "management issue" beyond their concern, or may have viewed problems as insurmountable, the transformational manager leads subordinates to view problems as challenges that they can and will meet and conquer. The manager engages and empowers subordinates to take personal responsibility for helping to solve problems.[48]

ENGAGING IN DEVELOPMENTAL CONSIDERATION When managers engage in developmental consideration, they not only perform the consideration behaviours described earlier, such as demonstrating true concern for the well-being of subordinates, but go one step further. The manager goes out of his or her way to support and encourage subordinates, giving them opportunities to enhance their skills and capabilities and to grow and excel on the job.[49] Heinrich von Pierer engages in developmental consideration in numerous ways, such as providing counselling sessions with a psychologist for managers who are having a hard time adapting to the changes at Siemens and sponsoring hiking trips to stimulate employees to think and work in new ways.[50]

All organizations, no matter how large or small, successful or unsuccessful, can benefit when their managers engage in transformational leadership. The benefits of transformational leadership, however, are often most apparent when an organization is in trouble, as indicated in this "Managing Globally."

Managing Globally

Transformational Leadership in South Korea

In 1989, when Lee Hun-Jo became chief executive of the once-successful Korean electrical appliance and electronics company Goldstar, the company was headed for ruin. Global and domestic market share was slipping, quality was declining, and even rank-and-file employees realized that bankruptcy was imminent if things did not change. Less than 10 years after Lee took over, Goldstar (renamed LG Electronics Co. in 1994) recovered its spot as the top producer of washing machines, refrigerators, and colour TVs in South Korea. LG Electronics also is gaining ground globally in the areas of liquid-crystal displays and semiconductors.[51]

Lee realized from the start that nothing short of a major transformation would turn LG Electronics' fortunes around. As he put it, "You have to transform human beings ... If you can't change your people, you can't change your organization. If you can't do that, you can't reach your goal."[52]

Lee's vision for LG Electronics included its being a top performer domestically and globally. He also envisioned dramatic changes for the organization's structure and culture. Like many Korean companies, LG Electronics had a relatively rigid hierarchy with decision making centralized at the top and a culture that respected authority and tradition. Lee's vision included decentralization of decision making and a culture supportive of efficiency, effectiveness, and innovation. In numerous face-to-face meetings, Lee enthusiastically communicated his vision throughout LG Electronics, made many changes to support it, and has even taken symbolic steps to communicate that things are changing. Rather than wearing the conservative neckties favoured by Korean top managers, Lee wears radiantly coloured ties and refuses to sit in the traditionally honoured spots reserved for the chief executive in meetings with managers.

Lee intellectually stimulates his subordinates in multiple ways. He has opened new paths of communication between nonmanagerial employees and managers, and has openly shared the company's problems with employees and made them feel responsible for helping to solve them. Decision making has been decentralized, and all employees are encouraged to feel responsible for coming up with improvements, ideas for new products, and ways to increase quality. LG Electronics traditionally took products developed by foreign competitors, such as the Japanese, and tried to copy and customize them for the Korean marketplace. Part of Lee's vision is for LG Electronics to come up with its own innovative products. He made product development engineers feel responsible for doing this and sent them out to talk to LG Electronics' customers to see what they really wanted. As a result of this intellectual stimulation, LG Electronics now has an innovative and best-selling product on its hands—a refrigerator specially designed to keep kimchi (Korea's national dish of pickled and fermented cabbage and radishes) fresh smelling and tasting for much longer than is possible in a conventional refrigerator.

Lee also engages in developmental consideration. He has taken dramatic steps to improve management relations with the union, and has not only shared information with union leaders but also has encouraged them to meet with him whenever they have ideas for improving things at LG Electronics.[53] He wants his employees to reach their full potential and is doing whatever he can think of to help them do that. Lee also reads extensively about the latest advances in management thought and practice in the United States and other countries, to help himself be an effective manager and leader. All in all, Lee seems to be just the kind of leader LG Electronics needed to regain its position as a top-performing global organization—a transformational leader.

The evidence supporting the superiority of transformational leadership is overwhelmingly impressive. For example, studies of Canadian, American, and German military officers found, at every level, that transformational leaders were considered more effective than their transactional counterparts.[54] Professor Jane Howell (at the Richard Ivey School of Business at the University of Western Ontario) and her colleagues studied 250 executives and managers at a major financial-services company and found that "transformational leaders had 34 percent higher business unit performance results than other types of leaders."[55] Studies also find that transformational leadership is more strongly correlated with lower turnover rates, higher productivity, and higher employee satisfaction than transactional leadership.[56]

Tips for Managers

Transformational Leadership

1. Let subordinates know how their own jobs contribute to organizational effectiveness and stress the importance of high performance.
2. Help subordinates learn new skills and develop on the job.
3. Have a vision of how much better things can be in your organization and enthusiastically communicate your vision throughout the organization.
4. Share organizational problems and challenges with subordinates and engage them to help solve the problems and meet the challenges.
5. Take a personal interest in your subordinates and inspire them to accomplish as much as they can.

Gender and Leadership

Do men and women lead differently?

National Post
CEO Scorecard
www.nationalpostbusiness.
com/datamining/ceo/
ceo.asp

The increasing number of women entering the ranks of management as well as the problems some women face in their efforts to be hired as managers or promoted into management positions have prompted researchers to explore the relationship between gender and leadership. Although relatively more women are in management positions today than there were ten years ago, relatively few women are in top management and, in some organizations, even in middle management. Although women make up 45 percent of the labour force in Canada, they fill only 32 percent of managerial roles, and only 12 percent of the senior management roles. Half of Canada's companies have no women in the senior ranks at all.[57] Of National Post's Top 150 CEOs of 2000, only two were women.

When women do advance to top-management positions, special attention is often focused on the fact that they are women, such as when Bobbi Gaunt was named to head Ford Motor Co. of Canada and Maureen Kempston Darkes was named to head General Motors of Canada.

A widespread stereotype of women is that they are nurturing, supportive, and concerned with interpersonal relations. Men are stereotypically viewed as being

Linda Hasenfratz, COO of Guelph, ON-based Linamar Corporation, will likely one day succeed her father Frank as chair and CEO of the company. Meanwhile, although she has worked in many positions including on the shop floor, some of Linamar's employees have questioned a woman's ability to lead in the male-dominated automotive parts industry.

directive and focused on task accomplishment. Such stereotypes suggest that women tend to be more relationship oriented as managers and engage in more consideration behaviours, whereas men are more task oriented and engage in more initiating structure behaviours. Does the behaviour of actual male and female managers bear out these stereotypes? Do female managers lead in different ways than males? Are male or female managers more effective as leaders?

Research suggests that male managers and female managers who have leadership positions in organizations behave in similar ways.[58] Women do not engage in more consideration than men, and men do not engage in more initiating structure than women. Research does suggest, however, that leadership style may vary between women and men. Women tend to be somewhat more participative as leaders than men, involving subordinates in decision making and seeking their input.[59] Male managers tend to be less participative than female managers, making more decisions on their own and wanting to do things their own way.

There are at least two reasons why female managers may be more participative as leaders than male managers.[60] First, subordinates may try to resist the influence of female managers more than they do the influence of male managers. Some subordinates may never have reported to a woman before, some may inappropriately see management roles as being more appropriate for men than for women, and some may just resist being led by a woman. To overcome this resistance and encourage subordinates' trust and respect, female managers may adopt a participative approach.

A second reason why female managers may be more participative is that they sometimes have better interpersonal skills than male managers.[61] A participative approach to leadership requires high levels of interaction and involvement between a manager and his or her subordinates, sensitivity to subordinates' feelings, and the ability to make decisions that may be unpopular with subordinates but necessary for goal attainment. Good interpersonal skills may help female managers have the effective interactions with their subordinates that are crucial to a participative approach.[62] To the extent that male managers have more difficulty managing interpersonal relationships, they may shy away from the high levels of interaction with subordinates that are necessary for true participation.

The key finding from research on leader behaviours, however, is that male and female managers do *not* differ significantly in their propensities to perform different leader behaviours. Even though they may be more participative, female managers do not engage in more consideration or less initiating structure than male managers.

Perhaps a question even more important than whether male and female managers differ in the leadership behaviours they perform is whether they differ in effectiveness. Consistent with the findings for leader behaviours, research suggests that across different kinds of organizational settings, male and female managers tend to be *equally* effective as leaders.[63] Thus, there is no logical basis for stereotypes favouring male managers and leaders or for the existence of the glass ceiling (an invisible barrier that seems to prevent women from advancing as far as they should in some organizations). Because women and men are equally effective as leaders, the increasing number of women in the workforce should result in a larger pool of highly qualified candidates for management positions in organizations, ultimately enhancing organizational effectiveness.[64]

Chapter Summary

THE NATURE OF LEADERSHIP

- Personal Leadership Style and Managerial Tasks
- Leadership Styles Across Cultures
- Power: The Key to Leadership
- Empowerment: An Ingredient in Modern Management

TRAIT AND BEHAVIOUR MODELS OF LEADERSHIP

- The Trait Model
- The Behaviour Model

CONTINGENCY MODELS OF LEADERSHIP

- Fiedler's Contingency Model
- Hersey–Blanchard's Situational Leadership Theory
- Path–Goal Theory
- The Leader Substitutes Model
- Bringing it All Together

TRANSACTIONAL AND TRANSFORMATIONAL LEADERSHIP

GENDER AND LEADERSHIP

Summary and Review

THE NATURE OF LEADERSHIP   Leadership is the process by which a person exerts influence over other people and inspires, motivates, and directs their activities to help achieve group or organizational goals. Leaders are able to influence others because they possess power. The five types of power available to managers are legitimate power, reward power, coercive power, expert power, and referent power. Many managers are using empowerment as a tool to increase their effectiveness as leaders.

TRAIT AND BEHAVIOUR MODELS OF LEADERSHIP   The trait model of leadership describes personal characteristics or traits that contribute to effective leadership. However, some managers who possess these traits are not effective leaders, and some managers who do not possess all the traits are nevertheless effective leaders. The behaviour model of leadership describes two kinds of behaviour that most leaders engage in: consideration and initiating structure.

CONTINGENCY MODELS OF LEADERSHIP   Contingency models take into account the complexity surrounding leadership and the role of the situation in determining whether a manager is an effective or ineffective leader. Fiedler's contingency model explains why managers may be effective leaders in one situation and ineffective in another. According to Fiedler's model, relationship-oriented leaders are most effective in situations that are moderately favourable for leading, and task-oriented leaders are most effective in situations that are very favourable or very unfavourable for leading. Hersey–Blanchard's situational leadership theory examines the need for leaders to adjust their style to match their followers' ability and motivation. For some subordinates it is necessary to give clear and specific directions, while for others, it may be appropriate for the manager to be laissez-faire in approach. House's path–goal theory describes how effective managers motivate their subordinates by determining what outcomes their subordinates want, rewarding subordinates with these outcomes when they achieve their goals and perform at a high level, and clarifying the paths to goal attainment. Managers can engage in four different kinds of behaviours to motivate subordinates: directive behaviours, supportive behaviours, participative behaviours, or achievement-oriented behaviours. The leader substitutes model suggests that sometimes managers do not have to play a leadership role because their subordinates perform highly without the manager having to exert influence over them.

TRANSACTIONAL AND TRANSFORMATIONAL LEADERSHIP Transactional leaders generally only get their subordinates to meet expectations. Transformational leadership occurs when managers have dramatic effects on their subordinates and on the organization as a whole and inspire and energize subordinates to solve problems and improve performance. These effects include making subordinates aware of the importance of their own jobs and high performance, making subordinates aware of their own needs for personal growth, development, and accomplishment, and motivating subordinates to work for the good of the organization and not just their own personal gain. Managers can engage in transformational leadership by being charismatic leaders, by stimulating subordinates intellectually, and by engaging in developmental consideration. Transformational managers also often engage in transactional leadership by using their reward and coercive powers to encourage high performance.

GENDER AND LEADERSHIP   Female and male managers do not differ in the leadership behaviours that they perform, contrary to stereotypes suggesting that women are more relationship oriented and men more task oriented. Female managers sometimes are more participative than male managers, however. Research has found that women and men are equally effective as managers and leaders.

Management in Action

Topics for Discussion and Action

1. Describe the steps managers can take to increase their power and ability to be effective leaders.

2. Think of specific situations in which it might be especially important for a manager to engage in consideration and in initiating structure.

3. Interview an actual manager to find out how the three situational characteristics that Fiedler identified are affecting the manager's ability to provide leadership.

4. For your current job or for a future job that you expect to hold, describe what your supervisor could do to strongly motivate you to be a top performer.

5. Discuss why managers might want to change the behaviours they engage in, given their situation, their subordinates, and the nature of the work being done. Do you think managers are able to change their leadership behaviours readily? Why or why not?

6. Discuss why substitutes for leadership can contribute to organizational effectiveness.

7. Describe what transformational leadership is, and explain how managers can engage in it.

8. Find an example of a company that has dramatically turned its fortunes around and improved its performance. Determine whether a transformational manager was behind the turnaround and, if so, what this manager did.

9. Discuss why some people still think that men make better managers than women even though research indicates that men and women are equally effective as managers and leaders.

Building Management Skills

Analyzing Failures of Leadership

Think about a situation you are familiar with in which a leader was very ineffective. Then answer the following questions.

1. What sources of power did this leader have? Did the leader have enough power to influence his or her followers?

2. What kinds of behaviours did this leader engage in? Were they appropriate for the situation? Why or why not?

3. From what you know, do you think this leader was a task-oriented leader or a relationship-oriented leader? How favourable was this leader's situation for leading?

4. What steps did this leader take to motivate his or her followers? Were these steps appropriate or inappropriate? Why?

5. What signs, if any, did this leader show of being a transformational leader?

Small Group Breakout Exercise

Improving Leadership Effectiveness

Form groups of three to five people, and appoint one member as the spokesperson who will communicate your findings and conclusions to the whole class when called on by the instructor. Then discuss the following scenario.

You are a team of human resource consultants who have been hired by Carla Caruso, an entrepreneur who started her own interior decorating business. At first, she worked on her own as an independent contractor. Then, because of a dramatic increase in the number of new homes being built, she decided to form her own company.

She hired a secretary/ bookkeeper and 4 interior decorators. Caruso still does decorating jobs herself and has adopted a hands-off approach to leading the 4 decorators because she feels that interior design is a very personal, creative endeavour. Rather than paying the decorators on some kind of commission basis, she pays them a higher-than-average salary so that they are motivated to do what's best for their customers, not what will result in higher billings and commissions.

Caruso thought everything was going smoothly until customer complaints started coming in. These complaints were about the decorators being hard to reach, promising unrealistic delivery times, being late for or failing to keep appointments, and being impatient and rude when customers had trouble making up their minds. Caruso knows that her decorators are competent people and is concerned that she is not effectively leading and managing them. She has asked for your advice.

1. What advice can you give Caruso either to increase her power or to use her existing power more effectively?

2. Does Caruso seem to be performing appropriate leader behaviours in this situation? What advice can you give her about the kinds of behaviours she should perform?

3. How can Caruso increase the decorators' motivation to deliver high-quality customer service?

4. Would you advise Caruso to try to engage in transformational leadership in this situation? If not, why not? If so, what steps would you advise her to take?

Exploring the World Wide Web

Specific Assignment

Many CEOs are highly visible leaders in their companies and industries. One such CEO is Mogens Smed of Calgary-based Smed International. Scan the company's Web site (www.smednet.com/ frameset.html). Click on "News and Stories," then on "November 15, 2000—History's in, pigeon droppings are out" to learn more about Smed. Then click on "Community" to learn more about the various contributions the company makes to community efforts.

1. How would you characterize Mogens Smed's personal leadership style?

2. In what ways does Smed encourage community activism?

3. How might Smed be considered a transformational leader?

General Assignment

Find the Web site of a company that provides information on the company's missions, goals, and values, the company's top managers and their personal leadership styles. How might the company's missions, goals, and values impact the process of leadership in this company?

ManagementCase

Cynthia Trudell: Leading in a Man's World

Cynthia Trudell, who was born in Saint John, NB, received her Ph.D. in physical science from the University of Windsor, specializing in photo chemistry—the study of gases on objects.[65] However, the slow pace and isolation of academic life convinced her to take a job in industry. Today Trudell is a member of the Automotive Hall of Fame and several US publications have referred to her as one of the top women executives in the United States.

Trudell started at Ford Motor Co. of Canada's engine plant in Windsor in 1979. Two years later, she was the senior engineering supervisor at General Motor Canada's transmission plant in Windsor, later rising to superintendent of manufacturing there. From that start, Trudell held a variety of positions within General Motors, her last as chair and president of Saturn Corp. between 1999 and 2001. When she was appointed head of Saturn, she became the first woman ever to head a fully integrated subsidiary of a North American auto maker. In April 2001, she left General Motors to become president of Brunswick Corporation's Sea Ray Group, where she heads a staff of 5000 and nine plants. Sea Ray is the largest manufacturer of powerboats in the world, and its products include the Sea Ray, Baja and Boston Whaler brands.

Trudell is a study in determination. At 19, she chose her life's mantra: "When I'm dying, and they're burying me, I want to be able to shake my fist and scream back at them, 'I lived, I laughed, I learned and I loved.'" When she was appointed president of Saturn, a *New York Times* reporter commented: "Now the world's largest auto maker is about to put a true car guy in charge of its Saturn division—only the car guy is a woman."

As she started her challenge at Saturn, she recognized that she would have to turn the division into a profitable unit. And that if she didn't deliver the results, she probably shouldn't be there.

Trudell is clear about who she is as a leader. She finds bureaucracy a waste of time: "It doesn't make money for you." She gets frustrated when she thinks she knows the right way to do something and others stand in the way. Therefore, the appointment to Saturn suited her. Saturn was known for its relatively flat hierarchy and cooperative relations between union and management.

The Saturn culture values open dialogue, something that Trudell values as well. She doesn't feel that her opening position in dealing with employees is to say, "This is the way we're going to do it." Instead, she recognizes the need to explain her point of view patiently, and to win support. Still, she recognizes that sometimes as a leader, a person has to be tough. "You can't be emotional, unless you're passionate. But if you overuse that, that loses its impact on people. Sometimes you have to show a little bit of anger because that 'stun guns' people."

She was openly supportive of Rick Wagoner, who took over as chief executive of GM in summer 2000, because she thought he supported a consensus style of management. But she also knew this would be a different style of management at GM, and that some senior executives would resist. She was clear about how things should be handled to reach a more consen-

sual style in the organization, though. "That means doing some tough stuff. It means saying, 'If you don't change your behaviour, you don't fit.'"

Trudell often relies on intuition to guide her, and believes anyone can learn to use their intuition. She suggests that decision makers should write down both what their gut and their brain are telling them, and then follow the outcome of a decision to see which gave better guidance. "People who are good at risk management are people who can get their gut helping to feed their brain. Intuition means that your senses are out there all the time. I have seen men, all of a sudden, have an intuition they didn't even know existed. If you always take the easy road, because that's what the brain says, because we'll rationalize, then people never realize their fullest potential."

One of Trudell's challenges has been to work effectively with labour unions. She has certainly earned their respect, if not their admiration. She was inspired early on in her career by a general manager she worked under who worked hard to establish better relationships with unionized employees. From that, she says, "I saw that the people who made the product were the people we all needed to support. They were the ones who made the money for us and everybody else was high-priced overhead."

Rick Chene of the Canadian Auto Workers (CAW) says that their relationship was generally positive when he worked with her at Windsor. When she tried to introduce lean manufacturing in Windsor, the fights with the CAW were bitter, and there were many disagreements. But Chene noted that Trudell "would never get bent out of shape. She'd move onto other issues." When she left Windsor to move to her next position, Chene and other union executives "made sure to say good-bye—a practice that … is far from universal." Chene suggested that if Trudell were given the opportunity by senior management to work in her own style with union members, "I was under the impression that Cynthia could be a catalyst for improving relations with workers. But not given the opportunity, she'd be another typical GM manager."

At the time of her departure from Saturn, little explanation was given about whether she made the move herself or whether she was encouraged to move elsewhere. Her own comment at the time was, "The opportunity presented itself and I probably would have never even thought of it had it not been there." Both Saturn and Sea Ray are located in Knoxville, Tennessee.

George W. Buckley, Brunswick's chairman and chief executive officer, in announcing her appointment said, "Her technical expertise, knowledge of systems and platforms, her strong brand management skills and experience with dealer channels, plus her focus on product quality, are ideally suited to make a tremendous impact at Sea Ray."

Questions

1. In what ways does Cynthia Trudell try to exert influence over her employees? Why has she been able to exert this influence?

2. How would you describe Trudell's personal leadership style?

3. How would you apply the different leadership theories to Trudell's beliefs about management?

ManagementCase
In the News

From the Pages of *The National Post*
M&M Founder Carving Bigger Slice of Market: Specialty Meats

When Mac Voisin, who is known as the "Baron of Barbecuing," was building his M and M Meat Shops franchise network, one of the golden rules he developed was to weed out all the hard-nosed entrepreneurs, a strategy that has kept the rebels out and conformists in line.

It has allowed the self-made man to grow M and M Meat Shops into a solid operation that consists of 300 stores across Canada with sales approaching $300-million.

"[The hiring strategy] is really a personality test and what it tells us is if the person is too entrepreneurial or not entrepreneurial enough. Both extremes can cause us a whole lot of grief," said the 51-year-old Mr. Voisin, who began the business 20 years ago in Kitchener, Ont., and developed the hiring concept following a handful of unprofitable outlets.

"If they're too entrepreneurial they'll want to sell their own product and work their own hours. If they're not entrepreneurial enough, we're going to have to hold their hands, they're going to phone us all the time and keep to the store instead of being out in the community," he said. "We're looking for a happy medium."

With record sales, the company has plans to become a 500-store franchise by 2006, and an expansion into the United States has not been ruled out.

In the 1980s, Mr. Voisin left the construction business to start M and M Meat Shops with brother-in-law Mark Nowak. The big joke, he says, was that at the time anybody with a pulse and a pocketbook could buy a franchise. The lack of careful consideration resulted in poor service as squabbles between owners and franchisees resulted in lower margins.

Mr. Voisin wanted to do things differently and spent a lot of time investing in people, management and a work ethic that went beyond what a lot of other companies did.

For instance, Mr. Voisin has a fax line reserved for franchisees who want to take their concerns directly to the president. He made a commitment to respond within 24 hours and has lived up to it.

Every two years, Mr. Voisin does a friendship tour, visiting store owners from North Delta, B.C., to Pierrefonds, Que. At head office, he is known to take employees along on these tours on a moment's notice.

All sales staff are required to undergo a four-month training course in customer service. The company also fosters a strong philanthropic spirit, raising nearly $5-million for the Crohn's and Colitis Foundation of Canada over the last 12 years. It was a cause Mr. Voisin independently sought to support simply because it was a little known charity.

The company's congenial approach has earned it several national awards, including the first Canadian Franchise Association award for distinction in 1992, when M and M Meat Shops beat out iconic chains McDonald's and Burger King. "From the very beginning they looked at things very strategically," said Richard Cunningham, the trade group's president. "They did a lot of training with their management team and they were quick to go in and solve a problem before it escalated into any kind of serious level."

The idea for M and M Meat Shops was inspired out of hosting barbecues. Mr. Voisin said he was frustrated with the lack of specialty meats sold in the grocery stores. The company struggled in the first few years, but in the early 1990s it rounded a corner after introducing smaller packaged items like chicken Kiev and veal Swiss.

"We really did poorly in the first five years," Mr. Voisin said. "We never really got any outside help and we just stumbled along. Our biggest challenge was understanding the importance of the expense sheet. Entrepreneurs tend to be very sales-oriented and they don't spend a lot of time trying to figure out how to control costs."

As the company grew, he began to step back from the day-to-day operations and expanded his senior management team to include industry veterans. Sales began to jump because of a rise in microwave sales, advances in flash freezing technology and an influx of women re-entering the workforce. The company even survived the arrival of big-box competition. Loblaw Cos. Ltd., for example, generated more than $2-billion last year from its popular President's Choice specialty labels. "We really weren't greatly impacted. [Loblaws] has probably helped and hindered us. They created more awareness for us, but on the other hand they could take some customers away," he said.

Mr. Voisin said retirement is a long way away and he always sees himself playing some type of role in the company. "I'll still visit stores and run regional meetings. I'm really the custodian of the fun culture we've developed. We believe if you're having fun people will want to stick around."

Source: K. Hanson, "M&M Founder Carving Bigger Slice of Market: Specialty Meats," *Financial Post (National Post)*, October 17, 2000, p. C5.

Questions

1. How would you describe Mac Voisin's personal leadership style?

2. What leadership behaviours does Voisin engage in?

3. Is Voisin a transformational leader? Why or why not?

Chapter fourteen

Groups and Teams

Learning Objectives

1. Explain why groups and teams are key contributors to organizational effectiveness.

2. Identify the different types of groups and teams that help managers and organizations achieve their goals.

3. Explain how different elements of group dynamics influence the functioning and effectiveness of groups and teams.

4. Explain why it is important for groups and teams to have a balance of conformity and deviance and a moderate level of cohesiveness.

5. Describe how managers can motivate group members to achieve organizational goals and reduce social loafing in groups and teams.

A Case in Contrast

Teams Work Wonders at Willow Manufacturing

Willow Manufacturing (www.willowcnc.com), a Toronto-based supplier of precision components, used to experience flaring tempers in its workplace often.[1] "Years ago we had all kinds of problems in our plant. Workplace violence was very much a part of our culture here, unfortunately, because of very lax hiring," says Willow's president, Dennis Wild. Managers created a "tough-boy" environment where they brow-beat staff while employees engaged in theft and arguments. The macho attitude of the plant was also not paying off: For many years, Willow was an unorganized, money-losing business.

Willow was incorporated in 1954 at its original location on Willow Ave. in the east end of Toronto. As the company grew over the years, so did its management team, until there were seven levels of management. These layers of management led to inefficient processes that caused lost time and money.

The plant itself was an unpleasant place to work; an inch-thick oil residue coated every surface. The factory was also noisy and smoky, which set the tone for poor employee morale and many internal disputes. The company came close to bankruptcy several times.

By the mid-1990s, Wild decided that it was time to restructure Willow to make it a better place to work, and to improve its financial situation. One of the key approaches to the turnaround was to create a team environment at Willow. Today, if you walked into Willow you would have trouble figuring out who was in charge. Everyone, from Wild on down, wears the same-style uniform. All members of the team are viewed as being equally important, which is why Willow removes status distinctions by having everyone wear the same clothing.

To enhance team interaction, Willow's managers were given training in how to create more

Willow Manufacturing went from unorganized, money-losing business to success after Dennis Wild, the company's president, introduced effective teamwork into the workplace.

teamwork. Management attitudes were changed as well, with an emphasis on removing the "us–them" attitude among employees and managers. Managers were also trained to coach and facilitate rather than to boss and manage.

Wild notes that to transform the company, some major housecleaning was in order. Under his direction, the company "hauled all the old emotional skeletons out of the closet and got staff to resolve many long-term conflicts."

Once the personal issues were resolved, Willow tackled inefficient manufacturing processes. Staff members were divided into teams that redesigned procedures, then submitted their ideas to another team that would further streamline the procedures. The teams were helping each other create better manufacturing processes.

In going through changes, Willow engaged in what's known as a "*kaizen* blitz," an attempt to create lean manufacturing systems in as short a period as possible. This put further pressure on Willow's teams. Therefore, at the end of each day, the teams met to evaluate the day's work and create a to-do list for the next day. Often, the teams were engaged in hour-by-hour planning.

Wild found that the system worked well. "It allowed us to implement improvements and make progress before we even had time to create barriers to the ideas. The key was the involvement of all employees, so that the processes we documented were sound and accepted by the people who had to use them."

Willow's vice-president, Linda Snow, says that the intensity and adrenaline rush of the *kaizen* blitz helped to create the successful team environment that's now part of Willow. "It was a self-imposed test in which we began to believe in our ability as a team and see how far we could stretch the improvement envelope in a short time."

The teamwork did not end once new procedures were put in place. Today, employees are consulted before a new piece of equipment is purchased. They also decide which shifts and hours they will work, giving them some control over balance between work and family.

Wild suggests that teamwork is essential to the company's success. "We've got a great group of people and they are the ones that are driving all of these changes, not me. It's the team that's driving the system. That is what all manufacturers need to do if they want to stay in business." ●

Overview

Dennis Wild and Willow Manufacturing are not alone in the shift toward using groups and teams to produce goods and services that better meet customers' needs. Companies such as Zellers, Xerox Canada, Dofasco, Toyota Canada, Westinghouse Canada, and Sears Canada are all relying on teams to help them gain a competitive advantage.[2] A 1994 Conference Board of Canada report found that over 80 percent of its 109 respondents used teams in the workplace,[3] a rate similar to that of US organizations.[4] In this chapter, we look in detail at how groups and teams can contribute to organizational effectiveness, and at the types of groups and teams used in organizations. We discuss how different elements of group dynamics influence the functioning and effectiveness of groups, and we describe how managers can motivate group members to achieve organizational goals and reduce social loafing in groups and teams. By the end of this chapter, you will appreciate why the effective management of groups and teams is a key ingredient for organizational performance and a source of competitive advantage. ●

group Two or more people who interact with each other to accomplish certain goals or meet certain needs.

team A group whose members work intensely with each other to achieve a specific, common goal or objective.

Groups, Teams, and Organizational Effectiveness

A **group** may be defined as two or more people who interact with each other to accomplish certain goals or meet certain needs.[5] A **team** is a group whose members work *intensely* with each other to achieve a specific common goal or objective. As these definitions imply, all teams are groups but not all groups are teams. The two characteristics that distinguish teams from groups are the *intensity* with which team members work together and the presence of a *specific, overriding team goal or objective.*

As described in the "Case in Contrast," members of the cross-functional teams at Willow worked intensely together to achieve the specific objective of developing a better and more productive working environment. In contrast, the accountants who work in a small CPA firm are a group: They may interact with each other to achieve goals, such as keeping up-to-date on the latest changes in accounting rules and regulations, maintaining a smoothly functioning office, satisfying clients, and attracting new clients, but they are not a team because they do not work intensely with each other. Each accountant concentrates on serving the needs of his or her own clients.

Because teams undergo some of the same processes as groups, there will be times in this chapter when what we say about groups applies to teams as well. As you might imagine, because members of teams work intensely together, teams can sometimes be difficult to form, and it may take time for members to learn how to work together effectively. Groups and teams can help an organization gain a competitive advantage because they can (1) enhance its performance, (2) increase its responsiveness to customers, (3) increase innovation, and (4) increase employees' motivation and satisfaction (see Figure 14.1). In this section, we look at each of these contributions.

Groups and Teams as Performance Enhancers

One of the main advantages of using groups is the opportunity to obtain a type of **synergy**: People working in a group are able to produce more or higher-quality outputs than would have been produced if each person had worked separately and all their individual efforts had been combined. The essence of synergy is captured in the saying, "The whole is more than the sum of its parts." Factors that can contribute to synergy in groups include the ability of group members to bounce ideas off one another, to correct each other's mistakes, to solve problems immediately as they arise, and to bring a diverse knowledge base to bear on a problem or goal. For instance, one of the challenges of Molson's chief operating officer, Dan O'Neill, has been to revitalize the company's heavily criticized recent ad strategies. O'Neill has rebuilt the company's national marketing team. However, he still faces the challenge of bringing "the new national team together with the 'really independent' regional marketing teams and 'develop synergies.'"[6] His ultimate

synergy Performance gains that result when individuals and departments coordinate their actions.

Figure 14.1

Groups' and Teams' Contributions to Organizational Effectiveness

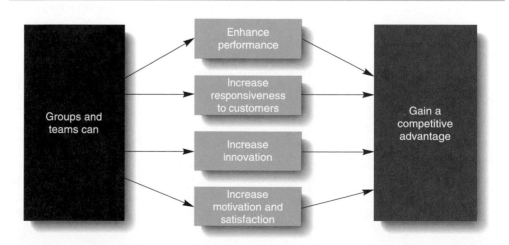

goal is to get the teams working so well together that Molson's can centralize marketing strategies while regionalizing their execution.

To take advantage of the potential for synergy in groups, managers need to make sure that groups are composed of members who have complementary skills and knowledge relevant to the group's work. Managers also need to give groups enough autonomy so that the groups, rather than the manager, are solving problems and determining how to achieve goals and objectives, as is true in the cross-functional teams at Willow. To promote synergy, managers need to empower their subordinates and be coaches, guides, and resources for groups, while refraining from playing a more directive or supervisory role. The potential for synergy in groups may be the reason why more and more managers are incorporating empowerment in their personal leadership styles (see Chapter 13). Managers can also make sure that the workplace is designed to facilitate teamwork, as Steelcase Canada does in this "Management Insight."

Management Insight

Creating Workplaces That Encourage Teamwork

How do you design a workplace that shows that teamwork really matters? Markham, ON-based Steelcase Canada (www.steelcase.com) chose to create office space that would support teamwork, and "transform the ways people work."[7] The company started by removing private offices, so that not even Steelcase Canada's president, Jim Mitchell, has a private office. He, his direct reports, and their secretaries share open offices. Some sales employees don't have offices at all, setting up their cordless phones, laptops and portable trolleys with files in open workspace.

When redesigning the Markham facility, managers at Steelcase were determined to create space that "[satisfied] teams first, then individuals." The company's president sees this as completely different from old organizational styles. "The old organizational paradigm for corporations was based on the military model of command and control," Mitchell says. Steelcase even exhibited this in its food facilities: Factory workers and administrators had separate cafeterias before the renovation. The new space is "organized around networks of trust and social monitoring."

The company is now designed around a hub, where the operating divisions are organized, and there is space for casual interaction, as well as coffee and meals. Walls are made of glass, letting everyone see the work that the company does, including its manufacturing department.

While Steelcase's layout facilitates teamwork, there are areas set aside so that private meetings can be held without disruption. One of the architects in charge of the project noted that, overall, "The merging of the diverse aspects of the headquarter facilities creates an environment where the shared activities of all of these groups is productive for the organization."

One further benefit to Steelcase: When customers visit, they can see Steelcase's products in use.

Groups, Teams, and Responsiveness to Customers

Being responsive to customers is not always easy. In manufacturing organizations, for example, customers' needs and desires for new and improved products have to be balanced against engineering constraints, production costs and feasibilities, government safety regulations, and marketing challenges. Being responsive to customers often requires the wide variety of skills and expertise found in different departments and at different levels in an organization's hierarchy. Sometimes employees at lower levels in the hierarchy, such as sales representatives for a computer company, are closest to customers and most attuned to their needs. However, lower-level employees like salespeople often lack the technical expertise needed to come up with new product ideas; such expertise is found in the research and development department. Bringing salespeople, research and development experts, and members of other departments together in a group or cross-functional team can enhance responsiveness to customers. Consequently, when managers form a team, they need to make sure that the diversity of expertise and knowledge needed to be responsive to customers exists within the team; this is why cross-functional teams are so popular.

In a cross-functional team, the expertise and knowledge that are housed in different organizational departments are brought together in the skills and knowledge of the team members. Managers of high-performing organizations are careful to determine which types of expertise and knowledge are required for teams to be responsive to customers, and they use this information in forming teams.

Teams and Innovation

Innovation is the creative development of new products, new technologies, new services, or even new organizational structures. Often, an individual working alone does not possess the extensive and diverse set of skills, knowledge, and expertise frequently required for successful innovation. Managers can better encourage innovation by creating teams of diverse individuals who together have the knowledge relevant to a particular type of innovation, rather than by relying on individuals working alone.

Using teams to innovate has other advantages as well. First, team members can often uncover each other's errors or false assumptions; an individual acting alone would not be able to do this. Second, team members can critique each other's approaches when need be and build on each other's strengths while compensating for weaknesses, one of the advantages of devil's advocacy and dialectical inquiry discussed in Chapter 6.

To further promote innovation, managers are well advised to empower teams and make their members fully responsible and accountable for the innovation process. The manager's role is to provide guidance, assistance, coaching, and the resources team members need, and not to direct or supervise their activities closely. To speed innovation, managers also need to form teams in which each member brings some unique resource to the team, such as engineering prowess, knowledge of production, marketing expertise, or financial savvy. Successful innovation sometimes requires that managers form teams with members from different countries and cultures, as indicated in this "Managing Globally."

Managing Globally

Cross-Cultural Team's Innovation Yields the 1996 Honda Civic

Ron Shriver, a manager and engineer at Honda's East Liberty, Ohio factory, played a prominent role in the development of Honda's 1992 Civic model (www.honda.com). When the model first came out, rather than basking in glory, Shriver was concerned. Many of the Civic's features, including heat vents for the rear seats and a more powerful engine, had raised its price at a time when car sales were falling in both North America and Japan. Shriver realized that innovation was needed for the 1996 model and that costs had to be cut to keep the price low, but without sacrificing quality.

Shriver formed a 12-person team whose members came from Honda's most significant departments to determine how to reduce costs for the 1996 model. Unbeknownst to Shriver, Honda's president in Japan, Nobuhiko Kawamoto, had come to a similar conclusion: The strong yen and slumping demand meant that Honda had to lower costs. Hiroyuki Itoh, the manager and chief engineer for the Civic in Japan, formed his own team to determine how to innovate for the 1996 Civic.

Within a few months, Shriver's and Itoh's teams were merged to form a cross-cultural team to identify innovative changes to the Civic that would cut costs but not turn off customers. In search of ways to reduce costs, the new team of both Japanese and American managers took a hands-on approach and talked to all people and groups who affected costs, such as engineers, factory workers, and suppliers. Jodie Kavanagh, a Honda employee working in the paint shop in Liberty, Ohio, for example, suggested a change that resulted in $1.86 million in savings. Suppliers also had a major input into the process, and agreements on specifications were reached with low-cost US suppliers, who replaced their more expensive Japanese counterparts. As a result of the team's efforts, the price of the 1996 Civic was only marginally higher than the price of the 1992 model, even though it was bigger, peppier, and had many new features.[8]

Groups and Teams as Motivators

How might teams be motivators?

Managers often decide to form groups and teams to accomplish organizational goals, then find that using groups and teams brings additional benefits. Members of groups, and especially members of teams (because of the higher intensity of interaction in teams), are likely to be more highly motivated and satisfied than they would have been while working on their own. The experience of working alongside other highly charged and motivated people can be very stimulating. In addition, working on a team can be very motivating: Team members more readily see how their efforts and expertise directly contribute to the achievement of team and organizational goals, and they feel personally responsible for the outcomes or results of their work. This has been the case at Willow Manufacturing, for instance.

At Burnaby, BC-based Dominion Directory Information Services, Inc.™ teamwork is everything. The company publishes yellow and white telephone directories in BC, Alberta, Ontario and Quebec as well as online at SuperPages.ca. Teamwork is a necessity in their business and has led to a high degree of quality in the many innovative products and services the company provides.

The increased motivation and satisfaction that can accompany the use of teams can also lead to other outcomes, such as lower turnover. Working in a group or team can also satisfy organizational members' needs for social interaction and feeling connected to other people. For workers who perform highly stressful jobs (such as hospital emergency and operating room staff), group membership can be an important source of social support and motivation. Family members or friends may not be able to fully understand or appreciate some sources of work stress that these group members experience firsthand. Moreover, group members may cope better with work stressors when they are able to share them with other members of their group. In addition, groups often devise techniques to relieve stress, such as the telling of jokes among hospital operating room staff.

Why do managers in all kinds of organizations rely so heavily on groups and teams? Effectively managed groups and teams can help managers in their quest for high performance, responsiveness to customers, and employee motivation. Before explaining how managers can effectively manage groups, however, we will describe the types of groups that are formed in organizations.

Types of Groups and Teams

formal group A group that managers establish to achieve organizational goals.

To achieve their goals of high performance, responsiveness to customers, innovation, and employee motivation, managers can form various types of groups and teams. **Formal groups** are groups that managers establish to achieve organizational goals. We just described two types of formal work groups: cross-functional teams, used at Willow, and cross-cultural teams, used at Honda. (Recall that cross-functional teams are teams composed of members from different departments and cross-cultural teams are teams composed of members from different cultures or countries.) As you will see, some of the groups discussed in this section also can be considered cross-functional (if they are composed of members from different departments) or cross-cultural (if they are composed of members from different countries or cultures).

informal group A group that managers or non-managerial employees form to help achieve their own goals or meet their own needs.

Sometimes organizational members–managers or nonmanagers–form groups because they feel that groups will help them achieve their own goals or meet their own needs (for example, the need for social interaction). Groups formed in this way are **informal groups**. Four nurses who work in a hospital and have lunch together twice a week constitute an informal group. Below, we describe important types of formal groups that can affect organizational performance.

The Top-Management Team

top-management team A group composed of the CEO, the president, and the heads of the most important departments.

A central concern of the CEO and president of a company is to form a **top-management team** to help the organization achieve its mission and goals. Top-management teams are responsible for developing the strategies that produce an organization's competitive advantage; most have between five and seven members. In forming their top-management teams, CEOs are well advised to stress diversity–in expertise, skills, knowledge, and experience. Thus, many top-management teams are cross-functional teams: They are composed of members from different departments such as finance, marketing, production, and engineering. Diversity helps ensure that the top-management team will have all the backgrounds and resources it needs to make good decisions. Diversity also helps guard against *groupthink*, faulty group decision making that results when group members strive for agreement at the expense of an accurate assessment of the situation (see both below and Chapter 6 for further discussion of groupthink).

edgeflow Inc.
www.edgeflow.com/

Sometimes the management team is almost more important than the idea for the company. Last year, Ottawa-based edgeflow Inc., a photonics company, raised $8.5 million from two venture capital firms on the strength of its team, rather than its ideas. Founders Wes Biggs, a former executive at Newbridge Networks Corp. (now Alcatel Canada) and Jacques Bissinger, the founder of Siemens AG's Ottawa technology innovation centre, partnered with two members of California-based Sierra Ventures, Stefan Mazur and Jeff Drazan. Mazur knew both Biggs and Bissinger from previous dealings. "We had what they considered to be the important attributes. We were known entities in the Ottawa area. We could attract key talent. The optical networking space had high growth and high opportunities for success," Biggs said.[9] In explaining why Sierra Ventures funded edgeflow Inc., Drazan said, "What we funded was not so much an idea as a collection of really talented people. And they've developed a business opportunity that we think is very interesting, and built a nice team around themselves to start with." Only time will tell whether edgeflow will be successful, but the team's talent will certainly get it off to a good start.

Research and Development Teams

Managers in pharmaceuticals, computers, electronics, electronic imaging, and other high-tech industries often create **research and development teams** to develop new products. Managers select R&D team members on the basis of their expertise and experience in a certain area. Sometimes R&D teams are cross-functional teams with members from departments such as engineering, marketing, and production in addition to members from the research and development department.

Command Groups

Subordinates who report to the same supervisor compose a **command group**. When top managers design an organization's structure and establish reporting relationships and a chain of command, they are essentially creating command groups. Command groups, often called *departments* or *units*, perform a significant amount of the work in many organizations. In order to have command groups that help an organization gain a competitive advantage, managers need to motivate group members to perform at a high level, and managers need to be effective leaders. Examples of command groups include the salespeople in The Bay who report to the same supervisor, the employees of a small swimming pool sales and maintenance company who report to a general manager, the telephone operators at the ManuLife insurance company who report to the same supervisor, and workers on an automobile assembly line at Ford Canada who report to the same first-line manager.

Task Forces

Managers form **task forces** to accomplish specific goals or solve problems in a certain time period; task forces are sometimes called *ad hoc committees*. When Vancouver-Island based Myra Falls copper and zinc mine was purchased in 1998 by Swedish-controlled Boliden Ltd., the mine had been facing labour strife for years.[10] Boliden sent over a new mine manager to help get things in order. His first job was to set up five task forces geared to key problem areas. For instance, the ground support task force found that the previous owners had neglected a number of safety problems. The task forces' recommendations were implemented, and $15 million worth of improvements were done. This sent a strong signal to employees that the new management team was concerned about its employees. Task forces can be a valuable tool for busy managers who do not have the time to explore an important issue in depth on their own.

Sometimes managers need to form task forces whose work, so to speak, is never done. The task force may address a long-term or enduring problem or issue facing an organization, such as how to contribute most usefully to the local community or how to make sure that the organization provides opportunities for potential employees with disabilities. Task forces that are relatively permanent are often referred to as *standing committees*. Membership in standing committees changes over time. Members may have, for example, a two- or three-year term on the committee, and memberships expire at varying times so that there are always some members with experience on the committee. Managers often form and maintain standing committees to make sure that important issues continue to be addressed.

Self-Managed Work Teams

Self-managed (or self-directed) work teams are teams in which team members are empowered and have the responsibility and autonomy to complete identifiable pieces of work. On a day-to-day basis, team members decide what the team will do, how it will do it, and which team members will perform which specific tasks.[11] Managers provide self-managed work teams with their overall goals (such as assembling defect-free computer keyboards) but let team members decide how to meet those goals. Managers usually form self-managed work teams to improve quality, increase motivation and satisfaction, and lower costs. Often, by creating self-managed work teams, they combine tasks that individuals working separately used to perform, so the team is responsible for the whole set of tasks that yield an identifiable output or end product. The Conference Board of Canada found that self-directed work teams are used in a variety of manufacturing (such as the auto industry, chemicals, equipment repair) and service environments (such as hotels, banks, and airlines).[12] The "Management Insight" describes how a self-managed team works at Langley Memorial Hospital in BC.

Management Insight

Self-Managed Teams at Langley Memorial Reduce Management Costs

Langley Memorial Hospital, in Langley, BC, has organized its materiel services department as a self-managed team.[13] The team, consisting of three department buyers plus 18 other full- and part-time staff for all other services, is responsible for managing inventory, adjusting the workload, and improving customer service. Staff members are encouraged to participate in decision making and implementing ideas. Because the team is self-managed, there is less direct supervision of staff. Departmental performance is measured by outcome indicators such as inventory level, inventory turnover rates, inhouse service levels, and lost time.

Staff members compare data with previous periods "to look at trends, incremental changes, and performance indicators that compare how well [they] are doing compared with targeted benchmarks."

The hospital has undergone a variety of changes in recent years, moving from a "top down" approach to having groups of clinical and support teams. As a consequence, departmental management has been reduced by 75 percent. Thus, the move to self-managed teams has dramatically reduced management costs for the hospital.

Managers can take a number of steps to ensure that self-managed work teams are effective and that they help an organization gain a competitive advantage:[14]

- Give teams enough responsibility and autonomy to be truly self-managing. Refrain from telling team members what to do or solving problems for them even if you (as a manager) know what should be done.

- Make sure that a team's work is sufficiently complex so that it entails a number of different steps or procedures that must be performed and results in some kind of finished end product.

- Carefully select members of self-managed work teams. Team members should have the diversity of skills needed to complete the team's work, have the ability to work with others, and want to be part of a team.

- As a manager, realize that your role with respect to self-managed work teams calls for guidance, coaching, and supporting, not supervising. You are a resource for teams to turn to when needed.

- Analyze what type of training team members need, and provide it. Working in a self-managed work team often requires that employees have more extensive technical and interpersonal skills.

Managers in a wide variety of organizations have found that self-managed work teams help the organization achieve its goals.[15] However, self-managed work teams can run into trouble. Members are often reluctant to discipline one another by withholding bonuses from members who are not performing up to par or by firing members.[16]

They are also reluctant to evaluate each other's performance and determine pay levels. One reason for team members' discomfort may be the close personal relationships they sometimes develop with each other. In addition, sometimes members of self-managed work teams actually take longer to accomplish tasks, such as when team members have difficulties coordinating their efforts.

Virtual Teams

virtual team A team whose members rarely or never meet face to face and interact by using various forms of information technology such as e-mail, computer networks, telephones, faxes, and video conferences.

Virtual teams are teams whose members rarely or never meet face to face and interact by using various forms of information technology such as e-mail, computer networks, telephones, faxes, and video conferences. As organizations become increasingly global and have operations in far-flung regions of the world, and as the need for specialized knowledge increases due to advances in technology, virtual teams allow managers to create teams to solve problems or explore opportunities without being limited by the need for team members to be working in the same geographic location.[17]

Take the case of an organization that has manufacturing facilities in Australia, Canada, the United States, and Mexico, and which is encountering a quality problem in a complex manufacturing process. Each of its manufacturing facilities has a quality control team that is headed by a quality control manager. The vice-president for production does not try to solve the problem by forming and leading a team at one of the four manufacturing facilities; instead, she forms and leads a virtual team composed of the quality control managers of the four plants and the plants' general managers. Team members communicate via e-mail and video-conferencing, and a wide array of knowledge and experience is brought to bear to solve the problem.

The principal advantage of virtual teams is that they enable managers to disregard geographic distances and form teams whose members have the knowledge, expertise, and experience to tackle a particular problem or take advantage of a specific opportunity.[18] Virtual teams can include members who are not employees of the organization itself; a virtual team might include members of an organization that is used for outsourcing. More and more companies—including Hewlett-Packard, Price-Waterhouse, and Eastman Kodak—are either using or exploring the use of virtual teams.[19] The "Management Insight" shows some of the challenges faced by companies that use virtual teams.

Management Insight

Virtual Teams Require Planning

Virtual teams have access to all kinds of technology to help members be productive: phone, fax, modem, Internet, e-mail and video-conference calls can all help team members dispersed across the city, the country or the world to interact with each other and stay on top of a project.[20] Nevertheless, the human element still matters. Teams that work on building trust early on tend to have better relationships and are more productive. And communication, even off-topic communication, helps members learn a little about each other as individuals, building up that trust.

Doug Jennings, a Vancouver-based performance consultant with IBM Canada, works on a virtual team with nine other colleagues, the rest of whom are in

Toronto. The team has conference calls twice a month, and meets in person several times a year.

Virtual team members face some of the same challenges as face-to-face teams, but they often have to resolve their differences online. They still need a leader, a common purpose, and ways to hold each other mutually accountable for achieving the team's goals.

Doug Harrison, vice-president and managing director of Ryder Integrated Logistics in Mississauga, Ontario, feels that his company has been transformed by using virtual teams to serve clients. Ryder provides outsourced logistics for such blue-chip clients as General Motors, Chrysler, Northern Telecom and Hewlett–Packard. It's been a challenge for managers, of course, since they are responsible for everyone on the team, not just people in their own department. The benefit, however, is that the teams allow "a much quicker response time to the market so we don't have to worry about following these departmental hierarchies," Harrison says.

Getting this to work at Ryder required new skills and new thinking for everyone. "We spent a lot of time training people and coaching our management to get out of their old thought processes of operating a hierarchical organization and start thinking about this team environment."

Not everyone likes a virtual environment, however. Jim Cantrell, manager of sales operations at Xerox, equipped his salesforce with laptops and sent them off as mobile workers. He says, "It wasn't the right thing to do for our employees ... I want to go out there and see my reps. I want to touch them."

Beware! Teams Aren't Always the Answer

When should we use teams?

Though we have given lots of information about how teams are used in the workplace, teams are not always the best way to get work done. Because teams have increased communication demands, more conflicts to manage, and need more meetings, the benefits of using teams have to exceed the costs.

In trying to determine whether a team is appropriate to the situation, consider the following:[21]

- If the work can be better performed by an individual, then it is not necessary to form a team.

- Can the team provide more value than the individual? For instance, new-car dealer service departments have introduced teams that link customer service personnel, mechanics, parts specialists, and sales representatives. These teams can better manage customer needs.

- Are there interdependent tasks, so that employees have to rely on each other to get work completed? Teamwork often makes interdependent work go more smoothly.

Some other situations where organizations would find teams more useful include: "When work processes cut across functional lines; when speed is important (and complex relationships are involved); when the organization mirrors a complex, differentiated and rapidly changing market environment; when innovation and learning have priority; when the tasks that have to be done require online integration of highly interdependent performers."[22]

Group Dynamics

The ways in which groups function and, ultimately, group effectiveness hinge on a number of group characteristics and processes known collectively as group dynamics. In this section, we discuss five key elements of group dynamics: group size, tasks, and roles; group leadership; group development; group norms; and group cohesiveness.

Group Size, Tasks, and Roles

Managers need to take group size, group tasks, and group roles into account as they create and maintain high-performing groups and teams.

GROUP SIZE   The number of members in a group can be an important determinant of members' motivation and commitment and of group performance. There are several advantages to keeping a group relatively small—between two and nine members. Compared with members of large groups, members of small groups tend to (1) interact more with each other and find it easier to coordinate their efforts, (2) be more motivated, satisfied, and committed, (3) find it easier to share information, and (4) be better able to see the importance of their personal contributions for group success. Recognizing these advantages, Nathan Myhrvold, senior vice-president for advanced technology at Microsoft Corporation, has found that eight is the ideal size for the types of R&D teams he forms to develop new software.[23] A disadvantage of small rather than large groups is that members of small groups have fewer resources available to accomplish their goals.

Large groups—with 10 or more members—also offer some advantages. They have at their disposal more resources to achieve group goals than do small groups. These resources include the knowledge, experience, skills, and abilities of group members as well as their actual time and effort. Large groups also enable managers to obtain the advantages stemming from the **division of labour**—splitting the work to be performed into particular tasks and assigning tasks to individual workers. Workers who specialize in particular tasks are likely to become skilled at performing those tasks and contribute significantly to high group performance.

The disadvantages of large groups include the problems of communication and coordination and the lower levels of motivation, satisfaction, and commitment that members of large groups sometimes experience. It is clearly more difficult to share information with and coordinate the activities of, say, 16 people rather than 8 people. Moreover, members of large groups might not feel that their efforts are really needed and sometimes might not even feel a part of the group.

In deciding on the appropriate size for any group, managers attempt to gain the advantages of small group size while at the same time forming groups with sufficient resources to accomplish their goals and have a well-developed division of labour. As a general rule of thumb, groups should have no more members than necessary to achieve a division of labour and provide the resources needed to achieve group goals. In R&D teams, for example, group size is too large when (1) members spend more time communicating what they know to others rather than applying what they know to solve problems and create new products, (2) individual productivity decreases, and (3) group performance suffers.[24]

GROUP TASKS   The appropriate size of a high-performing group is affected by the kinds of tasks the group is to perform. An important characteristic of group tasks that affects performance is **task interdependence**, the degree to which the work performed by one member of a group influences the work performed by other members.[25] As task interdependence increases, group members need to interact more frequently and intensely with each other, and their efforts have to be more closely coordinated if they are to perform at a high level. Management expert James D. Thompson identified three types of task interdependence: pooled, sequential, and reciprocal (see Figure 14.2).[26]

POOLED TASK INTERDEPENDENCE   **Pooled task interdependence** exists when group members make separate and independent contributions to

---

division of labour
Splitting the work to be performed into particular tasks and assigning tasks to individual workers.

task interdependence
The degree to which the work performed by one member of a group influences the work performed by other members.

pooled task interdependence
The task interdependence that exists when group members make separate and independent contributions to group performance.

Figure 14.2
Types of Task Interdependence

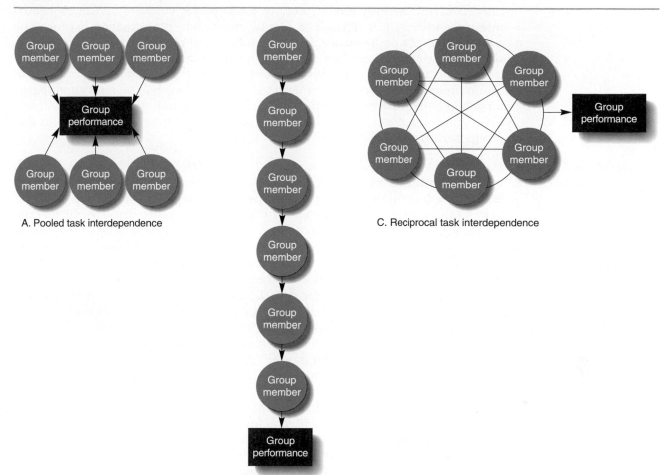

A. Pooled task interdependence

B. Sequential task interdependence

C. Reciprocal task interdependence

group performance; overall group performance is the sum of the performances of the individual members (see Figure 14.2A). Examples of groups that have pooled task interdependence include a group of teachers in an elementary school, a group of salespeople in a department store, a group of secretaries in an office, and a group of custodians in an office building. In these examples, group performance—whether it be the number of children who are taught and the quality of their education, the dollar value of sales, the amount of secretarial work completed, or the number of offices that are cleaned—is determined by summing the individual contributions of group members.

For groups with pooled interdependence, managers should determine the appropriate group size primarily from the amount of work to be accomplished. Large groups can be effective because group members work independently and do not have to interact frequently with each other. Motivation in groups with pooled interdependence will be highest when managers reward group members for their individual performance.

sequential task interdependence

The task interdependence that exists when group members must perform specific tasks in a predetermined order.

SEQUENTIAL TASK INTERDEPENDENCE Sequential task interdependence exists when group members must perform specific tasks in a predetermined order; certain tasks have to be performed before others, and what one worker does affects the work of others (see Figure 14.2B). Assembly lines and mass-production processes are characterized by sequential task interdependence.

When group members are sequentially interdependent, group size is usually dictated by the needs of the production process—for example, the number of steps needed in an assembly line to produce a CD player efficiently. With sequential interdependence, it is difficult to identify individual performance because one group member's performance depends on how well others perform their tasks. A slow worker at the start of an assembly line, for example, causes all workers farther down the line to work slowly. Thus, managers are often advised to reward group members for *group* performance. Group members will be motivated to perform highly because each member will benefit if the group performs well. In addition, group members may put pressure on poor performers to improve so that group performance and rewards do not suffer.

reciprocal task interdependence

The task interdependence that exists when the work performed by each group member is fully dependent on the work performed by other group members.

RECIPROCAL TASK INTERDEPENDENCE Reciprocal task **interdependence** exists when the work performed by each group member is fully dependent on the work performed by other group members; group members have to share information, interact intensely with each other, and coordinate their efforts in order for the group to achieve its goals (see Figure 14.2C). In general, reciprocal task interdependence characterizes the operation of teams, rather than other kinds of groups. The task interdependence of R&D teams, top-management teams, and many self-managed work teams is reciprocal.

When group members are reciprocally interdependent, managers are advised to keep group size relatively small because of the need to coordinate team members' activities. Communication difficulties can arise in teams with reciprocally interdependent tasks, because team members need to interact frequently with one another and be available when needed. As group size increases, communication difficulties increase and can impair team performance.

When a group's members are reciprocally interdependent, managers also are advised to reward group members on the basis of group performance. Individual levels of performance are often difficult for managers to identify, and group-based rewards help ensure that group members will be motivated to perform at a high level and make valuable contributions to the group. Of course, if a manager can identify instances of individual performance in such groups, they too can be rewarded to maintain high levels of motivation. Microsoft and many other companies reward group members both for their individual performance and for the performance of their group.

group role A set of behaviours and tasks that a member of a group is expected to perform because of his or her position in the group.

GROUP ROLES A **group role** is a set of behaviours and tasks that a member of a group is expected to perform because of his or her position in the group. Members of cross-functional teams, for example, are expected to perform roles relevant to their special areas of expertise. At a greeting card manufacturer such as Hallmark Cards, the role of writers on the cross-functional team is to create verses for new cards, the role of artists is to draw illustrations, and the role of designers is to bring verse and artwork together to create an attractive and appealing card. The roles of members of top-management teams are shaped primarily by their areas of expertise—production, marketing, finance, research and development—but members of top-management teams also typically draw on their broad expertise as planners and strategists.

task-oriented roles

Roles performed by group members to make sure the task gets done.

maintenance roles

Roles performed by group members to make sure there are good relations amongst group members.

Beyond the simple roles that each person fulfills in order to complete the task at hand, two major kinds of roles need to be discussed: **task-oriented roles** and **maintenance roles**. Task-oriented roles are performed by group members to make sure that the group accomplishes its tasks. Maintenance roles are carried out to make sure that team members have good relationships. For teams to be effective, there needs to be some balance between task orientation and relationship maintenance. Table 14.1 identifies a number of task-oriented and maintenance roles that you might find in a team.

Table 14.1
Roles Required for Effective Group Functioning

	Function	Description	Example
Roles that build task accomplishment	Initiating	Stating the goal or problem, making proposals about how to work on it, setting time limits.	"Let's set up an agenda for discussing each of the problems we have to consider."
	Seeking information and opinions	Asking group members for specific factual information related to the task or problem, or for their opinions about it.	"What do you think would be the best approach to this, Jack?"
	Providing information and opinions	Sharing information or opinions related to the task or problems.	"I worked on a similar problem last year and found. . . ."
	Clarifying	Helping one another understand ideas and suggestions that come up in the group.	"What you mean, Sue, is that we could. . .?"
	Elaborating	Building on one another's ideas and suggestions.	"Building on Don's idea, I think we could. . . ."
	Summarizing	Reviewing the points covered by the group and the different ideas stated so that decisions can be based on full information.	Appointing a recorder to take notes on a blackboard.
	Consensus testing	Periodic testing about whether the group is nearing a decision or needs to continue discussion.	"Is the group ready to decide about this?"
Roles that build and maintain a group	Harmonizing	Mediating conflict among other members, reconciling disagreements, relieving tensions.	"Don, I don't think you and Sue really see the question that differently."
	Compromising	Admitting error at times of group conflict.	"Well, I'd be willing to change if you provided some help on. . . ."
	Gatekeeping	Making sure all members have a chance to express their ideas and feelings and preventing members from being interrupted.	"Sue, we haven't heard from you on this issue."
	Encouraging	Helping a group member make his or her point. Establishing a climate of acceptance in the group.	"I think what you started to say is important, Jack. Please continue."

Source: D. Ancona, T. Kochan, M. Scully, J. Van Maanen, D.E. Westney, "Team Processes," in *Managing for the Future* (Cincinnati, OH: South-Western College Publishing, 1996), p. 9.

In forming groups and teams, managers need to communicate clearly to group members the expectations for their roles in the group, what is required of them, and how the different roles in the group fit together to accomplish group goals. Managers also need to realize that group roles change and evolve as a group's tasks and goals change and as group members gain experience and knowledge. Thus, to get the performance gains that come from experience or "learning by doing," managers should encourage group members to take the initiative to assume additional responsibilities as they see fit and modify their assigned roles. This process, called **role making**, can enhance individual and group performance.

In self-managed work teams and some other groups, group members themselves are responsible for creating and assigning roles. Many self-managed work teams also pick their own team leaders. When group members create their own roles, managers should be available in an advisory capacity, helping group members effectively settle conflicts and disagreements. At Johnsonville Foods, for example, the position titles of first-line managers were changed to "advisory coach" to reflect the managers' new role vis-à-vis the self-managed work teams they oversee.[27]

role making Taking the initiative to modify an assigned role by assuming additional responsibilities.

Johnsonville Foods
www.johnsonville.com/

Group Leadership

All groups and teams need leadership. Indeed, as we discussed in detail in Chapter 13, effective leadership is a key ingredient for high-performing groups, teams, and organizations. Sometimes managers assume the leadership role, as is the case in many command groups and top-management teams. Or a manager may appoint a member of a group who is not a manager to be group leader or chairperson, as is the case in a task force or standing committee. In other cases, group or team members may choose their own leaders, or a leader may emerge naturally as group members work together to achieve group goals. When managers empower members of self-managed work teams, they often let group members choose their own leaders. Some self-managed work teams find it effective to rotate the leadership role among their members. Whether leaders of groups and teams are managers or not, and whether they are appointed by managers or emerge naturally in a group, they play an important role in ensuring that groups and teams perform up to their potential.

Group Development Over Time

Do teams just naturally work well together?

THE FIVE STAGE GROUP DEVELOPMENT MODEL   Although every group's development over time is somewhat unique, researchers have identified five stages of group development that many groups seem to pass through (see Figure 14.3).[28] In the first stage, *forming*, members try to get to know each other and reach a common understanding of what the group is trying to accomplish and how group members should behave. During this stage, managers should strive to make each member feel like a valued part of the group.

In the second stage, *storming*, group members experience conflict and disagreements because some members do not wish to submit to the demands of other group members. Disputes may arise over who should lead the group. Self-managed work teams can be particularly vulnerable during the storming stage. Managers need to keep an eye on groups at this stage to make sure that conflict does not get out of hand.

During the third stage, *norming*, close ties between group members develop, and feelings of friendship and camaraderie emerge. Group members arrive at a consensus about what goals they should be seeking to achieve and how group members should behave toward one another.

In the fourth stage, *performing*, the real work of the group gets accomplished. Depending on the type of group in question, managers need to take different steps at this stage to help ensure that groups are effective. Managers of command groups need to make sure that group members are motivated and that they are effectively leading group members. Managers overseeing self-managed work teams have to empower team members and make sure that teams are given enough responsibility and autonomy at the performing stage.

The last stage, *adjourning*, applies only to groups that eventually are disbanded, such as task forces. During adjourning, a group is dispersed. Sometimes, adjourning takes place when a group completes a finished product, such as when a task

Figure 14.3
Five Stages of Group Development

force evaluating the pros and cons of providing onsite childcare produces a report supporting its recommendation.

Managers need a flexible approach to group development and need to keep attuned to the different needs and requirements of groups at the various stages.[29] Above all else, and regardless of the stage of development, managers need to think of themselves as *resources* for groups. Thus, managers always should be striving to find ways to help groups and teams function more effectively.

Do teams exert the same amount of energy throughout their task?

UCLA: Connie Gersick www.anderson.ucla.edu/

THE PUNCTUATED EQUILIBRIUM MODEL Professor Connie Gersick of UCLA developed the punctuated equilibrium model to account for what she observed after watching numerous groups: Groups do not develop in a universal sequence of stages.[30] The punctuated equilibrium model suggests that groups with deadlines have their own unique sequence of action (or inaction): (1) The first meeting sets the group's direction; (2) this is followed by the first phase of group activity, which is one of inertia; (3) at the end of the first phase a transition takes place; this transition occurs when the group has used up exactly half its allotted time; (4) the transition results in major changes; (5) after the major changes, a second phase of inertia follows the transition; and (6) the group's last meeting is characterized by markedly accelerated activity.[31] This pattern is shown in Figure 14.4.

The model suggests that at the group's first meeting, the patterns and assumptions by which the group will operate get set. This pattern becomes "written in stone" and is usually not re-examined during the first half of the group's life. The first half of the group's life is characterized by inertia: either the group stands still or it becomes locked into a fixed course of action. You have no doubt encountered this in your own groups: During the first half of a project that has a deadline, team members don't seem overly concerned about getting the task done.

At some point, however, the group recognizes that work needs to get completed. Gersick found that all groups experienced a transition at exactly the same point: precisely halfway between their first meeting and their official deadline. This was the point where group members realized that they needed to "get moving."

At this point, Phase 1 ends and the group enters a transition phase where the members make all kinds of changes, drop old patterns, and adopt new perspectives. During this transition, the group sets a revised direction for Phase 2, which

Figure 14.4
Punctuated Equilibrium Model

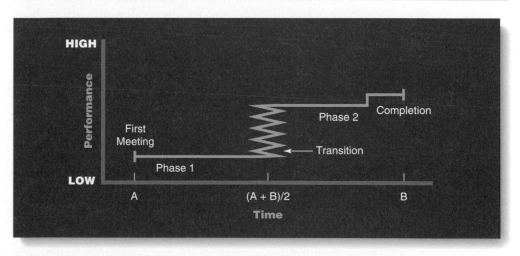

Source: Based on C.J.G. Gersick, "Time and Transition in Work Teams: Toward a New Model of Group Development," *Academy of Management Journal*, March 1988, pp. 9–41. Copyright 2001 by Acad of Mgmt. Reproduced with permission of Acad of Mgmt in the format Textbook via Copyright Clearance Center.

is a new equilibrium period or period of inertia. During Phase 2, the group carries out plans created during the transition period. The group puts in a final burst of activity to finish its work at its final meeting.

In summary, the punctuated equilibrium model characterizes groups as having long periods of inertia with a few brief periods of revolutionary change and activity. The high bursts of activity are triggered when group members become aware of time and deadlines. The punctuated equilibrium model is consistent with the five stage group development model, in that it suggests that groups begin by combining the forming and norming stages, they then go through a period of low performing. In the transition between Phases 1 and 2 they enter a period of storming, which is then followed by a period of high performing. Finally, the group adjourns. Keep in mind that the punctuated equilibrium model more appropriately describes temporary task groups that are working under a time-constrained deadline.

Group Norms

All groups, whether top-management teams, self-managed work teams, or command groups, need to control their members' behaviour to ensure that the group performs well and meets its goals. Assigning roles to each group member is one way to control behaviour in groups. Another important way in which groups influence members' behaviour is through the development and enforcement of group norms.[32] **Group norms** are shared guidelines or rules for behaviour that most group members follow. Groups develop norms for a wide variety of behaviours, including working hours, the sharing of information among group members, how certain group tasks should be performed, and even how members of a group should dress.

group norms Shared guidelines or rules for behaviour that most group members follow.

Managers should encourage members of a group to develop norms that contribute to group performance and the attainment of group goals. For example, group norms that dictate that each member of a cross-functional team should always be available for the rest of the team when his or her input is needed, return phone calls as soon as possible, inform other team members of travel plans, and give team members a phone number at which he or she can be reached when travelling on business, help to ensure that the team is efficient, performs highly, and achieves its goals. A norm in a command group of secretaries that dictates that secretaries who have a light workload in any given week should assist secretaries with heavier workloads helps to ensure that the group completes all assignments in a timely and efficient manner. And a norm in a top-management team that dictates that team members should always consult with each other before making major decisions helps to ensure that good decisions are made with a minimum of errors.

CONFORMITY AND DEVIANCE Group members conform to norms for three reasons: (1) They want to obtain rewards and avoid punishments; (2) they want to imitate group members whom they like and admire; and (3) they have internalized the norm and believe it is the right and proper way to behave.[33] Consider the case of Robert King, who conformed to his department's norm of attending a fund-raiser for a community food bank. King's conformity could be due to (1) his desire to be a member of the group in good standing and to have friendly relationships with other group members (rewards), (2) his copying the behaviour of other members of the department whom he respects and who always attend the fund-raiser (imitating other group members), or (3) his belief in the merits of supporting the activities of the food bank (believing that to be the right and proper way to behave).

Failure to conform, or deviance, occurs when a member of a group violates a group norm. Deviance signals that a group is not controlling one of its members' behaviours. Groups generally respond to members who behave deviantly in one of three ways:[34]

1. The group might try to get the member to change his or her deviant ways and conform to the norm. Group members might try to convince the member of the need to conform, or they might ignore or even punish the deviant.

2. The group might expel the member.

3. The group might change the norm to be consistent with the member's behaviour.

That last alternative suggests that some deviant behaviour can be functional for groups. Deviance is functional for a group when it causes group members to stop and evaluate norms that may be dysfunctional but that are taken for granted by the group. Often, group members do not think about why they behave in a certain way or why they follow certain norms. Deviance can cause group members to reflect on their norms and change them when appropriate.

Take the case of a group of receptionists in a beauty salon who followed the norm that all appointments would be handwritten in an appointment book and at the end of each day the receptionist on duty would enter the appointments into the salon's computer system, which was used to print out the hairdressers' daily schedules. One day, a receptionist decided to enter appointments directly into the computer system at the time they were being made, bypassing the appointment book. This deviant behaviour caused the other receptionists to think about why they were using the appointment book at all since appointments always could be entered into the computer directly. After consulting with the owner of the salon, the group changed its norm. Now appointments are entered directly into the computer, which saves time and cuts down on scheduling errors.

ENCOURAGING A BALANCE OF CONFORMITY AND DEVIANCE

In order for groups and teams to be effective and help an organization gain a competitive advantage, they need to have the right balance of conformity and deviance (see Figure 14.5). A group needs a certain level of conformity to ensure that it can control members' behaviour and channel it in the direction of high performance and group goal accomplishment. A group also needs a certain level of deviance to ensure that dysfunctional norms are discarded and replaced with functional ones. Balancing conformity and deviance is a pressing concern for all groups, whether they are top-management teams, R&D teams, command groups, or self-managed work teams.

In the top-management team comprising the four co-presidents who manage the Nordstrom chain of department stores, for example, it is important for team members to conform to group norms stressing open and frequent communication, lively debate, and attendance at the team's weekly meetings.[35] It is equally important, however, for team members to deviate from norms dictating the kinds of merchandise that the co-presidents routinely select for sale in Nordstrom stores when they discover new and innovative merchandise lines that may increase customer satisfaction.

The extent of conformity and reactions to deviance within groups are determined by group members themselves. The three bases for conformity described above are powerful forces that more often than not result in group members' conforming to norms. Sometimes these forces are so strong that deviance rarely occurs in groups, and when it does, it is stamped out.

Managers can take several steps to ensure that there is enough tolerance of deviance in groups so that group members are willing to deviate from dysfunctional norms and, when deviance occurs in their group, reflect on the appropriateness of the violated norm and change the norm if necessary. First, managers can be role models for the groups and teams they oversee. When managers encourage and

Nordstrom
http://store.nordstrom.com/

Figure 14.5
Balancing Conformity and Deviance in Groups

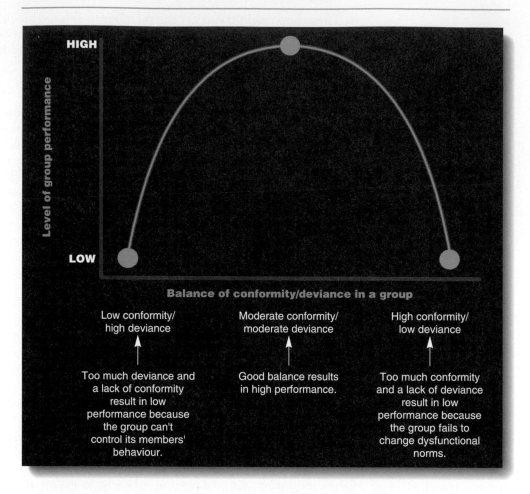

accept employees' suggestions for changes in procedures, do not rigidly insist that tasks be accomplished in a certain way, and admit when a norm that they once supported is no longer functional, they signal to group members that conformity should not come at the expense of needed changes and improvements. Second, managers should let employees know that there are always ways to improve group processes and performance levels and thus opportunities to replace existing norms with norms that will better enable a group to achieve its goals and perform at a high level. Third, managers should encourage members of groups and teams to assess periodically the appropriateness of their existing norms.

Group Cohesiveness

group cohesiveness

The degree to which members are attracted or loyal to a group.

Another important element of group dynamics that affects group performance and effectiveness is **group cohesiveness**, the degree to which members are attracted or loyal to their group or team.[36] When group cohesiveness is high, individuals strongly value their group membership, find the group very appealing, and have strong desires to remain part of the group. When group cohesiveness is low, group members do not find their group particularly appealing and have little desire to retain their group membership. Research suggests that managers should strive to have a moderate level of cohesiveness in the groups and teams they manage because that is most likely to contribute to an organization's competitive advantage.

Why is cohesiveness important?

CONSEQUENCES OF GROUP COHESIVENESS   There are three major consequences of group cohesiveness: level of participation within a group, level of conformity to group norms, and emphasis on group goal accomplishment (see Figure 14.6).[37]

LEVEL OF PARTICIPATION WITHIN A GROUP   As group cohesiveness increases, the extent of group members' participation within the group increases. Participation contributes to group effectiveness because group members are actively involved in the group, ensure that group tasks get accomplished, readily share information with each other, and have frequent and open communication (the important topic of communication is covered in depth in Chapter 15).

A moderate level of group cohesiveness helps to ensure that group members actively participate in the group and communicate effectively with each other. The reason why managers may not want to encourage high levels of cohesiveness is illustrated by the example of two cross-functional teams responsible for developing new toys. Members of the highly cohesive Team Alpha have lengthy meetings that usually start with non-work-related conversations and jokes, meet more often than most of the other cross-functional teams in the company, and spend a good portion of their time communicating the ins and outs of their department's contribution to toy development to other team members. Members of the moderately cohesive Team Beta generally have efficient meetings in which ideas are communicated and discussed as needed, do not meet more often than necessary, and share the ins and outs of their expertise with each other to the extent that it is needed for the development process. Teams Alpha and Beta have both developed some top-selling toys. However, it generally takes Team Alpha 30 percent longer than Team Beta to do so. This is why too much cohesiveness can be too much of a good thing.

LEVEL OF CONFORMITY TO GROUP NORMS   Increasing levels of group cohesiveness result in increasing levels of conformity to group norms, and, when cohesiveness becomes high, there may be so little deviance in groups that group members conform to norms even when they are dysfunctional. In contrast, low cohesiveness can result in too much deviance and can undermine the ability of a group to control its members' behaviours to get things done. Groups need a

Figure 14.6
Sources and Consequences of Group Cohesiveness

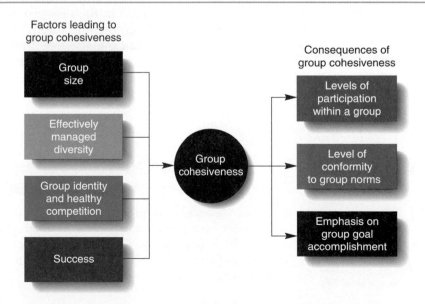

balance of conformity and deviance, so a moderate level of cohesiveness often yields the best outcome.

EMPHASIS ON GROUP GOAL ACCOMPLISHMENT   As group cohesiveness increases, emphasis on group goal accomplishment also increases within a group. Very strong emphasis on group goal accomplishment does not, however, always lead to organizational effectiveness. For an organization to be effective and gain a competitive advantage, it is important for the different groups and teams in the organization to cooperate with each other and be motivated to achieve *organizational* goals, even if doing so sometimes comes at the expense of the achievement of group goals. A moderate level of cohesiveness motivates group members to accomplish both group and organizational goals. High levels of cohesiveness can cause group members to focus so strongly on group goal accomplishment that they strive to achieve group goals no matter what—even when doing so jeopardizes organizational performance.

How can groups become more cohesive?

FACTORS LEADING TO GROUP COHESIVENESS   Four factors affect group cohesiveness (see Figure 14.6).[38] By influencing these *determinants of group cohesiveness*, managers can raise or lower the level of cohesiveness to promote moderate levels of cohesiveness in groups and teams.

GROUP SIZE   As we mentioned earlier, members of small groups tend to be more motivated and committed than members of large groups. Thus, to promote cohesiveness in groups, when feasible, managers should form groups that are small to medium in size (between around 2 and 15 members). If a group is low in cohesiveness and large in size, managers might want to consider the feasibility of dividing the group into two and assigning different tasks and goals to the two newly formed groups.

EFFECTIVELY MANAGED DIVERSITY   In general, people tend to like and get along with others who are similar to themselves. It is easier to communicate with someone, for example, who shares your values, has a similar background, and has had similar experiences. However, as discussed in Chapter 5, diversity in groups, teams, and organizations can help an organization gain a competitive advantage. Diverse groups often come up with more innovative and creative ideas. One reason why cross-functional teams are so popular in organizations like Hallmark Cards is that the diversity in expertise represented in the teams results in higher levels of team performance.

In forming groups and teams, managers need to make sure that the diversity in knowledge, experience, expertise, and other characteristics necessary for group goal accomplishment is represented in the new groups. Managers then have to make sure that this diversity in group membership is effectively managed so that groups will be cohesive. We discussed the effective management of diversity in detail in Chapter 5, and the following "Focus on Diversity" provides additional insight into the steps managers can take to ensure that diverse groups and teams are cohesive.

Focus on Diversity

Promoting Cohesiveness in a Diverse Team at Mercedes–Benz

Andreas Renschler is president of Mercedes–Benz US International Inc. (www.mercedes-benz.com), which in 1997 produced Mercedes' first sport-utility vehicle (the M-Class sport-utility vehicle) at a plant in Vance, Alabama. Mercedes–Benz CEO Helmut Werner committed more than $1.5 billion to the project, which he hopes will move Mercedes to the front of the global market for utility vehicles. The new car plant is Mercedes' first major foreign manufacturing facility outside Germany and embodies Werner's global cost-cutting strategy for Mercedes–Benz.

Renschler had a daunting task–to develop the new vehicle, design the factory and manufacturing process, and recruit and motivate the workforce. His goal was to find and use the most efficient manufacturing processes, and he assembled a diverse top-management team to help him meet this challenge. The team is made up of managers from various countries, including the United States, Germany, and Canada, who gained their experience in companies such as Ford, Nissan, General Motors, and Toyota.[39] Together, team members debate issues such as the best way to design the factory and which manufacturing processes to use.

Given the diverse nature of team members, Renschler recognized early on the need to take steps to build group cohesiveness. To foster trust and camaraderie, he had team members, including himself, participate in three-day wilderness adventures in the Austrian Alps, where they climbed cliffs and rafted down icy rivers. He encourages the development of personal bonds and cohesiveness in his team through his own informal and gregarious style and by socializing with team members. He openly communicates with team members and expects the same from them and is never one to stand on ceremony or adopt Mercedes' traditional formalities.

Signs that Renschler's efforts to build cohesiveness in his top-management team are working come from the productive way in which team members debate ideas. They often disagree with each other but end up making a decision that all team members can support.[40] And Renschler's approach seems to be paying off: In 1998, the plant increased its capacity to meet the high demand for the M-Class sport-utility vehicle.[41]

GROUP IDENTITY AND HEALTHY COMPETITION When group cohesiveness is low, managers often can increase it by encouraging groups to develop their own identities or personalities and to engage in healthy competition. Or managers can encourage team-building exercises. For instance, TELUS, Starbucks, and Coca-Cola have asked Conrad Cone, director of Vancouver-based Pacific Adventure Learning, to organize workshops to create better teams in their companies. Cone notes that, "With the Internet, e-mail and the phone, you're seeing more and more people who work together but are split geographically. It's called the split-team syndrome and gradually it creates misinterpretations and mistrust."[42] The programs are one to five days in length, and range from "death-taunting afternoons on the side of a mountain to quiet, calm self-esteem workshops in [the] boardroom."

Pacific Adventure Learning
www.pacificadventure.org/

If groups are too cohesive, managers can try to decrease cohesiveness by promoting organizational (rather than group) identity and making the organization as a whole the focus of groups' efforts. Organizational identity can be promoted by making group members feel that they are valued members of the organization as a whole and by stressing cooperation across groups to promote the achievement of organizational goals. Excessive levels of cohesiveness also can be reduced by reducing or eliminating competition between groups and rewarding cooperation.

SUCCESS When it comes to promoting group cohesiveness, there is more than a grain of truth to the saying that "Nothing succeeds like success." As groups become more successful, they become increasingly attractive to their members, and their cohesiveness tends to increase. When cohesiveness is low, managers can increase cohesiveness by making sure that a group can achieve some noticeable and visible successes.

Managing Groups and Teams for High Performance

Now that you have a good understanding of why groups and teams are so important for organizations, the types of groups that managers create, and group dynamics, we consider additional steps that managers can take to make sure groups and teams perform highly and contribute to organizational effectiveness. Managers striving to have top-performing groups and teams need to (1) motivate group members to work toward the achievement of organizational goals, (2) prevent groupthink, (3) reduce social loafing, and (4) help groups to manage conflict effectively.

Motivating Group Members to Achieve Organizational Goals

Managers can motivate members of groups and teams to achieve organizational goals and create a competitive advantage by making sure that the members themselves benefit when the group or team performs highly. If members of a self-managed work team know that they will receive a percentage of any cost savings discovered and implemented in the team, they probably will strive to cut costs. For example, Canadian Tire offers team incentives to employees of its gas bars. "Secret" retail shoppers visit the outlets on a regular basis, and score them on such factors as cleanliness, manner in which the transaction was processed, and the types of products offered, using a 100-point scoring system. Scores above a particular threshold provide additional compensation that is shared by the team. Xerox Canada, through its XTRA program, rewards districts for achieving profit and customer satisfaction targets. Everyone in the district shares equally in the bonuses.

Xerox Canada
www.xerox.ca/

Managers often rely on some combination of individual and group-based incentives to motivate members of groups and teams to work toward the achievement of organizational goals and a competitive advantage. When individual performance within a group can be assessed, pay is often determined by individual performance or by both individual and group performance. When individual performance within a group cannot be assessed accurately, then group performance should be the key determinant of pay levels. A Conference Board of Canada study of teams in the workplace found that managers are not necessarily good at constructing team rewards, however. The most commonly used incentive to acknowledge teamwork was recognition, including "small financial rewards, plaques, ceremonies, publicity in company newspapers, and celebrations of success at company gatherings," used by well over half of the companies surveyed.[43] Team cash bonuses were given by only 25 percent of the surveyed companies, and only 17 percent of companies rewarded their teams through gainsharing.[44] One additional consideration when deciding whether and how to reward team members is the effect of pay dispersion on team performance. Research by Nancy Langton of UBC shows that when there is a large discrepancy in wages among group members, collaboration is lowered.[45]

Other benefits that managers can make available to group members when a group performs highly, in addition to monetary rewards, include extra resources such as equipment and computer software, awards and other forms of recognition, and choice future work assignments. For example, members of self-managed work teams that develop new software at companies like Microsoft often value working on interesting and important projects; members of teams that perform highly are rewarded with interesting and important new projects.

Preventing Groupthink

We have been focusing on the steps that managers can take to encourage high levels of performance in groups. Managers, however, need to be aware of an important downside to group and team work: the potentials for groupthink, social

groupthink A pattern of faulty and biased decision making that occurs in groups whose members strive for agreement among themselves at the expense of accurately assessing information relevant to a decision.

loafing, and conflict, all of which can reduce group performance. **Groupthink** occurs when group members become so focused on reaching agreement that they stop examining alternative courses of action and try to prevent the full expression of deviant, minority, or unpopular views within the group. The group pressure to conform causes a deterioration in an individual's mental efficiency, reality testing, and moral judgment.[46]

The symptoms of groupthink include: [47]

- *Illusion of invulnerability*: Group members become overconfident among themselves, allowing them to take extraordinary risks.

- *Assumption of morality*: Group members believe highly in the moral rightness of the group's objectives and do not feel the need to debate the ethics of their actions.

- *Rationalized resistance.* Group members rationalize any resistance to the assumptions they have made. No matter how strongly the evidence may contradict their basic assumptions, members behave so as to reinforce those assumptions continually.

- *Peer pressure.* Members apply direct pressures on those who momentarily express doubts about any of the group's shared views or who question the validity of arguments supporting the alternative favoured by the majority.

- *Minimized doubts.* Those members who have doubts or hold differing points of view seek to avoid deviating from what appears to be group consensus by keeping silent about misgivings and even minimizing to themselves the importance of their doubts.

- *Illusion of unanimity.* If someone doesn't speak, it's assumed that he or she is in full accord. In other words, abstention becomes viewed as a "Yes" vote.

Groupthink does not affect all groups. It seems to occur most often where there is a clear group identity, where members hold a positive image of their group that they want to protect, and where the group perceives an outside threat to this positive image.[48] Groupthink is less about preventing dissent amongst group members and more about ways for a group to protect its positive image.

Groupthink can be minimized.[49] Group leaders need to play an impartial role, actively seek input from all members and avoid expressing their own opinions early on in the discussion. One group member could be appointed to the role of devil's advocate, explicitly challenging the majority position and offering a different perspective. The group should also actively seek out discussion of diverse alternatives, and consider the negative sides of all alternatives. By doing so, the group is less likely to prevent dissenting views and more likely to gain an objective evaluation of each alternative.

Reducing Social Loafing in Groups

social loafing The tendency of individuals to put forth less effort when they work in groups than when they work alone.

Social loafing is the tendency of individuals to put forth less effort when they work in groups than when they work alone.[50] Have you ever watched one or two group members who never seemed to be pulling their weight?

Social loafing can occur in all kinds of groups and teams and in all kinds of organizations. It can result in lower group performance and may even prevent a group from attaining its goals. Fortunately, managers can take steps to reduce social loafing, and sometimes completely eliminate it; we will look at three.

1. *Make individual contributions to a group identifiable.*
Some people may engage in social loafing when they work in groups because they think that they can hide in the crowd—that no one will notice if they put forth less effort than they should. Other people may think that if they put forth high levels of effort and make substantial contributions to the group, their contribution will

not be noticed and they will receive no rewards for their work—so why should they bother?[51]

One way in which managers can effectively eliminate social loafing is by making individual contributions to a group identifiable so that group members perceive that low and high levels of effort will be noticed and individual contributions evaluated.[52] Managers can accomplish this by assigning specific tasks to group members and holding them accountable for their completion.

2. *Emphasize the valuable contributions of individual members.*
Another reason why social loafing may occur is that people sometimes think that their efforts are unnecessary or unimportant when they work in a group. They feel that the group will accomplish its goals and perform at an acceptable level whether or not they personally perform at a high level. To counteract this belief, when managers form groups, they should assign individuals to groups on the basis of the valuable contributions that *each* person can make to the group as a whole. Clearly communicating to group members why each of their contributions is valuable to the group is an effective means by which managers and group members themselves can reduce or eliminate social loafing.[53]

3. *Keep group size at an appropriate level.*
Group size is related to the causes of social loafing we just described. As size increases, identifying individual contributions becomes increasingly difficult, and members are increasingly likely to think that their individual contributions are not very important. To overcome this, managers should form groups with no more members than are needed to accomplish group goals and perform highly.[54]

Helping Groups to Manage Conflict Effectively

At some point or other, practically all groups experience conflict either within the group (intragroup conflict) or with other groups (intergroup conflict). In Chapter 16, we discuss conflict in depth and explore ways to manage it effectively. As you will learn there, managers can take several steps to help groups manage conflict and disagreements.

Tips for Managers

Group Dynamics and Managing Groups and Teams for High Performance

1. Make sure that members of groups and teams personally benefit when the group or team performs highly.

2. Form groups and teams with no more members than are necessary to achieve group and team goals.

3. Reward members of groups whose tasks are characterized by pooled task interdependence based upon individual performance.

4. Reward members of groups or teams whose tasks are characterized by sequential task interdependence based upon group performance.

5. Reward team members whose tasks are characterized by reciprocal task interdependence based upon team performance or a combination of individual and team performance (if individual performance can be identified).

6. Clearly communicate to members of groups and teams the expectations for their roles and how the different roles in the group fit together.

7. Encourage group and team members to assess periodically the appropriateness of existing norms.

Chapter Summary

GROUPS, TEAMS, AND ORGANIZATIONAL EFFECTIVENESS

- Groups and Teams as Performance Enhancers
- Groups, Teams, and Responsiveness to Customers
- Teams and Innovation
- Groups and Teams as Motivators

TYPES OF GROUPS AND TEAMS

- The Top-Management Team
- Research and Development Teams
- Command Groups
- Task Forces
- Self-Managed Work Teams
- Virtual Teams
- Beware! Teams Aren't Always the Answer

GROUP DYNAMICS

- Group Size, Tasks, and Roles
- Group Leadership
- Group Development Over Time
- Group Norms
- Group Cohesiveness

MANAGING GROUPS AND TEAMS FOR HIGH PERFORMANCE

- Motivating Group Members to Achieve Organizational Goals
- Preventing Groupthink
- Reducing Social Loafing in Groups
- Helping Groups to Manage Conflict Effectively

Summary and Review

GROUPS, TEAMS, AND ORGANIZATIONAL EFFECTIVENESS

A group is two or more people who interact with each other to accomplish certain goals or meet certain needs. A team is a group whose members work intensely with each other to achieve a specific common goal or objective. Groups and teams can contribute to organizational effectiveness by enhancing performance, increasing responsiveness to customers, increasing innovation, and being a source of motivation for their members.

TYPES OF GROUPS AND TEAMS

Formal groups are groups that managers establish to achieve organizational goals; they include cross-functional teams, cross-cultural teams, top-management teams, research and development teams, command groups, task forces, self-managed work teams, and virtual teams. Informal groups are groups that employees form because they feel that the groups will help them achieve their own goals or meet their needs. Teams may not always be the answer to achieving a goal, however.

GROUP DYNAMICS

Key elements of group dynamics are group size, tasks, and roles; group leadership; group development; group norms; and group cohesiveness. The advantages and disadvantages of large and small groups suggest that managers should form groups with no more members than are needed to provide the group with the human resources it needs to achieve its goals and use a division of labour. The type of task interdependence that characterizes a group's work gives managers a clue about the appropriate size of the group. A group role is a set of behaviours and tasks that a member of a group is expected to perform because of his or her position in the group. All groups and teams need leadership.

Five stages of development that many groups pass through are forming, storming, norming, performing, and adjourning. Punctuated equilibrium tells us that groups become most involved in their task when half the allocated time has passed.

Group norms are shared rules for behaviour that most group members follow. To be effective, groups need a balance of conformity and deviance. Conformity allows a group to control its members' behaviour in order to achieve group goals; deviance provides the impetus for needed change.

Group cohesiveness is the attractiveness of a group or team to its members. As group cohesiveness increases, so, too, do the level of participation and communication within a group, the level of conformity to group norms, and the emphasis on group goal accomplishment. Managers should strive to achieve a moderate level of group cohesiveness in the groups and teams they manage.

MANAGING GROUPS AND TEAMS FOR HIGH PERFORMANCE

To make sure that groups and teams perform highly, managers need to motivate group members to work toward the achievement of organizational goals, prevent groupthink, reduce social loafing, and help groups to manage conflict effectively. Managers can motivate members of groups and teams to work toward the achievement of organizational goals by making sure that members personally benefit when their group or team performs highly.

Management in Action

Topics for Discussion and Action

1. Why do all organizations need to rely on groups and teams to achieve their goals and gain a competitive advantage?

2. Interview one or more managers in an organization in your local community to identify the types of groups and teams that the organization uses to achieve its goals.

3. Think about a group of which you are a member, and describe your group's current stage of development. Does the development of this group seem to be following the forming-storming-norming-performing-adjourning stages described in the chapter?

4. Think about a group of employees who work in a McDonald's restaurant. What type of task interdependence characterizes this group? What potential problems in the group should the restaurant manager be aware of and take steps to avoid?

5. Discuss the reasons why too much conformity can hurt groups and their organizations.

6. Why do some groups have very low levels of cohesiveness?

7. Imagine that you are the manager of a hotel. What steps will you take to reduce social loafing by members of the cleaning staff who are responsible for keeping all common areas and guest rooms spotless?

Building Management Skills

Diagnosing Group Failures

Think about the last dissatisfying or discouraging experience you had as a member of a group or team. Perhaps the group did not accomplish its goals, perhaps group members could agree about nothing, or perhaps there was too much social loafing. Now answer the following questions.

1. What type of group was this?

2. Were group members motivated to achieve group goals? Why or why not?

3. How large was the group, what type of task interdependence existed in the group, and what group roles did members play?

4. What were the group's norms? How much conformity and deviance existed in the group?

5. How cohesive was the group? Why do you think the group's cohesiveness was at this level? What consequences did this level of group cohesiveness have for the group and its members?

6. Was social loafing a problem in this group? Why or why not?

7. What could the group's leader or manager have done differently to increase group effectiveness?

8. What could group members have done differently to increase group effectiveness?

Small Group Breakout Exercise

Creating a Cross-Functional Team

Form groups of three or four people, and appoint one member as the spokesperson who will communicate your findings to the whole class when called on by the instructor. Then discuss the following scenario.

You are a group of managers in charge of food services for a large university. Recently, a survey of students, faculty, and staff was conducted to evaluate customer satisfaction with the food services provided by the university's eight cafeterias. The results were disappointing, to put it mildly. Complaints ranged from dissatisfaction with the type and range of meals and snacks provided, operating hours, and food temperature, to unresponsiveness to current concerns about the importance of low-fat/high-fibre diets and the preferences of vegetarians. You have decided to form a cross-functional team to further evaluate reactions to the food services and to develop a proposal for changes to be made to increase customer satisfaction.

1. Indicate who should be on this important cross-functional team and why.

2. Describe the goals the team should be striving to achieve.

3. Describe the different roles team members will need to perform.

4. Describe the steps you will take to help ensure that the team has a good balance between conformity and deviance and a moderate level of cohesiveness.

Exploring the World Wide Web

Specific Assignment

Many companies are committed to the use of teams, including Sears Canada. Scan Sears' Web site to learn more about this company (www.sears.ca/e/info/info.htm). Then click on "Corporate Information," "Careers at Sears" and "Mission, Vision & Values."

1. What principles or values underlie Sears' use of teams?

2. How does Sears use teams to build employee commitment?

General Assignment

Find the Web site of a company that relies heavily on teams to accomplish its goals. What kinds of teams does this company use? What steps do managers take to ensure that team members are motivated to perform at a high level?

ManagementCase

Teams Manage AES (With the Help of a Few Managers)

In the late 1970s, Dennis W. Bakke and R.W. Sant founded AES Corporation, a power company that sells electricity to public utilities and steam to industrial corporations. Since the early days, AES's revenues have been increasing, on average, about 23 percent per year, annual profits have reached the $155 million mark, and the company has grown to 1500 employees. AES has only four levels in its corporate hierarchy: workers, plant managers, division managers, and corporate managers. There are no corporate departments or managers in charge of areas such as purchasing, finance, human resources, or operations. Who oversees such activities? They are all handled by volunteer teams formed by plant managers and composed of rank-and-file workers. In a nutshell, AES appears to be a well-managed company with a minimum of managers and many teams.[55]

Do workers in an electric power plant make million-dollar investment decisions or negotiate major contracts with suppliers? This is exactly what is done at AES. Jeff Hatch, an employee in the Montville, Connecticut plant who performs activities such as unloading coal from barges, and Joe Oddo, a maintenance technician at the plant, are both part of a voluntary team that manages the plant's $51 million investment fund. Other teams of technicians handle the purchasing of materials ranging from mops to turbines, and teams of engineers arrange financing for new plants. Multimillion-dollar contracts normally negotiated by CEOs are handled by teams of engineers as well. New employees are hired by teams with diverse members ranging from pipe fitters to accountants.

Why does AES manage with teams (and without many managers)? According to Bakke and Sant, four core values underlie this unique approach to management— integrity, social responsibility, fairness, and fun. Observes Sant, "Fun is when you're intellectually excited and you are interacting with others .... It's the struggle, and even the failures that go with it, that makes work fun."[56]

AES has experienced its share of failures as well as successes. In 1992, seven workers falsified emission-control reports at the Shady Point, Oklahoma plant. When managers discovered and reported this violation to the authorities, the result was a $194 000 fine. Why did the violation occur? Sometimes team members feel so responsible for what happens at AES that they are afraid to admit when they make a mistake. The Shady Point workers who falsified the reports had been afraid they would be fired when managers realized emissions were high.

When problems like this occur, managers interpret them as a signal that AES's values are not coming through. Bakke and Sant felt so personally responsible for not getting AES's values across to the plant's employees that they reduced their own bonuses by over 50 percent in 1992. To avoid a recurrence of this kind of problem, they also made it clear to employees in the plant that they can trust managers to stand by them even when they make a mistake.

True to the spirit of social responsibility, a team of employees in the Montville, Connecticut plant determined how much carbon dioxide the plant would release into the environment in the foreseeable future. The team then had thousands of trees planted in Guatemala to offset the omissions, to the tune of $3.1 million.

Making high-powered decisions can be stressful for AES employees. Paul Burdick, for example, described how he felt when, after being on the job as a mechanical engineer at AES for only a few months, he had major responsibility in a team to complete a $1.55 billion purchase of coal: "I'd never negotiated anything before, save for a used car ... I was afraid to make some of the decisions." He found the experience very motivating, challenging, and energizing, however, while also feeling intense pressure to do "right" by other AES employees. As Burdick suggests, such intellectual stimulation has "a flip side ... You're given a lot of leeway and a lot of rope. You can use it to climb or you can hang yourself."[57]

Evidence that most employees might actually enjoy the stimulation of making important decisions and being responsible for them (and do not find it overly stressful) is provided by the fact that AES's turnover rate is less than one percent. Nevertheless, suppliers, financiers, and company presidents often balk at having to negotiate and deal with rank-and-file workers in order to do business with AES. As Sant puts it, "Outside parties clearly are frustrated at having to deal with people who have more authority than top management. So many people want to come to the CEO, but we generally back off and say, 'It's up to these guys. You've just got to work these relationships.'"

What does coal handler Jeff Hatch think about this innovative use of teams at AES? "Who would have thought I'd be reading the *Wall Street Journal* every day and second-guessing Alan Greenspan? ... It definitely makes it a lot more fun to show up for work every day."[58]

Questions

1. What are the advantages of AES's innovative use of teams?

2. What are the potential disadvantages of having teams of work-ers rather than managers make most of the important decisions?

3. Do you think Sant and Bakke's approach to managing AES would work in other companies? Why or why not?

ManagementCase

In the News

From the Pages of *The Ottawa Citizen*
Team Building Adventures More Than Game

When 40 employees from Hewlett-Packard's technology-finance division gathered in late November for a retreat at Chateau Montebello, they spent four days engaged in a variety of activities—discussing corporate strategy, upgrading their customer-support skills and navigating their way across a river infested with piranhas.

Piranha-infested rivers?

OK, so the flesh-eating fish were fictitious and the river turned out to be a harmless sandpit. But organizers of the retreat are hopeful that this make-believe adventure, in which colleagues had to help each other across a fake river using barrels and planks of plywood, will play a crucial role in the company's efforts to encourage teamwork and improve communication among its employees.

"We learned, as individuals, the value of communication, and how important it is to acknowledge the strengths that everyone brings to the group," said participant Lilie Venditti, who, when not sidestepping around imaginary piranhas or defusing fake bombs, manages Hewlett-Packard's Canadian Business Centre.

"These exercises really brought us closer together," she said. "Once we got back ... I noticed that people were more open with each other."

These mock adventure games, in which groups of employees are forced to rely on each other to overcome adverse challenges, might seem like an unorthodox way to train personnel, but the concept is catching on with an increasing number of Canadian companies, who, wanting to foster teamwork and trust among employees, are forsaking traditional classroom-style lectures in favour of hands-on learning.

"When you have a talking head, be it on video or in front of a class, there's a low level of retention," said John Cross, vice-president, human resources, for Hewlett-Packard Canada Ltd. "We find that experiential learning is a far, far better learning experience. People tend to remember things through stories and this is a story that they can recall."

Stuart Robertson, a physical-education professor at Champlain College and veteran outdoor educator, put it even more simply: "You can sit in a classroom and talk all you want about downhill skiing," he said. "But you can't teach someone to ski without taking them on to a mountain."

Mr. Robertson, who is also an adjunct professor at Concordia University's department of exercise science, recently signed on to develop and facilitate team-building adventure programs for Atmosp(here) Communications, a Montreal firm that has built a reputation as an event planner but is now focusing its attention on experiential learning, through a new division entitled Naviquest.

Atmosp(here) Communications founder Jason Katz, who organized the Hewlett-Packard program, is working feverishly to build up his company's client base, convinced that corporations are ready to offer their employees more hands-on training. The company's program has just been accredited by Emploi Quebec—making it eligible under the provincial law requiring corporations to spend one per cent of their total salary on training and development programs each year. And the company is expected to launch a flagship outdoor-adventure centre at Hotel l'Esterel in the Laurentians next spring.

Working with Mr. Robertson and fellow outdoor educator Keith Wilkinson, Mr. Katz's company has crafted a series of activities that draw on the skills that employees need to develop in order to become more productive in the workplace. Challenges might include working together to defuse an imaginary bomb or getting a whole team of employees through an electrified spider web.

"Our goal is to put employees into situations that they have to conquer together; they need to find the best path in order to complete the task or defuse the situation, and that often means finding better ways of communicating with each other," Mr. Katz said.

"The activities may last only 20 minutes, but they are metaphors for what happens in life," Mr. Robertson added.

"While the impact of such programs is often difficult to measure, a growing body of literature suggests that companies benefit greatly when putting their employees through experiential-type learning activities," said Dan Romano, who oversees corporate training programs for H2O Adventures. He cites one survey that indicates companies can expect a 30-percent increase in productivity and a significant drop in employee absenteeism in the six months following the program.

"The investment comes back to these companies," he said. "It's often a question of how companies cannot afford to do this."

Starting out as a kayak company offering white-water rafting adventures along the Rouge River in Western Quebec, H2O Adventures began courting corporate clients about three years ago. Today, that slice of their business is growing exponentially and now represents about two-thirds of the company's total revenue.

Mr. Romano said some corporate executives are skeptical about the idea, mistaking the programs as nothing more than fun and games. And participants often enter with reservations of their own. "When they hear that there is a learning component to it, they think they'll be forced to sit through a lecture, where they will be told how to perform," he said.

A typical program often lasts anywhere from three hours to a full day, but can be tailored to cover up to an entire week. The two companies' client lists include corporations like Pfizer Canada Inc., Bristol-Myers Squibb Co., Future Electronics, London Life Insurance Company and hi-tech startups Hyperchip Inc. and Zero-Knowledge Systems. Mr. Romano said it is no coincidence that his company's list of clients includes a high proportion of firms in the technology and pharmaceutical industries—not only do company heads from those milieus tend to be more progressive in their thinking, and thus more apt to try unorthodox training methods, but Mr. Romano said those industries are also most vulnerable to losing employees through corporate raiding.

"In the high-tech industry, for example, where staff are continuously being headhunted, and where the knowledge and ability inside an employee's head is the most valuable asset they have, it behooves them to have a really good team-building program in place, in order to develop a really loyal staff," he said.

But Steven Appelbaum, a management professor at Concordia's John Molson School of Business, cautions companies not to rely too much on off-site team-building programs, saying the lessons learned through simulated games and activities rarely translate into better working habits at the office. "The problem is that (these activities) do not correlate back to the workplace."

Employees participate in these activities "because they know it's what their managers want, so they get along with each other and play the role that's expected of them," he said. "But then, when they get back to the office on Monday morning, they put their armour back on and go back to their old patterns."

Instead, Mr. Appelbaum suggests companies that want to keep their employees motivated need to concentrate on old-fashioned, textbook style management techniques, such as opening communication channels and involving personnel in decision-making processes.

"It's the structures and behaviour of the organization that are the critical factors that determine whether you can get people to play ball for you, not whether your employees can rely on each other in a game," he said. "If an organization creates an environment where people feel empowered, where they feel motivated and where they are involved in making decisions, then you don't have to do all of this extra stuff."

But those involved in organizing experiential-learning programs disagree, insisting that the lessons learned do in fact translate back to the workplace. Activities are followed by debriefing sessions, where participants have a chance to analyse the skills they relied upon to complete their tasks. And Atmosp(here) Communications runs followup sessions back at the client's office within a month of the program.

"If we just ran these scenarios and left it at that, it could be considered fun and games," Mr. Robertson said. "But we go back to these people and help them transfer what they learned to the workplace."

"A lot of the success ends up being anecdotal," Hewlett-Packard's Mr. Cross admitted. "But clearly, relationships among employees tend to be stronger and communication is better."

Source: D. Cassoff, "Team Building Adventures More Than Game: Experts Disagree on the Usefulness of Mock Adventures Used to Motivate Employees," *The Ottawa Citizen*, December 26, 2000, p. F6.

Questions

1. What strategies does IBM Canada use to help develop teamwork?

2. There is clearly a debate regarding the usefulness of off-site teambuilding exercises. To what extent do you think these kinds of programs might be useful for teambuilding?

Chapter fifteen

Communication

Learning Objectives

1. Explain why effective communication helps an organization gain a competitive advantage.

2. Describe the communication process, and explain the role of perception in communication.

3. Define information richness, and describe the information richness of communication media available to managers.

4. Describe the communication networks that exist in groups and teams.

5. Explain how advances in technology have given managers new options for managing communication.

6. Describe important communication skills that individuals need as senders and as receivers of messages.

A Case in Contrast

The Importance of Good Communication Skills

Both managers and employees at Owen Sound, ON-based RBW Graphics (www.transcontinental-gtc.com) pride themselves on the family atmosphere of the company.[1] Brian Reid, general manager, speaks to every employee he encounters whenever he walks around the plant.

Good communication among management and employees is a hallmark of the company, and that attitude pays off. The company has consistently been on the leading edge of technology in the printing industry, as far back as 1927.

RBW empowers its staff to make decisions and act upon them. The average employee has worked there for 18 years. And though there have been several organizing attempts by unions (including a drive in 1999), there has never been a union at the plant.

"I believe our employees have more say with the current structure than they would with unions," says Reid. The company has never laid off a full-time employee. In agreeing with Reid, press technician Brad Fritzsch says, "I think the unions haven't been successful here because of the way we operate. Management does a pretty good job at trying to address all the people's concerns, and there are a number of sub-committees that provide for good communication."

Among RBW's committees are a Joint Health and Safety Committee, a Shop Committee and a Social Committee. Employees volunteer to serve on the committees and they are responsible for exchanging information and investigating, recommending and implementing solutions, policies and events to improve the working and personal lives of the employees.

Because of good communication in the plant, the company has been able to achieve work structures that might have been difficult in other companies. For instance, in 1997 RBW switched

At RBW Graphics, good communication empowers employees and creates a work environment that both employees and managers appreciate.

Vancouver's city managers failed to consult with their staff before abolishing the four-day workweek that had been in place for 22 years. Employees staged a seven-week strike because they could not reach agreement with the city.

to a 12-hour shift system, making the company a seven-day-a-week, 24-hour-a-day operation. The decision to do this was investigated and voted on by the staff. Therefore, even though the impact was great, the transition was well received.

Bill Hiscox, a pressroom technician, says the atmosphere on the shop floor is "just like being in a small town." He adds, "It's a good family company and they really look after us well." The admiration is mutual, however. When Transcontinental Printing, RBW's parent corporation, won a coveted six-year contract to print *Time Canada* magazine in 1999, Wayne Newson, the company's president, noted that "the most gratifying thing to us is that we did not get this contract on price. We had to be competitive but it really came down to the capabilities of our plant in Owen Sound. We won the business based on our people and our competencies."

While RBW exemplifies good communication among managers and employees, not all employers treat their employees so well. When Canadian Union of Public Employees (CUPE) (www.cupebc.ca) Local 15, which represents the City of Vancouver's inside workers, went on strike in early October 2000, the workers were responding to a long-simmering feud with the city's managers. In late April 1998, the city council had announced, without consulting its staff, that it would abolish its 22-year-old program of four-day workweeks, effective September 1, 1998. The program was very popular with the staff.

Within two weeks of the city's announcement, negative response from employees became widespread. Some resigned from the staff-appreciation committee, others withdrew voluntary services, and/or wrote anguished letters to councillors "about the emotional and financial impact it would have on them, city hall and the community if the city returned to more traditional work schedules." Then-city manager Ken Dobell showed no sympathy to the employees' complaints. He simply remarked that "the rest of the world is on a five-day workweek and the city is out of step." In other words, he refused to listen to his employees' concerns.

Two years later, city employees were still upset. Two dozen managers and professional staff had quit during that period, double the normal quit rate for the city. In October 2000, the CUPE workers went on strike for seven weeks because they could not reach agreement with the city on the four-day workweek. At issue was the fact that the city would not communicate with its employees to resolve difficulties with the way the four-day workweek was implemented at City Hall. Though early on in the debate the city claimed that there had been widespread complaints about disruptions caused by the four-day workweek, during the strike city manager Judy Rogers said there was only "anecdotal evidence of dissatisfaction among business leaders with irregular city hours."

Employees were not offered the opportunity to address alleged concerns while still preserving their flextime schedules. Dave Amy, an engineering technician, explained, "I worked with the developers who brought the complaints [about flextime] forward to council, and yes, they had some reasons to complain. But those were small issues that could very well have been worked out. It didn't need to come down to this." ●

Overview

As should be clear from the "Case in Contrast," ineffective communication is detrimental for managers, workers, and organizations; it can lead to poor performance, strained interpersonal relations, poor service, and dissatisfied customers. Managers at all levels need to be good communicators in order for an organization to be effective and gain a competitive advantage.

In this chapter, we describe the nature of communication and the communication process and explain why it is so important for all managers and their subordinates to be effective communicators. We describe the communication media available to managers and the factors they need to consider in selecting a communication medium for each message they send. We consider the communication networks that organizational members rely on, and we explore how advances in information technology are expanding managers' communication options. We describe the communication skills that help individuals be effective senders and receivers of messages. By the end of this chapter, you will have a good appreciation of the nature of communication and the steps that all organizational members can take to ensure that they are effective communicators. ●

Communication in Organizations

communication

The sharing of information between two or more individuals or groups to reach a common understanding.

Communication is the sharing of information between two or more individuals or groups to reach a common understanding.[2] From the "Case in Contrast," it is clear that some organizations are more effective at doing this than others. RBW encourages employees and managers to work together on solutions to problems. The City of Vancouver simply imposed a decision that would affect the personal lives of many of its employees.

The Importance of Good Communication

Is good communication really all that important?

In Chapter 1, we explained that in order for an organization to gain a competitive advantage, managers must strive to increase efficiency, quality, responsiveness to customers, and innovation. Good communication is essential for reaching each of these four goals and thus is a necessity for gaining a competitive advantage.

Managers can *increase efficiency* by updating the production process to take advantage of new and more efficient technologies and by training workers to operate the new technologies and expand their skills. Good communication is necessary for managers to learn about new technologies, implement them in their organizations, and train workers in how to use them. Similarly, *improving quality* hinges on effective communication. Managers need to communicate to all members of an organization the meaning and importance of high quality and the routes to attaining it. Subordinates need to communicate to their superiors quality problems and suggestions for increasing quality, and members of self-managed work teams need to share with each other their ideas for improving quality.

Good communication can also help to increase *responsiveness to customers.* When the organizational members who are closest to customers, such as salespeople in department stores and tellers in banks, are empowered to communicate customers' needs and desires to managers, managers are better able to respond to these needs. Managers, in turn, must communicate with other organizational members to determine how best to respond to changing customer preferences.

Innovation, which often takes place in cross-functional teams, also requires effective communication. Members of a cross-functional team developing a new kind of compact disc player, for example, must effectively communicate with each other to develop a disc player that customers will want, that will be of high quality, and that can be produced efficiently. Members of the team also must communicate with managers to secure the resources they need to develop the disc player and must keep managers informed of progress on the project.

Effective communication is necessary for managers and all other members of an organization to increase efficiency, quality, responsiveness to customers, and innovation, and thus gain a competitive advantage for their organization. Managers therefore must have a good understanding of the communication process if they are to perform effectively. Ed Clark seems to know how to communicate effectively, as this "Management Insight" shows.

Management Insight

TD Canada Trust's New Boss Likes to Talk

TD Canada Trust is a new bank, and it has a new president.[3] The bank (created from a merger of Toronto-Dominion Bank and Canada Trust) is headed by Ed Clark, the former head of Canada Trust. Many say that he's the right person to lead the merged workforces: he comes from a bank known for its customer service and customer loyalty.

Clark is trying to make sure that the merger goes well, for both new and old customers. In his first year, he's visiting branches throughout the country, just to listen to employees and customers alike. "I want to know what people are thinking so we can improve what we are trying to achieve. If we need to change things, we will."

Clark knows that eventually branches will be closed, and there will be some layoffs, although he's not sure of exact numbers at the start of his term. The merger began in February 2000 and won't be completed until 2003. He's trying to do the merger differently than a US-style merger where branches are closed immediately.

"We want to take our customers and carry our employees through the merger process, because in the end we're trying to produce a retail bank that starts with the customers and works backwards, rather than with the shareholders and works forwards."

To do this, communication is key. Employees find learning new systems difficult, and he wants to keep morale up. Customers notice that things are moving more slowly, and service isn't as good as they expect. So Clark visits the branches, taking a notebook and pencil with him, and chats with the customers in the lineups and the tellers at their tills.

His communication style is definitely working: TD Canada Trust started increasing its market share shortly after the merger.

sender The person or group wishing to share information.

message The information that a sender wants to share.

encoding Translating a message into understandable symbols or language.

noise Anything that hampers any stage of the communication process.

receiver The person or group for which a message is intended.

medium The pathway through which an encoded message is transmitted to a receiver.

decoding Interpreting and trying to make sense of a message.

The Communication Process

The communication process consists of two phases. In the *transmission phase*, information is shared between two or more individuals or groups. In the *feedback phase*, a common understanding is reached. In both phases, a number of distinct stages must occur for communication to take place (see Figure 15.1).[4]

Starting the transmission phase, the **sender**, the person or group wishing to share information with some other person or group, decides on the **message**, what information to communicate. Then the sender translates the message into symbols or language, a process called **encoding**; often messages are encoded into words. **Noise** is a general term that refers to anything that hampers any stage of the communication process. In the "Case in Contrast," City Manager Dobell's failure to pay attention and listen to employee concerns about how a change in the workweek would affect their lives was a source of noise.

Once encoded, a message is transmitted through a medium to the **receiver**, the person or group for which the message is intended. A **medium** is simply the pathway—such as a phone call, a letter, a memo, or face-to-face communication in a meeting—through which an encoded message is transmitted to a receiver. At the next stage, the receiver interprets and tries to make sense of the message, a process called **decoding**. This is a critical point in communication.

The feedback phase is begun by the receiver (who becomes a sender). The receiver decides what message to send to the original sender (who becomes a receiver), encodes it, and transmits it through a chosen medium (see Figure 15.1).

Figure 15.1
The Communication Process

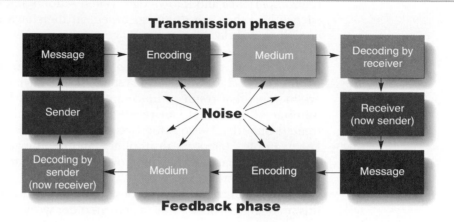

The message might contain a confirmation that the original message was received and understood, a restatement of the original message to make sure that it was correctly interpreted, or a request for more information. The original sender decodes the message and makes sure that a common understanding has been reached. If the original sender determines that a common understanding has not been reached, sender and receiver cycle through the whole process as many times as needed to reach a common understanding. As the "Case in Contrast" indicates, failure to listen to employees prevents many managers from receiving feedback and reaching a common understanding with their employees. Feedback eliminates misunderstandings, ensures that messages are correctly interpreted, and enables senders and receivers to reach a common understanding.

The encoding of messages into words, written or spoken, is **verbal communication**. We also encode messages without using written or spoken language. **Nonverbal communication** shares information by means of facial expressions (smiling, raising an eyebrow, frowning, dropping one's jaw), body language (posture, gestures, nods, shrugs), and even style of dress (casual, formal, conservative, trendy). Walk into Toronto-based Willow Manufacturing and you'll find everyone who works there, even President Dennis Wild, wearing the same-style uniform.[5] That's one way the company conveys that everyone at Willow is part of the team, and equally important.

As Wild realizes, nonverbal communication can reinforce verbal communication. Just as a warm and genuine smile can back up words of appreciation for a job well done, a concerned facial expression can back up words of sympathy for a personal problem. In such cases, the congruence between verbal and nonverbal communication helps to ensure that a common understanding is reached.

Sometimes when members of an organization decide not to express a message verbally, they inadvertently express it nonverbally. People tend to have less control over nonverbal communication, and often a verbal message that is withheld gets expressed through body language or facial expressions. A manager who agrees to a proposal that she or he actually is not in favour of may unintentionally communicate disfavour by grimacing.

verbal communication

The encoding of messages into words, either written or spoken.

nonverbal communication

The encoding of messages by means of facial expressions, body language, and styles of dress.

The Role of Perception in Communication

Perception plays a central role in communication and affects both transmission and feedback. In Chapter 11, we defined *perception* as the process through which people select, organize, and interpret sensory input to give meaning and order to the world around them. We mentioned that perception is inherently subjective and influenced by people's personalities, values, attitudes, and moods as well as by their experience and knowledge. When senders and receivers communicate with each other, they are doing so based on their own subjective perceptions. The encoding and decoding of messages and even the choice of a medium hinge on the perceptions of senders and receivers.

In addition, perceptual biases can hamper effective communication. Recall from Chapter 5 that biases are systematic tendencies to use information about others in ways that result in inaccurate perceptions. In Chapter 5, we described a number of *biases* that can result in diverse members of an organization being treated unfairly. These same biases also can lead to ineffective communication. For example, stereotypes—simplified and often inaccurate beliefs about the characteristics of particular groups of people—can interfere with the encoding and decoding of messages.

Suppose a manager stereotypes older workers as being fearful of change. When this manager encodes a message to an older worker about an upcoming change in the organization, the extent of the change may be downplayed so as not to make the older worker feel stressed. The older worker, however, fears change no more than younger colleagues fear it and decodes the message to mean that hardly any changes are going to be made. The older worker fails to prepare adequately for the change, and performance subsequently suffers because of lack of preparation for the change. Clearly, the ineffective communication was due to the manager's inaccurate assumptions about older workers. Instead of relying on stereotypes, effective managers strive to perceive other people accurately by focusing on their actual behaviours, knowledge, skills, and abilities. Accurate perceptions, in turn, contribute to effective communication.

The Dangers of Ineffective Communication

Because managers must communicate with others to perform their various roles and tasks, managers spend most of their time communicating, whether in meetings, in telephone conversations, through e-mail, or in face-to-face interactions. Indeed, some experts estimate that managers spend approximately 85 percent of their time engaged in some form of communication.[6] So important is effective communication that managers cannot just be concerned that they themselves are effective communicators; they also have to help their subordinates be effective communicators. When all members of an organization are able to communicate effectively with each other and with people outside the organization, the organization is much more likely to perform highly and gain a competitive advantage.

When managers and other members of an organization are ineffective communicators, organizational performance suffers, and any competitive advantage the organization might have is likely to be lost. Moreover, poor communication sometimes can be downright dangerous and even lead to tragic and unnecessary loss of human life. For example, communication problems in the cockpit of airplanes and between flight crews and air traffic controllers can lead to deadly consequences. On September 26, 1997, a Garuda Airlines Airbus crashed into a highland jungle in Indonesia, killing all 234 passengers and crew aboard. The control tower first instructed the pilot to turn right, and then requested a confirmation of a left turn. When the pilot, a bit confused, replied "Confirm turning left? We are starting turning right now," the controller replied, "OK. Continue turning right." Immediately thereafter the plane smashed into trees and exploded.[7]

Unfortunately, errors like this one are not isolated events. A safety group at NASA tracked over 6000 unsafe flying incidents and found that communication difficulties caused approximately 529 of them.[8]

Information Richness and Communication Media

To be effective communicators, managers (and other members of an organization) need to select an appropriate communication medium for *each* message they send. Should a change in procedures be communicated to subordinates in a memo or sent as e-mail? Should a congratulatory message about a major accomplishment be communicated in a letter, in a phone call, or over lunch? Should a layoff announcement be made in a memo or at a plant meeting? Should the members of a purchasing team travel to Europe to cement a major agreement with a new supplier, or should they do so through faxes? Managers deal with these questions day in and day out.

There is no one best communication medium for managers to rely on. In choosing a communication medium for any message, managers need to consider three factors.

information richness

The amount of information that a communication medium can carry and the extent to which the medium enables sender and receiver to reach a common understanding.

The first and most important is the level of **information richness** that is needed. Information richness is the amount of information a communication medium can carry and the extent to which the medium enables sender and receiver to reach a common understanding.[9] The communication media that managers use vary in their information richness (see Figure 15.2).[10] Media high in information richness are able to carry a lot of information and generally enable receivers and senders to come to a common understanding.

The second factor that managers need to take into account in selecting a communication medium is the time needed for communication, because managers' and other organizational members' time is valuable. Managers at United Parcel Service, for example, dramatically reduced the amount of time they spent communicating with colleagues in Germany and England by using video conferences instead of face-to-face communication, which required travel overseas.[11]

The third factor that affects the choice of a communication medium is the *need for a paper or electronic trail,* or some kind of written documentation that a message was sent and received. A manager may wish to document in writing, for example, that a subordinate was given a formal warning about excessive lateness.

In the remainder of this section, we examine four types of communication media that vary along these three dimensions: information richness, time, and need for a paper or electronic trail.[12]

Figure 15.2
The Information Richness of Communication Media

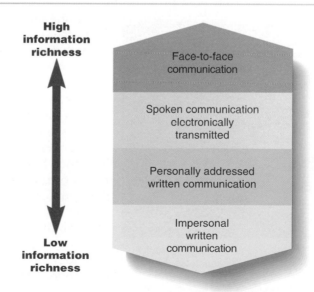

High information richness

Low information richness

Face-to-face communication

Spoken communication electronically transmitted

Personally addressed written communication

Impersonal written communication

Face-to-Face Communication

Face-to-face communication is the medium that is highest in information richness. When managers communicate face to face, they not only can take advantage of verbal communication but also can interpret each other's nonverbal signals such as facial expressions and body language. A look of concern or puzzlement can sometimes tell more than a thousand words, and managers can respond to these nonverbal signals on the spot. Face-to-face communication also enables managers to receive instant feedback. Points of confusion, ambiguity, or misunderstanding can be resolved, and managers can cycle through the communication process as many times as they need to, to reach a common understanding.

management by wandering around

A face-to-face communication technique in which a manager walks around a work area and talks informally with employees about issues and concerns.

Management by wandering around (MBWA) is a face-to-face communication technique that many managers at all levels in an organization find effective.[13] Rather than scheduling formal meetings with subordinates, managers walk around work areas and talk informally with employees about issues and concerns that both employees and managers may have. These informal conversations provide managers and subordinates with important information and at the same time foster the development of positive relationships. William Hewlett and David Packard, founders and former top managers of Hewlett-Packard, found management by wandering around to be a highly effective way of communicating with their employees.

Because face-to-face communication is highest in information richness, you might think that it should always be the medium of choice for managers. This is not the case, however, because of the amount of time it takes and the lack of a paper or electronic trail resulting from it. For messages that are important, personal, or likely to be misunderstood, it is often well worth managers' time to use face-to-face communication and, if need be, supplement it with some form of written communication documenting the message.

Advances in information technology are providing managers with new and convenient alternative communication media for face-to-face communication. Many organizations are using *video conferences* to capture some of the advantages of face-to-face communication (such as access to facial expressions), while saving time and money because managers in different locations do not have to travel to meet with one another. During a video conference, managers in two or more locations communicate with each other over large TV or video screens; they not only hear each other but also see each other throughout the meeting.

In addition to saving travel costs, video conferences can speed up decisions, shorten new product development time, and lead to more efficient meetings. Some managers have found that meetings are 20 to 30 percent shorter when they use video conferences instead of face-to-face meetings.[14]

Videoconferencing can also be used to provide services to clients that might not otherwise be available. In BC's pulp and paper industry, teleconferencing can be used to save time for clients. "People buy logs, but they like to see them first. And if you can save a guy a four- or five-hour trip in his pickup truck to see a log, it's a lot more beneficial," says Doug Baleshda, owner of Kamloops, BC-based 135 Services Ltd., a distributor of videoconference products.[15]

The telemedicine centre at Memorial University connects about 250 sites in Newfoundland to provide such services as cardiological testing, nuclear medicine and radiology, clinical consultations, and continuing medical education.[16] More recently, Andrea Battcock, the associ-

Video conferencing allows for face-to-face communication between two or more people. It also saves on travel costs and the time involved to fly to other locations.

ate director of administration and development for the Telemedicine and Educational Technology Resource Agency (TETRA) at Memorial University in St. John's, has been conducting a "tele-psychiatry" project, comparing psychiatric assessments of children done face-to-face versus via video-conference sessions. The diagnosis and treatment recommendations were almost identical in either session, and when the study connected children in Corner Brook, Newfoundland, with the Janeway Child Health Centre in St. John's 700 km away, it was a winning situation for parents and the province. Video-conference setup costs are about $90 for a one-and-a-half hour session. Transportation costs for the family to come to St. John's from Corner Brook would have been about $2500. Children who could not be treated before because of lack of access or the tremendous cost can now be diagnosed with much greater ease. Advances like these have made Newfoundland a leader in the field of telemedicine.

Spoken Communication Electronically Transmitted

After face-to-face communication, spoken communication electronically transmitted over phone lines is second-highest in information richness (see Figure 15.2). Although managers communicating over the telephone do not have access to body language and facial expressions, they do have access to the tone of voice in which a message is delivered, the parts of the message the sender emphasizes, and the general manner in which the message is spoken, in addition to the actual words themselves. Thus, telephone conversations have the capacity to convey extensive amounts of information. Managers also can ensure that mutual understanding is reached because they can get quick feedback over the phone and can answer questions.

Richmond, BC-based Boston Pizza International Inc., which was founded in 1963, today has more than 139 stores throughout Canada and the United States. As the company expanded, founder Jim Treliving and co-owner George Melville were concerned about trying to maintain a local presence with their staff spread so far apart. "We were concerned that as we grew an internal bureaucracy would form," Melville says.[17] To alleviate this, senior members from each office take part in a weekly teleconference on Monday mornings at 9 a.m. "It keeps everyone involved and informed," Melville explains. It also helps with team building, so that everyone in the company feels that they are an important part of the success of the company.

Voice mail systems and answering machines also allow managers to send and receive verbal electronic messages over telephone lines. Such systems are obviously a necessity when managers or employees are frequently out of the office, and those on the road are well advised to check their voice mail periodically.

Personally Addressed Written Communication

Lower than electronically transmitted verbal communication in information richness is personally addressed written communication (see Figure 15.2). One of the advantages of face-to-face communication and verbal communication electronically transmitted is that they both tend to demand attention, which helps ensure that receivers pay attention. Personally addressed written communication such as a memo or letter also has this advantage. Because it is addressed to a particular person, the chances are good that the person will actually pay attention to (and read) it. Moreover, the sender can write the message in a way that the receiver is most likely to understand. Like voice mail, written communication does not enable a receiver to have his or her questions answered immediately, but when messages are clearly written and feedback is provided, common understandings can still be reached.

Even if managers use face-to-face communication, a follow-up in writing is often needed for messages that are important or complicated and need to be referred to later on. This is precisely what Karen Stracker, a hospital administrator, did when she needed to tell one of her subordinates about an important change in the way the hospital would be handling denials of insurance benefits. Stracker met with the subordinate and described the changes face to face. Once she was sure that the subordinate understood them, she handed her a sheet of instructions to follow, which essentially summarized the information they had discussed.

E-mail also fits into this category of communication media because senders and receivers are communicating through personally addressed written words. The words are appearing on their personal computer screens, however, rather than on pieces of paper. E-mail is becoming so widespread in the business world that managers are even developing their own e-mail etiquette. For instance, messages in capital letters are often perceived as being shouted or screamed. Here are some guidelines from polite e-mailers: Always punctuate messages; do not ramble on or say more than you need to; do not act as though you do not understand something when in fact you do understand it; and pay attention to spelling and format (put a memo in memo form).

Would you consider telecommuting?

The growing popularity of e-mail has enabled many workers and managers to become *telecommuters*, people who are employed by organizations and work out of offices in their own homes. There are approximately 1 million telecommuters in Canada and this is expected to increase to 1.5 million by the end of 2001.[18] Brampton, ON-based Nortel Networks operates one of the biggest telecommuting programs in Canada.[19] Nearly 30 percent of its workforce telecommutes to some extent. The Bank of Canada introduced a pilot project for telecommuting in 1997, and by the end of 1999 telecommuting had become part of the bank's corporate culture. IBM Canada initiated a telecommuting program in the early 1990s and currently about 2500 of its employees are involved in the program.[20]

A recent Ekos Research study found that 55 percent of Canadians want to telecommute, and 43 percent would leave their current jobs if offered one where telecommuting were a possibility. Of those surveyed, 33 percent said they would choose the opportunity to telecommute rather than a 10-percent raise. Other researchers looking at teleworking in Canada have found that it results in increased productivity,[21] decreased stress,[22] better customer service to customers and clients,[23] reduced turnover[24] and decreased absenteeism.[25]

Not all employees embrace the idea of telecommuting, however. Some workers complain that they miss out on important meetings and informal interactions that lead to new policies and ideas. They also miss the social contacts that occur at work. Teleworking can decrease commitment to the organization,[26] increase feelings of isolation[27] and burnout,[28] and make it more difficult for employees to function as team players.[29]

While the growing use of e-mail has enabled better communication within organizations, not all benefits have been positive. Some employees sexually harass co-workers through e-mail, and employees often find their electronic mailboxes clogged with junk mail. In a recent survey, over half of the organizations surveyed acknowledged some problems with their e-mail systems.[30]

To avoid these and other costly forms of e-mail abuse, managers need to develop a clear policy specifying what company e-mail can and should be used for and what is out of bounds. Managers also should clearly communicate this policy to all members of an organization, as well as describing the procedures that

Sally McNeil, a manager at Compaq Canada, knows that her telecommuting employees can feel disconnected from the workplace sometimes. She tries to call them once a week to offer support, and makes sure that they receive e-mails about office events and parties.

will be used when e-mail abuse is suspected and the consequences that will result when e-mail abuse is confirmed. The increasing use of voice mail and e-mail in companies large and small has led to some ethical concerns, as depicted in the following "Ethics in Action."

Ethics in Action

Eavesdropping on Voice Mail and E-Mail

Should managers listen to their subordinates' voice mail messages? Should they read their employees e-mail? Many employees who currently use voice mail and e-mail would probably answer this question with an emphatic "No!" Just as workers do not expect their bosses to eavesdrop on their telephone conversations, intercepting voice mail messages without the consent of the receiver seems to be unethical and an invasion of privacy. Some managers evidently feel differently, however. Over 20 percent of managers contacted for a recent survey indicated that they monitored their subordinates' voice mail, e-mail, or computer files. Some of these managers contend that because the systems the employees are using are company owned or are paid for with company funds, managers should have access to the information contained on them.

National Post writer Jonathan Kay recently interviewed an employee who was fired for forwarding dirty jokes to clients via e-mail.[31] Kay called the man Fred Jones, since he didn't want to be identified. Jones sold network computers for a living and during this employment had received consistently good performance reviews and always received top bonuses. Jones believed he sent the jokes only to the clients he thought would like them, and assumed that a client would tell him if he or she did not. Unbeknownst to him, however, a client had complained to the company about the dirty jokes and after the company investigated, they fired Jones. Jones still doesn't completely understand why he was fired. He feels his e-mail was private, and no different from telling jokes at the water cooler.

Current law may be on the side of employers, however, at least in some instances. In Canada, employee information, including e-mails they send, is not necessarily private. The Federal Privacy and Access to Information Acts, in place since 1983, apply to all federal government departments, most federal agencies, and some federal crown corporations. These acts limit the collection, use and disclosure of personal information, and, for the person who is protected, provide rights of access to that information. All ten provinces, as well as the Yukon and Northwest Territories, have similar coverage for public sector employees. In 2001, the Personal Information Protection and Electronic Documents Act extended privacy legislation to federally regulated industries, including banking, telecommunications, and transportation However, many private sector employees are still not covered by privacy legislation. Only Quebec's privacy act applies to the entire private sector.

The ethics of listening to other people's voice mail or reading their e-mail are likely to be a growing concern for many managers. While no comparable Canadian data are available, a recent survey of over 2000 large American firms found that 38 percent reported that they "store and review" employee e-mail messages. This was up from 27 percent in 1999 and just 15 percent in 1997.[32] The Ontario, Manitoba, and British Columbia governments have told their employees that e-mail will be monitored if abuse is suspected. The governments' positions are that the Internet and e-mail should only be used for business purposes.

Impersonal Written Communication

Impersonal written communication is lowest in information richness and is well suited for messages that need to reach a large number of receivers. Because such messages are not addressed to particular receivers, feedback is unlikely, so managers must make sure that messages sent by this medium are written clearly in language that all receivers will understand.

Managers often find company newsletters useful vehicles for reaching large numbers of employees. Many managers give their newsletters catchy names to spark employee interest and also to inject a bit of humour into the workplace. Managers at the pork-sausage maker Bob Evans Farms Inc. called their newsletter "The Squealer" for many years but recently changed the title to "The Homesteader" to reflect the company's broadened line of products.[33]

Managers can use impersonal written communication for various types of messages, including rules, regulations, policies, newsworthy information, and announcements of changes in procedures or the arrival of new organizational members. Impersonal written communication also can be used to communicate instructions about how to use machinery or how to process work orders or customer requests. For these kinds of messages, the paper trail left by this communication medium can be invaluable for employees.

Bob Evans Farms
www.bobevans.com/

Communication Networks

Although various communication media are utilized, communication in organizations tends to flow in certain patterns. The pathways along which information flows in groups and teams and throughout an organization are called **communication networks**. The type of communication network that exists in a group depends on the nature of the group's tasks and the extent to which group members need to communicate with each other in order to achieve group goals.

communication networks The pathways along which information flows in groups and teams and throughout the organization.

Communication Networks in Groups and Teams

As you learned in Chapter 14, groups and teams–cross-functional teams, top-management teams, command groups, self-managed work teams, and task forces–are the building blocks of organizations. Four kinds of communication networks can develop in groups and teams: the wheel, the chain, the circle, and the all-channel network (see Figure 15.3).

WHEEL NETWORK   In a wheel network, information flows to and from one central member of the group. Other group members do not need to communicate with each other to perform highly, and the group can accomplish its goals by directing all communication to and from the central member. Wheel networks are often found in command groups with pooled task interdependence. Picture a group of taxicab drivers who report to the same dispatcher, who is also their supervisor. Each driver needs to communicate with the dispatcher, but the drivers do not need to communicate with each other. In groups such as this, the wheel network results in efficient communication, saving time without compromising performance. Though found in groups, wheel networks are not found in teams because they do not allow for the intense interactions characteristic of teamwork.

CHAIN NETWORK   In a chain network, members communicate with each other in a predetermined sequence. Chain networks are found in groups with sequential task interdependence, such as in assembly-line groups. When group work has to be performed in a predetermined order, the chain network is often found because group members need to communicate with those whose work

Figure 15.3
Communication Networks in Groups and Teams

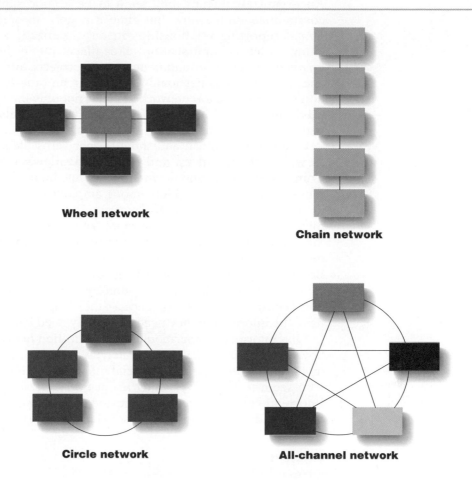

directly precedes and follows their own. Like wheel networks, chain networks tend not to exist in teams because of the limited amount of interaction among team members.

CIRCLE NETWORK   In a circle network, group members communicate with others who are similar to them in experiences, beliefs, areas of expertise, background, office location, or even where they sit when the group meets. Members of task forces and standing committees, for example, tend to communicate with others who have similar experiences or backgrounds. People also tend to communicate with people whose offices are next to their own. Like wheel and chain networks, circle networks are most often found in groups that are not teams.

ALL-CHANNEL NETWORK   An all-channel network is found in teams. It is characterized by high levels of communication: Every team member communicates with every other team member. Top-management teams, cross-functional teams, and self-managed work teams frequently have all-channel networks. The reciprocal task interdependence often present in such teams requires information flows in all directions. Computer software specially designed for use by work groups can help maintain effective communication in teams with all-channel networks because it provides team members with an efficient way to share information with each other.

Organizational Communication Networks

An organization chart may seem to be a good summary of an organization's communication network, but often it is not. An organization chart summarizes *formal* reporting relationships in an organization and the formal pathways along which communication takes place. Often, however, communication is *informal* and flows around issues, goals, projects, and ideas instead of moving up and down the organizational hierarchy in an orderly fashion. Thus, an organization's communication network includes not only the formal communication pathways summarized in an organizational chart but also informal communication pathways along which a great deal of communication takes place (see Figure 15.4)

Communication can and should occur across departments and groups as well as within them and up and down and sideways in the corporate hierarchy. Communication up and down the corporate hierarchy is often called vertical communication. Communication among employees at the same level in the hierarchy or sideways is called *horizontal* communication. Managers obviously cannot determine in advance what an organization's communication network will be, nor should they try to. Instead, to accomplish goals and perform at a high level, organizational members should be free to communicate with whomever they need to contact. Because organizational goals change over time, so too do organizational communication networks. Informal communication networks can contribute to an organization's competitive advantage because they help ensure that organizational members have the information they need when they need it to accomplish their goals.

One informal organizational communication network along which information flows quickly (if not always accurately) is the grapevine. The **grapevine** is an informal network along which unofficial information flows.[34] People in an organization who seem to know everything about everyone are prominent in the grapevine. Information spread over the grapevine can be on issues of either a business nature (an impending takeover) or a personal nature (the CEO's separation from his wife).

grapevine An informal communication network along which unofficial information flows.

Figure 15.4

Formal and Informal Communication Networks in an Organization

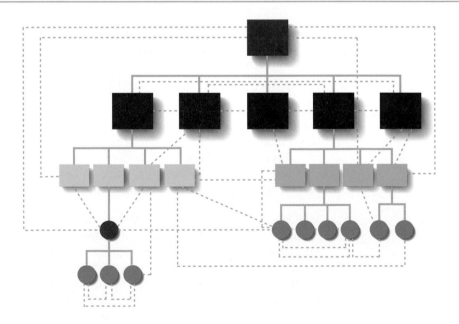

——— Formal pathways of communication summarized in an organizational chart

----- Informal pathways along which a great deal of communication takes place

Technical Advances in Communication

Exciting advances in information technology are dramatically increasing managers' abilities to communicate with others as well as to access information quickly to make decisions. Three advances that are having major impacts on managerial communication are the Internet, intranets, and groupware.

The Internet

Internet A global system of computer networks.

The **Internet** is a global system of computer networks that is easy to join and is used by employees of organizations around the world to communicate inside and outside their companies. Approximately two-thirds of Canadians have access to the Internet, and three-quarters of adult Canadians agree that the Internet is an essential part of life today.[35]

Managers and companies use the Internet for a variety of communication purposes. They can use e-mail to communicate with suppliers and contractors in order to maintain appropriate inventory levels and keep them informed of progress on projects and changes in schedules or to communicate within a company, including to and from offices distant from corporate headquarters. They can use the company's Web site to advertise to potential customers, to sell goods and services to customers, to provide the general public with information about the company, and to recruit new employees.[36] They can also use the Internet to obtain information about other companies including competitors.

Intranets

intranet A companywide system of computer networks.

Growing numbers of managers are finding that the technology on which the Internet is based enables them to improve communication within their own companies by creating a new type of communication medium. These managers are using the technology that allows for information sharing over the Internet to share information within their own companies through company networks called **intranets**. Intranets are being used not just in high-tech companies such as Sun Microsystems and Digital Equipment but also in companies such as Chevron, Goodyear, Levi Strauss, Pfizer, DaimlerChrysler, Motorola, and Ford.[37]

Intranets allow employees to have many kinds of information at their fingertips (or keyboards). Directories, phone books, manuals, inventory figures, product specifications, information about customers, biographies of top managers and the board of directors, global sales figures, minutes from meetings, annual reports, delivery schedules, and up-to-the minute revenue, cost, and profit figures are just a few examples of the kinds of information that can be shared through intranets. Intranets can be accessed with different kinds of computers so that all members of an organization can be linked together. Intranets are protected from unwanted intrusions by hackers or by competitors with firewall security systems that request users to provide passwords and other pieces of identification before being able to access the intranet.[38] How managers can develop, implement, and benefit from intranets is illustrated by Ottawa-based MDS Nordion, a leading producer of medical isotopes for the diagnosis and treatment of cancer and heart disease. The company uses its intranet to help keep employee morale high. It does this through a practice called "speak-ups," where employees submit to management anonymous questions that are answered on the company's intranet. The employees engage in this exercise frequently, asking questions about salaries, and even the company's decision to hold the annual Christmas party in January. "Once you start letting people speak their minds, and others see that they don't get burned, word spreads," Debi King, vice-president of human resources, notes.[39]

The advantage of intranets lies in their versatility as a communication medium. They can be used for different purposes by people who may have little expertise in computer software and programming. While some managers complain that the

MDS Nordion
www.mds.nordion.com/

Internet is too crowded and employees spend too much time surfing the Web, informed managers are realizing that the use of Internet technology to create their own computer networks may be one of the Internet's biggest contributions to organizational effectiveness.

Groupware

groupware Computer software that enables members of groups and teams to share information with each other.

Groupware is computer software such as Lotus Notes and Digital Equipment's Linkworks that enables members of groups and teams to share information with each other to improve their communication and performance. Managers at the Bank of Montreal and other organizations have had success in introducing groupware into their organizations; managers at the advertising agency Young & Rubicam and other organizations have encountered considerable resistance to groupware.[40] Even in companies where the introduction of groupware has been successful, some employees resist using it. Some clerical and secretarial workers at the Bank of Montreal, for example, were dismayed to find that their neat and accurate files were being consolidated into computer files that would be accessible to many of their co-workers.

Managers are most likely to be able to use groupware successfully in their organizations as a communication medium when certain conditions are met:[41]

1. The work is group or team based, and members are rewarded, at least in part, for group performance.

2. Groupware has the full support of top management.

3. The culture of the organization stresses flexibility and knowledge sharing, and the organization does not have a rigid hierarchy of authority.

4. Groupware is being used for a specific purpose and is viewed as a tool for group or team members to use to work more effectively together, not as a personal source of power or advantage.

5. Employees receive adequate training in the use of computers and groupware.[42]

Employees are likely to resist using groupware and managers are likely to have a difficult time implementing it when people are working primarily on their own and are rewarded for their own individual performance.[43] Under these circumstances, information is often viewed as a source of power, and people are reluctant to share information with others by means of groupware.

In order for an organization to gain a competitive advantage, managers need to keep up to date on advances in information technology such as groupware, intranets, and the Internet. But managers should not adopt these or other advances without first considering carefully how the advance in question might improve communication and performance in their particular groups, teams, or whole organization. Some managers have not learned the importance of making communication easy for their customers, as this "Management Insight" shows. They may need to re-think the media they provide for communication access.

Management Insight

Is Anybody Out There?

Companies that try to attract business through their Web sites may be making communication more difficult for their customers.[44] Amazon.com and E-Bay have no phone numbers listed for head office and no 1-800 number listed either. Nike.com instructs its customers to send e-mail if they have questions, suggesting that the e-mails should have complete sentences without complex, multi-clause sentences.

Some companies do list customer service lines, such as the Web sites for Just White Shirts & Black Socks Inc. and HMV Canada Music Stores Ltd., but many other Web sites do not. Or they make it difficult to find the number.

Professor Michael Parent, of the Richard Ivey School of Business at the University of Western Ontario, says that making it difficult to contact a company indicates poor customer relationship management. "Making it difficult to contact companies is a form of corporate arrogance."

Some on-line companies may have been trying to provide customers with a complete online experience, while others relied on e-mail to save costs. David Daniels, of Jupiter Media Metrix, says that "most customers want real-time contact, but their e-mails are not replied to fast enough." His firm, which does Internet research, found that 55 percent of consumers expect an e-mail response within six hours. But one-third of companies took three or more days to reply to messages.

Daniels says he expects that the phone will make a comeback for companies dealing with customers. "E-mail is not efficient enough."

Tips for Managers

Information Richness and Communication Media

1. For messages that are important, personal, or likely to be misunderstood, consider using face-to-face communication or video conferences.

2. Consider using video conferences instead of face-to-face meetings to save time and travel costs.

3. Frequently check voice mail when out of the office.

4. For messages that are complex and need to be referred to later on, use written communication either alone or in conjunction with face-to-face communication, verbal communication electronically transmitted, or video conferences.

5. Develop a clear policy specifying what company e-mail can and cannot be used for and communicate this policy to all organizational members.

Developing Communication Skills

There are various kinds of barriers to effective communication in organizations. Some barriers have their origins in senders. When messages are unclear, incomplete, or difficult to understand, when they are sent over an inappropriate medium, or when no provision for feedback is made, communication suffers. Other communication barriers have their origins in receivers. When receivers pay no attention to or do not listen to messages or when they make no effort to understand the meaning of a message, communication is likely to be ineffective.

To overcome these barriers and effectively communicate with others, managers (as well as other organizational members) must possess or develop certain communication skills. Some of these skills are particularly important when managers send messages; others are critical when managers receive messages. These skills help ensure that managers will be able to share information, will have the information they need to make good decisions and take action, and will be able to reach a common understanding with others.

Table 15.1

Seven Communication Skills for Managers as Senders of Messages

- Send messages that are clear and complete.
- Encode messages in symbols that the receiver understands.
- Select a medium that is appropriate for the message.
- Select a medium that the receiver monitors.
- Avoid filtering and information distortion.
- Ensure that a feedback mechanism is built into messages.
- Provide accurate information to ensure that misleading rumours are not spread.

Communication Skills for Senders

How can you improve your communication skills?

Organizational effectiveness depends on organizational members being able to effectively send messages to people both inside and outside an organization. Table 15.1 summarizes seven communication skills that help ensure that when individuals send messages, they are properly understood and the transmission phase of the communication process is effective. Let's see what each skill entails.

SEND CLEAR AND COMPLETE MESSAGES   Individuals need to learn how to send a message that is clear and complete. A message is clear when it is easy for the receiver to understand and interpret, and it is complete when it contains all the information that the sender and receiver need to reach a common understanding. In striving to send messages that are both clear and complete, managers must learn to anticipate how receivers will interpret messages, and adjust messages to eliminate sources of misunderstanding or confusion.

ENCODE MESSAGES IN SYMBOLS THE RECEIVER UNDER-STANDS   Individuals need to appreciate that when they encode messages, they should use symbols or language that the receiver understands. When sending messages in English to receivers whose native language is not English, for example, it is important to use commonplace vocabulary and to avoid clichés that, when translated, may make little sense and in some cases are either comical or insulting.

jargon Specialized language that members of an occupation, group, or organization develop to facilitate communication among themselves.

   Jargon, specialized language that members of an occupation, group, or organization develop to facilitate communication among themselves, should never be used to communicate with people outside the occupation, group, or organization. For example, truck drivers refer to senior-citizen drivers as "double-knits," compact cars as "rollerskates," highway dividing lines as "paints," double or triple freight trailers as "pups," and orange barrels around road construction areas as "Schneider eggs." Using this jargon among themselves results in effective communication because they know precisely what is being referred to. But if a truck driver used this language to send a message (such as "That rollerskate can't stay off the paint") to a receiver who did not drive trucks, the receiver would be without a clue about what the message meant.[45]

SELECT A MEDIUM APPROPRIATE FOR THE MESSAGE   As you have learned, when relying on verbal communication, individuals can choose from a variety of communication media, including face-to-face communication in person, written letters, memos, newsletters, phone conversations, e-mail, voice mail, faxes, and video conferences. When choosing among these media, individuals need to take into account the level of information richness required, time constraints, and the need for a paper or electronic trail. A primary concern in choosing an appropriate medium is the nature of the message. Is it personal, important, nonroutine, and likely to be misunderstood and in need of further clarification? If it is, face-to-face communication is likely to be in order.

SELECT A MEDIUM THAT THE RECEIVER MONITORS   Another factor that individuals need to take into account when selecting a communication medium is whether the medium is one that the receiver monitors. Individuals differ in the communication media they pay attention to. Many people simply select the medium that they themselves use the most and are most comfortable with, but doing this can often lead to ineffective communication. Those who dislike telephone conversations and face-to-face interactions may prefer to use e-mail, sending many e-mail messages every day and checking their own e-mail every few hours. Those who prefer to communicate with people in person or over the phone may have e-mail addresses but rarely use e-mail and forget to check for e-mail messages. No matter how much an individual likes e-mail, sending an e-mail message to someone else who never checks his or her e-mail is futile. Learning which individuals like things in writing and which prefer face-to-face interactions and then using the appropriate medium enhances the chance that receivers will actually receive and pay attention to messages.

A related consideration is whether receivers have disabilities that limit their ability to decode certain kinds of messages. A blind receiver, for example, cannot read a written message. Managers should ensure that their employees with disabilities have resources available to communicate effectively with others, as the following "Focus on Diversity" highlights.

Focus on Diversity

Options in Communication
Media for the Deaf

In the past, certain kinds of jobs were off limits for deaf people. Seven years ago, William Hughes was in precisely this situation: he was denied a position as an auditor because he could not use the telephone. Now, however, Hughes is an auditor at the Pension Benefit Guaranty Corporation (a US federal agency) because managers in that organization made sure that he has access to advanced communication technology that enables him to use the telephone, faxes, and e-mail to communicate with company auditors, insurers, and lawyers. He uses the telephone lines to communicate by means of a text-typewriter that has a screen and a keyboard on which senders can type messages. The message travels along the phone lines to special operators called communications assistants, who translate the typed message into a text that receivers can listen to. Receivers' spoken replies are translated into typewritten text by the communication assistants and appear on the sender's screen. The communication assistant relays messages back and forth to each sender and receiver.

Danny Delcambre, owner, manager, and head chef of Delcambre's Ragin' Cajun Restaurant in Seattle, is hearing impaired and uses a text-typewriter to make reservations, to take catering orders for gumbo and blackened fish, and to order special foods from K Paul's, a famous New Orleans restaurant. The majority of Ragin' Cajun's employees are also deaf, but they too are able to communicate effectively with each other and with customers because of Delcambre's responsiveness to their special needs.

These advances in media not only enable the deaf to communicate effectively but also let them be more independent and less stigmatized by their disability. As Sue Decker, who is AT&T's (www.att.com) marketing and outreach programs manager and is hearing impaired, indicated, e-mail "levels the playing field for me ... When I communicate through e-mail, there is no reference to my hearing impairment. I look and act no differently from any other e-mailer."[46] To fully utilize the talents of hearing-impaired employees and employees with other kinds of disabilities, managers must ensure that they take advantage of advances in communication media such as the text-typewriter and e-mail.

filtering Withholding part of a message out of the mistaken belief that the receiver does not need or will not want the information.

AVOID FILTERING AND INFORMATION DISTORTION Filtering occurs when senders withhold part of a message because they (mistakenly) think that the receiver does not need the information or will not want to receive it. Filtering can occur at all levels in an organization and in both vertical and horizontal communication. As described in Chapter 8, rank-and-file workers may filter messages they send to first-line managers, first-line managers may filter messages to middle managers, and middle managers may filter messages to top managers. Such filtering is most likely to take place when messages contain bad news or problems that subordinates are afraid they will be blamed for. Recall from the "Management Case" at the end of Chapter 14 that workers at AES Corporation's Shady Point, Oklahoma, plant not only failed to tell managers that emissions were high but even falsified emission-control reports so that managers would not find out.

information distortion Changes in the meaning of a message as the message passes through a series of senders and receivers.

Information distortion occurs when the meaning of a message changes as the message passes through a series of senders and receivers. Some information distortion is accidental—due to faulty encoding and decoding or to a lack of feedback. Other information distortion is deliberate. Senders may alter a message to make themselves or their groups look good and to receive special treatment.

Managers themselves should avoid filtering and distorting information. But how can they eliminate these barriers to effective communication throughout their organization? They need to establish trust throughout the organization. Subordinates who trust their managers believe that they will not be blamed for things beyond their control and will be treated fairly. Managers who trust their subordinates provide them with clear and complete information and do not hold things back.

INCLUDE A FEEDBACK MECHANISM IN MESSAGES Because feedback is essential for effective communication, individuals should build a feedback mechanism into the messages they send. They either should include a request for feedback or indicate when and how they will follow up on the message to make sure that it was received and understood. When writing letters and memos or sending faxes, one can request that the receiver respond with comments and suggestions in a letter, memo, or fax; schedule a meeting to discuss the issue; or follow up with a phone call. Building feedback mechanisms such as these into messages, ensures that messages are received and understood.

rumours Unofficial pieces of information of interest to organizational members but with no identifiable source.

PROVIDE ACCURATE INFORMATION Rumours are unofficial pieces of information of interest to organizational members but with no identifiable source. Rumours spread quickly once they are started, and usually they concern topics that organizational members think are important, interesting, or amusing. Rumours, however, can be misleading and can cause harm to individual employees and to an organization when they are false, malicious, or unfounded. Managers can halt the spread of misleading rumours by providing organizational members with accurate information on matters that concern them.

Communication Skills for Receivers

Senders also receive messages, and thus they must possess or develop communication skills that allow them to be effective receivers of messages. Table 15.2 summarizes three of these important skills, which we examine in greater detail.

Table 15.2
Three Communication Skills for Managers as
Receivers of Messages

- Pay attention.
- Be a good listener.
- Be empathetic.

PAY ATTENTION   When individuals are overloaded and forced to think about several things at once, they sometimes do not pay sufficient attention to the messages they receive. To be effective, however, individuals should always pay attention to messages they receive, no matter how busy they are. For example, when discussing a project with a subordinate, an effective manager focuses on the project and not on an upcoming meeting with his or her own boss. Similarly, when individuals are reading written forms of communication, they should focus their attention on understanding what they are reading; they should not be sidetracked into thinking about other issues.

BE A GOOD LISTENER   Part of being a good communicator is being a good listener. This is an essential communication skill for all organizational members. Being a good listener is surprisingly more difficult than you might realize, however. The average person speaks at a rate of 125 to 200 words per minute, but the average listener can effectively process up to 400 words per minute. Therefore listeners are often thinking about other things at the same time that a person is speaking.

It is important to engage in active listening, which requires paying attention, interpreting, and remembering what was said. Active listening requires making a conscious effort to hear what a person is saying, and interpreting it to see that it makes sense. Being a good listener is an essential communication skill in many different kinds of organizations, from small businesses to large corporations.

Organizational members can practise the following behaviours to become active listeners:[47]

How can you become a better listener?

1. *Make eye contact.* Eye contact lets the speaker know that you're paying attention, and it also lets you pick up nonverbal cues.

2. *Exhibit affirmative head nods and appropriate facial expressions.* By nodding your head and making appropriate facial expressions you further show the speaker that you are listening.

3. *Avoid distracting actions or gestures.* Don't look at your watch, shuffle papers, play with your pencil, or engage in similar distractions when you are listening to someone talk. These actions suggest to the speaker that you're bored or uninterested. The actions also mean that you probably aren't paying full attention to what's being said.

4. *Ask questions.* The critical listener analyzes what he or she hears and asks questions. Asking questions provides clarification, and reduces ambiguity, leading to greater understanding. It also assures the speaker that you're listening.

5. *Paraphrase.* Paraphrasing means restating in your own words what the speaker has said. The effective listener uses phrases like: "What I hear you saying is..." or "Do you mean ... ?" Paraphrasing is a check on whether you're listening carefully and accurately.

6. *Avoid interrupting the speaker.* Interruptions can cause the speaker to lose his or her train of thought and cause the listener to jump to erroneous conclusions based on incomplete information.

7. *Don't overtalk.* Most of us prefer talking to listening. However, a good listener knows the importance of taking turns in a conversation.

8. *Make smooth transitions between the roles of speaker and listener.* The effective listener knows how to make the transition from listener to speaker roles, and then back to being a listener. It's important to listen rather than planning what you are going to say next.

BE EMPATHETIC   Receivers are empathetic when they try to understand how the sender feels and try to interpret a message from the sender's perspective, rather than viewing a message from only their own point of view. Marcia Mazulo, chief psychologist in a school district in the Maritimes, recently learned this lesson after interacting with Karen George, a new psychologist on her staff. George was distraught after meeting with the parent of a child she had been working with extensively. The parent was difficult to talk to and argumentative and was not supportive of her own child. George told Mazulo how upset she was, and Mazulo responded by reminding George that she was a professional and that dealing with such a situation was part of her job. This feedback upset George further and caused her to storm out of the room.

In hindsight, Mazulo realized that her response had been inappropriate. She had failed to empathize with George, who had spent so much time with the child and was deeply concerned about the child's well-being. Instead of dismissing George's concerns, Mazulo realized, she should have tried to understand how George felt and given her some support and advice for dealing positively with the situation.

Understanding Linguistic Styles

Consider the following scenarios:

- A manager from Toronto is having a conversation with a manager from Saskatchewan. The Saskatchewan manager never seems to get a chance to talk. He keeps waiting for a pause to signal his turn to talk, but the Toronto manager never pauses long enough. The Toronto manager wonders why the Saskatchewan manager does not say much. He feels uncomfortable when he pauses and the Saskatchewan manager says nothing, so he starts talking again.
- Elizabeth compliments Bob on his presentation to upper management and asks Bob what he thought of her presentation. Bob launches into a lengthy critique of Elizabeth's presentation and describes how he would have handled it differently. This is hardly the response Elizabeth expected.
- Catherine shares with fellow members of a self-managed work team a new way to cut costs. Michael, another team member, thinks her idea is a good one and encourages the rest of the team to support it. Catherine is quietly pleased by Michael's support. The group implements "Michael's" suggestion, and it is written up as such in the company newsletter.
- Robert was recently promoted and transferred from his company's Halifax office to its headquarters in Ottawa. Robert is perplexed because he never seems to get a chance to talk in management meetings; someone else always seems to get the floor. Robert's new boss wonders whether Robert's new responsibilities are too much for him, although Robert's supervisor in Halifax rated him highly and said he is a real "go-getter." Robert is timid in management meetings and rarely says a word.

What do these scenarios have in common? Essentially, they all describe situations in which a misunderstanding of linguistic styles leads to a breakdown in communication. The scenarios are based on the research of linguist Deborah Tannen, who describes **linguistic style** as a person's characteristic way of speaking. Elements of linguistic style include tone of voice, speed, volume, use of pauses,

linguistic style A person's characteristic way of speaking.

directness or indirectness, choice of words, credit-taking, and use of questions, jokes, and other manners of speech.[48] When people's linguistic styles differ and these differences are not understood, ineffective communication is likely.

Differences in linguistic style can be a particularly insidious source of communication problems because linguistic style is often taken for granted. People rarely think about their own linguistic styles and often are unaware of how linguistic styles can differ. Although there are regional differences in linguistic style, much more dramatic differences in linguistic style occur cross-culturally.

CROSS-CULTURAL DIFFERENCES   Managers from Japan tend to be more formal in their conversations and more deferential toward upper-level managers and people with high status than are managers from Canada. Japanese managers do not mind extensive pauses in conversations when they are thinking things through or when they think that further conversation might be detrimental. Canadian managers, in contrast, find very lengthy pauses disconcerting and feel obligated to talk to fill the silence.[49]

Another cross-cultural difference in linguistic style concerns the appropriate physical distance separating speakers and listeners in business-oriented conversations.[50] The distance between speakers and listeners is greater in Canada, for example, than it is in Brazil or Saudi Arabia. Citizens of different countries also vary in how direct or indirect they are in conversations and in the extent to which they take individual credit for accomplishments. Japanese culture, with its collectivist or group orientation, tends to encourage linguistic styles in which group rather than individual accomplishments are emphasized. The opposite tends to be true in the United States, where Americans proudly reel off their accomplishments.

These and other cross-cultural differences in linguistic style can and often do lead to misunderstandings. Communication misunderstandings and problems can be overcome if managers make themselves familiar with cross-cultural differences in linguistic styles. Before managers communicate with people from abroad, they should try to find out as much as they can about the aspects of linguistic style that are specific to the country or culture in question. Expatriate managers who have lived in the country in question for an extended period of time can be good sources of information about linguistic styles because they are likely to have experienced firsthand some of the differences that citizens of a country are not aware of. Finding out as much as possible about cultural differences also can help managers learn about differences in linguistic styles, for the two are often closely linked.

Differences in linguistic style may come from early childhood, when girls and boys are inclined to play with members of their own sex. Girls tend to play in small groups, noting how they are similar to each other. Boys tend to emphasize status differences, challenging each other and relying on a leader to emerge.

GENDER DIFFERENCES Thinking back on the four scenarios that open this section, you may be wondering why Bob launched into a lengthy critique of Elizabeth's presentation after she paid him a routine compliment on his presentation, or you may be wondering why Michael got the credit for Catherine's idea in the self-managed work team. Research conducted by Tannen and other linguists indicates that the linguistic styles of men and women differ in practically every culture or language.[51] Men and women take their own linguistic styles for granted and thus do not realize when they are talking with someone of the opposite sex that gender differences in style may lead to ineffective communication.

In Canada and the United States, women tend to downplay differences between people, are not overly concerned about receiving credit for their own accomplishments, and want to make everyone feel more or less on an equal footing so that even poor performers or low-status individuals feel valued. Men, in contrast, tend to emphasize their own superiority and are not reluctant to acknowledge differences in status. These differences in linguistic style led Elizabeth to routinely compliment Bob on his presentation even though she thought that he had not done a particularly good job. She asked him how her presentation was so that he could reciprocate and give her a routine compliment, putting them on an equal footing. Bob took Elizabeth's compliment and question about her own presentation as an opportunity to confirm his superiority, never realizing that all she was expecting was a routine compliment. Similarly, Michael's enthusiastic support for Catherine's cost-cutting idea and her apparent surrender of ownership of the idea after she had described it led team members to assume incorrectly that the idea was Michael's.[52]

Do some women try to prove that they are better than everyone else, and are some men unconcerned about taking credit for ideas and accomplishments? Of course. The gender differences in linguistic style that Tannen and other linguists have uncovered are general tendencies evident in many women and men but not in all women and men.

Where do gender differences in linguistic style come from? Tannen suggests that they develop from early childhood on. Girls and boys tend to play with children of their own gender, and the ways in which girls and boys play are quite different. Girls play in small groups, engage in a lot of close conversation, emphasize how similar they are to each other, and view boastfulness negatively. Boys play in large groups, emphasize status differences, expect leaders to emerge who boss others around, and give each other challenges to try to meet. These differences in styles of play and interaction result in differences in linguistic styles when boys and girls grow up and communicate as adults. The ways in which men communicate emphasize status differences and play up relative strengths; the ways in which women communicate emphasize similarities and downplay individual strengths.[53]

MANAGING DIFFERENCES IN LINGUISTIC STYLES Managers should not expect to change people's linguistic styles and should not try to. Instead, to be effective, managers need to understand differences in linguistic styles. Knowing, for example, that some women are reluctant to speak up in meetings, not because they have nothing to contribute but because of their linguistic style, should lead managers to ensure that these women have a chance to talk. And a manager who knows that certain people are reluctant to take credit for ideas can be extra careful to give credit where it is deserved. Knowing that some individuals are slower to speak up, or that they wait for cues to jump into a conversation, managers can be more proactive about inviting quiet members to speak up. As Tannen points out, "Talk is the lifeblood of managerial work, and understanding that different people have different ways of saying what they mean will make it possible to take advantage of the talents of people with a broad range of linguistic styles."[54]

Tips for Managers

Sending and Receiving Messages

1. Make sure that the messages you send are clear, complete, encoded in symbols the receiver will understand, and sent over a medium the receiver monitors.

2. Establish a sense of trust in your organization to discourage filtering and information distortion.

3. Send your messages in a way that will ensure that you receive feedback.

4. Pay attention to the messages you receive, be a good listener, and try to understand the sender's perspective.

5. Be attuned to differences in linguistic style and try to understand the ways they affect communication in your organization.

Summary and Review

Chapter Summary

COMMUNICATION IN ORGANIZATIONS

- The Importance of Good Communication
- The Communication Process
- The Role of Perception in Communication
- The Dangers of Ineffective Communication

INFORMATION RICHNESS AND COMMUNICATION MEDIA

- Face-to-Face Communication
- Spoken Communication Electronically Transmitted
- Personally Addressed Written Communication
- Impersonal Written Communication

COMMUNICATION IN ORGANIZATIONS Communication is the sharing of information between two or more individuals or groups to reach a common understanding. Good communication is necessary for an organization to gain a competitive advantage. Communication occurs in a cyclical process that entails two phases: transmission and feedback.

INFORMATION RICHNESS AND COMMUNICATION MEDIA Information richness is the amount of information a communication medium can carry and the extent to which the medium enables the sender and receiver to reach a common understanding. Four categories of communication media in descending order of information richness are face-to-face communication (includes video conferences), spoken communication electronically transmitted (includes voice mail), personally addressed written communication (includes e-mail), and impersonal written communication.

COMMUNICATION NETWORKS Communication networks are the pathways along which information flows in an organization. Four communication networks found in groups and teams are the wheel, the chain, the circle, and the all-channel network. An organizational chart summarizes formal pathways of communication, but communication in organizations is often informal, as is true of communication by means of the grapevine.

TECHNOLOGICAL ADVANCES IN COMMUNICATION The Internet is a global system of computer networks that managers around the world use to communicate within and outside their companies. Intranets are internal communication networks that managers can create to improve communication, performance, and customer service. Intranets use the technology that the Internet is based on. Groupware is computer software that enables members of groups and teams to share information with each other to improve their communication and performance.

DEVELOPING COMMUNICATION SKILLS There are various barriers to effective communication in organizations. To overcome these barriers and effectively communicate with others, individuals must possess or develop certain

COMMUNICATION NETWORKS

- Communication Networks in Groups and Teams
- Organizational Communication Networks

TECHNOLOGICAL ADVANCES IN COMMUNICATION

- The Internet
- Intranets
- Groupware

DEVELOPING COMMUNICATION SKILLS

- Communication Skills for Senders
- Communication Skills for Receivers
- Understanding Linguistic Styles

communication skills. As senders of messages, individuals should send messages that are clear and complete, encode messages in symbols the receiver understands, choose a medium that is appropriate for the message and monitored by the receiver, avoid filtering and information distortion, include a feedback mechanism in the message, and provide accurate information to ensure that misleading rumours are not spread. Communication skills for individuals as receivers of messages include paying attention, being a good listener, and being empathetic. Understanding linguistic styles is also an essential communication skill. Linguistic styles can vary by geographic region, gender, and country or culture. When these differences are not understood, ineffective communication can occur.

Management in Action

Topics for Discussion and Action

1. Interview a manager in an organization in your community to determine with whom he or she communicates on a typical day and what communication media he or she uses.

2. Which medium (or media) do you think would be appropriate for each of the following kinds of messages that a subordinate could receive from his or her boss: (a) a raise, (b) not receiving a promotion, (c) an error in a report prepared by the subordinate, (d) additional job responsibilities, and (e) the schedule for company holidays for the upcoming year? Explain your choices.

3. Discuss the pros and cons of using the Internet to conduct business transactions such as purchasing goods and services.

4. Why do some organizational members resist using groupware?

5. Why do some managers find it difficult to be good listeners?

6. Explain why subordinates might filter and distort information about problems and performance shortfalls when communicating with their bosses.

7. Explain why differences in linguistic style, when not understood by senders and receivers of messages, can lead to ineffective communication.

Building Management Skills

Diagnosing Ineffective Communication

Think about the last time you experienced very ineffective communication with another person—someone you work with, a classmate, a friend, a member of your family. Describe the incident. Then answer the following questions.

1. Why was your communication ineffective in this incident?

2. What stages of the communication process were particularly problematic and why?

3. Describe any filtering or information distortion that occurred.

4. Do you think differences in linguistic styles adversely affected the communication that took place? Why or why not?

5. How could you have handled this situation differently so that communication would have been effective?

Small Group Breakout Exercise

Reducing Resistance to Advances in Information Technology

Form groups of three or four people, and appoint one member as the spokesperson who will communicate your findings to the whole class when called on by the instructor. Then discuss the following scenario.

You are a team of managers working for a large travel agency. The recent increase in airline prices and decrease in clients planning exotic holidays has led to concern by employees about the security of their jobs. The CEO is seen by the employees as being remote and noncommunicative. You know that very few employees will be laid off, but employees will be asked to consider ways to do their jobs more efficiently. You want to calm fears and also get employees focused on turning the business around. You are meeting today to develop strategies to communicate the changes to the employees.

1. You want to determine the extent of employee concern. How will you show that you are actively listening to their concerns?

2. What media will you use as part of your strategy to improve communications? What justifications do you have for using these media?

3. What role will e-mail have in your communication strategy?

Exploring the World Wide Web

Specific Assignment

Many companies use the World Wide Web to communicate with prospective employees, including the Ford Motor Company. Scan Ford Canada's Web site (www.ford.ca) to learn more about this company and the kinds of information it communicates to prospective employees through its Web site. Then click on "Career Centre." Click on the various selections in this location of the Web site, such as "Ford in Canada," "Career Starting Points," "Empowerment, Diversity, Teamwork" and "Sharing in the Rewards."

1. What kinds of information does Ford communicate to prospective employees through its Web site?

2. How might providing this information on the World Wide Web help Ford Canada attract new employees?

General Assignment

Find the Web site of a company that you know very little about. Scan the Web site of this company. Do you think it effectively communicates important information about the company? Why or why not? Can you think of anything that customers or prospective employees might want to see on the Web site that is not currently there? Is there anything on the Web site that you think should not be there?

ManagementCase

In the News

From the Pages of *The Globe and Mail*
Stinging Office E-Mail Lights 'Firestorm'

The only things missing from the office memo were expletives. It had everything else. There were lines berating employees for not caring about the company. There were words in all capital letters like "SICK" and "NO LONGER." There were threats of layoffs and hiring freezes and a shutdown of the employee gym.

The memo was sent by e-mail on March 13 [2001] by the chief executive officer of Cerner Corp., which develops software for the health care industry and is based in Kansas City, Mo., with 3100 employees around the world. Originally intended only for 400 or so company managers, it quickly took on a life of its own.

The e-mail message was leaked and posted on Yahoo. Its belligerent tone surprised thousands of readers, including analysts and investors. In the stock market, the valuation of the company, which was $1.5-billion (US) on March 20, plummeted 22 per cent in three days.

Now Neal Patterson, the 51 year-old CEO, variously described by people who know him as "arrogant," "candid" and "passionate," says he wishes he had never hit the send button.

"I was trying to start a fire," he said. "I lit a match, and I started a firestorm."

That's not hard to do in the internet age, when all kinds of messages in cyberspace are capable of stirring reactions and moving markets.

But in this case, Mr. Patterson was certainly not trying to manipulate the market; he was simply looking to crack the whip on his troops.

That sometimes requires sharp language, he said, and his employees know how to take it with a grain of salt.

Business professors and market analysts apparently need more convincing. They are criticizing not only Mr. Patterson's angry tone, but also his mode of communication.

Mr. Patterson ran afoul of two cardinal rules for modern managers, they say. Never try to hold large-scale discussions over e-mail. And never, ever, use the company e-mail system to convey sensitive information or controversial ideas to more than a handful of trusted lieutenants. Not unless you want the whole world looking over your shoulder, that is.

In Mr. Patterson's case, this is what the world saw:

"We are getting less than 40 hours of work from a large number of our K.C.-based EMPLOYEES. The parking lot is sparsely used at 8 a.m.; likewise at 5 p.m. As managers —you either do not know what your EMPLOYEES are doing; or you do not CARE. You have created expectations on the work effort which allowed this to happen inside Cerner, creating a very unhealthy environment. In either case, you have a problem and you will fix it or I will replace you.

"NEVER in my career have I allowed a team which worked for me to think they had a 40-hour job. I have allowed YOU to create a culture which is permitting this. NO LONGER."

Mr. Patterson went on to list six potential punishments, including laying off 5 per cent of the staff in Kansas City. "Hell will freeze over," he vowed, before he would dole out more employee benefits. The parking lot would be his yardstick of success, he said; it should be "substantially full" at 7:30 a.m. and 6:30 p.m. on weekdays and half full on Saturdays. "You have two weeks," he said. "Tick, tock."

That message, management experts say, created an atmosphere of fear without specifying what, if anything, was actually going wrong at the company. Moreover, it established a simplistic gauge of success—measuring worker productivity by the number of cars in a parking lot is like judging a book by its word count.

"It puts you at war with your employees and with your basic tendencies in human nature," said Jeffrey Pfeffer, a professor at the Stanford University Graduate School of Business. "It's the corporate equivalent of whips and ropes and chains."

But the more costly error was releasing such an inflammatory memo to a wide audience. Whenever a company does that these days, it is practically inviting a recipient to relay it to friends or even corporate rivals. At that point, a message of even the mildest interest to others will start churning through the farthest corners of the internet.

"I would not advocate the use of e-mail for a problem-solving discussion," said Ralph Biggadike, a professor at the Columbia University Graduate School of Business. "E-mail does not really promote dialogue."

For Cerner, it apparently promoted a market upheaval. On March 22, the day after the memo was posted on the Cerner message board on Yahoo, trading in Cerner's shares, which typically runs at about 650 000 a day, shot up to 1.2 million shares. The following day, volume surged to four million. In three days, the stock price fell to US$34 from US$44.

Stephen Savas, an analyst with Goldman Sachs, said the memo got overblown. "But it did raise two real questions for investors. One: Has anything potentially changed at Cerner to cause such a seemingly violent reaction? And two: Is this a CEO that investors are comfortable with?"

Source: E. Wong, "Stinging Office E-Mail Lights 'Firestorm,'" *The Globe and Mail*, April 9, 2001, p. M1. Copyright 2001 by the *New York Times* Co. Reprinted by permission, April 9, 2001.

Questions

1. How might Neal Patterson have more effectively communicated his message to his managers?
2. What were the particular problems associated with sending this kind of message via e-mail?

ManagementCase

In the News

From the Pages of *The Globe and Mail*
Out of Sight, Not Out of Mind

Maria Ierfino is learning to decipher the moods of her staff members—sentiments of sadness, frustration, joy or anger—based on their voices alone. She has no choice: three of them work miles away, from home offices.

"We do a lot of virtual hugging," says Ms. Ierfino, the marketing leader at BCE Corporate Services in Montreal. "I listen for people's moods over the phone and what members of my team are going through."

Managing people who work at home is evolving into an art form. It's very different from managing people face-to-face.

Virtual workers may be out of sight, but to be effective, managers must ensure their teleworkers are not out of mind, say telework consultants and observers.

Because managers are one of the few points of contact for teleworkers, they are becoming the emotional, social and professional bridge between them and the organizations they work for.

Janet Salaff, a sociology professor at the University of Toronto who focuses on telecommuting, or teleworking, says managers are responsible for including people who work from home in conference calls, office meetings and annual parties.

"One of the biggest complaints from teleworkers is that they didn't know there was a Christmas party," she says.

The success of telework arrangements heavily depends on whether the job can be done well from home. But adequate management is also important, Ms. Salaff says.

"If managers communicate too much, it is a nuisance. Teleworkers want to control their time and space. But if managers communicate too little, their workers might feel ignored."

Phil Montero is a teleworker consultant in Andover, Mass., who is known on his Web site, youcanworkfromanywhere.com, as "the Mobile Man." He says many telework arrangements fail because those who work from home start to feel isolated and ignored.

"It wouldn't hurt if managers worked from home occasionally so they can relate to their workers and understand their needs better."

Sally McNeil, a Compaq Canada manager who supervises two of her 10 employees from a distance, says being aware of isolation and other concerns can be as difficult as measuring teleworkers' performance.

"If someone has a problem in the office, I can often tell from their body language. I miss that with teleworking," says the director of technology and sales support for Compaq in Markham, Ont.

Ms. McNeil says the two teleworkers visit the office once a week, which is a big help. And when there is an office event or party, she e-mails her whole team the news.

Ms. McNeil says the scenario is much easier when the worker is a senior staff member—someone who has enough experience and office contacts to thrive alone. But even in those cases, new management techniques are required.

"I have to make an effort to find out things. I'm very much a manager who walks around and talks to people in the office. I have to work at staying connected with my tele-workers," she says.

To accomplish this, she e-mails her distant workers regularly but calls them on the phone only about once a week, so as not to encroach on their time.

Ms. Ierfino, who worked on Bell Canada's first telework program in the 1980s, has also tried to strike a balance. She conducts one-hour weekly conference calls with her at-home workers and full-day meetings once every two months with her whole team, either in Montreal or Toronto, where most of her telecommuters live.

But she relies on them to contact her too. "My teleworkers often call me if they are having a bad day. You learn to listen to understand what they are going through."

Source: N. Southworth, "Out of Sight, Not Out of Mind: Managers Must Learn to Keep Teleworkers in the Loop," *The Globe and Mail*, April 25, 2001, p. M1.

Questions

1. What communication disadvantages for managers, employees, and the organization as a whole are there to telecommuting?

2. What can a manager do to improve communication for employees who telecommute? What can telecommuters do to improve communication flow if they telecommute?

Chapter sixteen

Organizational Conflict, Negotiation, and Politics

Learning Objectives

1. Explain why conflict arises, and identify the types and sources of conflict in organizations.

2. Describe conflict management strategies that managers can use to resolve conflict effectively.

3. Describe negotiation strategies that managers can use to resolve conflict through integrative bargaining.

4. Explain why managers need to be attuned to organizational politics, and describe the political strategies that managers can use to become politically skilled.

A Case in Contrast

The Power of Political Skills

When two of Canada's largest banks, the Bank of Montreal (www.bmo.com) and Royal Bank (www.royalbank.com), announced in early 1998 their plan to merge, no one could have been more surprised than Bay Street's keenest analysts.[1] Though such a move would surely require careful scrutiny by the competition bureau, CEOs Matthew Barrett of BMO and John Cleghorn of Royal did not seem interested in managing the politics of such an announcement. Instead, they "acted as though their merger was a fait accompli, and treated with indifference the public's concern about branch closures and job losses."

Ten months after their announcement, the two men seemed to realize that managing the optics of their planned merger was as important as figuring out how to merge the two workforces. It was only then that they put some specifics in writing to try to calm the growing concerns of both consumers and the federal government. However, when they announced that the merger would result in a 10-percent reduction in service charges, more money for loans to small and medium-sized business, and 500 additional outlets, Barrett and Cleghorn seemed more desperate than convincing.

The actions of Barrett and Cleghorn show that the two men did not think about the politics of their actions in announcing the merger. Rather than building up support quietly behind the scenes, and making sure to address consumer concerns immediately, they tried to bully the merger through.

At the time of the BMO–Royal Bank announcement, lawyer Harold MacKay was heading a task force on financial services that was due to be tabled later that year. Some analysts suggest that the banks tried to force the hands of both Finance Minister Paul Martin and Harold MacKay.

"Matt sweet-talked John and they both jumped the gun," one investment banker said.

"They took the high-risk gamble and decided to spring it on Paul, because if they went to Ottawa privately he would have told them to wait for MacKay. They decided it might be worth getting Paul angry, if they could force the government's hand and push it through." He blames Barrett. "This is definitely Matt's style. He's a swashbuckler."

Effective political skills can make a big difference in bank merger outcomes. John Cleghorn of Royal Bank and Matthew Barrett of Bank of Montreal (both shown at top) could not convince the federal government of the appropriateness of merging their banks. However, Charlie Baillie of TD Bank and Ed Clark of Canada Trust (both shown at bottom) completed an effective merger after taking more care in playing politics.

By the end of 1998, consumers were completely up in arms about the proposed bank mergers, with 51 percent saying that they believed the mergers were motivated by greed. Meanwhile the banks' CEOs continued to lobby behind the scenes to get Martin to approve the mergers. Nevertheless, Martin told the bankers that he would not approve the merger, putting to an end the nearly year-long battle to create bigger banks for Canada.

Charlie Baillie, CEO of Toronto-Dominion Bank (TD) (www.td.com), and Al Flood, CEO of Canadian Imperial Bank of Commerce (CIBC) (www.cibc.com), announced their own merger plans shortly after Barrett and Cleghorn's announcement. The two met the same angry consumer outbursts from consumers and politicians, and the same reaction from Martin.

Baillie quickly learned from the political mistakes that the banks had made in their first merger attempts. The same day the mergers were turned down, Baillie phoned Martin Broughton, chairman of British American Tobacco PLC, to discuss an exclusive deal to buy Canada Trust. Baillie made the decision to deal directly with BAT, rather than with BAT's Canadian subsidiary, Imasco Ltd. This made it possible to keep the dealings quiet, avoiding an auction by TD's competitors. TD knew it was unlikely to win a bidding war against the other banks.

TD officials notified the Finance Department of plans to buy Canada Trust from Imasco Ltd. almost as soon as they started engaging in talks with British American Tobacco Co., the company's owner. Kym Robertson, a TD spokesperson, said, "We informed Finance when we began negotiations and we kept them apprised as a courtesy. We certainly weren't seeking approval at that time. But we did keep them informed about how things were evolving."

Bureaucrats from the Ministry of Finance went over the deal in detail with TD officials more than six months before it was announced. They also discussed with the bank how to overcome possible objections, including job losses resulting from the takeover. Two weeks before the deal was announced, Baillie and his executives met directly with Martin to outline their plans. And in a further political move to ease possible objections, they also met in advance with Liberal MPs from London, Ontario, where Canada Trust was founded, to offer assurances that the city would not lose any of its 2000 jobs.

When Baillie publicly announced his takeover bid for Canada Trust in August 1999, he was able to report that the government supported the move. He also included detailed promises of longer hours, better service, and a plan to treat laid-off employees fairly. Public opposition to the merger never really occurred and Martin approved the merger within six months after Baillie went public.

Baillie, who is described as "soft-spoken and professorial," explained why he handled the two mergers differently: "With the last one, I was reacting because the two other banks got together and they were going to be so large. I felt the only recourse we had was to try and get as close to them as we could, and so we went ahead." Baillie is credited with making all the right political moves in carrying off the merger with Canada Trust.   ●

Overview

Charlie Baillie was successful in his second attempt to merge Toronto-Dominion bank with a partner because he effectively used his power to influence others and to bring about changes that allowed him to achieve his goals. Matthew Barrett and John Cleghorn did not effectively use their power, and in fact were accused of bullying to try to get their merger through. In Chapter 13, we described how managers, as leaders, exert influence over other people to achieve group and organizational goals and how managers' sources of power enable them to exert such influence. In this chapter, we describe why managers need to develop the skills necessary to manage organizational conflict and politics if they are going to be effective and achieve their goals.

First, we describe conflict and the strategies that managers can use to resolve it effectively. We discuss one major conflict resolution technique, negotiation, in detail, outlining the steps managers can take to be good negotiators. Second, we describe organizational politics and the political strategies that managers can use to expand their power and use it effectively. By the end of this chapter, you will appreciate why managers must develop the skills necessary to manage these important organizational processes if they are to be effective and achieve organizational goals. ●

Organizational Conflict

organizational conflict

The discord that arises when the goals, interests, or values of different individuals or groups are incompatible and those individuals or groups block or thwart each other's attempts to achieve their objectives.

Organizational conflict is the discord that arises when the goals, interests, or values of different individuals or groups are incompatible and those individuals or groups block or thwart each other's attempts to achieve their objectives.[2] The "Case in Contrast" describes the conflict that existed between the CEOs of some of Canada's largest banks, and consumers and the federal government because of the incompatible interests and goals of managers and bank customers. Conflict is an inevitable part of organizational life because the goals of different stakeholders such as managers and workers are often incompatible. Organizational conflict also can exist between departments and divisions that compete for resources or even between managers who may be competing for promotion to the next level in the organizational hierarchy. An extreme example of conflict between brothers who founded one of the larger private grocery conglomerates in Canada is profiled in this "Management Insight."

Management Insight

Conflict at McCain Foods

For 37 years, Wallace McCain and his older brother Harrison headed Florenceville, NB-based McCain Foods Ltd. (www.mccain.com). The company had started out selling french fries and together the brothers had built a multinational grocery empire from those humble beginnings.[3] That partnership came to an end in August 1993, after *The Financial Post* called Wallace's son, Michael, "The leading candidate to become the potato king." This reference to Michael as successor started what many called "the feud of the century."

The public rift between the two brothers came as somewhat of a surprise. From the time they had founded McCain Foods in 1956, "one brother never made a decision without consulting the other." Their offices in Florenceville were linked by an unlocked door. The two complemented each other well. Harrison was an outgoing salesman, while Wallace, quieter than his brother, was the number cruncher who managed the books. Together the two built the firm from first-year sales of $152 678 to over $5 billion in 1998. While the core of the business was still french fries, there were also non-food subsidiaries that included a large trucking division and a national courier company.

The brothers' feud continues to this day. What triggered it was conflict over who would head McCain Foods after the brothers stepped down. Though the brothers had privately been at odds over succession for years, their differences had not been made public. Wallace favoured his son Michael as his successor. Harrison tried to convince other family members that Wallace and his sons would cut the other McCains out of the business. When they finally could not come to a resolution, the dispute ended up in a New Brunswick arbitration court. Wallace McCain was kicked out as co-CEO, though he still remains part owner and a member of the board. Subsequently, Wallace moved to Toronto to become chairman of competitor Maple Leaf Foods Ltd. Harrison also fired his nephew, Michael, who then joined his father at Maple Leaf, becoming president and CEO in 1999. More than four years after the feud went public, Harrison acknowledged, "There are still strained relations in our family holding company. I wish I could say the bitterness is all gone, but that would be an overstatement."

How is the level of conflict related to performance?

As the McCain case illustrates, it is important for managers to develop the skills necessary to manage conflict effectively. In addition, the level of conflict present in an organization has important implications for organizational performance. Figure 16.1 illustrates the relationship between organizational conflict and performance. At point A, there is little or no conflict and organizational performance suffers. Lack of conflict in an organization often signals that managers emphasize conformity at the expense of new ideas, are resistant to change, and strive for agreement rather than effective decision making. As the level of conflict increases from point A to point B, organizational effectiveness is likely to increase. When an organization has an optimum level of conflict (point B), managers are likely to be open to, and encourage, a variety of perspectives, look for ways to improve organizational functioning and effectiveness, and view debates and disagreements as a necessary ingredient for effective decision making. As the level of conflict increases from point B to point C, conflict escalates to the point where organizational performance suffers. When an organization has a dysfunctionally high level of conflict, managers are likely to waste organizational resources to achieve their own ends, to be more concerned about winning political battles than about doing

Figure 16.1
The Effect of Conflict on Organizational Performance

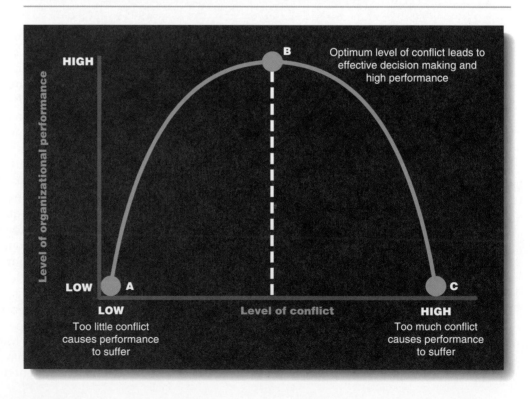

what will lead to a competitive advantage for their organization, and to try to get even with their opponents rather than make good decisions.

Conflict is a force that needs to be managed rather than eliminated.[4] Managers should never try to eliminate all conflict but rather should try to keep conflict at a moderate and functional level to promote change efforts that benefit the organization. To manage conflict, it is important for managers to understand the types and sources of conflict and to be familiar with certain strategies that can be effective in dealing with it.

Types of Conflict

There are several types of conflict in organizations: interpersonal, intragroup, intergroup, and interorganizational (see Figure 16.2).[5] Understanding how these types differ can help managers to deal with conflict.

INTERPERSONAL CONFLICT Interpersonal conflict is conflict between individual members of an organization, occurring because of differences in their goals or values. Two managers may experience interpersonal conflict when their values concerning protection of the environment differ. One manager may argue that the organization should do only what is required by law. The other manager may counter that the organization should invest in equipment to reduce emissions even though the organization's current level of emissions is below the legal limit.

INTRAGROUP CONFLICT Intragroup conflict is conflict that arises within a group, team, or department. When members of the marketing department in a clothing company disagree about how they should spend budgeted advertising dollars for a new line of men's designer jeans, they are experiencing intragroup conflict. Some of the members want to spend all the money on advertisements in magazines. Others want to devote half of the money to billboards and ads in city buses and subways.

INTERGROUP CONFLICT Intergroup conflict is conflict that occurs between groups, teams, or departments. R&D departments, for example, sometimes experience intergroup conflict with production departments. Members of the R&D department may develop a new product that they think production can make inexpensively by using existing manufacturing capabilities. Members of the production department, however, may disagree and believe that the costs of making the product will be high. Managers of departments usually play a key role in managing intergroup conflicts such as this.

Figure 16.2
Types of Conflict in Organizations

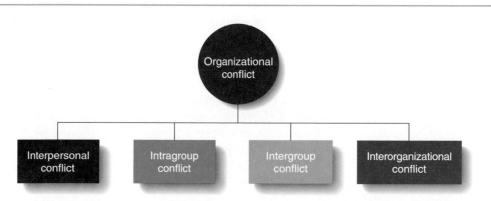

INTERORGANIZATIONAL CONFLICT　Interorganizational conflict is conflict that arises across organizations. Sometimes interorganizational conflict arises when members of one organization feel that another organization is not behaving ethically and is threatening the well-being of certain stakeholder groups. In this "Ethics in Action," environmental groups are concerned about what a new resort will do to the environment, while native groups feel that they have not been dealt with fairly by governments in the past.

Ethics in Action

Cayoosh Resort

Olympic gold medallist Nancy Greene-Raine's hopes of building a ski resort in Lillooet, British Columbia have not gone as smoothly as her athletic competitions once did.[6] Green-Raine's business, NGR Resort Consultants Inc., has spent years trying to gain permission to build Cayoosh Resort, a $500 million investment that would create 1000 jobs.

Lillooet could use an infusion of new business. The economy has long been driven by the forest industry, BC Rail, and BC Hydro, but those industries' contributions to the community are in decline. A local veneer plant and a lumber business are struggling to survive.

Greene-Raine and her husband, Al Raine, believe that Cayoosh Resort could be a smaller version of Whistler, with better snow conditions and more sunshine. From the start, however, the developers have faced critics. Vancouver-based environmental groups say that the resort would destroy the grizzly bear habitat and threaten a pristine valley.

Besides the environmental groups, resource developments in British Columbia generally require support from First Nations. In this case, that means getting the backing of the St'at'imc Nation, which includes 11 bands. The bands have objected to the development proposal, and have threatened road blockades if it proceeds.

Though unemployment levels reach more than 70 percent in most native villages, the bands do not believe they stand to gain anything from the proposed resort. Chief Gary John said the St'at'imc Nation has received almost nothing from the mining, logging, and hydro developments in the region. "When Hydro came in, when BC Rail came in, they said we'll make sure there's work for you, you'll benefit. But it never happened. Hundreds of thousands of cubic metres of timber have left this community, and nothing has come into our hands."

Raine is actually sympathetic to native concerns. "The issue turns around the lack of trust," he said. "There's 90 years of failure by the federal government to address issues First Nations have been bringing forward. In 1911, the chiefs signed a declaration stating their claim to the territory—and they are still waiting for that to be dealt with."

NGR offered to pay the St'at'imc for lease of the land. By the eleventh year in operation, payments were projected to total $400 000 a year and when the area was fully developed payments would exceed $1 million annually. The St'at'imc rejected the proposal and refused to negotiate with NGR. "The only thing that would get talks going," John said, "would be if Cabinet ministers from Ottawa and Victoria came to discuss 'the big picture,' which involves BC Rail, BC Hydro, and the sharing of resource revenues. Canada and British Columbia are very wealthy. They should be sharing some of that wealth, instead of leaving us in this welfare state." If NGR's development is to succeed, Greene-Raine and her husband have considerable interorganizational conflict to manage and ethical issues to resolve.

Sources of Conflict

Conflict in organizations springs from a variety of sources. The ones that we examine here are incompatible goals and time horizons, overlapping authority, task interdependencies, incompatible evaluation or reward systems, scarce resources, and status inconsistencies (see Figure 16.3).[7]

INCOMPATIBLE GOALS AND TIME HORIZONS   Recall from Chapter 8 that an important managerial activity is organizing people and tasks into departments and divisions to accomplish an organization's goals. Almost inevitably, this grouping results in the creation of departments and divisions that have incompatible goals and time horizons, and the result can be conflict. Production and production managers, for example, usually concentrate on efficiency and cost cutting; they have a relatively short time horizon and focus on producing quality goods or services in a timely and efficient manner. In contrast, marketing and marketing managers focus on sales and responsiveness to customers. Their time horizon is longer than that of production because they are trying to be responsive not only to customers' needs today but also to their changing needs in the future in order to build long-term customer loyalty. These fundamental differences between marketing and production are often breeding grounds for conflict.

Suppose production is behind schedule in its plan to produce a specialized product for a key customer. The marketing manager believes that the delay will reduce sales of the product and therefore insists that the product must be delivered on time even if saving the production schedule means increasing costs by paying production workers overtime. The production manager says that she will happily schedule overtime if marketing will pay for it. Both managers' positions are reasonable from the perspective of their own departments, and conflict is likely.

OVERLAPPING AUTHORITY   When two or more managers, departments, or functions claim authority for the same activities or tasks, conflict is likely.[8] For instance, in the earlier "Management Insight" both Harrison and Wallace McCain felt that they had sole authority to determine who would succeed them in heading the business.

Figure 16.3
Sources of Conflict in Organizations

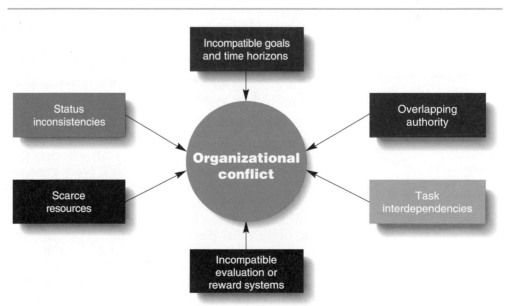

TASK INTERDEPENDENCIES   Have you ever been assigned a group project for one of your classes and one group member consistently failed to get things done on time? This probably created some conflict in your group because other group members were dependent on the late member's contributions to complete the project. Whenever individuals, groups, teams, or departments are interdependent, the potential for conflict exists.[9] Managers of marketing and production with differing goals and time horizons come into conflict precisely because the departments are interdependent. Marketing is dependent on production for the goods it markets and sells, and production is dependent on marketing for creating demand for the things it makes.

INCOMPATIBLE EVALUATION OR REWARD SYSTEMS   The way in which interdependent groups, teams, or departments are evaluated and rewarded can be another source of conflict.[10] Production managers are evaluated and rewarded for their success in staying within budget or lowering costs while maintaining quality. So they are reluctant to take any steps that will increase costs, such as paying workers high overtime rates to finish a late order for an important customer. Marketing managers, in contrast, are evaluated and rewarded for their success in generating sales and customer satisfaction. So they often think that overtime wages are a small price to pay for responsiveness to customers. Thus, conflict between production and marketing is rarely unexpected.

SCARCE RESOURCES   Management is the process of acquiring, developing, protecting, and utilizing the resources that allow an organization to be efficient and effective (see Chapter 1). When resources are scarce, management is all the more difficult and conflict is likely.[11] When resources are scarce, divisional managers, for example, may be in conflict over who has access to financial capital, and organizational members at all levels may be in conflict over who gets raises and promotions.

STATUS INCONSISTENCIES   The fact that some individuals, groups, teams, or departments within an organization are more highly regarded than others in the organization can also create conflict. In some restaurants, for example, the chefs have relatively higher status than the people who wait on tables. Nevertheless, the chefs receive customer orders from the wait staff, and the wait staff can return to the chefs food that they or their customers think is not acceptable. This status inconsistency—high-status chefs taking orders from low-status wait staff—can be the source of considerable conflict between chefs and wait staff. It is for this reason that in some restaurants the wait staff puts orders on a spindle, thereby reducing the amount of direct order-giving from the wait staff to the chefs.[12]

Conflict Management Strategies

International Association for Conflict Management www.iacm-conflict.org/

The behaviours for handling conflict fall along two dimensions: *cooperativeness* (the degree to which one party attempts to satisfy the other party's concerns) and *assertiveness* (the degree to which one party attempts to satisfy his or her own concerns).[13] This can be seen in Figure 16.4. From these two dimensions emerge five conflict-handling behaviours: *avoiding, competing, compromising, accommodating,* and *collaborating.* Some people avoid conflict by trying to withdraw from it. Competing occurs when one person tries to satisfy his or her own interests, without regard to the interests of the other party. Compromise is possible when each party is concerned about its own goal accomplishment and the goal accomplishment of the other party and is willing to engage in a give-and-take exchange and to make concessions until a reasonable resolution of the conflict is reached. Accommodation occurs when one person tries to please the other person by putting the other's interests ahead of

Figure 16.4
Dimensions of Conflict-Handling Behaviours

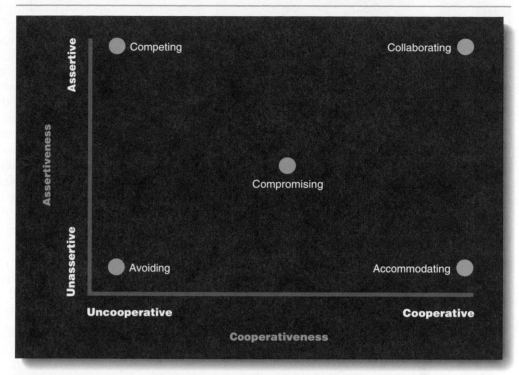

Source: K.W. Thomas, "Conflict and Negotiation Processess in Organizations," in M.D. Dunnette and L.M. Hough (eds.), *Handbook of Industrial and Oganizational Psychology*, 2nd ed., vol. 3 (Palo Alto, CA: Consulting Psychologists Press, 1992), p. 668. With permission. Copyright 2001 by Acad of Mgmt. Reproduced with permission of Acad of Mgmt in the format Textbook via Copyright Clearance Center.

one's own. Collaboration is a way of handling conflict in which the parties to a conflict try to satisfy their goals without making any concessions and instead come up with a way to resolve their differences that leaves them both better off.

If an organization is to achieve its goals, managers must be able to resolve conflicts in a functional manner. *Functional conflict resolution* means that the conflict is settled by compromise or by collaboration between the parties in conflict. When the parties to a conflict are willing to cooperate with each other and devise a solution that each finds acceptable (through compromise or collaboration), an organization is more likely to achieve its goals. Conflict management strategies that managers can use to ensure that conflicts are resolved in a functional manner focus on individuals and on the organization as a whole. Below, we describe four strategies that focus on individuals: increasing awareness of the sources of conflict, increasing diversity awareness and skills, practising job rotation or temporary assignments, and using permanent transfers or dismissals when necessary. We also describe two strategies that focus on the organization as a whole: changing an organization's structure or culture, and directly altering the source of conflict.

STRATEGIES FOCUSED ON INDIVIDUALS

INCREASING AWARENESS OF THE SOURCES OF CONFLICT   Sometimes conflict arises because of communication problems and interpersonal misunderstandings. For example, differences in linguistic styles (see Chapter 15) may lead some men in work teams to talk more, and take more credit for ideas, than women in those teams. These communication differences can result in conflict when the men incorrectly assume that the women are uninterested or less capable because they participate less, and the women incorrectly assume that the men are being

One of the issues in the dispute between the nurses in British Columbia and the Health Employers Association is whether nurses are paid enough. Another one that BC Nurses Union president Debra McPherson raises is the chronic under-staffing that hospitals seem unwilling to address.

bossy and are not interested in their ideas because they seem to do all the talking. By increasing people's awareness of this source of conflict, managers can help to resolve conflict functionally. And once men and women realize that the source of their conflict is differences in linguistic styles, they can take steps to interact with each other more effectively. The men can give the women more of a chance to provide input, and the women can be more proactive in providing this input.

Sometimes personalities clash in an organization. In these situations, too, managers can help resolve conflicts functionally by increasing organizational members' awareness of the source of their difficulties. For example, some people who are not inclined to take risks may come into conflict with those who are prone to taking risks. The non-risk-takers might complain that those who welcome risk propose outlandish ideas without justification, while the risk-takers complain that their innovative ideas are always getting shot down. When both types of people are made aware that their conflicts are due to fundamental differences in their ways of approaching problems, they will likely be better able to cooperate to come up with innovative ideas that entail only moderate levels of risk.

INCREASING DIVERSITY AWARENESS AND SKILLS   Interpersonal conflicts also can arise because of diversity. Older workers may feel uncomfortable or resentful about reporting to a younger supervisor, a Chinese Canadian may feel singled out in a group of white workers, or a female top manager may feel that members of her predominantly male top-management team band together whenever one of them disagrees with a proposal of hers. Whether these feelings are justified or not, they are likely to cause recurring conflicts. Many of the techniques we described in Chapter 5 to increase diversity awareness and skills can help managers effectively manage diversity and resolve conflicts that have their origins in differences between organizational members. Better understanding of First Nations issues and ways to resolve these conflicts are certainly needed to resolve a number of issues facing businesses in British Columbia and other parts of Canada, as evidenced by the previous "Ethics in Action."

PRACTISING JOB ROTATION OR TEMPORARY ASSIGNMENTS   Sometimes conflicts arise because individual organizational members simply do not have a good understanding of the work activities and demands that others in an organization face. A financial analyst, for example, may be required to submit monthly reports to a member of the accounting department. These reports have a low priority for the analyst, and she typically turns them in a couple of days late. On the due date, the accountant always calls up the financial analyst, and conflict ensues as the accountant describes in detail why she must have the reports on time and the financial analyst describes everything else she needs to do. In situations such as this, job rotation or temporary assignments, which expand organizational members' knowledge base and appreciation of other departments, can be a useful way of resolving the conflict. If the financial analyst spends some time working in the accounting department, she may better appreciate the need for timely reports. Similarly, a temporary assignment in the finance department may help the accountant realize the demands a financial analyst faces and the need to streamline unnecessary aspects of reporting.

USING PERMANENT TRANSFERS OR DISMISSALS WHEN NECESSARY
Sometimes when other conflict resolution strategies do not work, managers may need to take more drastic steps, including permanent transfers or dismissals.

Suppose two first-line managers who work in the same department are always at each other's throats; frequent bitter conflicts arise between them even though they both seem to get along well with the other people they work with. No matter what their supervisor does to increase their understanding of each other, these conflicts keep occurring. In this case, the supervisor may want to transfer one or both managers so that they do not have to interact as frequently.

When dysfunctionally high levels of conflict occur among top managers who cannot resolve their differences and understand each other, it may be necessary for one of them to leave the company. This is what happened at McCain Foods.

STRATEGIES FOCUSED ON THE WHOLE ORGANIZATION

CHANGING AN ORGANIZATION'S STRUCTURE OR CULTURE Conflict can signal the need for changes in an organization's structure or culture. Sometimes, managers can effectively resolve conflict by changing the organizational structure they use to group people and tasks.[14] As an organization grows, for example, the *functional structure* that was effective when the organization was small may cease to be effective, and a shift to a *product structure* might effectively resolve conflicts (see Chapter 8).

Hallmark
www.hallmark.com/

Managers also can effectively resolve conflicts by increasing levels of integration in an organization. At Hallmark Cards, managers used cross-functional teams to speed new card development and resolve conflicts between different departments. When a writer and an artist have a conflict over the appropriateness of the artist's illustrations, they do not pass criticisms back and forth from the editorial department to the art department, because now they are on the same team and can directly resolve the issue on the spot.

Sometimes managers may need to take steps to change an organization's culture to resolve conflict (see Chapter 9). Norms and values in an organizational culture might inadvertently promote dysfunctionally high levels of conflict that are difficult to resolve. For instance, norms that stress respect for formal authority may create conflict that is difficult to resolve when an organization creates self-managed work teams. Values stressing individual competition may make it difficult to resolve conflicts when organizational members need to put others' interests ahead of their own. In circumstances such as these, taking steps to change norms and values can be an effective conflict resolution strategy.

ALTERING THE SOURCE OF CONFLICT When conflict is due to overlapping authority, incompatible evaluation or reward systems, and status inconsistencies, managers can sometimes effectively resolve the conflict by directly altering the source of conflict—the overlapping authority, the evaluation or reward system, or the status inconsistency. For example, managers can clarify the chain of command and reassign tasks and responsibilities to resolve conflicts due to overlapping authority.

Tips for Managers

Handling Conflict

1. Try to handle conflicts by compromise or collaboration.

2. Analyze how differences among parties to a conflict (such as in linguistic styles, personality, age, or gender) may be contributing to misunderstandings and conflict.

3. Consider using job rotation or temporary assignments to help your subordinates understand the work activities and demands of other organizational members.

4. Analyze the extent to which conflict in your organization is due to a faulty organizational structure or a dysfunctional culture.

Negotiation Strategies for Integrative Bargaining

negotiation A method of conflict resolution in which the parties in conflict consider various alternative ways to allocate resources to each other in order to come up with a solution acceptable to them all.

distributive negotiation Adversarial negotiation in which the parties in conflict compete to win the most resources while conceding as little as possible.

integrative bargaining Cooperative negotiation in which the parties in conflict work together to achieve a resolution that is good for them all.

CARSTAR Canada
www.carstarcanada.com/
CGU Group Canada
www.cgu.ca/

A particularly important conflict resolution technique for managers and other organizational members to use in situations in which the parties to a conflict have approximately equal levels of power is negotiation. During **negotiation**, the parties to a conflict try to come up with a solution acceptable to themselves by considering various alternative ways to allocate resources to each other.[15]

There are two major types of negotiation—distributive negotiation and integrative bargaining.[16] In **distributive negotiation**, the parties perceive that they have a "fixed pie" of resources that they need to divide up.[17] They take a competitive, adversarial stance. Each party realizes that he or she must concede something but is out to get the lion's share of resources.[18] The parties see no need to interact with each other in the future and do not care if their interpersonal relationship is damaged or destroyed by their competitive negotiations.[19]

In **integrative bargaining**, the parties perceive that they might be able to increase the resource pie by trying to come up with a creative solution to the conflict. They do not view the conflict competitively, as a win-or-lose situation; instead, they view it cooperatively, as a win–win situation in which all parties can gain. Integrative bargaining is characterized by trust, information sharing, and the desire of all parties to achieve a good resolution of the conflict.[20]

CARSTAR Automotive Canada, a chain of collision shops, and Scarborough, ON-based CGU Group Canada Ltd. worked out their own win–win solution in 2000.[21] Traditionally, insurance agents and body shop owners are natural enemies: body shop owners want to make profit from doing auto repairs, and insurance agents want to keep claim costs down. The two share a common customer too—one who wants a car repaired properly. The two forged an agreement, with CARSTAR promising to keep average repair costs down and CGU promising to send more business to the body shop franchise. The agreement is likely to be a win for consumers too, who should find their claims handled faster and more easily.

There are five strategies that managers in all kinds of organizations can rely on to facilitate integrative bargaining and avoid distributive negotiation: emphasizing superordinate goals; focusing on the problem, not the people; focusing on interests, not demands; creating new options for joint gain; and focusing on what is fair.[22]

superordinate goals Goals that all parties in conflict agree to regardless of the source of their conflicts.

EMPHASIZING SUPERORDINATE GOALS   **Superordinate goals** are goals that all parties agree to regardless of the source of their conflict. Increasing organizational effectiveness, increasing responsiveness to customers, and gaining a competitive advantage are just a few of the many superordinate goals that members of an organization can emphasize during integrative bargaining. Superordinate goals help parties in conflict to keep in mind the big picture and the fact that they are working together for a larger purpose or goal despite their disagreements. CARSTAR and CGU recognized that they were both servicing the same customer, and that doing so together would smooth out the relationships.

FOCUSING ON THE PROBLEM, NOT THE PEOPLE   People who are in conflict may not be able to resist the temptation to focus on the shortcomings and weaknesses of the other party or parties, thereby personalizing the conflict. Instead of attacking the problem, the parties to the conflict attack each other. This approach is inconsistent with integrative bargaining and can easily lead the parties into distributive negotiation. All parties to a conflict need to keep focused on the problem or on the source of the conflict and avoid the temptation to discredit each other. CARSTAR and CGU recognized that unhappy clients served neither the insurer or the body shop.

FOCUSING ON INTERESTS, NOT DEMANDS   Demands are *what* a person wants; interests are *why* the person wants them. When two people are in conflict, it is unlikely that the demands of both can be met. Their underlying interests can be met, however, and meeting them is what integrative bargaining is all about. CGU wanted to keep costs down, and CARSTAR was interested in building up the business. Together they were able to achieve their goals. One of the criticisms leveled against Debra McPherson was that she focused more on demands than interests in trying to gain a new contract for British Columbia nurses, as shown in this "Management Insight."

Management Insight

Debra McPherson and the BC Nurses' Union

When Debra McPherson, president of the British Columbia Nurses' Union (BCNU) (www.bcnu.org), was growing up in Fort Osborne Barracks, Winnipeg, she was surrounded by the sons and daughters of lawyers and doctors in her small classroom.[23] "I was glad we all wore uniforms because I didn't have the clothes to compete. I learned early on that I couldn't compete with people on that kind of level," she says.

That formative experience has no doubt coloured her working experiences. Today, head of the 25 000-member union, she is seen as an uncompromising person, one who stands her ground.

McPherson points out that she needs to be firm, otherwise nurses would be treated even more poorly than they already are. In leading the current job action against hospitals in British Columbia, she tells administrators and the public alike that nurses should have a say in how healthcare is delivered, and that wages need to be a lot better than what's been offered. "Why should I be paid less than a freaking plumber?" she asks.

McPherson is on a mission to earn more respect for nurses. She claims that "the image of nurses as Florence Nightingales only perpetuates them being abused by administrators who don't want to pay them what they are worth and who demand of them overtime that would be unacceptable anywhere else."

Although union members traditionally have been white men earning salaries above the minimum wage, unions have become less popular with this group of workers, while becoming more popular with women. Virtually all of the 100-percent increase in union membership since 1967 has come from women.[24] Women believe that belonging to a union will help improve their working conditions, pay, benefits, and job security.

McPherson, for her part, feels that the union is the only hope that nurses have to get better working conditions and pay. She sees hospital management "as oppressors and as barriers to good health management practices."

CREATING NEW OPTIONS FOR JOINT GAIN   Once the parties to a conflict focus on their interests, they are on the road toward achieving creative solutions that will benefit them all. This win–win scenario means that rather than having a fixed set of alternatives from which to choose, the parties can come up with new alternatives that might even expand the resource pie.

FOCUSING ON WHAT IS FAIR   Focusing on what is fair is consistent with the principle of distributive justice, which emphasizes the fair distribution of outcomes based on the meaningful contributions that people make to organizations (see Chapter 5). It is likely that parties in conflict will disagree on certain points and prefer different alternatives that each party feels may better serve his or her own interests or maximize his or her own outcomes. Emphasizing fairness and distributive justice will help the parties come to a mutual agreement about what is the best solution to the problem.

When managers pursue those five strategies and encourage other organizational members to do so, they are more likely to resolve their conflicts effectively, through integrative bargaining. In addition, throughout the negotiation process, managers and other organizational members need to be aware of, and on their guard against, the biases that can lead to faulty decision making (see Chapter 6).[25]

Tips for Managers

Negotiation

1. Whenever feasible, use integrative bargaining rather than distributive negotiation.

2. To help ensure that conflicts are effectively resolved through integrative bargaining, emphasize superordinate goals, focus on the problem not the people, focus on interests not demands, create new options for joint gain, and focus on what is fair.

Organizational Politics

organizational politics
Activities that managers engage in to increase their power and to use power effectively to achieve their goals and overcome resistance or opposition.

political strategies
Tactics that managers use to increase their power and to use power effectively to influence and gain the support of other people while overcoming resistance or opposition.

Managers must develop the skills necessary to manage organizational conflict in order for an organization to be effective. Suppose, however, that top managers are in conflict over the best strategy for an organization to pursue or the best structure to adopt to utilize organizational resources efficiently. In such situations, resolving conflict is often difficult, and the parties to the conflict resort to organizational politics and political strategies to try to resolve the conflict in their favour.

Organizational politics are the activities that managers (and other members of an organization) engage in to increase their power and to use power effectively to achieve their goals and overcome resistance or opposition. Managers often engage in organizational politics to resolve conflicts in their favour.

Political strategies are the specific tactics that managers (and other members of an organization) use to increase their power and to use power effectively to influence and gain the support of other people while overcoming resistance or opposition. Political strategies are especially important when managers are planning and implementing major changes in an organization: Managers not only need to gain support for their change initiatives and influence organizational members to behave in new ways but also must overcome often-strong opposition from people who feel threatened by the change and prefer the status quo. By increasing their power, managers are better able to make needed changes. In addition to moving to increase their power, managers also must make sure that they use their power in a way that actually does enable them to influence others.

The Importance of Organizational Politics

The term *politics* has a negative connotation for many people. Some may think that managers who are "political" are individuals who have risen to the top not because of their own merit and capabilities but because of "whom they know." Or they may think that "political" managers are self-interested and wield power to benefit themselves, not their organization. There is a grain of truth to this negative interpretation. Some managers do appear to misuse their power for personal benefit at the expense of their organization's effectiveness. Recall, for example, from the "Case in Contrast" in Chapter 13 how George Irwin misused his power as CEO of Irwin Toy by favouring one member of the marketing department and not listening to other senior managers. He and the marketing employee worked on products that the others in the company did not support.

Nevertheless, organizational politics are often a positive force. Managers striving to make needed changes are likely to encounter resistance from individuals and groups who feel threatened and wish to preserve the status quo. Effective managers engage in politics to gain support for and implement needed changes. Similarly, managers often face resistance from other managers who disagree with their goals for a group or for the organization and also disagree with what they are trying to accomplish. Engaging in organizational politics can help managers overcome this resistance and achieve their goals.

Indeed, managers cannot afford to ignore organizational politics. Everyone engages in politics to a degree—other managers, co-workers, and subordinates, as well as people outside an organization such as suppliers. Those who try to ignore politics might as well bury their heads in the sand because in all likelihood they will be unable to gain support for their initiatives and goals.

Political Strategies for Increasing Power

How could I increase my power in an organization?

Managers who use political strategies to increase their power are better able to influence others to work toward the achievement of group and organizational goals. By controlling uncertainty, making themselves irreplaceable, being in a central position, generating resources, and building alliances, managers can increase their power (see Figure 16.5).[26] We next look at each of these strategies.

CONTROLLING UNCERTAINTY   Uncertainty is a threat for individuals, groups, and whole organizations and can interfere with effective performance and goal attainment.[27] For example, uncertainty about job security is threatening for many workers and may cause top performers (who have the best chance of finding another job) to quit and take a more secure position with another organization. When an R&D department faces uncertainty about customer preferences, its members may waste valuable resources to develop a product, such as smokeless cigarettes, which customers do not want. When top managers face uncertainty about global demand, they may fail to export products to countries that want them and thus lose a source of competitive advantage.

Managers who are able to control and reduce uncertainty for other managers, teams, departments, and the organization as a whole are likely to see their power increase.[28] Managers of labour unions gain power when they can eliminate uncertainty over job security for workers. Marketing and sales managers gain power when they can eliminate uncertainty for other departments such as R&D by accurately forecasting customers' changing preferences. Top managers gain power when they are knowledgeable about global demand for an organization's products. Managers who are able to control uncertainty are likely to be in demand and sought after by other organizations.

MAKING ONESELF IRREPLACEABLE   Managers gain power when they have valuable knowledge and expertise that allow them to perform activities that no one else can handle. This is the essence of being irreplaceable.[29] The more central these activities are to organizational effectiveness, the more power managers gain from being irreplaceable.

Figure 16.5
Political Strategies for Increasing Power

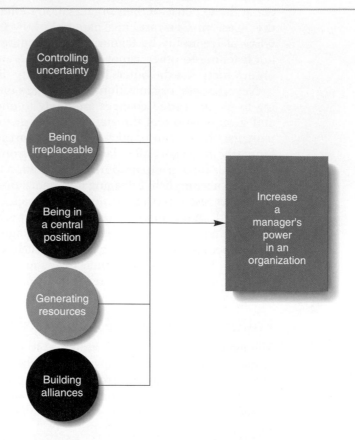

BEING IN A CENTRAL POSITION   Managers in central positions are responsible for activities that are directly connected to an organization's goals and sources of competitive advantage and often are located in central positions in important communication networks in an organization.[30] Managers in central positions have control over crucial organizational activities and initiatives and have access to important information. Other organizational members are dependent on them for their knowledge, expertise, advice, and support, and the success of the organization as a whole is seen as riding on these managers. These consequences of being in a central position are likely to increase managers' power.

Managers who are outstanding performers, have a wide knowledge base, and have made important and visible contributions to their organizations are likely to be offered central positions that will increase their power.

GENERATING RESOURCES   Organizations need three kinds of resources to be effective: (1) input resources such as raw materials, skilled workers, and financial capital, (2) technical resources such as machinery and computers, and (3) knowledge resources such as marketing or engineering expertise. To the extent that a manager is able to generate one or more of these kinds of resources for an organization, that manager's power is likely to increase.[31] In universities, for example, professors who are able to win large research grants from associations such as the Social Sciences and Humanities Research Council gain power because of the financial resources they are generating for their departments and for the university as a whole.

Social Sciences
and Humanities
Research Council
www.sshrc.ca/

BUILDING ALLIANCES When managers build alliances, they develop mutually beneficial relationships with people both inside and outside the organization. The two parties to an alliance support one another because doing so is in their best interests, and both parties benefit from the alliance. Alliances provide a manager with power because they provide the manager with support for his or her initiatives. The partner to the alliance provides support because he or she knows that the manager will reciprocate when the partner needs support. Alliances can help managers achieve their goals and implement needed changes in organizations because they increase managers' levels of power.

Recall from the "Case in Contrast" that Charlie Baillie took great pains to gain the support of the federal government before announcing his proposed takeover of Canada Trust. This is the essence of building alliances. Baillie was able to build alliances with the Finance Department and MPs because he helped them to see why the merger would be in their own best interests. He reassured the MPs from London, Ontario that their citizens would not lose their jobs.

Many powerful top managers focus on building alliances not only inside their organizations but also with individuals, groups, and organizations in the task and general environments on which their organizations are dependent for resources. These individuals, groups, and organizations enter into alliances with managers because doing so is in their best interests and they know that they can count on the managers' support when they need it.

ROB Magazine:
Peter Godsoe
www.robmagazine.com/
archive/98ROBseptember/
html/moving_target.html

Peter Godsoe used most of these strategies on his way to becoming CEO of Scotiabank.[32] When he was put in charge of the bank's lending in the United States and Latin America, he made the operation his own by giving it a new name: the Western Hemisphere International Regional Office (WHIRO). At the time, he reported to Scott McDonald, who was viewed as a potential successor to then-CEO Ced Ritchie. Godsoe wanted the job, however. So for five years, while heading WHIRO, he built "a loyal following by making WHIRO the hot shop." To develop the unit's culture, Godsoe developed cartoons, WHIRO hero awards, a crest, jackets and a Latin motto that translated: "If you don't have a hernia, you're not pulling your weight." Soon, every time another organizational division was created, Godsoe ending up heading it. McDonald ended up leaving the bank, and Godsoe did eventually replace Ritchie.

Political Strategies for Exercising Power

Politically skilled managers not only have a good understanding of, and ability to use, those five strategies to increase their power; they also have a good appreciation of strategies for exercising their power. These strategies generally focus on how managers can use their power unobtrusively, as did Charlie Baillie in the "Case in Contrast."[33] When a manager exercises power *unobtrusively*, other members of the organization may not be aware that the manager is using his or her power to influence them. They may think that they support the manager for a variety of reasons: because they believe that doing so is a rational or logical thing to do, because they believe that doing so is in their own best interests, or because they believe that the position or decision that the manager is advocating is legitimate or appropriate.

The unobtrusive use of power may seem devious, but managers typically use this strategy to bring about change and achieve organizational goals. Matthew Barrett and John Cleghorn, by contrast, tried to use their power as a bullying tactic to force the government to agree to the mergers. What they needed to do instead was to gain support of consumers and the federal government. Political strategies for exercising power to gain the support and concurrence of others include relying on objective information, bringing in an outside expert, controlling the agenda, and making everyone a winner (see Figure 16.6).[34]

Figure 16.6
Political Strategies for Exercising Power

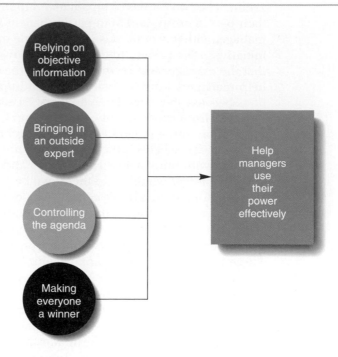

RELYING ON OBJECTIVE INFORMATION   Managers require the support of others to achieve their goals, implement changes, and overcome opposition. One way for a manager to gain this support and overcome opposition is to rely on objective information that supports the manager's initiatives. Reliance on objective information leads others to support the manager because of the facts; objective information causes others to believe that what the manager is proposing is the proper course of action. By relying on objective information, politically skilled managers unobtrusively exercise their power to influence others.

BRINGING IN AN OUTSIDE EXPERT   Bringing in an outside expert to support a proposal or decision can, at times, provide managers with some of the same benefits that the use of objective information does. It lends credibility to a manager's initiatives and causes others to believe that what the manager is proposing is the appropriate or rational thing to do.

Although you might think that consultants and other outside experts are "neutral" or "objective," they sometimes are hired by managers who want them to support a certain position or decision in an organization. Particularly when managers are facing strong opposition from others who fear that a decision will harm their or their departments' interests, they may bring in an outside expert who they hope will be perceived as a neutral observer to lend credibility and objectivity to the managers' point of view. The support of an outside expert may cause others to believe that a decision is indeed the right one. Of course, sometimes consultants and other outside experts really are brought into organizations to be objective and provide managers with guidance on the appropriate course of action to take.

CONTROLLING THE AGENDA   Managers also can exercise power unobtrusively by controlling the agenda—influencing what alternatives are considered or even whether a decision is made.[35] Charlie Baillie did this by keeping federal officials involved at all points during his merger talks, and making sure that he could address their concerns before they arose. When managers influence the alternatives that are considered, they can make sure that each considered alternative is acceptable to them and that undesirable alternatives are not in the feasible set. In a hiring context, for example, managers can exert their power unobtrusively by ensuring that job candidates whom they do not find acceptable do not make their way onto the list of finalists for an open position. They do this by, for example, making sure that these candidates' drawbacks or deficiencies are communicated to everyone involved in making the hiring decision. When three finalists for an open position are discussed and evaluated in a hiring meeting, a manager may seem to exert little power or influence and just go along with what the rest of the group wants. However, the manager may have exerted power in the hiring process unobtrusively, by controlling which candidates made it to the final stage.

Sometimes managers can prevent a decision from being made. A manager in charge of a community relations committee, for example, may not favour a proposal for the organization to become more involved in local youth groups such as the Boy Scouts and the Girl Guides. The manager can exert influence in this situation by not including the proposal on the agenda for the committee's next meeting. Alternatively, the manager could place the proposal at the end of the agenda for the meeting and feel confident that the committee will run out of time and not get to the last items on the agenda because that is what always happens. Either not including the proposal or putting it at the end of the agenda enables the manager to exercise power unobtrusively. Committee members do not perceive this manager as trying to influence them to turn down the proposal. Rather, he or she has made the proposal into a non-issue that is not even considered.

MAKING EVERYONE A WINNER Often, politically skilled managers are able to exercise their power unobtrusively because they make sure that everyone whose support they need benefits personally from providing that support. By making everyone a winner, a manager is able to influence other organizational members because these members see supporting the manager to be in their best interest.

Tips for Managers

Political Strategies

1. Determine the major sources of uncertainty for your work group and organization and take steps to help control these sources of uncertainty.

2. Try to develop skills or expertise that are crucial to your organization and not possessed by other organizational members.

3. Determine which resources are crucial for your organization and try to help generate these resources.

4. Build alliances with powerful organizational members to gain support for your ideas.

5. Whenever possible, use objective information to support positions that you advocate.

Chapter Summary

ORGANIZATIONAL CONFLICT

• Types of Conflict

• Sources of Conflict

• Conflict Management Strategies

NEGOTIATION STRATEGIES FOR INTEGRATIVE BARGAINING

ORGANIZATIONAL POLITICS

• The Importance of Organizational Politics

• Political Strategies for Increasing Power

• Political Strategies for Exercising Power

Summary and Review

ORGANIZATIONAL CONFLICT   Organizational conflict is the discord that arises when the goals, interests, or values of different individuals or groups are incompatible and those individuals or groups block or thwart each other's attempts to achieve their objectives. Four types of conflict arising in organizations are interpersonal conflict, intragroup conflict, intergroup conflict, and interorganizational conflict. Sources of conflict in organizations include incompatible goals and time horizons, overlapping authority, task interdependencies, incompatible evaluation or reward systems, scarce resources, and status inconsistencies. Conflict management strategies focused on individuals include increasing awareness of the sources of conflict, increasing diversity awareness and skills, practising job rotation or temporary assignments, and using permanent transfers or dismissals when necessary. Strategies focused on the whole organization include changing an organization's structure or culture and altering the source of conflict.

NEGOTIATION STRATEGIES FOR INTEGRATIVE BARGAINING
Negotiation is a conflict resolution technique used when parties to a conflict have approximately equal levels of power and try to come up with an acceptable way to allocate resources to each other. In distributive negotiation, the parties perceive that there is a fixed level of resources for them to allocate, and each competes to receive as much as possible at the expense of the others, not caring about their relationship in the future. In integrative bargaining, the parties perceive that they may be able to increase the resource pie by coming up with a creative solution to the conflict, trusting each other, and cooperating with each other to achieve a win–win resolution. Five strategies that managers can use to facilitate integrative bargaining are to: emphasize superordinate goals; focus on the problem, not the people; focus on interests, not demands; create new options for joint gain; and focus on what is fair.

ORGANIZATIONAL POLITICS   Organizational politics are the activities that managers (and other members of an organization) engage in to increase their power and to use power effectively to achieve their goals and overcome resistance or opposition. Effective managers realize that politics can be a positive force that enables them to make needed changes in an organization. Five important political strategies for increasing power are controlling uncertainty, making oneself irreplaceable, being in a central position, generating resources, and building alliances. Political strategies for effectively exercising power focus on how to use power unobtrusively and include relying on objective information, bringing in an outside expert, controlling the agenda, and making everyone a winner.

Management in Action

Topics for Discussion and Action

1. Discuss why too little conflict in an organization can be just as detrimental as too much conflict.

2. Interview a manager in a local organization to determine the kinds of conflicts that occur in that manager's organization and the strategies that are used to manage them.

3. Why is integrative bargaining a more effective way of resolving conflicts than distributive negotiation?

4. Why do organizational politics affect practically every organization? Why do effective managers need good political skills?

5. What steps can managers take to ensure that organizational politics are a positive force leading to a competitive advantage, not a negative force leading to personal advantage at the expense of organizational goal attainment?

6. Think of a member of an organization whom you know and who is particularly powerful. What political strategies does this person use to increase his or her power?

7. Why is it best to use power unobtrusively? How are people likely to react to power that is exercised obtrusively?

Building Management Skills

Effective and Ineffective Conflict Resolution

Think about two recent conflicts that you had with other people: one conflict that you felt was effectively resolved (C1) and one that you felt was ineffectively resolved (C2). The other people involved could be co-workers, students, family members, friends, or members of an organization of which you are a member. Answer the following questions.

1. Briefly describe C1 and C2. What type of conflict was involved in each of these incidents?

2. What was the source of the conflict in C1 and in C2?

3. What conflict management strategies were used in C1 and in C2?

4. What could you have done differently to manage conflict in C2 more effectively?

5. How was conflict resolved in C1 and in C2?

Small Group Breakout Exercise

Negotiating a Solution

Form groups of three or four people. One member of your group will play the role of Jane Rister, one member will play the role of Michael Schwartz, and one or two members will be observer(s) and spokesperson(s) for your group.

Jane Rister and Michael Schwartz are assistant managers in a large department store. They report directly to the store manager. Today, they are meeting to discuss some important problems that they need to solve but about which they disagree.

The first problem hinges on the fact that either Rister or Schwartz needs to be on duty whenever the store is open. For the last six months, Rister has taken most of the least desirable hours (nights and weekends). They are planning their schedules for the next six months. Rister hoped Schwartz would take more of the undesirable times, but Schwartz has informed Rister that his wife has just gotten a nursing job that requires her to work weekends, so he needs to stay home weekends to take care of their infant daughter.

The second problem concerns a department manager who has had a hard time retaining salespeople in his department. The turnover rate in his department is twice that of the other departments in the store. Rister thinks the manager is ineffective and wants to fire him. Schwartz thinks the high turnover is a fluke and the manager is effective.

The last problem concerns Rister's and Schwartz's vacation schedules. Both managers want to take off the week of July 1, but one of them needs to be in the store whenever it is open.

1. The group members playing Rister and Schwartz assume their roles and negotiate a solution to these three problems.

2. Observers take notes on how Rister and Schwartz negotiate solutions to their problems.

3. Observers determine the extent to which Rister and Schwartz use distributive negotiation or integrative bargaining to resolve their conflicts.

4. When called on by the instructor, observers communicate to the rest of the class how Rister and Schwartz resolved their conflicts, whether they used distributive negotiation or integrative bargaining, and their actual solutions.

Exploring the World Wide Web

Specific Assignment

Companies and labour unions in Canada are often in negotiations about wages and other workplace issues. Go to the Canadian Labour Congress Web site (www.clc-ctc.ca/eng-index.html) and click on "Union News." Read through some of the actions that the Congress is currently engaged in. Then click on "Links," which will take you to links for a variety of Canada's labour unions. Choose one that is actively engaged in bargaining with an employer.

1. What is the union's position on the dispute?

2. What are the key items it is seeking for its members?

General Assignment

Find the Web site of a company that is currently engaged in bargaining with a union. What information does it provide about the negotiations? How persuasive are its positions? To what extent do its positions portray either an integrative or a distributive bargaining approach?

ManagementCase

In the News

From the Pages of *Canadian Press Newswire*
Unions Find Fertile Ground at Newspapers

The war between Canada's newspaper fiefdoms has many of the front-line troops diving for the cover of organized labour.

Unions have been organizing newsrooms, capitalizing on the uncertainty of a shifting industry where the likes of Conrad Black have built up empires.

Reporters and editors at Southam Inc.'s *Calgary Herald* said Yes last week to union representation after a drive that caught many in the traditionally anti-union city off guard.

Several other newsrooms — including the independent *Halifax Chronicle-Herald* and *Mail-Star* and Southam's *Regina Leader-Post*— have also organized.

The *Thunder Bay Chronicle-Journal*, owned by Thomson Newspapers Co. Ltd., recently negotiated its first contract, as did the *St. Catharines Standard*, another of Black's Southam properties.

Bob Hackett of Simon Fraser University's School of Communications says Black, who controls 58 Canadian dailies through the Southam and Hollinger chains, is cutting back at papers like the *Leader-Post* to finance his bigger properties.

"In smaller and medium markets they have no competition and they don't have to worry about producing exceptional journalism," Hackett says. "All they have to be is acceptable to keep the optimum number of readers and advertisers."

He says employees fear for their jobs, especially when they've seen 25 per cent of the workforce lopped off, as was the case in Regina two years ago.

"But in Calgary, and it's a very encouraging development to me, journalists are worried about questions of editorial integrity."

Certification at the *Herald* leaves the *Edmonton Journal*, *Saskatoon StarPhoenix* and new *National Post* as the only major Black-controlled papers without a union in the newsroom.

Orland French, a former reporter with the *Globe and Mail* and now visiting professor at the University of Regina journalism program, says Black's purchase of Southam and its marriage with Hollinger has stirred the business like never before.

"On many of those papers they've gone through a lot of turmoil in the past year or two with Hollinger taking over, and this is the survivors trying to maintain some kind of security," French says of the unionizing.

The Toronto Star recently made a hostile takeover bid for Sun Media, which owns 15 dailies. That merger would further concentrate ownership.

"It really frightens people," says Arnold Amber, Canadian director of The Newspaper Guild Canada. "Uncertainty leads people to seek co-operative protection, and in a work setting that's a union."

The ownership trend is putting new demands on unions to become defenders of newsroom independence, says Simon Fraser's Hackett.

"Now with the *National Post* out, how long can we sustain competition between two national papers? What if the *Globe and Mail* goes under or if there's a merger?

"Some people are talking about journalistic chill. If you work in Canada and you run afoul of Conrad Black, you've hardly got anywhere else to go."

The Guild's Amber says fears about concentrated ownership have been a common theme in recent union drives.

Don Babick, president and chief operating officer of Southam, dismisses the suggestion that journalistic integrity is being threatened, calling it "a nice ploy for the organizing drive."

"If someone is preaching the bogeyman of interference from the top, then that's totally unfounded," Babick says. "There is no evidence of that happening at our newspapers."

Whether there's a union or not, local editorial managers will still decide what appears in their newspapers, he says.

Babick sees the organizing drives more as a function of two aggressive unions, the Guild and the Communications, Energy and Paperworkers Union of Canada, looking to expand.

Calgary Herald publisher Ken King says a communication breakdown between senior management and staff during an era of rapid change was one factor that led to the organizing drive by the Communications union.

"It's one thing to have problems; it's another thing to be seen to seemingly ignore them," says King.

"I indicated to staff that I was very regretful and accepted the responsibility that was associated with that and acknowledged to them that their concerns had been validated in large part."

King says the *Herald* is overhauling its structure with a major emphasis on opening new channels of communication.

A union news release identified the key issues at the *Herald* as "unfair and arbitrary treatment by management as well as concerns about editorial integrity." The *Herald* responded by suing the union for defamation.

Union vice-president Gail Lem says wage inequalities were also an issue in Calgary—senior reporters earn about $65 000 a year but many in the newsroom make considerably less.

She says many employees believe they were left no choice but to organize because of the overwhelming size of their employer.

"It's not the old *Calgary Herald* any more," she says. "It's part of a big chain where unfortunately quality journalism sometimes takes a back seat to the bottom line."

Source: R. Curren, "Unions Find Fertile Ground at Newspapers," *Canadian Press Newswire*, November 8, 1998.

Questions

1. What are the sources of conflict at the various newspapers between publishers and the editors and reporters?

2. What strategies could be used to reduce the conflict?

3. What negotiation strategies could be used to reach agreement between the unions and the publishers?

ManagementCase

In the News

From the Pages of *Business Week*
Half a Loaf at Blimpie

Shortly after dawn on St. Patrick's Day, 1000 corned-beef sandwiches were trucked from Blimpie on Long Island to the American Stock Exchange in Lower Manhattan, passing dozens of Blimpie shops that were much closer. To the bleat of bagpipes, Chief Executive Anthony P. Conza rang the opening bell to herald his switch from the New York Stock Exchange. The traders devoured the subs, unaware of a strange truth: Conza was on the turf of "the other" Blimpie.

Long before Blimpie became America's No. 2 submarine-sandwich chain, Conza and co-founder Peter DeCarlo sliced the company in half. State by state, city by city, they divvied the nation in 1976 to resolve warring business philosophies. "It was like Monopoly," Conza says. Starting with 50 stores each, they began a grueling race. "I said I could

do it better, and he said he could do it better," DeCarlo explains. If size matters, Conza won: With 2000 stores and US$39 million in revenues, his publicly traded Blimpie International Inc. is about 10 times as big as DeCarlo's privately held Blimpie Associates.

But it's a hollow victory. Blimpie remains a bifurcated anomaly in a business that thrives on uniformity. Its divided status has throttled growth at the larger company and given it one of the more convoluted histories in the annals of Corporate America. And that's only the start of the problems caused by mishandling the Blimpie name. Investors in Blimpie International, too, have been left holding crumbs. Amid free-falling profits, they have questioned the multimillion-dollar payouts the company makes to its executives for rights to use the name overseas. The result: Shares have slid to

around US$3, down from US$16 two years ago. "I've never heard of such a ludicrous arrangement in all my life," says Wendy Liebmann, a New York retail consultant.

Indeed, even as Conza tries to bail his chain out by expanding abroad and developing new restaurants featuring tacos and pasta, he is hampered by the other Blimpie's control of Manhattan—a showcase serving everyone from Wall Streeters to tourists. "It's like I've invited people over for dinner," Conza says, "and they arrive at somebody else's house and eat their cooking."

For all the problems the name has caused, it was born innocently enough. In 1964, Conza and DeCarlo were 24—the best of friends, the most naive of businessmen. At a Halloween party in Hoboken, N.J., Conza, DeCarlo, and a third friend talked about starting a business. The product: the sub sandwich they had tried on the Jersey Shore. Thinking the name "sub" sounded like a greasy spoon, they rifled through the dictionary and stopped at "blimp."

They borrowed US$2000 from a friend of DeCarlo's in the textile business. DeCarlo, with a perpetual smile and a crushing handshake, sweet-talked suppliers. Conza, the shy son of a New York Stock Exchange runner, quit his clerking job at E.F. Hutton to handle the books. "He was the pencil man with patience," says David Pierro, whose three stores in Manhattan and New Jersey overlap both Blimpies. "Peter was the limo guy with US$1000 suits and checks bouncing all over the place."

Customers flooded in. And within a year, Blimpie sold its first franchise. While Conza sought to control Blimpie's fate, DeCarlo pushed to open anywhere a franchisee was interested. DeCarlo won, and both say that unbridled expansion ate up all their cash, forcing them to sell the stores they owned. They cashed in their cars and life-insurance policies. Both recall the last straw: Approaching the bridge from New Jersey to Manhattan, neither could come up with the 50¢ toll. Soon after that, they sliced Blimpie in half. Conza took Chicago. DeCarlo grabbed parts of California, Maryland, and Virginia. On it went. "I woke up one day to a call saying, 'Three of your stores are under Peter. Three are under Tony,'" recalls New York franchisee Joe Martignano. "It was like my parents split up."

Both soon floundered, and DeCarlo gave Conza his rights outside the Northeast in exchange for a cut of profits in those regions. Conza took Blimpie International public in 1983 but pumped money into a Southwestern-style chain that almost pulled him under. In 1987, he began selling huge subfranchises.

Since 1994, the strategy more than doubled sales.

But like divorced parents bickering over the kids, the two never stopped arguing. Conza has criticized the occasional sanitary violations of the New York stores. DeCarlo, who blames New York's aging real estate, demanded that Conza stop undercutting quality by selling prepackaged sandwiches at Southern gas stations. Conza ordered thousands of baseballs with the Blimpie logo for a promotion, but DeCarlo refused to buy any. Confusing customers further, they even have competing ad campaigns.

Amid the squabbling, archrival Subway closed in on Manhattan, forcing Conza and DeCarlo to unify. Conza's offer to buy the smaller Blimpie for US$40 million—about 10 times sales—was rebuffed. "The money wasn't right," DeCarlo says. But he sent emissaries to Conza's test kitchen to nibble on turkey, ham, and beef. They agreed on standardizing cold cuts but still diverge on cheese and bread. Nor can they settle on a menu. "They didn't have the chicken fajita I eat at home," gripes a Florida tourist, leaving a New York store.

The arrangement was tolerable until the mid-1990s, when Blimpie International ran out of territory in the U.S. With revenues limited to franchise fees and equipment sales, Conza looked overseas. But unlike most trademarks, which are registered to a corporation, "Blimpie" is owned by Conza, DeCarlo, and Chief Operating Officer David L. Siegel. Without control of the name, Blimpie couldn't raise money to go abroad.

To solve the problem in advance of a US$10 million offering in 1995, the company agreed to pay DeCarlo, who refused to give up his rights, 30% of the international profits. Conza and Siegel were advised to fork over the name for free by Miami investment banker Steven N.

Bronson. His firm, Barber & Bronson, a major Blimpie shareholder, sponsored the offering. But instead, the pair leased the name to Blimpie for 99 years. Last year, the chain paid them US$4.5 million to use the name abroad—a good deal more than the US$3.28 million it earned in profits. By 2002, they are to get US$3 million more for its use. "They wanted to maximize their personal wealth," Bronson says. "We had a problem with it. But it was better than leaving ownership with management."

Conza and Siegel, who own 31% and 15% of the stock, respectively, insist the arrangement is fair. "We've compromised our salaries and benefits to build the company," Siegel says. "Why should we give away our rights?" But the deal is a big reason Wall Street soured on the stock. "When management is taking money out the backdoor so a company can use its own name, something's rotten in Denmark," says analyst Michael D. Smith of brokerage Fahnestock & Co.

Worse, despite the hefty payments, Blimpie has made little dent abroad: So far, Conza has opened just 37 stores overseas. And profits, which sank 19% for the fiscal year ended June, 1997, were off a further 20% for the first three quarters of fiscal 1998. Blimpie's problems may have started with its name—but they surely don't end there.

Source: I.J. Dugan, "Half a Loaf at Blimpie," *Business Week*, August 10, 1998, pp. 43–44.

Questions

1. What are the sources of conflict between Anthony P. Conza and Peter DeCarlo?

2. How have Conza and DeCarlo tried to manage the conflict between them?

3. Have they been successful at managing conflict? Why or why not?

Organizational Change

Learning Objectives

1. Identify what is involved in managing organizational change.

2. Explain how managers could help to overcome resistance to change.

3. Explain the importance of changing the production system.

4. Describe the main features of total quality management and the challenges facing managers and organizations that seek to implement total quality management.

5. Describe how managers can improve the efficiency of an organization's production system.

6. Differentiate among just-in-time inventory, *kaizen*, and process reengineering.

7. Identify the managers' role in changing the organizational culture.

A Case in Contrast

Facing the Winds of Change

Until its dramatic drop in fortunes in the early spring of 2001, Brampton, ON-based Nortel Networks had been at the top of the list of Canada's "Most Profitable Businesses."[1] Both Nortel and its former CEO, John Roth, were routinely commended for several very successful years. The company was known as a leader in technological change.

In Roth's first year at the top of Nortel, he was able to report that the company had had its best year ever, posting both record profits and record sales. However, that wasn't good enough for Roth, and shortly afterwards he launched a major transformation of the company. His goal: to have Nortel become "a prime contractor in building a new and improved Internet." Roth set out to reinvent telecommunications, the world's biggest industry.

John Roth took a no-holds-barred approach at Nortel to take the company from being "a stodgy and slow-moving maker of phone switches—to the forefront of the networking business in record time." In doing so, the company claimed the Number 1 spot on several fronts, even beating out the AT&T spinoff star,

Moore Business Corporation's Ed Tyler did not appreciate how changes in technology might reduce the need for the business forms his company produced.

Lucent Technologies. Roth's strategy for this change was to buy his way to strength, rather than to develop it in-house. He started by buying Bay Networks for $10.4 billion in 1998. Then he bought (among other companies) Shasta Networks, Periphonics, Clarify, Qtera, CoreTek, Xros and Architel Systems.

Even though Roth announced his resignation in April 2001 as a result of Nortel's tumbling share prices, Nortel was still a much better company than it had been when Roth took over in 1997.

Oddly, Nortel faltered because it failed to research the marketplace adequately, even though that was something it had done incredibly well during its rise. While Roth will "always be remembered as an exceptional leader during the company's high-growth phase," neither he nor Nortel was prepared when the "telecommunications sector plunged into its own recession."

Even if Nortel's luck has run out for the moment, at least the company appreciated how adapting the organization to respond to changes in technology made sense. Toronto-

John Roth effectively led Nortel through one set of changes, but the collapse of technology stocks signaled the need for a new strategy and a new CEO at Nortel.

based Moore Business Corp. still has not really figured out how to respond to "The New Economy."[2] In 1997, Moore, a manufacturer of business forms and labels, was viewed as a solid company. Shares were trading at around $30, and its business was growing. Unfortunately, the company failed to consider how changing technology would put the manufacturer of business forms in a precarious position. Word processing programs and Web-based applications made the market for hard-copy forms that needed to be typed all but disappear. By December 2000, shares were trading at $3.95.

CEO Ed Tyler faced angry shareholders in April 2000, after share prices had slid for two years in a row. As one angry older shareholder said, "How is it possible that the people at the top don't have foresight?"

At one time, Moore stocks were considered to be "the bluest of blue-chips." Moore's slowness to adapt to change may have arisen because many of its current shareholders are older retirees who simply held onto their shares while the 118-year-old company declined. They didn't insist that management perform better, and so the company became complacent.

Thomas Kierans, chairman of the board of directors for Moore, acknowledged to shareholders that, "Sadly, the company's performance has been eroding for many years. Our industry is out of fashion these days." And then, perhaps in defeat, he noted, "We looked at selective asset sales and other structural changes. But it's not at all evident that any of these options is feasible."

Tyler resigned in disgrace in December 2000, and was replaced by Robert Burton. Burton's first challenge was to work on cutting costs. He reviewed all business lines, and considered selling non-essential assets, such as real estate. He was also considering closing some offices. As he noted, "The organization is top-heavy. The costs of this company are completely out of line with our revenue." One example of an out-of-line cost was the $1.4 million performance-based bonus given to Ed Tyler for his work in 2000, despite the company's floundering stock price. In spring 2001, Moore was even considering cutting research and development, indicating once again that it had not figured out a strategy to deal with change. ●

Overview

Managers and organizations face a variety of forces leading them towards change. These include technology, globalization, and increased competition. Successful leaders like John Roth are able to use their power effectively to influence others and to bring about changes that allow them to achieve their goals, while unsuccessful leaders like Ed Tyler do not appropriately engage in change.

John Roth may look as if he was a failure at change, but that view may be short-sighted. One of the reasons that Nortel needs to reinvent itself yet again, in spite of having just done so very recently, is that the telecommunications industry is entering a new era. There is no longer explosive growth in worldwide telecom markets worldwide. The industry is entering a slower-growth period that will see different companies come to prominence. So Roth led a very successful change, but may not have been the appropriate leader in the face of such industry changes.

To achieve superior quality, efficiency, responsiveness to customers, and innovation—the four building blocks of competitive advantage—managers at all levels in an organization must adopt state-of-the-art management techniques and practices that give them more control over the organization's activities. In this chapter, we look at how to manage change and overcome resistance to change. We also discuss various techniques that managers can use to effect change in different parts of the organization. By the end of this chapter, you will understand the vital role that change plays in building competitive advantage and creating a high-performing organization. ●

Managing Organizational Change

To be successful, managers need to be continually aware of their ability to respond to the environment, the needs of their customers and clients, and the demand for innovation. Organizational change can affect practically all aspects of organizational functioning, including organizational structure, culture, strategies, control systems, groups and teams, and the human resource management system, as well as critical organizational processes such as communication, motivation, and leadership. Organizational change can bring alterations in the ways managers carry out the critical tasks of planning, organizing, leading, and controlling and the ways they perform their managerial roles. To understand how widespread the need for change in Canadian organizations is, consider the findings of a 1999 study of 309 human resource executives across a variety of industries. One hundred percent of them reported that they were going through at least one of the following changes: mergers, acquisitions, divestitures, global competition, and management and/or organizational structure.[3]

Deciding how to change an organization is a complex matter, not least because change disrupts the status quo and poses a threat, prompting employees to resist attempts to alter work relationships and procedures. Organizational learning, the process through which managers try to increase organizational members' abilities to understand and appropriately respond to changing conditions (see Chapter 6), can be an important impetus for change and can help all members of an organization, including managers, effectively make decisions about needed changes.

Assessing the Need for Change

Assessing the need for change calls for two important activities: recognizing that there is a problem and identifying its source. As the "Case in Contrast" shows, when John Roth took over at Nortel, he immediately recognized the need to be a first-mover in telecommunications, and set out to do that. Sometimes the need for change is obvious, such as when an organization's performance is suffering. Often, however, managers have trouble determining that something is going wrong because problems develop gradually; organizational performance may slip for a number of years before it becomes obvious. This is what happened to Ed Tyler in the "Case in Contrast." Thus, during the first step in the change process, managers need to recognize that there is a problem that requires change.

When Wayne Sales took over as president and CEO of Canadian Tire, signs of the need for change were all over: The stock price had dropped $15 in the previous year, sales were dropping, and Home Hardware, Wal-Mart and Home Depot were taking away his customers.

Often, the problems that managers detect have produced a gap between desired performance and actual performance. To detect such a gap, managers need to look at performance measures—such as falling market share or profits, rising costs, or employees' failure to meet their established goals or stay within budgets—which indicate whether change is needed. These measures are provided by organizational control systems (discussed in Chapter 9).

To discover the source of the problem, managers need to look both inside and outside the organization. Outside the organization, they must examine how changes in environmental forces may be creating opportunities and threats that are affecting internal work relationships. Perhaps the emergence of low-cost foreign competitors has led to conflict among different departments that are trying to find new ways to gain a competitive advantage. Managers also need to look within the organization to see whether its structure and culture are causing problems between departments. Perhaps a company does not have the integrating mechanisms in place to allow different departments to respond to low-cost competition (see Chapter 8).

Lewin's Three-Stage Model of Change

Kurt Lewin identified a three step process that organizations could use to manage change successfully: *unfreeze* the status quo, *move* to a new state, and *refreeze* the new change to make it permanent.[4]

Organizations in their ordinary state reflect the status quo. To move toward a new state, unfreezing is necessary. Unfreezing, the process by which an organization overcomes the resistance to change, can occur in one of three ways, as shown in Figure 17.1. **Driving forces**, which direct behaviour away from the status quo, can be increased. **Restraining forces**, which hinder movement from the existing equilibrium, can be decreased. One can also combine the first two approaches.

Individuals generally resist change, and therefore managers must take steps to break down that resistance. They can increase the driving forces by promising new rewards or benefits if employees work towards the change. Managers can also remove some of the restraining forces. For instance, if employees fear change because they don't know how to use the new technology, training could be given to reduce that fear. When resistance to change is extremely high, managers may have to work on both the driving and the restraining forces for unfreezing to be successful.

Moving involves getting the change process itself underway. Once change has been implemented, the behaviours have to be refrozen so that they can be sustained over time. Otherwise, change is likely to be short-lived, and employees are likely to go back to the previous state. Refreezing balances the driving and restraining forces to prevent the old state from arising again.

driving forces Forces that direct behaviour away from the status quo.

restraining forces Forces that prevent movement away from the status quo.

Figure 17.1
Unfreezing the Status Quo

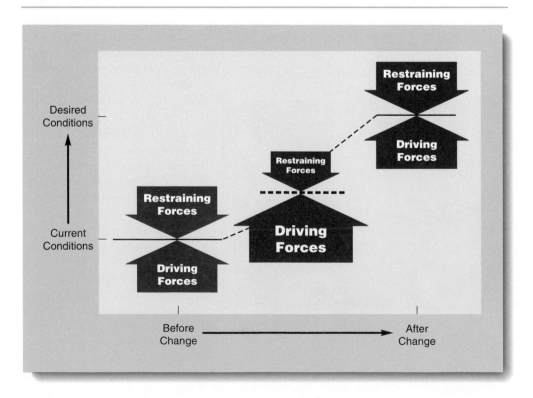

To refreeze the change, managers need to put permanent driving forces into place. For instance, the new bonus system could reinforce specific new changes. Over time, the norms of the employee work groups and managers will also help solidify the change if senior managers have sufficiently reinforced the new behaviour.

Resistance to Change

Individuals and organizations resist change, almost naturally, it would seem. Generally, once individuals have gotten into some routine, which they regard as the status quo, they feel comfortable with this state. Consider how you become unsettled when your routine has to change because of some new demand on your life. Or suppose you have enjoyed working with a set of people, and now you are being asked to move into another department.

Sometimes resistance to change is very immediate and explicit. Employees start complaining about a change, or they slow down their work. They may even threaten to go on strike if they are unionized. When employees voice their concerns, at least the manager can try to respond. Sometimes the resistance is not overt, however. Employees become less committed to their jobs, calling in sick, or becoming less motivated to do their work. This type of resistance is more difficult to combat, as it may take a while for the manager to recognize the employees' discontent.

It is possible to divide the sources of resistance to change into individual and organizational responses. Of course, these sources may overlap. At Deloitte & Touche, managers and employees alike initially had difficulty understanding some of the reasons for the company to change its culture, as this "Focus on Diversity" shows.

Focus on Diversity

Deloitte & Touche Looks for a More Humane Workplace

In the early 1990s, Deloitte & Touche noticed that although it was hiring significant numbers of women, they were leaving at much higher rates than men, and very few candidates for partnership were women.[5] At first, senior management at Deloitte & Touche concluded that this was not their problem, but society's or women's problem. In other words, managers refused to recognize that the problems were internal, and therefore refused to see the need for change.

After significant re-examination of the problem during the 1990s however, management came to see otherwise. In particular, they found that the company now had "a new generation of younger professionals, males and females alike, [that] shares the concerns that were initially raised by the women." Today, the company is trying to change the culture to make Deloitte & Touche better for all employees.

Toronto-based Deloitte & Touche Canada has been following the lead of its American parent in changing its workplace practices. David Laidley, the chair of Deloitte & Touche Canada, recognized the need for change: "If talented people are leaving, you've got to do something about it. It's a business imperative."

In 1998, Laidley and his senior managers launched the ART initiative for the Advancement and Retention of Talented people. One of the challenges of this initiative was getting women to talk, and men to listen. Some of the men felt that the women were "male-bashing," while some of the women who had "made it in a man's world" didn't recognize the problems other women were facing. The responses of these employees were typical reactions to attempts at organizational change.

Kathleen Christie, one of the first female partners at Deloitte & Touche Canada, and currently chief human resource officer, notes that the expectations of employees have changed over time. The younger generation, she says, are more team-oriented, expect their leaders to be good communicators, and are impatient with authoritarian managers. When asked whether Deloitte & Touche Canada is accommodating these changed expectations, she says that the company is making progress, though not as quickly as she might like.

One area where Deloitte & Touche Canada has made progress, however, is in the turnover rate. These days about 10 percent of employees leave voluntarily: 51 percent are men and 49 percent are women.

Individual Resistance to Change

The following summarizes five reasons why individuals may resist change.[6]

Why do individuals resist change?

HABIT   Human beings are creatures of habit and prefer to develop routines to make their lives easier. When confronted with change, habits can be disturbed, and this becomes a source of resistance.

SECURITY   People who have a high need for security are likely to resist change because they'll find their security threatened. For instance, when a company announces a layoff, employees may fear that they will lose their jobs. Even when companies simply announce that they are looking for new ways of doing jobs, employees can become fearful that jobs will be lost.

ECONOMIC FACTORS   If pay is tied to productivity, individuals could fear that change will lead to loss of income. For instance, when federal employees were told that new productivity measures would be introduced, this could have meant that bonuses would be harder to earn. When new technology is introduced into the workplace, employees might be worried that they won't learn it quickly enough, and that this could lead to a drop in bonuses.

FEAR OF THE UNKNOWN   Many people simply resist or fear the unknown. This means that they don't like to do new things because they don't want to look foolish, or they don't like the uncertainty of how the new procedures will work.

SELECTIVE INFORMATION PROCESSING   Individuals are often guilty of hearing only what they want to hear, and then responding on that basis. For instance, in the lengthy bus strike in Vancouver during the spring of 2001, union members were convinced that any change that management wanted to make to schedules meant that some of the current bus drivers would lose their jobs. More likely, it meant that fewer employees would be hired in the future, and thus this would decrease the size of the union in time, but that is different from current employees actually losing jobs.

CYNICISM   When individuals have been through a series of changes, they start to feel cynical that any form of change is really going to make a difference. Researchers found that four major things contributed to cynicism on the part of employees:[7]

- Feeling uninformed about what was happening;
- Lack of communication and respect from one's manager;
- Lack of communication and respect from one's union representative;
- Lack of opportunity for meaningful participation in decision making.

These same researchers also found that personality affected resistance to change: those with negative personalities were more likely to be cynical about change. They also found that cynicism about change often led to lower commitment, less satisfaction, and reduced motivation to work hard. In the "Management Insight," we see how Gilles Pansera, president of Industries Manufacturières Mégantic Inc., worked with his employees to overcome their resistance to change.

Management Insight

IMMI Overcomes Resistance to Change

When Gilles Pansera purchased Lac-Mégantic, QC-based Industries Manufacturières Mégantic Inc. (IMMI) in 1990 and became its president, the operation had been losing money for the previous 10 years.[8] Pansera believed that to achieve profitability the company had to retarget the market and upgrade machinery. After surveying his competitors, including one in Japan, he decided to concentrate on "doorskin" plywood. This product required a much more labour-intensive production process, however, and he needed to change his employees' habits.

Pansera quickly discovered that change was "a much harder proposal than expected." The employees had never been given any responsibility under the previous owners, and so even ones who had worked at IMMI for 20 years rarely knew anything about the complete operation of the plant.

Pansera's strategy for dealing with changes was to engage in full communication with his employees. This included showing the books to them, which he does every quarter. He believes that employees should know everything about the company. IMMI's unionized employees appreciated his openness. Shortly after Pansera took over, the employees agreed to renegotiate their collective agreement. In turn, Pansera agreed to end the private deals that the previous owners had made with favoured employees.

When Pansera decided to establish a total quality management program for IMMI, he produced an employee manual describing the new changes and procedures. Initially, employees resisted this change. Then Pansera discovered that 30 percent of the employees did not know how to read.

To handle this problem, Pansera scrapped the manual. Instead, with the support of the local school board, he started a program to teach literacy and basic mathematics to workers. Pansera spends $200 000 a year on staff training, which he considers to be a worthwhile investment.

Change at IMMI worked for two main reasons. First, Pansera communicated openly with employees. Second, Pansera dealt with employee resistance to change by helping people acquire the skills they needed to engage in change more comfortably. Both of these measures reduced employee resistance to change.

Organizational Resistance to Change

Why do organizations resist change?

Organizations, by their very nature, are conservative and actively resist change.[9] You have probably noticed this if you've ever made a suggestion to someone in an organization about how they might more effectively serve you as a customer or client. Six major sources of organizational resistance have been identified.[10]

STRUCTURAL INERTIA Organizations are structured for stability. Certain types of people are hired, and certain types of people get promoted into senior management positions. Thus, the organization continues to reproduce itself over and over again. When an organization faces change, structural inertia acts as a restraining force to maintain stability.

LIMITED FOCUS OF CHANGE   Organizations, particularly large ones, have a variety of interdependent subsystems. When one department introduces change, it often has an impact on other departments. For instance, the information technology unit may introduce new accounting software, without training everyone in how to use it. From their perspective this is a more effective piece of software, but others are comfortable with the system they've been using. Thus, organizations need to look at the big picture of change, rather than seeing how things are affected in just one of the subsystems.

GROUP INERTIA   Groups develop group norms, and may place pressure on individuals to resist change. For instance, an individual administrative assistant may welcome new changes, but if other administrative assistants in the organization together suggest that the changes are not acceptable, this may cause the individual to resist the change as well in order not to alienate others in the group.

THREAT TO EXPERTISE   When change occurs, those who were previously seen as experts may see that expertise threatened. For instance, information used to be concentrated in the hands of managers, but many organizations make information available more widely throughout the organization. Thus, some employees may develop expertise in certain areas that rivals their manager's expertise.

THREAT TO ESTABLISHED POWER RELATIONSHIPS   Within an organization there is a distribution of power, both between managers and employees, and across departments. Sometimes change can disrupt this power. For instance, the introduction of computer technology throughout the organization can reduce the power of the IT group. Similarly, moves to empower employees may reduce the power of supervisors and middle managers.

THREAT TO ESTABLISHED RESOURCE ALLOCATIONS   Change is viewed as a threat when one's resources might be cut. For instance, the Saturn division at General Motors had its resources significantly reduced when GM decided to invest more in its Oldsmobile division (before eventually closing that division). Saturn employees and management wondered about the fate of their division when their resources were cut.

Overcoming Resistance to Change

Change is not easily introduced in most workplaces, and for it to be successful, managers have to identify obstacles or sources of resistance to change. Managers must analyze the factors that may prevent the company from reaching its ideal future state. Obstacles to change are found at the corporate, divisional, departmental, and individual levels of the organization.

Corporate-level changes in an organization's strategy or structure, even seemingly trivial changes, may significantly affect how divisional and departmental managers behave. Suppose that to compete with low-cost foreign competitors, top managers decide to increase the resources spent on state-of-the-art machinery and reduce the resources spent on marketing or R&D. The power of manufacturing managers would increase, and the power of marketing and R&D managers would fall. This decision would alter the balance of power among departments and might lead to increased politics and conflict as departments start fighting to retain their status in the organization. An organization's present strategy and structure are powerful obstacles to change.

Organizational culture also can facilitate or obstruct change. Organizations with entrepreneurial, flexible cultures, such as high-tech companies, are much easier to change than are organizations with more rigid cultures such as those sometimes found in large bureaucratic organizations like the military or General Motors.

The same obstacles to change exist at the divisional and departmental levels as well. Division managers may differ in their attitudes toward the changes that top managers propose and will resist those changes if their interests and power seem threatened. Managers at all levels usually fight to protect their power and control over resources. Given that departments have different goals and time horizons, they may also react differently to the changes that other managers propose. When top managers are trying to reduce costs, for example, sales managers may resist attempts to cut back on sales expenditures if they believe that problems stem from manufacturing managers' inefficiencies.

At the individual level, too, people are often resistant to change because change brings uncertainty and uncertainty brings stress (see Chapter 11). For example, individuals may resist the introduction of a new technology because they are uncertain about their ability to learn it and effectively use it.

These obstacles make organizational change a slow process. Managers must recognize these potential obstacles to change and take them into consideration. Some obstacles can be overcome by improving communication so all organizational members are aware of the need for change and of the nature of the changes being made. Empowering employees and inviting them to participate in the planning for change also can help overcome resistance and allay employees' fears. In addition, managers can sometimes overcome resistance by using the integrative bargaining strategies discussed in Chapter 16. For example, emphasizing superordinate goals such as organizational effectiveness and gaining a competitive advantage can make organizational members who resist a change realize that the change is ultimately in everyone's best interests because it will increase organizational performance. The larger and more complex an organization is, the more complex is the change process. In the "Management Insight," we take a look at some of the difficulties of change in a unionized work environment.

Management Insight

Conducting Change in a Unionized Environment

When Paul Tellier took over as president and CEO of Montreal-based Canadian National Railway (CN) in the early 1990s, he had to make major changes to the railway. He started by reducing "the number of layers of management and abolished five vice-president posts, so that where formerly there were sometimes 10 layers of authority between the president and any line employee, there are now no more than five."[11] Managers thus had a broader scope of command. Communication was easier, with fewer levels through which messages had to travel.

Not all of the changes that Tellier made were easy, however. CN's unionized employees are represented by the Brotherhood of Maintenance of Way Employees, the International Brotherhood of Electrical Workers, Rail Canada Traffic Controllers, and the Canadian Auto Workers. Tellier recognized the difficulties he would face in convincing the unions that they would need to participate in change: "Managing change is first and foremost influencing mentalities: not the mentality of your customers so that they appreciate what you are trying to do, but the mentality of your employees so that they conform to the realities the customer must face."[12]

One of the mentalities Tellier had to change was the practice of "featherbedding."[13] Because of union contracts, CN was paying wages to 2000 employees whose jobs no longer existed and who therefore did not even report to work. Anyone who had worked at CN for eight years and whose job had disappeared was guaranteed their pay until they turned 65. The union contracts also stated that employees could not be transferred against their will. Therefore, CN was forced to do such things as hire new workers in Edmonton, while employees who were not needed in Moncton refused to move.

CN changed a number of work rules after a 1995 strike. For example, under the new agreement, employees receive 90 percent of their pay for six years, but workers who refuse to be transferred receive only 65 percent of their pay for two years.

Some of the employees are not happy with Tellier's changes. Cliff Hamilton, a CN train engineer, says, "I think it's a crime what's going on. They're taking money out of the pockets of Canadian workers and putting it in the hands of American shareholders." CN has also had some difficulty with the unions. In 1995, CN faced nine days of strikes and lockouts before Ottawa legislated the unions back to work. However, in August 1998, contract negotiations ended successfully without any strikes.

Despite these difficulties, CN has managed a remarkable turnaround while operating in a unionized environment. By March 1998, CN was two years ahead of schedule in efficiency improvements, as measured by its operating ratio (the percentage of each dollar of revenue needed to run the railway).[14] For the third quarter of 1999, CN posted an operating ratio of 71 percent, the best of any major North American railroad for that period. Tellier's structural change program has clearly resulted in a much more profitable railroad operation.

Two consultants who have worked with a number of Canadian organizations in recent years note four essential elements for managing change in a unionized environment:[15]

How can change be managed in a unionized environment?

- *An effective system for resolving day-to-day issues.* Employees should have alternatives to the formal grievance process so that they feel they can be heard easily. If the workplace is open to hearing workers' issues, this will underscore a commitment to participation and empowerment.
- *A jointly administered business education process.* Because union leaders and their members become uneasy about the effects of change on jobs, education can help employees understand the need for change. Making them more aware of company performance helps them better understand the decisions the company makes.
- *A jointly developed strategic vision for the organization.* Giving union members the opportunity to be involved in setting the vision lets them focus on *how* change can be made, rather than *whether* it should be made. The vision "should describe performance expectations, work design, organizational structure, the supply chain, governance, pay and rewards, technology, education and training, operating processes, employee involvement, employment security, and union–management roles and relations."[16]
- *A nontraditional, problem-solving method of negotiating collective agreements.* Managers need to create an atmosphere of tolerance and willingness to listen. Expanding the traditional scope of bargaining to include complex issues such as strategic plans is also helpful. While management resists bargaining over these issues, when they do, it communicates a commitment to working jointly with unionized employees.

Below we consider a variety of ways that organizations can introduce change, by either changing the production process or changing the culture.

Changing the Production System

More often than not, organizations try to achieve change by making changes in their production system. This happens through reengineering, restructuring, and quality programs. Organizations can also change strategies, which is often accomplished through mergers and acquisitions, or selling off parts of the existing organization. John Roth, for instance, accomplished change at Nortel through strategic acquisitions.

The attributes of an organization's outputs—their quality, cost, and features—are determined by the organization's production system.[17] Since an organization's ability to reduce costs and improve quality derives from its **production system**, managers need to devote considerable attention to constantly improving production systems. Managers have adopted many new techniques to improve production in recent years—such as total quality management and just-in-time inventory, discussed in detail later in this chapter.

The total quality management movement, for example, is concerned with designing production systems that produce high-quality outputs, thereby satisfying customer demands for product quality. By paying attention to the production system, managers can improve both quality and efficiency, thus reducing costs, which should satisfy both customers and shareholders (when companies are publicly held).

production system

The system that an organization uses to acquire inputs, convert the inputs into outputs, and dispose of the outputs.

Managing Change by Improving Quality

High-quality products are reliable, dependable, and satisfying; they do the job they were designed for and meet customer requirements.[18] Quality is a concept that can be applied to the products of both manufacturing and service organizations—goods such as a Toyota car or a McDonald's hamburger, or services such as Southwest Airlines flight service or customer service in a bank. Why do managers seek to control and improve the quality of their organization's products?[19] There are two reasons (see Figure 17.2).

First, customers usually prefer a higher-quality product to a lower-quality product. So an organization able to provide, *for the same price*, a product of higher quality than a competitor's product is serving its customers better—it is being more responsive to its customers.

The second reason for trying to boost product quality is that higher product quality can increase efficiency and thereby lower operating costs and boost profits. Many managers in Western companies did not appreciate this relationship until the mid-to-late 1980s. They were operating with the belief, now known to be incorrect, that improving product quality raised operating costs. This belief was based on the (mistaken) assumption that building quality into a product is expensive. By contrast, managers in many Japanese companies had long operated on the

Figure 17.2

The Impact of Increased Quality on Organizational Performance

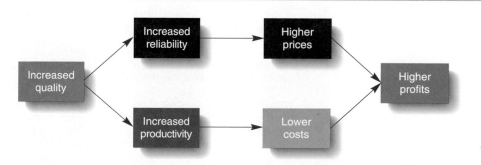

assumption that achieving high product quality lowered operating costs because of the effect of quality on employee productivity: Higher product quality means that less employee time is wasted in making defective products that must be discarded or in providing substandard services, and less time has to be spent in fixing mistakes. This translates into higher employee productivity, which means lower costs.

Total Quality Management

At the forefront of the drive to improve product quality is a technique known as total quality management.[20] **Total quality management (TQM)** focuses on improving the quality of an organization's products and services and stresses that all of an organization's functional activities should be directed toward this goal. Conceived as an organizationwide management program, TQM requires the cooperation of managers in every function of an organization if it is to succeed. The TQM concept was first developed by a number of American consultants, including the late W. Edwards Deming, Joseph Juran, and A.V. Feigenbaum.[21] Originally, these consultants won few converts in the United States but were enthusiastically embraced by the Japanese, who named their premier annual prize for manufacturing excellence after Deming. Deming identified 14 steps that should be part of any TQM program (see Table 17.1).[22]

In essence, to increase quality, Deming urged managers to develop strategic plans that state goals exactly and spell out how they will be achieved. He argued

total quality management A management technique that focuses on improving the quality of an organization's products and services.

TQM Magazine
www.emeraldinsight.com/
tqm.htm

Table 17.1
Deming's 14 Steps to Quality

1. Create constancy of purpose toward improvement of product and service, with the aim to become competitive, to stay in business, and to provide jobs.
2. Adopt the new philosophy. We are in a new economic age. Western management must awaken to the challenge, must learn its responsibilities, and must take on leadership for change.
3. Cease dependence on inspection to achieve quality. Eliminate the need for inspection on a mass basis by building quality into the product from the start.
4. End the practice of awarding business on the basis of price tag. Instead, minimize total cost.
5. Improve constantly and forever the system of production and service, to improve quality and productivity and thus constantly decrease costs.
6. Institute training on the job.
7. Institute leadership. The aim of leadership should be to help people and machines and gadgets do a better job. Leadership of management is in need of an overhaul, as well as leadership of production workers.
8. Drive out fear, so that everyone may work effectively for the company.
9. Break down barriers between departments. People in research, design, sales, and production must work as a team, to foresee problems of production and in use that may be encountered with the product or service.
10. Eliminate slogans, exhortations, and targets for the workforce asking for zero defects and new levels of productivity. Such exhortations only create adversarial relationships. The bulk of the causes of low quality and low productivity belongs to the system and thus lies beyond the power of the workforce.
11. (a) Eliminate work standards on the factory floor. Substitute leadership. (b) Eliminate management by objectives. Eliminate management by numbers, numerical goals. Substitute leadership.
12. (a) Remove barriers that rob the hourly worker of his or her right to pride of workmanship. The responsibility of supervisors must be changed from sheer numbers to quality. (b) Remove barriers that rob people in management and in engineering of their right to pride of workmanship.
13. Institute a vigorous program of education and self-improvement.
14. Put everybody in the company to work to accomplish the transformation. The transformation is everybody's job.

that managers should embrace the philosophy that mistakes, defects, and poor-quality materials are not acceptable and should be eliminated. He suggested that first-line managers be allowed to spend more time working with employees and providing them with the tools they need to do the job. He recommended that management create an environment in which employees will not be afraid to report problems or recommend improvements. He believed that output goals and targets needed to include not only numbers or quotas but also some notion of quality to promote the production of defect-free output. Deming also argued that management has the responsibility to train employees in new skills to keep pace with changes in the workplace. Furthermore, he believed that achieving better quality requires managers to develop organizational values and norms centred on improving quality and that every manager and worker in an organization must commit to the goal of quality.

From the early 1980s, as word of the remarkable production successes resulting from TQM practices spread, many Western managers began implementing TQM within their organizations. In some organizations the results have been nothing short of spectacular. For example, Toronto-based NRI Industries Inc., which takes tires and waste rubber and turns them into parts for the automotive industry, has used TQM to achieve an average of zero defective parts per million (ppm) for four of its five largest customers. Its ppm defects for its fifth-largest customer, DaimlerChrysler AG, is 28, which the company intends to improve even though DaimlerChrysler only requires the ppm defects to be 150. "What's good enough today in the auto business is not good enough tomorrow," says Greg Bavington, vice-president of operations.[23] NRI recently sent 15 of its middle managers to a training course to help them identify additional areas of improvement in their plant. Total quality management has been successfully introduced in both the private sector and the public sector. Private sector Canadian companies using TQM include Longueuil, QC-based Pratt & Whitney Canada, Toronto-based AMP, Markham, ON-based Steelcase Inc., and Cargill Limited. A commitment to TQM brought the province of New Brunswick a balanced budget in 1994. University of Alberta Hospitals and North York, Ontario's school board also successfully introduced TQM programs.[24]

NRI Industries Inc.
www.nriindustries.com/

European
Foundation for
Quality Management
www.efqm.org/

Despite the many TQM success stories, evidence is mounting that there is still a long way to go before Western managers widely accept TQM practices. A 1992 study by the American Quality Foundation found that only 20 percent of US companies regularly review the consequences of quality performance, compared with 70 percent of Japanese companies.[25] A survey of European companies by the European Foundation for Quality Management revealed that only 30 percent of European companies claimed to have adopted TQM practices, and a mere 5 or 10 percent said they were still actively pursuing TQM programs.[26] The European Foundation study also found that many TQM programs fail because of a lack of commitment by managers, who frequently talk up the importance of TQM but do not act on it.

Putting TQM Into Action: The Management Challenge

Given the mixed track record of TQM, what actions can managers take to increase the probability of successful implementation of a TQM program? A recent study of successful and unsuccessful implementations of TQM found that the managerial attitude toward TQM explained much of TQM's success or lack thereof.[27]

Managers who saw TQM as a way to increase the firm's business introduced the most widespread and successful implementations of TQM. Managers whose customers requested TQM, and who therefore focused on the importance of customer needs, introduced less extensive TQM programs. These managers were more likely to introduce TQM in a piecemeal fashion, and sought publicity for having a TQM program but were not fully committed to TQM as an overall business strategy. Workers in these firms were also less likely to see the value of TQM and did not find that it was introduced as a coherent strategy. Managers who were reluctant to introduce TQM and only did it under great pressure from customers had the least successful implementations of TQM.

The study concluded that those firms that introduced TQM as part of their strategic business plan to expand their business were more likely to initiate programs that were quite successful. Implementing TQM to please customers was not necessarily a wise strategic decision, because "if all firms conform to customers' specifications, conformance provides no competitive advantage."[28]

Managing Change by Improving Efficiency

Managers can also increase the efficiency of an organization's production system. The fewer the inputs required to produce a given output, the higher will be the efficiency of the production system. Managers can measure efficiency at the organizational level in two ways. The measure known as *total factor productivity* looks at how well an organization utilizes all of its resources—such as labour, capital, materials, and energy—to produce its outputs. It is expressed in the following equation:

$$\text{Total factor productivity} = \frac{\text{Outputs}}{\text{All inputs}}$$

The problem with total factor productivity is that each input is typically measured in different units: Labour's contribution to producing an output is measured by hours worked; the contribution of materials is measured by the amount consumed (for example, tonnes of iron ore required to make a tonne of steel); the contribution of energy is measured by the units of energy consumed (for example, kilowatt-hours), and so on. To compute total factor productivity, managers must convert all the inputs to a common unit, such as dollars, before they can work the equation.

Though sometimes a useful measure of efficiency overall, total factor productivity obscures the exact contribution of an individual input—such as labour—to the production of a given output. Consequently, most organizations focus on specific measures of efficiency, known as *partial productivity*, that measure the efficiency of an individual unit. For example, the efficiency of labour inputs is expressed as:

$$\text{Labour productivity} = \frac{\text{Outputs}}{\text{Direct labour}}$$

Labour productivity is most commonly used to draw efficiency comparisons between different organizations. For example, a 1994 study found that it took the average Japanese company in the automobile components industry half as many labour hours to produce a component part such as a car seat or exhaust system as the average British company.[29] Thus, the study concluded, Japanese companies use labour more efficiently than British companies.

The management of efficiency is an extremely important issue in most organizations, because increased efficiency lowers production costs, thereby allowing the organization to make a greater profit or to attract more customers by lowering its price. For example, in 1990 the price of the average personal computer sold in Canada was $4000; by 2001 the price was around $1200. This decrease occurred despite the fact that the features of the average personal computer increased during this time period (microprocessors became more powerful; memory increased; communication facilities such as built-in modems were added). Why was the decrease in price possible? The manufacturers of personal computers took several steps to boost their efficiency, which allowed them to lower their costs and prices yet still make a profit. At Compaq Computer, for example, managers redesigned personal computers so that they were easier to assemble; this reduced the time it took to assemble a ProLine desktop computer from 20.85 minutes in 1991 to 10.49 minutes by 1994, a significant increase in efficiency.[30]

Managers can boost efficiency in their organizations by focusing on TQM and a number of other factors.

Total Quality Management and Efficiency

Increased product quality, obtained through the adoption of a TQM program, can have a major positive impact on labour productivity: When quality rises, less employee time is wasted in making defective products that have to be discarded or in fixing defective products. Moreover, a major source of quality improvement can come from designing products that have fewer parts and are therefore relatively easy to assemble. Designing products with fewer parts also cuts down on total assembly time and increases efficiency.[31]

Just-in-Time Inventory and Efficiency

just-in-time inventory system A system in which parts or supplies arrive at an organization when they are needed, not before.

Just-in-time (JIT) inventory systems play a major role in the process of identifying and finding the source of defects in inputs. When an organization has a **just-in-time inventory system**, parts or supplies arrive at the organization when they are needed, not before. This system can be contrasted with a just-in-case view of inventory, which leads an organization to stockpile excess inputs in a warehouse just in case it needs them to meet sudden upturns in demand. Under a JIT inventory system, defective parts enter an organization's production system immediately; they are not warehoused for months before use. This means that defective inputs can be quickly spotted. Managers can then trace the problem to the supply source and fix it before more defective parts are produced. Just-in-time systems were originally developed in Japan during the 1950s and 1960s. As this "Managing Globally" explains, they were developed in an attempt to improve product quality.

Managing Globally

The *Kanban* System in Japan

The Japanese *kanban* system of just-in-time inventory was originally developed at the Toyota Motor Company (www.toyota.com) during the 1950s by a mechanical engineer, Ohno Taiichi. At the time, Taiichi was a middle manager in charge of a Toyota machine shop that produced component parts for Toyota's automobile assembly lines. In developing the *kanban* system, Taiichi was trying to achieve two goals. First, he wanted to reduce the costs associated with stockpiling inventory before it was used in an automobile assembly line. Second, and more important from his perspective, he wanted to improve the quality of Toyota's cars. Taiichi reasoned that achieving these goals required an improvement in the quality of component parts.

At the time, vast numbers of component parts were produced at once and stored in a warehouse until they were needed. Taiichi saw a major problem with this approach: A defective part might not be discovered for weeks or months, when the part was needed in the assembly process. But by that time, it might be too late to determine why the defect had occurred, and correcting the problem that had produced the defect would be difficult. Moreover, if the defect was due to the initial machine settings, the outcome was likely to be the production of large volumes of defective individual parts and enormous waste.

Taiichi decided to experiment with a new production system. Starting in his small machine shop, he developed a simple system of levers and pulleys that allowed him to reduce the time required to set up production machinery from hours to minutes and made the production of small lots of component parts economical. He then produced and sent component parts to the assembly line just as they were needed. The parts travelled from his machine shop to the assembly line in a small wheeled container known as a *kanban*. The assembly-line workers emptied the *kanban* and then sent the container back to Taiichi's machine shop. The return of the *kanban* container was the signal to produce another small batch of component parts, and so the process repeated itself.

Kanban boxes stacked at a Toyota plant ready to be taken to the production line for final assembly.

The system worked beautifully, and Taiichi was able to get rid of most of the warehouse space needed to store inventory. Moreover, the short production runs meant that defects in parts showed up at the assembly line almost immediately, which helped enormously in the process of identifying and eliminating the source of a defect. As a result, Taiichi's machine shop quickly gained a reputation for quality within Toyota.

Over the years, Taiichi was repeatedly promoted for his efforts (when he ended his career in the mid-1980s, he was Toyota's chief engineer) and given the authority to spread his *kanban* innovation, first within Toyota and then to Toyota's suppliers. During the 1970s, other companies in Japan copied Toyota's revolutionary *kanban* system. Much of the subsequent success of Japanese companies globally during the 1980s can be attributed to improvements in product quality brought about by the wide-scale adoption of the *kanban* system in Japan, a full decade before managers in Western companies imitated the idea.[32]

Although JIT systems, such as Toyota's *kanban* system, were originally developed as part of the effort to improve product quality, they have major implications for efficiency. Major cost savings can result from increasing inventory turnover and reducing inventory holding costs, such as warehousing and storage costs and the cost of capital tied up in inventory. Ford's switch to JIT systems in the 1980s, for example, reportedly bought the company a huge one-time saving of $4.65 billion, and inventory-holding costs have been reduced by one-third.

More recently, several service companies have adopted the JIT concept, often with great success. Wal-Mart uses JIT systems to replenish the stock in its stores at least twice a week. Many Wal-Mart stores receive daily deliveries. Wal-Mart's main competitors, Zellers and Sears, typically replenish their stock every two weeks. Wal-Mart can maintain the same service levels as these competitors but at one-fourth the inventory-holding cost, a major source of cost saving. Faster inventory turnover has helped Wal-Mart achieve an efficiency-based competitive advantage in the retailing industry.[33]

One drawback of JIT systems is that they leave an organization without a buffer stock of inventory.[34] Although buffer stocks of inventory can be expensive to store, they can help an organization when it is affected by shortages of inputs brought about by a disruption among suppliers (such as a labour dispute in a key supplier). Moreover, buffer stocks can help an organization respond quickly to increases in customer demand—that is, they can increase an organization's responsiveness to customers.

Because holding a buffer stock of inventory does have advantages, some early adopters of JIT systems have recently pulled back from a complete commitment to JIT.

Kaizen (Continuous Improvement) and Efficiency

kaizen An all-embracing operations management philosophy that emphasizes the need for continuous improvement in the efficiency of an organization's production system.

Kaizen is the Japanese term for an all-embracing operations management philosophy that emphasizes the need for continuous improvement in the efficiency of an organization's production system.[35] Unlike TQM or JIT, *kaizen* is not a specific operations management technique; rather, *kaizen* stresses the contribution to improving efficiency and quality that can come from numerous small, incremental improvements in production processes.

The central principle of *kaizen* is the elimination of waste: wasted materials, piles of excess inventory, time wasted when a production employee makes more moves than are necessary to complete a task because, for example, his or her machine is poorly positioned, and time wasted in activities that do not add value, such as moving parts from one machine to another. (See the discussion of scientific management theory in Chapter 2 for some historical background on these issues.) According to representatives from the Kaizen Institute, a European management consultancy, in the average factory for every second spent adding value by, for example, assembling a product, another 1000 seconds are spent not adding value.[36]

Kaizen Institute
www.kaizen-institute.com/

The *kaizen* philosophy emphasizes that managers and other employees should be taught to critically analyze all aspects of their organization's production system, to identify any sources of waste, and to suggest ways to eliminate waste. Often, self-managed work teams perform this analysis. They take time out once a week or once a month to analyze the design of their jobs and to suggest potential improvements to functional managers.[37]

Increasingly, as part of the *kaizen* process, managers are experimenting with changing facilities layouts to try to increase efficiency. In Ventra's plastics plant, located in Oakville, Ontario and profiled in the "Management Case," the application of *kaizen* resulted in a change in facilities layout that increased the need for a new plant and warehouse space while reducing costs.

The implementation of self-managed teams and facilities layouts, TQM, and JIT are all consistent with the *kaizen* approach: All seek to reduce wasted materials and time. Indeed, these techniques were originally developed by Toyota and other Japanese companies that had adopted the *kaizen* philosophy and were looking for specific ways to improve their production processes.

Process Reengineering and Efficiency

process reengineering The fundamental rethinking and radical redesign of business processes to achieve dramatic improvements in critical measures of performance such as cost, quality, service, and speed.

Think of the major activities of businesses as processes that take one or more kinds of inputs and create an output that is of value to the customer.[38] **Process reengineering** is the fundamental rethinking and radical redesign of business processes to achieve dramatic improvements in critical measures of performance such as cost, quality, service, and speed.[39] Order fulfillment, for example, can be thought of as a business process: Once a customer's order is received (the input), all the activities necessary to process the order are performed, and the ordered goods are delivered to the customer (the output).

Like *kaizen*, process reengineering can boost efficiency because it eliminates the time devoted to activities that do not add value. Unlike *kaizen*, with its emphasis on continuous incremental improvements, process reengineering is about redesigning business processes from scratch. It is concerned with the radical redesign of business processes, not incremental changes in those processes.

University of Waterloo researcher Neil Chandler and graduate student Howard Armitage found that Canadian companies reported higher success rates of completed reengineering projects than those reported by American firms. Of Canadian firms, 94 percent were at least moderately successful, while Ernst & Young's survey of US companies found a success rate of only 54 percent.[40] However, regarding measurable success, the Canadian findings raise some interesting issues. Of the companies that had completed a project, 32 percent experienced increased competitive advantage, 17 percent experienced increased profits, and 18 percent experienced an increase in the quality of their products and/or services. Stock prices increased for only 4 percent of the respondents,[41] suggesting that reengineering efforts do not appear to improve shareholder value. There also have been some notable failures in reengineering. In 1995, after several years and an investment of several million dollars, SaskTel ended its reengineering project due to widespread negative reactions from management and employees alike. Almost half of the 20 employees involved in reengineering took stress leave.[42]

Chandler's study also found that the most significant factor leading to a positive reengineering experience is top management support (78 percent), followed by keeping lines of communication open (44 percent), a strong project management team (41 percent), and appropriate leadership (41 percent).[43]

Tips for Managers

Changing the Production System

1. While managers must seek to improve the customer responsiveness of their organization by improving its production system, they must not offer a product whose cost becomes so high profits suffer.

2. Achieving superior quality and productivity requires the adoption of organizationwide philosophies such as *kaizen* and TQM.

3. Making these techniques work within an organization requires hard work and years of persistence from the managers, and a recognition of the ethical implications of these techniques for affected employees.

Changing Production Systems: Some Remaining Issues

Achieving quality and efficiency often requires a profound shift in management operations and in the culture of an organization. The message of both TQM and *kaizen* for improving operations management in the future is that all employees need to evaluate an organization's production system constantly in an ongoing and never-ending search for improvements. Many reports are appearing in the popular press about widespread disillusionment with TQM, JIT, *kaizen*, and reengineering. It is possible that many of the disillusioned organizations are those that failed to understand that implementing these systems requires a marked shift in organizational culture.[44] We discuss below the difficulties of changing organizational culture. None of these systems is a panacea that can be taken once like a pill to cure industrial ills. Making these techniques work within an organization can pose a significant challenge that calls for hard work and years of persistence by the sponsoring managers.

Managers also need to understand the ethical implications of the adoption of many of the production techniques discussed here. TQM, JIT, *kaizen*, and reengineering can all increase quality, efficiency, and responsiveness to customers, but they may do so at great cost to employees. Employees may see the demands of their job increase as the result of TQM or *kaizen*, or, worse, they may see themselves reengineered out of a job. Consider, for example, the incidents described in this "Ethics in Action."

Ethics in Action

The Human Cost of Improving Productivity

Toyota (www.toyota.com) may be the most productive automobile company in the world, but some of its gains have been achieved at a significant cost to its employees. Take Hisashi Tomiki, the leader of a four-man self-managed team in Toyota's huge Toyota City production plant, 200 miles south of Tokyo, Japan. Tomiki and his team work at a gruelling pace to build cowls (steel chambers onto which windshields and steering columns are attached). Consider this description of Tomiki at work:

In two minutes, Tomiki fits 24 metal pieces into designated slots on three welding machines, runs two large metal sheets through each of the machines (which weld on the parts), and fuses the two sheets together with two spot welds. There is little room for error. Once or twice an hour a mistake is made or a machine sticks, causing the next machine in line to stop. A yellow light flashes. Tomiki runs over. The squad must fix the part and work faster to catch up. A red button halts the production line if the problems are severe, but there is an unspoken rule against pushing it. Only once this day does Tomiki call in a special maintenance worker.[45]

The experience of workers like Tomiki makes many Western workers nervous about the spread of Japanese management techniques and reengineering. Thus, the problems highlighted in the "Ethics in Action" raise serious questions about the introduction of *kaizen* and reengineering: They may constitute a violation of basic ethics, principally because they may require some deception. With regard to *kaizen*, one must ask whether it is ethical to continually increase the demands placed on employees, regardless of the human cost in terms of job stress. It is obvious that the answer is no. Employees are important stakeholders in an organization, and their support is vital if the organization is to function effectively. What are the limits to *kaizen*; what kind of work pressures are legitimate, and what pressures are excessive? There is no clear answer to this question. Ultimately the issue comes down to the judgment of responsible managers acting ethically toward all their stakeholders.

Changing Organizational Culture

How do we change an organization's culture?

An organization's culture signals to employees what behaviour is appropriate, and what is not appropriate. It conveys to members what gets rewarded, what activities should receive particular attention, and even which departments or groups are perceived as more valued than others. Sometimes the organizational culture is what prevents an organization from making necessary changes in the workplace. For example, as previously mentioned, when Paul Tellier took over at Montreal-based Canadian National Railway (CN), he had to deal with a unionized workforce that was quite resistant to change. In fact, the unions had negotiated a practice of "featherbedding," where union members whose jobs had been abolished were still being paid, even though they weren't working. And even if CN had jobs for these employees in other provinces, the employees had the right to refuse a job if they didn't want to move.[46] These practices created great difficulties for Tellier when he first tried to turn CN around.

Organizations that want to move in a new direction must alter policies, structures, behaviours, and beliefs in order to get from how "we've always done it" to how things will be done in the future. Thus even the changes in the production system described above need to be carried out within the context of examining and changing an organization's culture.

Changing an organization's culture is not a trivial task, however, because it means establishing new policies, procedures and reward mechanisms. Individuals are likely to resist change, a topic we discussed earlier in the chapter.

Schein identifies five mechanisms that leaders can use to embed and reinforce an organization's culture.[47] These mechanisms are:

- *Attention.* Those things the leader directs the attention of his employees to (i.e., what is criticized, praised or asked about). These things communicate what the leader and the employee value.
- *Reactions to crises.* The reaction of the leader and managers to crisis conveys to employees the core values of the organization. For instance, when companies face financial difficulties, employees take from the message of downsizing that people don't matter in this organization.
- *Role modelling.* Leaders communicate to employees strong messages about their values through their actions. In other words, actions speak louder than words when employees are trying to determine what the culture of the organization is.
- *Allocation of rewards.* Rewards such as pay increases or promotions signal to employees how one succeeds in the organization.
- *Criteria for selection and dismissal.* The leader's decisions about what kinds of employees to recruit or dismiss sends a signal to all about what kinds of employees are valued.

In order to change the culture of the organization, managers need to look at how they recruit and dismiss, how they reward, what messages are sent from their actions, and what things they bring to employees' attention. Changes in these activities may well result in resistance, but successful change will require the consistent application of new procedures and rewards.

Summary and Review

MANAGING ORGANIZATIONAL CHANGE Managing organizational change is one of managers' most important and difficult tasks. Lewin's Three-Stage Model of Change explains the importance of unfreezing, moving, and refreezing in order to accomplish change.

RESISTANCE TO CHANGE Resistance to change is found at the corporate, divisional, departmental, and individual levels of the organization. Managers must be aware of the sources of change in order to overcome resistance to change.

OVERCOMING RESISTANCE TO CHANGE Change is not easily introduced in most workplaces, and for it to be successful, managers have to identify obstacles or sources of resistance to change. Managers must analyze the factors that may prevent the company from reaching its ideal future state.

CHANGING THE PRODUCTION SYSTEM Since the ability of a company to reduce costs and improve quality derives from its production system, managers need to devote considerable attention to improving production systems constantly. Managers have adopted many new techniques to improve production in recent years—such as total quality management, and just-in-time inventory.

Chapter Summary

MANAGING ORGANIZATIONAL CHANGE

- Assessing the Need for Change
- Lewin's Three-Stage Model of Change

RESISTANCE TO CHANGE

- Individual Resistance to Change

- Organizational Resistance to Change

OVERCOMING RESISTANCE TO CHANGE

CHANGING THE PRODUCTION SYSTEM

MANAGING CHANGE BY IMPROVING QUALITY

- Total Quality Management

- Putting TQM Into Action: The Management Challenge

MANAGING CHANGE BY IMPROVING EFFICIENCY

- Total Quality Management and Efficiency

- Just-in-Time Inventory and Efficiency

- Kaizen (Continuous Improvement) and Efficiency

- Process Reengineering and Efficiency

CHANGING PRODUCTION SYSTEMS: SOME REMAINING ISSUES

CHANGING ORGANIZATIONAL CULTURE

MANAGING CHANGE BY IMPROVING QUALITY Managers seek to improve the quality of their organization's output because doing so enables them to better serve customers, to raise prices, and to lower production costs. Total quality management focuses on improving the quality of an organization's products and services and stresses that all of an organization's operations should be directed toward this goal. Putting TQM into practice requires an organizationwide commitment to TQM, a strong customer focus, finding ways to measure quality, setting quality improvement goals, soliciting input from employees about how to improve product quality, identifying defects and tracing them to their source, introducing just-in-time inventory systems, getting suppliers to adopt TQM practices, designing products for ease of manufacture, and breaking down barriers between functional departments.

MANAGING CHANGE BY IMPROVING EFFICIENCY Improving efficiency requires one or more of the following: the introduction of a TQM program, the introduction of just-in-time inventory systems, the establishment of self-managed work teams, the institutionalization of a *kaizen* philosophy of continuous improvement within the organization, and process reengineering. Top management is responsible for setting the context within which efficiency improvements can take place by, for example, emphasizing the need for a *kaizen* philosophy. Functional-level managers bear prime responsibility for identifying and implementing efficiency-enhancing improvements in production systems.

CHANGING PRODUCTION SYSTEMS: SOME REMAINING ISSUES Achieving quality and efficiency often requires a profound shift in management operations and in the culture of an organization. The changes require that all employees constantly evaluate an organization's production system in an ongoing and never-ending search for improvements. Making these techniques work within an organization can pose a significant challenge that calls for hard work and years of persistence by the sponsoring managers. Managers also need to understand the ethical implications of changing the production system.

CHANGING ORGANIZATIONAL CULTURE An organization's culture signals to employees what behaviour is appropriate, and what is not appropriate. It conveys to members what gets rewarded, what activities should receive particular attention, and even which departments or groups are perceived as more valued than others. Organizations that want to move in a new direction must alter policies, structures, behaviours, and beliefs in order to get from how "we've always done it" to how things will be done in the future. In order to change the culture, managers need to pay attention to the messages they give to employees, be good role models, and make sure that they give appropriate rewards to encourage change.

Management in Action

Topics for Discussion and Action

1. What are the main obstacles to change?

2. Interview a manager about a change effort that he or she was involved in. What issues were involved? What problems were encountered? What was the outcome of the change process?

3. What difficulties do managers face when trying to introduce organizational change? How might they overcome some of these difficulties?

4. What are the main challenges to be overcome in implementing a successful total quality management program?

5. Widespread dissatisfaction with the results of TQM programs has been reported in the popular press. Why do you think TQM programs frequently fail to deliver their promised benefits?

6. What is efficiency, and what are some of the techniques that managers can use to increase it?

7. What, if any, are the ethical limitations to the aggressive implementation of the *kaizen* philosophy of continuous improvement?

Building Management Skills

Managing a Production System

Choose an organization with which you are familiar—one that you have worked in or patronized or one that has received extensive coverage in the popular press. The organization should be involved in only one industry or business. Answer these questions about the organization.

1. What is the output of the organization?

2. Describe the production system that the organization uses to produce this output.

3. Does its production system allow the organization to produce its output efficiently?

4. Try to identify improvements that might be made to the organization's production system to boost the organization's responsiveness to customers, quality, and efficiency.

Small Group Breakout Exercise

Reducing Resistance to Advances in Information Technology

Form groups of three or four people, and appoint one member as the spokesperson who will communicate your findings to the whole class when called on by the instructor. Then discuss the following scenario.

You are a team of managers in charge of information and communications in a large consumer products corporation. Your company has already implemented many advances in information technology. Managers and workers have access to voice mail, e-mail, the Internet, your company's own intranet, and groupware.

Many employees use the new technology, but the resistance of some is causing communication problems. For example, all managers have e-mail addresses and computers in their offices, but some refuse to turn their computers on, let alone send and receive e-mail. These managers feel that they should be able to communicate as they have always done—in person, over the phone, or in writing. Consequently, when managers who are unaware of their preferences send them e-mail messages, those messages are never retrieved.

Moreover, the resistant managers never read company news sent over e-mail. Another example of the resistance that your company is encountering concerns the use of groupware. Members of some work groups do not want to share information with others electronically.

Although you do not want to force people to use the technology, you want them at least to try it and give it a chance. You are meeting today to develop strategies for reducing resistance to the new technologies.

1. One resistant group of employees is made up of top managers. Some of them seem computer-phobic. They have never used, and do not want to start using, personal computers for any purpose, including communication. What steps will you take to get these managers to give their PCs a chance?

2. A second group of resistant employees consists of middle managers. Some middle managers resist using your company's intranet. Although these middle managers do not resist the technology per se and use their PCs for multiple purposes, including communication, they seem to distrust the intranet as a viable way to communicate and get things done. What steps will you take to get these middle managers to take advantage of the intranet?

3. A third group of resistant employees is made up of members of groups and teams who do not want to use the groupware that has been provided to them. You think that the groupware could improve their communication and performance, but they seem to think otherwise. What steps will you take to get these members of groups and teams to start using groupware?

Exploring the World Wide Web

Specific Assignment

Many companies are making major changes in their organizations to increase their effectiveness and gain a competitive advantage. One such company is IBM. Scan IBM's Web site to familiarize yourself with IBM's current initiatives (www.ibm.com/IBM). Click on "Employment," "IBM Workplace," and "Pay Dirt," and read the material provided on each Web page.

1. How would you characterize IBM's approach to change?

2. How does IBM encourage change?

General Assignment

Find the Web site of a company that is making major organizational changes. What are those changes? How are they being implemented? What kinds of obstacles to change do you think managers in this company may be encountering?

ManagementCase

Applying *Kaizen* to Improve Production at Ventra

Oakville, ON-based auto-parts company Ventra Group Inc. started using *kaizen* techniques in 1988.[48] Ventra faced overcapacity problems when it acquired Seeburn, a leading maker of car jacks. Seeburn needed a third plant, but instead, management opted to improve productivity through *kaizen*. Annual sales for Seeburn increased significantly as a result, rising from $45 million in annual sales in 1993, before *kaizen*, to $70 million in 1995.

Buoyed by the success at Seeburn, former president Frank Legate brought more *kaizen* culture to Ventra's Chatham, Ontario plastics plant in 1995, after Ventra lost a big contract to supply Ford's Mustang with tail-light lenses. The loss of the contract represented about 25 percent of the plastic plant's output. Significant layoffs resulted when the contract was lost. "The loss of the

Mustang contract is an incentive to make change to the organization. It highlights to people if we don't do things right, this is what the customer is going to do to us. Our jobs are at risk," noted Legate at the time.

The first major *kaizen* improvement eliminated the need for a costly new warehouse. To do this, hourly workers and management worked together to free up 900 square metres of space in their existing warehouse. Employees attached a red tag to every piece of equipment they felt was not needed to carry out production, and then management acted on their recommendations.

The second *kaizen* activity improved the Chatham plant's layout. Gary Nettleton, the plant's manufacturing manager, notes that this move was done to increase productivity. He estimated that hourly workers wasted about 75 percent of their work time on such things as "getting

presses ready for production runs, moving tools between presses and double handling of material." In other words, workers were preparing to work, rather than working.

Not everything has gone smoothly with Ventra's *kaizen* procedures, however. Plant manager Steve Hackney complained that "the problem is that the plant is 60 percent different on Thursday than Monday. The rate of change is schizophrenic here. There are just too many things to do in a day." Still, Hackney has been accommodating the changes. Some of the hourly workers resist change at all costs; they are referred to as hardliners. Legate doesn't view the hardliners as a problem, however.

"The hardliners are the most valuable. On the face of it, they're the most negative, but their bitches are really suggestions. The trick is to harness those suggestions."

Ventra's *kaizen* methods have had a positive impact on Ventra. For the first six months of fiscal 1999, after its latest round of changes, Ventra reported record revenue and earnings.

Questions

1. What changes did managers at Ventra make to the work system?

2. Why do you think the new work system was successful?

3. What sources of resistance to change were experienced at Ventra?

ManagementCase
In the News

From the Pages of *National Post*
In the Clutches of a Slowdown

It is going to be an uneasy Christmas for Canadian employees of DaimlerChrysler AG's embattled North American unit who must wait until February to hear if they will still have jobs after Chrysler announces its restructuring plan.

In 1924, Walter P. Chrysler made auto history by introducing the Chrysler Six, the world's first affordable car that incorporated four-wheel hydraulic brakes and a high-compression engine that had more power than all other comparable engines. A year later, he established Chrysler Corp., which expanded rapidly, closing the year with about 3000 dealers across the United States and an impressive US$17-million profit.

Since then, Chrysler has had its ups and downs. It managed to maintain growth throughout the Great Depression, for example, despite the cool public reception to the 1934 Airflow—a revolutionary vehicle with a teardrop front designed by Chrysler engineer Carl Breer and Orville Wright, the legendary aviator.

More recently, Lee Iacocca and a government bailout helped the automaker avoid bankruptcy in 1980, when a Middle East oil embargo and competition from fuel-efficient Japanese imports wreaked havoc with North American automakers. Chrysler dodged potential ruin again in the early Nineties by remaking itself as a nimble manufacturer of consumer favourites such as its LH series of sedans and Viper sports car.

Today, however, the North American icon, which merged with Daimler-Benz AG two years ago to create a global automotive powerhouse, faces what some insiders consider the biggest challenge of its rocky 76-year history.

"It's like a corporate version of The Perfect Storm. Too much hit us at once," says one U.S. manager who thinks even a heroic effort by the company's new German management team may not be enough to drive Chrysler out of the ditch.

Now that the U.S. auto bubble has burst, General Motors Corp., Ford Motor Co. and Chrysler are throttling back production to fight bloated inventories. This month, for example, the Big Three have trimmed overtime and idled operations that employ about 20 000 workers at assembly plants in Ontario and Quebec.

Plant shutdowns have a direct impact on the Big Three's earnings because automakers count revenues from new vehicles when they are built, not when they are sold. As a result, each of the Detroit trio has issued earnings warnings for the fourth quarter.

But Chrysler, which generated half of DaimlerChrysler's profits last year, is already deep in the red. The unit is expected to lose about US$1.25-billion in the fourth quarter, twice its US$512-million third-quarter loss, due to the combined effect of high product launch expenditures and stiffer competition in key market segments, which has forced the company, and its rivals, to rely on costly consumer incentives to keep vehicles moving off dealer lots. Although the division is still expected to post a small profit for 2000, next year could be a different story.

"We believe the competitive market environment will continue to intensify and that our underlying financial performance, particularly in the U.S., will reflect this," Juergen Schrempp, DaimlerChrysler chairman, said in a letter to shareholders this week. "Indeed, if the automobile industry, especially in the U.S., becomes weaker in 2001, we will face a year which is even more challenging than 2000."

According to industry watchers, Chrysler's latest financial crisis was set in motion a few years ago when executives of the company that started off with affordability as its goal miscalculated what consumers would pay.

"They really missed the boat three or four years ago," says Dennis DesRosiers, an automotive industry consultant who thinks the management team that generated record profits in the mid-Nineties began to believe their own headlines and let costs escalate.

"They were operating in a 3% to 5% price increase world at a time when consumers were wanting to pay less and less."

Mr. Schrempp also blames Chrysler's former management for the unit's sad state of affairs, which has reduced the value of the once-mighty company to zero in the eyes of shareholders and generated calls to break up the 1998 merger that was once billed as a "marriage made in heaven."

Indeed, Mr. Schrempp was outraged by a series of production cuts announced by Chrysler management in October after he told analysts the division's problems were under control and it would return to profitability in the fourth quarter.

That embarrassment led Mr. Schrempp—who has since admitted he always intended the merger to be a takeover—to take a chainsaw through Chrysler's headquarters last month. In what has been dubbed the Auburn Hills Massacre, James Holden, Chrysler boss, was told to hit the road and take his top sales, administrative and public relations executives along for the ride.

Under the new leadership of Dieter Zetsche, a Mercedes-Benz veteran and Wolfgang Bernhard, chief operating officer, the company is now firmly in the hands of German executives, who are working on a massive restructuring plan expected to be made public in February.

Mr. Schrempp has already laid the groundwork for a huge layoff, stating Chrysler is staffed for a company that owns 20% of the market, not the 14.5% it actually controls. As a result, Mr. Zetsche is expected to slash up to 20 000 jobs and close at least one of Chrysler's 13 assembly operations in Canada and the United States.

Although he says the goal "is to have as little negative impact on people as possible," Mr. Zetsche has warned the company's 125 000 employees to expect "painful" measures next year. He has already temporarily shut down plants for one-week periods to further cut production and ordered suppliers to cough up a 5% price reduction starting on Jan. 1, and find another 10% by 2003.

Mr. Zetsche freely admits the stakes are high for all concerned.

"Every job, including mine," is on the line, he told reporters this week, in his first meeting with media since being put behind the wheel at Chrysler. "And I am up for that."

According to union officials, the best that Canada's 14 000 unionized Chrysler workers can hope for is probably getting away with a few more temporary shutdowns at operations in Windsor and Brampton, Ont., and having overtime shifts "taken out of the production picture."

Industry watchers disagree over the worst-case scenario. But some say Chrysler's commercial van assembly operation in Windsor is high on the list of targets for permanent closure. Company insiders also think the Pillette Road operation, which employs about 2000 workers, is a "likely target to anyone who knows the history of the plant."

Buzz Hargrove, president of the Canadian Auto Workers union, says he would be "shocked" if Chrysler closed any plants, especially the Pillette operation, which is undergoing a $1.5-billion expansion meant to make it "the most versatile manufacturing plant on the face of the Earth."

The union boss thinks Mr. Zetsche is smart enough to take into account that Chrysler's Canadian production has increased from 394 000 units in 1990 to 797 000 last year because Canadian autoworkers are more efficient than their U.S. cousins.

But Mr. Hargrove is nervous because Mr. Zetsche may act in the short-term interest of shareholders or succumb to U.S. union pressure to let Canada feel most of the pain, something he says the Big Three have done before.

Whatever happens, union leaders on both sides of the border say they will not reopen contracts to help cut costs.

Mr. Zetsche, who says there are positive and negative issues associated with doing business in Canada, refuses to guarantee the Pillette plant's future, which now reportedly hinges on the Dodge MAXXcab, a luxury pickup/SUV concept vehicle in need of a home for mass production.

"There is nothing to tell you because no decision has been made," Mr. Zetsche told the Financial Post this week, adding he intends to rethink every dollar spent.

But that is the easy stuff, according to Mike Flynn, director of the Office for the Study of Automotive Transportation at the University of Michigan, who thinks fixing cultural problems will be much harder.

"There were two real problems with the merger right from the start," he says. "The first was that it never was a merger of equals, which made it a bit of a charade .... The second difficulty was that you were taking one of the more hierarchical car companies in the world and trying to integrate it with one of the least hierarchical car companies in the world."

Insiders say employee morale at DaimlerChrysler's head office in Stuttgart, Germany, has improved since Mr. Zetsche replaced Mr. Holden, because the general feeling is that the "overpaid Americans" would "rather play golf" than put in overtime to make the merger work.

But Mr. Zetsche faces serious morale problems in the United States, where angry managers think Daimler took advantage of Chrysler's cash reserves to acquire stakes in Mitsubishi Motors Corp. and Hyundai Motor Co. and then used U.S. executives as scapegoats when market conditions got tough.

According to some estimates, DaimlerChrysler's cash reserves are dwindling fast. Prior to its US$36-billion acquisition by Daimler-Benz in 1998, Chrysler had socked away about US$9-billion to ensure it would not go broke in a weak car market as it nearly did in 1980.

Source: T. Watson, "In the Clutches of a Slowdown: Plant Closures Might Loom in DaimlerChrysler's Future as the Carmaker Tries to Correct Past Management Errors, a Misread of What Consumers Wanted to Drive off the Lot and a Clash of Cultures from its Recent Merger," *Financial Post (National Post)*, December 23, 2000, p. D7.

Questions

1. What are some of the forces for change that DaimlerChrysler has faced over its lifetime?

2. In what ways have employees been involved in the changes at DaimlerChrysler?

3. What does DaimlerChrysler need to do to ensure that its managers and employees remain committed to change?

Integrated
Cases

IntegratedCase

For Wayne Sales, the past is always present. As chief executive of Canadian Tire Corp. since last summer, he can't just denounce everything that happened before he took over because he was among the architects of the retailer's plan to renovate old stores and build new ones.

But in two years that strategy, the legacy of Mr. Sales' predecessor, Steve Bachand, will have run its course. There will be 480 Canadian Tire stores in Canada and no room for any more. That could be a problem because any retailer that doesn't keep growing can wither and die.

The United States beckons, but Canadian Tire tried southern exposure twice in the last 20 years and lost a total of $350-million. As soon as talk turns to such a plan, anyone with institutional memory around head office in Toronto wags a finger and gives a warning.

But why not try again? After all, this is a different Canadian Tire since all those U.S. banners began arriving after the Canada-U.S. Free Trade Agreement was signed. "We withstood everything that North America could throw at us," said Mr. Sales. "Not only have we been survivors, we've grown market share. You have to play your game. It's a horrible mistake when you see some of our competitors try to out-Depot Home Depot, out-Wal-Mart Wal-Mart. This is the thing I love about Canadian Tire. We're so

unique in the marketplace. Canadians understand our format."

And yet after successfully defending itself, Canadian Tire began slipping last year. Mr. Bachand announced his retirement in January and the following month the company took a surprise $58.5-million writedown. "Canadian Tire was put in the penalty box," said Mr. Sales. "The stock was trading at the $29 range and then the day we announced the writedown went to $19. [Analysts] were blindsided and it became a surprise. I don't think it was a reaction to Steve retiring. CEOs retire all the time. For me, it was timing. There's a difference between information versus surprise."

For the next six months, the company conducted a global search before picking Mr. Sales, 50. The Virginia-born Mr. Sales is the third American to head Canadian Tire since Dean Muncaster was fired in 1985. Among those Mr. Sales beat out for the job was Andy Giancamilli, who has since resigned as president and chief operating officer of Kmart Corp., of Troy, Mich. "I came in a very difficult time, trying to refocus earnings momentum and giving it a strategy," said Mr. Sales.

Meanwhile, competition in Canada intensified. In the last five years, 120 big box stores have been built in Canada by Home Depot, Wal-Mart, Revy Home Centres and the rest. Canada has seen proportionately as much big-box growth in

those five years as the United States did in 15.

Under Mr. Sales, some aspects of the past are being de-emphasized. Mr. Sales has put on hold Mr. Bachand's four-year plan to have two hundred PartSource stores. He still likes the stand-alone PartSource outlets because they can capture heavy do-it-yourself auto parts users where Canadian Tire only has 11% of market share and commercially installed parts where Tire has no market share. PartSource also has a defensive advantage in keeping out U.S. retailers such as Auto Zone. "I don't want to send any signal that it is a bad business model," Mr. Sales said. "It is a very profitable business model."

But the capital outlay required is substantial and 50 new PartSource stores would increase annual revenue, now $5.2-billion, by only $100-million. For the time being, Mr. Sales has decided to invest instead in new distribution centres in Montreal and Calgary. (PartSource outlets are unlike Canadian Tire outlets that are owned by independent dealers. Local Canadian Tire dealers own three, the other 25 are franchise operations.) Substantially increased revenue from other sources seems unlikely. E-commerce was begun in 2000, but sales from the 12,000 items available online is difficult to predict.

So, if there are no new stores, where will future revenue growth come from? Mr. Sales has been

meeting with Canadian Tire 's controlling shareholder Martha Billes and the other members of the board of directors, aiming to produce a new strategy by Labour Day. He downplays expectations. "I don't think you're looking at a revolutionary strategic plan. To some, it'll be a yawner."

Canadian Tire went through a similar thought process in the past. In the late 1970s, the company believed it had run out of room east of the Rockies. In 1980, Canadian Tire expanded to British Columbia and lost money for years. In 1982, Canadian Tire bought a bankrupt chain in Texas and lost $250-million before the company bailed out in 1985. In the 1990s, a second, much smaller foray into the Northern Tier states caused a further loss of $100-million.

One thing is certain, Canadian Tire is unlikely to stray from its core business. Before joining Canadian Tire in 1992, Mr. Sales worked at Kmart in the United States for 25 years and has been distressed by Kmart's recent problems after it acquired too many unrelated companies.

Since taking over as chief executive Mr. Sales has replaced two officers, Ralph Trott, senior vice-president, business development, and John Rankin, senior vice-president, dealer relations, both of whom were part of the Bachand regime. He also reorganized the corporate structure into three divisions reporting to him: retail, credit cards and new business.

Mr. Sales is a more political and less prickly chief executive than Mr. Bachand. He will finish what they began together in terms of the building program but whatever the outcome of the strategic planning, three elements are already clear. First, he wants to improve in-store product availability, particularly on advertised specials. More inventory is not the answer; a just-in-time approach is. "There's this misconception that the higher the inventory the lower the out-of-stock position is. There's no correlation. When you have too much inventory you lose some degree of control. If I had one general complaint, on average, inventory is too heavy."

Second, he intends to take Canadian Tire in a new direction, one that permits less individuality among the dealers. To make his point, Mr. Sales cited his own travels in China where he soon grew tired of local food and yearned for the familiarity of a Big Mac. That has become his template for Canadian Tire; he wants every outlet to be as predictable as a McDonald's.

Some dealers are reluctant to cede autonomy. "They're beginning to use the 'm' word, mandatory. We're trying to seek the right balance. They do have a tendency to slow down the process, but in the end, they help you get it right, they help prevent costly mistakes. Customers will choose to shop where they feel they have personal relationships."

As part of the plan, Mr. Sales has targeted the 40 worst dealers. "If you can't make the trip you have to exit the organization," Mr. Sales has told them. "I have a stewardship of this triangle that I take very seriously and how Canadians think about Canadian Tire. The strength of this is limited to the weakest link that we have in the organization."

The third part of the strategy is improved customer service. Surveys found 75% of customers think Canadian Tire is as good as or better than its competitors, but only 19% say Canadian Tire is the best. In response, Mr. Sales has increased in-store staff training and product knowledge. Fifty 30-minute self-teaching courses were already available via the Internet to employees; within 18 months, there will be 250 such programs. "Consumers were confused about what Canadian Tire represented. We must deliver a constant shopping experience in format, pricing and product. We have to become absolutely the best at what customers tell us today we're pretty good at."

Source: R. McQueen, "Canadian Tire at Crossroads, Once Again: Retailer Haunted by Past Attempts at Strategic Growth," *Financial Post* (*National Post*), May 7, 2001, p. C7.

IntegratedCase

From the Pages of *National Post*
Firm Encounters
China Syndrome

When Ray Perez was at business school in Canada in the late 1980s, he dreamed of opening up new consumer markets.

After graduating in 1989, Mr Perez, 33, joined Kooshies Baby Products, the family concern. The Toronto-based enterprise had just launched a range of non-disposable nappies and Mr Perez was soon appointed to run the factory. Convinced of the products' international sales potential, he helped to open up markets in more than 40 countries.

In 1996, with help from the Canadian International Development Agency, Kooshies entered into a joint venture with Diqiu, a Changzhou state-owned enterprise that was famous across China for its dyeing and flannel cotton products. Kooshies had a 51 per cent stake in Changzhou Kooshies Garments. Mr Perez himself took on the task of establishing a factory in China and opening up the Chinese market.

Kooshies' first factory was located in the suburbs of Changzhou, which is in Jiangsu province, around 100 miles inland from Shanghai. It took several months longer than expected to get the plant up and running. "Production has been the least of my problems," says Mr Perez.

Instead, his headaches were caused by the failure of the joint venture set-up, the management team he inherited and the difficulty of selling products to the local market. Neither Mr Perez nor the Shanghai-based consultancy that had recommended Diqiu realised it was on the verge of bankruptcy. Having contributed the plant and supplies of textiles, Diqiu failed to provide the agreed financial investment so Mr Perez was forced to run the business with 40 per cent less operating capital than planned.

The joint venture struggled on for a year before Kooshies bought out Diqiu's stake. For the next year, Mr Perez ran the business as a wholly foreign-owned concern. Unable to access credit locally or from the Canadian operation, he kept Kooshies afloat by stipulating that all distributors had to pay up front in cash.

In retrospect, Mr Perez believes his biggest mistake was taking on a management team from Diqiu. "The state-owned enterprise gave me all the riff-raff, people who had just slept for 10 years", he recalls. When he arrived in Changzhou Mr Perez drew up a list of raw materials to be sourced locally. Diqiu's procurement managers assured him that many of the products were unavailable in China. At first he deferred to their experience but then, on regular trips to Shanghai, began to source the materials himself.

He started to fire the local managers and within two years they had all been replaced, mostly by people under 25. For Mr Perez, they were "people with fresh minds, uncorrupted and much easier to train." It was not easy finding suitable management staff. Few Changzhou residents can speak English, and negotiating through interpreters took longer than Mr Perez had imagined. Finding people with creative talent, such as designers, has also been difficult. It has been harder still to find staff he can trust; information that was supposed to remain secret, such as salesmen's commissions, has often become common knowledge across the business.

Building up domestic sales to just under half of total turnover has been an uphill struggle, says Mr Perez. Around 20m Chinese babies are born each year, but Mr Perez observes that "the figures are a lot more beautiful in theory than in reality".

With severely scaled-back resources, the marketing budget was minimal and Kooshies' promotion relied mainly on Mr Perez and one local assistant. Travelling around China, they managed to place Kooshies products in 200 department stores in 14 provinces within 18 months.

Initially, the company relied on local distributors in each province. Now it also sells direct to some 20 local department stores. This needs a team of sales staff and stores only pay when they have sold the products.

Operating as a wholly foreign-owned concern gave Mr Perez full

control, but he had no support. In August 1999, however, he teamed up with Chen Qiao Yu, the boss of a local private company that makes beach chairs for US retailers such as Wal-Mart. Mr Chen bought a 49 per cent stake in Changzhou Kooshies. Work began immediately on a new factory at Wujing, a small town near Changzhou.

In western markets, Kooshies promotes its products as environmentally friendly. Just 20 of Kooshies non-disposable nappies can replace up to 7,000 disposable nappies. However, the company has had to adapt its marketing strategy in China, a country without an independent green lobby. Environmental benefits are placed behind health and cost.

Kooshies Ultra, which Mr Perez describes as a "revolutionary diaper" made from cotton flannel, has been a poor seller in China. Flannel is Kooshies' main product in 45 countries around the world, including Hong Kong, but in China, "the flannel capital of the world", it is considered an inferior product and the preference is for brushed cotton.

In the venture's early days, business was hindered because Diqiu's contribution had included 100,000 metres of flannel, making it hard to change the product line.

Although hindered by a lack of resources, Kooshies has begun to customise products for the Chinese market. For example, while Canadian customers prefer nappies with a white waistband, Chinese pattern-makers warned Mr Perez that local consumers would associate white with funerals.

Even within China, product markets differ from one province to the next. For instance, popular western designs featuring big animal prints do not sell in most parts of China; people prefer softer traditional baby colours. Guangzhou and Shanghai, though, are more open to western designs.

Source: J. Gamble, "Firm Encounters China Syndrome," *Financial Post* (*National Post*), May 31, 2001, p. C2.

Glossary

A

ACCOMMODATIVE APPROACH
Moderate commitment to social responsibility; willingness to do more than the law requires if asked.

ACHIEVEMENT ORIENTATION
A worldview that values assertiveness, performance, success, and competition.

ADMINISTRATIVE MANAGEMENT
The study of how to create an organizational structure that leads to high efficiency and effectiveness.

ADMINISTRATIVE MODEL
An approach to decision making that explains why decision making is inherently uncertain and risky and why managers usually make satisficing rather than optimum decisions.

AGREEABLENESS The tendency to get along well with other people.

ALDERFER'S ERG THEORY The theory that three universal needs–for existence, relatedness, and growth–constitute a hierarchy of needs and motivate behaviour. Alderfer proposed that needs at more than one level can be motivational at the same time.

AMBIGUOUS INFORMATION
Information that can be interpreted in multiple and often conflicting ways.

ATTITUDE A collection of feelings and beliefs.

AUTHORITY The power to hold people accountable for their actions and to make decisions concerning the use of organizational resources.

B

BARRIERS TO ENTRY Factors that make it difficult and costly for an organization to enter a particular task environment or industry.

BEHAVIOURAL MANAGEMENT
The study of how managers should behave in order to motivate employees and encourage them to perform at high levels and be committed to the achievement of organizational goals.

BIAS The systematic tendency to use information about others in ways that result in inaccurate perceptions.

BOUNDARY SPANNING
Interacting with individuals and groups outside the organization to obtain valuable information from the task and general environments.

BOUNDARYLESS ORGANIZATION
An organization whose members are linked by computers, faxes, computer-aided design systems, and video teleconferencing and who rarely, if ever, see one another face-to-face.

BOUNDED RATIONALITY
Cognitive limitations that constrain one's ability to interpret, process, and act on information.

BRAINSTORMING A group problem-solving technique in which individuals meet face-to-face to generate and debate a wide variety of alternatives from which to make a decision.

BRAND LOYALTY Customers' preference for the products of organizations currently existing in the task environment.

BUREAUCRACY A formal system of organization and administration designed to ensure efficiency and effectiveness.

BUREAUCRATIC CONTROL
Control of behaviour by means of a comprehensive system of rules and standard operating procedures.

BUSINESS-LEVEL PLAN
Divisional managers' decisions pertaining to divisions' long-term goals, overall strategy, and structure.

BUSINESS-LEVEL STRATEGY
A plan that indicates how a division intends to compete against its rivals in an industry.

C

CAFETERIA-STYLE BENEFIT PLAN A plan from which employees can choose the benefits that they want.

CENTRALIZATION The concentration of authority at the top of the managerial hierarchy.

CHARISMATIC LEADER An enthusiastic, self-confident leader able to clearly communicate his or her vision of how good things could be.

CLAN CONTROL Control exerted on individuals and groups in an organization by shared values, norms, standards of behaviour, and expectations.

CLASSICAL DECISION-MAKING MODEL A prescriptive approach to decision making based on the assumption that the decision maker can identify and evaluate all possible alternatives and their consequences and rationally choose the most appropriate course of action.

CLOSED SYSTEM A system that is self-contained and thus not affected

535

by changes that occur in its external environment.

CODES OF ETHICS Formal standards and rules, based on beliefs about right or wrong, that managers can use to help themselves make appropriate decisions with regard to the interests of their stakeholders.

COERCIVE POWER The ability of a manager to punish others.

COLLECTIVE BARGAINING Negotiation between labour unions and managers to resolve conflicts and disputes about issues such as working hours, wages, benefits, working conditions, and job security.

COLLECTIVISM A worldview that values subordination of the individual to the goals of the group and adherence to the principle that people should be judged by their contribution to the group.

COMMAND ECONOMY An economic system in which the government owns all businesses and specifies which and how many goods and services are produced and the prices at which they are sold.

COMMAND GROUP A group composed of subordinates who report to the same supervisor; also called a department or unit.

COMMUNICATION The sharing of information between two or more individuals or groups to reach a common understanding.

COMMUNICATION NETWORKS The pathways along which information flows in groups and teams and throughout the organization.

COMPETITIVE ADVANTAGE The ability of one organization to outperform other organizations because it produces desired goods or services more efficiently and effectively than competitors do.

COMPETITORS Organizations that produce goods and services that are similar to a particular organization's goods and services.

CONCEPTUAL SKILLS The ability to analyze and diagnose a situation and to distinguish between cause and effect.

CONCURRENT CONTROL Control that gives managers immediate feedback on how efficiently inputs are being transformed into outputs so that managers can correct problems as they arise.

CONSCIENTIOUSNESS The tendency to be careful, scrupulous, and persevering.

CONSIDERATION Behaviour indicating that a manager trusts, respects, and cares about subordinates.

CONTINGENCY THEORY The idea that managers' choice of organizational structures and control systems depends on—is contingent on—characteristics of the external environment in which the organization operates.

CONTINUOUS-PROCESS TECHNOLOGY Technology that is almost totally mechanized and is based on the use of automated machines working in sequence and controlled through computers from a central monitoring station.

CONTROL SYSTEMS Formal target-setting, monitoring, evaluation, and feedback systems that provide managers with information about how well the organization's strategy and structure are working.

CONTROLLING Evaluating how well an organization is achieving its goals and taking action to maintain or improve performance; one of the four principal functions of management.

CORPORATE-LEVEL PLAN Top management's decisions pertaining to the organization's mission, overall strategy, and structure.

CORPORATE-LEVEL STRATEGY A plan that indicates in which industries and national markets an organization intends to compete.

CREATIVITY A decision maker's ability to discover original and novel ideas that lead to feasible alternative courses of action.

CROSS-FUNCTIONAL TEAM A group of managers from different departments brought together to perform organizational tasks.

CULTURE SHOCK The feelings of surprise and disorientation that people experience when they do not understand the values, folkways, and mores that guide behaviour in a culture.

CUSTOMERS Individuals and groups that buy the goods and services that an organization produces.

D

DATA Raw, unsummarized, and unanalyzed facts.

DECISION MAKING The process by which managers respond to opportunities and threats by analyzing options and making determinations about specific organizational goals and courses of action.

DECODING Interpreting and trying to make sense of a message.

DEFENSIVE APPROACH Minimal commitment to social responsibility; willingness to do what the law requires and no more.

DELPHI TECHNIQUE A decision-making technique in which group members do not meet face to face, but respond in writing to questions posed by the group leader.

DEMOGRAPHIC FORCES The outcomes of changes in, or changing attitudes toward, the characteristics of a population, such as age, gender, ethnic origin, race, sexual orientation, and social class.

DEPARTMENT A group of people who work together and possess similar skills or use the same knowledge, tools, or techniques to perform their jobs.

DEVELOPMENT Building the knowledge and skills of organizational members so that they will be prepared to take on new responsibilities and challenges.

DEVIL'S ADVOCACY Critical analysis of a preferred alternative, made in response to challenges raised by a group member who, playing the role of devil's advocate, defends unpopular or opposing alternatives for the sake of argument.

DIALECTICAL INQUIRY Critical analysis of two preferred alternatives in order to find an even better alternative for the organization to adopt.

DIFFERENTIATION STRATEGY Distinguishing an organization's products from the products of competitors in dimensions such as product design, quality, or after-sales service.

DISCIPLINE Obedience, energy, application, and other outward marks of respect for a superior's authority.

DISTRIBUTIVE JUSTICE A moral principle calling for the distribution of pay raises, promotions, and other organizational resources to be based on meaningful contributions that individuals have made and not on personal characteristics over which they have no control.

DISTRIBUTIVE NEGOTIATION Adversarial negotiation in which the parties in conflict compete to win the most resources while conceding as little as possible.

DISTRIBUTORS Organizations that help other organizations sell their goods or services to customers.

DIVERSIFICATION Expanding operations into a new business or industry and producing new goods or services.

DIVERSITY Differences among people in age, gender, race, ethnicity, religion, sexual orientation, socio-economic background, and capabilities/disabilities.

DIVISION A business unit that has its own set of managers and functions or departments and competes in a distinct industry.

DIVISION OF LABOUR Splitting the work to be performed into particular tasks and assigning tasks to individual workers.

DIVISIONAL MANAGERS Managers who control the various divisions of an organization.

DIVISIONAL STRUCTURE An organizational structure composed of separate business units within which are the functions that work together to produce a specific product for a specific customer.

DRIVING FORCES Forces that direct behaviour away from the status quo.

E

ECONOMIC FORCES Interest rates, inflation, unemployment, economic growth, and other factors that affect the general health and well-being of a nation or the regional economy of an organization.

ECONOMIES OF SCALE Cost advantages associated with large operations.

EFFECTIVENESS A measure of the appropriateness of the goals an organization is pursuing and of the degree to which the organization achieves those goals.

EFFICIENCY A measure of how well or productively resources are used to achieve a goal.

EMOTION-FOCUSED COPING The actions people take to deal with their stressful feelings and emotions.

EMOTIONAL INTELLIGENCE The ability to understand and manage one's own moods and emotions and the moods and emotions of other people.

EMPOWERMENT Expanding employees' tasks and responsibilities.

ENCODING Translating a message into understandable symbols or language.

ENTROPY The tendency of a system to lose its ability to control itself and thus to dissolve and disintegrate.

ENVIRONMENTAL CHANGE The degree to which forces in the task and general environments change and evolve over time.

EQUITY The justice, impartiality, and fairness to which all organizational members are entitled.

EQUITY THEORY A theory of motivation that focuses on people's perceptions of the fairness of their work outcomes relative to their work inputs.

ESCALATING COMMITMENT A source of cognitive bias resulting from the tendency to commit additional resources to a project even if evidence shows that the project is failing.

ESPRIT DE CORPS Shared feelings of comradeship, enthusiasm, or devotion to a common cause among members of a group.

ETHICAL DECISION A decision that reasonable or typical stakeholders would find acceptable because it aids stakeholders, the organization, or society.

ETHICS Moral principles or beliefs about what is right or wrong.

ETHICS OMBUDSMAN An ethics officer who monitors an organization's practices and procedures to be sure they are ethical.

EXPATRIATE MANAGERS Managers who go abroad to work for a global organization.

EXPECTANCY In expectancy theory, a perception about the extent to which effort will result in a certain level of performance.

EXPECTANCY THEORY The theory that motivation will be high when workers believe that high levels of effort will lead to high performance, and high performance will lead to the attainment of desired outcomes.

EXPERT POWER Power that is based in the special knowledge, skills, and expertise that a leader possesses.

EXPORTING Making products at home and selling them abroad.

EXTERNAL ENVRIONMENT The forces operating outside an organization that affect how the organization functions.

EXTERNAL LOCUS OF CONTROL The tendency to locate responsibility for one's fate within outside forces and to believe that one's own behaviour has little impact on outcomes.

EXTINCTION Curtailing the performance of dysfunctional behaviours by eliminating whatever is reinforcing them.

EXTRINSICALLY MOTIVATED BEHAVIOUR Behaviour that is performed to acquire material or social rewards or to avoid punishment.

EXTROVERSION The tendency to experience positive emotions and moods and to feel good about oneself and the rest of the world.

F

FEEDBACK CONTROL Control that gives managers information about customers' reactions to goods and services so that corrective action can be taken if necessary.

FEEDFORWARD CONTROL Control that allows managers to anticipate problems before they arise.

FILTERING Withholding part of a message out of the mistaken belief that the receiver does not need or will not want the information.

FIRST-LINE MANAGERS Managers who are responsible for the daily supervision of nonmanagerial employees.

FOCUSED DIFFERENTIATION STRATEGY Serving only one segment of the overall market and trying to be the most differentiated organization serving that segment.

FOCUSED LOW-COST STRATEGY Serving only one segment of the overall market and being the lowest-cost organization serving that segment.

FOLKWAYS The routine social conventions of everyday life.

FORMAL APPRAISAL An appraisal conducted at a set time during the year and based on performance dimensions and measures that were specified in advance.

FORMAL GROUP A group that managers establish to achieve organizational goals.

FRANCHISING Selling to a foreign organization the rights to use a brand name and operating know-how in return for a lump-sum payment and a share of the profits.

FREE-MARKET ECONOMY An economic system in which private enterprise controls production, and the interaction of supply and demand determines which and how many goods and services are produced and how much consumers pay for them.

FREE-TRADE DOCTRINE The idea that if each country specializes in the production of the goods and services that it can produce most efficiently, this will make the best use of global resources.

FTAA Free Trade Agreement of the Americas, seen as a logical extension of NAFTA, is intended to remove trade barriers across the Americas from the Arctic Circle to Cape Horn. The agreement is expected to be completed by 2005.

FUNCTION A unit or department in which people have the same skills or use the same resources to perform their jobs.

FUNCTIONAL MANAGERS Managers who supervise the various functions, such as manufacturing, accounting, and sales, within a division.

FUNCTIONAL STRUCTURE An organizational structure composed of all the departments that an organization requires to produce its goods or services.

FUNCTIONAL-LEVEL STRATEGY A plan that indicates how a function intends to achieve its goals.

FUNCTIONAL-LEVEL PLAN Functional managers' decisions pertaining to the goals that functional managers propose to pursue to help the division attain its business-level goals.

G

GATEKEEPING Deciding what information to allow into the organization and what information to keep out.

GATT General Agreement on Tariffs and Trade, signed by a number of countries in 1947 to help reduce trade barriers through lower tariffs. By 1994, 117 countries were party to the agreement.

GENERAL ENVIRONMENT The wide-ranging economic, technological, sociocultural, demographic, political and legal, and global forces that affect an organization and its task environment.

GEOGRAPHIC STRUCTURE An organizational structure in which each region of a country or area of the world is served by a self-contained division.

GLOBAL FORCES Outcomes of changes in international relationships, changes in nations' economic, political, and legal systems, and changes in technology, such as falling trade barriers, the growth of representative democracies, and reliable and instantaneous communication.

GLOBAL ORGANIZATIONS Organizations that operate and compete in more than one country.

GLOBAL OUTSOURCING The purchase of inputs from foreign suppliers, or the production of inputs abroad, to lower production costs and improve product quality or design.

GLOBAL STRATEGY Selling the same standardized product and using the same basic marketing approach in each national market.

GOAL A desired future outcome that an organization strives to achieve.

GOAL-SETTING THEORY A theory that focuses on identifying the types of goals that are most effective in producing high levels of motivation and performance and explaining why goals have these effects.

GRAPEVINE An informal communication network along which unofficial information flows.

GROUP Two or more people who interact with each other to accomplish certain goals or meet certain needs.

GROUP COHESIVENESS The degree to which members are attracted or loyal to a group.

GROUP NORMS Shared guidelines or rules for behaviour that most group members follow.

GROUP ROLE A set of behaviours and tasks that a member of a group is expected to perform because of his or her position in the group.

GROUPTHINK A pattern of faulty and biased decision making that occurs in groups whose members strive for agreement among themselves at the expense of accurately assessing information relevant to a decision.

GROUPWARE Computer software that enables members of groups and teams to share information with each other.

H

HAWTHORNE EFFECT The finding that a manager's behaviour or leadership approach can affect workers' level of performance.

HERZBERG'S MOTIVATOR–HYGIENE THEORY A need theory that distinguishes between motivator needs (related to the nature of the work itself) and hygiene needs (related to the physical and psychological context in which the work is performed). Herzberg proposes that motivator needs must be met in order for motivation and job satisfaction to be high.

HEURISTICS Rules of thumb that simplify decision making.

HIERARCHY OF AUTHORITY An organization's chain of command, specifying the relative authority of each manager.

HOSTILE WORK ENVIRONMENT SEXUAL HARASSMENT Telling lewd jokes, displaying pornography, making sexually oriented remarks about someone's personal appearance, and other sex-related actions that make the work environment unpleasant.

HUMAN RELATIONS MOVEMENT Advocates of the idea that supervisors be behaviourally trained to manage subordinates in ways that elicit their cooperation and increase their productivity.

HUMAN RESOURCE MANAGEMENT Activities that managers engage in to attract and retain employees and to ensure that they perform at a high level and contribute to the accomplishment of organizational goals.

HUMAN RESOURCE PLANNING Activities that managers engage in to forecast their current and future needs for human resources.

HUMAN SKILLS The ability to understand, alter, lead, and control the behaviour of other individuals and groups.

HYBRID STRUCTURE The structure of a large organization that has many divisions and simultaneously uses many different organizational structures.

I

ILLUSION OF CONTROL A source of cognitive bias resulting from the tendency to overestimate one's own ability to control activities and events.

IMPORTING Selling at home products that are made abroad.

INDIVIDUAL ETHICS Personal standards that govern how individuals interact with other people.

INDIVIDUALISM A worldview that values individual freedom and self-expression and adherence to the principle that people should be judged by their individual achievements rather than by their social background.

INDUSTRY LIFE CYCLE The changes that take place in an industry as it goes through the stages of birth, growth, shakeout, maturity, and decline.

INEQUITY Lack of fairness.

INFORMAL APPRAISAL An unscheduled appraisal of ongoing progress and areas for improvement.

INFORMAL GROUP A group that managers or nonmanagerial employees form to help achieve their own goals or meet their own needs.

INFORMAL ORGANIZATION The system of behavioural rules and norms that emerge in a group.

INFORMATION Data that are organized in a meaningful fashion.

INFORMATION DISTORTION Changes in the meaning of a message as the message passes through a series of senders and receivers.

INFORMATION RICHNESS The amount of information that a communication medium can carry and the extent to which the medium enables sender and receiver to reach a common understanding.

INFORMATION SYSTEM A system for acquiring, organizing, storing, manipulating, and transmitting information.

INFORMATION TECHNOLOGY The means by which information is acquired, organized, stored, manipulated, and transmitted.

INITIATING STRUCTURE Behaviour that managers engage in to ensure that work gets done, subordinates perform their jobs acceptably, and the organization is efficient and effective.

INITIATIVE The ability to act on one's own, without direction from a superior.

INNOVATION The process of creating new goods and services or developing better ways to produce or provide goods and services.

INPUT Anything a person contributes to his or her job or organization.

INSTRUMENTAL VALUE A personal conviction about modes of conduct or ways of behaving that an individual seeks to follow.

INSTRUMENTALITY In expectancy theory, a perception about the extent to which performance will result in the attainment of outcomes.

INTEGRATIVE BARGAINING Cooperative negotiation in which the parties in conflict work together to achieve a resolution that is good for them all.

INTERNAL ENVIRONMENT The forces operating within an organization and stemming from the organization's structure and culture.

INTERNAL LOCUS OF CONTROL The tendency to locate responsibility for one's fate within oneself.

INTERNET A global system of computer networks.

INTRANET A companywide system of computer networks.

INTRINSICALLY MOTIVATED BEHAVIOUR Behaviour that is performed for its own sake.

INTUITION Ability to make sound decisions based on one's past experience and immediate feelings about the information at hand.

J

JARGON Specialized language that members of an occupation, group, or organization develop to facilitate communication among themselves.

JOB ANALYSIS Identifying the tasks, duties, and responsibilities that make up a job and the knowledge, skills, and abilities needed to perform the job.

JOB DESIGN The process by which managers decide how to divide tasks into specific jobs.

JOB ENLARGEMENT Increasing the number of different tasks in a given job by changing the division of labour.

JOB ENRICHMENT Increasing the degree of responsibility a worker has over his or her job.

JOB SATISFACTION The collection of feelings and beliefs that managers have about their current jobs.

JOB SIMPLIFICATION Reducing the number of tasks that each worker performs.

JOB SPECIALIZATION The process by which a division of labour occurs as different workers specialize in different tasks over time.

JOINT VENTURE A strategic alliance among two or more companies that agree to establish jointly and share the ownership of a new business.

JUDGMENT Ability to develop a sound opinion based on one's evaluation of the importance of the information at hand.

JUST-IN-TIME INVENTORY SYSTEM A system in which parts or supplies arrive at an organization when they are needed, not before.

K

KAIZEN An all-embracing operations management philosophy that emphasizes the need for continuous improvement in the efficiency of an organization's production system.

L

LABOUR RELATIONS The activities that managers engage in to ensure that they have effective working relationships with the labour

unions that represent their employees' interests.

LATERAL MOVE A job change that entails no major changes in responsibility or authority levels.

LEADER An individual who is able to exert influence over other people to help achieve group or organizational goals.

LEADER–MEMBER RELATIONS The extent to which followers like, trust, and are loyal to their leader; a determinant of how favourable a situation is for leading.

LEADERSHIP The process by which an individual exerts influence over other people and inspires, motivates, and directs their activities to help achieve group or organizational goals.

LEADER SUBSTITUTE Characteristics of subordinates or characteristics of a situation or context that act in place of the influence of a leader and make leadership unnecessary.

LEADING Articulating a clear vision and energizing and enabling organizational members so that they understand the part they play in achieving organizational goals; one of the four principal functions of management.

LEARNING ORGANIZATION An organization in which managers try to maximize the ability of individuals and groups to think and behave creatively and thus maximize the potential for organizational learning to take place.

LEGITIMATE POWER The authority that a manager has by virtue of his or her position in an organization's hierarchy.

LICENSING Allowing a foreign organization to take charge of manufacturing and distributing a product in its country or world region in return for a negotiated fee.

LINE OF AUTHORITY The chain of command extending from the top to the bottom of an organization.

LINGUISTIC STYLE A person's characteristic way of speaking.

LONG-TERM ORIENTATION A worldview that values thrift and persistence in achieving goals.

LOW-COST STRATEGY Driving the organization's costs down below the costs of its rivals.

M

MAINTENANCE ROLES Roles performed by group members to make sure there are good relations amongst group members.

MANAGEMENT The planning, organizing, leading, and controlling of resources to achieve organizational goals effectively and efficiently.

MANAGEMENT BY OBJECTIVES A goal-setting process in which a manager and his or her subordinates negotiate specific goals and objectives for the subordinate to achieve and then periodically evaluate the extent to which the subordinate is achieving those goals.

MANAGEMENT BY WANDERING AROUND A face-to-face communication technique in which a manager walks around a work area and talks informally with employees about issues and concerns.

MANAGEMENT INFORMATION SYSTEM An information system that managers plan and design to provide themselves with the specific information they need.

MANAGEMENT SCIENCE THEORY An approach to management that uses rigorous quantitative techniques to help managers make maximum use of organizational resources.

MANAGER A person who is responsible for supervising the use of an organization's resources to achieve its goals.

MARKET STRUCTURE An organizational structure in which each kind of customer is served by a self-contained division; also called customer structure.

MASLOW'S HIERARCHY OF NEEDS An arrangement of five basic needs that, according to Maslow, motivate behaviour. Maslow proposed that the lowest level of unmet needs is the prime motivator and that only one level of needs is motivational at a time.

MASS-PRODUCTION TECHNOLOGY Technology that is based on the use of automated machines that are programmed to perform the same operations over and over.

MATRIX STRUCTURE An organizational structure that simultaneously groups people and resources by function and by product.

MECHANISTIC STRUCTURE An organizational structure in which authority is centralized, tasks and rules are clearly specified, and employees are closely supervised.

MEDIUM The pathway through which an encoded message is transmitted to a receiver.

MENTOR An experienced member of an organization who provides advice and guidance to a less-experienced worker.

MERIT PAY PLAN A compensation plan that bases pay on performance.

MESSAGE The information that a sender wants to share.

MIDDLE MANAGERS Managers who supervise first-line managers and are responsible for finding the best way to use resources to achieve organizational goals.

MISSION STATEMENT A broad declaration of an organization's purpose that identifies the organization's products and customers and distinguishes the organization from its competitors.

MIXED ECONOMY An economic system in which some sectors of the economy are left to private ownership and free-market mechanisms and others are owned by the government and subject to government planning.

MOOD A feeling or state of mind.

MORES Norms that are considered to be central to the functioning of society and to social life.

MOTIVATION Psychological forces that determine the direction of a person's behaviour in an organization, a person's level of effort, and a person's level of persistence.

MULTIDOMESTIC STRATEGY Customizing products and marketing strategies to specific national conditions.

N

NAFTA The North American Free Trade Agreement, which became effective on January 1, 1994, was designed to abolish the tariffs on 99 percent of the goods traded between Canada, the United States and Mexico by 2004.

NATIONAL CULTURE The set of values that a society considers important and the norms of behaviour that are approved or sanctioned in that society.

NEED A requirement or necessity for survival and well-being.

NEED FOR ACHIEVEMENT The extent to which an individual has a strong desire to perform challenging tasks well and to meet personal standards for excellence.

NEED FOR AFFILIATION The extent to which an individual is concerned about establishing and maintaining good interpersonal relations, being liked, and having other people get along.

NEED FOR POWER The extent to which an individual desires to control or influence others.

NEED THEORIES Theories of motivation that focus on what needs people are trying to satisfy at work and what outcomes will satisfy those needs.

NEEDS ASSESSMENT An assessment of which employees need training or development and what type of skills or knowledge they need to acquire.

NEGATIVE AFFECTIVITY The tendency to experience negative emotions and moods, to feel distressed, and to be critical of oneself and others.

NEGATIVE REINFORCEMENT Eliminating or removing undesired outcomes when people perform organizationally functional behaviours.

NEGOTIATION A method of conflict resolution in which the parties in conflict consider various alternative ways to allocate resources to each other in order to come up with a solution acceptable to them all.

NETWORK STRUCTURE A series of strategic alliances that an organization creates with suppliers, manufacturers, and distributors to produce and market a product.

NOISE Anything that hampers any stage of the communication process.

NOMINAL GROUP TECHNIQUE A decision-making technique in which group members write down ideas and solutions, read their suggestions to the whole group, and discuss and then rank the alternatives.

NONPROGRAMMED DECISION MAKING Nonroutine decision making that occurs in response to unusual, unpredictable opportunities and threats.

NONVERBAL COMMUNICATION The encoding of messages by means of facial expressions, body language, and styles of dress.

NORMS Unwritten rules and informal codes of conduct that prescribe how people should act in particular situations. In an organization, the standards of behaviour and common expectations that control the ways in which individuals and groups in an organization interact with each other and work to achieve organizational goals.

NURTURING ORIENTATION A worldview that values the quality of life, warm personal friendships, and services and care for the weak.

O

OBJECTIVE APPRAISAL An appraisal that is based on facts and is likely to be numerical.

OBSTRUCTIONIST APPROACH Disregard for social responsibility; willingness to engage in and cover up unethical and illegal behaviour.

ON-THE-JOB TRAINING Training that takes place in the work setting as employees perform their job tasks.

OPEN SYSTEM A system that takes in resources from its external environment and converts them into goods and services that are then sent back to that environment for purchase by customers.

OPENNESS TO EXPERIENCE The tendency to be original, have broad interests, be open to a wide range of stimuli, be daring, and take risks.

OPERATING BUDGET A budget that states how managers intend to use organizational resources to achieve organizational goals.

OPTIMUM DECISION The most appropriate decision in light of what managers believe to be the most desirable future consequences for their organization.

ORDER The methodical arrangement of positions to provide the organization with the greatest benefit and to provide employees with career opportunities.

ORGANIC STRUCTURE An organizational structure in which authority is decentralized to middle and first-line managers and tasks and roles are left ambiguous to encourage employees to cooperate and respond quickly to the unexpected.

ORGANIZATIONS Collections of people who work together and coordinate their actions to achieve goals.

ORGANIZATIONAL ARCHITECTURE The organizational structure, control systems, culture, and human resource management system that together

determine how efficiently and effectively organizational resources are used.

ORGANIZATIONAL BEHAVIOUR The study of the factors that have an impact on how individuals and groups respond to and act in organizations.

ORGANIZATIONAL BEHAVIOUR MODIFICATION The systematic application of operant conditioning techniques to promote the performance of organizationally functional behaviours and discourage the performance of dysfunctional behaviours.

ORGANIZATIONAL CITIZENSHIP BEHAVIOURS Behaviours that are not required of organizational members but that contribute to and are necessary for organizational efficiency, effectiveness, and gaining a competitive advantage.

ORGANIZATIONAL COMMITMENT The collection of feelings and beliefs that managers have about their organization as a whole.

ORGANIZATIONAL CONFLICT The discord that arises when the goals, interests, or values of different individuals or groups are incompatible and those individuals or groups block or thwart each other's attempts to achieve their objectives.

ORGANIZATIONAL CULTURE A system of shared meaning, held by organization members, that distinguishes the organization from other organizations.

ORGANIZATIONAL DESIGN The process by which managers make specific organizing choices that result in a particular kind of organizational structure.

ORGANIZATIONAL ENVIRONMENT The set of forces and conditions that operate beyond an organization's boundaries but affect a manager's ability to acquire and utilize resources.

ORGANIZATIONAL LEARNING The process through which managers seek to improve employees' desire and ability to understand and manage the organization and its task environment.

ORGANIZATIONAL PERFORMANCE A measure of how efficiently and effectively a manager uses resources to satisfy customers and achieve organizational goals.

ORGANIZATIONAL POLITICS Activities that managers engage in to increase their power and to use power effectively to achieve their goals and overcome resistance or opposition.

ORGANIZATIONAL SOCIALIZATION The process by which newcomers learn an organization's values and norms and acquire the work behaviours necessary to perform jobs effectively.

ORGANIZATIONAL STAKEHOLDERS Shareholders, employees, customers, suppliers, and others who have an interest, claim, or stake in an organization and in what it does.

ORGANIZATIONAL STRUCTURE A formal system of task and reporting relationships that coordinates and motivates organizational members so that they work together to achieve organizational goals.

ORGANIZING Structuring working relationships in a way that allows organizational members to work together to achieve organizational goals; one of the four principal functions of management.

OUTCOME Anything a person gets from a job or organization.

OUTSOURCING Using outside suppliers and manufacturers to produce goods and services.

OVERPAYMENT INEQUITY Inequity that exists when a person perceives that his or her own outcome/input ratio is greater than the ratio of a referent.

OVERT DISCRIMINATION Knowingly and willingly denying diverse individuals access to opportunities and outcomes in an organization.

P

PATH–GOAL THEORY A contingency model of leadership proposing that leaders can motivate subordinates by identifying their desired outcomes, rewarding them for high performance and the attainment of work goals with these desired outcomes, and clarifying for them the paths leading to attainment of work goals.

PAY LEVEL The relative position of an organization's pay incentives in comparison with those of other organizations in the same industry employing similar kinds of workers.

PAY STRUCTURE The arrangement of jobs into categories that reflect their relative importance to the organization and its goals, levels of skill required, and other characteristics.

PERCEPTION The process through which people select, organize, and interpret what they see, hear, touch, smell, and taste, to give meaning and order to the world around them.

PERFORMANCE APPRAISAL The evaluation of employees' job performance and contributions to their organization.

PERFORMANCE FEEDBACK The process through which managers share performance appraisal information with subordinates, give subordinates an opportunity to reflect on their own performance, and develop, with subordinates, plans for the future.

PERSONALITY TRAITS Enduring tendencies to feel, think, and act in certain ways.

PLANNING Identifying and selecting appropriate goals and courses of action; one of the four principal functions of management.

POLITICAL AND LEGAL FORCES Outcomes of changes in laws and regulations, such as the deregulation of industries, the privatization of organizations, and increased emphasis on environmental protection.

POLITICAL STRATEGIES Tactics that managers use to increase their power and to use power effectively to influence and gain the support of other people while overcoming resistance or opposition.

POOLED TASK INTERDEPENDENCE The task interdependence that exists when group members make separate and independent contributions to group performance.

POSITION POWER The amount of legitimate, reward, and coercive power that a leader has by virtue of his or her position in an organization; a determinant of how favourable a situation is for leading.

POSITIVE REINFORCEMENT Giving people outcomes they desire when they perform organizationally functional behaviours.

POTENTIAL COMPETITORS Organizations that presently are not in a task environment but could enter if they so chose.

POWER DISTANCE The degree to which societies accept the idea that inequalities in the power and well-being of their citizens are due to differences in individuals' physical and intellectual capabilities and heritage.

PRIOR HYPOTHESIS BIAS A cognitive bias resulting from the tendency to base decisions on strong prior beliefs even if evidence shows that those beliefs are wrong.

PRIVATELY HELD ORGANIZATIONS Companies whose shares are not available on the stock exchange but are privately held.

PROACTIVE APPROACH Strong commitment to social responsibility; eagerness to do more than the law requires and to use organizational resources to promote the interests of all organizational stakeholders.

PROBLEM-FOCUSED COPING The actions people take to deal directly with the source of their stress.

PROCEDURAL JUSTICE A moral principle calling for the use of fair procedures to determine how to distribute outcomes to organizational members.

PROCESS REENGINEERING The fundamental rethinking and radical redesign of business processes to achieve dramatic improvements in critical measures of performance such as cost, quality, service, and speed.

PRODUCT STRUCTURE An organizational structure in which each product line or business is handled by a self-contained division.

PRODUCT TEAM STRUCTURE An organizational structure in which employees are permanently assigned to a cross-functional team and report only to the product team manager or to one of his or her direct subordinates.

PRODUCTION BLOCKING A loss of productivity in brainstorming sessions due to the unstructured nature of brainstorming.

PRODUCTION SYSTEM The system that an organization uses to acquire inputs, convert the inputs into outputs, and dispose of the outputs.

PROFESSIONAL ETHICS Standards that govern how members of a profession are to make decisions when the way they should behave is not clear-cut.

PROGRAMMED DECISION MAKING Routine, virtually automatic decision making that follows established rules or guidelines.

PSYCHOLOGICAL CONTRACT An individual's beliefs or perceptions regarding the terms and conditions of an agreement to which that individual is party.

PUBLICLY HELD ORGANIZATIONS Companies whose shares are available on the stock exchange for public trading by brokers/dealers.

PUNISHMENT Administering an undesired or negative consequence when dysfunctional behaviour occurs.

Q

QUID PRO QUO SEXUAL HARASSMENT Asking or forcing an employee to perform sexual favours in exchange for some reward or to avoid negative consequences.

R

REAL-TIME INFORMATION Frequently updated information that reflects current conditions.

REALISTIC JOB PREVIEW An honest assessment of the advantages and disadvantages of a job and organization.

RECEIVER The person or group for which a message is intended.

RECIPROCAL TASK INTERDEPENDENCE The task interdependence that exists when the work performed by each group member is fully dependent on the work performed by other group members.

RECRUITMENT Activities that managers engage in to develop a pool of qualified candidates for open positions.

REFERENT POWER Power that comes from subordinates' and co-workers' respect, admiration, and loyalty.

REINFORCEMENT Anything that causes a given behaviour to be repeated or stopped.

REINFORCEMENT THEORY A motivation theory based on the relationship between a given behaviour and its consequence.

RELATED DIVERSIFICATION Entering a new business or industry to create a competitive advantage in one or more of an organization's existing divisions or businesses.

RELATIONSHIP-ORIENTED LEADERS Leaders whose primary concern is to develop good relationships with their subordinates and to be liked by them.

RELIABILITY The degree to which a tool or test measures the same thing each time it is used.

REPRESENTATIVE DEMOCRACY A political system in which representatives elected by citizens and legally accountable to the electorate form a government whose function is to make decisions on behalf of the electorate.

REPRESENTATIVENESS BIAS A cognitive bias resulting from the tendency to generalize inappropriately from a small sample or from a single vivid event or episode.

REPUTATION The esteem or high repute that individuals or organizations gain when they behave ethically.

RESEARCH AND DEVELOPMENT TEAM A team whose members have the expertise and experience needed to develop new products.

RESOURCES Assets such as people, machinery, raw materials, information, skills, and financial capital.

RESTRAINING FORCES Forces that prevent movement away from the status quo.

RESTRUCTURING Downsizing an organization by eliminating the jobs of large numbers of top, middle, and first-line managers and nonmanagerial employees.

REWARD POWER The ability of a manager to give or withhold tangible and intangible rewards.

RISK The degree of probability that the possible outcomes of a particular course of action will occur.

ROLE The specific tasks that a person is expected to perform because of the position he or she holds in an organization.

ROLE CONFLICT The conflict or friction that occurs when expected behaviours are at odds with each other.

ROLE MAKING Taking the initiative to modify an assigned role by assuming additional responsibilities.

ROLE OVERLOAD The condition of having too many responsibilities and activities to perform.

RULES Formal written instructions that specify actions to be taken under different circumstances to achieve specific goals.

RUMOURS Unofficial pieces of information of interest to organizational members but with no identifiable source.

S

SATISFICING Searching for and choosing an acceptable, or satisfactory, response to problems and opportunities, rather than trying to make the best decision.

SCENARIO PLANNING The generation of multiple forecasts of future conditions followed by an analysis of how to respond effectively to each of those conditions; also called contingency planning.

SCIENTIFIC MANAGEMENT The systematic study of relationships between people and tasks for the purpose of redesigning the work process to increase efficiency.

SELECTION The process that managers use to determine the relative qualifications of job applicants and their potential for performing well in a particular job.

SELF-EFFICACY A person's belief about his or her ability to perform a behaviour successfully.

SELF-ESTEEM The degree to which individuals feel good about themselves and their capabilities.

SELF-MANAGED (OR SELF-DIRECTED) WORK TEAMS Groups of employees who supervise their own activities and monitor the quality of the goods and services they provide.

SELF-REINFORCER Any desired or attractive outcome or reward that a person gives to himself or herself for good performance.

SENDER The person or group wishing to share information.

SEQUENTIAL TASK INTERDEPENDENCE The task interdependence that exists when group members must perform specific tasks in a predetermined order.

SEXUAL HARASSMENT Unwelcome behaviour of a sexual nature in the workplace that negatively affects the work environment or leads to adverse job-related consequences for the employee.

SHORT-TERM ORIENTATION A worldview that values personal stability or happiness and living for the present.

SITUATIONAL LEADERSHIP THEORY (SLT) A contingency model of leadership that focuses on the followers' readiness.

SMALL-BATCH TECHNOLOGY Technology that is used to produce small quantities of customized, one-of a-kind products and is based on the skills of people who work together in small groups.

SOCIAL AUDIT A tool that allows managers to analyze the profitability and social returns of socially responsible actions.

SOCIAL LOAFING The tendency of individuals to put forth less effort when they work in groups than when they work alone.

SOCIAL RESPONSIBILITY A manager's duty or obligation to make decisions that promote the welfare and well-being of stakeholders and society as a whole.

SOCIAL STRUCTURE The arrangement of relationships between individuals and groups in a society.

SOCIAL SUPPORT Emotional support provided by other people such as friends, relatives, and co-workers.

SOCIETAL ETHICS Standards that govern how members of a society are to deal with each other on issues such as fairness, justice, poverty, and the rights of the individual.

SOCIOCULTURAL FORCES Pressures emanating from the social structure of a country or society or from the national culture.

SPAN OF CONTROL The number of subordinates who report directly to a manager.

STANDARD OPERATING PROCEDURES Specific sets of written instructions about how to perform a certain aspect of a task.

STEADY-STATE CAREER A career consisting of the same kind of job during a large part of an individual's work life.

STEREOTYPE Simplistic and often inaccurate beliefs about the typical characteristics of particular groups of people.

STRATEGIC ALLIANCE An agreement in which managers pool or share their organization's resources and know-how with a foreign company, and the two organizations share the rewards and risks of starting a new venture.

STRATEGIC HUMAN RESOURCE MANAGEMENT The process by which managers design the components of a human resource management system to be consistent with each other, with other elements of organizational architecture, and with the organization's strategy and goals.

STRATEGY A cluster of decisions about what goals to pursue, what actions to take, and how to use resources to achieve goals.

STRATEGY FORMULATION Analysis of an organization's current situation followed by the development of strategies to accomplish its mission and achieve its goals.

STRESS A condition that individuals experience when they face important opportunities or threats and are uncertain about their ability to handle or deal with them effectively.

SUBJECTIVE APPRAISAL An appraisal that is based on perceptions of traits, behaviours, or results.

SUPERORDINATE GOALS Goals that all parties in conflict agree to regardless of the source of their conflicts.

SUPPLIERS Individuals and organizations that provide an organization with the input resources that it needs to produce goods and services.

SWOT ANALYSIS A planning exercise in which managers identify organizational strengths (S) and weaknesses (W), and environmental opportunities (O) and threats (T).

SYNERGY Performance gains that result when individuals and departments coordinate their actions.

SYSTEMATIC ERRORS Errors that people make over and over and that result in poor decision making.

T

TARIFF A tax that a government imposes on imported or, occasionally, exported goods.

TASK ENVIRONMENT The set of forces and conditions that originate with suppliers, distributors, customers, and competitors and affect |an organization's ability to obtain inputs and dispose of its outputs, because they influence managers on a daily basis.

TASK FORCE A committee of managers or nonmanagerial employees from various departments or divisions who meet to solve a specific, mutual problem; also called an ad hoc committee.

TASK INTERDEPENDENCE The degree to which the work performed by one member of a group influences the work performed by other members.

TASK STRUCTURE The extent to which the work to be performed is clear-cut so that a leader's subordinates know what needs to be accomplished and how to go about doing it; a determinant of how favourable a situation is for leading.

TASK-ORIENTED LEADERS Leaders whose primary concern is to ensure that subordinates perform at a high level.

TASK-ORIENTED ROLES Roles performed by group members to make sure the task gets done.

TEAM A group whose members work intensely with each other to achieve a specific, common goal or objective.

TECHNICAL SKILLS Job-specific knowledge and techniques that are required to perform an organizational role.

TECHNOLOGICAL FORCES Outcomes of changes in the technology that managers use to design, produce, or distribute goods and services.

TECHNOLOGY The combination of skills and equipment that managers use in the design, production, and distribution of goods and services.

TERMINAL VALUE A personal conviction about lifelong goals or objectives that an individual seeks to achieve.

THEORY X Negative assumptions about workers that lead to the conclusion that a manager's task is to supervise them closely and control their behaviour.

THEORY Y Positive assumptions about workers that lead to the conclusion that a manager's task is to create a work setting that encourages commitment to organizational goals and provides opportunities for workers to be imaginative and to exercise initiative and self-direction.

360-DEGREE APPRAISAL A performance appraisal by peers, subordinates, superiors, and sometimes clients who are in a position to evaluate a manager's performance.

TIME HORIZON The intended duration of a plan.

TOP-DOWN CHANGE Change that is implemented quickly throughout an organization by upper-level managers.

TOP-MANAGEMENT TEAM A group composed of the CEO, the president, and the heads of the most important departments.

TOP MANAGERS Managers who establish organizational goals, decide how departments should interact, and monitor the performance of middle managers.

TOTAL QUALITY MANAGEMENT A management technique that focuses on improving the quality of an organization's products and services.

TOTALITARIAN REGIME A political system in which a single party, individual, or group holds all political power and neither recognizes nor permits opposition.

TRAINING Teaching organizational members how to perform their current jobs and helping them acquire the knowledge and skills they need to be effective performers.

TRANSACTIONAL LEADERSHIP Leaders who guide their subordinates toward expected goals with no expectation of exceeding expected behaviour.

TRANSFORMATIONAL LEADERSHIP Leadership that makes subordinates aware of the importance of their jobs and performance to the organization and aware of their own needs for personal growth and that motivates subordinates to work for the good of the organization.

U

UNCERTAINTY Unpredictability.

UNCERTAINTY AVOIDANCE The degree to which societies are willing to tolerate uncertainty and risk.

UNDERPAYMENT INEQUITY Inequity that exists when a person perceives that his or her own outcome/input ratio is less than the ratio of a referent.

UNETHICAL DECISION A decision that a manager would prefer to disguise or hide from other people because it enables a company or a particular individual to gain at the expense of society or other stakeholders.

UNITY OF COMMAND A reporting relationship in which an employee receives orders from, and reports to, only one superior.

UNITY OF DIRECTION The singleness of purpose that makes possible the creation of one plan of action to guide managers and workers as they use organizational resources.

UNRELATED DIVERSIFICATION Entering a new industry or buying a company in a new industry that is not related in any way to an organization's current businesses or industries.

V

VALENCE In expectancy theory, how desirable each of the outcomes available from a job or organization is to a person.

VALIDITY The degree to which a tool or test measures what it purports to measure.

VALUE SYSTEM The terminal and instrumental values that are guiding principles in an individual's life.

VALUES Ideas about what a society believes to be good, right, desirable, or beautiful.

VERBAL COMMUNICATION The encoding of messages into words, either written or spoken.

VERTICAL INTEGRATION A strategy that allows an organization to create value by producing its own inputs or distributing and selling its own outputs.

VISION STATEMENT A broad declaration of the big picture of the organization and/or a statement of its dreams for the future.

VIRTUAL TEAM A team whose members rarely or never meet face to face and interact by using various forms of information technology such as e-mail, computer networks, telephones, faxes, and video conferences.

W

WHISTLE-BLOWER A person who reports illegal or unethical behaviour.

WHOLLY OWNED FOREIGN SUBSIDIARY Production operations established in a foreign country independent of any local direct involvement.

WTO World Treaty Organization, comprising 125 countries, determines and enforces policies regarding trade among member nations.

Endnotes

Chapter 1

1. "Case in Contrast" is based on C. Cattaneo, "WestJet CEO Fired to Head Off Revolt: WestJet Founder Feared Defections By Key Executives," *Financial Post (National Post)*, September 26, 2000, pp. C1, C2; P. Fitzpatrick, "Morale Uplifted as CEO Departs: WestJet Demands Resignation of Stephen Smith," *Financial Post (National Post)*, September 12, 2000, pp. C1, C11; and P. Verburg, "Prepare for Takeoff," *Canadian Business*, December 25, 2000, pp. 94–96.

2. G.R. Jones, *Organizational Theory* (Reading, MA: Addison-Wesley, 1995).

3. J.P. Campbell, "On the Nature of Organizational Effectiveness," in P.S. Goodman, J.M. Pennings, and Associates, *New Perspectives on Organizational Effectiveness* (San Francisco: Jossey-Bass, 1977).

4. "Management Insight" is based on P. Willcocks, "Yours and Mine? Can the New Owner of the Once-Troubled Myra Falls Copper and Zinc Mine Near Campbell River Forge a New Relationship with Workers and Their Union to Create a True Partnership?" *BC Business Magazine*, September 2000, pp. 114–120.

5. H. Fayol, *General and Industrial Management* (New York: IEEE Press, 1984).

6. P.F. Drucker, *Management Tasks, Responsibilities, and Practices* (New York: Harper and Row, 1974).

7. S. Adams, "Chips are Down for ATI's Diversification: Company Fighting to Maintain Share as Market Slows," *Financial Post (National Post)*, January 26, 2001, p. D3; R. Thompson, "Angry Investors Blast ATI Chiefs Over Stock Slump: Posts US$11.8M Profit. Competing Chip Maker Performing Better, Critics Say," *Financial Post (National Post)*, January 12, 2001, p. C5.

8. G. Dixon, "Clock Ticking for New CEOs," *Globe and Mail*, May 8, 2001.

9. J. Kotter, *The General Managers* (New York: Free Press, 1992).

10. C.P. Hales, "What Do Managers Do? A Critical Review of the Evidence," *Journal of Management Studies*, January 1986, pp. 88–115; A.I. Kraul, P.R. Pedigo, D.D. McKenna, and M.D. Dunnette, "The Role of the Manager: What's Really Important in Different Management Jobs," *Academy of Management Executive*, November 1989, pp. 286–93.

11. A.K. Gupta, "Contingency Perspectives on Strategic Leadership," in D.C. Hambrick (ed.), *The Executive Effect: Concepts and Methods for Studying Top Managers* (Greenwich, CT: JAI Press, 1988), pp. 147–78.

12. D.G. Ancona, "Top Management Teams: Preparing for the Revolution," in J.S. Carroll (ed.), *Applied Social Psychology and Organizational Settings* (Hillsdale, NJ: Erlbaum, 1990); D.C. Hambrick and P.A. Mason, "Upper Echelons: The Organization as a Reflection of its Top Managers," *Academy of Management Journal*, 9, 1984, pp. 193–206.

13. T.A. Mahony, T.H. Jerdee, and S.J. Carroll, "The Jobs of Management," *Industrial Relations*, 4, 1965, pp. 97–110; L. Gomez-Mejia, J. McCann, and R.C. Page, "The Structure of Managerial Behaviours and Rewards," *Industrial Relations*, 24, 1985, pp. 147–54.

14. K. Labich, "Making Over Middle Managers," *Fortune*, May 8, 1989, pp. 58–64.

15. "'Haves & Have-Nots': Canadians Look for Corporate Conscience," *Maclean's*, December 30, 1996/January 6, 1997, pp. 26, 37.

16. "'Haves & Have-Nots': Canadians Look for Corporate Conscience," *Maclean's*, December 30, 1996/January 6, 1997, pp. 26, 37.

17. "'Haves & Have-Nots': Canadians Look for Corporate Conscience," *Maclean's*, December 30, 1996/January 6, 1997, pp. 26, 37.

18. W.F. Cascio, "Downsizing: What Do We Know? What Have We Learned?" *Academy of Management Executive*, 7, 1993, p. 100.

19. T.H. Wagar, "Exploring the Consequences of Workforce Reduction," *Canadian Journal of Administrative Sciences*, December 1998, pp. 300–309.

20. S.R. Parker, T.D. Wall, and P.R. Jackson, "That's Not My Job: Developing Flexible Work Orientations," *Academy of Management Journal*, 40, 1997, pp. 899–929.

21. B. Dumaine, "The New Non-Manager," *Fortune*, February 22, 1993, pp. 80–84.

22. "Management Insight" based on P. Verburg, "Prepare for Takeoff," *Canadian Business*, December 25, 2000, pp. 94–96+.

23. R.H. Guest, "Of Time and the Foreman," *Personnel*, 32, 1955, pp. 478–86.

24. C.W.L. Hill, *Becoming a Manager: Mastery of a New Identity* (Boston: Harvard Business School Press, 1992).

25. H. Mintzberg, "The Manager's Job: Folklore and Fact," *Harvard Business Review*, July–August 1975, pp. 56–62.

26. H. Mintzberg, *The Nature of Managerial Work* (New York: Harper and Row, 1973).

27. H. Mintzberg, *The Nature of Managerial Work* (New York: Harper and Row, 1973).

28. R.L. Katz, "Skills of an Effective Administrator," *Harvard Business Review*, September–October 1974, pp. 90–102.

29. R.L. Katz, "Skills of an Effective Administrator," *Harvard Business Review*, September–October 1974, pp. 90–102.

30. C. Harris, "Prime Numbers: A Statistical Look at the Trends and Issues That Will Dominate Our Future," *The Financial Post*, November 15/17, 1997, p. P13.

31. J.A. Brander, *Government Policy Toward Business*, 3rd edition (Toronto: John Wiley & Sons, 2000), p. 380.

32. D. Jamieson and J. O'Mara, *Managing Workforce 2000: Gaining a Diversity Advantage* (San Francisco: Jossey-Bass, 1991).

33. "Focus on Diversity" is based on "Army Lags Behind Navy, Air Force in Attitudes Toward Women, Minorities: Report," *Canadian Press Newswire*, April 7, 2000.

34. T.H. Cox and S. Blake, "Managing Cultural Diversity: Implications for Organizational Competitiveness," *Academy of Management Executive*, August 1991, pp. 49–52.

35. A. Shama, "Management Under Fire: The Transformation of Management in the Soviet Union and Eastern Europe," *Academy of Management Executive*, 1993, pp. 22–35.

36. "Radio Canada and Montreal La Presse Sign Partnership Agreement," *Canadian Press Newswire*, January 20, 2001.

37. K. Seiders and L.L. Berry, "Service Fairness: What It Is and Why It Matters," *Academy of Management Executive*, 12, 1998, pp. 8–20.

38. "Managing Globally" is based on "Mountain Equipment Co-op Grapples with Human Rights," *The Vancouver Sun*, February 24, 2001, pp. F1, F12 and information at the company's Web site (www.mec.ca).

39. C. Anderson, "Values-Based Management," *Academy of Management Executive*, 11, 1997, pp. 25–46.

40. W.H. Shaw and V. Barry, *Moral Issues in Business*, 6th ed. (Belmont, CA: Wadsworth, 1995); T. Donaldson, *Corporations and Morality* (Englewood Cliffs, NJ: Prentice-Hall, 1982).

41. T. Tedesci, "Nesbitt Burns Procedures Investigated," *The Vancouver Sun*, April 7, 2001, pp. A1, A4; and D. DeCloet, "Industry Owes a Duty of Care," *The Vancouver Sun*, April 7, 2001, pp. D1, D6.

42. "Ethics in Action": How to Destroy a Charity's Reputation is based on "Executive Director of BC Lions Society Resigns Amidst Investigation," *Canadian Press Newswire*, September 20, 2000.

43. D.R. Tobin, *The Knowledge Enabled Organization* (New York: AMACOM, 1998).

44. "Canadian Productivity Rising Because of High Tech Investment, Says Conference Board," *Canadian Press Newswire*, November 30, 2000.

45. "Management Insight" is based on M. Guerriere and T. Kassum, "The Value of Automation: Adding Information Technology to Healthcare Delivery May Be the Key to Surviving a Human Resource Crisis," *Canadian Healthcare Manager*, December 2000, pp. 43–44.

Chapter 2

1. H. Ford, "Progressive Manufacture," *Encyclopedia Britannica*, 13th ed. (New York: Encyclopedia Co., 1926).

2. R. Edwards, *Contested Terrain: The Transformation of the Workplace in the Twentieth Century* (New York: Basic Books, 1979).

3. "Chrysler Takes Lead as Top Producer," *Plant*, October 24, 1994, p. 2.

4. A. Priddel, "Automakers Rejoice: Canadian Vehicle Production Soared 21% in 1999, but Sales Are Expected to Taper Off," *Financial Post (National Post)*, January 7, 2000, p. E7.

5. A. Priddel, "Automakers Rejoice: Canadian Vehicle Production Soared 21% in 1999, but Sales are Expected to Taper Off," *Financial Post (National Post)*, January 7, 2000, p. E7.

6. K. Dorrell, "We're Almost #1: Canada Pulling Ahead of Michigan as Car Production Capital," *Plant*, November 27, 2000, pp. 12–16.

7. A. Smith, *The Wealth of Nations* (London: Penguin, 1982).

8. A. Smith, *The Wealth of Nations* (London: Penguin, 1982), p. 110.

9. J.G. March and H.A. Simon, *Organizations* (New York: Wiley, 1958).

10. F.W. Taylor, *Shop Management* (New York: Harper, 1903); F.W. Taylor, *The Principles of Scientific Management* (New York: Harper, 1911).

11. L.W. Fry, "The Maligned F.W. Taylor: A Reply to His Many Critics," *Academy of Management Review*, 1, 1976, pp. 124–29.

12. J.A. Litterer, *The Emergence of Systematic Management as Shown By the Literature from 1870–1900* (New York: Garland, 1986).

13. H.R. Pollard, *Developments in Management Thought* (New York: Crane, 1974).

14. D. Wren, *The Evolution of Management Thought* (New York: Wiley, 1994), p. 134.

15. R. Edwards, *Contested Terrain: The Transformation of the Workplace in the Twentieth Century* (New York: Basic Books, 1979).

16. J.M. Staudenmaier, Jr., "Henry Ford's Big Flaw," *Invention and Technology*, 10, 1994, pp. 34–44.

17. H. Beynon, *Working for Ford* (London: Penguin, 1975).

18. F.W. Taylor, *The Principles of Scientific Management* (New York: Harper, 1911).

19. F.B. Gilbreth, *Primer of Scientific Management* (New York: Van Nostrand Reinhold, 1912).

20. F.B. Gilbreth, Jr., and E.G. Gilbreth, *Cheaper By the Dozen* (New York: Crowell, 1948).

21. D. Roy, "Efficiency and the Fix: Informal Intergroup Relations in a Piece Work Setting," *American Journal of Sociology*, 60, 1954, pp. 255–66.

22. M. Weber, *From Max Weber: Essays in Sociology*, H.H. Gerth and C.W. Mills (eds.), (New York: Oxford University Press, 1946); M. Weber, *Economy and Society*, G. Roth and C. Wittich (eds.), (Berkeley: University of California Press, 1978).

23. C. Perrow, *Complex Organizations*, 2nd ed. (Glenview IL: Scott, Foresman, 1979).

24. M. Weber, *From Max Weber: Essays in Sociology*, H.H. Gerth and C.W. Mills (eds.), (New York: Oxford University Press, 1946), p. 331.

25. See C. Perrow, *Complex Organizations*, 2nd ed. (Glenview IL: Scott, Foresman, 1979), Ch. 1, for a detailed discussion of these issues.

26. H. Fayol, *General and Industrial Management* (New York: IEEE Press, 1984).

27. "Management Insight" based on J. Beatty, "Women in Pants Can't Answer Telephones at Enquiry B.C.," *The Vancouver Sun*, February 1, 2001.

28. L.D. Parker, "Control in Organizational Life: The Contribution of Mary Parker Follett," *Academy of Management Review*, 9, 1984, pp. 736–45.

29. P. Graham, *M.P. Follett—Prophet of Management: A Celebration of Writings from the 1920s* (Boston: Harvard Business School Press, 1995).

30. M.P. Follett, *Creative Experience* (London: Longmans, 1924).

31. E. Mayo, *The Human Problems of Industrial Civilization* (New York: Macmillan, 1933); F.J. Roethlisberger and W.J. Dickson, *Management and the Worker* (Cambridge, MA: Harvard University Press, 1947).

32. D. Roy, "Banana Time: Job Satisfaction and Informal Interaction," *Human Organization*, 18, 1960, pp. 158–61.

33. For an analysis of the problems in determining cause from effect in the Hawthorne studies and in social settings in general, see A. Carey, "The Hawthorne Studies: A Radical Criticism," *American Sociological Review*, 33, 1967, pp. 403–16.

34. D. McGregor, *The Human Side of Enterprise* (New York: McGraw-Hill, 1960).

35. D. McGregor, *The Human Side of Enterprise* (New York: McGraw-Hill, 1960), p. 48.

36. W.E. Deming, *Out of the Crisis* (Cambridge, MA: MIT Press, 1986).

37. J.D. Thompson, *Organizations in Action* (New York: McGraw-Hill, 1967).

38. D. Katz and R.L. Kahn, *The Social Psychology of Organizations* (New York: Wiley, 1966); J.D. Thompson, *Organizations in Action* (New York: McGraw-Hill, 1967).

39. T. Burns and G.M. Stalker, *The Management of Innovation* (London: Tavistock, 1961); P.R. Lawrence and J.R. Lorsch, *Organization and Environment* (Boston: Graduate School of Business Administration, Harvard University, 1967).

40. T. Burns and G.M. Stalker, *The Management of Innovation* (London: Tavistock, 1961).

41. J. Levine. "Philips' Big Gamble," *Business Week*, August 5, 1991, pp. 34–36.

42. "Philips Fights the Flab," *The Economist*, April 7, 1992, pp. 73–74.

43. C.W.L. Hill and G.R. Jones, *Strategic Management: An Integrated Approach*, 3rd ed. (Boston: Houghton Mifflin, 1995).

Chapter 3

1. C. Cattaneo, "PetroCan Profit Rises Fourfold to $893M: Cash Flow Doubles. Cost Cutting and Strong Crude, Gas Prices Credited," *Financial Post (National Post)*, January 24, 2001, pp. C1, C9.

2. "Market Welcomes Petro-Can," *The Financial Post*, December 23/25, 1995, p. 23.

3. C. Cattaneo, "Petrocan Rids Itself of Pariah Legacy: Once Viewed as a Federal Government Invader, the Firm Is Now Accepted in its Home Town," *Financial Post (National Post)*, November 17, 1999, p. C8.

4. P. Foster, "Hopper's Last Stand Excerpt From Self-Serve: How Petro-Canada Pumped Canadians Dry," *Canadian Business*, September 1993, pp. 56–65.

5. "Petrocan's New Boss Angles for a Sell-Off: Company CEO James Stanford Says State Ownership Scares Off Investors," *Western Report*, October 4, 1993, p. 30.

6. "Petrocan's New Boss Angles for a Sell-Off: Company CEO James Stanford Says State Ownership Scares Off Investors," *Western Report*, October 4, 1993, p. 30.

7. C. Cattaneo, "Petrocan Rids Itself of Pariah Legacy: Once Viewed as a Federal Government Invader, the Firm Is Now Accepted in Its Home Town," *Financial Post (National Post)*, November 17, 1999, p. C8.

8. C. Howes, "Exxon Veteran Takes Petro-Can Helm: Stanford Retiring. No Idea When Ottawa Will Sell Its $1B Stake," *Financial Post (National Post)*, December 18, 1999, pp. D1, D9.

9. C. Cattaneo, "Petrocan Rids Itself of Pariah Legacy: Once Viewed as a Federal Government Invader, the Firm Is Now Accepted in Its Home Town," *Financial Post (National Post)*, November 17, 1999, p. C8.

10. C. Cattaneo, "Petrocan Rids Itself of Pariah Legacy: Once Viewed as a Federal Government Invader, The Firm Is Now Accepted in Its Home Town," *Financial Post (National Post)*, November 17, 1999, p. C8.

11. L.J. Bourgeois, "Strategy and Environment: A Conceptual Integration," *Academy of Management Review*, 5, 1985, pp. 25–39.

12. M.E. Porter, *Competitive Strategy* (New York: Free Press, 1980).

13. M.E. Porter, *Competitive Advantage* (New York: Free Press, 1985).

14. For views on barriers to entry from an economics perspective, see M.E. Porter, *Competitive Strategy* (New York: Free Press, 1980). For the sociological perspective, see J. Pfeffer and G.R. Salancik, *The External Control of Organization: A Resource Dependence Perspective* (New York: Harper and Row, 1978).

15. M.E. Porter, *Competitive Strategy* (New York: Free Press, 1980); J.E. Bain, *Barriers to New Competition* (Cambridge, MA: Harvard University Press, 1956); R.J. Gilbert, "Mobility Barriers and the Value of Incumbency," in R. Schmalensee and R.D. Willig (eds.), *Handbook of Industrial Organization*, vol. 1 (Amsterdam: North Holland, 1989).

16. C.W.L. Hill, "The Computer Industry: The New Industry of Industries," in C.W.L. Hill and G.R. Jones, *Strategic Management: An Integrated Approach*, 3rd ed. (Boston: Houghton Mifflin, 1995).

17. "Management Insight": It's Hard to Get into the Lottery Printing Business is taken from N. Boomer, "Playing to Win," *Canadian Printer*, November 1998, pp. 26–31.

18. J. Schumpeter, *Capitalism, Socialism and Democracy* (London: Macmillan, 1950), p. 68. Also see R.R. Winter and S.G. Winter, *An Evolutionary Theory of Economic Change* (Cambridge, MA: Harvard University Press, 1982).

19. P. Verburg, "The Fight for Your Phone Bill," *Canadian Business*, December 10, 1999, pp. 46–54.

20. Based on information in C. Potter, "Auto Accessory Supplier Slashes Costs, Time to Market," *Design Engineering*, November/December 2000, pp. 17–18.

21. N. Goodman, *An Introduction to Sociology* (New York: HarperCollins, 1991); C. Nakane, *Japanese Society* (Berkeley: University of California Press, 1970).

22. "The War Between the Sexes," *The Economist*, March 5, 1994, pp. 80–81; I. Ip, S. King, and G. Verdier, "Structural Influences on Participation Rates: A Canada–US Comparison," *Canadian Business Economics*, May 1999, pp. 25–41.

23. The Economist, *The Economist Book of Vital World Statistics* (New York: Random House, 1990).

24. For a detailed discussion of the importance of the structure of law as a factor explaining economic change and growth, see D.C. North, *Institutions, Institutional Change and Economic Performance* (Cambridge: Cambridge University Press, 1990).

25. "Management Insight": NB Power Faces Deregulation is based on "NB

Outlines Plans for Energy Competition but Says It's Not Deregulation," *Canadian Press Newswire*, January 30, 2001.

26. P. Verburg, "The Fight For Your Phone Bill," *Canadian Business*, December 10, 1999, pp. 46–54.

27. Chapters Code of Conduct is from Competition Tribunal, as appearing in J. McNish and M. Strauss, "A new Chapter opens in publishing," *The Globe and Mail*, May 15, 2001, pp. B1, B8. The information about the Chapters' settlement can be found on the Competition Tribunal Web site (www.ct-tc.gc.ca/english/welcome.html). The actual decision is located at www.ct-tc.gc.ca/english/cases/ct-2001-003/0031b.pdf.

28. R.B. Reich, *The Work of Nations* (New York: Knopf, 1991).

29. Jagdish Bhagwati, *Protectionism* (Cambridge, MA: MIT Press, 1988).

30. R.B. Duncan, "Characteristics of Organization Environment and Perceived Environment," *Administrative Science Quarterly*, 17, 1972, pp. 313–27.

31. J.S. Adams, "The Structure and Dynamics of Behaviour in Boundary Spanning Roles," in M.D. Dunnette (ed.), *The Handbook of Industrial and Organizational Psychology* (Chicago: Rand McNally, 1976).

32. R.H. Miles, *Macro Organizational Behaviour* (Santa Monica, CA: Goodyear, 1980).

33. For a discussion of sources of organizational inertia, see M.T. Hannan and J. Freeman, "Structural Inertia and Organizational Change," *American Sociological Review*, 49, 1984, pp. 149–64.

34. "Managing Diversity" is based on Canadian Companies Mentor Aboriginal Businesses: C. Petten, "Corporate Mentoring Assists Aboriginal Entrepreneurs," *Windspeaker*, August 2000, p. 16. Courtesy of *Windspeaker*, Canada's National Aboriginal News Source.

35. Not everyone agrees with this assessment. Some argue that organizations and individual managers have little impact on the environment. See M.T. Hannan and J. Freeman, "Structural Inertia and Organizational Change," *American Sociological Review*, 49, 1984, pp. 149–64.

36. "Mr Clean: Nortel Was a Mess When Jean Monty Arrived," *Canadian Business*, June 1996, pp. 59, 61+.

37. D. Olive, "In Beermaking, Two's a Crowd," *Financial Post (National Post)*, January 10, 2001, p. C2.

38. "Sleeman Poised for US Moves After Building Beer Company with Crafty Deals," *Canadian Press Newswire*, December 28, 2000.

39. "Sleeman Poised for US Moves After Building Beer Company with Crafty Deals," *Canadian Press Newswire*, December 28, 2000.

40. "Sleeman Poised for US Moves After Building Beer Company with Crafty Deals," *Canadian Press Newswire*, December 28, 2000.

41. "Smaller Brewers Want to Face Smaller Excise Tax Than Labatt and Molson," *Canadian Press Newswire*, September 19, 2000.

42. "Smaller Brewers Want to Face Smaller Excise Tax Than Labatt and Molson," *Canadian Press Newswire*, September 19, 2000.

43. "Smaller Brewers Want to Face Smaller Excise Tax Than Labatt and Molson," *Canadian Press Newswire*, September 19, 2000.

Chapter 4

1. J. Kirby, "From S to XXXL: Montreal Brothers Glenn and Greg Chamandy Left Behind the Kid's Clothing Small Time to Become T-Shirt Kings," *Canadian Business*, December 25, 2000, pp. 100–102+.

2. R. Gibbens, "Gildan Aims to Drive T-Shirt Sales Over $1B: Strategy Being Developed. Company Helped Knock Off Competitor Fruit of the Loom," *Financial Post (National Post)*, May 12, 2000, p. C4.

3. J. Kirby, "From S to XXXL: Montreal Brothers Glenn and Greg Chamandy Left Behind the Kid's Clothing Small Time to Become T-Shirt Kings," *Canadian Business*, December 25, 2000, pp. 100–102+.

4. D. Weimer, "A Killing in the Caymans?" *Business Week*, May 11, 1998, p. 50.

5. B. Copple, "Losing Their Shorts," *Forbes*, October 2, 2000, p. 60.

6. J. Kirby, "From S to XXXL: Montreal Brothers Glenn and Greg Chamandy Left Behind the Kid's Clothing Small Time to Become T-Shirt Kings," *Canadian Business*, December 25, 2000, pp. 100–102+.

7. J. Bhagwati, *Protectionism* (Cambridge, MA: MIT Press, 1988).

8. For a summary of these theories, see P. Krugman and M. Obstfeld, *International Economics: Theory and Policy* (New York: HarperCollins, 1991).
Also see C.W.L. Hill, *International Business* (Homewood, IL: Irwin, 1997), Chapter 4.

9. J. Brander, *Government Policy Toward Business*, 3rd edition (Toronto: John Wiley & Sons Canada), 2000.

10. C.A. Bartlett and S. Ghoshal, *Managing Across Borders* (Boston: Harvard Business School Press, 1989).

11. C. Arnst and G. Edmondson, "The Global Free For All," *Business Week*, September 26, 1994, pp. 118–26.

12. M. Jimenez, "Free Trade a Boon to Mexico: Fox," *National Post*, April 20, 2001, p. A14.

13. J. Brander, *Government Policy Toward Business*, 3rd edition. (Toronto: John Wiley & Sons Canada), 2000.

14. R. Dore, *Taking Japan Seriously: A Confusion Perspective on Leading Economic Issues* (Stanford, CA: Stanford University Press, 1987).

15. "Boeing's Worldwide Supplier Network," *Seattle Post-Intelligence*, April 9, 1994, p. 13.

16. P. Fitzpatrick, "Aerospace Industry Sees Silver Lining in Asian Crisis," *The Financial Post Daily*, January 23, 1998, p. 5.

17. I. Metthee, "Playing a Large Part," *Seattle Post-Intelligence*, April 9, 1994, p. 13.

18. "Managing Globally": Spectramind Phones You from New Delhi is based on D. McElroy, "Workers Know the Score," *Financial Post (National Post)*, May 28, 2001, p. C16.

19. W. Dawkins, "Revolution in Toyland," *Financial Times*, April 8, 1993, p. 9

20. T. Levitt, "The Globalization of Markets," *Harvard Business Review*, May–June 1983, pp. 92–102.

21. T. Deveny et al., "McWorld?" *Business Week*, October 13, 1986, pp. 78–86.

22. R. Wesson, *Modern Government–Democracy and Authoritarianism*, 2nd ed. (Englewood Cliffs, NJ: Prentice-Hall, 1992).

23. Nobel Prize-winning economist Douglas North makes this argument. See D.C. North, *Institutions, Institutional Change, and Economic Performance* (Cambridge: Cambridge University Press, 1990).

24. For an accessible discussion of the reasons for this, see M. Friedman and R. Friedman, *Free to Choose* (London: Penguin Books, 1990).

25. "Managing Globally": Coolbrands Takes Ice Cream to North Korea is based on O. Bertin, "Ice Cream Firm Warms to North Korea," *The Globe and Mail*, May 24, 2001, p. B7; P. Brieger, "Frozen Yogurt Crosses the DMZ," *Financial Post (National Post)*, July 20, 2001.

26. P.M. Sweezy and H. Magdoff, *The Dynamics of US Capitalism* (New York: Monthly Review Press, 1972).

27. The ideology is that of individualism, which dates back to Adam Smith, John Stuart Mill, and the like. See H.W. Spiegel, *The Growth of Economic Thought* (Durham, NC: Duke University Press, 1991).

28. P. Hofheinz, "Yes, You Can Win in Eastern Europe," *Fortune*, May 16, 1994, pp. 110–12.

29. T. Walker, "Crucial Stage of the Reform Program," *Financial Times*, November 18, 1993, sec. 3, p. 1.

30. M. Magnier, "Chiquita Bets Czechoslovakia Can Produce Banana Bonanza," *Journal of Commerce*, August 29, 1991, pp. 1, 3.

31. E.B. Tylor, *Primitive Culture* (London: Murray, 1871).

32. For details on the forces that shape culture, see C.W.L. Hill, *International Business* (Homewood, IL: Irwin, 1997), Chapter 2.

33. G. Hofstede, B. Neuijen, D.D. Ohayv, and G. Sanders, "Measuring Organizational Cultures: A Qualitative and Quantitative Study Across Twenty Cases," *Administrative Science Quarterly*, 35, 1990, pp. 286–316.

34. R. Bellah, *Habits of the Heart: Individualism and Commitment in American Life* (Berkeley: University of California Press, 1985).

35. G. Hofstede, "The Cultural Relativity of Organizational Practices and Theories," *Journal of International Business Studies*, Fall 1983, pp. 75–89.

36. G. Hofstede, B. Neuijen, D.D. Ohayv, and G. Sanders, "Measuring Organizational Cultures: A Qualitative and Quantitative Study Across Twenty Cases," *Administrative Science Quarterly*, 35, 1990, pp. 286–316.

37. R.E. Caves, *Multinational Enterprise and Economic Analysis* (Cambridge: Cambridge University Press, 1982).

38. B. Kogut, "Joint Ventures: Theoretical and Empirical Perspectives," *Strategic Management Journal*, 9, 1988, pp. 319–33.

39. "Managing Globally": How Scotiabank Moved to Latin America is based on "Scotiabank's Latin America Strategy Questioned," *Canadian Press Newswire*, April 13, 1999.

40. B. Marotte, "Banks Advised to Look to US," *The Globe and Mail*, May 15, 2001, p. B9.

41. K. Dorrell, "We're Almost #1: Canada Pulling Ahead of Michigan as Car Production Capital," *Plant*, November 27, 2000, pp. 12–16.

42. N. Hood and S. Young, *The Economics of the Multinational Enterprise* (London: Longman, 1979).

43. J. Bhagwati, *Protectionism* (Cambridge, MA: MIT Press, 1988).

44. M. Jimenez, "Free Trade a Boon to Mexico: Fox," *National Post*, April 20, 2001, p. A14.

45. "Free Trade or Foul," *The Economist*, June 4, 1994, p. 70. Also see P. Krugman and M. Obstfeld, *International Economics: Theory and Policy* (New York: HarperCollins, 1991).

46. "Ethics in Action": Maiwa Handprints Pays Third World Artisans More is based on A. Daniels, "Textile Importer Defends Artisans' Rights," *Vancouver Sun*, May 1, 2000, pp. C8, C10; *Maiwa: A Quiet Manifesto for the Preservation of Craft* (Vancouver: Maiwa, 2001); http://www.ethicsinaction.com/nominations/bcnominees.html#ongoingindividualbc); and http://www.maiwa.com/.

Chapter 5

1. N. Ramage, "Honesty Wins the Day: A Case Study in Effective Media Relations," *Marketing*, September 25, 2000, p. 7.

2. E. Gibbs, "Bridgestone Vows to Restore Battered Firestone Brand: President Apologizes. Plans to Overhaul US Subsidiary by End of the Year," *Financial Post (National Post)*, September 12, 2000, p. C13.

3. C.W. Wolf, "Bridgestone Has No Plans to Expand Tire Recall: Blames Ford for Crashes. Says Deficiencies in Explorer Caused Many Fatalities," *Financial Post (National Post)*, September 13, 2000, p. C11.

4. "Massive Tire Recall Sends Bridgestone Profits Skidding: Down 80%," *Financial Post (National Post)*, February 23, 2001, p. C10.

5. A. Harney, "Bridgestone Boss to Quit: Denies Move Related to Firestone Tire Recall in the US," *Financial Post (National Post)*, January 12, 2001, p. C10.

6. M. Ellis, "North American Slump Leads to Ford Earnings Slide: 33% Drop in Fourth Quarter. Sales Revenue For Canadian Operations Declines 5.7%," *Financial Post (National Post)*, January 19, 2001, p. C13.

7. "Ford Canada Posts Higher Sales Despite Bridgestone/Firestone Tire Scandal," *Canadian Press Newswire*, October 3, 2000.

8. J.A. Pearce, "The Company Mission as a Strategic Tool," *Sloan Management Review*, Spring 1982, pp. 15–24.

9. C.I. Barnard, *The Functions of the Executive* (Cambridge, MA: Harvard University Press, 1948).

10. R.E. Freeman, *Strategic Management: A Stakeholder Approach* (Marshfield, MA: Pitman, 1984).

11. T. Tedesco and S. Rubin, "FPI Plunges into Proxy War," *Financial Post (National Post)*, April 21, 2001, pp. D1, D6.

12. A. Stevens, "Boss's Brain Teaser: Accommodating Depressed Worker," *Wall Street Journal*, September 11, 1995, p. B1.

13. T.L. Beauchamp and N.E. Bowie (eds.), *Ethical Theory and Business* (Englewood Cliffs, NJ: Prentice-Hall, 1979); A. Macintyre, *After Virtue* (South Bend, IN: University of Notre Dame Press, 1981).

14. R.E. Goodin, "How to Determine Who Should Get What," *Ethics*, July 1975, pp. 310–21.

15. T.M. Jones, "Ethical Decision Making by Individuals in Organizations: An Issue Contingent Model," *Academy of Management Journal*, 16, 1991, pp. 366–95; G.F. Cavanaugh, D.J. Moberg, and M. Velasquez, "The Ethics of Organizational Politics," *Academy of Management Review*, 6, 1981, pp. 363–74.

16. L.K. Trevino, "Ethical Decision Making in Organizations: A Person–Situation Interactionist Model,"

Academy of Management Review, 11, 1986, pp. 601–17; W.H. Shaw and V. Barry, *Moral Issues in Business*, 6th ed. (Belmont, CA: Wadsworth, 1995).

17. A.S. Waterman, "On the Uses of Psychological Theory and Research in the Process of Ethical Inquiry," *Psychological Bulletin*, 103, no. 3, 1988, pp. 283–98.

18. www.shell.ca/code/values/ethics/ethics.html

19. "Corruption Still Tainting Asian Financial Picture, Study Says," *The Vancouver Sun*, March 20, 2001, p. D18.

20. "Canadian Firms Ink New Ethics Code [For International Operations]," *Plant*, October 6, 1997, p. 4.

21. C. Cattaneo, "Lingering Sudan Effect Likely to Tarnish Talisman," *Financial Post (National Post)*, February 24, 2000, pp. D1, D3.

22. "Talisman Shares Jump in Wake of Sudan Report," *Financial Post (National Post)*, February 16, 2000, p. C3.

23. C. Harrington, "Talisman Says Peacemaking Is the Business of Governments, Not Business," *Canadian Press Newswire*, February 17, 2000.

24. C. Harrington, "Talisman Says Peacemaking Is the Business of Governments, Not Business," *Canadian Press Newswire*, February 17, 2000.

25. M.S. Frankel, "Professional Codes: Why, How, and With What Impact?" *Ethics*, 8, 1989, pp. 109–15.

26. J. Van Maanen and S.R. Barley, "Occupational Communities: Culture and Control in Organizations," in B. Staw and L. Cummings (eds.), *Research in Organizational Behaviour*, vol. 6 (Greenwich, CT: JAI Press, 1984), pp. 287–365.

27. "Ethics in Action": How to Make Profits and Harm Clients is based on T. Tedesco, "Broker Shielded From Firing," *Financial Post (National Post)*, April 10, 2001, pp. C1, C10; D. DeCloet, "Punished Broker Acted as an Advisor to Watchdog," *Financial Post (National Post)*, May 16, 2001, p. C4.

28. T.M. Jones, "Ethical Decision Making by Individuals in Organizations: An Issue Contingent Model," *Academy of Management Journal*, 16, 1991, pp. 366–95.

29. J.R. Rest, *Moral Development: Advances in Research and Theory* (New York: Praeger, 1986).

30. "When It Comes to Ethics, Canadian Companies Are All Talk and Little Action, a Survey Shows," *Canadian Press Newswire*, February 17, 2000.

31. B. Victor and J.B. Cullen, "The Organizational Bases of Ethical Work Climates," *Administrative Science Quarterly*, 33, 1988, pp. 101–25.

32. H. Demsetz, "Towards a Theory of Property Rights," *American Economic Review*, 57, 1967, pp. 347–59.

33. K.M. Grace, "The Last Chapter Isn't Written: Misfortunes of Book Discounters Give Hope to Canada's Battered Independents," *Report Newsmagazine*, November 20, 2000, pp. 32–33.

34. L. McKnight, "Will the Sky Fall? Publishers Worry About Chapters' Survival," *Maclean's*, August 14, 2000, p. 33.

35. D. Hasselback, "BC Hydro Overcharging California Utilities, Report Says," *Financial Post (National Post)*, April 12, 2001, p. C4.

36. D. Baines, "BC Hydro Unit Cited for Blame in California's Electricity Crisis," *The Vancouver Sun*, April 12, 2001, pp. F1, F5.

37. D. Collins, "Organizational Harm, Legal Consequences and Stakeholder Retaliation," *Journal of Business Ethics*, 8, 1988, pp. 1–13.

38. S.W. Gellerman, "Why Good Managers Make Bad Decisions," in K.R. Andrews (ed.), *Ethics in Practice: Managing the Moral Corporation* (Boston: Harvard Business School Press, 1989).

39. L.K. Trevino, "Ethical Decision Making in Organizations," *Academy of Management Review*, 11, 1986, pp. 601–17.

40. M.S. Baucus and J.P. Near, "Can Illegal Corporate Behaviour Be Predicted? An Event History Analysis," *Academy of Management Journal*, 34, 1991, pp. 9–36.

41. J. Flynn and C. Del Valle, "Did Sears Take its Customers for a Ride?" *Business Week*, August 3, 1992, pp. 24–25.

42. C. Howes, "Ethics as More Than Just a Course: More Companies Are Promoting Ethical Practices in Work," *National Post*, October 28, 2000, p. D4.

43. C. Howes, "Ethics as More Than Just a Course: More Companies Are Promoting Ethical Practices in Work," *National Post*, October 28, 2000, p. D4.

44. C. Howes, "Ethics as More Than Just a Course: More Companies Are Promoting Ethical Practices in Work," *National Post*, October 28, 2000, p. D4.

45. P.E. Murphy, "Creating Ethical Corporate Structure," *Sloan Management Review*, Winter 1989, pp. 81–87.

46. G.R. Jones, *Organizational Theory: Text and Cases* (Reading, MA: Addison-Wesley, 1997).

47. "When It Comes to Ethics, Canadian Companies Are All Talk and Little Action, a Survey Shows," *Canadian Press Newswire*, February 17, 2000.

48. E. Gatewood and A.B. Carroll, "The Anatomy of Corporate Social Response," *Business Horizons*, September–October 1981, pp. 9–16.

49. M. Friedman, "A Friedman Doctrine: The Social Responsibility of Business Is to Increase Its Profits," *New York Times Magazine*, September 13, 1970, p. 33.

50. W.G. Ouchi, *Theory Z: How American Business Can Meet the Japanese Challenge* (Reading, MA: Addison-Wesley, 1981).

51. J.B. McGuire, A. Sundgren, and T. Schneewis, "Corporate Social Responsibility and Firm Financial Performance," *Academy of Management Review*, 31, 1988, pp. 854–72.

52. M. Friedman, "A Friedman Doctrine: The Social Responsibility of Business Is to Increase Its Profits," *New York Times Magazine*, September 13, 1970, pp. 32, 33, 122, 124, 126.

53. J.B. Dozier and M.P. Miceli, "Potential Predictors of Whistleblowing: A Prosocial Perspective," *Academy of Management Review*, 10, 1985, pp. 823–36; J.P. Near and M.P. Miceli, "Retaliation Against Whistleblowers: Predictors and Effects," *Journal of Applied Psychology*, 71, 1986, pp. 137–45.

54. Information in this paragraph based on "Ontario to Protect Employees Who Cooperate With Public Inquiries," *Canadian Press Newswire*, June 12, 2000.

55. E.D. Bowman, "Corporate Social Responsibility and the Investor," *Journal of Contemporary Business*, Winter 1973, pp. 49–58.

56. "Prejudice: Still on the Menu," *Business Week*, April 3, 1995, p. 42.

57. "Women Find the Top Jobs in Canada Easier to Get at U.S.-Owned Companies," *Vancouver Sun*, August 19, 1999, p. F5.

58. R. Folger and M.A. Konovsky, "Effects of Procedural and Distributive

Justice on Reactions to Pay Raise Decisions," *Academy of Management Journal*, 32, 1989, pp. 115–30; J. Greenberg, "Organizational Justice: Yesterday, Today, and Tomorrow," *Journal of Management*, 16, 1990, pp. 399–402.

59. G. Glynn, "Bank of Montreal Invests in Its Workers," *Workforce*, December 1997, pp. 30–38.

60. J. Greenberg, "Organizational Justice: Yesterday, Today, and Tomorrow," *Journal of Management*, 16, 1990, pp. 399–402.

61. "Management Insight" is based on "BioChem Faces Discrimination Suit," *Financial Post (National Post)*, July 11, 2000, p. C2.

62. D. Calleja, "Equity or Else," *Canadian Business*, March 19, 2001, p. 31.

63. G. Robinson and K. Dechant, "Building a Case for Business Diversity," *Academy of Management Executive*, 1997, pp. 3, 32–47.

64. K. Kalawsky, "US Group Wants Royal's Centura Buy Delayed: Alleges Takeover Target Discriminates Against Minorities," *Financial Post (National Post)*, April 10, 2001, p. C4.

65. H. Branswell, "When Nestlé Canada Said Last Month It Would No Longer Be Making Chocolate Bars in a Nut-Free Facility, Thousands Wrote in to Protest," *Canadian Press Newswire*, May 14, 2001.

66. H. Branswell, "When Nestlé Canada Said Last Month It Would No Longer Be Making Chocolate Bars in a Nut-Free Facility, Thousands Wrote in to Protest," *Canadian Press Newswire*, May 14, 2001.

67. E.D. Pulakos and K.N. Wexley, "The Relationship Among Perceptual Similarity, Sex, and Performance Ratings in Manager–Subordinate Dyads," *Academy of Management Journal*, 26, 1983, pp. 129–39.

68. S.T. Fiske and S.E. Taylor, *Social Cognition* (Reading, MA: Addison-Wesley, 1984).

69. S.T. Fiske and S.E. Taylor, *Social Cognition* (Reading, MA: Addison-Wesley, 1984).

70. B. Cheadle, "Health Canada Cited for Discrimination," *Canadian Press Newswire*, March 19, 1997.

71. A.P. Carnevale and S.C. Stone, "Diversity: Beyond the Golden Rule," *Training & Development*, October 1994, pp. 22–39.

72. B.A. Battaglia, "Skills for Managing Multicultural Teams," *Cultural Diversity at Work*, 4, 1992; A.P. Carnevale and S.C. Stone, "Diversity: Beyond the Golden Rule," *Training & Development*, October 1994, pp. 22–39.

73. "Selling Equity," *Financial Post Magazine*, September 1994, pp. 20–25.

74. "Study Shows Women Who Are Unhappy with Corporate Life Plan to Start Own Businesses," *Women in Management*, December/January 1999, pp. 1–3.

75. "Focus on Diversity": Sweetgrass Comes to the RCMP is based on M. O'Brien, "Heritage Room for Native Cadets," *The Leader-Post (Regina)*, December 5, 2000, p. A3.

76. J. Goddu, "Sexual Harassment Complaints Rise Dramatically," *Canadian Press Newswire*, March 6, 1998.

77. B. Carton, "Muscled Out? At Jenny Craig, Men Are Ones Who Claim Sex Discrimination," *Wall Street Journal*, November 29, 1994, pp. A1, A7.

78. P. Arab, "Sexual Harassment Ruled a Workplace Safety Hazard," *Canadian Press Newswire*, August 22, 1997.

79. R.L. Paetzold and A.M. O'Leary-Kelly, "Organizational Communication and the Legal Dimensions of Hostile Work Environment Sexual Harassment," in G.L. Kreps (ed.), *Sexual Harassment: Communication Implications* (Cresskill, NJ: Hampton Press, 1993).

80. M. Galen, J. Weber, and A.Z. Cuneo, "Sexual Harassment: Out of the Shadows," *Fortune*, October 28, 1991, pp. 30–31.

81. "Employers Underestimate Extent of Sexual Harassment, Report Says," *The Vancouver Sun*, March 8, 2001, p. D6.

82. A.M. O'Leary-Kelly, R.L. Paetzold, and R.W. Griffin, "Sexual Harassment as Aggressive Action: A Framework for Understanding Sexual Harassment" (paper presented at the annual meeting of the Academy of Management, Vancouver, August 1995).

83. "Employers Underestimate Extent of Sexual Harassment, Report Says," *The Vancouver Sun*, March 8, 2001, p. D6.

84. Information in this paragraph based on Ian Jack, "Magna Suit Spotlights Auto Industry Practices," *Financial Post Daily*, September 10, 1997, p. 1.

85. I. Jack, "Magna Suit Spotlights Auto Industry Practices," *Financial Post Daily*, September 10, 1997, p. 1.

86. S.J. Bresler and R. Thacker, "Four-Point Plan Helps Solve Harassment Problems," *HR Magazine*, May 1993, pp. 117–24.

87. "Racial Differences Discourage Mentors," *Wall Street Journal*, October 29, 1991, p. B1.

88. C. Purden, "Rising to the Challenge," *Report on Business Magazine*, June 2001, pp. 30-31.

Chapter 6

1. The CSI story is based on a real incident experienced by a consulting client of one of the authors of this text. The names of the company and individuals and dates involved have been changed.

2. H.A. Simon, *The New Science of Management* (Englewood Cliffs, NJ: Prentice-Hall, 1977).

3. One should be careful not to generalize too much here, however; for as Peter Senge has shown, programmed decisions rely on the implicit assumption that the environment is in a steady state. If environmental conditions change, then sticking to a routine decision rule can produce disastrous results. See P. Senge, *The Fifth Discipline: The Art and Practice of the Learning Organization* (New York: Doubleday, 1990).

4. H.A. Simon, *Administrative Behavior* (New York: Macmillan, 1947), p. 79.

5. H.A. Simon, *Models of Man* (New York: Wiley, 1957).

6. K.J. Arrow, *Aspects of the Theory of Risk Bearing* (Helsinki: Yrjo Johnssonis Saatio, 1965).

7. R.L. Daft and R.H. Lengel, "Organizational Information Requirements, Media Richness and Structural Design," *Management Science*, 32, 1986, pp. 554–71.

8. R. Cyert and J. March, *Behavioral Theory of the Firm* (Englewood Cliffs, NJ: Prentice-Hall, 1963).

9. J.G. March and H.A. Simon, *Organizations* (New York: Wiley, 1958).

10. H.A. Simon, "Making Management Decisions: The Role of Intuition and Emotion," *Academy of Management Executive*, 1, 1987, pp. 57–64.

11. B. Kelley, "A Day in the Life of a Card Shark," *Journal of Business Strategy*, Spring 1994, pp. 36–39.

12. M.H. Bazerman, *Judgment in Managerial Decision Making* (New York: Wiley, 1986). Also see H.A. Simon, *Administrative Behavior* (New York: Macmillan, 1947).

13. M.H. Bazerman, *Judgment in Managerial Decision Making* (New York: Wiley, 1986); G.P. Huber, *Managerial Decision Making* (Glenview, IL: Scott, Foresman, 1993); J.E. Russo and P.J. Schoemaker, *Decision Traps* (New York: Simon and Schuster, 1989).

14. M.D. Cohen, J.G. March, and J.P. Olsen, "A Garbage Can Model of Organizational Choice," *Administrative Science Quarterly*, 17, 1972, pp. 1–25.

15. M.D. Cohen, J.G. March, and J.P. Olsen, "A Garbage Can Model of Organizational Choice," *Administrative Science Quarterly*, 17, 1972, pp. 1–25.

16. M.H. Bazerman, *Judgment in Managerial Decision Making* (New York: Wiley, 1986).

17. P. Senge, *The Fifth Discipline: The Art and Practice of the Learning Organization* (New York: Doubleday, 1990).

18. E. de Bono, *Lateral Thinking* (London: Penguin, 1968); P. Senge, *The Fifth Discipline: The Art and Practice of the Learning Organization* (New York: Doubleday, 1990).

19. J.E. Russo and P.J. Schoemaker, *Decision Traps* (New York: Simon and Schuster, 1989).

20. M.H. Bazerman, *Judgment in Managerial Decision Making* (New York: Wiley, 1986).

21. J.E. Russo and P.J. Schoemaker, *Decision Traps* (New York: Simon and Schuster, 1989).

22. D. Kahneman and A. Tversky, "Judgment Under Uncertainty: Heuristics and Biases," *Science*, 185, 1974, pp. 1124–31.

23. C.R. Schwenk, "Cognitive Simplification Processes in Strategic Decision Making," *Strategic Management Journal*, 5, 1984, pp. 111–28.

24. "Management Insight" is based on G. Hamilton, "Log Home Builders Turn Pestilence Into Profit," *The Vancouver Sun*, April 10, 2001, pp. D1, D8.

25. An interesting example of the illusion of control is Richard Roll's hubris hypothesis of takeovers. See R. Roll, "The Hubris Hypothesis of Corporate

Takeovers," *Journal of Business*, 59, 1986, pp. 197–216.

26. B.M. Staw, "The Escalation of Commitment to a Course of Action," *Academy of Management Review*, 6, 1981, pp. 577–87.

27. J.E. Russo and P.J. Schoemaker, *Decision Traps* (New York: Simon and Schuster, 1989).

28. J.E. Russo and P.J. Schoemaker, *Decision Traps* (New York: Simon and Schuster, 1989).

29. I.L. Janis, *Groupthink: Psychological Studies of Policy Decisions and Disasters*, 2nd edition (Boston: Houghton Mifflin, 1982).

30. J.N. Choi and M.U. Kim, "The Organizational Application of Groupthink and its Limitations in Organizations," *Journal of Applied Psychology*, 84, 1999, pp. 297–306.

31. C. McCauley, "The Nature of Social Influence in Groupthink: Compliance and Internalization," *Journal of Personality and Social Psychology*, 57, 1989, pp. 250–260; P.E. Tetlock, R.S. Peterson, C. McGuire, S. Chang, and P. Feld, "Assessing Political Group Dynamics: A Test of the Groupthink Model," *Journal of Personality and Social Psychology*, 63, 1992, pp. 781–796; S. Graham, "A Review of Attribution Theory in Achievement Contexts," *Educational Psychology Review*, 3, 1991, pp. 5–39; and G. Moorhead and J.R. Montanari, "An Empirical Investigation of the Groupthink Phenomenon," *Human Relations*, 39, 1986, pp. 399–410.

32. J. Longley and D.G. Pruitt, "Groupthink: A Critique of Janis' Theory," in L. Wheeler (ed.), *Review of Personality and Social Psychology* (Newbury Park, CA: Sage, 1980), pp. 507–513; and J.A. Sniezek, "Groups Under Uncertainty: An Examination of Confidence in Group Decision Making," *Organizational Behavior and Human Decision Processes*, 52, 1992, pp. 124–155.

33. J.N. Choi and M.U. Kim, "The Organizational Application of Groupthink and its Limitations in Organizations," *Journal of Applied Psychology*, 84, 1999, pp. 297–306.

34. C.R. Schwenk, *The Essence of Strategic Decision Making* (Lexington, MA: Lexington Books, 1988).

35. See R.O. Mason, "A Dialectic Approach to Strategic Planning," *Management Science*, 13, 1969, pp. 403–14;

R.A. Cosier and J.C. Aplin, "A Critical View of Dialectic Inquiry in Strategic Planning," *Strategic Management Journal*, 1, 1980, pp. 343–56; I.I. Mitroff and R.O. Mason, "Structuring III–Structured Policy Issues: Further Explorations in a Methodology for Messy Problems," *Strategic Management Journal*, 1, 1980, pp. 331–42.

36. R.O. Mason, "A Dialectic Approach to Strategic Planning," *Management Science*, 13, 1969, pp. 403–14.

37. D.M. Schweiger and P.A. Finger, "The Comparative Effectiveness of Dialectic Inquiry and Devil's Advocacy," *Strategic Management Journal*, 5, 1984, pp. 335–50.

38. Mary C. Gentile, *Differences That Work: Organizational Excellence Through Diversity* (Boston: Harvard Business School Press, 1994).

39. "Management Insight" is based on A. Muoio, "Brainstorming at Switzerland's BrainStore: Building an Assembly Line for Ideas," *Financial Post (National Post)*, April 12, 2000, p. C15.

40. B. Hedberg, "How Organizations Learn and Unlearn," in W.H. Starbuck and P.C. Nystrom (eds.), *Handbook of Organizational Design*, vol. 1 (New York: Oxford University Press, 1981), pp. 1–27.

41. See P. Senge, *The Fifth Discipline: The Art and Practice of the Learning Organization* (New York: Doubleday, 1990).

42. See P. Senge, *The Fifth Discipline: The Art and Practice of the Learning Organization* (New York: Doubleday, 1990).

43. P.M. Senge, "The Leader's New Work: Building Learning Organizations," *Sloan Management Review*, Fall 1990, pp. 7–23.

44. P.M. Senge, "The Leader's New Work: Building Learning Organizations," *Sloan Management Review*, Fall 1990, pp. 7–23.

45. W. Kondro, "Canada in Creativity Crisis: Study," *National Post*, May 25, 2001, pp. A1, A12.

46. T.A. Stewart, "3M Fights Back," *Fortune*, February 5, 1996, pp. 94–99; and T.D. Schellhardt, "David in Goliath," *Wall Street Journal*, May 23, 1996, p. R14.

47. R.W. Woodman, J.E. Sawyer, and R.W. Griffin, "Towards a Theory of Organizational Creativity," *Academy of Management Review*, 18, 1993, pp. 293–321.

48. M. Ullmann, "Creativity Cubed: Burntsand Has Found a Novel Program to Motivate Its Most Creative Employees. Can It Work for You?" *SVN Canada*, February 2001, pp. B22–B23+.

49. T.J. Bouchard, Jr., J. Barsaloux, and G. Drauden, "Brainstorming Procedure, Group Size, and Sex as Determinants of Problem Solving Effectiveness of Individuals and Groups," *Journal of Applied Psychology*, 59, 1974, pp. 135–38.

50. M. Diehl and W. Stroebe, "Productivity Loss in Brainstorming Groups: Towards the Solution of a Riddle," *Journal of Personality and Social Psychology*, 53, 1987, pp. 497–509.

51. I. Edwards, "Office Intrigue: By Design, Consultants Have Workers Conspire to Create Business Environments Tailored to Getting the Job Done," *Financial Post Daily*, December 16, 1997, p. 25.

52. Information in this paragraph from G. Crone, "Electrifying Brainstorms," *Financial Post (National Post)*, July 3, 1999, p. D11.

53. D.H. Gustafson, R.K. Shulka, A. Delbecq, and W.G. Walster, "A Comparative Study of Differences in Subjective Likelihood Estimates Made By Individuals, Interacting Groups, Delphi Groups, and Nominal Groups," *Organizational Behavior and Human Performance*, 9, 1973, pp. 280–91.

54. N. Dalkey, *The Delphi Method: An Experimental Study of Group Decision Making* (Santa Monica, CA: Rand Corp., 1989).

55. T. Graham, "The Keys to the Middle Kingdom: Experts Will Tell You It Takes Years of Patient Effort to Crack the Chinese Market, But That's Not Always the Case," *Profit: The Magazine for Canadian Entrepreneurs*, December 1997/January 1998, p. 29.

56. E.S. Browning, "Computer Chip Project Brings Rivals Together, but the Cultures Clash," *Wall Street Journal*, April 3, 1994, pp. A1, A8.

57. N.B. Macintosh, *The Social Software of Accounting Information Systems* (New York: Wiley, 1995).

58. C.A. O'Reilly, "Variations in Decision Makers' Use of Information: The Impact of Quality and Accessibility," *Academy of Management Journal*, 25, 1982, pp. 756–71.

59. G. Stalk and T.H. Hout, *Competing Against Time* (New York: Free Press, 1990).

60. R. Cyert and J. March, *Behavioral Theory of the Firm* (Englewood Cliffs, NJ: Prentice-Hall, 1963).

61. E. Turban, *Decision Support and Expert Systems* (New York: Macmillan, 1988).

62. R.I. Benjamin and J. Blunt, "Critical IT Issues: The Next Ten Years," *Sloan Management Review*, Summer 1992, pp. 7–19; W.H. Davidow and M.S. Malone, *The Virtual Corporation* (New York: Harper Business, 1992).

63. P. Fitzpatrick, "Wacky WestJet's Winning Ways: Passengers Respond to Stunts That Include Races to Determine Who Leaves the Airplane First," *Financial Post (National Post)*, October 16, 2000, p. C1.

64. W.H. Davidow and M.S. Malone, *The Virtual Corporation* (New York: Harper Business, 1992).

65. From an interview conducted by C.W.L. Hill with a senior Boeing manager.

Chapter 7

1. B. Simon, "Upstart Cott Shakes Cola Kings," *Financial Times*, June 14, 1994, p. 18; "Coca-Cola Versus Pepsi-Cola and the Soft Drink Industry," *Harvard Business School Case* #9-391-179.

2. A. Levy, "Pepsi Ceding Cola War Victory to Rival Coke: Fails to Take Advantage of Leader's Stumbles," *Financial Post (National Post)*, January 19, 2000, p. C12.

3. "Cott Pays $72M US for Concord Beverage, Posts Profitable Quarter," *Canadian Press Newswire*, October 18, 2000.

4. A. Chandler, *Strategy and Structure: Chapters in the History of the American Enterprise* (Cambridge, MA: MIT Press, 1962).

5. M. Ingram, "Our Job Is to Be Better," *The Globe and Mail*, May 12, 2001, p. F3.

6. A. Chandler, *Strategy and Structure: Chapters in the History of the American Enterprise* (Cambridge, MA: MIT Press, 1962).

7. V. Pilieci, "The Lost Generation of Business Talent," *The Vancouver Sun*, May 2, 2001, pp. D1, D9.

8. F.J. Aguilar, "General Electric: Reg Jones and Jack Welch," in *General Managers in Action* (Oxford: Oxford University Press, 1992).

9. F.J. Aguilar, "General Electric: Reg Jones and Jack Welch," in *General Managers in Action* (Oxford: Oxford University Press, 1992).

10. F.J. Aguilar, "General Electric: Reg Jones and Jack Welch," in *General Managers in Action* (Oxford: Oxford University Press, 1992).

11. C.W. Hofer and D. Schendel, *Strategy Formulation: Analytical Concepts* (St. Paul, MN: West, 1978).

12. H. Fayol, *General and Industrial Management* (1884; New York: IEEE Press, 1984).

13. L. Iacocca, *Iacocca: An Autobiography* (New York: Bantam Books, 1984).

14. A. Lam, "The Entrepreneurial Bug Hits Business Students Before Graduation," *Business Sense*, 2000, p. 33.

15. H. Fayol, *General and Industrial Management* (1884; New York: IEEE Press, 1984), p. 18.

16. P. Wack, "Scenarios: Shooting the Rapids," *Harvard Business Review*, November–December 1985, pp. 139–50.

17. J.A. Pearce, "The Company Mission as a Strategic Tool," *Sloan Management Review*, Spring 1992, pp. 15–24.

18. P.C. Nutt and R.W. Backoff, "Crafting Vision," *Journal of Management Inquiry*, December 1997, p. 309.

19. D.F. Abell, *Defining the Business: The Starting Point of Strategic Planning* (Englewood Cliffs, NJ: Prentice-Hall, 1980).

20. www.worksafebc.com/corporate/about/goals/default.asp

21. "Focus on Diversity" is based on S. Bartlett, "Healing Centre Opens at General Hospital," *Windspeaker*, February 2000, p. 22; the Regina Health District's Web page, www.reginahealth.sk.ca; and "Native Healing Centre Officially Opens," *Regina Health District's News Release*, December 10, 1999.

22. G. Hamel and C.K. Prahalad, "Strategic Intent," *Harvard Business Review*, May–June 1989, pp. 63–73.

23. E.A. Locke, G.P. Latham, and M. Erez, "The Determinants of Goal Commitment," *Academy of Management Review*, 13, 1988, pp. 23–39.

24. K.R. Andrews, *The Concept of Corporate Strategy* (Homewood, IL: Irwin, 1971).

25. "Management Insight": Finning Narrows Its Focus is based on J.F. Shepard, "Renewing the Corporation,"

Canadian Business Review, v.23(3), 1996, pp. 25–26+.

26. W. Boei, "Ventures West Glad to Escape Dot-Com Meltdown Unscathed," *The Vancouver Sun*, May 30, 2001, p. D4.

27. P. MacKinnon, "Strategy 101," *Atlantic Progress*, March 2001, p. 65.

28. "Management Insight": E.D. Smith Want to Expand to the U.S. is based on O. Bertin, "E.D. Smith Caught in a Bit of a Jam," *The Globe and Mail*, April 23, 2001, p. B5.

29. M. McNeill, "Peak of the Market Buys Competitor," *Winnipeg Free Press*, June 2001, pp. B1, B3.

30. A. Wahl, "The Lessons of Lucent: The Competition's Screwups Offer Nortel a How-To Model," *Canadian Business*, February 19, 2001, pp. 39–40.

31. E. Penrose, *The Theory of the Growth of the Firm* (Oxford: Oxford University Press, 1959).

32. M.E. Porter, "From Competitive Advantage to Corporate Strategy," *Harvard Business Review*, 65, 1987, pp. 43–59.

33. D.J. Teece, "Economics of Scope and the Scope of the Enterprise," *Journal of Economic Behaviour and Organization*, 3, 1980, pp. 223–47.

34. M.E. Porter, *Competitive Advantage: Creating and Sustaining Superior Performance* (New York: Free Press, 1985).

35. For a review of the evidence see C.W.L. Hill and G.R. Jones, *Strategic Management: An Integrated Approach*, 3rd ed. (Boston: Houghton Mifflin, 1995), Chapter 10.

36. V. Ramanujam and P. Varadarajan, "Research on Corporate Diversification: A Synthesis," *Strategic Management Journal*, 10, 1989, pp. 523–51. Also see A. Shleifer and R.W. Vishny, "Takeovers in the 1960s and 1980s: Evidence and Implications," in R.P. Rumelt, D.E. Schendel, and D.J. Teece, *Fundamental Issues in Strategy* (Boston: Harvard Business School Press, 1994).

37. J.R. Williams, B.L. Paez, and L. Sanders, "Conglomerates Revisited," *Strategic Management Journal*, 9, 1988, pp. 403–14.

38. H. Shaw, "Fish, Dairy Units Sacrificed to Help Raise Cash for Baked Goods: Bestfoods Deal," *Financial Post (National Post)*, February 20, 2001, pp. C1, C6.

39. C.A. Bartlett and S. Ghoshal, *Managing Across Borders* (Boston: Harvard Business School Press, 1989).

40. C.K. Prahalad and Y.L. Doz, *The Multinational Mission* (New York: Free Press, 1987).

41. C.W.L. Hill, *International Business: Competing in the Global Economy* (Homewood, IL: Irwin, 1994), p. 490.

42. M.K. Perry, "Vertical Integration: Determinants and Effects," in R. Schmalensee and R.D. Willig, *Handbook of Industrial Organization*, Vol. 1 (New York: Elsevier Science Publishing, 1989).

43. T. Muris, D. Scheffman, and P. Spiller, "Strategy and Transaction Costs: The Organization of Distribution in the Carbonated Soft Drink Industry," *Journal of Economics and Management Strategy*, 1, 1992, pp. 77–97.

44. "Matsushita Electric Industrial (MEI) in 1987," *Harvard Business School Case* #388-144.

45. K. Deveny et al., "McWorld?" *Business Week*, October 13, 1986, pp. 78–86; "Slow Food," *The Economist*, February 3, 1990, p. 64.

46. P. Ghemawat, *Commitment: The Dynamic of Strategy* (New York: Free Press, 1991).

47. D. McMurdy, "The Human Cost of Mergers," *Maclean's*, November 20, 2000, p. 128.

48. M.E. Porter, *Competitive Strategy* (New York: Free Press, 1980).

49. C.W.L. Hill, "Differentiation Versus Low Cost or Differentiation and Low Cost: A Contingency Framework," *Academy of Management Review*, 13, 1988, pp. 401–12.

50. For details see J.P. Womack, D.T. Jones, and D. Roos, *The Machine That Changed the World* (New York: Rawson Associates, 1990).

51. M.E. Porter, *Competitive Strategy* (New York: Free Press, 1980).

52. C.W.L. Hill and G.R. Jones, *Strategic Management: An Integrated Approach*, 3rd ed. (Boston: Houghton Mifflin, 1995).

53. J.P. Womack, D.T. Jones, and D. Roos, *The Machine That Changed the World* (New York: Rawson Associates, 1990).

54. See D. Garvin, "What Does Product Quality Really Mean?" *Sloan Management Review*, 26, Fall 1984, pp. 25–44; P.B. Crosby, *Quality is Free* (New York: Mentor Books, 1980); and A. Gabor, *The Man Who Discovered Quality* (New York: Times Books, 1990).

Chapter 8

1. G. Cheesbrough, "Guidelines for Corporate Transformation," *Canadian Speeches*, v.13(1), 1999, pp. 56–60.

2. G. Cheesbrough, "Guidelines for Corporate Transformation," *Canadian Speeches*, v.13(1), 1999, pp. 56–60.

3. G. Cheesbrough, "Guidelines for Corporate Transformation," *Canadian Speeches*, v.13(1), 1999, pp. 56–60.

4. G. Cheesbrough, "Guidelines for Corporate Transformation," *Canadian Speeches*, v.13(1), 1999, pp. 56–60.

5. G. Cheesbrough, "Guidelines for Corporate Transformation," *Canadian Speeches*, v.13(1), 1999, pp. 56–60.

6. S. Heinrich, "Steering Altamira in a New Direction: Gordon Cheesbrough Has Set Out to Improve the Performance of the Mutual Fund Company and Win Back Lost Investors by Shifting the Focus from Single Star Managers to the Team Approach and by Introducing a Broader Range of Products, Such as Competitors' Funds," *Financial Post (National Post)*, November 28, 1998, p. D9.

7. G.R. Jones, *Organizational Theory: Text and Cases* (Reading, MA: Addison-Wesley, 1995).

8. J. Child, *Organization: A Guide for Managers and Administrators* (New York: Harper and Row, 1977).

9. P.R. Lawrence and J.W. Lorsch, *Organization and Environment* (Boston: Graduate School of Business Administration, Harvard University, 1967).

10. R. Duncan, "What Is the Right Organizational Design?" *Organizational Dynamics*, Winter 1979, pp. 59–80.

11. T. Burns and G.R. Stalker, *The Management of Innovation* (London: Tavistock, 1966).

12. D. Miller, "Strategy Making and Structure: Analysis and Implications for Performance," *Academy of Management Journal*, 30, 1987, pp. 7–32.

13. A.D. Chandler, *Strategy and Structure* (Cambridge, MA: MIT Press, 1962).

14. J. Stopford and L. Wells, *Managing the Multinational Enterprise* (London: Longman, 1972).

15. C. Perrow, *Organizational Analysis: A Sociological View* (Belmont, CA: Wadsworth, 1970).

16. J. Woodward, *Management and Technology* (London: Her Majesty's Stationery Office, 1958).

17. F.W. Taylor, *The Principles of Scientific Management* (New York: Harper, 1911).

18. R.W. Griffin, *Task Design: An Integrative Approach* (Glenview, IL: Scott, Foresman, 1982).

19. R.W. Griffin, *Task Design: An Integrative Approach* (Glenview, IL: Scott, Foresman, 1982).

20. J.R. Hackman and G.R. Oldham, *Work Redesign* (Reading, MA: Addison-Wesley, 1980).

21. J.R. Galbraith and R.K. Kazanjian, *Strategy Implementation: Structure, System, and Process*, 2d ed. (St. Paul, MN: West, 1986).

22. P.R. Lawrence and J.W. Lorsch, *Organization and Environment* (Boston: Graduate School of Business Administration, Harvard University, 1967).

23. G.R. Jones, *Organizational Theory: Text and Cases* (Reading, MA: Addison-Wesley, 1995).

24. P.R. Lawrence and J.W. Lorsch, *Organization and Environment* (Boston: Graduate School of Business Administration, Harvard University, 1967).

25. R.H. Hall, *Organizations: Structure and Process* (Englewood Cliffs, NJ: Prentice-Hall, 1972); R. Miles, *Macro Organizational Behaviour* (Santa Monica, CA: Goodyear, 1980).

26. A.D. Chandler, *Strategy and Structure* (Cambridge, MA: MIT Press, 1962).

27. G.R. Jones and C.W.L. Hill, "Transaction Cost Analysis of Strategy–Structure Choice," *Strategic Management Journal*, 9, 1988, pp. 159–72.

28. "Management Insight": Cascades Inc.'s Product Structure is based on L. Millan, "Who's Scoffing Now? The Lemaire Brothers Started Out Using Recycled Fibre in One Small Paper Mill in Rural Quebec," *Canadian Business*, March 27, 1998, pp. 74–77.

29. "Management Insight": From Geographic to Market Structure is based

on B. Critchley, "Royal Bank/DS Now Restructured," *Financial Post (National Post)*, February 10, 2000, p. D2.

30. S.M. Davis and P.R. Lawrence, *Matrix* (Reading, MA: Addison-Wesley, 1977); J.R. Galbraith, "Matrix Organization Designs: How to Combine Functional and Project Forms," *Business Horizons*, 14, 1971, pp. 29–40.

31. L.R. Burns, "Matrix Management in Hospitals: Testing Theories of Matrix Structure and Development," *Administrative Science Quarterly*, 34, 1989, pp. 349–68.

32. C.W.L. Hill, *International Business* (Homewood, IL: Irwin, 1997).

33. C.A. Bartlett and S. Ghoshal, *Transnational Management* (Homewood, IL: Irwin, 1992).

34. G.R. Jones, *Organizational Theory: Text and Cases* (Reading, MA: Addison-Wesley, 1995).

35. P. Blau, "A Formal Theory of Differentiation in Organizations," *American Sociological Review*, 35, 1970, pp. 684–95.

36. J. Child, *Organization: A Guide for Managers and Administrators* (New York: Harper and Row, 1977).

37. Information about Ducks Unlimited from "Salute! Celebrating the Progressive Employer [Advertising supplement]," *Benefits Canada*, March 1999, p. Insert 1–23.

38. P.M. Blau and R.A. Schoenherr, *The Structure of Organizations* (New York: Basic Books, 1971).

39. G.R. Jones, *Organizational Theory: Text and Cases* (Reading, MA: Addison-Wesley, 1995).

40. "P&G Divides to Rule," *Marketing*, March 23, 1995, p. 15.

41. B. Kogut, "Joint Ventures: Theoretical and Empirical Perspectives," *Strategic Management Journal*, 9, 1988, pp. 319–32.

42. "Focus on Diversity": Membertou Development Seeks Jobs for the Mi'kmaq is based on K. Cox, "Joint Ventures Key to Success for Cape Breton Reserve," *The Globe and Mail*, May 9, 2001, p. B12.

43. "Outsourcing," Advertising supplement in *PurchasingB2B*, October 2000, pp. Insert 1–12.

44. G. Crone, "Welcome to the Other Web: Loose Clusters, Not Rigid Contracts, Are the Future in Business,"

The Financial Post Daily, January 22, 1998, p. 11.

45. "Going Out for Business: As the Third-Party Logistics Boom Continues, Companies Must Learn to Manage the Outsourcing Relationship," *Materials Management & Distribution*, September 1996, pp. 38–39.

46. K. Mark, "Still Hot: Outsourcing Remains Solid Option for Many Companies," *Materials Management & Distribution*, September 1998, pp. 28, 30.

47. © 1996, Gareth R. Jones.

48. M. Meyer, "Culture Club," *Newsweek*, July 11, 1994, pp. 38–42.

Chapter 9

1. R.L. Rose, "After Turning Around Giddings and Lewis, Fife Is Turned Out Himself," *Wall Street Journal*, June 22, 1995, p. A1.

2. P.J. Spain and J.R. Talbot (eds.), *Hoover's Handbook of American Business* (Austin, TX: Reference Press, 1996). Note: IBM completed the acquisition of Informix in July 2001, and renamed it Ascential Software Corporation.

3. W.G. Ouchi, "Markets, Bureaucracies, and Clans," *Administrative Science Quarterly*, 25, 1980, pp. 129–141.

4. "Managing Globally" based on B. Whitmore, "Czech 'Laughing' Stock Rises," *The Edmonton Sun*, April 6, 2001, p. DR1; M. Gillings, "Czech-Made Skoda No Longer a Laughing-Stock," *The Financial Post Daily*, June 19, 1998, p. D18.

5. P. Lorange, M. Morton, and S. Ghoshal, *Strategic Control* (St. Paul, MN: West, 1986).

6. H. Koontz and R.W. Bradspies, "Managing Through Feedforward Control," *Business Horizons*, June 1972, pp. 25–36.

7. E.E. Lawler III and J.G. Rhode, *Information and Control in Organizations* (Pacific Palisades, CA: Goodyear, 1976).

8. C.W.L. Hill and G.R. Jones, *Strategic Management: An Integrated Approach*, 4th ed. (Boston: Houghton Mifflin, 1997).

9. W.G. Ouchi, "The Transmission of Control Through Organizational Hierarchy," *Academy of Management Journal*, 21, 1978, pp. 173–92.

10. W.G. Ouchi, "The Relationship Between Organizational Structure and

Organizational Control," *Administrative Science Quarterly*, 22, 1977, pp. 95–113.

11. W.G. Ouchi, "Markets, Bureaucracies, and Clans," *Administrative Science Quarterly*, 25, 1980, pp. 129–141.

12. W.H. Newman, *Constructive Control* (Englewood Cliffs, NJ: Prentice-Hall, 1975).

13. J.D. Thompson, *Organizations in Action* (New York: McGraw-Hill, 1967).

14. R.N. Anthony, *The Management Control Function* (Boston: Harvard Business School Press, 1988).

15. "Management Insight" is based on C. McLean, "Incorporating Safety into the Corporate Culture: Nacan Closes in on One Million Hours, No Lost-Time Claims," *Plant*, November 27, 2000, p. 17.

16. P. Fitzpatrick, "Wacky WestJet's Winning Ways: Passengers Respond to Stunts That Include Races to Determine Who Leaves the Airplane First," *Financial Post (National Post)*, October 16, 2000, p. C1.

17. "Management Insight": WestJet's Employees Control Costs is based on P. Fitzpatrick, "Wacky WestJet's Winning Ways: Passengers Respond to Stunts That Include Races to Determine Who Leaves the Airplane First," *National Post*, October 16, 2000, p. C1.

18. W.G. Ouchi, "Markets, Bureaucracies, and Clans," *Administrative Science Quarterly*, 25, 1980, pp. 129–141.

19. C.W.L. Hill and G.R. Jones, *Strategic Management: An Integrated Approach*, 4th ed. (Boston: Houghton Mifflin, 1997).

20. R. Simons, "Strategic Orientation and Top Management Attention to Control Systems," *Strategic Management Journal*, 12, 1991, pp. 49–62.

21. G. Schreyogg and H. Steinmann, "Strategic Control: A New Perspective," *Academy of Management Review*, 12, 1987, pp. 91–103.

22. B. Woolridge and S.W. Floyd, "The Strategy Process, Middle Management Involvement, and Organizational Performance," *Strategic Management Journal*, 11, 1990, pp. 231–41.

23. J.A. Alexander, "Adaptive Changes in Corporate Control Practices," *Academy of Management Journal*, 34, 1991, pp. 162–93.

24. "Ethics in Action": Scotia McLeod Looks to be a Conservative Blue Chip Safe House is based on D. DeCloet,

"Scotia Bid to Jump Off Percentage Treadmill," *Financial Post (National Post)*, May 16, 2001, p. C3.

25. C.W.L. Hill and G.R. Jones, *Strategic Management: An Integrated Approach*, 4th ed. (Boston: Houghton Mifflin, 1997).

26. G.H.B. Ross, "Revolution in Management Control," *Management Accounting*, 72, 1992, pp. 23–27.

27. P.F. Drucker, *The Practice of Management* (New York: Harper and Row, 1954).

28. S.J. Carroll and H.L. Tosi, *Management By Objectives: Applications and Research* (New York: Macmillan, 1973).

29. R. Rodgers and J.E. Hunter, "Impact of Management By Objectives on Organizational Productivity," *Journal of Applied Psychology*, 76, 1991, pp. 322–26.

30. M.B. Gavin, S.G. Green, and G.T. Fairhurst, "Managerial Control Strategies for Poor Performance Over Time and the Impact on Subordinate Reactions," *Organizational Behaviour and Human Decision Processes*, 63, 1995, pp. 207–21.

31. D.S. Pugh, D.J. Hickson, C.R. Hinings, and C. Turner, "Dimensions of Organizational Structure," *Administrative Science Quarterly*, 13, 1968, pp. 65–91.

32. P.M. Blau, *The Dynamics of Bureaucracy* (Chicago: University of Chicago Press, 1955).

33. See, for example, H.S. Becker, "Culture: A Sociological View," *Yale Review,* Summer 1982, pp. 513–527; and E.H. Schein, *Organizational Culture and Leadership* (San Francisco: Jossey-Bass, 1985), p. 168.

34. T.E. Deal and A.A. Kennedy, "Culture: A New Look Through Old Lenses," *Journal of Applied Behavioral Science,* November 1983, p. 501.

35. E.H. Schein, "Leadership and Organizational Culture," in F. Hesselbein, M. Goldsmith, and R. Beckhard (eds.), *The Leader of the Future* (San Francisco: Jossey-Bass, 1996), pp. 61–62.

36. W.G. Ouchi, "Markets, Bureaucracies, and Clans," *Administrative Science Quarterly*, 25, 1980, pp. 129–141; M. Lebas and J. Weigenstein, "Management Control: The Roles of Rules, Markets, and Culture," *Journal of Management Studies*, 23, 1986, pp. 259–72.

37. M. Rokeach, *The Nature of Human Values* (New York: Free Press, 1973).

38. D.C. Feldman, "The Development and Enforcement of Group Norms," *Academy of Management Review*, 9, 1984, pp. 47–53.

39. D. Yedlin, "Merging Corporate Cultures Not Always Easy," *Calgary Herald,* June 2, 2001, p. E1.

40. G.R. Jones, *Organizational Theory: Text and Cases* (Reading, MA: Addison-Wesley, 1995).

41. H. Schein, "The Role of the Founder in Creating Organizational Culture," *Organizational Dynamics*, 12, 1983, pp. 13–28.

42. J.M. George, "Personality, Affect, and Behaviour in Groups," *Journal of Applied Psychology*, 75, 1990, pp. 107–16.

43. J. Van Maanen, "Police Socialization: A Longitudinal Examination of Job Attitudes in an Urban Police Department," *Administrative Science Quarterly*, 20, 1975, pp. 207–28.

44. P.L. Berger and T. Luckman, *The Social Construction of Reality* (Garden City, NY: Anchor Books, 1967).

45. H.M. Trice and J.M. Beyer, "Studying Organizational Culture Through Rites and Ceremonials," *Academy of Management Review*, 9, 1984, pp. 653–69.

46. "Bonding and Brutality: Hazing Survives as a Way of Forging Loyalty to Groups Canadian Airborne Regiment," *Maclean's,* January 30, 1995, p. 18.

47. "Bonding and Brutality: Hazing Survives as a Way of Forging Loyalty to Groups Canadian Airborne Regiment," *Maclean's,* January 30, 1995, p. 18.

48. B. Ortega, "Wal-Mart's Meeting Is a Reason to Party," *Wall Street Journal*, June 3, 1994, p. A1.

49. C. Stephenson, "Corporate Values Drive Global Success at Lucent Technologies," *Canadian Speeches*, November/December 1999, pp. 23–27.

50. A. Rafaeli and M.G. Pratt, "Tailored Meanings: On the Meaning and Impact of Organizational Dress," *Academy of Management Review,* January 1993, pp. 32–55.

51. J. Greenwood, "Job One: When Bobbie Gaunt Became Ford of Canada President Earlier This Year, the Appointment Put a Spotlight on the New Rules of the Auto Industry: It's Less About Manufacturing These Days Than

About Marketing and Sales," *Financial Post Magazine,* June 1997, pp. 18–22.

52. D. Akin, "Big Blue Chills Out: A Canadian Executive Leads the Campaign to Turn IBM into Cool Blue," *Financial Post (National Post)*, October 11, 1999, pp. C1, C6

53. S. Mcgee, "Garish Jackets Add to Clamor of Chicago Pits," *Wall Street Journal,* July 31, 1995, p. C1.

54. T. Cole, "How to Stay Hired," *Report on Business Magazine,* March 1995, pp. 46–48.

55. K.E. Weick, *The Social Psychology of Organization* (Reading, MA: Addison-Wesley, 1979).

56. J. McCann, "Cutting the Crap," *National Post Business,* March 2001, pp. 47–57.

Chapter 10

1. "Management Insight": Recruiting Challenges at Two Small Companies is based on R. Wright, "21 Ways to Build Great People," *Profit: The Magazine for Canadian Entrepreneurs,* June 2000, pp. 122–132; and "Businesses Founded in Flush Times Deal with Looming Slowdown," *Canadian Press Newswire,* January 2, 2001.

2. Information on TD Bank based on H. Schachter, "Leading-Edge Learning: Banks Look for Results From Their Investments in Employee Education," *Canadian Banker,* v. 107(2), pp. 16–20+.

3. J.E. Butler, G.R. Ferris, and N.K. Napier, *Strategy and Human Resource Management* (Cincinnati, OH: Southwestern, 1991); P.M. Wright and G.C. McMahan, "Theoretical Perspectives for Strategic Human Resource Management," *Journal of Management,* 18, 1992, pp. 295–320.

4. J.B. Quinn, P. Anderson, and S. Finkelstein, "Managing Professional Intellect: Making the Most of the Best," *Harvard Business Review,* March–April 1996, pp. 71–80.

5. K. Harley, "Zero Churn," *Atlantic Progress,* May 2001, pp. 30–33.

6. J.B. Quinn, P. Anderson, and S. Finkelstein, "Managing Professional Intellect: Making the Most of the Best," *Harvard Business Review,* March–April 1996, pp. 71–80.

7. C.D. Fisher, L.F. Schoenfeldt, and J.B. Shaw, *Human Resource Management* (Boston: Houghton Mifflin, 1990).

8. P.M. Wright and G.C. McMahan, "Theoretical Perspectives for Strategic Human Resource Management," *Journal of Management,* 18, 1992, pp. 295–320.

9. L. Baird and I. Meshoulam, "Managing Two Fits for Strategic Human Resource Management," *Academy of Management Review,* 14, 1989, pp. 116–28; J. Milliman, M. Von Glinow, and M. Nathan, "Organizational Life Cycles and Strategic International Human Resource Management in Multinational Companies: Implications for Congruence Theory," *Academy of Management Review,* 16, 1991, pp. 318–39; R.S. Schuler and S.E. Jackson, "Linking Competitive Strategies with Human Resource Management Practices," *Academy of Management Executive,* 1, 1987, pp. 207–19; P.M. Wright and S.A. Snell, "Toward an Integrative View of Strategic Human Resource Management," *Human Resource Management Review,* 1, 1991, pp. 203–25.

10. R. Stogdill II, R. Mitchell, K. Thurston, and C. Del Valle, "Why AIDS Policy Must be a Special Policy," *Business Week,* February 1, 1993, pp. 53–54.

11. J.M. George, "AIDS/AIDS-Related Complex," in L. Peters, B. Greer, and S. Youngblood (eds.), *The Blackwell Encyclopedic Dictionary of Human Resource Management* (Oxford: Blackwell, 1997).

12. J.M. George, "AIDS/AIDS-Related Complex," in L. Peters, B. Greer, and S. Youngblood (eds.), *The Blackwell Encyclopedic Dictionary of Human Resource Management* (Oxford: Blackwell, 1997).

13. J.M. George, "AIDS/AIDS-Related Complex," in L. Peters, B. Greer, and S. Youngblood (eds.), *The Blackwell Encyclopedic Dictionary of Human Resource Management* (Oxford: Blackwell, 1997); R. Stogdill II, R. Mitchell, K. Thurston, and C. Del Valle, "Why AIDS Policy Must be a Special Policy," *Business Week,* February 1, 1993, pp. 53–54.

14. S.L. Rynes, "Recruitment, Job Choice, and Post-Hire Consequences: A Call for New Research Directions," in M.D. Dunnette and L.M. Hough (eds.), *Handbook of Industrial and Organizational Psychology,* vol. 2 (Palo Alto, CA: Consulting Psychologists Press, 1991), pp. 399–444.

15. M. Lewis, "BCE Appoints Alcan Recruit 'Chief Talent Officer,'" *Financial Post (National Post),* May 24, 2001, p. C11.

16. "Focus on Diversity" is based on C. Alphonso, "It's Not Just Students in the Hot Dog Suits: Theme Parks Are Now Recruiting Seniors and Parents," *The Globe and Mail,* Monday, April 23, 2001, p. B8.

17. "CIBC Outsources Human Resources Operations to EDS Canada in $227M Deal," *Canadian Press Newswire,* March 29, 2001.

18. R.J. Harvey, "Job Analysis," in M.D. Dunnette and L.M. Hough (eds.), *Handbook of Industrial and Organizational Psychology,* vol. 2 (Palo Alto, CA: Consulting Psychologists Press, 1991), pp. 71–163.

19. E.L. Levine, *Everything You Always Wanted to Know About Job Analysis: A Job Analysis Primer* (Tampa, FL: Mariner, 1983).

20. R.L. Mathis and J.H. Jackson, *Human Resource Management,* 7th ed. (St. Paul, MN: West, 1994).

21. E.J. McCormick, P.R. Jeanneret, and R.C. Mecham, *Position Analysis Questionnaire* (West Lafayette, IN: Occupational Research Center, Department of Psychological Sciences, Purdue University, 1969).

22. C.D. Fisher, L.F. Schoenfeldt, and J.B. Shaw, *Human Resource Management* (Boston: Houghton Mifflin, 1990); R.L. Mathis and J.H. Jackson, *Human Resource Management,* 7th ed. (St. Paul, MN: West, 1994); R.A. Noe, J.R. Hollenbeck, B. Gerhart, and P.M. Wright, *Human Resource Management: Gaining a Competitive Advantage* (Burr Ridge, IL: Irwin, 1994).

23. C.D. Fisher, L.F. Schoenfeldt, and J.B. Shaw, *Human Resource Management* (Boston: Houghton Mifflin, 1990); E.J. McCormick, *Job Analysis: Methods and Applications* (New York: American Management Association, 1979); E.J. McCormick and R. Jeannerette, "The Position Analysis Questionnaire," in S. Gael (ed.), *The Job Analysis Handbook for Business, Industry, and Government* (New York: Wiley, 1988); R.A. Noe, J.R. Hollenbeck, B. Gerhart, and P.M. Wright, *Human Resource Management: Gaining a Competitive Advantage* (Burr Ridge, IL: Irwin, 1994).

24. S.L. Rynes, "Recruitment, Job Choice, and Post-Hire Consequences:

A Call for New Research Directions," in M.D. Dunnette and L.M. Hough (eds.), *Handbook of Industrial and Organizational Psychology*, vol. 2 (Palo Alto, CA: Consulting Psychologists Press, 1991), pp. 399–444.

25. "Management Insight" is based on R. Wright, "21 Ways to Build Great People," *Profit: The Magazine for Canadian Entrepreneurs*, June 2000, pp. 122–132.

26. S.L. Premack and J.P. Wanous, "A Meta-Analysis of Realistic Job Preview Experiments," *Journal of Applied Psychology*, 70, 1985, pp. 706–19; J.P. Wanous, "Realistic Job Previews: Can a Procedure to Reduce Turnover Also Influence the Relationship Between Abilities and Performance?" *Personnel Psychology*, 31, 1978, pp. 249–58; J.P. Wanous, *Organizational Entry: Recruitment, Selection, and Socialization of Newcomers* (Reading, MA: Addison-Wesley, 1980).

27. See S.L. Robinson, M.S. Kraatz, and D.M. Rousseau, "Changing Obligations and the Psychological Contract: A Longitudinal Study," *Academy of Management Journal*, February 1994, pp. 137–152; and D.M. Rousseau, *Psychological Contracts in Organizations: Understanding Written and Unwritten Agreements* (Thousand Oaks, CA: Sage, 1995).

28. R.M. Guion, "Personnel Assessment, Selection, and Placement," in M.D. Dunnette and L.M. Hough (eds.), *Handbook of Industrial and Organizational Psychology*, vol. 2 (Palo Alto, CA: Consulting Psychologists Press, 1991), pp. 327–97.

29. R.A. Noe, J.R. Hollenbeck, B. Gerhart, and P.M. Wright, *Human Resource Management: Gaining a Competitive Advantage* (Burr Ridge, IL: Irwin, 1994); J.A. Wheeler and J.A. Gier, "Reliability and Validity of the Situational Interview for a Sales Position," *Journal of Applied Psychology*, 2, 1987, pp. 484–87.

30. R.A. Noe, J.R. Hollenbeck, B. Gerhart, and P.M. Wright, *Human Resource Management: Gaining a Competitive Advantage* (Burr Ridge, IL: Irwin, 1994).

31. "Management Insight" is based on R. Wright, "21 Ways to Build Great People," *Profit: The Magazine for Canadian Entrepreneurs*, June 2000, pp. 122–132.

32. "Wanted: Middle Managers, Audition Required," *Wall Street Journal*, December 28, 1995, p. A1.

33. R.B. Lieber, "The Fight to Legislate Incompetence Out of the Cockpit," *Fortune*, February 5, 1996, p. 30.

34. I. Gray, "Reference Checking Slips Through the Cracks: Companies Reluctant to Do More Than a Perfunctory Background Check Are Leaving Themselves Exposed," *The Financial Post*, September 27/29, 1997, p. 49.

35. M. Fitz-James, "Ruling Defines Discovery Without Lawsuit: Judge Opens Legal Loophole in Case of Ontario Anesthesiologist Who Wanted to See Negative Letters of Reference Written by Colleagues," *Medical Post*, December 5, 2000, p. 56.

36. I.L. Goldstein, "Training in Work Organizations," in M.D. Dunnette and L.M. Hough (eds.), *Handbook of Industrial and Organizational Psychology*, vol. 2 (Palo Alto, CA: Consulting Psychologists Press, 1991), pp. 507–619.

37. Examples in this paragraph taken from R. Ray, "Employers, Employees Embrace E-Learning," *The Globe and Mail*, May 25, 2001, p. E2.

38. M.B. Arthur, D.T. Hall, and B.S. Lawrence (eds.), *Handbook of Career Theory* (Cambridge: Cambridge University Press, 1989), p. 8.

39. S.L. McShane, *Canadian Organizational Behaviour*, 4th ed. (Whitby, ON: McGraw-Hill Ryerson, 2001), p. 548.

40. Luiza Chwialkowska, "Ottawa Plan Targets Jobs Crisis," *National Post*, June 18, 2001, p. A1.

41. See, for example, P.O. Benham, Jr., "Developing Organizational Talent: The Key to Performance and Productivity," *SAM Advanced Management Journal*, January 1993, pp. 34–39.

42. Information about Alcan and Hewlett-Packard based on L. Duxbury, L. Dyke, and N. Lam, "Career Development in the Federal Public Service: Building a World-Class Workforce," *Treasury Board of Canada*, January 1999.

43. S.P. Robbins and N. Langton, *Organizational Behaviour: Concepts, Controversies, Applications*, 2nd Canadian ed. (Toronto: Pearson Education Canada, 2001), p. 70.

44. Luiza Chwialkowska, "Ottawa Plan Targets Jobs Crisis," *National Post*, June 18, 2001, p. A1.

45. For further elaboration of these points see B. Moses, *Career Intelligence: Mastering the New Work and Personal Realities*, (Toronto: Stoddart, 1997).

46. C.D. Fisher, L.F. Schoenfeldt, and J.B. Shaw, *Human Resource Management* (Boston: Houghton Mifflin, 1990).

47. C.D. Fisher, L.F. Schoenfeldt, and J.B. Shaw, *Human Resource Management* (Boston: Houghton Mifflin, 1990); G.P. Latham and K.N. Wexley, *Increasing Productivity Through Performance Appraisal* (Reading, MA: Addison-Wesley, 1982).

48. "Management Insight" is based on R. Wright, "21 Ways to Build Great People," *Profit: The Magazine for Canadian Entrepreneurs*, June 2000, pp. 122–132.

49. T.A. DeCotiis, "An Analysis of the External Validity and Applied Relevance of Three Rating Formats," *Organizational Behavior and Human Performance*, 19, 1977, pp. 247–66; C.D. Fisher, L.F. Schoenfeldt, and J.B. Shaw, *Human Resource Management* (Boston: Houghton Mifflin, 1990).

50. T. Davis and M.J. Landa, "A Contrary Look at Employee Performance Appraisal," *Canadian Manager*, Fall 1999, pp. 18–19+.

51. L. Duxbury, L. Dyke, and N. Lam, "Career Development in the Federal Public Service: Building a World-Class Workforce," *Treasury Board of Canada*, January 1999.

52. M. MacKinnon, "Barrick's Munk Leads Pay Parade: $38.9M," *Canadian Press Newswire*, April 26, 1999.

53. David Berman, "A Bad Place to Be Boss. Lesson #1 for Canadian CEOs: Learn to Live on a Lot Less Than Your International Peers," *Canadian Business*, July 1997, pp. 17–19.

54. T. Hamilton, "Cisco CEO's Massive Pay Cut Described as Lesson for Roth," *Toronto Star*, April 26, 2001, pp. E1, E11.

55. S. Premack and J.E. Hunter, "Individual Unionization Decisions," *Psychological Bulletin*, 103, 1988, pp. 223–34.

56. R. Blumenstein, "Ohio Strike That is Crippling GM Plants Is Tied to Plan to Outsource Brake Work," *Wall Street Journal*, March 12, 1996, pp. A3, A4.

57. J. Hannah, "GM Workers Agree to End Strike," *Bryan–College Station Eagle*, March 23, 1996, p. A12.

58. R.W. Keidel, "Rethinking Organizational Design," *Academy of Management Executive*, 8, 1994, pp. 12–30.

59. "'Haves & Have-Nots': Canadians Look for Corporate Conscience," *Maclean's*, December 30, 1996/January 6, 1997, pp. 26, 37.

60. "Haves & Have-Nots": Canadians Look for Corporate Conscience," *Maclean's*, December 30, 1996/January 6, 1997, pp. 26, 37.

61. W.F. Cascio, "Downsizing: What Do We Know? What Have We Learned?" *Academy of Management Executive*, 7, 1993, p. 100.

62. "Shareholders Versus Job Holders. Do Corporations Have an Obligation to Provide Work? Or, Are They Solely Economic Units That Have No Social Function?" *Canada and the World Backgrounder*, October 1996, pp. 11–13.

63. "Work Option Plans Can Soften Blows of Layoffs," *The Financial Post*, May 4/6, 1996, p. 37.

64. S. McKay, "The Age Factor: If a Company Is Nothing Without Its Employees Who Make It Work, Then Surely Those With a Lifetime of Knowledge and Experience Must Count Among its Most Valuable Assets," *Financial Post 500*, 1998, pp, 72–82.

65. S. McKay, "The Age Factor: If a Company Is Nothing Without Its Employees Who Make It Work, Then Surely Those With a Lifetime of Knowledge and Experience Must Count Among Its Most Valuable Assets," *Financial Post 500*, 1998, pp. 72–82.

Chapter 11

1. Based on P. Kuitenbrouwer, "New Boss in Sharp Contrast: F. Anthony Comper. Incoming Bank of Montreal Chief Opposite of Flashy Barrett," *Financial Post (National Post)*, February 24, 1999, p. C4; K. Noble and J. Nicol, "Barrett Takes His Exit: The Bank of Montreal's Charismatic CEO Turns Down Two More Years at the Helm," *Maclean's*, March 8, 1999, p. 34; J. Nicol, "The Man Who Must Plot a New Course," *Maclean's*, March 8, 1999, p. 36; R. McQueen, "Long Shadows: Even in the Biggest Bank, the Institution Comes to Resemble Its CEO," *National Post Business*, June 2000, pp. 43–44; and J. Ivison, "Simple Steps Look Like Fast Footwork: BMO's Comper Does a Tapdance With

the [First-Quarter] Results," *Financial Post (National Post)*, February 28, 2001, p. C2.

2. C. Cattaneo, "WestJet CEO Fired to Head Off Revolt: WestJet Founder Feared Defections by Key Executives," *Financial Post (National Post)*, September 26, 2000, pp. C1, C2; P. Fitzpatrick, "Morale Uplifted as CEO Departs: WestJet Demands Resignation of Stephen Smith," *Financial Post (National Post)*, September 12, 2000, pp. C1, C11.

3. J.M. Digman, "Personality Structure: Emergence of the Five-Factor Model," *Annual Review of Psychology*, 41, 1990, pp. 417–40; R.R. McCrae and P.T. Costa, "Validation of the Five-Factor Model of Personality Across Instruments and Observers," *Journal of Personality and Social Psychology*, 52, 1987, pp. 81–90; R.R. McCrae and P.T. Costa, "Discriminant Validity of NEO–PIR Facet Scales," *Educational and Psychological Measurement*, 52, 1992, pp. 229–37.

4. J.M. Digman, "Personality Structure: Emergence of the Five-Factor Model," *Annual Review of Psychology*, 41, 1990, pp. 417–40; R.R. McCrae and P.T. Costa, "Validation of the Five-Factor Model of Personality Across Instruments and Observers," *Journal of Personality and Social Psychology*, 52, 1987, pp. 81–90; R.R. McCrae and P.T. Costa, "Discriminant Validity of NEO–PIR Facet Scales," *Educational and Psychological Measurement*, 52, 1992, pp. 229–37.

5. M.R. Barrick and M.K. Mount, "The Big Five Personality Dimensions and Job Performance: A Meta-Analysis," *Personnel Psychology*, 44, 1991, pp. 1–26.

6. D. Olive, "Twilight in Batawa: They Closed Tom Bata's Shoe Factory This Spring, Marking the End of a Company Town That Had Outlived Its Time," *National Post Business*, June 2000, pp. 60–66.

7. D. Baldwin, "Bata Founders View Laid Off Employees as Family," *Canadian Press Newswire*, October 20, 1999.

8. J.M. Digman, "Personality Structure: Emergence of the Five-Factor Model," *Annual Review of Psychology*, 41, 1990, pp. 417–40; R.R. McCrae and P.T. Costa, "Validation of the Five-Factor Model of Personality Across Instruments and Observers," *Journal of Personality and Social Psychology*, 52, 1987, pp. 81–90; R.R. McCrae and P.T. Costa, "Discriminant

Validity of NEO–PIR Facet Scales," *Educational and Psychological Measurement*, 52, 1992, pp. 229–37.

9. "Management Insight" is based on H. Ediriweera, "Boomers Adapt to Gen X Managers," *Silicon Valley North*, January 2001, p. 29.

10. J.B. Rotter, "Generalized Expectancies for Internal vs. External Control of Reinforcement," *Psychological Monographs*, 80, 1966, pp. 1–28; P. Spector, "Behaviors in Organizations as a Function of Employees' Locus of Control," *Psychological Bulletin*, 91, 1982, pp. 482–97.

11. A. Van den Broek, "Boyce Leads Change at Unilever," *Marketing Magazine*, October 2, 2000, p. 8.

12. J. Brockner, *Self-Esteem at Work* (Lexington, MA: Lexington Books, 1988).

13. D.C. McClelland, *Human Motivation* (Glenview, IL: Scott, Foresman, 1985); D.C. McClelland, "How Motives, Skills, and Values Determine What People Do," *American Psychologist*, 40, 1985, pp. 812–25; D.C. McClelland, "Managing Motivation to Expand Human Freedom," *American Psychologist*, 33, 1978, pp. 201–10.

14. D.G. Winter, *The Power Motive* (New York: Free Press, 1973).

15. M.J. Stahl, "Achievement, Power, and Managerial Motivation: Selecting Managerial Talent with the Job Choice Exercise," *Personnel Psychology*, 36, 1983, pp. 775–89; D.C. McClelland and D.H. Burnham, "Power Is the Great Motivator," *Harvard Business Review*, 54, 1976, pp. 100–10.

16. R.J. House, W.D. Spangler, and J. Woycke, "Personality and Charisma in the US Presidency: A Psychological Theory of Leader Effectiveness," *Administrative Science Quarterly*, 36, 1991, pp. 364–96.

17. M. Rokeach, *The Nature of Human Values* (New York: Free Press, 1973).

18. M. Rokeach, *The Nature of Human Values* (New York: Free Press, 1973).

19. M. Rokeach, *The Nature of Human Values* (New York: Free Press, 1973).

20. L. Kraar, "The Overseas Chinese: Lessons from the World's Most Dynamic Capitalists," *Fortune*, October 31, 1994, pp. 91–114.

21. P. Edgardio, "A New High-Tech Dynasty?" *Business Week*, August 15, 1994,

pp. 90–91; "Formosa Plastics Corp.: Company Says Pretax Profit Doubled in the First Quarter," *Wall Street Journal*, April 28, 1995, p. A1; L. Kraar, "The Overseas Chinese: Lessons from the World's Most Dynamic Capitalists," *Fortune*, October 31, 1994, pp. 91–114.

22. D.W. Organ, *Organizational Citizenship Behavior: The Good Soldier Syndrome* (Lexington, MA: Lexington Books, 1988).

23. J.M. George and A.P. Brief, "Feeling Good–Doing Good: A Conceptual Analysis of the Mood at Work–Organizational Spontaneity Relationship," *Psychological Bulletin*, 112, 1992, pp. 310–29.

24. W.H. Mobley, "Intermediate Linkages in the Relationship Between Job Satisfaction and Employee Turnover," *Journal of Applied Psychology*, 62, 1977, pp. 237–40.

25. "Managers View Workplace Changes More Positively Than Employees," *Wall Street Journal*, December 13, 1994, p. A1.

26. J.E. Mathieu and D.M. Zajac, "A Review and Meta-Analysis of the Antecedents, Correlates, and Consequences of Organizational Commitment," *Psychological Bulletin*, 108, 1990, pp. 171–94.

27. J. Heinzl, "Roche Macaulay President Fires Himself," *The Globe and Mail*, April 24, 2001, p. B4.

28. D. Watson and A. Tellegen, "Toward a Consensual Structure of Mood," *Psychological Bulletin*, 98, 1985, pp. 219–35.

29. D. Watson and A. Tellegen, "Toward a Consensual Structure of Mood," *Psychological Bulletin*, 98, 1985, pp. 219–35.

30. J.M. George, "The Role of Personality in Organizational Life: Issues and Evidence," *Journal of Management*, 18, 1992, pp. 185–213.

31. J.M. George and K. Bettenhausen, "Understanding Prosocial Behavior, Sales Performance, and Turnover: A Group Level Analysis in a Service Context," *Journal of Applied Psychology*, 75, 1990, pp. 698–709.

32. J.M. George and A.P. Brief, "Feeling Good–Doing Good: A Conceptual Analysis of the Mood at Work–Organizational Spontaneity Relationship," *Psychological Bulletin*, 112, 1992, pp. 310–29; A.M. Isen and R.A. Baron, "Positive Affect as a Factor in Organizational Behavior," in B.M. Staw and L.L. Cummings (eds.), *Research in Organizational Behavior*, vol. 13 (Greenwich, CT: JAI Press, 1991), pp. 1–53.

33. R.C. Sinclair, "Mood, Categorization Breadth, and Performance Appraisal: The Effects of Order of Information Acquisition and Affective State on Halo, Accuracy, Informational Retrieval, and Evaluations," *Organizational Behavior and Human Decision Processes*, 42, 1988, pp. 22–46.

34. T. Tillson, "Is Your Career Killing You?" *Canadian Business*, September 26, 1997, pp. 78–80+.

35. H.R. Schiffmann, *Sensation and Perception: An Integrated Approach* (New York: Wiley, 1990).

36. "Focus on Diversity": Exercisers Are "Better People" is based on A.M. Owens, "People Who Exercise Are More Highly Regarded: Study," *The National Post*, February 10, 2001, p. A2.

37. A.G. Greenwald and M. Banaji, "Implicit Social Cognition: Attitudes, Self-Esteem, and Stereotypes," *Psychological Review*, 102, 1995, pp. 4–27.

38. R.S. Lazarus, *Psychological Stress and Coping Processes* (New York: McGraw-Hill, 1966); R.S. Lazarus and S. Folkman, *Stress, Appraisal, and Coping* (New York: Springer, 1984); R.S. Lazarus, "Psychological Stress in the Workplace," in R. Crandall and P.L. Perrewe, *Occupational Stress: A Handbook* (Washington, DC: Taylor & Francis, 1995).

39. T. Tillson, "Is Your Career Killing You?" *Canadian Business*, September 26, 1997, pp. 78–80+.

40. D. Watson and J.W. Pennebaker, "Health Complaints, Stress, and Distress: Exploring the Central Role of Negative Affectivity," *Psychological Review*, 96, 1989, pp. 234–54.

41. D. Watson and A. Tellegen, "Toward a Consensual Structure of Mood," *Psychological Bulletin*, 98, 1985, pp. 219–35.

42. R.L. Kahn and P. Byosiere, "Stress in Organizations," in M.D. Dunnette and L.M. Hough (eds.), *Handbook of Industrial and Organizational Psychology*, 2d ed., vol. 3, (Palo Alto, CA: Consulting Psychologists Press, 1992), pp. 571–650; S. Jackson and R. Schuler, "A Meta-Analysis and Conceptual Critique of Research on Role Ambiguity and Role Conflict in Work Settings," *Organizational Behavior and Human Decision Processes*, 36, 1985, pp. 16–78.

43. R.L. Kahn and P. Byosiere, "Stress in Organizations," in M.D. Dunnette and L.M. Hough (eds.), *Handbook of Industrial and Organizational Psychology*, 2d ed., vol. 3, (Palo Alto, CA: Consulting Psychologists Press, 1992), pp. 571–650.

44. S. Folkman and R.S. Lazarus, "An Analysis of Coping in a Middle-Aged Community Sample," *Journal of Health and Social Behavior*, 21, 1980, pp. 219–39; S. Folkman and R.S. Lazarus, "If It Changes It Must Be a Process: Study of Emotion and Coping During Three Stages of a College Examination," *Journal of Personality and Social Psychology*, 48, 1985, pp. 150–70; S. Folkman and R.S. Lazarus, "Coping as a Mediator of Emotion," *Journal of Personality and Social Psychology*, 54, 1988, pp. 466–75.

45. S. Folkman and R.S. Lazarus, "An Analysis of Coping in a Middle-Aged Community Sample," *Journal of Health and Social Behavior*, 21, 1980, pp. 219–39.

46. A. Lakein, *How to Get Control of Your Time and Your Life* (New York: Wyden, 1973); J.C. Quick and J.D. Quick, *Organizational Stress and Preventive Management* (New York: McGraw-Hill, 1984).

47. G. Dreher and R. Ash, "A Comparative Study of Mentoring Among Men and Women in Managerial, Professional, and Technical Positions," *Journal of Applied Psychology*, 75, 1990, pp. 525–35; T.A. Scandura, "Mentorship and Career Mobility: An Empirical Investigation," *Journal of Organizational Behavior*, 13, 1992, pp. 169–74; D.B. Turban and T.W. Dougherty, "The Role of Protégé Personality in Receipt of Mentoring and Career Success," *Academy of Management Journal*, 37. 1994, pp. 688–702; W. Whitely, T.W. Dougherty, and G.F. Dreher, "Relationship of Career Mentoring and Socioeconomic Origin to Managers' and Professionals' Early Career Success," *Academy of Management Journal*, 34, 1991, pp. 331–51.

48. "Management Insight": Life Balance Improves Performance is based on D. Luckow, "Where Are They Now?" *Profit: The Magazine for Canadian Entrepreneurs*, April 2000, pp. 27-44.

49. J.C. Quick and J.D. Quick, *Organizational Stress and Preventive Management* (New York: McGraw-Hill, 1984).

50. R. Neff, "They Fly Through the Air With the Greatest of ... Ki?" *Business Week*, January 23, 1995, p. 60.

51. S. Cohen and T.A. Wills, "Stress, Social Support, and the Buffering Hypothesis," *Psychological Bulletin*, 98, 1985, pp. 310–57; I.G. Sarason, H.M. Levine, R.B. Basham, and B.R. Sarason, "Assessing Social Support: The Social Support Questionnaire," *Journal of Personality and Social Psychology*, 44, 1983, pp. 127–39.

52. T. Tillson, "Is Your Career Killing You?" *Canadian Business*, September 26, 1997, pp. 78–80+.

53. K.L. Alexander and S. Baker, "The New Life of O'Reilly," *Business Week*, June 13, 1994, pp. 64–66; K. Labich, "Is Herb Kelleher America's Best CEO?" *Fortune*, May 2, 1994, pp. 44–52; L. Smith, "Stamina: Who Has It, Why You Need It, How You Get It," *Fortune*, November 28, 1994, pp. 127–39.

54. L. Smith, "Stamina: Who Has It, Why You Need It, How You Get It," *Fortune*, November 28, 1994, pp. 127–39.

55. L. Smith, "Stamina: Who Has It, Why You Need It, How You Get It," *Fortune*, November 28, 1994, pp. 127–39.

Chapter 12

1. W. Bounds, "Kodak's CEO Got $1.7 Million Bonus in 1994 Despite Below-Target Profit," *Wall Street Journal*, March 13, 1995, p. B9; C.J. Cantoni, "Manager's Journal: A Waste of Human Resources," *Wall Street Journal*, May 15, 1995, p. A22; D. Defotis, "Kodak's Moment May Be Near," *Financial Post (National Post)*, August 12, 2000, p. C8; M. Maremont, "Kodak's New Focus," *Business Week*, January 30, 1995, pp. 62–68; P. Nulty, "Kodak Grabs for Growth Again," *Fortune*, May 16, 1994, pp. 76–78; B. Saporito, "The Eclipse of Mars," *Fortune*, November 28, 1994, p. 82.

2. B. Saporito, "The Eclipse of Mars," *Fortune*, November 28, 1994, p. 82.

3. R. Kanfer, "Motivation Theory and Industrial and Organizational Psychology," in M.D. Dunnette and L.M. Hough (eds.), *Handbook of Industrial and Organizational Psychology*, 2nd ed., vol. 1 (Palo Alto, CA: Consulting Psychologists Press, 1990), pp. 75–170.

4. A.H. Maslow, *Motivation and Personality* (New York: Harper and Row, 1954); J.P. Campbell and R.D. Pritchard, "Motivation Theory in Industrial and Organizational Psychology," in M.D. Dunnette (ed.), *Handbook of Industrial and Organizational Psychology* (Chicago: Rand McNally, 1976), pp. 63–130.

5. R. Kanfer, "Motivation Theory and Industrial and Organizational Psychology," in M.D. Dunnette and L.M. Hough (eds.), *Handbook of Industrial and Organizational Psychology*, 2d ed., vol. 1 (Palo Alto, CA: Consulting Psychologists Press, 1990), pp. 75–170.

6. S. Ronen, "An Underlying Structure of Motivational Need Taxonomies: A Cross-Cultural Confirmation," in H.C. Triandis, M.D. Dunnette, and L.M. Hough (eds.), *Handbook of Industrial and Organizational Psychology*, vol. 4 (Palo Alto, CA: Consulting Psychologists Press, 1994), pp. 241–69.

7. N.J. Adler, *International Dimensions of Organizational Behavior*, 2d ed. (Boston: P.W.S.-Kent, 1991); G. Hofstede, "Motivation, Leadership and Organization: Do American Theories Apply Abroad?" *Organizational Dynamics*, Summer 1980, pp. 42–63.

8. C.P. Alderfer, "An Empirical Test of a New Theory of Human Needs," *Organizational Behavior and Human Performance*, 4, 1969, pp. 142–75; C.P. Alderfer, *Existence, Relatedness, and Growth: Human Needs in Organizational Settings* (New York: Free Press, 1972); J.P. Campbell and R.D. Pritchard, "Motivation Theory in Industrial and Organizational Psychology," in M.D. Dunnette (ed.), *Handbook of Industrial and Organizational Psychology* (Chicago: Rand McNally, 1976), pp. 63–130.

9. R. Kanfer, "Motivation Theory and Industrial and Organizational Psychology," in M.D. Dunnette and L.M. Hough (eds.), *Handbook of Industrial and Organizational Psychology*, 2d ed., vol. 1 (Palo Alto, CA: Consulting Psychologists Press, 1990), pp. 75–170.

10. F. Herzberg, *Work and the Nature of Man* (Cleveland: World, 1966).

11. N. King, "Clarification and Evaluation of the Two-Factor Theory of Job Satisfaction," *Psychological Bulletin*, 74, 1970, pp. 18–31; E.A. Locke, "The Nature and Causes of Job Satisfaction," in M.D. Dunnette (ed.), *Handbook of Industrial and Organizational Psychology* (Chicago: Rand McNally, 1976), pp. 1297–1349.

12. "Management Insight": Treating People Right at Pazmac Enterprises is based on G. Bellett, "Firm's Secret to Success Lies in Treating Workers Right," *The Vancouver Sun*, March 21, 2001, pp. D7, D11.

13. T.R. Mitchell, "Expectancy-Value Models in Organizational Psychology," in N.T. Feather (ed.), *Expectations and Actions: Expectancy-Value Models in Psychology* (Hillsdale, NJ: Erlbaum, 1982), pp. 293–312; V.H. Vroom, *Work and Motivation* (New York: Wiley, 1964).

14. D. Milbank, "Long Viewed as Kaput, Many European Firms Seem to Be Reviving," *Wall Street Journal*, February 14, 1995, pp. A1, A8.

15. "Motorola Inc.: Company Is Chosen to Build Cellular System in Calcutta," *Wall Street Journal*, January 5, 1995, p. B4; "Motorola Inc. Plans to Increase Business With Chinese Ventures," *Wall Street Journal*, February 13, 1995, p. B11.

16. P. Engardio and G. DeGeorge, "Importing Enthusiasm," *Business Week/21st Century Capitalism*, 1994, pp. 122–23.

17. P. Engardio and G. DeGeorge, "Importing Enthusiasm," *Business Week/21st Century Capitalism*, 1994, pp. 122–23.

18. E.A. Locke and G.P. Latham, *A Theory of Goal Setting and Task Performance* (Englewood Cliffs, NJ: Prentice-Hall, 1990).

19. E.A. Locke and G.P. Latham, *A Theory of Goal Setting and Task Performance* (Englewood Cliffs, NJ: Prentice-Hall, 1990); J.J. Donovan and D.J. Radosevich, "The Moderating Role of Goal Commitment on the Goal Difficulty–Performance Relationship: A Meta-Analytic Review and Critical Analysis," *Journal of Applied Psychology*, 83, 1998, pp. 308–315; M.E. Tubbs, "Goal Setting: A Meta-Analytic Examination of the Empirical Evidence," *Journal of Applied Psychology*, 71, 1986, pp. 474–83.

20. E.A. Locke, K.N. Shaw, L.M. Saari, and G.P. Latham, "Goal Setting and Task Performance: 1969–1980," *Psychological Bulletin*, 90, 1981, pp. 125–52.

21. P.C. Earley, T. Connolly, and G. Ekegren, "Goals, Strategy Development,

and Task Performance: Some Limits on the Efficacy of Goal Setting," *Journal of Applied Psychology*, 74, 1989, pp. 24–33; R. Kanfer and P.L. Ackerman, "Motivation and Cognitive Abilities: An Integrative/Aptitude–Treatment Interaction Approach to Skill Acquisition," *Journal of Applied Psychology*, 74, 1989, pp. 657–90.

22. "Management Insight" is based on L. Perreaux, "When 'The Job Sucks,' Maple Leaf Raffles Trucks: Company Incentives at Slaughterhouse in Manitoba," *National Post*, May 19, 2001, p. A3.

23. F. Luthans and R. Kreitner, *Organizational Behavior Modification and Beyond* (Glenview, IL: Scott, Foresman, 1985); A.D. Stajkovic and F. Luthans, "A Meta-Analysis of the Effects of Organizational Behavior Modification on Task Performance, 1975–95," *Academy of Management Journal*, 40, 1997, pp. 1122–1149.

24. J.S. Adams, "Toward an Understanding of Inequity," *Journal of Abnormal and Social Psychology*, 67, 1963, pp. 422–36.

25. J.S. Adams, "Toward an Understanding of Inequity," *Journal of Abnormal and Social Psychology*, 67, 1963, pp. 422–36; J. Greenberg, "Approaching Equity and Avoiding Inequity in Groups and Organizations," in J. Greenberg and R.L. Cohen (eds.), *Equity and Justice in Social Behavior* (New York: Academic Press, 1982), pp. 389–435; J. Greenberg, "Equity and Workplace Status: A Field Experiment," *Journal of Applied Psychology*, 73, 1988, pp. 606–13; R.T. Mowday, "Equity Theory Predictions of Behavior in Organizations," in R.M. Steers and L.W. Porter (eds.), *Motivation and Work Behavior* (New York: McGraw-Hill, 1987), pp. 89–110.

26. E.E. Lawler III, *Pay and Organization Development* (Reading, MA: Addison-Wesley, 1981).

27. Based on S.E. Gross and J.P. Bacher, "The New Variable Pay Programs: How Some Succeed, Why Some Don't," *Compensation & Benefits Review*, January–February 1993, p. 51; and J.R. Schuster and P.K. Zingheim, "The New Variable Pay: Key Design Issues," *Compensation & Benefits Review*, March–April 1993, p. 28.

28. "Hope for Higher Pay: The Squeeze on Incomes Is Gradually Easing Up,"

Maclean's, November 25, 1996, pp. 100–101.

29. P. Booth, *Challenge and Change: Embracing the Team Concept*, Report 123–94, Conference Board of Canada, 1994, p. 18.

30. "Management Insight" is based on "Paying Workers Well Is Not Enough, Survey Finds," *Financial Post (National Post)*, May 16, 2001, p. C10.

31. E.E. Lawler III, *Pay and Organization Development* (Reading, MA: Addison-Wesley, 1981).

32. E.E. Lawler III, *Pay and Organization Development* (Reading, MA: Addison-Wesley, 1981).

33. E.E. Lawler III, *Pay and Organization Development* (Reading, MA: Addison-Wesley, 1981).

34. "Risk and Reward: More Canadian Companies Are Experimenting With Variable Pay," *Maclean's*, January 8, 1996, pp. 26–27.

35. C. Mandel, "Cash by the Numbers: The Vogue for 'Performance Incentives' Spreads to Primary Schools," *Alberta Report*, March 29, 1999, p. 33.

36. K. May, "New Pay Scheme Intended to Help Retain Canada's Top Bureaucrats," *Vancouver Sun*, August 3, 1999, p. A5.

37. "Management Insight" is based on R. Fife, "Censured Mandarins Got Bonuses: Performance Pay Given in Departments Lambasted by Auditor," *National Post*, May 24, 2001, p. A6.

38. A.J. Michels, "Dallas Semiconductor," *Fortune*, May 16, 1994, p. 81.

39. M. Betts, "Big Things Come in Small Buttons," *Computerworld*, August 3, 1992, p. 30.

40. M. Boslet, "Metal Buttons Toted by Crop Pickers Act as Mini Databases," *Wall Street Journal*, June 1, 1994, p. B3.

41. C.D. Fisher, L.F. Schoenfeldt, and J.B. Shaw, *Human Resource Management* (Boston: Houghton Mifflin, 1990); B.E. Graham-Moore and T.L. Ross, *Productivity Gainsharing* (Englewood Cliffs, NJ: Prentice-Hall, 1983); A.J. Geare, "Productivity from Scanlon Type Plans," *Academy of Management Review*, 1, 1976, pp. 99–108.

42. D. Beck, "Implementing a Gainsharing Plan: What Companies

Need to Know," *Compensation & Benefits Review*, January–February 1992, p. 23.

43. L. Ramsay, "Action Shifts from Salary to Incentives: Canadians Play Catch-Up. Pay for Performance Programs are Being Extended to Cover Entire Workforces," *Financial Post (National Post)*, February 5, 1999, p. C18.

44. R. Jacob, "Corporate Reputations," *Fortune*, March 6, 1995, pp. 54–64; J.R. Norman, "Choose Your Partners," *Forbes*, November 21, 1994, pp. 88–89; S. Tully, "Why to Go for Stretch Targets," *Fortune*, November 14, 1994, pp. 145–58.

45. S. Tully, "Why to Go for Stretch Targets," *Fortune*, November 14, 1994, pp. 145–58.

46. S. Tully, "Why to Go for Stretch Targets," *Fortune*, November 14, 1994, pp. 145–58.

Chapter 13

1. This "Case in Contrast" is based on K. Barker, "Dr Boss: Julia Levy Tells Kate Barker About Her Reluctant Transition From Scientist to CEO," *National Post Business*, July 2000, p. 33; D. Calleja, "Now We're in Business," *Canadian Business*, December, 25, 2000, pp. 119–120+; D. Hasselback, "QLT Soars as Sales Outlook Brightens: Shares Gain 35%. Potential Market Grows but Revenue Forecast Still Falls," *Financial Post (National Post)*, February 9, 2001, pp. D1, D2; I. MacNeill, "Entrepreneurs of the Year 2000," *B.C. Business Magazine*, September 2000, pp. 45, 47+; I. MacNeill, "Pacific Canada Entrepreneur of the Year," *B.C. Business Magazine*, October 2000, pp. 36–39; S. Silcoff, "Irwin Toy in Discussions With Potential Private Buyer: Negotiating Cash Offer," *Financial Post (National Post)*, February 28, 2001, pp. C1, C6; S. Silcoff, "There Is No Joy in Irwin Toy Land: Feud Involving Family Members Ended in Departure of Chief Executive," *Financial Post (National Post)*, December 11, 2000, pp. C1, C6; S. Silicoff, "Irwin Toy Bows Out as Publicly Traded Company," *Financial Post (National Post)*, May 24, 2001, p. C11; P. Verburg, "The Light Stuff: Julia Levy and QLT Phototherapeutics Inc. Have Spent 20 Years Perfecting a Light-Activated Cure for Elderly Blindness. It Could Mean Blockbuster Revenues, if They Can Master the Switch From Discovery to Manufacturing," *Canadian Business*,

February 7, 2000, pp. 66–70; P. Withers, "M(i)s-matched? Why So Few Women Seem to Be Taking Advantage of the High-Tech Bonanza," *B.C. Business Magazine*, October 2000, pp. 102–111.

2. G. Yukl, *Leadership in Organizations*, 2nd ed. (New York: Academic Press, 1989); R.M. Stogdill, *Handbook of Leadership: A Survey of the Literature* (New York: Free Press, 1974).

3. R. Calori and B. Dufour, "Management European Style," *Academy of Management Executive*, 9, no. 3, 1995, pp. 61–70.

4. R. Calori and B. Dufour, "Management European Style," *Academy of Management Executive*, 9, no. 3, 1995, pp. 61–70.

5. H. Mintzberg, *Power in and Around Organizations* (Englewood Cliffs, NJ: Prentice-Hall, 1983); J. Pfeffer, *Power in Organizations* (Marshfield, MA: Pitman, 1981).

6. R.P. French, Jr., and B. Raven, "The Bases of Social Power," in D. Cartwright and A.F. Zander (eds.), *Group Dynamics* (Evanston, IL: Row, Peterson, 1960), pp. 607–23.

7. J. Fierman, "Winning Ideas from Maverick Managers," *Fortune*, February 6, 1995, pp. 66–80.

8. J. Fierman, "Winning Ideas from Maverick Managers," *Fortune*, February 6, 1995, p. 70.

9. J.A. Lopez, "A Better Way? Setting Your Own Pay–And Other Unusual Compensation Plans," *Wall Street Journal*, April 13, 1994, p. R6; "Maverick: The Success Story Behind the World's Most Unusual Workplace," *HR Magazine*, April 1994, pp. 88–89; J. Pottinger, "Brazilian Maverick Reveals His Radical Recipe for Success," *Personnel Management*, September 1994, p. 71.

10. J. Fierman, "Winning Ideas from Maverick Managers," *Fortune*, February 6, 1995, pp. 66–80.

11. T.M. Burton, "Visionary's Reward: Combine 'Simple Ideas' and Some Failures; Result: Sweet Revenge," *Wall Street Journal*, February 3, 1995, pp. A1, A5.

12. L. Nakarmi, "A Flying Leap Toward the 21st Century? Pressure From Competitors and Seoul May Transform the Chaebol," *Business Week*, March 20, 1995, pp. 78–80.

13. J. Schaubroeck, J.R. Jones, and J.L. Xie, "Individual Differences in Utilizing Control to Cope With Job Demands: Effects on Susceptibility to Infectious Disease," *Journal of Applied Psychology*, 86, no. 2, 2001, pp. 265–278 and A.M. Owens, "Empowerment Can Make You Ill, Study Says," *The National Post*, April 30, 2001, pp. A1, A8.

14. "Delta Promotes Empowerment," *The Globe and Mail*, May 31, 1999, Advertising Supplement, p. C5.

15. B.M. Bass, *Bass and Stogdill's Handbook of Leadership: Theory, Research, and Managerial Applications*, 3rd ed. (New York: Free Press, 1990); R.J. House and M.L. Baetz, "Leadership: Some Empirical Generalizations and New Research Directions," in B.M. Staw and L.L. Cummings (eds.), *Research in Organizational Behavior*, vol. 1 (Greenwich, CT: JAI Press, 1979), pp. 341–423; S.A. Kirpatrick and E.A. Locke, "Leadership: Do Traits Matter?" *Academy of Management Executive*, 5, no. 2, 1991, pp. 48–60; G. Yukl, *Leadership in Organizations*, 2nd ed. (New York: Academic Press, 1989); G. Yukl and D.D. Van Fleet, "Theory and Research on Leadership in Organizations," in M.D. Dunnette and L.M. Hough (eds.), *Handbook of Industrial and Organizational Psychology*, 2nd ed., vol. 3 (Palo Alto, CA: Consulting Psychologists Press, 1992), pp. 147–97.

16. E.A. Fleishman, "Performance Assessment Based on an Empirically Derived Task Taxonomy," *Human Factors*, 9, 1967, pp. 349–66; E.A. Fleishman, "The Description of Supervisory Behavior," *Personnel Psychology*, 37, 1953, pp. 1–6; A.W. Halpin and B.J. Winer, "A Factorial Study of the Leader Behavior Descriptions," in R.M. Stogdill and A.I. Coons (eds.), *Leader Behavior: Its Description and Measurement* (Columbus Bureau of Business Research, Ohio State University, 1957); D. Tscheulin, "Leader Behavior Measurement in German Industry," *Journal of Applied Psychology*, 56, 1971, pp. 28–31.

17. A. Taylor III, "Why GM Leads the Pack in Europe," *Fortune*, May 17, 1993, pp. 83–86.

18. U. Gupta, "Starting Out: How Much? Figuring the Correct Amount of Capital for Starting a Business Can Be a Tough Balancing Act," *Wall Street Journal*, May 22, 1995, p. R7; R. Jacob, "How One Red Hot Retailer Wins Customer Loyalty," *Fortune*, July 10, 1995, pp. 72–79; "Staples Taps Hanaka from Lechmere Inc. to Become Its CEO," *Wall Street Journal*, July 29, 1994, p. B2.

19. T. King, "How a Hot Ad Agency, Undone by Arrogance, Lost Its Independence," *Wall Street Journal*, April 11, 1995, pp. A1, A5.

20. T. King, "How a Hot Ad Agency, Undone by Arrogance, Lost Its Independence," *Wall Street Journal*, April 11, 1995, p. A5.

21. T. King, "How a Hot Ad Agency, Undone by Arrogance, Lost Its Independence," *Wall Street Journal*, April 11, 1995, A1, A5.

22. E.A. Fleishman and E.F. Harris, "Patterns of Leadership Behavior Related to Employee Grievances and Turnover," *Personnel Psychology*, 15, 1962, pp. 43–56.

23. R. Likert, *New Patterns of Management* (New York: McGraw-Hill, 1961); N.C. Morse and E. Reimer, "The Experimental Change of a Major Organizational Variable," *Journal of Abnormal and Social Psychology*, 52, 1956, pp. 120–29.

24. R.R. Blake and J.S. Mouton, *The New Managerial Grid* (Houston: Gulf, 1978).

25. P. Hersey and K. Blanchard, *Management of Organizational Behavior: Utilizing Human Resources* (Englewood Cliffs, NJ: Prentice-Hall, 1982).

26. F.E. Fiedler, *A Theory of Leadership Effectiveness* (New York: McGraw-Hill, 1967); F.E. Fiedler, "The Contingency Model and the Dynamics of the Leadership Process," in L. Berkowitz (ed.), *Advances in Experimental Social Psychology* (New York: Academic Press, 1978).

27. R.J. House and M.L. Baetz, "Leadership: Some Empirical Generalizations and New Research Directions," in B.M. Staw and L.L. Cummings (eds.), *Research in Organizational Behavior*, vol. 1 (Greenwich, CT: JAI Press, 1979), pp. 341–423; L.H. Peters, D.D. Hartke, and J.T. Pohlmann, "Fiedler's Contingency Theory of Leadership: An Application of the Meta-Analysis Procedures of Schmidt and Hunter," *Psychological Bulletin*, 97, 1985, pp. 274–85; C.A. Schriesheim, B.J. Tepper, and L.A. Tetrault, "Least Preferred Co-Worker Score, Situational Control, and Leadership Effectiveness: A Meta-Analysis of Contingency Model

Performance Predictions," *Journal of Applied Psychology*, 79, 1994, pp. 561–73.

28. P. Hersey and K.H. Blanchard, "So You Want to Know Your Leadership Style?" *Training and Development Journal*, February 1974, pp. 1–15; and P. Hersey and K.H. Blanchard, *Management of Organizational Behavior: Utilizing Human Resources*, 6th ed. (Englewood Cliffs, NJ: Prentice Hall, 1993).

29. Cited in C.F. Fernandez and R.P. Vecchio, "Situational Leadership Theory Revisited: A Test of an Across-Jobs Perspective," *Leadership Quarterly*, vol. 8, no. 1, 1997, p. 67.

30. M.G. Evans, "The Effects of Supervisory Behavior on the Path–Goal Relationship," *Organizational Behavior and Human Performance*," 5, 1970, pp. 277–298; M.G. Evans, "Leadership and Motivation: A Core Concept," *Academy of Management Journal*, 13, 1970, pp. 91–102; R.J. House, "A Path–Goal Theory of Leader Effectiveness," *Administrative Science Quarterly*, September 1971, pp. 321–338; R.J. House and T.R. Mitchell, "Path–Goal Theory of Leadership," *Journal of Contemporary Business*, Autumn 1974, p. 86; M.G. Evans, "Leadership," in S. Kerr (ed.), *Organizational Behavior* (Columbus, OH: Grid Publishing, 1979); R.J. House, "Retrospective Comment," in L.E. Boone and D.D. Bowen (eds.), *The Great Writings in Management and Organizational Behavior*, 2nd ed. (New York: Random House, 1987), pp. 354–364; M.G. Evans, "Fuhrungstheorien, Weg-ziel-theorie," (trans. G. Reber), in A. Kieser, G. Reber, and R. Wunderer (eds). *Handworterbuch Der Fuhrung*, 2nd ed. (Stuttgart, Germany: Schaffer Poeschal Verlag, 1995), pp. 1075–1091; and J.C. Wofford and L.Z. Liska, "Path–Goal Theories of Leadership: A Meta-Analysis," *Journal of Management*, 19, 1993, pp. 857–76.

31. "Management Insight": Turnaround in the Forestry Industry is based on R. McQueen, "The Long Shadow of Tom Stephens: He Branded MacBlo's Crew as Losers, Then Made Them into Winners," *Financial Post (National Post)*, June 22, 1999, p. C1, C5.

32. R. McQueen, "The Long Shadow of Tom Stephens: He Branded MacBlo's Crew as Losers, Then Made Them Into Winners," *Financial Post (National Post)*, June 22, 1999, p. C1, C5.

33. S. Kerr and J.M. Jermier, "Substitutes for Leadership: Their Meaning and Measurement," *Organizational Behavior and Human Performance*, 22, 1978, pp. 375–403; P.M. Podsakoff, B.P. Niehoff, S.B. MacKenzie, and M.L. Williams, "Do Substitutes for Leadership Really Substitute for Leadership? An Empirical Examination of Kerr and Jermier's Situational Leadership Model," *Organizational Behavior and Human Decision Processes*, 54, 1993, pp. 1–44.

34. S. Kerr and J.M. Jermier, "Substitutes for Leadership: Their Meaning and Measurement," *Organizational Behavior and Human Performance*, 22, 1978, pp. 375–403; Podsakoff, Niehoff, MacKenzie, and Williams, "Do Substitutes for Leadership Really Substitute for Leadership?"

35. J.M. Howell and B.J. Avolio, "The Leverage of Leadership," in *Leadership: Achieving Exceptional Performance*, A Special Supplement Prepared by the Richard Ivey School of Business, *The Globe and Mail*, May 15, 1998, pp. C1, C2.

36. J.M. Howell and B.J. Avolio, "The Leverage of Leadership," in *Leadership: Achieving Exceptional Performance*, A Special Supplement Prepared by the Richard Ivey School of Business, *The Globe and Mail*, May 15, 1998, pp. C1, C2.

37. K. Miller, "Siemens Shapes Up," *Business Week*, May 1, 1995, pp. 52–53.

38. B.M. Bass, *Leadership and Performance Beyond Expectations* (New York: Free Press, 1985); B.M. Bass, *Bass and Stogdill's Handbook of Leadership: Theory, Research, and Managerial Applications*, 3rd ed. (New York: Free Press, 1990); G. Yukl and D.D. Van Fleet, "Theory and Research on Leadership in Organizations," in M.D. Dunnette and L.M. Hough (eds.), *Handbook of Industrial and Organizational Psychology*, 2nd ed., vol. 3 (Palo Alto, CA: Consulting Psychologists Press, 1992), pp. 147–97.

39. G.E. Schares, J.B. Levine, and P. Coy, "The New Generation at Siemens," *Business Week*, March 9, 1992, pp. 46–48.

40. K. Miller, "Siemens Shapes Up," *Business Week*, May 1, 1995, pp. 52–53.

41. K. Miller, "Siemens Shapes Up," *Business Week*, May 1, 1995, pp. 52–53.

42. J.A. Conger and R.N. Kanungo, "Behavioral Dimensions of Charismatic Leadership," in J.A. Conger, R.N. Kanungo, and Associates, *Charismatic Leadership* (San Francisco: Jossey-Bass, 1988).

43. A.L. Sprout, "Packard Bell," *Fortune*, June 12, 1995, p. 83.

44. J.A. Conger and R.N. Kanungo, *Charismatic Leadership in Organizations* (Thousand Oaks, CA: Sage, 1998).

45. "Building a Better Boss," *Maclean's*, September 30, 1996, p. 41.

46. J.M. Howell and P.J. Frost, "A Laboratory Study of Charismatic Leadership," *Organizational Behavior & Human Decision Processes*, 43, no. 2, April 1989, pp. 243–269.

47. "Building a Better Boss," *Maclean's*, September 30, 1996, p. 41.

48. B.M. Bass, *Leadership and Performance Beyond Expectations* (New York: Free Press, 1985); B.M. Bass, *Bass and Stogdill's Handbook of Leadership: Theory, Research, and Managerial Applications*, 3rd ed. (New York: Free Press, 1990); G. Yukl and D.D. Van Fleet, "Theory and Research on Leadership in Organizations," in M.D. Dunnette and L.M. Hough (eds.), *Handbook of Industrial and Organizational Psychology*, 2nd ed., vol. 3 (Palo Alto, CA: Consulting Psychologists Press, 1992), pp. 147–97.

49. B.M. Bass, *Leadership and Performance Beyond Expectations* (New York: Free Press, 1985); B.M. Bass, *Bass and Stogdill's Handbook of Leadership: Theory, Research, and Managerial Applications*, 3rd ed. (New York: Free Press, 1990); G. Yukl and D.D. Van Fleet, "Theory and Research on Leadership in Organizations," in M.D. Dunnette and L.M. Hough (eds.), *Handbook of Industrial and Organizational Psychology*, 2nd ed., vol. 3 (Palo Alto, CA: Consulting Psychologists Press, 1992), pp. 147–97.

50. K. Miller, "Siemens Shapes Up," *Business Week*, May 1, 1995, pp. 52–53.

51. "Combo Push From Goldstar, Zenith," *Dealerscope*, February 1995, p. 38; "L.G. Electronics Co.: South Korean Firm Raises 1995 Sales Target by 22.6%," *Wall Street Journal*, January 5, 1995, p. 10; L. Nakarmi, "Goldstar Is Burning Bright," *Business Week*, September 26, 1994, pp. 129–30.

52. L. Nakarmi, "Goldstar Is Burning Bright," *Business Week*, September 26, 1994, p. 129.

53. L. Nakarmi, "Goldstar Is Burning Bright," *Business Week*, September 26, 1994, p. 129.

54. Cited in B.M. Bass and B.J. Avolio, "Developing Transformational Leadership: 1992 and Beyond," *Journal of European Industrial Training,* January 1990, p. 23.

55. J.M. Howell and B.J. Avolio, "The Leverage of Leadership," in *Leadership: Achieving Exceptional Performance*, A Special Supplement Prepared by the Richard Ivey School of Business, *The Globe and Mail*, May 15, 1998, pp. C2.

56. B.M. Bass and B.J. Avolio, "Developing Transformational Leadership: 1992 and Beyond," *Journal of European Industrial Training,* January 1990, p. 23; and J.M. Howell and B.J. Avolio, "The Leverage of Leadership," in *Leadership: Achieving Exceptional Performance*, A Special Supplement Prepared by the Richard Ivey School of Business, *The Globe and Mail*, May 15, 1998, pp. C1, C2.

57. R. McQueen, "Glitter Girls No More," *National Post Business*, March 2001, p. 68.

58. A.H. Eagly and B.T. Johnson, "Gender and Leadership Style: A Meta-Analysis," *Psychological Bulletin*, 108, 1990, pp. 233–56.

59. A.H. Eagly and B.T. Johnson, "Gender and Leadership Style: A Meta-Analysis," *Psychological Bulletin*, 108, 1990, pp. 233–56.

60. A.H. Eagly and B.T. Johnson, "Gender and Leadership Style: A Meta-Analysis," *Psychological Bulletin*, 108, 1990, pp. 233–56.

61. A.H. Eagly and B.T. Johnson, "Gender and Leadership Style: A Meta-Analysis," *Psychological Bulletin*, 108, 1990, pp. 233–56.

62. A.H. Eagly and B.T. Johnson, "Gender and Leadership Style: A Meta-Analysis," *Psychological Bulletin*, 108, 1990, pp. 233–56.

63. A.H. Eagly, S.J. Karau, and M.G. Makhijani, "Gender and the Effectiveness of Leaders: A Meta-Analysis," *Psychological Bulletin*, 117, 1995, pp. 125–45.

64. A.H. Eagly, S.J. Karau, and M.G. Makhijani, "Gender and the Effectiveness of Leaders: A Meta-Analysis," *Psychological Bulletin*, 117, 1995, pp. 125–45.

65. I. Austen, "Problem Child [Can Cynthia Trudell Save Saturn?]," *Canadian Business*, March 26, 1999, pp. 22–31; M. Ellis, "Trudell Jumps Saturn Ship to Steer Sea Ray Boats: Highest-Ranking Woman Auto Exec Moves to Brunswick," *Financial Post (National Post)*, March 30, 2001, p. C10; R. McQueen, "Saturn Boss Aims to Make Difference: Trudell's Mantra: 'I lived, I laughed, I learned and I loved,'" *Financial Post (National Post)*, April 1, 2000, p. D1, D2; "Saturn Corporation's Trudell to Lead Sea Ray," Brunswick Corporation *Press Release*, March 29, 2001.

Chapter 14

1. "A Case in Contrast" is based on C. McLean, "Reinventing a Clean, Lean Manufacturing Machine: Willow Pulls Together as a Team to Survive in the Competitive Metal Working Industry," *Plant*, September 27, 1999, p. 13; B. Wheatley, "Innovation in ISO Registration," *CMA Management Accounting Magazine*, June 1998, p. 23; L. Wichmann, "Taking the Fight Out of Your Workplace Environment: Aggressive Behavior Costs Manufacturers Time and Money," *Plant*, May 8, 2000, p. 13.

2. W.R. Coradetti, "Teamwork Takes Time and a Lot of Energy," *HR Magazine*, June 1994, pp. 74–77; D. Fenn, "Service Teams That Work," *Inc.*, August 1995, p. 99; "Team Selling Catches On, but is Sales Really a Team Sport?" *Wall Street Journal*, March 29, 1994, p. A1.

3. P. Booth, *Challenge and Change: Embracing the Team Concept*. Report 123–94, Conference Board of Canada, 1994.

4. *Training Magazine*, October 1995, Lakewood Publications, Minneapolis, MN.

5. T.M. Mills, *The Sociology of Small Groups* (Englewood Cliffs, NJ: Prentice-Hall, 1967); M.E. Shaw, *Group Dynamics* (New York: McGraw-Hill, 1981).

6. J. MacDonald, "Captain Canadian: Molson's Top Man Leading His Charges Back to Winning Ways," *Canadian Packaging*, March 2000, pp. 13–15.

7. "Management Insight": Creating Workplaces that Encourage Teamwork is based on K. Rude, "Retrofitting a Community of Spaces: When Steelcase Canada Moved Its Toronto-area Operations Under One Roof, Quadrangle Architects Provided a Renovated Facility in Markham That Showcases the Latest Workplace Strategies," *Canadian Interiors*, January/February 2001, pp. 42–45.

8. E.H. Updike, D. Woodruff, and L. Armstrong, "Honda's Civic Lesson," *Business Week*, September 18, 1995, pp. 71–76.

9. J. Vardy, "If You Build It, They Will Come: Edgeflow Inc. Idea for Company Secondary to Recruitment," *Financial Post (National Post)*, November 30, 2000, p. C11.

10. P. Willcocks, "Yours and Mine? Can the New Owner of the Once-Troubled Myra Falls Copper and Zinc Mine Near Campbell River Forge a New Relationship with Workers and Their Union to Create a True Partnership?" *B.C. Business Magazine*, September 2000, pp. 114–120.

11. J.A. Pearce II and E.C. Ravlin, "The Design and Activation of Self-Regulating Work Groups," *Human Relations*, 11, 1987, pp. 751–82.

12. P. Booth, *Challenge and Change: Embracing the Team Concept*, Report 123-94, Conference Board of Canada, 1994.

13. "Management Insight" is based on L. Berglund, "So, You Think You're a Good Manager...Find Out for Sure With a Reverse Appraisal of Your Staff," *Modern Purchasing*, May 1998, p. 32.

14. B. Dumaine, "Who Needs a Boss?" *Fortune*, May 7, 1990, pp. 52–60; J.A. Pearce II and E.C. Ravlin, "The Design and Activation of Self-Regulating Work Groups," *Human Relations*, 11, 1987, pp. 751–82.

15. B. Dumaine, "Who Needs a Boss?" *Fortune*, May 7, 1990, pp. 52–60; A.R. Montebello and V.R. Buzzotta, "Work Teams That Work," *Training & Development*, March 1993, pp. 59–64.

16. T.D. Wall, N.J. Kemp, P.R. Jackson, and C.W. Clegg, "Outcomes of Autonomous Work Groups: A Long-Term Field Experiment," *Academy of Management Journal*, 29, 1986, pp. 280–304.

17. W.R. Pape, "Group Insurance," *Inc. (Inc. Technology Supplement)*, June 17, 1997, pp. 29–31; A.M. Townsend, S.M. DeMarie, and A.R. Hendrickson, "Are You Ready for Virtual Teams?" *HR Magazine*, September 1996, pp. 122–26; A.M. Townsend, S.M. DeMarie, and A.M. Hendrickson, "Virtual Teams: Technology and the Workplace of the

Future," *Academy of Management Executive*, 12, 3, 1998, pp. 17–29.

18. A.M. Townsend, S.M. DeMarie, and A.R. Hendrickson, "Are You Ready for Virtual Teams?" *HR Magazine*, September 1996, pp. 122–26.

19. W.R. Pape, "Group Insurance," *Inc. (Inc. Technology Supplement)*, June 17, 1997, pp. 29–31; A.M. Townsend, S.M. DeMarie, and A.R. Hendrickson, "Are You Ready for Virtual Teams?" *HR Magazine*, September 1996, pp. 122–26.

20. Based on Paul Luke, "Team Building on the Job No Passing Fancy," *The Edmonton Journal*, January 12, 1997, p. B5; S.L. Jarvenpaa, K. Knoll, D.E. Leidner, "Is Anybody Out There? Antecedents of Trust in Global Virtual Teams," *Journal of Management Information Science*, 14, 4, 1998, pp. 29–64; G. Crone, "Welcome to the Other Web: Loose Clusters, Not Rigid Contracts, are the Future in Business," *The Financial Post*, January 22, 1998, p. C11; Diana Kunde, "Modem Alone Can't Make Mobile Work Force Work: 'It Doesn't Make Sense for Everybody. You Have to Have Some Flexibility.'" *The Ottawa Citizen*, October 12, 1998, p. D6.

21. A.B. Drexler and R. Forrester, "Teamwork–Not Necessarily the Answer," *HR Magazine*, January 1998, pp. 55–58.

22. R. Forrester and A.B. Drexler, "A Model for Team-Based Organization Performance," *Academy of Management Executive*, August 1999, p. 47. See also S.A. Mohrman, with S.G. Cohen and A.M. Mohrman, Jr., *Designing Team-Based Organizations* (San Francisco: Jossey-Bass, 1995); and J.H. Shonk, *Team-Based Organizations* (Homewood, IL: Business One Irwin, 1992).

23. A. Deutschman, "The Managing Wisdom of High-Tech Superstars," *Fortune*, October 17, 1994, pp. 197–206.

24. A. Deutschman, "The Managing Wisdom of High-Tech Superstars," *Fortune*, October 17, 1994, pp. 197–206.

25. J.D. Thompson, *Organizations in Action* (New York: McGraw-Hill, 1967).

26. J.D. Thompson, *Organizations in Action* (New York: McGraw-Hill, 1967).

27. J.S. Lublin, "My Colleague, My Boss," *Wall Street Journal*, April 12, 1995, pp. R4, R12.

28. B.W. Tuckman, "Developmental Sequences in Small Groups," *Psychological Bulletin*, 63, 1965, pp. 384–99; B.W.

Tuckman and M.C. Jensen, "Stages of Small Group Development," *Group and Organizational Studies*, 2, 1977, pp. 419–27.

29. C.J.G. Gersick, "Time and Transition in Work Teams: Toward a New Model of Group Development," *Academy of Management Journal*, 31, March 1988, pp. 9–41; C.J.G. Gersick, "Marking Time: Predictable Transitions in Task Groups," *Academy of Management Journal*, 32, June 1989, pp. 274–309.

30. C.J.G. Gersick, "Time and Transition in Work Teams: Toward a New Model of Group Development," *Academy of Management Journal*, 31, March 1988, pp. 9–41; C.J.G. Gersick, "Marking Time: Predictable Transitions in Task Groups," *Academy of Management Journal*, 32, June 1989, pp. 274–309; E. Romanelli and M.L. Tushman, "Organizational Transformation as Punctuated Equilibrium: An Empirical Test," *Academy of Management Journal*, October 1994, pp. 1141–1166; and A. Seers and S. Woodruff, "Temporal Pacing in Task Forces: Group Development or Deadline Pressure?" *Journal of Management*, vol. 23, no. 2, 1997, pp. 169–87.

31. C.J.G. Gersick, "Time and Transition in Work Teams: Toward a New Model of Group Development," *Academy of Management Journal*, 31, March 1988, pp. 9–41.

32. J.R. Hackman, "Group Influences on Individuals in Organizations," in M.D. Dunnette and L.M. Hough (eds.), *Handbook of Industrial and Organizational Psychology*, 2nd ed., vol. 3 (Palo Alto, CA: Consulting Psychologists Press, 1992), pp. 199–267.

33. J.R. Hackman, "Group Influences on Individuals in Organizations," in M.D. Dunnette and L.M. Hough (eds.), *Handbook of Industrial and Organizational Psychology*, 2nd ed., vol. 3 (Palo Alto, CA: Consulting Psychologists Press, 1992), pp. 199–267.

34. J.R. Hackman, "Group Influences on Individuals in Organizations," in M.D. Dunnette and L.M. Hough (eds.), *Handbook of Industrial and Organizational Psychology*, 2nd ed., vol. 3 (Palo Alto, CA: Consulting Psychologists Press, 1992), pp. 199–267.

35. D.J. Yang, "Nordstrom's Gang of Four," *Business Week*, June 15, 1992, pp. 122–23.

36. L. Festinger, "Informal Social Communication," *Psychological Review*, 57, 1950, pp. 271–82; M.E. Shaw, *Group Dynamics* (New York: McGraw-Hill, 1981).

37. J.R. Hackman, "Group Influences on Individuals in Organizations," in M.D. Dunnette and L.M. Hough (eds.), *Handbook of Industrial and Organizational Psychology*, 2nd ed., vol. 3 (Palo Alto, CA: Consulting Psychologists Press, 1992), pp. 199–267; M.E. Shaw, *Group Dynamics* (New York: McGraw-Hill, 1981).

38. D. Cartwright, "The Nature of Group Cohesiveness," in D. Cartwright and A. Zander (eds.), *Group Dynamics*, 3rd ed. (New York: Harper and Row, 1968); L. Festinger, S. Schacter, and K. Black, *Social Pressures in Informal Groups* (New York: Harper and Row, 1950); M.E. Shaw, *Group Dynamics* (New York: McGraw-Hill, 1981).

39. D.A. Blackmon, "A Factory in Alabama Is the Merger in Microcosm," *Wall Street Journal*, May 5, 1998, pp. B1, B10.

40. D. Woodruff and K.L. Miller, "Mercedes' Maverick in Alabama," *Business Week*, September 11, 1995, pp. 64–65.

41. D.A. Blackmon, "A Factory in Alabama is the Merger in Microcosm," *Wall Street Journal*, May 5, 1998, pp. B1, B10.

42. N. Hulsman, "Fun Strictly Optional," *B.C. Business Magazine*, July 2000, p. 8.

43. P. Booth, *Challenge and Change: Embracing the Team Concept*, Report 123-94, Conference Board of Canada, 1994, pp. 14–15.

44. P. Booth, *Challenge and Change: Embracing the Team Concept*, Report 123-94, Conference Board of Canada, 1994, p. 14.

45. J. Pfeffer and N. Langton, "The Effect of Wage Dispersion on Satisfaction, Productivity, and Working Collaboratively: Evidence from College and University Faculty," *Administrative Science Quarterly*, 38, 1993, pp. 382–407.

46. I.L. Janis, *Groupthink* (Boston: Houghton Mifflin, 1982); W. Park, "A Review of Research on Groupthink," *Journal of Behavioral Decision Making*, July 1990, pp. 229–245; C.P. Neck and G. Moorhead, "Groupthink Remodeled: The Importance of Leadership, Time Pressure, and Methodical Decision Making Procedures," *Human Relations*, May 1995,

pp. 537–558; and J.N. Choi and M.U. Kim, "The Organizational Application of Groupthink and Its Limits in Organizations," *Journal of Applied Psychology*, April 1999, pp. 297–306.

47. I.L. Janis, *Groupthink* (Boston: Houghton Mifflin, 1982).

48. M.E. Turner and A.R. Pratkanis, "Mitigating Groupthink by Stimulating Constructive Conflict," in C. De Dreu and E. Van de Vliert (eds.), *Using Conflict in Organizations* (London: Sage, 1997), pp. 53–71.

49. See N.R.F. Maier, *Principles of Human Relations* (New York: John Wiley & Sons, 1952); I.L. Janis, *Groupthink: Psychological Studies of Policy Decisions and Fiascoes*, 2nd ed. (Boston: Houghton Mifflin, 1982); and C.R. Leana, "A Partial Test of Janis' Groupthink Model: Effects of Group Cohesiveness and Leader Behavior on Defective Decision Making," *Journal of Management*, Spring 1985, pp. 5–17.

50. P.C. Earley, "Social Loafing and Collectivism: A Comparison of the United States and the People's Republic of China," *Administrative Science Quarterly*, 34, 1989, pp. 565–81; J.M. George, "Extrinsic and Intrinsic Origins of Perceived Social Loafing in Organizations," *Academy of Management Journal*, 35, 1992, pp. 191–202; S.G. Harkins, B. Latane, and K. Williams, "Social Loafing: Allocating Effort or Taking It Easy," *Journal of Experimental Social Psychology*, 16, 1980, pp. 457–65; B. Latane, K.D. Williams, and S. Harkins, "Many Hands Make Light the Work: The Causes and Consequences of Social Loafing," *Journal of Personality and Social Psychology*, 37, 1979, pp. 822–32; J.A. Shepperd, "Productivity Loss in Performance Groups: A Motivation Analysis," *Psychological Bulletin*, 113, 1993, pp. 67–81.

51. J.M. George, "Extrinsic and Intrinsic Origins of Perceived Social Loafing in Organizations," *Academy of Management Journal*, 35, 1992, pp. 191–202; G.R. Jones, "Task Visibility, Free Riding, and Shirking: Explaining the Effect of Structure and Technology on Employee Behavior," *Academy of Management Review*, 9, 1984, pp. 684–95; K. Williams, S. Harkins, and B. Latane, "Identifiability as a Deterrent to Social Loafing: Two Cheering Experiments," *Journal of*

Personality and Social Psychology, 40, 1981, pp. 303–11.

52. S. Harkins and J. Jackson, "The Role of Evaluation in Eliminating Social Loafing," *Personality and Social Psychology Bulletin*, 11, 1985, pp. 457–65; N.L. Kerr and S.E. Bruun, "Ringelman Revisited: Alternative Explanations for the Social Loafing Effect," *Personality and Social Psychology Bulletin*, 7, 1981, pp. 224–31; K. Williams, S. Harkins, and B. Latane, "Identifiability as a Deterrent to Social Loafing: Two Cheering Experiments," *Journal of Personality and Social Psychology*, 40, 1981, pp. 303–11.

53. M.A. Brickner, S.G. Harkins, and T.M. Ostrom, "Effects of Personal Involvement: Thought-Provoking Implications for Social Loafing," *Journal of Personality and Social Psychology*, 51, 1986, pp. 763–69; S.G. Harkins and R.E. Petty, "The Effects of Task Difficulty and Task Uniqueness on Social Loafing," *Journal of Personality and Social Psychology*, 43, 1982, pp. 1214–29.

54. B. Latane, "Responsibility and Effort in Organizations," in P.S. Goodman (ed.), *Designing Effective Work Groups* (San Francisco: Jossey-Bass, 1986); B. Latane, K.D. Williams, and S. Harkins, "Many Hands Make Light the Work: The Causes and Consequences of Social Loafing," *Journal of Personality and Social Psychology*, 37, 1979, pp. 822–32; I.D. Steiner, *Group Process and Productivity* (New York: Academic Press, 1972).

55. B. Birchard, "Power to the People," *CFO*, March 1995, pp. 38–43.

56. A. Markels, "A Power Producer Is Intent on Giving Power to Its People," *Wall Street Journal*, July 3, 1995, pp. A1, A12.

57. A. Markels, "A Power Producer Is Intent on Giving Power to Its People," *Wall Street Journal*, July 3, 1995, pp. A1, A12.

58. A. Markels, "A Power Producer Is Intent on Giving Power to Its People," *Wall Street Journal*, July 3, 1995, pp. A1, A12.

Chapter 15

1. "A Case in Contrast" based on V. Hempsall, "Family Matters: Strong Employee Relations Help RBW Graphics Manage Change," *Canadian Printer*, June 1999, pp. 24–26; "Transcontinental Wins *Time Canada* Contract, Buys Plesman," *Canadian Printer*, October 1999, p. 14;

F. Bula, "City Staff Face Losing Four-Day Work Week," *The Vancouver Sun*, April 28, 1998, pp. B2, B3; F. Bula, "City's Plan to End 4-Day Week Sparks Backlash," *The Vancouver Sun*, May 15, 1998, pp. B1, B3; F. Bula, "Bid to Alter Work Week in City Shop for Repairs," *The Vancouver Sun*, May 26, 1998, pp. B1, B3; P. Brooke, "Civic Strike More About Time Than Money," *The Vancouver Sun*, November 1, 2000, p. A6.

2. C.A. O'Reilly and L.R. Pondy, "Organizational Communication," in S. Kerr (ed.), *Organizational Behavior* (Columbus, OH: Grid, 1979).

3. Gerry Bellett, "TD Canada Trust Boss Goes on Fact-Finding Mission: Ed Clark Studies Customer and Staff Relations First-Hand," *The Vancouver Sun*, Friday, June 15, 2001, pp. F7, F17.

4. E.M. Rogers and R. Agarwala-Rogers, *Communication in Organizations* (New York: Free Press, 1976).

5. B. Wheatley, "Innovation in ISO Registration [Kaizen Blitz]," *CMA Management Accounting Magazine*, June 1998, p. 23; C. McLean, "Reinventing a Clean, Lean Manufacturing Machine: Willow Pulls Together as a Team to Survive in the Competitive Metal Working Industry," *Plant*, September 27, 1999, p. 13.

6. D.A. Adams, P.A. Todd, and R.R. Nelson, "A Comparative Evaluation of the Impact of Electronic and Voice Mail on Organizational Communication," *Information & Management*, 24, 1993, pp. 9–21.

7. "Miscommunication Preceded Indonesian Air Crash," *The Associated Press Wire Service*, September 29, 1997.

8. "Miscommunications Plague Pilots and Air-Traffic Controllers," *Wall Street Journal*, August 22, 1995, p. A1.

9. R.L. Daft, R.H. Lengel, and L.K. Trevino, "Message Equivocality, Media Selection, and Manager Performance: Implications for Information Systems," *MIS Quarterly*, 11, 1987, pp. 355–66; R.L. Daft and R.H. Lengel, "Information Richness: A New Approach to Managerial Behavior and Organization Design," in B.M. Staw and L.L. Cummings (eds.), *Research in Organizational Behavior* (Greenwich, CT: JAI Press, 1984).

10. R.L. Daft, *Organization Theory and Design* (St. Paul, MN: West, 1992).

11. "Lights, Camera, Meeting: Teleconferencing Becomes a Time-Saving Tool," *Wall Street Journal*, February 21, 1995, p. A1.

12. R.L. Daft, *Organization Theory and Design* (St. Paul, MN: West, 1992).

13. T.J. Peters and R.H. Waterman, Jr., *In Search of Excellence* (New York: Harper and Row, 1982); T. Peters and N. Austin, *A Passion for Excellence: The Leadership Difference* (New York: Random House, 1985).

14. "Lights, Camera, Meeting: Teleconferencing Becomes a Time-Saving Tool," *Wall Street Journal*, February 21, 1995, p. A1.

15. M. MacMillan, "Do You See What I See? Desktop Videoconferencing, Long a Member of the 'Almost But Not Quite' Family of Products, May Finally Be Taking Off, Industry Insiders Say," *Computer Dealer News*, October 20, 2000, pp. 27–28.

16. M. Brady, "Troubled Children in Newfoundland Treated Via Video-Conference," *Financial Post (National Post)*, September 8, 1999, p. E4.

17. S.M. Boyce, "Two Friends Rolling in Dough: 70 Million Pies Served," *Financial Post (National Post)*, December 13, 2000, p. E7.

18. N. Southworth, "Informality Governs Most Telecommuters," *The Globe and Mail*, April 4, 2001, p. B11.

19. H. Scoffield, "Nortel Leaves Employees at Home," *The Globe and Mail*, May 27, 1998, p. B24.

20. S. Mingail, "Computing Telework's Trade-offs," *Financial Post (National Post)*, August 9, 1999, p. C8.

21. L. Arnold, "Geographical, Organisational and Social Implications of Teleworking–Emphasis on the Social Perspectives," paper presented at the 29th Annual Meeting of the Canadian Sociological and Anthropological Association, Calgary, Alberta, June 1994; K.S. Devine, L. Taylor, and K. Haryett, "The Impact of Teleworking on Canadian Employment," in D. Glenday, A. Duffy, and N. Pupo (eds.), *Good Jobs, Bad Jobs, No Jobs: The Uncertain Future of Employment in Canada* (New York: Harcourt Brace, 1997), pp. 211–22; C.A. Hamilton, "Telecommuting," *Personnel Journal*, April 1987, pp. 91–101; and I.U. Zeytinoglu, "Employment Conditions in Telework:

An Experiment in Ontario," Proceedings of the 30th Conference of the Canadian Industrial Relations Association, 1992, pp. 281–293.

22. L. Arnold, "Geographical, Organisational and Social Implications of Teleworking–Emphasis on the Social Perspectives," paper presented at the 29th Annual Meeting of the Canadian Sociological and Anthropological Association, Calgary, Alberta, June 1994.

23. I.U. Zeytinoglu, "Employment Conditions in Telework: An Experiment in Ontario," Proceedings of the 30th Conference of the Canadian Industrial Relations Association, 1992, pp. 281–93; and K.S. Devine, L. Taylor, and K. Haryett, "The Impact of Teleworking on Canadian Employment," in D. Glenday, A. Duffy, and N. Pupo (eds.), *Good Jobs, Bad Jobs, No Jobs: The Uncertain Future of Employment in Canada* (New York: Harcourt Brace, 1997), pp. 211–22.

24. I.U. Zeytinoglu, "Employment Conditions in Telework: An Experiment in Ontario," Proceedings of the 30th Conference of the Canadian Industrial Relations Association, 1992, pp. 281–93.

25. K.S. Devine, L. Taylor, and K. Haryett, "The Impact of Teleworking on Canadian Employment," in D. Glenday, A. Duffy, and N. Pupo (eds.), *Good Jobs, Bad Jobs, No Jobs: The Uncertain Future of Employment in Canada* (New York: Harcourt Brace, 1997), pp. 211–22; and C.A. Hamilton, "Telecommuting," *Personnel Journal*, April 1987, pp. 91–101.

26. K.S. Devine, L. Taylor, and K. Haryett, "The Impact of Teleworking on Canadian Employment," in D. Glenday, A. Duffy, and N. Pupo (eds.), *Good Jobs, Bad Jobs, No Jobs: The Uncertain Future of Employment in Canada* (New York: Harcourt Brace, 1997), pp. 211–22.

27. K.S. Devine, L. Taylor, and K. Haryett, "The Impact of Teleworking on Canadian Employment," in D. Glenday, A. Duffy, and N. Pupo (eds.), *Good Jobs, Bad Jobs, No Jobs: The Uncertain Future of Employment in Canada* (New York: Harcourt Brace, 1997), pp. 211–22.

28. C.A. Hamilton, "Telecommuting," *Personnel Journal*, April 1987, pp. 91–101.

29. L. Arnold, "Geographical, Organisational and Social Implications of Teleworking–Emphasis on the Social

Perspectives," paper presented at the 29th Annual Meeting of the Canadian Sociological and Anthropological Association, Calgary, Alberta, June 1994.

30. "E-Mail Abuse: Workers Discover High-Tech Ways to Cause Trouble in the Office," *Wall Street Journal*, November 22, 1994, p. A1; "E-Mail Alert: Companies Lag in Devising Policies on How It Should Be Used," *Wall Street Journal*, December 29, 1994, p. A1.

31. J. Kay, "Someone Will Watch Over Me: Think Your Office E-Mails Are Private? Think Again," *National Post Business*, January 2001, pp. 59–64.

32. "Ethics in Action": Eavesdropping on Voice Mail and E-mail is based on J. Kay, "Someone Will Watch Over Me: Think Your Office E-Mails Are Private? Think Again," *National Post Business*, January 2001, pp. 59–64.

33. "Employee-Newsletter Names Include the Good, the Bad, and the Boring," *Wall Street Journal*, July 18, 1995, p. A1.

34. O.W. Baskin and C.E. Aronoff, *Interpersonal Communication in Organizations* (Santa Monica, CA: Goodyear, 1989).

35. J. Osborne, "2001: The Internet. Faster, Higher, Stronger, Maybe," *Broadcaster*, January 2001, p. 29.

36. P.M. Eng, "Big Business on the Net? Not Yet," *Business Week*, June 26, 1995, pp. 100–101; GCCGroup, "Internet Functions," www.gccgroup.com/netfacts.htm.

37. M.J. Cronin, "Ford's Intranet Success," *Fortune*, March 30, 1998, p. 158; M.J. Cronin, "Intranets Reach the Factory Floor," *Fortune*, June 17, 1997, p. 122; A.L. Sprout, "The Internet Inside Your Company," *Fortune*, November 27, 1995, pp. 161–68; J.B. White, "Chrysler's Intranet: Promise vs. Reality," *Wall Street Journal*, May 13, 1997, pp. B1, B6.

38. M.J. Cronin, "Ford's Intranet Success," *Fortune*, March 30, 1998, p. 158; M.J. Cronin, "Intranets Reach the Factory Floor," *Fortune*, June 17, 1997, p. 122; A.L. Sprout, "The Internet Inside Your Company," *Fortune*, November 27, 1995, pp. 161–68; J.B. White, "Chrysler's Intranet: Promise vs. Reality," *Wall Street Journal*, May 13, 1997, pp. B1, B6.

39. P. Chisholm, "Redesigning Work: Enlightened Employers Are Trying to

Make Office Life More Creative, More Flexible, Less Stressful, Even Fun," *Maclean's*, March 5, 2001, p. 34.

40. G. Rifkin, "A Skeptic's Guide to Groupware," *Forbes ASAP*, 1995, pp. 76–91.

41. G. Rifkin, "A Skeptic's Guide to Groupware," *Forbes ASAP*, 1995, pp. 76–91.

42. G. Rifkin, "A Skeptic's Guide to Groupware," *Forbes ASAP*, 1995, pp. 76–91.

43. "Groupware Requires a Group Effort," *Business Week*, June 26, 1995, p. 154.

44. N. Southworth, "Phone Numbers Are Rare Breed on Web," *The Globe and Mail*, May 10, 2001, p. T4.

45. "On the Road," *Newsweek*, June 6, 1994, p. 8.

46. A. Wakizaka, "Faxes, E-Mail, Help the Deaf Get Office Jobs," *Wall Street Journal*, October 3, 1995, pp. B1, B5.

47. Based on S.P. Robbins and P.L. Hunsaker, *Training in Interpersonal Skills: TIPs for Managing People at Work*, 2nd ed. (Upper Saddle River, NJ: Prentice Hall, 1996), Chapter 3.

48. D. Tannen, "The Power of Talk," *Harvard Business Review*, September–October 1995, pp. 138–48; D. Tannen, *Talking from 9 to 5* (New York: Avon Books, 1995).

49. D. Tannen, "The Power of Talk," *Harvard Business Review*, September–October 1995, pp. 138–48; D. Tannen, *Talking from 9 to 5* (New York: Avon Books, 1995).

50. D. Tannen, "The Power of Talk," *Harvard Business Review*, September–October 1995, pp. 138–48; D. Tannen, *Talking from 9 to 5* (New York: Avon Books, 1995).

51. D. Tannen, "The Power of Talk," *Harvard Business Review*, September–October 1995, pp. 138–48.

52. D. Tannen, *Talking from 9 to 5* (New York: Avon Books, 1995).

53. D. Tannen, *Talking from 9 to 5* (New York: Avon Books, 1995).

54. D. Tannen, "The Power of Talk," *Harvard Business Review*, September–October 1995, pp. 138–48; D. Tannen, *Talking from 9 to 5* (New York: Avon Books, 1995).

Chapter 16

1. "Case in Contrast" based on D. DeCloet, "Warm, Cuddly Bank Mergers: How Do You Create a Megabank? Try Being Nice for a Change," *Canadian Business*, May 29, 2000, pp. 28–32; J. Greenwood, "TD Steals a March From Competitors: Nabbed CT Financial," *Financial Post (National Post)*, December 4, 1999, p. D8; G. McIntosh, "Feds Knew of Canada Trust Sale Months in Advance," *Canadian Press Newswire*, December 3, 1999; K. Noble, "Going Green: It Will Be the End of an Era if Ottawa Approves TD Bank's Purchase of Canada Trust," *Maclean's*, August 16, 1999, p. 40; B. Shecter, "Baillie Wins the Prize With His Master Strategy: Avoids Auction," *Financial Post (National Post)*, August 4, 1999, pp. C1, C4.

2. J.A. Litterer, "Conflict in Organizations: A Reexamination," *Academy of Management Journal*, 9, 1966, pp. 178–86; S.M. Schmidt and T.A. Kochan, "Conflict: Towards Conceptual Clarity," *Administrative Science Quarterly*, 13, 1972, pp. 359–70; R.H. Miles, *Macro Organizational Behavior* (Santa Monica, CA: Goodyear, 1980).

3. "Management Insight" is based on P. Kuitenbrouwer, "Simmer...Then Raise to a Boil: A Family Stew Over Succession at the McCain Foods Empire Spills Into the Courts," *Financial Post Daily*, February 2, 1998, p. 22; P. Newman, "Tales from a Mellower Harrison McCain: Four Years After Winning a Bitter Feud With His Brother, Harrison Acknowledges That 'Strained' Family Relations Still Exist," *Maclean's*, January 19, 1998, p. 50; G. Pitts, *In the Blood*, (Doubleday Canada, 2000), pp. 15–16.

4. S.P. Robbins, *Managing Organizational Conflict: A Nontraditional Approach* (Englewood Cliffs, NJ: Prentice-Hall, 1974); L. Coser, *The Functions of Social Conflict* (New York: Free Press, 1956).

5. L.L. Putnam and M.S. Poole, "Conflict and Negotiation," in F.M. Jablin, L.L. Putnam, K.H. Roberts, and L.W. Porter (eds.), *Handbook of Organizational Communication: An Interdisciplinary Perspective* (Newbury Park, CA: Sage, 1987), pp. 549–99.

6. "Management Insight" is based on M. Hume, "Trouble on Perfect Mountain," *National Post*, April 30, 2001, p. A17.

7. L.R. Pondy, "Organizational Conflict: Concepts and Models," *Administrative Science Quarterly*, 2, 1967, pp. 296–320; R.E. Walton and J.M. Dutton, "The Management of Interdepartmental Conflict: A Model and Review," *Administrative Science Quarterly*, 14, 1969, pp. 62–73.

8. G.R. Jones and J.E. Butler, "Managing Internal Corporate Entrepreneurship: An Agency Theory Perspective," *Journal of Management*, 18, 1992, pp. 733–49.

9. J.A. Wall, Jr., "Conflict and Its Management," *Journal of Management*, 21, 1995, pp. 515–58.

10. R.E. Walton and J.M. Dutton, "The Management of Interdepartmental Conflict: A Model and Review," *Administrative Science Quarterly*, 14, 1969, pp. 62–73.

11. L. R. Pondy, "Organizational Conflict: Concepts and Models," *Administrative Science Quarterly*, 2, 1967, pp. 296–320.

12. W.F. White, *Human Relations in the Restaurant Industry* (New York: McGraw-Hill, 1948).

13. K.W. Thomas, "Conflict and Negotiation Processes in Organizations," in M.D. Dunnette and L.M. Hough (eds.), *Handbook of Industrial and Organizational Psychology*, 2nd ed., vol. 3 (Palo Alto, CA: Consulting Psychologists Press, 1992), pp. 651–717.

14. P.R. Lawrence, L.B. Barnes, and J.W. Lorsch, *Organizational Behavior and Administration* (Homewood, IL: Irwin, 1976).

15. R.J. Lewicki and J.R. Litterer, *Negotiation* (Homewood, IL: Irwin, 1985); G.B. Northcraft and M.A. Neale, *Organizational Behavior* (Fort Worth, TX: Dryden, 1994); J.Z. Rubin and B.R. Brown, *The Social Psychology of Bargaining and Negotiation* (New York: Academic Press, 1975).

16. L. Thompson and R. Hastie, "Social Perception in Negotiation," *Organizational Behavior and Human Decision Processes*, 47, 1990, pp. 98–123.

17. K.W. Thomas, "Conflict and Negotiation Processes in Organizations," in M.D. Dunnette and L.M. Hough (eds.), *Handbook of Industrial and Organizational Psychology*, 2nd ed., vol. 3 (Palo Alto, CA: Consulting Psychologists Press, 1992), pp. 651–717.

18. R.J. Lewicki, S.E. Weiss, and D. Lewin, "Models of Conflict, Negotiation and Third Party Intervention: A Review

and Synthesis," *Journal of Organizational Behavior*, 13, 1992, pp. 209–52.

19. G.B. Northcraft and M.A. Neale, *Organizational Behavior* (Fort Worth, TX: Dryden, 1994).

20. R.J. Lewicki, S.E. Weiss, and D. Lewin, "Models of Conflict, Negotiation and Third Party Intervention"; G.B. Northcraft and M.A. Neale, *Organizational Behavior* (Fort Worth, TX: Dryden, 1994); D.G. Pruitt, "Integrative Agreements: Nature and Consequences," in M.H. Bazerman and R.J. Lewicki (eds.), *Negotiating in Organizations* (Beverly Hills, CA: Sage, 1983).

21. V. Spencer, "Insurers and Collision Shops: Driving Partnerships Forward," *Canadian Underwriter*, October 2000, pp. 80–81.

22. R. Fischer and W. Ury, *Getting to Yes* (Boston: Houghton Mifflin, 1981); G.B. Northcraft and M.A. Neale, *Organizational Behavior* (Fort Worth, TX: Dryden, 1994).

23. "Management Insight" is based on J. Lee, "Leader Takes a Hard Line," *The Vancouver Sun*, May 15, 2001, p. A10.

24. E. Akyeampong, "A Statistical Portrait of the Trade Union Movement," *Perspectives on Labour and Income*, Cat. No. 75-001-XPE, Winter, Ottawa, Statistics Canada.

25. P.J. Carnevale and D.G. Pruitt, "Negotiation and Mediation," *Annual Review of Psychology*, 43, 1992, pp. 531–82.

26. A.M. Pettigrew, *The Politics of Organizational Decision Making* (London: Tavistock, 1973); R.H. Miles, *Macro Organizational Behavior* (Santa Monica, CA: Goodyear, 1980).

27. D.J. Hickson, C.R. Hinings, C.A. Lee, R.E. Schneck, and D.J. Pennings, "A Strategic Contingencies Theory of Intraorganizational Power," *Administrative Science Quarterly*, 16, 1971, pp. 216–27; C.R. Hinings, D.J. Hickson, J.M. Pennings, and R.E. Schneck, "Structural Conditions of Interorganizational Power," *Administrative Science Quarterly*, 19, 1974, pp. 22–44; J. Pfeffer, *Power in Organizations* (Boston: Pitman, 1981).

28. J. Pfeffer, *Power in Organizations* (Boston: Pitman, 1981).

29. J. Pfeffer, *Power in Organizations* (Boston: Pitman, 1981).

30. M. Crozier, "Sources of Power of Lower Level Participants in Complex Organizations," *Administrative Science Quarterly*, 7, 1962, pp. 349–64; A.M. Pettigrew, "Information Control as a Power Resource," *Sociology*, 6, 1972, pp. 187–204.

31. J. Pfeffer, *Power in Organizations* (Boston: Pitman, 1981); G.R. Salancik and J. Pfeffer, "The Bases and Uses of Power in Organizational Decision Making," *Administrative Science Quarterly*, 19, 1974, pp. 453–73; J. Pfeffer and G.R. Salancik, *The External Control of Organizations: A Resource Dependence View* (New York: Harper and Row, 1978).

32. Information in this paragraph is based on R. McQueen, "Hard Truths: To Capture a Corner Office, You Have to Play Politics and Know When to Lie," *National Post Business*, September 2000, pp. 51–52.

33. J. Pfeffer, *Power in Organizations* (Boston: Pitman, 1981).

34. J. Pfeffer, *Power in Organizations* (Boston: Pitman, 1981).

35. J. Pfeffer, *Power in Organizations* (Boston: Pitman, 1981).

Chapter 17

1. Information on Nortel Networks is based on M. Ingram, "Roth's Approach Pushed Nortel to the Forefront," *The Globe and Mail*, May 12, 2001, p. B7; E. Reguly, "Did Strong-willed Board Help Ease Roth Out the Door?" *The Globe and Mail*, May 12, 2001, p. B6; D. Olive, *No Guts, No Glory: How Canada's Greatest CEOs Built Their Empires* (Whitby, ON: McGraw-Hill Ryerson, 2000).

2. Information on Moore is based on D. Steinhart, "US Headquarters to Bear the Brunt of Moore's Axe: Cutting 1,400 Jobs," *Financial Post (National Post)*, January 5, 2001, p. C5; "Business Form Company Moore Selling Carbonless Copy Paper Operation to Mead," *Canadian Press Newswire*, November 13, 2000; P. Kuitenbrouwer, "Angry Investors Slam Moore Boss: Blue Chip No More. Company Admits Strategic Options in Short Supply," *Financial Post (National Post)*, April 29, 2000, p. D4.

3. J. Lee, "Canadian Businesses Not Good at Adjusting, Survey Says," *The Vancouver Sun*, December 14, 1998, pp. C1–2.

4. K. Lewin, *Field Theory in Social Science* (New York: Harper & Row, 1951).

5. "Focus on Diversity" is based on J. Steed, "Company-Wide Effort Keeps Talent on Board," *Toronto Star*, May 6, 2001, p. B1.

6. S.P. Robbins and N. Langton, *Organizational Behaviour: Concepts, Controversies, Applications*, 2nd Canadian edition (Toronto: Pearson Education Canada, 2001), pp. 606–607.

7. A.E. Reichers, J.P. Wanous, and J.T. Austin, "Understanding and Managing Cynicism About Organizational Change," *Academy of Management Executive*, 11, 1997, pp. 48–59.

8. "Management Insight" is based on "Turnarounds of the Year," *Profit: The Magazine for Canadian Entrepreneurs*, December 1996/January 1997, pp. 64–71; and F. Shalom, "Doorway to the World: A Lac-Mégantic Company Couldn't Make It as a Toothpick-and-Clothespin Factory, So It Went Upscale, Becoming North America's Biggest Maker of Hardwood-Door Panels," *Montreal Gazette*, June 17, 1996, p. C8.

9. R.H. Hall, *Organizations: Structures, Processes, and Outcomes,* 4th ed. (Englewood Cliffs, NJ: Prentice Hall, 1987), p. 29.

10. D. Katz and R.L. Kahn, *The Social Psychology of Organizations,* 2nd ed. (New York: John Wiley & Sons, 1978), pp. 714–715.

11. P. Tellier, "Turning CN Around," *Canadian Business Review*, Spring 1995, pp. 31–32+.

12. P. Tellier, "Turning CN Around," *Canadian Business Review*, Spring 1995, pp. 31–32+.

13. Featherbedding discussion is based on "Back on the Rails: Years of Cutting Have Produced a Leaner and Meaner CN," *Maclean's*, January 13, 1997, pp. 36–38.

14. P. Fitzpatrick, "CN's Tellier Took Home $1.3M," *Financial Post Daily*, March 26, 1998, p. 6.

15. J.R. Stepp and T.J. Schneider, "Fostering Change in a Unionized Environment," *Canadian Business Review*, Summer 1995, pp. 13–16.

16. J.R. Stepp and T.J. Schneider, "Fostering Change in a Unionized Environment," *Canadian Business Review*, Summer 1995, pp. 13–16.

17. This is a central insight of the modern manufacturing literature. See R.H. Hayes

and S.C. Wheelwright, "Link Manufacturing Process and Product Life Cycles," *Harvard Business Review*, January–February 1979, pp. 127–36; R.H. Hayes and S.C. Wheelwright, "Competing Through Manufacturing," *Harvard Business Review*, January–February 1985, pp. 99–109.

18. The view of quality as reliability goes back to the work of Deming and Juran; see A. Gabor, *The Man Who Discovered Quality* (New York: Times Books, 1990).

19. See D. Garvin, "What Does Product Quality Really Mean?" *Sloan Management Review*, 26, Fall 1984, pp. 25–44; P.B. Crosby, *Quality Is Free* (New York: Mentor, 1980); A. Gabor, *The Man Who Discovered Quality* (New York: Times Books, 1990).

20. See J.W. Dean and D.E. Bowen, "Management Theory and Total Quality: Improving Research and Practice Through Theory Development," *Academy of Management Review*, 19, 1994, pp. 392–418.

21. For general background information see J.C. Anderson, M. Rungtusanatham, and R.G. Schroeder, "A Theory of Quality Management Underlying the Deming Management Method," *Academy of Management Review*, 19, 1994, pp. 472–509; "How to Build Quality," *The Economist*, September 23, 1989, pp. 91–92; A. Gabor, *The Man Who Discovered Quality* (New York: Times Books, 1990); P.B. Crosby, *Quality Is Free* (New York: Mentor, 1980).

22. W.E. Deming, "Improvement of Quality and Productivity Through Action by Management," *National Productivity Review*, 1, Winter 1981–82, pp. 12–22.

23. G. Keenan, "Lego: The Toy as Training Tool," *The Globe and Mail*, May 7, 1999, p. B25.

24. G. Arnaut, "The Taxpayer as Customer," in *The Total Quality Imperative*, an insert to *Report on Business*, January 1995.

25. J. Bowles, "Is American Management Really Committed to Quality?" *Management Review*, April 1992, pp. 42–46.

26. V. Houlder, "Two Steps Forward, One Step Back," *Financial Times*, October 31, 1994, p. 8.

27. T.Y. Choi and O.C. Behling, "Top Managers and TQM Success: One More Look After All These Years," *Academy of Management Executive*, 11, 1997, pp. 37–47.

28. T.Y. Choi and O.C. Behling, "Top Managers and TQM Success: One More Look After All These Years," *Academy of Management Executive*, 11, 1997, pp. 46.

29. J. Griffiths, "Europe's Manufacturing Quality and Productivity Still Lag Far Behind Japan's," *Financial Times*, November 4, 1994, p. 11.

30. S. McCartney, "Compaq Borrows Wal-Mart's Idea to Boost Production," *Wall Street Journal*, June 17, 1994, p. B4.

31. S.C. Wheelwright and K.B. Clark, *Managing New Product and Process Development* (New York: Free Press, 1993).

32. M.A. Cusumano, *The Japanese Automobile Industry* (Cambridge, MA: Harvard University Press, 1989); O. Taiichi, *Toyota Production System* (Cambridge, MA: Productivity Press, 1990; Japanese edition, 1978); J.P. Womack, D.T. Jones, and D. Roos, *The Machine That Changed the World* (New York: Macmillan, 1990).

33. G. Stalk and T.M. Hout, *Competing Against Time* (New York: Free Press, 1990).

34. For an interesting discussion of some other drawbacks of JIT and other "Japanese" manufacturing techniques, see S.M. Young, "A Framework for Successful Adoption and Performance of Japanese Manufacturing Practices in the United States," *Academy of Management Review*, 17, 1992, pp. 677–701.

35. M. Imai, *"Kaizen": The Key to Japan's Competitive Success* (New York: Random House, 1987).

36. R. Gourlay, "Back to Basics on the Factory Floor," *Financial Times*, January 4, 1994, p. 12.

37. S.M. Young, "A Framework for Successful Adoption and Performance of Japanese Manufacturing Practices in the United States," *Academy of Management Review*, 17, 1992, pp. 677–700.

38. M. Hammer and J. Champy, *Re-Engineering the Corporation* (New York: Harper Business, 1993), p. 35.

39. M. Hammer and J. Champy, *Re-Engineering the Corporation* (New York: Harper Business, 1993), p. 46.

40. N.D. Chander and H. Armitage, "An Assessment of Business Process Reengineering Among Canadian Organizations," Working Paper: University of Waterloo.

41. N.D. Chander and H. Armitage, "An Assessment of Business Process Reengineering Among Canadian Organizations," Working Paper: University of Waterloo.

42. "SaskTel Dials the Wrong Number; Employees Rebel at Being 'Re-engineered' by a Psychobabbling Yankee Consultant," *Western Report*, February 26, 1996, pp. 14–17; "The Ghost in the Machine (Re-engineering)," *Financial Post 500*, 1996, pp. 8, 16.

43. N.D. Chander and H. Armitage, "An Assessment of Business Process Reengineering Among Canadian Organizations," Working Paper: University of Waterloo.

44. For example, see V. Houlder, "Two Steps Forward, One Step Back," *Financial Times*, October 31, 1994, p. 8.; A.K. Naj, "Shifting Gears," *Wall Street Journal*, May 7, 1993, p. A1; D. Greising, "Quality: How to Make It Pay," *Business Week*, August 8, 1994, pp. 54–59.

45. L. Helm and M. Edid, "Life on the Line: Two Auto Workers Who Are Worlds Apart," *Business Week*, September 30, 1994, pp. 76–78.

46. Featherbedding discussion is based on "Back on the Rails: Years of Cutting Have Produced a Leaner and Meaner CN," *Maclean's*, January 13, 1997, pp. 36–38.

47. E. Schein, *Organizational Culture and Leadership* (San Francisco, CA: Jossey-Bass, 1985).

48. "Management Insight" is based on "The Kaizen Advantage: Japanese Term for the Unglamorous Techniques You Use to Get Continuous Manufacturing Improvements," *The Financial Post*, October 21/23, 1995, pp. 10–11; "Performance 500 Top 10," *Canadian Business 500*, June 1997, pp. 137–146; "Ventra Logs Record Results," *Financial Post (National Post)*, May 14, 1999, p. C2.

Photo Credits

Chapter 1

Page 3, Courtesy of Ernst & Young. From left to right–Donald Bell, Tim Morgan, Clive Beddoe, and Mark Hill; Page 3, Courtesy of *Canadian Press* CP. Photograph by Jeff McIntosh; Page 12, AP/Wide World Photos/ Jim Cooper; Page 23, Michael Rosenfeld/Tony Stone Images.

Chapter 2

Page 33, CORBIS/Austrian Archives; Page 33, Chad Ehlers/International Stock; Page 38, Corbis-Bettmann; Page 40, 20th Century Fox (Courtesy Kobal); Page 42, AP/Wide World Photos.

Chapter 3

Page 61, Courtesy of *The National Post*; Page 61, Courtesy of *Canadian Press* CP. Photograph by Jeff McIntosh; Page 66, Courtesy of the Associated Press AP. Photograph by Cliff Schiappa; Page 74, Courtesy of *Canadian Press* CP. Photograph by Frank Gunn.

Chapter 4

Page 91, Courtesy of Gildan Activewear; Page 91, Courtesy of *The Chicago Tribune*, photo by Alex Garcia; Page 95, Jon Chiasson/Liaison Agency Inc.; Page 100, Fritz Hoffmann/The Image Works; Page 113, Courtesy of *The Vancouver Sun*. Photograph by Bill Keay.

Chapter 5

Page 121, Courtesy of *Canadian Press* CP. Photograph by Cam Mcalpine; Page 121, Associated Press AP. Photograph by Luis Alvarez Stringer; Page 131, Courtesy of CP *Canadian Press* & Maclean's. Photograph by Peter Bregg/Maclean's Staff; Page 135, Courtesy McDonald's Corporation; Page 145, Courtesy of *The Leader-Post*.

Chapter 6

Page 155, Charly Franklin/FPG International LLC; Page 155, Telegraph Colour Library/FPG International LLC; Page 157, Courtesy of *The National Post*; Page 166, Paul S. Howell/Liaison Agency Inc.; Page 179, Courtesy of *The National Post*.

Chapter 7

Page 189, Sharon Hoogstraten; Page 189, Courtesy of CLEO Photography, Whitby Ontario; Page 192, Gary Beechey, BDS Studios; Page 207, Peter Blakely/SABA; Page 211, Courtesy of Sleeman Brewery.

Chapter 8

Page 224, Courtesy of *Canadian Press* TRSTR. Photograph by John Mahler Staff; Page 224, Courtesy of *Canadian Press* Maclean's. Photograph by Phill Snel Staff; Page 229, Bernard Boutrit/Woodfin Camp & Associates, Inc.; Page 243, Courtesy of the *Toronto Star*; Page 245, *Winnipeg Free Press*, May 7, 2001.

Chapter 9

Page 255, Christopher Bissel/Tony Stone Images; Page 255, Loren Santow/Tony Stone Images; Page 257, Scala/Art Resource, NY; Page 276, Courtesy of Southwest Airlines.

Chapter 10

Page 287, Courtesy of Comtek Advanced Structures Ltd.; Page 287, Courtesy of CLEO Photography, Whitby Ontario; Page 298, Sandor Fizli photographer. Atlantic Progress; Page 299, AP/Wide World Photos/Town Talk, Stephen Reed; Page 313, Richard Howard/Black Star.

Chapter 11

Page 323, Courtesy of *Canadian Press* TRSUN. Photograph by Alex Urosevic; Page 323, Photo courtesy of *The National Post*; Page 333, Courtesy of Taras Kovaliv ©; Page 335, Courtesy of the *Toronto Star*.

Chapter 12

Page 349, JamesLeynse/SABA; Page 349, Sharon Hoogstraten.; Page 353, Courtesy of *The Vancouver Sun*. Photograph by Bill Keay; Page 360, John Abbott; Page 369, James Schnepf/Liaison Agency Inc.

Chapter 13

Page 379, Courtesy of QLT; Page 379, Courtesy of *Canadian Press* TRSTR. Photograph by Ron Bull Staff; Page 383, Mark Segal/Index Stock; Page 401, Courtesy of *The National Post*.

Chapter 14

Page 409, Courtesy of Willow MFG. Ltd.; Page 414, Courtesy of Burnaby, BC-based Dominion Information Services Inc™.

Chapter 15

Page 443, Courtesy of RBW Graphics/Transcontinental; Page 443, Courtesy of *The Vancouver Sun*. Photograph by Ward Perrin; Page 450, Jon Feingersh/The Stock Market; Page 452, *The Globe and Mail*; Page 465, Ellen Senisi/The Image Works; Page 465, Bob Krist/Tony Stone Images.

Chapter 16

Page 475, Courtesy of *Canadian Press* CP. Photographer Kevin Frayery; Page 475, Courtesy of *Canadian Press* CP. Photograph by Rene Johnston; Page 484, Courtesy of *The Vancouver Sun*. Photograph by Stuart Davis.

Chapter 17

Page 501, Courtesy of *Canadian Press* CP. Photograph by Tom Hanson Staff; Page 501, Courtesy of *The National Post*; Page 503, Courtesy of *Canadian Press* CP/*Toronto Star*. Photograph by Andrew Stawicki; Page 516, Courtesy Toyota Motor Manufacturing, Kentucky, Inc.

Index
Name/Company/URL

A

3M: **www.3m.com**, 173, 375
135 Services Ltd., 450
ABC, 382
Abitibi Consolidated, 210
Abitibi-Price, 117
Adam, Sandy, 246
Adams, J. Stacy, 364
Adam Smith Institute:
    www.adamsmith.org.uk, 36
AES Corporation, 438–39, 462
Agere Systems Inc., 204
Agfa, 56
Agricultural Data Systems, 370
Airborne Regiment, 276
Air Canada: **www.aircanada.ca**,
    3, 4, 14, 66, 210
Air Ontario, 4
Aiwa Co., 98
Ajax, city of, 371
AJ Bus Lines, 139
Alberta Energy Company, 82
Alberta, provincial government,
    369
Alcan Aluminum, 126, 304
Alcatel Canada, 415
Alderfer, Clayton, 353, 354–55
Alexander, Pam, 344
Algoma Steel, 246
Algonquin Automotive, 72
Alliance of Manufacturers &
    Exporters Canada, 126
Altimira, 223–24
Amazon.com, 458
Amber, Arnold, 497
Amcor PET Packaging, 220
AMD, 64
American Management
    Association (AMA):
    www.amanet.org/index.htm,
    319
American Quality Foundation, 513
America Online, 64
AMP, 513
Amstrad, 207
Amy, Dave, 444
Angiotech Pharmaceuticals Inc.:
    www.angiotech.com,
    295–96
Appelbaum, Steven, 440
Apple Computer, 16, 65, 66, 208
Architel Systems, 501
Armitage, Howard, 518
Arthur Andersen, 5, 111, 275
Ascential Software Corporation,
    559n
ASEAN Holdings Inc., 344

Asper, Izzy, 152
Astley, Bob, 283
AT&T: **www.att.com**, 461
ATI, 8
Atlantic Opportunities Agency, 370
Atlantic Pearl, 339
Atmosph(here) Communications,
    439
Auto Zone, 530
Avaya Inc., 204
Avcorp Industries, 98, 371
Avenor Inc., 236
Avis, 109
Avon: **www.avon.com**, 12
Axworthy, Lloyd, 126, 127
Azarchs, Tanya, 110

B

Bachand, Steve, 530
Baillie, Charlie, 476, 491
Bakke, Dennis W., 438
Baleshda, Doug, 450
Bank of Canada, 294, 452
Bank of Montreal:
    www.bmo.com, 110, 111,
    144, 288, 323–24, 369, 458,
    475–76
Bank of Nova Scotia. *See*
    Scotiabank
Barber & Bronson, 499
Barrett, Matthew, 323–24, 475–76
Barron, Millard, 394
Bata, Sonja, 327
Bata, Tom, 327
Bavington, Greg, 513
Bay Networks, 501
Bazowsky, Dave, 7
BBM Human Resources
    Consultants:
    www.bbmcareerdev.com,
    304
BCE, 96, 293
BCE Corporate Services, 472
BC Employment Standards
    Branch:
    www.labour.gov.bc.ca/esb,
    44
BC Human Rights Commission:
    www.bchrc.gov.bc.ca, 44
BC Hydro, 131, 480
BC Lions Society for Childeren
    with Disabilities:
    www.lionssocietybc.bc.ca/,
    25
BC Liquor Control Board, 97
BC Rail, 480

Beatty, Perrin, 29
Beavis and Butt-Head, 162–63
Beddoe, Clive, 3, 4, 12, 14, 264
Bell Canada: **www.bell.ca**, 67, 75,
    117, 303, 319
Bell, Don, 3
Bell Nexxia:
    www.bellnexxia.com, 303
Benimadhu, Prem, 367
Bergman, Anita, 198
Bernhard, Wolfgang, 526
Bertelsmann:
    www.bertelsmann.com, 251
Bestfoods Baking Co., 206
Big 8, 220
Biggadike, Ralph, 471
Biggs, Wes, 415
Billes, Martha, 531
BioChem Pharma Inc., 138–39
Birney, Ross, 377
Bissinger, Jacques, 415
Black, Conrad, 497
Black's Harbour, 206
Blake, Robert, 389
Blanchard, Kenneth, 381, 389,
    392, 395
Blimpie, 498–99
Blohm, David, 285
BMO Nesbitt Burns, 24, 128
BMW, 212
Bob Evans Farms Inc.:
    www.bobevans.com, 454
Bob Jones Ranch, 371
Body Shop, The, 327
Boeing: **www.boeing.com**, 98,
    99, 255, 375
Boliden, 6–7, 416
Bombardier, 93, 173, 199
Bombay Company, 109
Boralex Inc., 236
Boston Beer Co., 86
Boston Pizza International Inc.:
    www.bostonpizza.com, 451
Boucher, Pat, 110
Bowman, Keith, 30
Boyce, Kevin: **www.unilever.ca/**
    corporate/index.html, 329
BrainNet, 171
BrainStore, 171–72
Branco Quilmes, 110
Branson, Richard, 275
Breer, Carl, 525
Brenneman, Rob, 62
Brewer, Earl, 290, 298
Bridgestone: **www.bridgestone-**
    firestone.com, 122
Bristol-Myers, 440
Bristol-Myers Squibb Co., 440

British American Tobacco PLC,
    476
British Columbia Nurses' Union
    (BCNU): **www.bcnu.org**, 487
Brock University, 276
Bronson, Steven N., 499
Brooks, Len, 13, 319
Brotherhood of Maintenance of
    Way Employees, 509
Brothers Markle Inc., 243, 247,
    253
Brunswick Corporation, 405, 406
Bryan, J.P., 394
Buckley, George W., 406
Burdick, Paul, 438
Burkhart, Amelia, 151
Burney, Derek, 382
Burns, Lorne, 30
Burns, Tom, 49, 50–51
Burton, Robert, 502
Burt, Tim, 245
Busch, Pauline, 145
Bush, George W., 97
Business Council on National
    Issues, 126
By Design, 130

C

Calaway Park, 293
Calgary Herald, 497
Calling Systems International
    (CSI), 155–57
Cameco, 82
Campbell, Gordon, 369
Campbell, Sandy, 264
Campbell Soup, 5
Canada 3000, 66
Canada Life, 367
Canada Life Assurance Co., 283
Canada, Ministry of Finance, 476
Canada Post:
    www.canadapost.ca/, 19
Canada's Wonderland, 293
Canada Trust:
    www.canadatrust.com,
    446, 476, 491
Canadian 88 Energy Corp, 394
Canadian Airlines, 79
Canadian Armed Forces, 21
Canadian Auto Workers:
    www.caw.ca, 34, 111, 315,
    405, 509, 526
Canadian Banking Ombudsman,
    128
Canadian Franchise Association,
    407

Canadian Human Rights Commission, 139, 141–42
Canadian Imperial Bank of Commerce (CIBC): **www.cibc.com**, 68, 294, 319, 476
Canadian International Development Agency (CIDA), 369, 370, 532
Canadian Labour Congress: **www.clc-ctc.ca/ eng-index.htm**l, 496
Canadian National Railway (CN), 13, 96, 98, 184, 294, 375, 509–10, 519
Canadian Nurses Association, 127
Canadian Occidental Petroleum Ltd., 131
Canadian Pacific Ltd., 184
Canadian Pacific Railway, 184, 294, 319
Canadian Radio-Television and Telecommunications Commission (CRTC), 29, 67
Canadian Red Cross, 158
Canadian Security and Intelligence Service, 175
Canadian Tire: **www.canadiantire.ca**, 279–80, 503, 530–31
Canadian Transportation Agency, 139
Canadian Union of Public Employees (CUPE): **www.cupe.ca**, 444
Canfor: **www.canfor.com**, 325
CanJam Trading Ltd., 339
CanJet, 66
Cantrell, Jim, 419
Cardinal Capital Management, 245
Cargill Limited, 513
Carleton University, 320
Carruthers, Sally, 385–86
CARSTAR Automotive Canada: **wwwcarstarcanada.com**, 486
Cascades Inc.: **www.cascades.com**, 236
Cassidy, 220
CBC, 12, 29, 205
Cedars, Lisa, 299
Celestica, 118, 310
Centura Banks Inc., 140
Cerner Corp., 471–72
CGU Group Canada Ltd.: **www.cgu.ca**, 486
Chamandy, Greg and Glenn, 91
Champlain College, 439
Chandler, Neil, 518
Chandran, Clarence, 296
Changzhou Kooshies Carments, 532
Chaplin, Charlie, 38
Chapters Inc.: **www.chapters.ca**, 20, 65, 75, 130–31
Cheesebrough, Gordon, 223–24
Chene, Rick, 405–406
Cheng Yu-tong, 331
Chen Qiao Yu, 533
Cherry Stix, 130
Chevron, 457

Chiat/Day, 388–89
Chiat, Jay, 388, 389
Chiquita, 105
Chretien, Jean, 29, 218
Chretien, Raymond, 382
Christian, Dan, 72
Christie, Kathleen, 506
Chrysler Canada, 241
Chrysler Corp.: **www.chryslercorp.com**: 34, 70, 34, 196, 247, 258, 419, 525
Chrysler, Walter P., 525
Churchill, Sir Winston, 152
Chysler, Walter, 34
Cisco Systems Canada, 302–303
Cisco Systems Inc., 204
Clarica, 283
Clarify, 501
Clark, Ed, 446
Clark, Glen, 158
Clarkson Centre for Business Ethics (University of Toronto): **www.mgmt.utoronto.ca/ CCBE**, 13, 319
Clearwater Fine Foods, 246
Clearwater Foods Ltd., 123
Cleghorn, John, 475–76
CNN, 95
Coca-Cola: **www.coca-cola**, 73, 189–90, 208, 212, 220, 431
Columbia University: Graduate School of Business, 471
Communication Incorporated (CI), 121
Communications Energy and Peperworkers Union of Canada, 29, 497
Compaq Canada, 452, 472
Compaq Computer, 66, 108, 514
Comper, Tony, 324
Competition Bureau: **www.competition.ic.gc.ca**, 20
Computer Associates, 100
Comtek Advanced Structures Ltd.: **www.comtekadvanced.com**, 290, 387–88
Concordia University, 439, 440
John Molson School of Business, 440
Condé Nast, 261
Cone, Conrad, 431
Conference Board of Canada: **www.conferenceboard.ca**, 25, 126, 147, 367, 410, 417, 432
Conger, Jay, 397
Connors Bros., 206
Conza, Anthony P., 498–99
CoolBrands International: **www.yogenfruz.com**, 103
Corel, 382
CoreTek, 501
Costco: **www.costco.com**, 208
Cotsonas, David, 394
Cott Corporation, 190, 208, 211–12, 220
Courier, Jim, 344
Cousins, Ian, 131
Cowpland, Doug, 382
Craft Brewers Association of British Columbia, 86
Creemore Springs Brewery Ltd., 86

Crevier, Guy, 22
Crockstad, Brenda, 180
Cross, John, 439, 440
Crystal Decisions, 18, 376–77
CSX, 376

D

Daimler-Benz AG, 525
DaimlerChrysler AG, 13, 72, 237, 457, 513, 525–27
Dallas Semiconductor Corp., 370
Daniel Edelman Inc., 162
Daniels, David, 459
Danier Leather Inc.: **www.danier.com**, 179
Dave's Army & Navy Store, 87
de Bono, Edward, 164
DeCarlo, Peter, 498–99
Decker, Sue, 461
Delcambre, Danny, 461
Dell Canada, 64–65, 65–66
Deloitte & Touche, 505–506
Deloitte & Touche Canada, 151, 247, 505–506
Deming, W. Edwards, 512
Department of National Defence, 174–75
DeSimone, Desi, 375
DesRosiers, Dennis, 526
De Zen, Vic, 218–19
Diavik Diamond Mines, 81
Digital Equipment, 457
Diqiu, 532
Disney, Roy, 185
Dobell, Ken, 444
Dofasco: **www.dofasco.ca**, 246, 410
Doig, Ian, 61
Dominion Directory Information Services, 386, 414
Dominion Securities. *See* Royal Bank/Dominion Securities
Domosys Corporation, 118
Domtar, 236
Dowsett, Diane, 296
Drazan, Jeff, 414
Drexel Point-Pepperell Inc., 92
Dry Plate Company, 56
Ducks Unlimited: **www.ducks.org**, 243
Dunlop, Al "Chainsaw", 393
DuPont, 109, 111, 147, 174, 274
DuPont Canada: **www.dupont.ca**, 263, 267, 374
Duxbury, Linda, 320

E

E.&J. Gallo Winery, 207
Eastman, George, 56
Eastman Kodak: **www.kodak.com**, 56, 247, 349–50, 357, 360, 361, 418
Eastman, Sharon, 155–57, 164, 167, 170
Eaton's: **www.eatons.com**, 66, 79, 81
E-Bay, 458
Edens, Ron, 57–58
edgeflow Inc.: **www.edgeflow.com**, 415

Edmonton Journal, 497
EDS Canada, 247, 294
E.D. Smith & Sons Ltd., 203–204
E.F. Hutton, 499
Eggleton, Art, 21
Eisner, Michael, 185, 186
Electronic Banking Inc., 57–58
Emmerson, David: **www.canfor.com/ 1400.asp**, 325
Emploi Quebec: **www.emploiquebec.net/ index.htm**, 439
Empresa Brasileira de Aeronautica SA, 21
Empresa Brasileira de Aeronautica SA (Embraer), 93
Enquiry BC, 43
Entwistle, Darren, 376
e-plastics.com, 151
Ernst & Young, 30, 518
eServices (Pvt.) Ltd., 99
European Foundation for Quality Management: **www.efqm.org**, 513
Evans, Martin, 392
Evans, Stephan, 472
Executive Decision Centre (Queen's University), 174
Exxon Corp., 62, 81

F

Fahnestock & Co., 499
Fahnestock and Co., 122
Falconbridge: **www.falconbridge.com**, 12
Fanoe, Thomas A., 87
Farley, Bill, 92
Fayol, Henri, 7, 40, 42–43
Federal Express: **www.fedex.com**, 26, 236
Feigenbaum, A.V., 512
Fiedler, Fred E., 381, 390–91, 395
Fields, Bill, 394
Fife, William, 255
Financial Post, 477
Finning, 201–202, 214
First, Tom, 284
Fisher, George, 56, 349–50, 357, 358, 360, 361
Fishery Producers International Ltd. (FPI), 123–24
Fleet Corporation, 162
Fletcher Challenge Canada, 117
Florio, Steven T., 261
Flynn, Mike, 376
Follett, Mary Parker, 44–45
Foot: Cone & Belding, 87
Foote, Cone & Belding, 88
Ford, Henry, 33–34, 38, 39, 47, 278
Ford Motor Company: **www.ford.com**, 33–34, 39, 48, 55, 70, 96, 98, 122, 160, 255, 405, 457, 525
Ford Motor Company of Canada Limited: **www.ford.ca**, 19, 122, 278, 400
Fox, Vicente, 112
Frances, Robert, 298

Franklin Motor Company, 38
French, Orland, 497
Fritzsch, Brad, 443
Frost, Peter, 398
Fruit of the Loom:
    www.fruit.com, 92, 98, 199
Fuji Film, 56
Fujitsu Ltd., 98
Future Electronics, 440

G

Gap: www.gap.com, 95
Garuda Airlines, 448
Gates, Bill, 158, 289, 327, 344
Gates, Terry, 263
Gaunt, Bobbi, 400
G.D. Searle, 208
GE Appliances, 279
General Electric: www.ge.com,
    48, 107, 118, 219, 319, 375
General Hospital (Regina), 198
General Instrument, 8
General Motors of Canada, 111,
    315, 346, 400, 405
General Motors Corp.:
    www.gm.com, 13, 34, 70, 72,
    81, 111, 243, 247, 419, 525
General Motors Europe, 388
Geogia-Pacific, 246
George, Karen, 464
George Weston Ltd., 19, 206
GE Plastics, 151
Gersick, Connie:
    www.anderson.ucla.edu,
    425–26
Gerstner, Lou, 327
Giancamilli, Andy, 530
Giddings and Lewis:
    www.giddings.com, 255
Gildemeister S.A.C., 202
Gilden Activewear Inc.:
    www.gildan.com, 91–92, 199
Girard, Bob, 122
Glaxo Wellcome, 174
Global Explorations Corp., 344
Global Gold, 130
Globe & Mail, 496
Godfrey, Paul, 12, 346
Godsoe, Paul;
    www.robmagazine.com/
    archive/98ROBseptember/
    html/moving_target.html,
    491
Goldman Sachs, 472
Goldstein, Stephen, 88, 89
Goodwin, Gary, 243
Goodyear: www.goodyear.com,
    116, 457
Graham, Terry, 176
Gray, John, 480
Greenarm Management, 290,
    298
Green, Diana, 151
Green-Raine, Nancy, 480
Grey, Ron, 30
Grocery Go-Pher, 196
Group Bull, 66
Gulf Canada Resources Ltd., 394,
    398
Gunderson, Dean, 168
Gunderson, Lori, 168

H

H20 Adventures:
    www.h20adventures.com,
    440
Haas, Robert D., 87, 88
Hackett, Bob, 497
Hackman, J.R., 230–31
Hackney, Steve, 524
Haldane, Bill, 128
Halifax Chronical-Herald, 497
Halifax Mail-Star, 497
Hallmark Canada, 485
Hallmark Cards:
    www.hallmark.com,
    241, 422
Hamilton, Cliff, 510
Hammond, Les, 344
Hampton Industries, 130
Hanes, 98, 199
Harbour, Andrea, 91
Hargrove, Buzz, 526
Harris Bankcorp, 111, 323
Harrison, Deborah, 276
Harrison, Doug, 419
Harton, Gordon, 87
Hasenfratz, Linda, 401
Hay Group, 30
HBO, 95
Health Canada, 142
Hersey, Paul, 381, 389, 392, 395
Herzberg, Frederick, 353, 355–56
Hewlett-Packard: www.hp.com,
    66, 241, 247, 282, 418, 419,
    439, 440, 450
Hewlett-Packard Canada, 304
Hewlett, William, 450
High Liner Foods, 319
Hilgert, Richard, 122
Hill, Mark, 3
Hilton Hotels, 109
Hiscox, Bill, 444
HMV Canada Music Stores Ltd.:
    www.hmv.com, 459
Hoffman, Charles E., 192
Hofstede, Gert, 106
Holden, James, 526
Home Depot, 5, 530
Honda: www.honda.com, 245,
    413–14
Hopper, Wilbert (Bill), 61–62, 79
Houle, Léo, 293
House, Robert, 392, 398
Howell, Jane, 398
Hudson's Bay Company:
    www.hbc.com, 19, 76,
    310, 394
Hughes, Louis, 388
Hughes, William, 461
Human Resources Development
    Canada: www.hrdc-
    drhc.gc.ca, 303–304, 369–70
Humber River Regional Hospital,
    300
Hunter, William, 295
Hushovd, Oyvind, 12
Husky Injection Molding Systems,
    278
Hutcheson, Jane, 288
Hydro-Québec:
    www.hydroquebec.com, 371
Hyperchip Inc., 440
Hyundai Motor Co., 386, 527

I

Iacocca, Lee, 196, 525
IBM: www.ibm.com, 66, 81, 98,
    118, 158, 176–77, 209–10,
    243, 279, 327, 385, 524
IBM Canada, 278, 294, 418, 452
Ierfino, Maria, 472, 473
Image Processing Systems Inc.,
    176
Imasco Ltd., 476
Imperial Oil, 174, 319
Inco, 319
Indigo Books & Music, Inc.:
    www.indigo.ca, 13, 20,
    65, 130
Industries Manufacturières
    Mégantic Inc. (IMMI), 507
Informix: www.informix.com,
    255–56
Ingari, Frank, 284
Ingersoll Rand, 118
Inner City/Community on the
    Move (ICP), 140
Innovative Staffing Solutions, 335
InSystems: www.insystems.com,
    296, 310, 318
Intel: www.intel.com, 5, 8, 64, 195
International Association for
    Conflict Management:
    www.iacm-conflict.org, 482
International Brotherhood of
    Electrical Workers:
    www.ibew.com, 509
Investment Dealers Association, 24
Investment Dealers Association
    (IDA), 128
Irwin, George, 379, 380, 381–82,
    489
Irwin Toy, 489
Irwin Toy Ltd.:
    www.irwintoy.com, 379, 380

J

Jack-in-the-Box, 334
Janeway Child Health Centre, 451
Jansen, Dan, 344
J.C. Penney Co., 88
JDS Uniphase, 13, 118, 266, 319
Jeffrey, Tracy, 196
Jemas, Bill, 162
Jennings, Doug, 418
Jennings, Robert, 382
Jenny Craig:
    www.jennycraig.com, 146
Jerilyn Wright and Associates, 174
Jobs, Steve, 16, 206
John Molson School of Business,
    440
Johnson, Donna, 162
Johnson, Ted, 29
Johnsonville Foods:
    www.johnsonville.com, 423
Julius Blum GmbH:
    www.blum.com, 357
Jung, Andrea, 12
Jupiter Media Matrix, 459
Juran, Joseph, 512
Just White Shirts & Black Socks
    Inc.: www.justwhite
    shirts.com, 459

K

Kahneman, Daniel, 167
Kahn, Robert, 48
Kaiswatum, Art, 144
Kaizaki Yoichiro, 122
Kaizen Institute: www.kaizen-
    institute.com, 517
Kanungo, Rabindra, 397
Kao Chin-yen, 331
Katz, Daniel, 48
Katz, Jason, 439
Kavanagh, Jodie, 414
Kavanagh, Michael, 18
Kawamata Katsuji, 168
Kawamoto Nobuhiko, 414
Kay, Jonathan, 453
Kelleher, Herb, 276, 344–45
Kelly Services:
    www.kellyservices.com, 293
Kempston Darkes, Maureen, 400
Kentucky Fried Chicken:
    www.kfc.com, 206, 334
Kerfoot, Greg, 376
Kesselring, Cindy, 58
Kidder, Mike, 156
Kierans, Thomas, 501
Kilpatrick, Jim, 247
King, Debi, 457
King, Ken, 497–98
King, Robert, 426
Kingston Township, 371
Kinnear, David, 220
Kmart Corp., 530, 531
KMPG: www.kpmg.ca, 30
Knowledge House:
    www.knowledgehouse.net,
    203
Kooshies Baby Products, 532–33
Kossw, Olav, 346
Kotler, Warren, 299
KPMG: www.kpmg.ca, 120
Kroc, Ray, 277
Kulhanek, Vratislav, 259
Kwon, Charlotte, 112, 113

L

Labatt Brewing Co.:
    www.labatt.ca, 67, 86
La Brasserie Seigneuriale, 86
Lagnado, Isaac, 88
Laidlaw Inc., 19
Laidley, David, 505
Lampe, John, 122
Langley Memorial Hospital, 417
Langton, Nancy, 432
La Presse, 22
Larose, Darren, 336
Larsson, Kjell, 6
Lasser, Charlie, 121
Latham, Gary, 360
Laurentian University, 336
Lawrence, Paul, 49
Lawton Partners Financial
    Planning Services, 245
LeBlanc, Steve, 362
Ledgers Canada, 246
Lee Hun Jo, 399–400
Lee, Matthew, 140
Lefebre, Dave, 327–28
Legate, Frank, 524

Lemaire, Laurent, 236
Lem, Gail, 498
Les-Méchins, 139
Lever, William, 94
Levi Straus & Co.: **www.levi.com**, 87–88, 124, 206–207, 457
Levi's USA, 88
Levy, Bob, 87
Levy, Julia, 379–80, 381, 385, 387, 388
Lewenza, Ken, 34
Lewin, Kurt, 504–505
Lewis, Robert, 382
Lexmark, 241
LG Electronics Co., 399–400
L'Heureux-Dubé, Claire, 152
Liebmann, Wendy, 498
Lightbridge Inc., 284–85
Linamar Corporation, 401
Livgroup Investments Ltd., 380
Loblaw Cos.: **www.loblaws.ca**, 190, 407
Locke, Ed, 360
Loehr, James, 344
London Life Insurance Company, 440
Loray, Carol, 383, 384
Lord, Bernard, 74
Lorsch, Jay, 49
Lucent Technologies: **www.lucent.com**, 204, 266, 277, 501
Lucky Goldstar, 21
Lunatex Inc., 299
Lute, Graham, 140

M

McBean, Marnie, 382
McCain Foods Ltd., 74, 477–78
McCain, Harrison, 477–78, 481
McCain, Michael, 477, 478
McCain, Wallace, 477–78, 481
McClelland, David, 329
MacDonald, Alison, 377
MacDonald Dettwiler & Associates (MDA), 174
Macdonald, John, 174
McDonald's: **www.mcdonalds.com**, 5, 50, 100, 109, 204, 206, 208, 209, 217, 228–30, 277, 302, 334
McDonald's Canada, 111
McDonald, Scott, 491
McDonald's Hamberger University: **www.mcdonalds.com/corporate/careers/hambuniv**, 302
MacDougall, Kathryn, 138
McDuff, Randolph, 128
McEachin and Associates, 300
McEachin, Richard, 300
MacFadyen, Alan, 62
McGillivray, Jacqui, 320
McGill University, 15, 397
McGrath, John, 293
McGrath, Ronan D., 192
McGraw-Hill Ryerson Canada, 175
MacGregor, Catherine, 44

McGregor, Douglas, 45–46
MacKay, Harold, 475
McLane, Andres, 224
Maclean's: **www.macleans.ca**, 382
McMann, Mary, 366
McMaster University, 334
Macmillan Bloedel (MacBlo): **www.weyerhaeuser.com**, 393–94
McNally, Al, 111
McNeil, Sally, 452, 472–73
McPherson, Debra, 487
MADD (Mothers Against Drunk Driving), 86
Magna Entertainment Corp., 66
Magna International: **www.magnaint.com**, 28, 147, 157, 275, 345–46
Maiwa Handprints: **www.maiwa.com**, 112, 113
Maldutis, Julius, 4
Mandela, Nelson, 152
Manitoba Hydro: **www.hydro.mb.ca**, 82
Manitoba Securities Commission: **www.msc.gov.mb.ca**, 24, 128, 257
Manley, John, 13, 319
Manulife, 398
Manulife Financial Corp, 283
Maple Leaf Foods Ltd., 362, 478
March of Dimes, 5
March, James, 159–62
Maritime Beer Co., 86
Maritime Telephone and Telegraph: **www.mtt.ca**, 319
Markle, Jack, 243, 253
Markle, Sam, 243, 253
Mars, 349–50, 351, 358
Mars, Forest, 349, 350, 357
Mars, John, 349, 350, 357
Martignano, Joe, 499
Martin, Kathleen, 334–35
Martin, Paul, 324, 475–76
Maslow, Abraham, 353–54
Mason, Steven, 375
Mathieson, Duncan, 62
Matsuka, John, 156
Matsushita, 51, 69, 206, 207, 208
Mattel: **www.mattel.com**, 100
Mayo, Elton, 45
Mazulo, Marcia, 464
Mazur, Stefan, 415
MCA Universal, 205
MDS Nordion: **www.mds.nordion.com**, 457
Mead, 375
Melville, George, 451
Membertou Development Corporation, 246
Memorial University: Telemedicine and Education Technology Resource Agency (TETRA), 450–51
Mercedes-Benz US International Inc.: **www.mercedes-benz.com**, 430–31
Mersch, Frank, 224
Metal Edge, 162
Mettler, Markus, 171, 172
Michael Stern Associates Inc., 319
Michaleski, Bob, 121

Michalowski, Vojtek, 328
Microsoft Corporation: **www.microsoft.com**, 64, 65, 108, 241, 252, 289–90, 327, 382, 420, 422, 432
Mill, John Stuart: 553n
Mills, Dennis, 345, 346
Milton, Robert, 210
Mintzberg, Henry: **www.management.mcgill.ca/people/faculty/profiles/mintzber.htm**, 15, 80
Mische, Justus, 383
Misura Inc., 346
Mitchell, Jim, 412
Mitsubishi Motors Corp, 527
Mleczko, Wink, 284
M and M Meat Shops, 406–407
Mobil: **www.mobil.com**, 385
Molson Inc., 67, 86, 369, 371, 398, 411
Molten Metal Technology Inc., 285
Monk, Timothy, 344
Montero, Phil, 450, 472
Moore Business Corp, 502
Moore, Peter, 389
More, Lauren, 122
Morgan, Tim, 3
Morgan, William, 344
Moses, Barbara: **www.bbmcareerdev.com**, 304
Motorola: **www.motorola.com**, 56, 100, 240, 359–60, 457
Mountain Equipment Co-op (MEC): **www.mec.ca**, 24, 130
Mouton, Janet, 389
MTV, 95
Mulholland, William, 323
Multimatic Investments Ltd., 158
Muncaster, Dean, 530
Mutual Group, 319
Myhrvold, Nathan, 420

N

Nacan Products, 263, 267
Nantucket Nectars: **www.juiceguys.com**, 284, 285
National Aeronautics and Space Administratioin (NASA), 158, 168, 170, 195, 448
National Parole Board, 139
National Post: **www.nationalpostbusiness.com**, 400, 453, 497
National Steel of Japan, 246
Natuzzi, 21
Naviquest, 439
NB Power: **www.nbpower.com**, 74
NBTel, 67
NEC, 66
Neilson Dairy, 206
Nesbitt Burns, 257
Nestlé Canada: **www.nestle.ca/english**, 140
Nettleton, Gary, 524
Newbridge Networks Corp., 319, 415
New Brunswick, province of, 513
Newhouse, S.I., 261
Newman, Jane, 388

Newson, Wayne, 444
Newspaper Guild Canada, 497
New York Times, 405
Nexen Inc., 131
Nike: **www.nike.com**, 98, 389
Nike.com, 458
Nissan, 72, 168
Nixon, Gordon, 238
Nokia, 118
Nordstrom: **http://store.nordstrom.com**, 427
Norris, Michael, 238
Norske Skog, 117
Nortel Networks Corporation: **www.nortelnetworks.com**, 13, 19, 82, 96, 98, 118, 123, 139, 173, 183, 194, 199, 266, 296, 313, 319, 320, 398, 452, 501, 511
Northern Telecom, 247, 419
North York, school board, 513
Nova Corporation, 274
Novartis AG, 171
Nowak, Mark, 406
NRI Industries, Inc.: **www.nriindustries.com**, 513
Nvidia, 8
N. Winter Consulting, 368

O

O'Brien, David, 184
Oddo, Joe, 438
Office for the Study of Automotive Transportation (University of Michigan), 526
Ohio State University, 388
Okanagan Spring Brewing: **www.okspring.com**, 86
Oldenburger, Scott, 362
Oldham's, G.R., 230–31
Omnicom Group Inc., 389
Ondrack, Dan, 386
O'Neill, Dan, 411
Onex Corporation, 19, 130
Ono Masatoshi, 122
Ontario Human Rights Commission (OHRC): **www.gov.on.ca/mczcr/english/about/ohrc.htm**, 152
Ontario Hydro, 369
Ontario Jockey Club, 66
Ontario Labour Relations Board, 146
Ontario, provincial government, 294
Ontario Securities Commission: **www.osc.gov.on.ca**, 224
Ontario Small Brewers Association, 86
Orser, Barbara, 147
Orton, Dave, 8
Osman, Mariana, 359
Ouchi, William, 273
Ovitz, Mike, 186

P

Pacific Adventure Learning: **www.pacificadventure.org**, 431

Pacifica Papers, 117
Pacific National Exhibition (PNE), 293
Packard Bell Computers, 397
Packard, David, 450
PanCanadian Petroleum: **www.pancanadian.ca**, 184
Pansera, Gilles, 507
Paperboard Industries International Inc., 236
Paquin, Pierre, 86
Parent, Michael, 459
Parke, Gary, 370
Parkesdale Farms, 370
PartSource, 530
Patterson, Neal, 471–72
Pattison, Jimmy, 152
Payne, Derek, 264
Pazmac Enterprises, 356
PCL, 82
PEAK Investment: **www.peakgroup.com**, 298
Peak of the Market, 204
Pedersen, Larry, 168
Péladeau, Karl, 12
Pelletier, Andrew, 130
Pelletier, Claude, 6
Pembina Pipeline: **www.pembina.com**, 121–22
Pencer, Gerald, 190
Pension Benefit Guaranty Corporation, 461
PepsiCo: **www.pepsi.com**, 73, 189–90, 205, 206, 212, 220
Perez, Ray, 532–33
Periphonics, 501
Perkins Paper Ltd., 236
Petro-Canada: **www.petro-canada.ca**, 61–62, 79, 319
Pfeffer, Jeffrey, 471
Pfizer, 457
Pfizer Canada Inc., 440
Philips NV: **www.philips.com**, 51–52, 69
Phillips, Joyce, 294
Pier 1 Imports, 109, 232–34
Pierer, Heinrich von, 396–97, 398
Pierro, David, 499
Pillsbury Canada Limited: **www.pillsbury.com/ world/Canada.asp**, 367, 368
Pitt, Romaine W.M., 300
Pizza Hut, 206, 334
Placer Dome, 82
Pollard Banknote, 67–68
Pollard, Laurie, 66
Pomeroy, Jay, 151
Porter, Michael, 202, 210, 211
Power Corp., 29
Pratt & Whitney Canada: **www.pwc.ca**, 513
Price-Waterhouse, 418
Primus Telecommunications Canada, 327–28
Procter & Gamble: **www.pg.com**, 98, 111, 150, 205, 244–45
Proximi-T Technologies de l'information Inc., 307
Putnam, Martin, 124

Q

QLT, 379–80
Qtera, 501
Quantum, 64
Quebecor: **www.quebecorworld.com**, 12, 205, 210
Queen's University: **www.queensu.ca**, 174
Quicken, 64
Qwest Corporation, 118

R

Rabinovitch, Robert, 12, 29
Radio-Canada, 22
Rafay, Reema, 335
Ragin' Cajun Restaurant, 461
Rail Canada Traffic Controllers, 509
Raine, Al, 480
Ralph Lauren, 88
Ramcharan, Dev, 327–28
Rankin, John, 531
Ransom, Mal, 397
RBW Graphics: **www.transcontinental gtc.com**, 443–44
RCMP, 144–45
Redland, Alan, 155, 156, 167, 170
Redwood Plastics, 386
Reeve, Pamela, 284, 285
Regina District Health Board, 198
Reid, Brian, 443
Reisman, Heather, 75, 130
Relph, Geoffrey, 279
Re/Max International Inc., 371
Renschler, Andreas, 430–31
Revy Home Centres, 530
Richard Ivey School of Business (University of Western Ontario): **www.ivey.uwo.ca**, 144, 459
Riedler, Fred E., 381
Risley, John, 123–24
Ritchie, Ced, 491
Robertson, Catherine, 43–44
Robertson, Kym, 476
Robertson, Stuart, 439
Robertson Telecom Inc., 43–44
Rob Evans Farms Inc., 454
Robinson, Peter, 24
Robinson, Sandra, 297
Roche, Geoffrey, 333
Roche Macaulay & Partners Advertising: **www.rochemacaulay.com**, 333
Roddick, Anita, 327
Roethlisberger, F.J., 45
Rogers AT&T Wireless, 192, 193
Rogers Cable, 192, 193
Rogers Cablesystems, 344
Rogers Communications: **www.rogers.com**, 17, 192–94, 277
Rogers Group, 377
Rogers, Judy, 444
Rogers Media, 193
Rogers, Ted, 17, 192, 277
Rokeach, Milton, 330

Rolland, 236
Roll, Richard: 556n
Romano, Dan, 440
Roots Air, 66, 67
Roots Canada: **www.roots.com**, 67
Ross, Donald, 86
Roth, John, 194, 199, 296, 313, 501, 503, 511
Rotman School of Management (University of Toronto), 386
Royal Airlines, 66
Royal Bank: **www.royalbank.com**, 82, 140, 238, 319, 475–76
Royal Bank/Dominion Securities: **www.rbds.com**, 238
Royal Dutch Shell. *See* Shell Canada
Royal Group Technologies, 218–19
Roy, Brad, 43–44
Roy, Raman, 99
Rubbermaid: **www.rubbermaid.com**, 241
Ryder Integrated Logistics, 247, 419

S

SADD (Students Against Destructive Decisions), 86–87
Safeway, 208
Sainsbury's, 190
Saint Mary's University: Department of Management, 14
St. Catharines Standard: **www.scstandard.com**, 487
Salaff, Janet, 472
Sales, Wayne, 279–80, 503, 530–31
Samsung, 386
Sanchez Vicario, Arantxa, 344
Sant, R.W., 438
Saskatoon Chemicals, 227
Saskatoon StarPhoenix, 497
SaskEnergy, 82
SaskTel: **www.sasktel.com**, 67, 518
Saturn Corp, 405
Saucier, Guylaine, 29
Saunders, Jim, 198
Savage, Gillian, 44
Scarlett, Steve, 356
Schell, Bernadette, 336
Schering and Hoescht, 21
Schneider, Peter, 185–86
Schnetzler, Nadja, 171
Schrempp, Juergen, 525, 526
Schrieder, Lowell, 293
Schumacher, Tom, 185
Schwartz, Gerry, 75, 130
Scotiabank, 110–11, 294, 319, 491
Scotia Capital Markets, 62
ScotiaMcLeod Inc., 224, 269
Scott, Tom, 284
Seagate Software, 376
Seagate Technologies: **www.seagate.com**, 64
Seagram's, 205, 206
Sea Ray Group, 405, 406
Sears, 131, 516 Roebuck & Co., 88
Sears Canada: **www.sears.ca/e/ info/info.htm**, 146, 410, 437

Seeburn, 524
Semco, 384–85
Semler, Ricardo, 384–85
Senge, Peter: 164: 172, 555n
Sharp, David, 144
Shasta Networks: **www.shastanetworks.com**, 501
Shaw Communications, 12
Shaw, Jim, 12
Shell Canada: **www.shell.ca**, 125, 126, 227, 319
Shell Chemical Holdings Inc., 219
Shell Co.: **www.shell.com**, 81, 196–97
Shepard, James, 201
Shiva Corp, 284
Siegel, David L., 499
Siemens AG: **www.siemens.com**, 176, 415
Sierra Ventures, 415
Simon Fraser University: School of Communications, 497
Simon, Herbert, 159–62
Sims, Mary-Woo, 44
Skoda Auto, 259
Sleeman Breweries: **www.sleeman.ca**, 67, 86
Sleeman, John, 86
Sloan, Alfred, 34
Smed International: **www.smednet.com**, 404
Smed, Mogens, 404
Smith, Adam: 36: 553n
Smith, Carol, 58
Smith, Fred, 236
Smith, Llewellyn, 203–204
Smith, Michael D., 499
Smith, Steve, 3, 4, 279, 325, 384
SNC Lavalin Group, 246
Snow, John, 376
Social Sciences and Humanities Researh Council **www.sshrc.ca**, 490
Sodexho Marriott Services, 246
Sony, 8, 51, 69
Southam Inc., 497
Southwest Airlines, 3, 276, 344
Sprott Securities Ltd., 91
Stalker, G.M., 49, 50–51
Stamp, Paddy, 146
Standard and Poor's, 110
Stanford, Jim, 62, 79, 111
Stanford University: Graduate School of Business, 471
Staples: **www.staples.com**, 388
Starbucks, 431
Statistics Canada: **www.statcan.ca**, 81
Status of Women Canada, 139
Steelcase Canada: **www.steelcase.com**, 412, 513
Steelcase Inc., 513
Stella Produce, 204
Stephens, Tom, 393
Stern, Michael, 319
Stora Enso, 117
Stracker, Karen, 452
Straka, Pavel, 300
Stretch-O-Rama, 130
Stride Rite, 313
Stroh, 86
Stronach, Belinda, 157, 345–47

Stronach, Frank, 66, 157, 158, 275, 345
Subway sandwich shops, 229–30
Sullivan, Mike, 29
Sun Life Assurance Co., 283
Sun Media, 497
Sun Microsystems: **www.sun.com**, 457
Supreme Court of Canada, 146, 152
Sutton Creations, 130
Symantec, 64
Syncrude Canada: **www.syncrude.com**, 82

T

TA Associates Inc., 224
Taco Bell, 77, 80, 206
Tactical Retail Solutions, 88
Taiichi Ohno, 515–16
Talisman Energy Inc., 127
Tannen, Deborah, 464, 466
Tarragon Oil and Gas, 174
Taylor, Frederick W.: **www.fordham.edu/halsall/ mod/1911taylor.htm**, 36–37, 39–40
TD Canada Trust: **www.tdcanadatrust.com**, 110, 446
Tellier, Paul, 509–10, 519
TELUS, 238, 431
Telus Corp.: **www.telus.com**, 67, 376
Thiokol, Morton, 158, 168, 170
Thompson, James, 48
Thompson, James D., 420
Thomson, Ken, 152
Thomson Newspapers Co. Ltd., 497
Thunder Bay Chronicle-Journal, 497
Time Canada, 443
Tomiki Hisashi, 519
Tommy Hilfiger, 88
Toronto Blue Jays: **www.bluejays.mlb.com**, 12
Toronto-Dominion Bank (TD): **www.td.com**, 82, 319, 446, 476
Toronto Star, 13, 205, 497
Tory, John H., 192, 344
Toshiba: **www.toshiba.com**, 66, 176

Tough Stuff, 162
Towers Perrin, 377
Townsend, William, 25
Toyota Canada, 258, 410
Toyota Motor Company: **www.toyota.com**, 72, 211, 212, 245, 515–16, 519
Toys 'R' Us, 95, 99–100
TransCanada PineLines, 274
Transcontinental Printing, 444
Transport Canada, 370
Treliving, Jim, 451
Trott, Ralph, 531
Trudell, Cynthia, 405–406
Tversky, Amos, 167
Twinpak, 220
Tyler, Ed, 501

U

UCLA, 425
Unilever, 94, 206
Unilever Canada: **www.unilever.ca**, 329
Union Pacific Railroad, 375
United Auto Workers, 315
United Nations, 152
United Parcel Service, 386, 449
United States National Highway Traffic Safety Administration, 122
United Way, 175
University of Alberta Hospitals, 513
University of British Columbia: **www.ubc.ca**, 295–96, 297, 385, 398, 432
University of Michigan, 389, 526
University of Pittsburgh Medical Center, 344
University of Regina: **www.uregina.ca**, 497
University of Toronto: **www.utoronto.ca**, 13, 146, 386, 392, 472
University of Waterloo: **www.uwaterloo.ca**, 518
University of Western Ontario, 398 Richard Ivey School of Business, 144, 459
UPM-Kymmene, 117
Upper Canada Brewing, 86

US Federal Energy Regulatory Commission, 131
Usinor, 246

V

VanCity Credit Union: **www.vancity.com**, 343
Vancouver, city of, 444
Venditti, Lilie, 439
Ventra, 517, 524–25
Ventures West: **www.ventureswest.com**, 202
Verreault Navigation, 139
Vestel, 8
Videotron, 205
Vinci, Leonardo da, 257
Viner, Anthony P., 192
Virgin Group: **www.virgin.com**, 275
Virtual Entertainment, 285
Voisin, Mac, 406–407
Volkswagen AG, 259
Volpe, Jeannot, 74
von Shack, Wesley, 151

W

Wagner, Terry, 14
Wagoner, Rick, 405–406
Waitt, Tom, 128, 257
Walker, Don, 346
Wal-Mart, 5, 76, 516, 530
Wal-Mart Canada: **www.walmart.com**, 130
Walt Disney Co., 185–86
Wang Y.C., 331
Watson, Ann, 293
Watson Wyatt Worldwide, 310
Waugh, Rick, 110
Weber, Max, 40–42, 43
Weiner, Lisa, 162
Weldwood of Canada, 82
Wendy's, 334
Werner, Helmut, 430
Werry, James, 269
Western Electric Company, 45
Western Hemisphere International Regional Office (WHIRO), 491
Westinghouse Canada, 410
WestJet: **www.westjet.com**, 3–4, 12, 14, 180, 264, 279, 325, 384

Weston, Galen, 206
Weyerhaeuser, 82, 393
Wharton School of Business: **www.wharton.upenn.edu/ doctoral/programs/ acct.html**, 392
White, Grace, 339
White, Philip, 255–56
Whyte, Patrick, 290, 387
Wiggins, John, 86
Wi-LAN Inc., 382
Wild, Dennis, 409–10, 447
Wiles, Barbara Ann, 58
Wilkinson, Keith, 440
Williams, Bob, 293
Williams, John, 370
Willow Manufacturing: **www.willowcnc.com**, 278, 409–10, 447
Winter, Nadine, 368
Woods, Ann, 371
Woodward, Joan, 227
Workers' Compensation Board of BC: **www.worksafebc.com**, 198
Worstman, Jeffrey, 179
Wright, Orville, 525
Wyatt Co., 332

X

Xerox: **www.xerox.com**, 77, 151, 203, 247, 419
Xerox Canada: **www.xerox.ca**, 410, 432
Xie Jia Lin, 386
Xros, 501

Y

Yamaha Motor Co., 98
York University: **www.yorku.ca**, 146, 147
Young & Rubicam, 458

Z

Zaghloul, Hatim, 382
Zellers: **www.hbc.com/zellers**, 76, 394, 410, 516
Zero-Knowledge Systems, 440
Zetsche, Dieter, 526

Subject

A

360-degree performance appraisals, 309–10
Aboriginal people
  and business mentoring, 81–82
  healthcare, 198
  joint ventures, 246
  and NGR Resort Consultants, 480
Access to Information Act, 453
Accommodation, conflict handling-behaviour, 482–83
Accommodative approach, to social responsibility, 134
Achievement, need for, 329
Achievement orientation, 107
Active listening, 463–64
Activity ratios, 266
Adding value, 208, 212–14
Ad hoc committees, 416
Adjourning stage, in group development, 424
Administrative decision-making model, 159–62
  and bounded rationality, 160
  and incomplete information, 160–61
  and satisficing, 161–63
Administrative management theory, 40–43
  defined, 40
  Fayol's principles of management, 42–43
  theory of bureaucracy, 41–42
Affiliation, need for, 329
Agreeableness, 326–27
Aircraft-parts manufacturing, 287–88
Alderfer's ERG theory, 354–55
Alliances, and organizational politics, 491
Appraisal. See Performance appraisal
Armed forces, diversity in, 21
Assumption of morality, 433
Attitudes
  and job satisfaction, 332–33
  managerial, 330
  and organizational commitment, 333
  and perception, 335
  stress and, 337
Authority
  allocation, 241–45
  centralization of, 244
  decentralization of, 243–44
  defined, 241
  expertise and knowledge as sources of, 44–45
  line of, 43
  in mechanistic structures, 50, 51
  in organic structures, 51, 52
  overlapping, 481
  and responsibility, 43

theory of bureaucracy and, 41–42
Autonomy, job, 231

B

Barriers of entry
  brand loyalty, 67
  defined, 66
  economies of scale, 66–67
  lottery ticket printing business, 67–68
  See also Market entry
Behavioural management theory, 43–47
  Follett and, 44–45
  Hawthorne studies, 45
  and human relations, 45–57
  Theory, X, 46–47
  Theory Y, 47
Behaviour anchored rating scale (BARS), 308
Behaviour appraisals, 306
Behaviour control
  bureaucratic control, 271–72
  direct supervision, 269–70
  management by objectives, 270–71
Behaviour observation scale (BOS), 308
Belongingness needs, 354
Benefits. See Pay, and benefits
Biases, 140–41, 335
  in ineffective communication, 448
  in performance appraisals, 309–310
Birth stage, of industry life cycle, 68–69
Bottling industry, 220
Boundary spanning
  communication activities, 80
  defined, 79
Boundary spanning roles
  establishing interorganizational relationships, 81
  gatekeeping and information processing, 81
  representing and protecting organization, 80–81
  scanning and monitoring environment, 81
Bounded rationality, 160
Brainstorming, 172, 174–75, 176–77
Brand loyalty, 66, 67, 68, 70, 100
Bribery, 126, 131
Bridgestone tire scandal, 122
British Columbia
  and e-mail abuse, 453
  fast-ferry project, 158
  forest industry, 393–94
  pay of politicians, 369
  pulp and paper industry, 450
  wine industry, 96–97

Budgets, operating, 267–68
Buffer stocks, 516
Bureaucracy
  defined, 41
  principles of, 41–42
Bureaucratic control, 271–72
Business-level plan, 193, 194
Business-level strategies, 193, 210–12
  differentiation strategy, 210–11
  focused differentiation strategy, 212
  focused low-cost strategy, 211–12
  low-cost strategies, 210
  output control, 266
  "stuck in the middle" problem, 211
Business school, 66

C

Cafeteria-style benefit plans, 313
Call servicing, 99
Canada
  dollar, 117
  global strategy, 117–18
  human rights legislation, 139
  leadership style, 382, 383
  national culture, 73
  newsprint industry, 117
  skills crisis, 303–304
  social structure, 72
  social trends, 73
  telecommunications industry, 117–18
  unionized workforce, 314–15
Canada-United States Free Trade Agreement (FTA), 96
Canadian armed forces, 21, 276
Canadian Human Rights Act, 139, 291
Career development. See Development
Car manufacturing
  brand loyalty in, 70
  controlling in, 258, 259
  Fordism, 34–35, 39
  Japanese manufacturers, 34, 111, 515–16
  revolutionary management approaches, 33–34
Central positions, and power, 490
Challenger space shuttle disaster, 158
Child labour, 130
China, 94, 102, 103, 104–105, 112
Churning accounts, 269
Clan control, 273
Classical decision-making model, 159
Classroom instruction, 301–302
Clerical mills, 57–58
Closed systems, 48

Codes
  of conduct, 75–76
  dress code, 43–44, 278
  of ethics, 125–29
  for new methods, 37
Coercive power, 384–85
Cognitive biases, 167–69
  avoiding, 169
  escalating commitment, 168–69
  illusion of control, 168
  prior bias hypothesis, 167
  representative bias, 168
Collaboration, conflict handling-behaviour, 483
Collective bargaining, 314, 315
Collectivism, 106
Colleges and universities, government funding, 65
Command
  and centralization, 43, 244
  and decentralization, 244–45
  unity of, 43
Command economy, 102
Commission pay, 269, 371
Common interest, 43
Communication
  active listening, 463–464
  cross-cultural differences in, 465
  defined, 445
  empathy in, 464
  gender differences in, 466, 483–85
  and hearing impaired, 461–62
  horizontal, 456
  and interpersonal conflict, 483–85
  linguistic styles in, 464–66
  nonverbal, 447
  and organizational structure, 242–43
  problem of ineffective, 448
  process, 446–47
  technical advances in, 457–58
  verbal, 447
Communication media
  electronically-transmitted spoken communication, 451
  face-to-face communication, 450–51
  impersonal written communication, 454
  personally addressed written communication, 451–54
  selection criteria, 449
Communication networks
  all-channel network, 455
  chain network, 454–55
  circle network, 455
  organizational, 456
  wheel network, 454
Communications industry, 117–119
Communications skills, 459–66
  for receivers, 462–64
  for senders, 460–62

Competing, conflict
  handling-behaviour, 482
Competition Act of 1986, 75
Competition laws and regulations
  healthcare, 67
  long-distance service, 67
Competitive advantage, 23
Competitors
  and barriers of entry, 66–67
  global task environment,
    100–101
  of not-for-profit organizations, 68
Complex mental models, and
  organizational learning, 172
Compromise, conflict
  handling-behaviour, 482
Conflict management strategies,
    482–85
  conflict-handling behaviours,
    482–83
  focused on individuals, 483–85
  focused on organization, 485
  See also Organizational conflict
Conscientiousness, 327
Contingency models, 389–95
  Fiedler's contingency model,
    390–91
  Hersey-Blanchard's situational
    leadership theory, 392
  leader substitutes models, 394
  path-goal theory, 292–93
Contingency theory, 49–51
Continuous process technology,
    227–28
Control
  behaviour, 269–72
  concurrent, 260
  feedback, 260
  feedforward, 259
  output, 265–68
  workplace safety, 263
Controlling, 9
  conservative culture and, 279
  efficiency evaluation, 257–58,
    261
  innovative culture and, 279
  monitoring employee
    behaviour, 258, 269–72
  nature of, 257
Control process, 260–63
Control systems, 78–79, 259–60
Conversion stage
  concurrent control, 260
  of open system, 48
Coordination
  and organizational structure,
    241–45
  output control, 266–67
Corporate-level plan, 193, 194
Corporate-level strategies, 203–10
  concentration on single
    business, 204
  diversification, 204–205
  E.D. Smith, 203–204
  international expansion,
    206–207
  related diversification, 205
  unrelated diversification,
    205–206
  vertical integration, 207–10
Cost reduction and savings,
    212–14, 220, 243, 261,
    264–65, 511–12, 515–16

Crafts production, 36
Creativity
  cross-cultural collaboration,
    175–77
  defined, 172
  group, 174–75
  individual, 173–74
  at Walt Disney, 185–86
Cross-functional team, 240–41
Cross-functional teams
  and conflict resolution, 485
  and management by objectives,
    271
Cross-functioning, 44
Culture shock 107–108
  See also Diversity; National
    culture; Organizational
    culture
Current ratio, 266
Customers
  global task environment, 100
  power of, 202
  responsiveness to, 213–14, 258,
    412–13, 445
  task environment, 65–66

D

Data, 177
Days sales outstanding, 266
Debt-to-asset ratio, 266
Decision making
  authority allocation and,
    243–45
  cognitive biases, 167–69
  conservative culture and, 278
  defined, 157
  identifying bias, 169
  information and, 179
  nature of, 157–58
  non-programmed, 159, 227
  programmed, 158–59, 227
  See also Group decision making
Decision-making models
  administrative model, 159–62
  classical model, 159
Decision-making process, 163–68
  recognizing need for decision,
    163–64
  generating alternatives, 164
  assessing alternatives, 164–65
  choosing among alternatives, 165
  implementing chosen
    alternative, 166
  learning from feedback, 166
Decline, as stage of industry life
  cycle, 70
Decoding, 446
Defensive approach, to social
  responsibility, 134
Delphi technique, 175
Demography, 73–74
Demutualization, 283
Denmark, 354
Departments
  as command groups, 416
  defined, 10
  government, 19–20
Deregulation, 74–75, 104
Development
  employee's responsibilities,
    304–305

as national issue, 303–304
  organization's responsibilities,
    304
  types of, 303
Devil's advocacy, 170–71, 333
Dialectical inquiry, 171
Differentiation strategy, 210–11
Direction setting
  hierarchies and, 186
  and plans, 195
Direct supervision, 269–70
Disabled worker, and
    employment equity, 292
Discipline, 43
Discrimination
  gender, 44
  overt, 141–42
  See also Employment equity
Dismissals, 484–85, 520
Distributive justice, 138
Distributive negotiation, 486
Distributors, 91–92
  global task environment,
    99–100
  power of large, 65
Diversification, 204–205
Diversity
  Canadian armed forces, 21
  Canadian workforce, 20, 136
  and communication styles, 143
  cross-cultural creative
    collaboration, 175–77,
    412–13
  culture and working styles, 143
  and decision making, 171–72
  defined, 136
  discriminatory behaviour and
    attitudes in workplace,
    140–43
  and distributive justice, 138
  flexible attitude, 143
  human rights legislation and, 139
  linguistic styles, 464–46
  needs and motivation, 354
  older workers, 293
  as organizational asset, 139–40
  and procedural justice, 139
  and RCMP, 144–45
  sex discrimination, 137, 138–39
  top-management commitment
    to, 144
  and workplace management,
    136–48
Diversity awareness programs, 142
Diversity education, 143–44
Diversity skills, 142–43, 484
Divestiture, 184
Divisional structures
  defined, 234
  geographic structure, 236–37
  market structure, 238
  product structure, 234–35
Division of labour
  and Fayol's principles, 43
  and job design, 228–30
  person-task relationships, 36–38
  scientific management and,
    36–37
Divisions
  coordinating functions, 241–45
  hierarchy of authority, 241–42
Downsizing, 13–14
  alternatives to, 319

at CBC, 29
  and morale, 319, 332–33
  and productivity, 319
  and profits, 319
  See also Restructuring
Dress code, 43–44, 278

E

Eastern Europe, 102, 103–105
Echo Boom generation, 88
Economic forces
  economic systems, 102–103
  global reforms, 104–105
  macroeconomic conditions,
    70–71
Economies of scale, 66
Education, formal, 303
Effectiveness, organizational, 5
Efficiency
  communication and, 444
  and creating value, 213
  improving, 514–18
  just-in-time inventory and,
    515–17
  kaizen and, 517
  order and, 43
  organizational, 5
  performance measure, 257, 261,
    514–15
  person-task relationships to,
    36–38
  process reengineering and,
    517–18
  Taylor's principles, 37
  total quality management and,
    515
Electronic brainstorming, 174–75
E-mail, 452–53, 471–72
Emotion-focused coping of stress
  meditation, 340
  physical exercise, 339–40
  social support, 340
Employee retention, 30
Employee stock options,
  universal, 376–77
Employment equity, 291–92
Employment Equity Act, 75, 139,
    291
Empowerment, 14, 386–87
  directive behaviours and, 392,
    393
  employee-centred behaviours
    and, 389
  initiating structure for, 389
  job-oriented behaviour and, 389
  leader-member relations and,
    391
  participative behaviours and, 393
  relationship-oriented leaders
    and, 390
  suitable candidates for, 386
  supportive behaviours and, 393
  task-oriented behaviours and,
    390
Encoding, 446
Environment. *See* Organizational
  environment; Organizational
  environment theory
Equity principle, 43
Equity theory
  conditions of equity, 363–64

inequity, 364
inputs and outcomes in, 363–64
restoring equity, 365–66
Escalating commitment, 168–69
Esprit de corps, 43
Esteem needs, 354
Ethical behaviour and dilemmas
child labour, 129
environmental protection, 112
fair business practices, 113
human rights, 112
Japanese management techniques and reengineering, 519
monitoring voice mail and e-mail, 453
output control systems, 268
pressure to increase performance and, 24–25
in recruiting, 296–97
self-interest and, 127, 128, 131–32
severance pay, 129
stakeholders' interests, 123–24, 131–32
suppliers and, 130–31
withholding negative information, 300
Ethical control systems, 132
Ethical culture, 133
Ethical decision, 124
Ethical standards
defining workers' rights, 39, 43–44
individual, 128–29
and open global environment, 112–13
professional, 127
and reputation of organizations, 25
societal, 125–26
Ethics
models, 125
promoting, 132–33
and social responsibility, 134–36
Ethics ombudsman, 132
E-Training, 302–303
European Union (EU), 76
Evaluation
of actual performance against chosen standards, 262
of complex, nonroutine activities, 262
designing measurement systems, 263
of division, as stand-alone responsibility centre, 268
financial measures, 265–66
incompatible system of, 482
of outputs and behaviours, 261–62
performance, 233
See also Performance appraisal
Excise tax, on beer, 86
Exercise, physical, 339–40, 344
Existence needs, 354, 355
Expectancy theory
expectancy, 356–57
and high performance, 358–60
instrumentality, 357–58
valence, 358

Experiential-learning programs, 431, 439–40
Exporting, 108–109
External environment
defined, 63
general environment, 70–76
task environment, 64–70
threats and opportunities, 63–64
External locus of control, 328
Extinction, and behaviour modification, 362–63
Extrinsically motivated behaviour, 351–52
Extroverts, 325, 344
Exxon Valdez disaster, 81

F

Favouritism, 380
"Featherbedding," 510
Federal Privacy Act, 453
Feedback, 166
job, 231
performance, 309–11
Fiedler's contingency model, 390–91
Filtering information, 438, 462
Financial performance measures, 265–66
Five forces model, analysis of threats, 202–203
Five-stage group development model, 424–25
Focused differentiation strategy, 212
Focused low-cost strategy, 211–12
Folkways, 105
Fordism
worker discontent, 39
work process, 33–34, 38
Forecasting, human resource needs, 292
Forest industry, 393–94
Forming stage, in group development, 424
France, 129
Franchising, 109
Free-market economy, 102
Free trade
agreements, 76
and BC wine industry, 96–97
doctrine, 94
effects on managers, 95–96
and garment industry, 91–92
Free Trade Agreement of the Americas (FTAA), 97
Function, defined, 193
Functional conflict resolution, 483
Functional-level plan, 193, 194
Functional-level strategies, 193
creating value, 212–14
Functional structure, 232–34

G

Gainsharing, 371
Gatekeeping, 81
General Agreement on Trade in Services (GATS), 94, 112, 119
General environment
defined, 64

demographic forces, 73–74
economic forces, 70–71
global forces, 76
political and legal forces, 74–75
sociocultural forces, 72–73
technological forces, 71–72
Generation X, 327–28
Geographic structure, 236–37
Germany, 101, 129
Global environment
competitive advantage in, 22
declining barriers of distance and culture, 94–95
impediments to, 111–13
increasing customer service in, 23–24
increasing efficiency in, 22–23
increasing innovation in, 23
increasing quality in, 23
open, 93
trade and investment liberalization, 93–94
Global expansion
as corporate strategy, 206–207
importing and exporting, 108–109
licensing and franchising, 109
Scotiabank in Latin America, 110–11
strategic alliances, 109–10
wholly owned foreign subsidiaries, 111
Global general environment, 101–108
economic forces, 102–103
political and legal forces, 101–102, 103–105
sociocultural forces, 105–108
Global strategy, 206–207
Global task environment, 97–101
competitors, 100–101
customers, 100
distributors, 99–100
suppliers, 98–99
Goals, 197
in control process, 260–61
defined, 191
developing, 198–99
incompatible, 481
management by objectives, 270
output standards, 266–67
specific and difficult, 267, 360–61
stretch, 267, 375–76
Goal-setting theory, 360–61
Government. *See* Political forces
Grapevine, 456
Greece, 354
Gross profit margin, 265–66
Group cohesiveness
conformity and, 429–30
defined, 429
diversity and, 430–31
excessive, 431
goal accomplishment and, 430
group identity and, 431
group participation, 429
group size and, 430
success and, 431
Group decision making, 169–71
devil advocacy and, 170–71
dialectical inquiry and, 171
diversity and, 171

groupthink, 169–70
Group development models
five-stage model, 424–25
punctuated equilibrium model, 425–26
Group dynamics
group cohesiveness, 428–31
group leadership, 424
group norms, 426–28
group roles, 422–23
group size, 420
group tasks, 420–22
Group norms
balancing conformity and deviance, 427–28
conformity and deviance, 426–28
defined, 426
Groups
ad hoc committees, 416
command, 416
defined, 410
formal, 415
informal, 415
leadership, 424
social loafing in, 433–34
standing committees, 416
Groups and teams
communication networks in, 454–55
difference between, 410–11
encouraging teamwork in, 412, 439–41
intergroup conflict, 479
intragroup conflict, 479
motivating, 432–34
as motivators, 414–15
and organizational effectiveness, 410–11
as performance enhancers, 411–12
and responsiveness to customers, 412–13
Group tasks, 420–22
pooled task interdependence, 420–21
reciprocal task interdependence, 422
sequential task interdependence, 421–22
Groupthink, 169–70
preventing, 415, 433–34
symptoms, 433
Groupware, 458
Growth needs, 354, 355
Growth stage, of industry life cycle, 69
Guanxi, 332

H

Hawthorne effect, 45
Hazing, 276
Hersey-Blanchard's situational leadership theory, 392
Herzberg's motivator-hygiene theory, 355–36
Heuristics, 167
Hierarchies
of authority, 241–42
centralized, 43, 50, 51, 244–45
conservative values and, 279

Hierarchies *(continued)*
    and decentralized authority, 52, 243–45
    flat organizations, 242
    and leadership, 186
    managerial, 12–14
    tall organizations, 242–43
Hierarchy of needs, 353–54
HIV-positive workers, 292
Hofstede's model of national culture
    achievement vs. nurturing orientation, 107
    individualism vs. collectivism, 106
    long-term vs. short-term orientation, 107
    power distance, 106–107
    uncertainty avoidance, 107
Hostile work environment sexual harassment, 147
Human relations movement, 45
Human resources, and organizational structure, 228
Human resources management
    components, 289–91
    defined, 289
    labour relations, 289, 291, 314–15
    legal environment, 291
    pay and benefits, 289, 290–91, 312–13
    performance appraisal and feedback, 289, 290, 305–12
    recruitment and selection, 289–90, 292–301
    strategic, 289
    training and development, 289, 290, 301–305
Hybrid organizational structure, 241
Hygiene needs, 355, 356

I

Illusion of control, 168
Illusion of invulnerability, 433
Illusion of unanimity, 433
Importing, 109
Incentives, performance, 37
    non-monetary compensation, 268
    pay, 362, 367–71
    remuneration of personnel, 43
    See also Motivation
India, 99
Individual ethics, 128–29
Individualism, 72–73, 106
Industrial Disputes Investigation Act, 314
Industry life cycle, 68–70
    birth stage, 68–69
    growth stage, 69
    shakeout stage, 69
    maturity stage, 70
    decline, 70
Informal organization, and work group behaviour, 45–46
Information
    ambiguous, 160
    attributes of useful, 177–78
    collecting and processing, 81, 179

completeness of, 178
defined, 177
distortion, 462
filtering, 438, 462
incomplete, 160–61
and management, 179
objective, 492
quality of, 177–78
relevance of, 178
richness, 449
timeliness of, 178
Information systems and technologies
    and Canadian healthcare crisis, 25–26
    information system, 179
    information technology, 179
    management information system, 48, 179
    and productivity, 25
    technological revolution, 180
Initiating structure, 389
Initiative
    and Fayol's principles, 43
    and worker participation, 44–45
Innovation, 213
    communication and, 445
    controlling and, 258
    cross-cultural collaboration, 175–76, 412–13
    deviance and, 427
    teams and, 413–14
Input, 352
Input stage
    feedforward control, 259–60
    of open system, 48
Instrumentality, 357–58
Instrumental values, 330
Insurance industry, 283
Integrative bargaining
    defined, 486
    distributive justice, 487–88
    focusing on interests, 487
    focusing on problem, 486
    negotiation strategies, 486–88
    options for joint gain, 487
    superordinate goals, 486
Intellectual property, 119
Intellectual stimulation, 343, 396, 399
Intergroup conflict, 479
Internal locus of control, 328–29
Internal structure, 79
Internet, 26, 457
Interorganizational conflict, 480
Interpersonal conflict, 479
Interviews, 297–99
    conducted by candidate, 299
    irrelevant questions, 298
    pre-employment interview, 298–99
    situational questions, 297
    unstructured interview, 298
Intragroup conflict, 479
Intranets, 457–58
Intrinsically motivated behaviour, 351–52
Introverts, 325
Intuition, 159
Inventory turnover, 266
Iran, 102
Iraq, 102

J

Japan, 73, 99, 100, 340, 354
    kaizen, 517
    kanban system, 515–16
    leadership styles, 383
    trade barriers, 112
Jargon, 462
Job analysis, 294
Job design
    assigning tasks to individual job, 229–30
    defined, 228
    and division of labour, 229
    and job characteristics model, 230–31
Job enlargement, 230
Job enrichment, 230
Job-hopping, 30
Job rotation, 484
Job satisfaction, 332, 332–33
Job simplification, 230
Job specialization. *See* Specialization, job
Joint venture, 110, 245, 246
Judgment, 159
Justice, model of ethics, 126
Just-in-time inventory, 515–17

K

Kaizan, 517
    blitz, 410
    and Ventra Group, 524–25
Kanban system, 515–16

L

Labour productivity, 514
Labour relations, 6–7, 289, 291, 314–15
    BC nurses union, 487
    Canadian National Railway, 519–20
    city of Vancouver, 444
    collective bargaining, 315
    newspaper industry, 497–98
    RBW Graphics, 443–444
Labour unions, 29, 65
    and public sector employees, 314
Large Scale Retail Store Law (Japan), 112
Lateral moves, 296
Layoffs. *See* Downsizing
Leadership, 8–9
    charismatic, 397–98
    conservative culture and, 279
    gender and, 400–401
    group, 424
    innovative culture and, 279
    at Irwin Toy, 379–80
    at LG Electronics, 399–400
    at Macmillan Bloedel, 394
    at M and M Meat Shops, 406–407
    nature of, 381
    and organizational behaviour, 44–47
    and power, 383–386
    at QLT, 379–8
    reaction to crises, 520

at Saturn Corp., 405–406
at Semco, 384–85
at Siemens AG, 396
situational characteristics and, 390–91
transactional, 396
transformational, 396–400
See also Personality traits
Leadership behaviours
    achievement-oriented, 393
    changing organizational culture, 520
    consideration, 388–89
    directive, 392
    employee-centred, 389
    participative, 393
    relationship oriented, 390
    supportive, 393
    task oriented, 390
Leadership models
    behaviour model, 388–89
    contingency models, 389–95
    leader substitutes, 394
    trait model, 387
Leadership style
    baby boomers, 327–28
    at Bank of Montreal, 323–24
    culture and, 382–83
    Generation, X, 327–28
    individualistic and top-down, 381–82
    personal, 381–82
    supportive, team-oriented, 381
Learning organization
    defined, 172
    group creativity and, 174–75
    individual creativity and, 173–74
Learning organization, cross-cultural brainstorming, 175–77
Legal forces, political forces and, 74–75
Leverage ratios, 266
Licensing, 109
Linguistic styles, 464–66
    cross-cultural differences, 465
    elements, 464–65
    gender differences, 466
    managing differences in, 466
Liquidity ratios, 266
Locus of control, 328–29
Long-term orientation, 107
Low-cost strategies, 210

M

Maintenance roles, 422
Malaysia, 100
Management
    applying principles of, 52
    by wandering around (MBWA), 450
    crisis, 81, 121–22
    defined, 5
    employee relations, 3–4
    labour relations, 6–7
    levels of, 10–12
    of organizational environment, 76–83
Management by objectives, 270–71

Management information system, 179

Management information systems, (MIS), 48

Management science theory, 47–48

Management theories. *See* under specific theories

Managerial functions, 7–8
controlling, 9
leading, 8–9
organizing, 8
planning, 7–8

Managerial roles
decisional roles, 17
identified by Mintzberg, 15
informational roles, 17
interpersonal roles, 15–17
tips form managers, 19

Managerial skills
conceptual skills, 17
human skills, 17–18
technical skills, 18

Managers
first-line, 10, 11, 78
middle, 10, 12, 78, 79
top, 11, 12
as agents of change, 82
boundary-spanning roles, 79–80
as coaches and facilitators, 44
controlling agenda, 492–93
defined, 5
divisional, 193, 194
effect of free trade on, 95–96
and environmental change, 77
and ethical dilemmas, 124–25, 136
expatriate, 108
and expert power, 489
and forecasting, 79
functional, 193
gatekeeping and information processing, 81
and macroeconomic conditions, 70–71
and national culture, 107–108
and organizational structure and control systems, 78–79
reducing impact of environmental forces, 77–78
representing and protecting organization, 80–81
as role models, 427–28
scanning and monitoring environment, 81
and social changes, 73

Manitoba, and e-mail abuse, 453

Maquiladoras, 112

Market entry
soft-drink industry, 189–90
as threat, 202
See also Barriers of entry

Market structure, 238

Maslow's hierarchy of needs, 353–54

Mass-production technology, 227

Matrix structure, 239–40

Maturity stage, of industry life cycle, 70

Mechanistic structures, 50, 51, 78–79

Meditation, 340

Medium, communication
appropriate, 460–61
defined, 446

Mentor, 339

Mergers and takeovers
BMO-Royal Bank abortive merger, 475–76
and cultural conflict in, 274, 526–27
Indigo-Chapters merger, 75
TD-Canada Trust takeover, 476
TD-CIBC abortive merger, 476

Merit pay plan, 368, 370–71

Message, feedback mechanism in, 462

Messages
accurate information, 462
clarity in, 460
defined, 446
understandable symbols in, 460

Mexico, 112

Minimized doubts, 433

Mission, 191, 197–98
statement, 191, 199

Mixed economy, 102

Monitoring
employee behaviour, 258
performance, 233
quality of goods and services, 258
task and general environments, 234
See also Control; Controlling

Moods, 330
and behaviour, 333–34
mood-swing patterns, 334
and perception, 335
stress and, 337

Moral rights, model of ethics, 126

Mores, 105–106

Motivation
at Eastman Kodak, 349–50
in groups, 432–34
and incentives, 361–62
and intellectual stimulation, 343, 396, 399
intrinsic and extrinsic sources of, 351–53
job satisfaction, 231
job training and expectancy, 359
at Maple Leaf Foods, 362
at Mars, 349–50
at Microsoft, 252
at Motorola, 359–60
nature of, 351–53
and organizational goals, 268, 352–53
and outcomes, 352
and path-goal theory, 392–93
pay and, 362, 367–71
raised performance standards, 262
specific and difficult goals, 360–61, 375–76
stress and, 337
stretch targets, 375–76
See also Behaviour control

Motivation theories
equity theory, 363–66
expectancy theory, 357–60
goal-setting theory, 360–61

need theories, 353–56
reinforcement theory, 361–63

Motivator needs, 355

Multidomestic strategy, 206–207

N

National culture
consumer tastes and preferences, 100
defined, 73
and global management, 107
Hofstede's model of, 106–108
values, 73

Needs assessment, 301, 302

Need theories
Alderfer's ERG theory, 354–55
Herzberg's motivator-hygiene theory, 355–36
Maslow's hierarchy of needs, 353–54
need, defined, 353

Negative affectivity, 326

Negative reinforcers, 362

Negotiation, 486
See also Integrative bargaining

Network structure, 245, 246–247

Nexus Generation. *See* Generation X

Noise, in communication process, 446

Nominal group technique, 175

Nonprogrammed decision making, 159, 227

Norms, 42, 105
and clan control, 273
and group cohesiveness, 429–30
and group conformity, 426–28
and work group influence, 45

North American Free Trade Agreement (NAFTA), 76, 96

North Korea, 103

Norway, 354

Nurturing orientation, 107

O

Obstructionist approach, to social responsibility, 134

Ontario, and e-mail abuse, 453

On-the-job training, 302

Openness to experience, 327

Open-systems, 48–49

Operating costs, 261

Operations management, 47

Optimum decision, 159

Organic structures, 51, 52
and innovative culture, 279
and organizational forces, 79

Organizational administration. *See* Administrative management theory

Organizational architecture, 225

Organizational behaviour modification, 363, 364

Organizational change
assessing need for, 503–504
and efficiency, 514–19
Lewin's three-stage model, 504–505
and organizational culture, 519–20

and production system, 511–19
and quality, 511–14
resistance to change, 505–508
in unionized environment, 509–10

Organizational conflict
at McCain Foods, 477–78
at Blimpie, 498–99
defined, 477
management strategies, 482–85
and organizational performance, 478–79
sources of, 481–82
types of, 479–80

Organizational control. *See* Controlling

Organizational culture
ceremonies and rites, 276–77
in conflict, 485
creating and sustaining, 273–74, 284–85, 520
and managerial action, 278–80
material symbols, 278
and organizational change, 519–20
socialization, 275–76
stories and language, 277–78
values of the founder, 274–75, 285

Organizational design, 225–41
divisional structure, 234–38
functional structure, 232–34
hybrid structure, 241
jobs, 228–231
matrix structure, 238–240
product team structure, 240–41

Organizational environment
assessing changes in, 77
brewing industry, 86–87
complexity of, 76–77
defined, 48, 63
as determinant of organizational structure, 226
external environment, 48, 50, 63
general environment, 70–76
internal environment, 64
management of, 76–83
rate of change in, 77
resources, 48
task environment, 64–70

Organizational environment theory, 48–51
contingency theory, 49–50
mechanistic structures, 50, 51
open-systems view, 48–49
organic structures, 51, 52

Organizational learning
defined, 172
principles of, 172–73

Organizational politics
defined, 488
as positive force, 489
strategies for exercising power, 491–93
strategies for increasing power, 489–91

Organizational stakeholders, and ethics, 123–25

Organizational structure, of management, 241–25

Organizational structures
defined, 40, 225
determinants of, 225–28

Organizational structures
  (continued)
  and managing environmental
    change, 78–79
  mechanistic, 50, 51
  organic, 51, 52
Organization citizenship
    behaviours (OCBs), 332
Organization learning, *See also*
    Learning organization
Organizations
  boundaryless, 246–247
  as closed-systems, 48
  defined, 5
  flat, 242
  global, 21, 92
  informal, 46
  tall, 242–43
  types of, 19–20
Organizing process, 8
Outcome
  and motivation, 352
  valence, 358
Output control, 265–68
  financial measures of
    performance, 265–66
  operating budgets, 267–68
  organizational goals, 266–67
  problems with, 268–69
Output stage
  feedback control, 260
  of open system, 48
Output standards, 261
Outside experts, 492
Outsourcing, 218, 247
  global, 91–92, 95–96, 98–99
  human resource needs, 293–94
Overpayment inequity, 365
Overseas Chinese, 331–32

P

Partial productivity, 514
Participatory approach, to
    controlling, 256, 401
Patents. *See* Intellectual property
Path-goal theory, 292–93
Pay, 289, 290–91
  and benefits, 313
  bonus plans, 369, 376–77
  CEOs, 313
  dispersion, 432
  for failed performance, 369–70
  level, 312
  merit, 367, 368–69
  merit plans, 370–71
  salary increases, 368–69
  structure, 312–13
PC 1003, 314
Peer appraisals, 309, 310
Peer pressure, 433
Perceptions
  accurate, 336
  in communication, 447–48
  in equity theory, 364
  influences on, 335
  stereotypes and, 334–35
Performance
  fianancial measures, 265–66
  organizational, 5
  tests, 299
  under stress, 337

Performance appraisal
  appraisers, 309–10
  defined, 305
  and feedback, 289, 290, 310–11
  formal, 310
  and human resources decisions,
    305–306
  informal, 310
  objective, 307
  types of, 305–308
Performance feedback
  defined, 305
  guidelines, 311
  subjective measures, 307–308
  suggestions for improvement, 310
Performing stage, in group
    development, 424
Permanent transfers, 484–85
Personal Information Protection
    and Electronic Documents
    Act, 453
Personality clash, 484
Personality tests, 299
Personality traits, 325–29
  achievement, need for, 329
  affiliation, need for, 329
  agreeableness, 326–27
  Belinda Stronach, 345–46
  of candidates of empowerment,
    386
  conscientiousness, 327
  defined, 325
  extroversion, 325–26
  locus of control, 328–29
  and managerial approaches, 320
  negative affectivity, 326
  openness to experience, 327
  power, need for, 329
  self-esteem, 329
Personal mastery, and
    organizational learning, 172
Person-task relationships, 36–38
Physiological needs, 354
Piece-rate pay, 370
Plan
  business-level, 193
  corporate-level, 193
  functional-level, 193
  qualities of effective, 196
  rolling, 194
  single-use, 195
  standing, 195
  time horizon of, 194
Planning
  conservative values and, 278
  consistency across
    organizational levels,
    193–94
  defined, 191
  human resource, 292–94
  innovative culture and, 278
  levels of, 192–94
  long-term vs. short-term
    approach, 383
  reasons for, 195–96
  role of managers, 194
  scenario, 196–97
Planning process, 7–8
  defining organization's business,
    191, 197–99
  strategy formulation, 199–214
  strategy implementation, 214
  steps in, 191–92

Political forces
  democratization, 103–104
  impediments to open global
    environment, 112, 118–19
  and legal forces, 74–75
Political strategies
  defined, 488
  See also Organizational politics
Pooled task interdependence,
    420–21
Portfolio strategy, 205
Position Analysis Questionnaire
    (PAQ), 294
Positive reinforcement, 361–62
Potential competitors, 66
Power
  coercive, 384–85
  expert, 385, 489
  legitimate, 383
  need for, 329
  position, 391
  referent, 385–86
  reward, 384, 385
  unobtrusive use of, 491–93
Power distance, 106
Prices
  and competition, 66
  price wars, 69, 202
Prior bias hypothesis, 167
Privacy legislation, 453
Privately held organizations, 19
Privatization, 75, 104
  of Petro-Canada, 61–62
  in United Kingdom, 102
Proactive approach, to social
    responsibility, 135
Problem-focused coping of stress
  mentoring, 339
  time management, 338–39
Procedural justice, 138
Process reengineering, 517–18
Production blocking, 174
Production line, 38
Production systems
  disillusionment with new
    production techniques, 518
  just-in-time inventory, 515–17
  kaizen (continuous
    improvement) and, 517
  reengineering, 517–18
  total quality management and,
    512–14, 515
Product structure, 234–35
Product team structure, 240–41,
    252
Professional ethics, 127
Profit, 265
Profit sharing, 264, 275, 371
Programmed decision making,
    158, 227
Publicly held organizations, 19
Public Service Staff Relations
    Act, 314
Punctuated equilibrium model,
    425–26
Punishment, 363, 384
  See also Coercive power

Q

Qualified privilege, 300
Quality

and cost savings, 511–14
  improving, 511–15
  product, 213
  total quality management,
    512–14
Quality standards, 261
Quantitative management, 47
Quebec, privacy legislation, 453
Quid pro quo sexual harassment,
    146

R

Rationalized resistance, 433
Real-time information, 178
Receiver, in communication
    process, 446
Recruitment
  defined, 292
  external recruiting, 295–96
  honesty in recruiting, 296–97
  internal recruiting, 297
  at Microsoft, 289
  at Nortel, 320
  planning process, 292–94
  and selection, 289–90, 292–301
  small companies, 295–96
  and sustaining organizational
    culture, 273
Red tape, 42
References, 299–300
Reinforcement theory
  and behaviour modification,
    363, 364
  extinction, 362–63
  negative reinforcement, 362
  positive reinforcement, 361–62
  punishment, 363
Related diversification, 205
Relatedness needs, 354, 355
Reliability, of selection tools,
    300–301
Representative bias, 168
Representative democracies, 101
Reputation, 25, 136
Resistance, rationalized, 433
Resistance to change, 505–508
  individual, 506–507
  organizational, 507–508
  overcoming, 508–10
Resources
  competition over, 482
  defined, 5
  generating, 490
  in organizational environment,
    48
Restructuring, 12–14
  at DaimlerChrysler, 526
  at Kodak, 56
Results appraisals, 307
Return on investment (ROI), 265
Risk, 160, 398
Rites of enhancement, 276–77
Rites of integration, 276
Rites of passage, 276
Role conflict, 337–38
Role making, 423
Role overload, 337–38
Role-play, 302
Rolling plan, 194
Rules, 42
Rumours, 462

S

Safety needs, 354
Salience effect, 141
Satisficing, 161–63
Scientific management
    clerical mills and, 57–58
    mechanization and pace of
        work, 38
    monotonous work process,
        37, 40
    worker discontent, 37
Scientific management theory,
    35–40
    defined, 36
    Gilbreths and, 40
    Taylor and, 36–39
Selection of job candidate
    background information, 297
    defined, 292
    interviews, 297–99
    and organizational culture, 520
    organizational culture and, 273,
        520
    process, 297–301
    references, 299–300
    reliability and validity of
        selection tools, 300–301
    testing and, 299
Self-actualization needs, 354
Self-appraisals, 309
Self-esteem, 329
Self-managed teams, 14, 416–18
Sender, in communication
    process, 446
Severance payments, 129
Sex discrimination, 137, 138–39
Sexual harassment
    defined, 146
    forms, 146–47
    measures for eradicating, 147
Shakeout stage, of industry life
    cycle, 69
Short-term orientation, 107
Similar-to-me effect, 140–41
Simulations, 302
Single-use plan, 195
Situational characteristics
    leader-member relations, 391
    leader style and, 391
    position power, 391
    task structure, 391
Skill variety, 230
Sleep
    disturbance, 337
    and increased stamina, 344
Small-batch technology, 227
Social audit, 136
Socialization, organizational,
    275–78
    ceremonies and rites, 276–77
    defined, 275
    material symbols, 278
    at McDonald's, 277–78
    stories and language, 278–79
Social loafing, 433–34
Social responsibility
    at AES Corporation, 438
    approaches, 134
    defined, 133
    forms of socially responsible
        behaviour, 134
    positive outcomes, 135–36

See also Ethical behaviour
    and dilemmas; Ethical
    standards
Social-status effect, 141
Social stratification, 72
Social structure, 72
Social support, 340, 414
Societal ethics, 125–26
Sociocultural forces, and general
    environment, 72–73
Soft-drink industry, 189–90
Soviet Union, 102
Span of control, 242
Specialization, job, 36, 38
Split-team syndrome, 431
Stability of tenure of personnel, 43
Stamina, physical, 344–45
Standard operating procedures
    (SOPs)
    and bureaucratic control,
        271–72
    codifying, 37
    defined, 42
    impediment to organizational
        learning, 272
    and organizational behaviour,
        42, 271–72
    slow decision making, 272
Standing committees, 416
Standing plan, 195
Status inconsistencies, 482
Stereotypes, 141, 334–35
Storming stage, in group
    development, 424
Strategic alliances, 109–10, 204,
    245–46
Strategy
    business-level, 193
    corporate-level, 193
    defined, 191
    as determinant of organizational
        structure, 226
    functional-level, 193
    global, 206, 207
    multidomestic, 206–207
    portfolio, 205
Strategy formulation, 199–214
    business-level, 210–12
    corporate-level, 203–10
    defined, 199
    five forces model, 202
    SWOT analysis, 200–202
Stress
    conflicting roles and, 337–38
    consequences of, 336–37
    and managers, 336
    role overload, 337, 338
    sources of managerial, 337–38
    uncertainty and, 336
Stress management
    emotion-focused coping,
        339–40
    problem-focused coping,
        338–39
Stretch targets, 267, 375–76
"Stuck in the middle" problem,
    211
Subsidiaries
    American, 19
    wholly owned foreign, 111
Substitute products, threat of,
    202
Supervisors, 10

Suppliers
    and ethical behaviour, 130–31
    global task environment, 98–99
    power of, 65, 202
    and product uniformity, 209
    sources and types of, 64–65
    of Xerox Corporation, 77
SWOT analysis, 200–202
Synergy, 49, 205, 411–12
Systematic errors, 167
Systems thinking, 173

T

Takeovers. See Mergers and
    takeovers
Tariff, 93
Task analyzability, 227
Task environment
    competitors, 66–67
    customers, 65–66
    defined, 63
    distributors, 65
    industry life cycle, 68–70
    suppliers, 64–65
Task forces, 416
Task identity, 231
Task interdependence
    conflict, 482
    defined, 420
    pooled, 420–21
    reciprocal, 422
    sequential, 421–22
Task-oriented roles, 422
Task significance, 231
Task variety, 227
Team building
    and employee selection, 298
    experiential-learning programs
        and, 439–41
    See also Group cohesiveness;
        Group dynamics
Team learning, 172
Teams
    appropriate utilization of, 419
    cross-functional, 413
    defined, 410
    fostering teamwork in, 412,
        439–41
    research and development,
        416, 420
    self-managed, 416–18, 423, 424
    top-management, 12, 77, 194, 415
    virtual, 418–19
    See also Group cohesiveness;
        Group dynamics; Groups;
        Groups and teams
Technology
    advances in communication and
        travel, 95
    computer-aided design, 72
    continuous process, 227–28
    defined, 71, 226
    degree of complexity, 227
    as determinant of organizational
        structure, 226–28
    and general environment, 71–72
    mass-production, 227
    small-batch, 227
    technological forces, 71
    See also Information systems and
        technologies

Telecommuting, 71, 452, 472–73
Teleconferencing, 71–72
Telephone conversations, 451
Temporary assignments, 484
Temporary workers, 293
Terminal values, 330
Testing, for aptitude, 299
Time-and-motion study, 37, 40
Time horizons, 383
    incompatible, 481
Time management, 338–39
Times-covered ratio, 266
Time standards, 261
Top-management
    commitment to diversity, 144
    team, 12, 77, 194, 415
Total factor productivity, 514
Totalitarian regimes, 101–102
Total quality management (TQM),
    47, 512–14, 515
Trademarks. See Intellectual
    property
Training, 289, 290, 301–303
    apprentice program at Comtek,
        287
    classroom, 301–302
    and development, 303–305
    and efficiency, 37
    e-training, 302–303
    and expectancy level, 357, 369
    experiential-learning programs,
        431, 439–40
    needs assessment, 301
    on-the-job training, 302
    performance appraisals and,
        306, 307
    types of, 301–303
Trait appraisals, 306
Transformational leadership
    charisma and, 397–98
    developmental consideration
        and, 398–99
    empowerment of subordinates,
        396–97
    intellectual stimulation and,
        396, 399
Turnover, staff
    and Fordism, 39
    See also Employee retention

U

Uncertainty
    controlling, 489
    and decision making, 160
Uncertainty avoidance, 107
Underpayment inequity, 365
Unethical decision, 124
United Kingdom, 101, 102, 129
United States, 101
    demography, 73, 74
    leadership style, 383
Universities. See Colleges and
    universities
Unrelated diversification, 205–206
Uruguay Round, 94
Utilitarian, model of ethics, 126

V

Valence, 358
Validity, of selection tools, 301

Value chain, 208
    in soft-drink industry, 189–90
Value, creating, 212–14, 220
Values, 105
    and clan control, 273
    of founder, 274–75, 285
    instrumental, 330
    managerial, 330
    of Overseas Chinese, 331–32
    and perception, 335
    system of, 331

    terminal, 330
Vertical integration, 207–10
Videoconferencing, 450–51
Vision, 191
    statement, 191

W

Web sites, 296, 457
Whistle-blower, 136

Women
    and clerical mills, 57–58
    leadership styles, 400–401
    linguistic style, 466
    pay and employment equity,
        138
    workforce participation, 73
Work experiences, varied,
    303
Workforce, diversity in, 20,
    |136

Workplace safety, 263
World Trade Organization
    (WTO), 76, 94

X

Xinyong, 332